THE CORRESPONDENCE OF
G. E. MORRISON
II
1912–1920

This was the cover picture of the *Illustrated London News* for 31 August 1912 which bore the caption 'The Political Adviser of the Chinese Republic and its first President: Dr G. E. Morrison – "Peking Morrison" – and Yuan Shih-kai.' Commenting on it many years later in a memorandum in which he recalled the world-wide reaction to his appointment by the Chinese Government in 1912, Morrison wrote, 'Some of the illustrated papers had my portrait, the most interesting being a faked representation of myself standing alongside of Yuan Shih-kai and directing his attention to a paper before him. This had been a snap-shot taken of the President and his Secretary Tsai Ting-kan. Tsai's head had been removed, and a fanciful one of mine inserted.'

THE CORRESPONDENCE OF
G.E.MORRISON

II

1912–1920

EDITED BY LO HUI-MIN

CAMBRIDGE UNIVERSITY PRESS
Cambridge
London · New York · Melbourne

CAMBRIDGE UNIVERSITY PRESS
Cambridge, New York, Melbourne, Madrid, Cape Town,
Singapore, São Paulo, Delhi, Mexico City

Cambridge University Press
The Edinburgh Building, Cambridge CB2 8RU, UK

Published in the United States of America by Cambridge University Press, New York

www.cambridge.org
Information on this title: www.cambridge.org/9781107414228

© Cambridge University Press 1978

This publication is in copyright. Subject to statutory exception
and to the provisions of relevant collective licensing agreements,
no reproduction of any part may take place without the written
permission of Cambridge University Press.

First published 1978
First paperback edition 2013

A catalogue record for this publication is available from the British Library

Library of Congress Cataloguing in Publication Data

Morrison, George Ernest, 1862–1920.
The correspondence of G. E. Morrison.

Includes index.
CONTENTS: v. 1. 1895–1912. v. 2. 1912–1920.
1. China–History–1900– –Sources. 2. Morrison, George Ernest, 1862–1920.
3. Journalists–Congresses.
I. Lo, Hui-min.
DS764.M67   951'.03   74-31806
ISBN 0 521 21561 7

ISBN 978-0-521-21561-9 Hardback
ISBN 978-1-107-41422-8 Paperback

Cambridge University Press has no responsibility for the persistence or
accuracy of URLs for external or third-party internet websites referred to in
this publication, and does not guarantee that any content on such websites is,
or will remain, accurate or appropriate.

NOTE

The editor would like to express his gratitude to the Australian Academy
of Humanities for a generous grant towards the cost of publishing this
volume.

Contents

	page
Preface	vii
Map	x
August 1912–September 1912	1
October 1912–March 1913	37
March 1913–July 1913	110
July 1913–October 1914	195
December 1914–August 1915	350
August 1915–June 1916	450
June 1916–June 1917	529
July 1917–November 1918	601
November 1918–May 1920	715
June 1920–December 1920	822
Glossary	829
Index	856

ERRATA

The following characters are to be substituted in these entries:

p.835: 翰 in 'Hanlin Yuan'
" 漢 in 'Hanyang'
p.837 曆 in 'Hung-li'
p.840 黌 in 'Kuo-she tang'
" 燾 in 'Kuo Sung-t'ao'
p.851 載 in 'Tsai-chen', 'Tsai-ch'un', 'Tsai-feng', 'Tsai-hsün', 'Tsai-i', 'Tsai-lan', 'Tsai-lien', 'Tsai-t'ao', 'Tsai-t'ien' and 'Tsai-tse'

Preface

The footnotes in these volumes are intended to be no more than a convenience to readers. The first mention of all identifiable persons and events, however familiar they might be to some, has a note, with only the briefest entry for the better-known Western ones. Mistakes and misprints in Volume I have been corrected, wherever possible, in the fuller notes, glossary, index and map in the present volume.

*

Every place mentioned in the text appears on the map, except places within cities and a few which we were unable to locate. Since available maps of the period are often conflicting and inaccurate in many details, the present map has been compiled from a great many sources. Each place has been checked against the co-ordinates in the Concordance to the 1:1,000,000 maps of China and Mongolia compiled by the Department of Defence of the United States Government, except for a few not appearing on those maps. An effort has been made to incorporate on this one map the changes in China's international and provincial boundaries since 1895. Changes that occurred before 1949 mostly affected the outlying provinces; those occurring within what used to be called China Proper are too minor to be recorded on a map of this nature. The more notable changes during the period were: the creation out of part of Szechwan and of Tibet of the Special District of Ch'uan-pien (1912, 1916) which, with some alterations, became the province of Sikang in 1928 and after 1949 lost its separate status; the creation in 1925 of Ningsia Province out of part of Kansu and of what is known as Inner Mongolia; and the creation of the Special Districts of Suiyuan (1913), Chahar (1914) and Jehol (1914), which all became provinces in 1928 but since 1949 have been divided between the Inner Mongolian Autonomous Region and Hopeh Province; and finally the boundary changes accompanying the secession of what was known as Outer Mongolia. Changes since 1949 are not recorded on this map. The names of provinces are entered as they were known in Morrison's time, i.e. Chihli but not Hopeh, and Fengtien, not Liaoning. These provincial names, as well as those of many better known cities and towns, are spelt according to the so-called Postal system of the time, while the others are in the Wade-Giles transliteration. The place names as they appear in the text, with their variant forms and earlier and later names, as well as the province in which each is to be found, are given in the glossary.

*

In addition to those whose assistance in the preparation and publication of these volumes I have acknowledged in the Preface in Volume I, I would like to record my gratitude to Enoki Kazuo, sometime Professor of Oriental History at the University of Tokyo, and his staff at the Morrison Library, otherwise known as the Tōyō Bunko, in Tokyo, for their great kindness in providing me with all possible facilities to work in this unique collection; to the editorial and publication staff of Cambridge University Press, particularly Francis Brooke, whose great care and thoroughness has made this volume much less imperfect than it otherwise would have been; and to Helen Bryant, who assisted me in preparing the map, glossary and index for these first two volumes.

CHINA 1895–1920

August 1912 – September 1912

On 1 August 1912, Morrison formally accepted the Chinese offer to become Political Adviser to the President of the Republic. The reaction to his appointment was not, as he told his friends, one of universal approval; it was mixed. Certainly there seemed to be no disagreement as to Morrison's suitability to fill such a post. China was heartily congratulated by foreign observers as well as by Chinese themselves for having secured his services. A great number of Morrison's friends and acquaintances, however, had serious reservations about his wisdom in accepting the Chinese offer. Among the host of congratulatory letters were many displaying doubt as to whether to congratulate him or commiserate with him on his new appointment.

Morrison had already given his reasons for leaving *The Times*; he spoke much more defensively, however, of his acceptance of the Chinese offer. Reuter's correspondent to whom he had confided his decision to leave China had, he claimed, indiscreetly leaked the news, and the Chinese, when they heard it, made Morrison the offer and persuaded him to stay. Morrison wrote little in his Diary about the events leading to his acceptance of the offer, and to judge from his wife's letters, even she was not aware of the details of the impending appointment until after everything had been arranged. Nevertheless, the fact that a man as careful as Morrison about money, who had finally decided to marry and assume greater financial responsibilities, should have abandoned suddenly and almost impulsively a good position without some guarantee of future security, seems to suggest that he probably had had prospects of employment with the Chinese Government. Certainly this was the feeling of his enemy and detractor, J. O. P. Bland, who said when writing to Chirol, an ally against their common adversary, that 'Morrison ought not to have suppressed the fact that he must at least have been hoping to get his Chinese appointment when he wrote [to Buckle] to express his intention of retiring [from *The Times*]'. 'The spontaneous invitation of the Chinese people', of which Ts'ai T'ing-kan wrote in the letter which opens this volume, had indeed been preceded by rather businesslike negotiations.

Morrison's appointment was widely reported. The man who for so long had made *The Times* famous for its Chinese news suddenly became himself headline news and the subject of comment. A leading German newspaper suggested that his appointment was a victory for England in China. In fact, however, the British Government had had no hand in his appointment, although the British Foreign Secretary, Sir Edward Grey, expressed his satisfaction to Morrison and made a point of seeing him when he returned to England.

Hopes for great things to come from Morrison's appointment were evident in articles which appeared in various magazines and newspapers. Morrison was openly spoken of in such terms as 'the man at the helm', 'pilot', and 'the man to lead China to her salvation'. The cover of the *Illustrated London News* (31 August 1912) featured an early photo-montage in which the head of Morrison was made to replace that of the figure standing behind the seated Chinese President, Yüan Shih-k'ai, offering him advice, implying that Morrison was now the power behind the new ruler in China.

Morrison himself seemed also to be rather confident of the good he could do for China in his new position. During his stay in England before taking up his appointment he embarked on his first public relations job for his new employer through interviews and writings, and at the same time tried to help China free herself from the bondage of the international financial consortium. Though he only partly succeeded in his first mission and completely failed in the second, the aura which his new fame brought him attracted a host of suppliants, some known to him and some not, asking for jobs and offering assistance of all kinds. Men like Sir Hiram Maxim, of 'rapid-firing gun' fame, by then in his early seventies, and another, a veteran general of the Afghan War, equally advanced in age, offered their services to help rejuvenate the old country, while the former Chief Justice of Hong Kong went so far as to threaten legal action in an attempt to compel the new Chinese government to employ him. Manufacturing and trading firms offered Morrison bribes and commissions for business openings. There was even an Englishman, William Ming, who was deluded into thinking himself a descendant of the Ming Dynasty overthrown by the Manchus 267 years before and sought Morrison's help in establishing a claim to the Chinese Throne. The bulk of such correspondence heralds the phenomenon of the post-1949 years, when for both her critics and her supporters, China became a source of livelihood. We have left out most of the congratulatory and begging letters, though they are by no means lacking in interest, being evidence both of Morrison's stature amongst his contemporaries and of how China appeared to many in the aftermath of the 1911 Revolution.

531. From Ts'ai T'ing-kan[1]

[Peking] 2 August 1912

My dear Dr Morrison,

Herewith the Document. It is neither an Agreement nor yet a Contract nor yet a Compact. It is a free and spontaneous invitation from the Government and People of the Chinese Republic to you who has kindly signified his consent and approval by the attachment of his signature. It is the most honourable invitation ever extended by China to any foreign gentleman and expressed in the most courteous language possible as shown by the characters.[2]

The President[3] sends you his best wishes.

Yours sincerely
Tsai Ting Kan

[1] Ts'ai T'ing-kan (1861–1935), at this time Yüan Shih-k'ai's English secretary and interpreter. He was one of the first group of Chinese students aged between 12 and 14 selected in 1872 to study in America where, in the first comprehensive programme of its kind, they were to spend twelve years going through primary school, high school and university, but whose stay was cut short by a change of government policy after nine years, and Ts'ai completed his studies at the Naval College at Taku near Tientsin upon his return to China. The outbreak of the First Sino-Japanese War (1894–5) found him commanding a squadron of torpedo boats which took part in the Battle of Weihaiwei, having serving under him Li Yüan-hung (q.v.), the future reluctant leader of the Wuchang Uprising and the first Republican Vice-President. A departmental head in the Ministry of the Navy at the outbreak of the Revolution in 1911, he entered the service of Yüan Shih-k'ai upon Yüan's accession to power, and in his vaguely defined role of confidential secretary he became in fact Yüan's Liaison Officer-at-Large with foreigners of all kinds, including diplomats. Because of his earlier connection with Li Yüan-hung, Ts'ai became Yüan's emissary to the revolutionaries in Wuchang after a provisional revolutionary government was set up there under Li. Morrison and Ts'ai T'ing-kan, who knew one another before 1911, came to be on very close terms at the outbreak of the Revolution when Ts'ai became one of Morrison's main sources of information on Palace and Government politics, and Morrison the vehicle of what Yüan Shih-k'ai, through Ts'ai T'ing-kan, sought to disseminate. It was largely due to Ts'ai's influence that Morrison was appointed Political Adviser. The correspondence between Ts'ai T'ing-kan and Morrison, sometimes amounting to several exchanges daily, is among the most voluminous in the Morrison papers. For his services to Yüan Shih-k'ai, Ts'ai T'ing-kan was rewarded with a Vice-Admiralship and in September 1913 was appointed Deputy Director-General of the Shui-wu ch'u, or Board of Revenue, of which he became Director-General in 1924, holding the post until January 1927. He also served briefly, from July to October 1926, as Foreign Minister. Something of a hand-maiden in the Yüan Shih-k'ai administration, Ts'ai played no significant role in Chinese politics after Yüan's death.

[2] The two characters in the original letter, *p'ing-jen* (see glossary), mean appointment by invitation.

[3] Yüan Shih-k'ai (1859–1916), the last Imperial Chancellor of the Manchu Dynasty. Some highlights of the culminating years of his career may be glimpsed in the pages of these volumes. He became Provisional President of the Chinese Republic on 10 March 1912 as a result of the compromise reached between himself and the revolutionaries under Sun Yat-sen. It was not however until 6 October of the following year that he was formally

Enclosure to Letter No. 531

This Agreement, made between the Government of the Republic of China, of the one part, and Dr. George Ernest Morrison, of the other part, Witnesseth as follows:

1. The Government of the Republic of China hereby engages the services of Dr. G. E. Morrison as Political Adviser to the President of the Republic of China, the appointment to be for a term of Five years, commencing from the date on which Dr. Morrison reports his arrival in Peking, on his return from Europe in the month of October next.

2. The Government of the Republic of China will pay to Dr. Morrison a salary of £3500 per annum, together with a house allowance of £250 per annum, and an allowance for a confidential secretary of £200 per annum, amounting in all to a sum of £3950 per annum, which shall be paid monthly by the Ministry of Finance into the account of Dr. G. E. Morrison with the Hongkong and Shanghai Banking Corporation in Peking at the current rate of exchange.

3. The Government of the Republic of China will provide Dr. G. E. Morrison at its own expense with the services of a competent Chinese translator.

4. The Government of the Republic of China will pay to Dr. G. E. Morrison the sum of £100 for his travelling expenses from England to Peking on taking up his appointment, and will pay to him a like sum for the expenses of his return journey on the full termination of his contract. The Government of the Republic of China will further provide Dr. G. E. Morrison with his travelling expenses should it have occasion to send him on any special mission.

5. Dr. G. E. Morrison wll be entitled to two months' leave of absence every year on full pay, to be taken at a time mutually convenient.

Signed between the Honourable Mr. Chao Ping-chün,[1] Secretary of State

---

elected President, though the distinction between the provisional and the substantive posts was of theoretical rather than practical significance to Yüan and his supporters, as indeed it was to his opponents.

[1] Chao Ping-chün (d. 1914), at this time Minister of the Interior (March 1912 – July 1913) was a fellow provincial and one of the staunchest supporters of Yüan Shih-k'ai, having served as Police Commissioner in Tientsin when Yüan was Viceroy of Chihli (1901–7). Removed from his post of Vice-Minister of the Interior (1905–9) on the dismissal of Yüan Shih-k'ai, he returned as Minister of the same portfolio upon Yüan Shih-k'ai's being recalled to form what turned out to be the last Imperial Cabinet. With the establishment of the Republic, Chao Ping-chün became the first Republican Minister of the Interior in the T'ang Shao-yi (q.v.) Cabinet (March–June 1912), on Yüan's nomination. He held the same post under Lu Cheng-hsiang (q.v.) who succeeded T'ang as Prime Minister in June 1912, and three weeks after the signing of Morrison's contract Chao became first Acting Prime Minister (20 August 1912) and then Prime Minister (9 September 1912), upon Lu's resignation. As Minister of the Interior he was responsible for many repressive measures against revolutionaries and revolutionary suspects, a policy culminating in the murder of Sung Chiao-jen (q.v.) on 20 March the following year, in which

for the Interior, for and on behalf of the Government of the Republic of China, and the said Dr. George Ernest Morrison, this first day of August of the First year of the Republic of China, One thousand nine hundred and twelve.

532. From Sahara Tokusuke[1]

Shanghai 3 August 1912

Dear Dr Morrison,

So after all you have accepted the post of an adviser to Chinese Republic. I don't know whether I have to congratulate you or not. But I know perfectly well that your responsibility is very great. I hope you will be really good adviser to push China to a proper course holding the propeller running properly. China is just like a *Titanic* confronting many iceburg.[2] I saw Dr. Iyenaga[3] the other day and I heard your very optimistic view on China.[4]

Chao was found to be directly involved. In the face of an outcry for his dismissal, he was allowed to resign, but Yüan made him instead *Tutu* of Chihli, in which post he died suddenly in February 1914. It was rumoured that he had been poisoned at Yüan Shih-k'ai's instigation.

[1] Sahara Tokusuke (1874-1932), Japanese journalist, at this time Editor of the *Shanghai Mercury*. He first went to China in 1900 as correspondent of the Tokyo *Jiji Shimpo*, and remained in Shanghai with the *Shanghai Mercury* until 1926. During his long sojourn in this Chinese city, he served not only as the eyes and ears of the Japanese authorities but also as their unofficial spokesman, and was actively engaged in furthering Japanese interests there. In 1926 he became Director of the Japanese organ in Manchuria, the *Shengching shih-pao* of Mukden, while working concurrently for the South Manchurian Railway Company. He twice represented Japan at conferences held by the Institute of Pacific Relations and was a defender of Japanese aggression in Manchuria.
[2] On the night of 14 April 1912 the White Star liner *Titanic*, then the largest and most luxurious afloat, sank with 1,513 of her passengers after striking an iceberg off Newfoundland while on her maiden voyage to New York.
[3] Iyenaga Toyokichi (1862-1936), Japanese publicist, who, to quote from his visiting card, was 'Professorial Lecturer in the University of Chicago'. He went to America in his early youth and studied law there. Later he also taught for a time at Columbia University. Seemingly a man of considerable eloquence, he spoke frequently in the cause of his country, defending in particular Japan's position in China to the American public. He was at this time on a visit to China and saw Morrison while in Peking. He was drowned in December 1936 while fishing in Lake Oneida (New York).
[4] Morrison's optimism was also noted and commented upon by many of his friends. Writing on 8 August 1912 to Sir Ernest Satow (q.v.), the former British Minister in Peking (1901-6), Dr Douglas Gray (q.v.), the physician to the British Legation in Peking, said, 'You will have noted Dr. Morrison's appointment as political adviser to the President. He gets £5,000 a year for five years, and allowance for two secretaries and house. He is quite the most optimistic foreigner out here as to the future course of events. It will be interesting to see how he gets on as a servant instead of as hitherto an independent unbiased observer who every now and then gave Yüan the benefit of his reflections.'

I am quite on the side of Dr. Iyenaga rather than yours. The most important thing for China at the present moment is that China should wake up to see how hopeless a condition she is in and to try to get out of that condition. In Japan we have done everything to place us to an equal footing with European nation for which many years hard works were involved and one leg of Count Okuma even![1] For China her tasks are more grave than those of Japan. It is really a very stupendously enormous task to do. And you are at her helm anyhow – so far you were a critic but you are now an actor on the stage or behind the scene. I hope you will succeed in your responsible task. So far I am concerned I am quite contented to be a fair critic and a recorder of facts. When the Republic will be recognized by the Powers I don't know but some of the Chinese newspapers in Shanghai has prophesized that your appointment as an adviser will lead to the recognition.[2] If not you will not be respected. The Tungmeng hui[3] people are simply trying to issue newspapers and so on. However, so far as their organs in Shanghai are concerned I do not place much credit on them. Rather their unofficial organs are much better that their official organ the *Ming Kuosinwan*.[4] As my family is away in

[1] Ōkuma Shigenobu (1838–1922), a leading Japanese politician in the late 19th and early 20th centuries. He was the founder and for many years the leader of the Rikken Kaishintō (Constitutional Progressive Party, better known by its shorter name, Progressive Party) one of the main political parties in modern Japan, and founder of the Tokyo Semmon Gakkō, which later became Waseda University. He held many important Cabinet posts from the time he first became Finance Minister in 1869, including two terms as Prime Minister, in 1898 and from 1914 to 1916. It was during the latter ministry that the famous Twenty-One Demands were presented to China. At the time of the incident (1889) to which Sahara here refers, Ōkuma was Foreign Minister (1888–9) in the Cabinet of Kuroda Kiyotaka (1840–1900). He lost a leg in an assassination attempt during the wave of public resentment at the revised treaties which he had concluded shortly before with various powers. Although a great improvement on former treaties, these provided for the appointment of foreign judges in Japan and were considered by many Japanese to be humiliating to their country. He was nevertheless held by others to be a patriot for having won back for Japan equality with the foreign Powers through these treaties.

[2] The Powers did not recognise the new Republic until May 1913 when the United States and Mexico led the way on 2 May, closely followed by Cuba on 4 May and Peru on 5 May. But it was not until 6 October 1913, following the election of Yüan Shih-k'ai as President, that other Powers followed suit. On that day Japan, Great Britain, Germany, France, Sweden, Belgium, Russia, Portugal, Holland, Austria, Italy and Denmark gave their recognition.

[3] The T'ung-meng hui, or Alliance Society, was the revolutionary party formed by Sun Yat-sen in Tokyo in July 1905, amalgamating the diverse revolutionary groups which had sprung up among Chinese students in Japan. As the organisation of the coordinated revolutionary forces, the T'ung-meng hui was responsible for the revolutionary activities which culminated in the Wuchang Uprising on 10 October 1911. Later, in August 1912, the T'ung-meng hui was merged with three other political parties to form the Kuomintang, a forerunner of the Chungkuo Kuomintang or Nationalist Party, which came into being on 10 October 1919 and assumed power in Nanking in 1927.

[4] *Min-kuo hsin-wen*, a Chinese language daily, printed in Shanghai.

Japan I am quite alone here and I may go up to Peking one of these days to see you personally to be more well informed than I am today.

With the kindest regards

Yours sincerely
T. Sahara

533. From W. H. Donald[1]

Shanghai 4 August [1912]

My Dear Doctor,

I am sorry I did not reply to your letter of the 20th ult. at once. There were certain moves going on here which I wanted you to try and counteract in Peking. I delayed writing (not expecting you to be leaving) to see them further develop before I fired off – and now, you are out of the capital.[2] It came to my knowledge some time ago that the Tung Ming-hui, with the full consent and approval of that pseudo-patriot, Sun Yat Sen,[3] were preparing

---

[1] William Henry Donald (1875–1946), an Australian journalist who went to Hong Kong in 1903 after having worked with newspapers in Sydney and Melbourne. He first joined the *China Mail*, of which he became Managing Director in 1906. It was in Hong Kong that Morrison made his acquaintance, and the two became firm friends. Later he became the correspondent of the *New York Herald* in China, and editor of the *Far Eastern Review*, which he had helped to found, but he resigned from the latter journal in 1920 because, under the influence of its proprietor, George Bronson Rea, it had adopted a pro-Japanese policy. Donald had been actively involved in Chinese politics from the very inception of his journalistic career in China. He was the vehicle by which the real version of Japan's Twenty-One Demands of 1915 was made known. As Director (1920–8) of the Bureau of Economic Information, which he organised at the invitation of the Chinese Government, he did much to counter the clamour for the international control of China. In 1928 he became adviser to General Chang Hsüeh-liang (q.v.), popularly known as the Young Marshal, who succeeded his father, Chang Tso-lin (q.v.), as the overlord of Manchuria in that year, and in 1934 adviser to Chiang Kai-shek (1887–1975). Because of these relations he played a part in securing the release of Chiang Kai-shek when Chiang was imprisoned by Chang Hsüeh-liang in what has become known as the 'Sian Incident' in December 1936. Donald remained in China until 1940 and was captured by the Japanese at Manila in 1941, remaining a prisoner until 1945. He died shortly after his return to China in November 1946. The allegation that he had drafted for Sun Yat-sen (q.v.) the first Republican Manifesto, and his association with Chiang Kai-shek in the 1930s as well as his defence of China against Japanese aggression, lent substance to the belief that Donald was a sympathiser and supporter of the Chinese Revolution. In his correspondence with Morrison, however, Donald is shown to have nourished a more vehement hostility towards the revolutionaries in these early years than is generally realised.

[2] Morrison left Peking for London on 6 August 1912, and returned to the Chinese capital early in October the same year.

[3] Sun Yat-sen (or Sun Wen) (1866–1925), Chinese revolutionary leader, revered as the 'Father of the Chinese Republic' since the party he founded came into power in 1928. He was elected Provisional President of the Republic on 29 December 1911, but resigned the post in favour of Yüan Shih-k'ai following the compromise which brought to an end the Manchu Dynasty. He remained however the leader of the revolutionary party and his struggle with Yüan Shih-k'ai appears intermittently throughout the pages of this volume.

to put him up for the Presidency at the forthcoming election. Sun Yat Sen poses as a man who has effaced himself for the sake of the country. Of course, I happen to know what that alleged self-effacement meant, since I was in the confidence of the crowd at the time that the deal was arranged to permit Yuan to have the Presidency. But I did not think the Tung Ming-hui would show their hand as early as they did. Their tactics have prevented any progress, and they have acted from the very first to embarrass Yüan Shih-kai. But it is no use going over all this to you. You know. The point I wish to bring out is this: That whilst Sun Yat Sen gives it out to the world that he is done with politics and is devoting his energies to the development of the natural resources – and whilst he also tries to persuade Peking that he is similarly employed – he is conspiring here with his bottle-washer coterie to become the President – that is the first President elected according to the Constitution – if there will be such a thing. In previous letters I tried to show you – perhaps in a hurried and ineffective way – that Sun is not the man he is alleged to be. You must know that he has no following of weighty people here. The men who ran the machine of revolution will have nothing to do with him. They did not even call on him. Never do mature men associate with him. The Cantonese guild will have nothing to do with him. Always he is surrounded by a crowd of half-baked, youthful rag-tag and bob-tail politicians (?). Save the mark! Sun has no brains to develop anything of a problem by himself. He is the willing instrument in the hands of a crowd of wire-pullers who have nothing to lose and everything to gain. They have Sun and Huang Hsin[1] in a house in Yates Road[2] and every day they congregate and plot and plan to oust Yuan. Well, as I told you before, they ultimately acquired the remains of the *China Gazette* for some $4,500, or Taels, I forget which. A few days before the deal was announced I said to Sun: 'I hear you have bought the *China Gazette*, or at least the Tung

---

[1] Huang Hsing (1874–1916), Chinese revolutionary leader educated in Japan. It was in the Japanese capital in 1903 that he founded the revolutionary society, the Hua-ch'ing hui (Society for the Revival of China) which merged in 1905 with Sun Yat-sen's organisation to become the T'ung-meng hui (Alliance Society). He was the organiser of the abortive uprising in Canton on 27 April 1911, the most daring undertaking by the revolutionaries before the uprising at Wuchang six months later. He became the Commander-in-Chief of the Republican forces in the Wuchang area after the October outbreak, and was made Minister of War, then the most important portfolio, and Chief of Staff, in the Provisional Government set up under Sun Yat-sen in Nanking in 1912. When the compromise was reached with Yüan Shih-k'ai by which the seat of government was moved from Nanking to Peking, Huang served briefly as Resident General in Nanking. An advocate of dealing with Yüan Shih-k'ai by constitutional rather than military means, his role in what has become known as the 'Second Revolution' (July–September 1913), was rather nominal, and his political life came to an end in 1914 when he went from Japan to the United States, where for two years he was cut off from the mainstream of Chinese politics. He died soon after his return to China in October 1916.

[2] A street in what was known as the Western Suburbs of Shanghai, then within the International Settlement.

Ming-hui has bought it.' 'No', replied Sun with a hesitating sort of smile, 'Ma Soo has bought it!' Ma Soo was a clerk in the China Merchants godown – then became private secretary to Sun at Nanking. He is a cross between a Frenchman and a Chinese, and once spelt his name Marceau. I looked Sun so steadily in the eye that the timid smile developed into a broad grin when I told him that he might palm that story off on others, but it would not do for me. The *China Gazette* was, of course, bought with the object of advancing the plans of those desirous of making Sun President. That was told me early after the purchase by Ma Soo himself (in confidence of course) and was bought to advance the party – despite the fact that Ma Soo had strenuously denied such a thing in the *North China Daily News* and the *China Press*. Why is the *North China* such a damned flabby paper as to be gulled by such an impossible squib as this Ma Soo? Well, Ma Soo came to me and tried to get me to assist him to run the paper, and to make a story short I told him I would not have anything to do with the rag if he gave me Taels 2,000 per month. Instead, I had been carrying on a campaign to down the Tung Ming-hui, through the *Shanghai Times*. That campaign started a few days before Sun landed in Shanghai from Kwangtung. I then tried to influence the Canton Guild to approach Sun as a body and urge him to suppress himself if he was really patriotic, and to permit the country to get upon its feet under Yuan. Well, they could not do that as a body but several agreed to individually impress that view upon Sun. But I thirsted to have a public whack at the Tung Ming-hui, and chance came my way when O'Shea,[1] the proprietor of the *Shanghai Times*, fell ill. He asked Pratt[2] to take over the editorial writing, and you can judge that I soon had heaps of subjects for Pratt. I set him after the Tung Ming-hui's scalp hot and strong, and we have been after it ever since. I do not know whether you have seen the [*Shanghai*] *Times* of late, but if not some day you might out of curiosity look a file over. We took the gloves off entirely – leastwise I kept mine on in the background and fired Pratt on. As he is of the same opinion as myself he fell readily to work, and still we go on.

Some few weeks ago, when the Tung Ming-hui made such a hopeless muddle of things in Peking and generally became discredited the party here had many secret meetings at which they were compelled to admit that the end was in sight unless they could devise some scheme to save their face and regain control. The brilliant thought came to someone that they should secure influence over all political parties to dissolve and reform as one party, and scarcely had the advantageous side of this presented itself to them than

[1] John O'Shea (b. 1869) an Irish journalist who began working in Shanghai in 1900 as a reporter for the *Shanghai Mercury*. In 1906 he became the Editor of the *Shanghai Times* and its owner in 1911.
Frederick Lionel Pratt (b. 1872), an Australian journalist, at this time the Editor of the *Shanghai Recorder*. He had worked in Hong Kong for many years for the *China Mail* and the *Hongkong Telegraph* before going to China in 1911.

Sun Yat Sen and Huang Hsin went to Wen Tsung Yao's[1] house (Wen had not even called on them) and asked his advice, etc. etc. They unfolded their scheme to Wen and eventually, putting their cards upon the table, urged him to try and get his (Wen's) party to dissolve. As soon as they had gone Wen came to see me and I urged him for all I was worth to give the Tung Ming-hui a wide berth and let them go to blazes. I pointed out the many reasons why the Tung Ming-hui needed some excuse to abolish itself, *but not its policy*, and, after pointing out that the party merely wanted to have all the others in its hands, etc., etc., Wen was convinced and went away. He let the whole matter lie for a week: he informed the leaders of his party, of course, what Sun and Huang were up to, but he did not call a meeting till a week had elapsed from the time of Sun's visit. At that meeting he advanced the arguments against the Tung Ming-hui, and the result was that the leaders declined the suggestion of the Tung Ming-hui and notified them that if the Tung crowd wished to dissolve they could do so and any 'respectable' members of the party might be permitted to join the other one.[2]

The Tung Ming-hui failed in its scheme, and then continued withdrawing its people from Cabinet office,[3] etc. Then they got the *China Gazette*, which

[1] Wen Tsung-yao (born 1876), Chinese Imperial official and Republican politician. Educated in America, he had served, after his return to China in 1903, as Secretary and Commissioner of Foreign Affairs to the Viceroy of Liangkwang at Canton, and later assisted T'ang Shao-yi in the negotiations with the British Government in India regarding Tibet. When the peace conference between the revolutionaries and the Manchu Government under Yüan Shih-k'ai was convened in Shanghai towards the end of 1911, he was a delegate representing the republicans of the south, and was appointed Foreign Affairs Commissioner in Shanghai by the Provisional Government in 1912. In the same year he became the co-founder, together with Ts'en Ch'un-hsüan (q.v.), of the Kuomin kungtang. He supported Ts'en's anti-Yüan stand, and became Director of the Foreign Affairs Bureau in the anti-monarchist military government set up under the leadership of Ts'en in Chaoch'ing, Kwangtung, on 1 May 1916. When T'ang Shao-yi resigned as the chief delegate of the southern republicans to the peace conference held in Shanghai in 1919 Wen was appointed to succeed him, but he soon retired from active politics after the failure of the Conference and lived in political obscurity until 1938, when he re-emerged to become President of the Legislative Council in the puppet government sponsored by the Japanese occupation army in Nanking under Liang Hung-chih (1883–1946). Two years later, in March 1940, when the so-called National Government was established in Nanking under Wang Ching-wei (1883–1944), amalgamating the hitherto puppet governments of the north and the south, Wen Tsung-yao became President of the Judicial Council.

[2] In the event, Wen's party, the Kuo-min kung-tang, did merge with the T'ung-meng hui to form the Kuomintang in January the following year, and Wen was elected one of the Directors of the new Party.

[3] The four T'ung-meng hui ministers in the first Republican cabinet under T'ang Shao-yi were Wang Ch'ung-hui (Justice), Ts'ai Yüan-p'ei (Education), Sung Chiao-jen (Agriculture and Forestry) and Wang Cheng-t'ing (q.v.) (acting for Ch'en Ch'i-mei (q.v.)) (Industry and Commerce). Following the resignation of the Prime Minister, T'ang Shao-yi, on 17 June 1912, Ch'en and Wang Ch'ung-hui submitted their resignation on 21 June, and Ts'ai, Sung and Wang Cheng-t'ing submitted theirs the next day.

they call the *China Republican*, and set out upon their campaign to glorify Sun and denounce Yuan. [...] When the paper came out the other local papers slobbered a bit, but the [Shanghai] *Times* did not. On the day following the issue of the *Republican*, the [Shanghai] *Times*, in an article referring to your appointment (enclosed) had a kick at the Tung Ming-hui, but the *Republican* editor (Ma Soo) did not notice it. But no reference was made to the advent of the paper at all, for as I knew what the policy was to be I decided to hold back from 'wishing it well' despite the tone of its opening leader, and to let fly at it later. The chance came sooner than I expected. I did not think the fools would display their hand so quickly – but so fired was the blood of the gang to get Yuan by the throat that they could not restrain themselves. They set out to defame him in the second leader, and continued in the third, and maybe the game will go on in the fourth. Well, in yesterday's issue they republished comments from the various papers and under the caption of the *Shanghai Times* put a great query mark. In the meantime I inspired Pratt to open out on them. As soon as I saw their second editorial I told Pratt to take the gloves off and denounce them, and he was in the middle of the article for Monday's paper, when we saw Saturday evening's issue with the query mark. I told him to use the same sort of mark as the caption for his editorial. He did so and I will enclose the article if I can catch this mail with it. If not I will post it next mail.[1]

Also I am having the articles translated from the *Republican* to be sent to the President at Peking by the *Tutu* of Chekiang.[2] Something has got to be done to squelch the Tung Ming-hui. I do not know your opinion, but you can see my feelings through this letter. I think Sun Yat Sen is an imposter – he, I must hasten to add, has never done anything to me, and we are good friends. But politically I won't stand for his imbecility, his downright wickedness, and his attempt to bluff the foreigners as well as the Chinese. He worked the opposition to the foreign loan merely as a political weapon to down Yuan, and his gang will do anything to using the long steel blade, or the bomb, to accomplish the same purpose.[3] They have to be held up; and

---

[1] None of the enclosures or articles referred to in this letter has been found.

[2] Chu Jui (1883–1916), Chinese soldier, leader of the Chekiang revolutionary forces that participated in the taking of Nanking from the Imperial forces in 1911. He became *Tutu*, or Military Governor, of Chekiang in July 1912, holding the post until April 1916, when he fled upon the declaration of the independence of the province by the republican forces, in opposition to Yüan Shih-k'ai's monarchical scheme. He also served concurrently as Civil Governor of Chekiang from July 1912 to September 1913.

[3] The republicans under Sun Yat-sen were strongly opposed to the loan which the Yüan Shih-k'ai government was then negotiating with foreign banks. They considered that the money thus secured would greatly strengthen the position of the Peking Government which was increasingly departing from the understanding reached between themselves and Yüan. The loan eventually obtained was strongly condemned by the Kuomintang-dominated Parliament, for having been concluded without its consent. This aggravated

for a long time I have been doing my little best, with the efficient aid of Pratt, to wring their withers. The amateur editor of the *Republican* who wishes to know what the [*Shanghai*] *Times* thinks of his production will know in the morning, and if he opens out in reply you will see the most glorious fight that has been witnessed since the days of the *Eatenswill Gazette*.[1] Now is the time to subscribe – a front seat before the show starts! But, we are enjoying it, as you may imagine, and if we cannot knock the arguments of the Tung Ming-hui endwise I will chuck up the game and go and crack stones.

Doctor, the whole damned thing is a wicked scandal. Sun Yat Sen, Huang Hsin, *et hoc*, ought to be booted neck and crop out of this Settlement and this country. Their game is to wreck the whole darned shooting match, and were it not for the fact that I am convinced that Sun is daily losing ground I would be apprehensive. I am now merely enjoying the fun of turning the Tung Ming-hui out of business, if I can, with the aid of Pratt and the S[*hanghai*] *Times* – a feeble hope.

You note their efforts in the papers herewith to defame Yuan, the man the leader of the Tung Ming-hui (S.Y.S.) declared that he would support as a loyal Chinaman. Why, Sun Yat Sen is a mere pitiful, uneducated, incapable charlatan! I say all that, too, simply because he exhibits his imbecility every time he opens his mouth. Believe me when I tell you I have no personal grudge against Sun, but when I see what his policy is doing to retard this splendid country, it makes my blood boil.

But enough! I wired you congratulations on behalf of myself and Pratt, Doctor, when we saw it announced that a definite offer had come to you. Pratt made some remarks in the [*Shanghai*] *Times*, and also I rushed round to get a picture of you for the *Far Eastern Review* July number – just publishing, so we will have you in the August number with a nice send off. Doctor – I am mighty glad. Words are useless to indicate what I feel.

The *N.C.D.N.* [*North China Daily News*] had a nice article, which I will enclose if I can find it.[2] I hope this does not bore you – but I wish you could have been in Peking just now to say a few words to the President on the

---

the friction between the north and south that finally led to the outbreak of the so-called 'Second Revolution' in July the following year, and to the dissolution of Parliament by Yüan Shih-k'ai.

1 An allusion to an episode in Charles Dickens' *Pickwick Papers* – an election fight between two political parties, the Blues and the Buffs, each with its organ, the *Eatanswill Gazette* and the *Eatanswill Independent*. The rival journals indulged in invectives of a scurrilous nature to smear each other, and the battle culminated in physical blows by the opposing editors in the local inn. In 1907 a journal devoted to Pickwickian humour, with the name *Eatanswill Gazette*, was published by the Eatanswill Club in Sudbury, Suffolk, the town which was thought to have been the model for Eatanswill. It ran to only four issues, from March 1907 to January 1908.

2 Not found.

subject of the gang here. However, we will try and capsize them ere you get back. I send best wishes for a lively holiday, and for a good time in the future.

Very sincerely
Donald W.H.

This letter is rushed off as fast as the machine can go to get the mail. Excuse incoherency. My regards to Miss Robin[1] if you see her.

534. From G. E. Buckle[2]

Personal　　　　　　　　　　　　　　　　　　　*The Times* 6 August 1912

My dear Morrison,

I do not know whether to congratulate you or not on the important news which you send me, and which reached us by cable a day or two before. As you have accepted Yuan Shih-kai's offer, I can only hope and trust that the result may answer your expectations. The salary and allowances are very handsome; and even if you only hold the post a short time it may well be worth your while to make the experiment. But you will remember that in a walk over Firle Beacon near Lewes[3] we discussed a similar offer or suggestion made to you by the Imperial Government, and I ventured to give you some reasons why you should pause before accepting. The change of constitution in China has not altered my views. But I earnestly hope that the event may prove that my views are entirely erroneous and unfounded, as they well may be, since you know China well at first hand, and *I* have merely a smattering of information at second hand.

I have some news for you in return for yours. I have resigned the Editorship, and shall be just leaving the office when this letter reaches you. I have served *The Times* for 32 years, 28½ as Editor, and I have reached the age at or about which all my predecessors, Barnes, Delane and Chenery[4] broke down and died. I begin to feel the strain more than I did, and I think it will be much better for the paper as well as for my health that a younger man should hand on the torch. My successor will be Geoffrey Robinson – an

---

[1] Jennie Wark Robin (1889–1923), whom Morrison was to marry three weeks later in England, had been his secretary since March 1911.

[2] George Earle Buckle (1854–1935), British journalist and author, Editor of *The Times* from 1884 to 1912. A Fellow of All Souls College, Oxford, he devoted himself in his retirement to scholarly pursuits, completing the *Life of Benjamin Disraeli* begun by his colleague, W. F. Monypenny (q.v.). He was also an editor of the letters of Queen Victoria.

[3] In his Diary for 6 August 1910, precisely two years to the day before this letter was written, Morrison recorded having taken a walk with Buckle, but merely commented, 'Very interesting talk,' without giving any details.

[4] All three were former Editors of *The Times*, Thomas Barnes (1785–1841) from 1817 to 1841, John Delane (1817–79) from 1841 to 1877, and Thomas Chenery (1826–84), Buckle's immediate predecessor, from 1877 to 1884.

admirable appointment.[1] I don't know whether you know him. He succeeded Monypenny[2] as Editor of the *J[ohannes]berg Star*, and was for some years *The Times* Correspondent in South Africa. For a year and a half he has been one of my assistants in the office, where he is both popular and respected. He is 37 years old – an Eton and Oxford man, and (like me) a Fellow of All Souls. He has been in the Colonial Office, and was for several years Milner's[3] Private Secretary in South Africa. He is very keen and alert, but has a cool head and good judgement. The traditions of the paper are safe with him.

It is a big wrench for me, but I avert my gaze from the past and look forward to a halfyear's holiday with my wife before thinking of finding other work. We sail for South Africa on Sept. 20th, and shall probably return in the spring by the East Coast, and take Italy on the way home. It sounds too good to be true.

So you see our pleasant association of many years in the service of *The Times* would have been broken on one side if it had not been on the other. I hope however that we may occasionally meet and exchange views, when the business of the Chinese Govt. or your pleasure brings you to London.

With all good wishes for your great venture, I am

Yours sincerely
G. E. Buckle

535. From G. D. Gray[4]

Kaifeng fu [Honan] 7 August 1912

My dear Morrison,

I had hoped to be back in Peking ere this but have yielded to the very urgent wishes of the *Tutuh*[5] to stay longer – for a few days but I will be back

[1] Geoffrey Robinson (1874–1944), also known by the name Dawson which he adopted in 1917, British journalist. He was selected by Northcliffe to succeed G. E. Buckle as Editor of *The Times* in 1912, a post he held until 1919, and again from 1922 to 1941. Previously he had served in the British Colonial Office from 1898 to 1901 when he became Private Secretary to Lord Milner in South Africa, and had been Editor of the *Johannesburg Star* from 1905 to 1910.

[2] William Flavelle Monypenny (1866–1912), British journalist and author, Assistant Editor of *The Times* from 1894 to 1899, when he was appointed Editor of the *Johannesburg Star*, a post he held with a short interruption until 1905. Commissioned to write the *Life of Benjamin Disraeli*, he died shortly after the appearance of the Second Volume, in November 1912, and the work was completed by G. E. Buckle.

[3] Alfred Milner (1854–1925), 1st Viscount, British colonial official and politician, High Commissioner for South Africa (1897–1905), and concurrently Governor for the Cape of Good Hope (1897–1901) and Governor of the Transvaal and Orange River Colony (1901–5). He later became a member of the War Cabinet (1916–18), Secretary of State for War (1918–19) and Secretary of State for the Colonies (1919–21).

[4] Following the shooting incident described in this letter and the scandal it aroused, Dr George Douglas Gray, physician to the British Legation in Peking (1902–26), was invited by the Chinese Government to go to Kaifeng-fu, the capital of Honan Province, to attend to the members of the Provincial Assembly wounded in the incident.

[5] Chang Chen-fang (b. 1865), Chinese Republican politician, *Tutu* of Honan (1912–14). He was a relative and a strong supporter of Yüan Shih-k'ai. The incident here described was

by the end of the week. I was a fool not to take your advice and name a big figure. C. F. Hsü the *Tutuh*'s Secretary came to me last night and said money was no object if I would only stay as the Deputies had been at the *Tutuh* to retain me for a month or more! This affair was a most curious one. The assembly was in session and a visit from the *Tutuh* was expected that day. He however was 'ill' and could not keep his promise but instead of him there appeared 5 or 6 men who walked in (the doors being all open as the day was hot) and at once began firing revolvers right and left wounding ten deputies and making a lot of misses. The assembly at once became blind with fear and bolted out through the opposite doors. Some of them jumped a wall and fell, severely bruising themselves! There were two soldiers on guard at the gate but they let the assailants through thinking they were an advance part of the *Tutuh*'s men. Later, hearing the firing they came up to the room and one got wounded while the other ran away. No one has any idea who the men were beyond thinking they were dismissed soldiers. Yesterday four arrests were made but on no proper grounds of suspicion. I went over the assembly and saw the bullet marks on the wall behind the Speaker's chair so they had evidently tried to get him. Three of the deputies are badly wounded but all are doing well. I find them a most intelligent lot of men who take their work seriously and are keen to discuss political problems. I operated on one man who had a smashed femur; he took the chloroform like a lamb. It was most amusing – the room was packed with deputies all discussing every stage of the proceedings and when the patient became conscious agan they quizzed him in the most amusing way as to what he had been dreaming about. They are all keen to know what the foreigners at Peking think of the political state, what sort of a man the Premier[1] is and if trouble is feared from the soldiers.

---

seen as an attempt by the *Tutu* and his followers to silence the Provincial Assembly, whose members, echoing the protests of the members of the National Assembly in Peking also criticised the loan negotiations Yüan Shih-k'ai was then conducting with the foreign powers. The public outcry against the shooting compelled Yüan to issue a Presidential Decree in which Chang was gently reprimanded. He was, however, removed from his post two years later because of his failure to suppress the activities of Pai Lang, or White Wolf (q.v.), and appointed a member of the newly-founded Political Council, a front organisation for his monarchical plan. Chang also became Governor of the newly-created Bank of Salt Revenue. A staunch monarchist, he was arrested in July 1917 for his part in Chang Hsün's abortive restoration attempt, but was soon pardoned by the Anfu Clique (q.v.) Government under Tuan Ch'i-jui (q.v.).

[1] The Prime Minister at this time was Lu Cheng-hsiang (1871–1949), who had been Foreign Minister in the first Republican cabinet under T'ang Shao-yi. On the departure of T'ang from Peking on 15 June 1912, Lu became Acting Prime Minister, then Prime Minister on 29 June, holding the post until some two weeks after his letter was written, on 22 August 1912. Lu had been repeatedly criticised, both in and outside Parliament, for his lack of knowledge and understanding of conditions in China, because since his first appointment to St Petersburg in 1892, until his recall after the formation of the first Republican cabinet, he had spent 17 out of 20 years abroad, serving among other posts

They don't quite understand the big loan[1] – as far as Honan is concerned they have ample funds to carry on. The harvests have been very good this year, fruit and vegetables are abundant and the people well fed and contented and happy. The soldiers are a scallywag looking lot of men, unkempt and evidently in no high state of discipline: they all have the queue still. I visited the *Tutuh* – a thin sallow man not very intelligent looking. He asked me all about the Ministers (Chinese) at Peking. I told him about your appointment and said I thought it was a fine thing as you knew China well and had visited every province. He said he did not altogether understand the reason of your being appointed! He is not in any close touch with the assembly and the Deputies have not as yet straightened it out in their minds as to why he did not pay his promised visit on the day the shooting took place.

I am being treated *en Prince* here – have a guard of ten soldiers and a fine suite of appartments with a good cook and attendance and free table. They have done the thing in style and I am most comfortable. The missionaries are all away summering. At Cheng Chou it was the same. I think this abandonment of mission work during the summer is a blot against Protestant missionaries when one compares them with Roman Catholics.

[...]

To see the crowded busy streets here, with the people all fat, industrious and happy looking one cannot but feel what a strength China has in her common illiterate working folk, all hard at it cultivating and buying and selling all day long, their minds occupied wth hard unremitting toil which they accept as their natural lot in life and seem to enjoy. Here are no strikes or compulsory Education or Labour parties or Suffragists such as Liberal Britain is now full of.

With salaams

Yours sincerely
Geo. Douglas Gray

---

as Minister to Holland (1905–7) and to Russia (1911). Yet despite his absences abroad, and also because of them, in that he was free from political entanglements, he was generally accepted by the various factions which controlled in turn the government in Peking. His background also enabled him to give a professional stamp to the Foreign Ministry which he headed intermittently between 1912 and 1920, winning for it the undeserved reputation of being a professional rather than a political department, unlike the other departments of the Cabinet, and he was regarded by many as a leader of what came to be known in the politics of those years as the 'Diplomatist Clique'. In 1919, as Foreign Minister, he led the Chinese delegation to the Paris Peace Conference, but resigned his portfolio in the face of criticism upon his return to China in 1920. In 1923, at his own request, he became Chinese Minister to Switzerland where he led the life of leisure he desired, until 1927, the year after the death of his Belgian wife, Bertha Bovy (q.v.). He then entered the monastery of St André in Bruges, Belgium, and died there as a Benedictine monk.

[1] This refers to the loan the Chinese Government was then negotiating with the powers. *See* p. 11 note 3.

536. From W. H. Donald

Shanghai 11 August 1912

My dear Doctor,

By last mail I sent you a hurried letter and several papers. [...] We are continuing the exposure of the Tung Ming-hui. In to-morrow we show how the campaign against Yuan Shih-kai was started and continued, and later we will go into the question of the Tung Ming-hui's standing in the country. I fancy the *Republican* must be squirming to-day on account of its inability to reply. It will squirm more to-morrow.

The exposure is disturbing the Tung Ming-hui, and I think it will compel them to alter their programme, or their procedure. Sun Yat Sen, who had no intention of going to Peking, may now go.[1] They are very sensitive to criticism.

Every one is sick of the way things are going and the sooner you can get back and advise Yuan to lop the heads off all obstructionists the better. What Yuan ought to do is to seize a big stick and [s]wipe the Tung Ming-hui and all its members on the head.

Best wishes for a good time.

Sincerely yours
W. H. Donald

537. From F. H. May[2]

Government House, Hong Kong 11 August 1912

Private

Dear Dr Morrison,

Many thanks for your letter of congratulation. It is with sincere pleasure that I am able to return the compliment by asking you to accept my best congratulations on the distinction you have won. It is a splendid achievement for the critic to be chosen out of the whole world as the trusted adviser. I only hope they will trust you.

The attack upon me has no political significance at all. The man was I am sure crazy although the Doctors who examined him at my instance pronounced him sane. Curiously enough he mixed up Fiji with South Africa

[1] At the invitation of Yüan Shih-k'ai, Sun Yat-sen went to Peking on 24 August 1912 and, as had previously been agreed upon between the two, was duly appointed by Yüan as Director-General of Railways. For the development of these Sun produced a grandiose scheme, blackening the map of China with a net of criss-cross lines, but he was apparently quite oblivious of how it was to be carried out. This scheme, which formed a large part of Sun's ideas for the modernisation of China, was held up to ridicule by many of his contemporaries and was regarded as evidence of his being an unpractical visionary.

[2] Francis Henry (later Sir Henry) May (1860–1922), British colonial official. He was at this time Governor of Hong Kong (1912–19) where he had begun his career as a cadet in 1881. Previously he had been Governor of Fiji and High Commissioner for the Western Pacific (1910–12).

(Fei chau in Cantonese) and thought that I was ex-governor of the Transvaal and had turned his compatriots out of that country.[1]

The situation in the Canton Province is very insecure. The Govt. really has no jurisdiction beyond the City of Canton and its surburbs. They are unable to get in the taxes, and while their expenditure runs to $2,000,000 a month their revenue is little over $1,000,000 a month. The old Manchu Govt. got $40,000,000 a year in revenue from the Province. It follows that the present Govt. is at its wit's end for money. They have attempted to meet their difficulties by an issue of un-guaranteed, unsecured paper to the extent of $18,000,000. This is now at a heavy discount and I really don't know how they can extricate themselves without the help of a loan. I believe that they would accept this even under guarantees of foreign supervision if they dared. But being weak, and indeed powerless beyond the City Walls, they fear the mob. Up to date the soldiery are able to obtain 20 cent pieces, issued by the Canton Mint, in exchange for most of the notes that come into their hands in pay. They are therefore still quiet. But how long this accommodation can be extended to them is doubtful. I have seen the Governor-General[2] and the Treasurer and the Governor General's Secretary. They are a poor lot giving little evidence of physical, moral, or intellectual strength. Unless they accept foreign assistance they can never rule the Canton Province. This Colony's interest is of course against any violent change. Trade is bad enough as things are without another upheaval to kill it altogether. One feels very much moved to help if one only had the opportunity of doing it.

You will have an anxious and busy time in trying to guide things into a right course. If at any time I can assist you please don't hesitate to ask for any help that you think I may be able to give you.

[...]

I hope the Chinese Govt. will have nothing to do with Sir F. Piggott.[3]

---

[1] An assassination attempt was made on May by a Chinese who, apparently misled by the Chinese character 'fei', which was used in both Fei-chi (Fiji) and Fei-chou (South Africa), took the two to be the same place. As May had just completed two years as Governor of Fiji before going to Hong Kong, he was held responsible by his would-be assassin for the misery and injustice which his compatriots were suffering in South Africa.

[2] Chang Ming-ch'i, Chinese Imperial official and Republican politician, Viceroy (or Governor-General) of Liangkwang at Canton since October 1910. He fled together with some of his staff to Hong Kong on 9 November 1911 following the outbreak of revolution in Canton. In October 1913 he re-entered official life serving the Republic under Yüan Shih-k'ai first as Civil Governor of Kwangsi, until July 1915, and then briefly as *Hsün-an-shih* (Governor) of Kwangtung, from July to October 1915.

[3] Sir Francis Taylor Piggott (1852–1925), British judge, Chief Justice of the Supreme Court of Hong Kong (1905–12). He sought unsuccessfully through Morrison to force through an appointment for himself as Adviser to the Chinese Government. The British Government, upon being consulted, recommended through the British Minister in Peking that Piggott should not be so employed. The many letters which Piggott addressed to Morrison, and through him to various members of the Chinese Government, reveal why he was objected to by the British authorities. Author of a number of works mainly based on

He is not a sound lawyer and I question whether he is sound in any sense.

Yours very sincerely
H. May

538. From J. C. Ferguson[1]

Peitaiho [Chihli] 12 August 1912

Dear Dr. Morrison,

You had left Peking before I had a chance to write you from this place to offer you my congratulations on your appointment as Political Adviser to President Yuan. He is said to be very considerate in his treatment of those who serve under him and you are likely to have on this line a comfortable term of years. As to the need for advice it is unlimited and you will not find that the Chinese are slow to take it when it is asked for. The only drawback is that it is often not asked for on questions where one is conscious of being able to do his best, but even in such circumstances, I have always felt that they know their own country best and are able to judge better than a foreigner what is practicable. You may have best wishes for success. If rumour and newspaper items are correct my best fears are also to be realized and you are not to return to Peking alone. So much the better, all of us worried men will say.

Yours sincerely
John C. Ferguson

---

colonial experience, and legal in nature, he also used the pseudonym 'Hope Dawlish' on occasions, as he did with his *Letters on the Chinese Constitution*, published in 1918.

[1] John Calvin Ferguson (1866–1945), an American adventurer with a remarkably long career in successive regimes in China, active for nearly a quarter of a century during the Manchu dynasty and for even longer during the Republican period. Going first to China as a missionary, he soon abandoned his calling and embarked on a career in which he successively and profitably dabbled in education, politics, journalism and art. Taking full advantage of the opportunities which the period of transition in China offered him, he exploited his foreign status by carrying out various small commissions for Chinese officials, thus enabling him to advertise himself widely as an 'adviser'. A successful dealer in curios, serving as middle-man for American collectors, museums and suppliers in China, he posed as an expert in Chinese bronzes and porcelain by lending his name to work done by Chinese scholars. Morrison called him an 'oily blackguard' whenever his name was mentioned, and described him shortly before he received his letter as 'the unctious "adviser" who has enriched himself by doing jackal work for the Chinese and who is the most universally distrusted man I know in China. He affects the possession of knowledge more than most men. Unquestionably he has had the opportunity of learning and of seeing much, but he is essentially untruthful and unscrupulous and thick-skinned as a rhinoceros.' This opinion was greatly reinforced as Morrison came to know Ferguson even better in later years. Ferguson was the recipient of many honours and decorations, including honorary doctorates from Boston University and the University of Southern California.

539. From C. W. Eliot[1]

Asticou, Maine [U.S.A.] 15 August 1912

Dear Dr. Morrison,

I read last evening in my paper that Mr. Rockhill[2] had been invited to become an Adviser on Foreign Affairs for the Chinese Republic; and I had previously read that you had been appointed Political Adviser to the President of the Republic.

I hasten to congratulate China and you on your selection as Political Adviser, and to express the hope that Mr. Rockhill will accept the invitation which has been given him. I remember your saying in your library at Peking that you were sure Mr. Rockhill would accept such an invitation; and I have a confident belief that your prediction will be fulfilled.

When I was in China I had two conversations with Mr. Tong,[3] both of some length, and in both I dealt with the subject of foreign advisers. After

[1] Charles William Eliot (1834-1926), American educationalist, President of Harvard (1869-1910) and a member of the governing body of the Carnegie Foundation. He was on a world tour (1911-12) and visited Morrison while in Peking.

[2] William Woodville Rockhill (1854-1914), American diplomat and scholar. Architect of the famous Open Door policy of the United States towards China, he became in 1905 United States Minister to China (1905-9). He was at the time of this letter Ambassador to Turkey, where he remained until the accession of Woodrow Wilson to the American Presidency the following year. Rockhill became a friend of Morrison when he first went to China in 1901 as the United States Special Envoy in connection with the Boxer Settlement negotiations, and when the Chinese Republic was established in 1912 Morrison suggested to Rockhill that he would be suitable as an adviser to the Chinese Republic. By 1914, however, when Rockhill had managed to persuade Yüan Shih-k'ai to give him an appointment, Morrison considered him so senile that he readily agreed with the then United States Minister to China, Paul Reinsch (q.v.), that it was a 'scandal' that such a man should have been employed. Rockhill died in Honolulu in December 1914, on his way to China from the United States.

[3] T'ang Shao-yi (1860-1938), Chinese Imperial official, provincial Governor and Republican politician, at the time Eliot met him in Peking Prime Minister of the first Republican cabinet. Educated in America, where he was sent by the Chinese Government in 1874, upon his return he joined the service of Yüan Shih-k'ai in Korea, becoming his right-hand man. His political fortunes from then until the advent of the Republic were closely linked with that of Yüan. He served during that period as one of China's chief spokesmen on foreign affairs, and in 1907 was appointed Governor of Fengtien Province. He followed Yüan into temporary political eclipse after 1909, but when Yüan was recalled to become Prime Minister in the Manchu Government after the Wuchang Uprising at the end of 1911, T'ang became his representative in the negotiations with the republicans in the south. It was at this time that T'ang's republican sympathies brought him into disagreement with his chief. But precisely because of these sympathies he were considered acceptable by the south as the first Prime Minister of the Republic. But dispute over the relative constitutional roles of the President and the Cabinet soon led T'ang, in June 1912, to his final break with Yüan. T'ang later became a leading figure in the successive rival governments set up by the republicans in the south, and during the Nationalist period he played a prominent but ineffectual role, supporting at various times factions in opposition to the authoritarian rule of Chiang Kai-shek. He was assassinated in Shanghai in 1938, allegedly by Chiang's secret agents.

my second interview with him, I wrote him from Tientsin the letter of which I enclose a copy; but shortly after, he retired from the government. As that letter contains a suggestion concerning the selection of foreign experts which I think may possibly be useful to you, I send it herewith. Now that you and Mr. Rockhill are likely to be in the service of China, the Chinese government need not find it so impossible as it has been in the past to select foreign experts of good capacity and character; but still it seems to me possible that you might like to have the assistance of a permanent body like the Trustees of the Carnegie Endowment for International Peace.

My party reached home last Saturday in good health and spirits, and I have now gone to work again in my own house by the sea, surrounded by a large family connection and many friends.

I look back with great pleasure and satisfaction on our journey through the East; but in retrospect nothing seems to me more delightful than the hour I spent with you in your library.

Sincerely yours
Charles W. Eliot

Enclosure to Letter No. 539: *C. W. Eliot to T'ang Shao-yi, Tientsin 1 May 1912*

My dear Sir,

In the conversation which I lately had the honour of holding with you, I endeavoured to describe as briefly as possible the measures which seem indispensable to success in procuring for the government of China proper credit in the money-lending markets of the world. I was not thinking of the immediate measures necessary for obtaining the loan of a sum of money sufficient to carry on the government for a year or eighteen months, but of those durable and far-reaching measures that would give the government a sure and ample income for decades and generations to come. To procure such an income, and hence the financial credit which is necessary to the independence and honour of China, I ventured to state that two measures were essential: (1) The Central Government must obtain by methods of taxation that have approved themselves to Western economists and statesmen an annual income sufficient for the present needs of the Republic, and likely to increase with the increasing prosperity of the country. (2) This income must be expended honestly and effectively on objects and in methods which have proved good in Western administrations.

To secure these two all-important ends, it is obvious that in the actual condition of the Chinese civil and military service foreign advisers must be procured and given enough authority to convince Western capitalists and governments that an adequate national income is going to be secured, and that it is to be spent in a modern, scientific way. When I had the privilege of talking with you at Shanghai and at Peking I understood you to think that foreign advisers were indispensable to the new Republican Government in the actual crisis, and should be employed by the Chinese Government itself for specified terms of years, without nomination by any foreign government or combination of governments. I beg to say that I agree very heartily with these views of yours. While I believe that many foreign experts should be employed with the utmost possible promptness, I also believe that it would be unwise for the government of China to accept such experts on the nomination of officials or representatives of the Great Powers. I have also been given to understand that the present Chinese government would find it very difficult to select competent and trustworthy foreign advisers, partly from lack of knowledge, and partly from lack of practice of judging the character and ability of individual foreigners.

As you know, I have already given to Colonel Tsai Ting-Kan, the interpreter to the President, the suggestion that the Trustees of the Carnegie Endowment for International Peace would be a very suitable body to nominate to the Chinese Government men selected from several Western nationalities (especially the smaller ones) who would be competent advisers in the several departments of the Republican Government needing such assistance.

At the conversation I had with the President on Friday last, through your good offices, it seemed to me that he had not then been put in possession of my suggestion, and, because of your silence, I was not sure that you fully apprehended the arguments I stated to the interpreter. I beg leave, therefore, to put before you in writing a description of the Carnegie Endowment for International Peace and of its Trustees.

In the first place, the Endowment has been incorporated by Congress as a permanent body of trustees, filling their own vacancies, possessed of a liberal income (£100,000 Sterling a year) intended to be perpetual, likely to endure for centuries, having for its main object the promotion of International Peace, but also proposing to promote those agencies and sentiments which make towards peace, such as education, religious toleration, public order, the cooperation of capital and labor in industries, equal laws, public justice, a permanent international tribunal, and all institutions which can cultivate good-will among men. The Trustees receive no salaries or other emoluments. Their efforts must necessarily be of an international sort. They must be impartial, independent, and disinterested, and their work must be laid out not for tomorrow, or for next year, but on far-reaching plans. The Trustees deal now with scholars, men of affairs, and statesmen in all the leading nations, and are acquainted with leading experts on all subjects in the principal Western nations. The Trustees are men of experience in educational, industrial, or governmental affairs; in support of this statement I need only cite the names of a few of the Trustees.

Elihu Root. Former Secretary of State. Now a Senator in Congress from the State of New York.[1]

Charlemagne Tower. Former Ambassador at Berlin.[2]

Oscar Straus. Former Ambassador at Constantinople and Secretary for Commerce and Labor in President Roosevelt's Cabinet.[3]

Henry S. Pritchett. Formerly Superintendent of the United States Coast Survey; then President of the Massachusetts Institute of Technology; now President of the Carnegie Foundation for Promoting the Higher Education.[4]

Robert M. Woodward. President of the Carnegie Institution for Promoting Scientific Research.[5]

Nicholas Murray Butler. President of Columbia University, New York.[6]

The gentlemen named above who have served as representatives of the American government in foreign countries are now simply private citizens. The Trustees of the Carnegie Endowment for International Peace are as impartial a body of men as can be imagined, and are recognized as such among all the Western nations; they are also competent as judges of men. Finally, they are all actuated by the friendliest sentiments towards China.

My suggestion was that the nominations made by the Trustees of the Carnegie Endowment should be subject to the veto of some representative of the Chinese government residing in Washington, either the Chinese

---

[1] Elihu Root (1845–1937), American lawyer and Republican politician. He was Secretary of War (1899–1903) under Presidents McKinley and Roosevelt, and in 1905 succeeded John Hay as Secretary of State, a post he held until 1909 when he was elected a senator for New York (1909–15). A friend of Andrew Carnegie, he served both as chairman and president of many of the Carnegie foundations.

[2] Charlemagne Tower (1848–1923), American diplomat and author. He was Ambassador to Germany (1902–8), having previously been Minister to Austria-Hungary (1897–9) and Ambassador to Russia (1899–1902).

[3] Oscar Solomon Straus (1850–1926), American lawyer and politician. He was twice the American representative in Turkey, as Minister (1887–9 and then 1898–1901) and Ambassador (1909–10). He also served as the American member of the Permanent Court of Arbitration at The Hague (1902), and from 1906 to 1909 was Secretary of Commerce and Labor under President Roosevelt.

[4] Henry Smith Pritchett (1857–1939), American astronomer and educationalist. He was Professor of Astronomy and Director of the Observatory of Washington University at St Louis (1883–97) before becoming Superintendent of the United States Coast and Geodetic Survey in 1897. In 1900 he was appointed President of Massachusetts Institute of Technology, and in 1906 President of the Carnegie Foundation for the Advancement of Teaching, a post he held until 1930.

[5] Robert Simpson Woodward (1849–1924), American scientist. He had worked as astronomer and geographer in the United States Geological Survey (1884–90), and the Coast and Geodetic Survey (1890–3), before becoming Professor of Mechanics and Mathematical Physics at Columbia University in 1893. He was appointed to the position here referred to in 1905, retaining it until 1920.

[6] Nicholas Murray Butler (1862–1947), American educator, President of Columbia University from 1901 to 1945. Prior to this he was Professor of Philosophy there (1899–1900). Among the many honours conferred upon him was the Chinese Grand Order of Jade in 1938.

Minister, or some person especially appointed for this work by the Chinese government.

I did not intend that this method of selecting foreign advisers should preclude the Government of China from selecting a few principal advisers quite of their own motion, – such as the general advisers for the President, for the Prime Minister, and for the Secretary for Foreign Affairs, whenever the Government could take such action with full knowledge of the true quality of the men selected; but I understood during my recent visit to Peking that the present government has full knowledge of very few men competent to serve as foreign advisers. Indeed, I heard the name of only one person whom Chinese and foreigners would alike regard as competent and altogether desirable as adviser to the President and his Cabinet. That name was William W. Rockhill.

From the conversations I have had with leading men in Peking, both Chinese and foreigners, during the ten days past (April 19th to 29th), I feel a strong conviction that if the President and Cabinet should now make two announcements *without consulting any foreign government or minister*, as follows – (1) We propose to invite William W. Rockhill to the service of the Chinese Government as General Adviser, and (2) we propose to ask the Carnegie Endowment for International Peace to select the numerous foreign experts whom the Chinese Government is conscious that it needs – the position of the Republic in regard to its capacity to borrow money and also in regard to recognition by foreign powers would immediately be much strengthened.

I expect to be in Tientsin for two weeks to come; and if at any time within this limit you desire to talk further with me concerning any of the measures herein proposed, I shall hold myself at your disposition in Peking.

I beg leave to add that I have not consulted the American Minister, or any other foreign official, about the proposals made in this letter. They proceed from an American private citizen experienced in educational administration and one of the Trustees of the Carnegie Endowment, namely, myself.

I am, with high regard

Sincerely yours
[C. W. Eliot]

540. From R. M. Collins[1]

[London] 27 August 1912

My dear Morrison:

Will you be good enough to accept my warmest congratulations upon your marriage which I read of in the morning papers.[2] Permit me to congratulate

[1] Robert Muirhead Collins (b. 1867), American journalist, at this time Chief of the Bureau of the Associated Press in London (1907–25). He had previously been a correspondent of Reuter and of the Associated Press in the Far East (1901–7). He came to know Morrison in Peking.

[2] Morrison's marriage on 26 August 1912 was reported in various papers including *The Times*, in which on 27 August there was a brief description of the ceremony.

you also on the appointment to the position of adviser to the Chinese Government. While from patriotic and perhaps narrow motives Americans would prefer to see one of their own nationality at the elbow of the President of the new republic, I know that from the standpoint of the interests of the Chinese themselves they have made the best choice possible.

I read with great interest your letter to *The Times*.[1] It is well that the Chinese have someone to speak for them at this juncture who knows the audience which he addresses and the features of the situation of interest and importance to foreigners. Chinese interests in Europe and America have suffered for some years because China's foreign representatives have not understood how to present China's case to the public when various important issues have arisen. While, of course, you, and in lesser degree some other correspondents in the East, have carried on this work the representatives of the government on the spot have a great advantage.

Whenever any question concerning the relations of Japan with China comes to the front, the Japanese diplomats abroad are thoroughly acquainted with all the facts and arguments which tend to support the Japanese side and leave no stone unturned to get them before the foreign public. Stevens[2] did great work for Japan along these lines in America during the Japan–China and Russo-Japanese war, as you know. Macleavy Brown[3] has lived so long in the East that apparently he is too much out of touch with European conditions to be very useful to the Chinese as a press agent.

[1] Morrison's letter to the Editor was published on 23 August 1912 under the title 'The Outlook in China. A Reply to Pessimists.' The *Evening News* described it as being 'indisputably the most important feature in this morning's papers', and the *Westminster Gazette* said that 'it should do China an immense service in Europe.' In a leader entitled 'Dr. Morrison on China', *The Times*, while admitting that the letter was 'a useful corrective to the exaggerated reports which have recently been current about the situation in China', went on to say: 'None the less, we are unable to share the complete optimism he displays with regard to the situation, and are afraid that China is by no means at the end of her troubles.'

[2] Durham White Stevens (1852–1908), American diplomat, first posted to Japan in 1873. He remained with the American Legation in Tokyo until 1884, when he resigned to enter the service of the Japanese government. He assisted various Japanese Foreign Ministers in the Treaty Revision negotiations, and also participated, as an adviser to the Japanese Delegation, in the Sino-Japanese negotiations regarding Korea. In 1887 he was sent by the Japanese Government to Washington as adviser to the Japanese Legation there and contributed to the successful conclusion of the subsequent Japanese–United States Treaty of 1889. He remained in the United States until 1900, when he was appointed Japanese Agent in Hawaii. In 1904 he was transferred to Korea as adviser to the government there, and was awarded the insignia of the First Class Rising Sun by the Japanese Emperor for his services. He was assassinated by Korean patriots in San Francisco for supporting the Japanese occupation rule in Korea.

[3] Sir John McLeavy Brown (1842–1926), British employee of the Imperial Chinese Maritime Customs, and for many years head of the Korean Customs (1898–1906). In 1906, at the age of 64, on Morrison's recommendation he was appointed Counsellor to the Chinese Legation in London, a post he held for twenty years until his death.

The memory of the newspaper reading public is short. Immediate statements regarding an Eastern topic, which may be thrashed out in the course of two or three days by the newspapers, are of far more value than such statements coming along a month or two after the topic has had the centre of the stage and been superseded by some other.

The English and American press is very well disposed toward China. Often it would only be too glad to be able to publish the Chinese statement of affairs, if such a statement could be obtained promptly. Unfortunately, the Chinese diplomatic service has been almost entirely lacking in knowledge of the exceedingly practical art of utilising Western newspapers. China's rivals have not been at all backward in that art. I hope under the new regime we may find the Chinese more appreciative of the fact that to meet the Western newspapers half-way will be as much to China's advantage as in the interests of the newspapers. Of course, any improvement of this sort could not be effected in a day.

Yours very truly
Robert M. Collins

541. To H. A. Gwynne[1]

[London September 1912]

My dear Gwynne,

Many thanks for your letter of September 7th 1914.[2]

I am staying on in London longer than I had expected in order to see Lord Morley[3] to-day and Sir Edward Grey[4] the following week. I think, however, it is probable I will leave for China on the 21st, Saturday, but if not, and I am still in London, it will give us both very great pleasure indeed to meet you and Mrs Gwynne.

I have been so rushed that I have not communicated yet with Pole-Carew.[5]

[1] Howell Arthur Gwynne (1865–1950), British journalist, at this time Editor of the *Morning Post* (1911–37), and previously Editor of the London *Standard* (1904–11). He became a close friend of Morrison while serving as Reuter's correspondent in Peking (January 1898 – May 1899).

[2] Gwynne's letter to which Morrison refers is not printed. Morrison's typed reply has the date '1914' added in ink, obviously a slip of the pen, where '1912' was intended.

[3] John Morley (1838–1923), 1st Viscount Morley of Blackburn, British politician, at this time Lord President of the Council. He had previously been Secretary of State for India (1905–10). Morrison met Morley in London in 1905, on which occasion Morley sought his opinion on the Indian opium trade with China. The discussion was said to have impressed Morley greatly and to have helped to shape Britain's subsequent policy on this much condemned traffic.

[4] Sir Edward Grey (1862–1933), later 1st Viscount Fallodon, British politician, at this time Secretary of State for Foreign Affairs (1906–16). He had sent a telegram to Morrison on 7 September asking for a meeting with him, and as a result Morrison, who had arranged to leave in the second week of September, delayed his departure from London.

[5] Lt.-Gen. Sir Reginald Pole Carew (1849–1924), British soldier. A veteran of the Afghan and South African wars, he was at this time a Member of the British House of Commons for Bodmin Division, Cornwall (1910–16).

The difficulty is this. I cannot conceive of the possibility of the Chinese giving an engagement such as he would like to our distinguished friend. At present the Chinese are very resentful of any interference. No Englishman can be employed, as you know, in the Northern Army in any capacity whatever, owing to the operation of the self-denying ordinance between England and Russia,[1] especially at the present juncture would it be difficult to convince the Chinese of the advantages of employing an English military man in such a capacity as that suggested by Pole-Carew.

We are getting into a position of considerable difficulty in China. We have followed a policy which has led us where we did not expect. The British Government gives exclusive support, to the exclusion of all other banking corporations, to the Hongkong & Shanghai Bank. Naturally the Bank takes every advantage of this privileged position. Resentment is felt by purely British bankers at this monopoly granted to a bank in which German influence is very marked. The other bankers who are as well informed as the H. & S. Bank, consider that they run no risk in lending money to China at the present juncture, yet they are prevented from granting it owing to the monopoly of the H. & S. Bank who demand terms which could never be acceded to by any self-respecting Chinese Government.

We have got into the way of talking in an airy maner of supervision over expenditure and foreign administration of the salt revenues. Such a claim is impossible. Besides, even if it were practicable, it means introducing international control under German headship into the salt collectorates, the most important of which are in the Yangtse Valley. Germany claims the right to have a German as head of any foreign government administration of the salt gabelle on the ground that England has an Englishman at the head of the Customs, and France a Frenchman at the head of the Post Office. What conceivable advantage could this be to England or English interests, although admittedly it would be an advantage to an Anglo-German Bank like the H. & S. Bank.

Look also at the way the Government are acting in connection with Tibet. Major W. F. O'Connor,[2] who was with Younghusband[3] in the Tibetan

---

[1] In an exchange of Notes in April 1899, Britain undertook not to seek concessions for her nationals north of the Great Wall, while Russia gave a similar undertaking concerning the Yangtse Valley.

[2] Lt.-Col. (later Sir) William Frederick Travers O'Connor (1870–1943), British soldier and colonial official. Seconded from the Political Department of the Indian Government to serve as Secretary and Interpreter to Sir Francis Edward Younghusband (q.v.) in the British invasion of Tibet (1903-4), he remained at Gyangtse, Tibet, when the British withdrew from Lhasa, with the title of Trade Agent (1904-8). At this time he was British Consul at Shiraz, Persia (1912-15). He subsequently became British Resident in Nepal (1918-20).

[3] Sir Francis Edward Younghusband (1863-1942), British soldier and colonial official. A graduate of Sandhurst, he entered the service of the British Government in India in 1900, and in 1906 was appointed Resident in Kashmir (1906-9). In 1903 he led the British

Expedition, desires the post of Consul General in Lhasa. I think it would be an excellent thing if we were to have a Consul General in Lhasa. I have always thought so. Presumably Russia will also have a Consul General, each Consulate having an official guard of its own Nationals. It would be a great advantage to our prestige in Nepal and on the frontier of India to know that there is a powerful British escort stationed in Lhasa. Russia is at present working for the autonomy of Mongolia. Japan is working for the recognition of her special rights in Manchuria. It has been an immense advantage to both Russia and Japan that England should seize this opportunity to interfere in the international administration of Tibet. The fact that England bound herself by a solemn agreement of the 8th of April 1906[1] not to interfere in the international administration of Tibet may be disregarded. Agreements are no more binding upon the British Government than they are binding upon the American Government. A discussion at the time of the negotiation of this Agreement took place in England as to whether China was the suzerain or sovereign power in Tibet. China recognises no such distinction. She claims to be the sovereign power. In the negotiations which led to the signature of the Adhesion Agreement, no reference whatever was made to her being [the] suzerain power. You can get the confirmation of this statement from C. W. Campbell,[2] whom you know well, and who was present at every one of the discussions that took place between the Chinese and Sir Ernest Satow[3] prior to the signature of the agreement. The reason of the British

---

invasion of Tibet, and occupied Lhasa until 1904. The subject of many books because of his exploits, he was also the author of a number of books on the religious faith to which he was attracted in later life. Among his published works was *Excellence-Worship. A Proposed Method by which the laity might...help...in satisfying the spiritual needs of the country and especially of...London* (London 1923).

[1] A convention of Six Articles signed by Britain and China concerning Tibet. It was signed on 27 April and not on 8 April 1906, the date Morrison gives here. This is referred to here as the Adhesion Agreement, as it modified and confirmed the Convention signed between Britain and Tibet on 7 September 1904. For details *see* J. V. A. MacMurray, *Treaties and Agreements With and Concerning China, 1894-1920* (New York 1921) Vol. 1, p. 581 *et seq.* Most treaties etc. between 1914 and 1920 mentioned in these notes can be found in this compilation, which is however far from being exhaustive; many treaties etc. are missing from it. In fact a more comprehensive compilation awaits an enterprising editor.

[2] Charles William Campbell (1861-1927), British consular official. He was, at the time referred to, Chinese Secretary in the British Legation in Peking, a post he held until his resignation from the service in 1911. He was living in retirement in London at the time this letter was written.

[3] Sir Ernest Satow (1843-1929), British diplomat, at the time referred to Minister to China (1900-6). He had previously been Minister in Tokyo (1895-1900) where he first went as a Student Interpreter in 1861. He was appointed a British delegate to the Hague Peace Conference in 1907, after leaving China. A man of scholarly bent, he devoted himself to writing during his retirement not far from Sidmouth where Morrison, shortly before his death there in 1920, was to meet him again. Satow was the author of *A Diplomat in Japan* (London 1921) and *A Guide to Diplomatic Practice* (London 1917-22).

Military expedition into Tibet was the weakness of Chinese authority there. The Tibetans had ignored the conditions of the agreement entered into between the Chinese Government, the sovereign power in Tibet, and the Indian Government, hence a punitive expedition became necessary. It was all the more necessary because the Tibetans, ignoring the sovereign power of China, had entered into negotiations with Russian subjects, inviting Russian intervention on their behalf and thus menacing British peace on the Indian frontier. The Dalai Lama,[1] that arch conspirator, was driven out of the country, an indemnity was exacted and that indemnity was paid by the sovereign country China. Surely it was a matter of common prudence that China should so act to prevent a repetition of such intrigues, such expeditions, such frontier dangers, such expenditures. When the British had withdrawn, the Chinese seized the first opportunity to establish their authority in the country. That arch intriguer, the Dalai Lama, again fled – this time to India, and he was deposed as a danger, a real and serious danger to the state. Before China has time to establish her position in Tibet on an unassailable basis, the revolution breaks out in China and the Tibetans rise and slay the Chinese garrison. Through the intervention, however, of the Nepalese, the Chinese garrison in Lhasa is rescued and promised safe-conduct through India back to China. In the meantime the Mongols are endeavouring to enter Tibet even through India to induce the Tibetans to make common cause with China [?Mongolia] and to look to Russia for their protection, and to the Russians to be the guardians of their autonomy. Arms are going into Tibet through Mongolia – Russian arms, Beardon rifles purchased in St Petersburg and carried through Urga across Mongolia and by Sining into Tibet. Now, having pledged ourselves not to interfere with the internal administration of Tibet, we have defined the terms upon which we will allow the Chinese to carry on the administration of that country. I find that owing to the internal dissensions in our own country we made an unsatisfactory agreement with Tibet and with China in 1904–6. We demand that China shall sign a new agreement with us, more favourable, and we declare that we will not recognise the Chinese Republic until that agreement has been signed; that is to say, we recognised the Government of an Empress Dowager[2] and of a

[1] Thub ldan rgya mtsho, otherwise Ah-wang-lo-pu-tsang-t'u-pu-tan-chia-ts'o-chi-chai-wang-chü-chüeh-le-lang-chieh (1876–1933), 13th Dalai Lama, Chief Lama of the Yellow Sect Buddhists and temporal ruler of Tibet. He fled from Lhasa when the British invaded Tibet in 1903. In 1908 he visited Peking shortly before the death of the Emperor Kuang-hsü and Empress-Dowager Tz'u-hsi. Fleeing to India at the outbreak of the 1911 Revolution, he was later reinstated by Yüan Shih-k'ai in October 1912, as the Ch'eng-shun-tsan-hua-hsi-t'ien-ta-shan-tzu-tsai-fo (or, 'Sincere and Loyal Propagator of Civilisation and Great, Righteous and Complacent Buddha of the Western Heavens').

[2] Hsiao-ch'in (1835–1908), better known as the Empress Dowager Tz'u-hsi. For nearly half a century she was the *de facto* ruler of China, from the death of her husband, the Emperor Hsien-feng, in 1861 until her own death in 1908. She is considered by many to have been the chief instigator of the events that took place in Peking in 1900.

number of inhuman savages who conducted the Boxer campaign and we will not recognise a Government which throughout the whole of this revolution has protected with the utmost faithfulness the lives and property of all foreigners, and which has, despite the immense internal revolution, carried out all its obligations with some minor and unimportant exceptions.[1] But this by the way. We have informed the Chinese that we will not recognise the Republic unless they have first signed with us an agreement regarding Tibet. We have thus convinced every Chinese that the policy of Japan in Manchuria, and of Russia in Mongolia is the guide of British policy in Tibet. We are to do in Tibet as those two friendly powers are doing in Manchuria and in Mongolia. Should confirmation be required of these views, the Chinese have only to read, as they do read, the views expressed by the chief Liberal organs, the *Daily News*, the *Daily Chronicle*, and the *Manchester Guardian*. Any further aggression desired by Japan in Manchuria or by Russia in Mongolia can be insured by these powers demanding that an agreement with Japanese or Russian policy must precede any recognition of the Chinese Republic. Why should the British Government so weaken the Chinese central authority? They refuse to permit financial assistance to be given to the Central Government on the ground of the Central Government's weakness, such weakness being due to its inability to obtain financial assistance. We are now still further weakening the central authority by impressing the Chinese, who largely supported the President Yuan Shih-kai because he was believed to command the confidence of foreign countries, especially England, that he does not possess that confidence. What then is to be the result of all this? I venture to suggest, firstly, that the recognition that we withhold from the Chinese Republic will be freely accorded by the United States Government; secondly, that the unfriendly action of the British Government in taking a leading part in closing the money markets of the world to China when China was in great financial embarrassment and in adding to that embarrassment will cause resentment throughout the whole country; thirdly, that our action with regard to Tibet will increase the resentment; fourthly, that the manifestation of that resentment will be a boycott such as the world has never yet seen, one compared with which the American boycott was unimportant.[2]

[G. E. Morrison]

[1] The British 'Government withheld recognition until 6 October 1913, after Yüan Shih-k'ai had been formally elected President of the Republic.
[2] Following the refusal by America to modify the Chinese exclusion clause in the new Commercial Treaty signed by China and the United States in 1903, a boycott movement against American goods was started in Canton and spread to other cities in China. This letter finishes abruptly here, without the usual ending. Morrison noted in the margin: 'rough draft, never sent I believe.'

542. To Lucy Gray[1]

[London] 9 September 1912

Dear Mrs. Gray,

I find that it will be impossible for us to be back before the beginning of October. I have to stay in London until Sir Edward Grey returns on the 19th, as he wishes to see me, and then we think of leaving on the 21st, so that we should not be in Peking before the 12th of October.

I have had an awful rush since I came to London, and I have not answered one-tenth of the letters I have received. Everyone wants a job. Apparently many think that I have come to England to look for men willing to serve the Chinese Government at a extravagant salary, and to advise on everything from Christian Science to the building of battleships. I have to see Lord Morley to-day, no doubt about the Tibetan question. The Government papers are attacking Sir Edward Grey very strongly for his extraordinary instructions to Sir John Jordan[2] to demand a new treaty with Tibet as a preliminary to the granting of recognition to the Chinese Republic. No doubt the other Powers in turn will make similar demands.

[...]

My appointment was universally approved, and all notices were favourable except one from Putnam Weale from Peking, who went out of his way to tell a deliberate lie, saying that the secretarial staff of Yuan Shih-kai had protested against my appointment *en masse*.[3] It is astonishing that the *Daily Telegraph* should continue to publish sensational messages from this irresponsible Jew. Wearne's[4] messages are very much appreciated in London.

[1] Lucy Gray, wife of Dr George Douglas Gray, the British Legation physician in Peking. She was, according to Morrison, one of the leading gossips in the Peking foreign community.

[2] Sir John Newell Jordan (1852-1925), British diplomat, Minister in Peking (1906-20). The 'Sir John' appearing frequently throughout the pages of this Volume, refers to Jordan, unless otherwise indicated.

[3] Putnam Weale was the *nom de plume* of Bertram Lenox Simpson (1877-1930), British journalist and author, at this time Special Correspondent of the *Daily Telegraph* in China. His message, entitled 'China's future: Dr. Morrison's post', was published in the *Daily Telegraph* on 14 August 1912. It read in part, 'The Chinese advisers and chiefs of the Presidential Secretariat waited on the President *en masse* and formally protested against the appointment of Dr. Morrison as political adviser to the Government. They maintained that, while departmental experts were needed, the country will not tolerate any alien being entrusted with any knowledge of general political affairs. In support of their contention, they advanced three long arguments, which it is inexpedient to publish. The underlying idea, however, was reasons of state. The President listened carefully, but reserved his reply. Chinese officials expect that...a compromise will be arranged.' It is interesting to note that Lenox Simpson himself later sought and obtained an appointment as an adviser to the Chinese Government, in which capacity he was assassinated in Tientsin in 1930. 'The correspondent of the *Daily Telegraph*', which appears frequently in this volume, refers to Simpson, unless otherwise indicated.

[4] A. E. Wearne (?b. 1875), Australian journalist, at this time Reuter's Correspondent in Peking. Until he volunteered to join the Allied forces at the front in 1915 he was the

Putnam Weale's, although they read interestingly, are not regarded seriously – as the Foreign Office said to me: 'It is only another lie from Putnam Weale'. The other day he telegraphed a statement which had to be officially contradicted. Every paper published the contradiction except the *Daily Telegraph* itself. When I came to London there was considerable anxiety among people as to the situation in China, Putnam Weale having telegraphed home for several days together sensational reports that the fate of China was trembling in the balance. *The Times* accordingly asked me to write them a letter over my own name, and this was published conspicuously on the 23rd of August. In a leaderette Braham expressed his dissent from the optimistic tone of my letter.[1] It was quite consistent that he should do so. But I will not bother you with such uninteresting talk.

[...]

Ever affectionately yours
[G. E. Morrison]

543. From W. Ming[2]

Private & Confidential 'Highworth', Hillfield Avenue, Crouch End, N., London 9 September 1912

Dear Sir,

By the courtesy of Mr Robin[3] of So[uth] Croydon I am able to address a letter to you upon a topic I have for some years endeavoured to find someone who would be in a position to afford me information and assistance. Through your name and work in China having lately been prominent in the papers I take the opportunity of approaching you, with a view to the idea I have in mind becoming more of the real, than hitherto imaginary. I will be as brief as possible and at the finish please do not consider me a fanatic, but one in good and sound mind. No doubt the sound of my name will recall to your recollection your association with China. From my earliest youth I have heard from my parents a continual reference to that disturbed unhappy country and I have always had – I know not why – one idea that I must have some sort of connection with it. I have heard my father many times say he ought to go over there, but with what idea I was never able to determine, only that he had more right than the then ruler. I have tried to trace my ancestors but have failed beyond my father's father who seems to

---

channel by which Morrison frequently released information from the Chinese Government to counteract hostile comments disseminated by other correspondents in China, such as David Fraser of *The Times* and Bertram Lenox Simpson of the *Daily Telegraph*.

[1] Dudley Disraeli Braham (1875–1951), British journalist, at this time Foreign Editor of *The Times* in succession to Valentine Chirol (q.v.). He was the author of a leader entitled 'Dr. Morrison on China', published in *The Times* on 23 August 1912. See p. 25 note 1.

[2] William Ming, a Londoner of whom little is known.

[3] Robert Robin, a New Zealander and Morrison's father-in-law, living at this time in Croydon, a London suburb.

have lived in the Country where he was known and called the 'Marquis' who came from foreign parts but nobody knew where. My brother, now dead, was, in facial appearance, absolutely Chinese. I have as a family possession a small painting of a seemingly superior person in Chinese attire. These facts will show you, and point, I think, to the possibility and perhaps probability that I am in a position to lay claim to being something more than a common British subject. How can I know? What can I do to find out? A story of romance may be the outcome of our history. If there be anything in it, I am quite ready to place myself at the disposal of anyone who has hitherto endeavoured to resuscitate the Ming dynasty[1] and I firmly believe that until that dynasty is again in power as it used to be, the present chaos in China will continue. Of course I do not mean that I would join in any rebel force against a Country friendly to the British Government, but to find a means to attain the end in a proper way. Do you know if the name of Ming is a common name in China or does it belong to only the nobility? If so, is there at the present time any representative of that dynasty? and who is he? Could I by some means communicate with whoever he may be? It is so difficult without someone who knows, as I take it, you in all probability know. Have I said sufficient to arouse your interest in me? I hope so. You Sir perhaps can show me how I could succeed in laying claim to my being something more than 'Mr Ming' and if so, both would be mutually benefitted. How is it to be done? I should be very glad to hear from you either before you leave for China, or after your arrival there. Apologising for the length of my letter and trust you will give it consideration.

I am, dear Sir

Yours faithfully
Wm. Ming

544. To D. D. Braham

[London] 11 September 1912

My dear Braham,

You must not be misled by the statements in Fraser's telegram of this morning.[2] He has been misled as to the terms of the loan contract. It was

---

[1] The Ming Dynasty lasted from 1368 to 1644 when it was brought to an end by the Manchus. The surname of the ruling family of the Ming Dynasty was Chu, of which fact Mr Ming was obviously unaware.

[2] David Stewart Fraser (1869–1953), British journalist and Morrison's successor as *Times* Correspondent in Peking. The telegram here referred to appeared in *The Times* of 11 September 1912 under the title 'The Chinese Loan. Difficulties of the New Scheme.' It concerned the loan which the Chinese Government with the help of Morrison had just concluded with the British financial group headed by Charles Birch Crisp ((1867–?1948), a British financier, founder of the Anglo-Russian Trust and the British Bank of Foreign Trade), hence known as the Crisp Loan. Subsequent mention of 'Fraser' refers to David Fraser, unless otherwise indicated.

signed, not on the 23rd of August, but on the 30th. It was a definite contract which in the main repeated word for word the terms of the Currency Loan Contract. The conditions were equally favourable to borrowers and to lenders. There was not one word in the contract about the establishment of a bank under foreign and Chinese auspices. Fraser seems to have a propensity for getting hold of the wrong end of the stick. I will endeavour to get you a copy of the contract so that you can see for yourself that it is a contract which ought to receive our support. The British Government, however, in the interests of the Six-Power group, will be compelled to demand its cancellation, and I understand that they are issuing instructions to Sir John Jordan to join with the ministers of the other five Powers in making this demand.[1] Where is this policy going to lead us? The sextuple agreement between the banks is terminable only on one year's notice. Addis[2] was in here yesterday, and he appears to me to regard with dismay the entanglement in which his bank is becoming involved. He tells me that the representatives of the six banks in Peking, including his own representative, Hillier,[3] agreed that no advance would be made by any one of the banks to the Chinese Government without the approval of the other five, but that he himself had put his foot down and stopped this. 'Fancy', he said, 'having the legitimate business of our bank subject to the veto of five hostile banks!'

We seem to be getting into an infernal muddle, and it is difficult to see what it may lead to. I should think that this policy must be extremely injurious to us.[4] The crude threat of Jordan that the British Government will not recognise the Chinese Republic until a new agreement has been signed regarding Tibet must be followed by similar threats on the part of the other Powers. Russian action in Mongolia and Japanese in Manchuria must make

[1] The Six-Power Group, which consisted of banks representing England, France, Germany, Japan, Russia and the United States, saw the Crisp Loan as a threat to its monopoly of foreign loans to the Chinese Government and forced China to cancel the agreement with Crisp, resulting in China's having to pay £150,000 in compensation. Morrison was indignant at what he described as the incomprehensible and injurious attitude of the British Government who had played the leading role in forcing the cancellation of the Crisp Loan to China.

[2] Charles (later Sir Charles) Stewart Addis (1861–1945), British banker, Manager of the Hongkong & Shanghai Banking Corporation in London (1905–21). A leading figure in British banking and financial circles, he later held, among many other posts, those of Director of the Bank of England (1918–32) and President of the Institute of Bankers (1919–21).

[3] Edward Guy Hillier (1857–1924), British banker, representative of the Hongkong & Shanghai Banking Corporation in Peking.

[4] Writing to Lovat Fraser on 10 September 1912 Morrison said, 'The British Government have wrecked this [Crisp] loan contract which would have been highly advantageous to British interests and would have helped to reorganise the Chinese Government at a critical time and they have done this in the interests of countries whose interests in China are not identical with our own.'

the Chinese despair. I would like to talk over this matter with you. I return to China on the 21st.

With best wishes to you

Yours sincerely
[G. E. Morrison]

545. To L. G. Fraser[1]

[London] 13 September 1912

My dear Fraser,

Your letter was only delivered at 6.30. I waited in a long time for it. I posted the corrections at 7.55 p.m.[2]

I hope I made it clear that you must be very careful in your references to the British Government. To you I can speak my mind, but to the Chinese I am always (and always will so continue) championing the British action, always endeavouring to make them realise that we British are their best friends, that we are a phenomenon among the nations, acting with scrupulous fidelity to our engagements, that where they, the Chinese come in conflict with the British, it is they, the Chinese, who are to blame. To you confidentially I can speak of the possibility of the boycott and of its real danger, but with the Chinese I would use every influence I possessed, even to the threat of resigning my post, to prevent the exercise of such a barbaric procedure. Please therefore make no reference to any boycott. The mere suggestion put into any article referring to me might have infinitely far reaching effects. I have always said and still believe that in the case of a boycott we should go to any length to prevent it, even to the length of crossing the frontier into Yunnan. I never will do anything to depreciate my own Government in the sight of the Chinese – quite the contrary. Thus in all my communications I lay stress upon the friendly attitude of the official people and the sympathy felt in the Foreign Office for China and the Chinese and the desire of our Government to see China strong and united and to assist in the attainment of that end.

I did not care to alter the personal praise of myself, but my wife hoped you would not mind leaving out about our marriage.

All good wishes to you. The best I can wish you is that you will find the same happiness in your wedded life that I have found in mine.

Very sincerely yours
[G. E. Morrison]

[1] Lovat George Fraser (1871–1926), British journalist, at this time on the editorial staff of the *Pall Mall Gazette*, and a contributor to *The Times*, for which paper he later became one of the chief leader-writers.

[2] This refers to an interview Morrison had with Lovat Fraser, who had previously sent Morrison a list of suggested questions on 11 September 1912. The interview was published in the *Pall Mall Gazette*, 'the paper of the moment' as Lovat Fraser described it, on the first page of its issue of 16 September 1912 under the title, 'Dr. Morrison on the New China.'

546. To Ts'ai T'ing-kan

[London] 21 September 1912

My dear Colonel,

I am leaving London to-morrow to return to China.

I enclose you a leading article from the *Manchester Guardian* of September 17th[1] based on the interview with me that was published in the *Pall Mall Gazette* the day before.

Many interesting letters have reached me since I came to England. This morning I received one from one who is probably the ablest political writer in Great Britain.[2] The letter is marked 'Private and Confidential' and the following is an extract from it:

> As no one has written in more critical terms regarding the Chinese Republic than I have done, perhaps you will allow me to add a word about the effect your visit has had upon English public Opinion regarding China. In view of my published articles about Chinese affairs, my testimony may at least be taken as quite impartial. I think your visit came at a very opportune moment, and though they may not know it, the President and the Chinese Government owe you a very deep debt of gratitude for what you have done while in England. You have placed the Republic in a far more favourable light, and have convinced people here that if it receives *early recognition*, it has every prospect of establishing a stable administration. In my own case, you have induced me to modify very largely, and in some respects to withdraw altogether my earlier criticisms. But I am not expressing my personal opinion only. From many quarters I hear that your published statements have made a deep impression, particularly in the City. The best proof, however, is to be found in the remarkable change of attitude in a large proportion of the British press. I am quite certain (and you know that no one in London has better opportunities of judging) that had it not been for your quiet work during the last few weeks, the attitude taken up by so many English journals regarding the ten-million loan would never have been adopted. If China is now more favourably regarded here, and if the Republic is likely to receive far more emphatic support – as assuredly it is – the change in public opinion is due to you. I fear China will never realise how much it owes you in this and similar matters.

I am glad to be able to give you this opinion, because this is a writer whose views more than those of anyone else I was hoping to modify.

With all good wishes to you

Ever faithfully yours
[G. E. Morrison]

[1] Not printed.
[2] The reference is to Lovat Fraser, whose letter that Morrison quotes here was dated 20 September 1912.

October 1912 – March 1913

The situation that awaited Morrison in Peking on his return from England to assume his duties as Political Adviser to the President of the Republic hardly merited the optimism he had so publicly aired about the country. The financial position on which the stability of the young Republic so much depended had not been improved by his intervention. If anything it had deteriorated. The consortium of foreign banks, whose control of China Morrison had tried to help break, had taken steps with the support of their governments to ensure that no other financial group, however powerful, could enter into purely financial dealings with China. Morrison had tried in vain to persuade the British Government to support one such loan to China by an exclusively British group headed by C. Birch Crisp. The British Government, under the influence of the Hongkong & Shanghai Banking Corporation, did exactly the opposite and more than any other government was responsible for frustrating China's efforts to find an alternative source of supply to relieve her financial stringencies. The British Government was in fact angered by what it regarded as Morrison's interference. Indeed, Morrison was considered to be the instigator of the whole dangerous exercise, so much so that Jordan, the British Minister in Peking, despite his indebtedness to Morrison, became openly antagonistic towards him. By jeopardising the goodwill and trust of the British Government so soon after becoming Political Adviser, Morrison lost the very effectiveness which the Chinese Government had sought through his appointment, namely as a sounding-board, moderating influence and contact between himself and the foreign powers. China suffered badly from the fiasco of the Crisp Loan. She was not only made to pay compensation to the consortium for her audacious attempt to break its monopoly of the money market, but the failure of the Crisp Loan lost her whatever little bargaining power she might have had.

Financial distress was not, however, the only serious crisis confronting China. The Mongols in Urga, dissatisfied with the misrule of the Manchu Government, seized upon the state of instability into which the Revolution had plunged China and, on Russian instigation and with her active support, started a revolt. In the south-western corner too, Britain, pressed by the Indian Government to consolidate the gains she had made following Younghusband's 1903 expedition into Tibet, went so far as to threaten non-recognition of the new Republic unless the Chinese Government acceded to her demands. Of the two, the Mongolian revolt proved to be the more serious. It threatened not only the vast frontier stretching from Western Manchuria to Sinkiang, but the very structure of the Republic. Given the freedom of the central authorities from dissension and financial worries, China might have been able to manoeuvre out of her difficulties. But her ability to deal with this upheaval was sapped by internal political divisions which were soon to flare up into open military conflict.

Having tried in vain to help China out of her financial troubles, Morrison took it upon himself as Political Adviser to solve her thorny border problems. He was particularly preoccupied with the events in Mongolia and made a special study of the question. This was to occupy him for many years, while the question remained unsolved. For reasons as much of space as of emphasis, we have limited our selection from his voluminous files touching on various aspects of this subject to a few examples affording a glimpse of the problem then facing China and of Morrison's attempts to solve it.

On the issue of Mongolia, probably more than on any other then bedevilling the young Republic, Morrison deplored the weakening of China's stand as a result of her internal dissension. Like most of the circle of his correspondents, he laid the blame on the republicans under Sun Yat-sen. His faith in Yüan Shih-k'ai as China's only hope had led him, while still Correspondent of *The Times*, to applaud Yüan's unconstitutional action in driving out the first Republican cabinet under T'ang Shao-yi – a decision which had destroyed what little chance there was for a democratic system of government. He now openly supported and indeed assisted Yüan in his assumption of autocratic rule. From this position it was only a short step to Morrison's later view that any action against Yüan's authority was an action against China. Obviously he did not view himself as a hired imperialist agent or collaborator with despotism. Instead he regarded himself as benevolently inclined towards China's resurgence and as a champion of a good cause which, if China was to survive, had to prevail. This stand, which pervades the whole of this volume, did not seem wrong or biassed to Morrison, as it might now seem to us with the benefit of hindsight. Many thoughtful and patriotic Chinese, caught as they were between imperialism and despotic rule, and beset by the same dilemma of having to make a choice, in fact often held the same view. The years leading up to, and immediately following the 1911 Revolution in particular, abound in events that left many Chinese lost in schizophrenic confusion.

This selection of Morrison's correspondence provides many such examples. A case in point was the *Supao* incident of 1903. Should a Chinese have rejoiced at the refusal by the authorities of the International Settlement in Shanghai to extradite the Chinese revolutionaries and thereby save their lives, or have resented this infringement on Chinese sovereign rights? Then again, in the *Tatsu Maru* case of 1908, should he have applauded the arrest of a

Japanese ship which was violating Chinese territorial waters, or have lamented the loss of the ammunition it was carrying for the Chinese revolutionary forces? In the early stages of the 1911 Revolution, there was the question of whether to welcome Japanese support for the republicans or to deplore their interference and attempts to widen and intensify the strife between the rival factions. Similarly, to Sun Yat-sen and his followers the concession to the Japanese in 1912 of partnership in the Han-yeh-p'ing mines in exchange for a Japanese loan was an exigency necessary for the stability and growth of the revolutionary forces, while to others it was a matter of pawning the birthright of the nation for mere expediency. In later sections of this Volume we shall come across other issues that caused divided loyalties for many Chinese. Even today it is not clear what the better of the alternative courses of action on such matters would have been; for Morrison and his contemporaries, when the issues were often shrouded by the smoke of propaganda, rumour or outright malicious fabrication, the choice must have been infinitely more difficult. If the knowledge of the dilemmas does not preclude us from passing judgment on the actors, it must surely help us to understand better the historical path taken by some of them in China's recent past. Limited though it is in many ways, Morrison's correspondence, being an uncensored record, probably gives a better idea of the contemporary scene than that which the recent rush of 'revolutionary' literature has created and would have us believe.

Apart from correspondence about the Mongolian problem, we have also had to omit much of that dealing in great detail with the Crisp and other foreign loan negotiations, the Tibetan question, the opium issue, and many other weighty topics of the day.

547. From Ts'ai T'ing-kan

[Peking] 16 October 1912

My dear Dr Morrison,

In this the first day of your sitting with a portion of the cabinet you have made a most favourable and profound impression. You *command* the attention of all and all spoke of you in the highest terms before the President who would very much like to have you stay to dinner – and he would have kept you were it not for Mrs Morrison.[1]

[...]

Yours sincerely
Tsai Ting Kan

[1] Recording his meeting with the Cabinet on 16 October 1912, Morrison wrote in his Diary: 'Yuan wanted me to stay to dinner – all ready but Mrs. was waiting for me. "You're only semi-independent now," he said.'

548. To Ts'ai T'ing-kan

Peking 18 October 1912

My dear Colonel Tsai,

Late last night when I was in bed, I received the following telegram from Mr Crisp:

'Grey replying question House Commons stated that Crisp Loan[1] was opposed because while negotiations were proceeding with the Six Powers Group we did not consider that China was free borrow elsewhere stop At meeting in city I stated that Grey was misleading House Commons and the proposals of Six Power Group were definitely rejected by Chinese Government on June 30 and China was therefore free to negotiate elsewhere stop Will you please clear up point by direct cable through medium *Daily Telegraph* Correspondent Peking.'

In reply I have caused the enclosed telegram[2] to be sent through Reuter's Agency, as coming from themselves. Obviously such a telegram should have greater publicity in this way than it would have if it had been sent through the *Daily Telegraph*, which is a paper of very little influence, and whose work has been wholly discounted owing to the disgraceful messages sent to it by Putnam Weale.

I have told Mr Wearne that if his people should object to his sending so long a message, I felt sure the Chinese Government would indemnify his Agency against any loss in the cost of the transmission of the message, but I hope that no such thing will be necessary, for the message is of considerable interest.

I have also told Mr Wearne that in return for his sending this message, I have given it to him exclusively, and that I hope he will frequently be prepared to be the channel of communication by which China can have her case stated to the world.

I am

Very sincerely yours
[G. E. Morrison]

[1] In reply to a series of questions in the House of Commons on the stand of the British Government in the matter of the Crisp Loan and the Six-Power Consortium's negotiations with the Chinese Government, Sir Edward Grey said that Britain's action had been taken in the interests of both British trade with China as well as Chinese trade. His questioners had expressed concern that Britain should have agreed to be merely one-sixth of the Group when the opportunity existed for her to supply loans to China on her own. They also expressed fear that the admission of Japan and Russia into the Group might enable those two powers to realise their ulterior designs on China.

[2] A Reuter's telegram, datelined Peking 18 October 1912 and published in *The Times* the following day, stated that the Chinese had expressed surprise at the British Government's opposition to the Crisp Loan. The Chinese pointed out that Hsiung Hsi-ling (q.v.), who was then Minister of Finance, before the signing of the preliminary contract on 13 July and again more emphatically before 30 August, sent a communication to the Six-Power Group definitely terminating the negotiations, which were not resumed in any form before the middle of September. In the Chinese view, therefore, China was quite free to negotiate with other lenders.

549. From D. S. Fraser

[Peking 20 October 1912]

Dear Morrison,

If you see the President tomorrow, it might be interesting to find out what reply has been received from the British Legation to the Wai wu pu's notification of the conclusion of the Crisp loan. Something has been done of an interesting nature. I have only got half the story.

Somebody said to me today, relative to your return, that there is a great opportunity now for you to do something to remove the acerbity between the Chinese and foreigners, or rather the bitterness of the Chinese towards us. Whatever the merits of the loan question, and however badly the Chinese may consider themselves to have been treated of late in various matters, nothing alters the fact that their affairs are largely affected by foreign powers. If they give way to resentment, they may make their own path more difficult, as well as that of the governments who have to deal with them. It could be serving all concerned if they were advised not to be so *difficile*. They are showing resentment in various small ways.

[...]

Yours
D.F.

550. To C. W. Campbell

[Peking] 24 October 1912

My dear Campbell,

Many thanks for your letter of October 31st.[1] I was delighted to get the catalogue of Jade curios.

You are very wise to make a hobby of collecting books. You really cannot go wrong. If you only compare the prices which the booksellers in England charge with those charged by German booksellers in Munich and Leipzig, you can see what are the possibilities. The prices in Germany today are those in England tomorrow.

[...]

I have taken up my new duties and I like the work very well indeed. I am well treated and I think I can be of some use. My chief difficulty is the hostility of Sir John Jordan who appears to regard me as a Chinese, although whatever success he has had since you left the Legation I think I can claim to have contributed to. I have never known our Legation to have been in such bad odour as it is at present. Yuan Shih-kai tells me that every time Sir John Jordan discusses affairs with him – whether it is a question of Yunnan or of Opium or of the Pekin Syndicate – he threatens that unless his claims are granted England will not recognise the Republic. It has come to this that the Chinese have made up their minds that England will not recognise the

[1] Not printed.

Republic. It is a dangerous game we are playing. If we boycott the Republic as we threaten to do, we will find a boycott movement in China compared with which the American boycott was nothing.

Very sincerely yours
[G. E. Morrison]

551. From G. Pereira[1]

Kuei-yang Fu, Kuei-chou 24 October 1912

Dear Morrison,

I arrived here by a new route via Huang-tsao pa and Kuei-hua T'ing. Things are very peaceful in this province, as they called in Yunnanese troops, who now run the show. The *Tu-Tu* was the commander of the regiment sent, T'ang-chi-yao[2] by name, aged 27 or 28. Two years ago he was a student in Japan. He is only a dummy, and reported to be run by the Commander of the Yunnanese troops. Everywhere I find youthful officials of the student class, generally under 30, who are ignorant of how to run the show. All the officials here were young officers or students, but as they found difficulties accumulating, especially financial, they were obliged to call in Kuo-tzu-hai[3]

---

[1] Lt.-Col. George Edward Pereira (1865-1923), British soldier, Military Attaché to the British Legation in Peking (1904-10). At this time he was on a journey of exploration in west and south-west China.

[2] T'ang Chi-yao (?1882-1927), Chinese soldier and Republican politician. A graduate of the Shikan Gakkō (Japanese Military Academy), he joined the T'ung-meng hui, the revolutionary society led by Sun Yat-sen, while a student in Tokyo. Soon after the outbreak of the Wuchang Uprising, he participated in the revolt that overthrew the Manchu provincial authorities in Yunnan-fu (later known as Kunming) and then led the republican army to neighbouring Kweichow Province, of which he became *Tutu* and concurrently Civil Governor on 26 April 1912. In September the following year he succeeded Ts'ai O as *Tutu* of Yunnan, while retaining the military governorship of Kweichow until 1916. From 1913 until his overthrow by his subordinate officers in February 1927, three months before his death, Yunnan, and to a lesser extent Kweichow, was to be his political and military base from which he played a prominent part in the affairs of the Republic. Though he was unable to prevent the defeat of the Republicans by Yüan Shih-k'ai's forces in the so-called 'Second Revolution' (July-September 1913), the anti-Yüan standard raised in Yunnan-fu under his nominal leadership in December 1915 gained the support of all the disaffected elements. In consequence he was partly responsible for forcing Yüan to abandon his monarchical scheme. Because of his army, he was very much courted by Sun Yat-sen, and together with the Kwangsi forces under Lu Yung-t'ing (q.v.) his forces became an important element in the Military Government set up by Sun Yat-sen in Canton in 1917. However he chose to follow an independent line preserving his own military power, and for this reason was accused by Sun's followers of harbouring selfish ambitions. Under his rule, which was continued by his successor Lung Yün (1888-1962), Yunnan became virtually a semi-independent state within China, a situation which, though somewhat modified during the war with Japan (1937-45), only came to an end with Lung's removal in 1945.

[3] Probably Kuo Ch'ung-kuang, who was formally appointed Director of the Bureau of Civil Affairs of Kweichow Province in June 1913. He also served briefly as Commissioner for Western Kweichow.

(formerly Wu-hu *Tao-t'ai*) to help them as Min-cheng-ssu.[1] The financial outlook for the provinces is certainly not good, the late Government flooded the market with notes to the value of 700,000 or 800,000 taels, and the present lot have supplemented this by issuing a million's worth of dollar notes. The trades people fight shy of them, but the Government insist on their accepting them at par, and, if they refuse, punish with fine and imprisonment. [...]

Yours very sincerely
George Pereira

552. To J. N. Jordan

Peking 1 November 1912

Dear Sir John,

Your remarks to me this afternoon following upon your attitude on the last occasion I called on you have given me great and undeserved pain. For 15 years I have known you, and in whatever capacity I could, I have defended you and supported you both in *The Times* and elsewhere. In London, in a published interview, I spoke of your work with praise,[2] as I have always done since I first worked for you, urging that you be appointed to your present post.

I cannot object to your criticising or disagreeing with what I said in London, but I do strongly protest against your suggestion that I am responsible for the publication of articles in the *Peking Daily News* by the British subject, Eugene Chen,[3] who ought to have been arrested and deported. Such a

[1] Bureau of Civil Affairs. The Chinese term for this bureau changed many times during the Republican period.

[2] This refers to Morrison's widely publicised interview with Lovat Fraser published in the *Pall Mall Gazette* on 16 September 1912. In it Morrison spoke thus of Jordan: 'We have in Sir John Jordan a Minister whose sympathies are with the Chinese people, who has spent much of his life among them, who is personally intimate with the President...'

[3] Ch'en Yu-jen or, to foreigners, Eugene Ch'en (1878–1944). Known as a 'revolutionary diplomat', he was born and brought up in Trinidad. He first went to China in 1912 and from then on until his death 32 years later, in 1944, he was in the front line of his native country's politics, always as a radical. Trained as a lawyer, he was at this time a Legal Adviser in the Ministry of Communications, but also wrote regularly for English-language newspapers in Peking, and later became Editor of the *Peking Gazette*. His outspoken articles brought him many difficulties and twice landed him in gaol. In 1917 he was imprisoned for his attack on the Tuan Ch'i-jui (q.v.) Government's secret dealings with Japan but was saved from more serious consequences by President Li Yüan-hung's dismissal of Tuan. He was imprisoned again in 1925 for his criticism of Chang Tso-lin the Manchurian warlord, then in control in Peking, but his life was saved by the timely arrival of the troops of Chang's rival, Feng Yü-hsiang (1882–1948). Ch'en Yu-jen was four times Foreign Minister, three of these in radical faction governments: in 1926 in the anti-Peking Government set up by Sun Yat-sen in Canton, in 1927 in the Wuhan Government, and in 1933 in the Fukien People's Government; and in between, briefly in 1931 in the Central Government in Nanking. As Foreign Minister in the Government in Wuhan, it was he who negotiated the retrocession to China of British concessions in Hankow and

suggestion seems to me the most unjust that has ever been brought against me in my career.

I arrived in London on August 19th, when, in consequence of telegrams from Peking there was much alarm, the papers issuing daily posters announcing impending Civil War in China. *The Times* on the 21st asked me to write an article over my own name rebutting these statements. I did so on the 22nd, and my letter was published on the 23rd,[1] on which day I saw Crisp for the first time. On the 26th I was married, on the 29th I saw Crisp for the second time, and on the 30th he signed the Loan contract.

In the meantime I had seen McLeavy Brown, and we both agreed that the terms of the Crisp Loan were favourable to China. For you must know that the best offer China had had for money was from George Jamieson,[2] who was requiring 7 per cent at 85 for monies lent on the security – an ample security of the unissued bonds of the Tientsin–Pukow Railway British Section.[3] Crisp

---

Kiukiang, the only such diplomatic victory China can claim to have won over an imperialist power during the whole Republican period. Ch'en was asked to join the Nationalist Government in Nanking when war broke out against Japan in 1937, but he refused to serve under Chiang Kai-shek. He fell into the hands of the Japanese in Hong Kong when the island was taken by Japanese forces in 1941, and was removed to Shanghai where he not only resisted but attacked both the Japanese authorities and their Chinese collaborators in the face of their pressure on him to join the puppet regime. Ch'en was responsible for some of the most famous documents in Republican Chinese history. The most important documents presented by the Chinese delegation at the Paris Peace Conference were from his pen, and it was he who in 1924 wrote Sun Yat-sen's declaration to the world against British imperialism, and again he who drafted Sun's famous letter to the Soviet Union shortly before Sun's death in March the following year. In 1933, as Foreign Minister in the short-lived People's Government set up in Fukien, he was the author of an appeal addressed to Ignacy Paderewski, Gerhart Hauptmann, George Bernard Shaw, Romain Rolland, Upton Sinclair and other leading intellectuals of the day, to enlist the support of international opinion. Ch'en made Morrison's acquaintance soon after his arrival in Peking and became a frequent visitor at his house. Morrison often criticised and tried to moderate what he regarded as Ch'en's intemperate language and, as is seen from this letter, he more than once suggested that Ch'en should be arrested and deported as a British subject for attacking the British Government. Yet he readily came to Ch'en's defence when Ch'en was arrested in 1917, and appealed to the British Legation to bring pressure to bear to have him released. In spite of his criticism and drastic pruning of Ch'en's drafts of the documents China presented to the Paris Peace Conference in 1919, two examples of which are printed in this volume (*see* pp. 728–55), Morrison greatly admired Ch'en as a man for his ability, and particularly for his patriotism.

[1] This refers to Morrison's letter to the Editor of *The Times* on 23 August 1912 published under the title 'Dr Morrison on China'. *See* p. 25 note 1.

[2] George Jamieson (1843–1920), British consular official. He was Consul-General in Shanghai when in 1899 he resigned to become the representative of the British and Chinese Corporation Limited, the newly-founded organisation of the leading British trading and industrial interests seeking railway and other concessions in China.

[3] The Tientsin–Pukow (originally Tientsin–Chinkiang) Railway, was one of five railway concessions extracted from China in 1898 by the British Government. The railway was then divided into two sections by admitting the participation of the Deutsch-Asiatische

was to lend at 5% 89, and was prepared to advance at once for the urgent needs of the Government £500,000 Treasury Bonds on the same terms as the £1,800,000 had been advanced by the Sextuple Banks.

I am convinced that I did what was right for British interests. I am convinced that in giving support to an attempt to break down the monopoly, the highly injurious monopoly as I believe it to be, of the Hongkong and Shanghai Bank, I was doing right. You yourself, shortly before I left Peking, had spoken to me with the utmost bitterness against Mayers[1] and Hillier, and had written, you told me, fully to the F.O., complaining of their action in financing the German section of the Tientsin–Pukow railway, and in subsequently refusing to give financial assistance to Tuckey's line,[2] whereby they had made it inevitable that this important trunk-line would become a German railway under a German Chief Engineer.

At the F.O. Gregory[3] told me that the exclusive support given to the H. & S. Bank had exposed the F.O. to constant attacks and protests from British Banks whose directors were not 4/9 German as is the case in the H. & S. Bank.

I believed then, and I still believe, that in assisting a purely British group like Crisp's with Lloyd's Bank and other British Banks, to obtain a footing in China, from which they have been hitherto excluded, I was doing a service to genuine British interests.

The discrimination shown, for example in China, against the Chartered Bank, a purely British owned bank, in favour of a cosmopolitan bank like the H. & S. Bank, 4 of whose directors are Germans, has been for years the subject of adverse comment. Adverse also has been the comment on the exclusive support given to the B[ritish] & C[hinese] Corporation in railway construction, whereby the Shanghai–Nanking Railway was delayed construction for years.

I claim, therefore, that in assisting to introduce new British interests into China, however humble was the part I played in doing so, I was doing a service to the British, and therefore increasing the influence of the British Legation in China.

Bank as a result of Germany's claiming Shantung as her sphere of influence. The German section ran from Tientsin to the southern border of Shantung, from which point to Pukow became the British section.

[1] Sydney Francis Mayers (1873–1934), British consular official and commercial representative. He first went to China as a Student Interpreter in 1895 and served as an Assistant in the Chinese Secretary's office at the British Legation in Peking from September 1901 to June 1909. Leaving the consular service he joined the British and Chinese Corporation in January 1910, succeeding J. O. P. Bland as its representative in China. He compiled a *List of Chinese Higher Officials* while serving with the British Legation in Peking.

[2] So-called because T. W. T. Tuckey was the British engineer in charge of the British section of the Tientsin-Pukow Railway.

[3] John Duncan Gregory (1878–1951), British diplomat, who subsequently became Assistant Under-Secretary of State for Foreign Affairs (1925–8), was at this time a Junior Assistant Clerk in the Foreign Office.

To suggest, however, that my action impaired British interests as shown by certain scurrilous attacks made in the *Peking Daily News*, and to imply that my action inspired this scurrility, seems to me quite cruelly unjust.

If the Chinese have shown any ill-feeling against the Legation, I am afraid that other causes have contributed to this ill-feeling.

[...]

In London I could hear nothing to justify the F.O. subservience to the H. & S. Bank. Certainly the public have no special interest in supporting the policy of giving this bank exclusive support.

In May 1911 the H. & S. Bank issued in London a Japanese loan of £11,000,000 at 95. Today those bonds stand at 82¼.

But I am wandering from my conclusion.

Since I have been in Peking I have always done what I could to help to make things pleasanter between the Chinese and our Legation, and that will always continue to be my endeavour. I nurse the belief that I can do much to remove misunderstanding, but any hope of doing so becomes impossible if I am to be exposed to such suggestions regarding 'remarkable coincidences' as those you made to me. It seemed to me both to-day and the last occasion I came to see you, that you treated me as if I were a Chinese hostile to British interests instead of a patriotic Australian who can swear with truth that he has been a loyal friend to you and to the Legation for nearly sixteen years. During all these years I have never felt that anything said to me was so unjust as your observations this afternoon. You will, under the circumstances, excuse my writing to you at this length. The last person I could wish to misunderstand me is the British Minister, for whom I have always entertained so deepseated a friendship.

Very sincerely yours
G. E. Morrison

P.S.

After re-reading this letter I have to add two observations. In the first I wish to say that before McLeavy Brown or I gave either of us any support to the Crisp negotiations, we ascertained from the F.O. (and I subsequently had this confirmed from others, especially from Mr. George Lloyd, M.P.,[1] of Lloyd's Bank) that Crisp was a man of the highest character and standing, that he had rendered valuable services to Russia, and had assisted materially in cementing Anglo-Russian friendship.

[...]

G.E.M.

[1] George Ambrose Lloyd (1879–1941), later 1st Baron Lloyd of Doldran. A Member of the House of Commons (1910–18), he became a Director of Lloyd's Bank Limited in 1912 but resigned in November 1918 upon his appointment as Governor of Bombay. He rejoined the Board in 1924, when he also became again a Member of Parliament (1924–5), but in the following year he once more resigned from the Board of the Bank to take up the post of British High Commissioner for Egypt and the Sudan (1925–9). He became Secretary of State for the Colonies in 1940.

553. From J. N. Jordan

Peking 2 November 1912

My dear Morrison,

I regret that I am unable to reply at any length to your letter of yesterday as it raises many controversial points which it would be undesirable for me to discuss. I gladly acknowledge that our relations during the past 15 years have always been extremely friendly and I cordially reciprocate the hope that they will continue to be so.

But I cannot endorse your action in the Crisp loan and it is notorious that this Loan was the avowed cause of the inspired newspaper campaign against Sir Edward Grey and myself as the local exponent of British policy.

There are, so far as I know, no misunderstandings between this Legation and the Chinese Government – there are clear-cut issues involving questions of policy and interpretation of Treaties in which our position is, in my opinion, founded on justice and reason.

[...]

Yours very sincerely
J. N. Jordan

[...]

554. From T. A. Rustad[1]

Chinwangtao, Chili 5 November 1912

Dear Doctor Morrison,

When I arrived in Peking on August 9th, on my way from Urga to Shanghai, I called at your place and learned that you had allready left for London. I met Mr. Larson[2] on the plateau a few days before I reached Kalgan and he told me you wished me to call. I am sorry I did not see you. When we arrived in Urga on the 27th of September 1911, the manchu *Amban* San-*Ta-Jen*[3] was in charge of the place. We called on him with our

---

[1] A Norwegian in the employ of the British and American Tobacco Company, operating in Mongolia. The spelling in this letter is as in the original.

[2] Frans August Larson (b. 1870), Swedish missionary and trader, formerly Agent of the British and Foreign Bible Society in Mongolia, where he lived for many years and travelled widely. He was appointed on Morrison's recommendation Adviser on Mongolian Affairs by the Chinese Government in 1913, and as such served as China's emissary to the Mongols in Urga, as well as to various groups of uncommitted Mongols in other parts of Mongolia. He recounted his experiences in an autobiography entitled *Larson, Duke of Mongolia* (Boston, 1930), which was translated into many languages, including German, in which language the book appeared under the more explicit and less grandiloquent title *Die Mongolei und mein Leben mit den Mongolen* (Berlin n.d.)

[3] Santo, also known as San Liu-ch'iao (b. 1876), Mongol Bannerman, the *Amban* (Administrator) at Urga from October 1909 until he was driven away by the Mongols during the revolt in Urga in 1911. He later became the Deputy Garrison Commander at Mukden, and then at Chinchou in Fengtien Province. He served the Republic by becoming, in 1920, Director of the Bureau of Appointments in the Prime Minister's Office in Peking, and in December the following year he became Director of the Bureau in charge of

passports, which he looked over, but he did not even ask us in, but left us standing outside the *Yamen*. I just mention this to show you what kind of a man he was. He was too big for his boots. His predecessor[1] treated the mongols well and there would not have been any revolt at all except for the contempteous way in which San-*Ta-Jen* looked down upon the mongols. Princes and all. The mongols were obliged to do something, or else that man would have squeeced the very life out of them. The mongol declaration of independance was not an outcome of the Chinese revolution against the manchu government. There would have been a revolution in Mongolia just the same. Only the chinese revolution precipitated the affair. Han-Ta-Wang,[2] Hai-Shun-Gung[3] and one of the high Lamas had allready been to St. Petersburg to appeal to the russian authorities for protection against the Manchu *Amban*. The visit was without any apparent effect. Han-Ta-Wang was obliged to stay away from Urga, the *Amban* did his best to get him, and several times ordered him back without any result. The mongols have got horses that every year they dedicate to the Living-God. These horses are brought into Urga during the summer festival, when horse-racing etc takes place. Well the *Amban* with his soldiers took these horses by force from the mongols and branded them with his own brand saying that they were to be used only by the army hereafter. Well you can imagine what effect that had on the mongols, who are very religious, in their way. The *amban* taxed every little bit that the mongols produced and needed. The building of the barraks near Urga, just about 3 miles to the East of the town was also done with mongol money. There were some fine trees in a certain valley near Urga that the mongols thought a lot of. Well the first thing the *Amban* did was to cut down these trees and use them in the barrack buildings. The *Amban* in fact did everything that he knew the mongols did not like. He sat on them, properly speaking. Treated them just like animals, not as well as he treated his own overfed ponies. The mongols are very peaceful people, but it was more than any human being could stand. Those that had any valuables were put

---

Chinese labourers who had been sent to France during the First World War. In 1924 he was made a member of the Council of the Generals, and later joined Chang Tso-lin, the Manchurian warlord, as one of his advisers. Santo was versed in the writing of classical Chinese poems. *Ta-jen* may be roughly translated as 'His Excellency', by which Chinese officials were addressed.

[1] Yen-chih was Santo's predecessor at Urga from June 1905 to October 1909.

[2] Han-ta chin-wang, chief of Khalka, the richest of the four Mongolian provinces that took part in the revolt against the Manchu Government in 1911. He twice led a mission to Russia to appeal for protection from the Czar, and as a result of the second mission I. Ia. Korostovetz (q.v.) was sent as Special Russian Envoy to Urga. This led to the signing on 3 November 1912 of the Urga Convention between Russia and the Mongolian government in Urga.

[3] Hai-san-kung, Kharchin Prince, who assisted the Da Lama (q.v.) in organising the revolt against China in 1911. He was at this time a Counsellor to the Ministry of the Interior in the Urga Government and was regarded as the leader of the pro-Chinese party at Urga.

in prison and what they had was taken away from them. I have heard hundred of stories of how he managed to get what they had, but it would serve no good to repeat them. I suppose you know most of them. Well the behaviour of the *Amban* was the cause of the Mongol rising against the government of China. The leaders were, The Living Budha, Ta-Lama,[1] Nam-Serai-Gung,[2] (now, Na-Wang), Han-Ta-Wang, Da-Lay-Bess,[3] Hay-Shun-Gung and several others, whose names I do not know. The noted robber and murderer Tock-Tan-Tai-Ching[4] was also on the Living-Gods side. He came into Urga soon after the Manchu *Amban* had left and behaved himself very well. The mongols say that he did bad things against the *Amban*, just because the *Amban* was so hard on the mongols, and they consider him as a patriote. Hay-Shun-Gung was the man who obliged this former robber-chief to keep straight. This robber has about 60 permanent followers. When the mongols sent troops over to Khobdo[5] then some of Tock-Tan-Tai-Ching's men went over with the soldiers, and were, I was told, more or less in charge of that expedition. Some of this robber chief's men were also sent to the east, towards Tsi-tsi-khar[6] etc. He himself has been in Urga most of the time. The Living God gave him a title signifying 'not afraid of anybody'. The men in north Mongolia against this new rule, were Sain-Noying-Khan[7] and Tsa-Tsek-Ta-Khan.[8] Tsa-Tsek-Ta-Khan 'died' about the first of June, many said he was poisoned by the God. About this time the mongols started collecting duty on all goods coming from China. The charge was five per cent *ad valorum* on most things and ten percent on Wine and Tobacco. No charge was made against our shipment, and no charge were made against imports by russians. As you know the russian troops helped the mongols to disarm the Hsuanhua-fu troops[9] that were stationed in Urga. The russians also sent troops down from Kiachta, but these only stayed a couple of weeks and then returned. After-wards about 100 cossacks came, which raised the garrison to about 300 in all. Mostly mounted troops. They also had a couple of mashine rifles and they gave instruction to mongols how to use those they

[1] Tsening Chimet, who as the Da Lama was head of the Lama *Yamen* in Urga and Chief of the Lamas under the supreme headship of the Bogdo.
[2] Namsarai or Nam-serai Wang, a Mongol Prince, at the time Minister of Justice in the Urga government.
[3] Da Lai Bese, or Da Lai Wang, a Mongol Prince, at the time Minister of War in the Urga government.
[4] Tok-tan-tai-chi, literally meaning *hung hu-tzu* (Redbeard or brigand). This name was given by Rustad to a famous *hung hu-tzu* leader who was commander-in-chief of Mongol forces in Urga in 1913.
[5] A region in the north-west of Mongolia to the north of the Altai Mountains.
[6] A town on the River Nen in Heilungkiang, some 150 miles north-west of Harbin.
[7] This refers to the Khan of the Sain Noin tribes, Namnan-Surun. In 1912 he succeeded the Da Lama Tsening Chimet, as head of the Mongolian Cabinet.
[8] Jasaktu Khan, at the time Deputy Minister of Justice in the Urga Government.
[9] The Chinese troops stationed at Hsüan-hua, a town situated between Kalgan and Peking.

had taken from the Chinese troops. The Mongols also had russian instructers teaching them to march and shoot. These men were quartered over at the chinese barracks and all wore russian uniforms. Some of them were Buriats,[1] but the officer in charge of them was a russian. Ten of them alltogether. They also fixed up a kind of blue uniform with caps for the mongol soldiers to wear, but otherwise they did not teach them much. They could not do any muscetry as the mongols had very little amunition. 5000 old Burdanc rifles were sold to them by the russians. Later a german came and took an order for 10,000 rifles with 500 rounds amunition each. Half of this lot was delivered in Urga and the other half came in from Manchuria, where the german firm has an agency. I was told at the time that the russian consul in Urga Mr Louba[2] got some commission on this sale. Towards the end of June when I was preparing to leave for China, there arrived two Finnish professors in Urga. They came from the University in Helsingfors. The one in charge Mr Ramstedt[3] had been in Mongolia before and spoke the language. He was a personal friend of Hai-Shun-Gung. One day he came round and brought me a letter written by Hai-Shun-Gung to the British Minister in Peking. Mr Ramstedt told me Hai-Shun-Gung had told him to ask me to take it down as he did not trust the russian mail. I told him I was in Urga for business only and that we could not do it. He took the letter back with him. But the next day he came back together with Hay-Shun-Gung and again asked me if I would take that letter down to the British Minister. I again told them that I could not do that, but if they would address the letter to another private man, who could if he wished communicate the content to the minister I would then take it. That is how I brought a letter down for Liutenant Binsted[4] of the british army in Peking who came through Urga in

[1] The Buriats, many of whom were Lamaists, were a Mongolian tribe in Siberia. A number of them were sent by the Russian government to Mongolia to incite the native populace against Manchu rule when the Chinese Revolution broke out in 1911.

[2] Victor Fedorovich Louba, Russian consular official. Student Interpreter and Secretary in the Russian Consulate in Urga from 1891 to 1899, he became Consul there in 1905, and returned in 1912 after having served in Harbin and Uliassutai. In 1915 he was transferred to the Russian Consulate in Kobdo.

[3] G. J. Ramstedt (1873–1950), Finnish scholar, who was at this time in Mongolia, first went there in 1898, remaining until 1901 studying the language of the Khalka Mongols. In 1917 he became Professor at Helsinki University, and in 1919 was sent as Finnish Chargé d'Affaires to Japan, where he remained until 1929. He then returned to his post at Helsinki University, retiring in 1941. In 1943 he became the President of the Finno-Ougrienne Society. He was the author of a number of works on Mongolian language and pronunciation and also of a book on Korean grammar.

[4] G. C. Binsteed (d. 1917), British soldier, of whom D. D. Braham wrote to Morrison on 26 January 1912: 'a Lieutenant Binsteed is wandering around Asiatic Russia and sending us articles, some of which we hope to publish. He may get as far as Peking, and if so he will call on you.' Apparently a gifted linguist, Binsteed, drawing on his own experience as well as information from books in many languages, including Russian, helped Morrison to compile a long and detailed memorandum on Mongolia, which Morrison sent to

February last. The letter simply asked him to find out if the Mongol declaration of independance had reached the Minister in Peking and asking for an answer. It also said that since the deliverance from the manchues the mongols had started schools of their own and that everything was peacefull in and around Urga. After this first meeting with Hai-Shung-Gung he used to come round quite often. He is a man who has travelled a lot. He has been all over china and speaks chinese just like a native. He told me he has worked for the deliverance of Mongolia from the manchu joke for many years. He would have Mongolia absolutely independant. We used to have discussions on the subject. He was not for the russians, on the contrary he was very suspicious of them and watched their movements very carefully. He said he know that there existed a party in Russia that wanted to make the Desert of Gobi the frontier between China and Russia. Russia only wanted north Mongolia together under one government. He said he knew the russians were against the southern mongols joining the north, because it would interfere with their plan. He however was working to get the whole of Mongolia together. He is a real patriote, nothing mean about him. He has got his ideal and is working for it. None of his sons will become Lama he told me. He asked me if I could induce some rich british company to come up and open up mines and help them to start a bank of their own etc. He promised me that if I could get together an english company he would show me a place where more gold could be found, than in any of the mines at present worked or rather controled by the russian. There is a rumour up there that the mongols know about another mine that has never been worked but that they keep in secret. Those Mining experts that the last *Amban*[1] sent round the country to try and find the mine had mongol guides with them and naturally they led them all round, except where the gold was to be found. The *Amban* tried by force to get the mongols to tell, but Han-Ta-Wang in whose territory the rich goldfield has been found has forbidden his men to talk about it, and the mongols are absolutely devoted to their princes. Well Hai-Shun-Gung says that he will give that concession to any Company that has the support of the British Government. His idea is to create an english interest in Mongolia so that the claims of Russia may be balanced. He would invite all nations to come and settle in mongolia. There is plenty of room he says, and he is certainly right. If a company could be got together for the working of the mine in question the mongols would only ask as part in the gains, Ten procent of the profits. The company would have to pay two or three mongol controllers for looking after mongol interests, and Tls 30, a month would be charged for each mongol soldier that the company would

---

Lu Cheng-hsiang and Ts'ai T'ing-kan in order to aid the Chinese Government in formulating its Mongolian policy. It is not printed in this selection. Binsteed was still young when killed in action during the European War.   [1] Santo.

want, for use of guarding the mine and act as escort to shipments of gold. He would himself do everything in his power to promote the interests of such a British mining Company in Mongolia. Hai-Shun-Gung asked me to get him a man, a forreigner to run the telegraph for them in Urga and other places in Mongolia, but I told him that it would be a very wise thing to leave the telegraph alone, as several nations were interested in it and it would perhaps be used by Russia as excuse to use armed intervention if they the mongols took over the working of the telegraph. Hai-Shun-Gung further told me that if no nation outside of Russia would recognize their independance, he would then go to the Hague conference and try to get the sympathy of the powers. Hai-Shun-Gung is the only man of the new Mongol government that realy does anything. The rest of them just drink and let things go as they best can, and leaves everything to Hai-Shun-Gung. He takes no salary and spends his own money. He wants the mongols to be treated like human beings that is all he works for he says. He is sincere all right, but I am afraid the Russians will get the best of him in the long run. The russians up there since the revolution have been working their hardest to get the mongols to order all the chinese away from Mongolia. But the mongols do not want the chinese to leave. They understand quite well that the russians cannot supply them with articles they need as well and as cheap as the chinese can. The russians have succeeded in getting the mongols to forbid the chinese to trade in the interior. The chinese are not now allowed to go and buy up skins etc as they used to do. That is all done by russian traders now. Some russian made a private loan to Na-Wang of One Million Roubles. Security in the russian gold mine district. The mongol princes owes the Ta-Ching Bank in Urga about 600,000 taels. And over three times that amount is owed by mongol princes and others to the chinese merchants in Urga. The living God alone is said to have debts outstanding to merchants in Urga for about Tls. 500,000 by himself alone. Since the revolution nobody has paid any debts, but extra ordinary to say the Ta-Ching Bank notes are still good in Urga only 5 percent lower than a Rouble and there is a lot of Chinese small coin in circulation. Twelve copper cents go to a ten cent piece. The mongols are much afraid of the russian notes because some Japs over in Harbin sent a whole bunch over in that direction, and most of the notes were very good immitations. I believe that if Hai-Shun-Gung could be explained the situation properly, he would rather go together with China than risk to be annexed by Russia, sooner or later. The living God is impossible, he is illiterate and does not know what he is doing he is half blind too. The rest of his followers are all mostly ignorent and only follow him because he is God, to them. Hai-Shun-Gung is now in Khobdo, but Sosita-Gung is in Urga watching things for him. If there is anything special you would like to know about Urga or that part of Mongolia I shall only be too glad to be of any service to you. I was there for 10 months and I know most of the people up there. We have one of our men stationed in Urga. His name is Mamen, he is a cousin of mine, we came out together.

Yours sincerely
T. A. Rustad

555. To Ts'ai T'ing-kan

[Peking] 14 November 1912

My dear Colonel,

[...]

I am delighted to hear that there is a possibility of Mr Sun Pao-chi accepting the post of Foreign Minister.[2] No appointment could be wiser. He has quite exceptional qualifications, for he speaks excellent French, which is the language of diplomacy. He has been Minister to France and Germany and in both countries he created a most favourable impression. He has held high territorial position in China as Governor of Shantung and the speech he delivered at the opening of the Provincial Assembly created a profound impression upon students of modern Chinese History. Everything is in his favour. He is *persona grata* at all the Legations and his pleasant and suave manner makes him personally popular. I do hope that he can be induced to accept the post.

In the meantime the protest will, no doubt, be formulated against Russian action in Mongolia and then further negotiations can be opened with the Russian Government with a view to the reconsideration of their position *vis-à-vis* the Mongols, a position which the Russian Government claims is due to the unwillingness of the Chinese Government to negotiate with them in the past.

I hope that public opinion is being assuaged by the resignation of Mr M. T. Liang.[3] The correspondents telegraphing home about his resignation made

[1] O. Mamen, a Norwegian in the service of the British American Tobacco Company in Urga.
[2] Sun Pao-ch'i (1867–1931), Chinese Imperial official, Provincial Governor and Republican politician. Son of an Imperial Tutor and a relative by marriage of I-k'uang (Prince Ch'ing) (1836–1916), he had been Minister to France (1902–5) and to Germany (1907–8) and was Governor of Shantung Province at the time of the 1911 Revolution, when he briefly declared the Province independent. He was mentioned as a possible successor as Foreign Minister to Liang Ju-hao (q.v.), whose resignation was only officially gazetted the day after this letter was written, but in the event Lu Cheng-hsiang was appointed. However Sun succeeded Lu Cheng-hsiang as Foreign Minister in September 1913, holding the post until January 1915 when he was in turn succeeded by Lu. While Foreign Minister, Sun acted as Prime Minister from February to May 1914, and was Prime Minister for some seven months ten years later, from January to July 1924.
[3] Liang Ju-hao (b. 1860) or Liang Mou-t'ing (hence M. T. Liang, by which name he was known to foreigners), served briefly as Foreign Minister from 16 September to 15 November 1912. One of a group of Chinese students sent to study in the United States in 1874, he served after his return to China with an engineering degree, as Managing-Director of the Imperial Northern Chinese Railways, Customs *Taotai* in Tientsin (1907), and Chief Secretary to Hsi-liang (1853–1917), Viceroy of Manchuria (1908–9). He was proposed

remarks upon his being a brilliant Chinese scholar as well as a fine English scholar. This would counteract the erroneous impression created by the unfortunate telegram from Mr Fraser in which he ventured to say that the Foreign Minister could not read his own language.[1]

With kind regards

Very sincerely yours
[G. E. Morrison]

556. To Turner[2]

[Peking] 15 November 1912

My dear Turner,

Your letter of the 10th August has remained a disgracefully long time unanswered, but, believe me, there was no letter I received since my appointment that gave me greater pleasure.

Not only have I been appointed Political Adviser, the work of which gives

---

as Minister of Communications in the T'ang Shao-yi Cabinet in 1912, but his nomination was rejected by Parliament. He participated in the Washington Conference in 1921 as a technical adviser to the Chinese delegation but otherwise played no prominent part in subsequent national politics.

[1] In a telegram announcing the appointment of Liang Ju-hao, published in *The Times* on 17 September 1912 under the title 'New Chinese Foreign Minister', Fraser wrote: 'The selection is remarkable, as the new Minister is unable to read the Chinese language, though he is well educated from the Western point of view.' A correction was subsequently published in *The Times* on 15 November 1912 which stated: 'Information to this effect [Liang's inability to read Chinese] was given to our Correspondent, who, however, now finds that it is unfounded, and regrets that it should have been given currency.'

[2] A positive identification has not been possible since the letter of 10 August 1912, to which this is a reply, cannot be traced. It could be either Peter Turner or George Turner, but more likely the latter. Peter Turner, whom Morrison described in his Diary in familiar terms as a 'likeable rogue', was the builder of Morrison's house in Peking. Morrison met him again in Toronto, where Turner was with the Bank of Montreal, in January 1919 on his way to the Paris Peace Conference, and of whom he wrote in his Diary on 23 January 1919: 'Peter Turner, a powerfully built man of the same age as myself but physically stronger than three of me...He has £2000 a year. Peter always claimed that he was a nephew of Jabez B. Snowball, Lt. Gov. New Brunswick 1902–7.' George Turner was a British financier, who, according to Sir Charles Addis, the Manager of the Hongkong & Shanghai Banking Corporation in London, in his letter of 7 April 1908 to J. O. P. Bland, then the representative in China of the British and Chinese Corporation, was 'the author of the damaging statements which have regularly appeared in the *Financial News* and other newspapers on the occasion of every new issue of a Chinese Loan...He came out to China sometime in the Eighties, went up to Peking and obtained, as he thought, orders for Railway material....(probably tricked by *Mafoo*, posing as a Mandarin)...I met him, then, and a decent man he was, but his failure to implement these documents, has turned to gall, and for years past he has been bombarding the Foreign Office, the British & Chinese Corporation and the Press. He has probably persuaded himself by this time...that he has wrongs to be redressed, and the deaf ear turned by the Foreign Office and the B & C has probably put him a little beside himself...I am inclined to think that the best course for us to pursue is to do nothing' (Bland Papers, Thomas Fisher Rare Book Library, University of Toronto).

me the greatest possible interest and pleasure, but I have followed your example and got married.

[...]

There is no chance of my being knighted – none whatever. At one time there was some such talk, but those honours are reserved for Jews, Railway Conductors and loyal Britishers who sing 'God Save the King' in broken English like Carl Mayer[1] and the Abrahams, Isaacs and Jacobs.

With kind regards

Yours very sincerely
[G. E. Morrison]

557. To Ts'ai T'ing-kan

[Peking] 22 November 1912

My dear Colonel,

[...]

To-day I have been very busy talking to different people and trying to arrange with the Russo-Asiatic Bank a meeting in London between Mr. Crisp and Mr. Addis.

That a compromise will be effected I have no doubt whatever, but one must try and arrange a settlement that will not impair the dignity of any of the parties concerned, especially the dignity of the Minister of Finance.

It seems to me most important that the Banks should reconcile their differences before they come to an agreement with the Chinese Government and before Crisp comes to an agreement as to relinquishing the advantages conferred upon him by Article 14 of his loan contract.[2]

The financial position itself, as shown by the Customs collection, is satisfactory. This year will be the record year. Although in the Memorandum submitted to the President by Mr. Aglen[3] there was an error made by the Powers by which the liabilities were understated by £204,000, Mr. Aglen's estimate on the other side of the available balance was too moderate and he

[1] Sir Carl Meyer (1851–1922), 1st Bart., German-born British financier. Born in Hamburg, Germany, he later moved to England and became a JP of Essex and a Lieutenant of the City of London. He was a Director of the National Bank of Egypt, Chairman of the London Committee of De Beers, and a Director of the Hongkong & Shanghai Banking Corporation as well as of the British and Chinese Corporation. He was created a Baronet in 1910.

[2] Article 14 of the Crisp Loan Agreement bound the Chinese Government not to issue any other external loan on any more favourable terms than those contained in the Crisp Agreement until the whole of the Loan had been issued to the public. It also required the Chinese Government to give preference to the Crisp Financial Group if further foreign capital was required for the duration of the Loan.

[3] Francis (later Sir Francis) Arthur Aglen (1869–1932), British employee of the Chinese Maritime Customs, which he joined in 1888. In 1912 he was appointed Inspector-General succeeding Sir Robert Hart on the latter's death. He was dismissed by the Chinese Government on 1 February 1927 for refusing to implement the policy of the Tariff Commission, then headed by Liang Shih-yi (q.v.), and A. H. F. Edwards was appointed Acting Inspector-General in his place.

will have nearly Two Million Taels more than he stated in the memorandum. Then he has made no allowance in his estimate for the American Indemnity moneys which have to be returned for this year. It works out that instead of China requiring before December 31st of this year to meet arrears of the Boxer Indemnity to the amount of £3,500,000 the total payment she requires to make will be less than £2,000,000 – a very important difference.

You, no doubt, know that *The Times* published fully the telegrams communicated by Mr. Lew Yuk Lin.[1] There was an unfortunate error in the telegram categorically denying the story of the Mongolian massacres, but it did not impair the general sense of the passage. *The Times* published it prominently on the front page. That is one thing, every good English paper, more especially *The Times*, is always willing to hear both sides, and I hope that so long as I am here I will be able to help to correct erroneous statements.

The *Peking Daily News* has been very effective the last few days. The tone of its articles is more effective because they are more temperate: it is argumentative without being personal. Several Ministers have spoken to me of the change in tone. I think much credit is due to Mr. Eugene Ch'en[2] for modifying the vehemence of his articles when he found that they were causing irritation and annoyance. It is so important to have friendly relations with all the foreign Ministers in Peking.

The Foreign Minister[3] has created a very favourable impression and I think there is little doubt that he can come to an agreement with Russia which would be satisfactory to the Chinese people. With the situation in Europe as it is Russia cannot wish to get into any entanglement out here and I believe that by a friendly interchange of views many misunderstandings might be removed.

[...]

My best wishes to you

Very sincerely yours
[G. E. Morrison]

[...]

[1] Liu Yü-lin (b. 1862), at this time Chinese Minister in London (September 1910 – June 1914). Previously he had been Consul-General in Australia and in Singapore. After he returned from England he became Commissioner for the Salt Gabelle and for Maritime Customs in his native Kwangtung Province. He later joined the Military Government set up by Sun Yat-sen in Canton.

[2] Morrison had earlier written to Ts'ai T'ing-kan asking him to use his influence with Ch'en Yu-jen to moderate his criticism of the Powers and the banks they supported. He also wrote to Ch'en himself on 6 November 1912 about Ch'en's article on the Powers' attitude to the Crisp Loan: 'I do not think that you are being kept informed as to the very serious financial situation that has arisen in England and the absolute necessity, if bankruptcy is to be avoided, of coming again into friendly relations with all the Powers and with different Banks. I do not think you realise how enormous is the irritation caused by the articles in your paper, which are taken to be the expressions of the opinion of the Chinese Government. This is no time to create friction but it is the time to try and remove all possible causes of friction and that I know is the ardent desire of the President himself.'

[3] Lu Cheng-hsiang.

558. To J. N. Jordan

[Peking] 23 November 1912

Dear Sir John,

[...]

I have just had a visit from Mr C. C. Wu,[1] son of Wu Ting Fang,[2] who is a Barrister at Law of Lincoln's Inn. He brought with him Mr Lo[3] who is just back from Merton, Oxford. I am asking Rose[4] to come over and meet

[1] Wu Ch'ao-shu (or Wu Ch'ao-ch'u, hence 'C. C. Wu') (1887–1934), Chinese diplomat and Republican politician. Educated in America and Britain, he was at this time Director of the Treaty Department in the Foreign Ministry. He remained with the Peking Government as a Counsellor in the Foreign Ministry and in the Prime Minister's Office until July 1917, when he left Peking to join the government which was set up by Sun Yat-sen in Canton, and became Vice-Minister of Foreign Affairs, while his father, Wu T'ing-fang (q.v.), was the Minister. In 1919 he led the southern group of the Chinese Delegation to the Paris Peace Conference, and in March 1923 he was made Foreign Minister in the southern Government succeeding his father who had died the previous year. He was active in the months preceding the formal establishment of the Nationalist Government in Nanking in 1928, serving, among other posts, as a mediator between the rival factions of the Kuomintang in Wuhan and Nanking, and in the same year became the first envoy from the Nationalist Government to the United States. Upon his return to China in 1931 he was appointed President of the Legislative Council, a post he held until his death.

[2] Wu T'ing-fang (1842–1922), Chinese diplomat and Republican politician. A British-trained lawyer, he abandoned his practice in Hong Kong to join the diplomatic service under Li Hung-chang, and in 1897 became Chinese Minister to Washington (1897–1902 and 1907–9). The Wuchang Uprising in 1911 found him on the side of the Republicans of the south, and he became their representative in the subsequent negotiations, and was later made Minister of Justice in the Provisional Government set up by Sun Yat-sen in Nanking in 1912. He became Foreign Minister in Tuan Ch'i-jui's Cabinet in November 1916 and he was made Acting Prime Minister on 23 May the following year when Tuan was dismissed by Li Yüan-hung. But less than a month later, on 12 June, he resigned in protest against Li's decision to dissolve Parliament, and left to join Sun Yat-sen's government in the south, holding, among other posts, intermittently the portfolio of Foreign Minister until his death in 1922. However, he exercised little influence on policy-making during those years.

[3] Possibly Lo Ch'ang, who was at this time Secretary to the Minister of Communications and who subsequently held various diplomatic and government posts, including that of Commissioner for Foreign Affairs in Shantung Province in 1915, and Consul-General in Singapore (1918–19), in London (1919–21) and in Ottawa (1923–5).

[4] Charles Archibald Walker Rose (1879–1961), British consular official. From Student Interpreter in 1898 he rose to become Commercial Secretary of the British Legation in Peking in 1918, in which position he remained until his resignation in 1921. His penchant for ballroom-dancing, apparently to the neglect of his duties while holding this last post, won him the label from Morrison of 'Professor of Dancing and Deportment in the Dept. of Commerce'. Rose was at this time a First-Class Assistant attached to the Chinese Secretariat in the British Legation in Peking. After his retirement from the consular service he became a Director of the Chartered bank of India, Australia and China. In 1928, as a Trustee of the Morrison Papers, he strongly opposed the publication of the Morrison Diaries edited by J. B. Capper, on the grounds that the events they recorded were at the time too politically sensitive.

them on Monday. There is going to be quite a community of English graduates in Peking. Perhaps Rose might be able to bring them all together. You might suggest this to him. I shall be glad to help in this direction.

The Government are trying to take advantage of the Urga incident to make the people understand that if they had been united such an act could not have been committed. I am quite sure that they have not the remotest intention of carrying out any military operations. I pointed out to the President the positions on the map and I reminded him of the way that China in the past has neglected her frontiers. I mentioned the case of Ulugchat where China had a garrison of 4 men. I also reminded him that at Urga China had before the troubles an available force of 250, whereas Russia had, within easy access of Urga, a body of not less than 125,000. I am trying to get the newspapers to discuss this question with more calmness. I think that in the *Peking Daily News* there will be no recurrence of the insensate articles that have been published in the past.

[...]

Very sincerely yours
[G. E. Morrison]

559. To Ts'ai T'ing-kan

[Peking] 27 November 1912

My dear Colonel,

In explanation of the accompanying Memorandum,[1] I may tell you that the first communication was submitted when China was in the throes of the Boxer Rebellion. You will remember that the Siege in Peking began on the 20th June 1900 and terminated on the 14th of August. On the 15th of December of the same year[2] an agreement – which I was the means of divulging to the world – was entered into between Monsieur Korostovetz,[3] who was then

---

[1] Not found.
[2] According to Rockhill in his *Treaties and Conventions with or concerning China and Korea 1894-1904* (Washington 1904, p. 201), with information probably supplied by Morrison who had been helping Rockhill, as he later helped MacMurray, with the compilations of these treaties, the date of signature of the Convention referred to was 11 November 1900. The Instrument signed by Korostovetz (q.v.) and Chou Mien (q.v.) bears the date of 30 January 1901. *See* MacMurray, *op. cit.*, Vol. I p. 329.
[3] Ivan Iakovlevich Korostovetz, Russian diplomat. He was at the time referred to Foreign Affairs Secretary at Port Arthur, under Admiral Alexeiev, and was one of the Russian delegates with Count de Witte at the Portsmouth Peace Conference. Vice-Director of the Oriental Section in the Russian Ministry of Foreign Affairs, he became in 1908, upon the death of Dmitri Pokotilov, Russian Minister in Peking. He held this post until his appointment, which was a direct result of Han-ta Chin-wang's mission to Russia, as Russian Special Envoy to Mongolia at Urga, where he arrived in September 1911. He was responsible for the so-called Urga Convention signed on 3 November 1912. Korostovetz was the author of a book on the Portsmouth Treaty published in London in 1920, and a book on Mongolia, *Von Cinggis Khan zur Sowjetrepublik; eine kurze Geschichte der Mongolei unter besonderer Berücksichtigung der neuesten Zeit* (Berlin and Leipzig 1926).

the Russian Secretary of Foreign Affairs in the Port Arthur Administration, and Chou Mien,[1] who was then the delegate of Tseng Chi the Tartar General at Mukden.[2] This agreement was published in *The Times* on the 3rd of January 1901 and created as great a sensation as must have created the recent Mongolian Convention signed on the 3rd November last.[3]

It was in fear of the impairment of the territorial integrity of China that induced Mr Secretary Hay[4] to hand the Note of the 18th February 1901 to the Chinese Minister at Washington.[5]

The communication of the 10th of February 1904[6] explains itself, as does that of the 15th of January 1905.[7] The exchange of the Notes of the 15th of November 1908 also required no comment.[8]

[1] The Chinese representative in the Chinese Eastern Railway. Later he became one of the largest land-owners in the Manchurian province of Heilungkiang.

[2] Tseng-ch'i, a Manchu Bannerman, was Tartar-General of Mukden from March 1899 to August 1900, when he was removed from the post as a result of protests by the Powers following Morrison's exposure of the Treaty of 11 November 1900 that bore his and Admiral Alexeiev's names. He was reinstated to the post on Russian insistence in March 1901, however, and retained it until April 1905. His reinstatement was in fact specifically stipulated, and formed Article 10 of the so-called Preliminary Agreement regarding Manchuria, signed by Korostovetz and Chou Mien on 30 January 1901, which replaced that of 11 November 1900. It read, 'The Tartar-General Tseng-ch'i is to remain for four years in office in this province to reorganize public affairs after the late disturbances.'

[3] A reference to a Convention signed at Urga on 3 November 1911 by the newly-established Mongolian Government and I. Ia. Korostovetz, the Special Russian Envoy. The 'Mongolian Convention' and 'Korostovetz Convention', mentioned in the pages of this volume refer to this Convention unless otherwise indicated.

[4] John Milton Hay (1838–1905), American politician and diplomat. Starting his career as private secretary to Abraham Lincoln (1809–65), 16th U.S. President, he entered the diplomatic service in 1865 as a junior secretary in the American Legation in Paris, rising to become Ambassador to the Court of St James in 1987. Made Secretary of State the following year by William McKinley, he retained the position under Theodore Roosevelt and died in office. One of the acts with which his name is associated was his proposal in 1899 to the Great Powers with an interest in China of the so-called 'Open Door policy', which was made famous by its failure.

[5] The Chinese Minister at the time referred to was Wu T'ing-fang. The Note was a remonstrance against the proposed expedition by Field-Marshal von Waldersee, Commander-in-Chief of the Allied Expedition Forces in China, into the interior of the province of Chihli. It was not addressed directly to the various governments, but was sent by Edwin Hurd Conger (1843–1907), the then United States Minister in Peking (1898–1905), to the envoys of the various Powers in Peking.

[6] A reference to the Note the State Department addressed to various Powers on 10 February 1904, proposing a guarantee of the neutrality and integrity of China during the Russo-Japanese War.

[7] This seems to refer to the Circular Note addressed by Russia to the Powers on 14 January 1905, concerning the alleged breach of neutrality by China during the Russo-Japanese War. Accordingly the American Legation in Peking was instructed by John Hay, the American Secretary of State, to make enquiries.

[8] Morrison seems to be referring to the Exchange of Notes between Japan and the United States declaring their policy in the Far East, which took place, however, on 30 November, not 15 November 1908.

You will, therefore, see from the Memorandum attached that an opportunity is given now to remind the United States of the policy which was declared to be the cardinal policy of their Government, not once but on repeated occasions between 1900 and 1908.

Unfortunately, the American Government is not as faithful to fulfil its engagements as it is to make them. You will remember that by the United States Treaty with Corea of May 22nd 1882, Art. I provided that:—

> 'If other Powers deal unjustly or oppressively with Corea, the United States Government will exercise their good offices, on being informed of the case, to bring about an amicable arrangement, thus showing their friendly feelings.'

The way America showed her friendly feelings in this case to Corea was in being the first to recognise every act of aggression committed by Japan against Corea: being the first to recognise the annexation of Corea: the first to withdraw her diplomatic representative from Corea and to consent to all relations with Corea being entrusted to the Japanese Government.[1]

I should think the time was very opportune for drawing the attention of the United States Government to its various declarations. It could, of course, discreetly become known in the European Press when this was done. I could easily arrange to have a suitable message communicated to the foreign papers.

With kind regards

Very sincerely yours
[G. E. Morrison]

560. To Liu Yü-lin

[Peking] 29 November 1912

Dear Mr Lew,

I have to draw your attention to the injury frequently done to the credit and to the fair name of China by the publication in English papers of articles or telegrams from interested sources such as, for example, St Petersburg, conveying incorrect information regarding China's actions, and to point out to you the need of correcting these erroneous statements, as soon as possible after they have been given publicity.

A famous French writer once said that 'a lie given currency for only 24

---

[1] The United States was the first country to condone Japan's first steps towards the annexation of Korea, by withdrawing her Legation there on 24 November 1905, only a week after the conclusion of the treaty by which Japan was to take over control of the foreign relations of Korea. The United States' hasty abandonment of Korea was described by Willard Straight (1880–1918), then a Secretary in the Legation, as 'like the stampede of rats from a sinking ship' (*see* A. W. Griswold, *The Far Eastern Policy of the United States*, New Haven 1938, p. 136). In 1910 she was also among the first to recognise the formal annexation of the country by Japan.

hours can often be of great service to a State', and that seems to be the view of foreign policy conspicuously followed by the Russian Government.

For example *The Times* of October 9th published a telegram from St Petersburg headed 'Massacres by Chinese in Eastern Mongolia'. No knowledge of this injurious telegram reached my Government until the arrival of the English mail nearly three weeks afterwards. The categorical contradiction you published in *The Times* of the 30th October materially counteracted the evil done by the injurious telegram, but it would have been much more effective if the correction had been published in *The Times* of the 10th or 11th October. And here I may remark that the telegram as published of this particular correction omitted the words 'none of' in the third line of the second paragraph, which should have read 'None of Yuan Shih-kai's troops' but which actually read 'Yuan Shih-kai's troops are stationed' – an essential difference. The rest of the telegram, however, containing a categorical denial of the alleged massacres was quite effective.

In future you should never allow injurious messages or statements of this kind to pass without the earliest contradiction. If, owing to the absence of special information, you should be unable to reply at once – if possible in the next issue of the paper – you should telegraph the gist of the objectionable article to Peking and I will see that an effective reply is at once cabled to you.

You should send your telegram in these cases in plain English, because then you can condense it by omitting obvious words in the ordinary way of sending messages of telegraphic brevity. If the message is not of extreme urgency you can send it at 'deferred rates' costing one half ordinary rates. Another way that you could also arrange is to have the messages requiring contradiction sent out by Reuter's Agency to their Agent in Peking. You could probably make an arrangement with them whereby this could be done at very little cost indeed, or, perhaps at no cost at all.

In *The Times* of the 9th November a semi-official explanation is published from St Petersburg, speaking of the Mongolian Convention, in which it is specifically stated that the 'Convention applies to Northern and Western Mongolia'. This information would have been of value to my Government. It is of the highest importance that every effort should be made by you to prevent the dissemination of misleading messages injurious to the credit of our Country.

Similar instructions are being sent to our Ministers in France, Germany, Russia and America.

I have the honour to be etc. etc.

[Lu Cheng-hsiang][1]

[1] This letter, addressed to the Chinese Minister in London in the name of Lu Cheng-hsiang, was drafted by Morrison. The memorandum Morrison prepared on the same subject to be sent to the Chinese Ministers in France, Germany, Russia and the United States is not printed.

561. To Ts'ai T'ing-kan

[Peking] 6 December 1912

My dear Admiral,[1]

Yesterday afternoon I had a visit from Mr C. C. Wu (son of Dr Wu Ting-fang) of the Foreign Office, telling me that he had been appointed to take charge of the Treaty Revision Department of the Foreign Office and that the previous afternoon he had been given by Mr Lu Cheng-hsiang the reply I had written with regard to Tibet.[2] He produced the original letter with my manuscript corrections. I am afraid we are now face to face with considerable further delay in sending a reply to the Note of the 17th of August last.

Mr Wu has written a pamphlet called *What are we in Tibet?* in which he argues that China's rights in Tibet are sovereign rights and not suzerain rights. It contains Latin quotations and is an ingenious study for a Debating Society. On account of this pamphlet Mr Lu has entrusted him apparently with the preparation of the reply. Unfortunately Mr Wu has not seen the *Blue Books* regarding Tibet. He has not had time to look through the papers.

He takes the view that there should be no historical summary in the reply sent to the British Government but that the reply should be based upon arguments derived from Treaties.

What I fear is that this delay if continued much longer and no reply be sent to a communication dated the 17th August, or a reply only be sent hair-splitting, the British Government may enter into direct relations with the Dalai Lama in the same way the Russian Government have entered into direct relations with the Hutukhutu in Urga.[3]

If the Chinese Government desire to raise the question of suzerain or sovereign in their reply to the British Note, this can easily be done in a few sentences. China does not consent to her position in Tibet being regarded as other than that of a sovereign Power.

I have nearly finished the Mongolian report and hope to send you in some notes tomorrow morning. The 4 articles of Mr Kroupensky's proposed agreement have also been given to Mr Wu.[4]

[...]

With kind regards
[G. E. Morrison]

[1] Ts'ai T'ing-kan was gazetted a Rear-Admiral on 20 November 1912.
[2] Britain had sent a Note on 17 August 1912 stating that China's acceptance of Britain's position regarding Tibet was a necessary condition for the recognition of the Chinese Republic by the British Government. The reply which Morrison drafted on behalf of China is not printed.
[3] Jebtsun Damba Khutukhtu (1870–1924), also referred to as the Bogdo Khan, the Bogdo Lama, Ba Ga Da Lama or the 'Living Buddha.' He was made head of the government which the Khalka Mongols established in Urga following their revolt against the Manchu Government in 1911.
[4] On 3 December 1912, as a result of the Urga Convention, Russia put forward a proposal comprising four articles as a basis for an agreement between Russia and China on the

562. To Ts'ai T'ing-kan

[Peking] 14 December 1912

My dear Admiral,

[...]

Yesterday the meeting of Bankers was to be held in Paris, but I have not yet heard the result. The Bankers here, however, tell me that there is no prospect of their advancing money to China under the conditions proposed by the Minister of Finance. However, we will know within a day or two what has been the result. You see difficulties are being added to difficulties. No Government can afford to treat a neighbouring friendly Power like England in the way that China is doing. Surely the Minister of Foreign Affairs must realise how the British Government feel when they have to reply to a question in the House of Commons that no reply has been sent to a despatch sent to the Chinese Government on the 17th of August.

Being kept entirely in the dark, I, of course, know nothing as to what is passing between the Minister of Foreign Affairs and the Russian Minister with regard to the question of Mongolia. I cannot help hearing outside that there is no prospect of an Agreement: that the Korostovetz Agreement at Urga will be ratified by the Russian Government and that the effect of insane suggestions, such as those of Sun Yat Sen, as to preparing an Expedition to march on Moscow and St Petersburg, must have the direct effect of increasing the Russian Guards in Mongolia and of preparations being made to increase the Russian Guards in Western China. The Chinese do not seem to be aware that at the present moment both Kashgar and Ili are in the military occupation of Russia and that the New Dominion is absolutely at Russia's mercy.[1] Yesterday I had a letter from Kashgaria. As you know there is an excellent Russian road from this Russian railway into Kashgar City, where there is a well equipped Russian force of 750 men, Infantry, Cavalry and Artillery, and within 8 days' march there are at least 20,000 men, a number which it is estimated could be increased within 3 months to a fully equipped force of 120,000. Andijan, the terminus of the Russian Railway, is quite close to the Chinese border and from that point it is only one day and a half to Tashkent.

---

question of Mongolia. This was conveyed to the Chinese Foreign Ministry through Wu Ch'ao-shu by Basil N. Kroupensky, at this time Russian Minister to China (1911–16) and later Russian Ambassador to Japan (1916–1922). The proposal became the basis of a Declaration by the two countries and an Exchange of Notes on 5 November the following year.

[1] A certain Mussulman named Effendi, a Russian subject and dealer in false passsports, had been attacked by Chinese soldiers and villagers in Kherah near Khotan because of his refusal to answer a summons by the local Chinese authorities. The Russian Government, which was pressing China for the revision of the 1881 St Petersburg Treaty, used this incident and the necessity of protecting her subjects as a pretext to send troops into China and occupy Chinese frontier towns. This was done despite China's assurance of compensation should the case be proved as the Russians alleged.

[...]

You will excuse my writing to you so frankly but it is better that you should know as quickly as possible how things appear to be going to one who sees them from outside.

With kind regards

Very sincerely yours
[G. E. Morrison]

563. To O. M. Green[1]

[Peking] 21 December 1912

My dear Green,

[...]

I have been wanting for some time past to write to you at some length on the British position in China and our waning influence.

I cannot, of course, take any exception to your criticism of my action in regard to the Crisp loan, although I think that your comments are unjust and that you ignore many important considerations. [...]

I cannot see why any Englishman should condemn a policy which is beneficial to British trade and to British Bankers of high standing, such as those who have been associated with Mr Crisp. It seems to me inexplicable that those British Bankers must be injured in order that some prospective benefit may be conferred upon Russians, Japanese and Germans.

The facts of the Crisp Loan as I know them are these: – You know that I had intended to leave China and go back to Australia. I had become engaged and my wife that was to be and I had decided to leave China and go back to our own country. My fiancee left for England on the 10th July with this knowledge. Naturally after this I took little interest in affairs and I was not aware that a preliminary contract had been signed on the 13th July by Hsiung Hsi-ling,[2] the Minister of Finance, and

---

[1] Owen Mortimer Green, British journalist and author, at this time Editor of the *North China Daily News and Herald*, the leading English language newspaper in China. He was also the *Times* Correspondent in Shanghai. Author of a number of books on China of his time, he later joined the London *Observer* as a writer on Chinese affairs.

[2] Hsiung Hsi-ling (1870–1942), Chinese Imperial official and Republican politician. He was Finance Minister in the first T'ang Shao-yi Cabinet, a post he held until the day after the signature of the loan contract here referred to. An opportunist appearing as a moderate political and social reformer, he was proposed by Yüan Shih-k'ai with the approval of the members of the Kuomintang who formed the majority in the parliament, as Prime Minister in July 1913 to succeed Chao Ping-chün, following the murder of Sung Chiao-jen. He then proceeded to form the so-called 'Cabinet of first-class talent' by including many of those who were regarded as enlightened conservatives, of varying shades of eminent grey. As Prime Minister it was he who counter-signed Yüan's decree cancelling the credentials of the Kuomintang members, thus bringing to an end China's attempt at parliamentary democracy. After he was forced to resign in February 1914 he was given a series of appointments, among them the directorship of the National Petroleum Bureau,

Mr Birchal.[1] This I only learnt subsequently after I had accepted the post that I now hold. Having accepted this post on August 1st I arranged to go home to England at once, say good-bye to *The Times*, get married and come back. I left for England on August 6th. Before leaving Peking the President told me of this preliminary contract, of negotiations that were proceeding then in London and of his desire that I should enquire into the *bona fides* of one Jackson,[2] whose agent had signed the preliminary contract.

On my arrival in London I put myself into communication with the Counsellor of the Chinese Legation, Sir John McLeavy Brown, a shrewd man of high integrity, and I learned from him that Mr Jackson, who was an American, had through Mr. Harry Brittain,[3] a well known Englishman who organised the Imperial Press Conference, been the means of approaching in regard to a loan Mr. C. Birch Crisp. As a result of my enquiries Mr. Jackson took no further part in the negotiations.

Of Mr. Crisp I enquired at the Foreign Office and I learned that he was a man of high character, who had rendered important services to Russia and had materially assisted in the Anglo-Russian *rapprochement*. From the Bankers, for example, the head of Lloyd's Bank, Mr George Lloyd, M.P., I heard similar recommendations. There can be no queston of the standing of Mr. Crisp. To compare him to his disparagement with Sir Carl Meyer, Bart, – the most active of the Directors of the Hongkong and Shanghai Bank, a Hamburg Israelite who bought his baronetcy, and is a man to whom no such words as integrity or high standing could be applied – seems to me to be unjust.

At this time the Chinese Legation in London, having been informed of the definite rupture with the Sextuple Group, had ceased loan negotiations except with Mr George Jamieson, the representative of one of the Hongkong

---

in which position he greatly enriched himself. This enabled him to devote himself to public and private charity work, with many of which organisations his name thereafter became frequently connected. In 1928, on the approach of the Nationalist forces of Yen Hsi-shan (1883-1960) and Pai Chung-hsi (1894-1966), he became a member of the committee to which General Chang Tso-lin handed over the peace-keeping duties of the city before he withdrew from Peking, a mark of honour to a 'do-gooder' but also a measure of the political impotence which characterised the last twenty-odd years of his life.

[1] Edward Frank Birchal (1852-1920), British financial broker. He signed with Hsiung Hsi-ling the Preliminary Agreement for the Crisp Loan on 2 July 1912, as agent of the Jackson International Financial Syndicate. He was also the agent in China of the London financial brokers Dunn Fischer & Company, Marconi and many other foreign financial and industrial firms.

[2] Probably Abraham Wendell Jackson, Jnr (b. 1855), American financier. He was head of the Jackson International Financial Syndicate, a principal in the Preliminary Agreement for the Crisp Loan.

[3] Harry (later Sir Harry) Ernest Brittain (1873-1974), a man of multiple roles and remarkable longevity, dying in his 101st year. He was, among other things, a director of more than twenty newspapers and journals, and was the initiator and organiser of the Imperial Press Conference which took place in 1909.

and Shanghai Bank subsidiary Companies, namely the Central China Railways, who was demanding 7% for a loan to be secured upon the unissued bonds of the Tientsin–Pukou Railway, which bonds he was to have the right of taking up at 85. Mr Crisp offered a loan of 5% at 89 nett. I thought and I still think these terms were advantageous to China. Time alone can show whether that view is a correct one or not. To speak of the terms as 'disastrous', when we know what very onerous terms have been imposed upon China in the past and were being imposed by the Sextuple Banks, seems to me unjust. China wanted the money badly: the terms were reasonable and she obtained the money from the best source in London.

Then began this policy of recrimination. The Hongkong Bank, although Mr. Addis himself told me that if he were free he would take up the loan on the Crisp terms, did its best to prevent a quotation being granted to the Crisp Loan. Mr. Crisp has retaliated by attacking the Hongkong Bank wherever possible, and he is an able man who speaks well although nothing could have been more foolish than his speech of October 15th,[1] which you were perfectly right to condemn and which we have all condemned.

Since Mr. Crisp signed this contract he has more than fulfilled all the conditions required by the contract. He has acted well. When it was intimated to him that the Chinese Government desired to re-enter into negotiations with the Sextuple Banks he offered to co-operate with the Banks and he offered to assist the Chinese in every way he could and he has done so. The terms he has arranged with them for withdrawing his opposition to the flotation of any loan before the 30th September of next year are most reasonable. It seems to me unfortunate that the loan actions of Mr. Crisp should be condemned because the preliminary contract in China was signed by a man whose actions have been condemned. Captain Kirton[2] has taken no part in the loan: he does not appear in it in any way except that he, on behalf of Jackson, induced Birchal, who had before, as Agent of a well-known firm Dunn Fischer & Co, been the means of obtaining a loan for China, to sign the preliminary contract in Peking. In a letter signed by Kirton and Y. C. Tong[3] and submitted recently to the President these two

[1] In his address to a meeting of the Anglo-Russian Bank, which appeared in *The Times* on 16 October 1912, Crisp was reported to have said that he could find no justification for the notion that a loan issued by the Hongkong & Shanghai Banking Corporation should be necessarily reliable and desirable to investors. He accused the British Foreign Office of supporting the proposition that the Hongkong & Shanghai Banking Corporation should have a monopoly of loans to China.

[2] Walter Kirton, British journalist and businessman. He was Managing Editor of the *National Review*, and a partner in the China Conservation & Development Company Limited, registered in Hong Kong. He had tried to enlist Morrison's support in various schemes.

[3] T'ang Yüan-chang, Chinese Imperial official. A returned student from America and a relative of T'ang Shao-yi, he was Chairman of the China Conservation and Development Company, of which A. Wendell Jackson, a principal of the Crisp Loan, as well as Walter

financiers declare that they have not received *one cent* from the proceeds of the loan and I think this is probable. Birchal himself received $\frac{1}{2}$%, which presumably he has to share with others and this is paid out of $1\frac{3}{8}$% which was the price for which Jackson sold his rights to the Syndicate in London.

Now, China having made arrangements with Crisp and having resumed negotiations with the Sextuple Group, finds herself befooled by the Sextuple Group, or rather by the Russian section of it. The Sextuple Group is an unworkable combination. The interests of the 6 Powers are not identical. Since these negotiations have been in progress Russia has signed the Mongolian protocol and Agreement and has submitted demands in Peking which give Russia rights in Mongolia almost as ample as those she has in her own territory of Siberia.

You will excuse the discursive way in which I am writing to you but I am only throwing out these statements to you for you to consider, because you are the Editor of the chief paper in the Far East and you are a man on whose judgment most English people, including myself, out here rely and you are in a position to render great service to the British community by informing them from the fulness of knowledge.

Our Government policy with regard to Chinese finance may be a wise one or not, but I think it is beyond dispute that our policy has inflicted serious injury to British interests. If it is too much to say that the policy of the British Legation as at present conducted in Peking is the blocking of British enterprise, it cannot be disputed that the result of their action can be so described. We cannot point to a single success since the Revolution began and yet we took a predominant part in assisting the Revolution, and had we been guided by a wiser Minister, we ought to be the Power who had gained material advantages in China.

Let us go back to banking and the signature of the Anglo-Belgian loan agreement of March 14th.[1] Indisputably the Chinese committed a blunder in signing this agreement but the part we took in condemning this action really punished not the Chinese nor the Belgians but the British. Although the British section of the Anglo-Belgian Loan comprised British people of the highest standing our Legation treated the representatives of those English Bankers as if they were adventurers of low repute and not the agents of men of the highest standing in the City of London. This is our policy. Our

---

Kirton, were partners. In 1913 he was removed by Yüan Shih-k'ai as Director of Telegraphs in Shanghai. Believing himself a victim of unfair accusation he sought through Morrison to have his name cleared, declaring himself to be a firm supporter of Yüan and his policy.

[1] This refers to a loan signed on 14 March 1913 by Chou Tzu-ch'i (q.v.) and the representatives of the Banque Sino-Belge, Robert Devos and Henry P. Rosen, for a loan of £1,000,000. This loan is also referred to as the Anglo-Belgian Loan because of British interests in the International Financial Syndicate which the Banque Sino-Belge represented.

treatment of Major Barnes[1] (whose father[2] was for many years one of the Directors of the Hongkong and Shanghai Bank) could not be more hostile if he represented anti-British interests. It is regrettable, but it is true that no Banker's representative can secure even a hearing at our Legation unless he is attached to the Hongkong and Shanghai Bank. As a result of our action we succeeded in blocking the Anglo-Belgian loan, Germany, France and America naturally finding no difficulty in supporting our Legation in inflicting an injury on British interests. What has been the result? China gave compensation to the Belgians who had suffered, but she did not give compensation to the British who had suffered. To the Belgians she granted the most important railway contract[3] ever given in China, the right to construct a main trunk railway traversing China in its greatest width from Haichow in Kiangsu to the Great Wall near Suchowfu, with the ultimate right of extension to Kashgar and Ili. Moreover the Belgians were compensated also by the Russians and were given one-third of the Russian share of the Sextuple loan agreement. What have the British got? Why, even in a dispute in connection with the Tongshan Engineering College all the energies of our Legation from the 11th June to the 20th October were devoted to an effort to obtain compensation for two British Professors[4] of £100 each, and after all our threatening and bullying we accepted less than had been offered to us before the controversy began, and now when there is a vacancy in this British College an American is appointed.

Can you point to a single British success of recent years in China? Shansi University was a purely British Institution conducted by Englishmen of high class.[5] They have been entirely excluded. Even before the Revolution the

[1] Major Ernest Barnes, formerly of the Indian Army, left on being promoted to the Indian Political Service. He was at this time the agent in China of C. Birch Crisp.
[2] Frederick Dallas Barnes (1842–99), British businessman. He first went to China in 1860 to work for the Peninsular & Oriental Company, whose representative in Shanghai he was for many years, later becoming its Managing Director.
[3] This refers to the contract for the Lu-k'ou-ch'iao (Peking)–Hankow Railway granted to the Belgian firm of Société Financière et Industrielle Belge en Chine, and signed on 27 May 1897.
[4] The two British teachers at the T'ang-shan College were Thomas and Cormack, who had claimed compensation for their dismissal by its Chinese Director. The settlement was reached through Morrison's intervention.
[5] What is here referred to as Shansi University was the foreign component of the institute of higher education that was founded in Shansi Province after the Boxer Uprising, the other component part being Chinese, under Chinese control. The foreign section was founded in 1902 with Boxer Indemnity funds by Timothy Richard (1845–1919) a missionary who first went to China in 1870. Richard became Chancellor while Moir Duncan (?1861–1906), an Oxford graduate, became the first Principal. Duncan was succeeded on his death in 1906 by Louis R. O. Bevan as Acting Principal. Then in 1907 William E. Soothill (q.v.), who later became Professor of Chinese at Oxford, was appointed Principal, remaining in this position until the University was handed over in June 1911 to the Provincial Government of Shansi, four months before the Wuchang Uprising. It was claimed by Soothill and others that the University then came under German influence under its

University had become chiefly German. The whole tendency in Peking is to exclude British Professors and put in French Professors. Look at the attack upon the Union Medical College in Peking – a British Institution with a large staff of foreign Professors – all but three of whom are British. Here you have the finest medical college in China, and yet the Chinese in retaliation have decided that the College shall not have the right to grant degrees but shall be treated as a High School for special subjects. And our Legation remonstrance conveyed in the most tactless I should say insulting manner in pidgin by our Chinese Secretary confirms the Chinese in their determination.

Look at the parlous condition of the Pekin Syndicate![1] Look at the case of the Sir John Lister Kaye concession,[2] of the Ssechwan Mining Concession of Archibald Little![3] What success has come to us? Throughout this Revolution who is it who obtained advantages? The Germans and the Japanese. In the list which is before me of goods supplied to the Chinese during the Revolution the Germans figure for amounts running into hundreds of thousands of Pounds and the Japanese to an almost equal extent. The Germans have obtained all manner of rights and advantages, even to the monopoly of the antimony output of Honan province. It is almost certain, Sir John Jordan himself tells me, that the Tientsin–Pukou Railway will, owing to the unpatriotic action of the Hongkong and Shanghai Bank and its German Directors, become a German main Trunk railway, despite all we have done in obtaining the right of contract and despite the fact that it was we who fought for the concession.

Take the case of Opium. We claim from the Chinese Government 25,100 Taels compensation for the burning of the 7 chests of Opium at Anching.[4]

---

new Principal, Hu Chün, a returned student from Germany, who completely changed its policies, causing all foreign teachers to leave. Morrison must have meant British when he spoke of 'high class Englishmen' since Richard and Bevan were Welsh, and Duncan Scottish.

[1] A British Syndicate which through their General Agent Angelo Luzzatti had obtained mining concessions in Shansi Province in May 1898, in dubious circumstances. These concessions became the object of a prolonged dispute between the Chinese and British Governments, as indeed were the concessions of Sir John Lister-Kaye (q.v.) and of Archibald John Little (q.v.), mentioned here by Morrison. These concessions were the topic of comment by correspondents in Volume I of this selection.

[2] Sir John Pepys Lister-Kaye (1853–1924), British financier and concession hunter, whose mining concessions, which became the subject of a long drawn-out dispute with the Chinese Government, were in Anhwei Province.

[3] Archibald John Little, a British businessman who had diverse concessions in Szechwan Province. He was the founder of the Upper Yangtze Steam Navigation Company Limited and the Kiang-fei-t'ing Mining Company Limited in Szechwan.

[4] This refers to the burning on 2 October 1912 of seven cases of Indian opium imported by British merchants, as a result of which the British Government, through their Consul-General in Shanghai, threatened reprisals and a gunboat was brought up the river to An-ch'ing in support of their claims for compensation.

There is not the remotest chance of the Chinese paying this amount. Sir Everard Fraser[1] considers that not only should this claim be paid but that the Chinese Government should pay compensation for the loss of 300 chests per month which would normally enter the province but whose entry is prevented by the action of the Provincial Authorities. Sir Everard argues that China should establish its honour throughout the world and compensate these Indian merchants who hold these vast supplies of Opium in Shanghai and Hongkong amounting in value to 12 or 15 million Pounds. Can anyone conceive that it is to the advantage of British merchants selling British manufactures that China in its present impoverished state should spend these vast sums on opium smoke? Sir Everard tells me that the value of this opium, estimated at a continuance of the present rates will at the end of this year be £15,000,000. Can any sane man conceive the possibility of China's paying this money voluntarily or of any British Government compelling her to pay it by force? Instead of attacking China with regard to opium, surely it would be wiser to point out facts to those opium dealers in Shanghai, some of whom, like the Sassoons,[2] are, it is alleged, Bagdad Jews of low origin who invest a considerable portion of their profits in brothels. Sir Everard tells me that we are face to face with a serious financial crisis in Shanghai caused by the locking up in unsaleable opium of huge advances made by the Hongkong Bank and other Banks. He tells me that the Hongkong Bank is involved to the amount of nearly One Million Sterling. I thought that they were involved to an even larger amount. There is no possible chance of this opium being sold in China and we may nag at the Chinese and bully them but they know that we have no intention of compelling the country to absorb this opium.

As an Englishman I deplore the difficulties and losses in which our fatuity is involving us in China. We are being fooled all round. [...]

We ought to be the predominant Power in China, for our interests enormously outweigh those of any other country, but in our insane support of one Banking Group we have striven to subordinate our interests to the level of that of the weakest of the Six Powers.

Years ago I spoke in *The Times* about the danger of giving a monopoly of support to one Bank or one Corporation. The B[ritish] and C[hinese] Corporation held up the construction of the Shanghai–Nanking Railway for 5 years, and then built a railway from the construction of which they obtained enormous profits. Did this firm act with any reason or justice? Take the case of the Hsinminfu–Aigun Railway. There again British enterprise was

[1] Sir Everard Duncan Home Fraser (1859–1922), British consular official, at this time Consul-General in Shanghai (1911–22).
[2] British merchants of Baghdad Jewish origin, the largest dealers in opium in China, from which they also branched into shipping, banking and politics. Many members of the Sassoon family were knighted for their activities in these various fields. (*See also* p. 127 note 2.)

blocked by our Legation. Our Legation is perpetually opposing British interests. Even in the case of the individual, why should our Legation go out of its way to asperse the character of Sir Francis Piggott, who has held the office of Chief Justice in a British Colony and thus aspersed the character of the profession in which he rose to high offices.

In the case of the Quadruple Group advances Rump,[1] a German, was made Auditor, with the full approval of the Hongkong and Shanghai Bank. Now, when an Englishman, J. H. Macoun,[2] is offered the appointment of Accountant in connection with the Sextuple Group new loan, the Bankers, including the Hongkong and Shanghai Bank, oppose the appointment and means have to be found to induce Macoum to refuse an offer which he had already accepted. The Hongkong and Shanghai Bank is an excellently conducted Institution and its staff are worthy of all praise. This cannot admit of dispute, but it is equally indisputable that the four German firms whose representatives have a seat each on the Court of Directors are the German firms who were principally instrumental in establishing in China the Deutsch-Asiatische Bank, which has been the chief competitor of the Hongkong and Shanghai Bank, and which has financed during the recent loan negotiations German firms who have been working for German interests in opposition to British interests. In London Addis told me that he did not approve altogether of the policy of his representative in Peking[3] and he cited a specific case in which a short time before he (Addis) had to act in opposition to the other five Banks. He said that all Six Banks had agreed, with the full consent of Hillier and of Mayers, that no Bank should make any advances to the Chinese provincial or Central Authorities without the sanction of the other five. In other words he said legitimate business of the Bank in which they had been engaged for 20 years was to be subject to the veto of 5 Banks whose interests were in many cases hostile.

In fine, can a single instance of success be cited to justify the present policy of our Legation in Peking. Our prestige is vanishing, our interests are suffering everywhere. We are being befooled by the foreign members of the Sextuple Group. Because of the supposed harmony and supposed frankness

[1] As a condition of the loan the Powers involved insisted that a certain number of foreigners be nominated to various positions of a supervisory nature, and C. Rump, a German, was appointed as an auditor. Morrison regarded this appointment as another German victory and a setback for Britain in China. At the end of his Diary for 1912, he wrote: 'Germans are employed, Barse in Shipping, Hackman in Arsenals, Rumpe as Auditor – our only success is Morrison and his appt. was notoriously opposed by the British Legation.' It is not clear whether he was recording what someone else had said to him or his own opinion.

[2] J. H. Macoun, a British employee of the Chinese Maritime Customs, which he joined in 1888, was at this time Customs Commissioner at Nanking. He was proposed as auditor in connection with the Six-Power Loan and had accepted the offer, but was asked to withdraw when opposition was raised by the representatives of the Five-Power Group.

[3] Edward Guy Hillier.

with which the six powers are acting, Sir John Jordan, who is the most honest and simple-minded of men, will believe any story told him by his foreign colleagues. Long ago Kroupensky read him what he called the main features of the Urga Protocol, with the result that Sir John telegraphed home to Sir Edward Grey, who agreed with Sir John that they were innocuous. Now that they are published can any reasonable man consider them innocuous?

You know that Russia has a guard of 750 men in Kashgar City and has occupied the road from the Russian Turkestan railway near Tashkent to Kashgar City by Russian guards. You know that Ili is also in virtual Russian occupation. You know also that all loan negotiations with the Sextuple Group are blocked by the Russian representative De Hoyer[1] on the ground that Russia cannot be a party to the lending of money to China that might be used in military preparations against Russia! And yet we still pin our faith to the Sextuple Group and consider that it is to our advantage to support Russia's action in that group and to block every British financial interest unless it be represented by the Hongkong and Shanghai Bank.

I am sure you will treat this letter with the utmost confidence and secrecy. I have only embodied in it what I could tell you *viva voce* had I the advantage of being in Shanghai. Why do you not come to Peking for a short visit and discuss things on the spot. Personally I am an optimist but I must confess that I regard the British position here with dismay and I think that every possible effort should be made to rectify the blunders our Government and our Legation are making, whether due to indifference or incompetence.

My best wishes to you

Very sincerely yours
[G. E. Morrison]

P.S. Drop me a line please in acknowledgment if you will be so good.

564. From O. M. Green

Shanghai 27 December 1912

My dear Morrison,

I have not time now to answer your most interesting letter in detail but send you at once the line of acknowledgement you asked for. Also I must apologize for not replying to your former letter. [...]

Now about your letter to-day. One thing I must say, namely that Russia's action in Mongolia has taken a good deal of the heart out of one's feeling for the Sextuple Group. I believe that if the loan had gone through in March the Urga convention would not have followed. As it is, it becomes difficult to see how Russia can be checked now. Against this does Russia still oppose the military expenditure of the loan business? I was assured in more than one quarter that that had been disposed of by the Paris Conference in June, that

---

[1] L. de Hoyer, Manager of the Russo-Chinese Bank.

is to say that all political complexion – apart of course from what there must be in high finance – had been taken from the negotiations.

For the moment, however, I will say no more except of course to ask you to treat the little I have said in the same secrecy as I treat yours. I think it very possible that I may come to Peking shortly. Should I do so and bring my wife with me, do you think Mrs Morrison would play with her a little while I am closeted with the great ones?

All the compliments of the season

Yours sincerely
Owen M. Green

565. To Ts'ai T'ing-kan

[Peking] 31 December 1912

My dear Admiral,

[...]

This morning I had a long visit from Count Sforza, the Italian Minister.[1] Although the interests of Italy in China are not very great, though they are constantly becoming greater, Italy is one of the great Powers of Europe and has a very important voice in the European Concert. It is, therefore, always advisable to maintain as friendly relations as possible with the Italian Minister, especially as he is really anxious to cultivate friendly relations with your country and is inspired by a genuine admiration for the President.

Count Sforza was much flattered, as was the Italian Government, by the offer made by the President to engage the services of the famous financier Count Luzzatti.[2] As you know, Count Luzzatti was unable to consider the offer owing to his advanced age. He is unquestionably the greatest financier in the world. At that time I told the Italian Minister that I thought it exceedingly likely that the Chinese Government would at some future date endeavour to secure the services of a high class Italian financier to assist in the reorganisation of China's finances. I said that I thought it would be a wise thing if Count Sforza would ascertain the names of famous Italians who had been trained under Count Luzzatti and who had a European reputation, in the event of the President desiring to approach the Italian Government again with regard to the engagement of an Italian financier.

[1] Carlo Sforza (1872–1952), Italian diplomat and politician, who was to play a prominent role in his country's affairs before the advent of fascism and after the Second World War, serving several times as Foreign Minister. He was Italian Minister to China from 1911 to 1915 and was on friendly terms with Morrison while in Peking.

[2] Luigi Luzzatti (1841–1931), Italian politician. He had been Foreign Minister (1891–2 and 1896–8) and Prime Minister (1910–11). In his Diary for 3 July 1911 Morrison wrote, 'Giuseppe Brambilla came to see me *re* Financial Adviser. Luigi Luzzatti, ex-Finance Minister and ex-Prime Minister about 60 speaks fluent but bad French and reads English German, has accepted nomination Ottoman debt, would probably like to come to China – can this be worked? Count Sforza says that Italy can now bring pressure upon Germany, that relations are better.'

On Saturday Count Sforza received a long letter from the Marquis di San Giuliano,[1] the Minister of Foreign Affairs submitting to him the names of three Italians, any one of whom could render services which would reflect credit upon the country of his birth. All three are members of the Italian Parliament. All three are men of distinction and of suitable age. For their integrity and disinterestedness the Italian Government would vouch. Their names are as follows:

> Professor G. Abignente, Member of Parliament, President of the General Budget Committee (a position which in Italy confers rank equal to that of a Cabinet Minister).[2]
> Professor L. Rossi, Member of Parliament, once Under-Secretary of State and till his recent resignation Commissioner General for Emigration[3] (the post of Commissioner General for Emigration is considered in Italy to be one of primary importance: it is now occupied by Count Gallina,[4] once Italian Minister in Peking and till lately Italian Ambassador in Paris).
> L. Wollenborg, Member of Parliament, has been Minister of Finance.[5]

On Thursday morning Count Sforza is going to pay his New Year call upon the President. He will then speak to the President and thank him for having made the offer regarding Count Luzzatti. No doubt the President will then express his regret that this famous man, whose name is so familiar to him, was unable to entertain the proposal to enter the services of the Chinese Government at a period when his advice could be of such immense importance to the new Republic. Count Sforza will then, no doubt, speak about other men of equal ability but not men who have had the opportunity of making so great a reputation as Count Luzzatti, and you could, no doubt, prime the President as to how suitably to speak of these men.

These things count a great deal at the present time when it is so important that early recognition shall be given to the Chinese Government. A few friendly words from Count Sforza telling of the interest that the President is taking in Italy and in Italian financiers, whose names were familiar to him,

---

[1] Antonio Paterno Castello, Marquese di San Giuliano (1852–1914), Italian politician and advocate of Italy's colonial expansion in Africa. He became Italy's Foreign Minister for the third time in March 1910, a post he held until his death in October 1914.

[2] Giovanni Abignente (1854–1915), Italian legal historian, son of the politician Filippo Abignente (1814–87).

[3] Luigi Rossi (b. 1867), Italian scholar and politician, at this time Professor of Constitutional Law at the University of Bologna (1891–1924), later professor of Comparative Public Law at the University of Rome. He was a Member of Parliament from 1922–6, and also served as Minister of Colonies (1919–21) and Minister of Justice (1921–2).

[4] Giovanni Gallina was Italian Minister to China from 1902 to 1904.

[5] Leone Wollenborg (1859–1922), Italian economist and politician. He was a Member of Parliament (1892–1913) and founder of Rural Cooperation (1885–1904). In 1901 he became Minister of Finance, but soon resigned because of his refusal to alter his reform measures which were regarded by his colleagues as too radical.

would have the effect at any rate of winning Italy to the side of early recognition.

With all good wishes to you for the New Year

Very sincerely yours
[G. E. Morrison]

566. To Ts'ai T'ing-kan

[Peking] 2 January 1913

My dear Admiral,

I came up yesterday to the Reception but not feeling well, I did not stay long enough to see you. It was a fine show and I hope was gratifying to the President.

[...]

The news in Reuter's telegram about Tibet is ominous.[1] The refusal of the Foreign Office to negotiate a new agreement with England must give England an excuse for negotiation directly with the Dalai Lama. If China is to cease to incur all kinds of difficulties the Foreign Office must learn your prompt and business like methods and must answer their communications with promptitude.

England sent her proposal about Tibet on August 17th.[2] The reply to this proposal was only handed in to the British Government on the 23rd December. No country can refuse to negotiate a friendly agreement with a friendly country. There is no surrender of rights in coming to an agreement. On the contrary if the agreement is wisely negotiated there may be an affirmation of rights which have not previously been recognised.

Look, too, in the case of Opium. Last Saturday, the 28th December, the Foreign Office handed in to the British Legation the reply, having reference to Mr Acland's speech in the House of Commons,[3] which I drafted and which

[1] This refers to an article which appeared in *The Times* on 12 December 1912 reporting China's reply to the British Note of 17 August 1912. In her reply China was reported to have told the British Government that she considered the existing Agreement sufficient and requiring no re-negotiation. While China had no intention of converting Tibet into a Province and while it was her desire to preserve the traditional system of Tibetan Government, she considered it her right to send troops into Tibet 'to preserve peace and order throughout the vast territory'. It was this reply that David Fraser, the *Times*' Peking Correspondent, described as 'truculent'.

[2] The British proposal of 17 August set down a basis for an agreement with China regarding Tibet. According to this proposal Britain would recognise China's suzerainty over Tibet on condition that China did not interfere in the internal administration of Tibet or station an unlimited number of troops in Lhasa or other parts of Tibet. Such an agreement, the British Note insisted, was a necessary precondition of Britain's recognition of the Chinese Republic and until such an agreement was arrived at, communication between China and Tibet via India was to remain closed.

[3] Francis Dyke Acland (1874–1939), at this time Under-Secretary of State for Foreign Affairs (1911–16). On 14 October 1912, William Wedgwood Benn (later 1st Viscount Stansgate), (1877–1960), at the time Junior Lord of the Treasury (1910–15), answering

you sent to the Foreign Office on the 25th of October. Published at that date it was an effective reply which would have checked many misstatements in the English Press, but those misstatements have already done the mischief. Published now it is antiquated.

Very sincerely yours
[G. E. Morrison]

567. To Ts'ai T'ing-kan

[Peking] 11 January 1913

My dear Admiral,

I enclose you two other memoranda,[1] which I have kept on separate sheets for convenient reading.

With kind regards

Very sincerely yours
[G. E. Morrison]

Enclosure to Letter No. 567: *Memorandum regarding Tibet, 11 January 1913*

It is I believe an open secret that the British Legation do not expect to have any further dealing in connection with the Tibetan question. That is to say, that the matter has been taken out of the hands of the British Minister in Peking.

The British Government regard the present condition as impossible. They have asked China to enter into an Agreement regarding Tibet. $4\frac{1}{2}$ months after sending in their request they receive a reply from the Chinese Government stating that no agreement is necessary.

What inevitably must happen is that the British Government, finding it impossible to get into agreement with the Chinese Government in this matter, will enter into direct relations with the Dalai Lama.

The Times, which is the chief paper of Great Britain, has suggested a certain active policy in Tibet. Such suggestions as a rule are followed by action. What *The Times* says today the Government does tomorrow. *The Times* are so closely in touch with the Government that they are constantly employed to give an indication of what the Government policy will be. Therefore *The Times* article must be taken as a warning. I would not be surprised any day to read in the Reuter's telegram that by arrangement with Russia England had sent a special Envoy to Lhassa to negotiate a Trade Convention with the Lhassa Government.

To try and prevent any hasty action of this kind it is necessary to act

---

a question on behalf of Acland in the House of Commons, said that there was evidence that the Central Government in Peking was unable to force the discontinuance of poppy cultivation in the provinces, and there was evidence that China had failed to carry out Article 1 of the Anglo-Chinese Treaty of May 1911 which provided for the progressive diminution of poppy cultivation throughout the country. For details *see Hansard 1912*, Vol. XLII, p. 756.

[1] One of these, on 'Boxer Indemnity Arrears', of the same date, is not printed.

quickly. Last evening Reuter's Correspondent telegraphed abroad that it was incorrect to consider that because China had stated in her reply that no agreement was in her opinion required, that she was unwilling to enter into an agreement. The telegram stated that Reuter had high authority for expressing the opinion that the Chinese Government would be prepared to discuss in a friendly spirit an agreement with England with regard to Tibet. Thus a way has been prepared and I hope it may be that the British Government will not act immediately, though, as I have said it is very possible that they may do so.

Clearly, it is essential that the Minister of Foreign Affairs should inform the British Minister that the Note sent in by him on the 23rd December is not China's final word on the subject. That England in her despatch of the 17th August stated the English case, China in her reply stated China's case and now the Chinese Government would be prepared to discuss in a friendly spirit a working agreement strengthening the friendship of the two countries and removing any possible cause of misunderstanding arising from the altered situation in Tibet – for it is impossible to deny that the situation is altered.

I cannot imagine that the British Government desire any policy of activity in Tibet, but jealous of the dignity of the Nation, they cannot consent to having despatches of the very highest importance treated as they have been treated in connection with this controversy.

I think you will be doing a wise act if you can induce Mr Lu Cheng-hsiang to consider the situation in the light of present knowledge.

568. From C. W. Campbell

Kent [England] 12 January 1913

Private

My dear Morrison,

I am greatly interested in your letter of Dec. 24 received yesterday.[1] [...]

Why should Jordan be hostile to you? I think you are mistaking his narrow, haggling, cannot-see-the-forest-for-the-trees treatment of British interests for personal hostility. The man cannot help himself. He is a mere clerk, a cautious clerk who is intent [on] only one thing – the retention of his post with its, for him, large emoluments, as long as he can keep it. Every action of his is guided by that consideration, first and foremost and all the time. Everyone who can do him harm, if they care to do it, will be carefully studied; everyone who cannot will be bullied if bullying suits his book. I shall never forget the mean way in which he put up with all Addison's[2] insolences

---

[1] Morrison's letter to Campbell, dated 24 December 1912, is not printed.
[2] Joseph (later Sir Joseph) Addison (1879–1953), British diplomat. He joined the Foreign Office in 1903, and in 1908 was posted as Acting Second Secretary in Peking, where he remained until 1910.

and bullied Vickers'[1] man for not doing the same. That's a thing of which I was actual witness. I heard Jordan threaten the man and I could hardly believe my ears. Well it may interest you to hear that now he has no more persistent detractors in this country than A.[2] and the German:[3] and if they had much influence (which they have not) Jordan would be in retirement by this. I speak to very few myself about the man, and then only in answer to direct questions. Sir E. Grey is his friend – his only friend in the F.O. I am told – and I can quite understand that while the pots are boiling so furiously all around Sir E. is anxious to keep the Chinese pot stirred by the same hand – Jordan is cautious, and that is the quality most required at this moment by the F.O.

You know my views about opium. I have always held that the British Govt. ought to have nothing to do with opium – no more than they have to do with spirits or strychnine – in China; and, outside the China Association, I find that very few who are competent to express an opinion defend our connection with opium *in China*. Jordan has no opinion which is not that prevailing in British trade circles! That means to say he may have his own opinion, but it does not pay him to express it.

My dear fellow you must expect the British public to regard you henceforth with deep suspicion. While you were on *The Times* you were a person who had to be reckoned with, and therefore you were courted; but now you are, if anything, in the opposite camp and are to be opposed and thwarted.

I am watching Yuan's progress with the deepest interest. When I am asked, as I am asked repeatedly, what I think of the Chinese Republic, I answer that the Chinese Republic at present is one man, and that while he lasts, and I hope he will last long, I have considerable confidence that the Chinese Republic will pursue a sensible and orderly rational course. It is just like Jordan to hold the 'recognition' stick over Yuan's head; but all Y. has to do in order to get recognition is to get the finances into order, pay debts, and establish a reliable budget of income and expenditure. As soon as he pays his way recognition will come; the financiers will see to that. Don't let the Chinese think of boycotts if you can help it: such things can only do harm to China and everybody else. England will recognise the Republic soon enough, if the Republic establishes a reputation. So far as I can judge Yuan is rapidly gaining the confidence of the financial world; and if he succeeds,

---

[1] H. Beaumont Donaldson, a former foreman of the British manufacturing firm Armstrong, he became in 1908 the representative of Vickers Sons & Maxim Limited in China.

[2] Addison.

[3] Campbell is probably referring to William (later Sir William) Grenfell Max-Müller (1867–1945), British diplomat, son of the German-born scholar Friedrich Max-Müller (1823–1900). He was Counsellor at the British Legation in Peking (1909–10) and acting as Chargé d'Affaires in Jordan's absence.

the Republic is established. Tong's escapade[1] was a rude shock, the effects of which still linger; and Yuan must bear this in mind.

I do not like this separate action of Russia in Mongolia. Well-informed people here say that Japan and Russia are acting in common and that the Japs knew of this Mongolian treaty before it was concluded. I doubt it. I have pointed out in an authoritative quarter that it is really a serious step that Russia has taken, which cannot fail to lead to other serious steps by other powers. I understood that Russia was brought into the Sextuple Group to obviate separate action of this kind.

Well I must stop. I have not seen Liu Yuk lin for an age, but the last time I spoke to him I gathered that he is still unpaid; which is really a scandal. He does not complain and only speaks of it to people like myself, but it is well-known in the City, and does not help 'recognition'.

A happy New Year to Mrs Morrison and yourself from both of us

Yours sincerely
C. W. Campbell

569. To Ts'ai T'ing-kan

[Peking] 24 January 1913

My dear Admiral,

[...]

I hear that the Russians are again pressing for the payment of the Indemnity Arrears. Obviously the policy of Russia at the present time is to involve China in all possible embarrassment, and in this policy Russia is supported by the active co-operation of France. Violent attacks upon China are being made every day in the *Journal de Pékin* – a French paper, which in a special degree receives the support of the French and Russian Legations. Surely the Foreign Minister ought to draw the attention of the French Government to the attacks daily formulated in this paper, which are calculated to create a breach of the friendly relations of the two countries. Today an excellent letter signed by Mr Liang Shih-yi[2] is published in that paper.

[1] This refers to an attack on T'ang Shao-yi by a would-be assassin on board the ship in which T'ang was travelling from Tientsin to Shanghai, after he resigned his post of Prime Minister. The attempt was seen as having been made at Yüan's instigation.

[2] Liang Shih-yi (1869–1933), Imperial official and Republican politician. He had one of the most successful political careers of his time by virtue of his hold over the financial and industrial resources of the country as much as his political ability, which enabled him time and again to return to power after temporary eclipses in different regimes. First entering upon an official career under the patronage of T'ang Shao-yi, whom he served as Secretary during the negotiation of the Sino-British Treaty of 1906 regarding Tibet, he became Director of the newly created Central Railway Administration in 1907, when T'ang became the Vice-Minister of Communications. In the same year he helped to found the Chiao-t'ung (Communications) Bank and began to extend his control over China's Railway system which led eventually to his becoming the leader of what was known as the 'Communication Clique'. A member of the inner circle of Yüan Shih-k'ai, to whom

It gives the lie direct to statements made in the paper and does so with much skill in a most courteous manner.

[...]

I am watching closely the present critical situation regarding the Sextuple Banks. Interesting developments may be expected. It is much to be desired that the Sextuple Group should be broken up. We ought to know something more this evening. It would be interesting for you to get a copy of the contract signed on the 18th of January by Mr Hsiung Hsi-ling and Mr Bouchard[1] for

---

T'ang Shao-yi had earlier introduced him, long before the rift occurred between T'ang and Yüan, he assisted Yüan to draft the Abdication Decree for the Manchu Emperor. He sided with Yüan when T'ang Shao-yi broke with Yüan by resigning his Prime Ministership in June 1912. By that time Liang had become Yüan's Chief Secretary, and in this position he wielded a power greater than that of any Cabinet Minister, including the Prime Minister, whose careers in fact he helped to make and unmake. His political control enabled him to strengthen his hold over finance and industry. He had himself appointed General Manager of the Chiao-t'ung Bank which then came completely under his control and he appointed his followers and supporters to take charge of various railway lines. In May 1914 he became Director-General of the Board of Revenue and of the Bureau of Domestic Loans. He helped to establish two other banks, one of which, the Yen-yeh Bank (Bank of Salt Revenue), controlled one of China's most important revenues. In 1915 he launched into war-profiteering by founding a company to recruit Chinese labour for France, a dealing which was much criticized at the time. So powerful was he and so closely connected with the important policy decisions of Yüan's administration that he was described as Yüan's 'evil genius'. As a result, following Yüan's death in June 1916 after the abortive monarchical attempt, Liang became one of the men wanted on criminal charges by the new Government. His grip over finance and industry however, was so strong that his position was little affected, and barely a year later, in July 1917, because of his financial support to Tuan Ch'i-jui, he once more came into power and the order for his arrest was rescinded. He returned in fact to become Speaker of the National Assembly in the Anfu Clique dominated Government, and in December 1921 he was made Prime Minister with the support of the Manchurian warlord Chang Tso-lin. Before his death in 1933, Liang was twice more on the wanted list for arrest – in May 1922 by the Chihli Clique controlled Government, and in 1928 by the Kuomintang Government – but each time he returned with his influence little impaired. Such were Liang's deeds and so notorious his reputation that in 1946, some eleven years after his death, there appeared a two-volume chronology of his life and work entitled *San-shui Liang Yen-sun hsien-sheng nien-p'u*, ostensibly compiled and published by his 'disciples' (*Feng-kang chi-nien ti-tzu*) but more probably the work of Ts'en Hsüeh-lü. Its purpose was obviously to whitewash him and in its attempt to present Liang as everything that he had not been and everything that he ought to have been, in order to keep up with the times and to curry favour with the Nationalists by then in power, the book is one of the more conspicuous examples of how history is bent for a particular purpose by manipulation of so-called historical records. The writing of modern Chinese history lamentably abounds in such examples of distortion.

[1] Possibly Raoul-Paul Alexandre Bouchard (1851–1916), French soldier. In 1913 Bouchard was co-founder with A. J. Pernotte of the Banque Industrielle de Chine, in which various prominent French politicians, such as André-Marcel Berthelot (q.v.), were involved. As Director-General of the Bank, Pernotte entered into an agreement with Hsiung Hsi-ling on 9 October 1913 for a loan of 150,000,000 francs to China, which was known as the Chinese Government 5% Industrial Gold Loan of 1914. Although Bouchard had con-

an Industrial Bank, the capital for which is to be provided as to one-third by China and two-thirds by French Capitalists. With this contract in his pocket, Mr Bouchard will now go home and endeavour to raise the money. It is quite astonishing that a contract of this kind should be signed wth a man of the standing of Mr Bouchard. Surely Mr Hsiung Hsi-ling ought to ascertain who the man is with whom he has entered into this contract. With this hole and corner way of carrying on negotiations China is bound to get herself, as she has got herself in the past, into difficulties.

[...]

The President was quite right in the construction he had put upon the action of the Sextuple Banks. It was not the European situation which had influenced them: it was the subservience to Russia's policy in Mongolia.

The outlook in Europe seems now quite hopeful. Turkey will surrender Adrianople and I think all chance of War has now been averted, but, of course, many questions have still to be settled.

[...]

Very sincerely yours
[G. E. Morrison]

570. To A. E. Wearne

[Peking] 25 January 1913

My dear Wearne,

Thanks for the copy of your telegram. I would suggest that it would be better to make it clear that Russia at present entirely dominates the situation. The paper[1] which is known to enjoy the confidence of the Russian and French Legations makes no secret that no loan negotiations can be satisfactorily concluded until Russia's demands with regard to Mongolia are satisfied. In other words the condition in China is imperilled by the action of the Powers in giving their support to Russian policy: There can be no conceivable advantage to England that Russia should obtain possession of Outer Mongolia, yet English policy out here is being subordinated to Russia's policy. The French Government are compelled to do whatever they are bidden by the Russian Government. The French Minister is acting purely in the interests of the Russian Legation. As the *Peking Daily News* said yesterday France is the catspaw. France has very little interest in China, whereas Germany, England, Japan and America have enormous interests.

The news telegraphed by you that China is on the brink of a precipice would be welcome news in Russia and France and would have no deterring influence. The point that seems to me to require emphasis is that it is not in *British* interests that China should be driven into this extremity.

There is no use in attacking the French Minister for what France is doing

---

ferred upon him the Chevalier d'Industrie by the French Government for his Chinese enterprises, he had a somewhat dubious reputation in China itself.

[1] A reference to the *Journal de Pékin*, edited by Marcel van Lerberghe (q.v.).

because he is only acting under the instructions of the French Foreign Office, who are virtually under the orders of the Russian Government, but it is fair to point out to Englishmen how seriously British interests are being jeopardised by French action.

Surely Hillier realises the danger into which we are being led – and Cordes[1] also.

In the case of war material, as you know the Germans and the Japanese are interested exclusively.

I gather from our Legation that there are 2 points which China has not agreed to the satisfaction of the British Legation, namely, first, as to the appointment of the Auditors and secondly as to the payment of the losses sustained during the Revolution. Conty[2] and Ijuin[3] arranged that these payments were to cover all losses sustained throughout the revolutionary districts, which would include Peking, Paotingfu, Tsinanfu, Shihchiachuang and Tientsin. The Chinese claim that it shall only include losses sustained in the area of military operations which would cover only Nanking and Wuchang.

I would suggest that you ascertain from Aglen the exact amount paid over to the Powers on account of the arrears of the Boxer Indemnity, stating the amount in Taels and in sterling: also that you obtain from him the exact amount of the Customs collection for 1912 and the rate of exchange at which the Tael is to be considered. I would then help you to make a very interesting comparison of the revenue of China in 1912 and the previous years.

I return your telegram, with many thanks.

Very sincerely yours
[G. E. Morrison]

[1] Heinrich Cordes, formerly Chinese Secretary to the German Legation in Peking. He left the diplomatic service after the Boxer Uprising to become the representative in China of the Deutsch-Asiatische Bank.

[2] Alexandre Robert Conty, French diplomat. He succeeded Pierre de Margerie (1861–1942) as French Minister in May 1912, a post he held until August 1917 when he was recalled at the request of the Chinese Government for his repeated rudeness and undiplomatic behaviour in his dealings with them.

[3] Ijūin Hikokichi (1864–1924), Japanese diplomat and politician who saw long service in China. He was Consul, then Consul-General in Tientsin (1901–6) and Minister in Peking (1908–13). He later served as Ambassador to Italy (1916–20) and as a Japanese delegate to the Paris Peace Conference. In 1923 he became Foreign Minister in the second Yamamoto Cabinet. Ijūin was a son-in-law of Ōkubo Toshimichi (1831–78) and a brother-in-law of Makino Nobuaki (q.v.). Morrison, in spite of his criticism of Ijūin's poor English, which made communication between them very difficult, considered himself a friend of his, and it was through Ijūin that negotiations for the sale of his library to Japan first started.

571. From W. Ming

'Highworth', Hillfield Avenue,
Crouch End, N., London 5 February 1913

Dear Sir,

The rushing life in this 20th Century must be my excuse for not replying to your letter of the 20th Dec. sooner.[1] I beg however now to thank you for it. You ask me for my photo. I enclose one for your acceptance. I regret however the face is not minus the moustache to comply with your idea of my being clean shaved – perhaps some kinsman may like me all the better for being 'up to date' in this respect. I also regret that I am free from birthmarks, if the possession of any is an advantage in deciding my destiny and personality, otherwise I am pleased to say I am pure blooded. I very much wish I could send you the painting I have – which I mentioned in my letter of some notability of the Chinese Empire, but that of course is impossible. I was not aware that any or all the representatives of the Ming dynasty reside in Nanking. That is one of my difficulties in being able to locate where my grandfather actually came from. Doubtless there are books of history in China which we here do not possess, therefore it would not be so difficult for anyone in China obtaining some sort of information about events which – as near as I can calculate – took place say about 110 years ago when those of the Ming dynasty were either expelled, or for political reasons found it more convenient to leave 'on their own'. I have discovered over here a gentleman who has written a book entitled *Recent Events & Present Policies in China* a newspaper cutting of the notice I enclose.[2] I placed myself in communication with Mr. Bland and he kindly replied by letter in which he informed me that the Mings have a direct and recognised descendant in the person of the Marquis Chu in China and the gentleman who could give information about the Marquis is Mr. E. Backhouse,[3] Shieh Fu Ma Ta Chieh, Peking (that is

---

[1] Replying to the letter from William Ming printed in this selection as No. 543, p. 32, Morrison wrote on 20 December 1912 to enquire whether Mr Ming had any physical characteristic which had induced him to think that he was a descendant of the Ming Dynasty, and asked him for a photograph. So earnest was Mr Ming that he was quite unaware of Morrison's very apparent sarcasm in his letter to which this is a reply.

[2] The enclosure referred to has not been found. John Otway Percy Bland (1863-1945) was the author of *Recent Events & Present Policies in China* (London, 1912), in which he strongly criticised the Chinese Republic. His hostility towards what he called Young China was to become intensified with the years, and permeated his many books and articles on China.

[3] Later Sir Edmund Backhouse (1873-1944), 2nd Bart, British scholar and adventurer, resident in China since 1898. Best known as the co-author with J. O. P. Bland of *China under the Empress Dowager* (London 1910) (and later of *Annals and Memoirs of the Court of Peking*, London 1914), in which half-knowledge was interlaced and embellished with daring fabrication, Backhouse had come to be regarded by his contemporaries as an authority on things Chinese, particularly affairs of the Court. After his failure to influence the selection committee for the Chair of Chinese at Oxford in his favour with the promise of the gift of his collection of books and manuscripts, he returned to settle in Peking where he remained until his death, in destitution. In 1943, at the request of Dr Reinhard

as clear as I can make the writing out to be). I have not communicated with this gentleman I am relying upon your goodself. Do you know, or heard of him? Is it possible in your position to get into touch – without the fear of losing your head – with the Marquis Chu? If not could I approach him? As you say it would be interesting if an Englishman could be found who could claim the Throne of the Ming Emperors. If my theory is correct then I should not claim to be a pure Englishman. To claim the Throne is not my idea. That would be too tall an order, but what I am most anxious to know is who am I? and what am I? By the information I gave you in my former letter I think you will recognise I have reason for doubt. If my grandfather *was* a Marquis, then I am entitled to that honour. If he possessed anything of value either in lands or money which by any chance could now be recoverable then I am open to advance my claims – Surely there must be some records – if what I suggest is true – of a Marquis Ming disappearing from China about the time I name. The Marquis Chu no doubt would know. If the aim I have in view is insupportable and useless, then I may be of some use here in England to the Marquis Chu or any other recognised, or unrecognised descendant bearing my name if only I could place myself at their disposal. I know you must be a busy man and I regret troubling you so much but anything you may do on my behalf to the furtherance of my interests in the object I have in view you will not be forgotten.

Trusting yourself and wife are well

Yours faithfully
Wm. Ming

572. To E. G. Hillier

[Peking] 7 February 1913

My dear Hillier,

A confidential telegram received from Berlin last night states that the German Government will never consent to an Englishman being appointed to the Salt Gabelle.[1] It is perfectly certain that the British Government will

---

Hoeppli (1893–1973), Swiss parasitologist, a Professor at the Hsieh-ho i-hsüeh yüan (Union Medical College) and at the time honorary Swiss Consul in Peking, he produced two volumes of memoirs entitled *The Dead Past* and *Décadence Mandchoue*. In these works, copies of which were given to the Australian National Library through the good offices of Alastair Morrison, the son of G. E. Morrison and friend of Dr Hoeppli, Backhouse freely indulged in compensating the unfulfilled promise of his learning with sexual fantasies and imaginary intimacy with the famous and notorious of his day.

[1] The banks of the Five-Power Consortium which demanded the Salt revenue as a security for their loan, stipulated as a condition the appointment of a foreign Inspector-General of Salt Revenue. After lengthy bargaining among the Powers themselves, Sir Richard Morris Dane (1854–1940) was appointed to the post, which he held from 1913 to 1918. Dane had served, before going to China, as Inspector-General of Excise and Salt in India (1907–9).

never consent to oppose the nomination or appointment of an Italian in the Audit or Loan Department. The political situation in Europe would not permit at the present time any irritation being caused by England to the Italian people such as would be caused if the appointment of Signor Rossi were to be opposed by England.

A trustworthy friend of mine who was at the Russian Legation yesterday was told contemptuously that the British Minister had changed his mind four times since the 21st of January. I do not know, of course, to what he referred.

Imagine the sardonic humour of the Russian Minister in complaining that China had shown ill feeling to Russia by not appointing a Russian as Adviser. Presumably Mr Kroupensky desires China to appoint a Russian as Adviser in Mongolian affairs.

No one can blame Russia for the part she has played. As Kroupensky said, he is here to work for Russia and not for China. Apparently the British Government's policy is to assist Russia, to assist the intrigues of Dorjieff[1] and to place in jeopardy our best commercial interests in China in order that Russia may be given time to consolidate her position at Urga.

In the meantime things are in about as hopeless a muddle as they well could be. I will be coming along to see you to have a talk over affairs.

With kind regards

Very sincerely yours
[G. E. Morrison]

573. From E. de Cartier[2]

Chingkiang [Kiangsu] 18 February 1913

My dear Morrison,

Just a word to say that I have had a very pleasant trip so far.

All along the railway line Peking to Hankow I saw abundant proofs of prosperity.

I lunched with Li Yuan Hung[3] at Wuchang. He showed me all courtesy

---

[1] Avgan Dorjieff (also spelt Dorjeev, Dorjieiv, etc.) (1876–1933), Russian-born Buriat Mongol adventurer. He sought to unite Tibet and Mongolia into an empire headed by the Dalai Lama, under the protection of the Russian Czar. His reputed conspiracy was for many years a matter of great concern to the British Government in India, and the subject of discussion between the British and Russian Governments.

[2] Baron Emile de Cartier de Marchienne (1871–1946), Belgian diplomat. He had become a friend of Morrison while serving as Secretary with the Belgian Legation in Peking in 1899. He was at this time Belgian Minister to China (1910–16). In 1917 he went as Minister to the USA and in 1919 Morrison saw him there briefly when passing through America on his way to the Paris Conference. De Cartier became the first Belgian Ambassador to Washington in 1920, and Ambassador to London in 1927.

[3] Li Yüan-hung (1864–1928), Chinese soldier and Republican politician. Reluctant leader of the Republican forces after the Wuchang Uprising in 1911, he became Vice-President

possible and seemed convinced that Yuan Shih Kai would be elected in April. He has managed to keep his troops in order so far – I also saw Sun Wu[1] and a few other young bloods – to all of whom I sang the praises of Yuan Shih Kai's statesmanship and ability under present difficult circumstances. They all seemed astonished at 5½ as rate of interest.[2] I explained to them that Austria had borrowed at practically 6¼% on her Treasury Bills and Bulgaria and Greece had paid 6%. I spent half a day at Kiukiang which Hankow thought was very bobbery. I found it perfectly quiet, and went about the native city which was as dull as ditch water. From all I hear the Yangtze valley is quite quiet, and trade very prosperous everywhere, beating even last year's records – *ce qui me cause un veritable plaisir* – I was told that a majority of Hupeh's nominees are friends of Yuan Shih Kai.

Remember me kindly to Mrs. Morrison and believe me always yours very sincerely

E. de Cartier

---

of the Republic, first under Sun Yat-sen and then under Yüan Shih-k'ai, remaining *Tutu* of his native Hupeh Province until December 1913, some ten months after this letter was written, when he was compelled to abandon his power base and go to Peking. No less a person than Tuan Ch'i-jui, one of Yüan Shih-k'ai's chief lieutenants and the Minister of War, was sent to dislodge him, and to occupy his position briefly until it was filled by another of Yüan's trusted men Tuan Chih-kuei (q.v.). In Peking Li was held a virtual prisoner until Yüan's death in June 1916, when he inherited the Presidency. But the entrenched warlord forces led by Tuan Ch'i-jui, by then Prime Minister, were too strong for him, and his first term as President came to an abrupt end after a game struggle on the night of 30 June 1917, following the coup by Chang Hsün, whom Li had called in to help as a mediator with the northern *Tuchuns*. Five years later, in June 1922, Li was again enticed out of retirement to become for the second time President, but he was no more than a puppet of the Chihli warlords then in control of Peking. His reign again came to an unhappy end, barely a year later, in June 1923. On this occasion he was detained for many hours at Tientsin Railway Station by Wang Ch'eng-pin (1874–1936), at the time Civil Governor of Chihli (1923–4), and it was only after he had handed over the Presidential Seal to his captor that he was allowed to return to the protection of the French Concession, where he died five years later.

[1] Sun Wu (?1877–1940), Chinese Republican politician. A leader of the Wuchang Uprising of 10 October 1911, he served as Director of Military Affairs in the Government set up by the revolutionaries in Wuchang, but soon faded into political insignificance after the initial revolutionary outburst. He was appointed to a number of sinecures, including, in October 1914, membership of the Council of Generals, and in December 1915, membership of the Political Consultative Council which Yüan Shih-k'ai had set up the previous year, under the chairmanship of Li Yüan-hung, to aid his monarchical scheme.

[2] De Cartier seems to be referring to the loan China was then negotiating with the Five-Power Consortium. The interest for the loan, the Agreement for which was not signed until 26 April, was 5%. De Cartier, in his attempt to defend Yüan's position, chose to ignore the political implications of the Loan which were behind the opposition of the southern republicans to it.

574. To D. D. Braham

[Peking] 18 February 1913

Private

My dear Braham,

Several times I have begun a letter to you but I have put it aside finding that it tended to become a controversial letter taking exception to the work of David Fraser, my successor in Peking. Seeing that it was I who recommended him for the post, it seemed rather absurd that I should be criticizing the views of one whose views I had presumably ascertained before recommending you to appoint him. Unfortunately I hardly ever see Fraser though our personal relations are quite friendly. He does not care to associate with the Chinese or those employed by the Chinese for fear, I imagine, of hearing the other side of the question. I only mention this because I regret that I can be of no service to *The Times* so long as your Correspondent finds it unwise to communicate with me.

When, for example, I was asked to communicate that important Urga Convention signed on November 3rd (not on October 21st as your St Petersburg Correspondent puts it, giving it the old style Russian date), I would naturally have liked to give it to *The Times*, but if I had done so what would have been the effect? David Fraser would have described the agreement in *The Times* as an 'innocuous' agreement, as he did in his letter to the *North China Daily News* and I would have been blamed for having inspired him with that view.

Accordingly at the desire of the Chinese I gave the documents to Reuter's Correspondent. You, however, did not publish it, but 6 days later you published an imperfect summary of it which was telegraphed back to you from St Petersburg, where it was derived from a telegram containing the Reuter's message sent from London.

I arrived back in Peking on the 12th of October and began my work at once. I find the work exceedingly interesting and most instructive. To one who has been a Correspondent the work is of quite special interest, because I have access to information which from a news point of view, is profoundly interesting.

I see the President frequently and try and give him some encouragement in the difficult work he has undertaken. He has not always been wisely advised. The class of foreigner who has hitherto been employed by the Chinese is the sort of man who tells the Chinese what they wish to hear rather than the straightforward truth. I may not advise wisely but at least I tell the President the truth and point out the difficulties of certain courses of action.

On my return I found the Legation in a state of nervous unrest in consequence of the Crisp loan. There had been foolish articles in the *Peking Daily News*, a semi-official organ here in Peking, which had caused Sir John great mental turmoil, but I very quickly caused the suppression of such foolish articles, helped to a change of policy and at any rate removed the sources of friction. At present the Editor of the paper is a clever young Englishman named George Woodhead,[1] co-editor with Montague Bell[2] of the *China Year Book*, a book which you no doubt, as we all do, find indispensable.

The question of Tibet has caused a good deal of acrimony and ill feeling. You will remember that the original British Note was sent to China on the 17th of August. I have no doubt you have a copy of this document, but in case you have not I enclose you one.[3] No reply had been sent to this note before I returned to Peking. The first thing I did was to urge the President to reply at once to the British despatch and to express the willingness of China to enter into a friendly arrangement with England with regard to Tibet. A review of the case from the Chinese standpoint was prepared in calm and reasonable language which seemed to me to be unobjectionable but this was never sent to the Legation. Unfortunately in November there came here a young English-trained barrister, a son of Dr. Wu Ting-fang,[4] who had written a pamphlet on *What are we in Tibet?* To him was entrusted the reply to the British Government. The reply that he prepared disregarded the reasoned statement drawn up before his arrival. It was an unsatisfactory reply, for it argued that no agreement with England was necessary since the case was covered by existing treaties and conventions. I enclose you a copy of this Note. By no means can this be called a 'truculent' document as it was described by Lovat Fraser.[5]

[1] Henry George Wandesforde Woodhead (1883-1959), British journalist and author, who in 1914 became Editor of the *Peking and Tientsin Times*, a post he held until 1930, and later Editor of *Oriental Affairs* (1933-4). After being briefly detained by the Japanese when they occupied Shanghai in 1942, he was repatriated to England where he became head of the Far Eastern Reference Section of the Ministry of Information of the British Government. Woodhead went to Hong Kong after the Second World War and became *Times* Correspondent there from 1946 to 1948, and Editor of the *Far East Trade* from 1950 to 1954. In 1911 he launched, together with H. T. Montague Bell (q.v.), the *China Year Book*, of which he was Editor from 1912 to 1939. Morrison, who had early taken an interest in Woodhead's career and frequently given him assistance, was indignant when Woodhead, without the consent of the Chinese Government which had a financial interest in the *China Year Book*, sold in 1919 a half-share of this annual publication to the Japanese, at a time when, in the wake of the Versailles Treaty, Japanese aggression in China was particularly resented. Among the many books written by him are his memoirs, *A Journalist in China* (London, 1934), re-published under the title *Adventures in Far Eastern Journalism* in Tokyo in 1935.
[2] Henry Thorburn Montague Bell (1873-1949), British journalist, co-founder and co-editor with George Woodhead of the *China Year Book*, was a nephew of the former Manager of *The Times*, C. F. Moberly Bell (1847-1911). He was the *Times* Correspondent in South Africa before going in 1906 to China to become the Editor of the leading British paper in the Far East, the *North China Daily News and Herald* of Shanghai (1906-11). Later he became Managing Director and Chief Editor of the *Near East and India*, and was the proprietor of the *Near East Year Book* and the *Annual Register* until 1947.
[3] Not printed.   [4] Wu Ch'ao-shu.   [5] *See* p. 75 note 1.

This unsatisfactory reply was sent in to the British Legation on the 23rd of December. Reuter sent you a correct summary of it and described it as being 'courteous and firm', which it unquestionably was. Whether it was a wise reply is another matter. Privately I may tell you that the President himself did not see this reply. When he saw it he was not satisfied. He saw that he could not refuse to enter into a friendly arrangement with England. Accordingly he caused to be written a despatch, which David Fraser in his telegram of January 14th described as 'an informal communication'. It was correctly sent by Reuter. I also enclose you a copy of this note,[1] from which you will see that the document was in no sense an informal communication. It was an ordinary official despatch from the Foreign Office in Peking to the British Minister.

Fraser's telegram urged that the question of Tibet should not be reopened, but if it should not be reopened it means that Great Britain can never give recognition to the Chinese Government because in the British despatch of the 17th of August intimation was conveyed to China that agreement on the lines laid down by England must be a condition precedent to the recognition by Great Britain of the Chinese Republic.

The present situation in Tibet is one that no Englishman can regard without concern. Yuan Shih-kai is in frequent communication with the Dalai Lama. From what I know I have no shadow of a doubt but that an agreement satisfactory to Great Britain could be come to, but in the meantime two things are happening. There is a considerable Chinese force of something like 700 Chinese soldiers, Chinese officials and their followers under the Chinese *Amban* sequestered in the Chumbi valley. Yuan Shih-kai desires to send them money for their relief – to enable them at any rate to buy food and winter clothing. Sir John Jordan declines to allow money to be sent to them through India for this purpose, but will allow money to be sent to them through India to enable them to remove from Tibet and come back to China via India. A voluntary evacuation of Tibet of this kind could not be consented to by the Chinese. They would prefer that every one of these men should perish.

That is one thing. The other is the agreement between Tibet and Mongolia. You have, no doubt, the full text of the agreement. You will know of the intrigues of Dorjeieff, the Russian Buriat, who was the cause of the Younghusband Expedition, whose policy has led China in recent years into serious conflict with Russia, with Great Britain and, what you seem to overlook, with France, for very serious complications were caused by the killing by Tibetan followers of the Dalai Lama of French Missionaries on the borders of Ssuchuan.

All that, however, is a small matter compared with the very serious matter of the importation of arms into Tibet. I spoke about this to

---

[1] Not printed.

Lord Crewe[1] but he said he had no information from Sir John Jordan. Arms are coming in in very large quantities indeed, mostly modern Russian rifles. They come from Kiakhta to Urga and are there received by Tibetan delegates. My friend, F. A. Larson of the British and Foreign Bible Society, who left Urga on the 8th of December in charge of representatives of certain Mongol Princes in Urga who desire to formally repudiate the treaty with the Bogdo Khan (or Hutukhtu) saw one train long of 1,000 (one thousand) camels come into Urga loaded with the latest Russian rifles and ammunition, which were then distributed, partly to representatives of outer Mongolia but mainly among delegates from Tibet. They go by the main road into Tibet without any difficulty whatever. The arms now being used against the Chinese in Western Ssuchuan are partly rifles captured from the Chinese, but mainly Russian Berdan rifles.

Russia finds an easy pretext for sending arms into Mongolia, as she declares that military preparations are being made by the Chinese to attack Outer Mongolia. She, therefore, is arming, in accordance with her agreement, the Outer Mongols against Chinese retaliation. That China has no such intention of proceeding to Outer Mongolia, no one knows better than the Russian Military Attaché in Peking. But the excuse is a clever one and the market for Russian rifles is a good one.

Russian action in Mongolia does not, I imagine, directly concern Great Britain, but indirectly it is of very great consequence indeed, for you must remember that Mongols who live on the Mongolian border which borders on the province of Chihli and on the border of Manchuria have made it known, no doubt from interested motives, that Great Britain and Russia are acting in accord in protecting Mongolia and Tibet and that these two great Nations are privy to the Mongolian Tibetan agreement. Statements made at rare intervals in the House of Commons denying these suggestions can do little to counteract the evidence furnished by the Mongols themselves.

That the Mongols were badly treated by certain Chinese Officials in the last few years cannot be disputed. Most of the trouble in Outer Mongolia can be laid at the door of the *Amban* Santo, a Manchu (or to be strictly accurate a Mongol Bannerman) who ought to be executed, just as most of the trouble of recent years in Tibet can be attributed to the action of the *Amban*, or rather the Assistant *Amban* Chang Yin-tang,[2] the truculent

[1] Robert Offley Ashburton Crewe-Milnes (1858–1945), Marquess of Crewe. British politician, he held many Cabinet posts, and was Ambassador to Paris (1922–8). He was at this time Secretary of State for India (1910–15).

[2] Chang Yin-t'ang, Chinese diplomat. A *chü-jen*, he was the brother of Chang Yin-huan (1837–1900), Chinese Minister to the United States (1885–6) and Yamen Minister who was exiled to Sinkiang for his part in the Reform Movement of 1898 and murdered there during the Boxer Uprising in 1900. Chang Yin-t'ang was Secretary to T'ang Shao-yi when T'ang was appointed Special Commissioner to the Tibetan negotiations in 1905. In October of that year Chang, as Chinese Special Commissioner, took over from T'ang

Chinese who is now Minister in Washington. No doubt if you see O'Connor he will have much to tell you of the way this man used to treat the Tibetans.

In Outer Mongolia the number of Princes who have given in their adherence to the Russian Mongolian Treaty is not great. The chief force in compelling the Treaty, and the chief of the Mission to St. Petersburg is a man I know well, the Hanta Chin Wang, a man of considerable force of character. He is at present called Minister of Foreign Affairs and is well known in Peking. He has often been in my house. His son died here from consumption. I have often told Yuan Shih-kai that the Hanta Chin Wang was driven into Rebellion. But the fact remains that the condition of the country under the Republican Government would have immeasurably improved. There can, I think, be no doubt as to that.

What the Chinese feel so keenly is that at the very time they were themselves condemning that method of administration which had caused dissatisfaction in Urga, the Russians stepped in and separated the Urga Aimaks from China altogether.

Under such curious impressions is the Hanta Chin Wang, or was the Hanta Chin Wang, that he has sent to ask me if I would give him the address of C. W. Campbell in London, an Englishman whom he knows, because he proposes to go to England there to ask for recognition by the British Government and to invite C. W. Campbell to be his foreign Adviser. Such a position would, of course, never be permitted to any Englishman and his belief that such a position could be given to an Englishman shows how he has been misled by his Russian friends. At present attached to his office in Urga is a Russian named Mushuitin, who corresponds with the *Novoe Vremya*, a man of disreputable antecedents who embezzled funds of the Russo-Chinese Bank in, I think, Irkutsk, who got in touch with Toktantaichi, the famous robber chief and brought him by the Russian Railway from Manchuria to Kiakhta and thence by road to Urga. The Toktan taichi is now the Commander in Chief of the Mongolian troops – a man of courage, a really famous brigand. He assisted the Russians during the Russo-Japanese war.

Those Japanese whom I know in Peking, and many of them I know intimately, with the Councillor of Embassy[1] I have, for example, been on

---

the Calcutta negotiations regarding Tibet, and in 1908 was a signatory to the Tibet Trade Regulations drawn up in Calcutta on 20 April that year. He was recalled to take up the post of Counsellor with the Waiwu pu in October 1908, and became Chinese Minister to Washington in 1909, remaining there until June 1913. Upon his return to Peking he was proposed by Yüan Shih-k'ai as the Chinese representative to a conference on Tibet which Jordan, the British Minister, was suggesting should take place in India. Chang's nomination, however, was rejected by Jordan, who alleged that Chang had caused too much trouble during the previous negotiations in India (1906-8), and Ch'en I-fan was appointed in his place.

[1] Mizuno Kōkichi (1873-1914), Japanese diplomat, Consul-General in Chefoo during the Russo-Japanese War (1904-5) and later at Hankow. He was at this time Counsellor at the Japanese Legation in Peking, where he died suddenly four months later, on 30 May.

intimate terms for 15 years, view with apprehension Russian action in Mongolia. It has certainly far exceeded in aggressiveness anything they had contemplated. What they fear is the arming of the Mongols along the Manchurian border of the Japanese sphere of influence.

On the other hand it is noteworthy that Russian action has had the effect of bringing China and Japan closer together than they had been since 1904. That 'common language' feeling is becoming more marked every day. I see evidence of it everywhere and this *rapprochement*, which is becoming quite marked, is viewed with some concern by the Russian Legation. I am confident that if you will watch carefully you will see continuously increasing evidence of the existence of Japanese influence in China. I give you one example, which, no doubt, has been telegraphed to you.

You know that for some time past negotiations have been proceeding between the Japanese Government and the Great Northern Telegraph Company, the Eastern Extension Telegraph Co. and the Chinese Government with regard to the surrender by the Great Northern Telegraph Company of its exclusive rights to land cables in China. That exclusive right has been waived on 4 different occasions by the Great Northern Telegraph Company with the consent of the Chinese Government – with England, Holland, America and with France. Now Japan desired similar privileges and she was prepared to give certain compensatory advantages in return. The Chinese have gladly conceded to the Japanese all their wishes without asking for any compensation, although some of us thought that she ought to have taken the opportunity of bringing forward the question of the Dalny customs and the establishment of the Tsingtau Customs Agreement of 1st December 1905 at Dalny.[1]

Among the men associated with Yuan Shih-kai no one is on more intimate terms with the President than Colonel Banzai,[2] a Japanese who had been

[1] This refers to an Agreement dated 1 December 1905, signed by the then German Minister in Peking, Alfons Mumm von Schwarzenstein and Robert Hart, Inspector-General of the Imperial Chinese Maritime Customs, amending the Agreement regarding the establishment of a Chinese Customs office in the German-leased territory of Tsingtao dated 17 April 1904. Morrison more than once suggested that, in order to overcome the difficulties which the Japanese authorities had raised, the agreement between China and Germany should be used as a basis for a similar arrangement between the Chinese and Japanese Governments regarding the port of Talien (Dairen) in the Leased Territory of Kwantung Peninsula in South Manchuria, which was transferred from Russia to Japan in accordance with the terms of the Portsmouth Treaty.

[2] Banzai Rihachirō (b. 1870), Japanese soldier who, like Aoki Nobuzumi (q.v.), was one of the Japanese officials with the longest connection with China. First going there in 1902 as Assistant to Aoki when the latter was Military Attaché with the Japanese Legation in Peking, he soon established himself as a capable intelligence officer, and his reports from Manchuria in 1903 greatly helped the Japanese General Staff in planning Japan's strategy in the subsequent Russo-Japanese War. Banzai's formal relationship with Yüan Shih-k'ai dated back to 1904 when he became Military Adviser to Yüan, then Viceroy of Chihli Province, and he remained with him until 1908, a few months before Yüan's dismissal by

associated with him for nearly 15 years. The President constantly speaks to me of the need of improving good relations between China and Japan. This is the more interesting to note because, as you know, Yuan Shih-kai was for years the most determined opponent Japan had in China, ever since, in fact, the War of 1894–5. Japan is known to have serious financial difficulties. Many of her prominent Merchants are owed large sums by the Chinese – sums amounting to millions sterling. Where the money is owed to the Yokohama Specie Bank the Bank is perfectly willing to postpone repayment. Where the money is owed to merchants like Okura or the Mitsui Bussan Kaisha, the Kawasaki Dock Yard, the Taiwan Bank and others, it is obviously the desire that repayment should be made without delay.[1] China is prepared to make that repayment as soon as she obtains her Reorganisation Loan. The Japanese, therefore, view with apprehension this policy to which they have been induced to give their adherence, of delaying or preventing China from obtaining the Reorganisation Loan.

With regard now to Opium, I must say that in all the years I have been associated with *The Times* I have never read in its columns articles that seemed to me more unjust, more misleading or more untrue than the articles by David Fraser on the Opium question of the 24th and 28th of January.[2] From an extensive correspondence in the *Central China Post*

Tsai-feng (1883–1951), the Prince Regent. After spending two years in France, Banzai was asked by the Japanese Government, on the outbreak of the Wuchang Uprising, to proceed to China, and from then on until his resignation in 1927 as Military Adviser to the then Peking Government, his residence in Peking became the Japanese intelligence headquarters in China. From there, under his tutelage, emerged men who subsequently won notoriety for the part they played in Japan's aggression in China. Amongst them were Doihara Kenji (1883–1948), Itagaki Seishirō (1885–1948) and Okamura Yasuji (b. 1884). On his retirement, Banzai was made a member of the Japanese House of Peers as a reward for his work in China. He continued to visit China frequently, and in spite of his retirement still served unoffiically as an adviser to the Japanese Government on Chinese affairs.

[1] Morrison compiled several detailed lists of China's debts to the Japanese firms here referred to, but they are not printed. For a note on the founder of Ōkura & Company, Ōkura Kihachirō, see p. 396 note 2.

[2] David Fraser's two articles on the opium question were published in *The Times* in two instalments under the titles 'China and her Treaty Obligations' (24 January 1913), and 'Growth and Consumption in China' (28 January 1913). In them he quoted selectively and out of context from letters written by missionaries in various provinces published in the *China Post*, and from an article by A. H. Smith (q.v.), to accuse China of violating the Opium Agreement signed by her with Britain on 8 May 1911. By this Agreement Britain undertook to reduce the importation of Indian opium into China to the point where it would cease completely in 1917, on condition that China would reduce and eventually abolish native cultivation of the opium poppy. The Agreement further stipulated that during this period Indian opium should be allowed to be transported throughout China with no additional transit duties. Fraser's articles formed the basis of a *Times* leader on 28 January 1913, which said that although Britain could not now depart from the definite policy she had adopted, and was unable to force Indian opium on China 'even in

(whose editor Brailsford, a very competent New Zealander, did such excellent work during the Revolution, being in fact the sole source from which information came from Hankow), it was established that the cultivation of the poppy was largely decreasing in China.[1] Several hundred letters were obtained from various Missionaries, Consuls and others in various parts of the Opium growing Provinces. The immense majority of the replies were favourable, and you must remember that these replies were received during the year past, some in the earlier months when conditions were less favourable than they are at present. Fraser read that published correspondence and picked out 14 reports from 9 provinces, written by missionaries who speak only of the condition of their own immediate neighbourhood, all of which reports were unfavourable and showed that the growth of the poppy in these districts was increasing.

Having put these into your paper he has given the impression that they were indicative of the conditions throughout the whole of China, with the result that your leader writer commits you to the misstatement that 'in many provinces the native opium traffic is steadily growing once more'. The Editor of the paper was himself the first to protest against the misleading statements published by *The Times*.

---

pursuance of our treaty rights', there was no doubt that 'Great Britain has been tricked by China', who was merely 'replacing Indian opium by the *far more deleterious* indigenous product.' Whereas 'there can be no doubt that the efforts to stop the production and use of opium in China have behind them a good deal of genuine moral fervour', the writer was 'constrained to add' that from the evidence furnished by David Fraser's articles, 'all the Chinese crusaders against opium are not animated by the lofty principles they expound with so much zeal. A large proportion of them are merely actuated by an anti-foreign prejudice which resents the right of Great Britain to import Indian opium.'

[1] John Annesley Brailsford, New Zealand journalist, at this time Editor of the English-language newspaper in Hankow, the *Central China Post*. It was he who had furnished Morrison with details of the events surrounding the Wuchang Uprising when Morrison visited Hankow soon after the event in 1911. Brailsford was indignant when the gist of Fraser's articles and the leader published in *The Times* was telegraphed back to China. In an interview published in the *China Press* in Shanghai on 2 February 1913 he professed disbelief that the *Times* Peking Correspondent could 'have sent home a report that the opium traffic in China was increasing in many provinces', when all the correspondence which the *Central China Post* had received from missionaries and others in various parts of China testified to the contrary. On 17 February 1913, after he had read in full David Fraser's articles as well as the *Times* leader, he published in his own paper a leader entitled '*The Times* and Opium' condemning the London daily and its Correspondent in Peking, pointing out the misquotations which Fraser had culled from the *Central China Post* and on which he had partly based his accusation against China. Brailsford described Fraser's accusation as 'a mischievous and reckless misstatement,' and denounced '*The Times* and its correspondent in Peking' for having 'blundered and blundered badly in their efforts to make out a case against the Chinese Government.' Referring to *The Times*' accusation of anti-foreign prejudice, Brailsford commented with the words which were reproduced in full by the *Peking Daily News*, quoted below in this letter.

E. T. Williams,[1] the First Secretary of the American Legation, has been making an independent report, the gist of which will no doubt be telegraphed to you. You will gather from it that he received no evidence which could confirm your view that the growth of the poppy was increasing in China – very much to the contrary. No one pretends that the cultivation of the poppy has wholly ceased, but that it has decreased enormously abundant evidence shows.

I cannot understand how you can argue that the Central Government is paralysed. The Opium Agreement is not a simple agreement. It is said that Sir Edward Grey once observed that you could drive a carriage and pair through every clause in it. The object of the agreement was to put down opium smoking and poppy cultivation. China is to suppress opium smoking and to regulate the retail trade in opium – *vide* Art. 7.[2]

You argue first that the agreement is being broken. Secondly that it is broken by the Provinces and not by the Central Government. Thirdly that the Central Government desire to prevent the Provinces from breaking the Agreement but that it is unable to do so because it is so weak as to be practically 'paralysed'.

I contend that your argument is misleading. If the conditions were such as you describe how has China been able to go along at all since the Revolution broke out on the 10th of October 1911? Just think how paltry are the increased debts that China has contracted during the last 6 months. The Central Government is preventing the Provinces from incurring further debt. The Central Government is establishing its own nominees in every Province in China. No doubt only last week you received a telegram telling you of the conjoint message sent to the Central Government by the *Tutuhs* of Ssuchuan, Yunnan, Kwangsi and Kweichou, the 4 most distant Provinces. Every day the Central Government is becoming stronger. The Central Government supports the Provinces in their opium action. Where there is defiance of the law, open defiance, namely in the cultivation of the poppy by the peasants, there have been in several places conflicts between the soldiers sent to enforce the law and the peasants who have continued the cultivation in defiance of the law and peasants have been killed. I doubt whether a dozen have been killed in all. Who can possibly blame the Chinese for this? No one pretends in China that opium smoking has ceased. All that can be claimed is that there has been an enormous diminuation in the use of opium.

[1] Edward Thomas Williams (1854–1944), American diplomat, at this time Secretary to the American Legation in Peking (1911–13). In the following year he was appointed Chief of the Far Eastern Division in the State Department, a post he held until 1918, when he became Assistant Professor of Oriental Languages at the University of California.
[2] A reference to Article 7 of the Agreement Relating to Opium of 8 May 1911, signed by Sir John Jordan, the British Minister, and Tsou Chia-lai, then Chinese Foreign Minister (1910–11).

You argue that the huge stocks of opium in Shanghai and Hongkong are unsaleable. They were unsaleable at the prices put upon opium by the merchants and dealers. That they are not unsaleable is an unfortunate truth. Stocks are being reduced daily. Present stocks are 28,000 chests and they are being sold at the rate of 1,000 per month.

You say that compensation will have to be paid by somebody or to somebody. What for? No compensation can be paid for the cessation of the India–China opium traffic, a traffic which the House of Commons called 'morally indefensible' and which you describe as 'obnoxious'.

You have got it into your head that huge stocks of opium in Shanghai and Hongkong upon which large sums have been advanced by British and foreign Banks, are unsaleable, but surely you can learn that it is not so.

You argue that the Banks are involved in very heavy loss. Ring up the Chartered Bank and the Hongkong Bank and ask them if this is the case. They are interested to the amount of more than £1,000,000 sterling. Ask them if they have lost or if they expect to lose a dollar, and hear what they say. As the writer of the *Peking Daily News* in a strong article today says:—

> 'The opium farmer whose poppies are ruthlessly uprooted by local officials cannot understand why his opium is to be destroyed while the importation and consumption of Indian opium still continues. It is only to be expected of human nature that the continuance of the Indian importation until the last acre of poppy in the province has been uprooted should arouse fierce resentment and discontent in the breasts of those against whom the Government adopts rigorous measures of repression. Until the importation and sale of the Indian drug are totally prohibited the Chinese opium farmer will never believe that the Government's orders for the suppression of poppy culture are final and cannot longer be disregarded. This is the whole secret of the "anti-foreign prejudice" and resentment of Great Britain's right to import Indian opium. The anti-opium crusade owes the astounding success it has already achieved solely to the desire of the nation finally to rid itself of a great moral curse. The erstwhile opium farmer, who sees the drug soaring to a price which would yield him a profit of nearly 400% may be excused if he feels "anti-foreign prejudice" against an alien power which continues to import opium into his district while he himself may no longer produce it.'

The opium in Shanghai and Hongkong at present unsold has cost in India £7,500,000. To this amount has to be added the cost of freight and insurance, the total thereby being increased to about £8,000,000, this being the maximum, and this amount is being reduced at the rate of 1,000 chests per month. Surely you are not ignorant that negotiations are far advanced for the Chinese Government to take over the whole of this amount and then sell it themselves in accordance with the system in force by the Japanese

Government monopoly in Formosa. I have no doubt that these negotiations will be completed and that nobody will lose. But you think otherwise, it may be because you have not been kept informed of the negotiations which the Indian Government apparently seem to consider are proceeding satisfactorily. It is purely a question of finance, but this is not regarded as insuperable. It offers indeed tempting chances to the Bankers.

But my letter is already prodigiously lengthy. I will write to you about the Loan later and about the foreign Advisers. I regret that you have not a correspondent here with whom I could discuss affairs and exchange ideas, but you can well imagine my present difficulty.[1]

I hope that you are keeping well and are flourishing. Please remember me kindly to Lovat Fraser, and, with best wishes,

Believe me

Very sincerely yours
[G. E. Morrison]

575. From A. H. Smith[2]

T'ung Chou [Chihli] 22 February 1913

Dear Dr. Morrison,

Thank you very much for your kind note.[3] I do not happen to see *The Times*, and was quite unaware till the other day that my article had figured in international politics. If I had foreseen that I should have added a sentence or two to what I wrote. I send you a letter which you can forward to *The Times* with anything of your own which will add weight to the criticism which as you say is almost universal. I hope you are serving the Chinese Government in a way sufficiently effective to balance the loss of your steady hand in *The Times* Correspondence – but the latter is in the open, and the

---

[1] Replying to Morrison on 7 March, Braham thanked him for his 'long and interesting letter', and with reference to Morrison's criticism of David Fraser, said: 'David Fraser's work I cannot, of course, discuss with you, and you will quite understand why if you think how you would have regarded it if Chirol had discussed your work with your predecessor in your present post. All I will say is that we have every confidence that David Fraser's views, however they may differ from yours, are reached in perfectly good faith after weighing all sides....as you recall yourself, it was you that recommended that he should go out and understudy you in the first place. You wouldn't have done that had you not had absolute confidence in his fair-mindedness and his intelligence'.

[2] Arthur Henderson Smith (1845–1932), American missionary and author. He first went to China in 1872 as a member of the American Board of Commissioners of Foreign Missions, and worked in Tientsin until 1880. He then went to P'ang-chuang in Shantung, from where he moved to T'ung-chou, near Peking. He was the author of *Chinese Characteristics*, published in New York in 1894.

[3] Morrison's letter to Smith, dated 22 February 1913, is not printed. In it Morrison called Smith's attention to the way in which his article, published in the *Peking Daily News* under the title 'Can the Republic Enforce Its Laws?', had been used by David Fraser, and suggested to Smith that he should write to the Editor of *The Times* to correct the mis interpretation made of it.

former is not. I am going to Peking next week to Dr. Mott's[1] meetings. I shall be glad to see you during the latter part of the week when meetings are not so strenuous. I am to stay at the Chao Kung fu with Dr. and Mrs. Goodrich.[2] With renewed thanks I remain most cordially yours

Arthur H. Smith

Enclosure to Letter No. 575: *A. H. Smith to the Editor of* THE TIMES,[3] *T'ung Chou, Peking 22 February 1913*

To the Editor of the London *Times*:

I have only recently learned (through the republication in Peking of a Leader from your columns) of the use which has been made of an article which I contributed to the *North China Daily News* more than three months ago, entitled: 'Can the Republic Enforce Its Laws?'

In that article I pointed out specific cases of official collusion with the illicit sale of opium, and raised the question (a most pressing one in the United States) whether a Republic can efficiently enforce its own laws as a Monarchy can so easily do. The object in view was especially to spur Chinese officials, now sensitive to Western opinion, to do their duty in such cases as were pointed out as an evidence of national good faith.

I was *not* reporting on conditions in general throughout China, nor on conditions anywhere, except in the places described and others like them. I did *not* say that the Chinese Republic *can not* enforce its Laws, for it has shown in a convincing way (more especially in the months since my article was written) that it *can* do so and *will*. Perhaps no other Government was ever in greater difficulties than the Chinese Republic has been during the first year of its existence. It deserves the commendation of every friend of the

---

[1] John R. Mott (1865–1955), an American missionary long connected with the Y.M.C.A. movement, of which he was successively Student Secretary (1888–1915), Foreign Secretary (1898–1915) and General Secretary (1915–31). In 1948 he became Honorary President of the World Council of Churches. He visited China frequently and in 1913 was offered by President Wilson, but declined, the appointment of United States Minister to China.

[2] Dr Chauncey Goodrich (1836–1925), a missionary with the American Board of Commissioners of Foreign Missions, who first went to China in 1865. He later directed the Gordon Missionary Theological Seminary in T'ung-chou from 1873 to 1911. Dr and Mrs Goodrich were the parents of Luther Carrington Goodrich (b. 1894), for many years Professor of Chinese History at Columbia University and Joint General Editor with Fang Chao-ying, of the *Dictionary of Ming Biography* (New York 1976).

[3] This letter from A. H. Smith was forwarded by Morrison to *The Times*, and was published in that paper on 12 March 1913, not in the usual 'To the Editor of *The Times*' column, but as a news item entitled 'Opium Growing and China'. The first paragraph and the last sentence were omitted, and there was an expression of regret that the paper had 'placed upon Dr. Smith's article an interpretation which he disclaims'. The Editor went on to say 'He [Smith] justified his questioning whether the Republic could enforce its laws by citing specific cases of official connivance with opium smuggling, and the construction we placed upon this seems to us to have been a very natural one'.

progress of the Human Race, for (like its Manchu predecessor) it has done more to cope with this gigantic curse than has ever been done elsewhere in history. To me it seems most unjust that China should be treated as a criminal for putting up a stout fight against the Black Smoke.[1]

[A. H. Smith]

576. To D. D. Braham

[Peking] 14 March 1913

Private

My dear Braham,

Since I last wrote you there have been developments in three directions, namely, in the extension of the *entente* with Japan, in the extended military activity of the Mongols under Russian instigation and in the Loan question.

Professor Ariga[2] arrived in Peking on the 8th March. He has been appointed for five months Adviser in International Law with the special duty of helping to frame the Constitution.

At the beginning of my service I advised Yuan Shih-kai to offer an appointment to Professor Ariga, who is understood to hold in the world the position formerly held by de Martens,[3] the Russian jurist. When the appointment was offered to Ariga he refused it on the ground of ill health. Undoubtedly his health is frail, but his real reason for refusing was the feeling then held by many Japanese that they ought not to be associated in the establishment of the Republican Government of China.

Yuan Shih-kai at first was opposed to sanctioning this offer on the ground that Ariga came from a country essentially monarchical and he feared that his appointment, especially in connection with the drafting of the constitution, might strengthen the fears of the Chinese who were suggesting that Yuan Shih-kai himself was aspiring to monarchical powers. He thought it would be wiser to appoint a Frenchman. I then suggested the name of Georges Padoux[4] who had rendered excellent service in the revision of the Code in Siam. Difficulties were interposed and neither project came to anything.

[1] 'Black Smoke', a literal translation of the Chinese term for opium.
[2] Ariga Nagao (1860–1921), Japanese jurist. He was appointed Legal Adviser to the Chinese Government at Morrison's suggestion, and held the post until his death. He had previously been Professor of International Law at Tokyo Imperial University.
[3] Frederic Frommhold de Martens (1845–1909), Russian diplomat and authority on international law. Legal Adviser to the Russian Foreign Office, he represented his country at many international conferences.
[4] Georges Padoux, French diplomat, and an authority on Muslim law. He was appointed auditor in connection with the Six Power Loan. Before going to China he had served for many years in Tunisia, followed by a term as Legal Adviser in Siam, where he had re-drafted the penal code. In his Diary entry for 28 May 1913 Morrison wrote, 'Padoux, the "Auditor", is a jurist, therefore appointed Auditor...I recommended him as a Legal Adviser since he is a distinguished jurist: the Chinese offered him the post of Auditor. Apparently he has accepted.'

Then later I was asked to arrange for the appointment of an American Professor and this has been done through Dr. Chas W. Eliot, formerly President of Harvard, one of the Trustees of the Carnegie Endowment for International Peace. An American has been appointed, named Francis Johnson Goodnow.[1] You will find his record in *Who's Who in America*. In the telegram sent to Dr. Eliot he was enjoined to select a man who had a special knowledge of the French Constitution. Telegrams state that Professor Goodnow has such knowledge. While I am speaking of legal appointments I may mention that the present Minister of Foreign Affairs,[2] who has spent the greater part of his life in Europe, on his own responsibility – failing to remember the incompetence of the previous Belgian legal adviser[3] – consented to appoint the Belgian jurist de Codt[4] as Legal Adviser to the Ministry of Foreign Affairs. De Codt has had experience in Egypt. It is an unnecessary appointment. He is married to a daughter of the late Rolin-Jacquemyns[5] who was once General Adviser to the King of Siam.

But to return to Ariga. It was learned recently that he had reconsidered his refusal. An offer was repeated to him through Count Okuma and he accepted it. His appointment is interesting because a considerable proportion of the Chinese who will have seats in the Senate and in the House of Representatives both of which meet in April, will be former students of Ariga's. It is early yet to know how many of the representatives will be Japanese-trained: Ariga himself estimates that certainly not less than 2 in 5 will have been at College in Japan. A complete list of the high Metropolitan and Provincial Officials in China and Provincial and Parliamentary representatives who have been educated in Japan would surprise you.

[1] Francis Johnson Goodnow (1859–1939), American educationalist. He was Professor of Administrative Law and Political Science at Columbia University when he was appointed Legal Adviser to the Chinese Government in March 1913, in connection with the drafting of the Constitution. He resigned to become President of Johns Hopkins University the following year (1914–29), but visited China in 1915 on which occasion he wrote a memorandum at the request of the Government on the relative merits of a Monarchy and a Republic. This memorandum was used by Yüan and his followers to support Yüan's monarchical scheme.

[2] Lu Cheng-hsiang.

[3] Chevalier E. d'Oplinter Wouters, Belgian jurist. He was the first foreign legal adviser appointed by the Chinese Government and served in that capacity with the Tsungli Yamen from 1896 to 1901.

[4] Henri de Codt, Belgian jurist, who was appointed to the position referred to here in 1912. He had previously spent twelve years in Egypt where he acquired a specialised knowledge of Mixed Court procedures and operation. In October 1913 he was sent by the Chinese Government to Shanghai to make a study of the Mixed Court there. According to Morrison, his most characteristic expression was: 'I know nothing'.

[5] Gustave Rolin-Jacquemyns (1835–1902), Belgian lawyer and politician, founder of the Institute of International Law (1873), Member of Parliament (1878) and Minister of the Interior from 1878 to 1884. In 1891 he became Adviser to Siam, where he assisted in reorganising that country's administration.

Sun Yat Sen is at present in Japan.[1] No feature of Far Eastern Affairs is more remarkable than the honour shown to this arch-Republican, whose views are shared by nearly all Chinese who have been educated in Japan and whose views, therefore, must be held by a very large number of Japanese students with whom these men are associated. He has been entertained by Prince Katsura,[2] by Matsugata,[3] by the Chief Bankers, high Court dignitaries, Cabinet Ministers, and has been treated with probably greater honour than has ever before been shown to the representative of any other country not of Princely rank.

A Sino-Japanese Society has been formed in Peking. It is estimated that in the Capital there are 2,000 Chinese who have been in Japan. The Press in China is very largely in the hands of Japanese-trained Chinese and Japanese papers in China have become as sympathetic towards China as they were formerly critical. The change is marked. Mr. Ijuin, the Minister in Peking, who enjoys high favour among the Chinese, shortly returns to Tokyo where his wife's brother, Baron Motono,[4] is the new Minister of

[1] After visiting Peking on Yüan Shih-k'ai's invitation, and there being appointed by Yüan Director of Railways, Sun Yat-sen went on to visit Japan in connection with his railway scheme, and he was warmly received by Japanese political and industrial leaders there. He hurried back to China a week after this letter was written, following the assassination of one of his chief political lieutenants, Sung Chiao-jen, on 20 March 1913 in Shanghai.

[2] Katsura Tarō (1847–1913), Japanese soldier and politician. He was thrice Prime Minister, first from 1901 to 1906, within which term the Russo-Japanese War, which raised Japan to the rank of a world power, was fought and won; during his second term from 1908 to 1911, Japan formally annexed Korea, and his third term of office came soon after the Chinese Revolution (1912–13). Katsura had been Commander-in-Chief of the Third Division during the first Sino-Japanese War (1894–5), and in 1896 led the Japanese forces in the occupation of Taiwan, becoming the island's first Governor-General. In 1898 he was recalled to become Minister of War, a portfolio he retained in the three successive cabinets (1898–1901) of Itō Hirobumi (1841–1909), Ōkuma Shigenōbu and Yamagata Aritomo (q.v.). In this capacity he was responsible for sending Japanese expeditionary forces to China following the Boxer Uprising. He laid the foundation of the Rikken Dōshi-kai (Constitutional Comrades Association) which after his death became the Kensei-kai (Constitutional Politics Association) under the leadership of Katō Takaaki (Kōmei) (q.v.).

[3] Matsukata Masayoshi (1835–1924), Japanese politician, twice Japanese Prime Minister (May 1891 – August 1892, and September 1896 – January 1898), and seven times Finance Minister, from the first Itō to his own second Cabinet, and again in the second Yamagata Cabinet. It was he who introduced the paper money system and the gold standard into Japan. He was created a Prince in 1922 for his contribution to Japan's financial administration, and remained until the end of his life an influential figure in Japanese finance and politics.

[4] No doubt he meant Makino. Ijūin's wife Yoshiko was a daughter of Ōkubo Toshimichi, the leading statesman of the early Meiji era, and a sister of Makino Nobuaki (1862–1949) who became Foreign Minister in February 1913. Motono Ichirō (1862–1918), a French educated Japanese diplomat, formerly Japanese Minister to Belgium (1898–1901), France (1901–6), and Russia (1906–16), was also a Foreign Minister – in the Terauchi Cabinet, from May 1916 to July 1918. In this last post he formulated Japan's

Foreign Affairs, and he will there retain his rank as Minister Plenipotentiary will act as Adviser in Chinese affairs. His successor, Yamaza,[1] is a well known advocate of the policy of intimate relations with China.

The Japanese view with anxiety the possible closing by Spheres of Influence of the market in China, that market which Ijuin in a noteworthy speech lately described as a 'Heaven-sent market for Japanese goods'. They view with concern the loss of Mongolia and the financial danger with which China is now menaced by the dominating action of Russia supported by France and England.

[...] The question of Mongolia causes increasing anxiety. I enclose you two reports,[2] the first written on the 20th of November and the second on the 12th of December, by a competent witness named F. A. Larson, who was at the time a resident in Urga. He is a Swede, who probably knows Mongolia better than any other man. He was Agent for the British and Foreign Bible Society and has not had many chances of education, but he is a shrewd and truthful man and I think will be of some service to the Chinese Government who have recently given him an appointment in the department of Mongolian and Tibetan affairs. These two reports are confidential, of course, but may be of use to you. Larson was with me yesterday. He has now gone back to Mongolia to meet three Mongol Princes who, with their followers, have been detained in Urga but have been now permitted to leave and having been supplied with money, are returning to Inner Mongolia.

On February 19th you published a telegram from St Petersburg stating that the Russian Government had seconded for service in Mongolia as Military Instructors two Colonels, 15 other officers and 42 non-commissioned officers. These, no doubt, are in addition to the Russian officers already in Urga or who have accompanied the expedition to Darg Angar. At present the Mongol forces consist of well mounted active men accustomed to the chase, hardy and fearless. Under proper guidance they can undoubtedly become a powerful force. The Russians are, I am afraid, inciting the Mongols to attack the Chinese because they know that if the Mongols were to have any success at all, all Mongol States along the Chinese frontier, who are now wavering in their allegiance, would throw in their lot with the victors. This morning Yuan Shih-kai showed me a report from Urga which stated that the Russian Government had advanced the Urga Government a considerable

---

China policy during the ascendancy of the Anfu Clique Government under Tuan Ch'i-jui, particularly with regard to the question of the Shantung Leased Territory which was to become the cardinal issue between the Chinese and Japanese Delegations at the Paris Peace Conference in 1919.

[1] Yamaza Enjirō (1866–1914), Japanese diplomat who became Minister to China in June 1913. A convivial drinker, he was conspicuous at diplomatic and government receptions for his high-spirited behaviour, which Morrison in his Diary attributed to the influence of alcohol. He died suddenly on 28 May 1914 on the eve of his recall to Japan. His death, which occurred a mere five days after that of Mizuno Kōkichi on 23 May, led to rumours that they had both been poisoned by Yüan Shih-k'ai. [2] Not printed.

Loan and had supplied them with three batteries of quick-firing guns and twenty machine guns. The Minister of Foreign Affairs had asked Kroupensky if the report were true and Kroupensky had admitted that it was true.

Writing to you on February 25th[1] I told you of the departure from Urga on January 30th of a force of 600 Khalka Mongols with some Russian Officers. They swore they would 'reach Kalgan or die'. Their first objective was the Imperial pasture lands in the Mongol State of Darg Angar, the chief breeding ground in Mongolia of horses and camels, whose tribesmen were among the first to support the Urga Government. They are already in Darg Angar. Almost at the same time another force of 1,000 Eastern Mongols belonging to the command of Tok-tan-tai-chi left for the same state, and now a letter from Urga dated the 15th of February tells us that another body of 4,000 men from the 2 Western Aimaks round about Uliassutai, who have been for some time in Urga undergoing Russian drill, have left there to join the two preceding detachments at Darg Angar, where apparently they will concentrate.

The Telegraph line from Kalgan to Urga, has in a distance of 600 miles, 3 telegraph stations. The Urga station is already operated by Russians. The next station, Turin, 150 miles nearer Peking is nominally under the Chinese and one of their foreign employees, a Dane named Langeback,[2] is at the present moment there. Yesterday he telegraphed to say that under orders from Urga the Mongols at Turin were instructed not to give him or his men any supplies whatever and he will therefore be compelled to return to Peking. This station will then presumably be operated by Russians. The next Station, 150 miles nearer Peking, is called Ude. Immediately east of this is Darg Angar, the Mongol State where the Mongol forces are assembling.

The route then from Urga to Kalgan is, as to two-thirds, under independent Mongols, the remaining third passes through territory which is at present colonised by Chinese. It is these Chinese who stand in danger of being attacked by the Mongols.

No doubt you will have read in the telegrams about the mission sent by the Bogdo Khan to Barga and the formal assent of the Barga Mongols to the Urga Convention. This conveys very little, yet it is of great importance because Barga (on C. W. Campbell's map, China No. 1, 1904,[3] this is written Barhut) is the territory of which Hailar, an important town on the Trans-Manchurian Railway, is the chief town. It extends to the border of

[1] Not printed.
[2] H. Langeback, Danish employee of the Chinese Telegraph and Telephone Administration. He was formerly Superintendent of Telegraphs in Tientsin before being sent to Mongolia, and was on intimate terms with Kroupensky (q.v.), Russian Minister to Peking (1911–16).
[3] This refers to the report made by Charles William Campbell entitled *A Journey in Mongolia* (*with a map*) and published as a Command Paper, China No. 1 (1904), C.D. 1874.

Heilung-chiang Province along the Aigun River and for a considerable distance south of Hailar and it includes the Kulun Nor, Manchuli Station etc. C. W. Campbell has passed through this territory accompanied by Larson. The Mongols of Urga and all the Chinese communities within their borders, including Hailar, have been expelled.

It seems certain that Russia will build a railway from Lake Baikal to Kiakhta on the frontier and by permission of the Mongols will extend this railway to Urga. Russian activity in Mongolia is bound to cause China increasing anxiety. It would be well for China if this activity were confined to Mongolia.

Urga is at present garrisoned by 750 Russians. A body of 250 Russians are also in Uliassutai. A Russian Consul is stationed at Kobdo[1] and on the pretext that the Chinese are preparing an expedition at Kucheng (a trade centre where various roads converge) 4 days east of Urumchi, the Capital of Sinkiang, for an alleged advance on Kobdo, the Russians have sent a comparatively strong force to Kobdo. They also occupy Chuguchak. Mongolia, therefore, can be regarded as lost to China. China for some time nursed the hope that the area of Mongolia might be restricted, but recent Russian activity is increasing its area not reducing it.

Further round the outskirts of China, bordering on Mongolia, is the territory of Kuldja. Kuldja is virtually in Russian occupation. Russia maintains in the chief town a Consular guard of 750 men, a number which can in a few days be increased twenty-fold. Kashgar also has a Russian garrison, or so called Consular guard, of 750 men, a number which also can be indefinitely increased, for a road into Kashgar from Russian territory near Tashkent is available for wheeled traffic. Macartney[2] writing to me from Kashgar expresses some anxiety as to the reason for this continued occupation when all is quiet.

Whether it is of advantage to the British Government in India that Russian activity should be extended into Kashgaria and become there as

---

[1] Mikhail Nikolaevich Kuzminsky, Russian consular official. He had served as Secretary and Interpreter in the Russian Consulate in Urga (1905, 1907–10), Uliassutai (1906) and Harbin (1911), before being appointed Consul in Kobdo in 1912. He was transferred to Sharasume in 1915.

[2] Sir George Halliday Macartney (1867–1945), British diplomat. He entered the service of the Indian Government in 1888, and became Special Assistant to the Resident in Kashmir in 1893, in which capacity he was primarily responsible for Chinese affairs. In 1896 he was seconded to the Anglo-Russian Pamir Boundary Commission. His knowledge of Chinese frontier provinces led to his appointment as British Consul in Kashgar in 1908, and Consul-General in 1910, a post he held until 1918. Son of Samuel Halliday Macartney (1833–1906), who entered the Chinese service in 1862 and who in 1876 accompanied Kuo Sung-t'ao (1818–91) the first Chinese Minister in England, where he remained as a Counsellor at the Chinese Legation in London until his death, the younger Macartney was born in Nanking when his father was Director of the Chinese Arsenal there (1865–75).

effective as it is in Kuldja to the north of the Tienshan mountains is, no doubt, a question that was considered by our Government when they gave their support to that Russian policy which has involved us in our present entanglement in China.

And this brings me to the question of the Loan. The Russian Minister here has stated consistently that China's agreement with the Urga Convention must be a condition precedent to the signature of a Loan contract. In a Note left by Kroupensky at the Foreign Office here, the gist of which was telegraphed to you by Reuter, he stated that Russia must insist upon the payment of the arrears of the Boxer Indemnity: that Chinese military preparations – he described them as 'Chinese mobilization' – indicated that China had abundance of money to spend and therefore she could not plead poverty for not meeting her indemnity obligations, but he added that if China would recognise the *fait accompli* of the Urga Convention Russia would not press China for payment of the Boxer Indemnity but would allow her to take her own time. Both Russians and French here have said repeatedly, both officially and unofficially, as well as in the Press, that China would not be allowed to obtain any foreign loan until the Mongolian question had been settled. Settlement meant, of course, the acquiescence of China in the independence of Mongolia and recognition of Russia's rights acquired under the Urga protocol. This fact has to be remembered when one wishes to understand why there has been the interminable delay in signing the loan contract.

But I must leave this loan question to another time. However I send you a copy of the letter which was sent on the 11th in Chinese by the Minister of Finance to E. G. Hillier, the head of the Hongkong and Shanghai Bank.

Surely you cannot regard with satisfaction the outcome of these loan negotiations and the muddle in which we have landed ourselves through lack of foresight and pusillanimity. Had Sir John not weakly turned round the loan negotiations would have been completed on February 5th.

You know that Germany declined to acquiesce in the nomination of an Englishman as the head of the foreign staff of the Salt Gabelle unless England gave an engagement that she would agree to the appointment of a German Engineer in Chief over the whole Tientsin–Pukou Railway. Subsequently she gave way and agreed to an Englishman being nominated to the salt gabelle, but our Foreign office do not seem to be aware that before consenting the German Legation satisfied itself that the Chinese Government could not accept the proposed change. Sir John is so overwrought and unstrung that he is really not fit to be conducting such important negotiations. We have done nothing but blunder.

With kind regards

Very sincerely yours
[G. E. Morrison]

577. From M. M. Yates[1]

Santa Barbara, Calif[ornia, USA] 14 March 1913

My dear Sir,

For five months I have had an envelope addrest to you, hoping to write, but being very busy with a very important subject in our Country of these U.S. I have neglected all else. No doubt one so well informed upon political matters of the U.S. as you are, fully understands our peril. Our Traitor Presidents and, Traitor politicians, have sold our country to the Jesuit Roman Catholics for their votes, and are almost beyond all sense and reason over their very effective work. Everyone of the parties to the deal ought to be hung, or put out of bodily life, for, of all sins that curse the world that of a Traitor to the land of his birth, and his forbears, is the worst, we are even humiliated with the spectacle of the so-called Popes Army, the Knights of Columbus said to number over Two Hundred Thousand armed equipt and drilled men, which their leaders declare are for the purpose of maintaining their hold upon the U.S. while our regular army only numbers about Eighty Thousand, and a large per cent of them are Catholics, and most of the Officers of the Army and Navy are also. The Catholic political Organisation has been steadily at this grasp upon our government for over forty years, but like all Jesuit work, it is done under cover of secrecy, and now they are establishing churches, or mission work among all outlying Countries in order to boast of conquering the whole world. They have established a firm grip over the ignorant Negroes of the south U.S. and will soon have them under control, as they have with our Indians of the U.S. But what I am hurrying to lay before you at this time is that they are reaching out to China and Japan, with the determination to conquer them owing to the famine and wars of those Countries, and their terrible distress. If the Catholics cannot conquer them in any other way, they will give them money, and take anything they can get. I have seen it repeatedly in the Papers, that Count Boni de Castelane most solemnly promises the Pope, to turn over the Chinese to his rule, if he will absolve his marriage to Anna Gould, is it not ridiculous to make such a traffic in humanity.[2] I had rather see all the

[1] Unable to identify.
[2] Anna Gould (?1875-1961) was the youngest daughter of Jay (Jason) Gould (1836-92), the American railway tycoon who, by a series of dubious dealings in railway shares, had accumulated a vast fortune which was estimated in 1872 at $25,000,000, before he gained the control of railway systems in Missouri, Texas, Kansas, New York and elsewhere, as well as the Western Union Telegraph Company, and the newspaper, the New York *World*. In 1894 Anna met, and the following year married, Marie-Ernest-Paul Boniface, Marquis de Castellane (1867-1932). In doing so she became one of a generation of American heiresses who married into the European aristocracy, a predecessor being Jeannette Jerome (1854-1921) who had married Lord Randolph Churchill (1849-94) in 1873. The couple built for themselves a pink marble palace by the Bois de Boulogne, the 'chateau des Marais', also known as the Palais Rose. This Palace, which was to come again into headline news half a century later when it was used as the venue for a conference of the Foreign

Chinese and Japanese in the Ocean going down under the depths, than forced into a life of abject slavery to support Catholics, and lately I saw in the papers that the Mikado of Japan was expecting to visit the Pope. That, if true, would look as tho something is being done. I had that the Chinese and Japanese too shrewd to ever be taken in by the Catholics as it was they that created the exclusion act in the U.S. that drove the Chinese out, and after almost getting Japan and the U.S. into a war, they let up a little, but they are to be very active in April this year, to exclude and drive out Japanese. I believe you must be in a position to warn the Chinese nation, and I hope also, the Japanese, that Americans need and want their laboring class here. We need their labor as sorely as they need our money. Yet, the Catholics thru their hold upon our government have steadily prevented it, and we americans are tied down to either do our own labor, or let it go undone. Foods are excessively high because there is not an adequate supply produced. The Catholic immigrants have been run into the U.S. by the millions, yet they are kept herded in the large cities, ready to vote (illegally), as they do not comply with law, to aid Catholic projects. They boldly announce that they will make America Catholic. But the people have a 'Free Press' now after 35 yrs of Catholic Controlled Press, so that people did not know what was being done against them. We have got a big struggle ahead of us. I beg you to warn the Chinese not to allow one single Catholic, priest, church, convert, or school, upon their soil. If they do, from that hour their freedom, liberty, and Country will be gradually taken from them. I fear the Chinese nation is doomed any how, as money sharks are as bad about stealing a

---

Ministers of the Great Powers after the Second World War, was, during the couple's occupancy, the scene of constant and glittering gatherings of the international aristocratic set. So lavish was their style of entertainment that by the time Anna parted from her husband in 1906 it was estimated that they had spent some $10,000,000 of the Gould fortune. In 1908 Anna married the cousin of the Marquis de Castellane, the Prince de Sagan, Duc de Talleyrand-Périgord (d. 1937), and after his death she went to live in her father's gothic-style mansion at Tarringtown in New York, which is now preserved as a historical monument, returning to Paris only shortly before her death in 1961. The Marquis de Castellane, whose circumstances were greatly reduced after the departure of his wife with their three children, had to turn to journalism and to selling antiques, the collection of which had been a hobby in his more affluent days, for a living. Among several volumes of his autobiographical writings is one published in Paris in 1925, entitled *L'art d'être pauvre, mémoires*. A man of strong political views, the Marquis expressed himself in an unambiguous manner on the major divisive issues in France of his day, such as the Dreyfus Affair, the Moroccan crisis and the question of the separation of Church and State, in the last of which he, as a staunch Catholic, was among the most vehement opponents. It is not clear how the Marquis de Castellane could have made the offer to the Vatican here reported. What is known is that his request to the Vatican for the dissolution of his marriage was refused, and the union was terminated by a civil divorce in 1906. The article, 'Boxeurs et sociétés secrètes en Chine' (*Revue des Deux Mondes*, August 1900), which he wrote at the height of European frenzy, shows him, however, to have been a much less fanatical person than the writer of this letter implied.

nation, as Catholics are, perhaps I am making a blunder in frankly stating this case to you. But even tho you be a devout Catholic, your soul, before almighty supreme force, will tell you that it is (next to being a Traitor to ones land of their birth), a greater Crime than War, to Steal ones Country by secret Jesuit schemes, and may the hand of retribution fall upon any and all who plot ruin of innocent people. Will you do me the great favour to acknowledge the receipt of this, even tho you cannot write a single sentence. I sent you some 'Free Press' papers, and would send you more if you can get them.

Dr M. M. Yates

578. From L. G. Fraser

Slough [Buckinghamshire, England] 19 March 1913

My dear Morrison,

I shall be glad if you will send me a line to tell me what is really going on at your end of the world. It is most difficult to arrive at the truth here. About Mongolia, I have taken the line that China will not offer active resistance, but the telegrams from St Petersburg about Chinese preparations are most persistent. I have said in the *P.M.G.* [*Pall Mall Gazette*] again and again that the Russian statements cannot be very trustworthy, and have pointed out that no news of warlike measures ever comes from Peking.

I did what I could to present the cause of China fairly in a leader in *The Times* of March the 7th called 'A Hitch in the Chinese Loan'.[1] I hope you saw it. At the same time, it really does seem now that the defection of the United States group announced this morning will smash up the scheme altogether.[2] I shall be glad to know what you think. I have not seen Murray Stewart[3] or Addis or Birch Crisp for a very long time, and so do not know what is going on here. The F.O. people have repeatedly told us that the loan will go through all right, but this does not now seem possible. Germany is financially in a very bad way, and the whole European situation is full of uncertainty. This must militate against your getting the money you want.

[1] The leader stated that a 'clerical error' in the last communication from the Ministers of the Six Powers had led China to believe that under the loan conditions foreigners appointed to various Government departments were to be the directors of these departments whilst China had agreed to the nomination of advisers only. The leader continued: 'the control instituted should not be allowed to extend to political objects, nor should there be any undue meddling with Chinese internal administration.'

[2] The American Group withdrew from the Six Power Consortium following objections by the newly elected President Woodrow Wilson to American participation in the China Loan. This news was reported by the *Times* correspondent in Washington and published in the paper on 18 March under the title 'Dr Wilson and the Six Power Loan.'

[3] A British business man from Hong Kong and Chairman of the China Association there as well as a member of the Hong Kong Legislative Council. He was a correspondent for *The Times* while in the colony.

The constitutional troubles in Japan have further filled people here with much misgiving.

I should also really like to know what your people are going to do about Tibet, and what is the meaning of the troops who seem to be still assembling on the Eastern Tibetan border. My impression is that the Government here are more in favour of a Resident at Lhasa than they were some time ago. At the same time, I doubt whether they will really do anything. The reason is that the situation in Southern Persia is so bad that the F.O. begin to recognise that they will have to make some sort of a move there. This seems to be their private conclusion, but it is not yet reflected in the conventional answers to questions about Persia asked in Parliament. They will not touch Persia and Tibet simultaneously.

You might tell me whether you are still hopeful about the 25 million loan, or whether you propose to revert to the policy of an open market.

Please give my kind regards to Mrs. Morrison, and believe me

Yours sincerely
Lovat Fraser

March 1913 – July 1913

The conflict between the old forces centred on Yüan Shih-k'ai in the North and the republicans in the South came into the open with the murder of Sung Chiao-jen. Sung was the leader of the Kuomintang in the newly elected parliament at the time of his assassination. A fervent advocate of parliamentary democracy who placed great faith in ousting Yüan and his military clique by constitutional means, he had been responsible after the overthrow of T'ang Shao-yi's cabinet of which he was a member, for re-organising the T'ung-meng hui, or Alliance Society, and merging it with three other parties with little or no republican conviction into a new party, the Kuomintang or Nationalist Party. This incongruous agglomeration succeeded, in spite of threats and bribery by Yüan Shih-k'ai, in emerging as the majority party in the new parliament elected on limited franchise in 1913. Believers in parliamentary democracy such as Sung and his colleagues, prominent amongst whom was Huang Hsing, second in importance only to Sun Yat-sen in the Kuomintang hierarchy, set about enlisting Yüan Shih-k'ai's followers and appointees in the Cabinet as members of their party, instead of fighting for the right of their party to form a government. In so doing they merely gave the party an inflated image of its own strength, and thereby won the reputation of having transformed the principle of 'party cabinet' into that of 'cabinet party'. Yet in spite of the factionalism of the new party which rendered it a comparatively harmless and naive opposition, Yüan was disturbed by Sung and his colleagues who, with a good deal of noise, vowed to overthrow his regime. Hence the murder of Sung, in many ways the ablest of the Kuomintang leaders.

When evidence was made public pointing directly to Yüan Shih-k'ai's closest associate, Chao Ping-chün, then concurrently Prime Minister and Minister for the Interior, as the chief instigator of the assassination, there was a cry for vengeance. Sun Yat-sen and his followers, who had until then counselled co-operation with Yüan, advocated a resort to military action when deprived of getting a hearing by constitutional means.

The republicans, however, were as weak militarily as they were in disarray politically. They could hardly claim to possess an armed force of their own beyond a small number of disaffected elements in the army, of indifferent loyalty. The popular support upon which the first revolutionary tide had been carried and on which Sun Yat-sen and his followers depended, had lost much of its impetus as the populace at large became confused by the compromise Sun Yat-sen had struck with Yüan Shih-k'ai and by the events which followed. The result was that to many the new anti-Yüan stance appeared to be mere political in-fighting or jockeying for position, rather than a continuation of the revolution, which had ended for most people with the overthrow of the Manchu dynasty. The defection of the so-called 'moderates' and right-wing elements, whom Sung and his T'ung-meng hui colleagues had press-ganged into the Kuomintang, to form the growing ranks of the 'third force' (to be called, like conservative parties in many countries, the 'progressive party'), helped to strengthen the scepticism prevailing throughout the country. No amount of revolutionary rhetoric by Sun and his followers could dispel it.

The majority of publications – mostly of Kuomintang origin – covering this period pictures the nation in ferment, ready to rise in unison to slay the dragon and to avenge Sung's murder, and gives a somewhat misleading impression of the contemporary scene. With the support of the 'third force' Yüan quietly ignored the threats of the Kuomintang in and outside parliament and proceeded to conclude the large reorganisation loan with the Five-Power Consortium which his government sorely needed in order, among other things, to buy or crush the opposition. Whatever Morrison's attitude to the assassination, and notwithstanding his refusal to serve on the proposed commission of enquiry, he was energetic in his attempts to suppress the bad publicity resulting from the murder. Through his relationship with his former press colleagues and with the English language press in Shanghai and other cities in China, he tried to bolster the image of Yüan and the Central Government which was essential for the purposes of the much-needed foreign loan. Furthermore, he attempted to use his influence with the head of the Police Force of the International Settlement in Shanghai to oust dissenters who were hiding under the protection of foreign jurisdiction. In spite of these weighty diversions, however, Morrison's paramount concern continued to be the Mongolian problem, about which he wrote many lengthy memoranda for the Chinese government.

579. From K'ung T'ien-tseng[1]

Shanghai 23 March 1913

Dear Dr. Morrison,

[...]

Shanghai is much agitated over the murder of Mr. Sung[2] and the radicals are again bitterly dissatisfied with President Yuan's talk again of a northern campaign, not knowing what it means. Most of the leading men support the re-election of the present President, but a certain section of the chief political party here is against the idea. One paper published in English[3] (you know which I mean) is violently anti-Yuan and has published many foolish articles which will injure not Yuan but the Republic. We try to reason with the Editor but he is as obstinate as a mule. He wants to put up somebody – but who he is he would not mention, but mentally we know who he is. He thinks he is doing a great service by giving these insensate attacks on Yuan, not knowing what an asset he is to the country just now. The trouble with these people is that they cannot place the country before parties, and advocate

[1] K'ung T'ien-tseng (d. 1916), Chinese journalist. An overseas Chinese from Malaya who claimed to be a direct descendant of Confucius, K'ung was at this time Editor of an English language journal in Shanghai, the *Republican Advocate*, which Li Teng-hui (1872–1947), a Yale graduate and later the President of Futan University in Shanghai, was Editor-in-chief.

[2] Sung Chiao-jen (1882–1913), Chinese Republican politician. A returned student from Japan, he was a prominent figure in the T'ung-meng hui founded in Tokyo in 1905 under the leadership of Sun Yat-sen. An able organiser, Sung was the moving spirit behind the establishment of the Provisional Government in Nanking and the election of Sun as its President in December 1911. When the T'ung-meng hui merged with other parties to become the Kuomintang in 1912, he was delegated by Sun to act as the chief executive of the new party, which became the majority party in the first parliament in Peking, and in this capacity he was indefatigable in preaching parliamentary democracy. After he and three of his Kuomintang colleagues withdrew from the first Republican Cabinet following the resignation of the Prime Minister T'ang Shao-yi in June 1912, he went on a lecturing tour through the Yangtse Provinces, criticising Yüan Shih-k'ai's administration which he stigmatised as a threat to the democratic system. His speeches had a rousing effect on the people in the south, and greatly disturbed the Peking Government. It was while on his way to Peking for the re-opening of Parliament after his lecturing tour that he was shot by an assassin at Shanghai Railway Station on 20 March 1913, dying two days later. The evidence for the murder, when it came to light, pointed to the direct involvement of Chao Ping-chün, then Minister of the Interior, and his Secretary Hung Shu-tsu (q.v.). This revelation shocked the nation and immediately widened the existing rift between the southern Republicans and Yüan's administration, eventually leading to what became known as the 'Second Revolution'.

[3] The *China Republican*, a Kuomintang organ in Shanghai, was closed down in 1913 on Morrison's suggestion by the French authorities in the French Concession in Shanghai, where the office of the paper was located. Its publisher, Ma Soo (or Marceau), of Chinese and French parentage, was deported from China, while its contributing Editor, Chesney Duncan (q.v.), was threatened with prosecution. Ma Soo later went to England and there published a newsletter in support of Sun Yat-sen's cause.

destruction without suggesting constructive measures. Our paper[1] tries to hold sane views on all political matters, and refrain from indulging [in] unnecessary attacks upon the Government because they tend to weaken our cause, but the radicals would not have it suspecting we are pro-Yuan, not knowing that we are standing for what is best – for the welfare of the country, irrespective of parties. These are my private views, and of course you will keep them to yourself because I belong to no party just now considering such premature.

The funeral of Mr. Sung took place just now. It was a most impressive one being quite modern, free from all the paraphernalia indispensable to Chinese processions. I met the deceased gentleman but once. He appeared to me quite a capable and good man. It is a pity the murderer was not caught at the time of the dastardly act. A reward of $5000 has been offered for his arrest. I have visited the scene of the murder, and am surprised that he could have escaped.[2]

With kind regards

Yours sincerely
T. C. K'ung

I hope you approve of my defence of the Republic against J. O. P. Bland's attacks.[3]

[1] *Republican Advocate*.
[2] The assassin, Wu Shih-ying (or Wu Ming-fu), and his accomplice Ying K'uei-ch'eng (or Ying Kuei-hsiang) were in fact apprehended in the house of Ying K'uei-ch'eng in the International Settlement in Shanghai on the day this letter was written. Wu Shih-ying died mysteriously in prison a month later, having been murdered, it was suspected, by an agent of the Chinese Government in its attempt to suppress any incriminating evidence that he might produce. Ying K'uei-ch'eng, after being handed over to the Chinese authorities, managed to escape from jail on 25 July, allegedly with the connivance of the Garrison-Commander, Admiral Cheng Ju-cheng (q.v.), who had arrived in Shanghai some two weeks earlier.
[3] This refers to a letter to the Editor of the *North China Daily News* which K'ung T'ien-tseng wrote on 14 September 1912 defending Morrison against Bland's attack on his letter published in *The Times* on 23 August 1912 under the heading 'The Outlook in China. A Reply to Pessimists. Dr. Morrison's views'. Bland, writing under the pen-name of 'Fairplay', questioned whether Morrison would be as optimistic about China's future as he had expressed himself in his letter had he not been in the service of the Chinese Government. K'ung in his letter contrasted Morrison with 'a class of foreigners who can blow hot and cold at the same time and serve as weather-cocks as long as they are paid for the service.' He maintained that Morrison, long before this, while still *Times* Correspondent in China, had 'always taken an optimistic view of this country, and he has not spoken or written merely to please'.

580. To Ts'ai T'ing-kan

Peking 27 March 1913

My dear Admiral,

I enclose you various papers [...]¹

I would urge that undue importance be not given to the messages of Putnam Weale. They really carry very little weight – in fact none at all among serious people. It would be very inadvisable to take action regarding them other than that I have suggested, which is:

(1) that Mr Henningsen² be instructed to see Putnam Weale and give him due warning:

(2) That the Minister of Foreign Affairs should in an informal manner give to the British Minister copies of Putnam Weale's telegrams, and draw his attention to their mischievous nature. At the same time Mr Lu Cheng-hsiang can refer to the British Order in Council,³ and he might ask whether this cannot be extended to cover offences such as that to which he is drawing the British Minister's attention.

With kind regards

Very sincerely yours
[G. E. Morrison]

Enclosure to Letter No. 580: *Memorandum regarding the Transmission of Seditious Messages to the European Press, with Special Reference to the two enclosed Telegrams sent by the* DAILY TELEGRAPH *Correspondent, Mr B. L. Simpson (Putnam Weale), on the afternoon of the 23rd March* [*1913*]

For a long time past the correspondent of the *Daily Telegraph* has been sending to his paper messages which constitute a systematic attack upon the present Government of China and upon the character and good faith of the high Chinese authorities, especially the President Yuan Shih-kai, and which are couched in terms that would not be tolerated in any other country in the world. Unfortunately, this correspondent is simply a notoriety hunter. He is paid a fee for each message. He is quite irresponsible, and only seeks to make a sensation. If official attention be given to his messages, they would assume an importance which they do not deserve. They are read as interesting messages: they in no way influence public opinion. For they are so violent in tone, so inaccurate and contradictory, that they carry no weight among the serious people in England.

¹ Only two of the enclosures are printed.
² H. F. Henningsen, Danish employee of the Chinese Telephone and Telegraph Administration, at this time Superintendent of the Peking Office.
³ The Order in Council, London, 11 February 1907, provided for the punishment by payment of security for good behaviour or by deportation of any person guilty of printing, publishing or selling seditious matter, seditious matter being defined as 'matter calculated to excite tumult or disorder or to excite enmity between His Majesty's subjects and the Government of China or the Government of Corea'.

I would suggest that the Minister of Foreign Affairs draw informally the attention of the British Legation to this action of a British subject, as being injurious to public decorum and calculated to impair the harmonious relations of the two countries. Should such attacks be made in England against the person of the Sovereign, the perpetrator, if he were alien, would be expelled from the country, or, if he were an Englishman, would be severely punished. When *The Times* published articles reflecting upon the Government of Russia, in a manner which was resented by that Government, *The Times* Correspondent in St Petersburg, Mr D. D. Braham, was deported.[1] No such action can be contemplated in Mr Simpson's case. He is really not worth deporting. He would then pose as a 'martyr', a 'victim of the autocratic government of the President'. Similarly, if his messages are refused for transmission, he would proclaim himself a martyr, his paper would defend him, and his attacks, which would then be written, would be more violent than his telegrams.

There is no special provision in the Treaties between China and England for dealing with such offences. Nor do the Orders in Council of the British Government quite cover the case. The British Government, by the order in Council of February 11th, 1907, of which I enclose a copy, deals with the publication of seditious matter in the China Treaty Ports by British subjects, and does not cover the case of the transmissions of seditious telegrams to a paper published in England. Action would in this case have to be taken in England. It is not worth while. Still it is imperative that the attention of Sir John Jordan should be drawn to these telegrams.

The Chinese Telegraph authorities can decline to transmit such seditious messages, but before taking this step, it would be advisable for the Director General of Telegraphs to send Mr Henningsen to see the *Daily Telegraph* correspondent, and give him due warning. There is nothing the correspondent would like better than to be made a martyr, and to think that his messages were so highly important that the Chinese Government were compelled to take action to try and stop him.

The International Telegraph Convention of June 11th, 1908, provides for the stopping of the transmission of such messages, but China is a signatory to that Convention. China is even in a stronger position to deal with the messages than she would be if she were a signatory to the Convention, but

---

[1] Braham was arrested and expelled from Russia on 28 May 1903. No specific charge was laid against him, but it was rather 'the hostile tone of the correspondence and of *The Times* in general' that was objected to. This at least was the complaint of the notorious Vyacheslar Konstantinovich Plehve (?1846-1904), Russian Minister of the Interior at the time and former Prosecutor in St Petersburg, Director of State Police, Governor and suppressor of Finland and persecutor of peasants, workers, Jews and Armenians. Morrison's attacks on Russia's activities in China, greatly intensified in the months preceding the outbreak of the Russo-Japanese War (1904-5), had greatly irritated the Russian Government, and had contributed largely to Braham's expulsion.

I repeat it would be unwise to take any action that would make the Correspondent appear as a martyr or as a man to whose vapourings serious attention is given.

I enclose two copies [...] of the original text of Mr Simpson's two telegrams of March 23rd, together with copies of their reproduction in plain English.[1]

(I) *23 March 1913, 3.20 p.m., Peking*

No more fatal and far-reaching thing for China, dashing the fair hopes which had just been raised by President Wilson's message,[2] could have occurred than the cruel assassination at Shanghai of Sung Chiao-jen, the leader of the Kuo ming Tang Party, a patriot and scholar who was universally esteemed. *There is not the slightest doubt but that he was shot by order*[3] and there is probably also a plan to kill General Huang Shing and General Chen Chi-mei,[4] who represent the militant element of the radical

---

[1] Only the latter are printed.
[2] In his annual report to Congress on 3 December 1912 President Wilson expressed the sympathy of the American people to China on her 'assumption of the republican principle,' and stated: 'During the formative constitutional stage, and pending definitive action by the assembly, as expressive of the popular will, and the hoped-for establishment of a stable republican form of government capable of fulfilling its international obligations, the United States is, according to precedent maintaining full and friendly *de facto* relations with the Provisional Government.' The Chinese Government was given to understand that formal recognition would be accorded to her as soon as the National Assembly was convened. This greatly heartened Yüan's followers who regarded the message as an expression of official recognition of the new Republic by the United States, at a time when such recognition by the Powers was very much sought by Yüan's administration.
[3] Simpson's assertion, which Morrison here underlined and condemned, turned out to be a good surmise, as was revealed in the subsequent hearing in the Mixed Court in the International Settlement, before a representative of the Chinese Government and British and French consular officials.
[4] Huang Hsing, who was with Sung Chiao-jen when Sung was assassinated, took refuge in Japan after the failure of the 'Second Revolution', and, as has been mentioned already in an earlier note, went to the United States in 1914 and died a natural death on his return to China in 1916. Ch'en Ch'i-mei (1876–1916), who returned to China after remaining for a year in Japan following the Second Revolution, actively continued the anti-Yüan campaign, and was assassinated by an agent of Yüan Shih-k'ai in Shanghai on 18 May 1916. Ch'en had joined the T'ung-meng hui when he first went to Japan in 1906, and had soon after returned to China to become one of the most active underground workers. In November 1911 he led the republican forces in the occupation of Shanghai, and he became the city's first *Tutu*. He was appointed Minister of Industry and Commerce in the first Republican Cabinet under T'ang Shao-yi, but did not take up the post, and he was compelled to give up his post of *Tutu* of Shanghai by Yüan Shih-k'ai in August 1912. He was at Sung Chiao-jen's death-bed, and three months later led the unsuccessful attempt at the seizure of the Shanghai Arsenal in the so-called 'Second Revolution'. On his return to China in 1915, he was responsible for the assassi-

South and control the Kuo Ming Tang or united Nationalists, who number 368 members out of a total of 546 in the coming Parliament and who are devoted to two leading ideas, viz, a party Cabinet, and Provincial rights as opposed to Yuan Shih-kai's ideal of a Peking dictatorship. This crime must therefore solely be looked at from the effect it produced on the Convocation of Parliament which is fixed for 8th April. Already 174 members had assembled here, upwards of 100 belonging to the Kuo Ming Tang. Yesterday on hearing the news of the murder Huang Shing and Sun Yat-sen said they would on no conditions come to Peking. Scores of Kuo Ming Tang members departed and the belief is strengthening that the whole party will assemble at Nanking which will produce an unparalleled position. It is noteworthy that the Kuo Ming Tang party is determined to vote for the essential chapters of the Constitution and President in the manner they decided would be most expedient. This is precisely what Yuan Shih-kai is determined to defeat at all costs. The recent voyage to the South of the Chief Presidential Secretary, Liang Shih-yi,[1] aroused the deepest concern. It was held to be particularly sinister, for despite the constantly published statement that Yuan Shih-kai does not seek re-election to the Presidency and that he is tired of public life, it is known, on the contrary, that he has accumulated large sums of specie, – a sort of Spandau fund[2] – to deal with future contingencies. The deepest pessimism reigns for days in all diplomatic quarters. The time when the government of China by assassin and dagger was possible is long past: the resumption of such methods must inevitably precipitate civil strife.

Putnam Weale

---

nation of Ch'eng Ju-ch'eng (q.v.), Yüan's Garrison-Commander in Shanghai, and in December the following year tried unsuccessfully to incite a naval revolt by seizing the Chinese gun-boat *Chao-ho*, then stationed on the Huangpu River in Shanghai. He therefore became one of Yüan's most hated enemies. Ch'en Ch'i-mei was the patron of Chiang Kai-shek, who served under him in Shanghai, and Chiang in turn became the patron of his two nephews, the brothers Ch'en Kuo-fu (1892–1951) and Ch'en Li-fu (b. 1900), who were to play an important role in the Kuomintang and subsequent Republican politics.

[1] Liang Shih-yi's visit to his native Kwangtung province in March 1913, ostensibly for the celebration of his father's 70th birthday, was regarded with suspicion by many who saw his trip as an attempt to prepare Kwangtung, then under the control of the Kuomintang, for the forthcoming conflict with the Kuomintang. The dismissal of Hu Han-min, the *Tutu*, barely three months after the murder of Sung Chiao-jen, strengthened the belief that there was more to Liang's visit to the south than he had let it be known. As it eventuated, Kwangtung was to become Yüan's stronghold under Lung Chi-kuang (q.v.) for the next three years until Lung's dismissal in December 1916.

[2] By virtue of legislation passed on 11 November 1871, following the Franco-Prussian War, the Imperial War Chest of £6,000,000 in gold was kept in reserve by the Bismarck Government for war purposes in a maximum-security fortress at Spandau near Berlin.

(II) *23 March 1913, 5.10 p.m., Peking*

In view of the latest assassination it is interesting to record the crimes which have never been explained since the outbreak of the Revolution: General Wuluching, commanding the sixth division, was shot in the night in a tent at Shihchia-chuang – about a day's distance from Peking, because he was believed to be about to march on the Capital.[1] General Liangpi commanding the Imperial Guard was decoyed to a Restaurant in Peking and bombed on returning home.[2] Premier Tong Shao-yi was confronted with a revolver on board a ship in Tientsin but the assassin was overpowered.[3] General Cheng Chen-wu and General Fang-wei were snared to Peking and denounced telegraphically and they were ordered to be shot without trial by police, on manufactured evidence.[4] Many smaller, unknown men have shared the same fate. Putnam Weale

581. To Ts'ai T'ing-kan

[Peking] 4 April 1913

Very confidential

My dear Admiral,

The Belgian Minister sent over yesterday Père Rutten[5] to see me with regard to the serious anxiety in which all the Belgian Missionaries are in that territory of Kwei Hua Ch'eng between Kwei Hua Ch'eng and Kalgan,

[1] General Wu Lu-chen (1879–1911), Chinese soldier, who joined the T'ung-meng hui while a military student in Japan. When it became known that he was conspiring with General Chang Shao-tseng (q.v.) of Lanchow to attack Peking while Yin-chang (1860–?1928), the Manchu Minister of War, was away directing operations at the front, the Court tried to forestall this move by removing him from the strategic point of Shihchia-chuang and appointing him on 4 November 1911 Governor of Shansi Province. It was there that he was assassinated two days later by Government agents.

[2] Liang-pi (1877–1912), a Manchu general trained in Japan and a grandson of I-li-pu (?1771–1843), Viceroy of Liangkiang during the first Sino-British War (1839–42). Liang-pi was the leading spirit in the monarchist faction which came to be formed at Court after the outbreak of the Revolution, opposing the course of compromise with the revolutionaries which Yüan Shih-k'ai was then negotiating. For this stand he was assassinated on 26 January 1912.   [3] See p. 79 note 1.

[4] On 15 August 1912 General Chang Chen-wu, who had earlier been invited to Peking, after being entertained by Tuan Ch'i-jui at the Hotel Wagon-Lits in the Legation Quarter, was waylaid by Government soldiers who were lying in wait, and together with another Republican general, Fang Wei, was summarily tried by a military court and shot on the order of Yüan Shih-k'ai, on manufactured evidence said to have been furnished him by Li Yüan-hung. The incident created a furore and the Parliament then in session threatened a censure motion demanding evidence which, however, was not produced. The matter was allowed to subside only after long wrangling between the Government and Parliament which finally gave way at the prospect of national unity with the imminent arrival of Sun Yat-sen in Peking.

[5] A Belgian Catholic missionary in Inner Mongolia.

owing to the incorporation in the Chinese troops of brigands, whose depredations the Catholics assisted to suppress, and who are now threatening the Catholics in retaliation.

The chief Chinese Christian of all, Tuan Jung, President of the Hsien i Huei of Hing-ho,[1] about whom the Belgian Minister spoke to the President, has been removed to Kwei Hua Ch'eng and is there imprisoned among the criminals. He has not been judged and he can neither defend himself nor bring witnesses to testify on his behalf. He is so tightly manacled and shackled that the iron has worn through the flesh and exposed the bone both of his feet and ankles. He is given only a basin of millet a day and Père Rutten says that he does not think the unfortunate man will long survive his treatment.

What I would like to point out is this. It is the French Legation which is the Protector of the Catholic Missionaries in China, with the exception of the German missionaries who are under the German Legation and Italian Catholics who are under Italian or French protection as they like. All Belgians are under French protection. This case, therefore, should, strictly speaking, be brought forward by the French Legation who, as you can well imagine, would only be too glad to exaggerate its importance and lay stress upon the condition of the country which rendered such things possible. It was to avoid this that the Belgian Minister himself took up the matter. It is not desirable at the present time that there should be any foreign interference with Chinese administration. Nothing the French and Russians would like better than that circumstances should arise on the Mongolian border which would give them a pretext for causing China difficulties. The best way to avoid this is by having an enquiry quickly addressed to the authorities in Kwei Hua Cheng with regard to this Tuan Jung and also with regard to the condition of the troops who are 'protecting' the various Christian communities. These communities number nearly 400. There are 140 Belgian priests who, as I have said, are under French protection (because France is the protector of the Catholic religion and all these priests have received their pass-ports from the French Legation, not from the Belgian) and there are 100,000 Chinese Catholics.

Since the Belgian Minister submitted the case to the President he does not like to take the matter elsewhere naturally, and yet everyone must know that the President has got a thousand other things to think about.

[...]

That big fat man whom you introduced to the President the other day, Mr. Roy Anderson,[2] has gone to Shanghai to see the heads of the Kuo Min tang,

---

[1] The District Consultative Assembly. Hing-ho or Hsing-ho is a town near the eastern border of what later became Suiyuan Province, east of Chi-ning and west of Chang-chia-k'ou.

[2] An American born of missionary parents in Hangchow and brought up in China speaking fluent Chinese. He later became the representative of the Standard Oil Company in China,

whom he knows well. His visit will, I am sure, have the effect of improving their good opinion of the President.

Today I have been busy sending to *The Times* a statement correcting some very curious mis-statements of fact published in *The Times* of the 7th of March. If you were in London you would have corrected those mis-statements on the spot, but Mr Lew Yuk-lin does not seem to attach importance to them. One particular mis-statement was a very alarming one regarding 'General Chang Hsun[1] and his 30,000 troops on the flank of the Tientsin-Pukou Railway'. I wrote to *The Times* and told them that the total number of General Chang Hsun's men was only 8,000, that they were a well disciplined body and that it was not advisable that they should be moved from where they are seeing that they are keeping order in a thickly populated and important district.

With kind regards

Very sincerely yours
[G. E. Morrison]

582. From C. Clementi Smith[2]

[Wheathampstead, Hertfordshire, England] 5 April 1913

My dear Morrison,

[...]

I have not written to you, feeling that you must have your time so fully occupied that you ought not to be bothered with even an additional letter. Then, too, I have nothing of any special information to write about. But my interest in the Far East continues to be vastly greater than anything that has been happening in the Near East, and the more I think the more rotten British policy appears.

---

and was active in Republican politics, having close connections with various members of the Kuomintang, and running errands between them and the Peking Government. Anderson later served as an adviser to Li Ch'un (q.v.) the Military Governor of Kiangsu.

[1] Chang Hsün (1854-1923), Chinese soldier, at this time stationed at Yen-chou in Shantung Province, to which place he had retreated when Nanking fell to the Republican forces in 1911. Because of the reputation of his troops for fierceness, it was very much feared by foreigners that he might at any time disrupt the important line of communication, the Tientsin-Pukow Railway, linking the lower Yangtse and the Chinese capital. The number of his troops was greatly exaggerated, and in order to put down speculation Morrison wrote to ask Chou Tzu-ch'i, then Governor of Shantung, who on 3 April 1913 replied that the correct number was 12,000 (*see* p. 141).

[2] Sir Cecil Clementi Smith (1840-1916), British colonial official. Formerly Governor and Commander-in-Chief of the Straits Settlements (1887-93), he was said to have been offered but to have declined the post of British Minister to Peking in 1896. He headed the British Delegation to the International Opium Conference in Shanghai in 1909 and to that in The Hague in 1911. He was the father of Beatrice Brownrigg (q.v.), a close friend of Morrison.

I am really glad to see the line the new President of the United States has taken as regards China.[1] It will, I hope, bring about the smashing of this ridiculous Consortium of the Powers, and that our Government will realize – if they can ever learn anything – that politics and finance should not be mixed up together.

We are, of course, looking anxiously forward to April 8th.[2] I cannot help thinking that the National Council is not likely to assemble in full force. Even if it does not, will it not be rather a danger than a help towards consolidating the Government in China.

Please give *mes hommages* to your Wife, and with hearty good wishes for success in your extremely difficult position.

Believe me

Yours very sincerely
Cecil Clementi Smith

583. To D. D. Braham

[Peking] 11 April 1913

Private

My dear Braham,

I enclose you a paper I have received from a friend of mine Captain Perry-Ayscough,[3] written from Urga on the 24th of March from the residence of Korostovetz himself.

[...]

The question of Mongolia is assuming a slightly better complexion. The most powerful of the pro-Russian Mongols, the Bagada Lama was, he

[1] A reference to the withdrawal of the American Banking Group from the Six Power Consortium. Wilson's action was interpreted at the time and by subsequent historians as an expression of the lofty ideals of the new President who did not wish to involve America in any undertaking that might impair China's sovereign rights. But evidence revealed since by American documented sources, in particular the Straight Papers, point not to Wilson's idealism as mentioned here in prompting the American withdrawal, but rather to the fact that the American Group found itself unable, in view of the current state of the financial market at home, to take up its portion of the loan then under negotiation with the Chinese Government, and so persuaded President Wilson to furnish them with an excuse to extricate themselves from the engagement. The American banks then diverted their funds to the more profitable market in South America.

[2] 8 April 1913 was the date set for the opening of Parliament. The American Government had earlier announced that they would recognise the Chinese Republic upon Parliament being convened.

[3] Henry George Charles Perry-Ayscough, British employee of the Chinese Post Office, a District Deputy Postmaster. His articles on Mongolia, which Morrison sent to Braham, were not published in *The Times*.

considers, badly treated by the Russians in Harbin when he went there on a special mission[1] and he has returned to Urga full of wrath. I would not be surprised if there were a repudiation of the Urga Convention of the 3rd of November by the very Mongols who were induced to sign it. Another Prince of some importance – the Wutai – who under the old Regime was driven from his territory north of Taonanfu and fled to Urga has returned with 800 men and will in the next few days tender his allegiance to the Republican Government. More than one of the men mentioned in Perry-Ayscough's article as having been attached to the mission to Russia, are to my own knowledge in close communication with the Government here.

Russia has shown some concern at the sudden *rapprochement* between China and Japan. As you no doubt know the Japanese Government have now undertaken to act as mediators and try and bring about a friendly understanding between China and Russia regarding Mongolia. The Russian Legation here is also somewhat concerned at the Declaration of the German Government with regard to Mongolia and also at the action of America. I think the chances of an understanding have distinctly improved since I wrote to you last.

[...]

The opening of Parliament passed off well. You will have noted that a few days before the Correspondent of the *Daily Telegraph* telegraphed to London that there would be no Assembly of Parliament: that the Kuo Min Tang were leaving Peking by scores and would hold a Parliament of their own in Nanking. I am sorry Fraser[2] did not think it worth while being present at the Opening, because he could have written a picturesque account of the Ceremony, although everything was very quiet.[3]

Yuan Shih-kai moved into the Palace last Sunday and of course my office moved with him. I now have a delightful office close to the lake, looking across to the little island where the Emperor Kwang Hsu was confined after the *coup d'Etat* of 1898.[4] The lake swarms with wild duck. I was with the President on Wednesday: he was in extraordinarily good spirits. Appa-

---

[1] In a memorandum on Mongolia dated 7 April 1913, which is not printed, Morrison wrote that the Bagada Lama, a pro-Russian Mongol, might because of the incident be persuaded to renounce his Russian allegiance and influence others to do the same.

[2] David Fraser.

[3] Morrison was being somewhat unfair in making this criticism for, during his 17 years as *Times* correspondent in China, he often absented himself from colourful and memorable occasions, a description of which would have been fascinating not only to his contemporaries but to readers of history.

[4] Kuang-hsü, the reign (1875–1908) title of Tsai-t'ien (1871–1908). Following a *coup d'état* on 22 September 1898 by the Empress-Dowager which put an end to the Reform Movement led by K'ang Yu-wei (q.v.), he was confined on Ying-t'ai, the island mentioned here, in the Palace precincts.

rently it is only the Shanghai Community who are perturbed in China at the present time. They have lost their heads altogether.[1]

With all good wishes to you

Very sincerely yours
[G. E. Morrison]

[...]

584. To D. D. Braham

[Peking] 15 April 1913

Private & Confidential

My dear Braham,

In my letter last Friday I mentioned that the Japanese Government were endeavouring to bring about a friendly understanding between China and Russia with regard to Mongolia.

The present situation causes serious anxiety to the Japanese. Statements made by the Chinese Foreign Office to the Russian Legation denying emphatically that China has any aggressive intentions in regard to Mongolia and denying that Chinese troops are being sent to attack the Mongols are not credited by the Russian Minister. Whether his refusal to believe is genuine or no of course we cannot tell. The fact remains that troops, unless required for Police work, in Inner Mongolia, are not being sent to Mongolia. The statement made by Colonel Brissaud des Maillets[2] to Reuter's correspondent, namely, that the troops are being sent only for police purposes to Inner Mongolia, is a correct statement. Fantastic stories about China's mobilisation etc. along the borders of Mongolia and Northern Manchuria are published in St Petersburg papers and no doubt to some extent are credited by the Russian Government and unless this misunderstanding can be removed the difficulties which are already great may become insuperable.

The Japanese Government are rendering assistance in this way. On the 2nd of April the Minister of Foreign Affairs asked the Japanese Minister here[3] (of course you can well imagine that the suggestion so to act came originally from the Japanese themselves) if China were to make a formal declaration to the Japanese Government that she had no aggressive intentions either in Mongolia or in Northern Manchuria, the Japanese Legation

[1] This refers to the agitation in Shanghai following the murder of Sung Chiao-jen.
[2] Georges Henri Brissaud-Desmaillets (1869–1948), French soldier, formerly French Military Attaché in China and Korea (1903–5). He was appointed Adviser to the Chinese Ministry of War in 1912, but left China soon after the outbreak of the European War, fought battles in Alsace and was made a full general in December 1916. After retiring from active service in 1931 he stood unsuccessfully for Parliament as a Radical Socialist.
[3] Ijūin Hikokichi.

would communicate this to the Russian Government. The Japanese Minister said he would do so if China would communicate an exact statement of all Chinese troops stationed along the frontiers of Mongolia and Northern Manchuria. This statement detailing the Chinese forces in the territory named was handed to the Japanese Legation on the 5th of April. It was considered by them to be a correct statement for it was confirmed by the independent knowledge of their Military Attaché Major-General Aoki.[1] Accordingly on the 8th of April Mr. Midzuno, who was acting for Mr. Ijuin, the Minister, who was ill, handed to Mr. Kroupensky, the Russian Minister in Peking, a formal declaration on the part of the Chinese Government affirming that this was a correct statement and that they had no intention of carrying out any aggressive or hostile policy against the Mongols or against the Russians.

On the 9th of April an identical communication was made by Baron Motono[2] in Japan to the Russian Ambassador.[3] We await the reply with interest.

A difficulty has been raised, however, in this way. Germany has declared that whatever rights and privileges are obtained by Russia in Mongolia, she will expect also to be conceded to her under the Favoured Nation treatment. Now such Favoured Nation treatment can only come into operation if an Agreement be made between China and Russia regarding Mongolia; because Germany will demand this from China Russia may therefore find it wiser to remain in direct relations with Mongolia and thus prevent any advantages that she may obtain there from being shared by others.

It is suggested that the basis of discussion between China and Russia should be the proposals in four Articles submitted by Mr. Kroupensky to the Foreign Minister here on the 3rd of December.[4] I have always thought that this communication was one which lent itself to compromise. Negotiations on this basis were, as you can well imagine, very difficult before Parliament assembled. I think they are not now so difficult and yesterday I gave

[1] Aoki Nobuzumi (1859–1924), Japanese soldier, who saw long service in China. In 1911 he became for the fourth time Japanese Military Attaché in Peking. A former friend and adviser of Yüan Shih-k'ai, he was ordered by the Japanese General Staff towards the end of 1915 to go to Shanghai to help the southern Republicans in their attempt to overthrow Yüan. He was assisted on this mission by Lt.-Col. (later General) Matsui Iwane (1878–1948), Japanese Commander-in-Chief in Central China at the outbreak of the Sino-Japanese War in 1937 who was hanged in 1948 as a war criminal, being held responsible for the Massacre of Nanking when the city fell to his forces in 1937. In January 1917 Aoki became Military Adviser to the Chinese Government, a post he retained until shortly before his death in 1924. He was succeeded by Banzai Rihachirō.
[2] Morrison no doubt meant Makino Nobuaki, Japanese Foreign Minister from February 1913 to April 1914 in the first Yamamoto Cabinet. See p. 101 note 4.
[3] Nicylas Malewsky-Malewitch, Russia Ambassador to Japan until 1916, when he was succeeded by Basil Kroupensky.
[4] For the Four Articles see Morrison's Memorandum regarding Mongolia of 10 June 1913, enclosed in Letter No. 619, Morrison to Ts'ai T'ing-kan, 1 July 1913, p. 174.

a copy of the communication to the Japanese Legation with, of course, the knowledge of the Chinese.

Naturally the Chinese would like to have approval of their action in endeavouring to come to an agreement expressed in *The Times*. I do not know what view you take but I am quite sure that if you agree with me that it would be to the advantage of everyone that the Mongolian question should be settled amicably – at any rate such is the desire of our Japanese allies – you will help towards an agreement.

With best wishes

Very sincerely yours
[G. E. Morrison]

585. From T. C. Taylor[1]

[London] 17 April 1913

Dear Dr. Morrison,

It is possible you may have heard my name in connection with the anti-opium movement of which I have been the accredited Parliamentary representative for six or seven years past, that is to say I constantly meet the Anti-Opium Board and frequently use the opportunities I have for seeing those Ministers of the Crown who are specially interested in the opium question. I was the mover of the 1907 resolution in the House of Commons and on my own account went to China to learn more about it on the spot in the winter of 1907–8. Unfortunately you were then away or I should have called upon you there.

It has been increasingly evident for nine months past that the crisis in China must soon come. So far back as June last in the Indian Budget debate in the House of Commons I protested against the then authorised planting of 200,000 acres of poppy in India last autumn. The India office now admit I was right and I have great hopes that they will at least fall in with my oft

---

[1] Theodore Cooke Taylor (1850–1952), British politician, industrialist and social reformer, Member of the House of Commons for the East (Radcliffe-cum-Farnworth) Division of Lancashire from 1900, and head of a family firm of woollen textile manufacturers. He started in 1892 a scheme of profit-sharing with his employees and was an active advocate of the principle of profit-sharing and labour co-partnership. As Parliamentary spokesman for the Anti-Opium Board he moved a resolution in the House of Commons in 1907 that the Indo-Chinese opium traffic, 'morally indefensible', should be stopped. He visited China on a fact-finding tour in 1907–8, and carried on his campaign both in and outside Parliament, rising to China's defence when the Indian Government tried to put pressure on the Home Government to abrogate the Opium Agreement of 1911 on the grounds that China had violated the Agreement. In a letter to the Editor of the London *Daily Telegraph* in January 1913, Taylor wrote: 'As a Lancashire Member of Parliament, I ask that the Government should encourage the production of cotton in India in place of opium which for two generations we have been producing in India wherewith to poison and ruin our (otherwise) customers in China for cotton and other useful goods.' We have spelt out in full the many abbreviated words used in this letter.

pressed plea that they would cease planting or authorising planting on Government account in British India. Indeed as you are probably aware for four months past it has been mainly a question of the stocks in Shanghai. Foreseeing this I have repeatedly urged (in private) upon the Government that China must not be compelled or even allowed to pay for these stocks. I am quite certain that British public opinion would not sanction it. For months past I have been urging the Government to formally and finally release China from the opium treaty bondage. In pursuance of this after a long talk with Lord Crewe in the middle of February, I took a private deputation to him to represent this view, at which he was good enough to inform us privately that the Chinese Government had actually proposed to purchase the Shanghai stocks on terms. At once we told him we were sure public opinion here would never endorse such a shameful ending to perhaps the most (continuingly) disgraceful chapter in British history. He did not agree with or differ from us – in point of fact I am confident he agrees with us. Of course Grey has been absolutely absorbed for months past with the Balkan question and I have seen less of him than usual. But when I found out about three weeks ago that Acland (Under Sec. for Foreign Affairs) was disposed (in private) to defend such a thing on the ground that it was none of our proposing or pressing but that China of her own free will and (as he suggested) because perhaps she had 'a bad conscience at having "Broken the treaty" '! had *volunteered* to get the opium dealers out of their difficulty. To my thinking that theory would never go down either in this country or anywhere else as *fact*.

Now please Dr Morrison write and tell me how far this has any *foundation*, if any, in fact. It is really *necessary* that I should know. I believe I possess the confidence not only of the anti-opium people but of the Government also. I have only one object and that is to get the opium habit stopped as quickly as possible. It is for that reason that I have defended Grey's *pari passu* policy up to the point when the production had become so enormously profitable in China as to make the position of the Chinese Government in rigidly suppressing production intolerable so long as she is compelled to admit the foreign article. I steadily maintain and am sure the House of Commons will back me that seeing the India Government have got many millions sterling more than they thought they were bargaining for in 1907, and seeing China's great and many difficulties, she should be released without paying a single cent. I know the dealers have recently made enormous profits and have excellent reason to believe that the dealers have made a perfect ring or 'trust' of the Indian article for China. They have even bought some back from the Chinese to make more money. Of course they are now smuggling it into China and the stocks are declining in Shanghai I understand, but that should be stopped. I should have made a parliamentary row over the Anking (*Flora*) incident but have done my best to keep quiet the critics of the

Government in order to get the Government to release China *without public* pressure. I am (as a Britisher) so *ashamed of the whole business*. I only wrote the article in the *Contemporary Review* (sending you under separate cover)[1] when I began to see the Government would need pressure. I am sorry Grey has been so absorbed lately by the *Near* East. Acland only today, while reiterating that this offer has been of China's free will *not at all under pressure from us* (!) has now told me he believes she has withdrawn it. I told him I hope it is true. But it must not be repeated. We really don't want the disgrace of *really pressing China* to buy what she is decapitating her subjects for producing. It would be as great a disgrace to us as an injury to her. And the really most wicked part of it would be the temptation that once in the opium business *as a Government* China would find it so profitable as to tempt her to continue. Of course I know that she is bargaining to get freedom from the treaty obligation, but she must and may have that without paying such a terrible price for it. In fact so far as I can see, China is not aware how strong public opinion here is against the traffic. We have of course a young Sassoon[2] in the House and also Keswick the younger.[3] But even with

[1] A reference to the article entitled 'Opium: A Live Question,' published in the *Contemporary Review*, Vol. CIII, 1913. In it Taylor urged the immediate cessation of the Indo-Chinese opium traffic and the prohibition of opium planting in India, replacing the drug with cotton. 'Let us stop the production and stop the hateful compulsion upon a regenerate China struggling to be free. Nothing less is consistent with the thrice recorded condemnation of this traffic by the House of Commons as "morally indefensible." Nothing less can satisfy the conscience of the British public'. Referring to 'the opium dealers [who] are calling for their pound of flesh', he said, 'The Chinese have long memories. Would it not then be well, even in our own interest, that we should at last be just to China? Is it worth haggling about it any longer?'

[2] Philip Albert Gustave David (later Sir Philip) Sassoon (1888–1939), 3rd Bart., British politician, maternal grandson of Baron Gustave de Rothschild, and grandson of Sir Albert Abdullah Sassoon (1818–96) 1st Bart., who because of his wealth was known as the 'Indian Rothschild' and who was responsible for extending his business empire to China, making the house of Sassoon one of the leading dealers in opium. Philip Albert Gustave David, referred to here as the 'younger Sassoon', was educated at Eton and Oxford and in 1912, on the death of his father, Edward Albert (1856–1912), succeeded to the Baronetcy and to his seat in the House of Commons for the same constituency of Hythe, a seat he was to retain for 27 years until his death. In 1915 he became Private Secretary to Field-Marshal Sir Douglas Haig, in which position he remained until the end of the war. He was twice Under-Secretary of State for Air (1924–9 and 1932–7) and was well known as a social figure and patron of the arts, being a Trustee of the National Gallery, the Tate Gallery and other well-known collections.

[3] Henry Keswick (1870–1928), British trader and politician, son of William Keswick (1835–1912), who as the head of Jardine & Company and Matheson & Company, and President of the China Association and the London Chamber of Commerce, was the leading China merchant of his time. William Keswick's firms, founded on the opium trade, were to expand into a commercial empire consisting of banking, shipping, manufacturing, railways, mining and numerous other fields of activity, extending beyond the borders of China, and to this day the firm under various names remains the leading financial and political force in the British colony of Hong Kong. Henry, referred to here as the younger

Rees[1] thrown in they don't count for much. I know well the chief figures on both front benches in the House of Commons and don't believe there is a single one of them favourable to the traffic.

Now here was my list of proposals to the Government:
1. Stop sales in India for the present
2. Stop growing
3. Release China.

No. 1 was done about Xmas. No. 2 virtually decided upon. No. 3 *must be done*. We have got a private Member's day for discussing this question, May 7th, Wednesday and want to get the Government to announce the right decision then.[2] As to who is to pay for the stocks my reply is, let the

---

Keswick, was educated at Eton and Cambridge, and worked for many years in China and Hong Kong in his father's firms. Amongst his many other positions, he served as Chairman of the Municipal Council and also of the Chamber of Commerce in Shanghai, as a member of the Legislative and Executive Councils in Hong Kong, Chairman of Directors of the Hongkong & Shanghai Banking Corporation and the first Chairman of the Far Eastern Section of the London Chamber of Commerce. In 1912, upon the death of his father, he succeeded to his seat in the House of Commons for the Epsom Division of Surrey, retaining it until 1918. Two of his three sons, Sir William Johnston Keswick (b. 1903) and Sir John Henry Keswick (b. 1906), have been among Britain's foremost financiers and businessmen.

[1] Sir John David Rees (1854-1922), 1st Bart., British politician, a Member of the House of Commons since 1908. Joining the Indian Civil Service in 1875, he became Private Secretary to three Governors of Madras, and British Resident in Travancore and Cochin, and was a member of the Governor-General of India's Council (1895-1900) before he retired from the service in 1901. A Director of many companies, some of which dealt in Indian opium, he was the principal spokesman for Indian opium growers and traders in the British House of Commons.

[2] In the debate that took place in the House of Commons on Wednesday 7 May 1913 Towyn Jones, a Member from Wales, making the opium issue the topic of his maiden speech, proposed that the House should reaffirm its previous resolution that the traffic in the drug was 'morally indefensible' and that Britain should release China from her treaty obligations to admit the Indian drug, and set China free to prohibit importation of the stock of opium. He was opposed by Henry Keswick, representing British opium interests in China, and Sir J. D. Rees, representing Indian interests, while Edmund Harvey, a Member for Liverpool, and T. C. Taylor, spoke in support. The lengthy debate ended with Mr Jones withdrawing his motion on the vague assurance of Edwin Samuel Montagu (1879-1924), Under-Secretary of State for India (1910-14), that the Government would consider measures to reduce the traffic with a view to having it brought to an end at the earliest possible time. During the course of the debate Henry Keswick, speaking with the experience of 'nineteen years in China', said that 'in dealing with an Oriental country', one must not 'start from the plane which is parallel to the plane of this House... but start from the Oriental point of view.' In the light of this, he asserted, opium 'is no more an evil than the taking of a glass of beer or a glass of wine'. 'It merely provided the ordinary man in the street in China with some small relief in the course of his work.' He professed incomprehension that opium dens should be so described, because he knew from his personal experience that 'they are not worse...than the ordinary house in which the Chinaman lives'. On being questioned as to whether he would allow his own sons to smoke opium, he said his answer was 'No', but he went on: 'I have tried it myself, and it

Owners take them away at once from China (on condition there is no more sold by the Government in India till all these stocks are sold) and sell them in the other markets yet remaining (barring our Colonies which will have to go out of the business too), viz. Tonking, Siam, Java, Borneo etc. They will still make a profit but if not we must not make China pay – rather Great Britain or India.

Now one thing more. I have just heard on apparently *good authority* that '*Yuan Shih Kai's own private fields in Honan are planted with poppy.*' I trust you will be able to get me an absolute and truthful denial of this on the highest authority. I am also writing Yuan himself – though I don't like to do so, but I must be able to deny this if I truly can in the debate May 7th if it is brought up. Please wire 'True' or 'False' to Taylors, Batley, before May 7th.

Yours faithfully
Theo. C. Taylor

P.S. Dr Cormack[1] Peking Med. College knows me. I should be glad of a frank reply to this in *China's interests*. It is possible I may not be able to get off a letter to Yuan by this post.

586. From Chang Yü-chün[2]

Peking 17 April 1913

Dear Sir,

It was very kind of you to accept my visit yesterday to talk about the proposals which I am to bring forward to your Country. It is, of course, as we believe, a little early for us to send a delegate to make any proposal to

---

made me very ill indeed. At the same time I may remind the hon. Gentleman that those who smoke opium in the Far East are vegetarians to a very great degree. I am a mere man, who eats meat, and I drink a glass of port wine, and I also take whisky. If he asks whether, in due course, the three sons, which I now have the honour to possess, will drink port wine, whisky, or beer, or anything of that nature, I shall be very glad to inform him that I shall look forward to their doing so with discretion.' For the full debate, see *Hansard* 1913, Vol. LII, Cols. 2150–94.

[1] James Grieve Cormack (b. 1864), British medical missionary who, upon graduating from Edinburgh University joined the China Inland Mission (1891–9). Working as a medical missionary first in Shanghai in 1905, then in Hankow in 1906, he joined in 1910 the staff of the Union Medical College in Peking becoming its Principal in 1913. Morrison, in a letter to Cormack dated 19 December 1913, complaining about being charged 'Harley Street fees' in Peking wrote: 'In calling upon me to pay such high charges I presume you can maintain that I can afford to pay them and that the fees paid do not go into your pockets but into the coffers of the Mission.'

[2] Lt.-Gen. Chang Yü-chün (other name Chi-shih) invariably anglicised his name as L. Chang. The initial 'L' may have stood for an adopted European name which is not, however, spelt out. A native of Hunan Province, he was at this time serving as Military Counsellor to Yüan Shih-k'ai. He was also involved in the opium prohibition movement.

your people since the native production of our country has not yet been completely suppressed. But it is, we think, a very dangerous time for China as she is so young at present, and does not desire to have any misunderstanding between China and Britain, and moreover, we are earnest in hoping that England may help China in some way. So it is very necessary to have the misrepresentations, which were caused by this opium prohibition work, removed and good feeling be sown among these two peoples.

We have much remaining to be done among ourselves. We do not dare to ask for the immediate stopping of Indian Opium during this time. But we are sure that the difficulties concerning the prohibition of opium among Chinese, such as the obstinate resistance of the poppy-planting farmers, the joint movements against the opium laws made by the bad gentry, the smugglings of the merchants, the defiances of the opium smokers aganst the orders to give up their habits, the interventions made by the British Minister and Consuls against the strict prohibition in the various Provinces, the permission given to the opium selling shops in the Ports, Settlements and Concessions, and some others, are all due to the continuance of the Indian Opium Trade. The going up of the gun-boat to Anking has caused much bad feeling among Chinese people, and the threatening of the British Minister with the Recognition of China has also created much bad feeling. All these matters are not good for the relations between nation and nation. We are anxious to have them removed or stopped for ever. China has become a Republic. She is hereafter going on to seek from all over the world that which she had not in the past. She also hopes that the world will treat her with the same heart and mind as other nations are to be dealt with.

No opium trade can continue any longer hereafter as China has awakened and the younger people are all keen to attain a good position for their own country. Why should Britain insist in trading in China with opium which she does not want while there are many many other things might be traded in? All written above are what I intend to propose to your people. Beside, I shall show many of the latest reports of the Provinces concerning the opium prohibition.

Excuse me for troubling you too long!

With my best wishes

I am

Yours faithfully
L. Chang

What we want to propose at this time

(1) To ask for helping China to be freed from the Treaty-obligation to receive opium, so that she might suppress the opium, no matter whether it is self-produced or imported, in the same way.

(2) To remove the opium stocks from Shanghai to any other lands out of China.
(3) To examine Chinese matters very carefully and never to rely only upon papers which are constantly misled by in some other directions to make untrue reports and cruel criticisms, so that true feeling of Chinese can be got and good understanding and mutual benefit might be obtained.

587. From J. Murdoch[1]

Kagoshima, Japan 18 April 1913

My dear Dr. Morrison,

You are the busiest of men, I know, and so I will plunge *in medias res* at once.

Two years or so ago, I ventured to trespass on your kindness and good nature by asking you about the possibilities of my finding something to do as a 'dominee' in China. Then the great Upheaval came along; and the Chinese had vastly more important matters to attend to than colleges and foreign professors.

Now that things are on a stable and assured basis, however, foreign 'dominees' may again come into demand by-and-by. The Central Govt. is not rich at present, I know. But that is only for the time; ample funds will soon be at its disposal. And what about the Provincial Colleges?

I should be extremely glad to find a scholastic post in the new Republic. A Chair of European *and* Japanese History, for choice; for History has been my life-long hobby. But failing that teaching English or English Literature wd. suit me very well.

The last Vol. of Japanese History I issued,[2] while heartily welcomed by progressive Japanese, has got me into serious trouble with the Conserva-

---

[1] James Murdoch (1856–1921), British scholar. A graduate of Aberdeen University, where he later became Assistant Professor of Greek (1880–1) and of Oxford, he was Headmaster of Maryborough Grammar School in Queensland, Australia (1881–5) and Second Master at Brisbane Grammar School (1885–8). In 1888 he went as a journalist to China to investigate the condition of coolies and in 1889 to Japan, where his report on the condition of coalminers in Kyūshū, published in the *Japan Gazette*, caused a stir. From that year until 1919, when he returned to Australia to become Professor of Oriental Studies at Sydney University, he remained in Japan teaching and writing except for a brief absence in 1893 when he joined a group of Australians who set out for Paraguay in an abortive attempt to found a Utopian community there. In 1903 he started *A History of Japan* with the cooperation of a Japanese scholar, Yamagata Isō. Morrison had met Murdoch in Japan on his return to China from Europe in 1900, and described him in his Diary entry of 4 March as a 'wild Scotchman, distinguished double-honour man at Aberdeen, scholar of Worcester, Oxford, in Germany and Paris, philosopher and traveller who had been a high-school headmaster at the age of 25'.

[2] The second volume of Murdoch's *A History of Japan* was published in Kobe, Japan, in 1903, and the third volume, edited by Joseph Henry Longford (1849–1925), and L. M. C. Hall, was not published until 1926, by K. Paul, Trench, Trübner & Company, London.

tives, and the ultra-divine descent party. As these latter are dominant in Educational work, I fear there is no more chance of employment for me in Japan. Vol. III of my History is now finished; and I shd. like to issue that from China, if possible.

The death of the old Emperor[1] seems to be a turning-point in the history of the country. So long as he lived the Chōshu and Satsuma bureaucracy[2] occupied an impregnable position, and constitutionalism was moribund. In Feb. last the Bureaucracy got hit very shrewdly. Before this, there had been friction between the Army and the Navy magnates. Then, the Chōshu men had for long been eliminating Satsuma men from all important offices. And last of all the Chōshu men quarrelled among themselves, Katsura and Yamagata[3] being at serious variance. The result was the overthrow of the Bureaucratic Katsura ministry.[4] Katsura got driven to making a political party of his own.[5] He is said to be quite sick of the venture, for he is trying to mix oil and water. Besides, he is said to be physically wrong; and it is not likely that his success as a party-leader will be great. As for the Seiyukai, many of its members are quite discredited, and it may have difficulty in holding together.

The third double-headed party,[6] led by Inukai[7] and Ozaki would have

[1] Mutsuhito, Emperor Meiji of Japan (1852–1912), whose reign (1866–1912) saw the emergence of modern Japan, had died on 30 July the previous year.
[2] The Chōshū and Satsuma were the two main Japanese feudal clans which played a leading role in the overthrow of the Tokugawa Shogunate and the restoration of Imperial power in 1868, and who dominated the Japanese political scene during the Meiji era. Prominent members of the Chōshū clan were Itō Hirobumi, Inoue Kaoru (1835–1915), Kido Kōin (1833–77) and Yamagata Aritomo, and of the Satsuma clan Saigō Takamori (1827–77) and his brother Tsugumichi (1843–1902), Matsukata Masayoshi and Kuroda Kiyotaka.
[3] Yamagata Aritomo (1838–1922), Japanese soldier and politician. A Chōshū clansman, he was the first military man to become Prime Minister, in 1889, a post he held for a second time in 1898. His stipulation that the portfolios of the army and navy should be held by men in active service was responsible for the creation of the military clique, or *Gunbatsu*, in Japanese politics.
[4] The third Katsura Cabinet, which came into being in December 1912, was overthrown two months later, in February 1913. The party he organised was the Rikken Dōshikai.
[5] Katsura Tarō laid the foundations of the Rikken Dōshikai, which became the Kenseikai after his death, under the leadership of Katō Takaaki (q.v.).
[6] A reference to the Rikken Kokumintō (Constitutional Nationalist Party), formed by a break-away group from the Kenseitō and reorganised in 1913 under the leadership of Inukai Tsuyoshi.
[7] Inukai Tsuyoshi (1855–1932), Japanese politician. A journalist before entering politics as a member of the Rikken Kaishintō in the Diet in 1890, he held the seat until his death. A supporter of Ōkuma Shigenobu, he became in 1913 Leader of the party Rikken Kokumintō opposing the Katsura Cabinet which he helped to bring down that same year. His political ability and influence were not reflected in his Ministerial offices, which were brief and infrequent. He was for two weeks Minister of Education in the first Ōkuma Cabinet in 1898, and it was not until 1923 that he again held office, this time as Minister of Communications for four months in the second cabinet of Yamamoto Gombē (1852–1933).

possibly swept the board, if they cd. have forced a dissolution of the Diet in March.[1] All the younger men are inclined to support this party. Inukai and Ozaki are very sympathetic towards China and urge their followers to watch her closely – and learn from her. Events in China have had a very considerable influence in Japan. Japan is face to face with the over-population question. With the British colonies and the U.S. closed to her emigrants, Manchuria becomes of increasing consequence to her. Ten years hence there may be trouble. At present there is not much risk. Komura[2] was extremely adventurous and aggressive; the source of his success was sheer audacity. The present foreign Minister[3] is just his reverse; and the Cabinet has its hands more than full of domestic problems. For a generation Japan can venture on no armed conflict with any strong power; the financial effort would break her back utterly. Even as it is the people at large are getting very restive under the load of taxation. The last war[4] has provided them with a very bitter lesson; and they have come to detest the mention of war. The only party that might venture upon a war wd. be the Katsura party; and even then wd. only face it as a last desperate resource. Even a Chinese boycott of Japanese trade has now got its terrors, for the question of exports is an all-important

---

He held the same portfolio again for nearly a year in the Katō Cabinet in 1924. In 1929 upon the death of Tanaka Giichi (1863–1929) he became the leader of the Seiyūkai and was appointed two years later, in December 1931, concurrently Prime Minister and Foreign Minister. His assassination five months later, on 15 May 1932, marked the end of party-orientated parliamentary government and the beginning of the domination of Japanese politics by militarists. An early collaborator with Ōkuma in an expansionist policy for Japan, Inukai was involved in movements against the established governments in China and Korea and in this connection became a supporter of Sun Yat-sen. His attitude towards the Chinese Revolution can, however, be best summed up by the reply he is said to have angrily made upon being approached by Sun to become one of his advisers, that no one except the Japanese Emperor could dare to command his services.

[1] Ozaki Yukio (1858–1954), Japanese politician, known as 'the Father of Parliamentary Politics' in Japan, having had a parliamentary career lasting nearly half a century from the time of his first election in 1890. Trained in the natural sciences, he became a journalist before entering politics. He was Minister of Education in the 1898 Cabinet of Ōkuma and Itagaki Taisuke (1837–1919), Mayor of Tokyo (1904), and Minister of Justice in the Ōkuma cabinet (1915).

[2] Komura Jutarō (1855–1911), Japanese diplomat and politician. A graduate of what subsequently became Tokyo University, and of Harvard University, he entered Japan's diplomatic service on the recommendation of Mutsu Munemitsu (1844–97), and was successively Secretary to the Japanese Legation in China (1893), Minister to Korea (1895–7), and to the United States (1898–1900). He represented Japan at the Boxer Settlement negotiations in 1901, and as Foreign Minister (1901–5) in the first Katsura cabinet he concluded the Anglo-Japanese Alliance in 1902 and represented his country at the Portsmouth Conference. He became Minister to London in 1906 and on his return to Japan was made Foreign Minister (1908–11) in the second Katsura cabinet, in which capacity he completed the annexation of Korea.

[3] Makino Nobuaki.

[4] The Russo-Japanese War of 1904–5.

one. The reception given to Dr. Sun Yat-sen was significant; the Japanese *don't* wish to quarrel with China at present.

But I'm afraid all this will tire you.

With all best wishes

Very respectfully yours
Jas. Murdoch

P.S. Teaching history to young Chinese republicans wd. be most congenial work. It would be possible to enlarge on the blessings of liberty, as well as on the supreme importance of order and a sense of responsibility. Mill's Essay *On Liberty* is a forbidden book in Japan!

588. From I. Ia. Korostovetz

Urga 19 April 1913

Dear Dr Morrison,

[...] I will probably leave Urga on or about the 1st May, perhaps earlier, at least they promised me. My position here is a trying one in every respect and the Mongols very difficult people to deal with. I have made my best to satisfy both sides that is my own people and the Government of Urga but have hardly succeeded. The treaty has been signed nearly six months ago and according to my opinion is not enforced yet and perhaps will not be. The new Consul General Miller[1] must arrive in a fortnight and will continue my work, but on what lines and in what direction I do not venture to say.

I hope China will not be so foolish to begin a war, it would be a second mistake especially now that we see that things can be arranged peacefully if the Peking Government makes concessions and meets a little the legitimate and modest proposals of Russia. I regret that they have lost so much time and allowed things to drift to the present point. Let us hope that they will come to an acceptable agreement for the benefit of the three interested parties.

Sending you my best wishes I remain yours

Very sincerely
Korostovetz

I suppose your situation must not be an easy one even with a Republican Government.

[1] Aleksander Iakovlevich Miller, Russian Consul-General in Urga 1913–16.

589 From T. M. Ainscough[1]

Chengtu [Szechwan] 22 April 1913

My dear Doctor Morrison,

[...]

The political situation here is rather complicated & interesting. Hu,[2] the *Tutu*, an apparently progressive man & decent sort, unfortunately for himself is a member of the Kung Ho Tang,[3] which is in a minority in the province. The Kuo min Tang seem to be doing their best to render his life not worth living and it is reported that a number of officials are about to be changed. The old Wai Wu Sze[4] has resigned on his election as member of the Assembly. His boast used to be that 'even if he had no other talents, he knew how to obstruct the Foreigner', so Porter[5] is rather pleased now that the Wai Chiow Pu are sending another man down from Peking. The Consulate House question is temporarily settled and Porter has just leased the best *Kung Kuan*[6] in Chengtu and is amusing himself by laying out the garden.

The native papers state today that a telegram has been received from Tachienlu stating that Hsiang Cheng has fallen and the Tibetans are submitting in large numbers. This, however, is as yet unconfirmed. There is a great row on with regard to the finances of the Tibet Expedition. Chengtu says Yin *Tutu*[7] has had a million Taels. Yin replies that he has only received half that amount, says that the balance must have leaked out between

---

[1] Thomas M. Ainscough. Morrison, in a letter to Braham of 9 May 1913 enclosing Ainscough's reports described him as 'a Shanghai merchant with a passion for travelling. He is a merchant of superior class, the representative of Bradford Dyers Association'. The following year he was appointed Special Commissioner of the Board of Trade to report on conditions and prospects of British trade in China.

[2] Hu Ching-yi (1877–1925), Chinese soldier. A graduate of Japan's military academy, the Shikan Gakkō, he had been Acting *Tutu* of his native Szechwan Province since July 1912, but was gazetted *Tutu* on 13 June 1913, holding the post until May 1915. He was then appointed a member of the Political Consultative Council set up by Yüan Shih-k'ai in August of that year.

[3] Republican Party.

[4] Presumably he was referring to the head of the provincial Foreign Affairs Bureau who at the time of this letter was K'o Hung-lieh. His resignation was formally gazetted on the 17th of August.

[5] Harold Porter (1879–1938), British consular official, at this time Acting Consul-General in Chengtu. As officiating Consul then Consul at Harbin (1917–22), he also served, from September 1918 to April 1919, as Commercial Commissioner for Siberia. In 1929 he resigned his post of Consul-General in Hankow (August 1927 – January 1929) to become General Manager of the Pekin Syndicate.

[6] A large residential mansion.

[7] Yin Ch'ang-heng (b. 1884), Chinese soldier. A graduate of Japan's Military Academy, the Shikan Gakkō, he became *Tutu* of his native Szechwan Province when the province declared its independence after the Wuchang Uprising. He was formally appointed Special Commissioner of the Ch'uan-pien District (later Sikang Province) in June the following year, holding the post until January 1914.

Chengtu and Tachienlu, and loudly calls for the Auditors. From all accounts Yin dare not leave Tachienlu on account of the feud which exists between Chao Erh Feng's[1] veterans (the *Pien Chun*) and Yin's modern Republican troops (*Lu Chun*). From chats I have had with various people such as merchants, Inn proprietors, Chinese gentlemen I have met in the road, etc, the enthusiasm for the new Republic appears to be waning, and it is being borne in on the country people that they are in a worse state than they were before. Hot headed students from Japan seem to be ruling the roost in Chengtu. Japanese influence is everywhere before one's eyes in the awful rococo govt buildings that are springing up everywhere. Thank Heaven they have no hold on the trade, but content themselves with peddling medicines and cheap gewgaws.

I am still keen on holding to my original route, although much will depend upon my own efforts to conciliate Yin *Tutu*. I am receiving plenty of discouragement from people here, but I always remember your advice:—

'Go ahead. Difficulties disappear as you confront them.'

With kind regards and many thanks for looking after these small literary efforts for me.

Yours very sincerely
T. M. Ainscough

590. From Ts'ai T'ing-kan

Peking 27 April 1913

My dear Doctor,

I herewith send you a translation of an article on Sung Chiao Jen – the Chinese article is not yet published. Will you make the most of it but publishing it in a condensed form which you think will make the greatest impression and clear the atmosphere?[2]

It is not a request of *mine* but you *are* requested to do so. [...]

Yrs sincerely
Tsai Ting Kan

[1] Chao Erh-feng, until his death on 27 November 1911, had been Acting Viceroy of Szechwan, succeeding his brother Chao Erh-hsün (q.v.), and concurrently Special Commissioner of the Ch'uan-pien District.

[2] The article has not been found, but in his Diary entry for 28 April Morrison wrote: 'Tsai sent me an article upon Sung Chiao-jen – a vague and stupid one – without any dates or consecutiveness. A characteristic Chinese document, which I ruthlessly suppressed!' In a letter to Ts'ai the next day, however, Morrison wrote: 'I have been carefully through the history of Sung Chiao-jen and will see what use can be made of it.'

591. From Ts'ai T'ing-kan

Peking 29 April 1913

Dear Doctor,

This is a telegram prepared by Liang Shih-yi. It is also to be utilized by you for the Correspondents if you so think fit.

Tsai

Enclosure to Letter No. 592:

In the course of yesterday's Sitting, the Senate adopted by a majority of 102 out of a total of 171 votes, the following resolution:—

> 'The Senate considering that the Government has negotiated the Great Loan without having obtained the approval of the Provisional Parliament and that in consequence it has given its signature illegally, holds the Loan Contract to be absolutely null'.

In spite of this motion the Government maintains that it had, in the course of a meeting, held within closed doors, of the 27th December 1912, obtained the full compliance of the Provisional Parliament: five particularly important articles of the contract scheme were in fact separately voted on at this meeting, whilst 16 other paragraphs containing the substance of the supplementary stipulations were approved *en bloc*. The motion of the Senate is considered as the result of party tactics, a move intended to alarm European opinion. The Government however consider that they need not take any notice of it. The Laws actually in force make it obligatory for the two Chambers to open and close their deliberations at the same time. Now the Chamber of Deputies is not yet legally constituted. The Nationalist party, which has a large majority in the Senate, wish to make use of this circumstance to mislead Europe and to pass off in Europe the vote of an opposition group passed off there[1] for that of the Parliament and of the Nation.

The Government propose always, as soon as the two Chambers are conducting their deliberations together, to go before them and to furnish them with all necessary explanations.

592. To Ts'ai T'ing-kan

[Peking] 1 May 1913

My dear Admiral,

[...]

Rumours are widely current in Legation quarters that the President is going to resign. I have been asked several times today if it is true. I scoffed

---

[1] This telegram was edited by Morrison and in this sentence, after inserting the phrase 'to pass off', he failed to delete 'passed off there', the words in the original draft.

at the idea. The President is there to save the country, and that is what he intends doing in face of the opposition of the Kuo Ming tang.

With best wishes

Sincerely yours
[G. E. Morrison]

593. To Ts'ai T'ing-kan

[Peking] 5 May 1913

My dear Admiral,

Many thanks for sending me the translation of Mr Hung Shu chu's telegram to the President, Vice President and other high officials.[1] I will see that it is given to the Correspondents.

You ask me for a list of prominent personages, Associations, Colleges and Chambers of Commerce in various countries and you remind me of a list you sent me some time ago. I am afraid that I have no record of such a list. I will come over tomorrow morning about 10 o'clock and then we can arrange how this can best be done. I will look through my papers in the meantime and see if I can find any record of this. In thinking of this matter before I came to the conclusion that the most advantageous way to distribute a paper of this kind was through the Legations abroad. It would be necessary to know first how many papers are to be thus distributed and what proportion would be given to each country. There is no difficulty about sending them direct to the Foreign Offices of the different countries and to the Ministries dealing with trade and commerce. There is one question, however, which it seems to me would have to be looked into very carefully indeed, namely, the supervision of the utterances of the *Peking Daily News*. Mr Woodhead is an excellent journalist who writes with great ability and

[1] Hung Shu-tsu (?1858–1919), Chinese Imperial and Republican official. A great-grandson of Hung Liang-chi (1746–1809), the famous scholar of the Ch'ing Dynasty, he had served as secretary to Liu Ming-ch'uan (1836–1896), Governor of Fukien and Taiwan (1884–91) and then to Yü Lien-san, Governor of Hunan (1898–1902). In 1912 he became secretary to Chao Ping-chün when Chao was made Minister of the Interior in the first Republican Cabinet. Hung escaped to the German-leased territory in Tsingtao following Sung Chiao-jen's murder, in which he and Chao were directly implicated. In 1916 he moved to live under an assumed name in the International Settlement in Shanghai, but was discovered and arrested in April 1917 and handed over to the Chinese authorities. He was tried and executed in Peking in April 1919. The telegram here referred to was a circular telegram Hung sent from Tsingtao on 3 May 1913, addressed to the President, the Vice-President, the Prime Minister's Office, the Ministry of Justice and the *Tutu* of Kiangsi as well as those of other provinces. In it he denied having given orders for the assassination and maintained that Chao Ping-chün and the Government had nothing to do with the affair. The telegram has been interpreted as having been sent at the suggestion of the Peking Government in exchange for the Government's refraining from pressing further for Hung's extradition from Tsingtao. For the telegram see *Ko-ming wen-hsien (Archives of the Revolution)* (Taipei 1968), Vol. 42, pp. 225–6.

facility, but his best friends could not pretend that what he wrote was always wise, conciliatory or calculated to make the task of the President and of the Minister of Foreign Affairs a more agreeable one. I think that if the paper is to be supported by the Government, as is evidently the intention, that one of those very able young officials of the Foreign Office, such as Mr. Wellington Koo or one of similar training, should read the Leaders before consenting to their insertion. This I know is what is always done in the case of papers in foreign countries which are employed to represent, more or less officially, the views of the authorities. It is absolutely essential that Mr Woodhead should cease to write in the impetuosity of youth. His leader on Friday last, for example, speaking of the 'death-knell of the pretentions of the Kuomintang' only causes friction, for there are members of the Kuomintang who are heartily in sympathy with the Government and it is not wise to embitter them by hasty words of this kind.

I think it was an excellent idea sending Mr Wearne down to see for himself with regard to the allegations made against the President.[1] A very clear statement, showing how untruthful the whole charge was will be telegraphed tomorrow to London so that it may appear in the papers before the debate begins in the House of Commons.

I received last night a long letter from Mr. Theodore C. Taylor[2] who is to move the resolution in the House of Commons the day after tomorrow asking me to telegraph to him a categorical yes or no with regard to the charge brought against the President. You have acted very well in arranging that a most effective reply shall be sent. Mr Taylor is the man who moved the famous resolution in the House of Commons, which was carried unanimously, without a single contrary voice, that the Indo-Chinese Opium traffic is 'morally indefensible'.

[...]

When I come tomorrow I will bring Mr Taylor's letter with me. Mr Lu Cheng-hsiang will now seize this very fortunate opportunity to bring before the notice of the British Government Art 9 of the Opium Agreement of the 8th of May 1911 which provides that:

'Should it appear on subsequent experience desirable at any time during the unexpired period of seven years to modify this agreement or any part thereof, it may be revised by mutual consent of the two high contracting parties'.

It may be interesting to you to know that I personally will be very proud if

---

[1] In his Diary entry for 6 May 1913 Morrison mentioned Theodore C. Taylor's allegation that opium poppy was planted in the President's private estates. Accordingly Wearne and Kirton were sent to Chang-te-fu: 'Special train. Take nothing. Food would be provided. Young Yuan had been telegraphed to. They went. On arrival 3 a.m. no word. Yuan could not see them – bad eyes. True. Lost face and hence treated with scant respect.'

[2] This refers to Letter No. 585, p. 125.

Mr Taylor's resolution in the Commons on Wednesday is successful because in telegraphing to *The Times* on the 8th of May of 1911 I used these words: 'This means the end of the Indo-China Opium traffic within 2 years.'[1] The two years end on Thursday. It would be very curious if the words were to come true.

Very sincerely yours
[G. E. Morrison]

594. To L. G. Fraser

[Peking] 6 May 1913

My dear Fraser,

I had intended writing you a few days ago with regard to the loan but as it seemed certain that the final contract would be signed on the evening of the 25th of April I thought you would not care to have stale news, and even now what I have to say cannot be of much interest to you because long before you receive this letter you will have learned by cable much more than I can tell you through the post.

[...]

I have no time to write to you as I should like regarding other questions, especially about Mongolia. I had a letter from Korostovetz a few days ago in which he spoke reasonably of a prospect of settlement.[2] His letter covered a long communication from a friend of mine who has been travelling in Mongolia, an earlier letter from whom I sent to Braham.[3]

[...] Could I refer to your Article in the *Observer* of the 31st of March. What you write is always interesting, always informing and suggestive. You, however, seem to me to attach undue importance to messages from Peking sent by Putnam Weale. Putnam Weale writes with great ability and with a temperateness which is lacking in his telegrams. He telegraphs nearly every day. He does not pretend to confine himself to facts. He endeavours to convey to Europe the impression that is formed in his mind in Peking by reading reports chiefly I must say from untrustworthy sources. You see this man, who is a very able man and a brilliant linguist, has so acted that the Chinese have no dealings with him. He knows no prominent Chinese and is not admitted to any foreign Legation that I know of and certainly is never treated with any confidence. He therefore has difficulty in getting facts

---

[1] In a special article entitled 'China and Indian Opium. The Position Today', published in *The Times* on 18 April 1911, Morrison stated that 'There is widespread confidence that within one year, or at most within two years, the Indo-Chinese opium trade will no longer be in existence.' This prediction was singled out in a leader in the paper the next day, and again in another leader on 9 May 1911 which commented that Morrison's prediction was 'probably well justified'.

[2] This refers to Letter No. 588, p. 134.

[3] A reference to articles by H. G. C. Perry-Ayscough which were forwarded by Morrison to D. D. Braham but were not published.

upon which to form his impressions. His work generally is singularly inaccurate, I think the most inaccurate work that has ever been sent from Peking in my time except to Japanese papers. I am speaking, you understand, of his telegrams, not of his letters which are nearly always of serious importance.

Since you like to be very accurate I would point out to you two or three errors in your article. You should write 'Kuomintang' not 'Kuo ming tang'. Surely it is an exaggeration to speak of prominent politicians as 'finding a sudden end wth uncommon frequency'. Political assassinations both during and since the Revolution have been extremely rare and attempts at assassination have also been exceedingly rare! In the case of Tong Shao-yi, he was undoubtedly threatened as you say but there was no question of running away: he returned to Tientsin to clear up the matter, remained there a few days, and then continued his journey to Shanghai and Canton. At the present moment he is in Canton and has been there for many months past. You are quite in error to speak of his having been under the protection of British bayonets, except for the few days following the threat. I think also you are misinformed with regard to the reason for the disagreement between Tong Shao-yi and Yuan Shih-kai and your information with regard to Chang Hsun requires revision. This latter is in command of a body of 8000 well drilled men at a point (Yenchow fu) on the Tientsin–Pukou railway in the South of Shantung Province. You speak of 30,000 men, but as I have explained to Braham, he has only 8,000. I cannot learn that he is a disturbing factor. My information is quite the contrary. Only a few days ago I had a letter from the Governor of Shantung Province[1] who had just returned from staying with Chang Hsun, and his letter bore testimony to the good work done by Chang Hsun.

I have to close in a hurry. If ever I can be of any service to you please don't hesitate to write to me. China and her future, especially the future of Tibet and Mongolia, interest me enormously.

I have just finished a report on Mongolia.[2] How I wish you were here to talk over matters with me. Why don't you come out?

Best wishes to you

Very sincerely yours
[G. E. Morrison]

[1] Chou Tzu-ch'i. In his letter dated 3 April 1913 he told Morrison that he had inspected Chang Hsün's troops in Yen-chou-fu, and went on to say: 'Shantung is in good order and the people is enjoying their peaceful life. The only thing we need very badly is rain. We have not been blessed by rain since spring. Opium plantation is entirely suppressed within this province and we hope that the importation will be stopt immediately.'
[2] Not printed.

595. Telegram from Chang Hsün to the President, Yüan Shih-k'ai[1]

Yen Chow [Shantung] 7 May 1913

Taotai Chang Hung-shun, an old friend of mine, with two men surnamed Wu and Sung just came to Yen Chow and told me that they were ordered by Huan Hsing to come and make arrangement with me. They stated that the forthcoming struggle was due to the difference over the loan question and the Sung case. They offered me an enormous amount of money and asked me to follow them in opposing the Central Government. I at once refused their proposals with strong words and expelled them immediately out of Yen Chow. They were not allowed to stay to prevent unexpected misfortunes.

Chang Hsun

596. To C. W. Eliot

[Peking] 13 May 1913

Dear Dr. Eliot,

I must apologise for not having answered your long letter of August 15th 1912 before this. I am ashamed to read the date on it, but that letter was of the greatest assistance to the President, because by some accident the letter which you had written to Mr. Tong Shao-yi on the 1st of May had been lost. Your letter to me contained a copy of it, and it was the procedure explained in that letter which was followed by the Chinese in asking you to select a Professor who could be attached to the Committee for drafting the Constitution.

There had been a proposal that a French Professor should be appointed to this office. I am glad to think that the Chinese decided that it was wiser to appoint an American Professor who had a special knowledge of the French Constitution.

Your selection has given universal satisfaction. Professor Goodnow arrived here a few days ago and has immediately won the regard of everyone whom he has met whether Chinese or foreign. Some little delay is inevitable in getting things into working order but I am sure that he will not be impatient and that he will soon find that he is engaged on a task worthy of his great ability and experience.

We are passing through a critical time but the outlook every day becomes clearer and the influence of the President is every day becoming greater. He is acting consistently with moderation and firmness. Among his followers he has always inspired great devotion. His good work is now being acknowledged even by those who previously looked upon him with suspicion and who feared that he was aspiring to monarchical or dictatorial

[1] Morrison in his Diary entry for 8 May 1913 wrote: 'Yuan Shih-k'ai sent me a telegram he had received from Chang Hsün who has been tampered with by emissaries from Huang Hsing.'

power. His declaration in reply to President Woodrow Wilson, in which he so unequivocally delivered himself regarding Republican Government, has done much to disarm the criticism of those who were antagonistic to him.[1]

Trade is flourishing and harvest prospects are generally good.

With kind regards
Believe me

Very sincerely yours
[G. E. Morrison]

597. To I. Ia. Korostovetz

[Peking] 13 May 1913

Dear Mr Korostovetz,

I am grateful to you not only for your letter of the 19th of April but also for your kindness in forwarding to me the long letter from Perry-Ayscough written after his journey to Uliasutai. Both this letter and a former one, which I think he showed you before sending it to me, I have condensed as much as possible and forwarded to *The Times* with the request that they should give them publicity.

I cannot, however, be sure that they will be published because there are many claims upon the space of *The Times* and these articles, although the subject of them is interesting especially to those who make a study of Mongolia, may not appeal to an Editor whose columns are crowded with news from South Eastern Europe.

Mongolia is a country which has always possessed great fascination for me although I have only here and there touched upon its borders, but ever since you began to make history in Urga I have been reading all the material I can get regarding this interesting subject. With the help of an English Officer who knows Russian,[2] I have also had prepared for me a *précis* of the reports by many Russian writers upon Mongolia. I have found great difficulty in getting a succinct account of the methods of Government and of the divisions, as well as the history of Mongolia, but I think I have at last succeeded in preparing such an epitome and last week I sent copies of the memorandum I had written – historical, geographical and ethnographical, non-political – to the President and to the Ministers of Foreign Affairs.

---

[1] In a message to President Wilson, Yüan Shih-k'ai, thanking him for the recognition of China by the United States Government, said: 'Though unfamiliar with the republican form of government the Chinese people are yet fully convinced of the soundness of the principle which underlies it and which is so luminously represented by your glorious Commonwealth. The sole aim of the Government which they have established therefore, is and will be to preserve this form of government and to perfect its workings to the end that they may enjoy its unalloyed blessings, prosperity and happiness within, through union of law and liberty and peace and friendship without, through the faithful execution of all established obligations.' [2] G. C. Binsteed. *See* p. 50 note 4.

For a long time past I have read in Russian papers and have seen telegrams in *The Times* describing Chinese military preparations against Mongolia. To the best of my knowledge and belief no policy of military adventure was ever contemplated by China in Mongolia. Troops were moved to some of the frontier places in Inner Mongolia but their numbers were insignificant and their object was none other than the policing of districts which are admittedly Chinese and where disturbances might have led to international complications.

That friendly adjustment of the dispute between your country and China regarding Mongolia is desired by every thoughtful Chinese I have no doubt whatever. It is admitted that under the Manchu *Amban* Santo the Mongols of Khalkha were unquestionably ill treated, their prejudices disregarded, their religious convictions slighted, but with the reformed Government it was intended that all such methods of maladministration should cease.

I think it was your intervention at this precise time when China was animated with the best intentions towards Mongolia that caused so much resentment in China.

Things here are becoming more tranquil. There was some excitement at the time of the completion of the Quintuple Loan but things are quieter now. There was talk of a military expedition, just as there was talk in the papers a short time ago with regard to a military expedition that was to advance through Mongolia to Moscow and St Petersburg. It had the same basis of fact.

There are not many changes here since you left Peking. I do not often see your successor[1] for my work now is quite different from what it was when I was a Correspondent. The work is pleasant. I have plenty to do and I have seen nothing to shake the optimism which I have always felt as to the future of the country.

Please give my kind regards to Mme. Korostovetz. With my best wishes and again thanking you for your letter

Believe me

Very sincerely yours
[G. E. Morrison]

[1] Basil N. Kroupensky.

598. To Ts'ai T'ing-kan[1]

[Peking] 19 May 1913

Memorandum Regarding a Proposition for the Creation of a Chinese Daily Newspaper

Mr T. F. Millard,[2] the Editor of a paper published in Shanghai enjoying American financial support and known as *The China Press*, who describes himself as 'an American journalist of great experience and high reputation, who is known to be a sincere friend of China of long standing and who is on close terms of friendship and acquaintance with high officials of the United States Government and prominent persons in America and elsewhere', submits a claim to the Chinese Government whereby in return for ample compensation being given to him by means of a 'strictly private agreement', he will found in Shanghai a Chinese newspaper with the 'object of preserving China from the sinister designs of more than one of the great Powers and from Chinese Politicians and foreign interests who scheme to keep the various parts of the country divided.'

Mr Millard declares that China is in a precarious position which has been becoming more acute for several years. This contention can be disputed. Mr Millard contends that the agitation in China is conducted by money obtained from party organisations, and 'in some instances by funds supplied by the Peking Government', but Mr Millard does not make it clear why the Peking Government should supply funds to subsidise papers hostile to itself.

Mr Millard alleges that the Chinese Press of Central and South China is almost without exception hostile to the Peking administration. This allegation can be disputed. Mr Millard considers that if a Chinese newspaper were to be founded by him in Shanghai, to be under his supervision, despite his ignorance of the Chinese script, 'ways and means to weld public opinion could be put into operation by which it would be possible to unite the

---

[1] The covering letter for this memorandum has not been found, but in his Diary entry for 23 May 1913 Morrison wrote: 'Tsai T'ing-kan telephoned me approving of my memo *re* Millard.'

[2] Thomas Franklin Fairfax Millard (1868–1942), American journalist and publisher. He had worked for many American newspapers in various parts of the world before going to China, where he founded and became Editor of the *China Press*, published from 1911 to 1917. In 1917 he founded *Millard's Review*, the name of which was later changed to *China Weekly Review*. Millard had close connections with the Kuomintang who came to power in Nanking in 1927, and was said to have received a subsidy from them. He also served from 1929 to 1935 as an adviser to the Kuomintang government. Both for political and personal reasons, Morrison took a great dislike to Millard, who more than once appealed to him for support in various projects, but whose letters Morrison usually ignored without even acknowledging them. Millard's proposal, which forms the subject of this memorandum, is not printed.

different parts of the country into one great nation'. For this purpose a large and influential newspaper in the Chinese language is required. It is to be published by Mr Millard in the foreign settlement of Shanghai. It is to be under American protection. Its management is to be American. In support of this proposal Mr Millard, omitting reference to the Chinese Exclusion Laws in force in the United States, advances the view that the United States of America is traditionally a friend of the Chinese nation, and that inasmuch as the American–Chinese newspaper cannot be deterred by any outside considerations from promoting the true interests of China, such a newspaper under American auspices and American protection can support the Peking administration.

The advantages of this course, Mr Millard points out, will be found in the fact that the Peking Government can, when convenient, disclaim responsibility for the utterances of the proposed newspaper published as it will be in a foreign settlement. But I venture to ask how can the Peking Government disclaim responsibility when it is known – as it assuredly will be known – that it was the Central Government which founded this paper, which made a written agreement with it, purchasing its support for a monthly payment of money?

My opinion having been asked as to the advantage or otherwise of such a scheme, I say unhesitatingly that it is one that cannot be too severely condemned. The Chinese are a commercial people who will buy the best and cheapest article submitted to them. Mr Millard says that the paper he proposes to establish will be superior to any paper ever printed in the Chinese language. Such a paper will pay. Such a paper requires no financial assistance – no Government subsidy. It is merely a business proposition. There are many people who would subscribe money to found a paper of this kind.

Mr Millard proposes to establish a paper costing Tls 100,000. He says that the Company of which he is a Manager will provide the capital, but he asks the Chinese Government to contribute towards this capital a sum of 60,000 Tls within two weeks of the signing of the secret contract which accompanies his memorandum.[1] The 60,000 Tls. are the equivalent of 5,000 taels per month to be paid by the Chinese Government towards the expenses of running the newspaper for one year. Payment must be made in advance 'owing to the precarious tenure of the Chinese Government' and the contract shall continue for three years.

The disadvantages of such a proposal are many and obvious. It will be impossible to keep this contract secret. On the contrary it is certain that for business reasons the widest publicity will be given to the fact that the paper is subsidised by the Peking Government. Who is to sign such a contract binding upon the Chinese Government? The Peking Government are asked to place themselves unreservedly in the hands of Mr Millard and to trust him

[1] Not printed.

entirely to support their views, Mr Millard being wholly ignorant of the Chinese language both written and spoken. Suppose Mr Millard should fail to carry out his contract what redress has the Chinese Government? Who is to come into the Court at the American Consulate-General in Shanghai and proclaim to the world the terms of this contract, by which Mr Millard is bound to support the policy of the Government? The American Government is at present admittedly friendly to the Chinese Government but sooner or later questions must arise regarding Asiatic exclusion, for example, in which differences of view will have to be maintained. Is Mr Millard in that case to forget his American nationality and to support the Chinese Government or is he to support his own Government, for he is still an American editing an American paper under American protection? What will the world think of such a contract having been entered into by a Government like the new Government of China? The scheme is unworthy of a self-respecting Government. Its disclosure will be injurious to the good name of the country. Truth will prevail in China. Assuming that there has been some opposition on the part of certain Chinese newspapers subsidised by political parties, is the Government so weak or lacking in dignity that it has to meet this opposition by subsidising a foreign protected Chinese newspaper to counteract such influence?

I would point out that the letter of Mr Millard is somewhat confusing. Mr Millard by his contract undertakes to publish at the beginning 6,000 copies daily, to be increased within six months to an issue of 10,000 copies daily. He undertakes to instal machinery capable of printing 250,000 copies daily. Mr Millard assumes that the cost of production of such a newspaper will be from 15,000 to 150,000 Taels per month according to the circulation, but Mr Millard has omitted to state that the profits of a paper are derived not from its circulation but from its advertisements. The larger the circulation the larger the income from advertisements. A paper that would be a failure with a circulation of 10,000 copies a day would have an immense revenue when it had a circulation of 200,000 copies a day.

If Mr Millard is conscientiously supporting the Government he will still continue to support the Government. If his support is only to be bought with money then his adherence is of no advantage to the Government.

In conclusion I would suggest that the reply to be given to Mr Millard be that 'The Government thank Mr Millard for the proposals which he has so kindly elaborated in his letter: the Chinese Government regret that the proposed draft contract cannot at present be entertained but the Chinese Government wish every success to the Chinese paper which Mr Millard proposes to establish with foreign capital in Shanghai.'

599. To Hsieh Tsan-t'ai[1]

[Peking] 22 May 1913

My dear Mr Tse,

Your letter of the 16th May came in last night, together with the copy of the letter you have addressed to the President recommending the employment of Sir Hiram Maxim,[2] aged 73, as Adviser to the Chinese Government to assist them in the manufacture of weapons of destruction. Do you really think that such a man is needed in China at the present time?

The fact that Sir Hiram Maxim has rendered himself conspicuous by his violent attacks upon missionary effort in China I do not now refer to. What I, as a well-wisher of the country, desire to see is its industrial development and the cessation of the insensate expenditure of money upon weapons of all kinds. China has been the dumping ground of rifles for the last 25 years. In no year during the last 25, even during the years following the Boxer troubles when the importation of arms was forbidden, has a less amount than 65,000 rifles *per annum* been imported, and of course in some years this number has been enormously exceeded. Millions and millions of Pounds sterling have been wasted upon arms. You can find every kind of rifle in the world in different sections of the Chinese territory. This has been the source of China's weakness.

Surely what China needs now is industrial development – the building of railways, of roads, improving canals and waterways, the construction of telegraphs, the improvement of sanitation. Surely some effort should be made to stop the appalling destruction of life that takes place annually in the flood areas of the Huai river, where famines are incessant and where this

[1] Hsieh Tsan-t'ai (b. 1872), an Australian-born Chinese. In 1903 he helped to found in Hong Kong the English-language newspaper, *South China Morning Post*, and became its compradore. He also worked for various foreign firms. It was in Hong Kong that he came into contact with revolutionaries and reformers of all creeds and colours, whose causes he variously espoused, and was involved in the abortive uprising in Canton in 1895. Although Morrison described Hsieh as a 'humbug', and repeatedly ridiculed him, he has been regarded as a hero from among the Overseas Chinese of the 1911 Revolution, for the support he gave to Sun Yat-sen and his followers.

[2] Sir Hiram Stevens Maxim (1840–1916), British engineer and inventor whose rapid firing gun with automatic action was adopted by the British Army (1889) and Navy (1892). Born in the United States, he became a naturalised British subject in 1900 and was knighted in 1901. In a letter to Hsieh Tsan-t'ai dated 14 April 1913, a copy of which Hsieh enclosed in his letter to Morrison dated 16 May 1913 (neither of which are printed), Sir Hiram wrote that he had long been in strong sympathy with the Chinese and would like to finish up his career by making himself useful to them. 'I could do a great deal', he said, 'if the Chinese would give me the opportunity. I am regarded as the greatest expert on fire-arms in the world....Notwithstanding that I am an old man I am still very active and able to do a lot of work....I am in a position to furnish China with all the rifles she may require at extremely low prices. I know the Rothschilds very well and also other great capitalists and in the event of the Chinese wishing to borrow in London I could place the loan on very reasonable terms, certainly quite as favourable as anyone else would be able to do.'

appalling destruction of life is preventable if river conservancy were to be taken in hand.

I hope you will consider the matter more carefully and consider whether the conditions in China which require the constant begging of charity from abroad and which are remediable could not be improved rather than that millions should be spent in purchasing through Sir Hiram Maxim a new patter rifle of a larger bore.

Please write to me again soon and
With best wishes
Believe me

Very sincerely yours
[G. E. Morrison]

600. From F. L. Pratt

Shanghai 25 May 1913

Private & Confidential

Dear Dr. Morrison,

The political situation here is as you are aware very interesting, and you may care to know that I have begun to play a little part in it. For some months past I have been a sort of unofficial adviser to Mr. Ivan Chen, the Commissioner for Trade and Foreign Affairs.[1] A few days ago Mr. Chen suggested that it would be a good idea if I took steps to find out what is really going on among the malcontents. He very shrewdly considered that enquiries coming from a newspaper correspondent would be more likely to elicit trustworthy information than a Chinese detective force which might be in the pay of the malcontents. The idea appealed to me as an excellent one, and I at once began to organize a force. I got hold of a Japanese detective and told him that I was anxious to obtain completer news for the papers in Europe that I represented than I could get from ordinary sources. He told me that he could keep me well informed and that he would employ certain Chinese whom he knew were in a position to obtain the news I wanted. Already he has supplied us with some items of interest and I really believe that when the organization is in working order, Mr. Chen's idea will conduce to the advantage of the Government.

[1] Ch'en I-fan, better known to foreigners as Ivan Chen, Chinese diplomat. A barrister of Lincoln's Inn, he had worked as Interpreter and then Counsellor in the Chinese Legation in London before returning to China. He was at this time Foreign Affairs Commissioner for Kiangsu Province (15 April–14 June 1913) when he was appointed as Special Commissioner for Tibetan Affairs. He represented China at the Simla Conference and signed on China's behalf the Simla Convention on 27 April 1914, for which he was rebuked by the Chinese Government. He was later given a sinecure post as Presidential Adviser.

I told the detective that I was particularly anxious for news on the following points: –

Whether the Government was strengthening the troops here or taking any other action in view of a possible rising.
How the Commissioner of Foreign Affairs is really disposed towards the Government.
If any arms and ammunition have been purchased locally lately and if so by and from whom.
What Sun Yat-sen, Huang Hsin and Chen Chi-mei are doing. Are they holding meetings.
Is Mr. Miyasaki,[1] or any of the other Japanese ex-army officers who advised Sun Yat-sen in 1912, taking any part in the present movement.
Does it appear that the movement in the direction of civil war is supported by any considerable section of the troops around Shanghai.
Can I safely telegraph to my papers that there is little prospect of civil war.

Of course, the first two questions are intended to mislead him as to the real object of the enquiries.

What do you think of the scheme. If it be properly worked I think that it will be of real value, as I agree with Mr. Chen that information would more readily be given for newspaper purposes abroad than to Government investigators. Personally I take the deepest interest in this. I am a Yuanite and sincerely believe that this factious opposition to him on the part of the Radical wing of the Kuomintang is endangering the country. For the men in opposition I have no sort of respect. They seem to me to be statesmen *pour rire* when they are not self-seekers.

I was wondering if, in the event of any startling news coming in, it would be well to arrange a code so that I might communicate with you by telegraph direct. It is possible that messages sent by Mr. Chen through the ordinary official channels may leak out, but I take it that any message from myself to you would be in less danger. If you think such a course necessary or desirable I will draw up a code.

There is I think no impropriety in my suggesting to you that the services that Mr. Ivan Chen is rendering to the Government here should be kept in

---

[1] Miyazaki Torazō (1870–1922), a Japanese adventurer who devoted his life to furthering Japanese interests in neighbouring Asian countries, particularly China, by fomenting revolts against the established governments and thereby promoting the increasing dependence of these people on Japanese leadership. In 1898 he was sent by Ōkuma Shigenobu, then Japanese Prime Minister and Foreign Minister, to report on the organisation and activities of secret societies in China and South-East Asia, and was involved in the Philippines Revolt of 1898–9 and the Waichow (Hui-chou) Revolt in Canton engineered by Sun Yat-sen in 1900. After the Wuchang Uprising in 1911, Miyazaki went again with his comrades to China, serving both as adviser to Sun Yat-sen and at the same time as unofficial go-between for the Republicans in the south and the Japanese Government.

mind. He has had a most delicate mission, both *vis-à-vis* foreigners and these agitators and he has throughout shown the most consummate tact. There is always a possibility of the men who are doing good work at places remote from the centre of things being forgotten, and I think that it is not improper that I should bring to your notice the services of an official who has been ably and loyally working in the interests of the Government.

Allow me to congratulate you upon the high decoration which the Government has conferred upon you.[1]

The view that you take of the contents of this letter will be awaited by me with the very deepest interest.

Yours very sincerely
[F. Lionel Pratt]

P.S. I have *not* told Donald about this.

601. To Ts'ai T'ing-kan

[Peking] 27 May 1913

My dear Admiral,

Some time when you are free I should like to have a talk with you. I envy your having so much to do while I am given very little opportunity of doing anything.

From the information in my possession I have made a memorandum about Pienma,[2] and I believe that the time is opportune for taking up this frontier question. I am confident that it could be better done now than at any other time and it would be a triumph for the President to settle not only the Mongolian and Tibetan questions but at the same time the vexed Yunnan frontier question.

There is a saying that one cannot make bricks without straw and I cannot get sufficient data from the Foreign Office to make a memorandum of any serious use. Dr Chang[3] said that an elaborate statement had been prepared by the authorities in Yunnan Province, but I do not know whether it has arrived yet in Peking or not. I wrote to Dr Chang asking him whether I could have a copy (of course in Chinese) but he was out when my letter reached the Wai Chiao-pu and I have not yet had a reply.

I have a strong impression that it would be possible to make a good bargain with regard to the Yunnan frontier. India wants the frontier question settled.

---

[1] Morrison was awarded the Second Class Order of the *Chia-ho*, or 'Plentiful Crop', a decoration which, as he recorded in his Diary of 22 June 1913, he did not value a 'brass farthing'.
[2] Not printed.
[3] Probably Chang I-shu (b. 1885), Chinese diplomat. A returned student from France, he became Director of the Foreign Affairs Bureau of Yunnan Province from June 1912, and in April 1914 was appointed Foreign Affairs Commissioner of the province, a post he held until April the following year, and again from October 1916 to 1926. He later served as a Chinese member of the Municipal Council of the French Concession in Shanghai.

For a distance of nearly 220 miles, through a country largely occupied by semi-civilised mountain races of primitive habits, the frontier is undelimited. The absence of boundary marks is a perennial source of trouble.

The British Government have suggested as boundary the water shed between the two rivers Irawaddy and Salwin. It so happens that the British have claimed sovereignty over territory in certain places east of this watershed, and the Chinese have enjoyed sovereignty in other places to the west of the watershed. The proposal of the British Government was regarded by them as in the nature of a compromise. Unfortunately this boundary line brings Pienma, to which territory China has admittedly superior claims, within the British border. Pienma is a collection of three small villages of some 23 grass thatched huts. The action of the British Government in occupying the hill, upon which these villages are situated, has created in Yunnan an impression very adverse to Great Britain. Much bitterness has been the result. The people in Yunnan have set their hearts upon the recovery of Pienma, which is now in British military occupation.

It seems to me, but I repeat that I have no authority for saying so – it is only my impression – that the British Government being so anxious to have the frontier question settled so as to prevent constant friction between the two countries, might be willing to withdraw from Pienma in return for a definite engagement being made with regard to the delimitation of the rest of the boundary. Believing this, I think it would be wise to take up this question with the British Government as soon as Sir John leaves for England. Sir John is leaving on the 6th June and it would be no use his taking up the case before his departure. Mr Alston,[1] however, coming fresh from the Foreign Office would be very competent to handle the matter.

As an alternative, I would suggest that at the same time as the Tibetan question is settled by conference in India, the Yunnan frontier question might be settled and Mr Ivan Chen, who is well acquainted with the subject, might be appointed as Envoy to arrange a settlement with the Indian and British Governments. He could then go to Darjeeling at the same time as Mr Wen Tsung-yao[2] or whoever might be the delegate with regard to Tibet and the two delegates while acting separately could assist each other.

Yesterday the British Legation informed Reuter's correspondent of the

---

[1] Francis Beilby Alston (1869-1929), British diplomat. Acting Counsellor at the British Legation in Peking from January to July 1912 and May 1913, he returned to become Chargé d'Affaires in Jordan's absence from June to November 1913. He was again Acting Counsellor in June 1916, and Chargé d'Affaires from November 1916 to October 1917. In 1920 he succeeded Jordan as British Minister to China, holding the post until 1922. Morrison had a poor opinion of Alston and was strongly opposed to his possible appointment as Minister to Peking. In writing to the Chinese, however, Morrison obviously felt that loyalty to the British Government demanded suppression of his own personal feelings towards Alston.

[2] Wen Tsung-yao, the predecessor of Ch'en I-fan as Foreign Affairs Commissioner for Kiangsu Province, was formerly Deputy *Amban* in Lhasa. *See also* p. 10 note 1.

transference of the negotiations to Darjeeling. They also informed Mr Wearne of the astonishing results achieved in the provinces of Hunan and Anhui with regard to the suppression of the poppy. Travelling from end to end of these Provinces, the British representatives (Messrs Wilton,[1] King[2] and Rose[3]) could find no trace of the poppy, although it was the poppy season. This information was telegraphed home last night. I assisted Mr Wearne to draft the telegram and coupled with the information regarding the proposed conference at Darjeeling and the assurance that negotiations between China and Russia with regard to Mongolia are following a favourable course, the message will create a very excellent impression in Great Britain.

This week too the question with Japan regarding the reduced Customs Tariff on the Manchurian Railway will be signed and China will immediately after propose the establishment of the Maritime Customs in Dalny under the same terms as those under which the Maritime Customs operate in Tsingtau.

For the efficient way in which effect has been given to the wishes of the President in all these foreign questions, Mr Lu Cheng-hsiang deserves great credit. This frontier question settled, China has then opportunity to propose that increase in the Customs revenue which is absolutely essential for the adequate financing of the State. The time, I repeat, is opportune for negotiating a settlement of the Yunnan Boundary.

My reports from Mongolia regarding the condition of the Chinese troops beyond Kalgan and the way they are fleeing from the Mongol *Hunghutzes* are very serious indeed. There seems to be a panic among them. You will remember I sent you a note I had received from Mr Larson about the 200 soldiers at Pangchiang. These men fled when they heard of the approach of the Mongols, burning their stores and abandoning those which they had not time to burn. Of course the Mongols are to a great advantage in being accustomed to the country and in being able to move about so quickly. They

---

[1] Ernest Colville Collins Wilton (1807–1952), British consular official. He was appointed one of the British Special Opium Commissioners (1912–14, 1914–15) who, by virtue of the Opium Agreement between China and Britain of 1911, were required to report on the condition of the opium cultivation prohibition in the provinces. As Consul at Tengyueh in 1906 he had helped to prepare the way for the Calcutta negotiations regarding Tibet, and early in 1908 was made head of the British delegation, and was one of the signatories to the Agreement between Great Britain, China and Tibet Amending the Trade Regulations in Tibet of 5 December 1893, signed at Calcutta on 20 April 1908. He left the consular service in 1923 to become Chief Inspector of the Salt Gabelle, a post he held until 1926.

[2] Louis Magrath King (1886–1949), British consular official, whose career was mainly involved with Tibetan affairs. He was stationed at Tachienlu from 1913 to 1916 to observe Chinese activities in Tibet during the Simla Conference. After serving with the Chinese Labour Corps in France during the latter part of the European War, he returned to take up Special Service on the Tibetan frontier and retired in 1924 as Consul in Tachienlu.

[3] Charles Archibald Walker Rose, at this time representing the Foreign Office at the Tripartite Conference on Tibet at Simla.

are not only well mounted, but Mr Larson estimates that the 200 *Hunghutzes* who came to near Pangchiang have among them 2,000 horses. The rapidity of movement is quite remarkable. One day they were 70 *li* north of Pangchiang and the next day they were 70 *li* south of Pangchiang having moved 140 *li* throughout the night.

To come back to where I started, can I not get work to do? I could, I know, render material help in the settlement of the Yunnan frontier question, but I am kept more in the dark now, I am sorry to say, than I used to be when I was a Correspondent. You must be much overworked. I wish I could help you in some way.

With all good wishes

Very sincerely yours
[G. E. Morrison]

602. From Ts'ai T'ing-kan

[Peking] 27 May 1913

My dear Doctor,

Your suggestions[1] are excellent and I will have the document translated for the information and guidance of the President.

You say you have no work. I like to know what you call your memo[2] if [you] do not think it is work of the first order.

I have been worked so much lately that I have not had leisure to suggest work for you. This I admit, but men of our type can never be idle – not even in our graves. I have not yet approached the President about our little conference but I know it is high time.

With best wishes

Yours sincerely
Tsai Ting Kan

603. From Ts'ai T'ing-kan

[Peking] 28 May 1913

My dear Doctor,

I brought you the Decoration[3] but you were out – too modest to receive it in person.

Let me congratulate you heartily.

Sincerely
Tsai Ting Kan

[1] A reference to the suggestions contained in Letter No. 601 Morrison to Ts'ai T'ing-kan, 27 May 1913.
[2] This refers to a lengthy memorandum on Mongolia, a copy of which Morrison sent to Lu Cheng-hsiang, the Foreign Minister, and to Ts'ai T'ing-kan, on 7 May 1913. It is not printed. [3] *See* p. 151 note 1.

604. From G. T. B. Davis to Yüan Shih-k'ai[1]

[Melbourne, Victoria, Australia] 29 May 1913

Sir,

As an American citizen I have been travelling through Australasia, and have been delighted at the manner in which the request for prayer for the future welfare of China has been responded to by the Christian people of Australia and New Zealand. I believe God is going to answer in a wonderful way the prayers that have ascended to His Throne throughout not only Australasia, but throughout Great Britain and America and other lands.

But there is another spiritual force which has been the foundation of the prosperity and power of Western nations, and which will determine the destiny of the Chinese Republic. I refer to the Bible. Western nations are strong or weak just in proportion to the way in which the populace read and love this Book, and live out its principles. Centuries ago Italy had an opportunity to become a great world-empire. They kept the Bible from the people and it became a second-rate nation. Spain and France had the same opportunity, lost it for the same reason, and they too became second-rate nations. In Germany Luther arose, and gave the Bible to more than half her people and as a result Germany is to-day far more powerful than France or Spain or Italy. In Great Britain the Bible is read and loved even more than in Germany, and as the result she has become a mighty world-empire. When Queen Victoria was asked the secret of Britain's greatness she replied, 'It lies in that Book', pointing to the Bible. The secret of the greatness of my own land, The United States of America, also lies in their love for the Bible. And America and Great Britain are the two most powerful nations in the world to-day simply because the people of those lands read this Book, and endeavour to carry out its teaching. So when China gets the Bible, she may and doubtless will, become the greatest nation the world has ever seen.

I was delighted recently to read about your giving copies of the New Testament to the high officials in the *Yamens* throughout the province of Shang-Tung a few years ago. What you, Sir, did in that province, The Pocket Testament League proposes to do throughout the entire Republic of China. Our plan is to send by post a copy of the Chinese New Testament to each public official, each University student, each post-office official and employee, each military and naval official, each soldier and sailor, each policeman and fireman and all public servants throughout China. And all this is to be done without cost to the Chinese Republic. With each copy of the Chinese New Testament, we plan to send a brief history of the Pocket Testament League showing how people throughout the world are reading a chapter of the Bible daily, and carrying the Testaments with them.

[1] George T. B. Davis, American missionary, International Secretary of the Pocket Testament League. The letter was addressed to Yüan through Morrison, but he does not seem to have forwarded it.

We hope also to send with each New Testament a pamphlet giving the views of President Woodrow Wilson and King George V, and other American Presidents and British Sovereigns, regarding the Bible as the secret of individual and national peace and prosperity.

But in order to make the plan most effective in promoting the future prosperity of the Republic of China, we wish to include with each New Testament a letter from you suggesting that those who receive the Testament should read it daily and diligently, and should make the book their constant companion. Such a letter from you, Sir, would add lustre to your rule over the Chinese Republic, and would prove a means of inestimable and ever-lasting blessing to the great Chinese nation.

I am now *en route* to Zurich, Switzerland, to address the Seventh World's Sunday School Convention on the world-wide work of the Pocket Testament League. This World's Convention represents about 20,000,000 Sunday School Teachers and Scholars in many lands. I wish to tell the Convention of our plan for giving New Testaments to the public officials and public servants of China.

I desire also to make the announcement to that Convention that the President of the Chinese Republic favours the plan of giving new Testaments to the public officials of China. Hence may I ask you, Sir, to cable me to the following address: –

George Davis, care Doctor George Bailey, President World's Sunday School Association, Zurich, Switzerland.

The Convention lasts from July 8th, to July 15th. Please cable by July 8th if possible.

[...]

I take pleasure in sending under separate cover a copy of *The Pocket Testament League*, a book giving an account of how the movement is spreading through the world.

I have the honour to be, Sir

Your most Obedient Servant
[George T. B. Davis]

605. To Ts'ai T'ing-kan

Peking 2 June 1913

Dear Admiral,

[...] Your people sent me an admirable translation of the Pienma papers. The more I read of this question, the more I am certain an adjustment can be made wholly favourable to China.

The great difficulty is the obscurity due to the overloading of the papers with unimportant geographical details. I will make it all clear in my memorandum. I am certain it can be arranged and that now is the time to arrange it.

The *Shun Tien Shih Pao* which is friendly with the Kuomingtang Japanese returned students published yesterday the 6 articles of the proposed agreement regarding Mongolia. It was undoubtedly a wise act to lay the case before Parliament but unfortunately no sufficient explanation was given of the circumstances. To all men who have spoken to me I have pointed out that the agreement reflects much credit upon the Government who have recovered for China rights which most people including nearly all the foreigners believed had been for ever lost.

A clear exposition of the

1. rights Russia had under former treaties;
2. rights obtained by Russia by virtue of the action in assisting in the Independence of Mongolia;
3. rights obtained under the Protocol and agreement with the so called Independent Mongolia where Mongolia was referred to, that is all Mongolia not 'Outer Mongolia' only;
4. rights recovered by the new agreement the rights of Sovereignty, the limitation of Mongolia to mean 'Outer Mongolia only';

would convince any reasonable man that the Government have protected the interests of their country in a manner that does them the highest honour.

A message summarising what the Government have done published in all the European papers on Saturday has created a very favourable impression indeed.[1]

One word in conclusion – our greatest Chinese scholar is Edmund Backhouse. Writing to me yesterday he says having frequently recently spoken to the same effect, 'The decrees now emanating from the Head of the state are noble in language, models of style, devoid of the hyperbole of the old Regime.'

Ever faithfully yours
[G. E. Morrison]

[1] The message was also published in *The Times* on 31 May 1913 under the title 'Mongolian Autonomy. Russo-Chinese Agreement'. By this Agreement China undertook not to interfere in the autonomy of Outer Mongolia, and to help prevent settlement by those other than Mongols in Outer Mongolia. In return Russia recognised both Outer and Inner Mongolia as an integral part of China and undertook to respect China's status there.

606. To F. L. Pratt

[Peking] 2 June 1913

My dear Pratt,

Domestic affairs have claimed my attention for the last few days[1] and this must be my excuse for delaying to answer your letter of the 25th of May. [...]

I fully agree with what you say about Mr. Ivan Chen. Curiously enough I have been urging that he should be entrusted with the negotiation of the settlement of the Yunnan frontier question. He has a better knowledge of the subject than most men and he is a man, as you say, of great tact and one who is *persona grata* with British people. Everyone admits than he has done admirably in Shanghai. I am confident the President more than anyone else appreciates the work that he has done.

Your scheme is excellent and you ought to be able to render real service by obtaining the information which you have set out to find.

The opposition is deplorable but things are looking a little better. Naturally I am most interested in foreign affairs and I cannot view without concern the unfortunate attitude of Parliament towards the Mongolian Agreement.[2] This agreement is a real success for China – quite an unusual diplomatic success, due perhaps not so much to astuteness on the side of the Chinese negotiators as to conciliation on the part of the Russians, for the Russians are in a position of overmastering force. No better terms could possibly have been got even by a powerful country and for China, so deplorably weak, with its whole frontier line from Manchuria to Kashgaria exposed to Russian menace, the success is a very real one. Yet I am told by men here that there is talk of Parliament's insisting upon the cancellation of the Urga Convention of November last,[3] and there are others – the hot-blooded young men who are the first to flee for protection to the foreign settlements when any trouble threatens – who are even urging a military expedition to Urga. This would mean the end of China outside the Wall.

I shall be glad if you will communicate with me by telegraph and would use the code you suggest. It might be of real use to the people whom I serve. [...]

Very sincerely yours
[G. E. Morrison]

[1] Morrison's first child, Ian Ernest McLeavy (named after his godfather Sir John McLeavy Brown), was born on 31 May 1913. He died in 1950 while covering the Korean War as a correspondent for *The Times*.
[2] The Mongolian Agreement was strongly criticised by Parliament, which refused to ratify it. It was also strongly condemned by the Republicans in the South, who accused the Government of selling out to Russia.
[3] This refers to the Convention signed by Korostovetz and the Mongols in Urga on 3 November 1912.

607. From Hsieh Tsan-t'ai

Hong Kong 2 June 1913

Private

My dear Dr. Morrison,

Your letter of the 22nd May received, and contents noted.

Do not believe for one moment that I agree with Sir Hiram Maxim's views regarding Religion, and neither do I sympathise with his attacks upon missionary effort in China.

Christianity has done incalculable good to China, and Christianity as a religion has come to China to stay. But, of course, it will be necessary to preach Christianity on a broader basis and on more scientific lines, before it can be universally adopted as a religion in China. There must be Religious Toleration, and Christianity must go hand in hand with the Teachings of Confucius. One deals with the present, and the other with the hereafter, and both have come to stay.

China awaits her 'Luther', a wise and Godly man, who will establish an Independent Christian Church, and preach a 'New Christianity', which will be understood and followed by her 500,000,000.

You are a God-fearing and conscientious man, and must acknowledge that Almighty God has preserved the peace-loving Chinese race for a purpose. And, what is that purpose.

It is plain to every thinker and moralist that that purpose is – 'Universal Peace and the Brotherhood of Man'.

China, a country whose morality and very existence as a nation to day, is based upon *Filial Piety*, will certainly play a leading part in this great movement; but, some will laugh and ask how is it possible in her present state of weakness and unpreparedness?

Well, China must arm herself and put her house in order but, how is this possible, unless she is well armed and powerful so as to be able to prevent the mischievous interference of her wicked neighbours.

China's neighbours will not allow her to work out her destiny in peace. It is not the way of the world, as you well know.

It is, therefore, imperative that China should become a powerful nation, if she expects to take a leading part in the Universal Peace Movement, and to make herself heard in the Counsels of the world.

The Chinese being a peace-loving people are morally fit to undertake this task, and I am positively certain that China would not use her strength for the conquest and absorption of her neighbours, let alone embarking on the mad career of the conquest of the world.

A strong China stands for Universal Peace; but, a weak China will be a bone of contention, and is certain to lead to race hatred and terrible wars between the White and Yellow races.

You should, therefore, try your best to help China to become strong and powerful, so as to enable her to take her proper place amongst the nations of the world.

Sir Hiram Maxim thinks as I do, regarding the future of China and the Chinese, and this is why he has so earnestly declared to me his willingness to finish up his career by making himself very useful to the Chinese. I admire his perception, and foresight, which is remarkable.

He believes as I do that only a strong China can be a sufficient guarantee of the Peace of the World.

The mightiest powers of to-day are Great Britain and Germany, and they owe their present position to their immense armies and formidable fleets. Where would they be without their armies and fleets?

Please remember that I am not a supporter of militarism.

I am anxious to see all the nations disarmed, and hope to see the day, when all international disputes will be settled by arbitration.

Only when China possesses a big Army and a big Navy, will the Great Powers listen to those noble men, who are now strenuously advocating disarmament.

At present, all talk of Universal Disarmament and Universal Peace is premature. Our first step is to educate and civilize all the savage races of the world. Before this is done, it is folly to talk of the Brotherhood of Men. Side by side with her Educational and Industrial efforts to reach the goal of her ambition, China should arm in order to protect herself from outside aggression.

I agree with you that China now needs industrial development – the building of railways, of roads, improving canals and waterways, the construction of telegraphs, the improvement of sanitation, etc., but, how is all this possible unless China is well armed and strong enough to maintain peace and good order, in spite of the jealousy and the selfish and aggressive designs of her neighbours? You must agree that China is obliged to arm for self protection and immunity from molestation. I do not advocate a policy of bloated armaments.

A strong Army and strong Navy are the only guarantees of peace, nowadays, and China should always remember this.

As soon as China is able to protect herself from internal rebellion and outside aggression, she will certainly take the lead in advocating Universal Disarmament.

I don't think it can do any harm in recommending Sir Hiram Maxim as an Adviser in Firearms to the Chinese Government. The Chinese Government will know how to appreciate the value of his advice, notwithstanding his attacks upon missionary effort in China, as they will know that it is only one of his idiosyncrasies, which can be effectually governed and regulated by the latest 'Gem' safety valve!

China must overhaul and regulate the output of her arsenals, and she must also call in and send to the scrap heap all obsolete guns and rifles, and in this work she needs the services of an expert Adviser.

China is already ordering ships, guns, and rifles from the German Krupp and certain Austrian Establishments, and is bound to increase these orders as time flies, and it can do no harm to advise the Chinese Government to extend its patronage to British Firms with Sir Hiram Maxim's advice. I hope you understand me.

China will only order what she needs for self protection and you may rest assured that she will not use a single shot in a wanton career of slaughter and aggression.

You know the Chinese so well that I am sure you agree with me.

With kind regards and best wishes, and hoping to hear from you again soon

Yours very sincerely
Tse Tsan-tai

P.S. If you do not agree with my views, please tell me, in confidence, why you do not agree, and kindly give me your reasons. Please reply, if possible, by return mail.

Tse

608. To Ts'ai T'ing-kan

[Peking] 7 June 1913

My dear Admiral,

So little have I done to deserve it that the recent honour[1] conferred upon me by His Excellency the President has put me in an embarrassment. For I have not been able adequately to express my thanks for this unexpected honour.

Will you on the first occasion thank on my behalf the President for so graciously giving me this honour? I can only express the hope that opportunity may be given to me to show that the confidence was not misplaced. And will you also thank the Minister of Finance, His Excellency Chou Hsueh-hsi[2] for so generously suggesting my name for this honour and will

---

[1] A reference to the Second Class Order of the 'Plentiful Crop'. See p. 151 note 1.
[2] Chou Hsüeh-hsi (1866–1947), Chinese Republican politician. He succeeded Chou Tzu-ch'i as Minister of Finance on 5 March 1913 and instituted many changes, including the dismissal of Chang Hu (q.v.), the Vice-Minister in Charge of the Salt Administration, though the dismissal was not gazetted until 20 June 1915. This action was strongly condemned by Morrison. A native of Anhwei Province, Chou became a member of the Anfu Clique of which his fellow provincials formed the nucleus. The son of Chou Fu (1837–1921), the former Viceroy of Liangkiang (1904–6), he had received a traditional education gaining a *chü-jen* degree in 1895. China's defeat in the first Sino-Japanese War (1894–5) diverted him from a bureaucratic career to new enterprises that were then springing up,

you also let me thank you my kind hearted and loyal friend for this last service you have rendered me of services that cannot be numbered.

And with all good wishes, believe me

Ever faithfully yours
G.E.M.

609. From F. L. Pratt

Shanghai 9 June 1913

My dear Dr. Morrison,

[...]

I am very glad to see that the opinion I had formed in regard to the Mongolian problem with the incomplete information available to me was confirmed by you with your fuller knowledge. If China is ever to be a nation of consequence, her publicists will have speedily to learn that patriotism must be set before partisanship. That lesson has certainly not yet been learnt. The opposition to the Agreement with Russia in regard to Mongolia is undoubtedly caused by the personal opposition to Yuan. What I mean is that if a Kuomingtang Cabinet had proposed this solution of the problem, it would have been lauded as a wonderful achievement – as it is. Personally I am beginning to despair of any real settlement of the difficulties that beset China other than a Dictatorship. The opinion I have always held and still hold is that a constitutional monarchy is the best possible form of Government that the genius of man has yet evolved. The Chinese Republic seems to me to be an unnecessarily violent change from the old order under which China at all events attained a high state of civilization while our forebears were decked in woad and stone axe represented Law with a capital L. From all I can learn most of the Chinese who really think for themselves, are not particularly in love with the Republican form of Government.

Oscar Wilde says:—

> Albeit nurtured in democracy,
> And liking best that state republican
> Where every man is kinglike and no man
> Is crowned above his fellows, yet I see,
> Spite of this modern fret for Liberty,
> Better the rule of One, whom all obey,
> Than to let clamorous demagogues betray
> Our freedom with the kiss of anarchy.[1]

---

and he became a noted industrialist in Northern China during the Republican period, active in many fields including mining, textiles, and cement and water works. His two short terms as Minister of Finance (July 1912–May 1913, and March 1915–April 1916) were conspicuous for his provincial nepotism. Although he did not formally resign until 4 September, by the time this letter was written Chou had already been granted leave of absence (16 May) and Liang Shih-yi was acting in his stead.

[1] The first eight lines of a sonnet entitled 'Libertatis Sacra Fames'.

The authority is unhappily tainted, but of the wisdom of his utterance there can be no doubt. The advanced wing of the Kuomingtang, I am convinced, have absolutely no regard for the well-being of their country. It is interesting to remember that the *China Republican*, which voices the views of the Sun Yat-sen, Huang Hsin, Chen Chi-mei combination, began its attacks upon Yuan Shih-kai in its second issue on August, 1912. It was started for the purpose of vilifying Yuan's Government and paving the way for a frenzied public appeal to Sun to come out again and 'sacrifice' himself by consenting to stand as President. Such an appeal was actually made to him not long since – by the *China Republican*, but the public was singularly unresponsive.

It may be well to explain my position *vis-à-vis* Sun and his gang. Rea,[1] the owner of the *Far Eastern Review* and Donald, are Secretaries to the Railway Corporation. I, however, have absolutely nothing to do with Sun or his Corporation, and I have carefully avoided even meeting the man. In my opinion he is a menace to China. Donald knows what my sentiments are in this connection and there is a sort of tacit agreement between us that the affiliation between the *Far Eastern Review* and Sun does not extend to me. Still, it is more than probable that D. would not like my actively working against Sun, and that is the reason that I asked you to keep my first letter on the subject confidential. It is not that I am in any way ashamed of what I am doing, but Donald is my dearest friend and I would not lose his friendship for anything. Later on, when things have settled down, I will tell him myself.

In some ways I think it would be almost worth while for the Government to have a real Intelligence Bureau organised in Shanghai, apart from anything of the kind they may have now. At present we are only spending $200 a month over the service and naturally no great results can be expected. But if a Bureau, ostensibly a newspaper correspondent's enterprise, were organised to keep watch upon the Kuomingtang leaders and find out what negotiations were being carried on by the provinces to secure money or munitions, I really think that it would prove of service to the Government. Of course, in making the suggestion I lay myself open to the charge that I have an axe to grind, and, as I like frankness, I have. After twenty years of press work nothing would please me better than to enter the Government service in some capacity, *if* I could earn my salt. I believe that I could do

[1] George Bronson Rea (1869–1936), American journalist and adventurer, founder of the *Far Eastern Review* in 1904. He attached himself to Sun Yat-sen after Sun became President of the Provisional Government in Nanking and served as one of the many then greatly inflated and vaguely-defined 'advisers', and was appointed by Sun Secretary of the Railway Corporation, of which Sun was briefly Director-General. In 1920 the *Far Eastern Review*, or rather George Bronson Rea, after receiving a subsidy from the Japanese Government, took a pro-Japanese line, and W. H. Donald, who had been a partner and Editor, cut his association with the periodical. In 1932, when the Manchu puppet government under P'u-yi (q.v.) was established, Rea became 'Counsellor' to its Foreign Ministry and wrote in support of the new regime.

useful work with such a Bureau as I have suggested and it probably would not cost more than about $1000 or $1200 a month. However, in any event we will keep on as we are going and if anything develops later on so much the better.

[...]

Yours very sincerely
F. Lionel Pratt

[...]

610. From Ts'ai T'ing-kan

Peking 10 June 1913

My dear Doctor,

The President said there was no need of your thanking him but that he should thank you for all your help. No man, he said, deserves more than you and he hopes to do more too.

He is suffering from stomach trouble for these two days. Dr. Wang says he is improving.

Yours sincerely
Tsai Ting Kan

611. From Ts'ao Chia-hsiang[1]

Peking 10 June 1913

Dear Doctor,

Herewith translation of a newspaper article which the President wishes to publish in the foreign press.[2]

Will you please attend to it?

Yours sincerely
Tsao Kai Cheong

Enclosure to Letter No. 611: *Political Parties*

Political Parties are composed of the citizens of the country. As it is considered that with individual strength the object of benefiting the country and people cannot be fully attained, it is necessary that a large number of people be collected to work for the same goal. Politicians are all citizens and though the designations of their respective parties are different, they are representing the opinion of a large number of the country people, and to whatever parties they may belong, there exists not the slightest discrepancy of opinion among them in respect of their natural duties in the matter of equality, freedom and protection of the people. The politicians in China who assume the designation of 'Nationalists' (Kuomingtang)

[1] *See* p. 222 note 1.
[2] Morrison noted in the margin: 'Received 10/6/1913. Suppressed as wholly unworthy. I'd never be a party to the publication of such a foolish undignified diatribe. That it should emanate from the President's Office is evidence itself of the evil influences with which the President is surrounded. – G. E. Morrison.'

are apparently following the principle of developing the people's rights and livings and are regarded to have cherished the right idea. They appear to be on the same standing with the Nationalists of foreign countries and consequently we believe in the fact that they represent the opinion of a section of the fellow-countrymen. But it greatly astonishes us when we go carefully into their actions and it makes the Nationalists of other countries ashamed to be members of a party of the same designation as that in China. Kuangtung and Hunan provinces are the native provinces of Sun Wen and Huang Hsing respectively, the leaders of the Kuomingtang, where they have the largest number of followers but these followers in these two provinces mercilessly and inhumanely persecute the people, commit extortions and all sorts of oppressions that they can contrive, with the result that the people are labouring under great hardships and some of them are compelled to remove to places of safety. Shanghai and Hongkong have almost formed the rendezvous for the people from Canton and Hunan and it is amazing to hear that they remove [themselves] to avoid the cruelty of the Kuomingtang. It is even said that the despotic and cruel rule in the two provinces is not restricted by the principle adopted by the *Tang*.[1] The two provinces are actually the bases of the Kuomingtang and no one other than a member of the *Tang* can aspire to any of the official positions there. Members are enlisted by means of cruel methods, and as soon as one joins the *Tang*, it follows that one possesses the special privilege of entering into an official post and oppressing the people but one is subject to persecution if one does not join the *Tang*. In this manner the Kuomingtang draws together a large number of desperadoes under its banner. They use ill-gotten money to establish newspaper offices which express preposterous views and official posts are given to ill-disposed adherents of the *Tang* who resort to dangerous attitude. In fact he who joins the *Tang* is respected but he who leaves the *Tang* is despised and the word Equality is far away from its intention. One thing that is much more surprising is the fact that one is always intimidated by pistol and bomb if one is inclined to quit the *Tang* after joining it. In some cases even the family has been threatened and involved. But all men have conscience. There are many who adhere to the Kuomingtang, inspired with the motive of obtaining big sum of money and great power, but there are always those who feel uneasy in their minds and anxious to leave the *Tang*, but they could not but suffer pains in their hearts and submit simply because of the pistol and the bomb. Where then is 'Freedom'? There are other provinces where such state of affairs also prevail but in those provinces in which Kuomingtang has no influence, such ridiculous thing is not heard of, and the public entertain no enmity against the *Tang*. So far as the influence of the Kuomingtang in China is concerned, it extends to places which form only a part of the whole country, but in those places where its influence is felt there exists the most

[1] *Tang*, meaning party or clique, refers here to Kuomintang.

bitterness against it. As the *Tang* is inhumane it deserves no sympathy and it cannot represent the true opinion of the people in China. Chinese citizens with any common sense do not associate with the members of the Kuomingtang in mischievous acts, and no one approves of the action of the *Tang* at all. Dangers lurk in every part of the country and in each and every case of assassination when details are gone into, the said *Tang* is invariably found to be implicated. This accounts for the fact that a 'Rioters Party' is said to be existent in China, and this appears not to be an exaggeration, but it behooves those who are interested in Chinese affairs not to regard the actions of the Kuomingtang [as] having any connection with the people. The attitude adopted by the Kuomingtang in China is just the opposite views of the general public. The students of political affairs studying the Chinese politics in this light will not be misled by unscrupulous talks.

612. To Ts'ai T'ing-kan

Peking 11 June 1913

My dear Admiral,
    Many thanks for your very kind note.[1]
    I am really sorry to learn that the President has been unwell. It is to me wonderful how he has sustained his strength in all that stress of work. No man who had not a dauntless heart and nerves of steel could have done what he has done during the past eighteen months. Everywhere I hear approval of the Mandate removing the *Tutu* of Kiangsi.[2]
[...]

Very sincerely yours
[G. E. Morrison]

[...]

[1] This refers to Letter No. 610, Ts'ai T'ing-kan to Morrison, 10 June 1913.
[2] Li Lieh-chün (1882–1946), Chinese soldier. A graduate of the Shikan Gakkō, he was converted to the revolutionary cause while teaching in a provincial military academy in Yunnan. He was appointed *Tutu* of Kiangsi in January 1912 and on 5 May 1913, nine days before this letter was written, he, together with his fellow *Tutus* of Anhwei, Hunan and Kwangtung, publicly denounced the Central Government for its complicity in the murder of Sung Chiao-jen and for its conclusion of a foreign loan without parliamentary approval. As a result he was removed by Yüan Shih-k'ai on 9 June, and in the ensuing abortive 'Second Revolution', Li was at the head of the southern republican forces, but on his defeat escaped to France. Returning to China in 1915 he was in time to join the anti-Yüan forces then being gathered under T'ang Chi-yao, the *Tutu* of Yünnan, in opposition to Yüan Shih-k'ai's monarchical scheme. After Yüan's death, Li continued to be active in the republican cause and was appointed by Chiang Kai-shek, whom he supported against his left-wing opponents, Governor of Kiangsi in 1927. He was prominent in the early days of the Nationalist Government in Nanking, siding always with Chiang Kai-shek, but in spite of this, and of the fact that his name continued to figure prominently in the list of Kuomintang officials, his role was by then essentially one of an elder statesman, with little actual power.

613. From T. M. Ainscough

The Salt Wells, Yen Yüan Hsien, [Szechwan] 24 June 1913
Dear Dr. Morrison,
[...] Please excuse indelible pencil but ink is not easy to handle when travelling.

I had a delightful time in Chien Ch'ang. [...] The Revolution in the Chien Ch'ang valley seems to have been rather a complicated affair and the work of bandits rather than revolutionaries. The well known brigand Chang Yu Tang[1] collected a gang of men round Huili Chou and marched up to Ningyüan, badly handling Dr Legendre[2] and Lieut. Dessiner[3] on the way. They were not only anti-Manchu, but also anti-foreign and openly anarchical. For days the city was besieged, the *Hsien*[4] was murdered, but the *Fu*[5] (named Wang) held his own and finally defeated them with great slaughter on Lushan – the mountain across the lake. The leaders were crucified and put to death by *ling chih*[6] and no quarter whatever was given to their followers. As it happened the few students that were in the valley had sided with the rebels, intending to use them as a Revolutionary force. With the Revolutionary party in power at Chengtu the question then arose – Had the *Fu* done his duty in suppressing bandits, or had he been a traitor to the Revolutionary cause in putting down genuine Revolutionaries? The matter was referred to Peking, and it was finally decided that Chang Yu Tang was an outlaw and that the *Fu* had done his duty. Meanwhile the Chengtu students wishing to avenge their members who had suffered during the trouble sent down a *Hsüan Fu Shih*[7] named Ch'en to investigate the whole affair, and he put to death several men who had done excellent work in helping the *Fu* to maintain law and order – among them a prominent Church member of the Mission. Wellwood[8] tried hard to save his life, but the *Fu* was powerless in the face of superior authority in Chengtu, and although Wellwood went to Chengtu, the man was executed while Wellwood was away.

The next trouble occurred with the troops. There were no *Lu Chün*[9] in the valley and the Ningyüan garrison were nothing more than a set of robbers under the command of a Mohammedan – Ma Yi-Ting.[10] They looted the city twice – the last time during March of this year. Finally the Govt appointed

[1] Unable to identify.
[2] Aimé François Legendre (b. 1867), French doctor and author. He was head of a French scientific mission to the West of China and director of a medical school in Szechwan. Among his published works was a description of the Lolo tribes in south-west China with whom he had lived for some time.   [3] Unable to identify.
[4] Here meaning the District Magistrate.   [5] Here meaning the District Prefect.
[6] Punishment by slow dismemberment of the body before beheading.
[7] Pacification Commissioner.
[8] An American missionary with the Baptist Foreign Missionary Society in Szechwan.
[9] Literally meaning infantry. Here the reference is to the new army modelled on Western lines.   [10] Unable to identify.

General Liao[1] from Yünnan to the command of all the *Han Chün*[2] in the province. Liao arrived in Ningyüan with only 30 men, but was a man of such strong character that he dismissed Ma and forced his army to disband. I had two long talks with Liao, who impressed me very favourably. He has had 30 years service in all parts of Yunnan and defended the Railway during the troubles. He has now resigned owing to the fact that Chengtu will neither supply him with men or money. Unless good troops are sent down shortly the Lolo trouble in the valley will be a most serious matter in the autumn when the tribes break out again.

[...]

Yours very sincerely
T. M. Ainscough

614. To O. M. Green

[Peking] 24 June 1913

My dear Green,

[...] With regard to the Mongol question, I do not think that you are quite just. Yuan Shih-kai, as you know, submitted the proposed text of the Russo-Mongolian Agreement,[3] so far as it had been agreed to, to the Lower House. Professor Bryce[4] is my authority for saying that in so doing he acted wisely and constitutionally. The Lower House recognise that the Agreement recovers for them much that they had apparently lost by the Urga Agreement, but unquestionably the Agreement is vague and there are several phrases in it that require elucidation. No such thing as a draft agreement was submitted by the Assembly. Asked for their opinion the Assembly gave their opinion, and I must say that the views they expressed – and they are before me as I write – are not unreasonable. For your private information I may tell you that they are mainly as follows:—

They ask that the Agreement shall contain a revision clause similar to Art. 15 of the 1881 Treaty with Russia. I am sure if that were inserted the agreement would be signed as it stands.

The Urga Convention spoke of 'Mongolia'. The revised agreement speaks of '*Mongolie Extérieure*'. The Chinese Special Committee ask what is Outer Mongolia and they suggest that it includes only the four *Aimaks* of Khalkha. The Russians require that it shall include Urianghai and Kobdo.

---

[1] Unable to identify. [2] Here the army of provincial units is meant.
[3] See p. 157 note 1.
[4] James Bryce (1838–1922), later 1st Viscount Bryce of Dechmont, British politician and educator. He was Regius Professor of Law at Oxford (1870–93) and from 1880 to 1907 a Member of the British House of Commons, serving as Under-Secretary of State for Foreign Affairs (1886) and Chief Secretary for Ireland (1905–6). In 1907 he became British Ambassador to Washington, and after leaving this post in 1913 visited Peking, where he and Morrison met.

Here there is not a very serious difference. It was feared that Russia would insist upon Bargut also being included.

Then with regard to the Consular Guards, China asks that the maximum strength of the guards should be stated and they ask that in Art. 8 of the protocol which provides for the establishment of Consulates wherever agreed upon between Russia and the Mongolian Government, the words 'Chinese Government' shall be substituted for the words 'Mongolian Government'. In Art. 4 for the words '*Autorité centrale*' the Chinese ask that they shall be altered to '*Les Autorités*'.

Obviously the question is a difficult one, for the *Hutukhtu* declared his independence in December 1911, whereas Russia, while speaking of him as Sovereign, has only admitted Mongolia's right to '*régime autonome*'.

Russia gets everything that she requires and China asks that there shall be certain elucidations (of the text of the proposed agreement) to prevent misunderstanding in the future. To attack China for so doing does not seem to me fair. You could assist the conclusion of an agreement, whereas the tone of the telegrams from Peking would indicate that you wished to prevent an agreement being arrived at. If you were here I would gladly show you all the papers but as you are not I can only send you these few lines which may help to a better understanding.

One thing in conclusion. Fraser in *The Times* condemns China for having disclosed that Great Britain was willing to have a Conference in Darjeeling regarding Tibet.[1] It was no secret although it was treated as secret by the Chinese, yet the Chinese are being blamed for the act of the Legation.

With all good wishes to you

Very sincerely yours
[G. E. Morrison]

615. To Ts'ai T'ing-kan

[Peking] 25 June 1913

My dear Admiral,

There has been a misunderstanding with regard to Tibet and to the mission of Mr. Ivan Chen which ought to be removed as soon as possible. It is no doubt due to the illness of Mr Lu Cheng-hsiang[2] and to the necessity that has arisen for removing the *Tutu* of Canton, Mr. Hu Han-ming.[3]

[1] In a telegram dated 29 May and entitled 'Chinese Ambitions in Tibet', published in *The Times* the following day, David Fraser said: 'With their customary lack of formality, the Chinese have published, within 24 hours of receiving a verbal suggestion from the British Minister, a statement that the question of a conference at Darjiling on Tibetan affairs is under consideration.'

[2] In face of criticism in and outside Parliament of the Agreement with Russia regarding Mongolia, Lu Cheng-hsiang absented himself from office on the excuse of illness. His official resignation was gazetted on 4 September, when he was succeeded by Sun Pao-ch'i.

[3] Hu Han-min (1879–1936), Chinese Republican politician, a follower of Sun Yat-sen, whose Secretary he became. He was elected *Tutu* of Kwangtung in November 1911,

As you know, the British Government have invited – I believe that is the correct term – the Chinese Government to send a delegate or delegates to India, there to confer with delegates from Great Britain and Tibet as to a final settlement of the vexed Tibetan question. No better choice of a delegate could have been made than Mr. Ivan Chen. Mr. Alston himself told the President how welcome Mr. Chen would be, because he speaks such admirable English, he knows the question so thoroughly having been Chargé d'Affaires in London when the negotiations took place previously with the British Government, and because he has in Shanghai fulfilled a difficult position with conspicuous ability.[1]

The British Government having been informed that Mr. Ivan Chen was to be China's representative at the negotiations in India, have now learned of the appointment of Mr. Hu Han-ming and Mr. Ivan Chen as 'pacificators of Tibet'. They have been told that the functions of 'pacificator' entrusted to these two officials are identically the same as those given during the Revolution to those Chinese Officials who were sent to the different Provinces of China Proper.[2]

Obviously the action of the President in removing Mr. Hu Han-ming was a wise one, for the removal of Mr. Hu Han-ming from Canton had become imperative. To prevent any misunderstanding it is necessary to note that the British Government are as much dissatisfied with Mr. Hu Han-ming as are the Chinese Cabinet, for he has never ceased to cause trouble between the Chinese and the British since he took up the post for which he was not fitted.

---

but did not take up the post until April 1913. Yüan Shih-k'ai removed him two months later, on 14 June, and appointed him Special Commissioner for Tibetan Affairs (otherwise translated as 'Pacification Commissioner'), an appointment which was designed by the Government as a ruse for his removal from Canton and which, as was to be expected, he did not take up. As leader of a right-wing faction in the Kuomintang, he played a prominent if somewhat ineffectual role in the Republican Government set up first in Canton in 1925 after the death of Sun Yat-sen, and then in Nanking in 1927. He was a victim of Chiang Kai-shek's political manoeuvrings when Chiang, in an attempt to make himself President and to set the left and right wings of the party against each other, put him under house arrest in February 1931 for his opposition to the scheme. This action immediately served to unite the diverse, discontented elements in the party, who rallied behind a common anti-Chiang front. But Chiang was by then too entrenched to be affected by this combined opposition, and Hu upon his release in September was allowed to retire to Hong Kong where he died five years later, long since a spent force. The misunderstanding to which Morrison here refers was due to the fact that both Ch'en I-fan and Hu Han-min were appointed to the same post on the same day (14 June 1913).

[1] This refers to Ch'en I-fan's term as Foreign Commissioner in Shanghai from April to June 1913.
[2] Posts of Special Commissioner with various titles were created frequently during the Peking period of the Republican regime. They were mostly for political expediency and were often sinecures. The English translation Morrison gives here is of the Chinese term *Hsuan-fu shih*, for which *see* Glossary. In the case of the appointment of Ch'en I-fan, the expression simply meant the Chinese Representative in the negotiations with the British over Tibet.

The British Government will refuse therefore to have Mr. Hu Han-ming as negotiator. The President I am sure knows this and of course the appointment of Mr. Hu Han-ming to Tibet was simply a diplomatic measure to get rid of a troublesome official for there is no likelihood whatever of his proceeding to Tibet.

Then another point to be made clear is the repeated declaration of Sir Edward Grey that no Chinese Officials will be permitted to proceed into Tibet via India until an agreement regarding Tibet has been arranged.[1] There should be no difficulty in coming to this agreement, but in order to prevent misunderstanding it is necessary that the British Government should be informed as early as possible that Mr. Ivan Chen has been appointed China's delegate to the Conference in India, where he will be entrusted not only with the Tibetan question but also with the Yunnan frontier question. He will presumably be given the rank of Special Envoy so as to ensure his receiving high consideration from the Indian Government. If that be done as quickly as possible the Foreign Minister could, in a covering note, inform the British Government that the question of the pacification of Tibet referred to in the Presidential Mandate was to take place *after* the agreement with England had been come to.

England asks that Tibet shall not be treated as a Province of China, but the Chinese Government themselves do not desire to treat Tibet as a dependency or as a Province of China but on an equality with the rest of China as one of the five divisions of the Chinese race.

The British Government ask that pending negotiations military operations shall cease. As a matter of fact these have ceased for the Chinese forces on the frontier of Ssuchuan have been victorious and the Presidential mandate ordered a cessation of hostilities. There is therefore no bar to the coming to an agreement except this misunderstanding about the 'pacification' mission of Messrs Hu Han-ming and Ivan Chen, which can be at once removed if official information be conveyed to the British Legation that Mr. Ivan Chen has been appointed Special Envoy to proceed to India entrusted with authority to settle the questions at issue.

You who have done so much to help China in her foreign relations could, I am sure, represent this case to the President. Somewhat heated messages are passing from the British Government to the Legation regarding this question and it would be wise as quickly as possible to remove any cause of misunderstanding.

Believe me

Very sincerely yours
[G. E. Morrison]

[1] See p. 75 note 2.

616. To W. H. Wilkinson[1]

[Peking] 27 June 1913

My dear Wilkinson,

[...]

I have always thought it was a shame that services such as you rendered to the Indian Government should have been unrewarded. That your services were appreciated I have known for a long time and all your friends have for a long time past expected that you would receive an Indian decoration.[2]

Sir Richard Dane has now come to Peking to begin the reorganisation of the salt gabelle. He seems to be under some misapprehension as to conditions in China, for he had expected that in travelling about he could have had many opportunities of big game shooting. This he finds is not the case. He has now to help the Chinese to produce from the salt for the use of the Central Government $1,250,000 monthly. So far the only salt collectorate that has sent in any figures at all is that of Lanchow of the Lianghuai collectorate which shows that an expenditure of $217,000 produced a collection of $189,000 – figures which were not satisfactory to the Inspector General.

I wonder when we are going to meet. I am longing to take a trip away from Peking.

Very sincerely yours
[G. E. Morrison]

617. From the Cabinet

Peking 30 June 1913

To Dr. Morrison,

We have received instructions from the President as follows:—

'Premier Chao Ping-chün has petitioned that from the time of the Sung Murder case the public opinion has been so divided, and that he proposed to follow the example of European and American countries and requested the President to appoint a committee comprising of Chinese and foreigners of high moral standing and well versed in law to thoroughly investigate into the case and to report the same. As Dr. Wu Ting-fang and Dr. Morrison are both well versed in Chinese and foreign law, I hereby appoint them to fully investigate into the case and report.'

[1] Probably Walter Hugh John Wilkinson, who later took the name Wilkinson-Guillemard (1874–1939), British colonial official. He was with the India Civil Service from 1897 to 1929, serving as British Envoy to Nepal from 1924 to 1929.

[2] In a letter to Morrison dated 5 June 1913, to which this is a reply, Wilkinson, after quoting from a letter he had received from Sir Arthur MacMahon (q.v.), then Indian Foreign Secretary, remarked: 'I replied that I had ventured to hope that this letter "would prove to be the prelude to more overt recognition" – but I have had no answer to this shameless hint!'

Having received the above, besides notifying Dr. Wu, we are sending you a copy of his petition for your information and hope that you will carry out the instructions.

We are

Yrs etc.
The Cabinet

Enclosure to Letter No. 617: *Petition by Premier Chao to the President*

From the time when the Sun[g] Murder case took place rumours have been so widely spread that the people have been mislead. After the publication of the evidence although those of ordinary intelligence would be convinced that this was not sufficient to implicate the Government, still there are meddlesome people who would even use this as a means for stirring up trouble. Now the country is not in a stable condition and the minds of the people are easily disturbed. If actions are not taken with immediate decision the people would take the shadow for substance and would be in a disorderly condition any time. The Government has barely time to preserve order, how can it then further its plans for reorganization.

The European and American nations in regard to important and difficult cases have often requested learn-scholars and famous men to make investigations for materials of arbitration. I, Ping Chün, would like to follow the example and request your Excellency to appoint a committee comprising Foreigners and Chinese of high moral standing and well versed in law, to thoroughly investigate this case and to report the same: Whether this ought to be done or not, I earnestly beg for your Excellency's decision.

618. To Ts'ai T'ing-kan

[Peking] 1 July 1913

My dear Admiral,

You might like to read the enclosed and if it is any use to you for reference please have it copied and then return it to me. I have put down the different facts so far as I know them regarding the Russo-Mongolian Agreement but I cannot, of course, pretend to have full knowledge.

I enclose you the Chinese text[1] of the Agreement which the President was so kind as to give me and which I gather is very difficult indeed to understand. The French text in places is also somewhat obscure. A Belgian Jurist of repute[2] is employed by the Foreign Office but I understand that he is not allowed to have access to such documents as these. Had he been consulted he might have suggested that certain of the French words used, such as *bons offices*, are unsafe words to be used in an agreement of this nature.

[1] Not printed. [2] Henri de Codt.

French is the most lucid of all languages but some of the French in this Agreement is quite difficult to translate.
[...]
With kind regards

Very sincerely yours
[G. E. Morrison]

Enclosure to Letter No. 618: *Memorandum re Mongolia, 10 June 1913*

So much that is inaccurate has been written about Mongolia that it would be well to summarise the events in their order.

In December 1911 Mongol officials in Urga who had been subjected to persecution on the part of the Chinese officials, induced the *Hutukhtu* to proclaim the independence of Mongolia. He could, of course only proclaim the independence of that portion of Mongolia which owed allegiance to him. By no means did this comprise all Mongolia. It did not even comprise Outer Mongolia nor even all Khalkha. Correctly it may be held to have comprised portion of the four *Aimaks* of Khalkha.

Prominent among the leaders of the Revolution was the Hanta Chinwang, a Khalkha Prince who had special reason to complain of his treatment at the hands of the Chinese, and who had conducted a Mission to Russia to appeal for protection from the Czar.[1] After the declaration of independence he became the Foreign Minister. Subsequent to the Coronation he proceeded a second time to Russia, this time to plead for Recognition. His mission found favour. Recognition was promised and a Russian Special Envoy, M. Korostovetz, who had recently been Minister to Peking was sent to Urga to give effect to the promise and on the 3rd November 1912 he signed the Agreement and Protocol, whereby in return for assisting Mongolia to maintain her autonomous regime Russia obtained far-reaching commercial advantages throughout Mongolia. The terms of the Convention and of the protocol have been published in a British parliamentary paper (No. 1, 1913).

Attention to several points in this Agreement. Firstly. The *Hutukhtu* is spoken of as the 'Sovereign of the Mongol people'. Nowhere is reference made to 'independence', the words used being 'autonomous regime'. Reference is made to the 'national and historic Constitution of their country, in the maintenance of which Russia will give her assistance'. The expulsion of the Chinese from Urga is described as 'putting an end to the old relations between Mongolia and China.'

The Agreement and Protocol spoke of 'Mongolia'. A few days later, however, a Russian semi-official communique announced that only 'Outer Mongolia' was referred to. At Urga the Russian Minister himself is quoted as saying that 'Outer Mongolia' consisted of the 4 *Aimaks* of Khalkha, but, said the Minister, Russia would also require some territory outside of Khal-

[1] *See* p. 48 note 2.

kha to be included, namely Urianghai and Kobdo. After the signature of the agreement the Russians gave to the world the sense of the agreement in which the best complexion was put upon it in favour of Russia but for a long time the protocol was kept secret. It was only when Reuter published the full text in the papers that it was seen how very far reaching were the rights and privileges which Russia had obtained in Mongolia.

No sooner had the agreement been signed than efforts were made by emissaries of the *Hutukhtu*, acting it was naturally supposed at the instigation of the Russians, to induce the Barga Mongols to join with Urga. The importance of this step can be realised by glancing at a good map of Mongolia, where it will be seen that Barga comprises the territory of which Hailar is the chief town, extends as far as the Khingan Mountains, is bounded by the Aigun River and is traversed by a railway in Russian military occupation.

In December 1912 it was announced that the Barhuts (Mongols of Barga) had thrown in their lot with the Mongols of Urga and recognised the sovereignty of the *Hutukhtu*. Outer Mongolia, therefore, included at this time a stretch of what was formerly China, from the Khingan Mountains right across to the neighbourhood of Kuldja, a territory as large as the 18 provinces of China proper.

But in the meantime the Russian Government had expressed their willingness to discuss the Mongolia question with China and to come to an agreement defining the respective relations to Mongolia of the two countries.

On December 3rd 1912, Mr. Kroupensky handed the following note to the Chinese Foreign Minister, Lu Cheng-hsiang.

To prevent further misunderstandig as to the Suzerainty of China in Mongolia and the relations of Russia towards Mongolia and also to definitely settle basis of Mongolian autonomy the following articles are proposed: –

1. China agrees that no administrative change shall take place in Mongolia in either its political administration or racial customs: that the Mongolians within their own territory shall have the special privilege and power of defending their land and maintaining the peace of their realm as well as the power to organise their military and police forces: that no foreigners shall be allowed to colonise in Mongolia, the Chinese being included among the foreigners.

2. Russia agrees that the territorial integrity (entity?) of Mongolia shall be strictly observed: that no Russian troops shall be sent to Mongolia: but that in the sending of Consulate Guards it shall not be necessary for Russia to give the Chinese Government any previous notice.

3. China desiring to restore former conditions in Mongolia shall make known publicly her willingness to permit Russian mediation in the

negotiations between her (China) and Mongolia, as to their relations to each other and as to the delimitation of the territorial frontier and also as to rightful development of Mongolian autonomy.

4. The rights and privileges of Russian subjects and Russian trade in Mongolia shall be incorporated in the supplementary Agreement to this Agreement – the same rights and privileges as are defined in the Agreement signed on the 21st October[1] by the mutual consent of Russia and Mongolia.

This became the basis of the new agreement, upon which negotiations when they were reopened have since continued. Negotiations were really reopened through the good offices of the Japanese who viewed with alarm the widening breach between China and Russia. Aggression in Mongolia was bound to be felt in Manchuria compelling corresponding action on the part of Japan. But the time for such action was inopportune. Every Japanese interest was therefore set in motion to bring about a *rapprochement*. Negotiations were begun and were continued through March, April and May, a tentative agreement being finally come to, of which the following is the text –

China and Russia with the object of obviating misunderstandings which might possibly arise from the present situation in Mongolia have agreed to conclude an agreement upon the following bases.

1. Russia recognises Mongolia to be an integral part of the territory of China and hereby undertakes not to seek to interrupt the continuity of its territorial integrity. Russia further undertakes to respect China's rights of every description which heretofore have existed in consequence of this territorial integrity.

2. China undertakes not to modify the local and historical autonomy of Outer Mongolia and to grant to the Mongols of Outer Mongolia who are responsible for the defence and for the maintenance of good order throughout the territory, the exclusive right of maintaining their own military organisation and police as well as the right not to allow the colonisation of their lands by any other people than Mongol subjects.

3. Russia on its part undertakes that with the exception of Consulate Guards it will not dispatch troops to Outer Mongolia and also undertakes not to carry out colonization of the lands of Outer Mongolia and not to allow itself to be represented by other institutions than the consulates permitted by the treaties.

4. China desiring to use her authority in Outer Mongolia in a peaceful manner declares herself disposed to accept the assistance (good offices) of Russia in order to establish on the above bases the principles of its relations with Outer Mongolia and so that the Central Authority of this

---

[1] The reference is to the Korostovetz Convention signed on 3 November 1912, or 21 October according to the Russian calendar.

region should recognize its historic character of being a local authority of a part of Chinese territory.

5. The Government of China out of consideration for the good offices of the Russian Government agrees to give to Russian subjects in Outer Mongolia the commercial privileges to be enumerated here below (here are set forth 17 clauses).

6. Hereafter in the case of agreements between Russia and the authorities of this country relating to changes in the international relationships of that region it is necessary that China and Russia negotiate direct and only after the Chinese Government has given its consent shall they become effective.

The 17 articles referred to in article 5 are the 17 articles of the Urga protocol.

It cannot be disputed that the proposed Agreement is creditable to the skill of the Chinese Negotiators. Unquestionably China has recovered much ground that she appeared to have irretrievably lost in Urga. Before authorising signature the President, acting in accordance with the provisions of the provisional constitution, submitted the terms of the proposed agreement to Parliament.

Accordingly on May 30th the Foreign Minister appeared before the Lower House and read to them the text of the proposed agreement. It was decided before giving assent that a Special Committee of 21 men should be appointed to consider the subject and report thereon.

Both this Special Committee of the House and a Special Committee of the Kuomintang discussed the proposed Agreement clause by clause. They discussed it in a reasonable spirit and as a result of their deliberations they have suggested certain modifications not of the sense so much as elucidations of the wording and the prevention of difficulties in the future. Their suggestions or proposals are rather optional than essential: they are reasonable in themselves and to any outsider would appear easy of acceptance by Russia if properly explained to her. For Russia retains intact the Protocol of the 3rd Nov. 1912 and her Minister is reported to have declared that 'all else matters little'.

China has ground for believing herself harshly treated. It is admitted that under the late Manchu Regime a foolish policy harshly executed by the Manchu *Amban* San To gave the Mongols ground for dissatisfaction and drove many individuals among them into rebellion; under the new Government these grievances were about to be remedied: the status of Mongolia was raised, the Mongols were proclaimed on a footing of equality with the other four sections of the Chinese race and were given equal rights under the Republic. Precisely at this point the Russians stepped in and encouraged, if they did not inspire, the movement of revolt which led to the declaration of independence. It is natural that China should feel aggrieved at the high-handed way in which she has been treated by Russia and should look with suspicion upon all agreements projected with Russia. Removal of possible grounds for misunderstanding is at the root of the suggestions made by the Special Committee who propose either that the modifications be embodied in the Agreement or be inserted in an exchange of Notes.

In the first place the Special Committee suggest that the Agreement should contain a Revision clause similar to that in Article 15 of the Russo-Chinese Treaty of 1881[1] providing for the Revision of the Commercial Articles of the Treaty after 10 years. Revision clauses are found in many Treaties between China and Foreign Powers and in many cases are even more comprehensive in their terms than the clause which they ask should be inserted in this Treaty.

Take now the text clause by clause.

Article 1. No change is suggested.

Article 2. The Chinese would like to alter the two last words, 'Mongol subjects' into 'Chinese citizens' but they admit that such alteration would beg the whole question and would never be acceded to by Russia. China asks how is the 'historic local autonomy' to be defined? What period of Mongol history is to be selected as historic? Historically China has the right of superior control over the military and the police. The *Amban* had this right. If this right be denied what is to prevent the Mongols from turning their arms against China. If China is denied this right then *local autonomy* becomes *political autonomy* which is independence. While it is true that the Urga Convention described the *Hutukhtu* as 'the sovereign of the Mongol people' nowhere in either the Agreement or the Protocol is reference made to *independence*, the words used being 'autonomous regime' or 'national and historic constitution'.

China asks: What is Outer Mongolia? What are its boundaries? China claims that this geographical expression shall include only the four *Aimaks* of Khalkha. The Russians maintain that it includes also Urianghai and Kobdo.

Urianghai has always been ignored by the Chinese Government. No Chinese troops are or ever have been stationed there. Kobdo is a destroyed town – destroyed in August 1912: all Chinese were either killed or expelled, the *Amban* Pu Jun[2] being himself escorted to the Russian frontier whence he returned to China via the Siberian Railway. China can only recover Kobdo as a result of a victorious war over the Mongols assisted by Russia. Kobdo is within easy access of the Russian border and of large bodies of Russian

[1] Article XV of the Sino-Russian Treaty signed at St Petersburg on 12/24 February 1881, and ratified there on 7/10 August the same year, stipulated that the Treaty would remain in force for a period of ten years unless request for its revision was made by either contracting party.

[2] An Imperial clansman, P'u-jun was Administrator at Kobdo from April 1908 to July 1911, when Sa-yin-t'u was appointed to succeed him but did not take up the post.

troops. To reach Kobdo China will have to transport troops across the desert to Hami and Kucheng whence transport will be in the highest degree difficult through a country devoid of habitation and of firewood and in a great part of the year devoid also of fodder and water.

Article 3. China desires to know how many Consular Guards? There must be a limit to the number. Russia can establish by agreement with the Government of Mongolia (Art 8 of the protocol) an indefinite number of Consulates. If she can guard them by an indefinite number of troops Russia can occupy the country in a military sense. China desires to limit the number in any one consulate to 60. Russia states that at some posts she has fewer than this number, at others more. The number, she says, must be determined by local conditions. (Russia has 750 guards at Kuldja and 750 in Kashgar, varying numbers of 500 and upwards at Urga, 250 at Uliasutai, 60 at Kobdo, 250 at Chuguchak and a varying number at Urumchi (Ti hua fu).)

Article 4. China presumes that *central authority* here refers to the *Hutukhtu* and suggests an alternative to *The Authorities*. By the wording of the article only one of the officials is a Chinese official, namely the *Hutukhtu*, whereas the Chinese wish all the officials to be Chinese officials. The *Hutukhtu* only recognise a Central authority in Mongolia: they cannot give tacit recognition of his declaration of independence. They want to have direct relationship with the authorities of Mongolia *not* mediate relationship through the *Hutukhtu*.

Article 5. The suggestion is made that the words 'successful result of' should precede the words 'good offices' of the Russian Government. Otherwise the Chinese plead that they are rewarding promises only.

The sequence is

Mongolia has declared her independence.

Russia has recognised Mongolian rights of autonomy.

China is now to reward Russia for using her good offices in inducing Mongolia to cancel her independence. China cannot employ force to recover possession since in such an event Russia has engaged to support Mongolia.

Article 6. China wants the clause to cover all treaties affecting Mongolia not only those modifying the established regime. In the case of the protocol China asks for a clearer definition of the establishment of Consulates and of 'factories' under Consuls or under Russian merchants. China desires that the appointment of Consuls as provided for in Art. 8 shall be done after agreement with the Government of China *not* after agreement with the Mongolian Government.

Now the question is being asked 'Is it not better to leave the Mongolian Agreement unfinished and proceed with a settlement of the Tibetan question?' The Chinese know the danger of delay but think that perhaps they could get better terms with regard to Mongolia if they had first come to an Agreement with England regarding Tibet.

I cannot accept this view. The suggestions made by the Special Committee are reasonable and if properly submitted to the Russian Legation it is probable that some or all of them might be accepted by the Russians. But if they are rejected it would even then be better to sign the Agreement than leave it any longer open. Conditions along the frontier of Mongolia are becoming daily worse. Quite a small body of Mongol *Hunghutzes* are dislocating the trade of the whole of Mongolia, the trade, that is, with China not the trade with Russia, which latter is actually benefitting by the condition of unrest that will certainly continue in an increasingly aggravated form until an agreement has been come to with Russia. Facts however disagreeable, must be looked in the face. Mongolia is at the mercy of Russia, Urga is virtually in Russian military occupation. Russian instigation can increase the present unrest in Mongolia to a degree still more alarming than at present. It would be well to 'agree with thine adversary quickly whilst thou art in the way with him'.

Postscript July 14, 1913.

The terms of the Agreement were approved by the Lower House by a majority of 30. But they have not yet been discussed by the Senate.

Delay has been fatal.

Cf. Kroupensky's visit yesterday to Lu Cheng-hsiang in hospital.[1]

619. To C. D. Bruce[2]

[Peking] 2 July 1913

Private & Confidential

My dear Bruce,

Yesterday the President sent for me to discuss earnestly with me the present condition of affairs in Shanghai. He asked me questions which I really was unable to answer not being fully informed. Questions especially about extradition: about Shanghai as a sanctuary for bomb manufacturers and

[1] During his visit to Lu Cheng-hsiang in hospital on 13 July, Kroupensky submitted to Lu more exacting demands than those contained in the six articles discussed in this Memorandum.

[2] Clarence Dalrymple Bruce (1862-1934), British soldier, at this time Police Commissioner in the International Settlement in Shanghai. He played an important role in helping to frustrate the attempt by the southern republicans to capture Shanghai from Yüan's control during the 'Second Revolution'. In 1914, on Morrison's recommendation, Bruce became Police Adviser to the Peking Government, but left the post soon after the outbreak of the European War. He was reinstated to his former position again through Morrison's efforts, after the war.

instigators to assassination euphemistically called 'Political Offenders', and, incidentally about the status of the Mixed Court.

I said that the man who could best give him information would be my friend Colonel Bruce. He asked me would I write to you confidentially on my own account to ask your counsel and advice, and hence the motive of this letter. Incidentally I took the opportunity of saying that the Chinese Government would be fortunate if they could take into their service a man of your experience and special knowledge who could organise a police service capable of dealing with the present dangerous situation. He seemed to regard the suggestion with approval, but, of course, it is too early yet to know what could be done. We shall have to communicate with each other much more fully and must together think out a scheme that I could lay before him.

I am sure that you will be willing to help him in this matter. Of course he knows that you are in the service of the Municipal Council and that you would not dream of doing anything that would be regarded with disfavour by your employers.

He seems to have an earnest desire to have things regularised in Shanghai. He does not know what to do. The facts as stated to him are that Shanghai has become the sanctuary of those engaged in plotting against the present Government. He has evidence that the men (of course I speak to you very confidentially) who took part in the recent attempted revolution in Hankow went under Japanese protection to Shanghai.[1] He is told that there is no doubt that the attack upon the Arsenal was organised by Chen Chi-mei.[2] Evidence, which is described as convincing, has been furnished to him alleging that Chen Chi-mei was the instigator of the assassination of Hsu Pao-shan.[3] In Shanghai bombs are being constantly manufactured in the foreign Concession under Japanese protection. Little is said when they are seized but frequently bombs are being seized at Taku and Tientsin whose origin has been Shanghai.

How is the matter to be dealt with – that is his question? What steps can he take to assist or to call upon the authorities to assist in suppressing a traffic of so nefarious a kind and so essentially dangerous? The Chinese here allege that Shanghai is the centre of the bomb trade. His attention had been drawn

[1] The reference is to Ning T'iao-yüan and Hsiung Yüeh-shan, who were arrested in a Japanese-owned hotel in the German concession in Hankow on 26 June 1913, accused of anti-Government activities.

[2] The Republican forces under Ch'en Ch'i-mei made an unsuccessful attempt at the seizure of the Shanghai Arsenal on 28 May 1913.

[3] Hsü Pao-shan (d. 1913), Chinese soldier, commonly known as 'Tiger Hsü' for his reputed ruthlessness. Garrison Commander at Yangchow and a supporter of Yüan Shih-k'ai, he was regarded as an arch-enemy by the republicans in the south. A connoisseur of porcelain, he was killed on 24 May 1913 by a bomb concealed in a box he thought to contain a valuable specimen, sent to him by his assassin, Huang Fu-sheng (?1882–1948).

to the recent bomb manufacturing case in Shanghai in which two Japanese, Matsukawa and Saiki, were implicated and to the very unsatisfactory termination of that case, the charge being dismissed and the accused being deported to Japan.

What steps can be suggested to remedy such an obvious miscarriage of justice?

We discussed also the question of the Mixed Court.[1] At the present time the Mixed Court Magistrate was appointed by the Consular Body, but obviously this was a temporary procedure rendered necessary by the conditions during the Revolutionary upheaval and the absence of any recognised government. I said for years a grievance that had specially been brought to my notice as a correspondent was the inferior standing of the Mixed Court Magistrate, the official appointed to this post by the Chinese being a man of such rank that he had no jurisdiction or authority over Chinese officials: that the remedy suggested had been the raising of the status of the position and the appointment to it of a responsible official of high character and of adequate rank. I gathered from him that there would be no difficulty about doing this. But of course no such appointment can be made until the Diplomatic Body has authorised the Consular Body to revert to the procedure prior to the Revolution.

Can you suggest anything that would be to the advantage both of the foreigners and of the Chinese? There is no disposition or intention to alter the status of Shanghai, but there must be some way by which the present anomalous condition of things such as that revealed by the Bomb manufacturing case, could be improved.

I told the President that after Christmas you were leaving the service of the Municipal Council and that perhaps you might be induced to enter the Chinese Government service. Would you mind telling me in confidence and quite frankly what would your views be in this matter, namely as to the duties, emoluments and time of service and when would your services be available. Please do not base any hopes upon the realisation of any such scheme, for I am only in a position where I can suggest – I cannot insist. I believe, however, that it might be possible to induce the Chinese to make you an offer. As you can well imagine it would be less difficult so to influence them if I could give them, through you, advice and counsel and some

[1] A Mixed Court with a Chinese Magistrate and foreign Assessors had been set up in the International Settlement to deal with cases in which Chinese were involved. The Chinese Government had long considered the practice needed to be amended, particularly after the *Supao* case of 1903 (see Volume I of the *Correspondence*), when the Manchu Government sought unsuccessfully to extradite the revolutionaries Tsou Jung (1885–1905) and Chang Ping-lin (1868–1936). The Yüan Shih-k'ai Government, in an attempt to suppress the activities of revolutionaries in the International Settlement, also pressed for changes in the procedure, to deprive political offenders of protection in the foreign concessions.

assistance at the present difficult time – advice as to how to proceed – suggestions as to how to act to remove these dangers of assassination which are very real dangers indeed especially from bombs.

There is an opportunity at the present time of making reforms and I believe any practical suggestion now made to the President would be acted upon.

Of course what you write I will treat with much discretion and confidentially, for I realise your position, but I think in this case foreign and Chinese interests coincide and any suggestions based upon your experience as chief of the Police in the Foreign Community which you can make to the Chinese might, if acted upon, be of material advantage to the foreign community.

With all good wishes to you

Very sincerely yours
[G. E. Morrison]

620. To Ts'ai T'ing-kan

[Peking] 4 July 1913

My dear Admiral,

Would you mind reading the enclosed and giving me your views privately?

Dr Wu Ting-fang tells me that he suggested a Special Commission and in order that it might be considered impartial he suggested that a foreigner should be attached to it. But he tells me that his idea was the appointment of a Special Commission such as that which for some months held an enquiry into the Marconi case in England.[1] In that enquiry the commission consisted of 15 members (6 Liberals, 6 Unionists, 2 Nationalists and 1 Labourite) and all were Englishmen. There never has been a case in which in any foreign country one who was not a native of the country has been given a place on the Commission.

Dr Wu Ting-fang seems to agree with this view and thinks that perhaps it would not add to the dignity of the country if a foreigner were attached to the Commission. It would be a reflexion, I think, upon the honour of the country for it is absurd even to suggest that there is no Chinese to be found who would not be impartial.

[1] On 11 October 1912 a Select Committee of the British Parliament was set up to investigate an agreement made between the British Government and the Marconi Telegraphic Company, and specifically to investigate charges against three Ministers for their involvement with the Marconi Company. The allegation was made that a large Government contract had been granted to the English branch of the company through the influence of Sir Rufus Isaacs, the Attorney-General and brother of the company's Managing Director. The allegation was found to be unproven, as were the charges of corruption against the three Ministers who were shareholders in the American branch of the company. Lloyd George was one of the three Ministers involved. The incident was made use of by the Conservative Opposition and aroused a great deal of political passion and dissension both in and outside the British Parliament.

You will find that foreigners will ridicule the idea of a foreigner sitting on a Chinese commission to enquire into the acts of the Chinese Prime Minister. Just imagine what a howl of indignation there would have been if a French judge had been given a seat on the Marconi Commission.

So please read the enclosed and give me the benefit of your advice.

Yours very sincerely
[G. E. Morrison]

621. To The Cabinet

[Peking] 4 July 1913

Gentlemen,

I have to acknowledge the receipt of your letter of the 30th June enclosing a memorial from H.E. the Prime Minister with regard to the disquieting effect of certain slanderous charges published in some sections of the Press regarding the case of the regrettable assassination of Mr. Sung Chiao-jen.

I have also seen H.E. Dr Wu Ting-fang and have consulted with him with regard to the case.

At all times I have the desire to serve the best interests of the country by whom I have the honour to be now employed and in accordance with this desire I venture to make the following observations.

Public men in every country have to pay the penalty of their high position by subjection to press criticism – the higher the position the greater the penalty – that is to say the more severe and searching is public criticism of their acts. There is no exception to this rule. In England and America press criticism is especially outspoken, in the case of America much more so than in England. As a rule Ministers have no redress. Experience shows that it is wiser to ignore charges animated by party spirit such as those given hasty currency in the Sung Chiao-jen case. In the passion created by this assassination of one who had held high office and who was personally the friend of many prominent Chinese suggestions were made and charges were levelled aganst high authorities which calmer reason showed to be wholly unjustified.

No charges against the Prime Minister worthy of consideration have been made in any foreign papers other than in *The China Republican* a Chinese owned newspaper published in English in Shanghai. No English or American paper has suggested that the Prime Minister has been implicated in this crime. No paper of any repute published on the Continent of Europe has, so far as I know, made any such charge. The character of the Prime Minister so far as I can learn from European papers is unblemished.

It is therefore supererogatory for Mr Chao Ping-chun to refute charges which, as regards the foreign press, have never been made.

In compliance, however, with the desire of Mr Chao Ping-chun the President has decreed that a Commission of Enquiry, to which I should be attached, should be held under the presidency of Dr Wu Ting-fang to investigate and report. While I appreciate the honour thus shown to me I hope it will not be thought that I desire to evade any work entrusted to me if I point out how undesirable it is in the interests of China that an enquiry of this delicate nature involving the character of one of its statesmen should be held in the official presence of a foreigner. These vague and intangible charges or rather suggestions and innuendoes are purely a domestic concern of China itself and of the Chinese people. Commissions, as Mr Chao Ping-chun states, have frequently been instituted in foreign countries to investigate charges brought against public men, but I believe I am right in saying that no instance has ever been known where a foreigner has been attached to such a Commission.

In the recent enquiry in England into certain transactions regarding Shares, in which the conduct of three Ministers was impugned, a Special Committee of 15 members of Parliament, composed of Members of all political parties, was appointed by the Crown to hear evidence and make an elaborate report.[1] Similarly in France in the case of the Panama scandals:[2] similarly in Russia over the Port Arthur surrender,[3] but no instance can be found where in Russia an Englishman sat on the tribunal, or in France a Russian was one of the Commission.

It is therefore specially undesirable that in China under its new conditions a procedure should be followed which would never be permitted in any other country.

The fact that Mr Chao Ping-chun the Prime Minister desires to have the case investigated by an impartial Tribunal is the best possible evidence that he is innocent, but if such an enquiry as that suggested is to be held, where is it to end? Not only will the Prime Minister have to be examined, but other prominent statesmen in the south will also have to appear and to explain public acts and to produce evidence rebutting other vague and intangible charges in which they themselves have become involved.

I submit that for the dignity of the country and for the honour of the Chinese people it would be unwise to hold such an enquiry at the present time.[4]

[1] *See* p. 183 note 1.

[2] In 1889 the Panama Company failed, and the shareholders appealed to the Government to institute an enquiry. Ferdinand de Lesseps and five Ministers and former Ministers as well as five deputies were charged with corruption. It was alleged that the deputies had been bribed by a Jewish financier, who was found dead during the enquiry.

[3] The surrender of Port Arthur by the Russian forces on 2 January 1905 during the Russo-Japanese War (1904–5), was accompanied by suspicions that it was a result of Japanese bribery of the Russian Commander, Anatoli Mikhailovich Stoessel (1848–1915). *See* Volume I, Letter No. 186, Morrison to James, 31 January 1905, p. 289, note 1.

[4] In the event the Special Commission was never convened, possibly due to Morrison's representations.

It is inevitable that in the heat of a revolutionary movement where passions have run so strongly, that charges and counter-charges should be made, recriminations and counter-recriminations. If all attacks upon the character of high authorities are to be subject to public enquiry serious delay will be caused to the business of the State and serious injury to its good name.

Should, however, it be still considered desirable that a Special Commission be appointed to investigate the case, no person could be found to preside over its deliberations with greater dignity than Dr Wu Ting-fang, who is not only held in high repute throughout China but bears a name honoured throughout the world. To Englishmen and Americans such an appointment would be specially acceptable because Dr Wu Ting-fang was educated in London. He has had the best legal training possible, is a barrister at law of Lincoln's Inn in London and he has twice been the distinguished Minister of China in Washington.

I beg that you will submit these views to His Excellency the Prime Minister.

I have the honour to be, Gentlemen

Your obedient servant
[G. E. Morrison]

622. From Ts'ai T'ing-kan

[Peking] 4 July 1913

My dear Doctor,

I concur in every word that you have written and endorse your views totally.

Let the honour rest in the suggestion that you be a member of the Commission, not further. In these heated times you may be blamed whatever the result of the enquiry.

I suggest that if the parties are really anxious to show impartiality they should invite both Chinese and Foreign correspondents to attend the enquiry (if in open court) so that full publicity and calm criticism be given to the world. This may act as a wholesome check to warped passion.

With best wishes

Yours sincerely
Tsai Ting kan

623. From C. D. Bruce

Shanghai 8 July 1913

My dear Morrison,

Your letter[1] reached me on Saturday as we were leaving on board a house boat to spend Sunday up river. Having carefully considered all you say I will

---

[1] Printed as Letter No. 619.

now do my best to answer your questions and to throw some light upon affairs in Shanghai for the information of the President.

You will I feel sure understand that my present position to no small extent ties my tongue. So long as I am serving the International Council there is a great deal that may not be said. No man of any sense can be for six years head of the International Police here and not be more fully in touch with Chinese affairs than almost any foreigner in China. During the last two I have been closely in touch with the leaders of what is called the Southern Party and with men of all shades of opinion and class, but until I leave the Council's service, my lips must be more or less sealed. I will however speak as freely as may be to you.

Not knowing how much the President hears about the status of Shanghai I may be giving both him and you stale information, at the same time at the risk of doing so it is better to endeavour to make all the points plain. No doubt you have a copy of your letter to me so it will save time if I answer in paragraphs.

If I am too brief or not sufficiently clear it is easy for you to ask for further information upon any particular point later on.

Your para 1.

Extradition: Meaning I take it the rendition of Chinese the Government want in political cases; is guided solely by the rule that before a summons or warrant is allowed to be made good the person charged must have a *prima facie* case made out against him in the Mixed Court before a foreign assessor — usually the British — and a Chinese magistrate. The latter hardly counts as if the British assessor is not satisfied that a *prima facie* case has been established the Magistrate can do little. It is up to me as C.S.P.[1] to bring the case before whichever Assessor I select. Naturally they usually come before the British Assessor. In July's *Municipal Gazette* my Police report for June, reference is made to these points as a matter for comment in the Huang Hsing case.

Sanctuary: (also alluded to by me in same report). The question of Sanctuary is equally clear. Unless a Chinaman is faced in the Mixed Court by his assessors or by sufficiently credible witnesses of high standing when he is charged with an offence, even by the Central Government, he will not be handed over until a *prima facie* case is made out, in the meantime sanctuary is secured to him.

Political offenders: Or as you term them bombers and instigators of assassination are equally secure unless a *prima facie* case is made out against them upon the particular charge.

One suggestion I would make is that the President should not allow the Huang Hsing incident to be repeated.[2] It did considerable harm to the

---

[1] Chief Superintendent of Police.
[2] In retaliation to the demand made by Sun Yat-sen and Huang Hsing to bring to justice the plotters of Sung Chiao-jen's murder, the Peking Government ordered Huang Hsing to

Central Government. Instead of acting as it did the Government should retain one of our high class firms of lawyers – Hanson, McNeil, and Jones, for choice, not Drummond's[1] firm – give them full particulars of the charge, furnish them with the true facts of the case and trust them. The government may then obtain what it desires and if the charges are *bona fide* the prisoner will be handed over without delay.

Status of Mixed Court: Since the Revolution and the partial taking over of the Mixed Court by the Council's police under instructions from the Consular Body the Court has improved in efficiency 50%: also in favour with Chinese litigants of all classes excepting the one class which previously used to bribe the Chinese magistrates (I speak plainly as no end is served by mincing matters). Any attempt at reintroducing the old conditions would therefore be met with almost general opposition. The present senior Chinese magistrate, Kuan by name,[2] is a nominee of the Consular body. He was the best choice under the circumstances (Pao-I the former senior magistrate having decamped with $60,000 shortage at the time of the revolution). Kuan has done what is wanted of him satisfactorily, but is a man of no character whatever, nor any more honest than most Chinese of his class would be if placed in such a position. Since he was nominated under the new conditions he receives a regular salary from the Mixed Court funds through the Consular body and the Council, and has little chance of peculation or of accepting bribes. The other three Chinese magistrates are decent people enough of their kind but in no sense of the word the equals in class of the Foreign Assessors. Whether a really able Chinese magistrate would care about the position I cannot say. So long as extra-territoriality does not even loom in the far distant future as likely to be abolished, just so long will the administration of the Mixed Court practically rest with the foreign Assessors. At present it is much better for the sake of justice all round that it should be so.

Your second para refers to myself so is left until other matters have been dealt with.

In your third para you refer to any help that I can give to the President and

---

be present at the local court in Peking to answer the allegation that he was behind assasination plots against prominent Peking Government officials. Huang made an appearance before the Mixed Court in Shanghai on 11 June 1913 to state that he would appear whenever the Court received the evidence against him from Peking. But no further requests were received from the Government and the matter was allowed to drop.

[1] William Venn Drummond (?1842–1915), British lawyer with a practice in Shanghai. He had formerly been Acting British Crown Advocate in that city. Morrison, in his Diary entry for 17 March 1913, described him as 'the champion bore in China'. As early as 1901 Drummond, in writing to Morrison, had predicted that the first emperor of a new Chinese dynasty would be Yüan Shih-k'ai.

[2] Kuan Chiung, more commonly known as Kuan Chiung-chih, Chinese judge, Magistrate of the Mixed Court in Shanghai from 1911 to 1927.

to my present position with the Municipal Council. Subject to what has already been said the answer to your appeal is this letter. The latter embodies the experience of six years as chief of Police and controller of the Secret Service Department, also of nearly fifteen years residence in China.

Your fourth para (page 2) refers again to the sanctuary which Shanghai is said to offer to plotters and to anti-government men such as Chen Chi-mei and others. Also to the backing afforded to these people by the Japanese. I have already said all there is to say regarding the sanctuary question as it presents itself to the community here. As to Chen Chi-mei, he is an arch plotter and the attack on the Arsenal may or may not have been his handiwork. I can only say that we were given due warning of its coming off and I cannot understand why this should have been done had he or his party been the aggressors. That both he and Loh Wei-sen[1] were instrumental in having Genl Hsu Pao-shan blown up may be true. Far be it from me to attempt to defend them: at the same time we cannot forget the murder of Sung and that China is still China. That Shanghai is one of the arteries through which Bombs enter China and that the Japanese are very closely connected with the trade is of course well known to me, but of this I cannot say more at present. The International Police have done their best to locate this traffic for months past. Only a few weeks back they eventually succeeded in bringing home their guilt (as we believe) to certain Japanese only to have all their efforts frustrated and their labour utterly thrown away by the attitude of the Japanese Consul General. I have made a special report to the Council upon this case and although I do not hope for much success over the matter have done all that is possible to bring home their responsibility to the Japanese Consulate.

Your paras 5 and 6 continue to refer to this matter but I cannot suggest anything further beyond thinking that a very straight diplomatic protest ought to be made to the new Japanese Minister in Peking,[2] citing this as a case of gross miscarriage of justice. Why should the President not have this done?

Your para 7 refers again to the Mixed Court. There is nothing I can add which would throw any further light upon the status of that court.

In your para 8 you mention the status of Shanghai itself and in this connection it may be advisable to say a word. So far as the carrying out of arrests and keeping undesirables under watch the Municipal police are terribly handicapped by the hopelessly corrupt and inefficient administration of the adjoining districts of Chapei and Paoshan and Pootung. As you of course are aware one of their head police officials was shot four days ago at Nanking

---

[1] Probably Lo Wei-hsin, a graduate of Waseda University in Tokyo. He had been a Secretary in the Ministry of the Interior in the Provisional Government at Nanking in 1912. Later he was to participate in the anti-Yüan movement in his native province of Chekiang, and became in 1916 a member of the Provincial Legislative Assembly.

[2] Yamaza Enjirō.

for being in possession of bombs and seditious literature: he probably deserved all he got but it shows the class of man with whom we are in contact. If the President desires the International Settlement to help him, by far the best means he can take to effect his object would be to extend for another five miles all round Shanghai the administrative area under the Municipal Council and the jurisdiction of the International Police. I do not advocate this because I wish for settlement extension but simply because I know it would add vastly to the suppression of crime in the area referred to. Personally I have all the responsibility and work I want as matters at present stand in Shanghai.

Your para 9 and para 2 [...] refer to myself and I will now answer them.

My engagement with the Municipal Council can terminate about the New Year and I am prepared to accept an offer from the President to enter the service of the Chinese Government upon the following terms.

That I am to organise and carry through as its chief a system tending to place the Police of the whole country upon a sound modernised basis, including the creation of a Criminal Investigation Department dealing with all matters usually pertaining to such a department in Europe. That I am to receive a three years agreement renewable at the end of that time or terminable by either party to it. The salary to be: for the first year £2500 (two thousand five hundred pounds) sterling payable *per mensem*, half in sterling, half in Taels at the current rate of exchange. The second year £2700 (two thousand seven hundred pounds). For the third year £2900 (two thousand nine hundred pounds). For each subsequent year £3000 (three thousand pounds). That I receive in addition House rent allowance and all travelling expenses incurred in the course of my work. My present salary is as I think you know nearly £2000 a year. The organization of an efficient Police Force for China is not a difficult matter in the sense that the material is good. Where the difficulty lies is in the non-existence, at present, of a reliable trustworthy officer class. This deficiency can only be overcome by time and would necessitate, at first, the appointment of a certain number of Foreigners to help to create and train the native class of officer.

My time, should I be given the opportunity, would for the first three years be taken up somewhat as follows. The first year by studying the existing system and seeing for myself the material to hand in the various provinces and provincial capitals: also in organizing a Criminal Investigation Department. The second year in drafting a reorganized scheme, creating various training schools and in gradually getting a general level of procedure in Police matters. The third year should see the scheme in working order, and the President better informed about provincial doings and what is passing at a distance from Peking than ever before.

The above is naturally only a brief outline of what my aim would be should I be offered and accept the appointment.

That I am lucky enough to have had experience in Police Work in China and of the training of Chinese such as few foreigners have ever previously had you are aware.

I honestly believe I could very materially assist the President in restoring law and order throughout the country. That I will endeavour to the utmost of my power so to do, if I am asked to try, you I think will bear me out in saying.

I must apologise for not having this letter type-written but I have never taught myself that useful accomplishment and cannot make use of any of my clerks or stenographer on this occasion.

With very kind regards
I am

Always yours sincerely
C. D. Bruce

624. To Ts'ai T'ing-kan

[Peking] 12 July 1913

My dear Admiral,

[...]

I send you [...] a memorandum regarding the contract signed on the 4th of July by Dr. Sun Wen with Lord ffrench,[1] the witnesses being Dr. Wang Chung-hui[2] and our friend Mr. Wan Bing-chun.[3]

---

[1] Charles Austin Thomas Robert John Joseph ffrench (1868–1955), 6th Baron, British Agent for Pauling & Co. He signed with Sun Yat-sen on 4 July 1913 a Preliminary Contract Providing for the Financing and Construction of the Railway from Canton to Chungking with Extension to Lanchow, which the Yüan Shih-k'ai Government refused to ratify after Sun was dismissed as Director-General of Railways, following the 'Second Revolution'.

[2] Wang Ch'ung-hui (1881–1958), Chinese Republican politician and jurist. He had studied Law in America, England and Germany and translated the Civil Code of the last country into English; published in 1907 it became the standard English version. He first met Sun Yat-sen in America and later became one of his closest collaborators. When Sun was elected President of the Provisional Government set up in Nanking in 1912 Wang became Foreign Minister. Later he was to hold many high cabinet posts both in the Peking regime, serving as Acting Prime Minister in 1922, and later in the Nationalist regime in Nanking, where he was, inter alia, Foreign Minister (1937–40), Secretary-General of the Supreme National Defence Council (1942–6) and a Judge in the International Court of Justice at The Hague (1931–6). He was one of the few Chinese officials whom Morrison held in high esteem.

[3] Wen Ping-chung (d. 1916), Chinese Imperial official. A returned student from America, he was at this time a Secretary in the Ministry of Foreign Affairs. He had previously been a Secretary and Interpreter to Tuan-fang (1861–1911) former Viceroy of Liangkiang at Nanking (1906–9) who was killed by his soldiers while proceeding to take up his post of Acting Viceroy of Szechwan in January 1912. Wen then worked for the republicans in Nanking in the Bureau of Foreign Affairs, and was for this reason criticised by Ts'ai

When the contract was brought to me yesterday I said that I must speak of this to Admiral Tsai the Pacificator, and Lord ffrench said he hoped that I would do so.

It seems to me that on a common aim like this a junction could be effected between the Government and the Railway Commission and much ill feeling be removed.

I would suggest that with your approval both these notes should be translated confidentially by Mr. Ju[1] into Chinese and be handed to the President.

Dr. Sun Wen sent a message to me expressing the hope that I would give the scheme my support. Conscientiously I can do so for I have repeatedly in past years – long before ever I thought of entering the Chinese Government service – urged that this method of railway construction should be introduced into China. Abundant instances could be given to prove that this method of construction has been advantageous in countries so dissimilar as Russia, France, Australia, Africa, Canada and South America.

With all good wishes

Very sincerely yours
[G. E. Morrison]

625. From S. P. Cockerell[2]

[London] 12 July 1913

Private

My dear Doctor,

Many thanks for your letter. It was a real pleasure to me to hear that you had a son and my cable to you was something more than a conventional expression of delight. It pleased me to think how elated you and Mrs Morrison would be, and I share, as I expect you do, the Chinese view that the birth of a son is a thing above all to be rejoiced at. It makes life worth living. News of Chinese politics is very scarce – which is perhaps a blessing considering the misleading stuff some of the newspapers get. Bland is on the

---

T'ing-kan for his shifting loyalties. In 1916 he was assassinated while working as a compradore for a foreign firm in Shanghai. He was the maternal uncle of the three Sung (Soong) sisters, Ai-ling (Mme K'ung Hsiang-hsi), Ch'ing-ling (Mme Sun Yat-sen) and Mei-ling (Mme Chiang Kai-shek).

[1] The message is not printed. Ju Jen-ho (or Ju Jung-hao, as he himself spelt it) was Morrison's Chinese translator and liaison officer in the Presidential Office. An enlarged and revised version of the message drafted by Morrison was published in the *New York Times* on 6 August 1913 over the signature of 'Ts'ai T'ing-kan, Private Secretary to the President'.

[2] Samuel Pepys Cockerell (1880–1915), British diplomat and financial agent. He resigned from the Foreign Office in 1910, and was at this time working as a representative of C. Birch Crisp & Co. He enlisted in the army at the outbreak of the European War, and died in Egypt in March 1915.

move again, both in the *National* and in *The Times*,[1] with his unquenchable desire to sneer. Such articles do have an effect, and it is a great pity *The Times* should allow itself to publish such things. It applauds Sir E. G.[2] for 'saving China from bankruptcy' and then publishes articles calculated to damage Chinese credit. A stockbroker friend of mine came to me yesterday and told me he was worried, as he had just put a friend into New Chinese [Loan] and if the friend saw the *Times* article he was likely to be much perturbed. Things in the City have been as bad as can be, worse, so say greyheaded old men, than they have ever been. There has been one unceasing fall in the price of securities, good as well as bad. [...] There is little prospect of great improvement until next year; some wise men say it will not come for a year. If China begins borrowing again in the open market I think she will find it extremely difficult and she will have to pay very dearly. The only news available as to her position is that for the first six months of 1913 receipts are $51 million against expenditure of $168 showing a deficit of $117 million, and it is said that the $51 million includes $18 million from the Provinces of which only $2 million has actually been received. This of course is ruin if it is going on. Are the Provincial payments coming in any better now that Yuan Shih Kai has some available funds and increasing powers? If so it is a pity we hear nothing about it. What, too, is Sir Robert Dane[3] making of the Salt Gabelle? If he has anything like a satisfactory report to make it might surely be worth while considering the expediency of publishing it. At the same time it is very necessary to consider carefully what is published and what not. The London market is very tricky. It is a great pity the Chinese Govt. have not a Financial Agent here really in touch with the City. It seems that such a man might do much to build up Chinese credit, and to prevent Chinese credit from being upset. The real measure of Chinese credit is our loan, which is essentially and above all others based upon faith in the Chinese Govt. At present, in spite of the five Powers guarantee etc etc of the New Loan, both are being dealt in at the same price (taking coupons into consideration) and that seems to me a hopeful sign for China if she will live up to it. It is very generally considered that China was abominably squeezed over the Reorg[anisation] Loan. The price of issue, at the time it was brought out, was a purely fictitious one not based on business considerations and did great damage to the market at a time when it was little able to stand it. 'If I can buy the Chinese Loan, with its guarantees etc, at a price to yield me £5.10.0 per cent why should I buy –

---

[1] In concert with David Fraser, *The Times* Correspondent in Peking, J. O. P. Bland did his best to paint a black picture of China, aiming at undermining the confidence of British investors. This he did most strongly in an article published in the *National Review*, entitled 'Chinese Loans and the British Investor' (Vol. 61, 1913, p. 869–77), and in a shorter article in a similar vein published in *The Times* on 11 July entitled 'Chinese Borrowings. The British Government and the Investor.'

[2] Sir Edward Grey.   [3] Sir Richard Dane.

which will not yield me as much' was a common question. It did much in this way to bring down the price of everything else. It is a great pity, by the way, that we hear nothing specific of Chinese Railway earnings which I believe are proving so very good. In fact all the good about China is hidden away in a cloud of mystery and silence; while the obviously bad things are advertised far and wide by the pessimists. It is a great pity.

[...]

Yours very sincerely
S. P. Cockerell

July 1913 – October 1914

Although militarily insignificant and politically isolated, the Kuomintang, through the rather empty revolutionary rhetoric of its members, provided the pretext Yüan Shih-k'ai was seeking for a showdown. He chose to strike before his enemies had time to move and form their ranks. Not only did he not punish the assassins of Sung Chiao-jen; but on the contrary, Chao Ping-chün, the chief plotter, after resigning his posts in the cabinet was given the important Military-Governorship of the metropolitan province of Chihli, a position held not long before by Yüan himself. Yüan also removed the four remaining provincial governors of Kuomintang allegiance and installed his own men. This act, aimed at eliminating completely the little influence the Kuomintang had in the southern provinces, compelled the republican forces, though largely dispersed and in great disarray, to put up a fight under the leadership of the dismissed Governor of Kiangsi, Li Lieh-chün. As was to be expected, the republicans proved no match for Yüan's forces, who quickly overran the rebellious provinces of Anhwei, Kiangsu, Kiangsi, Hunan, Kwangtung and Fukien. Nanking, the capital of the first and short-lived Provisional Republican Government under Sun Yat-sen, was sacked by the troops of Chang Hsün, an event which came close to causing an international incident when it was discovered that among the thousands killed were three Japanese. The Kuomintang's attempted uprising in Shanghai proved equally unsuccessful. The fighting, though sporadic, wrought great damage across the provinces. It lasted barely two months, from the second week of July 1913 to the beginning of September of that year, and became known as the 'Second Revolution'.

After this precipitate end, those who could escaped to Japan or to foreign settlements in Shanghai, while a great many were glad either to be bought over or to be allowed to repent. Unable to lay hands on those who had fled overseas, the government endeavoured to round up those who had sought refuge in the foreign concessions. Morrison the Political Adviser, who had earlier worked for the expulsion of Yüan's opponents from the international settlements in Shanghai, now did his best to help his master hunt down the wanted men.

The sequel to the republican debacle is well known. Having defeated his enemies in the field, Yüan Shih-k'ai lost no time in launching an attack on the political front. He proscribed the Kuomintang and forced its members, on pain of persecution and imprisonment, to recant. More than four hundred from both Houses of Parliament were deprived of their parliamentary membership because of their Kuomintang affiliations and connections. Parliament, unable to function through lack of a quorum, was brought to inevitable dissolution although Yüan, shrewd as he was, had manoeuvred to have himself elected President by this body before he showed it his long-nourished contempt. The correspondence here reveals how Yüan's henchmen, even before Parliament was completely dead and properly buried, were already preparing moves to enable him to realise his monarchical ambition.

While this drama was being enacted both surreptitiously and overtly, Morrison made a short visit to England in June 1914. Though it was primarily for private reasons, he tried to justify the visit to his employers by the need 'to see what can be done to remove false impressions due to incorrect statements published in the European press with regard to China and to the policy of the President'. Indeed, as we have already noted, Morrison, with his journalistic background, was particularly sensitive to bad publicity both abroad and in China, since the Peking government and above all Yüan were his special concerns. His desire to find ways to combat or remedy this situation led, on the one hand, to the suggestion of subsidising a foreign news agency, in this case Reuter, with a view to securing more favourable reporting, and on the other, to the censorship measures which Morrison helped to formulate.

In the short time that he was in England, Morrison devoted considerable energy to improving the image of his employers. He gave an interview which, by his account, was, or should have been, read by no less than 'three-and-a-half million people'. He also addressed a large gathering of politicians, financiers and other prominent personalities. He sought in addition to influence opinion through his personal connections and contacts. He risked his own credibility to make his story credible, and indeed more than once spoke with tongue in cheek. Little wonder, therefore, that his detractors became numerous and vociferous. We publish here a semi-literate letter addressed to him by a London domiciled Chinese, illustrating how the man whose appointment had been applauded along the whole spectrum of Chinese opinion had lost much goodwill through his partisanship in less than two years. On the other hand, it can certainly be argued to Morrison's credit that, although by this time his dissatisfaction with his role as Political Adviser to the Chinese President had become widely known, he was able to suppress his private grievances in the interests of duty. But there is no doubt that Morrison, either unaware of the monarchical conspiracy being prepared, or not taking it seriously, inadvertently helped to encourage his august master in his imperial dreams by gilding his public image and thus misleading him about the strength of his own position.

626. From Hsieh Tsan-t'ai

Hong Kong July[1] 1913

My dear Dr. Morrison,

You have not sent me your reply to my last letter?[2]

I am so sorry that civil war has broken out in China and I pray for the sake of China and the Chinese that it will soon be ended. Let us hope that the 'bath of blood' will bring forth men fitted in every way to govern and watch over the destinies of this great Country.

I am confident that you will seize every opportunity to help in quickly ending this fratricidal strife.

There is nothing I so much abhor as to see Chinese killing Chinese in a senseless Civil War.

I sincerely hope that President Yuan Shih Kai will be true to the people who have made him President, and that he will always act constitutionally and keep in mind that great and good man, George Washington, the First President of the United States.

I am sorry for Dr. Sun Yat Sen and his friends, but their down-fall has not surprised me. I could see that it was coming.

I gave Dr. Sun and others friendly advice on different occasions but it appears that my advice has been unheeded. I formed my opinion of these men years ago, and this is why I have studiously avoided all political parties and societies. Ever since the 1895 Affair,[3] I have been working independently, and it has always been my aim to work for union and cooperation amongst the various political parties in the great Movement for freeing the Chinese from their Manchu Tartar yoke.

I belong to no political party, but am only a humble citizen, in spite of the fact that I have been working for twenty five years for the Independence of the Chinese.

I have tried my best to help China and the Chinese and after all, I think it is best to be a humble citizen.

With kindest regards and best wishes and hoping to hear from you soon

Yours very sincerely
Tse Tsan Tai

[1] No day was given, but judging by the contents of the letter, it was after 12 July, the day Li Lieh-chün signalled the beginning of the 'Second Revolution' by declaring at Hukow the independence of Kiangsi.
[2] A reference to Letter No. 607, Hsieh Tsan-t'ai to Morrison, 2 June 1913.
[3] The reference is to the abortive uprising engineered by Sun Yat-sen which took place in Canton on 26 October 1895. Sun managed to escape to Hong Kong and from there to Japan and England where the famous incident of his abduction by the Chinese Legation in London took place in October of the following year.

627. From F. L. Pratt

Shanghai 18 July 1913

My dear Dr. Morrison,

Many thanks for your letter of July 8th.[1] I was really a little worried because I feared that it was possible that my letter containing the code had fallen into the wrong hands.

We are here in the midst of excursions and alarums. To-day I advised Chen[2] to wire to you to arrange that official telegrams of a reassuring nature should be sent here from Peking for distribution to the foreign and Chinese press. You see the position is this: The Kuomintang crowd publish all sorts of telegrams announcing glorious victories for the rebels and that province after province has joined in the movement. This sort of thing is very likely to have some effect in winning over waverers and I really think that a publicity campaign – as the Americans call it – would serve a very important purpose.

As far as I can learn there is no enthusiasm among the Chinese here for the rebels, but as you know there are always a number of people sitting on the fence ready to jump on whichever side seems most desirable. These people would probably be more impressed by official telegrams announcing in moderate language successes gained by the loyalists in Kiangsi and Northern Kiangsu.

Personally I do not believe that the movement will go very far. The rebels are relying upon the assistance of Chang Hsun and Chu Jui and they say that Tiger Hsu's brother[3] at Yangchow has already joined them. It would seem extremely doubtful that Chu Jui will join, and it seems hardly believable that Chang Hsun would join with a mob for which he has so supreme a contempt.

Of course foreign opinion here is dead against the rising. Business has had its end knocked in. There are all sorts of rumours about assistance being given by the Japanese. There must be some fire to account for such volumes of smoke, but it would obviously be impossible for Japan officially to support the rebellion. That Japanese individuals are taking part in the movement seems however to be beyond doubt.

[...]
With best wishes

Yours very sincerely
F. Lionel Pratt

[1] Not found.
[2] Ch'en I-fan. Although his term as Foreign Affairs Commissioner for Kiangsi Province ended officially upon his appointment as Special Commissioner for Tibetan Affairs on 14 June 1913, he was obviously still in Shanghai when this letter was written.
[3] Hsü Pao-chen, younger brother of Hsü Pao-shan.

628. From F. L. Pratt

Shanghai 22 July 1913

Dear Dr. Morrison,

A man came in to see me to-day with some rather extraordinary information which I send on to you for what it may be worth. He is a former satellite of General Po or Pah or whatever he calls himself, I mean the man who was *Tutuh* of Anhui.[1] He says that he has a copy of a plan of campaign supplied to Sun Yat-sen by the Japanese, both military and financial. The man in question wants to sell this information to the Central Government. The blackguard is of course after money mainly, but I think it quite probable that he may have some information that would be valuable to the Government. In times like these one must not be too particular about one's agents and it may be that the Government would care to enter into negotiations with the man. If so please let me know either by letter or wire. [...]

What I was going to wire to you about was the matter of which I spoke in my last. The Kuomingtang papers certainly influence public opinion by their lies about the progress the Southerners are making. If the Government had a Press Bureau here to receive and to distribute to foreign and to Chinese papers official bulletins showing the real position it would do an immense amount of good. This idea is really well worth following up.

Public opinion here is dead against the rebels, I mean Chinese public opinion as well as foreign. Yuan is generally commended for having had the pluck to bring this miserable gang of Settlement skulkers into the open. What we are all hoping now is that he does not adopt any more half measures, but leaves the opposition so badly whipped that it will not dare to whimper for years.

[...]

Yours very sincerely
F. Lionel Pratt

[...]

[1] Po (or Pai) Wen-wei (?1874–1947), Chinese soldier. He took part in the capture of Nanking from the Imperial forces in 1911 and became Acting *Tutu* of his native province of Anhwei in April the following year. He was removed in February 1913 by Yüan Shih-k'ai, who appointed him Special Commissioner of the Kansu and Shensi Border Area, but he refused to take up the post. In fact on the day before this letter was written Po declared Anhwei Province independent, an independence which was however short-lived, and Ni Ssu-ch'ung (q.v.) was ordered three days later, on 27 July, to take over from him the military and civil administration of the province. After the defeat of the republican forces in September, Po fled to Japan with Sun and many of his followers. He re-emerged after the establishment of the Nationalist Government in Nanking in 1928 and figured prominently in the ranks of the diverse anti-Chiang Kai-shek factions within the Kuomintang. For this reason he held only sinecure posts in the Chiang-dominated regime for the remainder of his life.

629. To Ts'ai T'ing-kan

[Peking] 25 July 1913

My dear Admiral,

I still think it would create an excellent impression if the Government were to recognise the validity of contracts signed by the Railway Board[1] under their charter.

That charter was cancelled very properly immediately after the declarations of the foolish and ungrateful Dr. Sun Yat Sen.[2] But the opinion I find everywhere, held at any rate by the British newspapers of Great Britain, who publish today the fact of the Cancellation, is that the Central Government would be well advised to approve of the contract and that the Wai Chiao-pu would be well advised so to notify the British Legation.

The functions of the Railway Board can now be transferred to the Ministry of Communications who can be so instructed.

I would suggest that the Wai Chiao-pu notify the British Legation that the functions of the Railway Board have been transferred to the Chiao tung pu.[3]

Yours very sincerely
[G. E. Morrison]

630. From C. D. Jameson[4] to E. T. Williams

Peking 25 July 1913

Dear Mr Williams,

The following incidents occurred while I was in Shanghai between July 6th and 12th and on July 16th, also in Tientsin on July 22nd, the possible significance of which did not occur to me at the time.

[1] A reference to the railway contract made between the Chinese Government and the British firm of Pauling & Co., and signed by Sun Yat-sen and Lord ffrench. See Letter No. 624, p. 191.
[2] Following the murder of Sung Chiao-jen, Sun Yat-sen made a number of pronouncements. On 26 April he sent a circular telegram to various authorities in China urging the severe punishment of the conspirators in Sung's murder, and on 2 May he sent an appeal through his former teacher, Dr Cantlie (q.v.), asking the people and governments of various countries to stop their banks lending money to support the Peking Government war purpose. Then on 21 July Sun sent another circular telegram demanding the resignation of Yüan Shih-k'ai to avoid civil war. In retaliation Yüan dismissed Sun from his post of Director-General of Railways two days later on 23 July 1913.
[3] Ministry of Communications.
[4] C. D. Jameson (b. 1855), American civil engineer. He was appointed Chief Engineer in connection with the Huai River Conservancy project under the general control of Chang Chien (1853–1926), a Republican politician and entrepreneur who had served as Minister of Agriculture and Forestry and later as Minister of Agriculture and Commerce. This letter, to E. T. Williams, the Secretary of the American Legation in Peking, was given by him to Morrison, doubtless for him to show to Yüan Shih-k'ai.

There were many English speaking Chinese in and out the Astor House in Shanghai, and some of these knew me, at least by name, although unknown to me, and several times, on the dates above mentioned, made conversation with me regarding the proposed Conservancy of the Huai River region. All of these interviews finally touched upon the condition of the Yellow River, the danger of its coming south again, what course it would probably follow, where the break was most liable to occur and what would be the result.[1] As this is a subject to which I have given much thought during the last two years, and as two of these people claimed to have been along the Yellow River lately, near Khaifeng fu, I talked quite freely with them.

I arrived in Tientsin on the morning of July 23rd, and while sitting in the lobby of the Astor House a young Chinese introduced himself to me on the subject of Conservancy and we talked some half an hour. In a few minutes we were on the subject of the possibilities of a break in the Yellow River dykes and the probable results.

In thinking over these interviews I fear there may be some serious result. You understand that it might be a most simple thing to cut the south dyke of the Yellow River, inundate the whole country to the south and break both the Pukow Railway and the Grand Canal. This could be done in one night with dynamite. The leaders of the rebellion are desperate men who are risking all on one chance and would stop at nothing. The Government should take no chances and the Yellow River banks should be most carefully guarded.

I can inform President Yuan of the above facts or you may, whichever you

[1] The breaching of river dykes was a long recognised warfare tactic in both Chinese history and fiction, and the Yellow River in particular had always offered great potential as a destructive weapon because of the immense devastation wrought by the periodic natural breaching of its banks. Its most recent change of course had occurred in July 1855 when it broke out north of K'ai-feng in Honan Province and flowed northwards following the course of the Ta-ch'ing Ho into the Gulf of Pechihli or the Po Hai. One of the consequences was that the Grand Canal, which had been the main route of supply from the rich Yangtse Valley to the Capital, became badly silted up and was greatly handicapped as the main artery it had once been. In spite of repeated efforts to divert water from the Yellow River into the Grand Canal in order to make it navigable again, the Canal never regained its pre-eminent position as a water highway. The direct result was the development of coastal steamship transportation, on which the Government increasingly came to depend for the transport of supplies from the south. This interest led eventually to the founding, under Government sponsorship, of the China Merchants' Steam Navigation Company (Lun-ch'uan chao-shang-chü) in 1872. While the efforts to divert water from the Yellow River failed to revive the Grand Canal, they frequently resulted in the flooding of large areas of rich farmland and the death and suffering of innumerable people living in the large triangular area of Honan, Shantung, Anhwei and Kiangsu, between the old course in the south and the new course to the north. On 9 June 1938, in an attempt to hold back the onrush of the invading Japanese Army after the fall of K'ai-feng four days previously, the banks of the River west of the city were deliberately breached. This drastic measure, though it succeeded in delaying the advance of the enemy, also resulted in great loss of life to the inhabitants.

think best. I consider these interviews more than a coincidence and of a serious nature.

Yours very truly
C. D. Jameson

631. To Ts'ai T'ing-kan

[Peking] 25 July 1913

My dear Admiral,

You will remember that some time ago Mongol emissaries came to Peking making certain proposals regarding the return to China of various Mongol officials and their followers. One of the clauses of the simple conditions proposed was that the agreement should be witnessed by Larson and myself. You will remember that I said I was quite willing to be a witness.

Since then the emissaries returned to Urga, and they are now back in Peking. The result of this work is embodied in the accompanying memorandum. Knowing how overworked you are, I have had this memorandum translated into Chinese by a friend of mine, Mr. Tseng Kuang-chuan,[1] who helped me during many years when I was *Times* correspondent, and who is now at leisure. He is an exceedingly clever man as you know. Thus I send you the memorandum in both Chinese and English.[2] It has taken two days longer to prepare owing to the absence of my Secretary. I hope it may be of some service.

All good wishes to you. Things are looking splendid for the President, and all the Legations I have spoken to are confident of his complete success.

Ever faithfully yours
[G. E. Morrison]

P.S. I am afraid it was not very neatly copied. Please excuse, as I did not want to delay.

Enclosure to Letter No. 631: *Memorandum regarding Mongolia 'and safe conduct to Mongol officials desiring to return to China*

Many of the Mongols who have taken part in the Declaration of Independence of Outer Mongolia, realising now how fatally they have been deluded

---

[1] Tseng Kuang-ch'üan, the grandson of Tseng Kuo-fan (q.v.), and the adopted son of Tseng Chi-tze (1839–90), better known to foreigners as Marquis Tseng, formerly Chinese Minister to France and England (1878–86). Tseng Kuang-ch'üan was Secretary and interpreter to Li Hung-chang during the Boxer settlement negotiations, and Chinese Minister to Korea from 1904 to 1906. He was Grain *Taotai* of Yunnan at the outbreak of the 1911 Revolution, and escaped by way of Indo-China to Peking where, unable to get a job in the new regime, he worked as interpreter and compradore for various concession-seekers. Morrison knew Tseng well from his *Times* Correspondent days, at which time Tseng frequently helped him with Chinese language material. He was a frequent visitor to Morrison's house and was often referred to by Morrison as 'little Tseng' or 'clever sleevedog Tseng' in his Diary. [2] Only the English version is printed here.

by Russian instigation, are eager to return to China. Even among the Ministers and high officials of the Urga Government there are those who still remain loyal to China. If safe conduct were guaranteed him, even a Mongol so active under Russian sway as the ex-hung hutza Toktan tai chi, would return to his district near Western Manchuria, and as he is at present Commander-in-Chief of the Mongol forces in Urga his return would be a serious blow to Russian policy in Mongolia.

Two confidential emissaries have been to see me, both Mongols, both speaking good Chinese. They have just returned from Urga, and are in close touch with Prince Na Yen Tu,[1] the Prince Khalachin, General Li Ting-yu,[2] and others. They are both well known to Mr. Larson, and are regarded by him as trustworthy men. It is unnecessary to point out how great would be the advantage to the Government if an agreement were come to with the Mongols themselves, especially with the prominent Mongols of Urga, and with those Mongols who are controlling bodies of mounted troops now operating between Kwei Hua Cheng and Kalgan and Dolon nor, and if in consequence of that agreement the Chinese troops now in Mongolia could be recalled inside the wall, and be despatched southwards to quell the insurrection in the Yang-tse. That such an agreement is possible I have no doubt.

In the beginning of this year Mongol emissaries from Urga proposed certain conditions, by agreement with which a number of Mongols and their families and following in Urga would return to China. Conditions proposed were easy of acceptance. They referred mainly to the prevention of the cultivation of Mongol lands by Chinese unless with Mongol consent, to the retention by Mongols of their ranks, to the re-building of the Palace and other buildings of Wu tai and the restoration of his rank, to a question of Mongols having their own officials, and to a question of expenses. Virtually the conditions had for their object the guarantee of protection of their lives and property.

The return of these Mongols to China – and every day the number of them is increasing – will have one highly important result. The world will see that Mongols, whom the Russians represented as being clamorous for Russian protection from Chinese oppression, are anxious to escape from that protection and return to their kinsmen. The return will falsify Russian misrepresentations.

[1] Na-yen-t'u, a Mongol Bannerman. He and Liang-pi were the most intransigent members at a meeting called by the Court to decide on the policy towards the revolutionaries after the Wuchang Uprising. He, however, later served the Republic in various high positions, including that of Deputy President of the Senate, member of the Political Consultative Council set up by Yüan in 1914, and member of the National Rehabilitation Council of 1925.

[2] Li T'ing-yü, Chinese soldier. After the outbreak of the 'Second Revolution' he was appointed the Deputy Garrison Commander of Kiukiang, and later became the Garrison Commander of Southern Kiangsi Province.

The Mongols who desire to return to Chinese allegiance are prominent men. Among them is the Prime Minister, Bagada Lama, who some months ago went to Harbin and was compelled by the Russians to return to Urga. He was accompanied by the Bintu wang, who also was ordered by the Russians back to Urga, where shortly afterwards he died, poisoned, it is believed, by the pro-Russian party who knew of his desire to return to China. Another who is anxious to return is the eldest son of Hai san kung, who is the leader of the Pro-Chinese Mongols of Urga.

More important, however, is the actual withdrawal from Urga of Na Bei-leh, the Vice Minister of War in the Government of Urga. He is at present on his way back to China accompanied by his family and his followers. On the 21st July he was at Ude, and telegraphed that he was leaving next day for Pang Chuang, and he asked that arrangements should be made for his safe conduct through the Chinese lines to Kalgan.

At Pang Chuang China has 1500 troops. Na Bei-leh will camp some distance from them, and will not enter their lines until after a guarantee has been given to him of safety for himself and his belongings. Obviously it is of great importance that this guarantee be given, and that he should be given not only safe conduct but be shown every honour.

Na Bei-leh is a Kharchin Mongol whose home is near Bintu wang. He controls in all some 1000 Mongol troops of whom 200 were sent on ahead some time ago. These 200 men have caused much trouble, but the blame rests with the Chinese troops almost as much as with the Mongols.

Some three months ago a force of 200 Chinese soldiers from Kuei Hua Cheng were sent to guard the Telegraph Station. They were badly selected. Mr. Larson was living at Pang Chuang at the time, and he wrote to me and said that the men would do no work, that they would not obey their officers, that there was no discipline. He warned me that the men were quite demoralised, and would certainly run away at the first appearance of any Mongols. And this is exactly what happened. No sooner had Na Bei-leh's 200 men arrived in the neighbourhood of Pang Chuang on their return to Kalgan, than the 200 Chinese soldiers incontinently fled abandoning their stores and ammunition. They had not seen the enemy: they did not fire a shot.

Seeing how easy it was to put the Chinese soldiers to flight, the troops of Na Bei-leh swelled with pride, and began to raid and pillage. They got out of hand, but they will obey the Prince and can be restored to order.

At present the 1500 Chinese soldiers at Pang Chuang are partly cut off from Kalgan. They do not move out of camp. They would be better employed in China, where they understand the country and its conditions.

Na Bei-leh and his followers desire to pass through their lines. Suppose violence were done them and they were robbed or wounded or killed, the effect would be disastrous throughout all Inner Mongolia. On the other hand suppose safe conduct were given them and honour shown them, the effect would be far-reaching. Orders would be issued to the Mongol troops operating between Kwei Hua-Cheng and Kalgan instructing them to remain inactive and they could return home quietly, and the Chinese troops who number a good many thousands could be withdrawn from Mongolia and sent off south to the area of insurrection.

I have been asked by the Mongols to bring the matter to the direct knowledge of His Excellency the President, with a request that instructions may be sent to the Chinese troops on the Mongol frontier to give every help and assistance to Na Bei-leh and his family and retainers to pass safely to Peking so that untoward accidents may be prevented.

I may conclude by saying that General Li Ting-yu the Chief of Staff of Prince Na Yen-tu is fully informed of all the circumstances, but he has gone south somewhat unexpectedly.

These Mongol emissaries, three in number, are by arrangement previously made entitled to their salary and expenses. Their salaries are $200 a month each. There is plenty of money allotted for this service lying in the Bank at Kalgan to the order of Mr. Larson. Since General Li Ting-yu is away I have advised Mr. Larson to pay these men what they are entitled to, and obtain the requisite receipts, which can then be handed to General Li Ting-yu on his return.

632. From Violet Markham[1]

Chesterfield [Derbyshire, England] 25 July 1913

Dear Dr. Morrison,

I am sending a line to say I hope to leave Moscow for Mukden by the Wagon Lits train on Wednesday August 27th. Will you do me a kindness? The papers are full of revolutions and riots in China and all kinds of excitements. These things are invariably exaggerated and so far I am not in the least minded to upset my plans on account of them.

But if you do get involved in a real row (and I understand there is nothing of the 'Gentlemen of the Guard fire first if it please you' spirit about a Chinese upset) perhaps you would send me word to Chang Chung[2] if in

---

[1] Violet Rosa Markham (later Mrs James Carruthers) (1872–1959), British social worker and author. She recorded her visit to China in 1913 in her autobiography *Return Passage* (London, 1953): 'In spite of poverty, dirt and a standard of life we should regard as deplorable I felt that life in China as I saw it in 1913 approximated much more truly to the ideal of democracy than anything which existed in England and America' (pp. 112–13).... 'In the autumn of 1913...the Chinese Republic, under its vigorous President, Yuan Shih-kai, was eighteen months old. Europeans I met spoke gloomily of the new regime, but whatever its failures it appears in retrospect as a halcyon period of peace and prosperity compared with all that was to follow' (pp. 114–15).

[2] Ch'ang-ch'un was a town in Kirin Province in Manchuria on the Mukden–Harbin Railway. In 1932 its name was changed to Hsin-ching when it became the capital of the 'Manchukuo' Government. It reverted to its original name in 1945.

your opinion it's better not to come south. In that case I would go on to Vladivostock and so to Japan.

But I am not nervous and hope nothing of the kind will be necessary. Still if there *is* trouble I know itinerant ladies are not very welcome personalities in a country.

I hope the son and heir flourishes. I am looking forward so much to seeing you again. Kind regards to Mrs. Morrison and yourself

Sincerely yours
Violet Markham

633. From Sahara Tokusuke

Shanghai 30 July 1913

My dear Dr. Morrison,

In viewing the present situation I advocated no compromise but the necessity of fighting out the dispute to the bitter ends. And Yuan did by this time. Then the other side has almost totally collapsed.

I do not believe in the Republic of China. I do believe in proper constitutional monarchy, as I told you in the beginning of 1912. If Yuan is really wishing to have a strong China it is much better for him to see a good opportunity and ask Hsuantung[1] to become the Emperor of China again and Yuan should be content with the Imperial Chancellor! If so he will be noted down in history as a good and loyal subject of his master. Human life is quite a short duration. To secure a strong China with a stable government it is much better to readopt the Constitutional Monarchy. Even with the great Tseng Kuo-fang[2] he did not usurp the Throne, though he was able to do so

---

[1] The reign (1909–11) title of P'u-yi (1906–67), the last Emperor of the Manchu Dynasty. The son of Tsai-feng, younger brother of the Kuang-hsü Emperor Tsai-t'ien (1871–1908), P'u-yi, not yet three, was made Emperor upon Kuang-hsü's death, but was forced to abdicate on 12 February 1912. On 1 July 1917 he was restored to the throne in a *coup d'état* staged by Chang Hsün, but the melodrama lasted barely a week. In October 1924 he was made to vacate the Palaces within the Forbidden City on the order of General Feng Yü-hsiang and became a refugee in the Japanese Legation in Peking, from which he escaped to Tientsin in February the following year. In November 1931, with the assistance of the Japanese Secret Service chief, Doihara Kenji, he escaped to Manchuria where he became the Head of the Puppet Government of 'Manchukuo' set up by the Japanese on 1 March 1932. After the Japanese surrender in August 1945, P'u-yi became a prisoner of the Soviet occupation forces and in August 1950 was handed over to the Chinese Government. After a prison term during which he served also as a gardener, he was released in 1959, and later worked with the National Political Library and Historical Materials Research Committee. His autobiography, said to have been written while he was undergoing re-education, is entitled *Wo-ti ch'ien-pan-sheng* (*The First Half of my Life*), appearing in an English translation published in Peking (1964–5) under the title *From Emperor to Citizen: The Autobiography of Aisin-Gioro Pu Yi*.

[2] Tseng Kuo-fan (1811–72), Chinese Imperial official and Viceroy. He was said to have rejected suggestions made to him to seize the reins of Government from the Manchus during the Taiping Revolution (1850–66). On the contrary, he helped to save the Manchu

at that time, if he ever has chosen. The reason why Tseng Kuo-fang thought it better to be loyal to his Imperial master was that the system is the best to adapt a monarchy.

China has too much of debts but once everything undesirable be properly cleared it is not much to be anxious to make China rich as it used to be.

[...]

Yours sincerely
T. Sahara

634. To C. D. Bruce

[Peking] 1 August 1913

My dear Bruce,

You are having stirring times in Shanghai. The Government has every reason to be well satisfied both with the Municipal Council and with the Consular Body and as a matter of fact is well satisfied.

[...]

The President cannot understand Japanese action in this crisis. He asks why are the Japanese papers so hostile to him? Why are so many Japanese taking part in the Revolution? Messages from Hongkong stated that nearly 400 Japanese are associated with the Kwantung rebels. The outgoing Minister, Ijuin, and the incoming Minister, Yamaza, both protest that the policy of Japan towards China has undergone no change, but it is very significant that the paper which has been most vehement in calling upon Japan to make a change is the *Mainichi*. It is the paper which most strenuously attacked Ijuin and has urged upon the Japanese Government to make the change. Yamaza arrived in Peking last Saturday and he brought with him in his private Car the correspondent of the *Mainichi*.[1] Surely there is something suspicious about that.

With all good wishes to you

Very sincerely yours
[G. E. Morrison]

Dynasty. An arch-conservative, he was idolised by Chiang Kai-shek and his teachings and the philosophy of the Ming neo-Confucian scholar Wang Yang-ming (1472–1528) were the tenets of the New Life Movement Chiang launched in February 1934, in which blind obedience to one's superiors was held to be the cardinal virtue.

[1] The particular correspondent referred to has not been identified, but the regular correspondent of the *Osaka Mainichi* in Peking at this time was Teshima Sutematsu (1863–1924) who had been the paper's correspondent in Peking since 1905, and held the post until 1915. He had previously been a consular official in China.

635. From C. D. Bruce

Shanghai 1 August 1913

My dear Morrison,

Your letter and enclosures[1] to hand.

When you get this the back of the trouble round here will be broken. Our swashbucklers have fled or are going.[2]

They have been treated perhaps better than they deserved, but the reason that guided those in authority mainly was our fear for retaliation upon defenceless foreigners in the interior.

It has been a strenuous fortnight and Shanghai bombarded hardly knows itself.

There has been no humbug about the danger and it might have been far worse.

So far as the North is concerned the whole situation was saved by the attitude of the ships who covered the Arsenal.

Had the latter place fallen I would not like to say what would have happened. Yuan owes the garrison a deep debt of gratitude. The aftermath round here will cause considerable trouble and danger unless handled with tact and firmness.

It would be advisable to give the Consular body control of a 5 mile zone, *pro-tem* any how: within that, disarm all troops of any kind or keep them out.

Whether Chapei should come under Municipal control later on is a detail. The local so called armed Chapei Volunteers and Police are the present danger.

The Japanese Admiral in supreme command has been rather a pill.[3] The other Admirals naturally kept away. The whole of the South wants a concerted and firm control and Yuan should make Nanking a strong fortified base for some time to come.

The sooner he gets a police force in being the better for the country, so tell me when I shall be wanted!

Am rather short of sleep otherwise well as I hope you both are.

Always yours sincerely
C. D. Bruce

[1] Not printed.
[2] The reference is to revolutionaries, Ch'en Ch'i-mei and his followers.
[3] The reference is to Nawa Matahachirō (1863–1928), at the time referred to Commander of Japan's Third Fleet (1912–14). He had taken part in both the Sino-Japanese and Russo-Japanese Wars and later became Commander-in-chief of the Second Fleet (1915), of Yokosuka Naval Base (1917) and was made a full admiral in 1918. His reputed drinking habits combined with his government's instructions to him to assist the defeated revolutionaries had presumably made him unattractive to someone of Bruce's political sympathies.

636. To Ts'ai T'ing-kan

[Peking] 5 August 1913

My dear Admiral,

I have received from Mr. Ju a message which he has asked me to put into telegraphic form which is to be sent in your name to the *New York Times*.[1] I have accordingly written out a message having altered the draft somewhat so as to make it what I believe will be more acceptable to American readers. I understand this kind of work because it has been my special study for many years. We could not in the message put in names like Li Hsun,[2] Ou-Yang Wu,[3] Cheng Ting-hsun[4] and others without explaining who they are. In my message I have put things in as favourable a light as I can.

[...]

Then there is another point, now that I am writing to you, which I may speak to you about. Large rewards have been offered for Huang Hsing, Chen Chi-mei and others. So far Sun Yat Sen's name has not been mentioned. You know nothing kills like ridicule. Would it not make Sun Yat Sen look ridiculous if a reward were offered for him not of a high amount, but of a very small amount, say $150 Mex. Such an announcement would excite amusement all over the world and would show the contempt which the Government have for this misguided man. On Friday as soon as I heard that he had left for Hong Kong I wrote to the Minister of Foreign Affairs urging that the British Government should at once be approached with a

---

[1] The message is not printed. An enlarged and revised version of the message, drafted by Morrison, was published on the front page of the *New York Times* on 6 August 1913 over the signature of 'Ts'ai T'ing-kan, Private Secretary to the President', and under the heading 'Will Never Rest till Revolt is Crushed, says Yuan Shih-kai in Message to *Times*'.

[2] Li Ch'un (1871–1920), Chinese soldier. A Division Commander under Feng Kuo-chang (q.v.), he led the northern forces against the southern republicans in Kiangsi after the outbreak of the 'Second Revolution', and in September 1913 replaced Ou-yang Wu, whose forces he had defeated, as Military Governor of Kiangsi Province. In August 1917 upon Feng Kuo-chang's becoming Acting President of the Republic, he took over Feng's post of Military Governor of Kiangsu Province, and until his death in October 1920 held the lower Yangtse for the Chihli Clique of warlords of which he was a leading member.

[3] Ou-yang Wu, Chinese soldier. A graduate of the Shikan Gakkō, he was Special Military Commissioner of Kiangsi Province after the outbreak of the 'Second Revolution'. He became Acting *Tutu* in June 1913, and was formally elected by the Provincial Assembly of Kiangsi as *Tutu* on the day Li Lieh-chün declared the independence of the province at Hukow. He fled after his forces were defeated by those of Li Ch'un, who took Nan-ch'ang on 15 August 1913. He was later apprehended, but was released after he recanted.

[4] Ch'en T'ing-hsün, leader of the Secret Society at Kiukiang. He was set up by his followers as a local military commander, at the outbreak of the 'Second Revolution', and was later appointed by the Peking Government as Garrison-Commander of Nan-k'ang in Kiangsi Province on 1 August 1913, four days before this letter was written. He then became Garrison-Commander of Northern Kiangsi, a post he held until May the following year.

request that Sun Yat Sen should not be permitted to land in Hong Kong since he was engaged in open rebellion against a country friendly to England.
With best wishes

Very sincerely yours
[G. E. Morrison]

637. To Ts'ai T'ing-kan

[Peking] 5 August 1913

My dear Admiral,

I do not know whether you have read the letter that was sent to me by Mr. Ju as a proposed draft for a telegram to the *New York Times*. You will notice in the draft as amended by me that I have left out all reference to 'China's bankruptcy'. I cannot urge too strongly the unwisdom of ever making any reference from an official source as to the bankruptcy of the country. I thought carefully over the telegram and I hope you will approve of it. Just as I was writing to you I was interrupted and I forgot to note this.

Very sincerely yours
[G. E. Morrison]

Have you seen the Budget in 14 volumes. It is a quite extraordinary compilation, the most absurd budget ever published.[1]

638. To Ts'ai T'ing-kan

[Peking] 19 August 1913

My dear Admiral,

I send you the extract from the speech made by Lord Morley with regard to Tibet.[2] Obviously the procedure now proposed by the British Government, namely of a Conference between the Chinese and Tibetans under British auspices, has developed from the unfortunate act of China in appealing to the Government of India to mediate with regard to Tibet, as stated in the third sentence. I assume that this statement is correct. If it is not, the statement ought to be challenged.

[...]

A long telegram sent by Mr Wearne to London reviewing the rebellion

[1] A reference to the first budget produced by the Republican Government. It was held to ridicule for its irrelevance and voluminous detail, which was quite unrelated to the actual financial situation.

[2] The extract (not printed) was from a speech made during a debate on Persia and Tibet in the British House of Lords on 28 July 1913, the full text of which is printed in *Parliamentary Debates (Lords)* 1913, Vol. XIV, pp. 1436-8. Morley, who was then Lord President of the Council, after reviewing the developments in Tibet since the Chinese Revolution, as he saw them, told the House that a tripartite conference between China, India and Tibet was soon to commence in Simla as a result (and this was the 'third sentence' mentioned in Morrison's letter) of an appeal by the Chinese and Tibetans to the Government of India to mediate.

and Japanese participation therein has been telegraphed back in full to Tokyo and to Peking. The Japanese Government are busy once more in giving explanations of conduct which is very difficult to explain. The telegram has had, I am sure, an excellent effect, for being sent to a British Agency it laid special stress on the injury being done to British trade and to Hongkong by the agitation of leaders in the rebellion who are now finding sanctuary in Japan.

With all good wishes

Very sincerely yours
[G. E. Morrison]

Enclosure to Letter No. 638: *Telegram of 15 August 1913 sent to Reuter's Agency, London*[1]

Ijuin left today after distinguished service China great honour Chinese other Guards Honour representatives every foreign Legation now Peking departure widely regretted for despite assurances given Japanese Government impossible ignore mistrust widely felt among Chinese foreigners at recent change policy Japan stop Attitude Japanese Government admittedly correct but fact cannot overlooked that with every movement preceding and during recent Rebellion Japanese provided arms Japanese associated intimately every leader in every engagement even now deposed Tutu Liliehchun Kiangsi who prime mover rebellion in flight to south province is accompanied his Japanese adviser Captain Aoyagi[2] no doubt large proportion Japanese associated disturbance adventurers but in view powerful control which Japanese Government exercises over nationals in China it considered certain they could not taken this active part had their Government desired prevent stop At present most militant leaders among rebels finding sanctuary Japan where Sunyatsen noisiest agitator in interviews declares will continue campaign until Yuanshihkai down fallen as downfell Manchu dynasty stop What foreign diplomatists Peking wonder is what advantage revolution been to Japan what advantage to Japan to succour rebel leaders what advantage to England

[1] This telegram was drafted by Morrison, who wrote: 'Wearne came in. The Japanese had had his (that is mine) telegram of Aug. 15 cabled back to him. It had created a bad impression for Japan in Europe said Matsudaira.' (Matsudaira Tsuneo (1877–1949) was then Second Secretary in the Japanese Legation in Peking.) This telegram was enclosed not with his letter of 19 August but of 20 August, to Ts'ai T'ing-kan (not printed).

[2] Aoyagi Katsutoshi (1879–1934), Japanese soldier and adventurer. He had taken part in the Russo-Japanese War, and after retiring from the army in 1910 devoted himself to subversive activities against neighbouring governments under the slogan of Pan-Asianism, which had become the creed of the Japanese extreme right. In 1912 he became an adviser to Li Lieh-chün, the *Tutu* of Kiangsi, and took part in the 'Second Revolution'. He escaped with Li to Japan after its failure and set up a military academy in Tokyo for the training of Chinese students, among whom was Chiang Kai-shek. In 1915 Aoyagi was to return to China to lend his support to the revolts in Inner Mongolia and western Manchuria.

British traders Hongkong that Chinese agitators from sanctuary in Japan are stirring strife first in Yangtse valley now Canton to detriment British trade vast injury Hongkong.

639. From Sahara Tokusuke

Shanghai 26 August 1913

Dear Dr. Morrison,

Many thanks for yours of Aug. 21st.[1] Nanking is still fighting against the Northerners but it will soon be ended.

The other day I had a very interesting conversation with a prominent Chinese who is quite a Republican. He told me both Dr. Sun Yat sen and Huang Hsin are having no more influence amongst the Kuomingtang and their career is finished, especially it is the case with Huang Hsin. China, he told me, will become Egypt and Yuan Shih-kai be Emir Pasha and nothing else.[2] China's financial autonomy is now impossible. Therefore he would not stay in China any more but will spend his life abroad. He said quite sadly that his cause was defeated and lost for ever.

Such a short conversation with a prominent Kuomingtang gentry who has nothing to do with the present rebellion was very interesting to hear. There is something in it, anyhow, I should say.

I do not expect you will give me any view at all as you hold a position in Peking. However I write you not expecting any view of yours but simply to forward you anything useful for your reference, as a student of Chinese problems.

If there be any good opportunity it is the best for Yuan Shih-kai to restore Emperor Hsuan tung to his throne because such will make the only difficult elements in China the Loyalists impossible to say anything against him. A few friends who have more or less loyalists tendency have told me that if Yuan will adopt that policy their cause will be lost. I write all these confidentially, as you know of.

I am only a mere student of Chinese problem and from my long experience in China I write this for your reference.

With the kindest regards to you and your good lady and your baby

Yours very sincerely
T. Sahara

[1] Not found.
[2] Sahara must have meant Ismail Pasha (1830–95) who, as Khedive of Egypt (1863–79), became the prey of European concession-hunters and swindlers on account of his grandiose projects and extravagant tastes. This led eventually to the sale, in 1875, of Egypt's share of the Suez Canal, to foreign intervention and the subsequent loss of his country's independence.

640. From W. W. Rockhill

Litchfield, Connecticut, U.S.A. 31 August 1913

My dear Morrison,

[...]

I have had rather strenuous times since arriving in Constantinople, though we are not directly interested in political affairs in Turkey and can watch with some complacency the mess that Europe has managed to make of Balkan affairs, and the collapse of European control in that part of the world. Conditions in Turkey are very like those in China, the same causes have brought about the same effects and may have the same consequences – though in China I am inclined to think that the end may be brighter – much brighter than in Turkey.

The Wilson administration has removed from the diplomatic service all the older men to make place for politicians of its party to pay off political debts. My successor – a New York Jew of German birth,[1] has been appointed, and I have only to continue in the service long enough to go back to Constantinople to present my letters of recall, pack up my belongings and leave – all of which will be accomplished by the middle of November – after which I shall have to find a means of earning a livelihood (not an easy task for a man of my age for what knowledge and experience I have is of little use except to the government). I have one or two schemes in hand but I do not know if they will work out. The one I like the most – though it will only give me temporary work – is to visit Mongolia, China and Japan and study present conditions and future prospects but I must first ascertain if I can get the money support that the trip will require, and if the public is willing to have my letters. I am greatly disturbed over the present policy (or rather lack of policy) of the U.S. as regards China and the Far East – though I feel convinced it cannot long endure. I think I can form an impartial opinion on most matters in China and perhaps assist in creating a new current and a stronger one in favour of China – Yuan's China, not Sun Wen's. If anything comes of my scheme I will let you know as I shall want to see you a good deal if I come back to Peking. Please keep all this to yourself for the time being as my scheme may not materialize.

I am sorry your work is not proving satisfactory, but with Orientals one must expect just what you are finding. I also recall old Sir Robert's[2] remark that what success he had had with the Chinese was the result of his persistent

---

[1] The reference is to Henry Morgenthau (1856–1946), American lawyer and diplomat. Born in Germany of Jewish parents, he migrated to the United States with his family when he was nine years old. He succeeded Rockhill as American Ambassador in Constantinople in 1913, holding the post until 1916. Among his several volumes of autobiography is *Ambassador Morgenthau's Story* (New York 1918), recording his three years' term in Turkey.

[2] Sir Robert Hart (1835–1911), who had been British Inspector General of the Imperial Chinese Maritime Customs from 1863 until his death.

efforts in a given and never changing direction – or words to that effect – I feel sure you can and will do likewise.

Did you ever receive a copy of the book Hirth and I brought out through the Academy of Sciences of St Petersburg?[1] I sent it to you or rather asked that a copy be sent you directly from the Academy. I am working at my spare moments on a supplementary work to this one – it is on the Relations and Trade of China with the Eastern Archipelago, and the coasts of the Indian Ocean during the fourteenth century (the Yüan dynasty). I have it already in pretty good shape.[2]

I hope you have not had to sell your library – I know how you loved it, you would miss it terribly not only now but later on in life.

[...]

Always very affectionately yours

W. W. Rockhill

641. To C. D. Bruce

[Peking] 4 September 1913

My dear Bruce,

I spoke to the President this morning about calling you up to Peking at the end of the month. There will be no difficulty about this. I would suggest your getting together all the information you can with regard to the suppression of disturbances and your suggestions so that you can be prepared to answer any questions that the President may put to you. In fact as I pointed out to the President one of the advantages of your coming would be that he could cross examine you for his own information.

Very sincerely yours

[G. E. Morrison]

642. From J. B. Capper[3]

S.S. *Kutwo* – approaching Shanghai 10 September 1913

Dear Mrs. Morrison – and Morrison,

We send you both our most hearty thanks for all your kindness and lavish

---

[1] Friedrich Hirth (1845-1927), American scholar and for 27 years an employee of the Imperial Chinese Maritime Customs (1870-97). He became a Professor of Chinese History at Columbia University in 1902 holding the chair there until 1917. The book referred to here, of which Rockhill was co-author, is entitled *Chao Ju-kua: his work on the Chinese and Arab trade in the twelfth and thirteenth centuries, entitled Chu-fan chih* (St Petersburg, 1911).

[2] This was published in Vol. XIV of *T'oung Pao* (1913), entitled 'Notes on the Relations and Trade of China with the Eastern Archipelago and the Coasts of the Indian Ocean during the Fourteenth Century'.

[3] John Brainerd Capper (1855-1936), British journalist. He was the Principal Assistant Editor of *The Times* from 1884 until his retirement in 1912. He visited China in 1913 and was a guest of Morrison's in Peking. It was Capper who undertook after Morrison's

hospitality, which did so much to make our stay in Peking the delightful time that it was from beginning to end.

Our journey to Hankow was not specially comfortable and we often sighed for the luxury we had left behind us, but it was interesting and we arrived only half an hour late. The bridges that had been washed away were a great sight as we passed. We caught Sunday night's Jardine steamer and came right on.

The port of Nanking is a sad sight – all in ruins and roofless – burnt out. It was like the pictures of the Messina earthquake.[1] We passed close in shore and saw a lot of Chang Hsun's blue uniformed desperadoes drawn up on shore and many other troops. We have had the accounts of European eye witnesses of the nameless horrors attending the sacking of Nanking – after Chang Hsun had given a written promise to a European deputation that nothing of the kind should occur. Dr. – (I forget his name) Macklin,[2] I think, a Nanking resident – went to him to complain and taxed him with his breach of faith holding his written guarantee up to him and he said, I am told, 'Yes it's all true enough: you can take me out and shoot me!' Three Japanese ships were there besides the British *Flora* and other war vessels. We would have landed to see things closer if we could; but we did not stop at the port itself, but some water higher up the river. I am told that Yuan-Shih-kai is bitterly hated, in all these parts. But I had better not meddle in domestic 'politics'.

Again we thank you heartily. I hope you are all three quite well and enjoying your Peking home. Our kind remembrances please to Miss MacGlade.[3]

Yours very sincerely
J. B. Capper

---

death and on Valentine Chirol's suggestion, to edit Morrison's Diary for publication by the London publishing firm of Constable. The first volumes of the edited Diary for the years 1899 to 1901, when submitted to the trustees of Morrison's estate (of whom Sir Miles Lampson (q.v.), later Lord Killearn, then British Minister in China, was one) were considered by them too politically sensitive to be published at that time, and the project on which Capper had spent some six years of his retirement was abandoned. Nanking, which Capper describes in his letter, fell to the troops of Chang Hsün on 1 September 1913.

[1] The reference is to the earthquake which occurred on 28 December 1908, totally destroying this Sicilian city and killing almost 80,000 people, half the city's population.

[2] W. E. Macklin, Canadian missionary and author, the first member of the American Foreign Christian Missionary Society to be sent to China. He was supposed to have been an adviser to Sun Yat-sen while Sun was President of the Provisional Government in Nanking.

[3] Miss A. B. MacGlade, at this time Morrison's secretary.

643. To W. Ming[1]

[Peking] 13 September 1913

Dear Mr. Ming,

I have been so overworked lately that I have, I am sorry to say, neglected to acknowledge the receipt of the photograph you were good enough to send me. It is an excellent photograph but the most careful scrutiny cannot disclose any traces of any Mongol features.

I regret to say that the Marquis Chu is at present not in Peking. Various enquiries are being made for his address by his anxious creditors. Mr. Hu Han-ming,[2] whose name you have sent me, is a Cantonese. I was not aware that he was any relation to the Ming dynasty. If so, your family have no reason to be proud of this disreputable journalist. Dr. Sun Yat-sen has a great friend in London, Dr. James Cantlie of Harley Street.[3] You no doubt, could obtain his address from him and he would also be able to inform you whether in his opinion Dr. Sun Yat-sen would support your claims to the throne of the Ming Emperors. Dr. Sun Yat-sen is understood to have somewhat Republican views and to have opposed the Manchu dynasty, but I do not know if he has declared himself as an avowed opponent of the Ming dynasty.

It is kind of you to promise not to forget me should you recover the throne of your Ancestors. Lately a son has been born to me and it would indeed be a great pleasure if I could bequeath to him a marquisate.

Again thanking you for the photograph,

I am

Very faithfully yours
[G. E. Morrison]

[1] This letter is in reply to two letters from William Ming dated 5 February 1913 (printed as Letter No. 571, p. 83) and 21 August 1913 (not printed). In this last letter, Mr. Ming wrote: 'Some time ago I spoke to a Chinaman who told me that...the Government of China must have in their possession money or estate formerly belonging to the person, who I first introduced to you in my narrative, as one who was called the Marquis, my grandfather. This information you may be sure has whetted my appetite in this matter – I must do something further.' 'China,' he observed, 'by the papers, seems still to be in a state of chaos and unrest and I have no doubt it will remain so until someone with European strength and enlightenment can be found to restore peace and prosperity to the country – I am ready to do my best in this! or to assist others to that end.' He also asked Morrison to send him 'a photo of, or the actual crest of the Ming Dynasty'.

[2] The family name of 'Hu Han-ming' (Hu Han-min) who had just been dislodged as the Military Governor of Kwangtung and at the time a refugee in Japan, was 'Hu' and not 'Ming', of which Mr Ming was obviously unaware.

[3] James (later Sir James) Cantlie (1851–1926), British medical practitioner. He first went to China in 1887 and was Dean of the College of Medicine in Hong Kong (1889–96), where he had taught Sun Yat-sen. He returned to England in 1896 and set up a practice in Harley Street, round the corner from the Chinese Legation in Portland Place where Sun Yat-sen had been abducted by Manchu officials on 11 October 1896, and Cantlie had helped to secure his release. Dr Cantlie was a consulting surgeon to the Seamen's

644. From Liang Cheng[1]

Hong Kong 17 September 1913

Dear Dr. Morrison,

You will be interested to know the action of President Yuan in the execution of the Police Commissioner Chen King Wa[2] of Canton is highly applauded by all classes of Cantonese high and low. This shows we have in the President a strong man thoroughly understanding the peculiar condition of Quantung provinces. We are living in a highly troublesome time – those republican cranks, pretenders of patriots, but really every one of them have their selfish aims – thinks China since a republic affords them every liberty to disturb the power of the country to defy the commands of the Central Government for the list [least] little thing that doesn't please their foolish and inexperienced heads. The only way to teach them subordination and prevent further treason is whole sale execution. The merchants and better class of the people are thoroughly sick of these peace-disturbers. If the President will continue to show a strong hand – even arbitrary action in that line – it will be welcomed. Such action may seem strange to European civilization. I am the last person to advocate the suppression of individual and judicial rights. But one must not forget we are Chinese and *must* be treated accordingly.

I am living here temporarily on account of the unsettled condition in the main land and principally on account of my children's schooling. Whenever I can be of any service to you please command me.

Yours sincerely
Chentung Liang Cheng

Hospital Society, and the founder and first President (1921-3) of the Royal Society of Tropical Medicine and Hygiene.

[1] Liang Cheng, otherwise known as Sir Chentung Liang, Chinese diplomat. He was knighted in his capacity of First Secretary to Chang Yin-huan on a mission to England in 1897. Liang was Chinese Minister to the United States (1902-7) and to Germany (1910-12). He retired to live in Hong Kong after the establishment of the new regime in China.

[2] The Cantonese pronunciation of Ch'en Ching-hua (d. 1913), Chinese Imperial official. A *chü-jen* or Provincial Graduate, he had served under the Manchus as a magistrate in various districts of Kwangsi Province, and joined the staff of Chang Ming-ch'i, when Chang became the Viceroy of Liangkwang at Canton in October 1910. As Commissioner of Police, Ch'en was suspected of conspiring with the republicans who had appointed him to the position. He was executed by Lung Ch'i-kuang when Lung was appointed by Yüan Shih-k'ai to succeed Ch'en Chiung-ming (q.v.) as *Tutu* of Kwangtung in August 1913. Long after his death Ch'en was remembered by the residents of Canton for his energetic measures against bandits, ruffians and gamblers, and for his unusual integrity.

645. To Sahara Tokusuke[1]

Peking 26 September 1913

Dear Mr. Sahara,

Many thanks for your letter of the 25th of August. Your suggestions are certainly startling and I do not know whether you are speaking jocularly or seriously when you suggest that the Emperor Hsuantung should be restored to the throne.

All Englishmen here take a very serious view indeed of the Japanese action in provoking this disturbance in the Yangtse Valley which has so seriously interfered with British trade. Surely the dismemberment of China, which is now being worked for by so large a number of Japanese, cannot be to the ultimate advantage of Japan and certainly such action spells only disaster to Great Britain which is the Ally of Japan. Japanese took part in the defence of Nanking – that is now officially admitted, but the people who are punished are the Chinese because they are not sufficiently strong to resent such action.

I do not know what opinion you have formed about the Changli incident[2] but I am told confidentially that the reports to Europe by the foreign Legations in Peking stigmatise the killing of the five Chinese Police as a brutal act of murder. Not a single shot was fired by the Chinese. Some of the Chinese who were killed were lying down. Travellers from Japan bring back most alarming reports as to the growth of the revolutionary movement in Japan. One prominent foreign official who has been to investigate on the spot has offered to wager that within 5 years there will be a revolution in Japan and he has formed the opinion that Japan's policy of provocation in China is designed to divert attention from the serious conditions in Japan itself. I have no idea what truth there can be in this. I tell it to you very confidentially and would like to know your opinion. For some time past people have been asking why is it that every Chinese who comes back from Japan comes back a revolutionary, while a very large proportion acquire in Japan views that are really anarchist? Who has influenced them in these views?

Please treat what I have told you in strict confidence.
With kind regards

Very sincerely yours
[G. E. Morrison]

[1] This letter was probably never sent, for it has written across it 'Cancelled' in Morrison's hand.
[2] The incident referred to took place on 11 September 1913 at Ch'ang-li on the Peking–Mukden Railway, south of Shanhaikwan in Chihli Province.

646. To Ts'ai T'ing-kan

[Peking] 26 September 1913

My dear Admiral,

[...]

The day before yesterday I had a visit from Na Beileh who is actually the vice-minister of War in the present Urga Government. As you know, largely owing to the mediation of Mr. Larson, he has returned to China together with his followers. Orders given by the President ensured him safe conduct and a cordial reception on his returning to the Chinese lines. So impressed has he been with his reception that he is anxious now to bring quickly back to China the numerous followers of his who have been waiting outside the Chahar district to see how their Prince had been received. Today I had a visit from another Mongol,[1] an intelligent young man with an excellent knowledge of Chinese who is a Secretary in the Home Office in Urga. He only left Urga on the 11th of September and has come round to Peking via Siberia. He is the eldest son of the Hai San Kung, who is the leader of the pro-Chinese party in Urga. Important information has been brought back by him but he has to act with extreme caution for fear that the knowledge that he has returned to China and that his father is anxious to return may induce the Russians to impose difficulties upon his father. He asks that certain treatment should be accorded to him.[2] To make quite clear what he requires he has written out in Chinese the proposals which he desires to bring before the notice of the High Authorities. In a separate sheet enclosed in this letter I roughly mention what he has done and some information that he has brought.[3] No doubt you would be so kind as to see that it is brought before the notice of the President, because it seems very important that the Mongol Government in Urga should be weakened as quickly as possible by the secession of many of its followers.

Just now I have returned from seeing Mr. Suttor[4] off by the train. Many Japanese were at the station. Every day we English people have the conviction forced upon us that the Japanese are endeavouring to create disturbances in China in order to divert attention from the very serious condition of affairs now prevailing in Japan. It is as certain as anything can be that there will be a revolution in Japan within measurable time. One high autho-

[1] Hai Yung-pu.
[2] According to the memorandum (not printed) which Morrison wrote about the visit, among the conditions Hai-san-kung laid down for his return to China were a promotion in rank and an increase in allowance, a large residence and travelling expenses to Peking. Absolute secrecy was to be maintained with regard to these arrangments.
[3] Not printed.
[4] John Bligh Suttor (b. 1859), an Australian official who since 1903 had been Trade Commissioner for the New South Wales Government in East Asia, stationed in Kobe, Japan. He had previously worked as Resident Engineer on the New South Wales Railways for over twenty years.

rity who has just come back from Japan tells me that he is prepared to wager that within five years there will be a revolution in Japan. The Emperor[1] has lost his sanctity. He is no longer revered by the people as a god. Education has grown amazingly and Japanese who before took no interest in their public affairs are now demanding that they should be given a voice in the government of their own country: that they who are the tax payers should know why they are being taxed, for what purpose the taxes are being applied and how far they are being wisely applied. Speaking broadly, there are 53 million people in Japan, of whom one and a half million only have the right to vote – less than 3%. The present excitement in Japan is being engineered by the military party who are the conservative party who desire to see the retention of things as they are, in order to divert the attention of those Japanese who, discontented with things as they are, are demanding the removal of the present Government, the effecting of reforms, adequate representation and reduction of the enormous burdens of expenditure upon arms and armaments. It is no exaggeration to say that the country is on the verge of bankruptcy. Of their 275,000,000 of foreign debts more than half are owed in Great Britain and in Germany and every interest in those two countries must be used to prevent Japan embarking upon a War of adventure in China which would finally wreck her finances and bring ruin to her country.

This evening I am sending home a message to the European papers regarding Japan, for it is only by the influence of public opinion as expressed in the European papers that Japan can be compelled to alter the policy upon which she is now embarking in China. The growth of feeling against Japan among all countries is really a marked feature. The Prime Minister of Australia[2] in a public speech has declared that in the event of war between Japan and America Australia would range herself on the side of America. Australians view with alarm this aggressive movement of Japan in China for such movements interfere with trade and commerce in which British, and to an increasing extent the Australian section of the British people, are vitally interested.

[1] Yoshihito (1876-1926), the third son of the Meiji Emperor Mutsuhito (1852-1912), succeeded his father in 1912 as the Taishō Emperor. His mental illness, which was already serious long before his enthronement in 1915, became so grave that his son Hirohito (b. 1901) was appointed Regent in 1921, five years before his death.

[2] Joseph (later Sir Joseph) Cook (1860-1947), Australian politician, began his political career as a Labor member of the State Legislative Assembly of New South Wales, but soon broke away and became an anti-Laborite. In 1909 he led his party to form a Coalition Government with Alfred Deakin (1856-1919) and became Minister of Defence. He was Prime Minister in 1913-14. In 1917 he joined the Coalition Government under William Morris Hughes (1864-1952) and was one of Australia's delegates to the Peace Conference where Australia took a leading stand against Japan's demands for racial equality. He became in 1921 Australian High Commissioner in London, holding the post until 1927.

Such views as these I will embody in a telegram which the Reuter Agency will, no doubt, be glad to send home to Europe this evening.

[...]

With best wishes

Very sincerely yours
[G. E. Morrison]

647. From W. H. Donald

Peking 7 October 1913

Dear Doctor,

I have just received the enclosed from Mr Suttor's office in Kobe. It is the extract mentioned by you a few days ago. While regretting extremely that someone has undoubtedly used an extract from some personal letter of mine discussing conditions in China, I am glad that it is not as I was led to believe. When speaking to Mr Suttor he led me to believe that a scurrilous attack had been made, and naturally I began to wonder what it all meant. I do not correspond on politics with anyone in Australia, and never do I enter into scurrility. Sight of this extract shows that it is not as bad as I imagined and suggests it is out of a letter I wrote sometime in May or early June to Mr Nall, the Chief News Editor of the *Daily Telegraph* – an old friend of mine. I was writing him privately on conditions in China and it appears that he must have handed the letter to someone who saw a chance of earning 10/- from the *Bulletin*.

I deeply regret that an extract should have been made from a personal and private letter. The act itself is rotten, and had the para. been anywhere else than in the *Bulletin* I would have felt it more deeply than I do – and I deplore this publication very much on account of the annoyance it may give you personally. Anyway it teaches me a lesson, and not even to give anyone an accurate idea of things will I again commit myself to paper. I ceased discussing politics even with Pratt on account of the misunderstandings which arise from letters. However, that is nothing – what I wish to say is that I am sorry that the para. should have been published, and that I hope you will not invest it with more seriousness than it really deserves. I feel that it does not make any reflection on you, but that it indicates that circumstances here are such that your services cannot be used properly – which of course is undoubtedly true.

One error occurs in the extract and that is with regard to the £250 – the copyist or the printer turned a 1 into a 2, apparently.

In a case like this words are idle. I am more annoyed than you can be that this should be published – but what can one do when some unprincipled person takes a private letter and uses it? All that is left me to do is to express deep regret, and to hope that you will not let what has been printed influence you to a belief that it is serious.

Believe me sincerely sorry

W. H. Donald

Enclosure to Letter No. 647: *Extract from The Sydney Bulletin, 31 July 1913*

Item from the revelations of W. H. Donald, the well-known Australian pressman, representing the *New York Herald* in Pekin, in a recent letter to a Sydney friend: 'I see Dr Morrison daily, and he does not know whether to be tired of his job or not. He has a hard time of it. Advice is easy to give: the Chinaman listens to advice, but will do what he thinks he wants to do. Morrison feels that, frequently. During the Revolution, he asked me, in Shanghai, why I did not enter the service of the Government. They were then offering me £250 a month. My reply was that, once a man entered the paid service of a Chinese his influence was gone. Morrison scoffed – now he admits it. Bitter proof. As *Times* correspondent he had twice the prestige and three times the influence.'

648. To Ts'ao Chia-hsiang[1]

[Peking] 8 October 1913

Dear Captain Tsao,

The extract which I herewith return[2] is, as I suspected when writing to you on the 3rd of October, an extract from a leading article published in *The Times* on September 9th. It is based upon the telegram, an extract of which I gave you on October 3rd sent from Peking by Mr. David Fraser on September 5th and published in *The Times* of September 6th. An extract such as that enclosed does not convey the full importance of the leader of *The Times* of the 8th of September, for that leader was mainly a semi-official intimation to the Japanese to restrain themselves. The leader says: –

'To us the murder of Mr. Abe[3] seems more deplorable than the Nanking

---

[1] Ts'ao Chia-hsiang, or, as he signed himself Tsao Kai-cheong, Chinese naval officer, later Rear-Admiral, at this time serving in the Secretariat of the President's Office as the secretary of Liang Shih-yi, the Chief Secretary of Yüan Shih-k'ai. He was to become Vice-Minister of the Navy in 1915, a post he held until July 1917.

[2] Not printed.

[3] Abe Moritarō (1872–1913), Japanese diplomat, at the time Director of the Bureau of Political Affairs in the Foreign Ministry (1912–13). On 5 September 1913 he was murdered by a young Japanese fanatic after a demonstration organised by the right-wing nationalist elements under the leadership of Tōyama Mitsuru (1855–1944), Inukai Tsuyoshi, Ōi Kentaro (1833–1922) and others, calling upon the Japanese Government to take a firmer stand against China following the death of three Japanese who were killed during the seizure of Nanking by Chang Hsün's troops on 1 September, here referred

outrage because if the motive assigned is correct, it means that the restraints of the last 50 years in Japan are weakening and that the tides of popular passion are less capable of control than they were during the Meiji era.'

The leader goes on to say

'After all the problem which confronts Japan in China is almost identical with that which has to be faced by the rest of the Great Powers. Every nation which has extensive commercial and financial relations with China is chiefly concerned to assist in restoring as soon as possible a strong and stable Government in the Republic. By common consent – and despite some recent unfavourable symptoms – the man best qualified to evolve order in China is Yuan Shih K'ai. He can only achieve his purpose if he is assured of external support. A Japanese naval demonstration against China at this juncture, followed by the seizure of Chinese territory, would probably bring about the President's downfall in the very moment of his victory over the rebels. At the same time it must be admitted that Yuan Shih-kai has not been fortunate in his choice of instruments, and his subordinates (referring specially to General Chang Hsun) have of late done a good deal to weaken his own position.'

The Chinese paper then in quoting the extract which was published in other papers has acted correctly. It would have been better of course if they could have got the whole leader but no blame can attach to them for acting as they have done. After all one must remember that in Great Britain there is the utmost freedom of public utterance. One must not forget that the criticism in *The Times* of the present British Government is much more hostile, much more severe, than any criticism that has ever been published in that paper of the Government of Yuan Shih Kai. When you read *The Times* regularly you will be astonished at the vehemence with which it attacks the responsible leaders of Great Britain, such as, especially, Mr Asquith[1] the Prime Minister and Mr Lloyd George,[2] the Chancellor of the Exchequer, who hold the two highest offices under the British Crown.

I presume that the President was naturally concerned because the Leader appeared to indicate that the British Government might delay giving their

---

to as 'the Nanking outrage', which was seen by Japanese right-wing extremists as a result of the weakness of Japan's China policy. Immediately after Abe's assassination, his murderer, seated on a map of China, committed suicide by disembowelment, letting his blood flow in such a way as to obliterate Mongolia and Manchuria.

[1] Herbert Henry Asquith (1852–1928), later 1st Earl of Oxford and Asquith, British politician. Leader of the Liberal Party and a Member of the House of Commons since 1886, he was Prime Minister from 1908 to 1916.

[2] David Lloyd George (1863–1945), British politician, a member of the House of Commons from 1890 till his death. He was Chancellor of the Exchequer from 1908 to 1915, and in 1916 succeeded Asquith as Prime Minister (1916–22).

official recognition to the Chinese Republic, but now that recognition has been given this concern no longer can affect him.[1] It must be remembered, too, that *The Times* has consistently supported President Yuan Shih-kai, although their correspondent in Peking has not done so, but his information is so imperfect and his messages show such a lack of knowledge and of judgment that they are ceasing to carry weight in Great Britain.

Very sincerely yours
[G. E. Morrison]

649. From R. F. Johnston[2]

[London] 9 October 1913

My dear Morrison,

I arrived in London on the 6th and took your 3 Chinese books to Luzac[3] on the following day. I made him give me a receipt for them.

I find myself stirred by none of the emotions which ought to stir me on returning to the homeland after an absence of fifteen years. I feel gloomy and depressed, partly perhaps because the weather is atrocious and partly because I am a stranger to everything and everyone, and feel very little inclination to make anybody's acquaintance. I have just seen (in the newspapers) that Walter[4] has got the promotion for which he has long been agitating. I have not yet called at the Colonial Office, so I do not yet know whether Walter's departure from Weihaiwei will affect my leave in any way. It may make it necessary for me to let the Colonial Office know – sooner than I had intended – that I have had enough of the service and wish to clear out. Of course if they would promote Lockhart[5] too, and offer me the

[1] Britain had recognised China the previous day, 7 October.
[2] Reginald (later Sir Reginald) Fleming Johnston (1874–1938), British colonial official and author. Entering the Hong Kong Civil Service in 1898, he was at the time District Officer and Magistrate in the British-leased territory of Weihaiwei (1906–17). In 1919 he became tutor in English to P'u-yi, the deposed Emperor of the Manchu Dynasty, but after the Japanese took P'u-yi into their 'protection', following his being ordered out of the Palace in the Forbidden City by Feng Yü-hsiang in 1924, Johnston left his service. In 1927 he returned to Weihaiwei to become British Commissioner (1927–1930), and in 1931 was appointed Professor of Chinese at the School of Oriental and African Studies, University of London. Among his published works are his memoirs recording the time he spent with P'u-yi in the Palace in Peking, entitled *Twilight in the Forbidden City*, published in London in 1934. In 1935 he visited his ex-pupil, who had by then become Emperor of the Puppet Government of 'Manchukuo'.
[3] Luzac & Co., a firm of booksellers in London dealing mainly with oriental publications, founded by the Dutch-born Cornelis Gerbrand Luzac (1862–1903).
[4] Robert Walter (d. 1959), British colonial official, until 1913 Secretary to the British administration at Weihaiwei. He was then transferred to the British Colonies in the West Indies, serving as Secretary for British Honduras (1914–20), Administrator of Dominica (1920–3) and in 1923 became Administrator of St Vincent.
[5] Sir James Haldane Stewart Lockhart (1858–1937), British colonial official. He was Commissioner for the British-leased territory of Weihaiwei for nearly twenty years from 1902 to 1921. He had previously been Colonial Secretary in Hong Kong (1895–1902).

Commissionership, I should be inclined to take it, as it is practically a sinecure and would leave me with plenty of time to myself. But it is highly improbable that Lockhart's billet will fall to me; and failing that the best thing I can do is to leave the service and carry out my intention of settling down to a literary life on the slopes of the Western Hills. I have been thinking over what you suggested to me – that I might get some sort of employment under the Chinese Government, and I appreciate what you said about it; but it is difficult to see what sort of job I should be competent to undertake. Perhaps I might do occasional odd jobs for them: I should be glad to do so for nothing if the work were congenial. I have long regarded China as my home: and my present visit to England is only helping to confirm that attitude. I am delighted to see from this morning's papers that the Chinese Republic has been recognised. I hope things will go smoothly now. The least our Government should do for you now is to give you a decoration: and I hope they will do so. Let me know if I can do anything for you here.

Yours very sincerely
R. F. Johnston

650. From Sahara Tokusuke

Shanghai 13 October 1913

Dear Dr. Morrison,

After all the President was elected but will there be peace.[1] The fact is that it is only a veiled military despotism in existence and not a Republic in any sense. On the day of the inauguration of the President Prince Pu-lun[2] has sent in a congratulatory address for the Emperor Hsuan-tung while the President has replied His Majesty quite cordially with full respect as his late ruler. Please understand that I am not any enemy to anybody. However I do sincerely consider it is the best solution for China to restore the Emperor to the Throne again whenever there be a chance as that will be the

---

[1] Under threats and coercion, the Parliament, after three ballots, formally elected Yüan Shih-k'ai as President on 6 October 1913.

[2] P'u-lun (d. 1927), Manchu Imperial Clansman. A grandson of Min-ning (1782–1850), Emperor Tao-kuang, during whose reign the first Opium War was fought (1838–42), P'u-lun was twice a candidate for the Manchu throne, in 1875 and in 1908, but both times was by-passed because of the opposition of the Empress-Dowager Tz'u-hsi. Instead he became an officially appointed 'people's spokesman' during both the Empire and the Republic. He was made President of the Senate (Tzu-cheng yüan), China's first Parliament, when it came into being in 1907, a post he held until shortly before the outbreak of the 1911 Revolution. After the abdication of the young Emperor Hsüan-t'ung (P'u-yi) and the advent of the Republic, he alone of the high Manchu officials chose to remain in Peking where he represented the former Imperial House at all Republican functions, and was the recipient of Republican honours and decorations. In 1915 he was appointed by Yüan Shih-k'ai to be the President of the Political Consultative Council, which Yüan had set up to aid his monarchical scheme. In 1925 he was made a member of the Provisional Political Consultative Council, the last 'Parliament' before the overthrow of the Peking regime by the Kuomintang in 1928.

only way to preserve China as a state. Though Yuan Shih-kai be enjoying the best of his health yet a mortal person can not be expected for ever. After him who will carry out the state affairs. It is better to have a good system behind him under an Imperial rule. I never changed my views since the revolution was started. It is not wise to hush things up but it is better to carry it out in good opportune occasion. This is my conviction and belief for China. I do wish the existence of China as a state for ever. Therefore I do maintain this view. I do not know how our government is considering the situation in China but I do express my views to you as a student of things Chinese since 1899.

With the kindest regards to Mrs Morrison and your goodself as well as to your son and heir

Yours always sincerely
T. Sahara

651. To Madame Yüan Shih-k'ai

[Peking] 13 October 1913

Dear Madam,

Last evening to my delight I received from you a gift of 30 pots of lovely flowers. I write now to thank you most gratefully for the beautiful gift which you have so graciously sent me. May I at the same time offer you my respectful congratulations on the occasion of your birthday and express the hope that you may live for many years in the enjoyment of health, happiness and prosperity, witnessing the epoch-making success achieved by your distinguished husband in the high office to which he has been called by his fellow countrymen amid the acclamations of the whole world.

Believe me

Very gratefully yours
[G. E. Morrison]

652. To Wu Ch'ao-shu

[Peking] 14 October 1913

Dear Mr. Wu,

Do you not think it would be a wise thing if some reply could be sent to the strictures of *The Times*, evidently written by Mr. J. O. P. Bland, condemning the Young China Party for the dilatoriness in the procedure of the drafting of the Constitution?[1]

[1] *The Times*, in a leader entitled 'China and the Powers' published on 10 October to mark the inauguration that day of Yüan Shih-k'ai as the first Republican President, said: 'During the two years which have elapsed since the successful revolutionary outbreak at Wuchang, Young China has displayed none of the qualities requisite to organize new forms of government by the people, or even for the people. The earlier work of the National

I do not think that any reasonable man can consider that there has been undue delay. So fast is the work and of such far reaching and epoch making importance that it is preposterous to expect that the work could have been accomplished in a few weeks. Do you think you could find time to write me a short resume of what has been done, privately of course, I would not use your name?[1] I would then cause a summary to be telegraphed to the European papers. No details, only the main features of when the work began, what has been finished and what yet remains to be done.

It is unfortunate that at the present time when important negotiations are proceeding in Simla that there should be this misrepresentation. You could, I think, materially help to strengthen the position by giving me a brief summary, such as I suggest.

Of course it would be still more effective if you could yourself write a letter to *The Times*, but obviously you are precluded from doing so by your being a member of the Constitution Drafting Committee.

Very sincerely yours
[G. E. Morrison]

653. To Ts'ao Chia-hsiang

[Peking] 14 October 1913

Dear Captain Tsao,

Negotiations I understand opened on Monday in Simla for the settlement of the Tibetan question between China, England and Tibet. It is announced in the papers that telegrams have been exchanged between the President and the Dalai Lama on the occasion of the Inauguration of the President. It would have a very important bearing upon the Conference if those telegrams could be published. Do you think you could obtain them for me? I am sure the President would realise the importance of making known to the world such a friendly interchange of messages at the present time. It would have a marked effect upon the Conference in Simla and would strengthen the hands of Mr Ivan Chen. If the messages could be given to me I could arrange to have them put into proper telegraphic form and published throughout the world. It would be wise to lose no time if the most telling effect is to be obtained.

With best wishes

Very sincerely yours
[G. E. Morrison]

---

and Provincial Assemblies was never constructive; the recent record of the Parliament at Peking has grievously disappointed those who looked to Young China for efficiency and unselfish patriotism. It has been a purely partisan struggle for place and power, a record of sordid intrigues, tempered by assassination. It has not even succeeded in drafting a Constitution...'

[1] Wu Ch'ao-shu replied to Morrison's letter on the same day enclosing a résumé of the work done by the Committee drafting the Constitution. This is not printed.

654. To D. D. Braham

Peking 17 October 1913

My dear Braham,

Your letter of the 2nd of October has just come in. [...]

The Times Leader chiding Young China for 'having displayed none of the qualities requisite to organise new forms of popular government and for not having even succeeded in drafting a constitution' caused some surprise here. It seemed to many of us a hasty judgment. The Committee for drafting the Constitution only began its work on the 21st of July. [...] So very rarely has any reference been made in *The Times* to anything that has been done by the Constitution Committee that you cannot be blamed for making such a comment, but the opinion that I have gathered from the Professors here is that an extraordinary amount of work has been accomplished with very little friction indeed.

A synopsis of the work done by the Constitution Committee will be given to the Press in the course of the next few days. I hope that it may induce you to reconsider your judgment.

The Mongolian negotiations have been proceeding for some time past but the point on which they have not yet come to an agreement is the most important of all. Some hope is held out by the Russian Minister that his Government will agree to the recognition by his Government of Mongolia as a *partie intégrante* of China.[1] The Chinese nurse the hope that the Russian Government will agree. I have little confidence myself that they will do so but we ought to know today or tomorrow, for the Russian Minister on Wednesday said that he expected the reply to come through last night.

With best wishes

Yours sincerely
[G. E. Morrison]

655. To Ts'ao Chia-hsiang

[Peking] 21 October 1913

Dear Captain Tsao,

I wonder do you know Mr Liang Shih-yi well enough to ask him about the following:— It is very important that China should not be misrepresented in the British papers. Strong attacks having been made against China, especially with regard to her failure to draft a Constitution and suggestions having been made that the Constitution drafting is a farce, it is necessary to

[1] By Article I of a Declaration signed on 5 November 1913 by Sun Pao-ch'i, Chinese Foreign Minister, and Basil Kroupensky, Russian Minister in Peking, 'Russia recognizes that Outer Mongolia is under the suzerainty of China,' while in point II of a note accompanying this Declaration addressed by Kroupensky to Sun Pao-ch'i, the Russian Minister pledged on behalf of his Government that 'Russia recognizes that the territory of Outer Mongolia forms a part of the territory of China.'

rebut these charges. Accordingly I have prepared a statement, a copy of which I enclose,[1] which I propose to ask Reuter to telegraph home to England. Reuters is conducted on business lines and it may be that this message will not readily sell in England. The cost of transmitting it to England will be about $300.

On several occasions when Reuter has been asked to send messages of this kind we have informed Reuter's correspondent that in the event of his people losing money by the message the loss will be made good to them by the Chinese. We want to do the same in this case. Reuter's correspondent when sending the message would at the same time telegraph that in the event of their sustaining any loss in connection with this message the Chinese will defray the cost.

So far Reuter has never asked for any refund. The total amount that China might be asked to refund would be something less than $300.

Could you ask Mr Liang Shih-yi if I will be authorised to inform Reuters that in the event of their sustaining any loss this amount will be refunded to them.

You will see that it is a very important message, written out with great care in telegraphic English, very much condensed. If the Government were to send this message to their Legation in London asking them to distribute it it would cost considerably over $1000. Sending it in this way it costs less than one-third and may cost nothing.

If Admiral Tsai has come back then there will be no need to ask Mr Liang Shih-yi. You could ask Admiral Tsai, but as I want to have it telegraphed to London this afternoon or evening I should be much obliged if you would ask Mr Liang Shih-yi if he will authorise me to send it.

With best wishes to you

Very sincerely yours
[G. E. Morrison]

656. To Hsiung Hsi-ling[2]

[Peking] 21 October 1913

Dear Mr. Hsiung,

I am writing to you about a matter which is, I am sure you will agree, of high importance. It concerns Mongolia.

Some time ago an agreement was made with Mr. Larson, a Swede, who has a larger knowledge of Mongolia than that possessed by any other person, whereby he entered the service of the Chinese Government for a term of years. His contract was signed with General Li Ting Yu. By a supplementary agreement General Li instructed Mr. Larson to arrange for the withdrawal from Outer Mongolia of as many Mongols of high position as he could. He was to do all he could to induce the Mongols to preserve their friendliness

[1] Not printed. [2] At this time Prime Minister (31 July 1913 – 12 February 1914).

with China. He was to advise on all Mongolian matters. In pursuance of this scheme various high officials have, through his instrumentality, returned to China, for example, Abugaida wan has returned to his home 300 *li* from Dolon Nor and has been raised in rank. Na Beileh has, as Your Excellency knows, recently returned to China, has been received by the President and has been raised to the rank of Na Wang. Su Kung has also returned but there are still remaining in Urga various high Authorities who would like to return to China. Among those the most friendly to China is the Hai San Kung and it is about him that I now write. He is still in Urga. He wants to return to China. His son is in Peking at the present time. He speaks excellent Chinese and could in half an hour explain more to you than could be done by writing many letters. Could I ask you to see the Hai San Kung's son and Mr. Larson. If you could give them an interview they would tell you much of the situation of Outer Mongolia and would, I think, be of real assistance in making things more clear. Once before Your Excellency had arranged to see Mr. Larson but owing to some mistake the engagement was never kept.

It is very important that the Hai San Kung should return to Peking but to induce him to return he would require to know how he was to be received. His friend the Bintu Wang, who showed marked friendliness to China, was killed in Urga. The son of the Hai San Kung returned to Peking on the 23rd of September. He is a trustworthy and intelligent man and if Your Excellency could find time to see him and Mr. Larson together I think you would find it of great interest. I could easily instruct them to call upon you at whatever hour would be convenient to you.

With my best wishes for your success

Believe me

Very sincerely yours
[G. E. Morrison]

657. To Ts'ao Chia-hsiang

[Peking] 27 October 1913

Dear Captain Tsao,

I send you herewith *The China Republican* for October the 20th which contains a leading article entitled 'Yuan as Autocrat'.[1] Such articles ought not to be permitted. The recent rebellion, which caused such wide-spread distress, was largely due to the incitement of this venomous paper.

The article has been effectively dealt with by Mr Woodhead in the *Peking Gazette* of Saturday. The Foreign Office ought at once to take steps to have the paper suppressed. I am quite sure that the French Minister would give instructions for the publication of the paper to be forbidden in the French concession and for the responsible editor to be extradited, as such articles are a direct incitement to rebellion. They are designed to inflame the

[1] Not found.

ignorant against the Government which has been formally recognised by France and by all other countries.

It is an open secret that the Leader writer is an Englishman named Chesney Duncan.[1] Steps should be taken to have the writer dealt with according to the provisions of the British Order in Council. Procedure must be taken through the proper channel. The Foreign Minister must approach the English and French Legations in Peking. The Commissioner for Foreign Affairs in Shanghai must bring the matter officially to the notice of the French and British Consuls in Shanghai.

Infinite injury can be done when such seditious articles are permitted. If the Government will only take proper constitutional steps further publications can be prevented.

When you see the President you might please mention to him that yesterday the Prime Minister received in a very cordial manner Mr Larson, the Swede who was able to give recent information regarding Mongolia, of which he has greater knowedge perhaps than any other man living, and the son of the Hai San Kung a prominent official in Urga who desires to return to China. The Prime Minister will, no doubt, report the interview to the President. I only wish to say that Mr Larson has been in to tell me how gratified the Mongols have been at the sympathetic hearing they received from the Prime Minister.

With kind regards

Very sincerely yours
[G. E. Morrison]

658. To Sun Pao-ch'i[2]

[Peking] 28 October 1913

Dear Mr. Sun,

Might I express to Your Excellency the great satisfaction with which all who are interested in the strengthening of China's friendly relations with foreign countries are witnessing the success which is attending your efforts since you assumed the onerous post of Minister of Foreign Affairs.

It is clearly the policy of Your Excellency to encourage friendly relations with all countries in order that when the important question arises of obtaining their assent to the revision of the tariff and the increase in the Customs duties all countries may show a sympathetic spirit towards the proposals made to them.

In this connection could I make a small suggestion to you? It concerns

---

[1] Chesney Duncan (b. 1854), British journalist, who had had wide professional experience in many Asian countries before settling in Shanghai, where he worked closely with the southern republicans and was credited with having written manifestos for Sun Yat-sen. At this time he was a contributing Editor of the *China Republican*.

[2] At this time Foreign Minister (11 September 1913 – 1 May 1914).

Italy, a country whose interests in China are admittedly not of first importance, but yet a country which is one of the great Powers of Europe. Some little time ago the Chinese Government proposed to engage the services of the famous financier Signor Luzzatti as financial Adviser to China. Too old to accept the appointment for himself, Signor Luzzatti offered to render what help he could as Adviser in Europe. Some little time later the Chinese Government, through the Italian Legation in Peking arranged to engage the services of another famous financial expert, Signor Rossi in connection with the Quintuple loan. Owing to the opposition of certain powers effect could not be given to this appointment. Then it was proposed – I do not know whether the proposal came from the Chinese Government or from the Italian Legation – to engage the services of a well known Italian, Baron Guido Vitale,[1] who has been for many years Chinese Secretary of the Italian Legation in Peking, in some position connected with the Foreign Office. Baron Vitale is a remarkable linguist who knows Mongol as well as Chinese and some 15 or more other languages. I understand that His Excellency your predecessor[2] suggested that Baron Vitale be offered the post of chief foreign Interpreter attached to the Foreign Office at a salary of $1000 per month, but Baron Vitale declined the offer on the ground that the remuneration was inadequate. The Italian Government were disappointed that what they thought to be an inadequate salary and a post which they considered to be of less dignity than that given to employees from other countries should have been offered to an Italian. Yet it must be admitted that the pay for the work thus contemplated was an adequate one and was in fact considerably higher than that allotted, for example, to the Chinese Secretary of the British Legation.

Now I learn confidentially that the Italian Government believe that they have not been treated in this matter with the consideration to which they think they are entitled. It is only a small matter of course, but it is probable that Count Sforza will refer to it at your first meeting, of course in a friendly spirit.

I know that if your Excellency could see fit to do so, it would be very gratifying to the Italian Government if a position were offered to Baron Vitale with a more dignified title than that of Chief Interpreter in the Wai Chiao Pu and with a more adequate salary.

Your Excellency could, no doubt, think of some title which would be more

[1] Guido Amedo Vitale (1872–1918), Italian diplomat and educationalist, a graduate of the Istituto Orientale di Napoli. He had come to know Morrison while serving as Secretary–Interpreter at the Italian Legation in Peking, a post he took up in 1892. They were on friendly terms until Morrison published in *The Times* the fact that Vitale, though no name was mentioned, had translated the expression 'the concert of Powers' into 'some kind of musical entertainment' in Chinese. He was the author of *Chinese Folklore, Pechinese Rhymes* (Peking 1896) and *Chinese Merry Tales* (Peking 1901).
[2] Lu Cheng-hsiang.

satisfactory to Italian pride than that of Interpreter, and a salary larger than $1000 a month. I am confident that the offer of a salary of $16,000 a year would be regarded as a friendly act by the Italian Minister. In the meantime Baron Vitale has been appointed Professor at the Oriental School in Rome[1] and I understand it is exceedingly unlikely that he would accept any offer made to him to return to Peking, but there is no doubt that it would be a compliment which would be much appreciated by the Italians if an offer were made to him of, say, $16,000 a year. It could be pointed out to the Italian Minister that this was the same salary for which the well-known French Officer, Colonel Brissaud Desmaillets, had consented to serve the Chinese Government.

I only venture to write you these few lines because your Excellency will then be prepared when, as I expect, Count Sforza, the Italian Minister, brings up the subject at your weekly interview.

Again allow me to offer you my congratulations, and
Believe me

Very sincerely yours
[G. E. Morrison]

659. To Ts'ao Chia-hsiang

[Peking] 29 October 1913

Dear Captain Tsao,

Mr Leo Meng-leng[2] came to see me this morning regarding the President and the limitation of his powers proposed by the Constitution Committee and left me a well written paper with the request that I would see it was published. It was necessary to see Professor Goodnow because he had helped to revise the paper but I have been unable to get in communication with him. I have been twice to his house but he is apparently taking a day off.

When you see Mr Liang Shih-yi I wish you could have a little talk with him about the need of China's stating her case more quickly than she is in the habit of doing. Take the case of Mongolia. The Russian Legation has communicated to all the correspondents the terms of the Note and of the Declaration. She has done so in a way beneficial to Russia but prejudicial to China. Advantage is taken by unfriendly correspondents to make use of such

[1] Vitale had been Professor of Chinese at the Istituto Orientale di Napoli, of which he became Director in 1913. He was not a professor at the Istituto del Medio ed Estremo Oriente in Rome, a different institution.
[2] Jao Meng-jen, Chinese Republican politician. A Barrister of Lincoln's Inn, he was at this time a member of the Bureau of Codification. In his Diary entry for 30 October 1913 Morrison described him as 'a highly incompetent young man' who seemed to know 'as little Chinese as he does English'. He became a member for his native Kiangsi Province in the caretaker Senate in November 1917, and in 1920 was briefly (from February to August) Deputy Director-General of the Currency Bureau.

information. Correspondents who are friendly with China desire to hear China's side of these negotiations but nothing is communicated to them. If China wants to have her case in Mongolia stated fairly in the English papers and in the papers in China it is absolutely essential that I be given the French text of the Agreement entered into between Russia and China regarding Mongolia. I would not use the text until the agreement had been signed but it is necessary that I should have it in my possession in order that I may have it translated and prepared for telegraphic purposes so that no time is lost in having it transmitted to Europe immediately after signature.

You no doubt read the Shanghai papers and you can see how prejudicial it is to China that reports regarding this agreement from Russian sources should be published in the papers and no refutation given to them by the Chinese.

It is not for curiosity that I wish to see the agreement but it is because if I have the agreement I can use it to the advantage of the country in whose service I am.

What is the use of using this information after the misleading report has already been published? A reader sees in the paper an account of the Mongolian Agreement. It does not say that this report is derived from Russian sources but he sees that the report is favourable to the Russians. What is the use of publishing another report subsequently on the same subject? No one will read it. Anyone seeing it will say that he had read it before. Throughout these Mongolian negotiations not a single word favourable to China has appeared in the European papers because all the information comes from Russia. So long as China conceals information from those who could use it to the best advantage she must suffer prejudice. It is the same with regard to Tibet.

With best wishes to you

Very sincerely yours
[G. E. Morrison]

660. To Jao Meng-jen

[Peking] 30 October 1913

Dear Mr Leo,

I send you herewith 2 copies of the paper which you brought me yesterday, together with the original.[1]

I have had a long talk with Professor Goodnow and I cannot but think that it would be wise if he were to be asked by the President to draw up a detailed statement, supported by arguments, in favour of the contention of the President that his powers under the draft constitution have been dangerously restricted.

[1] Not found, but its contents may be inferred from the previous letter, No. 659.

Another copy of the paper I am sending to the *Peking Gazette* and I would suggest that you have the paper translated and communicated to the Chinese Press.[1]

With kind regards

Very sincerely yours
[G. E. Morrison]

Enclosure to Letter No. 660: *Paper by Professor F. J. Goodnow*

The system of government proposed by the draft Constitution, which has just been completed by the Committee of Parliament, is 'Cabinet Government' pure and simple. It has been said of the President of the French Republic, which has adopted this form of government, that he neither reigns, as does the King of Great Britain, nor governs, as does the President of the United States. If this Constitution is adopted, the President of the Republic of China will occupy a position of impotence similar to that occupied by the President of the French Republic.

This will be his position, since practically all power of appointing ministers of state is taken from him. In the first place, the constitution provides that the appointment of the Prime Minister, although presumably to be made by the President, shall be approved by the House of Representatives. In the second place it provides that the President shall remove ministers with regard to whom a vote of lack of confidence has been expressed by the House of Representatives. It will therefore be necessary that the President appoint Ministers, other than the Prime Minister, only with the approval of the Prime Minister.

The first effect of the adoption of this system of Cabinet Government will then be the concentration of all power in the hands of ministers, who, if they are not the appointed of the House of Representatives, must continue to be acceptable to them. For at any time, no matter how critical, and for any cause, no matter how trivial, the House of Representatives may pass the fatal vote of lack of confidence in the Ministers which will oblige the President to dismiss them from office. It is, of course, true that the President may theoretically, once during a Session, dissolve the House of Representatives. But inasmuch as in order to dissolve it, the President must obtain the consent of the Senate, to be given by a two-thirds vote, this right is theoretical rather than actual. For if we are to judge from French experience, which the drafting committee has apparently had in mind in making this provision, such a right of dissolution, so limited, is no protection to the Executive against captious and inconsiderate action on the part of the House. The French President may, with the consent of the French Senate, dissolve the French Chamber of Deputies. But although this consent is to be given only by a majority vote,

---

[1] The paper by Goodnow which Morrison sent to the *Peking Gazette* was published in that newspaper on 31 October 1913, and is printed below.

the French President has dissolved the Chamber of Deputies only once in the history of the Republic, namely in 1877.[1]

The probable result of the adoption of Cabinet Government in China, if we may judge from the experience of foreign nations, will be that the new government, to which the system will be applied, will be highly unstable and that reasonable continuity of policy will be difficult if not impossible of attainment. Short lived ministries, based on conditions between small party groups, may be expected to follow one another with somewhat the same rapidity which characterises the politics of France and Italy.

It can hardly be doubted that every well wisher of China will deplore the action of the Committee in adopting the Cabinet system if it is to have these results. For at this most critical time in the history of the country, what is needed perhaps more than anything else is stability and continuity of policy. That China will in the near future need to make more loans can hardly be doubted. That these loans must be made by foreign bankers is inevitable. That these bankers will be willing to loan large sums of money to the country when they can not determine with reasonable certainty who in even a few months will be the possessors of political power, and thereby will control the expenditure of the proceeds of the loans, is hardly to be hoped.

But, entirely apart from the questions of foreign loans the adoption of Cabinet Government is to be regretted. There is so much reorganisation to be undertaken, so much constructive legislation of the greatest importance to the welfare of the country to be framed and passed, that one who has been hoping that the recent Revolution is in the immediate days to come going to be of benefit to the country can but face the future with dismay. Any political party which seriously advocates this Cabinet form of government for China at the present time will be assuming responsibilities of the gravest character.

661. To S. P. Cockerell

[Peking] 3 November 1913

My dear Cockerell,

Many thanks for your two long letters,[2] the first of which I have been an uncommonly long time in answering. [...]

Thanks for sending me the newspaper cuttings. I cannot agree with your views about Japan. On the evidence furnished to you, however, you could

[1] In 1877 Marie Edme Patrice Maurice de MacMahon (1808–93), the French President (1873–9), reproached his Prime Minister for his conduct of affairs in the Chamber of Deputies and requested the dissolution of the Chamber which immediately passed a motion of no confidence in the Ministry. The Senate was also dissolved and in the ensuing election the Government was defeated.

[2] Of the two letters mentioned here, only that of 12 July 1913 is printed. *See* Letter No. 625, p. 192.

not be blamed for drawing such conclusions. Putnam Weale who was the most hostile of Japan's critics returned from Japan an ardent advocate of Japan's policy in China. His change of front has given rise to much speculation. His telegrams are so outrageously exaggerated that it is surprising to see the *Pall Mall Gazette* paying any attention to them. You have only to look back over the past. The Rebellion which broke out on October 10th 1911 he foretold would be ended in two weeks. We 'in the know' knew that the President was going to give his adherence to the Republic. Putnam Weale in a picturesque message described him as 'fighting with his back to the wall for the Monarchy'. The recent rebellion in the Yangtse[1] he foretold would last for 10 years. It lasted for less than that number of weeks.

How can a man send home accurate information when he is not in touch with anyone in authority either foreign or Chinese and who is denied access to his own Legation!

I would say that the relations between China and Japan have never been more intimate and that the intimacy is growing. Long before the so-called humiliation of China by Japan it had been arranged by Sun Pao-chi in Japan that Japan was to be given these railway concessions in China which have only recently been published.[2]

There seems to be a considerable diminution in the suspicion formerly entertained by the Chinese for the Japanese. The Vice-Minister of Foreign Affairs, Tsao Ju-lin,[3] speaks Japanese admirably. He was for many years in

---

[1] A reference to the 'Second Revolution'.

[2] This refers to the concessions made by Sun Pao-ch'i on 5 October 1913 in an exchange of Notes with Yamaza Enjirō on railways in Manchuria and Inner Mongolia.

[3] Ts'ao Ju-lin (1876-1966), Chinese Republican politician, at this time Vice-Minister of Foreign Affairs (August 1913 – April 1916). A Law graduate from Japan, his whole career was closely linked with Japanese aggression in China. First entering the Chinese Foreign Ministry in 1905 as Interpreter, he quickly rose in that Department to become Vice-Minister in 1910. The 'golden boy' in the government dominated by Tuan Ch'i-jui during the heyday of the Anfu Clique, he served in turn and sometimes concurrently as Minister of Communications, of Foreign Affairs and of Finance. As new overlord of China's communications system and its financing, he gained for the faction of which he was leader the label of 'New Communication Clique', as distinct from the original 'Communication Clique' under the leadership of Liang Shih-yi, Chu Ch'i-ch'ien, Chou Tzu-ch'i and Yeh Kung-cho (q.v.). All his ministerial transactions concerned China's relations with Japan. It was he who negotiated the settlement following the death of three Japanese in Chang Hsün's attack on Nanking in 1913; and he was China's spokesman during the negotiations that followed the Twenty-One Demands. It was his plan to unite China by force with Japanese financial backing which resulted in transactions mortgaging to Japan some of China's most important resources. His marked Japanese sympathies eventually led him to be branded as an arch-villain in the eyes of his countrymen and he became the main target of a student protest in 1919 during what has become known as the 'May Fourth Movement'. In 1949 he escaped to Taiwan with the Nationalist Government, thence to Japan, and he later went to live in the United States, where he died. His memoirs published in Chinese depict him as he wanted himself to be known, rather than as he is known to have been.

Japan and his friends and associates among foreigners in Peking have always been Japanese. I think his influence has been used largely towards coming to a better understanding.

Our own position is not a satisfactory one. Alston does not seem to take his work very seriously so I am told. I very rarely see him.

[...]

Very sincerely yours
[G. E. Morrison]

662. To Yen Ho-ling[1]

[Peking] 4 November 1913

Dear Dr Yen,

I have written to Captain Tsao asking him to send you, if he still has it, the copy of the *China Republican* with its villainous attack upon the President. This appeared in the issue for October 20th. It was severely commented upon in the *Peking Gazette* in an excellent leader on October 25th. Both the article and the leader I sent in to the President's office. The leader points out that the proprietor of the paper, Mah Soo, is a French Eurasian: that the paper is published at 63 Rue du Consulat in the French Concession of Shanghai, and that the leader writer of the paper is an Englishman. I believe as a matter of fact his name is Chesney Duncan.

Mah Soo is a Chinese subject although of mixed parentage for he submitted to Chinese jurisdiction when proceedings were taken against his paper by the opium merchants in Shanghai. The English leader writer can be dealt with under Art. 5, Section I of the British Order in Council of February 1907.

Attacks are still continuing and they ought to be stopped. The paper is being distributed by the Chinese Post Office. Instructions ought at once to be given to the Postal authorities to refuse to permit this seditious paper to be circulated by the Chinese Post Office. All copies sent through the Post Office ought to be forfeited.

The French Legation is the one to whom protest should be addressed by the Foreign Office calling for the expulsion from the French Consulate of

---

[1] Yen Ho-ling (1879–1937), Chinese diplomat and educator, known to foreigners by his anglicised name of Hawkling L. Yen. A returned student from America, he was at this time a Secretary in the Ministry of Foreign Affairs (1913–16). In 1916 he became the Managing Editor of the *Chinese Social and Political Science Journal*, the organ of an association founded in that year by foreign-trained students, most of them from the United States, as well as some foreigners then working and living in Peking, Morrison among them. Yen was appointed a Technical Adviser with the Chinese Delegation to the Paris Peace Conference in 1919 and on his return became President of Tsinghua College, an institution founded with the surplus portion of the Boxer Indemnity Fund returned to China by the United States. He also served in many diplomatic posts and was Vice-Minister of Agriculture and Commerce in 1924 (July–September). He later taught at the Peking Normal University.

this seditious paper. More than any other man Mah Soo was responsible for the recent rebellion. Others have escaped. He remains to carry on his evil deeds.

With kind regards

Very sincerely yours
[G. E. Morrison]

663. From Ch'en I-fan

Simla 10 November 1913

Dear Dr Morrison,

I should have written to you long time ago, had I not been pressed by the work of the Conference.[1] I am here doing all the work myself and do not receive any outside assistance. On the point of my leaving Peking the present Foreign Minister[2] recommended Mr B. D. Bruce to me for service in Simla, but on arrival here some small difficulties were raised against his inclusion in my staff, and he was soon afterwards ordered to return to Darjeeling by the direct order of I.G.[3]

The first meeting of the Tibetan Conference was opened on the 13th, and the Tibetan claims were then handed in. They consisted of five items as follows:[4]

1. Independence of Tibet.
2. Extention of Tibetan territory including Kokonor and Batang and Litang.
3. The revision of the Trade Regulations of 1893 and 1908 with England without China.
4. No *Amban* in Lhasa.
5. Freedom of intercourse between Lamas in China with Tibet.
6. Compensation to Tibet for what damages done there by the Chinese soldiers.

To these I presented my counter-proposals on the 30th ultimo after consultation with my Government and they consisted of 7 items.

1. Chinese undertake not to convert Tibet in a Province.
2. Chinese must have an *Amban* with an escort of 2600 soldiers.
3. China shall be the only intermediary for any negotiations between Tibet and any foreign Power.

[1] The tripartite conference between China, Britain and Tibet then being held in Simla.
[2] Sun Pao-ch'i.
[3] B. D. Bruce, British employee of the Chinese Maritime Customs. His appointment as Adviser to Ch'en I-fan at the Simla conference was blocked by the British Legation, and Aglen, the Inspector-General of the Chinese Customs, was obliged to withdraw his nomination.
[4] Ch'en's original item no. 5 he later changed to no. 6 and inserted another no. 5.

4. Amnesty granted to all those who have been imprisoned on account of well known sympathy. (This claim looks insignificant, but if carried through means a great deal to China for there are still many sympathisers of China in Tibet.)
5. Clause 5 in the Tibetan claims can be discussed. (I want to use this as a lever for what I want in other respects.)
6. The Revisions of the Trade Regulations must be made with China on the basis of Art. IV of the Adhesion Convention of April 27th of 1903.
7. A rough claim of frontier delimitation includes Giamdu and Narguchuka.

As you will see there must be a great deal of bluff on both sides, we have to claim Giamdu, though I have not the tittle of reason to think that such a demand can be entertained for a moment. The reason that I did not put any claim for sovereignty over Tibet was simply because instead of gaining anything by that it would be supposed by the Indian Government that I had no intention of having the problem solved. I hope you can see your way of approving the course of action I have taken in this matter. I am alone here, but I am fighting several opponents whom I will not particularize until I am face to face with you.

All the papers here approve the strong action taken by our President in regard to the Opposition Party of the well known Kuomingtang.

Believe me

Yours very sincerely
Ivan Chen

If you want to see the Tibetan claims and our counter proposal, you can [ask the] Wai Chiao Pu for them.

I.C.

664. To E. G. Hillier

[Peking] 11 November 1913

My dear Hillier,

I have been with the President this morning and have had a long talk with him about many things of interest. There can be little doubt that now that he has taken authority he will impress his views upon all departments of Government. He asked me to do many things for him.

Is it possible for you, privately, to give me any help with regard to correcting the very misleading statements that are being disseminated by David Fraser with regard to the salt? On the very day of the President's Election Fraser states in *The Times* that 'The most fantastic pictures of Persian dishonesty and incapacity find their counterpart here'.[1] In *The Times* of October

[1] In an article in *The Times* of 7 October 1913, reporting Yüan Shih-k'ai's election to the Presidency the previous day, and entitled 'Chinese President Elected. The Provincial Unrest. Position of the Foreign Advisers', David Fraser wrote: 'Many foreign advisers have been engaged, but none have been able to exercise any really beneficial influence,

the 22nd he states 'The reorganisation of the salt gabelle, despite recent undertakings, continues to be impeded.' In the *North China Daily News* of November 1st he states 'As frequently stated in your columns the salt gabelle is exploded as a security for further borrowing. Sir Richard Dane's investigations confirm the contention that the year's revenue that can come from salt will not meet existing charges. There is no blinking the fact that at present only the merest fraction of the revenue estimated by the Chinese will be available to the Government and that enough to meet existing charges can only be obtained under foreign supervision after a long period of ceaseless struggle against adverse conditions.' In the *North China Daily News* on the 5th of November Fraser states that 'the only conditions under which a large loan can be floated would be for the Powers to take over the financial administration of China'.

Statements such as these are wholly injurious and misleading. Could you, privately, give me a statement which I could use, of course I would quote only the figures and not give my authority, which would show that the reorganisation of the Salt Gabelle is not being impeded? Sir Richard Dane spoke to me most enthusiastically of what he had been able to accomplish and what he expected to be able to accomplish. It is the wish of the Chinese, as I judge unmistakably from the President, to meet his wishes, to accept his advice and to carry out an effective reorganisation that will prevent any pretext for foreign intervention.

It is very unfortunate that at the present time such statements, which are practically the opposite of the truth, should be published by Fraser. They ought to be rebutted. Can you help me to rebut them?

With kind regards

Very sincerely yours
[G. E. Morrison]

665. From E. G. Hillier

Peking 12 November 1913

Confidential

My dear Morrison,

In reply to your letter of yesterday, I shall of course be very glad to give you any information which will assist you in correcting the unfavourable and,

---

partly because of Chinese conservatism and partly because good advice is not acceptable to those who are inspired with corrupt motives. The most fantastic pictures of Persian dishonesty and incapacity find their counterpart here, and the disruption which is overtaking Persia will inevitably overtake China unless the only possible remedy be employed – namely, the importation of foreign efficiency and straight-forwardness into the conduct of public affairs.'

in my opinion entirely false impression to be gathered from Fraser's reports. These might, and indeed would have been quite justified by the conditions prevailing a couple of months or more ago, but they are now quite out of date; and, in justice to the really serious efforts which the Chinese government has since made to introduce efficiency into the salt administration, I would be glad to see them contradicted. The working regulations now drawn up by Sir Richard Dane for the administration of the salt gabelle have been approved by the Minister of Finance,[1] and seem to us quite satisfactory. They secure adequate executive powers to the Chief Inspectorate, and already the collection of salt revenue is showing encouraging results. Up to the present date, speaking in round figures, the collection paid into the group's Banks in Tientsin is $2,500,000; in Chinan-fu $1,000,000; in Canton $500,000; in Hangchow, Foochow and Hankow probably about $1,000,000. This total of $5,000,000 represents a collection spread nominally over the period of five months from June to October, but actually only over half that period, since comparatively little was collected during June and July; it also of course leaves untouched the Liang-huai and other important salt centres in the interior, from which contributions may be expected later, when conditions have become more settled. In Tientsin alone, collection is proceeding at the rate of about $400,000 a week, so that from this source we may expect an average of nearly $2,000,000 a month. If the other places named can be relied on to contribute another $1,000,000 a month between them, an average total will be reached of $3,000,000 a month, or $36,000,000 a year. From this of course has to be deducted the cost of collection; and it has further to be borne in mind that the winter, being the season for salting vegetables and provisions, is a more active time for the salt trade than the summer. Making every reservation however, I consider that the outlook, thanks to the indomitable energy and high administrative ability of Sir Richard Dane, is great deal more encouraging than we should have dared to to predict a couple of months ago.

The actual liabilities of the Chinese government, chargeable on the salt are, in round figures:- two months' service of the indemnity (uncovered by the Maritime Customs) at £250,000 a month = $5,000,000; annual service of Crisp and other loans, say $7,500,000; service of reorganisation loan, $12,500,000; total $25,000,000 showing a substantial margin of estimated collection over liabilities.

With regard to the public, it will of course require more than mere estimates, based upon the collection of a couple of months, to remove the unfavourable impression produced by earlier reports. Nothing in fact will remove their deep rooted scepticism but actual results, extending over some months, published over the signature of Sir R. Dane; and my advice to the

[1] Hsiung Hsi-ling, at this time Prime Minister, was concurrently Minister of Finance (11 September 1913 – 9 February 1914).

Chinese government would be that they direct all their efforts to make his first report a successful one.

I have marked this letter as confidential, but the information it contains is of course at your disposal to make use of at your discretion; I only ask that, as promised in your letter under reply, you will treat its source as strictly confidential.

Yours sincerely
E. G. Hillier

666. From C. N. E. Eliot[1]

The University, Hongkong 12 November 1913

Dear Dr Morrison,

Very many thanks for the book. Yes, it is mine, only I cannot imagine how lit came to be found in Mrs Morrison's drawing room. Had it been found in the library I should not have been surprised, but I distinctly remember that Mrs Morrison was away from Peking at the time that I left, and that my attempts to say goodbye to her were in vain. I can only imagine that after the manner of a Chinese story, a portion of my spirit entered into the book, and caused it to execute a call on its own account.

I am also much obliged for your letter of Oct 24 about the University of Peking.[2] I had already heard that it has been reopened and therefore am not surprised at what you say. But still, a considerable number of students are sent abroad from different parts of China every year to study in Japan, America, or Europe. I certainly understood from the President that he would cause some of these students to be sent here, and if any convenient oppor-

---

[1] Sir Charles Norton Edgcumbe Eliot (1862–1931), British diplomat and scholar. He had served at various diplomatic posts, including those of Secretary at the British Embassy in Washington, and High Commissioner in Samoa (1899), and Zanzibar (1900–4), before becoming Vice-Chancellor of Sheffield University in 1905. In 1912 he became the first Principal of the University of Hong Kong, and in 1919 was made British Ambassador to Japan, holding the post until 1926. A Sanskrit and Turkish scholar, he was the author, *inter alia*, of a Finnish grammar, a book on Hinduism and Buddhism and many papers on marine biology. Morrison, writing to Ts'ai T'ing-kan (20 August 1913), said of him: 'Sir Charles is a very famous scholar who had a wonderful career at Oxford and afterwards in the Diplomatic service. Had he remained in the Diplomatic service he would now be an Ambassador. He is really a wonderful linguist knowing, I believe, 23 languages. Hongkong University was lucky to get such a man as principal.' Eliot made a point of spending several weeks every year working in Morrison's library in Peking.

[2] In an audience which Morrison had helped to secure for him with Yüan Shih-k'ai when Eliot was visiting his library in Peking in August 1913, Eliot was promised that Hong Kong University would be among the institutions to which students sponsored by the Chinese Government would be sent upon the inauguration of such a programme. Morrison, in his letter to which this was the reply, told Eliot that the Ministry of Education had decided to re-open Peking University, which had been closed. It was to function as a fully-fledged university with no immediate intention of using it as a preparatory institution for sending students abroad.

tunity presents itself, I hope you will remind him of the matter. You can assure him that both the Governor of this Colony[1] (who is Chancellor) and myself have no sympathy with revolutionary ideas, and we do our best to keep the students rather old fashioned in political and social matters.

The present position is extraordinarily interesting. I confess I do not understand it very clearly, for the Hongkong Press is not illuminating, but the really remarkable thing is that the dispersal of the Kuo Ming tang does not seem to have aroused any visible indignation or even protest.

With kindest regards

Yours very sincerely
C. Eliot

667. From G. Passeri[2] to T'ang Jui[3]

Peking 21 November 1913

Private & Confidential

Dear Sir,

With reference to the various conversations which I have had the pleasure to have with you with regard to the financial needs of China and its present and future relations with the Quintuple Group,[4] I now beg to express to you my views on the subject and the remedies that I think could be applied by us

[1] Sir Francis Henry May.
[2] G. Passeri, Italian Adviser to the Bank of China. In this capacity he was responsible, on 12 May 1916, for disobeying the moratorium ordered by Yüan Shih-k'ai, and thus saved the reputation of the Bank, an act which won for Chang Chia-ao (b. 1888), then Assistant Manager of the Shanghai Branch of the Bank, censure from the Government but credit from historians. In 1918, when Passeri helped to liquidate the Deutsch-Asiatische Bank, a course of action Morrison had long and persistently advocated, Morrison described him as a 'Damned crooked clever Italian knave, both lawyer and Chartered Accountant.' A copy of this letter to T'ang Jui (q.v.) was given by Passeri to Morrison, who also strongly resented the control exerted by this consortium of banks over China, and who had earlier tried unsuccessfully to help China free herself from it.
[3] T'ang Jui (or T'ang Chüeh-tun) (d. 1916), Chinese Republican politician. A native of Kwangtung Province and a fellow student of Liang Ch'i-ch'ao, he became Liang's political associate and, according to Liang's account, had taken part in the abortive uprising of 1900 in Wuchang, engineered by the reform leader T'ang Ts'ai-ch'ang (1867–1900). In August 1913 he became Deputy Governor of the Bank of China and Governor the following month, but was replaced by Sa Fu-mao (q.v.) in July 1914. In 1916 he was sent as an emissary by Liang Ch'i-ch'ao to Lu Yung-t'ing in Kwangsi, and successfully persuaded Lu to change his stand from that of a supporter to that of an opponent of Yüan's monarchical scheme. He then became Lu's representative to Lung Chi-kuang in an effort to persuade the Military Governor of Kwangtung to take the same stand, but was shot by Lung's subordinates on 12 April 1916 during the conference which had been called to finalise Kwangtung's declaration of independence from the Central Government.
[4] After the American withdrawal, the Group came to be known as the Five-Power or Quintuple Group.

in order to render the Republic free from a consortium, whose principal aim is a political one.

I have to admit that the present financial condition of China, the general economic situation of the Country and, what is more important, the past and present engagements with the Bankers of the Quintuple Group, would render impossible any attempt to escape from their grip at the present moment.

We are now surrounded by a circle of iron, which prevents us from obtaining any help from the world at large. In this circle of iron only a few could penetrate and are those who came to China to offer you small loans at conditions that were not always convenient, but that you had at times to accept as you had no choice. These people from whom you got these small loans were far from representing the real capitalists and, in most instances, were only the envoys of industrial and commercial enterprises, whose chief aim was to obtain an order for their products or a concession for the exploitation of China's natural riches. In only one instance, that of the Crisp Loan, can we find something in the nature of a serious proposal, although some of the persons connected with it out here in China were not all that could be desired to carry out successfully an enterprise that at that time meant a challenge to the political interests of the various nations interested in the Quintuple Group. But we must not forget that the attitude taken at that time by some of the Powers was so unpopular amongst the individuals of the various nationalities that the loan could have gone through had it been handled in a more appropriate manner, while you must not forget also that the attitude taken by the Foreign Governments would not be repeated to-day, because of its unpopularity at the time of the Crisp Loan and because the understanding that existed then amongst the Five Powers is far from being the same at present, that some of the most powerful nations have realised that they are playing into the hands of those that had no financial strength but great economical and political interests in China. It is a well known fact that some of the Powers have declared that they are ready to back up any other enterprise outside of the Quintuple Group if the loan does not come under the heading of 'reorganisation' and we must not forget that this decision was taken in order not to allow the continuation of a monopoly that may be termed disgraceful. Besides, and as a proof that the Quintuple Group are not sticking together at present as they were before, exists the fact that the negotiations for the second loan of £25,000,000, in which is embodied the Currency Loan of £10,000,000, were at first carried through by only three of the Banks: the British, the German and the French, without the knowledge of the other two, who were admitted into the Group only during the last few days. I could give you many more instances to persuade you that this circle of iron, which I have mentioned above, is beginning to show signs of weakness here and there, as it is a fact that, if the interests of the Quintuple Group Powers are not always those of China, it must be admitted that the interests in China of the Five Powers are in some cases in open conflict and if the differences were forgotten for a time they are liable to come up again, as they cannot always be smoothed down at will.

As far as I can see we should not look at the Quintuple Group of to-day as an insurmountable obstacle to our financial independence and, if this financial independence is still impossible to-day, there is no reason why we should not begin to work in order to obtain it in the future.

In other words China needs money at present very badly, it is a necessity to obtain a loan within three months and certainly nothing much can be done within three months towards our financial independence and we shall have, therefore, to negotiate again with the Quintuple Group.

The conditions that they impose on us are hard, impossible to accept and this for two reasons: first, because the banks are not anxious to lend us money, as the foreign money markets are and are going to be flooded with various loans; second, because we have so far not given any signs of contemplating the possibility of going ourselves out into the open market to approach directly the real capitalists.

We cannot do much towards counterbalancing the first of these reasons, but it is left entirely to us to act in such a manner as to show the Quintuple Group that we begin working for our financial independence.

Before going deeply into this matter, I wish to explain to you a few points in connection with the Quintuple Group, which may help you to understand a good many of my future arguments.

The Quintuple Group is, as you know very well, a consortium created chiefly for political interests. Every one of the Banks composing it has been backed up so far by its own Government, as the conditions of China were such as to render impossible any escape from such a monopoly. There is one point nevertheless which we must take into due consideration and of which we must try to make the best we can and that is that the Quintuple Group is far from representing the money market of the world and also that the money market of the world is not a slave of political interests. If we go carefully into the matter we will find that the Quintuple Group of Banks have no financial strength of their own and are only intermediary between China and the open money markets on a commission basis, a commission that is unluckily too heavy a burden on our national finances.

In consideration of this commission apparently they lend us their credit, but if we consider the matter carefully we may come to the conclusion that we could do without their assistance if we tried to do so.

In fact they would not float our loans if the security we offer was not sufficient to cover the risks, while the supervision that they demand on our expenditure is only insisted upon for political reasons. All that they do is to take our bonds fully secured and float them on the various markets and it is not only because of the name of the Banks of the Quintuple Group or the moral support of the Foreign Governments that the last Reorganisation was oversubscribed many times in Europe, but also because the security offered by China was quite a good enough guarantee for the investors. As a proof of what I am saying I may mention that the last Japanese Loan, although handled by strong Foreign Banks, with the approval of Foreign Governments, was only subscribed for a small fraction, while the bulk of it had to be taken up by the underwriting Banks.

There remains another fact which must have our attention which is to find out where is the money that is lent to China coming from: not certainly from Japan, not from Russia, but chiefly from France, England and Germany in the order given. And to whom does this money belong? In Europe a good deal of the national wealth is in the hands of private people and it is from these people that the money is obtained for us. And what do these private people care for the Russian interests in Mongolia, the Japanese interests in Manchuria, the British interests in Thibet, the German interests in Shantung and the French interests in Southern China? Do you not believe that if other 'independent' bankers could be made to handle our loans for our account these people would not just as readily subscribe? Many of the Banks belonging to the Quintuple Group are unknown in their own country, have no financial strength neither do they command the money markets and they have to seek for assistance themselves from those banks whose undertakings are merely financial ones and that they do not realise in many instances that they are backing up interests that are conflicting with those of the one Power to which their money is lent.

Having explained to you the above points in connection with the Quintuple Group, I may now proceed to express my proposal which I hope will meet with your approval.

As I have said already our present situation makes it compulsory for us to negotiate for another loan and at the present moment we cannot address ourselves to anybody else but the Quintuple Group, as we are not prepared to do otherwise.

After this new loan which will probably reach the amount of £25,000,000 I trust that there will be no more need for China of money under the heading of 'reorganisation', while it is pretty certain that we may require loans for other purposes and I believe that it would be a good plan to prepare from now the means to render ourselves independent from the Quintuple Group for future needs. I believe that what we ought to do without any loss of time is to send out to America and Europe a few gentlemen on a financial mission. By financial mission I do not mean one that ought to seek for loans from the very beginning, but a body of men of practical wisdom and knowledge of the conditions of China, who ought to go round the world to approach not only the financial authorities of the various Powers but, what is still more important, the biggest banking institutions and wealthy private banks and bankers. Their task ought to be to explain to these people the real conditions of our country, their relations with the Quintuple Group banks, the way we have been handicapped so far in obtaining financial help and try by these means to interest these independent financiers in the affairs of the Republic and to make them understand that it would be as much in their interests as in ours to deal directly instead of through the Quintuple Group, which makes of 'their' money a weapon to wound China in its most vital part. In the various capitals of foreign nations, leading commercial banks could be made to accept the agency of the Bank of China on the understanding that in case of need they ought to help us in floating our National Loans on the usual commission basis.

This financial mission should have, therefore, two distinct aims, one to approach directly the big money holders and make them sympathise with us, creating therefore in the various money markets a sympathetic feeling with China, the other to obtain the support of independent banks for our future needs. I believe that if this task could be entrusted to the right persons, who might with their knowledge of China's financial conditions and their businesslike proposals gain both the confidence and trust of the big financial men in America and Europe, a great step would be made towards our financial independence. Having perfected all the necessary arrangements and having paid over to the Bank of China the £10,000,000 out of the loan that we are just negotiating I do not see why in future it should not be possible for us to handle the loans of our Government and to float them in Europe with the help of our agents. There are a good many points in this connection which I wish to elucidate in order to reduce as much as possible the objections to my proposal, but before doing so I will mention the advantages, immediate and future, which we would obtain from the working of my scheme.

I daresay that the fact of the Chinese Government and the Bank of China sending out a financial mission would greatly impress the financial circles both in China and Europe: the first immediate advantage that we would obtain would probably be that the Quintuple Group, in seeing our earnestness to render ourselves independent, may lower their demands for the present loan and modify their conditions to such an extent as to render them acceptable to our Government.

Besides this advantage of a material character we would gain a great moral victory as we would show to the monopolists that we are beginning to wake up and are trying to get away from their clutches.

The advantages for our future financial welfare are quite plain and do not require much explanation: we would in fact be able to take full advantage of the whole of the offer of money existing in the world, instead of being tied down to a consortium that dictate their own terms.

I am sure that in reading this letter your impression will be that my proposal is very good, but that you are certainly afraid that it will be very difficult to carry out, as it may appear to you that I have forgotten that the Quintuple Group is backed by their own Governments and that if we should try to obtain money directly they would endeavour to make our plans a failure.

If that is your impression I can assure you that I have not forgotten either of these two points and that I quite anticipate what may happen.

To begin with I have to repeat here again that the Government's support to the Quintuple Group has been only given for the Reoganisation Loan or any other Loans that may come under this heading, while the same Governments have declared that they are willing to support any other financial enterprises in China for other purposes. If we obtain the £25,000,000 from the Quintuple Group now, in future we may not require any more money for the purpose and, even if we did, it should not be very difficult to make the new loans appear under another heading, as we must not forget that independent bankers in Europe and America will not demand a supervision of our expenditure, while of course they may ask a control of their security, but even this control will be of a very mild form as there are no political interests attached to it.

Should my plan be carried out two things may happen:

In the first place the Quintuple Group of Banks or rather every one of the five banks, seeing that we are trying to get independent capital and having no means whatever to prevent us from doing so, may make the best of the situation and be again what they were in the past, commercial enterprises looking for business where they can find it. In this case they would be more our friends than our enemies, as it would be in their interest to take even an indirect part in the flotations of new loans. This is of course a very optimistic view of the situation, but, knowing as I do the foreign banks in China, I quite expect that they would take this course, as when the worst comes to the worst they would not lose the chance to make money for reasons that do not exist any longer. In this case then, while our Agents in Europe and America would float our loans, the foreign banks in China would probably not only take up some of our bonds for account of their private clients, but would also I am sure offer their assistance to us to bring out the money from Europe for our account as they would certainly make money by it. It would be left to us to accept this offer or not and, as a proof that what I mention is very likely to happen, I give the instance of the Crisp Loan, when the Chartered Bank entrusted with the payment of it in China was confronted at first with the enmity of the other banks, while when the other banks saw that they could not prevent the Chartered Bank from carrying out their engagement they stepped out and asked and voluntarily offered assistance to the Chinese Government in this connection, assistance that was accepted in order to get the funds more readily from home. This shows exactly my point, that the Foreign Banks in China would not lose an opportunity when nothing better is left to them. I may mention in this connection quite confidently to you that it is to my knowledge that, while the Quintuple Group of Banks has agreed to stick together and not to offer or give any direct or indirect assistance to the Chinese Government in order to force you to accept their conditions for the first Reorganisation Loan, almost every one of the five banks did give direct or indirect assistance in the way of small loans, discounting of Chinese Government bonds etc., the money of which it was a well known fact was going to the Chinese Government. At the time, I may mention to you, very serious quarrels arose, but nothing came out of them, the only result being that the banks seeing that they could not prevent the others from making underhand dealings followed suit themselves and gave their assistance which they ought not to have given. Of these facts I can give you verbally all the particulars you like, particulars which would go to prove that the Quintuple Group stick together as long as China is willing to pass through their hands, but that almost every one of the banks of the Quintuple Group is quite ready to transact direct with us should the occasion come to do so.

In the second instance and I believe the one that you expect would take place, the Quintuple Group of Banks and their Governments would show fight if we were to try and get the money elsewhere. This fight might explicate itself in two ways: first they might try and frighten China diplomatically, second they may try to reduce our credit by talking against us and at the same time they may try to harm us in influencing the money markets.

You will readily understand after all that I have said that if we were to require new loans in the future we may easily pass them under other headings than 'reorganisation' and in this case any diplomatic interference would be absolutely groundless and surely the Home Governments are too serious and too self respecting to go against China without a reason as they would besides go against what they have declared, i.e. their readiness to back up any other enterprise outside the Quintuple Group if loans are not made for Reorganisation purposes.

With regard to the actions of the banks of the Quintuple Group themselves, they could not try to reduce our credit by denouncing our position, firstly because they would not by their action affect the securities we may offer for new loans, securities that should be open to inspection by the parties interested, secondly because it would not be in their interest to do so, as after all they would have by that time probably £50,000,000 of our obligations in their hands and any campaign against us would surely create a reduction in the value of their holdings or of those of their clients, while of course any sensible person would readily understand that the campaign against us is only made because we are trying to get the money elsewhere. And in this connection we must not forget that our Agents and friends in Europe and America would probably render this campaign useless by standing up for us.

Nor would the Banks of the Quintuple Group be in a position to influence the money markets against us, as their strength in foreign countries is very small, rather insignificant if compared with that of the Agents we may succeed in appointing for our Bank.

I hope I have succeeded in making the situation quite clear to you, but I do not deny that to a proposal like mine many objections may be raised, objections that do not come to my mind at the present moment, but which I am sure I would be in a position to answer successfully if submitted to me. I consider in fact my proposal of such a vital importance for the future of China that I beg of you to consider carefully my scheme and give me a list of remarks that you or your friends in the Ministry of Finance may consider of any help to the working of the plan.

[...]

Recommending my proposal to your careful consideration and that of the Minister of Finance,

I beg to remain

Yours faithfully
Passeri

668. From Ts'ai T'ing-kan

Peking 23 November 1913

My dear Morrison,

[...] The President asked about you yesterday and when I told him that you felt so easy about the situation you went to shoot ducks for a week in Pao-ting he was very pleased.

Sir John also enquired after you.

Yours sincerely
Tsai Ting kan

669. From O. M. Green

Shanghai 24 November 1913

Dear Morrison,

[...] People down here, or some of them, still have the Japanese scare; and if one looks far ahead and remembers that, in the event of China's being really developed and prosperous, Japan would take a very second place in the Far East, one can't be surprised. You will have seen from the paper the extraordinary panic which occurred last week round Kiangnan.[1] No one even the Chinese officials could understand it, and many people are saying 'Oh,

---

[1] A reference to the attack on the Kiangnan Arsenal in Shanghai, in which many Japanese took part.

Japan'. I must say I could not understand the alleged 'moderation' of Japan in respect of Nanking.[1] Fraser harped on it and so did *The Times*.[2] There is probably a lot inside of which I know nothing and evidently Chang Hsun's loyalty to Yuan was able to stand more strain than one had expected. But when one remembers all the circumstances of the case, that the Japanese were 'suspect' from the first, especially in connexion with the defence of Nanking and that they may almost have been said to lay themselves out to get killed – also that it was a time of civil war when such incidents are more or less inevitable, I do think the exceptional pressure they put at this very delicate point was unnecessarily harsh and most dangerous to the Central Government; and we had for us (considering our traditional friendship to Japan) a pretty strong leader, of which I wired a summary to *The Times*.[3]
[...]

Yours sincerely
O. M. Green

670. To Ku Wei-chün[4]

[Peking] 24 November 1913

Dear Dr. Koo,

With regard to our conversation the other day concerning the premature publication by Reuter's Agency of the text of a synopsis of the Russo-Mongolian Agreement, it may interest you to know that the full text of the

[1] Following the sacking of Nanking and the death of three of its Japanese residents, Japan made a very stringent series of demands, including the dismissal of Chang Hsün from the post of Military Governor of Kiangsu Province.

[2] In David Fraser's telegram of 14 September, published under the title: 'The Japanese demands. Full compliance by China. Policy of the Tokyo Cabinet' these words appeared: 'the present Japanese policy to China is unaggressive and Japan recognises that her interests are best served by the preservation of peace in China...'.

[3] The summary appeared in *The Times* of 27 September, entitled 'Misgivings in Shanghai'. It began: '*The North China Daily News*, which is traditionally friendly to Japan, protests most strongly against the extraordinary pressure which Japan is putting on China in respect of the incident at Nanking, where the killing of three Japanese, although the most regrettable, is the more easily condonable, in view of all the circumstances of the case, of all offences of which Japan complains.'

[4] Ku Wei-chün (b. 1887), Chinese diplomat and Republican politician, otherwise known as Wellington Koo. He was one of China's best-known and ablest representatives abroad during the Republican period, of both the Peking and Nanking governments. A graduate of Columbia University where his father-in-law, Tang Shao-yi, had been a student, he had probably one of the smoothest and most successful careers, becoming in 1915, at the age of 28, Chinese Minister to the United States, already by then one of China's most important diplomatic posts, within three years of his appointment as a Secretary in the Ministry of Foreign Affairs in Peking. He first came into international prominence as a delegate to the Paris Peace Conference where his pleading of China's case, though it was in vain, made a profound impression on those who witnessed it. After representing China again at the Washington Conference, he returned to Peking and

agreement was communicated by the Russian Government at St Petersburg on November the 8th to the Japanese and French Embassies. Presumably it was also communicated to the other Embassies but this I do not know for certain. This will explain what at the time did not seem clear to either of us – how it was that the Japanese had the full text of the Agreement. Mr. Kroupensky's suggestion that it was the Chinese who had communicated the text was an impudent piece of bluff.[1]

I have no doubt whatever that it was the Russian Legation in Peking who disclosed the text of the Agreement which they had undertaken not to publish until some time later.

With best wishes and hoping soon to have the privilege of another conversation with you

Very sincerely yours
[G. E. Morrison]

671. From C. S. Addis

London 25 November 1913

My dear Morrison,

It gave me great pleasure to receive your very kind letter [...][2]

The expulsion of the Kuo Ming t'ang must be justified by its success.[3] I take it from you such a course had become inevitable; but it was hazardous to risk sending back to their electors 300 disgraced men to foment disaffection in the south, and had the *coup d'état* failed...

---

remained there until the overthrow of the Peking regime in 1928, serving three times as Foreign Minister (August–November 1922; April 1923 – October 1924; October 1926 – June 1927), as well as Finance Minister (May–October 1926) and twice as Acting Prime Minister (July–September 1924 and October 1926 – June 1927). After the Kuomintang came into power in 1928, an order for his arrest for his role in the Peking regime was made, but was later rescinded. In 1931 he assumed a prominent role again as Foreign Minister in the Nanking Government, and proved himself an able advocate of China's cause after the Japanese seizure of Manchuria. From 1931 until his retirement as China's representative at the International Court of Justice in The Hague in 1967, he was Nanking's most prominent diplomat and held almost continuously three of China's most important diplomatic posts, those of Minister, then Ambassador to France (1932–40), Ambassador to Great Britain (1940–4) and to the United States (1946–56), and represented China at practically every major international conference during the period. Morrison first came to know Ku and had frequent contact with him while Ku was serving in Peking. They met again during the Paris Peace Conference.

[1] Morrison was indeed guilty of indiscretion, as is revealed in his Diary, in having leaked the contents of the Russo-Mongolian Agreement to A. E. Wearne, Reuter's Correspondent, and was very much embarrassed by it. This letter was his attempt to explain away his indiscretion. [2] Not found.

[3] On 4 November 1913 Yüan Shih-k'ai ordered the dissolution of the Kuomintang and the cancellation of the parliamentary credentials of the Kuomintang members. Over 400 members were affected and Parliament as a result ceased to function through lack of a quorum.

I believe we are all agreed here that the crux of the situation is the neglect of the Provinces to contribute to the Central exchequer. To that there are two policies. (a) to supply the Central Govt. with money in order to extend the revenue control and (b) to withhold further loans until the Provinces, seeing the Central Govt. confronted with bankruptcy, realize the necessity of remitting.

From a foreigner's point of view I regard the second of these two policies as being no policy at all, unless it be the policy of letting the ship drift and waiting to see what will happen. The difficulty in the way of policy (a) is the provision of adequate security but I do not think that difficulty should prove insurmountable unless some of the Powers elect to make it so.

I am so glad to hear Dane is doing well. He made an excellent impression here.

Best wishes for the coming year to you and Mrs Morrison, and, I am delighted to be able to add, to your family.

Believe me

Yours truly
C. Addis

672. To Ch'en Chin-t'ao[1]

Peking 26 November 1913

Private & Confidential

Dear Dr. Chen Chin-tao,

I send for your confidential information the memorandum which I have just sent in to the Prime Minister[2] and which, in a slightly modified form, I have also sent in as a memorandum for the President. I hope it meets with your approval.

With kind regards

Very sincerely yours
[G. E. Morrison]

---

[1] Ch'en Chin-t'ao (1870–1939), Chinese Imperial official and Republican politician. A returned student from America, he had worked in the Imperial Bank and on the Board of Finance under the Manchu Government and became Minister of Finance in the Provisional Republican Government established under Sun Yat-sen in 1912, and later Director-General of the Central Audit Office in Peking. In 1913, on Morrison's recommendation, he was sent to Europe as Financial Commissioner with a view to negotiate foreign loans, and upon his return became Minister of Finance in June 1916 in the Tuan Ch'i-jui cabinet and concurrently Director-General of the Salt Administration. In May 1917 he was the victim of a conspiracy said to have been engineered by Liang Shih-yi and was arrested on a charge of corruption, remaining in prison until February 1918. In 1920 Sun Yat-sen appointed him Minister of Finance in his Government in Canton but he did not take up the post. In 1925, however, he again served briefly as Finance Minister of the Peking regime in the Hsü Shih-ying Cabinet. He later taught at Tsinghua University in Peking and in 1938 joined the Puppet Government set up by the Japanese in Nanking under Liang Hung-chih, as Finance Minister, a post he held until his death.

[2] On the same day as this letter was written, Morrison also wrote to Hsiung Hsi-ling, the

Enclosure to Letter No. 672: *Memorandum Regarding the sending Abroad of a Financial Agent of the Chinese Government, 26th November, 1913*

Before referring to the sending abroad of Dr. Chen Chin-tao I would like again to draw attention to the need of preventing or minimising the injury so frequently done to the good name of China by hostile articles or telegrams published in the European Press.

I suggested to His Excellency the Prime Minister that instructions might be sent to the Chinese Ministers in England, France, Germany and Russia regarding the correction of injurious telegrams published in the European papers. I now learn from Mr. Hsiung Hsi-ling that this has been done. I gave as illustrations passages published in the London *Times*, which is the chief of the English newspapers. I pointed out how regrettable it was that there should be a delay in correcting such misstatements. Papers of the high standing of *The Times*, whose aim and object are to publish the truth, will always gladly publish corrections of misstatements to which they have inadvertently given currency.[1]

Injurious statements or messages published by responsible newspapers in Europe ought not to pass without contradiction. China sends Ministers to Europe to support the good name and credit of their country. Where statements appear in a paper of such power as *The Times* alleging, for example, as was done on October the 22nd last that China is 'preventing the Reorganisation of the Salt Gabelle', an authoritative contradiction should immediately be published by the Legation in London, and if they have no material at hand with which to contradict it, they should report the adverse comment to the Wai Chiao Pu who could furnish them with the material for a reply.

Adverse statements of this kind ought to be telegraphed to Peking in the words in which they are written condensed to telegraphic brevity. The cost of such transmission is quite unimportant. Such messages sent at 'deferred' rates are telegraphed to Peking at half price. Effective reply cannot be sent unless the exact words are known, for in the reply reference has to be made to the exact words.

The necessity of such action is obvious. In England, France, Germany, and to some extent in Russia, the Government is influenced by public opinion. Public opinion is guided by the Press. If that Press is misinformed serious injury can be done, especially to the credit of a country. In view of China's intention to negotiate a large foreign loan in Europe it is obviously

---

Prime Minister and Minister of Finance, repeating what he had embodied in the enclosed memorandum. The letter is not printed.

[1] The memorandum Morrison sent to Hsiung Hsi-ling on 14 November 1913 was entitled 'Memorandum regarding Injurious Statements in the European Press'. It is in substance a repetition of the first part of this memorandum, and is not printed.

essential that statements injurious to the credit of the country should not be published, or if they are published when erroneous should not be allowed to pass unchallenged.

I suggested that a brief memorandum embodying this suggestion might profitably be sent to the Ministers abroad and I now learn, as I have said, that this has been done.

The need of such action was obvious in view of the sending abroad of a Financial Agent of the Chinese Government. In this connection I desire to make certain suggestions.

In the first place Dr. Chen Chin-tao must be properly accredited. For the past year or more many Chinese have appeared in Europe proclaiming themselves representatives of the Chinese Government for financial affairs. These men have not always added to the credit of their country. One delegate lately sent to London who stayed there at a well known hotel took Chinese curios for sale and was indignant when the landlord of the hotel refused to allow them to be displayed for sale in the hotel corridor as curios are displayed in the entrance of the Hotel Wagons-lits in Peking.[1]

To be properly accredited I would suggest that in the first place the Wai Chiao-Pu should officially inform the British Minister and other Ministers concerned, but especially the British Minister, that Dr. Chen Chin-tao has, by Presidential Mandate, been appointed Financial Agent abroad with the rank of Minister Plenipotentiary and then I would suggest that His Excellency the Minister of Finance should accompany Dr. Chen Chin-tao to the British Legation and should personally request the British Legation to notify the British Foreign Office that Dr. Chen Chin-tao is proceeding to Europe duly authorised and accredited by the Chinese Government. In this way Dr. Chen Chin-tao will go to Europe with the honour befitting his post.

I would suggest that Dr. Chen Chin-tao be the direct representative of the Ministry of Finance – the financial agent of the Ministry of Finance. On his arrival in London he should at once be officially presented by the Chinese Minister to the British Foreign Office as the official representative of the Chinese Government, a similar procedure to be followed on his arrival at other foreign Capitals.

I would also suggest that while in Europe Dr. Chen should be kept very fully informed on the financial position in China so that he can answer questions first hand. In the past it has too often happened that information on Chinese affairs has reached the foreign banks before it has reached the

[1] A reference to Sung Fa-hsiang, or Far T. Sung. Morrison wrote in his Diary on 12 November 1913: 'Dr Chen Chin-tao came in. He is going to England as Financial Agent.... I told him of Far T. Sung and of his taking home 2000 dollars of curios, silks, porcelain, carpets etc. which he wanted to display at the Portland Hotel as the curio dealers display their wares in the Wagons-Lits.' Morrison elsewhere described him as a 'rascal and imposter'. For Sung's official career *see* p. 361 note 1.

Chinese Legation causing embarrassment to the Chinese representative who has to admit that certain information has not reached him.

Should the Government decide, while Dr. Chen Chin-tao is abroad, to send to Europe or to America any special delegate entrusted with some special loan affair, I would emphasise the importance of keeping Dr. Chen Chin-tao informed of the mission so as to prevent the confusion that has so often resulted in the past from having two missions abroad each one working independently of the other and each one therefore necessarily conflicting with the other.

The procedure I have outlined above is the ordinary procedure in sending abroad Financial Agents invested with high authority.

673. From H. de Reuter[1] to A. E. Wearne

London 27 November 1913

Dear Sir,

We have the pleasure to acknowledge receipt of your two letters of the 10th inst.,[2] both of which we have read with particular interest, and which, so far as they deal with matters outside mere editorial work, we reserve the discussion for a future date, when we have had time to study the valuable suggestions with which you have been good enough to favour us. Consequently we confine ourselves at the present moment to the treatment of the editorial questions raised in connection with which we invite your particular attention to the enclosed letter from our Chief Editor,[3] with whom we have discoursed the matter in its various aspects. It is important that you should penetrate yourself with our Chief Editor's remarks, because at your distance there are certain fundamental features of the case that escape both you and Dr Morrison. Our press is peculiar in its treatment of political questions, as it deals with news on the subject very much in accordance with what it believes to be the public fancy for the time being. With few exceptions, news from countries which are not immediately before the public eye, in consequence of stirring or sensational events, are more or less cold shouldered to make way for matters of relatively secondary value from places where events of this description occur, and receive accordingly the largest hospitality in the columns of the press.

People abroad, and even the most intelligent correspondents, often fail to realise these, it must be confessed, not very intelligible, or rather intelligent journalistic methods: but as we have to take things as we find them it would be folly to ignore what is daily present to our eyes, and attempt single-

---

[1] Auguste Julius Clemens Herbert de Reuter (1852–1915), Managing Director of Reuters Telegram Co. [2] Not printed.

[3] The letter to Herbert de Reuter from F. W. Dickinson, Managing Editor of Reuters Telegram Company, here referred to, dated 24 November 1913, is not printed.

handed to run atilt against the almost universal tendency of our press, and deliberately indulged in.

It is therefore hopeless to expect matters from countries like China to find an ample welcome in the column of the press here, unless a revolution or kindred sensation provide a condiment for the intelligence. Hence we lay stress on this irrepressible fact to prevent the disappointment arising for those unaware of, or who seek to ignore it.

We for our part naturally desire to improve our services to the utmost, by incorporating the intrinsically important matters that you and Dr Morrison would readily embody in the telegrams: but we feel it our duty to spare you and him the chagrin of finding much of the material wasted, in consequence of the attitude of the press, and to put you therefore on your guard against attempting what, in the circumstances, may be found difficult of achievement in the full sense of your expectations. If, on the other hand, you and Dr Morrison will take into account what the Chief Editor and our accompanying letter urge in this respect, we believe we can fruitfully serve China as well as the people of this country.

Thanking you for your esteemed report of the position
I remain

Yours faithfully
Herbert de Reuter

674. To Ts'ai T'ing-kan

Peking 28 November 1913

My dear Admiral,

I send you herewith two papers,[1] which I would ask you to bring before the notice of the President. Since Mr. Ju is with you working at the map I send them to you direct. Please read them and see that there is nothing in them that would conflict with your own views and knowledge.

The position in Mongolia is much worse than I have stated. Things are all right at Kweihuacheng and in Eastern Mongolia but towards the Kalgan end of the routes to Urga, to Dolon Nor and to Kweihuacheng things are very unsatisfactory indeed. The fact is large numbers of the Inner Mongols have been compelled to throw in their lot with the Outer Mongols. You will remember that some time ago Na Beileh returned to China bringing with him some of his own but leaving behind about 300 troops whom he wished

[1] Only one memorandum is printed here. It seems to have been inspired by Mizuno Kō-kichi, the counsellor at the Japanese Legation, for in his Diary of 26 November 1913 Morrison wrote: 'Visit from Midzuno who suggests the opening of Kweihuacheng, Kalgan, Dolon-nor, Chih Feng, Kai Lu, Taonanfu as trade marts open to Foreign Trade. Think idea good and wrote accordingly a memo which I will send in tomorrow.' The compiler of the chronological record of the life of Liang Shih-yi (*see* p. 79 note 2), however, attributed the idea of opening trade marts to Liang.

to send later to their homes near Hsinminfu, but there were delays in Peking and postponements and the result has been that the 300 troops have been compelled to join the Urga army of advance. Very few Mongolian soldiers have been killed. There has been very little actual fighting. The fact is the Mongols can stand the climate and the Chinese soldiers have not yet been acclimatised. You cannot fight when you are hungry and cold, are made panicky by the reports of the strength of your opponents, their fleetness of movement, their excellent equipment and the assistance that is being given to them by foreign officers!

However I need not say too much about this. The fact remains that Inner Mongolia is in a serious state. Russians are, as you see from the map, moving about in Inner Mongolia: Russian settlers are dwelling there. In addition to military measures it is necessary as quickly as possible to do some diplomatic act such as the opening of those six frontier trade marts which will strengthen the commercial interest of foreigners in Inner Mongolia so that foreigners will not regard with complacency any attempt by Russia to do in Inner Mongolia what she has done in Outer Mongolia.

With best wishes

Very sincerely yours
[G. E. Morrison]

Enclosure to Letter No. 674: *Memorandum* re *Mongolia, 28 November 1913*

I desire to point out the urgent need of taking steps to interest foreign countries in the retention by China of Inner Mongolia. Had the late Government voluntarily opened, as it was urged to do, Urga and Uliassutai to foreign trade and had it authorised foreign merchants to reside there for the purpose of trade, the occupation of Urga and of Uliassutai by Russian troops would have been rendered difficult if not impossible.

The conditions in Mongolia at the present time are most unsatisfactory. A condition of warfare exists along the frontier and Mongolian troops, consisting largely of troops from Urga itself and accompanied by field guns manned in some cases by Russian officers and in all cases by Mongols who have been trained by Russian officers are close to the border of China proper. Chinese troops have been fighting on the high tableland of Mongolia at a great disadvantage. They have had no previous experience of such fighting. They have had no previous experience of such immense mobility of movement as characterises the movements of the Mongolian troops. They are poorly provided with what is necessary to resist the severity of the climate. Outside of Kalgan on the roads to Urga and Dolon Nor in a large number of cases, some of which have been actually witnessed by foreigners, the Chinese troops have fled precipitately abandoning everything without firing a shot on the mere appearance of Mongols. On the other hand over large areas of Inner Mongolia the Chinese troops have been harrowing the friendly

Mongols. Reports of victories have certainly in many cases been victories over these unarmed peasants.

Apparently the Central Government are being often deceived as to the action of the troops in Inner Mongolia. Reports from independent sources confirm the charges that frequently Chinese troops on coming to an encampment of friendly Mongols have driven the Mongols from their tents and have used their woodwork and their furniture for firewood. What was done by the Chinese troops in Peking on the 29th of February last year has been done in various places throughout Inner Mongolia. At Tabol the Chinese soldiers even looted the property of Mr. Larson the Adviser on Mongolian Affairs. Only two weeks ago the Chinese troops stationed at Ta Wang Miao 30 *li* west of Tabol ran away without firing a shot. Chinese troops are now driven back to Shaberte 90 *li* from Kalgan on the road to Dolon Nor, only 30 *li* from the top of the Pass which leads from Kalgan on to the Mongol table-land. Climatic conditions are very severe, especially for those who are unaccustomed to such conditions.

Now I venture to point out this. Unless different methods can be adopted by the Chinese soldiers there will be the same trouble in Inner Mongolia that there has been in Outer Mongolia.

Russian settlers are living, although they have no treaty right to do so, in various parts of Inner Mongolia and they are affected by the disturbances. Many observers fear that they may ask for Russian protection and there is obvious danger in this.

To prevent Inner Mongolia from having the fate of Outer Mongolia it is obviously necessary to act so as to win back the sympathy of the Inner Mongols. To expel and to kill Outer Mongols who are raiding Inner Mongolia is justifiable, but to loot and kill friendly Mongols settled peaceably in Inner Mongolia is little short of madness, for reprisals then take place and the Chinese settlers are made to suffer as the Mongols have suffered. To retain the Inner Mongols they must be better treated than, or at least as well treated as, the Outer Mongols are treated by the Russians. At present the influence of the *Hutukhtu* who is their God is powerful in Inner Mongolia and he and his people are being well treated by the Russians. Russian officers have been active in Inner Mongolia and the conditions they report, namely that the Chinese soldiers treat the Mongols worse than cattle, may give the same pretext for Russian intervention as was given under the late dynasty by the unwise policy of the *Amban* Santo in Urga.

But while it is certain that the conditions are unsatisfactory it is equally certain that under the present government these conditions will be ameliorated and the Inner Mongols will be rendered so satisfied that instead of desiring to join the Outer Mongols and invite Russian assistance they will endeavour to wean the Outer Mongols from their dependence upon Russia.

Two ways suggest themselves for resisting the Russian advance. There is the military way and simultaneously there is the peaceful way of interesting foreigners in the trade of Inner Mongolia by creating a number of trade marts open to foreign trade and residence along the border of Inner Mongolia. The time is opportune for the Agreement regarding Outer Mongolia has been concluded and published to the world. I suggest that without any loss of time a Presidential Mandate should be issued declaring that with the object of promoting international trade Kuan Cheng tze, Kalgan, Dolon Nor, Ch'ih Fêng (Hata), K'ai Lu and Taonanfu, six important Chinese frontier towns are forthwith open to foreign trade and residence, according to regulations to be drawn up by the Minister of Home Affairs after consultation with the Minister of Foreign Affairs. Trade marts thus opened are on a wholly different footing from ports opened by Treaty with Foreign Powers. China retains all rights of every kind and herself draws up the Regulations giving foreigners the right of residence and of trade. The Maritime Customs can be instructed to open Customs Stations at these places so that there will be an increase in the Customs revenue which is now needed to meet China's financial obligations.

All Powers are interested in the Maritime Customs Revenue because of the Boxer Indemnity and of various large loans secured upon the Customs. All Powers are, therefore, interested in the retention by China of her Customs stations and of the territory served by those stations. Should these six stations be opened as I suggest all foreign powers will be interested in their retention by China for all time and similar action to that which has been so disastrous in Urga will be averted. Confidential reports show that during last year (and this year) Russian Officers disguised as Merchants or ordinary travellers have been investigating the conditions in Inner Mongolia with a view to action in the future similar to that taken in the past in Outer Mongolia.

It would be advisable to open all six places at the same time for it would be invidious to open Kweihuacheng and Kalgan only and might give the appearance of action against Russia, whereas if all 6 places were opened there would be no discrimination shown as against Russia or Japan. Objection may be raised on the ground that at first the chief foreigners to settle in some of the places would be Japanese but that is the case already. Japanese already reside in those places although they have no Treaty right to do so.

Precedents for the opening of such inland trade marts can be found in the case of Chinwangtao and of Tsinanfu. Chinwangtao was opened to foreign trade on the 15th December 1901 in deference to a memorial presented by the Wai Wu Pu, Kwang Hsü 24th year 3rd Moon 4th day.

As regards Kalgan it will be remembered that the Treaty between China and Russia regarding Ili signed at St. Petersburg 24th February 1881 provides in Article 13 that 'In the town of Kalgan Russian subjects can erect houses shops stores and other buildings on land which may be acquired either by purchase or by grant from the local Authorities.'

Other foreign Merchants – British German and Japanese – have also opened places for trade in Kalgan but it would be wise if this procedure were regularised in the way I have suggested.

Action should not be delayed. It cannot be known when tranquillity will be restored in Mongolia and in the meantime the opening can be declared and the preparations for establishing the Customs can be proceeded with. It is opportune to act now: a little later and difficulties may have arisen rendering such spontaneous action difficult.

675. From Ts'ai T'ing-kan

Peking 28 November 1913

My dear Doctor,
Thanks for letter and Memos.[1]
President will surely be pleased to peruse their contents.

He stated to me yesterday that he desires you to give him in short and suggestive paragraphs foreigners view of what China should do to make herself strong and prosperous; what is needful and urgent for the moment and when her house is in some order what further should be done. In fact to make out a policy of gradual development.

With best wishes

Yours sincerely
Tsai Ting kan

676. To Ts'ai T'ing-kan

[Peking] 29 November 1913

My dear Admiral,
I would like to draw your attention to the following suggestion and request that if you consider it worthy of consideration you communicate it both to the President and to the Prime Minister.

Now that the agreement between Russia and China regarding Mongolia has been signed it is opportune that steps should be taken to bring about peace in Inner Mongolia. Winter has come on, the conditions are extremely severe and there can be little doubt that there is a general desire on the part of both combatants that hostilities between the Mongols and the Chinese should discontinue.

At present Mr. F. A. Larson, the Adviser on Mongolian Affairs, is in Peking anxious to assist in bringing about peace. He has, as you know, a wider knowledge of Mongolia than is possessed by any other man. For 20 years he has been living in Mongolia travelling from one end of the country to the other, and is known personally or by name to every Mongol official in both Inner and Outer Mongolia. It was Mr. Larson who recently

[1] A reference to the preceding letter, No. 674, and enclosure.

went up to the border of Sunit and brought back Na Beileh (now Na Wang Yeh) to Peking.

This morning Mr. Larson received a letter from a trustworthy friend residing at Tabol where Mr. Larson himself lives, 250 *li* north of Kalgan, stating that he had received on Monday a visit from a Mongol Commander who said that the Mongols knew that peace had been declared and that the Mongols were no longer to fight on the cultivated land occupied by the Chinese peasants but they were to resist any movement of Chinese troops into the grass lands of Mongolia.

All indications point to the desire of the Mongols to have peace.

I suggest, therefore, that Mr. Larson, who is the man best competent for such a mission, should be instructed to proceed to Mongolia and act as intermediary arranging with the Mongol Leaders the terms under which they are willing to lay down their arms. He is prepared to leave at once and proceed to the neighbourhood of his home which is 250 *li* north of Kalgan. From there he will send letters to the Mongol leaders and arrange a Conference with them and hear what they have to say. Only good could come of such a mission as this. It is absolutely necessary that Mr. Larson should be instructed to go. He cannot go on his own responsibility for if so he would be exposed to the same indignity that he experienced before at the hands of some of the Chinese officers who openly spoke of him as a 'foreign devil' and hinted that the work that he was doing was none of his business.

Mr. Larson speaks Mongol fluently but does not speak Chinese well. It would be advantageous to him to have a trustworthy Chinese Interpreter. The one best suited for this would be Mr. Samuel Shen[1] who is now employed in the Telegraph Service and whose name is known to Mr. Hsiung Hsi-ling. He has previously been with Mr. Larson in Mongolia and understands conditions there and speaks English perfectly. Mr. Larson would also take with him one of the men of Na Wang Yeh. If it should be decided to send Mr. Larson to Mongolia instructions must be sent to the Chinese Generals at Kalgan that he is to be properly treated.

I hope this suggestion may bear fruit and that there may be as little delay as possible. Mr. Larson is ready to leave Peking at a few hours' notice.

With best wishes

Very sincerely yours
[G. E. Morrison]

[1] Most probably Shen Shou-chih, who was Director of Telegraphs in Jehol, of which Province Hsiung Hsi-ling was *Tutung* (Lieutenant-General) from April 1912 to July 1913.

677. From Chang Yü-chün[1]

Peking 2 December 1913

Dear Dr. Morrison,

I wonder whether you have any idea to help the President to pass over the dead lock of the present political situation as we regard that he is now in a position which is rather difficult to get out since the dissolution of the Kuomingtang and the unseating of the Kuomintang members from the Parliament.

It is of course a serious question whether the Parliament is of any, if any, use to the present China. But anyhow we have already come to a position which recklessly compels us to admit a representative government although the millions are still far away from such a standard. Some men are in favour with the policy of giving up the Parliamentary system for at least two or three years. It is, however, not very wise to take such a step because lest we shall be exposed to a condition which has be experienced by Mexico.

I have written some thing to advise the President to revive the Parliament by diminishing the number of the lower house by half, say; and by making the new Administrative Council to stand as the Senate. Of course I have not been well qualified to make any real good recommendation on political lines. I did so only according to what I thought best.

Chinese people are highly in a position to be educated as how to advance the country by graduate progress. Most of us do not even know what is a constitution and practically 90 per cent of the population are quite indifferent about governmental system. What is essential for the government is to promote the political knowledge of the people and get them interested in the political questions so as they might be properly guided to study it in a practical way. The condition of what the Government has done is only to tell the masses that to study the politics is a dangerous way for their own life. This is again the famous Emperess Dowager of the late Dynasty's default which was the fountain of the 1900 riot and also the root of the 1911 Revolution which she made in 1898.

I am afraid that I have made too much request to you. But I am in a position to understand that your valuable words are of great appreciation to the Repsident that I can not bear to restrain from committing myself to do so.

I am

Yours truly
L. Chang

[1] This letter is printed with its original mistakes, 'graduate' for 'gradual', 'Repsident' for 'President' etc.

678. To Ts'ao Chia-hsiang

[Peking] 3 December 1913

Dear Captain Tsao,

I send you herewith a memorandum regarding the suggested policy in Mongolia which I have drawn up for you incorporating suggestions made by Mr. Larson, the Adviser on Mongolian Affairs who is, as I have said in the report, the chief living authority on Mongolia.

I would be so much obliged if you would have it translated into Chinese and communicated to His Excellency the President.

The printed details regarding the Texas Rangers and the Canadian Mounted Police will be sent later.[1]

I think all we have said is simple and practical. I have condensed it as much as possible and have made it as simple as possible.

I have other memoranda which will be sent in shortly.

Very sincerely yours
[G. E. Morrison]

Enclosure to Letter No. 678: *Memorandum Regarding Mongolia, 3 December 1913*

In order to secure permanent peace in Inner Mongolia, the conditions of the country, climate and habits of the people must be taken into consideration.

Owing to the fact that the country is uncultivated, sparsely settled, the climate cold and dry and the people living in tents which can be moved at a very short notice, the regular Chinese troops, unaccustomed to these conditions, find themselves at great disadvantage and expense. In North West Canada and along the Mexican borders of the United States, where similar conditions prevail, special forces specially trained for police work known as the Canadian Mounted Police and the Texas Rangers have done excellent work. [...] Either of them would serve as an admirable model for a Chinese police on the Mongolian border.

A strong force on these lines is needed in Inner Mongolia – a large portion of it to be formed of friendly Cha'hars, the other portion of Chinese, recruited from young, strong farmers of good character and respectable families settled in Mongolia and already accustomed to the conditions of the country. Pay and equipment should be adequate to remove all temptation of looting or persecuting those whom they are engaged to protect. Organisation and training should, at least for the first two or three years, be entrusted if possible to competent foreigners – no less than eight or ten – who are used to similar work. Chinese officers from inside the Wall are not trained for such work nor are they used to the hardships of the Mongolian winter. But here comes in a difficulty. China some years ago

[1] Not printed.

entered into an engagement with Russia not to employ any foreigners in the Northern Army Administration. This engagement was directed specially against the employment of British Officers. It might be wise in this case to borrow for two or three years some American officers from the Texas Rangers. In any case the Texas Rangers or the Canadian Mounted Police should serve as the model for such an Organisation. With such a trained force in full operation the plains of Mongolia would soon be as safe and quiet as any other part of the Republic. It may be mentioned that in Persia the *gendarmerie* have been reorganised by Swedish Officers who have done their work tactfully and well. The suggestion is made that if American officers are not available some of these Swedish Officers might be engaged to re-organise the frontier police.

Administration: The old methods employed under the Manchu dynasty are not suited to present conditions in Mongolia. What is needed is a Council of the Mongols themselves held in Mongolia, say, north of Kalgan which should include all the head Princes of Inner Mongolia, such as Abugai Ta Wang, Durbet Wang etc. Among them also should be included Hai San Kung, at present in Urga, who has great organising ability and knowledge of both Mongols and Chinese. He has proved himself throughout the recent crisis a loyal subject of the Chinese Republic. His son could take his place till he arrived. To this Council Mr. Larson, who has a knowledge of Mongolia greater than that possessed by any other man Chinese or Foreign, could be attached as Adviser.

Probably none of these Princes, with the exception of Hai San Kung, would require any financial support.

The head Princes would not be required to stay permanently at the headquarters of the Council, but they could meet in conference once a year or oftener if necessary. At other times their places could be taken at headquarters by intelligent deputies to whom all questions could be referred. This Mongol Council should have the right to summon smaller Princes and Officials resident in the uncultivated areas of Mongolian territory and discuss with them the conditions under which improvements could be possible. Their proposals could then be sent to the Central Government for confirmation or rejection. This Mongol Council should also have the right to send members to Parliament. It should also have the right to decide all questions arising anywhere regarding the cultivation and colonisation of new territory: also it should have the right to control the policy system and be responsible for reporting immediately to the Central Government any disaffection that might lead to a breach of the peace of the Republic.

As far as possible the Mongol Council should keep the people of Mongolia informed as to the aims and laws of the Republican Government. All matters pertaining to military movements and training of troops should previously be agreed upon by the Central Government and the Mongol Council. Many other questions about the organisation etc. would naturally come up for discussion and would be subsequently referred to the Central Government. All such matters should be settled between the Council and the Central Government direct and not by the intervention of intermediaries.

The Mongols would soon learn that they are citizens of the Republic and that the interests of the Republic are their interests.

Communications: Owing to the lack of proper communications in Mongolia the Chinese soldiers have been greatly handicapped. No rapid movements are possible and Chinese merchants are compelled to pay exorbitant prices for transport. It is possible at a reasonable cost to improve these conditions. In the grass lands of Mongolia outside of the cultivated areas the roads are excellent. A railway should be constructed from Kalgan northwards over the pass to Chagon Horo where the grass lands begin. The distance is only 250 *li* and once this distance is passed there are good roads in every direction. From this point a motor car could, without difficulty, reach Dolon Nor in a day, the boundary between Inner and Outer Mongolia in two days and Urga in four days. The railway could at any time be extended in any direction. There are no engineering difficulties. The importance of a railway from Kalgan to this place on the main road to Kuei hua ting, Kalgan and Dolon Nor is obvious as at present the difficulty and expense of mounting the pass north of Kalgan are enormous. This short railway would be a boon to Chinese merchants as under the present conditions the difficulties of bringing goods to and from Kalgan are enormous. The course of this suggested railway has been surveyed by Mr. Lagerholm the Swedish Engineer. The maps of this survey are still in the hands of Mr. Lagerholm in Tientsin.

Education: The supreme need of the Mongols is Education. At present education along Western lines exists nowhere in Mongolia except in Urga and Uliassutai where schools have been opened by the Russians. One of the first reforms to be discussed by the Mongol Council would be education and the opening of preparatory schools throughout the country. High schools, with competent teachers, should be established by the Central Government at the headquarters of the proposed Mongol Council north of Kalgan. Mongols should be given the same educational advantages as are accorded to Chinese throughout the Republic. Foreign missionaries who give their time to education work should be encouraged. Modern educational books should be translated into Mongol. Mongols also need properly trained and intelligent doctors.

[...][1]

General Improvements: If Kalgan and other places in Inner Mongolia were opened immediately as foreign trade marts foreign commerce would increase, the country would prosper and foreign aggression be prevented.

[1] Here paragraphs on cattle-breeding are omitted.

Artesian wells should be bored in districts where there is plenty of grass but no water.

An agreement should be made whereby the Inner Mongols will have the same privileges of entering Urga and Outer Mongolia with their caravans as the Outer Mongols have of entering Kalgan. At present high duties are charged in Urga upon all goods leaving or entering Outer Mongolia unless they are Russian goods or under Russian control.

Russia has already opened a good Public School in Urga: also a hospital with a foreign doctor, and to cope with the terrible cattle sickness she has an establishment under a competent veterinary surgeon. She is about to construct a railway from the Siberian railway to Kiakhta which she will soon extend to Urga. Above all she gives protection to the Outer Mongols and to the preservation of peace and tranquillity. China must be prepared to do all this and more for the Inner Mongols so as to induce them to look upon the Republic as their home and not to seek elsewhere for help.

It is certain that the Living Buddha,[1] who has immense religious influence, being regarded as a God, will with Russian help endeavour to strengthen his political influence in Inner Mongolia.

The railway from Kalgan which has recently been opened to Tatung should be extended to Kuei hua ting and as already suggested the six frontier places of Kuei hua ting, Kalgan, Dolon Nor, Ch'ih Feng, Kai lu and Taonan-fu should be opened as trade marts open to foreign trade and residence.[2]

679. To J. B. Affleck[3]

[Peking] 9 December 1913

My dear Affleck,

Would you mind telling me to whom I ought to write in connection with an incident I have just witnessed of the brutal maltreatment by two Policemen, Nos 15 and 19, of a Chinese newspaper seller – a young boy of 18 or so.

When I was walking with Mr Cox of Reuters I saw the two Policemen cruelly beating this young fellow. They were holding him down on the ground, pulling him about by his pigtail. When we went up the Policemen said that he had committed some small offence, but even if he had committed a serious offence he ought not to have been treated in this way.

This occurred on the north side of the bridge across the moat just outside of the Italian Legation. A Chinese policeman came up and in quite a friendly way advised that the young man should go quietly with Policeman No 15 to the Police Office in the Eastern Part of the Legation Quarter. What happened there I do not know.

[1] The *Hutukhtu*. [2] *See* p. 258 note 1 and p. 275 note 2.
[3] John Barr Affleck (1878–1941), British consular official, at this time serving as accountant with the British Legation in Peking. He retired as Consul-General in Tientsin in August 1938.

So often these Policemen, taking advantage of their being employed by foreigners, are seen maltreating the Chinese that I think it would be a wise thing if an example were made in this case and the Policemen Nos 15 and 19 be hauled over the coals.

Yours very sincerely
[G. E. Morrison]

680. To C. D. Bruce

[Peking] 9 December 1913

My dear Bruce,

I feel ashamed to have left your letter[1] so long unanswered, but I have been very rushed. I am afraid that naturally you are waiting to hear from me before you write to me of your visit to Nanking. I will, with pleasure, communicate whatever you suggest to the President and will warmly support any scheme you suggest.

The crux of your letter is that the Civil Governor in Nanking[2] has shown himself so far either unwilling or powerless to support Admiral Tseng[3] in carrying out sound and effective reforms. The time is opportune for speaking to the President provided the President carries out what he promised me last week, namely that within one week he would remove Chang Hsun and 9000 of his troops. Every time I see the President I speak to him about Chang Hsun and the need of his removal. I am waiting with much curiosity to see whether he will carry out the promise he has so definitely made.

Things in Mongolia are in a bad way. China has 60,000 troops along the frontier and they are being held in check and persistently routed by some 3,000 Mongols. China has brought the trouble upon herself and has only herself to blame. I submitted an offer on behalf of Mr. Larson, the Adviser on Mongolian Affairs to proceed to Tabol near Kalgan, summon a Conference of the Mongolian Princes and endeavour to bring about peace. Mr Larson is confident that he could do so but his scheme has been blocked by the military who, so long as there is plunder and dollars and rewards for raiding innocent villagers, are anxious that the present situation should continue.

I am optimistic enough to hope that after having the affairs of Kiangsi

---

[1] Bruce's letter of 13 August is not printed.

[2] Han Kuo-chün (?1858–1942), Republican politician. He was at this time Civil Governor of his native Kiangsu Province (September 1913 – May 1914). He became Governor of the province again in June 1921, holding the post until 1925. He was Governor of Anhwei from July 1914 to July 1915.

[3] Cheng Ju-cheng (d. 1915), Chinese sailor, Rear-Admiral. He was appointed on 28 July 1913 Garrison Commander at Shanghai. His arrival in Shanghai on 3 July, combined with other political and military moves by the Peking Government, helped to precipitate the action of Li Lieh-chün at Hukow nine days after this letter. Cheng was later assassinated on 10 November 1915 by the southern republicans for his repressive measures against them.

and of the Yangtze mouth[1] put in order you may be called to Peking to organise a Police Service along the frontier of Mongolia. In the meantime the chief drain upon China's resources is the maintenance of the Chinese troops in Inner Mongolia. It is a loss both directly by payment and indirectly by the stoppage of all trade.

Please write to me again and I will promise not to be so long in answering next time.

With all good wishes

Very sincerely yours
[G. E. Morrison]

681. To Ku Wei-chün

[Peking] 16 December 1913

Dear Dr. Koo,

A long letter which I have just received from Professor Jeremiah W. Jenks,[2] enclosing a copy of a letter which he has written to the Wai Chiao-pu in which your name occurs, constrains me to write to you.

Surely under the new methods of Government it is time to discontinue the waste of money involved in the retention of information bureaus.

Until quite recently – perhaps it does so even to this day – the Wai Chiao-pu maintained a Press Bureau in Brussels called the Agence de l'Extreme Orient. The Agency received a subsidy not only from the Wai Chiao-pu but from the Ministry of Communications and from certain Provincial officials. The Agency was nominally managed by a Secretary of Legation named Wang Mou-tao.[3] It published and still publishes *La Revue Jaune*, a worthless Magazine that fills no purpose whatsoever other than to bring an undeserved subsidy to its publishers. This agency, which is actually controlled by a paid Belgian Journalist of inferior calibre, was subsidised to send communications to the Press in England and on the Continent. At one time six London Journals subscribed to it, none of first rate importance, but at present no London Journal will spare space for its communications.

[1] A reference to Yüan Shih-k'ai's cleaning-up operation after the 'Second Revolution'.
[2] Jeremiah Whipple Jenks (1856–1929), American economist. While Professor of Political Economy at Cornell (1891–1912), he was invited in 1904 by the Chinese Government to advise on monetary reform. The proposals he produced were strongly condemned by Morrison, who had a poor opinion of Jenks' integrity and ability. In the letter to Morrison dated 12 November 1913, enclosing a long letter which Jenks asked Morrison to forward to the Wai-chiao pu (Chinese Ministry of Foreign Affairs), Jenks appealed to him for assistance to enable him 'to do something to give the American people, through the press, accurate information regarding the situation in China, so far as I can secure it, and also to attempt, through suggestions to editors, to mould somewhat the mental attitude of the American people on that question,...provided,' he continued, 'I can be free from the annoyance of advancing money out of my own pocket every month and continual cabling.' Jenks' long letter to the Wai-chiao pu is not printed.
[3] At this time Second Secretary in the Chinese Legation in Brussels.

On the 9th of July 1910 these six London Journals each received a circular from the Agency purporting to be telegraphed to it from Peking and stating as follows:—

'There has been a jolly scandal in Peking. One knows now that the British Minister has been recalled and Dr. Morrison has been superseded. They have been associated with the head of Jardine Mathesons in an opium smuggling conspiracy in South China. Mr. Bredon[1] discovered the nice little game. He has just seized a large consignment of opium in Canton' and so on.

No paper ventured to publish this libellous statement. For this letter the Chinese Government was compelled to apologise both to Sir John Jordan and to myself. Still the Agency continues. Mr. Wang Mou-tao still holds an official position and the *Revue Jaune* is still published to the detriment of the good name of China.

For some time past I have been receiving every week a budget of feebly written copy, vulgarly known as 'piffle', issued by the Far Eastern Information Bureau, 15 Astor Place New York. One has just come in. Conducted by a Journalist[2] who has never been to China, this highly-paid Agency picks up scraps from telegrams sent from China by the newspaper Correspondents and paragraphs from papers published in the Far East, rehashes them and sells them to whatever newspapers are willing to buy such stuff.

I enclose you a copy of their last lucubration: '500 words. Editorial Suggestion. We sleep whilst others wake.' It is really an appeal to the American people to devote more attention to China. Surely it is not necessary for China to pay an American Journalist to write articles urging American manufacturers to devote more attention to China! American manufacturers can look after themselves. The 'Special Correspondence' dated Shanghai October 12th is simply a repetition of Reuter's message.

Professor Jenks, whom I know personally, appeals to me to induce you to provide a monthly sum for the retention of the bureau to which his name is given as director. I regret I cannot accede to his request. I think that every

[1] Sir Robert Edward Bredon (1846–1918), British employee of the Chinese Maritime Customs which he joined in 1873, retiring in 1897. In that same year he was recalled to China by his brother-in-law Sir Robert Hart to rejoin the service, and was appointed Deputy Inspector-General, with the understanding that he would take over Hart's position upon his death or retirement. The British Government, which had supported the plan, changed its mind, however. Because of an undertaking extracted from China in 1898 that Britain would have a say in the matter, Bredon was not appointed. As Deputy Inspector-General (1898–1908), however, he was allowed to act as Inspector-General (1908–10) during Hart's absence from China, but upon F. A. Aglen's being appointed to Hart's position upon Hart's death, Bredon was compensated with an appointment as Adviser to the Shui-wu ch'u (Chinese Board of Revenue).

[2] Earl Hamilton Smith, American journalist. He was employed as Editor in the Far Eastern Information Bureau which Jenks founded and directed with subsidies from the Chinese government through their legation in Washington.

dollar spent on such a bureau is a dollar wasted. To pay $1500 gold per month as a 'minimum sum' for the maintenance of such a bureau is not only an inexcusable waste of money but it is an undignified act unworthy of a Government like that of China. I am convinced that this Bureau should be closed down at once and that China should in her own interests make a rule never to waste money in this way.

Professor Jenks wants $300 gold a month for his services. In his own profession the Professor occupies a high position and the salary he asks for, were it for services rendered in the special subjects of which he is a master, would not be unreasonable but as payment for services in connection with the Press bureau any salary would be excessive. This is a higher salary than is paid to Reuter's Correspondent in Peking though Reuter sends out first hand news for the information of the whole world not the feeble and belated copy published by the Far Eastern Information Bureau.

Of nothing am I more convinced than that the system of subsidising foreign Press Bureaus is injurious to the good name of China. On my return to China in October of last year at a Cabinet Meeting at which I was present I was informed that a sum of money had been set apart for me wherewith to pay for messages that were to be sent to Europe for Publication. I said that no such money was needed. Correspondents are only too glad to send news for nothing, and as a matter of fact the many thousands of words sent at different times during the last year on behalf of the Chinese Government to the European Press have not cost the Chinese Government one cent.

I write to you confidentially and I am sure you will treat the letter in confidence. You are one of the ablest of the officials in China with a great career before you. You will, I am sure, see that the continuance of these Press bureaus conducted by paid aliens is injurious to the good name and prestige of your country.

China now has many Chinese who write a foreign language perfectly. Surely it is this class of man who ought to be employed as publicists and correspondents in foreign countries. A Chinese correspondent in London or in America can live well and move in good Society and meet all foreign Journalists on equal footing on an income of £600 per annum – $500 Mex. a month with certain allowances for travelling expenses. Japanese correspondents in Europe are paid a smaller salary than this.

The time has come when China ought to employ her own subjects as correspondents and should discontinue the subsidising of *La Revue Jaune* and of the Far Eastern Information Bureau and such like Organisations, which bring into ridicule the country that is known to pay for them.[1]

With kind regards

Very sincerely yours
[G. E. Morrison]

[1] In his reply dated 19 December 1913 Ku Wei-chün, thanking Morrison for his 'frank expression' of his views, said: 'This organization [the Far Eastern Information Bureau]

682. To Ijūin Hikokichi

[Peking] 27 December 1913

Private & Confidential

Dear Mr. Ijuin,

I take the opportunity of this Season to send to you and Mrs Ijuin the best wishes of my wife and of myself for your continued success, happiness and prosperity. We miss you greatly: we read with interest of your doings in Japan: we are confident that the day is not far distant when you will be called to still higher office in the service of your country.[1]

At the same time I am taking the liberty of writing to you frankly and confidentially in regard to a matter in which I am personally interested and regarding which I seek your advice and opinion. It concerns the disposal of my library, which has now reached such proportions as to be beyond my power to continue. My work with the Chinese demands so much time that I am forced to discontinue the hobby, the pursuit of which has given me so much pleasure and instruction during the past twenty years. From the beginning of next year I propose to regard my library as sufficiently complete and will only buy afterwards such books as may be needed to keep it up to date.

More than a year and a half ago Sir John Jordan told me that you had spoken to him with regard to the possibility of my library being acquired for Japan, either by the Government or by some public institution. About the same time I was spoken to with regard to the possibility of its being acquired by a wealthy Japanese nobleman, whose name was not disclosed to me. At that time I did contemplate selling the collection, having in view my return to Australia, but circumstances arose which, as you know, made me decide to remain in Peking and accept service under the Chinese Government.

At that time my library was not catalogued. Since I entered the Chinese service I have, with the assistance of three secretaries, worked incessantly at

---

was started by one of the then members of the Chinese Legation in Washington at a time when J. O. P. Bland was pouring forth his tirade of criticism against the Chinese Republic before American audiences. During the first few months it was supported by voluntary advances made by this official, and it is only recently that the Director of the Bureau has approached the Waichiao Pu for permanent support. A moderate sum has been remitted to it until the end of the current year. The question of maintaining it thereafter on the basis proposed by the Director is still under consideration. Your letter has come in time.'

[1] Ijūin left Peking in September as Japanese Minister under criticism for what many Japanese considered to be his over-conciliatory attitude towards Yüan Shih-k'ai's Government. He was later appointed Japanese Minister to Italy (1916–20), and became a member of the Japanese Delegation to the Paris Peace Conference in 1919. In September 1922 he was appointed Governor-General of the Japanese Leased Territory of Kwantung Peninsula, but was recalled in September the following year by Yamamoto Gombē to be Foreign Minister in his Cabinet. He held this post until his death in 1924.

the Index. It is now complete in 1600 typrewitten pages 11 × 8½ in. The work has been carefully done. Each book, fully described, has been properly entered under the name of the author, with cross references wherever necessary.

In the library also are many MSS, as for example the MS Journals of Lord Macartney's Embassy to China,[1] and I have also catalogued my prints and engravings of personages and scenes and views in China, a collection which has been described as unique in its completeness. My collection of maps is also unusually complete but it is not included in the index.

Although my library has been kept up to date, and I have continued to add to it almost daily, I find the work taxes my time and my energies to a degree that I am no longer able to sustain. The task in fact is too great for any one man. I have therefore decided to sell the collection, and my determination is known to certain American delegates who have recently been in Peking. No agreement has been come to, nor can I say that negotiations have been even yet entered into. All that has happened so far has been that I have been asked if I would be prepared to sell my library to an American institution and I have answered in the affirmative.

But while prepared to sell my library I would prefer, if it possibly can be arranged, to see my library permanently installed in the Far East. My work during the last twenty years has been wholly in the Far East. The library has grown up in the Far East. It deals almost exclusively with the Far East. If it were possible to retain it in the Far East, then I would indeed be glad, and this leads me to the object of my letter, which is to ask you, privately and confidentially, whether in your opinion there would be any prospect of my library being purchased in Japan.

It has been so formed that it could, without difficulty, continue to be kept up to date, and the books are so catalogued and arranged that any trained librarian could at once take charge of them.

As Your Excellency knows the library consists of books in foreign languages – it does not contain Japanese books.

If such a library were to go to Japan, I know it would be well looked after, and its value as a collection recognised, containing as it does so large a number of rare editions of historical value.

When asked by the American delegates what value I placed upon the library, I replied £40,000. I have been told by those I have consulted, that

[1] George Macartney Macartney (1737–1806), 1st Earl, British politician, Governor of Madras (1781–5). In 1792 he was sent by George III on a special mission to China with a view to the opening of China to British trade. The reply by Hung-li, the Ch'ien-lung Emperor (1711–99), to the message of George III borne by Macartney, has hitherto been cited by historians as an illustration of China's arrogance and by apologists of subsequent British aggression towards China as the main cause of Sino-British conflict. The journals of Macartney's embassy were among the more valuable items in Morrison's collection sold to Iwasaki Hisaya (q.v.) and are now housed in the Tōyō Bunko in Tokyo.

this is not an unreasonable sum, based as it is upon the fact that the library is the only one of its kind in the world, that its formation has required 20 years of unremitting work and that the great majority of the rare books were acquired in the days before interest in the Far East had been awakened and the value of books on China had been enhanced by the competition of American libraries. But if it were possible for the library to be retained in the Far East, where it could serve to some degree in recalling my associations with the Far East, I would be prepared to part with it for a less sum than this.

The library is housed in a fireproof building. It is insured at Lloyds, London for £25,000, a sum which is well below its real value. At any time I would be glad to allow it to be examined by a duly accredited expert who would know that the value of a specialized collection is always much greater than the aggregate value of the individual volume.

I do not know whether you saw it at the time, but in case you did not, I enclose the copy of a paper[1] published in the *North China Daily News* on the occasion of my expected retirement from Peking. It was written by Mr David Fraser my successor as Correspondent of *The Times*.

In conclusion I beg Your Excellency to excuse the freedom with which I have trespassed on your good nature in thus writing to you.

And with best wishes

I am

Very sincerely yours
[G. E. Morrison]

P.S. I have not told anyone in Peking, not even at your Legation, that I have written to you.

683. To Ts'ai T'ing-kan

[Peking] 12 January 1914

My dear Admiral,

If it is true that Russia has protested verbally against the opening of the Trade Marts the news is good, for it shows that the opening of these trade marts will interfere with Russia's aggressive policy.[2] It is now in the highest degree important that immediate steps should be taken to put the Presidential Mandate into effect. Instructions should be given to the Shui Wu Chu at once to take in hand the establishment in these seven places of branches of the Maritime Customs, so that without any loss of time the Government may begin to receive revenue from these places.

[1] Not printed.
[2] Following the suggestion made by Morrison in an attempt to forestall Russian designs, seven towns, five of them in Inner Mongolia, were opened to foreign trade by Presidential Decree on 8 January 1914. These were Kweihwacheng, Chang-chia-k'ou, Dolon Nor, Ch'ih-feng, T'ao-nan, Lung-k'ou and Hulutao.

It would then be easy to point out to the Russian Government should they make any further protest that the Trade Marts are opened in the interests of trade, that their opening has no political significance, that branches of the Maritime Customs are being established there and that inasmuch as the revenue of the Maritime Customs is now devoted to the payment of the Boxer Indemnity, in which the Russian Government is the most interested of the Powers, the Chinese Government are confident that the Russian Government will view the opening with satisfaction.

I am sure you will see the importance of taking this matter in hand as quickly as possible in the interests of international harmony and of the development of China's foreign trade.

With all good wishes

Very sincerely yours
[G. E. Morrison]

P.S. On the day of the opening I received a message from the Japanese Legation saying 'Hearty congratulations. Great success for China.' They evidently cordially approve of what has been done by the President.

684. To E. de Cartier

[Peking] 14 January 1914

My dear De Cartier,

I return you with many thanks the correspondence dated the 1st of December regarding the case of Tuan Jung and his unjust execution.[1] It is a horrible story of false accusation and of falsification of documents to secure the conviction of an innocent man. One such case as this published to the world is alone sufficient to postpone for twenty years any possibility of the abolition of extraterritoriality in China. I am very sorry indeed and I hope that you will induce the Wai Chiao Pu to pursue the case to its end.

With kind regards

Very sincerely yours
[G. E. Morrison]

[1] The enclosure has not been found, but the reference is to the incident which forms the subject of Morrison's letter to Ts'ai T'ing-kan of 4 April 1913, No. 581, p. 118.

685. To C. D. Bruce

[Peking] 16 January 1914

My dear Bruce,

Tomorrow Barton[1] and Captain Tsao Kai-cheong are leaving for Shanghai to make a confidential enquiry into the conditions there with regard to the terms upon which an extension can be granted.[2]

Briefly the case is this. The Community desire the extension. The Chinese here view the proposal favourably and the President, I am sure, desires to meet the wishes of the community but he has also to consider the wishes of his own people and it is quite certain that no extension of territory can be granted unless some disadvantages under which China now labours can be removed or adjusted.

The extension will be granted on the following conditions. I tell you this confidentially. You will, I know, use your knowledge with discretion and see what you can do to help.

1. Compensation for works already constructed in the extension, roads etc., and indemnity for loss sustained by the surrender of taxation. I understand there is no difficulty about this.

2. The taxation of the extension cannot be on the same footing as that of the present Settlement. At present China receives as land tax from the Settlement the equivalent of about $1 per English acre *per annum*. It is quite impossible that China can consent to receive so little for the extension which she is now granting. She will require to receive a proportion of the taxable value of the property. I see no reason why this should not be adjusted.

3. China will require to resume control of the Mixed Court, the present appointment of the Mixed Court Magistrate being a temporary measure of expediency. I understand that there will be no difficulty about this, especially if she will give every guarantee that she will appoint men not inferior to those already occupying the post.

4. There will have to be discussion as to the position of the Assessors, especially in connection with cases as between Chinese and Chinese and

[1] Sidney Barton (1876–1945), British consular official. First going to China in 1895, he was at this time Chinese Secretary at the British Legation in Peking (1911–22). In 1922 he became Consul-General in Shanghai, a post he held until 1929 when he was appointed British Minister to Abyssinia (1929–37). Morrison had a poor opinion of Barton's ability, and particularly deprecated his attitude towards the Chinese, among whom Barton spent 42 years, and whom he invariably called 'swine'.

[2] Following a demand by the Municipal Council of the International Settlement in Shanghai for an extension of the settlement's boundaries, Barton and Ts'ao were despatched to Shanghai to negotiate with the Municipal Council and the local Chinese authorities. Yüan Shih-k'ai was contemplating granting the extension in exchange for Chinese jurisdiction over the Chinese in the International Settlement, essential to his persecution of elements hostile to the Government. Later, Henri de Codt, the Belgian Legal Adviser, was sent down in connection with the Mixed Court, with a view to giving the Chinese authorities greater control over Chinese political offenders.

reconsiderations of the rules for the Mixed Court. I understand that the rules drawn up in 1906 by the Municipal Council are not at present considered sufficient by the Municipal Council, whereas the Chinese would consider that they were far beyond the original rules drawn up in 1869.[1]

5. The most Serious of all is the question of the harbouring in the Shanghai Settlement of criminals who can hardly, even by a technicality that would be counted in any Court of Law, be termed political offenders. This is a question that will have to be discussed. It is quite intolerable that the Settlement should be a Sanctuary for bomb throwers and those engaged in the manufacture of bombs. All civilised countries are agreed that a man engaged in attempting to do violence to the head of the State or to any of his family can in no sense be classed as a political offender.

6. Finally there is the question of Chinese representation upon the Municipal Council. Sir John Jordan when spoken to about this said he thought it was only fair and reasonable. 'Why not', he asked. Barton, who was present, pointed out that there would be many difficulties in the way of this being accomplished. I do not see why these difficulties cannot be overcome. Taxation without representation is a violation of the fundamental law of our Government. Sir John Jordan subsequently said that he thought at any rate there could be Chinese representation on the Municipal Council with regard to the Extention, but I feel pretty confident that this will not be considered sufficient by the Chinese. When the question came up in 1906 and when it was proposed that there should be a Chinese Consultative Committee, the rate-payers, on the ground that such a Committee was not provided for in the Land regulations, threw out the suggestion. It would make for harmony if there were Chinese on the Municipal Council. Certainly Chinese work well on Municipal Councils in Hong Kong, Singapore and elsewhere. If the Community desire extension they cannot expect to give nothing in return.

The President does not wish the mission of Captain Tsao to be too much advertised. He would wish it to be kept secret but obviously this will be difficult. Captain Tsao you met at my house. He is an exceedingly intelligent, fair minded man and he is looking forward with much pleasure to meeting you again in Shanghai. I would suggest that if you would be so kind you might bring him and Green together and have a friendly discussion over the whole case.

Barton is not of what might be called a conciliatory disposition and he takes the view that representation on the Municipal Council will never be granted. I cannot myself believe that this is the view of the Shanghai community.

If there is any information that I can give you with regard to other questions of the mission of Captain Tsao please do not hesitate to write to me and I will reply promptly. He has got all the case clearly written out and I think

This refers to the Land Regulations drawn up by the International Settlement authorities.

he understands it quite well. At any rate he goes down desiring to hear all sides so that he can make a perfectly fair and reasonable report to the President. He is not authorised to do anything more than report upon conditions and to suggest to the President a solution.

My wife is going home to England in the *Devanha* leaving Shanghai on the 24th March and I am coming down to see her off. I will therefore see you if all is well within two months from now.

With best wishes

Believe me

Very sincerely yours
[G. E. Morrison]

686. To Ts'ai T'ing-kan

[Peking] 24 January 1914

My dear Admiral,

I enclose you three memoranda,[1] together with an extract from J. B. Moore, one of the greatest living authorities on international law.[2]

I still have a memorandum to send you with regard to the reception of foreign representatives concerning which I consulted our friend Mr Rockhill,[3] but I really have no time to have it typed this morning. I will send it in to you on Monday.

I hope these memoranda will be of some service to you and that you will approve of them.

I have had a long conference with Mr Wellington Koo and I believe I am right in saying that he is of the same opinion as myself that the question of the Indemnities should be taken to the Hague. Neither he nor I spoke as to who should represent China other than that I expressed my strong opinion that a foreigner should not be employed. I think it most undignified for China to employ a Dr J. C. Ferguson to represent her at a Red Cross Conference in America, a John Forster to be her Consul General in London and a Jeremiah W. Jenks to farm out a fictitious information bureau at Washington, when there are so many able Chinese available for representing their country.

With all good wishes

Very sincerely yours
[G. E. Morrison]

[1] Only two are printed here.
[2] John Bassett Moore (1860–1947), American jurist. He was Professor of International Law and Diplomacy at Columbia University (1891–1924), a Member of the Hague Tribunal (1912–18), and Judge of the Permanent Court of International Justice (1921–8). The extract from Moore's work is not printed.
[3] W. W. Rockhill (q.v.) was then visiting Peking where he was seeking employment with the Chinese Government, having been obliged to retire as American Ambassador to Turkey upon Wilson's accession to the Presidency. The memorandum which Morrison wrote on the reception of foreign representatives is not printed.

Enclosure I to Letter No. 686: *Memorandum regarding employment of Mongol Cavalry in Honan Province, 24 January 1914*

The situation in Mongolia shows great improvement. The withdrawal of the Chinese soldiers has been welcomed by the people. It has been followed by fighting among the Mongols themselves. Molunga and Serembo and many of their followers from Eastern Mongolia have been captured after a struggle with Mongols from Urga and are at present in the camp of the Urga Mongols north of Tabol. Mr. Larson is now in Kalgan and will ascertain full particulars and will report later. Large numbers of Mongols have come over to the Chinese and there is no doubt that all those at present engaged outside of Kalgan, between Kalgan and Dolon Nor, would be glad to return to China provided adequate provision could be made for them. I understand that the Government are prepared to pay three months salary to Mongol soldiers who lay down their arms. The question now is what is to be done with these disbanded soldiers. Why not employ them during the months for which they are being paid?

From the Mongols who have returned to China and from those who are ready to return to China a powerful force could be formed of not less than 500 men, all of whom are good horsemen, good shots and accustomed to move rapidly over long distances. Every one of these men can speak Chinese. Na Beileh, who was the first of the prominent Mongols to come back to China, has experience of handling men of this kind who are his own countrymen and Na Beileh, who has been so abundantly rewarded by the President, is anxious to show his loyalty to the Chinese Government by assisting the Government at the present time in suppressing the White Wolf[1] in Honan. He is confident that if he were given a body of men and were sent down into Honan Province he would bring back the White Wolf dead or alive.

This scheme is one worthy of serious attention. Conditions in Honan Province, especially in the Southern parts, are as bad as they can be. Foreigners speak of the conditions there as 'China's shame' and a leading article in the *Peking Gazette* on Thursday last was written under this heading. Merchants in Hankow are clamouring for foreign intervention in suppressing the disturbances in Honan Province, which are ruining their trade.

[1] Pai Lang, literally 'White Wolf', was the popular name by which Pai Yung-ch'eng was known, and it was also used to refer to the revolt he led. A returned military student from Japan, Pai had earlier served under Wu Lu-chen, who was assassinated by agents of the Manchu Government on 7 November 1911. Pai Yung-ch'eng revolted against Yüan Shih-k'ai's Government in 1913 and for over a year defeated and evaded the troops sent to capture him. Chang Chen-fang, the Military Governor of Honan, the centre of White Wolf's activities, was dismissed for his failure to suppress the revolt, which, however, came to an end during 1914 in Shansi when Pai Yung-ch'eng mysteriously disappeared, reportedly killed. Although Pai's army was small, the revolt created a great stir among the populace and abroad, occurring as it did hard in the wake of the 'Second Revolution' and in the province regarded as the stronghold of Yüan Shih-k'ai.

Sir John Jordan has already submitted a complaint formulated by 21 British Merchants in Hankow urging Consular protection. Already one foreign missionary has been looted and it is to be feared that if the present conditions continue some foreigner will be killed and international complications will arise. Trustworthy foreigners strongly condemn the conduct of the Chinese soldiers in Honan. Trustworthy evidence shows that the soldiers send word in advance to the brigands telling them they are coming so as to give the brigands time to escape. Reports are then furnished to the Central Government of victories where there has been no fighting and injury is thereby done to the good name of the country. Every reason seems to indicate the advisability of employing a body of Mongol cavalry, well mounted and armed, accustomed to travel quickly in the roughest conditions, to chase down the White Wolf and his bands of brigands.

Enclosure II to Letter No. 686: *The Russo Mongolian Chinese Conference at Kiakhta, 24 January 1914*

Now that the two delegates[1] who will represent China at the Tripartite Conference – Russia, Mongolia, China – to be held at Kiakhta,[2] have been appointed I suggest that inasmuch as neither of these delegates has any local knowledge of the conditions in Mongolia they would be wise to confer with Mr. Larson, the Swedish Adviser, before setting out on their difficult

[1] A reference to Pi Kuei-fang (b. 1865) and Ch'en Lu (1878–1939). One of the few Russian-educated students who held a high post during the Republic, Pi Kuei-fang had served with the Chinese Imperial Legation in St Petersburg and as Consul-General in Vladivostok, before becoming Administrator of Tarbagatai District in Mongolia in May 1912. After attending the Kiakhta Conference, to which he was one of the two Chinese delegates, he was appointed concurrently Military and Civil Governor of Heilungkiang Province (May 1916 – June 1917). He then became a Presidential Adviser on military affairs, and in 1927 Director-General of Relief and Rehabilitation. Ch'en Lu was a returned student from France. He had also served in the diplomatic service under the Manchu Government, becoming Chief Secretary of the Ministry of Foreign Affairs in 1909, and was Director of its Political Bureau from 1910 to 1911. In 1913 he was appointed by the Republican Government Minister to Mexico, a post he held until the appointment here referred to. He then became Resident-General in Urga (June 1915 – August 1916). In May 1918 he was made Vice-Minister of Foreign Affairs and was Acting Minister during the absence of Lu Cheng-hsiang at the Paris Peace Conference. In 1920 he was appointed Chinese Minister to France, remaining there until 1927, during the greater part of which period he was said to have had to provide for the upkeep of the mission, the home Government being torn by civil strife and unable to remit funds. On his return to China, he resigned to set up a private legal practice in Shanghai, but re-emerged into politics by becoming Foreign Minister in the Puppet Government set up under Liang Hung-chih by the Japanese occupation forces in Nanking in March 1938. He was assassinated in February the following year.

[2] A conference between Russia, China and the Mongolian authorities at Urga was arranged to take place at Kiakhta, and it resulted in the Tripartite Agreement in regard to Outer Mongolia, signed on 7 June 1915 at Kiakhta.

mission. Mr. Larson's knowledge of Mongolia and the Mongols is unsurpassed. He has already rendered excellent service and he is anxious to continue to render such service to the Government which employs him.

Various questions will have to be settled at the Tripartite Conference. I venture to suggest that this is an opportunity that ought not to be lost for making an attempt to open Urga to international trade. It is well known that the Agreement between Russia and China regarding Mongolia has caused profound dissatisfaction and disappointment to the Mongols. They have practically lost their revenue. Trade has been interfered with. The expulsion of so many Chinese has caused them loss. They cannot get labour for the gold mines. Chinese cultivated the soil and grew vegetables and good stuff. This class of Chinese cultivator and colonist has been specially interfered with and the cost of living has accordingly increased. Expenses of administration have increased fourfold, while the revenue is being decreased. Owing to the difficulty of getting labour the yield from the gold mines has been greatly reduced – it has fallen to about one third. At the same time the Mongols are more in debt than ever, because they have wasted in the most foolish manner possible the money that they borrowed from Russia. They have built a gigantic standing Buddha at Urga and covered it with gold leaf. They have bought ten thousand Buddhas to surround this great image: they are now in treaty to purchase, at ten times its cost, an Elephant brought from the Zoological gardens at St Petersburg. All this extravagance has eaten up most of the two million dollars advanced by the Russian government.

Might I suggest that an arrangement should be proposed whereby a branch of the Chinese Customs could be established in Urga and a percentage of the revenue collected therefrom could be handed over to the Urga Government on the same principle that portion of the revenue collected by the Customs stations in Kiaochao and in Dalny is handed over to the local German and Japanese administrations respectively. Such an arrangement is, I believe, possible because the Mongols are extremely desirous of obtaining revenue and the Russians are equally desirous of seeing conditions established in Urga which would help to relieve the present financial difficulties of the Government which they are now protecting.

At present Article 2 of the Russo-Mongolian Protocol of November 3rd 1912 provides for absolute free trade for Russian subjects in Outer Mongolia. Other countries can and will claim similar privileges. Here then is a question of importance and of difficulty, the easiest solution of which is the one I have suggested. At present Outer Mongolia is under the *suzerainty* of China. This means that the Foreign Relations of Urga are under the control of the Chinese Government. If they are not under this control then China is not the Suzerain Power of Outer Mongolia. But the Chinese Russian Agreement definitely states that China is the Suzerain Power of Outer Mongolia. The Agreement moreover goes further and declares that

Outer Mongolia is part of Chinese territory. If it is part of Chinese Territory then China should be empowered to exercise authority there but she is not so empowered for Outer Mongolia is autonomous. Autonomy implies the right of levying her own Customs duties but Mongolia cannot levy Customs duties because by treaty with Russia she has bound herself not to and because other powers will require similar exemption. But China may not be included and Outer Mongolia may levy duties upon trade with Inner Mongolia and with China. Suppose Outer Mongolia does this then China, now that she has opened other trade marts along the border of Inner Mongolia, will be in a position to impose retaliatory treatment upon the trade of Outer Mongolia so that there will be

1. Either no trade and therefore no revenue;
2. or Trade only with foreign merchants and therefore again no revenue.

At present goods sent to Urga under Transit pass ought to be admitted without further payment, but suppose the Urga Government do not regard the Chinese Transit Pass, to whom will the foreign Governments look for redress? To China? How can they, seeing that China has been deprived of the right to exercise authority in Outer Mongolia. To Mongolia then? But this would mean an Agreement between Foreign Countries and Mongolia and definite treaty engagement between them. This would mean moreover the Recognition by other countries that Mongolia was not under the Suzerainty of China and that it was not a part of Chinese Territory. And it would mean much more, namely, the stationing by Foreign countries of diplomatic representatives at Urga, a policy that would be in a high degree unacceptable to Russia. Therefore Russia for her own sake will not encourage Mongolia in a policy which would give Mongolia direct intercourse with Foreign Countries. And this policy can best be prevented by coming to an Agreement regarding the opening of Urga to foreign trade and the establishment of a branch of the Maritime Customs and the allotment of a proportion of the revenue collected by it to the Government of Urga. This question is one that invites very serious attention.

Then there are more questions to be settled. The Conference will, no doubt, arrange for the issue by the Mongols of Outer Mongolia of a proclamation to all Mongols of Inner Mongolia promising them freedom from arrest and persecution. At present many Mongols of Inner Mongolia are afraid to come over to the Chinese for fear of being attacked by the Outer Mongols. Moreover in Urga large numbers of Inner Mongols who are friendly with China and willing to return to their former allegiance are being detained against their will. Complete freedom must be given to these people to return to their homes. Complete freedom of movement between Inner and Outer Mongols should also be provided for and no interference with the Camel traffic should be permitted. At present the camels of Inner Mongolia on reaching Outer Mongolia are often seized for the payment of taxes or for the service of officials. The traffic in arms of every kind should be absolutely forbidden. Extradition of bad characters should be provided for.

At present large sums are owed by the Mongols to Chinese merchants. These debts should be repaid.

China will appoint a resident in Urga. It is essential that on his staff should be men knowing Russian, Mongolian and English. In this connection I would remind the President that at the Bureau of Foreign Affairs in Kalgan there is not a single Chinese who can speak any foreign language and not a single official who even knows Mongolian.

The question of the Post Office is of high importance. Representations regarding the safeguarding of Chinese interests in the postal service have, I understand, been submitted by M. Piry,[1] the Postmaster General. Of no less importance is the question of the Telegraphs and in this connection I cannot too strongly urge that Mr. Henningsen who possesses an unrivalled knowledge of the Peking-Kalgan-Urga-Kiakhta telegraph line, should be consulted and asked to draw up a memorandum suggesting the adoption of a policy for safeguarding Chinese interests in this important telegraph line. The way that the recent Telegraph negotiations in Tokio were bungled by the Director General of Telegraphs in Peking, through sheer ignorance and incapacity, was most lamentable.[2] China lost every point of advantage. It would be wise to try and prevent a similar blundering when this important question is discussed at the Tripartite Conference in Kiakhta.

687. To Ku Wei-chün

Peking 27 January 1914

Dear Dr. Koo,

In view of the fact that tariff revision is one of the urgent questions which China will have to take up in the near future might I point out how unfortunate it is that the highly paid agency of Jeremiah W. Jenks should distribute such appallingly ignorant and incorrect statements as the following: –

[1] A. Théophile Piry (d. 1918), French employee of the Chinese Maritime Customs, which he joined in 1874. He became a Commissioner in 1896 and was appointed Postal Secretary and later Postmaster-General when the Posts and Telegraphs were separated from the Customs Administration, holding this appointment until his retirement in April 1917.

[2] Lung Chien-chang (b. 1872), Chinese Imperial official and Republican politician. He had served under the Manchus in various capacities in the Board of Posts and Communications, and as one of Liang Shih-yi's most trusted subordinates he continued to prosper under his patronage in the Republic, becoming Director-General of the Postal Administration. In 1914 he was made Civil Governor of Kweichow Province, holding the post until January 1916 when, as a supporter of Yüan's monarchical scheme, he was forced to flee to Hong Kong upon Kweichow's declaration of independence from the Central Government. In June 1917 however he re-emerged as Acting Minister of Communications in the cabinet of Li Ching-hsi (1860–1925), but he had held the post for barely two weeks when he was replaced by Ts'ao Ju-lin.

'Peking. October 20. Hon Sun Pao-chi, minister of foreign Affairs, today sounded the various foreign ministers in regard to China's desire to increase materially her customs duties, which are supposed to be five per cent, but which are as low as three per cent, in many instances due to the inability of the government to enforce fines. The present customs tariff has been in force since 1902, by virtue of a treaty with Great Britain and subsequent agreements with the several nations.

Legally speaking, China, as a full fledged nation, has a right to draw up and enforce her own customs tariff, modified only by the customary favoured nation treaties entered into by all countries. However, China's custom service has been in the hands of foreigners for nearly fifty years, and no tax on imports can be imposed by China without the sanction of treaties.'

There is hardly a single sentence in this that is not grotesquely misleading.

I shall be much interested if you will allow me to see the list of papers in which the lucubrations of Jeremiah W. Jenks are published. I presume that you are insisting that he shall send you cuttings from the papers to show what return China is receiving for the very large subsidy which is now being paid to him for the work of Mr. Hamilton Smith and the Office boy.

Have you noticed that in connection with China's default of £150,000 on the 13th December to the London City Safe Deposit Company (I forget the exact name) a most injurious statement is made in *The Times* putting all the blame upon China, and yet this statement has been allowed to pass unchallenged by Mr. Lew Yuk-lin who was fully aware of the facts that the default was due to the failure of the British Legation to forward the official notification from the Wai Chiao Pu to the British Foreign Office that the Dunn Fisher & Co. loan was officially recognised by the Chinese Government.

With kind regards

Very sincerely yours
[G. E. Morrison]

688. To H. Cockburn[1]

[Peking] 30 January 1914

My dear Cockburn,

I was delighted to get your letter dated the 22nd of December.[2] It is years since I heard from you. When I was last in England I did not know how to communicate with you and now I learn that you have written a novel. You

[1] Henry Cockburn (1859–1927), British consular official. He had been Chinese Secretary at the British Legation in Peking (1896–1906), then in 1906 British Consul-General in Korea, a post he held until his retirement from the service in 1909. Through an introduction by Morrison, he later joined the Pekin Syndicate. [2] Not printed.

have given me the title but you have written it so illegibly that no one in my household can [make] it out. Of course I will get a copy. I am sure it will be mighty interesting.[1]

My wife is going home to England in March by the P & O Steamer from Shanghai and I hope to come home later in the year when I shall assuredly try and break in upon you in your seclusion.

You say you never see anyone. I presume you mean no one from the Far East. As you know I have now got an appointment, with a five year's contract, as Political Adviser to the President of the Republic. The most satisfactory part of the appointment, next to the salary, is the title. Occasionally I have I think some influence with the President but I have many disappointments and I cannot see that the Chinese of the Republic are very different from the Chinese that we knew 15 years ago.

The Legation is very much changed since you were here. Barton who was a student in your time is now your successor. He takes a somewhat narrow view of things and so far I am afraid has chiefly to record a long series of failures. Sir John Jordan still works desperately hard, chiefly immersed in details concerning Consular reports from the Treaty Ports. We still have no policy and we still have to note the monotonous regularity with which our rivals are obtaining railway and other important concessions in China. We are still under the domination of the Hongkong and Shanghai Bank, the monopoly being stronger than ever. Our latest discovery was to find that the British and Chinese Corporation, who had got the concession for the Signan–Pukou line, had by an agreement in 1905 conceded 55% of their interest to France and Belgium.[2] There has been an outcry at this for the French asked for equal participation in the railway. They have gracefully withdrawn, however, and have been given in compensation huge railway concessions in south western and central China.

Of the men who were here in your time Hillier is still to the fore. He looks old and weather-beaten but is still a power. Sidney Mayers has got a fat appointment[3] and is very prosperous and more self important than ever. He struts as though the whole place belonged to him. Kroupensky was here the other evening to meet Rockhill and Mrs Rockhill who are here writing reports for the American Asiatic Association. [...]

Peking is transformed. You would hardly recognise the place. The main street is the Wang Fu Ching Ta Chieh. Many people call it 'Morrison' Street. I do everything I can to assist in the extended use of this title for it

---

[1] Cockburn's novel, *The Tresleys*, was published by Andrew Melrose, London, 1914.
[2] Britain conceded to France participation in the Hsin-yang–Pukow Railway Concession in an Agreement signed on 2 October 1905, in which, of the 100,000 company shares, 45,000 were held by the British group, 45,000 by the French group and 10,000 by the Belgian group.
[3] In 1910 Sidney Francis Mayers left the British consular service to become the representative in China of the British and Chinese Corporation.

gives an advertisement to my property. There is some talk of a Company buying out my site and erecting on it Morrison Mansions. My Library has increased about four fold in the last 8 years and I now have my collection housed in a fireproof building which is insured at Lloyds for $25,000. I am making a feeble effort to dispose of it. Some time ago I was asked if I would be prepared to sell it and I said that I would be. If I were to get the price that I ask for it I would be in a position to retire and go back to Australia. This is my great wish.

I am going to send you some photographs of our Kid one of these days.

All good wishes to you and Mrs Cockburn and mind you I will look you up when I come home even though you seem determined never to meet any one.

Very sincerely yours
[G. E. Morrison]

689. From F. E. Taylor[1]

Hankow [Hupeh] 2 February 1914

My dear Morrison,

[...]

When I called on Tuan Chi Jui,[2] I had a long talk with him and, among

[1] Francis Edward Taylor (b. 1855), British employee of the Chinese Maritime Customs, which he first joined in 1877. He was at this time Commissioner in Hankow (1913-14). He became Statistical Secretary of the Chinese Maritime Customs later the same year, holding the post until his resignation in 1919.

[2] Tuan Ch'i-jui (1865-1936), Chinese soldier. A collaborator of Yüan Shih-k'ai in Yüan's building up of a new Chinese Army, he became one of his chief lieutenants. He played a leading role in assisting Yüan to hasten the abdication of the Manchu Emperor, which duly took place a week later, on 12 February 1912, by heading an appeal to the Court, threatening to march on the Capital unless it agreed to a Republican form of Government. The following month, when the first Republican Government was formed, he became Minister of War on Yüan's nomination, and held down this position in spite of frequent Cabinet changes, except for a few months during 1915-16 when he voluntarily withdrew in disapproval of Yüan's monarchical scheme. So powerful was he by then that he was made Prime Minister upon being asked in April 1916 to return to the Government, and from then until the defeat in 1920 of the Anfu Clique he was the dominating figure in China, exercising a power not always beneficial for his country, particularly in his dealings with Japan on whose financial support he largely depended. In November 1924 he returned to become Chief Executor, a post he held until April 1926, but he was no longer to wield the influence he once did, and upon his removal he went back to live in the Japanese Concession in Tientsin and devoted himself to the study of Buddhism, like another leading figure of the Anfu Clique, Wang I-t'ang (q.v.) and many other disillusioned Chinese politicians. In spite of his past pro-Japanese record, he resisted Japan's pressure on him to participate in the puppet Government in occupied Northern China and in 1933 moved to Shanghai where he died three years later. Tuan was in Wuchang at the time referred to, having been sent there by Yüan Shih-k'ai early in December the previous year for the purpose of dislodging Li Yüan-hung, the Vice-President and Military Governor of

other things we discussed Tariff revision. He was sufficiently interested in my views to ask me to put them into writing, in order that they might be submitted to the President, and says he is taking the document with him to Peking. As is I suppose natural, I am very keen on my plan and I firmly believe in it, so that I should be glad if you would consider it and give it your support if you approve. The Chinese and English translations are not literal, but each is intended to appeal to its own side. I may say that every merchant and every Chinese to whom I have explained it approves. Personally I am convinced that it would lead to a great expansion of trade, and would strengthen the hands of the Central Government by enlisting the sympathies both of the commercial classes and the producers. With the disappearance of Salt barriers under Dane's reorganization, and the abolition of all Opium collecting stations, the time seems to have come when *Likin* can be killed easily; and only a man who has studied the question fully realises what a curse the thing is to the country.

Of course this scheme is put forward in my private capacity and not from a Commissioner of Customs. I have not consulted Aglen about it, because I am sure he would sit upon it. He will, as he always does, take the narrow departmental view that five cents of duty passing through his hands is more important than developing trade that will yield a larger revenue in the future. And I admit that my scheme would not only temporarily lower the Customs receipts, but would do away with the necessity of having Foreign Assistants at ports not in direct communication with foreign countries, since they would only be required where Import Duty is to be levied. The Chinese Assistants could do all that is required in the way of checking cargo with documents and in keeping returns for statistical purposes; and they might in time replace all foreigners except a few retained for inspecting duty. With a Pension Scheme in force this need not take many years.

It appears that at present the Central Government has to find the money for foreign obligations, getting little or no help from the provinces, and is compelled to push the country deeper and deeper into debt. Now the cancellation of the Boxer Indemnity payments would mean a distinct gain to the Central Govt; while the abolition of *Likin* would be no loss, since I imagine that little of the collection reaches Peking. To my mind, every way you look at it makes my scheme more attractive. It would relieve the Central Government and increase its prestige with the people, and would act as an

---

Hupeh. Li's remaining at his home base had been a cause of great concern for Yüan who now took advantage of his greatly strengthened position, resulting from the elimination of the southern republican forces of the Yangtse Valley in the 'Second Revolution', to compel Li to vacate his seat in Wuchang and go to Peking. Tuan Ch'i-jui, then Minister of War and the strong man of the Government, was given the mission. He was appointed Li's successor in Hupeh only as a formality, holding the post a mere three months before being relieved by another of Yüan's trusted lieutenants, Tuan Chih-kuei, the day before this letter was written.

immense stimulus to both domestic and foreign trade, while encouraging the development of industrial enterprises, mining, etc: These effects are certain. The only question is whether the thing can be put through in the face of those Governments who prefer to receive the cash and are but slightly interested in trade. I think it can if the foreign Press is discreetly worked; but of this you are a better judge than I can be. You might show the scheme to one of your influential Chinese friends and see how he regards it. I do not want to be advertised, but I have a not ignoble ambition to do something to leave my mark before I retire. I see Bredon has been writing a lot of stuff about Tariff revision, and I do not want to be thought as entering into competition with him!!!

[...]

Yours truly
F. E. Taylor

690. From C. D. Bruce

Shanghai 12 February 1914

My dear Morrison,

Thank you for yours about the White Wolf affair. Surely the Govt. must be realising the danger of the present situation to Chinese credit! I do not suggest for a moment that any sudden appearance on the spot of a foreigner will at once quiet things, but I do think that the fact of their sending their Police Adviser to help restore order and to point out what should be done would have a good effect. If the Legation think the matter sufficiently serious to send the Military Attaché to report obviously it is right that I should be on the spot first.

The shooting of the Japanese here was an unfortunate affair. So far as we know the shooting was done by detectives sent down by Ch'ang Hsun. It was certainly not done by Admiral Tseng's or Sah's[1] men. However, that does not matter much as the fact remains that the men were shot by Chinese Govt. detectives and I fear the Japanese have a good case. If Admiral Tsêng

[1] Sa Chen-ping (?1858–1951), Chinese sailor of Mongol descent, who during his long career served four different regimes. One of the earliest Chinese students, along with Yen Fu (q.v.) to attend the Royal Naval College at Greenwich, he became an Admiral and Commander-in-Chief of the fleet under the Manchu Dynasty, and fought on the side of the Imperial forces after the Wuchang Uprising. He became however a servant of the Republic as soon as it was established, and after some four years in Shanghai holding various posts, he became Minister of the Navy briefly in 1917, and again in 1919 (December 1919 – May 1921). He was Acting Prime Minister for some three months following the defeat of the Anfu Clique in May 1920, then returned to become Governor of his native Fukien Province in 1922, a post he held until 1927. In November 1933 he was press-ganged into becoming a member of the short-lived break-away Government set up in his home city of Foochow, and in 1949 became a Delegate to the People's Political Consultative Conference, and was elected a member of its National Committee. At the time referred to, Sa was Director-General of the Land and River Police in Shanghai.

can prove that the Japanese were in company with the revolutionary gang as Sah's detectives report, it will be difficult for the Japanese Consul General to do more than strongly object to such promiscuous shooting.

At present Mr. Ariyoshi's[1] attitude has been moderate.

The recent promotion of Mr. Yang Tcheng[2] has tended somewhat to making trouble between him and Admiral Tsêng as to their mutual control and jurisdiction. They both confide in me and I can see it may lead to difficulties. Tsêng has hitherto been the leading local official and now Yang as almost a *Tao-tai* has, perhaps unwittingly, sometimes handled matters which Tsêng thinks should be his work. As you know well it is one of the most difficult problems in China to get any officials to work together, but it would be a thousand pities if any idea of superseding Tsêng was to arise. He is without doubt a very exceptional Chinese. A doer not a talker – the white-est son of Han I have come across. If my *Gendarmerie* scheme goes through I want him at the head of it. He is wasted here.

You will have seen Green's leaders on the need for a *Gendarmerie*. I gave him the hint as it seemed time that the foreign press got to work upon the White Wolf scandal. At the same time I advised Mr. Yang to wire Peking to suggest that Reuter if willing should smooth the home public down about it. Putnam and others may be sending strong messages home for all we know.

[...]

Very sincerely yours
C. D. Bruce

691. To C. D. Bruce

Peking 16 February 1914

My dear Bruce,

I am very sorry to say that the President will not consent to your going to Honan Province. He says that he cannot possibly spare you from Shanghai at the present juncture and he asked me to make this communication to you. I am afraid that at the back of his head is the fear that he might lose face were he to send a foreigner attached to his soldiers who might see how little they were to be trusted and how shockingly they had been treating the people

---

[1] Ariyoshi Akira (1876-1937), Japanese diplomat, at this time Consul-General in Shanghai where he was to stay for some ten years (1909–20). In 1932 he returned to China as Minister, and became his country's first Ambassador to China when the Legation was elevated to an Embassy in May 1935.

[2] Yang Ch'eng, Chinese diplomat. At this time Foreign Affairs Commissioner in Shanghai (October 1913 – October 1915), he had formerly been Chinese Minister to Austria (December 1903 – April 1906) and concurrently to Germany (September 1905 – December 1906). In July 1926 he became Director-General of the Overseas Chinese Affairs Bureau.

whom they ought to protect. This, however, is my idea only and of course nothing like it has been said to me.
[...]

Very sincerely yours
[G. E. Morrison]

692. From C. D. Bruce

Shanghai 24 February [1914]

My dear Morrison,

The morning your letter[1] reached me about not going to 'White Wolf's' hunt I received another from General Feng Kuo chang the *Tutuh*,[2] saying I might go to Sinyang chow to join General Tuan Chi jui.

Genl Fêng has also wired *in re* but in the letter to me says it is no use waiting for an answer from Peking, you may as well go to Sinyang chow.

Perhaps if the President were informed that General Fêng thinks I should be of use and that General Tuan has no objection he might reconsider his decision and allow me to start for Sinyang chow.

Would you at any rate do what you can to get permission! I shall not give anything away he need not fear, but I can advise upon steps that are not only desirable but obvious to us foreigners. Besides don't you agree that the President's sending oneself would look as though he was in earnest about the suppression! I am informed privately that Northern troops as now being used, Honan, Anhwei, Chili and Shantung men will not do the work properly. They are too closely connected with the Brigands. Only other men such as Hunanese, Chekiang, etc. will succeed in promptly stamping out the rising. This is only natural from the Chinese point of view.

Nothing more yet about the Japanese shooting. One point it does bring to the fore once more, and both Admiral Tseng and self have often mentioned it, it is the very serious danger to the Govt. of allowing loose detectives from any province to come down here to work *inside* the Settlement unknown to Admirals Tseng or Sah. It was some of Chang Hsun's men who did this. Enclosed I send a C.I.D. scheme which both General Feng and Admiral Tsêng are strong on inaugurating. Peking gets it through Tsêng, but you may also like to speak about the prompt necessity for such an organization after perusing the memorandum.
[...]

Very sincerely yours
C. D. Bruce

[...]

[1] Morrison's letter of 16 February 1914, No. 691.
[2] At this time Military Governor of Kiangsu Province in which Shanghai is situated.

Enclosure to Letter No. 692: *Memorandum upon the Institution of a Central Criminal Investigation Department for China, February 1914*

The necessity for the institution of a modern Criminal Investigation Department (commonly known as the C.I.D.) has become a matter of vital necessity to the Chinese Government.

The condition of the Country since the Revolution of 1911 may be taken as sufficient proof of this statement. The political unrest during the last 2 years has to a very great extent been brought about by the facilities which persons of bad character have had, to move about unknown to the Central Government. From town to town and province to province such emissaries of Rebellion have passed, often unsuspected. This could not have happened had there been a properly organized detective department under Central control watching all such movements. The persons referred to come from various ranks of society. Many are known bad characters, others are less well known, but both they and the criminal brotherhood who have joined them, the murderers, would be murderers, and bomb manufacturers, have for the last two years made parts of China almost impossible for law abiding citizens to live in. These bad characters could never have caused so much mischief had their whereabouts been accurately known to the Central Police Authorities.

The constant keeping in touch with this class of person would be merely one item in the work. The energies of a properly organized C.I.D. would be made use of over a far wider sphere. The Detective net should stretch much further and should in time catch fish of all kinds. Referring to matters of less importance; the ordinary robber if allowed freedom of action can follow his trade over an extended area so long as his movements are not checked. He is here today and gone tomorrow. His crime accomplished, he quits the scene for new ground or makes for a neighbouring town to dispose of his booty, where being unknown to the local Police he poses as an innocent and inoffensive stranger.

It will be understood then that all the criminal classes from the treason-plotter to the lowest robber should come within the knowledge of a modern C.I.D. Its organization should be such as to embrace all those who live to prey upon honest people by fraud of any and every kind.

In Europe today order is so thoroughly well established that the crime of the country is hardly more than an annoyance. In China, if crime is allowed to get to a head it is capable of destroying the peace and prosperity of whole tracts of country. The mass of the people in their common moods are gentle submissive and disposed to be innocent. But for that very reason bold and successful criminals are dangerous in the extreme. It is true if it be said that for some years to come the stability of the Central Administration, the safety of many Government Officials, as well as the peace of the country depend upon the prompt organization of an up to date C.I.D.

Hitherto the want of such an organization in China has hardly been felt.

The old method of Police procedure has been to wait until a crime has occurred and then to proceed in search of the criminal. Under present conditions to continue such antiquated methods will bring untold mischief. The key to successful Detective work is the prevention of crime by the intelligent anticipation of events.

Another point which should be noted is that hitherto the Chinese so-called Police, or *Yamen* runners, have usually preyed upon and ill used the people. This is very wrong. To ensure success either in Detective or in ordinary Police work friendly relations with the common people of any town or district are essential. If either Detectives or the Police abuse their authority they can expect no help from the man in the street. Without such help in no part of the world can Police work with success. This is one of the reasons why any duplicating of Police duties such as their being employed to collect revenue or taxes is a fundamental error. Similarly to make Police act as soldiers or soldiers do ordinary Police work is a mistake. This is not to say that soldiers may not be used to uphold the authority of the Police. In Countries like China where distances are great and the provinces still in a very disturbed state it is probable that for some years to come a *gendarmerie* composed of Police with some military training will be found necessary. For Country districts and for work among an agricultural population locally enlisted Police, not soldiers, will obtain better results.

Before proceeding to outline the scheme for a C.I.D. throughout the provinces a few remarks upon the present conditions of detective work may be of use. So far as I am aware every Provincial Capital and in the Country the district headquarter has had its detective service. Some of these may have been fairly efficient but in most cases their great drawback was that they preyed upon the people and abused their authority. They also usually only commenced to work when the crime had been committed and the criminals possibly gone. Another reason which made the old fashioned efforts at detecting crime so hopeless is the universal habit of all Chinese to work in water tight compartments, that is to say, without any desire for or attempt at cooperation. The Police of one village or district never consider it necessary to do more than hunt criminals from their own boundaries. Neither was it any one's business to send information elsewhere of the fact that bad characters or robbers were known to be assembling near a certain village with the intention of moving across the borders of the district or province. Practically each local Police force worked in isolation and cooperation between two neighbouring forces was usually wanting. Coming to later years, it is known that considerable improvement has taken place both in method and in the personnel of the Police and detectives, especially in North China. The Police training School at Tientsin is an example of what is now being done to improve Police organization, but so far the movement is a very limited one. Another drawback has to be faced and it is the unsuitability of the

Chinese mode of life for ensuring cooperation. It is a well known fact and to be accounted for by the conditions under which every Chinaman has for centuries lived that he will not if he can possibly help it allow himself to be mixed up with any matter outside his own possible concerns. A Chinaman may have actually seen a robbery or even a murder committed, but he prefers to pass by on the other side. He may be needed as a witness but he will not speak except under compulsion. His testimony might furnish an important link to ensure an arrest, he withholds it and pleads ignorance. In a people so constituted it will be a very difficult matter to alter this attitude towards crime. But the necessity is vital if any detective organization is to flourish. As has already been remarked the essence of successful detective work is the rapid dissemination and reception of news from all quarters. From town to town, from district to district, province to province information must pass, and until the necessity for such cooperation is fully grasped success cannot crown the efforts of the Police.

Having endeavoured to give some idea of the present condition of C.I.D. work it is now time to discuss the question of the most suitable place for the Headquarters of the proposed new organization. The scheme about to be drawn up is as has already been stated chiefly, and to start with, for the Yangtze Valley and North of the River. To endeavour to commence on too ambitious a scale would merely be to court failure. The pressing need of the Government is to be in possession of full and early information of the movements of Political suspects and of all those who are still plotting against the President. Owing to its geographical situation and political condition the Yangtze Valley requires most careful watching. Shanghai being, so to speak, the gate of the Yangtze, through which place pass a very large proportion of persons 'wanted' by the Government, must be kept under close observation. So also should the two provinces of Kiangsu and Chekiang be. Between them they contain such important towns as Shanghai, Soochow, Chinkiang, Yangchow, Nanking, Hangchow, Ningpo, Taichow and Wenchow. The most important point to decide is the location of the Headquarters of the new C.I.D. organization. While there may be something to be said for the selection of more than one place I think that after due consideration it will be allowed that there remain only two places to chose between, and these are Shanghai and Nanking. The former has many points in its favour but there are reasons against its selection which in my opinion render the choice of Nanking the most suitable.

The presence of the Foreign Settlement at Shanghai might make the installation of a Government Detective Headquarters there a matter of some difficulty. As long as any feeling remains that the presence of a Central Detective Office might interfere with the action of the International Settlement and French Municipal Police so long would the work of the new C.I.D. be hampered, neither would the organization run as smoothly as it would at Nanking. Shanghai is now a days so closely connected by rail and telegraph with Nanking that for all practical purposes intercommunication is assured. Moreover and this point is worth emphasising Nanking is the provincial capital and as a C.I.D. headquarters for the Yangtze Valley with free intercourse with other towns and with other Provincial Officials, is better situated than is Shanghai. Such an organization as is suggested though to a certain extent independent of provincial control is more suitably located at a provincial capital. Is independent of any local Foreign difficulty from which Shanghai can never be quite free, also can, as it undoubtedly will, expand with much greater facility at Nanking than at Shanghai. Suitable land and buildings for any such organization as it is to be hoped the new C.I.D. will in a few years become are not forthcoming at Shanghai. At Nanking there is ample accomodation for any extension.

For the present then it is proposed to centre the C.I.D. at Nanking and to make it specially applicable to the Yangtze Valley, Kiangsu and Chekiang Provinces.

[...]

693. To J. K. Ohl[1]

Peking 5 March 1914

My dear Ohl,

It gave me mighty great pleasure to receive a letter from you, dated the 5th of December, telling me much news about our old friends. I shall always remember the years that we spent together in Peking. Believe me I am sincere when I say that I never could wish to have a more honourable colleague.

Things here are not doing well. What to do with the Army is the most serious problem with which China is confronted at the present time. All her earnings are being poured into the maw of the Army. To keep those hordes would tax the resources even of a rich State while the burden in China is almost insupportable.

Very little attention to China appears to be given in the European and American papers. Putnam Weale has long since been discredited. Recently even he has had to complain that his messages are being edited. He has screeched so long that even the *Daily Telegraph* readers have become impatient. Fraser, my successor on *The Times*, is restricted to 150 words a week. We are good friends but we do not discuss political affairs. Since he has taken the view that he should oppose everything that I ever supported and as any information I would give him would be used in the contrary

[1] Josiah Kingsley Ohl (d. 1920), American journalist, at this time on the editorial staff of the *New York Herald* (1913–18). He had previously been Correspondent for that paper in China, where he came to know Morrison, and in 1918 became its Editor-in-Chief and Managing Director.

sense to what I would desire, I have thought it better to refrain from any discussion with him upon affairs in China. [...]

The American Minister promises well.[1] To America has fallen some of the finest plums ever plucked in China. The Standard Oil deal, the Bethlehem Steel contract and the Huai River conservancy. You have, no doubt, heard that Japan has made the most advantageous contract that has ever been made in China or in any other country. Probably no finer gift has ever been made by one nation to another than the Hanyeping contract, by which Japan for a long period of years is to be sold the products of the Tayeh iron mines for $1.50 gold per ton. The concession carries with it many advantages, the stationing of troops at the Tayeh mines and the keeping open of communications between Tayeh and the river being not the least of them. This is not exactly a concession. It is a right insisted upon by Japan by virtue of her interest.

[...]

I suppose you have heard of the changes on the London *Times*. There is hardly a man on the paper whom I know. It is reported out here that even George Saunders,[2] the Paris Correspondent, one of the ablest correspondents in the world has left the paper. David Disraeli Braham,[3] whose real name it has been said is Abraham, has also left. It has likewise lost its parliamentary Editor. It was lucky that I left the paper when I did otherwise I might find myself at the present moment with a family to support and nothing to support them on.

Since I joined the Chinese service I have had more leisure to devote to my Library and I have during the past 15 months obtained a very large number of books and pamphlets needed to make the collection more complete. The catalogue has just been finished. You, no doubt, know that I propose now to sell the library. The burden of maintaining it is too great for me. Books on China are going up very quickly in value. As an illustration of the rapidly increasing value of these books I may mention that within the last few weeks I have been offered by European booksellers four books, the catalogue price of which was £40, £30, £25 and £25 and I was able to

[1] Paul Samuel Reinsch (1879-1923), American diplomat and educator. He was Professor of Political Science at the University of Wisconsin (1901-1913) when President Wilson appointed him American Minister to China in 1913, a post he held until August 1919. Upon completing his term of office he was made Adviser to the Chinese Government on a non-resident basis, and died in Shanghai while on a visit there. His interest in China began while he was teaching at Wisconsin, and he was the author of *Intellectual and Political Currents in the Far East* (Boston 1911). His experiences in China were recorded in his memoirs, *An American Diplomat in China* (London 1922).

[2] George Saunders, British journalist. He succeeded Valentine Chirol (q.v.) as *Times* Correspondent in Berlin in 1896 and in 1908 was appointed to succeed William Lavino as Paris Correspondent upon Lavino's death.

[3] D. D. Braham, who succeeded Valentine Chirol as Foreign Editor of *The Times* in 1912, left the paper in 1914 to become the Editor of the Sydney *Daily Telegraph*.

write back and say that all four books were already in my possession, perfect copies, which had cost me £2.18. for the lot. I have been having some correspondence with Japan on the subject.

[...]

Believe me

Ever your sincere friend
[G. E. Morrison]

694. To J. N. Jordan

[Peking, undated][1]

Dear Sir John,

I am leaving for Hongkong on Monday morning and as it may be one month or more before I return to Peking I would like to write you a few lines regarding the position to which we are drifting quickly in China.

As you know my own habit is one of optimism. For many years I have been studying things in China from the point of view of an observer, but I can no longer take any part in bringing my opinion to the notice of the public except in an indirect way which is not as effective as I could wish it. It is quite obvious to me that the situation is bad, that the situation must get worse, that it would be difficult to avoid a catastrophe and that the situation is due to the misguided policy – if policy it can be called, by which the British Government has given a monopoly of support to one corporation. The only hope for preventing the impending catastrophe is by breaking up the Consortium.

I do not think that you realise how intense is the bitterness caused by the action of the Government in giving support to one corporation only. That there is a slight change now must be admitted, but I have no doubt your Legation has long realised how difficult it has been to escape from the entanglements into which it has been inveigled, but having set forth on a policy which was not sufficiently considered – for even its best friends would not consider that Mr Alston[2] or Mr Gregory[3] had either the knowledge or the mentality to enable them to consider all the factors of such a complex situation when they led Sir Edward Grey into this policy – they could not have foreseen where it was to lead us.

Everyone must admit that the Hongkong Bank is a well-conducted Bank, but everyone must admit that it is largely under German influence. When it imposed its will upon the Foreign Office it did a wise stroke of business for itself but it inflicted a serious blow to British interests in the Far East.

[1] This draft letter is undated and was possibly never sent. From internal evidence it would seem to have been written some time between 12 and 16 March 1914, when Morrison left Peking for Shanghai and Hong Kong.   [2] Francis Beilby Alston.
[3] John Duncan Gregory.

At the end of 1912 China endeavoured to obtain money outside of the Quintuple Group.[1] She obtained a loan on very satisfactory terms – a loan as safe as the Bank of England to the investors, for it was a charge upon the Salt gabelle, which however badly administered could not fail to produce enough to meet the service of the loan. This loan was entered into with an Englishman of high class[2] who had rendered important service to the British Government. Negotiations were entered upon with the full approval of the Foreign Office. There was nothing in the way to block these negotiations further than that the British Government had committed itself to support, to the exclusion of all other groups, the Hongkong and Shanghai Bank. All the British Government need have done if they did not wish to support this loan, was not to have opposed it. What they did was to endeavour to ruin this Britisher and the public who had invested in his loan through British Banks of the highest standing, such as Lloyds Bank and others. The punishment meted out to him was an extremely severe one, yet he acted in perfect good faith and he has honourably fulfilled his obligations. Everyone associated with him was boycotted. The loan moneys were transferred to Peking by the Hongkong and Shanghai Bank. They made all the profits. The Chartered Bank was not – with the exception of one small case – even given an opportunity of tendering, but because the Chartered Bank was associated with it, although it is an absolutely British Bank which has rendered invaluable services to the British Government, the Bank's representative in Peking was boycotted, and almost incredible as it would seem Mr Cockerell,[3] who only joined Mr Crisp after the loan had been negotiated, was even boycotted by one who had been his school-mate at College and his mate in the Diplomatic service. All this was done at the behest of the Hongkong and Shanghai Bank.

Look even what happened also in the case of the other attempt by an important British Bank to oppose this deplorable monopoly. When the Belgian loan contract was signed on March the 14th 1912 it was signed on behalf of a British Bank and of a Belgian Bank. These two Banks undoubtedly acted in good faith. That China committed a blunder there is no doubt at all. I never agreed with the view that it was a breach of faith, but even assuming that it was a breach of faith, no breach of faith could be alleged against the British and the Belgian Bank. But the four Ministers took China severely to task and compelled China to relinquish the large

[1] The particular foreign financial consortium to which Morrison here refers was first set up in 1911 by the banks of England, France, Germany and the United States, and was known as the Four-Power Group. It then became the Six-Power or Sextuple Group with the inclusion of banks representing Japan and Russia. This in turn became the Five-Power or Quintuple Group on the withdrawal of the American banks in 1913. Strictly speaking, therefore, Morrison's use of the term Quintuple Group was wrong when speaking of events in 1912.   [2] The reference is to Charles Birch Crisp.
[3] Samuel Pepys Cockerell.

loan which was to follow the issue of the small loans. It was quite right to compel the cancellation of this transaction but the people who suffered by it were the British. In the interests of the Hongkong Bank was punished a purely British Corporation. Compensation was paid by the Chinese Government and look what an enormous compensation was given. Two great Trunk Railways[1] traversing China for a distance of more than 2,000 miles – Franco-Belgian, half French, half Belgian, the French being members of the Quadruple Group who had compelled China to cancel the contract with the British. The British got nothing out of it. They are entirely and absolutely excluded from any participation in these two Great Trunk lines either in supplying the material or in engineers or in any other way. Yet when the time came to obtain the money for the construction of this French and Belgian railway, a considerable amount of the money is obtained from England through the brokers of the Hongkong and Shanghai Bank. In other words the British so acted that they punished British people, put vast profits into the pockets of the French and of the Belgians and even provided the money for the purchase of Belgian and French material and the development of French and Belgian enterprises. Surely this is a matter worth thinking about.

Speaking to me the other day you complained of the dearth of English representatives of English manufacturing houses, but it is the policy of the British Government that has led to this dearth of reputable Englishmen. Our policy of giving a monopoly to one Corporation, our policy of boycotting – for that is what it has amounted to – a purely British Bank like the Chartered Bank – has had for its object the exclusion of reputable British financial representatives with the result that men of an inferior class largely of the adventurer type have come to Peking and are deceiving the Chinese Government by offering terms which they are quite unable to fulfil. That it is to the advantage of the Hongkong and Shanghai Bank to see the increase of the number of these adventurers cannot be disputed. The Bank knows that the effect of these pseudo financiers' missions is to cause China to delay the hope of being able to obtain money outside of the Consortium, to involve China in greater financial difficulties so that the terms subsequently demanded by the Consortium can be increasingly onerous.

The policy of England in China is absolutely opposed to that of France. England desires the maintenance of the integrity of China. England desires a strong and powerful China. France is working for her dismemberment and England is blindly assisting her in this policy. When a Frenchman is

[1] The reference to one line, that of the Peking–Hankow Railway, some 755 miles long, is clear. The other trunk line could only be the Tientsin–Pukow Railway, though it was half British, half German. It is also possible that he is referring to what was to become the Lung-hai Railway, from Hai-chou to Shansi, but this line, in which French and Belgian finance was involved, was still in an embryonic stage at this time.

urged by M. Conty[1] to leave the Customs and join the service of the Salt Gabelle the inducement held out to him when he complained that he would be receiving less salary in the Salt than he is now receiving in the Customs, is that China will shortly be under the financial control of the Foreign countries and that a Frenchman could expect to be Salt Commissioner for the province of Yunnan.

While the Consortium has been in existence every possible advantage has been lost by the British. Russia took advantage of the Consortium and by delaying the Quintuple loan was able to exact whatever terms she liked about Mongolia. Japan, Germany and France by refusing to sign the Quintuple Loan agreement except on terms were able to obtain a Chinese Government guarantee of all the bonds of the Commercial Guarantee Bank of Chihli which was established by a German with the approval of the German Legation, and by a Frenchman of the Banque de l'Indo Chine with the full approval of the French Legation, to take over the debts incurred by these three countries during the financial upheaval of a few years ago. Originally when Mr Crisp negotiated the loan with China, called after him, he was promised the establishment in China of an Industrial Bank similar to the Industrial Bank which he had established in Russia and which had been a great success. Nearly ruined by the British Government he was compelled to relinquish the idea of the establishment of this bank. But the French had no such scruples and they established the Bank with the full support of the Banque de l'Indo Chine and of the French Government.

Look at the success which has attended the Banque Industrielle. It is idle to pretend that this Bank is separate from the Banque de l'Indo Chine. When the arrangements were made for the erection of new bank premises in Peking the instructions given to the English Architect who is to do the building were that the building should comprise quarters for the Banque Industrielle. Yet at this time the Manager of the Banque de l'Indo Chine was telling Hillier that there was no connection with the two and was pretending to ridicule the pretensions of the Banque Industrielle. Surely we can no longer be blind to the fact that the Banque Industrielle has the support of the Banque de l'Indo Chine and of the French Legation. The concessions obtained by it are the most valuable ever given in China for industrial work and for railway work. Any attempt to compete with it on the part of an independent British firm or of an independent Anglo-French firm has been frustrated. The Anglo-French Syndicat de Yunnan had every reason to expect that they could obtain the concession for the railway from Yunnan to Chengtu. They had paramount claims. The French Minister even was prepared to support their claims but the British Government refused to give any support, or rather so postponed

---

[1] Alexandre Robert Conty, French Minister in Peking from 1912 to 1917 when he was recalled at China's request because of his alleged bullying behaviour.

any consideration of the matter that the French came quickly in and obtained the concession which nullified it of the railway from Yunnan to Chungking. For years it has been the hope of every Englishman that the British would retain some right in the railway from Yunnan to Chungking. It has now been given to the French through the influence of the Banque de l'Indo Chine supported by the French Legation, and the Syndicat de Yunnan is left in the air. The statement written by Mr Collins[1] is painful reading to any Englishman.

What single advantage have we gained by our support of the Consortium? It may be argued, as it was argued, that owing to the modification of our support by which industrial enterprises outside the Hongkong and Shanghai Bank would be given support by the British Government, Lord ffrench obtained a railway contract of high value. The Hongkong and Shanghai Bank bitterly opposed Lord ffrench and the scheme of building the railway by contract – there is no secret in that, they preferred that the railway should be constructed by their own people and you cannot blame them for this, in the most expensive way possible, as for example the method of construction departmentally associated with the name of the B & C Corporation. When Lord ffrench signed his contract for the construction of a railway from Canton to Chungking it only required quick support from the British Legation to have that contract ratified but the Legation kept waiting for instructions from the British Government, but the British Government refused to give its support, or rather again delayed endeavouring to discover some reason for not opposing it. The result was that events happened in China by which Sun Yat-sen was dismissed from office and the contract he had entered into was repudiated. In compensation, as it is called, Lord ffrench has been given the contract for the construction of a railway from Shashe to [   ][2] – whoever heard of this southern place? What Englishmen are going to put up money to build a railway to terminate in a French railway in the mountains of Kweichow Province leading nowhere? Besides the statement made in the papers of Shashe that it is a large city are misleading, for the railway begins from a small village on the Yangtse, on the other side of the river from Shashe. I venture to say that this railway will never be built or at any rate will not be built for many years to come. It follows no natural trade route. It contains immense difficulties and compared with the other railway projects that have been granted in China it is wholly unproductive. No one rejoices at this fact more than the H & S Bank.

While we have been giving our support to the Consortium and have excluded all British competition all other four members of the Consortium have seen the advantage to be gained by our stupidity to make profit for

---

[1] William F. Collins, a British Mining engineer with the Anglo-French Syndicat de Yunnan and the China Mining and Metal Company. He had supplied Morrison from time to time with information about the enterprises of the syndicate. The statement to which Morrison here refers is not printed.   [2] Blank in the original.

themselves. All the disastrous arms contracts which China was compelled to sign last year when in great straits for money her difficulties having been added to by the delay of the Consortium, were negotiated with the Deutsch-Asiatische Bank, to the profit of the Deutsch-Asiatische Bank and with the full approval of the German Legation who were affecting ignorance of the transactions which they were actively engaged in supporting. Only last week another of these transactions has been completed – A loan of Mks. 50,000,000 secured upon the land of the province of Kwangtung – a province in which we have paramount interests. This loan is negotiated by [   ][1] the head of Carlowitz and one of the Directors of the H & S Bank. It provides that one-third of the loan shall be supplied in arms and 2/3 in cash. The terms are onerous. They are immensely advantageous to the Germans and to the Deutsch-Asiatische Bank through whom the transaction is completed.

Taking advantage of British stupidity the French Group in the Consortium who have obtained all these valuable concessions through their Stalking Horse the Banque Industrielle have insisted that no further loan shall be obtained for China until China has agreed to pay the indirect claims submitted by the French Bank for losses alleged to have been incurred during the Revolution, and Japan supports that claim and Russia supports it. The Hongkong and Shanghai Bank has operations in China many times larger than those of the Banque de l'Indo Chine – probably ten times larger. Their claims for compensation come to about £3000, and I learn from Mr Hillier that according to Mr Ker[2] even that claim cannot be sustained. Yet the French Bank claims for its losses more than £300,000 and this claim must be settled before the French Group will take any part in advancing money to China. Japan's claim are even more outrageous. In the case of a drugseller in Tsinanfu in March 1912, the owner claims Tls 490,000 compensation. The Japanese Legation has reduced this claim to Tls. 70,000. There is little doubt that fair compensation would be a few hundred Taels. In the case of the paltry Japanese bookseller in Peking whose house was looted on the night of the 29th of February 1912, and whose losses could not have been more than a few hundred Dollars, the Japanese Legation are supporting his claim for $100,000 compensation and until such claims as these are settled no Quintuple loan with China will be permitted.

What then is the result of this? No reputable Bank can lend money to China because the H & S Bank has the monopoly. China cannot, therefore, obtain money in the open market or on any reasonable terms. She is driven to make disastrous loans, all the advantages of which go to our foreign competitors. No firms are more entitled to support than Armstrongs and Vickers,

[1] Blank in the original.
[2] William Pollock Ker (b. 1864), British consular official. After serving in various consular posts he became Commercial Attaché in the British Legation at Peking in 1909, where he remained until his appointment in July 1917 as Consul-General in Tientsin. He retired from the last position ten years later, in August 1927.

yet the British policy has brought it about that every possible advantage is given to their competitors in Germany and America to their exclusion. Even in the case of the Peking tramways British policy has brought it about that the concession which ought to have been given to the Shanghai Tramway Company has been given to the French Banque Industrielle. The Shanghai Tramways were prepared to pay an advance to China of $1,000,000 in connection with the tramways. It was a perfectly honourable and legitimate offer but on the ground that the British Government cannot countenance any such advance – because such payment savours of bribery – no support could be given to this tramway scheme and therefore the concession has been granted to the French to the entire exclusion of the British. It was an absolutely proper thing to offer this money. I have consulted independent authorities on this matter, such as Professor Goodnow,[1] and he is also of this opinion. Vested rights have to be bought out. There must be preliminary expenses connected with such a transaction and it is only right and fair that those expenses should be paid for. But this is an advance not coming from the H & S Bank and therefore must be opposed.

We cannot point to a single advantage we have gained from our association with the Consortium. We have brought China to the verge of ruin so that catastrophe can only be averted by a bold withdrawal first of our monopoly of support to a British Bank which is largely under German influence and secondly by our withdrawal from the Consortium. Huxley[2] has written that the chief difference he notices among men is not their liability to fall into error but their willingness to acknowledge these inevitable lapses.

The British Government have fallen into error. Their policy has been a disastrous failure. It now will have to be seen whether they will have the courage to acknowledge their failure and endeavour to retrieve it.

The present French Inspector of the Banque de l'Indo Chine[3] has laid it down as a policy which must be followed by the Consortium that all French claims must first be paid before France will either consent to join in any Quintuple loan to China or permit any tariff revision. The British must suffer and the Chinese must suffer until the French are paid.

We have now a great opportunity to break away from the Consortium not only to prevent disaster to China but to profit British enterprise and British industry.

[G. E. Morrison]

[1] Frank Goodnow.   [2] Thomas Henry Huxley (1825–95), British naturalist.
[3] Possibly H. M. R. Saint-Pierre.

695. From L. E. Broome[1]

Near Lo Shan Honan 13 April 1914

Dear Morrison,

[...]

The country in my vicinity (about 30-40 miles east of Hsin Yang Chou) is in a jumpy state after the late raid of White Wolf. My wife said that she had shown you my letters about it all so I need not repeat them.

But as a consequence, the inhabitants are very nervous and in a town like Lo Shan, of 15–20,000 inhabitants, the city gates are constantly being shut. Various *opéra bouffe* imitators of W.W.[2] have sprung up and earn an easy living robbing defenceless villages. I was told once that they had expressed an intention of looting my camp but nothing happened. Rotten luck, as it happened to be in a big temple, easily defensible and I waited for them with my 2 white men with 3 shot guns (buck shot) and could have blown them off the face of the earth with no chance of their being able to get at us behind a breast work of mill stones commanding the only entrance about 20 yards clear range.

You ask about the soldiery – why they are none – only a lot of coolies dressed as feeble imitations. They can neither march nor fight and their officers are feeble to the last degree. The non-com[missioned] seems to be of better stuff. I took some photos and if you care to see them Zumbrum has the negatives. I will return to Hsin Yang Chou in about a month's time and be able then to take things a bit easier. The Layman brothers[3] are all to the good and between us we are turning out first class work. My boss has seen fit to congratulate us, at any rate, tho' I says it, as shouldn't.

[...]

Yours ever
Louis Broome

696. To Ts'ai T'ing-kan

[Peking] 13 April 1914

My dear Admiral,

I send you herewith a memorandum which I wrote this morning on the China Merchants' Steam Navigation Company. I will send you later one dealing with Hankow and another with the Note question at Canton all for the information of the President.[4]

[1] Louis E. Broome, British railway engineer employed on the Pukow–Sinyang Railway.
[2] White Wolf.
[3] Morrison more than once observed in his Diary that many Chinese railways were being built by barbers, waiters and oddities of various European nationalities who knew nothing about railway construction until they undertook such work in China.
[4] During March and April 1914 Morrison made a fact-finding trip to Hankow, Canton and Shanghai, and on his return wrote lengthy memoranda on three pressing problems of the time: on the question of the redemption of Canton Notes, which successive authorities in Kwangtung Province had issued and which had become a serious embarrassment for

Messrs J. P. Bisset & Co. are a firm of good standing. Their partner Mr. Crossley[1] is now in Peking and I fancy you have seen him. They have been well recommended to me. It is necessary to enter into relations with some one who does not belong to the Hongkong and Shanghai Bank but who has the support of that powerful Bank, for the Hongkong Bank is not at liberty to enter into such relations with the cooperation of the Japanese, German, French and Russian Banks and this you by no means desire.

It may be that the Banque Industrielle de Chine is endeavouring to obtain a similar concession by lending the Chinese Government money. Should this be done and should this French Bank be given control of the Company there will be great indignation in England among the merchants and serious friction with the British Government. I think that is certain. They will base their protest upon the Declaration of China of February 11th 1898[2] and upon the fact that the C.M.S.N. Co has for nearly 40 years worked in harmonious cooperation with two British Companies. Should it now be turned over to a French or Franco-German Company the act will be regarded with great indignation. Of course I do not know whether this is the intention or not but the fact that the father of Mr. Wang,[3] the Compradore of the Banque Industrielle de Chine, one of the most prominent Directors of the C.M.S.N. Co. is now in Peking is thought to indicate a possible agreement with that Bank.

It gave me great pleasure to see your cheerful face today. I hope to have another paper ready tomorrow and the third the day after.

With best wishes

Very sincerely yours
[G. E. Morrison]

---

the trade and economy of the province; on the redevelopment of the Chinese city of Hankow, the responsibility for which Yüan Shih-k'ai had earlier entrusted to Yang Tu and later to Ting Shih-yuan (qq.v.). Only the third memorandum, on the China Merchants Steam Navigation Company, is printed here.

[1] A. G. Crossley was the Representative of J. P. Bisset & Co. in China.
[2] A reference to the declaration made by China on that date, recognising the Yangtse as a British sphere of influence.
[3] A reference to Wang Tz'u-ch'ang, otherwise Wang Ch'un-shan. As Mayor of Canton during the Liangkwang Vice-royalty (1889–95) of Li Han-chang (1821–99), the elder brother of Li Hung-chang (q.v.), and T'an Chung-lin (d. 1905), the father of the prominent Republican politician T'an Yen-k'ai (1879–1930), Wang was known as 'Wang Pan-ch'eng', or 'Half-city Wang', so wide-ranging were his interests and power. He was a close associate of Sheng Hsüan-huai (q.v.), and later became Manager of the China Merchants Steam Navigation Company which Sheng controlled. Wang Tz'u-ch'ang was the father of Wang K'e-min (1873–1945), at this time Manager of the Banque Industrielle de Chine, a joint Sino-French undertaking, who was to play a prominent role in subsequent Republican politics, serving, among other posts, as Governor of the Bank of China and Finance Minister in the Peking Government. He later became a collaborator with the Japanese invasion army in North China, and died in prison in Peking in December 1945, his life having previously been spared by a clemency order of Chiang Kai-shek, and his family went to live in Japan, where they now own one of Tokyo's better known Chinese restaurants.

Enclosure to Letter No 696: *Memorandum* re *the China Merchants' Steam Navigation Company, 13 April 1914*

The property of the China Merchants Steam Navigation Company is much more valuable than is generally known. They have valuable property at every Treaty Port in China and at every calling place on the Yangtse River. Their property in Shanghai alone has been valued by experts at Taels 12,000,000. So ample is their accommodation for shipping that at their wharves near the French Concession 23 ordinary river steamers can lie at the same time end to end. No wonder the Japanese were prepared to pay for this property alone the sum of Tls. 4,000,000. The property on which their offices are situated in the International Settlement is assessed at Tls. 1,200,000 and is actually worth 2,000,000 Tls, while they possess in addition immensely valuable wharves in Hongkew[1] and on the other side of the river. Twelve million taels is a conservative estimate of the total value of the Shanghai property. Of their property at other Treaty Ports a moderate estimate reckons the value at Tls. 8,000,000. Thus the probable value of the landed property of this Company is not less than Tls. 20,000,000.

The fleet of the Company consists of 30 steamers of a gross tonnage of 54,367 tons. Of their 30 ships, 21 are obsolete, being more than 20 years old some indeed being forty years and one even 44 years old. Only 9 date from 1896 to 1912. It is doubtful whether the market value of this fleet is more than £4 per ton. Its value is approximately 1,500,000 taels.

At least 40% of the ships are being run at a loss. Wasteful mismanagement is everywhere conspicuous. Never has the fleet been brought up to date. During the same period of years and with less advantages the British firm of Butterfield & Swire have assembled a fleet of 57 ships of a gross tonnage of 106,736 tons, of which only 13 date from prior to 1894 while 44 are modern ships constructed since 1895.

Under proper management immense profits are possible, yet at the present time the Company is being run at a loss. Dividends, however, are still being paid but on the last two occasions they have been paid in the form of shares in the Hanyang Iron Works, which have been distributed among the shareholders.

No wonder the Japanese covet such a property as this. No wonder they are prepared to make tempting offers to Sheng *Kung-pao*,[2] to Li Ching-

[1] A district in the north of Shanghai.
[2] Sheng Hsüan-huai (?1849–1916), Chinese Imperial official and entrepreneur, whose plan for the nationalisation of China's railways was the immediate cause of the anti-Government outbreak in 1911. Until his power was broken by Yüan Shih-k'ai it was unrivalled in some of China's leading industrial enterprises, including the China Merchants Steam Navigation Company. The power and influence he had exercised during the last years of the Manchu Dynasty were not dissimilar to those wielded by Liang Shih-yi in the subsequent Republican period.

fang[1] and to other shareholders. It would be a disaster if this property were to pass under the control of the Japanese. Sooner or later it would mean Japanese armed occupation of the various properties. Japanese now possess military control over the Tayeh Ironmines. Japanese control and guard when necessary the railway from Tayeh to the Yangtse river, while by virtue of these interests Japanese have erected in Hankow itself on Chinese territory barracks for two thousand Japanese troops. Were the property of the China Merchants Company to pass under the control of the Japanese it would be a national disaster. By none would it be regarded with more alarm than by the British whose two Shipping Companies have for nearly 40 years been working in harmonious cooperation with the Chinese Company.

Such a disaster must be prevented. The Company must remain Chinese under Chinese Government control. With effective up to date management the property can become one of great profit to the Government.

To obtain control of the Company will cost the Government £2,000,000. British cooperation will enable the Chinese Government to obtain this amount by loan on reasonable terms secured upon the landed property and fleet of the Company which would remain Chinese. The loan would be five per cent and could be repayable at a premium at as short a time as the Government deemed advisable. During the currency of the loan the management would have to be entrusted to the British firm who obtained the loan for the Chinese Government.

For some years past the well known British firm of J. P. Bisset & Co, whose compradore[2] is one of the Directors of the China Merchants, aware of the enormous losses and leakage due to ineffective management, have endeavoured to arrange for the reorganisation of the Company under their

[1] Li Ching-fang (1855–1934), adopted son of Li Hung-chang. He was Minister to London from 1907 to 1910, and at the time referred to was living in Shanghai. He was a shareholder in many industrial enterprises which his father had helped to set up.

[2] Chou Ch'ang-ling (or Chou Shou-ch'en) (1861–1959), Chinese Imperial official and businessman, better known by his anglicised name, Shouson Chow, and invariably addressed, after being knighted by George V in 1928, as 'Sir Shouson', to the extent that very few people remembered his original name. He was one of the earliest Chinese students sent to study in America in 1872, but his stay there was cut short after nine years, and he was sent to Korea, where he served briefly as Chinese Consul at Inchon until the outbreak of the Sino-Japanese War. He then became Managing-Director of the China Merchants Steam Navigation Company (1903–7), in 1907 Managing-Director of the Peking–Mukden Railway, and in the following year *Taotai* of Newchwang. At the outbreak of the Wuchang Uprising he resigned his post at the Chinese Foreign Ministry, where he was by then working, and moved to Hong Kong where he speedily and spectacularly established himself as a leading businessman. Besides being the Compradore of Bisset & Co., he extended his operations to practically every field, including such vital and growing utilities as electricity, telephone, tramways and ferry-boats, as well as entertainment, land-development, banking and overseas trading. By virtue of these and his charity works, he was made a Member of the Legislative and Executive Councils of the colony, and was the recipient of a knighthood.

management. They are promised the support of the Hongkong and Shanghai Bank and what is of great importance there is no doubt that this firm could secure the assistance in the underwriting of various of the rich Insurance Companies and of the British Ocean Steamship Companies trading between China and Great Britain in whose interests it is of such importance that the Company should remain Chinese.

At the present moment the Company consists of 40,000 shares the market value of which is 140 taels per share equal to 5,600,000 taels in all. Sheng *Kung-Pao* and Li Ching-fang, the former of whom holds 13,000 and the latter 4,000 shares are the two chief shareholders. In December 1912 the shareholders offered to sell their shares to the Chinese Government for Tls. 11,500,000, 8,000,000 for the shares (namely 200 taels for each share), 3,500,000 taels to pay off various debts incurred by the Company.

At the present time the Company owe the Hongkong and Shanghai Bank Tls. 1,500,000 repayable in 15 years, and have other liabilities to the amount of another 1,500,000 taels.

The Government can reasonably assess the value of the property at the price for which the shareholders were prepared to sell their shares in December 1912, namely 8,000,000 taels. This amount plus 3,000,000 needed to pay off their present obligations plus another 3,000,000 Taels needed for bringing the fleet up to date brings the total required to 14,000,000 taels (£2,000,000).

I have made careful enquiries and I am confident that this amount can be obtained and that it is very desirable to obtain it with as little delay as possible. I venture confidently to predict that the Government will be astonished and delighted at the profits that will be made when the Company has been reorganised. Its present mismanagement is injurious to the prestige of the country.

697. From F. L. Pratt

Shanghai 19 April 1914

Dear Dr. Morrison,

Things here are quiet at the moment, but there are all sorts of rumours going around as usual. That was a good haul that Admiral Tseng[1] made the other day, and no doubt he will be able to persuade his prisoners to give information that will be useful later on. He has I am told a most persuasive manner with rebels who fall into his hands.

A well informed Cantonese was telling me the other day that the chief danger lies in Canton. He said that *Tutuh* Lung[2] had no idea of the tyranny

[1] Ch'eng Ju-ch'eng, Garrison Commander of Shanghai. The 'haul' refers to his arrest of a large number of revolutionaries and suspects, many of whom were tortured, while others were summarily put to death.   [2] Lung Chi-kuang.

and brutality shown to the civil population by the soldiery, and that he had no idea of administration. The Civil Administrator[1] is said to be a protege of the *Tutuh* and consequently afraid to take the initiative in keeping the troops in order. If conditions are as bad as they are represented to be there is undoubtedly danger of trouble from this quarter.

[...]

Very sincerely
F. Lionel Pratt

698. To F. H. May

Peking 21 April 1914

Dear Sir Henry,

Since my return I have been busy communicating to the President both verbally and in writing the results of my enquiries down south. The President is alive to the danger of the continuance of the Note trouble in Canton and will, I think, make every effort to restore confidence.

Application was made to the Quintuple Banks for leave to apply some portion of the £2,000,000 set apart for the reorganisation of the Salt (Annexe F of the Loan Contract of 26th April 1913). The Bankers held a meeting and telegraphed home a joint message favouring the proposal. Both the French and the German Ministers, however, state that the Bourse regulations in Paris and Berlin are very stringent and that it will not be easy to obtain permission to divert the funds from the purpose for which they have been specifically set apart by the terms of this Annexe. I take it this means that France and Germany will not consent to the proposal. China is losing at present $8,000 a week in interest upon this £2,000,000 and it would appear as if she were to continue to lose this amount indefinitely.

No agreement has yet been come to with regard to the payment of the Indemnity claims already settled, for which £2,000,000 was allotted by the loan contract. China is losing not only the 2% interest upon this £2,000,000 but she will require to pay interest at the rate of 5% upon the total claims amounting to £3,250,000 from the date at which these liabilities were incurred.

Then China has a further difficulty. Her Salt revenue is coming in in a satisfactory way. At present she has, after meeting all charges $15,000,000 of Salt revenue lying to her credit in the Five Banks. No interest up to now has been paid upon this amount. She can only obtain a vague promise that

[1] Li K'ai-shen, at this time Acting Civil Administrator of Kwangtung Province (September 1913 – May 1914). He later became a member of the Political Consultative Council set up by Yüan Shih-k'ai. On the accession to the Presidency of his fellow-provincial from Hupeh, Li Yüan-hung, he became a Presidential Adviser, and in March 1917 was appointed Chinese Resident in Urga. In December 1921 he became the Director of the Preparatory Bureau for Local Self-Government in his native Hupeh Province.

interest from 1 to 1½% may be paid and the Banks are claiming that under Art. 5 of the Loan contract China must retain always in the Banks, without interest or at merely nominal interest, a sum sufficient to meet the service of all the loans secured upon the Salt for 18 months ahead, that is to say she must keep a sum of not less than $24,000,000 always in the Banks!

At present China is endeavouring to arrange for an adequate silver reserve as security for the Bank of China Notes to be issued in place of the depreciated currency in Canton Province. These notes at present circulate at par in Peking, in Shanghai and up the Yangtse Valley. I am told by foreign Bankers that the methods of the Bank of China are fairly sound.

At present I hope the Chinese will pay into the Chartered Bank in Hongkong a sum of not less than $10,000,000 as security against the new Note issue. A branch of the Bank of China will be established in Canton and I hope that its management will be entrusted to a competent foreigner.

Yesterday the Minister of Finance was in to see me and speaking of the three big public Works in Canton – the Electric Light, the Water Works and the Canton Cement Works – I told him that if there was adequate guarantee against future interference on the part of the Authorities there would be little difficulty in obtaining from Hongkong and Canton merchants a sum of probably not less than $3,000,000 for the purchase outright of these three works. I fancy he will telegraph an enquiry to Lau Chu-pak[1] whom he knows well. Opposition is bound to be encountered from the present *Tutu* whose brother[2] is the Director (the exceptionally incompetent Director) of the Cement Works. The President promises to send to Canton a competent man to take the place of the present *Tutu*. His present choice is Tsai Ao,[3] the former *Tutu* of Yunnan, one of the best of the younger men.

[1] The pronunciation in his native Kwangtung dialect of Liu Chu-p'o (1866–1922), Chinese businessman. He was active in local Hong Kong politics and education and was instrumental in the founding of Hong Kong University and the Hong Kong Chamber of Commerce. He became a Member of the Legislative Council of Hong Kong in 1914. The Hong Kong & Yaumati Ferry Company which operates services between the island and Kowloon was one of the many enterprises of the family, being founded by his son, Lau Tak-po.

[2] Lung Chi-kuang, *Tutu* of Kwangtung, had two younger brothers, Lung Ch'in-kuang (q.v.) and Lung Yü-kuang. Lung Ch'in-kuang at this time was Garrison Commander of Canton and Waichow (Huichow) until February 1916, when he was succeeded by his brother Lung Yü-kuang. Both of the younger brothers of Lung Chi-kuang were at this time living in Canton, and had control over various enterprises in the city including cement and electricity works.

[3] Ts'ai O (1882–1916), Chinese soldier. A graduate of the Shikan Gakkō, he became *Tutu* of Yunnan on the declaration of independence by the Province after the Wuchang Uprising, and remained in the position until September 1913, when he was succeeded by T'ang Chi-yao. Fear of his undoubted ability and leadership caused Yüan Shih-k'ai to recall him to Peking where he was kept a virtual prisoner and given various sinecure posts, including the directorship of Land Survey. At the end of 1915 Ts'ai succeeded in evading Yüan's surveillance and joining T'ang Chi-yao in Yunnan to oppose Yüan's

He has been well educated in Japan. He is young, vigorous and intelligent and I think that when you meet him you will form a very favourable opinion of him. Failing him, or in addition to him, the President will probably send to Canton Chang Ch'i-huan[1] of Kwangsi Province, also a competent man.

The President is in good spirits. I gave him a lurid picture of the danger of the continuance of the present unsettled conditions. He is fairly well informed as to the situation. His chief source of information is Liang,[2] the head of the Chiaotung Bank, a brother of Liang Shih-yi.

The other day I wrote to Lady May and I would like again to thank you and Lady May for the kind hospitality you showed me in Hongkong. With great pleasure I look back to my visit. My journey round was certainly instructive and the reports I was able to make to the President have been, I hope of some use.

With kind regards

Very sincerely yours
[G. E. Morrison]

699. From E. W. Thwing[3]

Peking 21 April 1914

Dear Dr. Morrison,

I was glad to receive your letter today, and to know that you are back in Peking. In regard to the opium condition in Shanghai and Hankow, I believe your correspondent has received a pretty correct view of conditions. As to

---

monarchical scheme, led the Republican army to invade Szechwan, becoming, after Yüan's death, the province's Military Governor on 24 June. Some three weeks later however, he was granted leave of absence on the discovery of throat cancer, and he died after three and a half months, on 8 November, while undergoing treatment in Japan. Ts'ai came to know Morrison while in Peking; they held each other in mutual respect, and Ts'ai from time to time sought Morrison's advice.

[1] Probably Chang Ch'i-huang (1877–1927), a native of Kweilin, Kwangsi Province. A *chin-shih*, he was appointed a Lt.-Gen. in 1912 and later became Political Adviser to General Wu P'ei-fu (1874–1939). In June 1922 he was appointed Governor of his native province, a post he held until March the following year. In the event Lung Chi-kuang was kept at the post and was only dismissed in June 1916, some three weeks after the death of Yüan Shih-k'ai.

[2] Liang Shih-hsü (b. 1879), the younger brother of Liang Shih-yi, a graduate in 1905 of the Canton Military Academy. He was made a Lt.-Gen. by Yüan Shih-k'ai in 1914, not, as the compilers of the chronology of Liang Shih-yi's life took care to point out, through his eldest brother's influence. This however remained only an honour; he was never in the army, but rather devoted himself to helping look after his brother's many enterprises, including the Chiaot'ung Bank.

[3] Edward Waite Thwing, an American missionary who was best known for his involvement in the anti-opium movement. He was ordained a Presbyterian Minister in 1892, did missionary work in South China from 1892 until 1895 and taught at the Christian College

Shanghai I know from personal investigation. The licensed shops have been increasing in a remarkable degree in the past few years. During 1911 there were 316 licenses issued in the foreign settlement of Shanghai, by the Shanghai Municipal Council. In 1912 the licensed opium shops were increased to 374, and in 1913 449 were officially reported. The reports this year indicate a further increase and it is also stated that morphia can be freely bought in the Settlement without hindrance. The news papers state that the Municipal Council has no intention of restricting this sale. The report of this Council, of March 9th, states that the total increase of license fees from shops has been during the past year T. 40,489. More than half of this surplus, T. 22,886, came from the increased licenses from opium shops. In addition to this reports indicate a thriving opium trade in the Settlement. The selling price of opium per chest has more than doubled during the past nine months, reaching the figure of T. 6830 per chest. I have received Chinese news papers, one of which advertized, I believe, twenty-seven opium shops. Reliable reports also indicate that many of the Chinese hotels rent their rooms to opium smokers, and that many opium smokers have come in from Soochow, Hangchow, and other interior cities to Shanghai where they can buy opium and indulge in their habit freely without interference from the authorities. Furthermore numbers of the poorer classes, who are victims to the opium habit, have come to Shanghai to secure the drug and continue their vice. In an editorial recently in the *China Press* it was claimed that the presence of the numbers of criminal classes was due to some extent because of the free sale of opium. Certainly Shanghai has earned the reputation, and with good reason, of being the largest opium smoking resort in the Far East. And this reflects upon all the Governments who have Consular officials in Shanghai. In view of China's earnest effort this condition certainly reflects upon Western civilization. Hongkong ranks second, and perhaps Hankow third. Opium is still sold in the French and Japanese Concessions in Tientsin. You may quote me in this matter. With kind regards.

Very sincerely yours
E. W. Thwing

[...]

in Canton from 1896 to 1898. After a period in Hawaii, where he was Superintendent of Chinese mission work, he returned to China and became General Secretary of the International Reform Bureau, the declared aim of which was to aid in the suppression of the opium traffic. He frequently appealed to Morrison for assistance in his work, but Morrison, who called him 'the professional agitator', had for some reason taken a strong dislike to him, and frequently put the word 'Reverend' in inverted commas when referring to him. In a letter to him of 22 May 1912, moreover, he declared Thwing was not to be admitted to his house and his servants were to eject him if he ventured near. Morrison's rebuke however seems not to have daunted Thwing and the two had more peaceable exchanges in later years.

700. To Ts'ai T'ing-kan

[Peking] 11 May 1914

My dear Admiral,

The attention of the President must be called at once to articles which are appearing in the *China Tribune* of Tientsin, a Japanese subsidised paper. These articles are written by an Englishman, Reginald Bate,[1] who is the Editor of the *China Times*, a paper in which he would not dare to publish such libellous statements. Mr. Sun Pao-chi should be instructed to take immediate action and draw the attention of the Japanese and of the British Legations to these articles, which are designed to impair the good relations of China with foreign countries.

In the case of the Englishman he can be punished under the Order in Council.

I enclose you the article which was published on Saturday.[2] It is out of all reason.

With all good wishes

Very sincerely yours
[G. E. Morrison]

701. To Ts'ai T'ing-kan

[Peking] 14 May 1914

My dear Admiral,

I think the time has come when I ought to go home to England in order to see what can be done to remove false impressions due to incorrect statements published in the European Press with regard to China and to the policy of the President. The annual meeting of the China Association was held on the 21st of April and the report of the Chairman, who has not been in China for many years, is quite misleading.[3] Especially is it unjust in what it says in regard to Sir Richard Dane and the obstruction which it alleges has been interposed in his work. We know this to be untrue and we know that Sir Richard is himself fully satisfied. It is wise that when I go home it

---

[1] A British journalist. He was the China Correspondent for the London *Daily Mail* and Editor of the English-language newspaper in Tientsin, the *China Times*.

[2] Not printed.

[3] Morrison surprisingly used the terms President and Chairman loosely, for the two offices in the China Association were quite different. The President of the Association at this time was George Jamieson, who had succeeded Sir Walter Caine Hillier (1849-1927), a former British consular official and Professor of Chinese at King's College, London. The Chairman of Committee of the Association was Frederick A. Anderson, a businessman and former resident of Shanghai. While in the British consular service in China Jamieson had made the financial administration of the country his special topic of study, and his knowledge had gained him employment with the British and Chinese Corporation, which he joined in 1899. He left China before Bland succeeded him as the Corporation's representative in China in 1906. Anderson had also left China many years before.

should not be thought that I was going home specially for any purpose connected with the Chinese Government. The time is opportune because by the terms of my contract I am entitled to a holiday and it is quite natural that I should go home in order to bring back my wife and child.

I would suggest, therefore, that it would be an advantage if I went to England with as little delay as possible, say, about the first week in June and that I should stay in England for a month or 6 weeks.

On my return I would suggest that it would be a great advantage if, instead of coming back by Siberia, I were to return by way of Canada and British Columbia. The Asiatic question is one of increasing importance to China and I could make enquiries and prepare a report that would be of value to the President. I can do this without attracting unnecessary attention and without its appearing that I had gone to Canada specially for this purpose, for as I am a Colonial myself it is natural that I should wish to visit Canada. I could obtain information more easily and quickly than it would be possible for the Chinese Consul to do because I have had many years' experience of that kind of enquiry when I was correspondent of the London *Times*. Besides I am well known in Canada and I would have excellent opportunities of speaking to the authorities.

From Canada I would come back to Japan and here again I would be in a position to make enquiries as to the revolutionaries which I could do more fully than if I were to go to Japan specially for that purpose. My visit would not be regarded as having any object other than the natural one that on returning to my post in Peking I should spend a few days in Japan with my wife and baby. I believe I could do good work and could make my holiday one that would be profitable to the President.

I would be so much obliged if you would consult with the President with regard to my project. Perhaps there are other things he might suggest which I could do for him while I was travelling round the world in this way.

I ought not to arrive too late in the summer in London because Parliament breaks up and all prominent Englishmen leave for their vacation, either to the country or to the Continent.

I propose to take my Confidential Secretary home with me as there will be much clerical work to do, and whether or no Miss MacGlade would have to return to England in October. I will engage a new Secretary in England.

Will you be so kind as to ascertain from the President when you have an opportunity what his views are with regard to my spending my holiday in this way?

Very sincerely yours
[G. E. Morrison]

702. To C. B. Stokes[1]

[Peking] 15 May 1914

Dear Major Stokes,

Yesterday in discussing the question of China's financial position you suggested that I might put into writing a few of the facts that I then cursorily mentioned.

I submit that China at the present time is not having her case fairly stated in the English papers. The reason, I think, is to be found chiefly in the expense of telegraphing from Peking to London. Correspondents are apt to send messages which are brief, trenchant and exciting rather than calm surveys of the situation which require more words and therefore are more costly.

My successor on *The Times*, David Fraser, relies I understand for his information chiefly upon the Manager of the Russo-Asiatic Bank, de Hoyer. I think he is frequently misled and that he would not be misled if he were to have intercourse with Chinese or with unprejudiced Englishmen. Telegraphing to *The Times* on the 28th August of last year he committed himself to the statement that

'Under the present chaotic conditions only a twentieth part of the estimated (Salt) revenue reaches Peking. It is now for the Government concerned to protect the interests of foreign investors by insisting that China shall fulfil the stipulations of the Reorganization Loan Agreement. With a few years' careful nursing under foreign administration the Gabelle ought to produce enough to meet the earlier claims and to provide a small margin towards the service of the Crisp loan. At some future time perhaps something may be available for the Reorganization loan but nothing material can be effected until the whole administration of the country has undergone transformation.'

At the time of sending this message had Fraser consulted the Hongkong and Shanghai Bank he would have learned that the revenue was coming in in a way that completely refuted his ill considered statement. Since then in order to appear consistent he has persisted in belittling the success attending the collection of the Salt revenue.

At the present time China's financial position is rather a subject for congratulation than for condemnation.

[...][2]

---

[1] Claude Bayfield Stokes (1875–1948), British soldier. He had served many years in India, and was at this time a General Staff Officer there. In his Diary of 14 May 1914 Morrison noted that Stokes was 'now head of Persian Section of Intelligence Dept. Simla.' He was on a visit to Peking when this letter was written. Stokes, who had been British Military Attaché in Teheran (1907–11) was to become Political Officer in Baku in 1919, and Chief British Commissioner in Trans-Caucasia (1920–1) during the Powers' intervention in Russia.

[2] Morrison went in great detail into how various loans were being paid off. This is omitted.

China can claim with truth to have made adequate provision for the meeting of her obligations. Yet at this time when the financial outlook is better than at any time since the Revolution broke out responsible men like the President of the China Association suggest the possibility of foreign intervention because of China's financial difficulties and Sir Ian Hamilton[1] sees in New Zealand signs of the impending dissolution of China. These deductions are based upon misleading premises.

As I have said all loans contracted prior to the Boxer year and the Boxer Indemnity of 1901 are secured upon and defrayed from the Maritime Customs revenue of China. For a time payments of the Indemnity and of the Indemnity alone were in default but the Powers, knowing that the difficulty was temporary only, were considerate and allowed China time for payment extending the time by one year and arrears bearing interest. All these arrears of payment and of interest were met in due course and the service of every loan and of the Indemnity secured upon the Customs had been punctually paid and is punctually paid at the end of each month. But in addition Mr Aglen, the able head of the Maritime Customs, considered that as the first six months of each year the charges are greater than in the second six months it would be wise for China to set apart from the Salt collection a sum of Tls. 480,000 per month in order to meet any possible deficiency from the Customs revenue. This amount then, as I have said, is paid over and the amount of three months' quota is retained by the Banks so that all reasonable provision has been made by China for meeting her obligations.

The annual meeting of the China Association was held on the 21st of April. At that meeting the Chairman hinted that there would be possible foreign intervention because of China's financial needs, yet on the 21st of April the Hongkong and Shanghai Bank already knew that there was a large surplus from the Salt collection lying to the credit of China with the Quintuple Banks. And on the 24th April Sir Richard Dane wrote to the Quintuple Banks to inform them that the 'Revenue appears to be coming in well' and that inasmuch as there was lying in the Group Banks at Shanghai at the end of March $13,973,980 he proposed to them that they could retain for the

[1] General Sir Ian Standish Monteith Hamilton (1853–1947), British soldier, who was attached to the Japanese Army during the Russo-Japanese War (1904–5) and who was at this time Commander-in-Chief in the Mediterranean and Inspector-General of Overseas Forces. Speaking at a civic reception in Auckland New Zealand, in May 1914, he emphasised that the Pacific was 'the meeting place not of nations but of continents', where 'it may be decided whether Europeans or Asiatics are going to decide the destinies of the world'. *The Times*, commenting on 14 May 1914 on the speech, said: 'If telegraphic reports are accurate, Sir Ian Hamilton had in his mind both the possible effects of disintegration in China upon neighbouring countries and the friction likely to be caused by the exclusion of Chinese and Japanese labour from the United States, Canada, Australia and other "European" communities. The economic and ethnic pressure of the hardworking, rice-eating, parsimonious "yellow" races upon British countries appeared to him a "real danger".'

meeting of various obligations up to the 30th of June 1915 the sum of $10,211,000 and to release at once the sum of $3,762,980. Replying on behalf of the Banks, Mr Hillier of the Hongkong and Shanghai Bank endeavoured to induce him to allow them to retain the Salt collection until it amounted to the sum of $23,896,000 but Sir Richard Dane brushed aside this unjust proposal and handed over to the Chinese the sum of Taels 2,700,000 being approximately the equivalent of $3,762,980, being surplus collection from the Salt revenue after providing for all possible payments for a long time hence.

I would venture to wager that no statement in any way like the foregoing has been sent to *The Times* by David Fraser conflicting as it does with his unfortunate essay of the 28th of August.

Very sincerely yours
[G. E. Morrison]

P.S. Two loans are extinguished this year, namely the 7% silver loan of £1,635,000 of 1894,[1] the final payment being made next November 1st, and the 6% Gold loan of £3,000,000 of 1895,[2] the final payment being due December 31st. Extinction sets free $2,400,000 of the Customs Revenue.

703. To E. G. Hillier

[Peking] 19 May 1914

My dear Hillier,

I am much obliged to you for allowing me to read Stephen's[3] letter. Something must be done to counteract the effect produced by the publication in Europe of sensational reports from the Correspondents in Peking. It is so

---

[1] Known as the 'Chinese Imperial Government seven per cent Silver Loan of 1894' from the Hongkong & Shanghai Banking Corporation, the contract was not signed until 26 January 1895.

[2] The contract for a six per cent loan of £3,000,000 was signed with the Hongkong & Shanghai Banking Corporation on 26 January 1895, the same day as the signing of the seven per cent silver loan (*see* previous note).

[3] A. G. Stephen, British banker, whom Morrison described as a 'very interesting stalwart Britisher,' was at this time Manager of the Hongkong & Shanghai Banking Corporation in Hong Kong. He had written to E. G. Hillier, the Bank's representative in Peking, on 12 May 1914, commenting on a letter he had received from Sir Charles Addis, Manager of the Bank of London. In his letter Addis wrote: 'The news from China is disquieting. The failure to cope with White Wolf in the country itself and the reported activity of the revolutionary emissaries in Japan and the U.S. are giving rise to grave anxiety. Any day people are thinking we may hear of some fresh outbreak and the result is that the general attitude of the market towards Chinese credit is deteriorating into suspicion and mistrust.' 'This,' Stephen commented, 'is very similar to what the *Morning Post* says and it seems to me that it is unduly pessimistic. What Addis thinks is of great importance to Chinese credit in London and it is a pity he has been so affected by the Jeremiahs of the Peking correspondents of the London dailies. We all know that things in China are not as we

expensive to telegraph to London that correspondents are apt to send sensational messages which require a few words rather than calm statements of fact which require many words.

If the truth could be given about China there would not be this anxiety in financial circles. The people at home do not seem to realise that money has been provided to meet China's obligations for a long time ahead. Nothing, so far as I know, has been sent home about the monies from the surplus Salt collection which have been paid over to the Chinese. No clear idea has been presented as to the exact amount of China's present outstanding indebtedness in connection with short term losses. Vague impressions are abroad that these amount to sums very much greater than we know them to be.

Your letter has convinced me that I will have to prepare a statement at once and have it telegraphed home stating officially what is the Chinese Government's view of the present condition and what is the actual financial situation. I will confer with you before seeing that it is sent.

In this connection I have written this morning privately to Hsu Un-yuan[1] to ask him to obtain permission from Chou Tsu-chi[2] to draw up a clear statement of the exact sums owed by China for these short term loans: the dates upon which payments were due and the interest that they are now bearing. If a clear and succinct statement of these liabilities could be made public and at the same time it could be made known that the Chinese Govern-

---

should like them but I think we are agreed that a serious rebellion is out of the question Were it not for his picturesque name I doubt if the operations of White Wolf would raise much attention in Europe and no one seems to give any prominence to the other side of the question, i.e. the prospect of splendid harvests, the record Customs collections and the splendid prospects of trade the construction of new railways will open up. I think it is high time that someone presented this side of the picture otherwise while they continue grousing in London the market will never look at Chinese loans.' Both of the letters quoted above were passed on to Morrison by Hillier.

[1] Hsü En-yüan (b. 1885), Chinese economist and Republican official. A graduate of the London School of Economics, he enjoyed a high reputation among British bankers prior to his return to China in 1910. As Vice-Director of the Bureau of Audit and later Governor of the Bank of China, he had frequent contact with Morrison who thought highly of his ability.

[2] Chou Tzu-ch'i (1868-1923), Chinese Republican politician. A returned student from America, he had begun his career in the diplomatic service. Vice-Minister of Finance in the last Imperial Cabinet formed by Yüan Shih-k'ai, he was appointed by Yüan as Military Governor of Shantung in 1912. In August 1913 he was recalled to Peking to serve first as Minister of Communications then as Minister of Finance, and then in April 1915 he became Minister of Agriculture and Commerce, a post he held until April the following year. After Yüan Shih-k'ai's death Chou went to Japan and thus escaped arrest for his complicity in Yüan's monarchical scheme. He was soon pardoned, however, along with his fellow conspirators and fellow members of the 'Communication Clique', Liang Shih-yi and Chu Ch'i-ch'ien and later became once more Minister of Finance (August 1919). In 1921 he was a Delegate to the Washington Conference. On his return he served briefly as Acting Prime Minister and concurrently Minister of Education (April-June 1922).

ment were negotiating a loan to convert all these high interest charges the effect would be reassuring.

Fraser in a telegram of the 28th of August last committed himself to a very unfortunate forecast of the financial position in China and to be consistent and not to make his message appear too ridiculous he has since concealed things which would show that his forecast was an unfortunate one.[1]

I return the letter herewith, with many thanks.

Yours in haste
[G. E. Morrison]

704. From T. A. Rustad

Kuei-Hua-Cheng, Shansi 20 May 1914

Dear Dr. Morrison,

I have been in these parts over six months now and I have several times thought of writing to you and tell you of what is going on in this district, but what came to my ears were from so unreliable sources that I did not think it worth while. Our new Tartar General or *Chiang-Chun* as he is called here, Pan-Che-Yin[2] is taking hold of things in quite an unusual energetic style and if he keeps it up we may yet see this district prosperous although it has suffered much from the last revolution but perhaps still more from the rapasious methods of our last Tartar General[3] and his helpers. I have not

---

[1] David Fraser's telegram, published in *The Times* on 29 August 1913, was entitled 'The Security for Chinese Loans. A Diplomatic Protest.' It read in part: 'It is now for the Governments concerned to protect the interests of foreign investors by insisting that China shall fulfil the stipulations of the reorganization loan agreement. After a few years' careful nursing under foreign administration the *gabelle* ought to produce enough to meet the earlier claims and to provide a small margin towards the service of the Crisp Loan; at some future time perhaps something may be available for the reorganization loan. But nothing material can be effected until the whole administration of the country has undergone a transformation and tranquillity has been permanently ensured.'

[2] P'an Chü-ying, Chinese soldier. He became Acting *Chiangchün* (Military Governor) for the Special District of Suiyuan (later Suiyuan Province) in April 1914. The title of *Chiangchün* was changed in July the same year to *Tut'ung*, and P'an held the post until his dismissal in October 1916.

[3] Chang Shao-tseng (?1869–1928), Chinese soldier and Republican politician. A returned student from Japan, he came into national prominence when, as the Commander of the 20th Division stationed at Lanchow at the outbreak of the Revolution, on 29 October 1911, together with Wu Lu-chen and Lan T'ien-wei (d. 1921), he appealed publicly for the abdication of the Manchu Emperor and the introduction of constitutional government. After the establishment of the Republic, he served as a mediator between the Yüan Shih-k'ai government and the southern republicans, and in October of that year was appointed *Chiangchün* of the Special District of Suiyuan, but was relieved of the post in April 1914, being suspected of having republican sympathies. After serving in the sinecure post of Presidential Adviser, he retired to Tientsin to devote himself to the study of Buddhism, remaining there until 1921. In that year he was invited back by Wu P'ei-fu, then the most powerful figure, to assist in mediating in the internecine warfare in Hunan and Hupeh. Chang became the Minister of War in October 1922 after Wu P'ei-fu himself

seen anything in the foreign newspapers, that I get, but I suppose you know that our late *Chiang-Chun* or his father was found smugling about 20 thousand ounzes of opium. It was found out at Yang-Kao, but I suppose our old *Chiang-Chun* will be able to put the responsability over on to somebody else. He confiscated a lot of opium while he was here and kept it all, what he burnt was brown sugar same as they burnt in Kalgan when the Tartar General over there even invited Mr. Twing [Thwing] to come and have a look. Over there they took the precaution to put some crackers in amongst the burning sugar so as to keep the people from getting too near. I have heard the story from a good source and I think it rather good as a joke on Mr. Twing. Here opium smuggling has been going on all the winter. The former Tartar General himself being in the business could not be hard on the others. The new general is taking things in another way. He burnt real opium here a few days ago and the natives are wondering what he is up to as he seems different from any official that has been in these parts. All the winter we have had armed parties going about the country robbing right and left but without killing anybody as far as I have heard. The robbers were all local people who had no other way of getting their food. Taxes and sur-taxes have been collected in this district untill at present it is believed that all the farmers are clean as wistles, but still the taxing goes on. I know by what we ourselves are paying that it must be terrible on the chinese. If the crops should not turn out much over the average there will be a serious outbreak round these parts and I suppose the new Tartar General will be blamed for it although he is only reaping the fruits of his precedessor's work. One band of robbers all farmers formerly under the direction of the new Magistrate in Salachi has been very busi this winter. I suppose you will think it extraordinary that a robber chief can be Magistrate but that is a fact and he is not the only robber chief in this district who is now dealing out justice. They have one in Uo-Lan-Hua or some other place to the north of here. The one in Salachi smokes opium all day long, I am told, and hears cases after midnight. Quite an unusual way of proceedure. Well his band got busi this winter and went over the Yellow-River and took prisoner one of the Mongol princes there. These robbers are only fourty in numbers but they know their business well. The man who asked them to cross the river and pay them for it was one of the Mongol prince's relatives. His idea was to get hold of the reigns of government. The robbers had the prince imprissoned in his own *Yamen* and would have killed him if he had sent for troops. One of the catholic missionaries in those parts finally intervened and got the robbers to leave. They are now farming again and will keep good as long as the tax officials leave them alone. Yes the overtaxation in this district

---

had turned down the post, holding it in successive Cabinets until January 1924, and serving concurrently for six months as Prime Minister, from January to June 1923. He then retired once more to Tientsin but remained an important member in the Chihli Clique and was assassinated four years later.

is said to be the real cause of all these small upraisings. The new Tartar General has already censured the head of the *Likin* here a man called Yu-Wei-To who formerly was a *Wen-Kuan*[1] in Tientsin, and prior to that he was a lottery ticket seller down there. He of course has not had any experience in taxing matters, just went ahead and asked whatever came into his head. When told that so and so had [   ][2] that on the same kind of goods for many years passed he would simply send for soldiers and have the man arrested or the goods confiscated. [...] Now some days ago I saw in the *Peking Gazette* that our Mr. Yu-Wei-To has informed Peking that he has collected $100,000 extra revenue which he will send in and on the strength of it the central government have promised him the 5th order of the Golden Stork and to pay him the allowance coming with it. Of course Yu-Wei-To can remit that money and more if he wanted to but the joke of the thing is that it said locally that he was not responsible for the offer of paying in $100,000 to the central government but that somebody else did it in his name and now our friend Yu-Wei-To is bound to see the matter through. If it is true I think it one of the best chinese jokes I have heard for some time. Our *likin* director is now sick and refuses to see anybody on business. Our own head dealer here is supposed to be a friend of him so I know what is going on from time to time. I have myself a little matter with him and although I have called a lot of times he does not want to see me, and I cannot blame the poor fellow. It is a well known fact that his predesessor took with him all the books in the *likin* stations round here and the new director had no records to go by. [...] I have tried to make foreigners come over here and do business, import or export, but with the excisting taxes they all say it is impossible. To buy Linseed, Grains hides etc. in this district is very cheap but when you have to pass the *likin* stations the price of the goods is doubled and before you get it to the railway it costs more than it can be bought for at Kalgan. This district suffered more than any other part of Shansi. Pao-Tou on the Yellow-River was taken and retaken a couple of times and looted every-time. There are still a lot of troops round here and although they are much better behaved than those round about Kalgan the natives would rather see them leave. One of our men travelled down from Ou-Lan-Hua in company with a chinese officer a Lieutenant I think. They spoke of the many robber bands and our man said he found it extraordinary that the troops did not finish them off when they were so many and the robbers so few and ill armed. Well said the officer the chinese soldiers is not such a big fool as some people think, suppose he were to go after the robbers strong and clean them out of the district, there would be no need for the soldiers to protect the inhabitants and the soldiers would then be disbanded. [...]

Yours sincerely
T. A. Rustad

[1] Literally, an official.   [2] Illegible.

705. To Ts'ai T'ing-kan

[Peking] 27 May 1914

My dear Admiral,

I enclose you the formal letter to H.E. the President. I feel sure that you will do everything that you can for me, for you have always been a friend to me and the greatest pleasure I have in being in China is being associated with you in the service of the great President.

There is much difficulty about this Note question[1] and the appointment of the foreigners. The Englishman was rejected by the French, Russian and Japanese. Then the German was rejected by the French and Russian. Now the question is can the Frenchman be appointed without the opposition of the Germans. Of all the unworkable combinations I have ever known that Quintuple arrangement seems to be the most unwieldy. It is very disheartening.

With best wishes to you

Very sincerely yours
[G. E. Morrison]

Enclosure to Letter No. 705: *To Yüan Shih-k'ai 27 May 1914*

Your Excellency,

By the terms of the contract under which I have the honour to be in Your Excellency's service, it was arranged that I was to be given two months' leave of absence each year, the time to be chosen as circumstances were favourable.

Last year while Your Excellency's work of reconstruction was continuing I took no leave at all. But this year the position is so favourable and the outlook so reassuring that I respectfully ask permission to proceed to England and to Canada to join my family. I make this application with the more confidence because the situation now seems to me better than it has ever been since I first came to China.

Under Your Excellency's wise guidance tranquillity has been established throughout the country, the financial position is one which enables the future to be faced without misgiving, railway and industrial development are being everywhere encouraged, while the relations of China with foreign

[1] The reference is to the question of the Canton Notes and the proposal for a Mixed Commission consisting of an equal number of Chinese and foreigners to supervise the redemption of some 32,000,000 dollars worth of banknotes which the Provincial Government had had printed in Japan for issue in Canton. Not only were the notes without security, but the blocks were not destroyed, and an unknown quantity of unauthorised notes were produced by the Japanese printers and came into circulation. As a result, public confidence in these notes was destroyed and bullion was being hoarded to the great detriment of internal and foreign trade. With the consent of the Powers concerned, it was decided in May 1914 that a portion of the Quintuple Loan secured by China the previous year should be used for the redemption of the notes.

countries are characterised by quite unusual friendliness, every outstanding question of importance having been settled by amicable agreement or being in process of amicable settlement.

Under these circumstances I venture to suggest that the time is opportunely chosen for me to submit my request to Your Excellency.

I am

Your Excellency's obedient servant
[G. E. Morrison]

706. To F. L. Pratt

[Peking] 10 June 1914

My dear Pratt,

I send you herewith an authentic document which the Chinese would like very much to have published. It is a letter which was written by Sun Yat-sen to Count Okuma and came into the possession of the authorities through the action of a friend of Sun Yat-sen's who has been associated with him for many years and is now dissatisfied.[1]

I understand that you are now editing the *North China Daily News* in the absence of Green. At any rate you might be the means of having the document published in the paper either in whole or in resumé. The translation requires correction in its English. It is an interesting document but it betrays the most astonishing ignorance of international affairs and apparently is

[1] This document was sent to Morrison by Ts'ai T'ing-kan, who wrote in his covering letter of 7 June 1914: 'I enclose two copies of the translation of a letter sent by Sun Wen to Ōkuma the Japanese Premier. Can you arrange to have the documents published in Shanghai as well as in London and still not have the secret divulged that the Chinese government or any Chinese person had anything to do with the matter?' Sun's letter, together with its original preface which was described by F. Lionel Pratt as another letter, was published by him in the *North China Herald* in its issue of 20 June 1914 (pp. 898–900) under the heading 'Sun Yat-sen's Patriotism. Astonishing Appeal to Japan. China for Sale', with sub-headings as well as a short editorial note which read: 'The following letters have reached us from a source in the *bona fides* of which we have every reason to believe. The first letter is from a prominent revolutionary.' Then the text as printed here followed. There were a few alterations. Ōkuma was not mentioned by name, but the words 'From Sun Yat-sen to a certain Premier,' were changed to 'Letter alleged to have been written by Dr. Sun Yat-sen to a high personage in Japan.' Long extracts from this version were quoted by Lyon Sharman in *Sun Yat-sen: His Life and its Meaning* (New York 1934). The purported original letter, found by Watanabe Ikujirō among Ōkuma's papers and published in his *Ōkuma Shigenobu* (Tokyo 1943), seems to have been written in Japanese. A Chinese version was printed by Wang Yün-sheng in his *Liu-shih nien lai Chung-kuo yü Jih-pen* (Tientsin 1933) (VI, pp. 34–8), but the letter has not appeared in any of the editions of the collected works of Sun Yat-sen so far published. The English translation printed here bears stylistic corrections in Ts'ai T'ing-kan's hand. It is a free rather than a literal translation, but in substance corresponds to the Japanese text Watanabe was alleged to have discovered.

written in entire ignorance of such a thing as that Favoured Nation Treatment is secured by all treaties.

If you have it published please do not disclose the source from which you obtained it. I am sure I can trust to your discretion in this matter. If you are unable to use it will you please return it to S.E. Lucas Esq., Manager Chartered Bank, Peking.

I am off tonight. All good wishes to you

Very sincerely yours
[G. E. Morrison]

Enclosure to Letter No. 706

For the past twelve years I have been pursuing the revolutionary course along with Dr. Sun. That I am still alive after what has occurred last year is something miraculous.[1] As our declared object was to preserve the integrity of our mother country so it is a matter of great surprise when my attention was drawn to a letter addressed to a certain Premier by Dr. Sun. The contents of the letter indicate in an unmistakable manner that he means to reduce China to a state of dependency such as that of India; indeed, he is to China as is Li Yuan Yun[2] was to Korea. The step he now takes is altogether against my cherished hopes, it is impossible for me to follow his lead any longer. I cause this letter to be published in order that members of our party may be acquainted with, and take into careful consideration, his recent astounding act. The letter is as follows:

From Dr. Sun Yat-sen 'To a certain Premier'

Sir,

I have the honour to bring to your notice the desirability for Japan to assist China in her efforts to reform, as the adoption of such a policy will tend to relieve the critical situation in the Far East. To recompense the assistance rendered by Japan, China is willing to thrown open her whole country to Japanese industrial and commercial enterprises. The two countries are so reciprocally dependent that when the proposed measures are carried into effect the result will be mutually advantageous. On the one hand, it will enable Japan to jump to the forefront of the world greatest powers and occupy a position similar to that of Great Britain; while on the other,

[1] This refers to the 'Second Revolution'.
[2] Li Yuan-yung (1858–1926), Korean politician who has been regarded as an arch-traitor by his countrymen, having been chiefly responsible for the signature in 1907 of the Seven-Article Agreement with Japan which turned Korea into a Japanese colony. In consequence, Li, who had previously held the portfolio of Education, was made Prime Minister in the new Korean Government. From this position he formalised the annexation by Japan of his country three years later. For his cooperation he was made a Baron by the Japanese Emperor, and in 1920, after the March 1st massacre (see p. 763 n. 1.) of his countrymen by the Japanese authorities, whom he supported, he was promoted to Marquis.

China will be able to preserve her integrity, develope her latent resources and become a rich country on the Continent of Asia. Thus Japan and China will then be in a position, with the assistance of each other, to maintain the peace of the world and to bring its civilization to a higher level. Such great work is indeed without a parallel in the chronologies of the world. The time is now ripe, and the opportunity thus accorded should not be lost. Therefore, I hope you will carefully consider the points enumerated below:

In the past days when China was suffering under the despotic rule of the late Ching Regime, people rose *en bloc* with a view to supersede the Absolute Monarchy with Republicanism. The Min Tang (i.e. the People's Party) holding in high respect humanitarian principles, sought to alleviate calamities caused by bloodshed by negotiating for peace which was arranged between the North and the South, and led to the abdication of the late Ching Emperor. Yuan was subsequently elected as the President of the Republic of China, and on assuming office he took an oath that he will forever observe the Constitution and remain loyal to the Republic of China. But since then he acted in direct contravention to the Constitution and against the right principles. Under the name of Republicanism he rules as a tyrant. Hence the people are very discontented and indignant, but they have no means to redress their grievances. Though he is more tyrannical than the House of Ching, his authority over the country is far less respected. This accounts for the repeated insurrections during the past two years. That the Min Tang will rise some day and the Revolution will reappear are foregone conclusions. But it is difficult to foretell when they can achieve success if they are devoid of help and dependent upon their own strength.

Should during the period of destruction a powerful nation were to offer assistance, the struggle would not be prolonged. Such assistance will not only prevent great internal sacrifices but will also remove foreign entanglements. As Japan is close to China and the prosperity or ruination of the one affects the other, it is but natural that the revolutionists should first seek aid from Japan. While during the period of construction, when the reform of administration, the training of the army, the encouragement of education and the development of industries are all taken in hand, talents must be borrowed from more advanced countries to render assistance. Considering that Japan and China are nations of the same race and same literature and that the former was also interested in the last revolution, there are weighty reasons for the revolutionists to look for help from Japan. After Japan has assisted China to reorganize her administration and religion and to develop her potential resources, the Governments and peoples of the two countries will be on much more intimate terms than between other countries. China will throw open all the trade centres in the country to Japanese labour and merchants and enable Japan to monopolize the commercial field in China. When the time comes, China will desire to free herself from the restrictions imposed by the former international dealings and to revise unfair treaties, she will need Japan's support in handling diplomatic questions. She will also depend on Japan's advice to reform her laws, judiciary and prison system. Moreover, Japan can facilitate the abolition of the extra-territoriality by giving her consent first. This will be beneficial to the Japanese because it will enable them to live in the interior of China. By the time China restores her control of the Customs, she will enter into a commercial alliance with Japan, whereby Japanese manufactures imported into China and Chinese raw materials imported into Japan will be exempted from paying duties. The prosperity of Japanese commerce and industry will go hand in hand with the development of the natural resources in China. Great Britain is composed of mere islets, her area is small, yet her influences have ever been in the ascendancy. It is scarcely necessary to mention that her influence is due to her acquisition of India as her great trading mart, and on this account the various Powers could not compete with her commercially. While the natural resources of Japan are practically exhausted and there are no field for further activities, China is large and rich with potential wealth yet to be developed. Japan could, therefore, without even incurring the trouble and expense of stationing troops, as Great Britain did in India, acquire big commercial mart in China. Thus the benefits that will accrue to her are doubly great. This is what I meant, as aforesaid, that she will leap to the forefront of the world greatest Powers.

Japan could, however, never aspire to such a position if she continues her present policy towards China. The reason is this: In governing China, Yuan ignores the trend of general friendship of Japan but he indulges in antagonism against her surreptitiously. Consequently in dealing with China, Japan will not be able to compete with other country even though she has equal opportunity. For instance, in negotiating the cases of Hanyehping, the China Merchants Steam Navigation Company and the Petroleum Concession in Yen Chang, either the Chinese Government procrastinated, or it instigated the people to rise in opposition, or it transferred rights originally conceded to Japan to some other country. China is now weak and her Government fears the good feelings between the Min Tang and Japan should increase so Yuan pretends to be eager to cultivate her goodwill, and at the same time practices the intrigues prevalent in the times of feudalism when one kingdom is played of against another. This is how China deals with Japan now, when China is stronger it is needless to say that Japan can only expect to get even worse treatment. Should Japan refuse to support China, the antagonism towards Japan will always be great while Yuan is in power. Even after that Government falls on its own accord, Japan cannot inspire the confidence of the Chinese people. For without that support the relations of the two countries can never be as satisfactory as they should, and they cannot share the benefit that will accrue.

Speaking from another standpoint, if the Chinese revolutionists are devoid of the support of a strong nation in connection with their campaign, longer time will be needed to achieve success, and after success is achieved they will fail to reform the administration and improve the diplomatic relations. On this account the revolutionists are now anxiously looking for support and Japan would reap enormous benefit if she were to give this support. This illustrates what I have said in the foregoing that the two countries are so reciprocally dependent [that] when the proposed measures are carried into effect the result will be mutually advantageous.

It is said that Japan cannot decide her policy concerning China without the consent of the British Government, but this is not an obstacle in the way. The real state of affairs in China has been recently exposed. When Yuan first took over his office he spent a good deal of money in inducing foreign correspondents in China to report favourable news and express favourable views on Chinese affairs, the news and opinions thus retailed were credited by the British Government. The public opinion in England, however, has since undergone a marked change, *The Times* stated recently that Yuan had not the ability to suppress disturbance and restore peace. Moreover Great Britain and France are on the most friendly terms, the French Government and people do not have any confidence in Yuan, as may be seen from the cancellation of the Government's guarantee for the French-Chinese Bank Loan.[1] The policy of the British Government towards China is 'perfect peace and order', but it has since discovered its mistake in believing that Yuan is capable of keeping peace and order and preserving the integrity of China, it is certain that it will now follow the example of France and assume a different attitude towards China. If Japan suggests a practical method of solving China's problem which would lead to permanent peace in China, the step is sure to receive the approval of Great Britain. Since the Japanese Government usually consult with Great Britain on international questions the latter also shapes her policy to meet the wishes of Japan.

It is my firm conviction that China can never have peace unless the governmental powers are in the hands of the Min Tang. The reasons are that, the Chinese are roughly divided into three classes, to wit, the official class, the Min Tang, and the masses. The last take no active part in politics. The official class do make energetic efforts to protect their personal interest but their energy only last as long as they are in power. As soon as they are out of power they will offer no resistance. Such was the conspicuous example of Yuan himself when he was dismissed by the ex-Prince Regent. Yuan considered himself fortunate for having escaped death and attempted nothing whatsoever to resist. The Min Tang, however, is composed of persons of different type; its members are fearless and determined to attain the end they have in view. Though the front ones, having to bear the brunt of the

[1] This probably refers to the '5% Industrial Gold Loan of 1914' signed on 9 October 1913.

misfortune, may fall, those behind will still forge ahead. They could not be suppressed even during the Ching Dynasty when they were ruthlessly dealt with by the authorities. Any one who has studied the conditions in China will realise that as long as the Min Tang fails to attain its object China will never have peace. Therefore it is perfectly clear that the preservation of peace in China depends on the solution of one and only one problem.

Though it is an extraordinary matter for a government to support the people of another country to overthrow their government, but extraordinary men accomplish extraordinary deeds in order to attain extraordinary results. You are the extraordinary man and this is the extraordinary opportunity so I dealt the matter at length.

I, Sun Wen, am the representitive of the Min Tang so I make bold to tell you what we hope for from Japan. Moreover if you consult history you will find that France supported America, Great Britain supported Spain and the United States supported Panama. The support of France was accorded on the ground of humanitarian principles, that of Great Britain for self-preservation in the Napoleonic campaign while the United States wanted to enjoy the facilities of the Panama Canal. By assisting the Chinese to overthrow their despotic government all the three merits as mentioned above will accrue to the country that accords the support; what is the fear then which prevents the proposal from being acted upon? It is scarcely necessary to mention the fact that in order to prevent diplomatic complications, secrecy and adroitness are necessary for carrying the matter to a successful issue.

I offer my opinion for the interest of the future of the Far East and entreat you to take it into your careful consideration and to enlighten me with your opinion.

Yours etc. etc.
Sun Wen

707. To Yüan Shih-k'ai

London 27 June 1914

Your Excellency,

I arrived in London on Tuesday morning after a somewhat fatiguing journey through St Petersburg and Berlin. The same afternoon I was interviewed by a correspondent of *The Times* and I enclose a copy of the published statement.[1] It is a correct statement revised by myself. I enclose some cuttings

---

[1] None of the enclosures mentioned is printed. This letter was sent to Yüan through Ts'a T'ing-kan. In his covering letter Morrison wrote: 'My mission has been successful so far and I hope the President will be well pleased with what I have done. As I have often said to you, what is the use of paying Press Agencies? Here at no cost to the Chinese Government at all – except at the cost of my expenses – China has had an admirable advertisement, published throughout the English Press, with the exception, of course, of the *Daily Telegraph*. *The Times* has acted well and as it is by far the most influential paper in

of the paragraphs written in consequence of what I said. In these cases I did not have an opportunity of revising the statement and therefore I am not responsible for their exact accuracy but the general sense is correct.

The immediate result of my interviews published in papers of an estimated aggregate circulation of not less than 3,500,000 (three million five hundred thousand) copies has been a rise in all Chinese securities amounting in all to a large sum. References to the confidence felt in my assurances I enclose, taken from various papers.[1]

The rise would have been still more satisfactory had it not been for the disastrous news yesterday published from Peking giving an account of the mutiny of the troops at Kalgan, the cruelty shown to women and children and the escape of the mutineers without punishment. *The Times* Correspondent states in the paragraph which I enclose that these disasters are symptomatic of the gravely unsettled state of China.[2]

Nothing could have been more unfortunate than for such an incident to have occurred at this juncture, for obviously it impairs the weight of the communications which I have made to the papers, but I learn however from influential friends in the City that it will not affect the value of my assurances. Today you will see that bonds have risen still further.

The net result so far of my visit has been a rise in the credit of the Chinese Government amounting in all to some millions of dollars.

A further detailed statement suggesting various measures that must be taken to improve China's credit and reputation I will send next week. I have said nothing except what I believe to be the truth.

I am

Your Excellency's obedient servant

[G. E. Morrison]

England I took special steps to see that the statement I made for it was textually correct. In the case of the other papers, of course, there was no time nor any need to revise the articles.' Morrison, in the interview published on 25 June 1914 under the title 'Dr Morrison on China. Aims of President Yuan. Official Point of View', said that when he left Peking the outlook seemed to him better than it had been at any time in his experience. Order was being maintained throughout the country, except for White Wolf, the revolutionaries were decreasing through lack of money, and Yüan Shih-k'ai had the situation well in hand. It was unjust to describe Yüan's administration as a reactionary autocracy. Yüan had not cut himself off from the Young China Party nor was he aiming at a family dynasty. It was the Young China Party, he said, who attempted too much. They tried to go in one step from the most ancient autocracy to the most advanced form of representative government known in the world. Their impetuosity had forced the President to intervene. Morrison went on to describe how well the President was surrounded and served by foreign-trained officials and ended by saying that the financial situation in China was on a much sounder footing than was generally known.   [1] Not printed.

[2] The report of the mutiny of soldiers at Kalgan on 24 June 1914 was published in *The Times* the following day under the title 'Revolt of Chinese soldiers. City sacked and burned. Escape of the Mutinists' and described the systematic looting and pillaging of the town by the mutinying troops.

708. From L. G. Fraser

Slough [Buckinghamshire England] 6 July 1914

Private

My dear Morrison,

Pray forgive a very hurried letter. The reason of my prolonged silence is that I was recalled from my wedding trip early last September to go into the Ulster question and I have been more or less immersed in Irish affairs ever since.

I have, however, written occasionally on Chinese affairs, in a rather cursory way, and I think I have done all that *The Times* has had (very little) on Far Eastern questions since that date. The view I have always urged on *The Times* is this – that President Yuan is the only man who can keep the country together, and that he is not doing so badly. I have been permitted to state this view again and again, and I may say that when I drew the attention of the Editor[1] and Steed[2] to Bland's article in Sunday's *Observer*[3] they both agreed that a steady but discriminating support should continue to be extended to the President.

I am going to write a leading article on *The Present Condition of China* within the next ten days or so.[4] It may not be quite so optimistic as you would like, but it will correct unduly pessimistic impressions. It is imperative, however, that I should see you first and go into the whole question thoroughly. [...]

Please understand quite clearly that *The Times* does not wish to attack he present administration in China, and does not care a straw about any deviations from the strict 'constitutional' path which the President may have found necessary. This attitude may not prevent occasional criticism of particular acts or minor lapses of your Govt, but the *general* support will, I am assured, continue to be given.

Yours always sincerely
Lovat Fraser

709. To W. E. Soothill[5]

London 7 July 1914

Dear Mr Soothill,

I am obliged to you for your letter of the 4th of July. I have never been able to accept the view that we have as a Nation done China much harm.

---

[1] Geoffrey Robinson.   [2] Henry Wickham Steed.
[3] In an article published in the *Observer* on 5 July 1914, under the title 'The Chinese Paradox. Puzzle for Students of History', Bland expressed doubts about the political and financial picture Morrison had drawn of China in his interview published in *The Times* on 25 June.   [4] The promised article did not appear.
[5] William Edward Soothill (1861–1935), British missionary who spent some twenty-five years in Wenchow, Chekiang Province, and was from 1907 to 1911 Principal of the European

It seems to me that the good we have done enormously outweighs the harm, if any, that we have done. I have never been able to understand why we should, in a wealthy country like China or in a country whose wealth is undeveloped owing to the neglect of her opportunities, found charities to assist in her education. It seems to me opposed to the national spirit, which we ought to do our best to encourage, that we should establish a University in Hankow. A University in Hongkong is a good thing, but I would wish to see the Chinese themselves take in hand their own education, with foreign help, of course.

Then as regards the Boxer Indemnity, it is wholly wrong in my opinion to condemn our action in that matter. Our claim was a just claim. We made nothing out of it and although we charge the Chinese 4% interest it must be remembered that China herself is a country which cannot obtain money at less than $5\frac{1}{2}$ to 6%.

I admire your disinterested efforts and I am very sorry indeed to hear that you have borne the expense for a year without salary. I know that your work in the case is done for the benefit of China. I should be glad to have a talk with you about the matter before I leave.

In the meantime would you be so kind as to give me the address of Sir Alexander Hosie. I am anxious to get into communication with him while I am in London.

Very sincerely yours
[G. E. Morrison]

710. From W. C. Wang[1]

Charing Cross [London] 8 July 1914

Dear Sir,

Though I am only a Chinaman, I am so proud for that the social education of China is so powerful and able to change the character of an European Dr. to that of a Chinaman exactly. It is surprised to read your address in

---

section of Shansi University. He was at this time engaged in a scheme to establish a University in central China using part of the Boxer Indemnity fund, and in a letter to Morrison dated 4 July 1914, asking for his support, Soothill wrote: 'If there are to be "spheres of influence" I am constantly urging that if Britain wants to retain the Yangtze valley as her "sphere", this can only be done by influencing the sphere *for its good*. There are many ways of doing so, and of these educational advancement is not the least. We have, as a nation, done China *much* harm. It is time, as a nation, that we did it some good.' Soothill became Professor of Chinese at Oxford in 1920, the position for which Edmund Backhouse (q.v.) also applied but failed to obtain notwithstanding the fact that he had given the University a great many rare Chinese books which he had obtained in the immediate aftermath of the Boxer Uprising. It was thought improper at the time that he should have made the gift when applying for the position.

[1] Unable to identify.

Daily Telegraph.[1] How resemble! as if every word is just utterred by a Chinaman, a China's fat and round faced mandarin.

I must die, you must die, and every man must die; China must be fallen, the Powers must be more prosperous, and the Earth must be catastrophic; but the souls last for ever.

Harmful and groundless as 'irreconcilables failed to repudiate China's foreign obligations' ect. and shamful and ridiculous as 'the President Yuan-Shih-Kai the most progressive ruler ever known in China' ect., are you an European Dr. not a China's bloodless mandarin? Are you a Chinaman's adviser among so called 'great jurists' Ariga and Goodnow not the famous former Correspondent of *The Times*, who had criticised Yuan-Shih-Kai's intimate friend Prince Ching?[2] I regret for the pens of yours and mine both. I am only sorry to say that your address published on a paper P. 3 but a news on same paper P. 11 this is as if your face is torn off.

But never mind, as you know well enough, as a rule, any man inverted into a Chinaman may enjoy the iron skined face comfortably.

I am

Your Chinese Obedient Servant
W. C. Wang

711. To L. G. Fraser

London 8 July 1914

My dear Fraser,

[...]

The general opinion of *The Times* leaders on China has been that they have been fair and quite sympathetic. It is pretty generally known that you have been the writer and you are known to be a man of calm and measured

[1] A reference to an address on 'The Present Position in China' given by Morrison to the members of the London Chamber of Commerce on 6 July 1914 and widely reported in the press, including *The Times* and the *Daily Telegraph*, the following day. Though he began by saying that he was not there as an advocate of the Chinese Government, Morrison went on to paint a rosy picture of Yüan Shih-k'ai's administration. 'No one,' he said, 'pretended that all China's difficulties were past, but they were less now than at any time since the Revolution. No one pretended that the campaign of calumny waged by a small remnant of irreconcilables had not had some effect, but the effect was diminishing.' His announcement that China was likely to open its mining resources to foreign capital and that a considerable proportion of what was saved from opium smoking might be spent in the future on British manufactures was greeted by his audience with approval.

[2] I-k'uang, Prince Ch'ing (1836–1916), Manchu Imperial Clansman, who became the dominant figure in the Manchu Court from 1898 after the death of Prince Kung, and Prime Minister in the first Cabinet under the Manchus in 1911. On that occasion Morrison wrote an article entitled 'China's First Prime Minister. Prince Ch'ing and his Record', which was published in *The Times* on 17 May 1911. In it Morrison strongly criticised Ch'ing, describing him as 'the most notorious figure in China' and claiming that his life story was 'the story of the most disastrous experience in the history of the Empire'.

judgment. Articles by Bland cause irritation because they are thought to be unjust. For example in the article in *The Observer* of last Sunday[1] he speaks about Kalgan as being one of the few cities which escaped looting at the time of the Revolution, speaks of it as an important city and says that it had been ruthlessly looted last Wednesday. What seems so unfair is this, that the telegram about the mutiny at Kalgan telegraphed by Donald, the Correspondent of the *New York Herald*, who is now acting for David Fraser, stated that there had been a mutiny of 5,000 troops, whereas next day he corrected this and said that the mutiny consisted of 200 to 400 men only. By no conceivable stretch of the imagination could it be said either that Kalgan is an important city or that it is one of the few cities which escaped looting before, and it is ridiculous to speak of a city being ruthlessly looted by a body of from 100 to 400 men. Chinese are notoriously inaccurate and I would question whether even 200 men took part in the looting.

I shall be seeing the India Office this week with regard to Tibet and I will then run over the case with you, but I have not come home here in any way to influence the English Press. I am home truly on leave, leave to which I was entitled last year but which the exigencies of the situation prevented me from taking. This year as all was going well I came home, yet I find the impression here is that China is in a worse condition now than it was last year. Putnam Weale is now entirely in the service of the small party of 'Irreconcilables'[2] who failed to bring about the second Revolution and his messages are almost grotesquely inaccurate.

All good wishes to you

Very sincerely yours
[G. E. Morrison]

712. To Ts'ai T'ing-kan

London 9 July 1914

My dear Admiral,

I enclose you a letter which I have addressed to His Excellency the President, which I hope you will have translated and communicated to him. I have spoken plainly but not as strongly as I ought to have done with regard to the impossible people to whom the Ministry of Finance have entrusted the obtaining of loans in Europe. Here in Europe when the President wants to get a 5% loan you have the Chinese Legation in Brussels authorising the signature of a loan with a disreputable German called Helfeld[3] about whom you can enquire at the German Bank in Peking, for a loan bearing interest at $8\frac{1}{3}$%.

[1] *See* p. 330 n. 3.   [2] A reference to the republicans under Sun Yat-sen.
[3] Alfred von Hellfeld. A Loan agreement was entered into between China and Hans von Hellfeld on behalf of Alfred von Hellfeld on 14 October 1913 and incorporated into a contract between Belgium and China dated 30 December 1913.

I enclose you the report of my speech from the *Morning Post* and a full report from the *Daily Telegraph*.[1] It has had the effect of enhancing China's credit but it is very important that everything should now be done to prevent such transactions as that of Chanless & Batouieff,[2] etc. It is impossible to exaggerate the injury that such things do.

The address that I gave to the London Chamber of Commerce has been very widely read not only in England but abroad and is being sent by the News Agencies all over the world. One of the prominent firms of London Sharebrokers considered that it was essential for the credit of China that my address should be published word for word. They asked that I should authorise a payment from the Chinese Government of £400 for this purpose. They were to send out 100,000 copies. I flatly refused. I said the Chinese Government would not pay a single cent for any such publicity. I knew very well that the brokers interested in China would take good care that the speech was published. *The Daily Telegraph* has a circulation of nearly 200,000 and it was published in full in that paper at no cost whatever to the Chinese Government.

I am now asked to address the Canadian Chamber of Commerce. I am seeing the India Office with regard to Tibet. I am having no holiday whatever. In fact I am working from early morning to late at night for everyone interested in China seems anxious to meet me.

I have been asked to speak before the Manchester Chamber of Commerce but it was not possible to arrange a date convenient to us both, besides I thought it was wiser to keep quiet for a little time for I thought it would be undignified for China if I were to be going about the country making speeches on her behalf.

You remember the lunch that we had with His Excellency the President when he authorised me to make a statement with regard to his desire to expedite the payments of the Boxer Indemnity. No statement I have made in London has had a better effect.

The great thing, however, standing out conspicuously is that we should all work together. I give instances in my despatch to the President but I might also give him another instance such as that of Mr George Bronson Rea, Editor of *The Far Eastern Review*, who is in London writing on official paper of the Ministry of Communications and is, I understand, being paid a salary as technical adviser to that Ministry. Everyone knows the name of Dr Hirai,[3] a member of the House of Peers in Japan, a distinguished railway

[1] A reference to his speech to the London Chamber of Commerce on 6 July. *See* p. 332 n. 1.
[2] For their identities, *see* enclosure.
[3] Hirai Seijirō (1856–1926), Japanese railway engineer, educated in Japan and America. After working as an engineer in mines and railways mostly in Hokkaido, he became Deputy Director-General of the Imperial Japanese Railway Administration in 1907, and was made a Peer in the following year. A member of the committee which helped to set up the South Manchurian Railway in 1906, he became in 1913 an adviser to the

engineer, but when the British Foreign Office asks who Mr Rea is Mr Lew Yuk-lin had to reply that he knew nothing whatever about him or about his mission, that he had never seen him.

At present in London there are some 28 Chinese loan contracts provincial and otherwise being offered to London banking houses, while everywhere I hear of the deplorable failure of China to meet her Treasury bills owing to big English firms like Vickers, Armstrongs and others.

I hope I have made everything quite clear. I leave for Canada on the 21st of August and have taken my passage. My wife and I often speak of you. We hope you are well and that everything is going well with our great President.

All good wishes to you

Very sincerely yours
[G. E. Morrison]

Enclosure to Letter No. 712: *To Yüan Shih-k'ai, London 9 July 1914*

His Excellency President Yuan Shih-kai

Your Excellency,

On Monday afternoon I addressed a large gathering of the London Chamber of Commerce on the subject of the present position in China. I enclose you a copy of the report as published in the London *Daily Telegraph*.

In my address I refuted the attacks made upon China's credit by the correspondent of the *Daily Telegraph* in Peking, by Mr Bland and others. It was one of the largest gatherings of the kind held in the City. Lord Southwark,[1] the Chairman of the London Chamber of Commerce, was in the Chair and many members of Parliament, both of the House of Commons and of the House of Lords were present. Among others who spoke was Sir Claude MacDonald, formerly Minister to Peking and later Ambassador to Japan.[2] Many congratulations have been sent to me upon the effect of my speech, which has been described as quite convincing. It would have been more effective if I had not been compelled to make reference to the recent

---

Chinese Government on railways, a post he held until 1926, shortly before his death. While in Peking he was President of the Association of Japanese Residents there.

[1] Richard Knight Causton (1843–1929), 1st Baron Southwark, British politician. A Liberal Member of the House of Commons (1880–5 and 1888–1910), he was Lord of the Treasury (1892–5), served as Liberal Whip from 1892 to 1905, and was Paymaster General from 1905 to 1910. He became President of the London Chamber of Commerce in 1913.

[2] Sir Claude Maxwell MacDonald (1862–1915), British soldier and diplomat. He was Minister to China from 1896 to 1900, and to Japan from 1900 to 1905, when he became the first British Ambassador to Japan on the raising of the Legation to an Embassy, a post he held until 1912. Morrison had had a close and friendly association with him during his time in Peking, but had a poor opinion of his capabilities, and referred to him privately as 'the Major'.

action of the Chinese Government with regard to finance. I said, what is the truth, that Your Excellency, aware of the injury that had been done to China in the past had now taken control of the Ministry of Finance and that in future no loan contract would be held valid unless it received Your Excellency's sanction.

Since I came to London the work I have done has had the effect of raising the value of all Chinese securities. The effect would have been still greater if it had not been for the deplorable action of the Chinese Government in giving options for loan contracts to unworthy foreigners of no standing whatsoever. In Tientsin there is a small firm named Chanless & Batouieff. Mr Chanless was formerly a clerk in the American Consulate General. He is a man of good character but of no financial standing soever. Mr Batouieff is a Russian Buriat. I am not even sure whether he can write English. He, of course, speaks it. I understand that Mr Batouieff has a dairy farm in Tientsin and sells milk. By some inconceivable act of folly this firm I find was given a three months' option to float a loan in Europe of £20,000,000 sterling. By no possible means could they have floated a loan of twenty thousand copper cash. Wherever I go among banking circles I hear of this ridiculous act which does discredit to China. Moreover I learn everywhere that when the first time limit expired instructions came from the Chinese Legation in Brussels extending the time for another month.

I would point out to your Excellency that all the big Banking people in London either have correspondents in the Far East or are in a position to learn what is the standing of firms in the Far East. To entrust an option of this kind to an obscure firm in Tientsin who sell milk causes ridicule and contempt and must in actual money have affected the credit of China to the extent of many hundreds of thousands pounds sterling.

Another loan hawked about London doing dishonour to China has been a contract entered into with a man[1] who was the fourth engineer of the Shanghai Municipality, who has no financial support whatever. Another also offered to the Banks is signed by an Englishman[2] who formerly lived in

[1] B. Leigh Newman, British adventurer, according to Morrison, 'formerly a junior assistant engineer or architect in the Shanghai Municipality, now preying on the Provincial Authorities, signed 9 contracts with the Provincial Authorities for sums between 3 and 5 millions sterling *each*! Has no backing, cannot, even to [E.S.] Lucas (q.v.), disclose the names of his "principals", he airily expresses his contentment at being able to pay his expenses from remittances sent to him by the provincial officials whom he is befooling. [...] Is represented in London by a swindler H. C. Twigge. His backers are Hudson's Consolidated Ltd. of London, probably the name being selected that might suggest to the unwary Hudson's Bay Company.'

[2] 'Colonel' John Peter Grant, Canadian engineer and adventurer. In 1918 on hearing of his appointment as purchaser in the Far East of war supplies for the British Government, Morrison in a letter of 10 August 1918 to Sir John Jordan, British Minister in Peking, outlined his career, describing him as 'no more a *Colonel* than I am, who was one of the hangers-on of Li Hung-chang and his corrupt entourage, and who attempted to execute

Hankow who has no reputation whatever and has no more chance of obtaining money in London than my Chinese Coolie would have of obtaining credit at the Hongkong and Shanghai Bank in Peking.

In the case of the 8% Nanking Provisional Bonds hawked about London by a German named Helfeld, who now calls himself Baron von Helfeld, a man of no financial standing whatsoever, whose record is a bad one, it means that China is paying $8\frac{1}{3}$% *per annum* for this loan money, the price being 5% at 87 redeemable at par in 4 years.

How can the Government expect to get a reasonable loan at 5% when contracts such as these bearing such exorbitant interest are entered into with foreigners of low repute who would not even be given a hearing by any reputable bankers in London? The British bankers think that China must be in desperate financial straits to resort to such extraordinary methods which bring ridicule upon the Government of China.

The only people who support Helfeld are the Chinese Legation in Brussels and a Publicity Bureau stationed in Brussells conducted by Wang Mou-tao, who formerly sent communications to the London Press which were so disgraceful and scandalous that no London paper will now take any notice of them. This Wang Mou-tao, the First Secretary[1] of the Legation, is the gentleman who your Excellency will remember charged Sir John Jordan and myself with being engaged in a 'great opium smuggling conspiracy'. For this calumny we were both given an official apology from the Chinese Government. For the Wai Chiao Pu to reappoint a man who can do such acts as these, to promote him to the post of First Secretary in Brussels and to pay him a high salary for conducting a news agency which only does injury to the country is most regrettable. I would suggest to your Excellency that Mr Wang Mou-tao be immediately recalled, that the Press Bureau called the 'Agence de l'Extrême Orient' which is quite useless, be suppressed and that all such transactions as those entered into with the Tientsin firm of

---

various swindles in China 1896–7...John Peter is a crook who has lived on his wits for years...During that time [1896–7] John Peter was accompanied by his wife, a notorious blackmailer...After failing in China the Grants went to Australia, and there in 1899, through Bernard R. Wise, who was himself of a questionable reputation although he had been President of the Union at Oxford, had been Attorney-General in N.S.W. and died only last year when Agent-General of N.S.W. in London – through Wise John Peter Grant nearly pulled off a swindle regarding alleged concessions of great value held by him in China, particulars of which Wise was not too ready to disclose. Less than two years ago John Peter again bobbed up in Canada, and nearly succeeded in obtaining large sums from Canadian speculators on the ground that he held through Lord Li Ching-fang, the adopted son of Li Hung-chang, exclusive concessions for railways and mines in the province of Anhui. Thinking I might know something of the case, one of the Canadians interested wrote to me for information, and I was then able to prevent an extensive swindle. The Canadian whom John Peter had inveigled into his bogus scheme lost £1,000, and is happy he did not lose many thousands.'

[1] Wang Mou-tao was Second not First Secretary.

Chanless & Batouieff, with Helfeld, with Newman, with Grant and other foreigners unknown to reputable Bankers should cease.

Then there is another point. The British Foreign Office finds here two representatives of the Chinese Government Mr Lew Yuk-lin and Dr Chen Chin-tao. Both are excellent men and both are working with every desire to serve their country but they are not working together and the Foreign Office tells me that when they ask Mr Lew of certain transactions of Dr Chen Chin-tao they are informed that Mr Lew knows nothing whatever about them, and when Dr Chen Chin-tao is asked about certain transactions of Mr Lew Yuk Lin's he has to reply that he is kept in complete ignorance regarding them. The Foreign Office ask why there should be two men of Plenipotentiary rank representing China in London and yet not working together. Such action conveys the impression that there is no united Government in China and that one half of the people have no trust or confidence in the other half.

I have repeatedly spoken to Your Excellency upon the need of having a Chinese Consul General in London. At present China is represented by an honorary Consul General named John Forster,[1] a man of no standing whatever, who was appointed by Lord Li Ching-fong.[2] He has a small business. He has neither social rank nor reputation and it is undignified for China to employ as her representative a man who had to answer serious charges brought against him in the law courts in connection with glass works at Haichow. It is a dishonour to a country which employs men of high standing like Professor Ariga, Professor Goodnow and Dr. Hirai and others that it should be officially represented in England by a Consul General like Mr Forster. I cannot too strongly impress upon Your Excellency the need of removing this man and of appointing a paid Chinese Consul General who would look after the interests of the Chinese in Great Britain. He would have to be a man of education and standing who would bring credit to the country.

With regard to Mr Lew Yuk-lin, I wish to state most emphatically that I have met in London all classes of people, a large number of whom know Mr Lew personally. They all agree in saying that as Minister Mr Lew Yuk-lin has acted well and honourably, that he has been scrupulously honest and that he has done much to uphold the dignity of the country. This is also the opinion given of him by my old friend Sir John McLeavy Brown.

In accordance with the wish of the Minister of Finance I have seen Mr Whitehead[3] of the Chartered Bank to endeavour to induce him to accept the

[1] A British businessman and adventurer who while in China was engaged in glass-making. In 1908 he was employed by the Chekiang gentry to assist in their negotiations with the Central Government and the British and Chinese Corporation who had earlier secured from the Central Government the concession for the Shanghai-Hangchow-Ningpo Railway.

[2] Li Ching-fang was Chinese Minister in London from May 1907 to December 1910.

[3] Thomas Henderson Whitehead (1851–1933), British banker. He worked in various capacities on the staff of the Chartered Bank of India, China and Australia in practically every

post of Director of the Bank of China, but it is quite certain that he will refuse this appointment. He is 63 years of age and he feels that at this age it would not be wise to take up a new appointment.

I have seen the President of the China Association[1] and I have seen a large number of the correspondents and of the representatives of the Press.

In London I hear nothing but condemnation of the mining regulations.[2] Money to large amounts would be available for developing the mining resources of China if regulations could be drafted enabling the employment of foreign capital. London is the centre of the capitalisation of the mining industry of many countries. In my speech and in my interviews I have said that the matter is now seriously engaging your Excellency's attention.

In London there is a small body of men, headed by Mah Soo, formerly Secretary to Dr Sun Yat-sen, endeavouring to influence the Press. Their only supporter is the Peking Correspondent of the *Daily Telegraph*. They need not be taken seriously, but so long as China is content to sign loan contracts with any foreigner, no matter what his previous reputation may be, who turns up in Peking and says he is in a position to obtain money in London, so long will China's credit remain discredited. Mah Soo does no injury to China. People here pay no attention to his words. Only one paper in fact publishes them and that is an obscure paper, but loan contracts like those I have referred to in the beginning of this letter do great injury to the country.

I have the honour to be

Your Excellency's obedient servant
[G. E. Morrison]

713. To Yüan Shih-k'ai

London 17 July 1914

His Excellency the President of the Chinese Republic
Your Excellency,

Statements are published in the English papers to the effect that China is now endeavouring to obtain a loan not of £8,000,000 but of £20,000,000. When quotations are put to Dr Chen Chin-tao, the financial Commissioner, he has to reply that he has no information. No information is sent to him which would enable him to answer questions put to him by English financiers. Powerful bankers in London wonder what purpose the mission of Dr. Chen

---

country in East Asia as well as in North America from 1874 on, became the Manager of the Hong Kong branch in 1883, and in 1902 the London Manager. He refused the Chinese offer, which eventually went to another Chartered Bank man, S. E. Lucas.

[1] Morrison must have meant Chairman rather than President, who was at this time F. A. Anderson whom he recorded in his Diary having met on 30 June 1914. *See* p. 313 note 3.

[2] A reference to the regulations governing the exploitation of mines promulgated on 11 March 1914.

Chin-tao serves seeing that the leader of it is kept in ignorance of what is going on in China.

Today the following statement for the Marconi Company is published in *The Times* and other papers:

> Marconi Company and China: Official Statement
>
> The Marconi Company yesterday issued the following statement: 'Negotiations have been pending between the Chinese Government and the Company for some time past for the erection of a number of wireless stations in China for internal and external telegraph services. On April 8 last the Chinese Government sent an official letter agreeing to authorize the Marconi Company to issue two million sterling Five per Cent Chinese Bonds in payment of the proposed stations.
>
> This document was filed at the British Legation at Peking, and the formal contract has been sent forward for approval and signature. The Company has every confidence that in due course the agreement will be signed and all mutual obligations fulfilled.'

In the absence of information I am bound to say that this telegram is creating an unfavourable impression, for the terms required by the Marconi Company are quite injurious to China. No English Banker is deceived by the statement of the Marconi Company that the Bonds are 5% (Five per cent) Bonds. Nominally they may be but the rate of discount makes them more than eight per cent.

Telegrams from Peking to *The Times* state that the Quintuple Bankers decline to negotiate a loan of £8,000,000 to enable China to pay off the short term loans on the ground that these loans were incurred by the Chinese Government in order to circumvent the Quintuple Group and that it is not right that the Quintuple Group should assist China to pay off loans incurred in opposition to the Quintuple Group. How far true this telegram is we do not know.

The London Bankers and big contractors and manufacturers complain that agents of the Chinese Government are endeavouring to negotiate the sale of Chinese Treasury Bills at rates of interest, which in the case of one loan of Telge and Schroeter, a German firm of arms dealers, amount to eighteen per cent.

Everywhere I hear the complaint that no effort has been made by the Chinese Government to meet Treasury Bills as they fall due. Prominent Banks and Members of Parliament ask me why is it that telegrams from Peking should announce that the Chinese Government are receiving large surpluses from the Salt administration when the Government are repudiating or expressing their inability to pay Treasury Bills as they mature in London. Cases cited to me are those of the two great English firms of Armstrongs and Vickers. The effect is injurious to the credit of China. The total amount is not great. The effect of paying them from current revenue would be of great value to China.

Your Excellency is, no doubt, aware that I have given interviews not only to English newspapers but to American correspondents. I enclose you the report cabled to New York and published in various American papers.[1] I have seen the Editors of the Chief London papers, many of whom I know personally. I have seen also the Chinese Editor of a paper called *The Chinese Review* which has been established here with a view of improving China's position. One thousand copies are printed. There are 50 subscribers and the remaining 950 numbers are distributed gratuitously. I cannot conceive that any good can be done by this Review. It is published once a month and contains no information that has not already been published in English papers. No English paper will publish news that has already been published in another paper.

The most powerful of the English papers is *The Times*, a paper with which I was connected for 17 years. It has the largest circulation of any of the high class papers in England. On behalf of *The Times* a proposal has been made to me to assist China by making known in a widely circulated issue the present condition and resources of the country. I will lay this matter before Your Excellency when I return to Peking. There is a much more sympathetic tone in the English papers with regard to China than there was before I arrived in London. Englishmen are only too anxious to see China prosperous and contented. They feel real sympathy with China and her difficulties and are really desirous that these difficulties should be overcome. Messages from the *Daily Telegraph* Correspondent in Peking still come almost daily attacking the Chinese Government but I do not think that these messages, which are never correct in fact and always erroneous in prophesy, do any serious injury to the country. On the other hand the presence in London of Chinese Treasury Bills which are not being redeemed when they fall due will continue to injure the credit of the Country.

I have the honour to be

Your Excellency's obedient servant
[G. E. Morrison]

[1] Morrison's optimistic views on the financial and political situation in China were also reported in the American press and were given prominence in the pages of the *New York Times* on 5 July. The enclosure is not printed.

714. To L. J. L. Dundas[1]

London 2 August 1914

Dear Lord Ronaldshay,

The President has telegraphed for me[2] and I am leaving Liverpool on Friday for Canada in the hope of being able to catch the *Empress* Steamer leaving Vancouver on August the 20th.

I am sorry that there will be no time for me to see you before I go. I am also sorry not to have seen Sir Edward Grey but I am grateful to you all the same for your kind offer to bring about a meeting, which would certainly have taken place if it had not been for this appalling upheaval.[3]

Serious alarm is naturally being felt by Yuan Shih-kai and in view of the certain shrinkage of the Customs revenue the financial outlook is black indeed. He fears specially Japan but I can see no reason for his fears. I will call in Japan on my way as it is his wish.

A prominent official in our Foreign Service tells me that Beilby Alston is to be our next Minister in Peking.[4] I daresay you know him. He is a pleasant Society man, but if he has any capacity he has on both occasions of his being Chargé d'Affaires in Peking been careful to conceal it. In my seventeen years in China he is the British Official in charge of our Legation in Peking who has created the greatest feeling of discontent among the English Community. He was wholly indifferent to his work and took no interest in it whatever. It was estimated in Peking that he spent five hours a day in the company of a lady and I believe it was the universal opinion, even among the Legation people, that he was the most incompetent noodle that had ever been given a post of responsibility in a Legation in Peking. I have sometimes thought that it would be a wise thing if the British Government were to appoint to the Legation in Peking a man of Indian experience. I do not know McMahon[5]

---

[1] Sir Laurence John Lumley Dundas (1876–1961), 2nd Earl of Ronaldshay, who had travelled extensively in Asia between 1900 and 1907. He later became Governor of Bengal (1917–22) and Secretary of State for India (1935–40) and Governor of Burma (1937–40). He was the author of books on Asia and of biographies of Curzon (1928) and Cromer (1932).

[2] Morrison was referring to a telegram he had just received from Chou Tzu-ch'i, the Minister of Finance, which read: 'I have received verbal instruction from the President as follows – "Whereas war has broken out in Europe and there may be trouble in Asia which affects its peace, Dr. Morrison is to watch the situation carefully and if he sees that it is serious, he is to return to Peking immediately to discuss matters."'

[3] A reference to the outbreak of the European War.

[4] In the event Jordan was to stay on in Peking as Minister until 1920. Only then was Beilby Alston appointed.

[5] Colonel Sir Arthur Henry McMahon (1862–1949), British soldier and colonial official. He served for thirty years in India, rising to become in 1911 Secretary to the Government of India Foreign Department (1911–14) and British High Commissioner for Egypt (1914–17). He was the British representative in the Tripartite Conference held in Simla (1913–14) between China, Britain and Tibet and was responsible for drawing up the boundary between China and India which bore his name, a boundary, however, which was never recognised by the Chinese Government.

but I should have thought that a man of that type, or Sir Frank Younghusband who has a knowledge of the frontier question, might render important services in such an extremely difficult post as Peking will be for the next few years.

I believe that the British Community in China – at any rate all British people whom I have spoken to inside or outside the Legation – would regard the appointment of an amiable nonentity like Alston to such a difficult post as a calamity.

I hope to be in Japan not later than the 3rd of September and I ought to be in Peking not later than the 10th of September. Should you ever care to write to me there I will be very glad indeed to answer as fully as I can any questions put to me.

As you know, the chief foreigner employed by the Chinese in connection with the Army is a Frenchman, Colonel Brissaud Desmaillets. The Chinese were induced to appoint him believing that the French Army is now in a higher state of efficiency than the German Army. Should events show that this is not the case and should the Germans show military superiority you may be quite sure that the Chinese will change accordingly the nationality of their military adviser.[1]

What I think is chiefly to be feared in China is the scarcity of money, the inability to pay troops and the consequent mutiny of those troops. On the other hand the knowledge that China will not be able to obtain any foreign financial assistance may lead to a more serious effort on the part of the Provinces to fulfil their obligations to the Central Government. It was difficult for the President to induce the Provinces to remit money to Peking when those Provinces were learning – often in an exaggerated and incorrect manner – that the Central Government was obtaining millions sterling from Europe on the security of the Provincial revenues.

With best wishes to you

Believe me

Very sincerely yours

[G. E. Morrison]

715. From W. E. Soothill

London 18 August 1914

Dear Dr Morrison,

Lest you should go back to China with a wrong opinion, and as your engagements seem too numerous for you to see me, I would like to refer to the two points you raised in your letter to me.[2]

[1] Colonel Brissaud-Desmaillets left China soon after the outbreak of the European War, and his place was later filled by Aoki Nobuzumi and then Banzai Rihachirō, following China's engagement to Japan which bound her to employ Japanese as military advisers. It was not until Chiang Kai-shek came to power that German military advisers were employed. [2] This refers to Morrison's letter to Soothill, No. 709.

I. That we as a nation have been sympathetic with China, and done her much good, there is no room for doubt, in mine, or any English mind. Neither is there room for doubt that in the mind of the rank and file Chinese our association with the Opium Trade hides much, if not all the good we believe we have done. My appeal to our Government was two-fold, one, that by the education of a number of China's future leaders in an atmosphere sympathetic with this country, the better side of our character might be understood to the *mutual* advantage of both countries; 2. that by such a process the material, as well as the moral, progress of both nations would be *mutually* advanced. It was not a case of founding a charity, nor would such an institution as was proposed have done anything but seek to develop China's national spirit – about which I am as keen as any one – for it was my purpose to seek an alliance with the Provincial College and failing that to have due representation of officials and gentry on the Board of Control. Moreover, the national spirit would have suffered no lack of development in the proposed University, for it is in Colleges under the influence of Christian men especially Englishmen where the national spirit has reached its best and safest expression.

Until recently it was hardly a question of whether there would be a University in Central China, but rather a question whether it would be a representative British Institution or merely another of the many already existing American ones. The Americans are doing a fine work, for which I have warm admiration. We are doing little. Their Universities are provided by Xtn [Christian] men for Xtn education, which cannot but be an enormous benefit to China. They will all ultimately come under Chinese control, as would the Institution I was working to evolve. Personally I should have aimed to build it on a broader basis and made it more thorough than the Americans.

II. As to the Boxer Indemnity, I have uttered never a word of condemnation of our action, but simply shewn that we are making a handsome profit and that we should lose nothing by assisting China to develop her resources thro' a well-equipped University. I have neither criticised or condemned. The figures were supplied to me by our Foreign Office, with authority to make what use of them I wished. On analysing them I made the discovery that we are making a profit of between two and three millions, and indirectly perhaps even more. There are other items also, altogether apart from the question of interest, and Sir Ernest Satow,[1] who arranged the Indemnity himself, was sufficiently impressed that he interviewed the Prime Minister[2] in our behalf.

Mr Lloyd George promised that if I took him £150,000 he would arrange a grant, which though not specifically named in figures, was clearly to be a

[1] Satow was at that time British Minister in Peking (1900–6).
[2] Herbert Henry Asquith.

like sum. He went further and promised that if I would take £50,000 he would arrange a liberal grant. Two weeks since I was to see him, and had in hand promises reaching nearly £120,000 entirely *conditional* on the Government grant. The Emperor of Germany has now blown my plans to the winds, as neither the private promises, nor Mr Lloyd George's, can be fulfilled.

So now, after three years' patient and depressing labour, I find that the one element which everybody in the world had omitted from his plans has come in and burst mine. Now I would not take the money out of the country if I could. We are fighting China's battle in Europe as well as our own.

So be it. I have put up the best fight for China in my power, most of the time single-handed, and have been knocked out with a blow from behind. I do not regret the effort, and don't believe my time and money have been wasted, although there is little to shew for them. I have deepened the interest of many in China, have reached the Prime Minister, Sir Edward Grey, Mr Lloyd George, and other members of the Cabinet; addressed a fine meeting of Members in the House of Commons; accompanied a first rate deputation to Mr Lloyd George and addressed him on China: 175 M.P.'s have been stirred sufficiently to pledge themselves to support a grant; and added sympathy with China has been effected in every leading Chamber of Commerce in the country; and several leading newspaper Editors have been, I hope, enlightened.

Now I must think of the future. I was approached for a Chair in America, and asked to lecture there. Also I have twice been asked to succeed Owen[1] here. But the time does not seem to have come when I am justified in settling down here, so I propose to make my way back to China at an early date, though in what capacity is not yet clear.

Inferring from your letter that you have misconceived my operations and object I have thought it worth while to explain.

Very sincerely yours
W. E. Soothill

Since writing this I learn you have left England so forward this to you at Peking.

716. To J. N. Jordan

Peking 16 September 1914

Dear Sir John,

I had a friendly talk with Yuan yesterday afternoon. He was in the best of spirits. In the course of our talk he expressed his wish to do all he could to evince his friendliness to England, and this gave me an opportunity of

---

[1] George Owen, British missionary of the London Missionary Society who, after having spent thirty-seven years in China, became Professor of Chinese at King's College, London, in 1908. He died in February 1914.

reminding him that he could not show his friendliness better than by reconsidering his attitude in regard to the Tibetan Convention.[1] We spoke of this for some time. He said he would instruct the Waichiaopu to confer with me, and I heard him give orders to Tsai Ting-kan to communicate with Sun Pao-chi. I may be mistaken, but I have the impression that I can induce Yuan to revise his judgment in this question, but before speaking to him again, I would be much obliged if you would tell me (for my own guidance) what is the procedure that the Chinese will have now to follow, assuming that they decide to sign the Convention. Where would it be signed, and by whom?

I have of course a full copy of the Convention and map initialled on April 27th by the three representatives at the Conference, and signed on July 3rd by the British and Tibetan representatives, the Chinese refraining. I have also copies of the essential correspondence.

I understand, as I have no doubt you have already done and will also impress the fact upon Yuan, that the text as signed on July 3rd is unalterable, and that no further negotiation with a hope to its alteration is permissible, that the Convention remains, and that China can either sign it or not sign it. If she signs it, she gains many privileges and advantages of which she is now deprived: if she does not sign it, she loses all opportunity of recovering those privileges and advantages.

The advantages to China of the Convention greatly outweigh the disadvantages, the chief of which in Yuan's eyes is the fear that he will be attacked in China for having inadequately safeguarded the interests of his country. I told him yesterday that when I spoke of this in London privately to influential people sympathetic with China, they, all knowing his strong position in China, scouted the idea that opposition on this score was worthy of consideration.

Since I think it is of great importance for China that this question should be settled as quickly as possible, I will be grateful for any assistance you can give me. Perhaps you would not mind if Wilton[2] were to speak to me about the procedure that has to be followed.

With kind regards

Very sincerely yours
[G. E. Morrison]

[1] The reference is to the Agreement signed by the representatives of China, Britain and Tibet in Simla on 27 April 1914. The Chinese Government refused to ratify the Treaty which Ch'en I-fan initialled on China's behalf.
[2] Ernest Colville Collins Wilton.

717. From Ting Shih-yüan[1]

Hankow [Hupeh] 28 September 1914

Dear Dr Morrison,

I trust that you have received my letter dated the 24th inst.[2]

I now beg to suggest that there should be a book printed, for private circulation among the officials, which, in a simplified form would cover all questions, without legal embroidery, of the existing laws, regulations and acts of this country. During the last eight months the necessity for such a book has been brought to my mind. It is not only needed by subordinates to myself, but by many of those who occupy positions superior to me. It is very necessary that the Central Government should prepare this, and I would emphasise the suggestion that it is eminently fitting that you, as Political Adviser, should bring this before the President, of course not mentioning my name in connection with the idea, for the laws of China are not understood by very many of those who have to do with their administration. I have also found that the returned student from Japan, who occupies an official position, has been taught Japanese law, and as a consequence tries to apply what he has assimilated of Japanese legal matters to the present Chinese laws, with the result that the force of our laws is rendered abortive. The same may be said of the officials who have been educated in England and America, they will reflect the English or American laws. This is not suitable to China, and does not cover the existing Chinese law. A concise epitome of the laws, in simple language, for the use of the officials, would be the means of avoiding many arguments and tiresome explanations such as it has been my lot to experience during the past eight months, and would terminate the present mistakes, and the fruitless controversy, rendering the actions of the Government officials uniform throughout the whole Republic. Of course a book of the nature suggested would require numerous changes and alterations every year in order that it might cover new conditions as they arise. In my opinion such a book of instructions would be the best method of ensuring cooperation among all officials, and I sincerely trust that you may

[1] Ting Shih-yüan (1879–1945), known to foreigners by his anglicised name of W. S. Y. Tinge, a returned student from England, at this time Customs *Taotai* of Hankow (January 1914 – July 1916) and concurrently Commissioner for Foreign Affairs for Hupeh Province (June 1914 – July 1916). He owed his rise in political fortune to his connection with Tuan Ch'i-jui, to whom he was once aide-de-camp. He became an active member of the Anfu Club when it was founded in 1918. On leaving Hankow he became Director of the Peking–Suiyuan Railway, and then of the Peking–Hankow Railway. He was on the wanted list after the Anfu Clique Government was ousted in 1920, but came back once more into the political scene with the return of Tuan Ch'i-jui. On the overthrow of the Peking regime in 1928, he retired to Ta-lien (Dairen) under Japanese protection, and like so many fellow members of the Anfu club became a collaborator of the Japanese occupation forces in China. He was sent as a representative to the League of Nations by the Puppet 'Manchukuo' Government set up by the Japanese in 1932, and on his return was made its Ambassador to Japan, a post he held until 1935.   [2] Not printed.

be able to bring about its creation and circulation among the officials of all grades, who sorely need it in the intelligent administration of China's laws, regulations and acts.

[...]

With best wishes to you and your wife and children at home

Very sincerely yours

W. S. Y. Tinge

718. From Tseng Tsung-chien[1]

Melbourne [Victoria, Australia] 12 October 1914

Dear Dr Morrison,

First of all allow me to thank you very heartily for a letter of introduction forwarded to me from Peking. Upon my arrival here at the beginning of July I was told you have gone to England and would not be back for some months or so, hence my silence. However after enjoying myself in reading the full report of your excellent speech in London, I have the news of your return to China. So I hasten to write this note.

Sir, I am very proud of having made your acquaintance in Peking. I would certainly look a fool if I had to tell people that I did not know you for wherever I go and whomever I meet the first question put to me is always that do you know 'our' Dr. Earnest Morrison. In addition to this fortune I have now the pleasure of knowing your brother and nephew who goes with the Expeditionary forces to fight for the Empire.[2] They are both charming and true gentlemen and are very kind to me.

Australia is certainly a happy country, the climate is good, business is better but the people is the best. The prestige of The Chinese Consulate is quite satisfactory thanks to all my predecessors. The position of Chinese in the Commonwealth is not envious but taking everything into consideration very little improvement could be made. Of course there are isolated cases which sometimes could and sometimes could not be helped. As we only get a certain class of Cantonese to come out here we can only hope to get certain kind of treatment. However there is at least one most unfair and unjust law existing that is some Chinese who are allowed to stay and do business

---

[1] Tseng Tsung-chien, or Tseng Tsung-kien as pronounced in his northern Fukien dialect, hence T. K. Tseng (b. 1881), Chinese diplomat and Republican politician. A graduate of Cambridge, he was appointed Chinese Consul-General to Australia in 1913, returning to China in August 1917. In 1925 he became Vice-Minister of Foreign Affairs and was appointed Chinese Minister to Sweden and Norway the following year. He survived the change of regime in China in 1928, and served in 1936 as Vice-Minister of Railways in the Nationalist Government in Nanking.

[2] He is doubtless referring to Dr Reginald H. Morrison, gynaecologist, the only brother of Morrison's living in Melbourne at the time, and to his son George Noel Irving ('Tim') (b. 1893) who had joined the First Division A.I.F. (Royal Highlanders).

here are denied the facility to bring their family out even for a visit from time to time, the result could not be beneficial to any party. As I am quite powerless in this direction, I sincerely hope that [on] your next visit to your Fatherland you will do your best [to] adjust this inhumane regulation.

I have not been to Sydney since your letter came, but am waiting the instruction from Government to pay a general visit to all Towns along both Western and Eastern coasts of the Commonwealth.

Since war broke out the mail from China is interrupted. There is very little news from home, the last alarm is that Japan had occupied Tsianfu. Australia is not so much affected by the European War, than by the serious drought with us. I shall not trouble you with further local news and beg to conclude my letter by thanking you once more.

Yours sincerely
T. K. Tseng

P.S. I am just learning to type please excuse the irregularities.

T.K.T.

December 1914 – August 1915

The outbreak of the European War, which cut short Morrison's stay in England, precipitated a serious crisis for China. Japan, whose encroachment on China, particularly in the Manchurian provinces, we have witnessed earlier in this selection, took the opportunity to make a further advance by establishing herself on the other side of the Gulf of Pechihli while the attention of all the Great Powers was diverted. This move was a repetition of the pattern of the 1894-5 Sino-Japanese War. Then, in a pincer movement against Northern China where the capital was situated, Japan had launched an attack on the Shantung promontory after seizing the Liaotung Peninsula. England's declaration of war on Germany provided Japan, as England's ally, with precisely the pretext she wanted.

Only four days after this declaration, on 8 August, the Japanese fleet made its appearance in strength off the coast of the German Leased Territory of Kiaochow. In anticipation of the Japanese move, discussions had been held in Chinese government circles as to the feasibility of China's declaring war on Germany to retrieve the territory forcibly seized by Germany in November 1897. The German Minister in Peking, who seemed to have guessed or to have feared Japan's intentions, also discussed with the Chinese the possibility of returning the Leased Territory to China. When rumour of this reached Tokyo, the Japanese Government hastened to warn China strongly against either course of action and 'counselled' her to continue the neutrality which she had announced on 6 August. However, on 15 August Japan served an ultimatum on Germany, giving her a week to surrender to her unconditionally the German-occupied territory in Shantung. Having received no reply by that time, Japan declared war on Germany.

At the time of the Japanese ultimatum, the Chinese government was told through the Chinese Minister in Tokyo that Japan was merely honouring her treaty obligation to England and had no territorial ambition of any kind in China. Now China was asked, following the precedent of the Russo-Japanese War of 1904-5, to declare a certain area of her territory a war zone and to withdraw her troops from Japan's intended points of landing to avoid a possible clash with Japanese forces. However, China was once more assured that, provided she observed her neutrality, Japan would return to her all her possessions including the Kiaochow Railway.

In the face of the joint pressure of Japan and Britain, China was helpless and acceded in the main to Japan's request. On 3 September, the day the Japanese landed in Shantung, China issued a statement, as she had done during the Russo-Japanese War ten years earlier, to the effect that she could no longer be held responsible for her neutrality, since she could no longer enforce that stand.

Having once obtained a foothold, the Japanese army advanced towards the heart of Shantung Province, instead of making a direct attack on the German Leased Territory and on its port, Tsingtao. On 26 September, completely disregarding the neutrality of China, it occupied the railway station of Wei-hsien which was not under German jurisdiction, and, ten days later, on 6 October, the railway station of Chi-nan, the provincial capital of Shantung. Not only were China's protests rejected, but she was warned that any resistance on her part would be regarded as aiding Japan's enemy, for which she would suffer serious consequences. Japan then imposed a curfew in the occupied zone, treating it as conquered territory.

Morrison did not seem to grasp the significance of Japan's moves when he arrived back in Peking in the middle of September. He was in fact quite pleased with the progress of England's ally, though at this time his fanatical prejudice against Germany was in no way as pronounced as it became later. It was not until the question of the control of the customs at Tsingtao arose, after the Japanese capture of the port in the second week of November, that Morrison was forced to take a more serious look at the implications of Japan's action.

The customs question, which occupies much space in the Morrison correspondence, proved to be an insignificant foretaste of what was to come. The Japanese Minister in Peking, Hioki Masu, who had been appointed shortly before the outbreak of the European war, went back to Japan for consultations before the fall of Tsingtao, and upon his return to China sought an interview with Yüan Shih-k'ai, which took place on 18 January 1915. On this occasion the Japanese, in violation of accepted diplomatic procedure, presented a list of Twenty-One Demands directly to the Chinese President, by-passing the Foreign Ministry. These were grouped under five headings and ranged from Shantung and Manchuria to the reorganisation of practically every branch of the Chinese Government, including its army and police forces. Compliance with these demands would have placed China virtually under Japan's direct control, yet Hioki, acting on instructions from his government, insisted upon China's acceptance, warning the President of the grave consequences that would ensue if the matter were not kept secret.

Morrison was stunned when with some difficulty he extracted from the Chinese the full text of the Demands. He fully realised the weakness of China's position and her dilemma. China could expect little help at that juncture, with the Great Powers so preoccupied with the war in Europe. But so outraged was he by the Demands and by the manner and circumstances of their presentation, that he believed their exposure might at least have some modifying influence on the Japanese Government and so enable China to escape with something less than the virtual surrender of her sovereignty. He was particularly shocked by what he termed 'the worst diplomatic turpitude' when Japan, upon her ultimatum becoming known, communicated a heavily pruned version of the Demands to friendly governments as well as to her ally England, omitting all the items she thought might offend their susceptibilities. The Demands were explained away as a friendly discussion of outstanding problems existing between the two countries. So successful was the Japanese ruse that it managed to convince most of the governments as well as world public opinion. *The Times* in fact launched a most vehement attack on China, accusing her, among many other things, of trying to sow discord among the allies. Morrison was convinced that world opinion would have been otherwise had China revealed the true story, and accordingly he persuaded the Chinese Government to overcome its fear and hesitation and expose Japan's duplicity. With the assistance of W. H. Donald, then acting *in loco* while *The Times*' regular Peking Correspondent was away on leave, he finally succeeded in making known the story as the world has since come to know it, and in so doing, brought upon himself a hate-campaign in the Japanese press.

We have left out the various versions of the Twenty-One Demands, the full text of which appears *inter alia* in J. V. A. MacMurray's *Treaties and Agreements with and Concerning China 1894–1919*, as well as the bulk of the material concerning the progress of the protracted negotiations, already dealt with in varying degrees of detail by other historians. The selection here aims rather to shed light on one hitherto neglected aspect, that of the actual exposure of the Demands, which was the turning point of the crisis.

Of the great bulk of material on China's financial plight, which remained a cardinal problem throughout the whole period covered by this selection, we have included only one letter from Morrison. There is however, a lengthy exchange between Morrison and Liang Shih-yi, Yüan Shih-k'ai's Chief Secretary who was considered by many to be his 'evil genius'. Liang's letter is a fair reflection of the official mind at the time, or rather of that of the most powerful clique behind the Chinese President; Morrison's contains a most comprehensive and frank analysis – in the opinion of the British Minister in Peking, 'a powerful indictment of Chinese policy' – which he probably would have wanted to convey to Yüan himself. In view of Japan's actions and of what was to follow, this document is of particular interest.

719. From F. A. Aglen

Peking 3 December 1914

My dear Morrison,

I send you enclosed for perusal two letters from Sugden, Chefoo Commissioner.[1] Please return them to me. As you know the Chefoo Breakwater, Sanchow, as a last despairing effort to resuscitate the moribund port, is only half measure without the railway to Wei hsien. And the two projects ought to have been taken in hand simultaneously. There is however with the advent of Japan on the seas an even more important political question, and as this is in your line, I send you the information for any use you think you may be able to make of it.

Personally I am convinced the Japanese mean to go ahead while they have the chance and that Chinese interests which in this case are also British interests, will be given small consideration. I am also convinced that whatever China attempts to do she must do off her own bat and that she can look for no support from Great Britain. The Govt. has decided to go ahead with the opening of Lung K'ou. Whether under present conditions and in ignorance of Japan's real intentions this is now a wise step it is difficult to say. The whole Shantung situation is nebulous in the extreme. I should like to have your views on the railway question.

Yours sincerely
F. A. Aglen

720. To J. W. R. Macleay[2]

Peking 11 December 1914

My dear Macleay,

The Japanese case regarding the Tsingtau Customs,[3] as stated to me by the Japanese, is as follows: – 'The procedure hitherto followed in connection with the Tsingtau Customs has been that the appointment was in the hands of the Maritime Customs Administration, that only one of German

---

[1] Arthur Henry Sugden (1863–1947), British employee of the Chinese Maritime Customs from 1883 to 1926. He succeeded F. J. Mayers as Commissioner in Lung-k'ou and Chefoo in 1914.

[2] James William Ronald (later Sir Ronald) Macleay (1870–1943), British diplomat. Appointed Counsellor with the British Legation in Peking in 1914, he returned to China as Minister in 1922 succeeding F. Beilby Alston, and remained there until 1926, when he was in turn succeeded by Sir Miles Lampson. He later became British Minister to Czechoslovakia (1927–9) and Ambassador to the Argentine (1930–3), where he had served as Minister from 1919 to 1922.

[3] As a result of the German refusal to comply with the Japanese request to surrender the German Leased Territory of Kiaochow in Shantung, Japan set up a blockade and landed troops in Shantung on 9 September 1914. This was followed by the occupation of Tsingtao two months later, on 7 November. Regarding herself as the rightful heir to all German interests there, Japan also claimed control of the port's Chinese Maritime Customs Station.

nationality could be appointed Commissioner, that his name had to be submitted first to the German Legation for approval, and that all the staff both indoor and outdoor had also to be of German nationality, but that in the case of those subordinate to the Commissioner, it was not necessary to submit their names to the Legation for approval.

'The Japanese having entered into possession of Tsingtau are entitled, they maintain, to the same rights and privileges regarding the Customs as were accorded to the Germans. To make assurances surer, before the fall of Tsingtau Tsao Yu-lin was informed by the Japanese Minister that the Customs after the capture would have to be placed under the administration of Japanese. After the fall, when it was necessary to appoint a Commissioner, Tsao Yu-Lin informed the Japanese Legation that the Chinese proposed to appoint Moorhead,[1] an English Commissioner of Customs from Mukden, as Commissioner. The Japanese objected, and the appointment was not proceeded with. Later Tsao Yu-lin informed the Japanese Legation that the Chinese proposed to appoint Kurosawa,[2] the Japanese Commissioner of Customs from Soochow, as Commissioner, and an Englishman as Deputy-Commissioner. Again the Japanese Legation objected, and the appointments were not proceeded with. Then, without consultation with the Japanese Legation and without any intimation being given to them previous to the appointment, the Chinese notified the Japanese Legation that Tachibana,[3] the Japanese Commissioner of Customs from Dalny, had been appointed.'

In the communication made by Mr Aglen to the Japanese Legation, the Japanese state that the desire is expressed that the procedure hitherto followed when Germans were in possession should now be continued while the Japanese are in possession. The Japanese contention is that all acts precedent to this communication show that the procedure hitherto followed in the case of the Germans has been disregarded in the case of the Japanese. They express dissatisfaction with the way the Chinese have acted in the matter. They affix the responsibility upon the Maritime Customs Administration.

[1] T. D. Moorehead, British employee of the Chinese Maritime Customs, in which service the family was represented by three generations, having been preceded by his father, R. B. Moorehead, and followed by his son.

[2] Kurosawa Reikichi (b. 1868) the first Japanese employee of the Chinese Maritime Customs, which he entered in 1899 on the recommendation of the then Japanese Minister in Peking, Yano Fumio (1850–1931). He had spent some ten years in America, from 1884 to 1894. He became a Commissioner of Customs in 1904 and was the first Commissioner at Dairen after the Russo-Japanese war. He later served as Commissioner at Yochow and Soochow.

[3] Tachibana Masaki (b. 1865), Japanese employee of the Chinese Maritime Customs, which he joined in 1900. A graduate of Tokyo Imperial University, he had taught at various Japanese colleges before going to China. He became Acting Deputy Commissioner in 1907 at An-tung, and Acting Commissioner at Dairen the following year. He was made a full Commissioner in 1914 and was officially appointed to his post in Tsingtao in September 1915.

I hope the case will be arranged, but apparently some umbrage has been caused which more care might have avoided.

To the Japanese it has been pointed out that the procedure now adopted by the Japanese will, if insisted upon, weaken the prestige and the authority of the Customs Administration: that the Customs are the trustees of foreign bondholders: that none of the monies collected are handled by the Chinese: that the whole of the revenues are applied to the payment in order of priority of the foreign loans secured upon the Customs and of the Boxer Indemnity, a considerable portion of which is Japanese: that there are already many Japanese in the Customs Service: that now more will have to be appointed because of the necessity of appointing Japanese indoor and outdoor staffs in Tsingtau: that in that case the recommendations of the Japanese Government will be welcomed, but that the men so appointed will have to be trained in the Chinese service and will have to rise through the grades of the service as Tachibana has risen, Kishimoto,[1] Kurosawa and others: and that it would be injurious to the service and be a most dangerous innovation if the Japanese Government were to appoint to the Chinese service a Japanese Commissioner over the heads of all Japanese who have been trained in the service.

With kind regards

Very sincerely yours
[G. E. Morrison]

721. From J. W. R. Macleay

Peking 12 December 1914

Confidential

My dear Morrison,

Many thanks for your letter of the 11th explaining the position in regard to the Tsingtao Customs business. As you can imagine I do not consider that the moment is opportune for us to intervene, but I thought that when Hioki[2] returns, as he is expected to do in the course of a day or so, I might mention the matter to him privately and point out that the appointment of

---

[1] Kishimoto Hirokichi (b. 1883), Japanese employee of the Chinese Maritime Customs, which he joined soon after graduating in 1905 from Tokyo Higher Commercial School. He had served in Chefoo, Shanghai and Tsingtao and later in the Administration's Chinese Secretariat in Peking.

[2] Hioki Masu (or Eki) (1861–1926), Japanese diplomat, who had served in China from 1900 to 1903, was appointed to succeed Yamaza Enjirō in July 1914 as Japanese Minister in Peking. After the Japanese seizure of the German Leased Territory in Shantung he was recalled by Katō for consultation, and returned with the Twenty-One Demands which he presented to Yüan Shih-k'ai on 18 January 1915. After leaving China in 1917, Hioki became Minister to Denmark, Norway and Sweden and was Ambassador to Germany from 1920 to 1924.

an outsider i.e. a person who is not a member of the Chinese Maritime Customs staff, might lead to serious international complications. I would suggest that the Japanese Legation could give a private hint to Aglen in the Chinese Govt. that a particular member of the Maritime Customs Staff – a Japanese of course – would be acceptable as Commissioner at Tsingtao and that it would be understood that the remainder of the staff at the port will be Japanese, following the precedent established during the German occupation and appointed by the I.G.

I agree with you in thinking that the matter has not been very tactfully handled by the Chinese Govt. but I believe Aglen's hands were forced and that he was not to blame.

I can hardly believe that the Japanese will risk the storm which the appointment of an outsider is sure to raise from the Powers who have a direct interest in the Maritime Customs revenue. It is probable that they have not fully considered the point.

Of course I am anxious to disabuse the Japanese Legation of the idea that we have interfered in the matter.

Yrs very sincerely
Ronald Macleay

722. To Chou Tzu-ch'i

Peking 14 December 1914

Private & Confidential

Dear Mr. Chow,

I am much obliged to you for your kind letter offering to keep me fully informed in connection with any questions regarding finance.[1] You have always been willing to help me, and I fully appreciate this further expression of your confidence.

Finance is the paramount question in China. The settlement of her foreign debts, and thereby the preventing of complications with foreign countries is a matter of the highest importance. Towards the solution of this problem all must work. Before we can grapple with the problem we must know exactly what is the problem. It is no good working in the dark or work-

[1] Morrison wrote on 31 October 1914 to Chou Tzu-ch'i, then Finance Minister, asking him to supply certain information about the outstanding loans China was owing to various foreign banks, to enable him 'to make out a Statement that would be easily understood by those who, like myself, have no banking training'. The information eventually supplied to him was considered by Morrison to be very incomplete, and he complained to Ts'ai T'ing-kan that Chou was trying to hide the real extent of China's indebtedness (Letter not printed). Correspondence on China's finance forms the great bulk of the Morrison Papers during these years but only an occasional such letter is printed in this selection.

ing in different directions, each one not knowing what the other is doing. The danger is a very real one – the danger, that is, of a foreign Debt Commission, and everyone must try and work to prevent such a misfortune to the country. Prevention can only be done by having a clear knowledge of what are the debts and by arranging some simple scheme for dealing with them equitably.

Look at what is happening. On the one hand Mr. Alfred Sze,[1] the new Chinese Minister to London, states in an interview published throughout the world, that the Chinese Government is able to meet punctually all its obligations, notwithstanding the curtailment of the Customs Revenue and the drop in exchange. Yet on the same day an official statement published in Peking by authority of the Chinese Government says: 'It is an open secret that the finances of China are in a state of chaos.' On the other hand there is the fact that during the last two years Treasury Bills given by the Chinese Government in payment of various foreign debts and obligations have been repeatedly dishonoured. Even on the same day that Mr. Sze was making this statement in London, the big English firm of Armstrongs received a telegram from Peking stating that the Chinese Government having no money were unable to meet Treasury Bills to the amount of £172,450, bearing interest at eight per cent, which fell due on November 30th. Statements that China is meeting her obligations do not mislead the European bankers who know on the contrary that China is not meeting these obligations.

Two dangers confront China. There is the danger of Japan, a powerful military country to whose chief merchants large sums of money are owing by the Chinese: and there is the French declared policy – or rather the policy enunciated by the French Minister in Peking – that the only hope for the financial salvation of China is the creation of a foreign Debt Commission to take charge of China's finances. Until we know clearly what is the exact amount owing, what rate of interest each debt is paying, and the date upon which each debt is due for payment, it is impossible to formulate any scheme for grappling in a systematic manner with these questions and thus avoiding these two dangers.

Before the present war China hoped to borrow money at 5% at 90,

[1] Shih Chao-chi (1877–1958), known to foreigners by his anglicised name Alfred Sze, Chinese diplomat and Republican politician. A returned student from America and a relative of T'ang Shao-yi, he served briefly as Minister of Communications in the first Republican Government in 1912 and as Foreign Minister in 1924, but was mainly known as a diplomat whose career had begun under the Manchus. In June 1914 he was appointed Chinese Minister in London, where he remained until November 1920, returning from 1929 to 1932, and was Chinese Minister to the United States from 1920 to 1929 and again from 1933 to 1935. In that year he became the first Chinese Ambassador and remained in the post until May 1937. He represented China at practically all the major international conferences, from the Paris Peace Conference in 1919 to the United Nations Conference in San Francisco in 1945.

receiving 84% net. Yet before the present war China was renewing Treasury Bills, and was making loans at rates varying from 6% to 18%. The firm of Telge and Schroeter (Tai lai),[1] whose compradore is the son of the Minister of the Navy, Mr. Liu Kuan-hsiung,[2] boasts to other foreigners that their last debt was renewed by the Chinese Government at 18%. This is of course compound interest, and it means that the debt is exactly doubled in four years.

This is no time for reproaching one another, or for casting blame or for crying about what has been done in the past. What has been done has been done. We are now looking to the future. Debts are outstanding – that is the fact. The question in which every Chinese and every foreigner worthy of trust is interested now is, what is the exact amount of each of these debts, what is the interest of each debt, and in what manner can payment be most economically effected? It is for this reason that I suggest the need of preparing a simple tabulated statement showing China's short term debts, and I am grateful to you for your kind offer which will help to make this statement complete. [...][3]

In the case of the Japanese the most serious item is a comparatively small debt. China is rich in iron, although there are no iron works in China. Japan has no iron, but has large iron works, and she is dependent for her iron supplies upon China. As Your Excellency knows, Japan has entire possession of the Pen-chih-hu Iron Mines in Fengtien, also of the Tayeh Iron Mines in Hupeh. She now expects to obtain possession of the Iron Mines along the Shantung Railway. Another of the most valuable of the iron deposits of China is the Tung-kuan-shan Iron Mines in Anhui, close to Wuhu, almost on the bank of the Yangtse River. On the 1st June, 1912, the Japanese firm, Mitsui Bussan Kaisha, advanced to the Government of the Province of Anhui the sum of Yen 200,000 secured upon these mines the debt to be repaid on 1st June, 1914. I am informed that this debt was not repaid, and that these iron mines, which are of high value to China by reason of their favourable situation in the very heart of the country close to the chief river, are now claimed to be Japanese property. Is this the case?

[...]

One fact in connection with these debts is apt to be overlooked. It is that all these debts are known more or less correctly to all foreign bankers, for

[1] The Chinese name of the firm.
[2] Liu Kuan-hsiung (b. 1858), Chinese sailor, a graduate of the Royal Naval College, Greenwich. At this time Minister of the Navy, he held down this post, with only a short absence, from 1912 to 1919 in spite of frequent Cabinet changes. Beginning his naval career under the Manchus, he became Vice-Minister of the Navy in the Provisional Government under Sun Yat-sen in Nanking, and was sent as a delegate to Peking to accompany Yüan Shih-k'ai to the southern capital. He then turned a staunch supporter of Yüan and later of Tuan Ch'i-jui and his Anfu Government.
[3] Morrison's review of China's indebtedness to various countries is omitted.

bankers, as Your Excellency knows, for their own protection, when debts are not paid, communicate freely with each other. Their duty is to watch closely the financial conditions of the country in which they are stationed, and when Treasury Bills are rejected in one country, it is known very quickly to the bankers of all other countries.

I believe that the small debts owing by China are less than is generally believed abroad. For that reason I believe that a clear and succinct statement, by which the various debts are grouped according to the various countries, would be of material assistance to His Excellency the President in grasping the situation and in knowing how to deal with it.

Every effort is being made – and wisely made – by His Excellency and by the Government to preserve friendly relations with the Japanese. The wisdom of such policy is obvious. In the great war which is now proceeding, the allied Powers of England, France, Russia and Japan will be overwhelmingly victorious, and although Japan is not taking a leading part in the conflict, she has rendered services of the highest value to England, to France and to Russia. Day and night every arsenal in Japan is working to supply guns and ammunition and military stores of all kinds to the Allies. Shiploads and trainloads are being sent to Europe. Even more important than the destruction of Germany's military power was the destruction of her naval power, and to this end Japan has rendered highly important services. More than one-third of her whole Navy is now at sea, assisting in the protection of the sea routes along which British troops from across the seas are being conveyed to Egypt and to Europe. If Tsingtau had remained a German naval base, British shipping on the coast of China could only have been carried on with great danger. Now, after a little more than four months of war, Germany has only four armed warships at sea. Every British trade route is open. Every German colony and possession outside of Germany with the exception of the German colonies in South Africa has been seized, and it is only a matter of time when all the German possessions in South Africa will also come under the British flag.

To this work the Japanese have contributed both directly and indirectly. Therefore the three Powers of France, England and Russia are under serious obligations to Japan. Therefore Japan can reasonably expect to receive the support of her Allies in the continuance of her policy in the Far East where she is unquestionably the chief military power. These facts are thoroughly appreciated by the Chinese Government who desire sincerely to improve in every way the friendly relations with Japan. To improve these relations, to prevent any establishment of a foreign Debt Commission approved by Japan, debts owing to prominent Japanese firms must be repaid.

And how can we repay these debts according to any system unless we know exactly what these debts are? How can you apply a remedy unless you know the illness? It is for that reason among others that I would urge that an attempt should quickly be made to prepare a complete and comprehensive statement of China's foreign debts.

Again I have to thank you for your kind offer to give me every assistance in preparing such a statement.

With best wishes

Believe me

Very sincerely yours
[G. E. Morrison]

723. To Ts'ai T'ing-kan

Peking 15 December 1914

My dear Admiral,

I am much obliged to you for drawing the attention of Mr. Chow Tzu-chi to the Memorandum I wrote on Short Term Loans.[1] Mr. Chow has written me a friendly letter offering to give me further information and I have written to him a reply, copy of which I herewith enclose.[2]

The most serious of recent events arising from the failure to meet financial obligations when they fall due has been the Japanese foreclosure on the Tung-kuan-shan Iron Mines. I refer to this in the Memorandum I have written to Mr. Chow. The statement is made by the Japanese. It may be that the statement is incorrect.

Mr. Hioki returns to Peking to-morrow, when no doubt representations will be made to him urging him to reconsider his attitude towards the Tsingtau Customs Commissionership. Interference of the kind proposed by Japan with the Customs Administration will cause many difficulties and will be highly injurious to the service in which foreign countries are interested as much as China is.

It is, I believe, certain that the Japanese will endeavour to obtain the reversion of the right accorded to the Germans on the 31st December, 1913, to continue the Tsingtau–Tsinanfu Railway to a point undetermined on the Peking–Hankow Railway, and to construct another railway from Kaomi south-westwards to the Tientsin–Pukow Railway. I have not yet seen this Agreement.[3] It would be advisable to get the Agreement so that we can study it and see what can be done to prevent the construction of Japanese railways into the interior of China. Chinese railways constructed by

---

[1] Not printed.   [2] This refers to the preceding letter, No. 722.
[3] An Exchange of Notes embodying an Agreement for the construction of a railway from Kaomi to Hanchuang, and of the so-called Tsinanfu–Shuntefu Railway, took place between Germany and China on 31 December 1913. Morrison later wrote a memorandum pointing out the harm which the concessions embodied in the Agreement would do to China and the danger of their exploitation by other countries, particularly Japan. This memorandum, entitled, 'Notes on the Shantung Railway Contract' and dated 9 April 1915, is not printed.

Japanese for China are one thing: Japanese railways constructed in China for Japan are another thing. I do not know whether the rights of China have in the Agreement referred to been adequately safeguarded or not.

You will see in my letter to Mr. Chow a reference to the new order given to the American Banknote Co. for another 10,000,000 notes of a face value not yet determined, but which cannot be less than $60,000,000, and if the same proportion is used as in previous orders, must amount to $100,000,000 face value.

In the Quintuple Loan Contract, Annex 'F' provided that a sum of $5,000,000 was to be set apart from the Loan for the establishment of a banking scheme to be approved by the Quintuple Banks in connection with the reorganisation of the Salt. Claim to the application of this money, was however withdrawn in a letter written by Mr. Chow Tzu-chi to the foreign bankers, dated May 14th last, the expenditure being described in his letter as 'unnecessary and undesirable'.

The creation of this new Salt Bank has been entrusted to Mr. Chang Chên-fang,[1] Governor of Honan Province in the time of White Wolf. I hope that he is aware of the correspondence between Mr. Chow Tzu-chi and the bankers to which I have made reference. At present the salt revenues are paid into the Bank of China, and by the Bank are paid in accordance with the terms of the Quintuple Loan Contract into the foreign banks.

I notice that the Bank of Industrial Development has been opened in Shanghai with much ceremony. It is bound to prosper exceedingly, its leading spirit being Mr. Far T. Sung, 'Inspector General of the Government Mints of China.'[2] The chief foreigner associated with the Bank appears to be Mr. M. E. B. Ezra,[3] a Bagdad Jew, who I understand has made some money in opium.

[1] See p. 14 n. 5.
[2] Sung Fa-hsiang (b. 1883), a returned student from America. He had taught Chemistry at Peking University before entering Government Service and held the position referred to here from 1914 to 1916. In 1917 he became English Secretary to the Acting President Feng Kuo-chang, and in 1919 Adviser in the Presidential Office under Hsü Shih-ch'ang. He was also involved in various banking and industrial enterprises. In 1928 he became Consul-General to Australia and in 1931 to the Dutch East Indies at Batavia.
[3] Nissim Ezra Benjamin Ezra (b. 1880), Jewish opium merchant and member of the Foreign Opium Combine in Shanghai. Born and educated in India, he went to Hong Kong in 1897 to join one of the leading opium dealers, E. D. Sassoon & Co. In 1908 he left the firm to establish his own business and in 1911 became the first foreigner to set up a retail opium shop in Hangchow, the provincial capital of Chekiang. He was involved in 1914 in the founding of the Bank of Industrial Development in Shanghai, and sought unsuccessfully to become its Foreign Manager. An active Zionist, he was in 1904 founder and publisher of the *Israel Messenger*, having been also a correspondent of the London *Jewish Chronicle* since 1900, and a contributor to the *Jewish Encyclopaedia* of New York. He was also Secretary of the Shanghai Zionist Association from 1900, and in that capacity in 1918 he obtained, through Morrison, the Chinese Government's pledge of support for the establishment of a Jewish homeland in Palestine.

Last evening I met General Munthe[1] at dinner, and he tells me that Germany has 'crushed' Russia and that Austria has also done 'extraordinarily well.' I presume that it is to such views as these, which are in direct conflict with all evidence, that Sir Robert Bredon refers in his published letter, wherein he states that 'the inhabitants of Peking are persuaded that the Germans are winning'.

It is a long time since I had the privilege of seeing you. I hope all is going well with you, and again thanking you

I am

Very sincerely yours
[G. E. Morrison]

724. From Ts'ai T'ing-kan

[Peking] 15 December 1914

Private & Confidential

My dear Doctor,

I thank you for your letter and enclosure.[2] If Mr. Chou had been more willing in giving information he alone as Finance Minister would have been benefited. No amount of confidence on our part can hide the true state of affairs and if anyone thinks he can he is not worthy of the President's confidence and trust.

It is evident to me that we must continue to play our part fearlessly and expose any concealment or corruption in order that the President may not be deceived.

When people know that we have set our hearts to such a duty we shall have plenty of offers of further information.

Yours sincerely
Tsai Ting Kan

725. To C. D. Bruce

[Peking] 28 December 1914

My dear Bruce,

[...]

My wife and I returned here on the 14th September. I have since had much to do but have made little progress. I have quite failed to induce the Chinese to accept the position in Tibet. They have everything to gain by

---

[1] J. W. N. Munthe, a Norwegian. Formerly an employee of the Imperial Chinese Maritime Customs, he later joined the staff of Yüan Shih-k'ai as a corporal in Yüan's new army at Hsiao-ch'ang and was promoted to the rank of Lt.-Gen. twenty years later, serving as a military and cavalry instructor.

[2] A reference to the copy of Morrison's letter to Chou Tzu-ch'i, No. 722.

signing the convention of the 3rd July.[1] They lose only one point; it is a question of boundary – the inclusion of Chiamdo in outer Tibet. Rather than remove their 2150 troops, now in Chiamdo, eastward into inner Tibet, they prefer not to sign the convention at all and so long as they do not sign it they are deprived, as you know, of all the advantages under the convention. They cannot send their *Amban* to Lhasa; they cannot resume intercourse with outer Tibet through India; they cannot recover possession of that territory, 56,000 square miles in area, as large as Shantung province, north of the Kwenlun mountains, which they were promised if they signed the convention of the 3rd July.

The President and many of his subordinates realise clearly what are the advantages and what are the disadvantages. The difficulty that is unsurmountable is the clamour that is feared would arise in Ssuchuan and Yunnan if there were to be any apparent surrender of China's territorial rights. In fact 'face-saving' again comes into the case. China is faring badly in Mongolia and the financial position is unsatisfactory. Money is coming in better but the short term debts are not being paid.

[...] We will all bear you in remembrance and hope to see you back in China safe and sound after a glorious campaign.[2]

With best wishes from my wife and myself

Yours very sincerely
[G. E. Morrison]

726. From A. H. Harris[3]

Newchwang [Fengtien] 5 January 1915

My dear Morrison,

I am sorry that circumstances did not admit of a further chat with you before you left. [...]

As to morphia and the opium smuggling in the north, why does not Dr Thwing come and study conditions here and publish results. There should be also a strong public movement to warn Japan from introducing into Shantung conditions that abound under her benevolent wing in Manchuria. She is a believer in the survival of the fittest and if by various means well known to you she can dispossess land owners and enfeeble youth, she does so but she does not like publicity. The results of her work in Korea speak

---

[1] The reference is to the Tripartite Convention signed at Simla on 3 July 1914.

[2] C. D. Bruce, who volunteered soon after the European war broke out, was taken prisoner in 1915. He survived the war and was responsible, after it ended, for the repatriation of German prisoners in Holland. He returned to China in 1920 to complete his unfinished term as Police Adviser in which capacity he had been employed by Yüan Shih-k'ai in 1914 on Morrison's recommendation.

[3] British employee of the Chinese Maritime Customs, at this time Commissioner at Newchwang.

very well for a certain line of conduct: what the Koreans have had to pay for the hold that Japan has on Korea is another question and of this nothing is said. Our position in India is due to quite another line of conduct.

You are of course aware that China has no standing on the S.M.R. [South Manchurian Railway] line. We know nothing of what comes and goes: not even in Newchwang except by the courtesy of the Company in supplying statistics. To remedy this state of affairs is almost impossible.

A surgical operation which would lop off from China all Manchuria and Mongolia would be a blessing in disguise. The Govt. has all and more than all it can manage to reorganise the 18 provinces plus the Sinkiang: but where is the bold man to dare suggest such a thing and the still bolder one to carry it out. Japan will never do it. 'Never' is too strong a word however; make it 'not yet'. It pays Japan to have things as they are: China pays: Japan governs – not too openly but, whenever she wishes to, most effectively.

Excuse a typed line: this letter is of course for yourself.
Kind regards

Yours sincerely
A. H. Harris

727. From Ts'ai T'ing-kan

Peking 28 January 1915

My dear Doctor,
[...]
Every day more of the conditions of the demands are being leaked out.[1] Your allies are very anxious that England and America should know nothing.

The Germans are flirting with the Japanese and the former have promised the latter that they can have a free hand in China. This means, I suppose that Japan has been bribed not to join the Allies in Europe.

[Ts'ai T'ing-kan]

728. To Ts'ai T'ing-kan

[Peking] 28 January 1915

My dear Admiral,
Many thanks for your note. I am sorry I cannot concur with your theory. I enclose you a short Memorandum in which I briefly give my views on the question.

With kind regards

Very sincerely yours
[G. E. Morrison]

[1] A reference to Japan's Twenty-One Demands.

P.S. I put my views separately so that you may consider them more easily. Did you read the letter signed 'One of the Citizens' in the *Gazette* this morning?[1] Such a letter shows the danger of inexact knowledge.

G.E.M.

Enclosure to Letter No. 728: *Memorandum, 28 January 1915*

It is unfortunate that secrecy is being maintained in regard to the Japanese demands. If complete secrecy had been maintained no evil would have resulted but there has been a leakage. What is true has been mixed with what is false with the result that the wildest rumours are current regarding alleged Japanese aggression, alleged infringement of China's sovereign rights, alleged infringement of China's territorial integrity. What is the truth, I do not know for I am in as complete ignorance as the man in the street.

Any theory based upon Japan's supposed unwillingness to disclose her policy to the British Government is a theory not worth consideration. Never have relations between England and Japan been more intimate than at present. Long before the war they were allies; they have continued the war as allies whereas the other Powers only became England's allies on the outbreak of war.

It is quite certain, although I have no information on the subject, that the British Government have been fully informed of the contents of the Japanese note to China and have been fully informed as to the intention of Japanese policy in China. I venture to think also that the British Government have satisfied themselves that Japan has no intention of departing from the policy of the Allies 'which is based upon the maintenance of the integrity of China with a view to the preservation of peace in the Far East'.

Any suggestion that Japan is courting the good will of Germany in opposition to the good will of the Allies is in my opinion a hypothesis that can find no support from any existing evidence.

Why would Japan seek the favour of Germany now when Germany has been stripped of her over-seas possessions, except those in South Africa, and when Germany is within measurable distance of being crushed as a great military power? Why did Japan not seek this good favour when Germany was yet believed to be an invincible military Power? Germany as a military factor in the Far East has ceased to exist. How can she then make any bargain with Japan regarding Japanese action in China in return for preventing Japanese troops from proceeding to Europe? What would deter Japan from sending troops to Europe is the want of money and the disinclination to treat her soldiers as mercenaries of another country.

To send one Japanese division to Europe would cost 33 million yen. This money would have to be provided by the Allies. What advantage would Japan gain by sending her troops to Europe?

[1] Material not available for identification.

In my opinion, it would be wise to permit the publication in the Press of the exact terms of the Japanese note. At present every correspondent is cabling to Europe and America messages in favour of China but these messages are all based upon the assumption that the demands of Japan are those to which popular rumour is giving currency. Surely it is dangerous for the peace of the country to allow such a condition of alarm to exist. It will surely strengthen China's position if the exact demands of Japan are made known. And as I said before it is unwise for China to accept the view that in this matter Japan has not fully and frankly informed her Ally, England, in accordance with the treaty existing between the two countries.

If England knows, it is almost certain that France and Russia also know, or at any rate if they desire to know I am confident that information will be given to them.

729. From Ts'ai T'ing-kan

[Peking] 28 January [1915]

Private

My dear Doctor,

You entirely misunderstand me when you say that Japan is courting Germany. It is Germany who is courting Japan and Japan has privately given out that Germany has said to her: We give Japan a free hand in China.

I think Japanese policy is to see the war in Europe carried to such an extent that every nation involved shall be crippled on land and sea for a long time. She would like to see herself senior partner in the alliance with England or any other power.

I am glad to learn that Japan has fully informed of the contents of the note to the British Government.[1] I understood from you the other day that she did not and that your Legation complained that we did not inform Britain of the contents.

The letter signed 'One of the citizens' is a silly thing. The *Gazette* should never have published it.

I have tried to learn the exact facts of the demand[s] but we are in the same position 'as the man in the street'.

The President sanctions your trip to Kalgan. I phoned you this afternoon but you had gone out. Thank you for your lucid memorandum.

Yours sincerely
Tsai Ting Kan

[1] This, as it turned out, was not the case.

730. From G. D. Gray

Peking 6 February 1915

My dear Morrison,

Many thanks for your article 'Japan's Morphia Trade with China' which I return herewith.[1] I have made some extracts for my summary and would propose to try and work up some more particulars and make a sufficiently strong article for the *Lancet* to make some stir about it.[2] This is the kind of 'stunt' they like to get hold of and it is a paper that is widely quoted and is in close touch with Parliament.

It would be a good thing to get special observations made in Fukien as to the import direct from Formosa. Perhaps most of the stuff made there goes to Japan for distribution.

[...]

The importation [of morphia] by smuggling is such an easy and simple affair that the Chinese Govt. could never hope to put it down by Customs examination alone. For instance the mixing of it in a consignment of flour (which I know has been done) would make it difficult of detection short of analysis, while the separating of it out from the flour on arrival at its destination is a simple matter of solution. If the Govt. could demand that all Morphia sold in China even for medicinal purposes be tinted some specific colour (say red or blue) which can be done without altering its therapeutical properties this would make it easier of detection on importation. Would it be possible to demand that there should be a consignees Register. If the Govt. could enter into negotiations with Foreign Powers in China asking that all foreign chemists be required to dispense it only on Doctor's prescriptions this would not be a difficult regulation to carry out in Foreign Concessions. The Poison Register kept by chemists in America and Europe is a well known thing. Then as far as Chinese Drug Shops outside Concessions are concerned the Govt. could easily deal with that especially if the Morphia is tinted. Appointments of Govt. analysts could be made (any foreign chemists would undertake it for retaining fees at no great expense) and these men could readily analyse suspicious samples seized by the Police. If properly gone about under clear well drawn up 'Regulations for the retail sale of Morphia' the Govt. could do much to stamp out the trade.

[...]

It would be a good thing to get a blow dealt at this growing Japanese new venture. I would like to see the whole thing publicly exposed and not kept in

[1] Not printed. Morrison later wrote an article under the same title, which is printed as the enclosure to Letter No. 919.
[2] No such article by Gray was published, though news items on the traffic of the drug appeared intermittently in the pages of the journal. In its issue of 9 June 1917 it printed an address by Wu Lien-te (q.v.), in his capacity of President of the Chinese National Medical Association, entitled 'The Menace of Morphine to China' which dealt with the subject much along the lines Gray had in mind.

confidential pigeon holes as seems so far to be the case. But the case will stand some further working up yet.

Yours sincerely
Douglas Gray

[...]

731. To J. N. Jordan

[Peking] 8 February 1915

Dear Sir John,

At Saturday's meeting there was a complete change in the attitude of Mr Hioki. Previously at his interview with the President and at his meetings with the Waichiao Pu Mr Hioki insisted in terms that were regarded by the Chinese as minatory upon the acceptance in principle of all the 21 demands. On Saturday afternoon he consented to discuss the demands in detail: he did more, he appeared to acquiesce in the insistence of Lu Cheng-hsiang that certain of the demands, namely those granting Japanese high officials authority in political affairs, in the military, in finance and in the police could not be accepted by China under any conditions whatever.

Of other clauses Lu Cheng-hsiang expressed his willingness to discuss them and admitted that some were possible of acceptance: some others were again possible of acceptance after revision by negotiation.

What has caused the change is not clear to the Chinese but on Saturday the President received a telegram from Petrograd from the Chinese Minister[1] saying that he had been informed at the Russian Foreign Office that Russia will approach Great Britain and France with a view to interrogating Japan regarding the negotiations with China.

It is interesting to note that Odagiri, speaking as he says in his private capacity, is urging the Chinese to make counter-proposals to the Japanese because he says the present negotiations are of a friendly nature and it is only fair that they should be to the advantage of both countries.

I was sorry that I could not get to the Anglo-Chinese Friendship Concert on Saturday evening, but I brought back with me from Tatung a very bad cold and this was not benefited by my long interview in the Palace on Friday where the temperature was like a furnace, the cold outside being Arctic.

With kind regards

Very sincerely yours
[G. E. Morrison]

[1] Liu Ching-jen, Chinese diplomat. Having served as Chargé at the Imperial Chinese Legation in St Petersburg, he became the first Republican Minister to Russia in September 1912, a post he held until after the outbreak of the Russian Revolution. He left the Russian capital in March 1918 and was appointed Senior Chinese Representative in Siberia. In September 1919 he was appointed Chinese Minister to Japan, but did not take up the post.

732. To Ts'ai T'ing-kan

Peking 11 February 1915

My dear Admiral,

[...]

Last night Donald sent 318 words to *The Times*, the longest telegram he has ever sent. He laid emphasis on the fact that the Chinese authorities still refuse to make any disclosure of the Japanese demands but he assures *The Times* that the facts he gives are to be relied on.[1]

A similar message was sent to the *N. China Daily News* and to the Associated Press in America so that there is now a clear understanding in responsible circles of the nature and extent of the Japanese demands.

Publicity of this kind – especially in carefully worded messages such as these – will be bound to have a restraining influence.

There is nothing more that I can do here at present that I can think of, and I believe I would be of some service if I were to go to Hankow and Shanghai and on my way back stay over at Tsinanfu.

Please let me know what you think when we meet tomorrow.

Very sincerely yours
[G. E. Morrison]

733. To Ts'ai T'ing-kan

[Peking] 11 February 1915

My dear Admiral,

It appears to me that your excellent letter[2] would be more forcible if you ended with the words 'the most favourable position in China'. At the present moment it would be better not to suggest that Japan lacks morality and I think the force of the letter would be impaired if you referred to financial stringency in Japan.

The Russian Government apparently does not consider that Japanese action is affecting Russian interests in China but obviously there is wide discrepancy between the demands actually submitted in Peking and the demands stated by Japan to have been submitted in Peking.

[1] A reference to a telegram published in *The Times* on 12 February 1915 under the title 'Outline of the Demands', listing the Japanese demands. The report made no mention of the Chinese refusal to disclose the demands but simply stated: 'The concessions demanded from China by Japan are not yet officially published, but they are reported to include the following:–' The veracity of the report was questioned by an editorial note immediately following the telegram which said: 'We understand that the demands presented by Japan to China were communicated in the course of last month to the British Foreign Office, and that the Russian French and United States Governments had also been informed of them. The desire of the Japanese Government to place its relations with China upon a well defined basis, appears to have been prompted in the first instance by the attitude taken up by the Chinese Government under German influence at the beginning of the war. Until a detailed and accurate account of the Japanese demands is available, judgment upon their scope and nature must be suspended.'   [2] Not found.

Personally I do not place much confidence in the expectation that Japan would not be able to obtain money for railway construction in China. Finance is very cosmopolitan; it thinks only of the pocket; men will lend money wherever they think the money will bring them a good return. The question is one often discussed in Peking. Prior to the European war the money lent by European countries to finance railways in China was lent on onerous conditions, the excuse given being that the methods of administration were such that it was necessary to make onerous conditions in order to safeguard the interests of the lender. Money was however lent to Japanese for the construction of the South Manchuria Railway on much more favourable terms because the Europeans believed that the railway would be well administered. I have frequently heard the opinion expressed that if the Japanese obtained concessions for the construction of railways in China they would obtain better financial terms in Europe than the Chinese would obtain for the construction of the same railways because of the difference in the methods of administration. However that is an opinion only and is not a certainty. It seems to me that reference to finance spoils the irony of the article which is well sustained down to the words 'more favourable position in China'.

The article makes it clear that the Japanese demands conflict with all their assurances and with their formal treaty engagements with other Powers as well as with China. The exposure is now fairly complete for detailed statements were sent last night not only to the London *Times*, but to the Associated Press in America drawing attention to the demands made by the Japanese and showing how they conflict with the interests of other countries in China as well as infringing upon Chinese sovereign rights and the maintenance of the *status quo*.

You will notice that the Franco-Japanese compact is technically called an 'Arrangement'.[1]

With kind regards

Yours very sincerely
[G. E. Morrison]

[1] A reference to the 'Agreement in regard to the Continent of Asia' signed in Paris on 10 June 1907 by Kurino Shin'ichirō (1851–1937) at the time Japanese Ambassador in Paris (1906–12), and Stéphan Jean-Marie Pichon (1857–1933), then the French Minister of Foreign Affairs and a former French Minister to China. By this Agreement the two countries, while agreeing to respect the independence and integrity of China and equal opportunities there for citizens of all nations, engaged 'to support each other for assuring the peace and security in the regions of the Chinese Empire adjacent to the territories where they have the rights of sovereignty, protection or occupation...with a view to maintaining the respective situation and the territorial rights of the two Contracting Parties in the Continent of Asia'.

734. To J. N. Jordan

[Peking] 15 February 1915

Dear Sir John,

I understand that *The Times* in a leader have expressed their view that the demands submitted by the Japanese are reasonable and are such that they can be accepted by the Chinese.[1] I would judge by this that *The Times* have accepted the Japanese Government's communication which asserts that the demands are innocuous and do not conflict with any engagement regarding the Open Door and equal opportunities in China.

In view of this statement I send you confidentially a careful translation of the full text of the Japanese note.[2] Should these demands be accepted the British will be for ever precluded from any mining venture in the Yangtse, in South Manchuria, Eastern Mongolia, Shantung and Fukien.

For years it has been urged that a base be obtained in the Chusan islands. This will become impossible if the demands are agreed to. Shantung is as large as England and Wales together with a population almost as large. For years we have been fighting Germany for exclusive rights in the Province: now those exclusive rights are to be transferred to Japan. If these demands are agreed to the whole situation in Eastern Asia undergoes profound modification.

[1] In a leader entitled 'Japanese Claims on China' published on 13 February 1915, *The Times* made use of the publication of the Japanese demands to deliver a strong attack on China. 'We are told,' it stated, 'that they [the Japanese demands] have caused a great commotion in Peking. There is nothing unusual about that. Commotion, genuine or feigned, is the ordinary result of all applications to Chinese authorities...it is important to bear in mind that the particulars which have reached us are not official, and that they come exclusively from Peking. News from Chinese informants is always suspect, and at the present time there are special reasons for accepting it with the utmost caution, through whatever channels it may reach Europe.' The leader went on to say: 'Her [China's] timidity has indeed baffled attempts to induce her to offer them any direct provocation, but she has readily yielded to German suggestions that, while Japan and Russia were engaged in other controversies, she need not show unreasonable assiduity or haste in fulfilling her agreements with these Powers...We must expect that the whole of this Oriental imitation of the "Reptile Press" will be worked at full pressure for the next few days, in order to flood Europe and America with distorted versions of the Japanese claims, and to comment upon them in such fashion as the Sino-Teuton publicists may think best calculated to create differences amongst the Allies. All news and all views which come from that quarter are tainted at the source...Even in the Peking version, which we published yesterday, these terms do not look harsh or unreasonable in principle...They do not in any way threaten the integrity of China, nor do they appear to violate the doctrines of "equality of opportunity" and of the "open door" as hitherto accepted by other Powers... The Okuma Government, like other Governments, must pay regard to different currents of public opinion. It cannot ignore the popular impatience with Chinese duplicity and tergiversation, but we believe it sincerely desires to use the present occasion for the object which the most sagacious of the Japanese statesmen have kept steadily before their eyes, and which England desires as earnestly as they – for clearing up definitely the whole position and establishing a firm and abiding general peace in the Far East.'
[2] Not printed.

I regret therefore that *The Times* should have been misinformed; it would have been better for them to have said nothing, but I presume that David Fraser has telegraphed from Tokio a statement given to him by the Japanese and this has been accepted by *The Times*,[1] although it conflicts with the more correct information cabled home by Donald.

With kind regards

Very sincerely yours
[G. E. Morrison]

735. From Ts'ai T'ing-kan

[Peking] 16 February 1915

My dear Doctor,

Do you think you can give me a copy of the note Japan has given to the British Government or the British Legation in Peking purporting to represent her articles of demand. Even an outline of such a note would be useful in guiding us as to what Japan would demand in secret and what she would demand in public.

Yours sincerely
Tsai Ting Kan

[1] David Fraser, in Tokyo when the Twenty-One Demands were presented, sent a message which was published in *The Times* on 12 February 1915: 'The secrecy enjoined on the Chinese,' it stated, 'gave rise to many fanciful versions of the demands, and doubtless German insinuations have led to further exaggeration of their significance.' It then went on to say: 'At the same time while it may be true that none affect the integrity of China, China has excuse for alarm in that her weakness and subjection to extraterritoriality present so many opportunities for intervention that she cannot contemplate with equanimity any serious extension of established foreign interests such as might be involved in complete acceptance of the Japanese proposals. Local politics are partly responsible for the step now taken by Japan. The present Government, recently defeated in the Diet and faced by an election and serious financial problems, finds itself impelled to pursue a forward foreign policy in accord with the loudly proclaimed popular demand. Thus, while it is true that the moment is propitious owing to the helplessness of China and the fact that the other Powers interested in her fate are engaged elsewhere, Japan is compelled by insistent internal necessities to take some action. Other foreign interests are closely affected by the Japanese demands, and particularly the British for activity by any one competitor in a field of enterprise necessarily limits the opportunities of the others. But in view of our relations with Japan, and particularly because of the valuable naval assistance she has recently rendered us, and is still rendering, it would be ungracious for Britain to put obstacles in the way of Japan's reasonable enough ambitions in China, always assuming that the demands would not, if acceded to by China, definitely violate the integrity of China or prevent equal commercial opportunity, or in some unforeseen way disturb the British position as already established.'

736. To Ts'ai T'ing-kan

[Peking] 16 February 1915

My dear Admiral,

It is just what I have been trying to do but I am assured that no communication was made here to the Legation in Peking. The Japanese Embassies did make communications to the American, British, French and Russian Governments and it is in consequence of these communications that *The Times* and *Le Temps* have accepted the view that the statement of the claims sent home by the correspondents from Peking has been exaggerated.

I think however that the matter has been cleared up for very full messages indeed have been sent both to *The Times* and to the Associated Press. *The Times* message last night was 380 words long.

A hopeful feature of the situation appears to be that Japan can only insist upon the eleven demands which she is understood to have communicated to Foreign Governments. In the interests of truth Donald has sent home most complete and correct messages, and these will I am sure convince *The Times* that they have been misled.

However I will see what I can do and let you know.

With best wishes

Very sincerely yours
[G. E. Morrison]

737. To H. W. Steed[1]

[Peking] 17 February 1915

Private

My dear Steed,

Long extracts from *The Times* Leader of the 12th[2] on the demands recently submitted by Japan have been cabled back to Peking and were cited on Monday by the Japanese Minister at his meeting with the Foreign Minister as evidence that in the opinion of the British Government the demands were

[1] Henry Wickham Steed (1871–1956), British journalist. Famous for his political crusades, he was at this time Foreign Editor of *The Times*, having succeeded D. D. Braham in this position the previous year. He had earlier been *The Times*' Own Correspondent in Rome (1897–1902), and in Vienna (1902–14). In 1919 he was appointed Editor of the paper succeeding Geoffrey Dawson, holding the post until November 1922 when he resigned upon the death of Lord Northcliffe. Then John Jacob Astor became the new proprietor, and Dawson was once more appointed to the editorial chair. Steed's memoirs, *Through Thirty Years* (New York, 1924), more a political record than personal recollections, are concerned essentially with European affairs. Morrison's name did not even appear, though the two had been allies in opposing the policy of the former Foreign Editor of *The Times*, Valentine Chirol. But judging by the tenor of the *Times* Leader on the Twenty-One Demands, Steed was far from seeing eye to eye with Morrison on many important issues in the Far East.   [2] *See* p. 371 n. 1.

reasonable and compatible with existing conventions. At the time your Leader was written it is probable that you were not in possession of the full text of the demands. Before this letter reaches you the necessity may have arisen to publish the demands in full, but in case it should not be necessary I send you for your confidential guidance a translation of the Note presented to the President on the 18th January.[1]

When the Note was presented the Chinese were threatened with reprisals should they disclose its terms. Having thus enforced China's maintenance of secrecy the Japanese proceeded to disclose a portion of the demands only and they have in consequence created a misleading impression abroad where they have stigmatised as 'wilfully exaggerated' the demands as cabled by the correspondents in Peking.

I gather that the Foreign Office were informed that the Japanese Government had submitted eleven demands. The Chinese have always been willing to negotiate these eleven demands. But the Japanese from the first have insisted that the whole 21 demands as embodied in the Note herewith enclosed, must be agreed to *en bloc*, no discussion of the separate articles being permitted until after this assent has been formally given.

Every Englishman in China recognises the difficulty of the British Government; the Chinese also recognise it and despite statements to the contrary, they have made no direct communication to the British Legation since the demands were first presented. You will see from the accompanying document that the statements have not been exaggerated and that the terms if agreed to are even more far-reaching than those the public have been permitted to learn. You will see that they exclude the British from any participation in mining enterprise, except with Japan's consent, in South Manchuria, Eastern Mongolia, Shantung, the Yangtse Valley and Fukien.

I would draw your attention to Section 4: –

'The Chinese Government agrees that no island, port and harbour along the coast shall be ceded or leased to any third Power.'

Provided this were made made a self-denying ordinance and the word 'other' were substituted for the word 'third' there would be no possible objection to this clause, although the reason of it is known to be inspired by the desire to prevent Britain from obtaining any foothold in the Chusan Archipelago, a course which has been advocated by many writers – with especial vigour by Sir Henry Norman[2] and quite recently by the Correspondent of the *Daily Telegraph*.

But the Preamble:—

'The Japanese Government and the Chinese Government with the object

[1] Not printed.
[2] Sir Henry Norman (1858–1939), British journalist and author, one-time Editor of the *Pall Mall Gazette*, and author of *People and Politics of the Far East* (London 1895).

of effectively protecting the territorial integrity of China agree to the following special articles'

is strenuously opposed. It is regarded by the Chinese as most dangerous. It is identical in intent with Article III of the Protocol signed in Seoul Korea on February 23rd, 1904:—

'The Imperial Government of Japan effectively guarantees the independence and territorial integrity of the Korean Empire.'

The Chinese argue that the Territorial Integrity of China may be threatened by internal disturbance (and in the past Japanese have admittedly taken a very active part in promoting and fostering internal disturbance) or by external aggression. If they sign this Preamble then Japan is furnished with the powers of a Protector. She can foment disturbance and then by virtue of this clause come into China and suppress the disturbance, and in that case, judging by the past history of Korea, she would remain in possession after the suppression.

Since the war began China has done her best to preserve her neutrality. German influence was powerful among the military, those officers – and there are many – who were trained in Europe as well as those trained in Japan having much confidence in the invincibility of German arms. They have however fast been disillusioned. German influence here is dead. Ridicule kills here as in Europe and the fact that the German Minister[1] had to sneak into China as the supercargo on a tramp steamer and that the German Consul in Hongkong, Voretzsch, was found to be living in the Hotel here under a false name as A. Nielson, the Swedish Consul, has done much to kill German influence in Peking.

As regards the alleged purchase of the two English papers in Peking, this surely is misleading. There are two English daily papers, the *Peking Daily News* and the *Peking Gazette*. The *Peking Gazette* is managed by an Englishman named Saunderson and is edited by a Chinese, Eugene Chen, who was born in Trinidad, a British subject, was educated in London and is on the Roll of English Solicitors. He is on terms of friendship with most of the Englishmen in Peking. Since he has edited the paper, which was formerly the property of the German bank, he has done his best to be impartial. He publishes fully every day every English, French and Russian telegrams as well as the German telegrams; he publishes every day an article from

[1] Paul von Hintze (1864-1941), German sailor and diplomat. He had served in the German Far Eastern Squadron from 1898 to 1902, becoming in that year Captain of the battleship *Kaiser Wilhelm*. In 1903 he was appointed Naval Attaché to the German Legation in St Petersburg, and was attached to the Czar in 1906. In 1911 he was recalled for supposed indiscretion. He was however promoted to Rear-Admiral, and sent in the same year as German Minister to Mexico. He remained there until 1914 when he was transferred to Peking. He left China after the declaration of war against Germany in August 1917 to become German Minister to Norway.

The Times, either a Leader or an article by your military correspondent, and I have heard no complaints from the English in Peking regarding the way in which he edits the paper.

The *Peking Daily News* is edited by Alexander Ramsay, a Scotch journalist, of whose loyalty there can be no question. He is the representative in Peking of the British Engineers' Association of which Douglas Vickers[1] was the Chairman and of which Wilfrid Stokes[2] is now the Chairman. The paper has never shown the smallest inclination to be hostile to the British, very much to the contrary. Its proprietor however is a Chinese named Chu Chi,[3] a Cantonese who lived for many years in Tsingtau and who is also the proprietor of a vernacular paper named the *Pei ching jih pao* which was for some time markedly pro-German in its sympathies. An extract from this paper, translated by Backhouse, attacking Great Britain was published in *The Times*. The attention of the English Legation has been called to its articles now and again but I understand that it is not considered worth while to interfere seeing that every day the paper publishes in Chinese the text of the very ample service supplied by Reuter.

Both English papers have discussed the Japanese demands, of course, and both have energetically opposed them, but in this they are only reflecting the views of most Englishmen in the Far East who see in the demands the most serious attack on the British position in the Far East ever yet attempted.

You must be having an anxious time in London. In China we are admirably served with news. Reuter has a very well organized Far Eastern Service and every day he distributes all over China the messages he receives from his own people in London, from the British Legation, the French Legation and the Russian Legation. One cannot praise too highly the service which this Agency has rendered to us since the outbreak of the war. Two months before the war began Reuter proposed to close down his Pacific service on the ground that it was losing money, but the Chinese Government, at my suggestion, came forward with a guarantee to indemnify it against loss so the Service was continued.

Then the war began and now the Service is of the highest value. On an average we get four foolscap pages of news, typewritten, by day, so that the news we receive by letter is often quite stale. Long extracts from speeches by our statesmen reach us *verbatim* and are distributed over China. Equal

[1] Douglas Vickers (1861–1937), British industrialist, Chairman of Vickers Limited (1918–26) and a Member of the British House of Commons (1918–22).
[2] Frederick (later Sir Frederick) Wilfred Scott Stokes (1860–1927), British engineer. In 1897 he became Managing Director of the British Manufacturing firm of Messrs. Ransomes and Rapier, becoming its Chairman in 1907. The gun which he designed and which bears his name, after being rejected in December 1914 was subsequently used in the trenches in 1915. He was President of the British Engineers Association (1915–17).
[3] Chu Ch'i (d. 1931), Chinese newspaper publisher, the proprietor of *Chinese Public Opinion*, and in 1909 of the *Peking Daily News* originally *Chinese Public Opinion*.

importance is given to the comments of *The Times*. Your Leader, of which I send you the extract as published in Peking, has caused much disquietude to the Chinese who hope that perhaps later you may be able to reconsider the terms of your condemnation.

With my best wishes to you. I read *The Times* religiously. It is doing glorious work.

Very sincerely yours
[G. E. Morrison]

738. To A. H. Harris[1]

[Peking] 19 February 1915

Dear Mr Harris,

[...]

The Japanese demands have caused grave disquiet here. They are worse even than the demands that have been published, more insidious and more comprehensive. Suggestions are now being made that they are to be enforced by an ultimatum: the moment that the ultimatum is received the demands will be telegraphed all over the world. They exclude all British or other foreigners from taking part in any mining enterprises in South Manchuria, Eastern Mongolia, Shantung, Fukien and the Yangtse Valley unless with Japanese consent, and yet *The Times* have been so misinformed as to describe them as not conflicting with any previous stipulation.

The fact is the Japanese having forced the Chinese to keep silence then disclosed a Bowdlerised version of the demands to the four friendly Powers. They have put us Englishmen in a very awkward position. With kind regards and many apologies

Very sincerely yours
[G. E. Morrison]

739. To H. W. Steed

[Peking] 24 February 1915

My dear Steed,

Last Wednesday I wrote to you a letter of which I herewith send a duplicate.[2] Unfortunately I did not stamp 'via Siberia' on the envelope and the letter has been sent to you via Suez and will not reach you until the end of March. I am very sorry about it.

In this letter I sent you a copy of the demands submitted by the Japanese Minister to the President on the 18th January. He handed in the documents

[1] A. H. Harris, British employee of the Chinese Maritime Customs, at this time Commissioner at Newchwang. In 1915 he was moved to Kowloon, and later served at Amoy and Canton.   [2] This refers to the letter printed above as No. 737.

in Japanese and in Chinese. The translation I now send you, with the exception of a few verbal alterations, is identical with the text I sent you last Wednesday. These alterations make the translation more correct; there was some obscurity in the Chinese text but at the meeting on Monday, Feb. 21st, the first meeting at which the Japanese Minister consented to discuss the terms separately, he explained certain ambiguities.

His explanation shows that with regard, for example, to Article 4 respecting the right of mining in South Manchuria and Eastern Mongolia the demand was not restricted to the opening of mines – a right which the Japanese already possessed by virtue of their Treaty – but the words are '*the mines*' and mean *all* the mines.

With regard to the 4th Section the Japanese Government refuses to consider this as a self-denying ordinance and emphasises that there could be no cession or lease to any Power other than the signatory to this agreement, namely to Japan.

In view of allegations set forth by the Japanese that the Chinese have been disseminating misleading information with regard to these demands, the President has had photographs taken of the actual documents submitted to him by the Japanese Minister and, should his good faith be challenged, copies will be sent to the friendly Powers.

I must apologise for troubling you so much but the Chinese, quite rightly, attach great weight and importance to what is said by *The Times* especially in its editorial columns. I therefore hope that you will not object to my sending to you these explanations.

Donald has kept you I understand well informed. To a degree rarely attained by a correspondent he is trusted by the Chinese and as he works in close harmony with both the Legation and the Chinese he has unusual opportunities of sending you a copy of the Text; I had of course previously given him a copy for his assistance.

Yours very sincerely
[G. E. Morrison]

740. To E. G. Hillier

[Peking] 25 February 1915

My dear Hillier,

I send you herewith a copy of the demands submitted to the President on the 16th January.[1] I enclose to you also on a separate sheet a copy of the proposals which the Japanese Government communicated to the friendly Powers, alleging that they were the proposals which they had submitted to China on the 18th and that any other statements were wilfully exaggerated, probably at the instigation of the Germans to create trouble between Japan and the friendly countries.[2]

[1] Not printed.   [2] Not printed.

When these two documents are read side by side one can come only to one conclusion, that there never has been a more disgraceful case of diplomatic turpitude than is shown here.

Please return me both papers after you have copied them.

Yours very sincerely
[G. E. Morrison]

741. From E. G. Hillier

Peking 26 February 1915

My dear Morrison,

I return herewith the text of the Japanese demands, original and expurgated, which you were kind enough to send me; very many thanks. Such a diplomatic exposure would of course be fatal to the prestige of any civilised country, but I am afraid it will not deter Japan from persisting in the attempt to extort all she can out of China at this most opportune moment. It can hardly do otherwise however than weaken Japan's position, and strengthen China's, and I hope that the gravest dangers of the situation may thereby have been averted.

Yours sincerely
E. G. Hillier

742. To Ts'ai T'ing-kan

Peking 26 February 1915

My dear Admiral,

I send you herewith a memorandum regarding the photographing of the document handed in to the President on January 18th by the Japanese Minister. In the enclosed memorandum I give you an excellent precedent.

I hope you will carry out your plan of photographing the anonymous letter addressed to the President a few days ago.[1] My wife is sure that the

[1] In his Diary of 24 February 1915, Morrison recorded '[Tsai T'ing-kan] sent me yesterday a German anonymous letter addressed to the President of which Jennie made me a translation warning him against the Japanese who were preparing to seize the Palace and urging him to shut the gates and be ready'. The translation, attached to a letter Morrison wrote to Ts'ai T'ing-kan on 24 February 1915, reads: 'Peking 19th February, 1915: Your Excellency: I have pretty sure information that an attempt against your person is being planned on the part of the Japanese Legation. Guards have been brought into the Legation and everything prepared. Put your Palace in a state of siege, station an adequate garrison on the walls, place guards and machine guns over the gates, barricade all the gates and prepare sand-bags for a rush on the principal gate. There is danger in delay. From one who has at heart the safety of your Person and the well-being of the Country.'

handwriting is not disguised. If the letter were reproduced in facsimile it would be easy enough to identify the writer.
[...]
With best wishes

Yours very sincerely
[G. E. Morrison]

Enclosure to Letter No. 742: *Memorandum regarding the photographing of a Certain Official Document, Peking 26 February 1915*

In reference to the excellent idea of having the documents submitted by the Japanese Minister on January 18th photographed, it may be pointed out that there is an interesting precedent for such an act of defence.

It will be recalled that in 1884 a state of war existed between Annam and France. It had existed since 1882 when, France having invaded Tongking, the rulers of Tongking invoked the assistance of the Chinese Black Flags.[1] The French underrated these enemies, attacked them in small force and were defeated. Later they renewed the operations with increased vigour.

At that time Tongking, which formed part of Annam, was regarded as under the suzerainty of China. For this reason the preliminary treaty of peace terminating these operations was signed at Tientsin by the Viceroy Li Hung-chang,[2] and the French Envoy, Captain Fournier.[3] This was on May 11th, 1884.

By the terms of this Treaty Li Hung-chang on behalf of China undertook to withdraw all Chinese troops from Tongking and to recognise the French Treaties with Annam, France at the same time undertaking to hold the frontier inviolate and to respect Chinese suzerainty.

[1] In 1882, when French troops attacked Tonkin, the Chinese troops in Kwangsi under Liu Yung-fu (1837–1917), in answer to an appeal from the ruler of Tonkin, went to his aid. Liu's troops fought under a black standard and hence won for themselves the name of 'Black Flags'. They were known for their bravery, and after the Peace treaty between China and France were sent to Formosa where Liu Yung-fu remained until the island was ceded to Japan in 1895.

[2] Li Hung-chang (1823–1901), Chinese Imperial official, Grand Secretary, and Viceroy of Chihli (or Metropolitan) Province from 1870 until his dismissal in 1895 after China's defeat by Japan, for which he was held to be responsible. He had been until then China's foremost and best known statesman, spoken of by some as one of the three greatest statesmen, in company with Bismarck and Gladstone, of the 19th century. In his Viceregal capacity in Tientsin, he was responsible for China's foreign relations and was thus blamed for all the unequal and humiliating treaties he signed on China's behalf during this period, including the Treaty here referred to. In 1900 he was recalled to be China's representative in the negotiation with the Powers of the Boxer Settlement, and was one of China's signatories to the Peace Protocol signed on 7 September 1901, two months to a day before his death.

[3] François Ernest Fournier (1842–1934), French sailor. As a naval Lietenant he represented France at the signing of the Tientsin Treaty with Li Hung-chang on 3 June 1884, for which he was promoted to Captain. He was made a Rear-Admiral and became Commander of the French Far Eastern Fleet in 1897, and in 1896 was promoted to Vice-Admiral and Commander of the French Fleet in the Mediterranean.

On the 17th May Captain Fournier, the French Representative, presented to Li Hung-chang a Memorandum naming the date upon which the fortresses in Tongking, which were then in Chinese occupation, were to be handed over to the French. But the Chinese pointed out that the dates specified were impracticable and that it was impossible within the time to carry out the withdrawal. Thereupon Captain Fournier erased the dates 'with his own hand'. The Memorandum was not signed by Li Hung-Chang. That was the Chinese story.

The French story was that the dates were not erased and that the Chinese had formally agreed to them. This contention implied that the document bore the signature of the Chinese Plenipotentiary.

Had the erasures been made or not? That was the question in dispute.

Li Hung-chang accordingly had the document photographed and distributed the photographs, which showed unmistakeably that the erasure had been made and that the document was not signed by the Viceroy.

Serious events followed. Although the document was not signed, the French proceeded to act as if it had been signed. The fortress of Langson was still in occupation of the Chinese and when the French troops under Colonel Dugenne[1] arrived there on the date which Captain Fournier had stated to his Government was fixed in the Memorandum, the Chinese had not yet received instructions and they asked for delay.

The French attacked them immediately, were defeated and forced to retire. The war between China and France ensued.

743. From Ts'ai T'ing-kan

[Peking] 27 February 1915

My dear Doctor,

The original documents containing the demands have been photographed.

Mr. Lu Ching Tsiang[2] told me last night that yesterday was the first time he had a hearty laugh since the negotiations. From what he said and what Mr. Tsao Ju Lin told me the Japanese have become more moderate and reasonable.

The gathering at the U.S. Legation last night was large, including Hsu Shi Chang,[3] and Ministers of the different Boards. After the dinner there was a smoking concert. The whole affair was rather successful.

As to the German letter sent to the President, His Excellency said since

[1] Alphonse Jules Dugenne (1841–87), French soldier. After serving in Algeria for some eight years he was sent to Tonkin in 1884 and took part in the Battle of Lanson, for which he was made a Lt.-Colonel. He was then sent with the French forces to Formosa, but returned in 1886 to Tonkin where he died the following year.
[2] Lu Cheng-hsiang.
[3] Hsü Shih-ch'ang (1855–1939), Chinese Imperial official, Grand Secretary, Grand Councillor and Republican politician, the first Viceroy of Manchuria (1907–9). He withdrew

the letter was addressed to him in person he thought it better not to have it published.¹ I will have a photograph of it made myself.

Yours sincerely
Tsai Ting Kan

[...]

744. To Ts'ai T'ing-kan

[Peking] 2 March 1915

My dear Admiral,

Might I suggest that you induce Eugene Chen to restrain himself? His pen is again outrunning his judgment. This morning he has a violent attack upon 'one Lindsay Russell',¹ President of the Japanese Society of New York. If this public man is of sufficient importance to be Chairman of the Japanese Society, (the Chairman of the corresponding Society in Great Britain is an ex-Ambassador)² his arguments may be controverted but to attack him on personal grounds and show ignorance of his personality is

---

from politics after the overthrow of the Manchu Dynasty, until May 1914 when, in response to an invitation by his erstwhile patron Yüan Shih-k'ai, he emerged to become Secretary of State (to which the post of Prime Minister had been changed in the new constitution promulgated as part of Yüan's monarchical scheme) holding this position with only a short interruption until April 1916. In 1918, as candidate of the Anfu Clique, he was elected President in succession to Feng Kuo-chang, and remained in the post until June 1922 when he was compelled to step down by the Chihli Clique militarists who replaced him with Li Yüan-hung. Hsü was reputed to have played a hand in the generous treatment by the Republican Government of the former Manchu Imperial family; and as an indication of his true loyalties he donned his old Ministerial costume from the Imperial days while serving as President of the Republic when he went to visit the deposed Emperor. After his retirement Hsü devoted himself to literary pursuits, including the study of Taoism, and was the sponsor of the photolithographic reproduction of the 15th century (1445) edition of the *Tao-tsang* (the Taoist Tripitaka) (Shanghai 1923-6), which was later reprinted in Taiwan.

¹ Lindsay Russell (d. 1949), American lawyer with a practice in both New York and London from 1895 to 1897. He was a founder in 1901 of the Pilgrims Society of London and New York, and in 1907 of the Japan Society of New York. He was best known for his role in promoting better relations between the United States and Japan and Italy, for which he was decorated by both governments. Russell was the author of a number of publications, and a contributor to *America to Japan: a symposium of papers by representative citizens of the United States on the relations between Japan and America and on the common interests of the two countries* (New York and London 1915). As Chairman of the Japan Society he frequently spoke up for Japan, and defended her position during the Twenty-One Demands crisis.

² The Chairman at this time (1913-18) was Col. Sir C. Wyndham Murray (1844-1928). A British soldier who had seen service in Afghanistan and Africa, he had been a Conservative Member of the British House of Commons from 1892 to 1906. Morrison may have meant Sir Claude M. MacDonald, the Vice-President, who was until 1912 British Ambassador to Japan. The President of the Japan Society had always, since its foundation in 1892, been the current Japanese Ambassador to the Court of St James.

only injurious to the critic. Eugene Chen abuses him in unmeasured terms, even stigmatising him as a fool. He will not realise that abuse is not argument. Lindsay Russell is a distinguished American, one of the leading lawyers in the United States, the Founder of the Pilgrims Society, almost as well known in England as he is in America.

Now that negotiations between Japan and China are following a more friendly course it is very necessary to keep the Press in restraint. Last night I was talking to one of the chief foreigners in Peking, probably the most distinguished member of the Foreign Diplomatic Body, a man very sympathetic with China who has a wide knowledge of foreign affairs, and he said that the danger that he foresaw was the unrestraint of the Chinese Press and the possibility that their intemperate attacks might provoke Japanese resentment.

It is only necessary to state the case calmly and temperately to obtain support; it is not necessary to indulge in violent abuse and recrimination.

Articles such as Putnam Weale is writing do no good to China. More than any other man he is responsible for the hostile attitude of some of the leading English papers during the last two years. As you know, the *Daily Telegraph* and the *Pall Mall Gazette*, two of our most influential papers published, day in day out, Putnam Weale's telegrams from Peking, which were most violently hostile to the President, under the headlines 'Chaos in China', 'Bankruptcy of China', 'Dismemberment of China', and such like.

That Putnam Weale would now support China speaks more for the wisdom of the Chinese Government than it does for the integrity of Putnam Weale and yet his first foreign article published by Eugene Chen has for its heading 'Partition sooner than domination'. An excellent reply to this article is written by Sheldon Ridge[1] in the *National Review* of the 27th February.

It is of high importance that the papers should be restrained and that they should adopt a more friendly and conciliatory attitude towards their powerful neighbour. Any arrogance or boastfulness, any expression indicating that Japan has been compelled to climb down is bound to lead to serious reaction and is bound to cause China difficulty in the future.

Best wishes

Yours very sincerely
[G. E. Morrison]

---

[1] Sheldon Ridge, British journalist, a graduate of Manchester and Leeds Universities, he first went to China in 1903, and became Assistant Editor of the *Shanghai Mercury* in 1906, and of its partner, the *Shanghai Times*, the following year. In 1908 he was appointed Editor of the *National Review*, a post he held until 1918, serving at the same time as a leader writer for the *Peking Daily News* and correspondent of the *China Press* in Shanghai. In 1918 he became a correspondent of the English language paper in Tientsin, the *North China Star*, and was in charge of its Peking bureau, as well as Peking Correspondent of the New York fortnightly journal, the *Nation*.

745. From Ts'ai T'ing-kan

Peking 2 March 1915

My dear Doctor,
   The world's mischief comes by 'over-doing'.
   The Germans sinned by over-doing.
   The Japanese sinned by over-doing.
   Eugene Ch'en is over-doing. I do not know what influence I have with him but I will send Mr. Tong[1] of our office to moderate him. I hate to handle a freak myself.

Yours sincerely
Tsai Ting Kan

746. To Ch'en Yu-jen

Peking 4 March 1915

Private

Dear Mr Chen,
   I am reading your articles with considerable anxiety. It seems to me, and apparently it seems also to others who have spoken to me, that you are doing your best to goad Japan into reprisals.
   Japan made a false step, public opinion has induced her to modify her demands, negotiations are now proceeding in a friendly manner, the hectoring policy has been at any rate for the time being discontinued.
   The violence of your attacks now can have only one result namely to furnish Japan with a pretext for obtaining compensation for 'loss of face'. One of the leading neutrals of Peking speaking to me on Monday said 'the danger from Japan seems now past but the danger will recur unless the "intemperate violence" of the *Gazette* can be restrained'.
   Abuse is not argument and I regret to see you employing your great gifts with such unneeded virulence. To criticise and refute the address of Lindsay Russell is only right and proper but to attack personally the distinguished American, Lindsay Russell, founder of the Pilgrims Society, estranges friends and injures the *Gazette*.
   'Words of guidance indicating a means of extricating herself from the grave position into which she has ostracised herself', to paraphrase some of your observations to-day, are regarded by the Japanese as arrogant impertinences and they, arguing that these are the expression of the opinion of responsible Chinese authorities, are bound to retaliate to the detriment of China.
   I hope you will not misunderstand me. I recognise your ardent patriotism

[1] Possibly Tung Hsien-kuang, or Hollington Tong, Chinese journalist and Republican politician. For a note on him *see* p. 713 n. 1.

and your fervent desire to assist the Government in the present crisis, but I believe I am expressing the opinion generally held by the foreign friends of China that unless you write with more restraint and with a higher sense of responsibility you will involve the Government in serious embarrassment.

When are you coming over to have a chat with me?

With best wishes

Very sincerely yours
[G. E. Morrison]

747. To Ts'ai T'ing-kan

[Peking] 9 March 1915

My dear Admiral,

Curiously enough after you left me this morning information reached me regarding Tsingtao and Pukou which shows the sagacity of the President in opening Pukou as a Treaty Port.[1] Pukou will largely take the place of Tsingtao. Chinese merchants have in the meantime forsaken Tsingtao and they declare emphatically that they will not return there unless the port is restored to China. In the meantime these merchants, many of whom are exceedingly well to do, contemplate opening at Pukou so that Tsingtao's loss will be Pukou's gain.

The export of the products of Shantung will thus take place via Pukou and not via Tsingtao to the advantage of the Chinese Government and to the special advantage of the Tsinan–Pukou Railway and of course to the special benefit of the port of Nanking within whose harbour limits I understand that Pukou will be included.

This news, which reached me from an authoritative source, struck me so forcibly that I have lost no time in sending it on to you.

With best wishes

Very sincerely yours
[G. E. Morrison]

748. To Ku Wei-chün

Peking 26 March 1915

Dear Dr. Koo,

It may interest you to know this. Some little time ago a friend of mine, an English correspondent,[2] asked Baron Kato[3] in Tokio what was meant by

[1] The southern terminus of the Tientsin–Pukow Railway, situated on the Northern bank of the Yangtse River opposite Nanking, Pukow was only formally opened as a Treaty Port on 1 June 1915.   [2] Probably David Fraser.
[3] Katō Takaaki (Kōmei) (1860–1926), at the time Japanese Foreign Minister (April 1914 – August 1915) in the second Ōkuma Cabinet.

the demand regarding the Han-Yeh-Ping Company, Article 2.¹ Baron Kato declared in reply that there were in the neighbourhood of the Tayeh iron deposits and of the Pinghsiang collieries certain other iron and coal deposits respectively and these Japan did not wish to be worked in competition with the mines in which she was interested.

The Foreign Minister went on to explain that Japan wished to define the area in each case in which such competition would be prevented and he spoke vaguely of 100 square *li* in each case. My friend is certain that he said 100 square *li* (equal 9 *li* by 9 *li*), and not 100 *li* square (equal 100 *li* by 100 *li*).

This is a very small sidelight but it may be of interest to you to know that such a statement was made, even privately, to an English correspondent of position.

I hope things are going on better.

With kind regards

Very sincerely yours
[G. E. Morrison]

749. To Ku Wei-chün

[Peking] 30 March 1915

Dear Dr. Koo,

I hope the negotiations regarding Manchuria² are proceeding harmoniously.

Some years ago when negotiations regarding the Chientao question³ were proceeding between Mr. Liang Tun-yen,⁴ who was then in the Foreign

---

[1] Article 2 in Group III of the Twenty-One Demands reads: 'The Chinese Government engage that, as a necessary measure for protection of the vested interests of Japanese capitalists, no mines in the neighbourhood of those owned by the Han-Yeh-Ping Company shall be permitted, without the consent of the said Company, to be worked by anyone other than the said Company: and further that whenever it is proposed to take any other measure which may likely affect the interests of the said Company directly or indirectly, the consent of the said Company shall first be obtained.' By an Exchange of Notes on 25 May 1915 the Chinese gave way to this Japanese demand regarding the Han-Yeh-Ping Company.

[2] A reference to the negotiations over Group II of the Twenty-One Demands which concerned Manchuria and Eastern Inner Mongolia.

[3] In August 1907 the Japanese Government, ostensibly in reply to a request from the Korean Government, sent a party of officials to take charge of Korean settlers in the delta region of the Tumen River – known by the Koreans and Japanese as 'Chientao' – in the north-east of the Chinese province of Kirin. This action by Japan provoked a nationwide protest, particularly by Chinese students in Japan. Two who were to play a prominent role at the birth of the Republic, Sung Chiao-jen and Wu Lu-chen, first made their name in the 'Chientao' incident. A settlement was not reached until 1909 when, in exchange for Japan's recognition of Chinese sovereignty in 'Chientao', the Chinese Government was forced to grant to Japan railways and other concessions in Manchuria.

[4] Liang Tun-yen (?1860–1924), Chinese Imperial official and Republican politician. One of the earliest students sent by the Chinese Government to study in America and a graduate

Office, and the Japanese Minister, Mr. Ijuin, I drew the attention of both negotiators to an Agreement very applicable for such conditions as those which were bound to arise in Chientao, an Agreement known as the Chiengmai Treaty.

On September 3rd, 1883, the British and Siamese signed a Treaty known as the Chiengmai Treaty, providing for the exercise of civil and criminal jurisdiction in all cases arising in North Siam between British subjects or in which British subjects were interested as complainants, accused, plaintiffs or defendants.

This Treaty was the fore-runner of those treaties which were subsequently signed by the British and Siamese and by the French and Siamese Governments, by which Siam recovered almost complete jurisdiction over foreign subjects in Siam.

You were not in Peking when the Chientao negotiations were in progress. It may interest you to read the text of the Treaty I then referred to. I herewith send you the essential clauses.[1] This Treaty worked wisely and effectively for $24\frac{1}{2}$ years until it was superseded by the more comprehensive treaty of the 10th March, 1909.[2]

With best wishes to you

Very sincerely yours
[G. E. Morrison]

---

of Yale. As Vice-Minister of Foreign Affairs (January 1909 – July 1910) he was China's representative at the 'Chientao' negotiations. He was named Foreign Minister in the Cabinets of both Prince Ch'ing and Yüan Shih-k'ai in 1911, but did not take up the post. A former Secretary in charge of Foreign Affairs under Chang Chih-tung (1837–1909), the Viceroy of Hukuang (1889–1907), Liang was known for his monarchical sympathies, and after the establishment of the the Republic took no further part in the Government until May 1914, when Yüan Shih-k'ai, in his attempt to realise his imperial ambition, appointed his friend Hsü Shih-ch'ang, a former Imperial Guardian, as his Secretary of State. Liang then became Minister of Communications, a post he held until April 1916, after the imperial scheme had been abandoned. He re-emerged to become Foreign Minister in Chang Hsün's Restoration government in July 1917, but when this failed he withdrew into political obscurity in Tientsin.

[1] Not found.

[2] The British–Siamese Treaty of 10 March 1909 was signed in Bangkok and ratified in London on 9 July the same year. It is not known to which 'essential clauses' of the Chiengmai Treaty Morrison was referring, since the enclosure was not found, but both the 1909 treaty with its Protocols and Notes exchanged between the two governments, as well as the Chiengmai Treaty of 3 September 1883, can be found in Hertslet's *Commercial Treaties* (London 1913).

750. From K'ung Hsiang-hsi[1]

Peking 3 April 1915

My dear Dr. Morrison,

Owing to illness I have been delayed in my preparation of the two statements enclosed,[2] and this morning when I telephoned asking for the privilege of another interview I learned to my regret that you were not in the city. As I leave Peking for Shansi Monday morning I leave the enclosed statements for you to use at your discretion, only asking that you will regard them as strictly private and confidential.

My address will be T'aikuhsien, Shansi, or in care of Miss Miner,[3] American Board Mission, Peking.

Regretting that I cannot see you again.[4]

I remain

Yours sincerely
H. H. Kung

Enclosure to Letter No. 750:

The present crisis in China brought about by Japan's great strategy impels all true patriots to put forth every effort to save the nation. It is in the hope

[1] K'ung Hsiang-hsi, better known to foreigners as H. H. Kung (1881-1967), Chinese Republican politician, whose early career is sketched in the enclosure to a letter dated 12 December 1915 from Robert Gailey to Morrison (No. 792 p. 477). He was a brother-in-law of Sun Yat-sen and of Chiang Kai-shek. The latter married Madame K'ung's youngest sister, Sung (or Soong) Mei-ling, in 1928. For twelve years (1933-1944) out of twenty years of Nationalist rule in Nanking K'ung served as China's Finance Minister, and he, Chiang and another brother-in-law, Sung Tzu-wen (or T. V. Soong) (q.v.), his wife's younger brother, virtually monopolised the posts of Prime Minister, Deputy Prime Minister and Acting Prime Minister, as well as Minister of Finance, thereby dominating the political, financial and economic scene in China. For this reason K'ung, Chiang and Sung in company with the Chen brothers, Kuo-fu and Li-fu, became known as 'the Four Grandee Families' controlling China during the period which ended in Communist supremacy in 1949.
[2] Only two pages of one of the enclosures have been traced, and these are printed below.
[3] Luella Miner, American missionary, President of North China Union Woman's College, Peking. In 1908, as President of the Association for the Protection of Women and Children, she sought Morrison's help in rescuing the well-known calligrapher Wu Chih-ying (Mrs. J. Lien Ch'üan) from official persecution for her suspected involvement with the revolutionary heroine Ch'iu Chin (1875-1907), who had been executed the previous year for her anti-Manchu activities.
[4] In his reply on 9 April 1915 Morrison wrote: 'I am so sorry that I was absent from Peking when you tried to communicate with me,... It was a great pleasure to me to meet you in Peking. What you said to me impressed me greatly and when an opportunity was given to me, I did not fail to discuss the interesting proposition suggested by you, without of course referring in any way to you. I gather that my colleague Admiral Tsai also had the advantage of a conversation with you. When you return to Peking I hope you will not fail to come and see me. The information contained in your two excellently written papers is of great interest to me.'

that the facts and proposals written below may help to unite the nation so that a solid front may be presented to our enemy that this statement is given. The writer is aware that in doing this he is laying himself open to suspicion on the part both of the government and the revolutionists, but the duty is plain to make any sacrifice, even though it prove in vain to try to serve our endangered country.

Japan dares to make her unreasonable demands and to send over her armies because she thinks China is not united. With spies in every important city of China and Chinese refugees in Japan who are supported by Japanese 'friends', supplied with funds and munitions of war from hidden sources, and guarded by Japanese police and special detectives, a ready-made revolt can be imported into any Chinese center where it may help Japan's schemes. It is not necessary that this revolt should be strong enough to overthrow the central government. It will serve Japan's purpose to have it create a disturbance in some place where she has property or where one or two Japanese can be mobbed for the good of their country. Then she can send her gunboats to protect her interests, and her troops can take possession of any place where her political strategy has paved the way. China may refuse to sign the twenty-one demands, but Japan's great continental scheme, which includes even India, will be only delayed, not thwarted, if she can nourish local insurrections or import ready-made ones. For the broad success of this scheme it is necessary that she have under her protection and influence prominent Chinese revolutionists or suspects. Many of them have been carried to Japan under Japanese protection. If the refugee has name, prestige, and the confidence of wealthy Chinese at home or abroad, contributions can be sent to him. This is double gain to the Japanese for it is not necessary for them to furnish so many funds to such an influential refugee, and exaggerated reports of his power and popularity, industriously circulated in Western lands through a subsidized press, will help hypnotize the world into the belief that it is necessary for the peace of the universe that Japan should police China. This means the domination of China in the end.

The name and prestige of Dr. Sun Yat-Sen are worth more to Japan than several divisions of an army. Since his arrival in that country from Formosa, to which place he withdrew during the second revolution, Dr. Sun has been flattered, supplied with a house and funds, and guarded as carefully as if he were an emperor. He moves about with seeming freedom, but always followed by detectives furnished by the Japanese Government. Every possible means is taken to keep him in the country. Less important personages are the ones to send to China to work out the details of Japan's schemes.

In order to thwart Japan's great strategy it is most important that Dr. Sun should leave Japan, as he seems to have many followers who will continue to give him moral and financial support as long as he remains in Japan. No other known revolutionist has sufficient prestige to command this support.

Japan can work her schemes far less easily through men who are universally believed to be seeking either name or wealth for themselves.[1]

[...]

The President has graciously granted an amnesty to all revolutionists who will confess their faults and pledge loyalty to the government, and many have accepted this offer, especially since the attack on Ch'ing-tao and the plain manifestation of Japanese designs on the country. Dr. Sun has made no declaration. The Japanese by showing him special attention and making him enticing promises are trying to prevent his leaving the country. Pride and a mistaken loyalty to long-cherished ideals or delusions make it extremely hard for Dr. Sun to accept the common terms of a general pardon under the present circumstances.

If President Yuan would write a personal letter to Dr. Sun urging his return to this country to work to accomplish the union of four hundred million Chinese against Japanese aggressions, it would greatly strengthen the government. If Dr. Sun came, however weak he may be, and however impractical his schemes, all his followers would be won with him to wholehearted support of the government. There would be no soil left in which Japan could sow her seeds of sedition. While there might be a difference of opinion as to the amount of strength which Dr. Sun could add to the government, there is no doubt that, deprived of this tool, the power of Japan for mischief-making would be greatly lessened.

Dr. Sun, though graciously invited to return, might refuse. In case he went to another country, Japan would lose her most valuable tool, if he remained in Japan and promoted her schemes against China in this crisis, after it was known that the President had invited him to return, he would lose the confidence of all truly patriotic Chinese and could no longer be 'worked' effectively by Japan. If Dr. Sun returns to China, and all factions work harmoniously to save the country, the name of President Yuan will shine with brighter lustre, and the world will learn to respect China and the Chinese. So China may escape the fate of Korea and Mexico. Dr. Sun should be given adequate protection, for if his personal safety should be endangered, whether the cause lay in China or Japan, Japan could find a hundred tools to take the place of the one she had lost, and would find a divided China ready to her hand.

The writer of this statement through American and other friends, had interviews with Dr. Sun in Shanghai before the second revolution (in which he was dissuaded from taking any active part) and in Tokyo during the past year, when the writer was engaged in religious work in that city. He is convinced through these interviews and others reported by American friends

---

[1] This statement appears to have consisted of three pages in close type, of which the second is missing. This footnote marks the end of the first page, while what follows forms the third page.

that Dr. Sun truly desires the good of his country, but because of some mistaken ideas he can easily be 'worked' by the Japanese. After the Japanese had invaded Shantung to attack Ch'ing-tao in reply to the remark 'You ought to be in Peking helping the President and your country,' Dr. Sun said, 'I have no power. It is not for me to say.' When conversing with an American friend on the situation in China he wept. Some think that his dangers and anxieties have affected his nervous system. The facts in regard to Japanese machinations and their manipulation of Dr. Sun are known to the writer through personal investigations and from reliable sources. He feels it his duty to report the situation to those who are in close connection with the government, and asks that what has been written be considered as strictly private and confidential.

751. To Ts'ai T'ing-kan

[Peking] 9 April 1915

My dear Admiral,

[...]

The Japanese are continuing their attacks upon me. They seem to think that I am in some degree responsible for the fact – the very interesting fact – that the entire British press is supporting China against the Japanese demands, including *The Times* which at the beginning was misled by the Japanese communications in Tokio, and the *Daily Telegraph* which for nearly two years has been attacking President Yuan and the Chinese authorities in the most violent manner. Excellent telegrams are being sent by Mr. David Fraser controverting the Japanese allegations.

In this connection it may interest you to know that in London on the 11th February when *The Times* received on the same day two contradictory messages, the correct from Donald in Peking, the misleading from Fraser in Tokio, they were in a difficulty and appealed to Mr. Alfred Sze[1] to throw light on the question. Unfortunately Mr. Sze was unable to do so; he could give no assistance or information. I am afraid that the reason was that he himself had been kept in ignorance.

The Times, unable to get information at the Chinese Legation, approached the Japanese Embassy, who gave them precisely the same information as that given to Fraser in Tokio. In these circumstances *The Times* accepted the Japanese statement which seemed to have confirmation, and regarded the statement telegraphed from Peking, of which they could get no confirmation in London, as exaggerated.

You see that Mr. Oishi,[2] the former leader of one of the chief parties in

---

[1] At this time Chinese Minister in London.
[2] Ōishi Masami (1855–1935), Japanese politician, advocate of an aggressive foreign policy for Japan. Over a period of more than forty years, until his retirement in 1915, he was

Japan, is urging that I be removed from my position with the Chinese Government and that a Japanese be appointed in my stead.

When I read such attacks as these upon a well-known Englishman like myself I sometimes wish I had signed a longer contract.

[...]

Very sincerely yours
[G. E. Morrison]

752. From Ts'ai T'ing-kan

[Peking] 24 April 1915

My dear Doctor,

The enclosed documents will give you a peep into the underworking of the Japanese who are in league with the rebels. If Sun Wen succeeds China is finished.

I have sent copies to Sir John. The correspondents may like to know something of what has been going on.

Yours sincerely
Tsai Ting Kan

Enclosure I to Letter No. 752: *Memorandum, 20 April 1915*

It has been reported that the Chinese rebels in Japan in the name of the 'Political Reform Party of the Republic of China' through the introduction of Kaichiro Yoshigawa,[1] a native of the District of Fukuoka, has obtained a loan of 3,000,000 yen from a wealthy merchant. It was decided that the revolution shall be completed within two months, that the first instalment of 1,000,000 yen should be paid in cash and that the balance should be made in the form of ammunitions to be supplied to the rebels at various places where the revolution is to start.

The Agreement between the two parties was drawn up in the beginning of April and was signed by Sun Wen, head of the revolutionists, Huang Yi ou,[2] representative and son of Huang Hsing, Chen Chi mei, Tai Tien

---

active in Japanese politics and helped to organise several political parties, the last being the Rikken Dōshikai in 1913. Immediately before that he was a member of the Kokumintō, the nationalist party.

[1] Yasukawa Keiichirō (1849–1934), Japanese industrialist, owner of coal mines in Fukuoka and a financial backer of Tōyama Mitsuru, the right-wing extremist adventurer. He played host to Sun Yat-sen when Sun visited Japan in 1913.

[2] Huang Yi-ou (b. 1893), the eldest son of Huang Hsing, he later worked in the Government set up by Sun Yat-sen in Kwangtung in 1917, and afterwards became a Councillor in the Tientsin Municipal Government when the city was made a Special Municipality. After the establishment of the Nationalist Government in Nanking in 1928 he was made a member of its Legislative Yüan.

chou,[1] Chu Cheng,[2] Wang Tung,[3] Li Keng yuan,[4] Hu Han ming, Hsiung

[1] The pen name of Tai Chi-t'ao or Tai Chuan-hsien (1891-1949), Chinese journalist and Republican politician. A Law graduate from Japan, on returning to China he was active in the anti-Government press, and after 1912 became a Private Secretary to Sun Yat-sen, remaining with him until 1925. One of the early students of Marxism, he was to become a strong opponent of cooperation between the Kuomintang and the Communist Party. Regarding himself, and being regarded by the right wing of the Kuomintang, as the authoritative interpreter of the teachings of Sun Yat-sen, he became the foremost anti-communist protagonist within the Kuomintang, and by associating himself with what became known as the 'Western Hills' Clique, the extreme right wing of the party, was a power behind Chiang Kai-shek's purge of Communists in 1927, and Chiang's domination in the subsequent Republican rule. As President of the Examination Yüan from its inception in 1928 until his resignation in 1948, he helped to impose strict ideological control over the civil service. He committed suicide, a disillusioned man, in Canton, shortly before the Kuomintang was swept by the Communist forces from Mainland China. At the time referred to he had fled to Japan, together with Sun and other revolutionaries, after the abortive 'Second Revolution'.

[2] Chu Cheng (1876-1951), Chinese journalist and Republican politician. He joined the T'ung-meng hui while studying Law in Japan, and later worked on pro-revolutionary Chinese-language newspapers in Singapore and Rangoon. On returning to China he was active in the revolutionary underground movement in his native Hupeh Province. He served briefly as Vice-Minister of the Interior in the Provisional Government set up by Sun Yat-sen in Nanking in 1912, and was to be Minister of the same portfolio in Sun's government in Canton in 1921. He was in charge of the Woosung Forts north of Shanghai during the 'Second Revolution' and on defeat escaped to Japan, where he was staying at the time referred to. In 1916 he returned to Shantung and with the support and under the cover of the Japanese occupation army in Shantung he assumed the title of Commander-in-Chief of the North-Eastern Army, which attacked Yüan Shih-k'ai's forces and occupied Weihsien and several other neighbouring towns. This became known as the Weihsien Insurrection. A rightist in the Kuomintang, Chu was a member of the so-called 'Western Hills' Clique, to which belonged the party's anti-Communist extremists who gathered together at the Western Hills outside Peking after Sun Yat-sen's death in 1925 to declare their opposition to cooperation between the Nationalist Party (Kuomintang) and the Communist Party, and to demand the expulsion of members of the latter. He had control of China's judicial system during the greater part of the Nationalist regime, from 1932 to 1948, as President of the Judicial Yüan, one of the five branches of the Central Government. In 1947, in order to give some semblance of democratic practice, he was asked to offer himself as an alternative candidate in the first Presidential election, in which Chiang Kai-shek was duly elected. He escaped the following year with the Nationalist Government to Taiwan where he died three years later.

[3] Wang T'ung, Chinese sailor, one of the earliest members of the Chung-hua Ko-ming tang organized by Sun Yat-sen in Tokyo in September 1913.

[4] Li Keng-yüan (1879-1965), Chinese soldier and Republican politician, a graduate of the Shikan Gakkō. On returning to China he became an instructor in the military academy in K'un-ming, and took part in the declaration of independence of his native Yunnan Province after the Wuchang Uprising and became the province's Deputy *Tutu*. He also participated in the anti-Yüan campaign of 1915-16, and after Yüan's death was appointed Governor of Shensi Province. He later served as an army commander in Kwangtung but retired to Shanghai after the Kwangsi troops under Ts'en Ch'un-hsüan, whom he supported, were defeated by those of Kwangtung in 1920. He entered the Peking Government in 1922 by becoming first Acting Minister then Minister of Agriculture and Commerce.

Ke wu,[1] Po Wen wei, Hsu Chung chih,[2] Hu Ying[3] and Tan Jen feng[4] (who had just arrived at Tokyo from the Straits Settlements), representing Tsen Chun

[1] Hsiung K'e-wu (b. 1881), Chinese soldier and Republican politician, a graduate of Japan's Shikan Gakkō. He participated in revolutionary uprisings against the Manchu Government and in 1915 took part in the campaign against Yüan's monarchical scheme. He became, in August 1916, Garrison Commander of Chungking, and in February 1919 Military Governor of his native Szechwan Province, a post he held until November the following year. Though one of the few Szechwanese military leaders who fought on the Republican front line, he was relegated to a sinecure position during the rule of the Nationalist Government in Nanking under Chiang Kai-shek and lived in retirement in his native province. There in 1949, on the approach of Communist forces, he pledged his support for the People's Republic, and has since served on military and administrative committees in the South-Western Region, of which Szechwan forms a part.

[2] Hsü Ch'ung-chih (?1887-1965), Chinese soldier and Republican politician, a grandson of Hsü Ying-k'uei (d. 1903), a Minister and the Viceroy of Fukien and Chekiang (1898-1903) under the Manchus. Hsü Ch'ung-chih was a graduate of the Shikan Gakkō. As a Commander of the Fukien forces he participated in the taking of Nanking after the Wuchang Uprising. He also took part in the 'Second Revolution', and fled to Japan after its failure. When the Kuomintang was reorganised in 1914 into the Chung-hua Ko-ming tang (Chinese Revolutionary Party) he became Director of its Military Affairs Bureau. During the anti-Yüan campaign in 1915 he returned to Shanghai and became the Chief of Staff under Ch'en Ch'i-mei, and was involved in the abortive naval uprising. In 1917 he joined the Government set up in Canton under Sun Yat-sen, in which he became a leading military figure until he was ousted in 1926 by his erstwhile subordinate, Chiang Kai-shek. After the overthrow of the Peking regime in 1928 and the establishment of the Nationalist Government in Nanking, to both of which he had made a large contribution, he was relegated to sinecures.

[3] Hu Ying (1884-1933), Republican politician. A founding member of the T'ung-meng hui, he became head of the Foreign Affairs Department in the Provisional Government set up in Wuchang after the successful uprising in that city in October 1911. In 1912 he was appointed *Tutu* of Shantung by the Republican Government set up in Nanking that year, but did not take up the post, the province being then under the military control of Peking. He was instead appointed by the Peking Government as Commissioner for the Colonisation of Tsinghai and Sinkiang Provinces.

[4] T'an Jen-feng (?1860-1920), Chinese Republican politician. A native of Hunan, he had worked after the Boxer Uprising with Secret Societies in his home province, and later in neighbouring Kiangsi and Kwangsi Provinces, for the overthrow of the Manchu regime. When discovered, he escaped arrest by going to Japan, where he joined the T'ung-meng hui. After spending two years in exile in South-East Asia planning attacks on the border provinces from Indo-China, he returned to help organise the Central China branch of the T'ung-meng hui which was responsible for the Wuchang Uprising of October 1911. He became Defence Commander of the city of Wuchang after the departure of Huang Hsing following the fall of Han-yang to the Northern troops and thereby stemmed the tide of defeat and saved the situation in central China. He became Army Commander in the Yangtse Valley after the establishment of the Republican Government in Nanking in 1912 and as a close associate and fellow-provincial of Sung Chiao-jen, became most vocal in the condemnation of Yüan Shih-k'ai after Sung's murder. He was also the strongest advocate, as opposed to Huang Hsing, of overthrowing the Peking regime by force. He fled to Japan after the failure of the 'Second Revolution'. As a man of strong views and quick temper, he disapproved of many of the measures of Sun Yat-sen, and shunned the Government Sun set up in Canton in 1917. He retired to Shanghai where he remained until his death.

hsuan,[1] Li Lieh chun and Chen Chiung ming.[2] There were over 20 signatures and seals. It was agreed that the loan was to be redeemed on the first opportunity after the revolution becomes a success. A payment of 7,000,000 yen was made in cash on the 4th instant and was taken over by Tan Jen feng, Hu Han ming, Hsiung Ke wu and Li Keng yuan. In the name of the 'Political Reform Party' Tan Jen feng was appointed *Great Tutuh* or Generalissimo of Kwangtung and Kwangsi with Hu Han ming as assistant; Hsiung Ke wu as *Great Tutuh* or Generalissimo of Szechuan, Yunnan and Kueichow with Li Keng yuan as assistant. They are now on their way to their respective destinations, each with over a hundred followers. Chen Chiung ming is to reside at Hongkong and from there to render assistance to the rebels.

Enclosure II to Letter No. 752: *A Translation of a Secret Agreement made between Sun Wen (Sun Yat Sen) and the Japanese*[3]

In order to preserve the peace in the Far East, it is necessary for China and Japan to enter into an offensive and defensive alliance whereby in

[1] Ts'en Ch'un-hsüan (1861–1933), Chinese Imperial official and Republican politician. The son of Ts'en Yü-ying (q.v.), he was one of the most prominent officials during the last years of the Manchu Dynasty, having served, among other posts, as Minister of Communications and Viceroy of Liangkwang (1903–6). First coming into prominence during the Boxer Uprising through his services to the Empress-Dowager Tz'u-hsi, he was the highest-ranking Imperial official to advocate abdication by the Manchu Emperor after the Wuchang Uprising, a course of action which was attributed by his detractors to his rivalry with Yüan Shih-k'ai rather than to republican convictions. After Yüan assumed the Presidency Ts'en became a leading figure in the republican opposition in the South, active in all the anti-Yüan campaigns from the 'Second Revolution' to the Constitutional Protection Movement in 1917. Under his leadership a government was set up in that year in Chao-ch'ing in Kwangtung. With the military support of Li Keng-yüan and Lu Jung-t'ing, his erstwhile subordinate, he came eventually to dominate the Military Government set up under the leadership of Sun Yat-sen in Canton, and replaced Sun as head of the Government in 1918 until the Kwangsi forces were defeated by those of Kwangtung in 1920. He then retired to Shanghai where he died thirteen years later.

[2] Ch'en Chiung-ming (1878–1933), Chinese soldier. He was appointed Governor of Kwangtung in June 1913 after Yüan Shih-k'ai had dismissed Hu Han-min from the post, but Ch'en was himself dismissed the following month for siding with the revolutionaries in the 'Second Revolution'. He spent the next two years in exile, mostly in Singapore, but returned to China at the end of 1915 after the province of Yunnan declared war on Yüan Shih-k'ai. After Yüan's death and the removal of his henchman Lung Chi-kuang from Canton, Ch'en helped Sun Yat-sen to set up the Military Government there in 1917, in which he became Chief-of-Staff and Minister of War. However, he revolted against Sun in 1922. Consequently he has been regarded by many as a traitor to the Revolution, and died in exile in Hong Kong. A man of great ability, Ch'en also sponsored numerous cultural activities with which many prominent Chinese intellectuals were connected, including Ch'en Tu-hsiu (1879–1942), founder and first leader of the Chinese Communist Party, Ch'en Kung-po (1892–1946), another founding member of the party and later a leading figure in the Wang Ching-wei (1883–1944) Puppet Government in Nanking, and Hu Shih (1891–1962) one of the leaders in the modern culture movement.

[3] This is a translation of the original Chinese text published in the *Ya-hsi-ya pao* on 18 April 1915. Its authority has been denied by Kuomintang sources.

case of war with any other nation or nations Japan shall supply the military force while China shall be responsible for the finances. It is impossible for the present Chinese Government to work hand in hand with the Japanese Government nor does the Japanese Government desire to cooperate with the former. Consequently Japanese politicians and merchants who have the peace of the Far East at heart are inclined to assist China in her reconstruction. For this object the following Agreement is entered into by the two parties:

1. Before an uprising is started, Terao,[1] Okura,[2] Tsuji Karoku[3] and their associates shall provide the necessary funds, weapons and military force, but the funds so provided must not exceed 1,500,000 yen and rifles not to exceed 100,000 pieces.

2. Before the uprising takes place the loan shall be temporarily secured by 10,000,000 yen worth of bonds to be issued by Sun (Sun Yat Sen). It shall however be secured afterwards by all the movable properties of the occupied territory. (See Article 14 of this Agreement)

[1] Terao Tōru (1858–1925), Japanese jurist. He had been a judge, an official in the Japanese Foreign Service, and a teacher of International Law at Tokyo Imperial University. He first came into contact with Chinese when he set up a school for young Chinese students who were attracted to Japan in great numbers after the Russo-Japanese War. Through this and through his connection with Miyazaki Torazō and Inukai Tsuyoshi he abandoned his university post to join the Provisional Government set up by Sun Yat-sen in Nanking after the Wuchang Uprising. As an Adviser he was largely responsible for the drafting of the Provisional Constitution which was formally promulgated by Sun on 11 March 1912. After the failure of the 'Second Revolution', a College of Law for Chinese students was established in Tokyo in February 1914 under the nominal patronage of Sun Yat-sen; and Terao, who was active throughout this period as a liaison between Sun and his Japanese supporters, was made Principal of the College.

[2] Ōkura Kihachirō (1837–1928), Japanese industrialist who, having set out as an apprentice, ended up one of Japan's wealthiest and most powerful men. His contact with China dated from 1874 when he was engaged in supplying the Japanese forces led by Saigō Tsugumichi in the invasion of Formosa. His business ventures in China, however, did not begin until twenty years later when, in 1902 at the age of 66, he began his continental adventure by making a loan to the Hanyang Iron Company. From that year until his death twenty-six years later at the age of 92 he built up a business and industrial empire in China, including coal and iron mining, timber, paper, oil, tanning, textiles, power and transportation, and farming, stretching from Hunan, Kiangsi and Hupeh in the south to Mongolia and Manchuria in the north. Among his many interests in China, two were particularly well known: his connection with the Han-Yeh-Ping Company which provided the basis of Group III of the Twenty-One Demands Japan presented to China in January 1915, and his control of the Pen-ch'i Iron Mine and Fu-shun Coal Mine in Southern Manchuria, two of China's richest and largest ore deposits. Using the method of joint enterprise, in which he provided the funds on the security of the resources in question, Ōkura came to exercise a penetrating influence over China's industry and finance. The fact that he had supplied ammunition and money to the southern Republicans under Sun Yat-sen in their struggle against the Central Government did not affect his relation with Peking, and on the occasion of his golden wedding anniversary, leading Chinese in diverse professions, from the head of state downwards, publicly joined in the celebration.

[3] Tsuji Karoku, Japanese soldier, a member of the Japanese General Staff.

3. The funds from the present loan and military force to be provided are for operations in the provinces South of the Yellow River viz; Yunnan, Kweichow, Hunan, Hupeh, Szechuen, Kiangsi, Anhwei, Kiangsu, Chekiang, Fukien, Kuangsi and Kuangtung. If it is intended to invade the Northern provinces North of the Yellow River, Tsuji Karoku and his associates shall participate with the revolutionists in all deliberations connected with such operations.

4. The Japanese Volunteer force shall be allowed from the date of their enrolment active service pay in accordance with the regulations of the Japanese Army. After the occupation of a place, the two parties will settle the mode of rewarding the meritorious and compensating the family of the killed, adopting the lost generous practice in vogue in China and Japan. In the case of the killed, compensation for each soldier shall, at the least, be more than 1000 yen.

5. Wherever the revolutionary army might be located the Japanese military officers accompanying these expeditions shall have the right to advise a continuation or cessation of operations.

6. After the revolutionary army has occupied a region and strengthened its defences, all industrial undertakings and railway construction and the like, not mentioned in the Treaties with other foreign powers shall be worked with joint capital together with the Japanese.

7. On the establishment of a new Government in China, all Japan's demands on China shall be recognised by the new Government as settled and binding.

8. All Japanese military officers holding the rank of Captain or higher ranks engaged by the Chinese revolutionary army shall have the privilege of being continued in their employment without a limit as to date and shall have the right to ask to be thus employed.

9. The loan shall be paid over in three instalments. The first instalment will be 400,000 yen, the second instalment [   ][1] yen and the third instalment [   ][2] yen. After the first instalment is paid over, Okura who advances the loan shall have the right to appoint men to supervise the expenditure of the money.

10. The Japanese shall undertake to deliver all arms and ammunition in the Districts of Jih Chao and Haichow (in Shantung and Kiangsu, South of Kiaochou).

11. The payment of the first instalment of the loan shall be made not later than three days after the signing of this Agreement.

12. All the employed Japanese military officers and Japanese volunteers are in duty bound to obey the orders of the commander of the revolutionary army.

13. The commander of the revolutionary army shall have the right to

[1] Blank in the original. [2] Blank in the original.

send back to Japan those Japanese military officers and Japanese volunteers who disobey his orders and their passage money shall not be paid if such decision meets with the approval of three or more of the Japanese who accompany the revolutionary force.

14. All the commissariat departments in the occupied territory must employ Japanese experts to cooperate in their management.

15. This Agreement takes effect immediately it is signed by the two parties.

The foregoing fifteen articles have been discussed several times between the two parties and signed by them in February. The first instalment of 400,000 yen has been paid according to the terms of this Agreement.

753. From Ts'ai T'ing-kan

[Peking] 1 May 1915

My dear Doctor,

I have much pleasure in returning your Agreement. The President has written on it this afternoon the words: 'After the completion of this agreement it shall be renewed for another five years.'[1] His private seal is affixed. Today is also the day in which the Chinese reply is given to the Japanese demands. The two facts will link themselves to your memory.

Yours sincerely
Tsai Ting Kan

754. To Ts'ai T'ing-kan

[Peking] 10 May 1915

My dear Admiral,

I have sent over to Mr. Ju the enclosed Memorandum asking him to translate it and send it in to the President.

This morning I have been informed that counsels are divided as to the expediency of sending in a detailed statement of China's case now or waiting until after the Treaty[2] has been signed.

In view of the fact that the Japanese statement has been published all over the world, any delay in sending in a counter statement would, I believe, be most unfortunate. I hope you will agree with me that the statement should be prepared and issued as quickly as possible.

[...]

[1] The Agreement set out the terms of Morrison's appointment as Political Adviser for five years from 1 August 1912. In accordance with the President's endorsement it was to be reviewed for another five years on 16 April 1917, and to be terminated on 30 September 1922.

[2] The Treaty embodying Japan's Twenty-One Demands was not signed until 25 May 1915.

I have tried several times to-day to get on to you on the telephone, but have not been successful.

Best wishes to you

Very sincerely yours
[G. E. Morrison]

Enclosure to Letter No. 754: *Memorandum urging the immediate publication of a detailed statement by the Chinese Government in reply to the statement by the Japanese Government already published throughout the world, 10 May 1915*

With regret I learn that there is hesitation on the part of the Wai Chiao Pu to issue a detailed statement recording the facts of the recent negotiations with the Japanese Government.

The reason given for this hesitation is the fear that such a communication may be distasteful to the Japanese Government.

To delay any longer the presentation to the world of China's case is to confirm the misleading impression that China has no case worth stating: its presentation would counteract the influence of the Japanese communiqué and would be in accordance with correct diplomatic procedure. The dignity and honour of the country demand that the case should be drawn up without delay and given at once the same widespread publicity as has been given to the Japanese statement.

I respectfully submit that this is the proper course to follow.

G. E. Morrison

755. From F. E. Taylor

Shanghai 14 May 1915

My dear Morrison,

I have heard nothing of you for too long. You must have had a strenuous time lately during the crisis, and I congratulate you on whatever share you had in guiding the Chinese to a settlement that seems to be much better than might have been. I presume that there may be modifications after the war, when others can take a hand in the game. I am told that the Japanese are very anti-British at heart, and their insolence in Kiaochow is said to be intolerable. They no doubt realise that we are the chief obstacle to their dream of Asiatic hegemony, and I expect that there will some day have to be a combination against them, or they will become too dangerous.

I send you a proof before publication of my Trade Report. You need not tell anyone that you have it, because it has not yet been passed by the Shui Wu Ch'u. But I know you are interested, and I should be glad of your criticisms and suggestions. The graphs that will be appended are quite novel and interesting. There are a few verbal alterations to be made before printing.

Feeling here against the Germans is now suddenly running very high, and they are being elbowed out of all clubs. Matters may go still further, as there is actually talk of driving them out of Shanghai!! All this comes about in consequence of the *Lusitania* incident,[1] which seems to me very British in its evidence of our dullness and want of imagination. Much worse and more shameful things for which there has been no excuse whatever have been quietly put up with. Atrocities in Belgium, bombardment of Scarborough and other towns, dropping of bombs on unfortified places, murders of women and children without military excuse, use of asphyxiating gas, poisoning of wells, etc, have all been merely characterised as 'frightfulness'; but because the Germans, after giving fair warning, succeed in sinking a steamer full of ammunition and supplies for their enemies, which they had no other means of stopping, the English get really angry at last. Well, the madder we get the better, so that is all to the good. We shall perhaps realise in time that we are fighting the ancient Goths disguised in a thin veneer of civilization which in time of peace more or less covers up their innate barbarism, and who are more of a nuisance and more of a danger in Europe than the Turks.

I am delighted to have my old job, and am very comfortable, though I should like to be more busy. Drop me a line when you have time.

Yours ever
F. E. Taylor

756. From J. A. C. Smith[2]

Yen an fu, Shenshi 19 May 1915

Dear Dr. Morrison,

I do not doubt you are a busy man these days when so much advice is needed. Still I know you are intensely interested in what is happening in the interior of this country as well, and possibly a line on Opium may not be out of place [...]

Opium growing was almost entirely abolished in this province of Shensi last year, and in the autumn, when it is sown in the Southern and more fertile part of the province, strict proclamations were issued forbidding its growth. In late February and early March, however, the people were given to understand (not by proclamation, but secretly) that they might grow it as freely as they liked, a heavy tax to be levied on the acreage. I personally met

---

[1] The S.S. *Lusitania*, a British passenger liner, was sunk on 7 May 1915 by a German submarine off the coast of Ireland resulting in great loss of life to citizens of many countries, including many Americans. The incident became a subject of fervent anti-German propaganda in America as well as among the Allied Powers.

[2] J. A. Creasey Smith, British missionary with the English Baptist Mission in Shensi. He was one of Morrison's sources of information on conditions in Shensi Province and surrounding districts.

two deputies sent by Lu Chien Chang[1] the *Chiang Chün*, to see Mr. Shorrock[2] the Senior English Missionary at Sianfu, to ask him to be silent about this matter and not report it to Minister or Consul, as Lu said he must do it to raise funds to pay his troops. Mr. Shorrock refused to make any promise of any nature regarding the matter – Spring sown poppy was now largely put in the ground and I personally have seen many thousands of *mou* of land growing it during this last few days.

About the 1st of May, new proclamations were issued threatening the direst penalties on all who grow it and ordering the instant plowing up of all sown. This after I had seen in the P[eking] & T[ientsin] Times a note of the impeachment of the Governor Lu of this province, for allowing its growth. The opium is still growing however and is being cultivated, the plants separated etc. This is not secretly, but openly done alongside the big main roads. This is evidently by orders of the Provincial Government for each *Hsien* or small town has its Opium Suppression Bureau, with soldiers and officials in abundance at their offices, many of them smoking the drug themselves, yet the opium grows within bowshot of the offices.

Lu Chien Chang is a very heavy smoker himself, he is reputed to consume 2 ozs daily. He certainly accepted a gift of 20,000 ozs from Chang Yün San,[3] Shensi's Brigadier-General and Ko lao hwei leader, when he arrived in Sianfu a year ago. Yesterday, in this city of Yen an fu, men were paraded on the streets with paper notices stuck on their backs and carrying gongs which they were beating, and accompanied by soldiers, a punishment for selling opium in small quantities – whilst well-to-do shop-keepers were heavily fined. Yet within 100 yards of the city wall opium is growing in abundance.

[...]

Kind regards to you. I trust you and your wife and son are well.

Sincerely yours
J. A. C. Smith

---

[1] Lu Chien-chang (1872–1918), Chinese soldier. As Garrison Commander in Shantung and then in Kwangtung under the Manchu Dynasty he was known for his strict anti-opium measures. He was a strong supporter of Yüan Shih-k'ai when Yüan became Republican President, and Lu became a Director of Yüan's martial Court and was responsible in that position for the death of many revolutionaries and revolutionary suspects. He was appointed Military Governor of Shensi Province in June 1914, but was defeated by anti-Yüan forces in June 1916 and compelled to flee the province. In June 1918, accused of inciting the bandits of Shansi and Shantung against the Manchurian army under Hsü Shu-cheng (q.v.), he was arrested and summarily shot by Hsü. His death was avenged by Feng Yü-hsiang, a relative by marriage, when, on 29 December 1925, Hsü was intercepted in a train on his way from Peking to Tientsin by Feng's troops, and put to death.

[2] The Rev. A. G. Shorrock, British missionary, head of the English Baptist Mission in Shensi.

[3] Garrison Commander of Northern Shensi from June 1914 to June 1915.

757. To F. E. Taylor

[Peking] 19 May 1915

My dear Taylor,

Some time ago I received a letter from you[1] in which you spoke of the vacancy in the Statistical Department, Shanghai, and expressed some doubt as to whether the post would be given to you. But here in Peking there was never any doubt at all that you would be asked to resume a post you had formerly filled with so much distinction.

On Sunday I was out snipe shooting with Aglen, and in the course of our walk he told me that you had just completed a most interesting Trade Report. In the morning when I went into Peking – I am now living in my cottage in the country – I found your letter and the proof sheets of your Report.

I think it is excellent in every way. But there are two matters which I wish you could find space to speak about, for your Report is primarily one of instruction to the Chinese. You say nothing about morphia. In discussing the reduction in the consumption of opium, you might, I suggest, profitably devote a few paragraphs to the condemnation of the traffic of morphia which is assuming such alarming dimensions. In 1913 evidence shows that to the Leased Territory alone Japanese dealers imported not less than $6\frac{1}{4}$ tons of the hydrochlorate of morphia. It was manufactured mainly in England but partly in Germany and Austria and was imported by registered post via the Siberian Railway to Kobe and Osaka.

The manufacture of morphia is becoming also an important industry in Formosa, where its extraction is being carried on under direct Government supervision. This morphia is wholly prepared for Chinese consumption. Moreover as one quarter to one half a grain is an average dose the number of doses which can be reckoned in tons is prodigious.

I am moreover informed that the entire stock of Persian opium available in the Far East was purchased by the Formosan Government.

That is one matter. Then there is another matter. You once more draw attention, as you frequently have done in the past, to the need of developing China's exports and to the need of railway construction in order to facilitate the movement of trade. You also draw attention to the large quantities of silver locked up in Shanghai and Hongkong. A project is now submitted to the Chinese Government by the Central China Railways, who have the concession for the construction of the Sinyang–Pukow Railway, whereby it is proposed in view of the impossibility of floating the Railway Loan in gold in Europe, to float it as a silver loan in China.

The scheme seems so worthy of support that you would do a service if you could give it a few words of encouragement, especially as such encouragement would be in harmony with the recommendations in your Report.

[...]

[1] Not printed.

Three months ago I spoke to the President about the need for taking some steps to induce the people to invest in Loans for the construction of their own railways, urging that Silver Loans should be raised in China and quotations be obtained on the Shanghai Stock Exchange, in order to bring into circulation the great accumulation of silver that, in default of remunerative investment, was being hoarded in the Shanghai Banks. A few words from you in this sense would be of great service just now.

I have enjoyed reading your Report very much. You will I hope, long continue in your present post and postpone indefinitely your return to Tasmania.

With best wishes and many thanks

Ever faithfully yours
[G. E. Morrison]

758. To E. M. Gull[1]

[Peking] 21 May 1915

My dear Gull,

Many thanks for your long letter of the 17th. It was very good of you to write to me so fully at the present time when you must have every minute occupied. I must congratulate you upon having so quickly qualified to fill the editorial chair of the most important British organ in Eastern Asia.

With regard to your suggestion that I should write an article on Chinese Finance, I am sorry that I cannot do so. Please just tell the *Guardian* that it is quite impossible for me to do so at the present time, though I am flattered by their request that I should do so.

The difficulty I find is this. Under Chou Tzu-chi there was a marked improvement in the conduct of the Ministry, but the new Minister, Chou Hsueh-hsi, although not an old man – he is not much above forty – has reverted to the old-time methods of the Chinese mandarin and is removing from office one by one the men who had acquired knowledge and experience under the previous Minister and is filling up the vacancies with his own henchmen and fellow-provincials.

To cite three instances of methods which I cannot condemn too strongly,

[1] Edward Manico Gull (b. 1883), British journalist, Correspondent of the *Manchester Guardian* in China. He also contributed to the American *New York Evening Post, Chicago Daily News,* and *Times Democrat*. He was at this time serving as Acting Editor of the *North China Daily News and Herald* during the absence of its regular Editor O. M. Green in 1915–16. He was also Editor of the *British Chamber of Commerce Journal* in Shanghai, which, according to Morrison, he helped to change from a 'rag' into a respectable publication. He was the author of a number of books published between 1933 and 1947 on Chinese economic problems and British interests in the Far East.

he has removed the highly competent head of the Salt Gabelle, Chang Hu;[1] he has removed the head of the Bank of China, F. M. Sah,[2] who was bringing the Bank to quite a marked state of efficiency, and he has removed the best financial commissioner in the provinces of China, Y.C. Chang,[3] who has been bravely fighting for the Central Government against much opposition in Wuhu.

To the posts vacated by these three men the new Minister has appointed highly incompetent officials whose only claim is that they are from the same province of Anhui.

This is most unsatisfactory and I could not write an article on finance without drawing attention to an evil system which I hoped had been abolished, and as I am in the service of the Chinese Government and render them all the help I can, it would be unseemly for me to attack them in an English newspaper. [...]

Very sincerely yours
[G. E. Morrison]

759. From A. H. Harris

Newchwang [Fengtien] 25 May 1915

My dear Morrison,

I must permit myself to send a line of congratulation to you and your colleagues on the wonders that you have done. You can justly feel a glow of pride that the ship of state has weathered the storm so well. Of course you are not yet out of the wood but some very useful clearing work has been done. I hope that Hankow mutterings will not bring down a storm.

Now that China seems to have secured a lease of sovereignty, albeit of a qualified kind, in these parts can she not consolidate it by sound and

[1] Chang Hu (b. 1875), Chinese Republican politician. He was appointed Vice-Minister of Finance and concurrently Director-General of the Salt Administration in September 1913. He was replaced in both positions by Kung Hsin-chan, a fellow provincial of the new Finance Minister, on 20 June 1915. In January 1919 he was re-appointed to his former post in the Salt Administration (January 1919 – October 1920), followed by two terms as Minister of Finance (December 1921 – March 1922 and August–November 1923).

[2] Sa Fu-mao (b. 1874), Chinese Imperial and Republican official. A graduate of Tientsin Naval College, he had served under the Manchu Dynasty as Acting Director-General of the Tao-ch'ing Railway and Director-General of Telegraphs at Canton. In July 1914 he succeeded T'ang Jui as Governor of the Bank of China but was replaced in that post by Li Shih-wei (d. 1927) on 12 April 1915, five weeks after Chou Hsüeh-hsi became Acting Minister of Finance. In July 1917 he was appointed Foreign Affairs Commissioner for Kiangsu, then in 1921 Director-General of the Mint in Shanghai, and later head of the Bureau of Industry in that city, holding both posts until 1922.

[3] Chang Yü-ch'üan, Customs Inspector of Wuhu from October 1913 to the end of March 1915. He was concurrently Foreign Affairs Commissioner of Anhwei Province. He was replaced in both positions by Hsü Ting-hsiang.

accepted Mixed Court regulations. Why is it that these hang fire? Does China think that their introduction would delay the abolition of ex-territoriality; and does she really think that ex-territoriality will be abolished!

Just as in 1905-8 her officials here did all in their power to hamper developments of these parts by foreign capital (witness only the absurd difficulties and restrictions at Mukden *re* residence and settlement) and with the disastrous results now seen, so now again she is putting off reforms that would, if introduced, consolidate her sovereign position. Take only mixed courts, currency reform under responsible expert advice, fixed civil list for her officials and adequate allowances.

This wonderful place here is of course a sort of no man's land: and I suppose awaits Japanese sovereignty before many material benefits come to it. Meanwhile the Chinese officials cling to what they can get and spend as little as they can; and who can really blame them however much one can see their short-comings and the great possibilities of the country. Japan will be in power one day and will make a fortune but there will be precious few foreigners living here in that day. Some 5 years will see the change of flag. Her military only 10 days ago were on the point of seizing the country up to Shanhaikuan!

Is America going to finance Japan? It looks something like it. Her great financier[1] is now in New York and his daughter living I believe, with the Schiffs.[2] If she does, there is a worse time awaiting China and all European interests and that too in the no[t] distant future. [...]

I suppose you saw Japan's morphia prohibition regulations for Manchuria! Nice look-see! [...]

Yours sincerely
A. H. Harris

[1] The reference is to Takata Shinzō (1852-1921), Japanese business man and financier, founder of Takata & Company, one of Japan's leading trading firms. He was at the time visiting New York, where his company had a branch office.

[2] Jacob Henry Schiff (1847-1920), American financier, related to two other well-known American Jewish financiers, being married to Theresa Loeb, the daughter of the head of Kuhn Loeb & Company in which Schiff became a partner, and father-in-law of Felix Warburg. He was also a Director of the Central Trust Company, Western Union Telegraph Company and of many other financial and industrial enterprises. He founded the Jewish Theological Seminary and the Semitic Museum in Harvard. His son, Mortimer Loeb Schiff (1877-1931), was also a financier and among other things a director of Kuhn Loeb & Company and of the Western Union Telegraph Company, as well as a member of the New York Stock Exchange.

760. To C. Clementi Smith

Peking 26 May 1915

My dear Sir Cecil,

It gave me great pleasure to receive your kind letter of 27th April.[1]

I quite agree with you that the title 'Excellent Crop' is an absurd one although it is a translation of the Chinese. The suggestion made by E. T. Williams, the American Secretary of the Legation, that the decoration should be styled 'the order of the Sheaf' was not accepted. In my case the decoration was given to me in June 1914.[2] I did not intend to make any application for permission to use it, but the Chinese noticing that I had not done so, officially communicated the fact of the Decoration to the Legation and the Legation made the application on my behalf.

We have been having a time of some anxiety. On the 18th January the Japanese submitted quite unexpectedly a series of 21 demands to the Chinese of a very comprehensive kind. They were submitted direct to the President, no previous intimation being given him that any such procedure was contemplated. The President was threatened with serious consequences if he disclosed their nature.

Having forced the Chinese to keep silence the Japanese then proceeded to disclose an expurgated version of the demands to the Ambassadors of England, France, Russia and America and to the Press correspondents as well as to the home Governments. No information was given to the British Minister in Peking by his Japanese colleague who throughout treated the British Legation as if it were the representative of an unfriendly, not of an allied, nation.

With the greatest difficulty the Chinese consented to allow the true version of the demands to become known. At first the Japanese deceived badly *The Times* correspondent, David Fraser, and through him *The Times* who accepted the untruthful Japanese statement and trounced the Chinese for their customary 'tergiversation'.

Gradually however the truth came out. Sir Edward Grey helped manfully to restrain the Japanese and the Agreement signed yesterday[3] was very much better than at one time seemed possible. The Chinese – at least the President does – know that they owe much to England in this case.

Here we wonder how long the alliance with Japan will survive after the war. Japanese militarism is the counterpart of German militarism. Every Japanese soldier, so we are told in Peking, from the highest to the lowest is imbued with the belief in the invincibility of German arms and inasmuch as a considerable proportion of Chinese military officers have come to a more

[1] Not printed.
[2] Morrison received the Chia-ho decoration twice, the first time, the Second Class of the order on 22 June 1913 (see p. 151 n.1), and the second time the First Class of the order on 21 September 1914.   [3] The Treaty embodying the Twenty-One Demands.

or less degree under the influence of German military officers or of Japanese military officers trained by German methods, it is not to be wondered at that in the army in China – such as it is – a feeling prevailed at the beginning that Germany would win.

That feeling has I believe as regards China long since been dispelled, but it still prevails in Japan and sometimes causes us some disquietude for we wonder if it is based upon information derived from Japanese observers at the front and whether they have learned things to our disadvantage of which we are kept in ignorance.

Japanese policy in China since the war began and her disregard of her treaty engagements with England are explicable if she believed that England would be defeated and would cease to be the great Power in the Far East. Only 10 days ago the Japanese lecturer at the Customs College here, Haraoka by name,[1] told his students that Germany would be victorious in the war, that Russia would shortly be demobilised and that England would be defeated!

As regards China things are not going well. Little if anything is accomplished. There is no constructive statesmanship, no continuity of purpose. An infinite number of things have to be done but all energy is devoted to the drawing up of interminable series of regulations. Reforms are spoken of, regulations to govern the reforms are drafted by the thousand and the people think that by the drafting of the regulations the reforms are accomplished.

Order is being fairly well maintained but there is still much brigandage outside the Great Wall and in the Canton Delta.

The Customs are doing well and the Salt is also yielding a good revenue but there is going to be a good deal of trouble about the salt – that is quite clear. A new Minister has been appointed,[2] a young man of the old school who in the old way is removing all men trained under his predecessor and is substituting untrained men from his own province. I have given him warning and he shows some alarm but he has already done injury and will, I am certain, come into conflict with the Quintuple Banks, Dane and the Legations.

Enemy trading still continues in China. It was inevitable seeing that the Hongkong and Shanghai Bank is so inextricably bound up with German trade in China, German trade is being kept alive in the interests of this Bank but now so much outcry is being raised that the policy is under reconsideration.

It is always one of the unexplained enigmas why the Chartered Bank, a purely British Bank, should be boycotted by the British Legation in China

[1] Haraoka Isamu. He joined the Chinese Maritime Customs as a language teacher in August 1911.
[2] Chou Hsüeh-hsi, who became Acting Minister of Finance on 5 March 1915, was appointed to the substantive post on 27 April 1915. He was at this time fifty years of age.

and a monopoly of support given to the H. and S. Bank who are responsible more than any other agency for the growth of German trade in China.

[...]

Perhaps you have heard that my engagement with the Chinese has been extended. When the Japanese seemed bent upon supplanting the Europeans with Japanese advisers it was proposed that my engagement, which does not terminate until 1917, should be extended another five years to 1922 and this arrangement was made on May 1st.

The Chinese treat me well. I do the best I can for them and I give all my energy to the task of inducing them to do things, to accomplish reforms, improve communications, develop their resources etc. and cease this everlasting drawing up of useless regulations.

I expect to be in England again this year, perhaps in October, when I sincerely hope that nothing will prevent our meeting.

[...]

Believe me

Ever faithfully yours
[G. E. Morrison]

761. From Ch'en I-fan

Shanghai 27 May 1915

Dear Dr Morrison,

I thank you very much for your letter of the 15th instant,[1] and I read with great interest the news contained therein.

I will be ready to respond to any call of the Central Government, as I have always been, although I have been, for some time, under the medical attention on account of the enlargement of some glands in my both arms.

In dealing with the Tibetan question, it seems to me that it is necessary for China to bear two points in mind: –

Firstly, that she should take up such attitude as will lead the Tibetans to think that the present Government of China is quite different from its predecessors and is quite prepared to show them as many favours as the Emperors Kang Hsi, Yung Ching and Kien Lung[2] who were the only Manchu Emperors they know of, in spite of millions upon millions of money China has spent on their account, and that if they can get something from China during the negotiations, it is that they got it out of China's own good will towards Tibet, and not through the pressure brought upon China by England on their behalf. In other words China must do nothing that will help to drive Tibet into the arms of England. The Tibetan question is, after all,

---

[1] Not found.
[2] The second, third and fourth Emperors of the Manchu Dynasty. K'ang-hsi was the reign (1654–1722) title of Hsüan-yeh, Yung-cheng the reign (1723–35) title of Yin-chen (1678–1735), and Ch'ien-lung the reign (1736–96) title of Hung-li (1711–99).

a question of influences. Whether the influence of China, or of England, shall predominate in Lhassa which is Tibet? That being so, it is very important to China to have her *Amban* in Lhassa as soon as possible, otherwise the little influence which China still has over a certain section of Lamas, for instance, the lamas of the great monastery of Drepong, will be gone too very quickly, and then Tibet will be lost to China for ever.

Secondly, that the existence of China as a great Power does not depend upon whether we can convert Tibet into a province, which is a mid-summer dream, or not, but upon how long China can have such a man as President Yuan to remain at the helm of the State. He is the only man in China that can give salvation to her, and every man in China shouuld assist him in settling all outstanding questions with foreign Powers so that he will have greater reputation abroad and will be able to enlist foreign sympathy on his side, of which the British one is the most important, because Great Britain is the predominating power in the world. Having succeeded in enlisting the necessary sympathy, China will then and then only, have time to breath and to consolidate her position internally. What we cannot do with Manchuria, Mongolia, and Tibet when we are really strong! History always repeats itself. What we should do at present, in regard to the three places, just mentioned above, should therefore be to get what we can with grace, and leave loopholes for our energy if, thank God, we can have it in the unknown future, which is bright, if, hereafter, every Chinese can love his country and his work in such a strenuous way as the President himself. It is a great pity to see that the really great president ploughs lonely in the field, to use the well-known phrase of Lord Rosebury.[1]

As I am fully aware of your views on this question, so I have ventured the above, and if there is anything which I have not made clear, please let me have an opportunity of explaining.

With kindest regards and hoping to hear from you again shortly

Yours very sincerely
Ivan Chen

762. To O. M. Green

[Peking] 27 May 1915

My dear Green,

[...]

What I am now writing to you about is this. When I was last in London the Advertising Manager of *The Times*, an Australian named Murray Allison,[2] spoke to me with regard to the publication by *The Times* of a China

---

[1] Archibald Philip Primrose (1847–1929), 5th Earl of Rosebery, British politician, Secretary of State for Foreign Affairs (1886 and 1892–4) and Liberal Prime Minister (1894–5).
[2] James Murray Allison (1877–1929), an Australian, Advertising Manager of *The Times* since 1908. He was the author of two collections of essays on advertising and the compiler of *Raemakers Cartoon History of the War* (London, 1919).

Supplement. The idea was that one supplement would be brought out as a trial and that if it should be a success the same arrangement should be made as is made by the Russian Government for a quarterly supplement to be devoted to China.

I thought the idea an excellent one and the cost suggested seemed to me reasonable and when I came back to Peking I spoke to the President and he at once expressed his approval. There would be therefore no difficulty in coming to an arrangement which would be to the advantage of both China and *The Times*.

The idea was not to have a supplement devoted to the praise of China and to a defence of her politically, but to gather together in a convenient form available information chiefly regarding the economic resources of the country. For a work of this kind, as you know, I have been collecting material for many years especially during the last year. My library now on all questions concerning the natural resources of the country is, I suppose, the most complete in existence. I told *The Times* that should it be decided upon to issue such a Supplement, I would be glad to give the full use of my library to anyone delegated to undertake the work.

I wrote a memorandum regarding it to Robinson[1] in which I made various suggestions as, for example, having the introduction written by Lord Bryce and as to the advantage of using the special knowledge of men like Sir Alexander Hosie.[2]

Since I came back to China I have heard nothing more of the project. I gather however from David Fraser that he is opposed to the publication of such a Supplement fearing that it might lead the Chinese to believe that they thereby acquired a certain influence with *The Times* which would modify in China's favour their view regarding the Far East. But such an erroneous conception as this could easily be prevented. I believe myself it is most desirable that such work should be done and when you are in London, if you should approve of the scheme, you might have an opportunity of speaking of it to the Editor or to the Manager or to Murray Allison himself.

It is only within the last year or two that I have realised how vast is the literature upon the resources of China and how easy it would be to prepare the Supplement, giving for example a comprehensive account of the mineral resources of the country, of its horticultural resources, of its botanical resources and so on. The most interesting work and I think perhaps the most

---

[1] Geoffrey Robinson (later Dawson), Editor of *The Times*.
[2] Sir Alexander Hosie (1853–1925), British consular official who before his retirement in 1912 had served as Commercial Attaché with the British Legation in Peking (1905–9) and as Consul-General in Tientsin (1909–12). In November 1919 he was recalled from retirement to serve for three months as a Special Attaché in Peking. In 1913, at the age of 60, he married Florence Soothill, the young daughter of the Rev. William Edward Soothill, an event which drew some lively comments from Morrison in his Diary.

valuable work done in China, is that done by Frank N. Meyer,[1] the Agent of the Agricultural Bureau of Washington, who has been for years collecting food plants and studying the timber trees of China from Peking right across to Kashgaria. His knowledge is quite encyclopaedic. He has written a book on the agriculture of China which the United States Government are hesitating to publish, fearing that it is incomplete. Such a work must always be incomplete but it is the most complete work of its kind that has ever been attempted and written with a knowledge that is absolutely unique.

I have told Meyer that if on his return to America next month he should find the State Department unwilling to publish his work because of its cost that I would see whether the necessary funds could not be provided from Peking.

I only mention all this to show that a Supplement devoted to the food products of China alone, to its huskless oats, to its huskless barley, to its infinite variety of cabbages and its extraordinary variety of fruit trees, would alone be of high value to English trade.

As you know, David Fraser does not take more than a passing interest in China and I fancy that his objection to such a supplement may be that he is unwilling to undertake such a task. The preparation of a supplement ought not to take more than three months and would not be a costly work.

Gull tells me that the *Manchester Guardian* is bringing out a special issue devoted to China. Interested as I am in the development of China I am glad to hear it and I hope that *The Times* may be induced to do likewise, so please bear this in mind when you get home.

[...] Probably before you reach England the arrangement will have been completed whereby press rates from China are reduced to little more than half what they are at present. [...] I was in favour of the change believing it would be to the advantage of China not only in permitting greater attention to be given to China by the newspaper press, but because China would directly earn a larger revenue from press messages than she is earning at the present moment. [...]

Very sincerely yours
[G. E. Morrison]

[1] Frank Nicholas Meyer (d. 1918), American agriculturalist. As the Agent of the United States Agricultural Bureau he had travelled extensively in China collecting plant specimens. He was the author of many books on his findings, among them *Chinese Plant Names* (New York 1911), *Economic Botanical Explorations in China* (Boston 1916) and *Forest Vandalism; Criminal Destruction of the Last Remnants of a Great Forest in North China* (Boston 1916).

763. To F. H. May

[Peking] 28 May 1915

My dear Sir Henry,

I have delayed for too long to acknowledge the receipt of your letter dated April 23rd,[1] for which I have to thank you.

I can see very little hope for the reform of the Land Tax unless the Government radically change their methods. The President has entrusted the work to Tsai Ao, formerly *Tutu* of Yunnan, who did good service during the Revolution.[2] He is an intelligent young man, educated in Japan, whom many of the Young China party regard as a future President of China. He speaks good Japanese but no other foreign language.

No sooner had his Bureau[3] been created than the Russian Minister notified the Chinese that should any foreigner be employed in an advisory capacity in connection with Land Revenue, the Russian Government would expect to be consulted. As a matter of fact Tsai Ao has appointed one Japanese to assist him: he is indoctrinated with a belief in Japan and he really knows nothing outside of Japan.

If Sir Richard Dane[4] could be employed he would render service of the greatest value to the Chinese. They are so unpractical and always do things in the wrong way and they have begun this Land Revenue reform in the most expensive and cumbrous way possible. If the scheme of Tsai Ao is carried out the cost to the Government will be enormous and no appreciable increase of revenue can be looked for for many years to come. As you say, until the Chinese will put their pride in their pocket and employ and give authority to foreigners they can never hope to reform their land tax and establish their country on a footing of equality with the independent countries of the world.

Many people must wonder how long China is going to retain even the measure of independence which she now possesses. Even when she employs a foreigner she is compelled to employ one according to his nationality, not according to his efficiency.

Tsai Ao had an interview with Sir Richard Dane but did not impress our Indian Administrator as having any really practical ideas which might lead to practical results.

The Chinese never will do the simple obvious thing but always will devise

---

[1] Not found.
[2] In an attempt to introduce a uniform system of land taxation in China, a land survey was ordered by the Government, and a Bureau set up with Ts'ai O as its Director-General. Morrison felt that such a survey would be both long and costly, and in a memorandum dated 28 September 1915 (not printed) suggested that the younger brother of Sir Richard Dane, Sir Louis Dane, who had had wide experience in India of land taxation methods, should be employed.
[3] The Bureau of Land Survey.
[4] Sir Louis Dane, the brother of Sir Richard, was no doubt intended.

the most cumbrous overburdened with regulations scheme possible, and I am afraid that Tsai Ao's scheme is no exception.

So far China has come fairly well out of the difficulty with Japan. An excellent translation of the Notes exchanged on the 25th[1] has been published by our local paper [...].

Will the Chinese learn their lesson? That is the question we are now asking ourselves. They ought never to have permitted themselves to get into such a condition of weakness as to require the support of the friendly Powers. To Sir Edward Grey the Chinese owe a great deal and they are, I believe – at any rate the President is – aware of the service that has been rendered to them by the British Government. The President has since been busy issuing homilies. I wish that the Government would cease this everlasting talk and proceed to action, not talk about carrying out reforms but actually carry them out.

A clearly expressed series of simple practical reforms that have to be carried out sooner or later – and the sooner the better – has been in the possession of the Government for some time. It now only remains to be seen whether actual work will be attempted and will be accomplished. From north to south there are things requiring to be done; conservancy in Newchwang and the Liao River, creation of a harbour at Hulutao, the draining of great flooded areas in the Metropolitan Province and in the Huai river Valley, the building of a break-water at Chefoo – to mention only three or four of these.

In the case of Chefoo the Chinese have been compelled to consent to the construction of a railway from Chefoo to Wei Hsien.[2] Nothing is more instructive than this. The need of saving the port of Chefoo to China by the construction of a railway from Chefoo to Wei Hsien has been obvious for 47 years and especially obvious since the rise of Tsingtau. Historically it is interesting to find that on the 13th July 1868, a petition was addressed by the British merchants of Chefoo to Sir Rutherford Alcock[3] urging him to press for the construction of a railway from Chefoo to Tsinanfu, the capital city of the province, and the appeal was renewed on the 4th November, 1875 and since then the suggestion must have been written about more than a hundred times. I was always speaking about it when I was *Times* Corre-

---

[1] A reference to the Notes exchanged between China and Japan on that day agreeing to Japan's Twenty-One Demands.
[2] The concession of the railway from Chefoo to Weihsien formed Article 3 in Group I of the Twenty-One Demands, and was granted by China on 25 May 1915. Article 2 of the Treaty exchanged on that day stated: 'The Chinese Government agrees that as regards the railway to be built by China herself from Chefoo to Lungkow to connect with the Kiaochow–Tsinanfu railway, if Germany abandons the privilege of financing the Chefoo–Weihsien line, China will approach Japanese capitalists to negotiate for a loan.'
[3] Sir Rutherford Alcock (1809–97), British consular official and diplomat, at the time referred to British Minister to China (1865–71). He was the second British Consul in Shanghai in 1844 succeeding George Balfour, and served later as Consul in Canton (1854), Consul-General in Japan (1858) and Minister to Japan (1859–65).

spondent, and since I came into my present service I have vainly urged the Chinese to construct this railway. Now they have to construct it under compulsion.

Order is being fairly well maintained except in two places namely outside the Great Wall and in the Canton Delta. In regard to the *Gendarmerie* the situation is this.

A man who was formerly in the service of the Chinese Outdoor Customs, a Norwegian named Munthe, who entered the service of the President as Cavalry Instructor, and who now holds the rank of Lieutenant-General, has been endeavouring to induce the President to establish a provincial *Gendarmerie* officered of course by Norwegians. The cost he estimates at 26,000,000 dollars *per annum*. No such sum is available. At present he has three officers undergoing a kind of training in Peking who are described as being in the police, one being Norwegian, one Swedish, and one Danish.

Some little time ago the President spoke to me about obtaining officers from one of the small Powers for the *Gendarmerie*. Having read in *The Times* and elsewhere of the excllent work done by the Swedish *Gendarmerie* in Persia, I suggested that he might place himself in communication with the Swedish Minister, Wallenberg.[1] He did so and the result was the engagement of General Hjalmarson.[2]

The conditions of his engagement are that he shall not be employed either in Manchuria or in Mongolia and that he shall be given an adequate measure of authority. He is now in Peking awaiting the Government's suggestion, having received six months leave from Persia, where he is *Instructeur-en-Chef* of the *Gendarmerie*. No sooner was his appointment announced than both the Russian and the Japanese Ministers remonstrated with the Chinese for appointing anyone outside of their respective nationalities. I understand that Hjalmarson will be employed in Honan Province, the President's own Province, but nothing has yet been determined and the whole scheme is vague and nebulous.

You will have heard all about the settlement of the opium question by which China will profit to the extent probably of not less than 24 million dollars.[3] It seems to me to be a common sense solution of the difficulty but it is one that is bound to be condemned by the Anti-opium party. In the meantime morphia is coming to China in immense quantities, evading the Cus-

[1] G. O. Wallenberg, Swedish diplomat, Minister to China since 1908. He was a brother of Knut Agathon Wallenberg (1853–1938), Sweden's Foreign Minister (1914–17), advocate of Swedish neutrality during the European war.

[2] Swedish soldier. He was especially recommended by Morrison, after C. D. Bruce volunteered for the European War, to help to organise a police force in Manchuria and Inner Mongolia, but the scheme was frustrated by protests from Japan and Russia.

[3] The settlement referred to was an 'Agreement Relating to the Suppression of the Illicit Sales of Native Opium in the Kiangsu, Kiangsi and Kwangtung Provinces', signed on 1 May 1915 by the Opium Merchants' Combines of Shanghai and of Hong Kong on the one hand and the Chinese Government on the other.

toms. In 1913 unimpeachable evidence showed that in Dalny alone 6¼ tons of hydrochlorate of morphia was imported; mostly made in England, it comes into China via Japan being sent to Japan in registered packets by the Siberian Railway. There it pays duty on entry and this duty is repaid on re-export to Manchuria. The money being paid into the Bank of Japan – the Government Bank – and repaid by them on presentation of an order from the Customs. Thus the whole transaction is one that is fostered by the Japanese Government who are one of the signatories to the Agreement which forbids the importation of morphia into China or of appliances connected with its use.

For a long time past I have been urging the Chinese to revise their mining regulations. They have been now revised on broad lines by the Swede[1] and the Englishman[2] who are the two chief advisers in the Mining Bureau but now the consent has to be got of the Minister and after that has been given the consent has to be got of the President with whom the fear of Japan is an obsession. When I spoke to him the other day about pressing forward the revision of the mining regulations – they have to be revised in accordance with the Mackay Convention of 1902[3] – he said 'if they are made too liberal then the Japanese will come in and seize all our mines'.

In the meantime he has been befooled by one of his chief men, Yang Tu,[4] into giving a monopoly in the production of antimony in the Province

[1] J. G. Anderssen, Swedish mining engineer. He became an adviser to the Mining Bureau in the Ministry of Agriculture and Commerce in 1914.
[2] Aubrey S. Wheler, British mining engineer from South Africa. He became an adviser to the Mining Bureau in the Ministry of Agriculture and Commerce in 1914.
[3] 'Convention of 5 September 1902 Respecting Commercial Relations between China and Great Britain', sometimes referred to by the name of the British representative, Sir James L. Mackay. Article IX of the Convention dealing with mining regulations reads in part: 'China will, with all expedition and earnestness, go into the whole question of Mining Rules and, selecting from the Rules of Great Britain, India, and other countries, regulations which seem applicable to the condition of China, she will recast her present Mining Rules in such a way as, while promoting the interests of Chinese subjects and not injuring in any way the sovereign rights of China, shall offer no impediment to the attraction of foreign capital or place foreign capitalists at a greater disadvantage than they would be under generally accepted foreign Regulations.'
[4] Yang Tu (1875-1931), Chinese Republican politician, at this time Deputy Director of the Bureau of National History, under his old teacher, the distinguished and unconventional scholar, Wang K'ai-yün (1833-1916), and a Member of the Political Consultative Council set up by Yüan Shih-k'ai to further his monarchical ambition. Yang, whose career was an outstanding example of unfulfilled promise in modern Chinese history, was best known as 'campaign manager' of Yüan's imperial scheme. Reared in traditional Chinese scholarship, he also sought to acquaint himself with Western learning in Japan, where he became a conspicuous figure in the capacity of Secretary of the Chinese Students' Union, to which body belonged many subsequently prominent men in the Republic. A convinced constitutional monarchist long before he met Yüan Shih-k'ai, Yang became, after the Wuchang Uprising in 1911, one of Yüan's emissaries to the republican South. Owing however to the political in-fighting among Yüan's entourage, his service brought

of Hunan to one Company, of which Yang Tu is the Director and chief shareholder. This has been done although it is a direct violation of the article in the French Treaty of 1858[1] which forbids the creation of any privileged society.

Professor Andersson, the Swede in the Mining Bureau, has just been in to see me; he is a very distinguished geologist, Director of the Geological Survey of Sweden, and he is one of the greatest living authorities on iron; he has done really important work since he came here. To-day he seems quite hopeful that the regulations will be passed. His English colleague, Wheler, on the other hand on Saturday was wholly discouraged. It is a difficult country to work for. The saying is trite but true that the Chinese are their own worst enemies.

It is a long and rambling letter I am sending you. Please forgive me and with best wishes,
  Believe me

Very sincerely yours
[G. E. Morrison]

764. To Ts'ai T'ing-kan

[Peking] 3 June 1915

My dear Admiral,

For a long time past we have discussed the need of devising some scheme whereby the large sums of silver hoarded in the banks in Shanghai may be drawn into circulation in China. These sums have accumulated because of the high price of gold owing to the European war and because of the difficulty of finding remunerative and safe investment in China.

A scheme was drawn up by Mr. Hillier, in conjunction with Mr. Mayers, which would permit railway construction on the Sinyang–Pukou line to continue by means of money raised by a silver loan pending the return to

---

him little reward beyond his appointment in 1913 as Commissioner for the Reconstruction of Hankow. But less than three months after this letter was written, his name was to become overnight a household word when, in August 1915, he proclaimed the establishment of the Ch'ou-an hui, or Peace Planning Society, to promote a monarchical system of government. But all his schemes came to nothing and his official career came to an end even before Yüan's death in June 1916. Thereafter Yang Tu's life story makes contradictory and pitiful reading. He became a member of the Kuomintang and a Buddhist, serving as Secretary to Tu Yüeh-sheng (1888–1951), the much-feared head of Shanghai's underworld and a collaborator of Chiang Kai-shek, and yet in the company of Lu Hsün (1881–1936), the foremost modern Chinese leftist writer, he became a member of the left-wing Freedom League. During the last years of his life he was obliged to eke out a living by selling his painting and calligraphy, signing himself 'Tiger Priest without a Monastery' (Hu-T'o-T'o, or Hu *dhâtu*), and died in penury of tuberculosis.

[1] Article XIV of the Sino-French Treaty signed at Tienstin on 27 June 1858, and ratified at Peking on 25 October 1860, stipulated that '*aucune société de commerce privilégiée ne pourra désormais s'établir en Chine, et il en sera de même de toute coalition organisée dans le but d'exercer un monopole sur le commerce*'.

normal conditions in Europe, when the silver loan so obtained would be converted into a gold loan. The terms of the loan contract already signed by the Chinese Government would remain unchanged except in the one particular that it would be a temporary silver loan, to be subsequently converted into a gold loan, instead of a gold loan.

Foreign bankers and brokers in Shanghai, insurance companies and Chinese investors approved of the scheme and it was accordingly submitted by the Agent of the British and Chinese Corporation to the Director-General of the Railway[1] on the 28th April. The scheme provided for the construction of the first section of the Sinyang–Pukou Railway. Bonds to the value of 7 million taels would be issued in Shanghai, bearing interest at 6%, such bonds to be converted later into 5% gold bonds.

The scheme was an attractive one. It was the most economical scheme possible under present conditions. If successful it would be followed by other similar loans of equal or larger amounts. It would permit the uninterrupted construction of a railway which would be of high importance to the Chinese people and to Chinese trade and commerce.

The scheme was accordingly submitted to Mr. Shen Yun-pei the Director-General of the Sinyang–Pukou Railway. Mr. Shen, being quite without knowledge of finance, referred the matter to the Chiaotung Pu[2] and they immediately found objections to it and after some delay submitted a counter-proposal to Mr. Mayers. The counter-proposal was designed with the idea of making the loan a gold one from the beginning and thus saving two flotations. It was duly referred to Shanghai, where it has been found to be quite impracticable. No agreement on the lines suggested by the Chiaotung Pu is possible. Moreover unfortunately, owing to the delay and to the failure of the Domestic Loan, the proposal made on April 28th cannot, I am given to understand, now be renewed. This means, I am afraid, the definite ending of any scheme of a silver railway loan; the railway will have to wait until conditions in Europe, a few years hence, are favourable for the flotation of a gold loan. In the meantime the silver will have to remain stocked in the banks of Shanghai, where it bears in the bulk of cases no interest.

I understand that one objection to the proposed loan is that if it were successful it would be a 'loss of face' to the Government, the Domestic Loan not having been a success. As a matter of fact the present Domestic Loan subscription list should have been closed on May 12th but it is still open. The effect of keeping it open is very injurious for it shows that the issue has been a failure. The price is accordingly steadily falling. The third

---

[1] Shen Yün-p'ei, Chinese Imperial official and Republican politician. He was appointed to the post here referred to in 1913, having been, since July 1909, Assistant Director-General of the Tientsin–Pukow Railway. One of the most active monarchists and supporters of Yüan Shih-k'ai's Imperial scheme, he became in 1915 President of the National Petition Association, set up to further Yüan's claim to the throne.

[2] Ministry of Communications.

year Domestic Loan is being sold in Peking at sixty-six dollars the bond of one hundred dollars, one firm here having bought ten thousand dollars' worth at this price the day before yesterday. This means estimating the period of redemption thirteen per cent interest. But a loan for railway construction or any other industrial purpose is much more attractive to the investor and is on quite a different footing from a purely Domestic Loan which is not to be employed for reproductive work.

I am sorry that the scheme has fallen through. A great deal of attention was given to it and a large number of foreigners and of foreign companies, in addition to wealthy Chinese would have invested in it and it would, I feel confident, have been a success.

I thought you might like to know how things stand.

Best wishes

Very sincerely yours
[G. E. Morrison]

765. From Ts'ai T'ing-kan

[Peking] 8 June 1915

My dear Doctor,

Mr. Liang Shih yi has sent me the enclosed with the request that you be kind enough to take measure to have [it] printed abroad, not in Peking.

I have read the document and it appears to me that you have to doctor it somewhat in spelling – in expression – and in condensation before you dispatch it.

With best wishes

Yours sincerely
Tsai Ting Kan

Enclosure to Letter No. 765: *Reflections on an inspired article in the* ASAHI SHIMBUN *of 22 November 1914*

To us it seems strange that, while Japan has won such a victory in diplomacy forcing China to yield to her many wholly unjustifiable demands by means of an Ultimatum, the Western Powers whose extensive interests in the Far East are now exposed to serious dangers and whose power the Japanese are secretly plotting to break down should show so little interest in the present situation. I have been much impressed by a very unusual article in the *Asahi Shimbun*, a leading Japanese newspaper, the principal contention of which is to the effect that it has not been Japan's settled policy to antagonize Germany. Upon reading this article carefully I have been much surprised by the motives of the Japanese Government and by their treacherousness and lack of faith towards their present European Allies, the article being evidently an inspired article. We people in the West, ignorant of the ultimate designs of the Japanese, have assumed an altogether too indifferent attitude in the relations between China and Japan. The entire article is very lengthy. We may give only the principal points as follows:

1) Assume that the Allies win in the present European war. In this case Russian influence will certainly dominate the Asiatic Mainland, thus inevitably coming into conflict with Japan. England will likewise double her efforts in developing her interests in China. Those Japanese who believe that Victorious England and Russia would welcome a strong and powerful Japan are mere idle dreamers. Among the Powers seeking expansion in the Far East Germany is the least dangerous. Besides she is powerful enough to check England's ambitions in this part of the world. Hence an alliance with Germany is the most advantageous to Japan. In taking the side against Germany in the present European war Japan has made a most serious blunder.

2) It may be safely predicted that in the coming few years there will be struggles between Japan and those Powers that have vital interests in the Far East. In case our demands which we shall have to make in the coming Peace Conference, are not agreed to by the Powers we shall be compelled to fight. It is our allied countries we have to fight against. Baron Kato once made the remark in the Imperial Diet that the allies of Japan are enemies to Japan's freedom of action. He certainly said the truth.

3) Had we formed an alliance with Germany in the beginning and not with England, we would already have acquired Manchuria and strategic positions in other parts of China.

4) We know it is a question of time that the Far East will be the centre of world's greatest struggles. Let us try to form an alliance with Germany, for if the allies win Japan is bound to suffer greatest disasters.

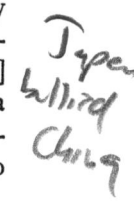

According to what I have cited above it is perfectly evident that the Japanese are inclined to turn away from their present allies and come to an understanding with Germany. Japan fears that the allies may be victorious in the present war and regrets that she did not see far enough in the beginning and blames herself for choosing to fight Germany. In this connection it may be worth while to point out the fact that in the formation of the Anglo-Japanese alliance Japan's main object was to secure financial assistance from England which she then was in need of. She had no sincere desire for friendship with the British people. Again the Anglo-Japanese Alliance and the subsequent conventions and agreements with Russia France and the United States all lay emphasis on the preservation of China's territorial integrity and the maintenance of the Open-Door. But were these compacts entered into by Japan for the love of China? Actions speak louder than words. While professing to act otherwise she has absorbed Korea, reputedly [?repeatedly] bullied China, and steadily encroached upon Chinese territory in Manchuria and elsewhere. In order not to be entirely dependent upon England's assistance she entered into an agreement with Russia which really amounted to an offensive alliance when she realized that her ambitions must clash with British interests in the Yangtse Valley. Outwardly Japan is England's ally, but secretly she has been working against her, because England is the power she is jealous of. If the allies win in the present war, England's power and influence in the Far East will be lessened, whereas if Germany wins she can act as check on England's ambitions in the Far East just as the author of the quoted article rightly has maintained.

It may be worth our while to examine Japan's motive in wishing for an alliance with Germany. Germany seeks primarily for economic opportunities in China, and not territorial expansion. Japan on the other hand realizing that economic conquest must be a slow process wants territorial possessions instead. She can easily come to an understanding with Germany on this basis if she can secure German assistance to dislodge the other powers from their present spheres of influence in China. On this point the Japanese Government and people all agree and the article quoted above simply gives expression to this general opinion. This contention can be substantiated by facts. During the siege of Tsingtau British soldiers who were fighting for the Japanese were treated with great indifference, while German merchants and captives were treated with every courtesy. This was deliberately done to please the Germans so as to pave the way for an early understanding with the German Government and for the consummation of the advocated German–Japanese Alliance.

When Japan took the opportunity and presented the 21 demands to China she deliberately defied the Anglo-Japanese Alliance and all subsequent conventions with other Powers. For all these treaties and conventions have as their principal provision the preservation of China's integrity. They insure equal commercial opportunities to all the Powers. The Powers in agreeing to this policy not merely intended to protect China's independence but saw clearly that any encroachment upon China's sovereignty would react unfavourably on all the other Powers having interest in China. The mutual jealousies of the Powers held back the selfish ambitions of all and was the most effective safeguard of China's influence. Japan, availing herself of the present opportunity, has now sought to depart from this policy. In short she wants to absorb China and unite the yellow races under her rule to fight the white races of the west. This has been the dream of many Japanese. They now want to try it.

In the opinion of the Japanese in order to establish a Monroe Doctrine in the Far East, it is necessary first to absorb China and in order to absorb China successfully she must first drive European influence out of China. In the eyes of the Japanese, the present European war is most welcome, because she knows she can act freely as the European Powers are all busily engaged. She is preparing for every emergency. She has in the recent negotiations with China insisted and obtained a sphere of influence in Inner

Mongolia, which gives her positions of strategic importance in the event of a war with Russia. The strongest power in the Far West is England and anything short of arms can hardly succeed to oust her out of China. Her strongest base now is Hongkong. In getting a foothold in Fukien Japan not only can cut off the connections between Hongkong and the Yangtze Valley but will completely isolate that small British Colony in China. Furthermore by possessing Fukien Japan is in a position to defy the United States, and threaten the Philippine islands. All these plans of the Japanese have been carried out successfully during the last few months while outwardly they still maintain that they have been sincere to their allies and faithful in the observance of their treaty obligations. Their position is so strengthened now that it is doubtful in the event of the allies being victorious, if they can do anything to alter the situation in the Far East.

If more proof is necessary to show Japan's lack of faith toward her ally I may cite another instance. The purpose that led British statesmen to agree to an Anglo-Indian alliance was their desire to insure the safety of the Indian Empire. Events have shown that this was a one-sided bargain and that the British Government has been outwitted. British people may recall the remarks addressed to Hindu students a few years ago in Tokyo by Count Okuma, now Premier, advocating Indian independence during the time of the nationalistic agitation in India. Public opinion was naturally aroused when their most trusted ally in the Far East encouraged rebellion in British Dominions. The Japanese seem to know fully the value of intriguing, and have adopted similar policy towards China, for it is a well known fact that Chinese rebels are given all the assistance and encouragement in Tokyo.

American trouble in China has been gradually taken away by the Japanese. Since the California Land Question[1] came into prominence it is generally known that if the Japanese had the necessary supply of funds war would have [been] declared on America long ago. This even the Americans know.

Now since they have obtained valuable concessions in China, they are in a much stronger position than they were even a year ago. War with America is not improbable. The standing army of the United States consists of not more than 100,000 men. In the event of a war with America the able-bodied Japanese in American territories can all be counted as effective fighting men. The Philippines can be taken in no time. Japanese troops can be transported to the American mainland by their war ships and once they get a good hold on the mainland the American army is bound to give way before the Japanese veterans. It is all within the scope of Japan's plans to occupy the Siberian railway thus driving Russia out of the Far East, and to take Hongkong and other British possessions in the Far East these projects must all be

---

[1] In response to a clamour to limit Japanese immigration, the State Government of California in 1913 introduced a law prohibiting Japanese immigrants from owning land, and limiting their tenure of it to three-year leases.

carried out in order to fully establish a Japanese Monroe Doctrine in the Far East, which the Japanese all fondly hope.

The Western countries know little of Japan and Japanese ways of doing things. They put too much faith in Japanese sense of honour and in written agreements, and there are people who still believe that Japanese means to observe in spirit and letter the Anglo-Japanese Alliance and the subsequent conventions Japan entered into with other Powers. These people ought to be undeceived if they know just what it indicates when they are told that the Far East soon will be the scene of world's bloodiest struggles. In my opinion China must be the case of this coming struggle in the Far East. For no matter which party in the present war wins the European countries will insist on a strict interpretation of the clause in those treaties guaranteeing equal opportunities to all and will rob China. Even if the Powers do not, Japan will avail herself of the opportunity and will try to conquer the Asiatic mainland. In a speech delivered in the Hibiya Park Count Okuma remarked that the balance of power in the Far East has broken down and that the Powers after the war will not be in a position to resist the Japanese. This remark sums up all I have said above about the present position in the Far East.

766. To Ts'ai T'ing-kan

Peking 9 June 1915

My dear Admiral,

In reference to your note yesterday accompanying the article from Mr. Liang Shih-yi, it would be of importance if Mr. Liang could give me the date of the article in the *Asahi* to which he refers and the extract itself either as it was printed in Japanese or in English.[1]

Was it a leading article or was it a letter addressed to the Editor?

The *Asahi* works in conjunction with the *London Times*, the London correspondent of the *Asahi* having access to *The Times* early news and *The Times* correspondent having a similar privilege in Tokio.

Moreover the *Asahi* was the most powerful advocate in Japan of the Anglo-Japanese alliance. If now it should have changed its policy as the article cited by Mr. Liang Shih-yi would indicate, the publication of the article with the exact date of its appearance would be of high value.

[...]

Very sincerely yours
[G. E. Morrison]

[1] Ts'ai T'ing-kan's reply of the following day is not printed. The date he gave for the publication of the article in the *Asahi* was 14 November 1914.

767. From Chang Min-chih[1]

Peking 17 June 1915

Dear Dr. Morrison,

[...]

With reference to the Chinese boycott of Japanese goods, as verbly mentioned by you the other day, I beg to inform you *privately* that on account of my journalistic position I am one of the active members of the Chinese National Goods Association in the Capital and we are doing our utmost efforts to make the movement going on as long as possible through peaceful and individual means for preventing official interference. What we are doing is to make every school boy and household wife to understand the coming Japs. danger to our Country because the recent negotiations amply showed that the cunning Japs. want to destroy our National existence and prevent our peaceful development under President Yuan. The Association issues no anti-Japs. pamphlet or public lecture but the members are performing their duties quietly and persistently. The Hunanese are doing very well at Changsha and other cities whilst the Cantonese are also effectively boycotting the Japs. goods at Canton.

The Association is going to publish a colloquial newspaper in Peking to be sold at one copper cent per copy and the chief object of this publication is to make the people always remember the date of 7th May as a 'National Disgrace Day' and the need of promoting the sale of Chinese goods. A new association has just been formed at Shanghai by Tang Shao-yi, Wu Ting-fang and other prominent Chinese partially for the same purpose in South China. My idea in writing this private letter to you is that there are certain Japs. goods can be replaced by British merchandize and I shall be very glad and am perfectly willing to work *gratis* if the newly-formed, pure British Chamber of Commerce at Shanghai wishes my co-operation in catching German and Japs. trades in North China because our assocation is closely connected with the Chinese General Chamber of Commerce. I have no doubt the Japs. will experience great difficulty to borrow British money after the war and certainly without British gold and Chinese markets, despite their military superiority over us, they cannot do us any serious harm as a Nation.

I will call in and see you at half past nine tomorrow morning.

C. L. Chang

[1] Chang Min-chih (otherwise Chung-liang hence his anglicised name Michie C. L. Chang), Chinese journalist and newspaper publisher. He was the founder and Managing Director of the Peking News Agency, and according to Morrison also served at different times as a correspondent of the *London and China Express* of London, the *North China Daily News* of Shanghai, the *Central China Post* of Hankow, the *South China Morning Post* of Hong Kong, the *China Times* of Tientsin and a paper in Singapore, besides some Chinese-language newspapers in various parts of China.

768. From Beatrice Brownrigg[1]

Maidenhead [Berkshire, England] 18 June [1915]

Dear Dr. Morrison,

I have just seen your letter to my father[2] – it is extremely interesting. I am so glad that the Chinese Government have extended your appointment both for your sake and for the sake of our relation with China. I am full of apprehension about the attitude of Japan. I wish we could have kept them out of the war. It is perfectly hateful that we should have given them an opportunity to criticize and condemn the action of a British colonel in the fighting at Tsingtau – of course the man ought to have been disgraced. I can't understand how he can have been recommended for a decoration, as decorations are not shovelled out like 'iron crosses'! His name must have been submitted by General Barnardiston?[3]...Of course the Japanese are first and last opportunists, and have no thoughts beyond their immediate advantage...

I have often remembered my time with you in Peking in the spring of 1901 since this war began, I remember all the accounts of German brutality, of German bestiality, of German treachery, etc. etc. that used to pour in from every quarter in those days – so the terrible history of the last ten months has not surprised me as it has surprised most people in this country. I think that much of German 'frightfulness' is now a policy of despair – the Germanic allies must recognise that. Even if it takes us years, we must win in the end because of our control of the sea. I wish I knew what you most wanted to hear about – the war is such a vast subject that it is impossible to compress any sort of general criticism into a letter. Moreover I am conscious of The Censor looking over my shoulder all the time!... The Grand Fleet is sick of inaction, and aching for a big fight, but I don't think the German High Sea Fleet will come out of their safe retreat – their submarines are most galling and most difficult to attack. We have been greatly hampered for want of Destroyers, but now we are increasing their number with rapidity. We have been amazingly successful in moving our troops backwards and forwards without disaster, so we need not think seriously of the losses of merchantmen and trawlers. We have got a huge army in France. I don't understand our tactics there – we keep a swaying line, and we have enormous

---

[1] Beatrice Brownrigg (née Clementi Smith) (d. 1952), wife of Admiral Sir Douglas Brownrigg. She first met Morrison when visiting Peking in 1901 and became his close friend and a frequent correspondent. She claimed in a letter published in *The Times* on 31 August 1937 that Morrison had asked her before his death to edit his papers.

[2] Sir Cecil Clementi Smith. Morrison's letter to him referred to here has not been found.

[3] Major-General Nathaniel Walter Barnardiston (1858–1919), British soldier. He was at this time Commander of British forces in North China and led the British contingent assisting the Japanese forces in the capture of Kiaochow from the Germans. He was rewarded for his services with the Order of the Second Class Rising Sun from the Japanese Emperor.

casualties, and the cry is always 'more shells more men'. My confidence in Sir John French[1] is rather on the wane, but I'm not in a position to criticize seriously. I see men from the fighting line, I get letters, and see letters, and the result is a mass of conflicting reports. Everybody sees the fighting from a different point of view, the infantry from the trenches the Artillery from the bases of attack, the Staff from Headquarters – you know what I mean? I suppose someday something decisive will occur, and then somebody will be able to say 'I told you so'! In the meantime except for the increasing expense of almost every necessity and the increase of taxation, life in England continues normal. Everybody works and there is very little 'play'. I teach my children, and failing masculine labour, work hard in my garden. We have also a small convalescent home in the village for wounded soldiers. Douglas[2] comes down once a week, otherwise he lives in London, he has very long hours at the Admiralty, 9.30 a.m. to 1.30 or 2 a.m.! he is a Chief Naval Censor, and says he has learnt more about the Press in the last ten months than most people learn in a lifetime! He loathes the whole Northcliffe[3] gang. Nobody has any regard for *The Times*, and I know many people who have given up taking it. If I begin to discuss the ex-government[4] (Radical) I shall never end, every member of the Cabinet ought to have been shot, first for the uupreparedness of the country for war and secondly for their blundering and corruption and pro-German bias during the months of war until the Coalition Government was made.[5] You can't imagine the muddling and mistakes and even now much more could be done if we only had an Oliver Cromwell[6] as a Dictator instead of that paltry old rogue Asquith! All the country should be under martial law and there should be a form of compulsory service, this ought to have been done directly war broke out. We are conducting the

[1] Field-Marshal Sir John Denton Pinkstone (later Viscount) French (1852–1925), 1st Earl of Ypres, British soldier. Chief of the Imperial General Staff (1911–14), at the outbreak of the European War he became Commander-in-Chief of the British Expeditionary Forces in France, but was removed soon after this letter was written because of his conduct of the war, and was appointed instead Commander-in-Chief of the troops stationed in the United Kingdom. After the war he became Lord Lieutenant of Ireland, a post he held until 1921.
[2] Rear-Admiral Sir Douglas Egremont Robert Brownrigg (1867–1939), 4th Bart, British sailor, at this time Chief Censor at the Admiralty. He had been Naval Attaché in Tokyo (1910–12), and married Beatrice Clementi Smith in 1896.
[3] Alfred Charles William Harmsworth (1865–1922), 1st Viscount Northcliffe of St Peter, British newspaper publisher, founder and owner of the London *Daily Mail* and since 1908 owner of *The Times*. He was a strong critic of the Liberal Government and its conduct of the war.
[4] The Liberal Government before its reorganisation in May 1915.
[5] The Liberal Government under Asquith was reorganised in May 1915 to admit the Conservatives under the leadership of Andrew Bonar Law (1858–1923) following the resignation of Lord Fisher, the First Sea Lord, as a result of the failure of the Dardanelles Campaign.
[6] Oliver Cromwell (1599–1658), the English revolutionary, soldier and politician.

whole business of the war in the most wildly extravagant way – pouring out money upon the class which pays no taxes as a sort of bribe to do what is wanted, instead of ordering them to serve their country, and there are 'strikes' here and 'strikes' there, till it makes me sick with rage. It is said that every country has the government it deserves. If this is true there was no need for the Germans to pray 'God punish England' – our government was sufficient punishment! Winston Churchill[1] never did a better thing than when he wrecked his Party and brought about his own downfall. He was too dangerous at the Admiralty, and really responsible for our terribly costly blunder at the Dardenelles. Lord Fisher,[2] thank Heaven! has also gone, and we have a very wise First Sea Lord in Sir Henry Jackson.[3]

I hope very much that you will come home in the autumn. I send you a photograph of my children. Please send me one of your baby – or are there two by now? I hope you all keep well? With kindest remembrances, and always good wishes for your welfare and happiness

Yours very sincerely
Beatrice Brownrigg

769. To Ts'ai T'ing-kan

[Peking] 30 June 1915

My dear Admiral,

You will no doubt know that negotiations have been re-opened regarding Tibet, or rather proposals were made on Friday, the 25th, by the representative of the Waichiao Pu to the British Minister indicating the concessions that China is prepared to make in order to give her adhesion to the Tibetan Convention.

This Convention was signed by England and Tibet on July 3rd, 1914, China withholding her consent, and although it would be agreeable to the British Government that the instrument should be completed by the signature of China, the consent of China is immaterial. This, I understand, is the British view.

From the British and Tibetan points of view the Convention is working satisfactorily, and China can agree to it or not as she chooses; it is only

---

[1] Winston Leonard Spencer Churchill (1874–1965) was dropped as First Lord of the Admiralty after the resignation of Lord Fisher, the First Sea Lord, in May 1915. As the initiator of the Dardanelles Campaign of that year, Churchill was blamed for its failure.

[2] John Arbuthnot Fisher (1841–1920), 1st Baron Kilverstone, British sailor and Admiral of the Fleet. First Sea Lord from 1904 to 1910, he was again appointed to the post in 1914 until his resignation in May 1915.

[3] Sir Henry Bradwardine Jackson (1855–1929), British sailor. A pioneer in the use of wireless telegraphy for the Navy, he was Chief of Staff of the Admiralty (1913–14), and succeeded Fisher as First Sea Lord in 1915. He became Admiral of the Fleet in 1919.

China who is the sufferer; her prestige and influence in Tibet have been gravely impaired, her trade with Outer Tibet has been lost, that large area – larger than Shantung Province – north of the Kuenlun mountains has been incorporated in Tibet and can only be recovered when China will reconsider her attitude and sign the Convention.

For reasons given I have always held the opinion that the British Government will not consent to the inclusion of Chiamdo in Inner Tibet. On the other hand I have always believed that the British Government would reconsider the question of Litang and Batang[1] and would be prepared to reconsider the boundary so as to recognise Litang and Batang as being within China proper and not in Inner Tibet.

Now the Waichiao Pu, having deliberated over the matter, have decided that they are prepared to withdraw the Chinese garrison from Chiamdo provided that certain compensatory advantages be given to them for so doing.

One has to do with Litang and Batang, about which I think an agreement is possible; another has to do with the inclusion of the territory north of the Kuenlun mountains in China proper, about which an agreement is, I think, possible; a third has reference to the cutting off from Outer Mongolia and its inclusion in Inner Mongolia of a large area south of the Kuenlun Mountains, a proposal which will never be agreed to; the fourth advantage asked for is that China should have the right of establishing agents at five specified places in Outer Tibet, namely, Chiamdo, Shigatse, Gyangtse, Gartok and Yatung.

If there is one thing more certain than another it is that the British Government will not consent to the establishment of these agencies, for in the view of the British Government the whole trouble in Tibet was caused by Chinese agents and they cannot consent to the restoration of the very officials whose unwise conduct in the past both towards the Tibetans and towards the British representatives brought about the present conditions in Tibet.

I was not consulted before these proposals were submitted to the British Legation. It is the rule of the Waichiao Pu never to consult any Foreign employee of the Chinese Government until after the step has been taken and usually not even then. As usual, therefore, I only learned of them after they had been presented, but I believe I am correctly interpreting the view of the British Government, as disclosed by its Tibetan policy since the beginning on August 17th, 1912, when I say that the proposals regarding the appointment of agents cannot be entertained. Similar proposals made during the course of the Tibetan negotiations met with a refusal.

China's troubles in Tibet were due to Lien Yu,[2] the *Amban*, to Chang Yin-tang, the Assistant *Amban*, and to other agents. The present Prime

[1] Two places in the Chamdo district which later formed part of the new province of Sikang.
[2] Lien-yü, Manchu Bannerman and official, *Amban* or Administrator of Tibet from October 1906 to March 1911.

Minister of Tibet was imprisoned by Lien Yu and his property confiscated. His robes and valuables were brought to Peking by Lien Yu and the knowledge of this fact does not tend to make the Prime Minister more conciliatory.

The action of Chang Yin-tang, his astonishing arrogance and insolence to the British officers in Tibet – Major O'Connor, Captain Bailey,[1] and Captain Campbell[2] – caused personal bitterness which cannot easily be eradicated. And when it is alleged that the Chinese Government will take care in the future that a superior class of officials shall be sent to Tibet, the Indian Government reply that all the agents whose overbearing conduct compelled British intervention in Tibet were rewarded on their return to China, as Santo, the *Amban* of Urga, was rewarded, whose maltreatment of the Mongols led to Russian intervention and the loss of Outer Mongolia.

Everything that one can learn by reading the Indian papers confirms the view that in the opinion of the Indian Government the trouble in Tibet was caused by Chinese Agents and that there could be no tranquillity if Chinese Agents were to be in a position to resume their activities.

Had the Waichiao Pu mentioned the subject before submitting their proposals to the British Legation I would have suggested to them the need of acting with the utmost circumspection in this matter of the agencies, for while the proposal looked innocent enough – five agents in trade centres, each with an escort of fifty men – the Indian Government would surely consider the matter from a different standpoint.

The Waichiao Pu forget that when the Dalai Lama was in Peking in the winter of 1908 there came here to visit him from India the Crown Prince of Sikkim[3] accompanied by Major O'Connor, one of the chief authorities on Tibet, whose treatment at the hands of Chang Yin-tang had caused indignation to the Indian Government. On their arrival they found that Chang Yin-tang was in charge of the Dalai Lama and that in pursuance of the policy of humiliation which he had carried out in Tibet he had appointed as personal caretaker of the Dalai Lama a young Cantonese named Lu, who was

[1] Frederick Marshman Bailey (1882–1967), British soldier and colonial official. He joined the Indian Political Department in 1905 and but for a brief period in 1915 was employed in work dealing with India's frontiers. He took part in the invasion of Tibet (1903–4) led by Younghusband, and made many exploratory expeditions between 1904 and 1911 in Tibet and Western China. After serving in Persia and India he became in 1932 Resident in Kashmir, and in 1935 British Minister in Nepal.

[2] W. L. Campbell, British soldier and colonial official. He succeeded C. A. Bell in 1905 as Assistant Political Officer in Chumbi District. The incident here referred to was said to have occurred in September 1906 when Chang Yin-t'ang, passing through the Chumbi Valley on his way to Lhasa, refused to call on Campbell and when Campbell called on him he was asked, but refused, to enter by a side door.

[3] The Maharajkumar of Sikkim visited Peking in 1908, accompanied by William Frederick Travers O'Connor, British Trade Agent at Gyangtse, Tibet. They called on the Dalai Lama, who was then paying a visit to the Chinese Emperor, at Wu-t'ai-shan and again in Peking.

for 12 years a shoemaker in Calcutta and whose humble position was well known to the Indian authorities and to the Dalai Lama.

Such a policy as this could only cause personal bitterness. It is remembered by the Indian Government who are now closely associated with the Government of the Dalai Lama, and I do not see how it is possible that the two Governments will ever consent to the restoration of conditions as regards the appointment of Trade or Consular Agents, or whatever the Agents are called, who think may be in a position to cause a recurrence of the disturbance and unrest along the Indian frontier which brought about British intervention on August 17th, 1912.

In studying this question the Waichiao Pu are apt to forget the conditions in the past and to pay too little attention to the policy of the Indian Government as disclosed on many occasions during the last three years. Yet if the Indian point of view is not understood how is it possible to re-open negotiations with any hope of success?

Very sincerely yours
[G. E. Morrison]

770. To Liang Shih-yi

Peking 12 July 1915

Dear Mr Liang,

I have to acknowledge the receipt of your long letter[1] commenting upon an article which appeared in the Japanese paper, the *Asahi Shimbun*, on November 14th, 1914, and I note your request to have it printed abroad and not in Peking.

I have studied the letter carefully and the impression it has left on my mind is one of great discouragement. I therefore take advantage of our long-standing friendship to write you fully my observations regarding it, asking you in advance to forgive me if I have unwittingly expressed my views too bluntly and too frankly. In serious questions such as those discussed in your letter interchange of views cannot be too frank and open. In no other way can misconceptions and misunderstandings be removed.

Your letter, I repeat, is most discouraging, written as it is by one of the most learned of Chinese statesmen. It seems to me to show a complete misconception of the relations between Japan and Great Britain and until such misconception has been removed any hope of a prudent guidance of China's foreign policy as it is affected by those relations is impossible.

Your letter is interesting and well written; it has been translated into excellent English but there is no paper in England known to me which would publish an article of this kind unless it were paid to do so and no paper in

---

[1] Morrison is referring to the enclosure to Letter No. 765 from Ts'ai T'ing-kan. It was not in fact a letter but an article written by Liang Shih-yi and translated by Ts'ai T'ing-kan, which Liang had wanted Morrison to have published.

England of any standing or influence would accept payment for the publication of an article so full of historical inaccuracies.

The article is based on a citation from the *Asahi*, one of the two chief organs in Japan which from the beginning advocated an alliance with Great Britain and have upheld steadfastly the alliance since it was entered into. The article comments upon the citation and expresses surprise or professes anxiety at the 'treacherousness and lack of faith shown by the Japanese Government towards France, Russia and England'. Evidence of this treachery is apparently found in the concessions recently wrung from the Chinese or in the concessions 'negotiation of which is postponed later' to be forced hereafter from China.

Far however from regarding the recent action of Japan with dissatisfaction, both France and Russia have given unmistakeable indication that they approve the policy of their ally. In their view, so far as one can ascertain it, a country which like China fails to better its methods of administration, which hesitates to develop its resources, makes no effort to follow the example set by its Eastern neighbour and after sixty years of bitter lessons still holds an inferior position among the nations, has had to pay the inevitable penalty of inertia.

What reason has France for dissatisfaction? Her official papers repeatedly have expressed their sympathy with Japan's policy in China. What reason has Russia to be dissatisfied? At some future date when the war is over it is possible that she will require in Northern Manchuria and Eastern Outer Mongolia the same rights and privileges regarding residence and rights of travel, police laws and taxation, mining rights and railway rights and other preferential treatment similar to those recently secured by Japan in South Manchuria and in Eastern Inner Mongolia. Pretext has also been given to Russia, should she desire to avail herself of it, to extend her influence already paramount over Western Hsinchiang north of the Tien Shan.

Both France and Russia have reason daily to be grateful for the assistance rendered by Japan in supplying them with the munitions of war needed for the vast operations in the West; both countries have daily reason to be grateful that Japan is able to assist in the carriage of the trade of the Far East with Europe and America when so many British overseas ships have been withdrawn from commerce and employed as transports to carry troops from every part of the British Empire to Western Europe, to Egypt and to the Dardanelles.

Has England any reason for dissatisfaction? From the outbreak of war Japan has acted with faithfulness to her alliance. She has given assistance of the most important kind. Immediately on the declaration of war she mobilised one third of her Navy and placed it at the service of her ally. Her ships have helped to sweep the German ships from off the seas. At the present moment there is not a single German ship, whether man-of-war, converted cruiser, or mercantile ship, to be found on any waters of the world except in the home waters under the immediate protection of German land defences. Yet before the war the German fleet was the second largest in the world and German merchant ships, second also in number in the world, were found on every sea. In assisting to destroy German overseas commerce the Japanese Navy has rendered at a cost of some millions of pounds sterling a service to her allies the importance of which cannot be overrated.

So too in the case of Tsingtau. In the destruction of Tsingtau as a German Naval base Japan rendered an unquestioned service to her ally, opening the way for the transference of British warships to European waters and permitting British merchant ships to continue their trading in and with the Far East without danger of molestation. Moreover in the opinion of English Statesmen the service thus rendered by Japan to her ally was in equal measure a service rendered by Japan to China, permitting as it did the undisturbed continuance of China's foreign trade, upholding the revenue of the Maritime Customs, and saving the country from otherwise inevitable bankruptcy.

Against services such as these is to be set the recent action of Japan in demanding from China rights of railway construction previously, in one case at least, granted to the British and in demanding preferential mining rights over large areas of China including the Yangtse Valley which may be described as the British sphere of influence. Not in justification of these demands but in elucidation of the British view regarding them I would point out:-

1 That the Japanese explanation protesting that in submitting their demands for railway construction they were unaware of any British prior rights, has been accepted by the British Government.

2 That the vast mass of British people interested in China conceive that the surest means of strengthening the Central Authority is the construction of railways in China.

3 That wherever in China railways are built, by whomsoever built, trade grows greatly and a fair proportion of that trade is secured by England.

4 That China's indifference or hostility to railway construction and the interminable delay in all railway negotiations and the absence of any definite railway policy give some justification to Japan for submitting her demands in so irregular a manner.

5 That, to cite once more an instance often cited, the appeal first made by the British in 1868 for the construction of a railway from Chefoo to Chinanfu was rejected and every attempt, beginning in 1875, since made by the British to provide the capital for the construction of this railway in order to save the port of Chefoo has been frustrated by the Chinese Government. No surprise therefore was manifested that Japan, who judging by experience would never by friendly negotiation secure the right to build this essential railway, should refuse to waste time in endless discussion.

6   That as regards mining enterprise in the Yangtse Valley the British have no reason to view the Japanese action with astonishment. Every attempt made by the British to open mines in the Yangtse Valley, to put capital into mines there, has been opposed by the Chinese Government. In the case of the Tung Kuan Shan iron deposits, a concession in which considerable sums of British money were lost owing to the opposition of the Chinese Government, the concession was bought out by the Chinese and then later mortgaged for a fraction of its value to the Japanese into whose possession it has now passed by foreclosure of mortgage.

What reason have the British to be dissatisfied with the extension of the Han Yeh Ping contract,[1] injurious as this contract has been to China? Through the blindness of her own officials China voluntarily negotiated with Japan this important contract. Ore from the Tayeh mines is of high value to Japan where it is required for the great steel works of Muroran in which the English firms of Armstrongs and Vickers are interested to the extent of nearly two millions of pounds sterling.

One can go further and ask what reason have the British to be satisfied with China's mining policy?

On September 5th, 1902, China undertook within one year to revise her mining regulations so as to permit the introduction of foreign capital. Five times since then has China revised the Regulations and each time made them more unacceptable. The Mining Regulations now in force are the most unreasonable and impracticable in the world. They are designed to exclude foreign capital and foreign enterprise, their effect is to keep the mining resources of the country primitive and undeveloped. The result has been that the Japanese do not trouble to obtain mining concessions subject to those regulations but within quite recent years have obtained undisputed possession or control of some of the finest iron mines and some of the best coal deposits in the whole of China. The Japanese coal mines at Fushun, near Mukden, are rapidly becoming among the most productive in the world.

In making these observations the point I wish to emphasise is this that inasmuch as China has in the past systematically obstructed British, French and American mining enterprise in China, notably in Shantung, Shansi, Yunnan and Ssuchuan, little sympathy is shown by British statesmen and writers for China when she is compelled to yield to force what she would never yield to reason, nor is Japan adversely criticised for realising that where mining is concerned the ordinary methods of diplomatic dealing involve waste of time and are of no avail.

[1] By an agreement signed on 2 December 1913 the Han-Yeh-Ping Company contracted a loan of 12,000,000 yen from the Japanese Government Iron Works and the Yokohama Specie Bank, using as a security the value of iron ore from the Company's mines. The loan was for the purpose of extending its yards and engineering works. On 25 May 1915 an Exchange of Notes between China and Japan confirmed the 'cooperation' of the Company and the Japanese capitalists.

In your article you say that in forming the Anglo-Japanese alliance the main object of Japan was to secure financial assistance from England. By this I presume you mean that Japan sought in the alliance the improvement of her commercial standing. It was a legitimate aspiration.

As you know, negotiations for the alliance proceeded for a long time. England was the first Power to recognise the patriotism, the ability, the efficiency and the strength of Japan. England was the first Power to grasp the fact that a mighty power had come into being in the Far East. And it was because England recognised Japan as a power of the future and it was because Japan regarded England as the greatest of world powers that the alliance was entered into in 1902 and was renewed and strengthened by two subsequent agreements.[1] It is well to recall the circumstances.

The first Agreement was signed at London on January 30th 1902, at a time when England was still at war in South Africa and was feeling severely the strain of long continued hostilities although the war was ending victoriously, and when admittedly there was increasing anxiety regarding European intervention. Hence the provision of Article Two: –

'In the event of one party being at war the other will maintain strict neutrality and use its efforts to prevent other Powers from joining in hostilities against its ally. In the event of any other Power or Powers joining, assistance will be given and the war will be conducted in common'.

The Agreement contained no reference to India. It was signed by Lord Lansdowne[2] and was to remain in force for five years. But two years before the expiry of this period, at the conclusion of the war between Russia and Japan, another Agreement was signed at London on August 12th, 1905, also by Lord Lansdowne, which greatly extended the scope of the first Agreement, each country now pledging itself to come to the assistance of its ally and not merely engaging to preserve strict neutrality.

This second Agreement provided for reciprocal recognition of Japan's paramount political military and economic interests in Korea and of Great Britain's paramount interest in the security of the Indian frontier. It was to remain in force for 10 years. Anyone conversant with the progress of the negotiations knows that it was first arranged that the duration of time during which the second Agreement was to remain in force was to be the same as the first Agreement, namely five years, but in the course of negotiation the Japanese expressed a desire to extend its operation for ten years and the compensatory advantage agreed upon was the clause relating to the Indian frontier. It had reference to the remotely possible contingency of an invasion of India by Russia.

[1] The Anglo-Japanese Alliance Treaty of 30 January 1902 was renewed on 12 August 1905 and again on 13 July 1911.
[2] Henry Charles Keith Petty-Fitzmaurice (1845–1927), 5th Marquis of Lansdowne, British politician. He was at the time Secretary of State for Foreign Affairs.

The time then for which this Agreement was to remain in force was ten years, but again some years before the expiry of this time, on July 13th, 1911, it was revised to meet the new conditions arising from the signature of Arbitration Treaties. Hence the insertion of Article 4: –

'Should either Contracting Party conclude a Treaty of Arbitration with a third Power it is agreed that neither Contracting Party shall be under obligation to go to war with the Power with whom such Treaty of Arbitration is in force.'

And since Korea in the meantime with the recognition of all countries had become Japanese, all reference to Korea was excluded.

English statesmen did not enter into this alliance blindfold but only after they had made the most careful study of the conditions in Japan. All parties were united in its favour as is shown by the fact that the first two Agreements were negotiated by Lord Lansdowne of the Conservative Government, one of the ablest of Indian Viceroys, while the third Agreement was negotiated by the Liberal Government with the full approval of the Cabinets of all the British self-governing colonies.

In China the hope is being encouraged that the alliance has been shaken. Any policy based upon such a supposition would lead to misfortune. No alliance ever yet entered into wholly escaped criticism, especially by a press so outspoken as that of Great Britain, but this alliance has met with less adverse criticism than any other Government act in England's history. It was entered into with full knowledge; it has rendered unquestioned service to both countries. It is still rendering service of the highest moment and any talk to the contrary is idle talk.

From the first the chief criticism directed against the alliance came from the members of the foreign communities in Japan. They opposed it as they had opposed the abolition of extra-territoriality in Japan, but their opposition was again disregarded. Criticism is still heard in the Far Eastern papers but I do not think that there is at present in public life in England a single statesman who does not consider that the alliance has been equally beneficial to Great Britain and to Japan. Some disadvantages may be recorded and are admitted but they weigh but little in the scale against the advantages. I am not aware of a single responsible public utterance that condemns the alliance. And British statesmen believe moreover that the alliance has been advantageous politically and commercially not only to Great Britain but to Greater Britain, to India, Australia and Canada.

Nowhere was the alliance more adversely commented upon than in certain papers in Australia. If the thesis of your letter could be sustained nowhere would the alliance be more condemned than in Australia at the present time. But so opportune have been the services rendered by Japan to Australia since the war began that the recent visit of the Japanese fleet to Australia has called forth a display of enthusiasm such as never before has been witnessed in the Commonwealth.[1]

Japan is a small island country of restricted natural resources but with an exceedingly efficient and patriotic population which is increasing by more than 700,000 *per annum*, wisely governed by men of action rather than by men of words. In an incredibly short space of time, profiting by the teaching of a large number of foreign assistants, she has raised herself to be one of the world's great military and naval powers, she has recovered her fiscal and judicial freedom, she has become one of the chief trading nations of the world. She has become independent of all foreign assistants. With magical speed she has created the third largest mercantile marine in the world and for this marine she can with truth claim that in efficiency and reliability it ranks with the best mercantile marine at present in existence.

By the growth of her industries Japan has become an important purchaser in the world's markets. She has become a manufacturing nation and the raw products required by her factories she is purchasing in ever increasing quantities from India, Australia, Canada and other British possessions. No Englishman therefore who gives the matter a thought can regret the growth in power and wealth of Japan or can withhold praise from the efficiency and ability with which it has been accomplished. And I regret to say that no Englishman can contrast the efficiency displayed in Japan, her successful striving to attain a higher place among the nations, with the inefficiency and indifference so widely observable in China, the appalling ignorance of the masses, the navy with its heterogeneous collection of useless ships, the costly and untrustworthy army, armed with every variety of rifle under heaven, the defective means of communication, the entire absence of roads, the confusion of currency, the financial chaos, the vast areas undrained where every year people perish by tens of thousands from famine and flood, both largely preventable by the exercise of those qualities by which Japan has been developed and Korea and Formosa have been transformed.

Your letter expresses the view that Japan contemplates obtaining the assistance of Germany to dislodge the other Powers from their present spheres of influence in China but in what way is that assistance to be given? Is it by German armies or by the German fleet? The performance of this miracle has been left too late. There are no German ships to carry German troops anywhere outside of Germany. And if Japan were to commit the inconceivable folly of waging war against her own allies she would within four weeks at most lose all her overseas trade and lose every overseas ship that she has upon the waters. Her success would be even less problematical than the contemplated march of Sun Yat Sen's army of five million men armed with paper cannon and paid with inconvertible paper money across Asia to Moscow and St Petersburg.

[1] A reference to the visit by a Japanese fleet to Australia in June 1915.

Does any man believe that Japanese statesmanship contemplates an alliance with an enemy-encircled Germany who has lost every possession she held in the world outside of Germany with the exception of certain districts in East Africa now fast falling to the British African forces?

But these are side issues, unprofitable speculations as to the future. Too much time is wasted in such idle thoughts. China must think of the present, of the danger confronting her, the danger of shutting her eyes to facts, the danger of looking to others for help that efforts of her own should render unnecessary. England, France, Russia and Japan are allies. What has happened in history where two Powers adjoin, one peopled by a powerful and aggressive race convinced that the extension of their civilisation confers unmixed blessing upon the defeated, and the other undefended, where little attempt is made to profit by western efficiency. What is to be the future of Mongolia and Kashgaria, of Yunnan and Kwangsi? Why should China, untaught by past experience, continue to nurse the hope that sooner or later some Power may take pity and interpose to prevent her from being forced to yield her rights to powerful and aggressive neighbours?

As the President has repeatedly proclaimed, China must look to herself for her own salvation. No help can come from outside. What Japan has done China ought to be able to do. What Siam has done China ought to be ashamed not to be able to accomplish. Siam had her great lesson in 1893. In that year her capital city was on its knees before the French fleet. She profited by that lesson. With the help of foreign assistants she put her house in order. Her struggle extorted the sympathy and admiration of the world. In 1907, within 14 years of her great humiliation, she had recovered her political, judicial, and financial freedom. One of the most prominent foreigners who assisted in her regeneration was a French jurist now in the service of China.[1] In Siam he was trusted and worked for the glory of his employers; in China he has been engaged for nearly two years and has never been consulted on any question whatever. Of his work in Siam he speaks with pride, of his sinecure in China it is an open secret that he speaks with disdain.

In 1860 Peking was occupied by foreign troops.[2] What did this lesson profit China? Writing in 1896 Lord Curzon,[3] who later become one of the most famous of Indian Viceroys and is now one of the foremost statesmen of the

[1] Georges Padoux.
[2] In October 1860, following the breakdown of the negotiations held at Tientsin, Anglo-French forces, after storming the Taku Forts, occupied Peking effecting large-scale destruction and pillage including the sacking and burning of the famous Yüan-ming yüan, the Summer Palace northwest of Peking.
[3] George Nathaniel Curzon (1859-1925), Marquis Curzon of Kedlestone, British politician. At the time referred to he was Parliamentary Under-Secretary of State for Foreign Affairs (1895-8) in the last Salisbury Cabinet. In 1899 he became Viceroy of India (1899-1905) during which time the British invasion of Tibet occurred. He served in various capacities in the British Government from 1915 to 1918, and became in 1919 Secretary of State for Foreign Affairs (1919-24).

world, lamented the fate of China, 'who in the last fifty years has lost Siam, Burma, Annam, Tongking, part of Manchuria, Formosa and Korea'.[1] And since 1896 Lord Curzon has not failed to observe that China has lost in all but name her sovereign control of South Manchuria, of North Manchuria, of Outer Mongolia and of Outer Tibet. Her control of Ili and of Kashgaria has become shadowy. Her sovereign control over Fukien and Shantung has been gravely infringed, she has lost her fiscal freedom, her telegraphic freedom, her financial freedom. She has lost the control of her Maritime Customs and of a considerable portion of her Native Customs. She has lost control of the Post Office and of the Salt Gabelle. Many of her most valuable mines have been alienated, most of her railways are pledged, the Peking *Octroi* have been hypothecated. Even in the appointment of foreign advisers the foreign Powers claim the right of interference. More than ever are foreign Powers unwilling to relinquish any measure of their extra-territorial privileges. This is an appalling record, a tale of woe that might make the bravest despair.

But even now it is not too late if work be begun at once. It is waste of time and energy to denounce the aggression of other powers for the denunciation falls on deaf ears. Wiser and more statesmanlike would it be to remove those conditions which invite foreign aggression.

What has been the history of China since 1860? From that war she learned no lesson. She has even forgotten that on November 24th, 1860, through the imbecility of her rulers she was deluded into tendering to Russia as a gift the fertile province of which Vladivostok is the chief city.

In 1874 China was spared the loss of Formosa largely by the friendly action of the British Minister in Peking. What lesson did China learn from this humiliation? Twenty years later as a result of a disastrous war she was compelled to surrender the island to Japan.[2]

In 1884–5 China, still helpless, suffered at the hands of France the destruction of the forts of Foochow and the blockade of Formosa. Peace was negotiated through Sir Robert Hart. Did China profit by this lesson?

In 1894–5 China, a large continental Power, was defeated in every engagement by the small island empire of Japan. Only 795 Japanese were killed during the whole campaign while the Chinese losses, although thirty-five times greater, were in all only 27,917. China was humiliated before the

[1] The source of the quotation here has not been traced, but in his book *The Problems of the Far East* published in London in 1894, Curzon had this to say: 'It is entirely during the last half, and mainly during the last quarter, of a century that Tonking, Annam and Cochin China have been wrested from the grasp of China by France, that Siam has repudiated her ancient allegiance, that Burma, once a vassal, has been absorbed into the British system, that the Liuchiu Islands, also a Tributary State, have been allowed to pass tacitly into the hands of Japan, that Korea has become a playground for the jealous rivalries of foreigners...'

[2] By the Treaty of Shimonoseki of 17 April 1895 China ceded to Japan the Island of Formosa together with all the islands appertaining or belonging to it.

world. To Li Hung-chang and his corrupt following she owed a large measure of her humiliation but no lesson was learned from this experience. Only within the last few weeks it is announced that the Chinese who assisted Li Hung-chang in the purchase of useless arms and became rich in consequence at the expense of his country, has been appointed Director of the Tientsin mint although he has no technical knowledge whatever.[1]

In 1900 the Boxer rebellion shook China to her foundations. Through the friendliness of the Powers, or rather through their jealousy of each other, China was given a new lease of life. She was to adopt western ways, to purify her administration, reform her currency and recast her mining laws. She was to become progressive and powerful.

In 1904–5[2] China was exposed to the humiliation before all the world of witnessing war between foreign countries waged on her soil and she powerless even to maintain her neutrality.

In 1914–5[3] once more China was to suffer the humiliation of witnessing war between foreign countries waged on her soil and she powerless even to maintain her neutrality.

The cumulative effect of great episodes like these has been the progressive alienation of sympathy from a country which has learned so little from the lessons of experience, a country which, endowed with every advantage of climate, with a people as intelligent, as industrious and as capable as any in the world, with matchless natural resources, with a flora unrivalled for its range and variety, with unequalled means of natural inland water communication, yet fritters away its energies upon useless missions, draws up elaborate schemes of reform and then shelves them, drafts reports and regulations of endless length and complexity, and all the time is reverting more closely to the methods of administration of finance and of taxation which in the past have been among the main factors in preventing China from occupying a place of dignity among the nations.

How can a country expect the benevolent sympathy of the world which after all these years has no modern representative government, no civil service, no security of office, no strategic railways, whose territory is traversed by railways voluntarily conceded, policed by the military of powerful neighbours, a country without a revenue system, without any simple system of taxation, without industries, without public works, a country which does not possess a single mile of modern high road, whose

---

[1] Chang Shih-heng, a native of Anhwei Province and a relative of Li Hung-chang, was appointed Director-General of the Mint in March 1915, holding the post until April the following year. He had served under the Manchus as Director of the Kiangnan Arsenal in Shanghai. Morrison recorded in his Diary on 23 June 1915 that Chang had been arms purchaser with Li Hung-chang and had been associated with Mandl, the agent of Krupp, 'to the enrichment of both'.

[2] A reference to the Russo-Japanese War (1904–5).

[3] A reference to the occupation of the German Leased Territory in Shantung by Japanese and British forces.

cities have the most primitive form of government known, a country which has no education system, although education is the basis of national strength, whose Minister of Education[1] is innocent of all knowledge of Western education, whose Minister of Finance[2] has no knowledge of Western finance although the financial problems of China are greater probably than in any other country.

Good finance is the very essence of good government. A great English statesman has said there is no better test of the condition of a people and the merits of a government than the state of the finances. 'Where was there a bad government' asked John Bright,[3] 'whose finances were in good order? Where was there a really good government whose finances were in bad order?'

A wise system of inland taxation, equitably adjusted, removing the burdens on trade, would hasten the day when the Powers will consent to an increase of the Customs duties. Methods now being re-introduced, imposed without system, harassing trade both domestic and foreign, will indefinitely postpone that day.

In the whole of China there is hardly a single enterprise which can be called a successful business enterprise. If successful at all – as for example the Hua Chang Antimony Company – it owes its success to Government favour in the remission of taxes or in the concession of a trade monopoly. If successful it lives at all times in the knowledge that the capricious change of officials may expose it to the danger of official extortion, the danger of being bled because it is successful. Hence the desire of Chinese merchants to have foreign capital associated in their enterprise in order to have foreign

---

[1] T'ang Hua-lung (1874–1918), Chinese Republican politician. Brought up with a traditional education, T'ang became a *Chin-shih* before he went to study in Japan. On his return to China in 1909 he became active in the constitutional movement then in the offing, and as a member of the Provincial Assembly of his native Hupeh Province, he was foremost among the provincial gentry in calling for the convening of a National Parliament. A constitutional monarchist, T'ang joined with Liang Ch'i-ch'ao and others after the establishment of the Republican Government and rallied in support of Yüan Shih-k'ai against the Republican revolutionaries under Sun Yat-sen. In spite of his criticism of Yüan's dissolution of the Parliament following the failure of the 'Second Revolution', he accepted the appointment of Minister of Education in May 1914 in the Hsü Shih-ch'ang Cabinet, still holding this post at the time of this letter. Two months later, however, he resigned in protest against Yüan's monarchical ambition, and his place was taken by Yüan's Chinese Secretary Chang I-lin (1867–1943). T'ang later gave support to Tuan Ch'i-jui and together with Liang Ch'i-ch'ao joined Tuan's Cabinet formed after Chang Hsün's restoration attempt in July 1917, becoming Minister of the Interior. In March 1918 he went on an overseas tour, and was assassinated in Victoria, Canada in September.

[2] Chou Hsüeh-hsi, who had been Minister of Finance from July 1912 to May 1913, held the same portfolio again from January 1915 to March 1916.

[3] John Bright (1811–89), British politician and social reformer, who, together with Richard Cobden (1804–65) was a leading representative of the emerging manufacturing class which became a force in British politics after the Reform Act of 1832.

protection against Government interference. With the exception of the Kalgan Railway not a single railway worthy of the name has been built in China by the Chinese, and on this railway the appointment of Co-Director was given to a learned Chinese who knew nothing whatever about railways, but who understood the practice, so widely prevalent in the railways of China, of the sale of office.

All those facts and many others that I have not space to refer to have to be borne in mind when one asks: –

1   Can China justify her claim to the sympathy of the world?

2   Is China preparing the way for the recovery of her fiscal freedom and for obtaining the assent of the Powers to the increase, so just and reasonable, of the Maritime Customs tariff?

3   Can China justify her claim to be heard at the Conference to be held at the conclusion of the present war? At the Conference following the Russo-Japanese war China asked to be heard but was denied a hearing. Has she a stronger claim to be heard now?

4   Has China done anything to justify her claim, which was favourably answered in the case of an inferior Power like Siam, to recover jurisdiction over foreigners in China? Is the re-institution of an archaic Censorate with all its powers of blackmail to be regarded as a reform or as a postponement of reform?[1] The abolition of the Censorate was hailed as a reform; its re-installation, so far as I can learn, is regarded as a reactionary step only less retrograde than would be the re-institution of Eunuchs.

Your letter cites the case of Korea and uses it as an argument against Japan. But such argument is no longer tenable. Japan's action in Korea is perhaps the strongest of all her claims to the benevolent consideration of the world. Before the Japanese occupation Korea was 'the worst governed country in the world', to quote Lord Curzon again, with its accumulated mass of abuses, the fearful extortion and misgovernment of its ruling classes, the sale of offices, the confusion of the court with the administration, the judicial oppression and negation of civil rights, the scandalous state of its currency, its communications and its native industry.

In the enforcement of Japanese rule there have been serious blemishes, notably the ruthless severity with which disaffection was crushed when some 16,000 Koreans suffered death and the persecution of the Korean

[1] The Censorate was an institution in Imperial China performing a supervisory function over the officialdom. Its members were sometimes described as the Emperor's eyes and ears, being supposedly endowed with the privilege not only of watching over the behaviour of officials but also of speaking out even against the ruler, a function which was however more theoretical than real. They were rather more often used by rival political factions to attack one another, and thus became a powerful check-and-balance tool for the ruler in safeguarding his (or her) authority. This institution, after undergoing some reform in 1906, was abolished with the passing of the Manchu Dynasty, but on 31 March 1914, in anticipation of the restoration of the monarchy, it was restored by Yüan Shih-k'ai under the name of the P'ing-cheng yüan, with the Su-cheng t'ing within it.

Christians charged with conspiring against the Resident General. But even this loss of life is insignificant compared with the loss of hundreds of thousands of Chinese lives sacrificed to famine or flood in China or to the devastating progress of the White Wolf or the equally devastating progress of the lawless troops following in his wake.

And against these blemishes can be set the good that Japan has done in Korea. She has transformed Korea, she has done for Korea what England has done for Egypt and Burma, what France has done for Tongking, what America has done for the Philippines. Even the most severe detractors of Japan, the American missionaries stationed in Korea, admit that never in their history have the Koreans been so well governed as at present, never have the people been so prosperous and contented. The people's welfare has been the first consideration of the Government. In every direction of public life the most far-reaching reforms have been effected, reasonable and equitable taxation, sanitation and public health, the building of roads, and railways, universal education, the administration of justice, improved cultivation of cotton and rice, silk and *ginseng*,[1] the opening of mines, the scientific fisheries, the re-afforestation that is changing the face of the peninsula.

Every observer I have met admits that Japanese Government in Korea has been an immeasurable gain to the Koreans themselves. Loose talkers are apt to speak of the destruction of British trade in Korea. Yet the value of British trade in Korea now is much greater than it was before the annexation. How could impoverished Koreans, the impoverished natives of a bankrupt country, afford to purchase British goods? With increasing prosperity every year has witnessed a larger demand for goods of British manufacture. In 1903 the whole trade of Korea, although the highest it had yet attained, was only valued at £2,827,381 and only seven British ships of a total tonnage of 15,115 took part in the trade. In 1913, the foreign trade of Korea – again the highest on record according to the British Consular Report – amounted to £10,450,375. British imports alone amounted to £921,019 and forty British ships of a total tonnage of 99,382 called at Korean ports.

Reading this you will begin to say that my letter is really a defence of Japan and of the Japanese alliance and not a defence of the country in whose service I have the honour to be. But this would be an unjust inference. I am writing to you the truth because you are a Chinese of high standing and because I am in Chinese employ. I cannot conceive that it is my duty because I am a so-called adviser to say nothing but sweet words and falsely encourage my employers in the belief that things are going well with China when as a fact the situation is one fraught with the gravest possibilities. I believe that what Japan has done China ought to be able to do. I believe that in shutting their minds to disagreeable facts the Chinese are drifting into danger from

[1] A plant whose root is said to have fortifying properties.

which escape as an independent nation will be impossible. I believe that the only hope of salvation lies in ceasing unworthy and pusillanimous make-believe, in ceasing to cry out for help which will not be given and in looking the situation bravely in the face and honestly attempting to profit by the blunders and the misdeeds of the past.

During the last three years China has lost in all but name Outer Mongolia and Outer Tibet, she has lost in all but name her sovereign influence in South Manchuria. In Eastern Inner Mongolia, in Shantung, and in Fuhkien, her independence of action has been gravely compromised and since the balance of power is an object of international policy in China as elsewhere, every advantage conceded by China to any other Power may give reasonable pretext for the presentation of similar demands by other Powers in other portions of Chinese territory. China can hope for no support from any other country. Reform must come from within if China is to obtain even the sympathy of other countries. The experience of Korea is being repeated in China, its teachings cannot be disregarded.

The disposition shown by China to look to America for active help is, so far as I can learn, a policy that meets with no encouragement from thoughtful Americans. No country is more friendly to China than America and of all classes in America no body of men has more generously testified its good-will and charity to China than the American missionaries who have worked for the uplift of China for nearly a century, who have erected colleges and hospitals for the service of the Chinese in nearly every province of its vast territory. But the Americans are a sensible hard-headed practical people with a devoted love of peace, who will give China every encouragement to set her house in order but who can never by any conceivable possibility take up arms to defend China against the consequence of her own misgovernment. A country whose love of peace prevented interposition in Mexico where hundreds of Americans were slain and hundreds of millions of dollars of American property were destroyed,[1] is unlikely openly to espouse the cause of China in order to prevent a possible extension of Japanese railway construction and a possible extension of Japanese mining development in China.

During the recent negotiations with Japan one of the American missionaries in Peking, a comparatively new arrival in China, drafted a petition to the President of the United States which he induced other missionaries to sign and which the Chinese Government at an expense of many thousands of dollars cabled to America.[2] Copies of this despatch were distributed by

---

[1] A reference to the revolutionary war of 1911–12 in Mexico in which many Americans lost their property and lives, and claims for compensation were lodged with the Mexican Government by the American Ambassador in April 1912.

[2] An appeal by a group of missionaries for assistance from the United States Government against Japanese aggression was sent by cable to President Wilson on Easter Day 1915. The signatories were led by Charles F. Hubbard, Minister of the Union Foreign Church and

the author among the correspondents, they reached even the Japanese correspondents who were told that the expense of the cable was being borne by the Chinese Government. The American Minister was kept in ignorance of this unwise and impolitic action until the message was already on the cable.

The President of the United States promptly suppressed the message, the violence of whose diction may be gauged from the sentence that 'Belgium's grievance against Germany, estimate it at its worst' (meaning the action of Germany in laying waste Belgium, in slaughtering men, women and children, in reducing to ashes the seats of learning) 'paled into insignificance compared with the crime of Japan in China', which it characterised as 'international highway robbery'.

One naturally asks what good end is served by an unbalanced despatch of this kind? The Japanese, always suspicious of their interference in politics, will scrutinise more closely the operations of American missionaries in Korea; when the time comes the Japanese, who never forget an injury, will remember that the Chinese Government paid the cost of sending so violent a despatch, in which Japan is described as an 'outlaw among nations', to the President of the United States. Many even now erroneously believe that the message was inspired by the Chinese Government and they will take note that the message, which asked the President to give it the widest publicity through the press, was promptly put in the waste paper basket.

Again one asks what conceivable advantage can China gain by paying an American journalist in Shanghai 15,000 dollars to proceed to America and attack Japan in the columns of the press open to his communications? Communications of the kind carry no weight because they are known to be paid for and are not the disinterested expression of independent opinion. No papers of influence will publish such communications. Least of all will the American Government be influenced by such methods. In America there is some hostility to Japanese immigration especially in the western states and this hostility is even more marked than is the opposition to Chinese immigration but so far as one can tell there is less likelihood of American interference between China and Japan than there was likelihood of American interference between Japan and Korea. Yet in the case of Korea America had entered into engagements which she had not entered into in the case of China.

In the Treaty between the United States and Korea signed at Seoul May 19th, 1883, the first article provides that:—

> If other powers deal unjustly or oppressively with Korea the United States will exert their good offices on being informed of the case to bring about an amicable arrangement, thus showing their friendly feelings.

---

included other well-known figures such as W. A. P. Martin, Chauncey Goodrich, H. H. Lowry, and Edward W. Thwing. According to Morrison the cable with every 'the' and 'and' totalled 5,100 words, and cost the Chinese Government, who had agreed to pay for it, 16,000 dollars.

Yet the first of all Powers to express approval of Japan's Convention of Suzerainty over Korea on November 17th, 1905,[1] was the United States and the Minister who urged his Government to take this step and give the lead to the other Powers was the late Mr Rockhill, one of the most distinguished of American Ministers and one of the men most sincerely sympathetic with China.[2]

For China to base her hope of salvation upon Agreements made between other Powers regarding the maintenance of the integrity of China and the doctrine of the Open Door is to build a house upon the sand. Such Agreements concern only the countries that signed them. Moreover, it is inconsistent for China to cite these Agreements in her defence now remembering that when they were entered into she resented them deeply and in some cases protested against them. For example, the Franco-Japanese arrangement, signed at Paris, June 10th, 1907[3] brought forth two months later a protest from the Chinese Government who, addressing the Governments of France and Japan, energetically and rightly affirmed that the maintenance of peace and security in Chinese territory which the two parties had stipulated to support was a sovereign responsibility of China who could not permit the interference of other Powers in assuring peace and security in her own territory.

A conciliatory reply was given but as *The Times* reported on August 24th, 1907: –

> 'China is far from satisfied. This last convention, made as have several other recent Agreements regarding China, between nations in complete disregard of China herself has deeply wounded the national pride. Perhaps China may learn from repeated lessons in time to appreciate how far reforms still require to be carried before the Government can be treated by other Powers on a footing of equality'.[4]

But to return to your letter. When you speak of Japan's defying the European Powers or defying America, what do you mean? Japan is of course stronger than Hongkong and the Philippines combined but to hold Hongkong or the Philippines Japan would require first to crush the might of Great Britain and America. You conceive the possibility of Japan, a country overburdened with national debt, being able to invade America because America has a standing army of only 100,000 men. Germany made the same miscalculation regarding England and spoke with derision of her 'contemptible little army of 100,000 men'. But England has already sent 750,000 troops against Germany besides the armies she has despatched to

[1] By Article II of the Convention signed by Japan and Korea on 17 November 1905 the Government of Japan took over the control of Korea's foreign relations.
[2] W. W. Rockhill was American Minister to China 1905-9.
[3] For the Franco-Japanese Agreement in regard to the Continent of Asia *see* p. 370 n. 1.
[4] A quotation from an article entitled 'The Franco-Japanese Convention Chinese Protest'.

Egypt and to the Dardanelles. And even if America had only 100,000 men Japan would require to send not less than 250,000 men to attack them conveyed in not less than 500 transports. She would require to use for this purpose every ship she has upon every ocean at home and abroad. To convey them she would require to employ her entire fleet for the Japanese fleet is smaller than the American fleet and she has no base or coaling station within several thousand miles of the American coast and no steam coal other than she can obtain in China. Such a scheme is not less fantastic than the mythical march of Sun Yat Sen's army to St Petersburg.

You refer to the case of India. Some years ago Count Okuma made a speech in Kobe in which he was reported to have spoken of the 200,000,000 people of India looking to Japan for salvation. Challenged as to the truth of the report the Count officially denied that he ever uttered any words capable of such interpretation or any sentiment antagonistic to the alliance, of which he declares himself an adherent, or any sentiment antagonistic to the British rule in India, of whose wisdom he declared himself a warm admirer. Your letter states that the 'purpose that led British statesmen to agree to an Anglo-Japanese alliance was their desire to insure the safety of the Indian Empire' and on this you comment that the alliance was a 'one-sided bargain and that the British Government has been outwitted'. Loose statements of this kind can only excite astonishment when uttered by statesmen of your high standing.

So too your statement that 'Japan has encouraged rebellion in British dominions'. But there has been no such thing as rebellion in British dominions unless you call the mutiny of 250 native soldiers in Singapore a rebellion. Germany dreamed that on the outbreak of war the natives of India would rise against their sovereign and overthrow British rule. But on the contrary never has such overwhelming evidence of the justice and beneficence of British rule in India been given as when on the outbreak of war offers of help poured in from every part of the Indian Empire, from Ceylon to the Himalayas, from the Persian Gulf to Burma. More than 250,000 Indian troops are now in the field and not less than three times as many more are ready to sacrifice their lives in the defence of the Mother country. Compared with such a striking fact as this the ill-considered utterance of a Japanese speaker eight years ago is unworthy of a passing thought.

Your letter concludes with the words 'The Far East will soon be the scene of the world's bloodiest struggle' and in your opinion 'China is to be the cause of this coming struggle'.

All things are possible in this world and it is conceivable that there may be a bloody struggle between the Powers for the possession of China. Much more probable is it however that there will be a friendly understanding between the Powers, a development of their policy of peaceful penetration especially in outlying areas where lawlessness prevails owing to incompetent administration, an increasing foreign pressure and an accelerated movement, long openly advocated by one of the Powers, towards financial control, the limitation of military expenditure and the compulsory application of the national funds to conservancy work and reproductive enterprise. All these movements will be hastened if in the meantime China does not abandon her present policy of procrastination, waiting for protection from outside which never will be given. China is big, rich with every blessing that can be given to a people except modern methods of administration. Her people under favoured conditions multiply with exceptional rapidity; she is indeed the most notable instance in history of a continuous extension of race co-existing with a continuous diminuation of empire. Is she to continue retrograding, effecting no adequate reform in internal affairs or foreign policy, devising no constructive policy but perpetually talking of the reforms to be accomplished in the future, everlastingly drawing up regulations and all the time ignoring the dangers of procrastination, the perils that in so many directions threaten her independence?

Believe me

Very sincerely yours
[G. E. Morrison]

771. To Ts'ai T'ing-kan

[Peking] 29 July 1915

My dear Admiral,

[...]

The Japanese are thoroughly alarmed at the extension of the boycott;[1] not its extension in China for I believe as a matter of fact the movement is dying out in China in obedience to Presidential orders, but in its extension in those wealthy possessions outside of China largely occupied by prosperous Chinese communities, in Siam, Burmah, the Dutch West Indies, Singapore, and the Straits, and the Philippines. The lesson is one that will not easily be forgotten.

I hope you do not find this weather too trying.

Best wishes to you

Very sincerely yours
[G. E. Morrison]

---

[1] A movement to boycott Japanese goods swept through the country following the publication of the Twenty-One Demands. The boycott spread to South-East Asia and persisted among the Chinese communities there long after it had died out in China itself.

772. From Beatrice Brownrigg

Maidenhead [Berkshire, England] 12 August 1915

Private

Dear Dr. Morrison,

Thank you very much for your long and interesting letter of the 18 July[1] which reached me yesterday, also a thousand thanks for the pictures of your boy. He looks splendid. I'm sure he is the greatest joy to you both. He must be very like you I think. I hope soon to hear of the safe arrival of a companion for him, and that your wife is quite strong again.

We continue in the greatest anxiety over the German advance in Russia, and some of us feel very acutely the apparent lack of initiative on the Western fighting line. It is extremely difficult to understand what we are doing in Flanders. Even senior officers who come home have no idea of what is happening except that which comes under their personal command. My impression is that our great General Staff is very poor, and we have no military genius like the Grand Duke,[2] or leader of men like Joffre.[3] Our men are incomparable – but they suffer from lack of experienced officers. We have a muddle instead of a government, and the War Office is controlled by men devoid of imagination. It is impossible to judge about the quality or quantity of information which is given to the Press unless one knows the whole facts. The Public has never ceased to resent the action of the Admiralty over the accident to the *Audacious* early in the war, but the truth has never been officially stated for reasons which it was impossible to betray.[4] The Admiralty has suppressed news, and always I think with good reasons, but it has never given false news. The War Office I know very little about, but I feel inclined to criticise the suppression of certain disasters and defeats, because I think it has helped to increase the extraordinary lethargy of this country towards the war. I am not in the smallest degree a pessimist

[1] Not printed.
[2] Nikolai Nikolaevich (1856–1929), Uncle of Nicholas II (1868–1918) and Grand Duke of Russia. He was appointed Commander-in-Chief of Russian forces at the outbreak of the European War in 1914 holding the post until September the following year, when Nicholas II himself assumed the supreme command. He was then sent to the Caucasus as Commander-in-Chief of Russian forces there. In 1917 he was re-appointed by Nicholas II to his previous post, but his appointment was cancelled by the provisional Government, and he remained in the Crimea until March 1919 when he left for France, to live at Antibes until his death.
[3] Joseph Jacques Césaire Joffre (1852–1931), French soldier. Victor of the first Battle of the Marne in 1914, he became Commander-in-Chief of the French Army in December 1915 but was relieved of his command after the Battle of the Somme in December 1916 and did not resume active service.
[4] The British battleship *Audacious* was sunk by a mine on 27 October 1914. The British Admiralty was so stunned by its loss that they tried to cover it up, and the full truth was not known until after the war.

and I have complete confidence in the ultimate success of the Allies, but I never regret the rare Air Raids with which we are visited because I hope they will rouse the non-combatants to realise that we are involved in the greatest war the world has ever known, that our National Security depends on the issue of the war. That fatal phrase 'Business as usual' has been the undoing of much enthusiastic energy which would have been so useful early in the war. Nothing should be 'as usual' – nor could it be if only the average Britisher had imagination instead of the insatiable demands of his stomach! To return to the subject of Air Raids – there has never been any damage to Woolwich Arsenal, or Liverpool Street Station. A street in Whitechapel was badly knocked about. The numbers of killed and wounded are always given correctly – the reason of suppressing the locality is that the aircraft are navigated by compasses, and if they know where they've dropped bombs they can correct their adventures for another time. It is quite evident from German accounts of these Raids that unless we publish the locality the enemy is nearly always quite wrong. We are having considerable success in destroying enemy submarines and it is evident that they are getting very anxious about this form of warfare and would like some excuse to give it up. The question of Cotton Contraband is agitating America and ourselves – I feel that our miserable government is greatly to blame for the question having reached a somewhat acute stage. At the beginning of the War the Foreign Office and Board of Trade changed their minds (?) every week as to what should be contraband or conditional contraband, and it is this vacillation which has aggravated America and other Neutrals. We had every right (and an excellent precedent in the action of the American Government during the war between the North and the South) to declare a close blockade, and to make cotton contraband, but we tried to satisfy everybody – and succeeded in satisfying nobody and undoubtedly lengthened the war. I have nothing but contempt for the Americans. They have allowed Germany to disregard every clause of the Hague Convention, to commit every description of bestiality, and have made no really vigorous protest, or warned Germany of what her relations with Neutral Nations will be after the war whatever the final issue. The Americans know that the Allies stand for the liberty of the civilised world and Germany for savage tyranny, and yet they say nothing beyond a mild explosion of anger at the loss of the *Lusitania*. To return to your letter, what you say about the battle of Neuve Chapelle is correct – it ought to have been a success, (we did succeed in taking some ground) but the attack failed for a variety of reasons and because some of the troops moved forward much faster than was expected; they were not supported by those in the rear, and they were shelled out of captured trenches by our own artillery. I can't help thinking that this sort of thing must be the fault of the Headquarter Staff. I believe it is much too large for one thing. It is absurd that on a front of 40–50 miles, and hundreds of thousands men we are arrested for some mysterous reasons from taking the vigorous offensive. I simply don't understand *what* we and the French are doing. We are moving in on Gallipoli, and have effected another landing which I hope will help. Please don't think that I am taking a depressing view of the position of the Allies. I have no doubt about the End, but I am utterly disgusted with the feebleness of the Government in conducting the war. We want a War Council instead of a Cabinet. We want National Service instead of this played-out voluntary system. We want a suppression of Trades Union Laws and Regulations. We want Martial Law. We are harassed and delayed on every side by hordes of small officials and all the clumsy machinery of 'Constitutional' Government. The King is afraid of his Ministers and has no initiative.

All that you say about the Japanese is most interesting – the Boycott has certainly had some effect. The exposure of corruption among the members of the government in Japan rather amuses me as you know it is nothing new. I once said something on this subject to Sir Claude MacDonald when I was in Japan, and he was most annoyed with me. I don't criticise it – it is not unknown in this country in the last ten years! Of course the Japanese will make use of the war to further their own ambitions but I cannot understand their policy in bullying China. There are frequent rumours that Yuan Shih Kai intends to found an imperial dynasty, but unless I hear it from you I don't believe it. I believe the best thing for China would be to restore the boy emperor – marry him to a Cantonese – with Yuan as the Power behind the Throne. What do you think?

I'm sorry our Legation is so badly represented in Diplomatic Circles – the women are almost as important as the men. I am amused to hear Lady Bredon[1] is still faithful to Putnam Weale otherwise Simpson – such a relationship ought to become legalised after so many years of fidelity!

I hope your nephews will be preserved from wounds illness and death. There is hardly a household of my acquaintance which is not in mourning, and racked with anxiety. I'm thankful that my only son is still a child. Do write to me again when you have time, and tell me about the new member of your family. With good wishes to you always

Yours ever sincerely
Beatrice Brownrigg

[1] A sister of Sir Robert Hart and wife of Sir Robert Bredon, for many years Deputy Inspector-General of the Imperial Chinese Maritime Customs.

August 1915 – June 1916

The monarchist movement, which had been intensifying its activities for some months, finally made its formal public appearance in the middle of August 1915, with the founding of the Ch'ou-an hui, or Peace Planning Society. Of the six whose names appeared in the Society's manifesto, one was China's earliest and most prominent anarchist; one was a well-known purveyor of modern Western thought in China, being the translator of Darwin, Huxley, John Stuart Mill and Spencer; three had been active figures in the early stages of the 1911 Revolution, while the prime mover of the whole scheme, Yang Tu, had been Vice-Minister of Education in the last Manchu Cabinet. The aim of the Society, according to its manifesto, was to promote discussion on the most suitable system of government in China. It made no secret, however, of where it stood on the matter. It not only analysed the reasons for the failure of the experiment in parliamentary government after the founding of the Republic, but quoted in its support from a memorandum prepared for the Chinese President by his American Legal Adviser, Francis Goodnow. This man, described as 'a great student of politics' of 'the senior republic of the world' and therefore 'more competent than others' to make a statement on the subject, had declared that 'it is of course not susceptible of doubt that a monarchy is better suited than a republic to China'.

While attracting a great deal of attention and becoming the focal point of public discussion for months to come, the Ch'ou-an hui's appearance and its explicit platform caused little surprise. Already at the end of 1913, soon after the debacle of the 'Second Revolution', Yüan's henchmen had started searching for ways of strengthening the presidential powers. This was followed by a rapid succession of measures emanating from legislative bodies set up by Yüan and manned by hand-picked 'delegates' to take the place of the dissolved parliament, such as the restitution of imperial titles and institutions as a prelude to the return to monarchical government. This trend culminated in the promulgation of a Constitution on 1 May 1914, which virtually made the President a dictator for life. Having thus far encountered no open opposition to what was represented as the will of the people through their 'elected representatives', the more extreme among these were emboldened to think that the time had come for a public movement to hasten the realisation of their scheme. Hence the foundation of the Peace Planning

Society which by its very name proclaimed that unless China adopted a monarchical system peace would not prevail.

The immediate pretext used by the sponsors of the Society for launching their open campaign was Goodnow's memorandum. Paul Reinsch, American Minister in Peking at the time, thought Goodnow should have had more political acumen than to make such a statement, but defended his innocence in the conspiracy. Goodnow himself tried to explain publicly that he was not the originator of the monarchist idea, that he was unaware of the use to which his statement would be put, that he was dealing with the question from a purely theoretical point of view and that he had been quoted out of context. Goodnow's denial was obviously made on the advice of his friends. When giving Morrison a copy of the memorandum in question, long before the matter surfaced, he had made clear his stand on the issue. While the Chinese masses did not understand what a president meant, he maintained, they knew what an emperor meant and would obey him willingly. Monarchy would also smooth the succession problem and avoid possible conflict and bloodshed. Goodnow certainly knew what he was doing when he gave his opinion on the subject and his views, as Morrison wrote at the time, were 'most explicit'.

Goodnow's memorandum notwithstanding, contemporary observers (and later historians) were puzzled by the timing of the monarchist campaign. China had hardly recovered from the shock of Japanese pressure over the Twenty-One Demands and the country was in ferment at the Government's acquiescence. Yüan himself, as Morrison recorded after one of his visits to the Chinese President, was 'hypnotized and paralysed by fear of Japan, like a frog in the presence of a snake'; and the snake was watching warily in case the frog tried to jump on to the imperial throne. Yüan's timing thus seemed tantamount to suicide. Morrison, however, provides us with a possible explanation when he wrote a few days after the above interview with his master that Yüan was 'evidently worried at the mess he is making of things and wishes to do something theatrical to retrieve his prestige'. When he wrote this Morrison was quite unaware of what was afoot; but his words were prophetic. The 'something theatrical' was precisely what the Ch'ou-an hui set out to perform.

Soon after the Society's formation in the middle of August, provincial authorities and military governors were instructed to 'consult' the 'people' and organisations under their jurisdiction as to their opinion on the question of the monarchy. With energetic official prompting, an enthusiastic and 'unanimous people's deliberation' was speedily reached in early November. The upshot was that a month later the Consultative Council, which was set up by Yüan for the purpose and which was handling a 'plebiscite' following on the provincial 'consultations', petitioned the President imploring him to yield to 'the unanimous wishes' of his subjects that he mount the imperial throne. In face of such 'overwhelming manifestations' Yüan modestly declared that he, 'a mere citizen among the four hundred million', would be wrong to reject the 'will of the people' and authorised preparations to proceed for the official enthronement on 9 February of the following year. Joint representations by Japan (who had earlier hinted approval), England and Russia against such a step did not deter him from his grandiose schemes.

In the meantime, from the south-western province of Yunnan came the first ominous rumblings. On 23 December 1915, the Provincia Governor, T'ang Chi-yao, issued a declaration warning Peking that unless the plan to establish the monarchy was cancelled and its sponsors punished, Yunnan would declare its independence. This is precisely what the province eventually did. The campaigns launched against the monarchists gathered under the banner of Yunnan all the disaffected elements, among them men like Ts'ai O (one of the most respected revolutionary leaders who had succeeded in escaping Yüan's surveillance), and Liang Ch'i-ch'ao (the erstwhile reform leader and one of China's best-known publicists). Yunnan was soon joined by its neighbours Kweichow and Kwangsi. It sent its army into Szechwan, which still pledged allegiance to the central government in Peking.

More serious to Yüan, however, was the threat posed by Japan from her occupied territory in Shantung. The Japanese were now not only implementing their repeated veiled threats to allow Chinese revolutionaries to operate from this base but were also sending their nationals to foment disturbances in the interior of the province. The Chinese provincial government was paralysed in the face of these activities. On the one hand it feared that the disturbances might invite Japanese intervention; on the other, that the arrest or killing of Japanese trouble-makers might provoke Japanese reprisals. It was another dilemma for a Chinese: whether to feel gratitude for Japan's assistance to her patriots or resentment at her duplicity.

The combined opposition grew daily more ominous as the enthronement date drew near. Yüan Shih-k'ai began to have second thoughts and finally, submitting to various pressures, decided on 23 February to postpone the enthronement indefinitely, two weeks after Morrison's outspoken condemnation of the monarchical plan (printed below as the enclosure to Letter No. 799) written significantly on 9 February, the day originally planned for the ceremony to take place. This decision was followed a month later, on 21 March 1916, by the abandonment of the monarchical restoration, again on the very day, as it so happened, that Morrison dated his memorandum advising this course of action. To the opposition from the growing ranks of the anti-monarchist forces was now added the resentment and grievances of those of his supporters who felt he had abandoned ship at the eleventh hour without giving them fair warning or guaranteeing their safety. Faced with this crisis, Yüan provided China with the best possible solution, as Morrison was later to describe it – his death, which occurred on 6 June 1916.

In this selection we have omitted many key documents such as Goodnow's memorandum, which can be found *inter alia* in the Papers of the State Department, *The Foreign Relations of the United States*, for 1915. Instead, we have given space to the story from the other side of the fighting line, including letters from a missionary in Szechwan and from an English business man who was hired by Yüan's secretary, Ts'ai T'ing-kan, through Morrison to spy on the movements of the Yunnan insurgents.

773. From Ts'ai T'ing-kan

Peking 17 August 1915

My dear Doctor,

I am privately sending you an interesting document[1] on the subject of which we had some talk a few days ago. I am sure the Government would like to have your views on the matter and an abstract treatment of the question of its own merits leaving out all personal element would increase the weight of your arguments.[2] The suitability of the form of government which will best ensure China's stability is *the* question. Will see you at 4.30 today at the President's office.

Yours sincerely
Tsai Ting Kan

774. To J. N. Jordan

Peking 20 August 1915

Private

Dear Sir John,

This is Goodnow's paper.[3] You will note on page 14 the paragraph which formed the text of the proclamation of the Chou An Hui.[4]

[1] This refers to a memorandum entitled 'Republic or Monarchy?' by F. J. Goodnow, former American Constitutional Adviser to China, and at the time President of Johns Hopkins University, in China on a visit.
[2] Morrison seems to have written a memorandum on the subject as Ts'ai T'ing-kan here requested. For, writing to Morrison from London on 3 October 1915, Tiao Ming-ch'ien (q.v.) said that he had heard Morrison 'had submitted to President Yuan a memorandum on the monarchical question differing from that of Dr. Frank J. Goodnow in the particular that you advocate a postponement of the contemplated momentous change.' No such memorandum before 3 October 1915 was found, but two of Morrison's later memoranda on the subject are printed below as the enclosure to Letter No. 799 and Letter No. 805.
[3] Goodnow's memorandum 'Republic or Monarchy?', not printed.
[4] The paragraph in question reads: 'It is of course not susceptible of doubt that a monarchy is better suited than a republic to China. China's history and traditions, her social and economic conditions, her relations with foreign powers all make it probable that the country would develop that constitutional government which it must develop if it is to preserve its independence as a state, more easily as a monarchy than as a republic.'

It is, I think, particularly unfortunate that a disquieting agitation of this kind should be started. The President is firmly in his seat; he ought to set himself to do work and justify his election and if he did work for a few years he could be entitled to support.

I have the lowest opinion of Yang Tu, especially for his operations in Hankow.

I enclose also for your confidential perusal a copy of a letter I recently addressed to Liang Shih-yi in reply to a communication given him to send me.[1] I have shown this to Macleay.

Liang Shih-yi says that after reading it he kept awake for two nights. It has been well translated by my confidential assistant in the President's office,[2] supervised by Tsai Ting-kan.

I am preparing also a detailed statement of what China has *not* done during the three years of my service.[3] I prepare these papers so that I can subsequently defend myself – so that it cannot be said of me what it may be said of others in similar position, that 'an adviser is one who tells you that what you are going to do is the proper thing to do!'

I saw the President on Tuesday and he seemed to me to be ill. He was asthmatic and complaining. He seemed to me to be unhappy and he somewhat plaintively said that he had more power when Viceroy than he now has as President.

Please return the papers to me when you have read them.

I am much worried for my wife feels the heat greatly, and the war news and now this mad scheme[4] of causing tumult in China are most disquieting.

Very sincerely yours

[G. E. Morrison]

775. From J. N. Jordan

Peking 23 August 1915

My dear Morrison,

I return herewith your letter to Liang Shih yi and hope I have not kept it too long. It is a powerful indictment of Chinese policy and should do some good if there is any disposition at all to listen to advice.

But China is of little account at present in view of the momentous events in Europe. It looks as if European civilization were trembling in the balance.

Yours sincerely

J. N. Jordan

[1] A reference to Letter No. 770 and the enclosure to Letter No. 765.
[2] Ju Jen-ho.
[3] Morrison wrote no less than three memoranda at different times on the subject, expressing disappointment and dissatisfaction. They appear in the Diary volumes.
[4] A reference to the monarchical scheme.

This Monarchical agitation is great nonsense and is, of course, a purely fictitious movement engineered by selfseekers. If there is trouble in China, the whole world will be in a turmoil and we have enough of that in all conscience already.

776. From H. A. Gwynne

London 23 August 1915

My dear Morrison,

Of course, I'll be god-father and very proud to be to boot.[1] I thank you for asking me and still more for the way you asked me. You are one of the faithful ones and I have not forgotten – hope I never shall, the many many kindnesses you have shown me. I hope this letter will come in time.

We are well in it here but the Germans don't even now understand us. We *mean* to win. Every effort of the smallest and most insignificant citizen here is directed to the one aim – beating the Germans. Never has the nation been more united and never has the determination of England been more pronounced. The Russian *débâcle*[2] only makes us set our teeth all the more and every man feels that he would rather die than live in a world controlled by Germans. We are, as usual, late in the field but we are coming on and when you get this letter I am sure compulsory service will be established here.

The fatal mistake the Germans make is to imagine that the world will submit to them. The European world submitted to Napoleon for a while because it would not help itself but as soon as it could, bang went Napoleon. So, too, only much more so, the world does not intend to submit to a civilization which is 200 years in arrears. And yet the benighted Germans do not even see that.

One of the most pathetic (and yet tragic) pictures of the war is the real honest grief of the Germans in Belgium that the Belgians do not like them. They really are puzzled. They truly believe that their *Kultur*[3] is so superior that inferior nations must run mad with joy to adopt it. They stand quite aghast as at the spectacle of a little nation disliking them and their version of

---

[1] Gwynne had been asked by Morrison to be the godfather of his second child, who was born the day after this letter was written, on 24 August – a boy later christened Alastair Robin Gwynne.

[2] A reference to the Russian collapse in Poland under the advance of General von Falkenhayn. Both Warsaw and Ivangorod fell on 5 August, followed by Novo Georg Iewsk two weeks later, on 19 August, and the battle began in the Pozcza Region on the very day this letter was written, followed by the fall of Brest Litowsk five days later. The retreat was explained away by Sergei Dmitrievich Sazanoff (1866–1927), the Russian Foreign Minister, as being due to the demoralising effect of German propaganda on the Russian troops. The Russian military set-back caused the first revolutionary agitation in the Duma the following month.

[3] 'Kultur, n. Civilization as conceived by the Germans. [G. = culture].' (*The Concise Oxford Dictionary of Current English.*)

civilization. There you have the true picture of the German and the whole essence of Germany's ideals.

Give my best regards to your wife – tell her that I shall be a proud man to become the god-father of any of your children. Good luck.

My wife sends her love to you all

Yours ever
H. A. Gwynne

777. From Hsieh Tsan-t'ai

Hong Kong 24 August 1915

Dear Dr. Morrison,

Newspaper Correspondents in the North say that President Yuan is making preparations to don the purple! Is this true? Do you approve of such a change? Don't you think the results will be disastrous!

I have just finished the rough draft of a new work in support of my book – *The Creation – The Real Situation of Eden and The Origin of the Chinese*.[1]

This book will contain convincing proofs (geological and scientific) of The Creation and the Deluge and it is my intention to publish it after this terrible war is ended. The title of the new book will be *Proofs of The Creation and The Deluge*. Hoping you are in the enjoyment of fine health and with kindest regards.

Yours very sincerely
Tse Tsan Tai

[...]

778. To Hsieh Tsan-t'ai

[Peking] 20 September 1915

Dear Mr. Tse,

I was much interested to receive your letter of the 24th August and to learn that you had written a new work on the *Creation and the Deluge*, and that you are going to publish it after this terrible war is ended. But why wait till then? A book of such absorbing interest ought to be published without any delay. In fact, on receiving your letter, I thought at once of telegraphing to you and asking you to delay no further: every hour is of importance.

I would suggest with regard to the title that you ought to lay emphasis on the fact that the work is by a Chinese philosopher. This I think is most important and I would suggest that it would be a friendly act if you were to dedicate your book to the Allied Rulers, sending each one of them a copy.

[1] The place and date of publication of this work have not been traced. The book to which this was a sequel was entitled *The Creation and Deluge*, of which too the place and date of publication have not been traced.

Their acknowledgements would give material assistance in making the book more widely known.

I have been waiting, with much expectation, for your pronouncement upon the activities of the Chou An Huei, who, I understand, are putting forward three proposals: –

1. That the President shall become Emperor.
2. That the President shall become Hereditary President.
3. That the President shall be Hereditary President *vis-à-vis* foreign countries and monarch in the eyes of his people.

Believe me

Very sincerely yours
[G. E. Morrison]

779. To Ts'ai T'ing-kan

[Peking] 28 September 1915

My dear Admiral,

I enclose you a memorandum regarding the suggested appointment of Sir Louis Dane in connection with the Land Tax. I hope I have made the case quite clear. It would have been interesting if I had developed the question and shown how the land system of the Punjab is so curiously similar to that of China, but that would be superfluous.

[...]

With best wishes to you

Yours very sincerely
[G. E. Morrison]

Enclosure to Letter No. 779: *Memorandum suggesting the appointment of an Indian administrator to introduce reform into the land tax, 28 September 1915*

I suggest that the time has come when the Government should seriously consider the advisability of applying later methods to the collection of the land revenues than those that prevailed during the preceding dynasty.

For this work it will be necessary to obtain the services of an expert trained for the work under analogous conditions. India alone can provide an administrator. In India the land revenue collected – although the country is of much smaller area than China and contains a much less numerous population – amounts to more than £22,000,000 *per annum*. The conditions of the two countries are in many respects analogous. It is this fact which has always enabled an administrator trained in India to adapt himself more readily to the conditions in China.

Of the provinces in India the province where the conditions regarding the holding and taxation of land most nearly resemble those of China is the Punjab, and the land tax system of the Punjab is the one which independent observers consider most easily applicable to the present conditions in China. No great changes are needed, only that guidance is required which, in the light of long experience under improved conditions in India, can show how the immense leakage which now takes place can be prevented.

In 1713, the Emperor Kang Hsi decreed that the land was to be fixed and immutable, but overwhelming evidence can be produced to show that the land tax is not fixed and is not immutable. By juggling with exchange it is increased in every case. Careful study over large areas in the interior shows that the amount paid by the taxpayer is not less than four times as much as the amount paid into the Treasury.

A well-known English consul, who is regarded as one of the chief authorities on China,[1] found in Ssuchuan, where he spent a year, that the additional charges imposed by the tax collectors increased the land tax in some districts to ten times its nominal charge.

In the Punjab the Government revenue is assessed not on each field or block, but on the whole of the land within the boundaries of what may roughly be called the *village*. The *village* is the unit of assessment. The Government has no dealings with individual cultivators; these small proprietors, associated together in village communities, are represented by an elected or hereditary head and are jointly responsible for the land tax from the entire village.

In China the tax-collector exacts what custom will tolerate from the taxpayer, the cost of collection, which may vary from 10 to 15 per cent, being added to the legal amount due. Instances can however be given where, for the purpose of increasing the levy, the tael is converted into cash at 2600 to the tael and then converted back into taels at 1100 cash to the tael, and then afterwards 50 per cent is added for the cost of collection.

Towards the settling of the land revenue the Chinese Government have taken the necessary step of ordering an accurate survey to be made of the country. Such a survey has been proceeding in India since 1805, that is to say for more than 110 years, and the work is not yet complete. It is a long and costly process. In China, with every desire to have the work accomplished quickly, it is doubtful if the survey can be completed within 30 years, and this survey means the constant expenditure of money. While this work is proceeding surely it would be prudent and remunerative to introduce those methods which experience in India has proved to be the most economical.

In China the system whose introduction is suggested will be that which brings about as small a change as possible; its chief feature will be its simplicity; all the people will be able to understand it. The system will see to it

---

[1] George Jamieson. He was author of *Revenue and Expenditure of the Chinese Empire* (1896), to which Morrison here makes reference. Elsewhere Morrison spoke slightingly of Jamieson and regarded his work as somewhat out of date. (*See* his letter to V. Chirol of 15 January 1910, *Correspondence*, Vol. I, p. 541.)

that the tax paid is reasonable and just and that the tax paid actually reaches the Treasury, checks being designed to prevent leakage.

In the case of the Salt tax, the harmonious co-operation of the Chinese authorities with a highly trained Indian administrator has succeeded in ensuring a certain and large revenue, the surplus of which is available for any future loan should borrowing be required.

In the case of the land tax an Indian official of equal experience should be invited to introduce, in harmonious co-operation with the Chinese authorities, a system which would effect the same result in the land tax as has been effected in the Salt Gabelle.

Such an administrator is, I believe, available, one whose knowledge of the land tax system of India is quite exceptional. The administrator I refer to is a younger brother of Sir Richard Dane, and one of the most distinguished of Indian administrators.

Sir Louis Dane G.C.I.E. was born in 1856. Entered the Indian Civil Service in 1876 and retired in 1913, having spent the greater part of his service in the Punjab. From 1892–1896 he settled the land taxation assessment of the large district of Peshawar, in the Punjab. From 1902–1908 he was Secretary to the Government of India in the Foreign Department, that is to say he was the Foreign Minister of India. During his tenure of office in the Viceroyalty of Lord Curzon, he conducted the highly important mission to Afghanistan and negotiated the Treaty of 1905. From 1908–1913 he was Governor of the Punjab, one of the most important of the high offices in India. He is now in retirement in England and would, I believe, be glad to come to China to emulate the success gained by his elder brother.

What I suggest is that Sir Louis Dane be invited to come to China under engagement for three years to recommend to the President those Indian methods by which the land revenue of China can be made more productive. There is reason to believe that under improved methods the land revenue paid to the Central Government would be increased threefold.

Objection might be made to the appointment by Mr. Kroupensky, the Russian Minister, on the ground of Article 4 of the Declaration of July 6th, 1895, by which China undertook never to grant to any foreign Power any right or privilege whatsoever in regard to the supervision of the administration whatsoever, but this is not a reasonable objection. Sir Louis Dane would not be supervising or administering revenue, he would simply, as an expert in land taxation, be giving to China the benefit of the knowledge which he had acquired during an administrative career of much distinction in India. Russia, at the present time bound to England by the alliance, could not reasonably object to the appointment of a distinguished Englishman, and would be still more unlikely to object to the appointment of a brother of Sir Richard Dane, whose relations with the Russian Legation have always been most cordial.

In the event of its being desired to come to an arrangement with Sir Louis Dane, preliminary work will have to be done by someone trained in land administration in China. In that case I would suggest that Mr R. F. Johnston, the Magistrate of Wei Hai Wei, a well-known Chinese scholar and one who has travelled widely in China, should be invited to join the service of the Government for two or three years in order to assist Sir Louis Dane.

In the meantime, should it be decided to consider this proposal, I would suggest that a confidential agent be instructed to discuss with Sir Richard Dane the possibility of engaging the services of his brother.

780. From O. M. Green

Bournemouth [Hampshire, England] 2 October 1915

Dear Morrison,

I hope you will excuse my rudeness in not answering your letter[1] before; but we had sailed before it reached Shanghai, [...].

I have not yet seen *The Times* people, but when I do, I will speak about the supplement,[2] if it's not too late. Geoffrey Robinson I have never yet met, but of course I know Steed well. Strictly between ourselves I do not fancy the Northcliffe influence has done *The Times* much good. It has developed a sort of waspish tone which a lot of people do not like, and the *Morning Post* is thought by many to be superior. I should be very glad to get back to England, but not to London where the journalist's conditions of life are more and more trying and wearing. Well, I've booked with the *N.D.C.N.*[3] for another three years anyway, and except for its being so far from England, a journalist has every reason to be proud of that job.

The war as seen from England is both more interesting and more perplexing than seen from China. On the one hand, we have certainly had a lot of successes, especially at sea, which never get into the papers. On the other, the way the Government has wasted and is wasting money is appalling. National service from the outset would have saved us millions. Now I think it is too late to introduce it as Labour – knowing very well that the main idea of national service would be to get cheaper work under military discipline, as opposed to trade union laxity – won't allow it, and Labour dictates most things now in this country. The Government is very unpopular all round – Lloyd George the one exception, and rapidly becoming a national hero! By all one can hear, he really deserves it. People speak of him as the future Conservative Prime Minister.

There has been a lot in the papers of late about China having an Emperor again. People ask me my opinion with a gravity quite out of proportion to the

[1] Printed here as Letter No. 762, dated 27 May 1915.
[2] A reference to a China Supplement published by the *North China Daily News*.
[3] The *North China Daily News*.

absurdity of the question (as if anyone would risk an opinion on such a point). But then the ignorance of people at home about China is mountainous. Most of them seem to think that one has to go about perpetually armed to the teeth for fear of being seized and tortured to death at a moment's notice. I lose no opportunity of extolling the virtues of old John Chinaman, which are surely far more numerous than his faults, and on the whole far more shining than those of many other nations.

With best wishes to yourself and Mrs. Morrison

Yours very sincerely
Owen M. Green

781. From R. F. Johnston

Weihaiwei [Shantung] 29 October 1915

Dear Morrison,

If you are very busy, I apologise in advance for writing to trouble you with a private matter; and if you feel inclined to curse me for a nuisance, just throw this letter into your w.p.b. and don't trouble to send a reply.

You probably know the series of books called 'The Home University Library' published by Williams and Norgate. I am writing for this series a monograph on the Chinese kingship – that is, the theory of monarchy in China as developed in the classical literature and in Chinese political tradition.

You of course know the old Chinese custom whereby distinguished persons from emperors downwards contribute prefaces to books written by other people; therefore there is nothing strange or presumptuous, from the Chinese point of view, in asking a Chinese public man, however exalted in rank he may be, to contribute a few words by way of preface to a book of the kind which I am preparing. What I want you to do, if you will be so very kind, is to have the enclosed memo explained to the President (perhaps he may be emperor by the time this reaches you!) in the hope that he may condescend to let me have a few words, in Chinese, which I could publish in facsimile, accompanied by my own translation, at the beginning of my book. If it is in his own handwriting, so much the better. I saw in a newspaper, a few days ago, that Yuan had given the correspondent of the *Manchester Guardian* a long letter to be published in the China supplement of that paper; and if he will do this for a foreign newspaper I do not think it would be unreasonable to expect him to write a few words for a book which (not on account of any merits of its own but because of the series in which it will appear) is pretty sure to reach a large and thoughtful section of the foreign reading public.

To save you any trouble in explaining the nature of the book I have written the accompanying memo, which perhaps you might give to some

English speaking secretary or other official who would be likely, at your request, to bring the matter to Yuan's notice in a tactful and persuasive manner!

Needless to say I shall be extremely grateful if you can help me in this matter. Possibly I ought to make my application through the legation; but my request is purely a private and unofficial one, and I much prefer that it should go through you.

Yours sincerely
R. F. Johnston

Enclosure to Letter No. 781: *Memorandum by R. F. Johnston*

The title of the book is *Kingship in China and its relation to Confucianism*.

It attempts to describe and explain the traditional Chinese theories relating to monarchic government as set forth in the classical literature, especially the [*Shu-ching, Shih-ching, Ch'un-ch'iu, Tso-chuan, Ta-hsüeh, Lun-yü, Chung-yung, Meng-tzu, Li-chi*].[1] The book attempts also to show how erroneous is the common Western idea that the Chinese monarchy of the past was an irresponsible despotism. It shows, on the contrary, that according to Confucian principles the powers and privileges of the monarch were strictly limited by his correlative duties and obligations; that he had the 'divine right' [*T'ien-ming*][2] to rule, *only so long as he fulfilled the human duty to rule well*; and that, in China, sovereignty ultimately rests with the Chinese people. It is shown that it is quite possible to establish a real constitutional monarchy without departing from the spirit of Confucian orthodoxy; and that the best hope for China's future progress (both social and political) lies in a loyal adherence to *and amplification of* the policy which is evidently that of the President himself – namely, to respect and keep in touch with the Confucian basis of Chinese civilization and with the ethical and political principles in which that civilization is rooted, while not hesitating to cut away all that is rotten and corrupt and to introduce all modifications and readjustments that may be necessary to meet modern requirements and to enable China to take her proper place among modern progressive nations.

R. F. Johnston

782. To Ts'ai T'ing-kan

[Peking] 29 October 1915

My dear Admiral,

[...]

Yesterday at 5.30 the Japanese Chargé d'Affaires supported by the British and Russian Ministers, made a communication to the Government regarding

[1] For the Chinese characters that were used in the original, *see* Glossary.
[2] *See* Glossary.

the establishment of the Monarchy.¹ You will no doubt have heard the exact words of the communication. It is most significant that the communication should be made now; it is most ominous. It shows how marked is becoming the tendency of the British and Russian Governments, engaged in the great struggle of Europe, to entrust the guidance of their policy in the Far East to Japan.

It seems to me that the time has come for China to reconsider her world attitude. I have written a short suggestion which I would like to discuss with you.²

[...]

With best wishes to you

Yours very sincerely
[G. E. Morrison]

783. From Ts'ai T'ing-kan

[Peking] 1 November 1915

My dear Doctor,

The President said this morning he must have or find a good excuse or pretext for going in.³

Find one for him and embody it in the memo, either signed or not as you please.

Yours sincerely
Tsai Ting Kan

¹ On 28 October 1915 Obata Yukichi (or Torikichi) (1873–1947), Counsellor at the Japanese Legation in Peking and at the time Chargé d'Affaires, accompanied by the British Minister, Sir John Jordan, and the Russian Minister, Basil Kroupensky, sought an interview with Lu Cheng-hsiang, the Chinese Foreign Minister, and 'advised' the Chinese Government in a *note verbale* to postpone the change to a monarchy. Obata, who had served as a consular official in Tientsin and other places in China as well as in Australia and England before taking up the present post, was known for his aggressiveness, fully shown during the negotiations over the Twenty-One Demands when he, rather than Hioki Masu, the Japanese Minister, was Japan's chief spokesman. In 1918 he returned to China as Minister, after serving for a period as Director of the Administrative Bureau in the Foreign Ministry, and in 1922 was a member of the joint Sino-Japanese Committee on Shantung. He later became Ambassador to Turkey (1925) and to Germany (1933). In 1931 he was made a member of the House of Peers and joined the Seiyūkai, and in February 1937 he was named as Foreign Minister in the cabinet of Hayashi Senjūrō (1876–1943), but did not take up the post.
² Morrison seems to be referring to the memorandum now forming the enclosure to his letter to Ts'ai T'ing-kan of 1 November 1915, printed here as No. 784.
³ Entering the War on the side of the Allies.

784. To Ts'ai T'ing-kan

[Peking] 1 November 1915

My dear Admiral,

I send you herewith the Memorandum. Every care must be taken not to give to the declaration any appearance of its being prompted by a desire to prevent the aggression of Japan. Facts must be faced. The Allies have for the time being ceded to Japan the foremost position in the Far East; their policy is apparently to be guided by Japan.

On Friday I caused it to be telegraphed by Reuter that the French Minister[1] associated himself with the Japanese advisory note, or whatever may be its diplomatic term. I assumed this to be the case and thought it well that it should be made known in order to prevent too strong an outburst of indignation against Japan. Just now I hear from David Fraser that the French Minister has received instructions to support his Allies and he will convey this intimation to the Waichiaopu probably this afternoon. I gather that the French Minister himself told Mr. Fraser this.

What I now fear is that Japan may seize the German and Austrian concessions in Tientsin and the German concession in Hankow which adjoins her own and has valuable harbour facilities.

Such action can, of course, be prevented if the course I suggest is followed. I earnestly hope that our mission can succeed.

With best wishes

Yours very sincerely
[G. E. Morrison]

Enclosure to Letter No. 784:

China has reached a critical period in her history. What is to be her policy for the future? During the summer the Emperor of Germany repeatedly assured his subjects that the war would be over in October. He believed that Russia was crushed and that the forces of Germany could then break their way through to Calais and to Great Britain. But his confidence has once more proved empty. If there is one thing certain it is that this war cannot end for another year. Many indeed there are who believe that the war will continue for two years longer.

In the meantime Japan every day is becoming richer, every day she is becoming stronger, every day her influence with the Allies is becoming more assured. More and more [it] is becoming apparent that the European Powers are willing to recognise Japan's predominant position in Far Eastern Asia. Even if Germany should be victorious in Europe Japan cannot be affected. So long as Britain's navy remains supreme no German ship can venture away from the protection of German land defences. Even if the British navy were defeated Japan's navy would still remain intact. Even if Germany were to

---
[1] Alexandre Maurice Conty.

send ships to attack Japan there is not a single coaling station left for Germany between Europe and Japan.

China is aware of the immense position Japan has obtained for herself among the foremost nations of the world. Is China to make no attempt to attain to a similar position?

Is China still to remain neutral? In 1904-5, China, unable to preserve her neutrality, was exposed to the humiliation of witnessing a great war waged on her territory. Again last year there was the spectacle, humiliating to all Chinese, of witnessing the advance through Chinese territory of a Japanese force marching to wrest from Germany territory which Germany had wrested from China by one of the most unjust acts perpetrated in her history.[1]

All China's troubles can be traced to German action in Tsingtau. Under the pretext of obtaining satisfaction for the murder in the interior of Shantung of two German priests, the German Emperor, having made arrangements to do so long before the date of the murder, seized Kiaochao and compelled China to sign agreements giving to Germany concessions in Shantung[2] which have impaired for ever China's sovereignty in that province. Germany's brutal act of aggression lost China the only harbour in Shantung and led to the loss of Port Arthur, with all its consequences, to the Boxer Rebellion, with all that it has cost China.

China has now an opportunity of recovering much that she has lost and of establishing her position in the sight of the world.

The time has come to make a decision. That decision must be come to quickly. China should renounce her neutrality and declaring that she is on the side of right and justice, should offer her support to the great Powers, England, France, Russia, Japan and Italy, and join with them in destroying for ever the power of evil of the German Empire. As one who has herself experienced oppression, she should stand before the world in support of the oppressed. China's trade is being ruined by the war and by the action of Germany: she should in her own interests do all that in her lies to bring that war to a conclusion.

The small State of Belgium, a country with which China has had the most friendly relations for many years past, has been ruthlessly crushed. Serbia is suffering a similar fate; the Turkish allies of Germany, instigated thereto by German officers, have committed the most appalling massacres known in the history of the world.

The President has read the harrowing stories of the crushing of Belgium, of the barbarities such as the sinking of the *Lusitania*, of the air raids on England, of the ruthless killing of women and children, and he still remains

---

[1] A reference to the Russo-Japanese War which was fought on Chinese territory, and to Japan's attack on the German Leased Territory of Kiaochow, when the Japanese army forcibly landed on Chinese territory.

[2] A reference to the Convention respecting the Lease of Kiaochow, signed on 3 March 1898.

neutral! Have the Chinese forgotten the part played by Germany in 1900 and the cruelties of German troops at Tsang Chow in this province and the slaughtering of innocent peasants. Have the Chinese forgotten the part played by Germany in imposing upon China the gigantic indemnity under the burden of which China is still groaning? Are the Chinese to forget what Germany has done in China? The time has come when China can recover much that she has lost and can establish her position for the future.

China must ally herself with England, France, Russia, Japan and Italy and declare war on Germany. The strongest reasons can be given for such a step:—

1. China champions the cause of the oppressed and raises her position among the nations.
2. She averts all danger of possible future aggression for no aggression is possible against an ally.
3. She will be allied with the Great Powers who are henceforth to dominate the world.
4. Of these Powers, England, France, Russia and Japan are the Powers that encircle China. Whatever happens they will see to it that no act of aggression can be committed against the allied friendly Power who came to their assistance while the war was at its height.
5. China will be given a seat at the conference to determine the conditions of peace. Should she remain neutral as at present she will never be given a hearing at any Peace Conference.
6. China will place her resources at the service of her Allies. These resources can be of material assistance, especially to Russia and Japan. Her arsenals can produce munitions of war. Immense quantities of military stores can be supplied. Money will pour into the country as it is pouring into Japan. China will be relieved of her financial difficulties. Dalny can become a port of entry for the vast military stores now being sent to Russia through Vladivostok.
7. China can confidently count on the support of the allied Powers in the recognition of the Monarchy.
8. China can confidently expect the approval of the allied Powers to the increase of her Customs, to the settlement of the Mongolian question, to the settlement of the Tibetan question and to the arrangement of many questions that will improve the condition of the people.
9. China will resume control of the Austrian and German concessions in Tientsin and of the German concession in Hankow. Is it possible to believe that these German concessions will be allowed by the Allies to remain in the possession of Germany?
10. China will cease for ever to pay the Boxer Indemnity due to Germany, the amount of which now outstanding is the mighty sum of more than

one hundred and fifty-five and a quarter million dollars at the present rate of exchange.
11. China will dismiss the German Legation and all German Consulates, will compel the Germans to withdraw from Shameen, giving in every case safe conduct by a Japanese ship to America.
12. Can the effect of such policy be other than good for the patriotic people of China? Will they not rejoice to see China revenge herself for the wrongs she has suffered in the past at the hands of Germany, for the humiliation her seizure of Kiaochiao has exposed her to? Will not attention be diverted from home affairs to the mighty triumph of the Government in allying itself with the great and friendly Powers of the World? Will not Chinese Financiers rejoice to think that the days of the Quintuple Bank alliance are ended and that China is within reasonable distance of recovering her fiscal freedom?

785. To Ts'ai T'ing-kan

[Peking] 5 November 1915

My dear Admiral,

The article in the *Peking Daily News* yesterday, urging China to join the Allies, was written by an American and represents, I believe, the views of the best Americans in Peking.

There is considerable indignation among the Allies, especially among the British, at the wrongful use made of the Chinese Governments Telegraphs by Dr. Krieger, the Correspondent of the *Ostasiatischer Lloyd*. Two days ago this mischievous man telegraphed for distribution by his Agency the lying allegation that it was England, not Japan, who took the lead in the opposition to the Monarchy and that it was England who induced Japan to make the communication of Oct. 28th.[1]

Surely the constant abuse by Germany of Chinese neutrality ever since the war began has been pretext enough for China to suspend diplomatic relations with the country which has involved China, and is involving China, in serious complications with friendly countries. The reply given by Sir Edward Grey regarding the use of Shameen,[2] Chinese territory, to carry on a press campaign against Great Britain was couched in the usual mild diplomatic form, but privately it is known how strong is the indignation of the British Government against the attitude of China in taking no steps to prevent the abuse of her neutrality by Germany.

[1] *See* p. 463 n. 1.
[2] Replying to a question in the House of Commons on 26 October 1915 on British jurisdiction in the territory of Shameen, leased from China at Canton, Sir Edward Grey said that although the territory was perpetually leased to Britain it was still a part of China; that British authorities there could not expel tenants of foreign nationality so long as they complied with the conditions of the lease, and that to expel German nationals by force would be an infringement of Chinese sovereignty.

Germany, scheming to cause disaffection among the Mahommedans of India and induce them to revolt against the British Government, is disseminating lying statements among the Mahommedans of China, especially of Far Western China. In doing so and in using Chinese to endeavour to smuggle arms into India, Germany is involving Chinese subjects in intrigues against Great Britain.

Recently, a well-known man belonging to one of the Legations in Peking has been making an independent enquiry regarding the feeling of the various Powers as to the likelihood of China's being given a voice at the Peace Conference following the war. The result of the enquiry was the unanimous expression of opinion that China, not being a belligerent, could not be given a hearing at any Conference.

The British Government seriously contemplated the ejection of the Germans from their concessions in China, but, as Sir Edward Grey explained, such action was held to be an infringement of China's rights, China being the sovereign of the soil where the concessions are situated.

Many ask the question, will the same restraint continue to mark the attitude of the other Powers?

With best wishes

Very sincerely yours
[G. E. Morrison]

786. To Ts'ai T'ing-kan

[Peking] 6 November 1915

Very Private

My dear Admiral,

I have reason to know that the American view in regard to the suspension of diplomatic relations with Germany coincides with my own.[1]

The only objection I have heard is the astonishingly slender one that the removal of Germans from the Customs would mean an increase of Japanese.

But the increase would be infinitesimal for there are French, British, American, Russian, Norwegian, Swedish, Danish, Belgian, Italian, Spanish, Portuguese nationalities to be selected from and the share to each would be very small indeed and largely temporary.

Questions are being asked as to what has become of the German crews

---

[1] On the question of China's participation in the European War on the side of the Allied Powers, Morrison kept in close contact with Americans and members of the American Legation, particularly Paul Reinsch the Minister. Reinsch gave his version of the story in his book *An American Diplomat in China* (London 1922).

'interned' at Nanking. It is believed that all have escaped and it is suggested that the Chinese authorities are responsible for the escape although they may not have assisted it.

Yours very truly
[G. E. Morrison]

787. To J. N. Jordan

Peking 10 November 1915

Dear Sir John,

Quite apart from the Short Term Loans which amount to several millions sterling, and the service whereof amounts to some hundreds of thousands of Pounds, China has to pay to Germany during 1916 for the service of Government Loans £1,445,000 equal to nearly £4,000 per day. [...]

I am sorry to see that Admiral Tseng has been killed.[1] Yesterday the President told me he was ordered to Canton to report on the Arsenal there.

Liang Tun-yen is bound to support the Germans. All or most or much of his money is on deposit in the Deutsch–Asiatische Bank.

Yesterday the President said to me: 'When I wished to join in the capture of Tsingtau, some of my generals – even some of my staff – who were under German influence and who had been educated in Germany, opposed the idea on the ground that Germany was our friend. I said to them it was Germany who in the most brutal manner obtained Tsingtau from us. We can now take back what Germany took from us on the most shallow pretext. They saw reason and agreed that my view was correct.'

As a matter of fact the President has such a forceful personality that he has no difficulty in inducing generals, or any other of his countrymen, in acquiescing in his wishes and agreeing that what he recommends is the wisest course to follow.

Yours very sincerely
G. E. Morrison

788. From Ts'ai T'ing-kan

Peking 29 November 1915

My dear Doctor,

I return this very interesting letter.[2] The President has ordered us to send

---

[1] Reference to Admiral Cheng Ju-cheng, Garrison Commander of Shanghai, who was assassinated by revolutionaries on the day this letter was written.

[2] Not found, but it undoubtedly refers to a letter from O'Malley Irwin on his discovery in Hupeh Province of the so-called dragon bone, referred to here as the 'wonderful fossil'. The 'discovery' was considered a good omen by Yüan Shih-k'ai and his supporters for Yüan to ascend the Chinese 'Dragon Throne'. The 'bone' turned out to be a fake. *See* Letter No. 797, p. 484.

a telegram to the Governor of Hupei to make inquiries and to give adequate protection to the wonderful fossil.

The letter ought to be published.

Yours sincerely
Tsai Ting Kan

789. To G. W. Prothero[1]

[Peking] 1 December 1915

Dear Dr. Prothero,

Last week I wrote you a hurried note in order to catch the mail. I said then and I now have to repeat that to my great regret circumstances have prevented me from fulfilling my wish to write a paper for the *Quarterly*.

My position has been a difficult one. I could not write a paper on China without speaking of Japan or of the monarchical movement or of the contemplated alliance with the Entente Powers and in each case the difficulties of treatment were insuperable.

The action of Japan in submitting to China on the 18th of January a series of demands, acceptance of which would have prejudiced the British position in China and at the same time communicating to the British Government a false copy of these demands from which the most objectionable clauses were omitted was an act of turpitude which has called forth widespread surprise and indignation. No account of China could have ignored this strange episode or have failed to condemn such a policy of chicanery.

Nor could one write a paper on China without speaking of the Monarchical Movement and with this movement I have no sympathy. I thought it unwise and ill-timed and likely to lead China into international entanglements. And I held strongly the opinion that the movement should be delayed until after the conclusion of the European War. While I could urge my views upon those in authority I could not write my disapproval in an English magazine.

On October 28, as you will have seen in the papers, the Japanese, British and Russian representatives tendered friendly counsel to China urging her to postpone the change to the monarchy until after the War, and a few days later the French Minister and still later the Italian Chargé d'Affaires joined in this representation.

[1] George (later Sir George) Walter Prothero (1848–1922), British scholar and Editor of the *Quarterly Review*. A History tutor at King's College and a University Lecturer in History at Cambridge, he became in 1894 the first Professor of Modern History at Edinburgh University. In 1899 he resigned the Chair to take over the Editorship of the *Quarterly Review* from his brother, Roland Edmund Prothero (q.v.) when the latter became Agent-in-Chief to the Duke of Bedford. George Prothero was editor for some twenty-three years, until his death. In 1919 he attended the Paris Peace Conference in the capacity of Historical Adviser to the Foreign Office. He became a regular correspondent of Morrison and saw a lot of him whenever Morrison was in London.

At the present time China is contemplating adhesion to the Entente. Russia, France and England favour this step, but the stumbling-block is Japan. In August of last year the Chinese Government desired to take part in the operations having for their object the ejection of the Germans from Tsingtao. The desire was communicated to the British Minister,[1] who advised China to take no action. In so many words he indicated that her co-operation was not needed. I was not in China at the time. The British Minister did not consult his Russian or French colleagues, did not even inform them of the Chinese offer. It is known that both regard his action as a diplomatic blunder. At the present time conditions in Asia render it advisable that China should join the Alliance. The advantages to the Entente Powers can hardly be exaggerated. China is regarded as a mighty power in Asia. She has a Mahommedan population numbering not less than 10,000,000. German intrigue is using every device to turn these Mahommedans against Great Britain in order to provoke or assist sympathetic Mahommedan unrest in India and in Persia. German intrigues in China can best be met by China's joining the Allies. This will mean the expulsion of all Germans from China, the seizure of German Concessions in the Treaty Ports, the cancellation of the German share of the Boxer Indemnity amounting to £13,500,000, and the suspension of payment of various Railway and Government Loans for the service of which and the Indemnity China is now paying – as you will have read in *The Times* – £6000 per day.

In order, however, to enter the Alliance China insists that she shall be invited to join by the four Powers, England, France, Russia and Japan. The President will not a second time expose himself to a rebuff such as he experienced in August of last year.

On November 6 it was made known to the British Government that China was prepared to take the steps that would lead to her joining the Alliance. Fear of Japan, and of what Japan might oppose, caused some delay when every day was of importance, but finally it was arranged that the English, French and Russian Ambassadors in Tokio should call upon the Japanese Foreign Minister and make conjoint representations urging the advisability of the Four Powers co-operating to invite China's adhesion to the Alliance. The advantages pointed out were not only the indirect advantages of removing for all time German influence in China, stopping German intrigues, which are menacing the peace of Asia, and wrecking German trade to the great advantage of Japanese trade, but the direct advantages of placing the arsenals and other resources of China at the service of Russia.

China has five arsenals, two of very considerable importance, the third of less importance, and two smaller ones. To improve the arsenals more modern machinery would be required and for their purchase loan monies would have to be obtained from the Powers interested. Japan, however, can claim special

[1] Sir John Jordan

interest in the chief arsenal and she is quite unwilling to see any other influence in the arsenals of China than her own.

You will remember that in the series of demands submitted to China on the 18th January emphasis was laid upon the advantage to China of Japanese co-operation in the extension and administration of the arsenals. (Japan has not yet given her answer to the proposals made by the Ambassadors. She views the move with suspicion. She is opposed to any improvement in the standing of China among the nations. She cannot view with equanimity the appearance of China at the Peace Conference following the War, a right which will be granted to China if she becomes a belligerent, but which will be denied her if she remains neutral.)

Suspicion has been further engendered in the Japanese mind by an unfortunate sentence in a communication made by Sir Edward Grey when submitting the views of the British Government to the Japanese Ambassador in London.[1] In regard to this question Sir Edward Grey referred to communications that had passed between the Chinese and the British. The Japanese suspect that negotiations had taken place between the British and the Chinese with the cognizance of the Russians and the French but without the knowledge of the Japanese Government. Much explanation has been necessary to remove this impression. The outlook at present is not good. China is prepared to come into the Alliance if invited to do so by the four Powers but Japan appears to be standing in the way, although it is difficult to believe that she would be a party to prevent help being granted to the three fighting nations of the Alliance.

If China should be invited, she will ask for three conditions:— (1) That her integrity be guaranteed, especially against any future reprisals on the part of Germany; (2) that she will enter into possession of the Concessions in Tientsin and Hankow, from which Germany is driven, and that these will not pass into the possession of the Allied Powers; her fear being that Japan might occupy the German concession in Hankow which adjoins the Japanese Concession, and (3) that more adequate measures may be taken to prevent foreign concessions from being the sanctuary from which Chinese rebels can plot against the State.

It is unfortunate there should be this delay. Every day is of importance, and this Japan knows well. For this delay gives the Germans time to set their machinery in motion in China and through the Press to incite the people against the policy of the Government. Before this letter reaches you, you will have heard the result. *The Times* is being kept exceptionally well-informed by its correspondent, a fellow-Australian of mine, named Mr. W. H. Donald. You need place little reliance upon what is said in the *Daily Telegraph*, as its

---

[1] Inoue Katsunosuke (1860–1929), Japanese diplomat, son-in-law of Inoue Kaoru, a leading politician of the Chōshū Clan. Inoue Katsunosuke was Japanese Ambassador to Britain from 1913 to 1916. He had previously been Minister to Belgium (1898), Germany (1898–1906), then Ambassador there (1906–8).

correspondent is denied access to any Legation in Peking and to any Chinese authority of substance.

There are many difficulties ahead. Japan has been, I am sure, difficult to manage. She has gained enormously by this war; her financial position has improved wonderfully; all her arsenals have been re-equipped since the war began and re-equipped at the expense of Europe. Balance of trade is in her favour; her shipping trade is reaping unexpected harvests. The longer the war continues the greater the advantage accruing to Japan. Japan has rendered many services since the war began and she will demand her price. That price, I am afraid, will have to be paid by China.

I would like to write you more fully, for I am sure you are much interested in the Far Eastern question – a very small question, it must be admitted, in comparison with the titanic struggle in Europe. We are following the course of the war with the keenest interest, but with absolute conviction as to its glorious ending. We have an admirable telegraph service, and it has been said by recent arrivals from England that in Peking we receive more news of the war than you do in London.

With kind regards

Very sincerely yours
[G. E. Morrison]

790. From T. A. Rustad[1]

Ho-kou, Shensi 5 December 1915

Dear Dr. Morrison,

I have now been over in this district since the middle of August and I have several times thought of writing to you, but as usual have only bad news as far as the state of this part of the country concerns, I have so far not thought it worthwhile to bother you.

[...] The general topic of conversation with businessmen and farmers with whom we come in contact, is always the numerous and high new taxes which are making it extremely difficult for farmers and Businessmen in this district to make both ends meet. In fact the Belgian missionaries tell me that there is a lot of people in this district, mostly farmers who can only afford one meal every-other day and many are even worse of. It is certain that these numerous new taxes and the way they are collected will sooner or later cause the people here to rise against the officials. Bands of brigands are increasing everywhere, as farmers without any means of making an honest living find themselves obliged to join the lawless robbers. Lately I had a letter from father J. Terstappen,[2] who lives at San-Tao-Ho about 300 *lis* north of Ninshiafu on the Yellow-river and he tells me that the brigands over there

---

[1] The spelling in this letter is as it was in the original.
[2] Belgian Catholic missionary working in Inner Mongolia.

move in bands of from 1000 to 2000 and that they have been engaged in battle by general Ma-Fu-Hsiang[1] who drove them away from Ning-Hsia-Fu territory over into territory which is under the jurisdiction of the Kuei-Hua-Cheng *Chiang-Chun*.[2] Troops from Pao-Tou who were over there did not dare to attack the brigands who have taken charge of that district and are squeecing the life out of the poor isolated farmers who make their living there. [...] Paotou now is a regular Opium-centre where dealers are selling and buying openly. Great profits are being made on the drug by everybody concerned in it and it is said that the Kuei-Hua-Cheng *Chiang-Chun* is getting his part of the loot. Great quantities of Opium is said to be stored by the secretary of the Mongol Prince Chungar, who lives only about 200 *lis* from this place, in Ordos territory. A new magistrate has now taken over the post in this place. His predecessor only kept the place for 5 months and is said to have retired with a good lump of money. The magistrates nowadays, never being sure of how long they may keep their places are obliged to make their little pile as soon as they can, to the detriment of the people over whom he rules. But nobody interferes and the magistrates have everything their own way as nobody dare to expose them for fear of the revenge that will certainly be lavished upon the man who would try and stop their squeecing. A realy funny incident occurred when a young man went to a magistrate near Hsi-Tsu-Mu informing the magistrate that the robbers were in his village pilaging and robbing the farmers. The magistrate answered by putting the young man in prison for spreading false rumours. That is a good illustration of how the magistrates run this country. [...] Nobody here takes any interest in the restauration of a monarchie with Yuan-Shih-Kai as Emperor, all they care for is the question of the ever increasing taxes and how they are going to make their living. A landed propriator was sent from here to Peking to act as

[1] Ma Fu-hsiang (1876-1932), Chinese soldier. He came from a Moslem family in Kansu Province which produced many well-known Republican figures who between them for many years controlled a large area of north-western China. Ma Fu-hsiang was the father of Ma Hung-k'uei (b. 1893), later Governor of Ningsia Province (1933-48) and uncle of Ma Hung-pin (1883-1960), Acting Governor of Kansu (1930-1) and Governor of Ningsia (1948-9). Ma Fu-hsiang first came to notice while serving under the Moslem General Tung Fu-hsiang (1839-1908), when he fought against the advancing Allied Forces in defence of Peking in 1900. On the fall of the city he became an escort for the Imperial party as it fled to Sian. After the establishment of the Republic, he was appointed Garrison Commander of Ningsia, and for the next ten years served in various capacities in the surrounding disturbed districts in Inner Mongolia. In 1921 he was appointed Military Governor to the Special District, later Province, of Suiyuan, holding the post until 1925 when Feng Yü-hsiang withdrew there after his defeat by Chang Tso-lin, and Ma was replaced by one of Feng's subordinates, Li Ming-chung. Ma cooperated with Feng Yü-hsiang until 1929, when Feng turned against Chiang Kai-shek. For his stand Ma was rewarded with the Governorship of Anhwei Province and membership of the Central Executive Committee of the Kuomintang. In the following year he became Chairman of the Mongolian and Tibetan Affairs Commission.

[2] P'an Chu-ying.

spokesman for this district of course after having received his instrnsuctio from the magistrate how to vote. Lately it was rumoured that the mongol Prince Chungar, whose territory starts on the opposite side of the river here, was against the restauration of the Monarchie and an order from the Kuei-Hua-Cheng *Chiang-Chun* ordered the local magistrate to go over and see the Prince and get to know why he refused to support the monarchical movement. As the said prince or rather his secretary who runs the business for this prince is said to be a man of his own opinions, the magistrate did not dare to go but sent the Chairman of the local chamber of Commerce to see the Prince. This man went over with a special letter from Peking which finally made the Prince and his secretary agree to supporting the new movement. The Prince then sent a petition to Peking asking for the restuaration of the Monarchie. In such way does the present government enlist the supports of influential men. The natives here fear that a change will make things even worse than they are now.

[...]

Yours sincerely
T. A. Rustad

791. To F. A. Aglen

Peking 7 December 1915

My dear Aglen,

[...]

On Saturday morning I had a visit from Kamei,[1] the editor of the *Shun Tien Shih Pao*, who has just returned from Japan. He is a man of some consequence. In Japanese he is quite an orator. He knows Baron Kato well. Kato spoke to him about the return of Tsingtau to China. He laid emphasis upon the alteration of conditions due to the refusal of Germany to listen to 'Japan's advice', which thereby brought upon Japan the necessity of expelling the Germans by force at a great expenditure of money and the spilling of much Japanese blood. Kamei said that the Japanese naturally desired to build a railway from Lungkow to Weihsien, but he thought that Japanese interests would be served by the construction of a railway from Chefoo to Weihsien. Japan would assuredly claim some right of interference in this construction, but he thought that it would be easy to arrange for the construction to be done by the British with the co-operation of the Japanese. His idea

---

[1] Kamei Rokurō (1871–1923), Japanese journalist. He first went to China in 1900 as Correspondent for the *Jiji Shimbun*, and became a frequent visitor to Morrison's house in Peking. An advocate of war against Russia, he assisted in the intelligence work of Aoki Nobuzumi, then Military Attaché with the Japanese Legation in Peking. In 1911 he succeeded Ueno Iwatarō (q.v.) as the Director of the *Shun-tien shih-pao* the Japanese Government-controlled Chinese-language newspaper in Peking. In that position he also played an important role as an unofficial spokesman and political go-between.

of co-operation, however, seemed to be that the British were to provide the capital and the Japanese were to do the construction.

Kurachi,[1] former Vice-Minister of Foreign Affairs in Japan, now Vice-President of the Sino-Japanese Development Co., came to me on Saturday afternoon, but I was out. I will see him to-day. I will also ask him over to lunch, and if he can come I will let you know and ask you to come over if you care to, although I am afraid you do not often go out to lunch, to meet him here and have a talk with him. He is a man of considerable influence.

Ginnell[2] came in to see me this morning, having seen Sir John Jordan on Saturday, who thought that British and Japanese co-operation was advisable. He said he would leave the matter in the hands of Macleay.

I spoke to Kamei about the appointing of the Japanese Customs officer from Osaka. He seemed to think it was due to misunderstanding. I read in the *Manchuria Daily News* an excellent article, evidently inspired by Tachibana. I hope the Japanese have reconsidered their attitude and that there will be no difficulty.

I will let you know if I hear anything regarding the railway.

With kind regards

Very sincerely yours
[G. E. Morrison]

[1] Kurachi Tetsukichi (1870–1944), Japanese diplomat and business entrepreneur who, after serving in China and elsewhere, was made Director of the Political Bureau in the Japanese Foreign Ministry in 1908, a post he held for four years assisting the successive Foreign Ministers, Hayashi Gonsuke (q.v.), Komura Jutarō (q.v.) and Uchida Yasuya (1865–1936) in the negotiations of the Anglo-Japanese Alliance, Russo-Japanese Agreement, Franco-Japanese Agreement, United States–Japanese Agreement, and the Korean Annexation Treaty. In 1912 he became Vice-Minister of Foreign Affairs, and in 1913, following the negotiations between Sun Yat-sen and Shibusawa Eiichi (q.v.) the leading Japanese businessman and industrialist, a joint Sino-Japanese enterprise, Chūgoku Kōgyō Kabushiki Kaisha (China Industrial Development Company Limited) was established, and Kurachi was appointed to take charge of the enterprise as Vice-President of the company, with Sun as nominal President. After the failure of the 'Second Revolution' the company was taken over by the Yüan Shih-k'ai Government and reorganised into Chū-Nichi Jitsugyō Kabushiki Kaisha, translated here as Sino-Japanese Industrial Development Company Ltd. Yang Shih-ch'i replaced Sun Yat-sen, while Kurachi remained in control of the new company as its Vice-President. The company, which had as its partners practically all the leading Japanese industrial and trading firms, including the South Manchurian Railway Company, Ōkura, Mitsubishi, Mitsui and many others, exercised extensive control over numerous Chinese enterprises in many parts of China, particularly in Manchuria and Shantung.

[2] James Ginnell, a British railway engineer.

792. From R. R. Gailey[1]

Peking 12 December 1915

Dear Dr. Morrison,

This is not the first time I have written to you when Chinese in whom I am interested were in trouble, or in danger of getting involved unjustly. It is the memory of your sympathy and promise of aid if necessary which prompts me to write again, though I hope that in this case there will be no need of intervention. I want you to be informed in regard to Mr. K'ung so that if any emergency should arise, there would be no delay in getting necessary information.

Mr K'ung tried twice to see you during his recent stay in Peking, but you were not at home. He wishes to acquaint you with the facts of this enclosed statement. Whether he would have told you in addition of recent family complications I do not know, but because of the investigations of this detective I think it is well to tell you, though Mr. K'ung told me in confidence. Mrs. K'ung[2] has a younger sister, Rosamonde,[3] who has recently returned from study in America. This impulsive girl has been enticed by Dr. Sun to marry him, his wife having been divorced for this purpose. This daughter was with her father in Shanghai, her mother having gone to Shansi to be with her daughter Mrs. K'ung in her confinement. The night that her mother returned to Shanghai the girl left for Japan with an emissary of Dr. Sun who had been sent there for her. Her parents were distressed beyond measure, and as soon as they could get a clue of their daughter's whereabouts, they followed her to Japan, but arrived too late, the marriage having already taken place. It was distress at this which caused Mr. Sung's serious illness, and called his daughter, Mrs. K'ung, to his bedside at Chingdao [Tsingtao]. The family feel very bitter against Dr. Sun for enticing this innocent enthusiastic daughter of an old friend to leave her home in this clandestine mélange, also for his faithlessness to the wife who had shared his trials, and whose children are older than the girl whom he recently married.[4]

[1] Robert R. Gailey, at this time American Secretary of the Young Men's Christian Association in Peking.
[2] The wife of K'ung Hsiang-hsi, Sung (or, as the family itself spelt it, Soong) Ai-ling (b. 1890) was the eldest of the six children of Charles Soong or Sung Chiao-shun (1866–1918), an American-trained missionary-turned-businessman and industrialist. She and her two younger sisters were educated at Wellesley College for Women in the United States.
[3] The English name of Sung Ch'ing-ling (b. 1892) or Madame Sun Yat-sen. She took a somewhat different political course from the rest of her family and relatives from 1927, after the emergence of Chiang Kai-shek, and was a prominent sponsor of many radical causes in the Nationalist period in China. She became one of the five Vice-Chairmen of the People's Republic of China in October 1949 when Mao Tse-tung was elected chairman.
[4] The first Madame Sun Yat-sen, Lu Mu-ch'en (1867–1952), gave birth to three children of whom Sun K'o (or Sun Fo) (b. 1891) was the youngest and best known. He occupied

If you think that this statement should be shown to Dr. Reinsch, will you inform him, or send to him yourself? I do not know whether he is acquainted with Mr. Kung.

Yours sincerely
[R. R. Gailey]

Enclosure to letter No. 792: *Statement in regard to Mr. & Mrs. H. H. K'ung*

Mr. K'ung Hsiang Hsi is a former student of the N.C. [North China] Union College located in T'ungchou. In 1901 he went to the United States where he took the degree of A.B. at Oberlin College, and of M.A. at Yale University. He returned to China as the representative of the Oberlin–Shansi Memorial Association, which supports educational work in Mr. K'ung's native place, T'aiku, Shansi. With this important educational work Mr. K'ung has been connected continuously since his return, with the exception of one year when he was granted leave of absence to take the position of head secretary of the Chinese Y.M.C.A. in Tokyo. Mr. K'ung's salary is paid by Oberlin College students, and he is recognized as their representative in China.

While Mr. K'ung was in the Y.M.C.A. work in Tokyo he became acquainted with Miss Regina Sung,[1] and married her in September, 1914. Since their return to China in the spring of 1915 they have been living in T'aiku, and have a little daughter born in September 1915.

The Sung family came, I think, from Macao. At least they are not Chinese subjects, but they lived many years in Shanghai, their daughters studied in the McTyeire School, and their sons in St. John's College, and all except the youngest, who are still in Shanghai, have studied, or are studying, in the United States.[2] Mr. Sung was an early friend of Dr. Sun Yat-sen, and the

---

many high posts in the Nationalist Government which came into being after his father's death in 1925, and served, *inter alia*, as Minister of Communications and of Finance, and in 1931 briefly and again in the last days of Nationalist rule on the mainland held the post of Prime Minister. For the greater part of this period (1932–48), however, he was head of the Li-fa yüan or Legislative Council, something of a sinecure but a post which many considered to be commensurate with his indifferent ability. He was the leader of a clique within the Kuomintang known as the T'ai-tzu p'ai (the 'Crown Prince' Clique) and typically he, the 'Crown Prince', was merely living under the shadow of the real ruler, Chiang Kai-shek. This clique attracted a number of the less successful members of officialdom, whose occasional outbursts of grievance as a result of failure to gain advancement smacked of a certain radicalism in the context of a party dominated by the extreme right in the Chinese political spectrum. It failed to serve as the bridge intended by Sun K'o between diverse elements within the Kuomintang, and partly through depletion of its ranks by death (of Wu Chao-shu and others) and by desertion (of Wu T'ieh-cheng (1888–1953) and others), the clique had ceased to be a political force long before the Kuomintang was swept from the Chinese mainland.

[1] The English name of Sung Ai-ling.
[2] Madame K'ung had three younger brothers, Sung Tzu-wen, Sung Tzu-liang and Sung Tzu-an. Of these Sung Tzu-wen, known to foreigners as T.V. Soong (1894–1971), was the most prominent. He was first educated at St. John's University, a Christian college in

families have long been acquainted. Miss Regina Sung after graduating from Wesleyan College in America returned to China, and was very popular in legation and official circles in Peking, where she lived with an aunt while her uncle Mr. Wen[1] held office in the Board of Foreign Affairs. After the Revolution took place and Dr. Sun arrived in Shanghai, she became his English secretary. She is a bright, talented woman, and assisted him not only in his English correspondence but in many other ways. Her father is a man of wealth, and when the Second Revolution was promoted, he was persecuted for money to finance it, and took refuge in Japan. Mrs. Sung is an earnest Christian woman, and as the family attended the Chinese Christian Church in Tokyo, Mr. K'ung became acquainted with the daughter and the marriage which ensued was the result of mutual attraction.

Dr. Sun did not favor this marriage. Mr. K'ung had never identified himself with the revolutionists, though offers had been made to him, and Dr. Sun doubtless felt that he might some time need again the services of his former very efficient secretary. For this and other reasons the break between Dr. Sun and the Sung family has been complete of late, and the old friendship has become an enmity. The Sung family returned to Shanghai. An important family affair, having no connection with politics, took Mr. Sung to Japan recently. He got back to Ch'ingtao ill, and Mrs. K'ung was summoned there from Shansi. He has since improved in health and returned to Shanghai.

Mr. and Mrs. K'ung got back to T'aiku Dec. 4th, and on the 6th Mr. K'ung wrote as follows: – 'A friend called on me yesterday to inform me that Mr. Yin, the chief of detectives from T'aiyuanfu was here on "Business" and also made inquiry into all my affairs and especially to find out about my wife's people. We are without a doubt suspected to be with the revolutionists that we despise, and there is no telling what is coming next. This afternoon the magistrate paid me a visit. I acquainted him with the fact that Yin is making inquiries, and he informed me that Yin is a bad and dangerous man, a big swindler, who has gotten many men into trouble. He was a *Hunghutze*, and now is the right hand man of the civil governor[2]. The magistrate thinks that Yin is not sent by the authorities but that he is trying to stir up trouble and thereby extract some money, a trick which he has used many a time effectively.' This letter was to a personal friend, and Mr. K'ung wrote, 'You at least know that we are absolutely innocent of all their suspicions.'

The writer was in Tokyo several months before Mr. K'ung married Miss Sung, and knows positively that this marriage did not unite Mr. K'ung with

Shanghai, and then at Harvard, graduating in 1915. He became Finance Minister in the Nationalist Government in 1925 and held the post almost continuously until 1933, when he was superseded by his brother-in-law, K'ung Hsiang-hsi. He was for long periods Acting Prime Minister and served as Foreign Minister from 1941 to 1945 and Prime Minister from 1945 to 1947. He went to live in the United States in 1949 and died in New York. [1] Wen Ping-chung.

[2] Chin Yung, Civil Governor (May 1914–July 1916), previously Director of Civil Affairs.

the revolutionists, but on the contrary removed Miss Sung from any connection with them. Mr. K'ung while in Tokyo loyally supported the government, a fact which can be proved, and at the sacrifice of personal popularity with some of the Chinese students.

793. From Ch'ien Wen-hsüan[1]

Yunnanfu [Yunnan] 10 January 1916

Dear Dr Morrison,

I regret to say that since I came here I have not been able to communicate to you except I sent you a telegram when I first arrived at Yunnanfu. It is because that all my energy and time have been devoted to the service which is quite new to me and further still I have tried my best to be friendly with all officials.

Not long after my arrival and on the 25th of December 1915 this province contemplated separation from present Government in case of restoring monarchy. The local authorities have threatened me to deliver all the Salt Revenue to them I refused to do and said all money is in Mr Bande's hand.[2]

Having received telegraphic instruction from C.I.[3] we have had a consultation with the Representatives of the *Tutuh* and the result is that we would do what we had been doing before. They have been very satisfied for giving subsidy as usual.

There is another great difficulty. As all soldiers who stationed everywhere in this province have been withdrawn the brigands fill their places, who plunder and rob. Not only salt merchants and travellers have suffered but our Tax-Collectors and *Weiyuans*[4] also have the greatest difficulty in keeping and transporting their treasures. What we can do for them is only asking the *Tutuh* to instruct the local authorities and militia to protect them. We issued a notice to ask the salt merchants to go on their business as before in order that our collection will not decrease.

I am a Chinese and have been badly threatened by the local authorities but they did not show any violence to Mr Bande, Foreign District Inspector. However I am willing to endure all hardships if they will come and be faithful to the service.

Hoping you are very well and have a happy New Year. Please give my best regards to Mrs Morrison and yourself.

Yours very sincerely
W. H. Chien

[1] Republican official, and a returned student from America, he was at this time Manager of the Branch Office of the Salt Administration in Kunming. He had previously been Supervising Director of Chinese Students in England.
[2] District Inspector of the Salt Administration in Yunnan.
[3] Chief Inspector i.e. Sir Richard Dane.   [4] Commissioners.

794. From R. F. Johnston

Weihaiwei [Shantung] 12 January 1916

My dear Morrison,

Very many thanks for your two letters of the 29th Dec. and 6 January, and for the 'Preface' which accompanied the latter.[1] It was most kind of you to interest yourself in the matter, the preface will serve my purpose quite well. I am sure Williams and Norgate[2] will be delighted. I will not have the book published till the Yunnan trouble is over. It obviously contains elements of great danger to the new dynasty, as the republicans will materially do all they can to support the movement. Moreover, you and I both know Yunnan well enough to realise the difficulties that the northern troops will have to cope with! The rebellion may last years, and be a constant drain on the slender resources of the central government. The Yunnan republicans have worded their manifesto very skilfully.[3] The breaking of the presidential oath is emphasised by them, very naturally, and it is perhaps the most unpleasant feature in the royalist proceedings. It seems to me that the President did not get out of the difficulty of the oath as well as he might have done. He might have done better to formally resign his position as President to begin with, and retire (as a matter of form) into private life. Then the presidential oath would no longer be his concern, and would no longer be technically binding on him. Thereafter he might have accepted the throne as a private individual. It might then have been plausibly argued that the presidential oath was binding only on Yuan as *Ta Tsung-tung*[4] not on Yuan as a mere ex-president. I suppose the President of the United States takes an oath to defend the Republican constitution; yet from the loyal and technical point of view I should think that if the Americans now chose to offer a royal crown to ex-President Roosevelt[5] and make him king of America, he might accept the offer without being regarded as a violator of his oath. This is only an idea that has occurred to me in view of the (very natural) adverse comments that have been made on Yuan's conduct in breaking his oath.

The people of these parts do not take the slightest interest in Peking politics, and the accession of the President to the throne leaves them quite cold. The 'elections' in this part of Shantung were a complete farce.

With heartiest greetings to yourself and your family

Yours very sincerely
R. F. Johnston

[1] This refers to a preface written by Yüan Shih-k'ai, which Morrison had secured at Johnston's request. *See* also Letter No. 781. Morrison's letters to Johnston are not printed.   [2] British publishers.

[3] A cable sent to Yüan Shih-k'ai on 23 December 1915 by the anti-monarchist party in Yunnan headed by T'ang Chi-yao and Jen K'o-cheng demanded that he should abandon his monarchical plan and punish its instigators, and stated that, failing a satisfactory reply by 25 December, Yunnan would immediately declare its independence. And this was what happened.   [4] Literal meaning, Great President, or simply President.

[5] Theodore Roosevelt (1858–1919), President of the United States from 1901 to 1909.

795. From A. J. Moore-Bennett[1]

Hong Kong 18 January 1916

Dear Dr Morrison,

I have been here – detained for a boat – for the past week and have run across to Canton and seen things and people.

Both in Nanking Shanghai and Canton I find very strong feeling against Mr Yuan Shih Kai and generally I feel that it will be almost impossible to hold the South down after the President ascends the throne.

Feeling seems most bitter and every single Chinese I have met be he rickshaw coolie or merchant prince is bitterly opposed to domination from Peking. Roy Anderson is in Canton now and every boat from Java, Singapore and the islands brings Chinese here who declare to me that they will give money and men to prevent Yuan making himself Emperor at their expense. I have preached the Gospel that now is not the time to rebel as rebellion will spell Japanese domination and Anderson has done the same but I fear it is all to no purpose, as they told me in Canton that if Yunnan could hold out until Yuan ascended the throne then on that day the S. and N. provinces will join together and secede from the North and endeavour to carry the campaign to get in all provinces S. and N. of the Yangtse.

Canton is a hive of industry and the biggest industrial city of China and seems to harbour very strong feelings against Yuan and Sir John Jordan who they claim supports him in his wickedness, of taxing trade but not helping trade or industry nor doing anything but feathering his nest. Shanghai seems to favour a Southern Republic with Li Yuan Huan[2] as President if he can be got out of Peking alive which people there seem to doubt.

One can never tell what China will do next and I do not venture a decided opinion except to say that appearances are strongly against a peaceful settlement. This letter is confidential although you may let Sir John know if you think fit as it might help me later with him. Wilton[3] in Canton seemed to know as little about internal affairs as the average treaty port man. With all good wishes to Mrs Morrison and yourself

Yours sincerely
Arthur J. Moore Bennett

[1] Arthur J. Moore-Bennett, British businessman. With a subsidy from Ts'ai T'ing-kan through the introduction of Morrison, he undertook to supply information on the political situation in Yunnan to the Chinese Government. The arrangement was soon to be terminated, however, because of what Morrison described as Moore-Bennett's being the 'incarnation of indiscretion'.
[2] Li Yüan-hung.
[3] Ernest Colville Collins Wilton, at the time British Acting Consul-General in Canton.

796. From A. J. Moore-Bennett

Shanghai 20 January 1916

Dear Dr Morrison,

This is my last chance of writing you without fear of censor before leaving.

I do feel that something might be done more than is being done, and I do feel that a prolonged campaign must mean the loss of China's independence and the loss of our prestige in China.

One of the French fathers from Yunnan is here passing through to France and he tells me that the people there would be passive if let alone but they must throw in their lot with the rebels or lose their heads. He said that the Lolos are maddened by the cruelties of the landlords and a very little is needed to make them rise and slay all the Yunnanese they can lay hands on – this fact might be of use to Yuan if matters could be arranged by defeating Tsai Ao but I am more than ever convinced that only by the North completely acquiescing to the will of the South can peace and non foreign intervention be arrived at.

Surely you can press this on Yuan, I am positive the suppression of Yunnan alone will not help matters, indeed today in a conversation with the leading Chinese banker here I was assured that the troops in both Kuangtung and Szechuan would never fight for Yuan unless a radical and far reaching change was made. To use his words the 'Provinces have to buy with their own money the whip Yuan uses to punish them with', and in my last trip I found a surprising frankness shown to me by the Yunnan troops in Kuangtung.

I cannot suggest it to Yuan – and I cannot ask you to but if a man China could really trust could have sufficient money at his disposal at a critical time – why then something might be done but I cannot see how anyone can do more than give news unless they are backed. Such backing might take the form of a draft in the Banque D'Indo-Chine Peking to be drawn against at Mongtse telegraphically so that unless it was used then the government would not lose by it. No receipts could well be given or got for money spent and the Government would have to give a *carte blanche* to whoever was nominated as it might be impossible to realize in any case – but a responsible foreigner is less likely to draw the cash and go over to the rebels than a Chinese – or alternatively some one might accompany the man as his compradore to acquiesce to the spending of the money.

If you see our Minister try to impress upon him – as I could never hope to – the seriousness of the situation and endeavour to let him see that I am doing this for our sake as much as for China as the entry of Japan means here today, Indo-China tomorrow and India the next day. After this time my letters must be conversational and news will be found interspersed with other matter.

I am not too hopeful but will do my best to persuade Yunnan to my way of thinking but affairs look hopeless. If a letter is sent to care of the Reverend Harding Chinese Inland Mission Chu-Ching Fu Yunnan or to The Rev. John Graham C.I.M. Yunnanfu they will fetch me *but they must not be addressed to me on the face.*

With all good wishes

Yours sincerely
A.

797. From J. O'Malley Irwin[1]

Tientsin 27 January 1916

My dear Morrison,

I am sorry to say that the Authorities at the British Museum have pronounced against the Fossil Theory. They have not yet made a final report and so far only say that the specimens submitted are of a very interesting and peculiar formation but are possible Stalagmites.

Personally I find it hard to believe that the things are anything but fossils but have to recognise that after all the people who say 'No' are in possession of special knowledge which I certainly lack. I am glad that I qualified my statement made in the *Far Eastern* [*Review*] and suggested the possibility of other formations. As I gave publicity to the Fossil Theory I am sending the following to Woodhead to publish in Saturday's issue of *P*[*eking*] *and T*[*ientsin*] *Times.*

'Those of your readers who may have been interested in the Article you reproduced from the *Far Eastern Review* may be interested to know that the British Museum Authorities have pronounced against the fossil theory. They have not yet made a final report and so far only say that the specimens submitted are of a very interesting and peculiar formation but are possibly stalagmites.'

Very sincerely yours
J. O'Malley Irwin

798. From Ts'ai T'ing-kan

[Peking] 7 February 1916

My dear Doctor,

The Emperor Elect will receive you this afternoon at 3.30. Will you be here at 3 or a little after?

Yours sincerely
Tsai Ting Kan

[1] A British journalist. *See* Letter No. 788, p. 469 n. 2.

799. To Ts'ai T'ing-kan

[Peking] 9 February 1916

My dear Admiral,

[...]

This afternoon I spent two hours with Mr. Liang Shih-yi. I wish my wife could have been present to have taken down in shorthand the ridiculous balderdash which the interpreter made Mr. Liang Shih-yi say to me. It is astonishing that Mr. Liang will not employ some clever young Cantonese with a mastery of English. Probably no man in China speaks more lucidly and suggestively than Mr. Liang, but his speech when delivered through Mr. Chen Lan[1] (an excellent gentleman, thoroughly honourable and trustworthy, and with a good knowledge of English relating to his own subject,) becomes jumbled and largely unintelligible.

The time was wasted. Much was lost and I sometimes was puzzled to know what was being spoken about. For Mr. Chen is not familiar with questions relating to Constitution and other abstract subjects.

Please do not think this is unfriendly to Chen who is a good friend of mine and one whose ability and character I greatly admire.

I enclose you the memorandum I have written. Will you kindly read it over, and then tomorrow morning we can discuss it so that we can act in agreement.

I gather from Mr. Liang that he is opposed to any abandonment of the Monarchy. He seemed to gather from the incorrect interpretation that I suggested a transference of power from the Chief Executive to the Parliament, but this is not my view. Very adequate authority must be retained by the Chief Executive but his responsibility must be shared by Parliament and his burden lightened.

Very sincerely yours
[G. E. Morrison]

Enclosure to Letter No. 799: *Memorandum of a recent visit to the Yangtse, Peking 9 February 1916*

In accordance with your Excellency's wishes I have just paid a visit to Hankow and the Yangtse, Nanking and Shanghai, going south by the Peking–Hankow Railway and returning by the Tientsin–Pukow Railway.

The journey was instructive. I met many people, Chinese and foreign, and had opportunities of inquiry and discussion. The result of my journey is so serious and so fully confirms the information that reached me before I left Peking that I venture to lay it before Your Excellency.

[1] The pronunciation in his native Kwangtung dialect of Ch'en Luan (?b. 1866), Chinese Republican official. A graduate from Queen's College in Hong Kong, he joined the Chinese Maritime Customs as a clerk in 1883, and served in various capacities including interpreter in the Sino-British negotiations over Tibet in 1904, and in 1906 became the Director of a school for trainees in the Customs Service. He was at the time referred to a Secretary in the Revenue Board, of which Liang Shih-yi was then Director-General and Ts'ai T'ing-kan Deputy Director-General.

Let me say at once that every man I met who spoke to me on the subject deplored the present situation in China and criticised adversely the monarchical policy which has precipitated the present outbreak. I met no man devoted to the interests of China who did not speak with indignation of the action of Your Excellency's Government in forcing despite all advice to the contrary the issue which has thrown the country into rebellion.

What was said to me varies in words but did not differ in substance. My questioners said to me:– 'As President of the Republic His Excellency Yuan had obtained as great personal power and as great personal devotion as was ever obtained by any ruler in the world. He had declared his adhesion to the Republic. It is true it was a Republic in name only and the President was really a military dictator, but Republic such as it was it opened the door to Republican institutions and we were content to wait until they were established. As President of the Republic he had received the ready recognition of all countries. With the great power entrusted to him it was hoped that he would be able to work for the good of the people, to improve the condition of the country, to reform the administration, to weed out the corrupt and inefficient officials of the ancient regime whose maladministration had brought China to a state of helplessness. It was hoped that he would be able to encourage the assistance of the enlightened, to build roads and railways, improve communications, devote attention to public works so that famine and floods might be prevented – that he would be able, in fact, to do something towards bringing China into line with the more highly developed countries of the world.'

This is what my questioners said to me and then they asked:– 'What has the powerful President accomplished? Has a single mile of highroad been built throughout China? Has any conservancy work been done? Have not tens of thousands of persons perished by preventible floods in Chihli, in the Huai River basin, in Kuangtung? Outside of Peking has the Government done anything to improve the condition of the people? Has taxation been lightened? Has currency confusion been reduced? Has any adequate effort been made to obtain the support of the educated classes of Chinese, educated, that is, in the western knowledge by which China can hope to compete with Western Powers? Where are the representative institutions? When tranquillity was restored were measures adopted for the good of the people or for the aggrandisement of the ruling family? In what respect does the Government of China now show advance upon the Government of China in the Ch'ing dynasty? In this year of 1916 what position does China, with its vast area and its vast population of intelligent beings hold among the nations? Is it conceivable that in a complex country like China the provinces can be held together by the same antiquated type of mandarins whose maladministration under the Ch'ing dynasty made China a scorn among the nations?'

If the people are well-governed, if there is just taxation and adequate protection given to life and property, the people will be contented, there will be no scope for agitators and the Japanese will not be listened to. But the conditions are such that Japanese interference is almost invited, and Japanese agitators or Chinese revolutionaries who contrast the conditions in Japan with the conditions in their own country find eager followers. Rebellion is endemic and must continue [to be] endemic until the condition of the people is improved. Piracy abounds in Kuangtung because legitimate means of trade are closed to the peasant. Brigands flourish in Mongolia because the administration is oppressive to the people, stifling their trade with overtaxation and giving them no redress from the depredations of the soldiers sent to 'protect' them. Vast areas are flooded and Chinese citizens perish by tens of thousands, famine stalks through the devastated districts, parents sell their children into slavery and nothing is done to remove the conditions bringing about these disasters, nothing except the drawing-up of interminable rules and regulations and the discussion of endless reports. No practical work is done. The people perish, and the officials who have practised the same archaic methods as of old are rewarded as of old.

No more intelligent people are found in the world than in Kuangtung. Large numbers of them have been educated abroad and realize what good government means. Can they be contented under the rule of an ex-brigand Miaotze[1] whose ideas of government are the ideas of the T'ang dynasty, who rules by bloodshed alone and who boasts to the foreign Consuls that since he has been in Canton he has lopped off two thousand heads of men who, it might be said, were better Chinese than himself. What service has he rendered towards the advancement of China? Even if he keeps order outwardly does he cause contentment? Controlling large revenues has he done one single act that has in any way contributed to the well-being of the province – to the improvement of the condition of the people? Does a ruler like Chang Hsun bring any contentment to the people? What is the condition of the province of Shensi under an official like Lu Chien-chang? Can the restoration of Chen Yi[2] to office be regarded except as a humiliation?

On the railway from P'u-k'ou northwards it was pitiful to see the beggars clamouring at the stations. People desired work but there was no work. The Sinyang-P'u-k'ou Railway, which would have brought prosperity and content into a large area now perennially suffering from famine, had been abandoned and the few workmen employed dismissed.

The position is gravely disquieting. It was the belief of nearly all those I met that Your Excellency cannot be correctly informed of the conditions in the country.

[1] A reference to the Military Governor of Kwangtung, Lung Chi-kuang, who was of the Miao minority from Yunnan.
[2] Ch'en, who had been Deputy Chief of General Staff, was appointed Civil Governor of Szechwan on 1 May 1915, and then Military Governor on 25 August.

In the opinion of those I met the root of the trouble has been the ill-advised and inopportune movement for the restoration of the monarchy and the bogus mandate ordered from the people purporting to represent the 'unanimous will of the people'.

Last summer every effort was made by those most interested in the maintenance of tranquillity in China to oppose the monarchical movement. We believed that the restoration of the monarchy was fraught with danger to the country – danger of domestic disturbance and of foreign interference. The British Minister more than once urged Mr Liang Shih-yi to use his influence with Your Excellency to stop the movement. Baron[1] Feng Kuo-ch'ang informs me that he gave similar advice. Not until some months later did the five allied Powers on October 28th give their advice urging the postponement of the monarchy. There was no loss of face in accepting the advice of five friendly Powers, but the advice was ignored and what was feared would happen has happened – the country torn with revolution and mighty Powers grimly watching, speculating on the profit they are to derive from the turmoil.

Every one in China has long known that the messages despatched from the provinces to Peking urging Your Excellency to ascend the throne were in most cases if not in all cases prepared by a small body of advisers in Peking and forwarded to the provinces to be retransmitted to Peking. Baron Feng Kuo-chang when asked by me why he did deceive the President by sending him a telegram urging him to ascend the throne replied in a loud voice so that all might hear 'because I was ordered to send that telegram. It was in accordance with the policy of the government. It was sent to Nanking by a special official who telegraphed it back to Peking in my name'.[2]

The publication in the foreign papers of the correspondence with the provinces has disclosed to the world the falseness and insincerity of the movement. To declare to the world that the monarchy is being re-established in deference to the unanimous mandate of the people is a mockery prejudicial to the good name and prestige of Your Excellency.

On the 14th of January Your Excellency seemed to have been informed that the Yunnan insurrection would be quelled in twenty days. The Rebellion may be suppressed by force, but the sentiment that inspired the rebellion cannot be suppressed by force. It has the sympathy if not the support of a large number of the people of China, even of the best-informed of the officials in Peking.

All the information I have been able to obtain convinces me that Your Excellency is misinformed when your advisers minimise the importance of

[1] As part of his monarchical plan, Yüan conferred on his supporters, as well as on those whose support he sought, the old Imperial titles, and Feng was one of six Dukes of the First Rank created on 21 December 1915.

[2] On 30 December Feng headed a telegram from four provincial military governors urging Yüan to ascend the throne. The other three were Lung Chi-kuang of Kwangtung, Ch'en Yi of Szechwan and T'ang Hsiang-ming of Hunan.

this movement. The State is in great danger. In only one way can this danger be averted that is by the definite abandonment of the monarchical restoration until after the conclusion of the present war and the will of the people can be ascertained, by the immediate institution of constitutional assemblies, the calling of Parliament and the creation of a responsible Cabinet with a responsible Prime Minister.

G. E. Morrison

800. From G. W. Prothero

London 14 February 1916

Dear Dr. Morrison,

I must have seemed remiss in not replying sooner to your most interesting letter of Dec. 1, which reached me some time ago, but I was very busy with the *Q.R.*[1] and other matters, and had to put it aside for a better opportunity. I am sorry you were unable to write something for the *Q.R.* but of course I fully understand the reasons which prevent it.

Nothing – or hardly anything – has been published here, so far as I know, respecting the negotiations of which you speak, and I have come across no one who knows anything about them. Of course, I have said nothing of what you tell me to anyone but one or two intimate and trustworthy friends. You say that I should probably hear the result before your letter reached me, but I have seen nothing in the papers, so I fear the negotiations have failed or are still dragging on fruitlessly. The conviction has gradually forced itself upon me, and many others – in fact on every one I know who has given any study to our foreign relations – that the F.O. is and has long been disastrously incompetent. The story of its failure in the Balkans and the mistaken concessions to Italy and Russia which had so much to do with that failure reveals a depth of ignorance and blindness and vacillation which is almost inconceivable; and if the F.O. has so dismally failed there, it is not surprising that it should fail in the Far East. Yet the country at large still believes in Grey; and his speech in the House the other day (about the Blockade of Germany) was so plausible, on the surface, as to have had the effect of persuasion on many Members who were previously hostile or suspicious.[2] Yet he evaded the real arguments throughout, and merely threw dust in the eyes of the public. If you ever come across the *English Review* read an article by Seton Watson[3] (who knows more about S.E. Europe than anyone in this

---

[1] The *Quarterly Review*. Morrison's letter to Prothero of 1 December 1915 is printed as No. 789.

[2] The reference is to a speech by Sir Edward Grey in the House of Commons on 26 January 1916, during the debate on Enemy Trade and the British Blockade. (*See Hansard*, 1916, Vol. LXXVIII, cols. 1311–27.)

[3] Robert William Seton-Watson (1879–1951), British scholar. Lecturer in East European History at King's College, London (1915–22), Masaryk Professor of Central European

country, except perhaps Wickham Steed) in the Febry. number, which contains a scathing attack – only too true – upon our policy in the Balkans and elsewhere. There is also an article in the Jan. *Q.R.* which I sent you, I think, or (if not) will send you, on the same subject, by another man well acquainted with that part of the world.[1] The chief point of interest there at present is Roumania; and her attitude, as well as that of Sweden, is naturally a source of anxiety. If both were to go in for the Central Powers, Russia would be knocked out; and it is undoubtedly on the cards that they both will – events elsewhere will probably decide but I know that the F.O. is much disturbed (as also is Russia) about Sweden; and the chief reason – in fact the only good reason – for not enforcing the blockade more stringently is this fear – So long as the Roumanians sit on the fence, I don't see how the Germans and Turks can spare enough men for a formidable attack on either Egypt or our force in Mesopotamia but if they joined the Germans our position in both areas would be very difficult. That seems to be the chief

---

History at London University (1922-45), and Professor of Czechoslovakian Studies at Oxford (1945-9). He was the founder and joint Editor of the *Slavonic Review* (1922-45). During the European War he worked in the Intelligence Bureau of the War Cabinet. In the Second World War he worked for the Foreign Research and Press Service (1939-40), and for the Political Intelligence Bureau of the Foreign Office (1940-2). His article, published in the *English Review*, February 1916, was entitled 'War of Liberation: The Failure of Sir Edward Grey' (Vol. XXII, pp. 135-61). Describing himself as 'one who before the war was a Liberal, but whom the war has forced to "scrap" one fond illusion or prejudice after another, and who is prepared to "scrap" many more things in his pursuit of an energetic and constructive Foreign Policy, as an indispensable aid to military success', he began with the question 'Have we a Foreign Policy today?', then went on to enumerate the failures of Grey's policy in the Balkans and concluded: 'No past service, however signal, can atone for the series of blunders from which we have tried to select the most flagrant. France and Germany and Russia are at present strewn with reputations which this war has wrecked, very often unjustly. Why should we alone adhere to homeopathic methods?' In the event Sir Edward Grey was replaced as Foreign Secretary by A. J. Balfour (q.v.) in December of that year, when Lloyd George took over from Asquith as Prime Minister.

[1] The article referred to in the January 1916 number of the *Quarterly Review* (pp. 164-87), entitled 'British Diplomacy in the Near East', was purported to be a review of five books on the Balkans, among them two by R. W. Seton-Watson, *The War and Democracy* (London 1914) and *Roumania and the Great War* (London 1915), and one by Noel Buxton M.P. entitled *The War and the Balkans* (London 1915). There was no discussion of the books, but instead the whole article was an attack on Sir Edward Grey's Balkan policy. 'Nothing would have courted failure so surely in dealing with the Balkan States as the indecision which characterized the diplomacy of the Entente Powers and especially of the British Government', the author said in conclusion. England, he maintained, had allowed herself to be deceived by Germany and even when the War broke out refused to recognize the importance of the Balkans. 'Thus when the Allies could have secured the support of the Neutral States, *they would not*. Months later, when the axioms of the Near East Question had been learned in the stern school of defeat, the Allies would, but *they could not*... The failure to understand the Near East Question has led to grave military difficulties; but the penalty of ignorance and indifference will unfortunately not end there.' The article was unsigned.

danger at present. That the domination of the Balkans and Turkey is really the ultimate and fundamental aim of Germany, I have long been convinced. The smashing of France and Russia was merely a necessary preliminary. They have not succeeded in this but they have reduced both practically to the defensive; and their next aim must be I think to reduce Russia completely. But, if we can hold back Sweden and Roumania, they will hardly succeed. Meanwhile, the most hopeful thing seems to be that the manufacture of munitions is at last becoming fairly satisfactory, and one may hope in the course of the summer to be nearly independent of the U.S. in this respect. This will relieve both the political and the financial situation considerably. But on all these matters you are doubtless at least as well informed as I am. Is there any chance that Mr. W. H. Donald would be able to write me an article about China? If you think so, it would be doing me a very great service if you would be good enough to ask him. I need hardly say that any further information you may find it possible to send me would be most gratefully received.

Yours sincerely
G. W. Prothero

801. To V. Petersen[1]

Peking 14 February 1916

My dear Petersen,
I duly received your letter enclosing the letter from Duke Lan.[2] I should

[1] Vilhelm Petersen, Danish engineer, employee of the Chinese Post and Telegraph Administration which he joined in 1902. He had served in various cities in China, and was Superintendent of the Peking office in 1910 and of the Tientsin office from 1910 to 1912. In that year the Administration became the Telegraph Bureau of the Ministry of Communications, and Petersen was appointed Inspecting Engineer. He had been responsible for the installation of the Telegraphs in Sinkiang Province. He was in Ti-hua when Morrison visited there and took him to see Tsai-lan.

[2] Tsai-lan, Manchu Imperial Clansman, a grandson of Min-ning, Emperor Tao-kuang (Hsüan-tsung) (1782–1850) and the third son of I-tsung (1831–89), whose estate outside Peking, the Ch'ing-hua Yüan, was appropriated as the site for Tsinghua College, built with the surplus of the Boxer Indemnity Funds returned by America. Tsai-lan and his two brothers, Tsai-lien and Tsai-i, were among the chief sponsors of the Boxer movement, and their death was demanded by the foreign representatives as a condition for the settlement after the Allied Powers occupied Peking in 1900. Instead, however, Tsai-lien, the eldest of the three, was reduced to a commoner, and the death sentences of Tsai-lan and Tsai-i were commuted to exile for life to Ili on the far western frontier of Sinkiang Province, or Chinese Turkestan. Morrison, on his journey across Central Asia in 1910, had met Tsai-lan in Urumchi (Tihua), the provincial capital of Sinkiang, where Tsai-lan was then living. Tsai-lan had sought Morrison's assistance in enabling him to return to Peking, but nothing came of this, and it was not until after the outbreak of the Revolution, following Tsai-lan's involvement in the abortive conspiracy to set up a new imperial government under the child Emperor Hsüan-t'ung in Sinkiang, that he managed to flee with his family via Urga to Manchuria, where he finally settled in Ninguta, in the north of Kirin Province (now in Heilungkiang Province), near the Russian border.

be very glad indeed if I could do anything to help the Duke to return to Peking, and I will certainly take action upon his letter. I do not believe that there would be any opposition to his return. Since it is rather difficult for me to write to him direct, would you kindly tell him that I have received his letter, I thank him very much, and I will see what can be done with regard to his appeal.

I remember with gratitude the kindness he showed me when I was in Tihuafu, and if I could do anything for him in return I would be very glad indeed.

So far as I know there is no opposition to his return. My own private opinion is that if the Duke were to come back quietly to Peking, there is not a soul here who would say anything. I certainly would say nothing, and I would be very glad indeed to see him. Owing to the War in Europe, Ministers here do not act in concert, and I do not think the old gentleman would incur any risk whatever in coming here. His exile was to the Sinkiang. If no opposition was made to his residence in Ninguta I do not see that any protest will be made against his coming to Peking.

When I learn anything, I will communicate with you again.

With best wishes to you

Sincerely yours
[G. E. Morrison]

Enclosure to Letter No. 801: *Translation of a letter from Tsai-lan to Morrison*

To Dr. Morrison,

I beg to state that I have neglected to see you for several years and in such an anxiety of your condition that I had often a dream of you. Certainly you would have a good habitation and you would have been so happy as I expected. It has been several autumns (years) since I arrived at the city of Ning. In such a lonely country, I have nothing good to state. Fortunately my health is good and it can well pacify your Honour's anxiety. But in the recent years, my age is becoming old; in my solitary life I had scarcely a pleasure. And in thinking of my old country, I often have a deep anxiety. Now fortunately is the time of the Emperor Yuan's enthronement, all those exiled are legally to be emancipated. I until now have been exiled for 15 years. In such an opportunity I have been fortunately to accept such a benevolent ceremony. By the way I beg you kindly to propose it for me in your convenience, so that the result can be effected as I am often favoured by you, so I venture to ask your kind assistance to accomplish the task so that I can return to my old land and will not be forever buried in the distant country. I should be forever grateful to you and notwithstanding with my hearty expectations. With my best compliments and regards etc.

Tsai Lan

802. From F. A. Aglen

Peking 4 March 1916

My dear Morrison,
 Mengtsz wires under date 3 March Laokai

'Situation Yunnan party reported critical owing to shortage of munitions of war. Last batch troops left Mengtsz for Kuangnan 29 February Li Lieh Chün[1] remains Mengtsz.'

If Lung Chin Kuang[2] can really be depended upon I think it would be well to await result of collision at Kwangnan before announcing abandonment of the monarchical plan. On the other hand, if the Yunnan party is really going to be given a hard knock the pro-monarchs will be very cock a hoop and will press hard to go ahead. Yuan will have to decide, of course, but abandonment will come better if he hoids the field. In any case I think he can afford to go slow.

Yours sincerely
F. A. Aglen

803. From A. J. Moore-Bennett

Haiphong [Tonkin] 6 March 1916

My dear Wife,[3]
 I have had a pretty bad trip from Hongkong where we left at dawn on Friday the 26th arriving at Hoihow on the 28th and being held up there until the 3rd inst when seeing no chance of the ship unloading I left on the French mail and arrived here on the 4th inst.

The stay allowed me to make some notes on the island which whilst very rich in all natural ways is a very hotbed of fever, malaria smuggling discontent and misrule and is I should think one of the worst governed prefectures in China today. Rubber is being planted and if properly worked would pay well, tin is mined but not seriously and silver also but the Japanese are the only ones who have really studied the island and they have just got a Japanese

[1] On the declaration of independence of Yunnan, the anti-Yüan forces there were organised into three armies. The first army, under Tsai O, went north to attack Szechwan while the second army under Li Lieh-chün proceeded east to Kwangsi, with the aim of attacking Kwangtung. The third army remained at the base in Kunming to hold Yunnan. The second army under Li Lieh-chün left Kunming for the front on 20 February 1916.
[2] Lung Chin-kuang, Garrison Commander of Canton and Waichow and brother of Lung Chi-kuang, Military Governor of Kwangtung. He was appointed by Yüan Shih-k'ai as Pacification Commissioner to Yunnan on 23 January 1916. This title was changed to Investigating Commissioner on 8 February, and Lung was ordered, together with his troops, to attack Yunnan. He was surrounded, however, and forced to surrender at Paise in Kwangsi Province on 12 March, a week after this letter was written, and compelled to declare in favour of the Republic.
[3] A code name Moore-Bennett used to address Morrison.

assistant to the Customs in and hope to become a dominating factor before long.

I told you in my last the Japanese Consul General for Yunnan[1] was with us and we became most friendly on the boat and he told me a great deal about this country's aspirations regarding China. Japan has at this time a Foreign Office representative in Yunnanfu which he is relieving and also he tells me that the Great General Staff have an officer and also an intelligence department man in Yunnan province besides the regular attaché which is at the front with the Northern Army and Mr Y. Hori (the consul) tells me that there are now some two hundred Japanese spread over Yunnan whilst others are coming in in every boat.

Mr Hori deprecates – as he informs me do the better educated Japanese – the thumping of the big stick to China as he believes in what he terms 'peaceful absorption' which he translated as meaning that if Japan can get ten or twenty thousand well educated Japanese traders per year spread over China then the day is not far removed when these men will constitute such a great political lever that no one of the powers will be able to interfere and Japan will have all the power to rule the land that a great army could give her. His mission is to find out and tell his Foreign Office whether the rebellion will succeed and he informs me that there is not a doubt but that General Tsai Ao is both a cleverer man, a more sincere patriot and a more honest ruler than Mr Yuan Shih Kai who he says is hated by the Japanese and Chinese alike for his crafty cunning and dishonest actions. Mr Hori seems singularly well acquainted with General Tsai's ambitions and movements and informs me that if the negotiation that Tsai is carrying on with the rich merchants and landed gentry of Honan, Hunan, Szechuan, Kuangtung and elsewhere is successful there will not be the slightest doubt that the rebellion will succeed as he says news reached him in Canton last week that the Northern Army are by no means all to be depended upon and if Tsai's *pourparlers* with the other provinces go through some at least of the Northern troops must come to the South.

Mr Hori informed me that Russia being sick with Great Britain for her failure in the Dardanelles and for the friction in Persia – which we have never heard of – had completed an agreement with Japan which would tend to give Russia and Japan the balance of power in Asia and that it was only natural for Japan to wish to safeguard her interests in China when it was only

[1] Hori Yoshiatsu (b. 1885), Japanese diplomat, at this time Consul in the Japanese Consulate-General in Canton, the jurisdiction of which included Yunnan. Although Japan obtained permission to open a consulate in Yunnan-fu in April 1916, in connection with which Hori Yoshiatsu had been despatched there, no official was stationed in Yunnan-fu until the appointment of Nihei Hyōji two years later. In 1926 Hori became counsellor in the Japanese Legation in Peking, and was many times Chargé d'Affaires (1926-8). In 1931 he was appointed Minister to Mexico (1931-6), holding concurrently the post of Minister to Costa Rica, Guatemala, Honduras and Nicaragua in 1935 (1935-6). He became, after his retirement, Managing Director of the news service, Dōmei.

too evident that China was incapable of ruling herself and equally the powers were incapable of adhering to any purposeful and just policy towards the country.

I asked Mr Hori if Mr Yuan Shih Kai made a drastic change at once and gave a constitution to the country and elected a president to the will of the country if China might not expect a new lease of [life] from the powers and he replied that it was most unlikely that China would do any such thing and if she did it would hardly be in Japan's interest to allow her to do so.

I pointed out to Mr Hori that if all he said was correct it was paramount to a declaration of suzerainty over China on the part of his government and he could hardly hope to hold to that position after the war when Britain would be in a position to send out an overpowering fleet but he pointed out that by the method of peaceful absorption the Japanese would be so friendly with the new Government that they would be willing to help to reap the benefits of her foresight.

Mr Hori's conversations lasted over several days and might not all interest you but the foregoing is the gist of his remarks and their general trend.

The French here who have been in Yunnan and have business connections inform me that Lung Si Kwaung[1] the Governor of Canton sent his brother to Mongtzu in order to try and stir up the people there against Tsai Ao but state that he had no luck owing to the fact that Tsai opened trade facilities for the Kochiu crowd and they are standing by him but it seems that the late Governor of Kueichou[2] is also an ambitious man and friction may arise if indeed it has not already done so between Tsai and he.

Mon. Pasquier[3] met me in the Hotel and informs me that Tsai is universally loved by the common people throughout the West but he is not sure if Tsai can get the other provinces to join him in time as he must have shells and munitions and needs their arsenals at once in order to succeed.

[...]

[1] Lung Chi-kuang.
[2] It is not clear whether Moore-Bennett is referring to Liu Hsien-shih (d. 1927), a follower of T'ang Chi-yao and a native of Kweichow who was Military Commissioner of the province from September 1913 until his dismissal by Yüan Shih-k'ai on 8 February 1916; or to Tai K'an, a returned student from Japan, and Civil Governor of the province from June 1913 until he was superseded by Lung Chien-chang in November 1914, and whose dismissal was formally gazetted in November the following year. Both Liu Hsien-shih and Tai K'an fought in the anti-monarchist ranks led by T'ang Chi-yao and Ts'ai O. After Yüan's death, Liu Hsien-shih was appointed Military Governor of Kweichow, and Tai K'an again the Civil Governor of Kweichow, in July 1916. Tai however, though reappointed Civil Governor of the province, was in fact away with his Yunnan and Kweichow armies in Szechwan, and Liu Hsien-shih took over concurrently the post of Civil Governor, holding both posts until 1920. Liu returned again to the Civil Governorship of the province in March 1923, after the Yünnan army, then in control of Kweichow, was forced to leave, and he remained in the post until January 1925.
[3] Monsignor Pierre-Victor Pasquier (b. 1848), Belgian missionary who joined the Missions Etrangères in 1870 and was sent to Kweichow in 1874. He died in Hong Kong.

I am informed that the Yunnanese closely follow every foreigner and watch him all day and all night so no man can foresee if I shall be able to locate the mines we need and if I do whether the Yunnanese will allow me to enter into negotiations to work them but I shall of course do my best.

[...]

Your affectionate husband
Arthur

804. To Ts'ai T'ing-kan

[Peking] 18 March 1916

My dear Admiral,

Will you kindly at the earliest opportunity convey to His Excellency the President my grateful thanks for the generous gift he has so graciously sent me through Mr. Hsü En-Yuan[1] of the Board of Audit.

Devoted as I am and as I have been for many years to the true interests of China I hope that I will always prove myself to be worthy of the confidence of His Excellency.

Earnestly I hope that His Excellency may be guided by the highest wisdom in adopting such measures of conciliation as will rescue the country from the Peril with which it is now menaced from the extension of the horrors of civil war and the ever-increasing danger of foreign intervention.

Best wishes

Very sincerely yours
[G. E. Morrison]

805. To Yüan Shih-k'ai

Memorandum re *Abandonment of Monarchy, 21 March 1916*[2]

Enquiries made in trustworthy quarters confirm the opinion I myself hold that the situation is rapidly increasing in gravity.

The secession of Kwangtung is believed to be imminent; there is intense and widespread dissatisfaction throughout the province at the barbarous methods of rule of Lung Chi-kuang.

When Kwangtung secedes Hunan, Kiangsi and other southern provinces will follow.

Formal request addressed to the Foreign Powers will then be made for the recognition of the seceded provinces as belligerents. It is certain that Japan will accord this recognition.

[1] In his Diary entry for 15 March 1916 Morrison wrote: 'The President has sent me through Hsu En-yuan [Deputy Director of the Board of Audit and Governor of the Bank of China] $1,000. Worthy Patron!'
[2] No covering letter has been found for this memorandum.

Trustworthy foreign reports contrast the orderly and humane conduct of the Yunnanese troops with the savage brutality of the Northern troops. To quote the words of an American missionary doctor writing from Suifu on February 17 to the chief English paper in China. 'Fellow missionaries who visited the battlefields report that the homes of the farmers were desecrated, rapine committed, farm-labourers tied and shot, houses burned ruthlessly, and the dead and dying Yunnan soldiers terribly mutilated' by the Northern soldiers.

Possibly greater dangers may be averted if the President at once issue a strong, clear mandate abandoning the Monarchy and magnanimously accepting the blame for the disastrous action of the Chou An Hui which has plunged the country into civil war.

The mandate should be worded without ambiguity and without reservation.

Recent mandates announcing the postponement of the Monarchy and the refusal to receive further positions in favour of the Monarchy, followed as they immediately were by fresh mandates creating orders of nobility, by continued preparations for the establishment of the Monarchy, and by the continued use of the style and title of Emperor, have aggravated the dangers of the present situation. There is bitter resentment at such transparent insincerity.

G. E. Morrison

806 From J. R. Muir[1]

Pengshanhsien, Sze[chwan] 28 March 1916

Dear Dr Morrison,

It is some time since I had the privilege of writing to you, but you will excuse this liberty I am sure as the occasion requires a letter. First let me congratulate you upon the very valuable service you have rendered humanity. It is not often given to any one man to exert the influence you have exerted in the recent turn of affairs in our beloved land of China. May your name go down in history as the man who removed a crown from an Emperor who was not particularly desired by his *quasi* subjects. We have probably done an injustice to the Adviser, no less than to the Chinese official, in the opinion that we have held that the advice given was very seldom acted upon. It is therefore all the more gratifying to read one day in our daily Reuters that Dr Morrison had advised the immediate cancellation of all plans for the Monarchy, and then to see in a day or two that the President had ordered that all the provinces be advised that the Monarchy they had voted to create was not desired!

[1] John R. Muir, a missionary with the China Inland Mission, stationed at Peng-shan Szechwan.

In these days prophets (true and false) are so common that it becomes odious to listen to the chorus of 'I told you so', but still it is with no little satisfaction that I recall what we wrote for the *Toronto Globe* some years ago. If I remember rightly I sent you a copy of the paper, but I have no assurance that it was read. For this I do not in any way blame a man who is called upon to read as much as you do. But if you wish now to see what I did write I may be able to find a copy of the *Toronto Globe* for December 26, 1913 in which there is an article on 'The Chinese Republic'. I closed the discussion with these words, 'The Chinese are thoroughly dissatisfied with the late Monarchy, and another Monarchy, even with a Chinese King (I ought to have written Emperor) would start another wave of opposition little, if any, weaker than the wave of 1911 that removed the Manchus.'

We have been told so often that an Occidental can never comprehend an Oriental that it ill behoves me to say that I understood them then, or that I understand them now. However there is one more idea in which I believe perfectly; namely, that a member of the official class in a land like China can never understand the people. They live so far apart that one can never approach the other. I have read a great deal about the present movement, but I have failed to see in any article I have read what I consider to be the real reasons why the monarchy has failed. In the final analysis it has not been a question of Republic *versus* Monarchy at all. If Mr Yuan was fully convinced that a Monarchy was the best for the country and that the people would accept a Monarchy he was doubtless right, but there are other elements which have been neglected and overlooked and it is these elements which have worked the present Revolution.

No one will believe throughout the whole world that Yuan Shih Kai did not desire the Monarchy. If he was sincere in his refusal he must be content now to be misunderstood as perhaps no one in this land of paradoxes has ever been misunderstood. The question might be readily asked 'Who would have refused?' In fact was it not quite natural for any being on earth to desire such a happy climax to the experiences of the past twenty years? If any man in this land was fitted to be Emperor he was the man, but...

Unfortunate as it may seem from any angle of view the fact remains that the years of the Republic have been very hard on the common people and the burden becomes increasingly heavy. It is useless for us to compile statistics showing that the prices of food-stuffs are little, if any, higher than they were seven years ago when we make our tables in dollars and taels. Salt may be selling (at the cent rate) for little more than it was, but the people who pay for it in 'cash' are sure that some one is robbing them. With salt, tobacco, sulphur, and whatnot being sold in official shops the people see no hope for themselves when the official tells them that they must pay a certain price. And when it comes to rebellion the people will hope for success that will bring down the price of salt! It is human nature. One of the first things that the Yunnanese did in Suifu was to cut down taxes one half. The report spread like wild-fire throughout the country.

To any student of economics at the present time it becomes apparent that literally, 'the rich are getting richer and the poor are getting poorer'. That such a condition spells disaster goes without saying. If Revolution had not come this year it would not have been delayed another decade whether we had Republic or Monarchy. What we mean by the above phrase is that the common people who receive and pay in 'cash' are receiving for their commodities and labour in some cases no more, and in any case little more, than they received seven years ago. But the man who deals in silver changes his silver at such a 'cash' rate that his wants are met about the same as they formerly were. In this we have one of the most pregnant causes of discontent. When we add to this the exchange rate of gold into silver the problem grows more complex for every one who reads knows that foreign interest, and salaries to foreign employees, are paid in gold and the common people 'foot the bill'. Even while we are enjoying the blessing of the high exchange that is all in our favor we view with alarm the exchange which gives us now about 40 cash for an American cent when we were content with 20 cash for the same amount a few years ago. The solution is 'Currency Reform'. If we had been given even a measure of proper reform up to last year the man we may still call Yuan Shih Kai might even now have been an Emperor.

Important as the matter of Currency Reform may seem, and I purposely put it first, there is another problem equally important. In the *Toronto Globe* article to which I have referred I tried to point out what seemed to me to be a very real spirit of Democracy among the Chinese people. To my mind they are in many ways far more democratic than any people I know, or have read about. It will not shock you to hear an American say that the United States is not 'Democratic'. I believe it to be a real 'Republic', but even a man like our beloved William Jennings Bryan[1] could not be a true Democrat in office in our land. So you will understand that I do not speak from the standpoint of a rabid Democrat. It would take too long for me to properly give my reasons for the belief. It has been stated by others, and you, yourself, have seen it again and again in your experience in China. Now whatever the causes that have brought it to pass the fact is that the measure of democracy enjoyed by the provinces before the exit of the Manchus has vanished. It is a matter of real grief to many a loyal Chinese. The loss of this liberty goes far through all

---

[1] William Jennings Bryan (1860–1925), American politician, member of the United States House of Representatives (1891–5) and unsuccessful Presidential candidate in 1896, 1900 and 1908. He became Secretary of State in 1913, holding the post until 1915. In 1925 he was one of the prosecuting lawyers in the case in which John T. Scopes, a teacher in Dayton, Tennessee, was indicted for teaching the Theory of Evolution to his classes. He was the author of *Letters to a Chinese official; being a western view of eastern civilization* (London and New York 1906), a reply to Lowes Goldsworthy Dickinson (1862-1932), the Cambridge don, author of *Letters from John Chinaman* (London 1901).

the avenues of life and many a man has been ready to say with Patrick Henry[1] of old, 'As for me: give me liberty, or give me death.'

It has appeared to some very well-informed writers that the real motive for the present Revolution was found in the embittered envy of a few of Yuan Shih Kai's former friends who had lost favour with him. That was only partially true. But it shows in its very statement wherein the truth lies. Beginning with the disaffection of Dr Sen, whose reported return to China is credited here,[2] there have been too many in all classes throughout China who have felt the loss of their liberty as citizens of this land. Disaffected officials in Peking are only a very small fraction of those who have felt it. It is well-nigh universal. Without the least question representative government is the only solution of that problem. No one knows better than we who have tried to organize churches among these people how impossible the idea of representative government appears. But it must be done. The provinces at least must feel that the iron hand of Peking is not held over them any more. We hear of three distinct countries; North, South and Middle, and I say, 'God forbid'. But the provinces will have their autonomy somehow or other if they must even set up separate governments. And without question it would then be found possible for them to govern themselves, so why not give it to them now.

I realize as I write this that it will be so long before this reaches you there will have already appeared reforms that will make the statement of these facts unnecessary, but you will bear with me. One more matter needs immediate attention. We have been wont to call the troops sent to the provinces 'Yuan's mercenaries'. It is most important that they be withdrawn. It was looked upon as an attempt to uphold the Monarchy when established and the provincial troops consider themselves very well able to establish and keep order. The plan in the United States by which government troops are only kept in regular forts and not permitted to interfere with affairs in any State, unless the Governor thereof requests assistance from the President (modified in extreme cases only), would seem to commend itself here. The Northern troops are royally hated wherever they go. Naturally they have had an inflated idea of their importance. They treat tradesmen with contempt – even to smashing wares without provocation and refuse to pay their just debts. Having no women of their own it is only expected that they will be immoral

[1] Patrick Henry (1736–99), American politician, a lawyer from Virginia who, together with Thomas Jefferson and Richard Henry Lee, initiated the Inter-Colonial Committee of Correspondence in 1773. As a member of the Continental Congress (1774–6) he moved resolutions to put the American colonies into a state of belligerency towards England with a speech containing the words quoted here at a speech held in Richmond in 1775.

[2] Sun Yat-sen, who fled to Japan in December 1914 after the failure of the 'Second Revolution', returned to Shanghai in April 1916 as the anti-Yüan movement gained momentum.

and, whereas a native soldier might find himself quite agreeable these outsiders are looked upon as insulting and their attentions are called 'rape'. As they received in some cases $10.00 a month while native soldiers received $5.00 the feeling toward them was only increased. They ought to be withdrawn at once.

These are some of the forces which worked together to undo the Monarchy. Without such causes as these the agitators would have found it impossible to create sufficient sentiment to cause rebellion. No people in the world are so fond of peace as the Chinese. Rebellion and confusion strike terror to the hearts of all. I write in the small city of Tanling some distance to the west of Pengshanhsien where I am now living with my family. The official to-day is in terror because of the reports of armed bands of robbers – the aftermath, or continuation, of the rebellion. All are eager to see these troubles leave them, and they are glad to a man, as far as I can tell, to see the official notices again declare that we have a Republic in name at least. For reasons beyond our powers to explain the idea of a Republic and Representative Government has come to stay. The better class understand and can discuss it intelligently, but even the common people are showing even eager interest in seeing the return of the Republic they so much desire.

Though my letter is already longer than it ought to be I have in mind one more subject to discuss. While there may have been a reasonable amount of wisdom in what I have written, that which I am about to say belongs to the realm of the visionary enthusiast. It is expected that the principle of 'Single Tax' will find its proper place only in the Millennium. But so thought my father and yours (when they thought at all about it) of the prohibition of the sale of intoxicants. So we may be permitted to expound theories even if the effort is wasted on an unsympathetic audience. I may say that when I first heard of 'Single Tax' from an enthusiastic crank when I was in my early 'teens' I considered it all nonsense. But one thing amazed me in later years. The simplicity of a tax system that could be understood by a boy! I never forgot what he said. It took me a great many years to give mental assent to it. But I venture to say that no honest mind in any land under any government existing, or to exist, could possibly fail to see that the only equitable, just and simple method of taxation is to tax the land alone.

If any man in China had the courage, not to say the honesty, to declare that all the cumbersome and burdensom system of taxation from salt to *likin* was to cease, it would work such a revolution in China toward the rulers of the land that we would have a New China without any question. The upper classes would be hard hit as they have been in England and that is just why we have little hope of seeing it, but they ought to be made to pay more; and indirectly in the adjustments of rents and leases that would inevitably follow they would recover all that they ought legitimately to have. While I say this I know all about foreign loans, preferred claims, etc., etc. which make it impossible, but at the same time I know that it could be done! Why not permit China to set the world an example that will startle every one? How I wish it might be!

These are some of the thoughts which fill one's mind away off here in a small corner of Western China at the time of this new crisis. Many of us can say that we truly love China and the Chinese people. Can it be that our love is even stronger than the love of those who to all appearances have been exploiting for their own ends? Sometimes it looks so to us and we long to see the teeming millions of this rich and fruitful land enjoy the blessings provided for them by an indulgent Providence. It might be so if there could be established a 'government of the people and by the people and for the people', one which would be one in fact as well as on paper.

Very respectfully yours
John R. Muir

[...]

I am back again in Pengshanhsien (permanent address) on April 8. This city is still in *status quo* at this date. There seems to be a rebellion, or armed marauder, movement coming toward us from the N.W. which may, or may not be, independent of the Yunnan movement. At present we cannot tell.

This was further delayed for fear that it might not get away from our city. However the mails are not interrupted. This city was attacked by robbers yesterday morning, April 10, but they did not get in. We hope for reinforcements from Chengtu, but fear the Governor has more than his hands full.

807. To G. W. Prothero

Peking 29 March 1916

Dear Dr. Prothero,

Your letter of February 14th reached me two weeks ago and the *Quarterly Review* Number that you were so kind as to send me arrived the day before yesterday.

[...]

You will have read in the telegrams that Yuan Shih-kai abandoned the Monarchy on Tuesday the 21st March. Since February 7th when I returned from the South I have been urging him to take this step. Chinese-like he failed to act boldly, but took half measures only trying first the effect of postponement. He was compelled to do finally what he ought to have done a long time before, namely abandon the movement.

With considerable misgiving we await the result. There is strong feeling against Yuan himself. He is not trusted. He is known to have inspired the Monarchy movement. The telegrams sent from Peking instructing the provincial authorities how to mould the people's will have been published and although their authenticity is denied they are known to be authentic and their publication has created a very bad impression indeed.

Now the South are clamouring for his abdication. Just as I write this I receive a telegram saying that the Swatow district has declared its independence.[1]

I will write again
Best wishes

Very sincerely yours
[G. E. Morrison]

808. To L. E. Broome

[Peking] 31 March 1916

My dear Broome,

[...]

You will have heard that the fossils discovered by Irwin at Ichang turned out to be stalagmites. Anderson,[2] the geologist here, associated with Pearson and Sons, ridiculed the idea of their being dragons, and his scepticism was endorsed by the British Museum. The discovery was looked upon as of good omen for the new reign. One can draw one's own conclusion from the fact that the dragons were dragons only in the imagination of the discoverers.

Things are going on very badly. Yuan Shih-kai will have the utmost difficulty in retaining his office. The feeling against him is very bitter, even in Peking, while in the South there seems to be an inflexible determination to compel him to abdicate. The Japanese here speak quite openly of a retirement, and seem to think that the question hardly admits of discussion. He is going, they say, and they speculate as to who will be his successor. Speaking to me the other night, a clever lady suggested that in the career of every great and successful man there comes a time when ambition gives way to vanity, and it was so in this case. Yuan had everything in the world that he could desire. He had restored a fair measure of order throughout the whole country, his word was law, he had at least as great control of China as had ever been obtained by any ruler, and, yet he goes and sacrifices everything for the sake of an empty bauble. His sons are much chagrined. I saw the eldest of them last Friday – a half-witted youth of 37, whom we always think of as a boy, and who has the intellectual development of 17.[3]

[1] The district in eastern Kwangtung of which Swatow was the chief city declared its independence against the Central Government in Peking on 28 March 1916.
[2] Robert van Vleck Anderson (1884–1949), American geologist who joined S. Pearson & Sons Limited in 1913, and remained with them until 1919 when he became United States Representative on the War Trade Board in Sweden.
[3] Yüan K'e-ting (or Yüan Yün-t'ai) (?b. 1877), the eldest son of Yüan Shih-k'ai. He had studied military science in Germany but, partly owing to a leg broken in a riding accident, never actually served in the army. He was credited with being one of the chief influences behind his father's monarchical scheme. Morrison always spoke disparagingly about him.

[...]

Write to me one of these days. I keep all your letters, and when you write a book later on, I will let you have the use of them to work up your material.

With best wishes to you

Ever faithfully yours
[G. E. Morrison]

809. To F. E. Taylor

[Peking] 31 March 1916

My dear Taylor,

I have before me your two letters of the 8th and 11th March.[1] It is shameful that I have been such a long time in answering them, but I have been in great embarrassment, having no secretary. Everything is in confusion.

I will send you a list of the later treaties signed since the outbreak of the revolution. China has signed many disastrous agreements since then. Her telegraph agreements seem to be specially injurious. On January 24th she signed a Telegraph Convention at Urga, the only advantage of which, but a very great one in the opinion of the Ministry at the time, was the absurd one that the Convention was signed in the first year of Hung Hsien.[2] In order to obtain the date inserted in this way, China was prepared to give away any advantage demanded of her. She thought that by having the Hung Hsien date inserted it meant the thin edge of the wedge, the tacit approval of Russia to the Empire, and the first step towards recognition. On Monday she signed a railway contract for the Harbin–Tsitsihar–Blagoveschenk Railway, Russian gauge, which will strengthen more than ever Russia's position in Northern Manchuria.[3] I should think the line will be of strategic importance, linking up the Trans-Manchurian Railway with the Amur Railway.

The future is very uncertain. Yuan has the support of the Diplomatic Body here, who, with the exception of the Japanese Legation, desire him to retain office. The Japanese speak openly of his retirement. They regard it as a foregone conclusion, and are wondering who will be his successor. General Aoki, whom I saw in Peking, thought that Hsu Shih-chang would be the most likely man. Other Japanese here regard Li Yuan-hung as the more probable, but the feeling that prevails in the Palace itself is that Yuan will be able to retain his position.

[1] Not printed.
[2] Hung-hsien was the reign title Yüan Shih-k'ai adopted in 1916. The convention here referred to was that signed by China, Russia and Outer Mongolia on 24 January 1916 concerning the installation of telegraph lines in Outer Mongolia.
[3] The Agreement was known as the Five per cent Gold Loan of 1916 for the Pin–Hei Railway, signed on 27 March 1916. By the Agreement Russia was to lend China 50,000,000 roubles to finance the construction of a railway linking Harbin with Heiho (or Aigun), situated on the Amur River opposite Blagovestchensk, with a branch line connecting Aigun and Tsitsihar.

You speak of my work in connection with the postponement. It was not postponement I urged, it was abandonment. I submitted my Memorial[1] as soon as I returned from Shanghai, and, in the strongest manner possible, I urged that there should be immediate abandonment of the monarchical movement, the summoning of Parliament, and the restoration of the Provincial Assembly. Other Counsellors urged less direct action, and that postponement should be attempted first. Liang Shih-yi urged this most strongly, and unfortunately his advice did prevail. Nothing could have been more unfortunate. Had the abandonment Mandate been issued with the postponement Mandate the President would have stood better before the country.
[...]

Very sincerely yours
[G. E. Morrison]

810 To G. W. Prothero

[Peking] 5 April 1916

Dear Dr. Prothero,
[...]
The situation here is serious. I doubt whether Yuan Shih-kai will be able to retain his post. He has been much shaken by recent events, his health is bad, he comes from a shortlived stock, he is thick-set and apoplectic, his life is not a healthy one, and he never spares himself. For more than four years past I have been urging him from time to time to undergo a course of massage, for his arteries are atheromatous, and he lives in considerable risk of an apoplectic seizure.

The movement against him has extended even during last week. The large and populous province of Szechuan has, by declaring its neutrality, virtually declared its independence of the Central Government. The situation in Kwangtung daily becomes more serious. It is dangerous to hazard conjectures in China, but, so far as I can see, the present outlook is as follows: – Kwangtung will declare its independence, and Hunan Province likewise. Virtually then the whole of the provinces of China will be held in Canton, under, I should expect, the Presidency of Liang Chi-chao, one of the great scholars of China, the most distinguished of the Chinese proscribed in September 1898.[2] Foremost among the resolutions to be passed by them will

---

[1] Morrison is referring to the enclosure to Letter No. 799.
[2] Liang Ch'i-ch'ao (1873–1929), Chinese scholar and Republican politician, who through his voluminous writings became one of the best known publicists in modern China. A pupil of K'ang Yu-wei, he collaborated with K'ang in initiating what has become known as the Reform Movement under the auspices of Emperor Kuang-hsü, a movement which was brought to an abrupt end in a *coup d'état* by the Empress-Dowager Tz'u-hsi on 21 September 1898. With the help of Hayashi Gonsuke, then Japanese Chargé d'Affaires in Peking, Liang escaped to Japan where through the journal he established he continued

be the demand that Yuan Shih-kai abdicate. Recognition will be asked for as belligerents, and, so far as we can tell, that recognition will be granted by Japan, unless the British Government is able to use its influence in favour of the Peking Government.

Undeniably there is a growing feeling among the Southern Chinese in favour of a *rapprochement* with Japan. Such a *rapprochement* is much to be desired. Japan is largely to blame for the growth of distrust against her in China. During the war between Japan and Russia the Japanese in the occupied territories of China treated the people so well, and their Government acted with such forbearance and wisdom, that there was an immense development of friendliness towards Japan in China. Then nothing was too good for the Japanese. No less than 23,000 Chinese students went to Japan to study, and nearly 2,000 Japanese were given employment by the Chinese Government.

A change gradually followed. The education given in Japan was of an inferior class. The Chinese were kept very much to themselves, and might almost be described as being segregated. The instruction given to them differed materially from that given to the Japanese, especially in the military schools. The Chinese students came under the influence of an inferior class of Japanese, and were infected with disloyalty. It became a saying in China (Yuan Shih-kai himself has given expression to such an opinion) that the Chinese student sent to England and to America to be educated returned a better patriot than when he went, but the Chinese student sent to Japan, in the immense majority of cases returned a revolutionary. Good feelings gradually passed away, and distrust took its place. Chinese students in large numbers returned from Japan, Japanese as their contracts expired were retired from the Chinese service. Demands in connection with Chientao, a district in Manchuria largely peopled by Koreans, increased the distrust. In this particular case Japan had as representative in Peking an able and far sighted man, named Ijuin (he has just been appointed Ambassador to Italy),

---

to preach the cause of constitutional monarchy, and became an opponent of the revolutionaries under Sun Yat-sen. After the establishment of the Republic he supported the regime of Yüan Shih-k'ai in Peking until Yüan launched his monarchical scheme. Liang was instrumental in persuading Lu Yung-t'ing to change his front and declare Kwangsi Province independent from the Central Government, and in establishing the Military Government under Ts'en Ch'un-hsüan. After Yüan's death, he cooperated with Tuan Ch'i-jui, serving briefly as Finance Minister from July to November 1917, and in 1919, with a large government subsidy, went as an official delegate to the Paris Peace Conference and made a tour of various European countries. This altered his previous admiration for Western civilisation. He also became a critic of Marxism which was beginning to make itself felt in Chinese intellectual circles in the wake of the May Fourth Movement which had occurred during his absence in Europe. By then however his pre-eminent position of intellectual leadership had been taken over by a new generation, though his scholarly writings still gained him an occasional hearing.

and under his guidance the Japanese Government consented to a compromise which contributed to a softening of the misunderstanding.

Other disputes arising subsequently were also settled by Mr. Ijuin in a way which helped towards a better understanding. Mr. Ijuin won the confidence of the Chinese in a larger measure than any other Japanese Minister in Peking in my time. He was a personal friend of Yuan Shih-kai, and all those who wished to see a *rapprochement* between China and Japan regretted his departure. He was succeeded by Yamaza in 1913, on whose death Hioki became Minister. Hioki, I believe, represents the same school of thought as Mr. Ijuin. He is a reasonable man of great ability, and a linguist of unusual gifts, who has a thorough knowledge of English. He was known to Sir John Jordan when still a minor official in Korea. I have known him since 1901. He negotiated, on behalf of his Government, the Commercial treaty with China of Oct. 8th 1903,[1] a treaty which followed the lines of the Mackay Treaty of Sept. 5th 1902. Unfortunately there is every indication that his Councillor of Legation, Obata,[2] represents what may be called the aggressive (the military) party in Japan. I am bound to say he is more admired by the Japanese here in Peking than is Hioki. It is difficult for a foreigner to understand the estimate formed by Japanese of the abilities of their own men, but my Japanese intimates here tell me that the views of Obata are more likely to prevail than those of Hioki. At any rate, under Obata the demands which have been made [were those] which have so greatly estranged China since the outbreak of the war. At the conference at which the demands submitted on the 18th January last year were discussed, it was quite noticeable how Obata seemed to dominate Hioki. Frequently Hioki would show a desire to be reasonable (that is from the Chinese point of view), when Obata would interfere and suggest a less friendly course, and to this in every case Hioki acceded.

For some time past there has been a violent campaign in certain sections of the Japanese press directed against England, especially against British diplomacy in China. These attacks invariably suggest that Yuan Shih-kai is the enemy of Japan, the chief obstructive to Japanese ambition, and that in this policy he is being supported by the British Minister and by myself. The attacks on me are quite persistent, and yet, when the time comes for me to publish my experience it will be seen how strongly and consistently I have urged the Chinese Government to endeavour to follow in the footsteps of Japan.

When I have heard attacks made upon the Japanese nation in regard to Korea I have pointed out to the Chinese what is the truth; that in the history of the world there has not been a more remarkable example of colonising genius and of administrative efficiency than has been shown by Japan in Korea. Lord Curzon was able to write in 1895 that Korea was the worst

---

[1] The Treaty in question was known as the Supplementary Treaty of Commerce and Navigation.   [2] Obata Yukichi (or Torikichi).

governed country in the world. If he were to see the country now, only 20 years later, he would be amazed at the progress. There have been blemishes, of course, in the administration. The cruelty with which the Japanese suppressed the so called 'rebellion'. The cruelty with which they punished a number of Korean Christians, including one man, at least, Baron Yun Chih-ho,[1] one of the most enlightened Koreans, and the extraction of the admissions of guilt from the accused under torture, were blemishes of the gravest kind, but against the evil done in these two cases can be weighed the good that Japan has done in the country, the improvement in every department of administration. She has reafforested the country. On 'Arbor Day' last year more than thirty million trees were planted, and no doubt an even greater number will have been planted this year. (By the way, reafforestation is one of the most pressing needs of China. For years we have been urging action to be taken.) It is interesting to note that I am writing to you on the first 'Arbor Day' established in China. By Mandate the day of the Spring Festival April 5th (the third day of the third moon) has been set apart for the planting of trees. The Mandate was issued on the 31st, and to-day is the first day. China is making some attempt now at afforestation, and has appointed an American as head of the Forestry Department,[2] and to that department a very competent Englishman, named William Purdom,[3] a trained collector, who has been some years in China, has been attached.

For some little time past Hioki has been acting here without the support of Obata, but now, to our regret, we learn that in a few days Obata will return to his former post. Such an appointment bodes no good for China, and yet the Chinese have only themselves to blame for having brought about a condition that enables Japanese aggression to succeed here.

[1] Yun Ch'i-ho (1867–1945), Korean publicist. He had studied in Japan, where he came to know Fukuzawa Yukichi (1834–1901) and Inukai Tsuyoshi, and in China, at the Anglo-Chinese College in Shanghai. In 1887 he became the first Korean Methodist Episcopalian and was sent to the United States to study at Vanderbilt University and Emory College. When he returned to Korea in 1897, after spending a period teaching English in Shanghai and touring Europe, he was appointed President of the Privy Council. He became Editor of a nationalist paper, the *Tongnip Sinmun* [*Independent News*] and was thus the object of Government disapproval. In 1906 he founded the Anglo-Korean School, and by means of his paper and his educational institution became active in the independence movement. In January 1912 he was one of the 105 prominent Koreans arrested after the discovery of an assassination plot against the new Japanese Resident-General of Korea, Terauchi Masatake (q.v.), the previous month, in what has become known as the '105 Incident'.

[2] Forsythe Sherfesee, American forestry expert who had worked for nine years as Director of Forestry in the Philippines before becoming Adviser to the Bureau of Forestry in the Chinese Ministry of Agriculture and Forestry in 1916.

[3] A British botanist who had trained and worked for many years in Kew Gardens, London, and was a collector for James Veitch & Sons and the Arnold Arboretum in the United States, before becoming an Adviser in the Chinese Ministry of Agriculture and Commerce.

The scheme for the entry of China into the Alliance, mismanaged as I fear it was by the British Legation and by the British Foreign Office, appears to have finally failed, and yet Kroupensky (the Russian Minister in Peking, who supported the movement, and has been transferred to Tokyo as Ambassador in place of the Russian Ambassador[1] who represented Russia when the proposal was made to Japan that she should combine with England, France and Russia, in inviting China to join the Alliance, and expel the Germans from China), said to me before his departure when I asked him whether there was any hope of the question being revived, that he had not lost hope. He seemed to think that there was a modification of Japan's attitude. That attitude he knows would be modified if the Allies were victorious or if only the belief gained ground that the Allies would be victorious. Hitherto the Japanese military party, trained under German traditions, have been impressed with the conviction of the invincibility of Germany.

To hark back to the withdrawal of Yuan Shih-kai. The Japanese even officially counsel his retirement. Speaking quite recently in an interview whose publication was authorised, Count Okuma, the Prime Minister, stated to the correspondent of the *Asahi*: 'If Yuan sincerely wants to secure the peace of China he should leave his present position and retire. I believe it would be the best policy for Yuan. Some people say that if Yuan retires there will be no capable man who can unify China, and the situation in the country will become all the more complicated, but that is a needless affair. If Yuan should retire, the present situation in China will become quieted down. As for the future, there will naturally be some way of managing it.'

Count Okuma has since denied that he spoke these words, but there is no shadow of doubt that these words were spoken by him. Confirmation reaches me from trustworthy sources in Japan that these are the views held by Count Okuma. It is significant also to note that when General Aoki (a distinguished General who has been many years in China, was the doyen of the military attachés in Peking, and was subsequently in command of the fortress of Port Arthur, and who has since been appointed military agent in China), it is significant to note that when Aoki was in Shanghai a high Chinese official (I have little doubt that this was Tang Shao-yi) said to him 'The chief obstructive to a *rapprochement* between Japan and China is Yuan Shih-kai, supported by the British Minister and by his English Advisers.' The significance of this statement is the disclosure that Tang Shao-yi was prepared to vent his hatred and revenge himself against Yuan by making a statement to the Japanese which he knew to be untrue, for he knows well both Sir John Jordan and myself, and knows well that both of us have always held the view that the only possible policy for China is one which will lead to a friendly *rapprochement* with her powerful and aggressive neighbour.

I am afraid that my letter has become somewhat discursive. Events follow

[1] Nicylas Malewsky-Maléwitch.

one another so quickly that by the time this reaches you much of the information in it may be of no value. Should there be any reason why you should wish ever to telegraph to me in Peking, the address 'Dr. Morrison, Peking' is sufficient, and by prefixing the word 'Deferred', the message comes through at half rates.

With kind regards

Very sincerely yours
[G. E. Morrison]

811. To Ts'ai T'ing-kan

[Peking] 6 April 1916

My dear Admiral,

In regard to my contract[1] the endorsement on which by His Excellency the President contains no date I would suggest that it would make the case clear and remove any possibility of misunderstanding if the enclosed clause were signed [by] Mr. Chu Chi-ch'ien[2] and by myself.

Your suggestion that this briefly worded clause be written on the back of the agreement in Chinese and English and signed by both parties, as was the first agreement, seems to me, the most simple solution possible.

If it could be done I would like for sentimental reasons that the date of the clause should be April 8th, for on that date my mother enters her 80th year.[3]

[1] Morrison, whose five-year contract with the Chinese Government was not due to expire until 1 August 1917, was nonetheless anxious to have it renewed as the clamour for Yüan Shih-k'ai's retirement grew more persistent. His contract was duly extended for 5 years, until 1922. The endorsement was dated, as requested, 8 April 1916.

[2] Chu Ch'i-ch'ien (1871–1964), Chinese Imperial official and Republican politician. A follower of Yüan Shih-k'ai, he became one of the leaders, together with Liang Shih-yi and Chou Tzu-ch'i, of the 'Communication Clique'. In 1913 Chu, who had earlier served as Minister of Communications, became Minister of the Interior when Chao Ping-chün was compelled to resign for his part in the assassination of Sung Chiao-jen. He held the post until shortly before Yüan's death in 1916. He was one of thirteen men the Republican South demanded to have punished for their roles in Yüan's monarchical scheme, but he was pardoned by the Anfu Government, which the 'Communication Clique' supported, and became Deputy Speaker in the Anfu-dominated House of Representatives. In December 1918 he was appointed Chief Delegate from the Peking Government to the Peace Conference held in Shanghai between the North and the South in February the following year, but he resigned in May, his place being taken by Wang I-t'ang, a leader of the Anfu Clique. Thereafter Chu played no further active role in politics, but devoted himself to various enterprises, including the Chung-hsing Coalmine in Shantung in which he and various other Peking politicians were shareholders. He was living in Peking when the People's Republic was established, and was made a member of a committee responsible for the improvement of parks in the Chinese capital.

[3] Morrison's mother, Rebecca Morrison (*née* Greenwood), was born in 1837, and died in 1932.

There is no hurry about having this done, but if whenever it is done it could be dated April 8th, it would be very pleasing.

Enclosed is the suggested wording.[1]

Very sincerely yours
[G. E. Morrison]

812. From Ting Shih-yüan

Hankow [Hupeh] 13 April 1916

My dear Dr Morrison,

At this busy time it has occurred to me that it might interest you to see the details of the work done during the past year, under my supervision, by the Public Works and Police Administration of Hankow.[2]

As you know, it is a Chinese custom whenever there is any unrest to keep in the public mind improvements of civil and national character. In other words, whenever a crisis occurs it is well to allow the people to observe a calm exterior on the part of the officials and to let them see that the ordinary routine is not disturbed in any manner, thereby creating confidence and allaying any spirit of unrest that may be in evidence.

This is what I am now doing in Hankow.

With best regards

Yours sincerely
W. S. Y. Tinge

813. To R. F. Johnston

[Peking] 14 April 1916

My dear Johnston,

Many thanks for your letter of the 5th.

[...]

I am profoundly dissatisfied with the way affairs are going on here. Yuan Shih-kai has made an awful mess of things, and I realise more than ever what a blunder I committed in joining his service with so much enthusiasm. My contract does not expire until the 30th Sept. 1922. I hate to be associated with a failure. When I joined the Chinese I had great confidence in the future, but for more than a year past I have been daily witnessing retrogression which I have been unable to check even in the humblest degree. Now it is too late. We have a weekly meeting of what is called a Political Conference.[3] We have met together six times, and have talked abundantly,

---

[1] Not printed.   [2] Not found.

[3] In an attempt to stem the tide of opposition, Yüan Shih-k'ai ordered that a weekly conference be held to discuss the pressing issues of the day, to be attended by the Cabinet Ministers and advisers. The first conference took place on 8 March 1916, and Morrison wrote in his Diary: 'Hopeless of course yet I came away somewhat cheered. The President who seemed to be feeling his burden addressed us. Things were to be done, not merely to

but accomplished nothing. At our last meeting the subject was the re-establishment of the Provincial Assemblies, a procedure which I have been urging for a long time past. I even ventured to suggest that if we did not hurry up there would soon be no provinces left in which to establish these bodies.

With best wishes
I am

Very sincerely yours
[G. E. Morrison]

814. From Ting Shih-yüan

Hankow [Hupeh] 20 April 1916

Personal

Dear Dr Morrison,

Your kind letter is to hand.[1] I am glad to hear that the situation is improving. I heard that you are one of the members to study the adjustment of political organization and also intend to propose to the Government to have the Provincial Assembly re-opened. In my opinion, if a talking shop opened at the provincial capital is not a good policy and cannot save the political situation, because a Chinese province is too big and cannot be popularly represented. But if a sort of local legislative council located at the place where a *Tao-Yin* can preside, is necessary and can obtain a sort of local opinion. Of course, I write these simply for your own reference without any other means.

With my kindest regards

Most sincerely yours
W. S. Y. Tinge

P.S. I use[d] to advocate the same, that is the Provincial Assembly between 1904–1905, but at present I realise my mistake.

815. To W. R. Hughes[2]

[Peking] 24 April 1916

My dear Hughes,

Many thanks for your letter of the 18th April[3] giving me a very full and lucid account of your difficulties. There is one sentence in your letter which seems to give the key. You say that 'no-one wants to quarrel with Japan, but

---

be written about being done. He might have taken a leaf from my Memorandum!' The meetings soon degenerated into a lengthy discussion of irrelevancies and time-wasting window-dressing, and were discontinued even before Yüan's death. [1] Not found.

[2] Willoughby R. Hughes (d. 1918), Australian civil engineer in charge of the Hulutao Harbour Development Scheme in which Morrison took an active interest and to which he gave his support in recommending acceptance of the project by the Chinese Government.

[3] Not printed.

on the other hand we are not going to be bullied by them'. Looking at the question from this distant point I would say that you fail to realise locally that Japan is the master of Newchwang, and that she is master by the consent – unwilling it may be, but tacit and actual none the less – of all her allies. What she insists upon will be done. It is no case of 'bullying'.

For more than a quarter of a century the Chinese have neglected the port of Newchwang, and it is idle for them now to try and act in any way which will appear as discrimination against Japan.

I perfectly understand your point, and I admire, as I have always done, the faithful way in which you serve your employers and do your duty, but there is a political aspect to this case which cannot be disregarded. The Japanese are more interested in Newchwang than are any other foreigners, and, as I said in my report, Newchwang is now as much a Japanese port as was Fusan before the annexation of Korea. I write to you very confidentially, and am sure that you will disclose nothing of what I say to you, but, so far as one can see at the present time, one of the conditions which Japan will ask for as her share of the spoils of victory will be recognition of her special position in China, and especially in Newchwang. Manchuria is now practically lost to China. The recent consent given by the Chinese Government to the pretensions of Russia and Japan: that no foreigner, not even a mining engineer, can be employed in Kirin or Heilungchiang, in any capacity connected with the Chinese Government, without the consent of Russia or Japan, has strengthened the position of Russia and Japan in that rich area which was, until little while ago, Chinese territory.

Every effort should be directed towards harmonious co-operation with the Japanese. It must be remembered that the Japanese have now obtained a valuable concession 50 miles west of Hsinminfu, and the coal that they obtain there will be exported from Newchwang. An engineer came to see me the other day who told me that he had just been devising plans for the S.M. Railway Co.,[1] whereby they may give shipping facilities in Dalny for 1200 tons of exports per hour, instead of 600 as at present. I have not before me the figures for Newchwang of last year, but the value of Japanese trade with China increased from 1908 to 1915 from $52\frac{1}{2}$ million taels to 134 million taels.

Please let me hear from you from time to time.

Very sincerely yours
[G. E. Morrison]

816. To J. R. Muir

[Peking] 27 April 1916

Dear Mr Muir,

Your long and interesting letter of the 28th March[2] reached me last evening. I was very much interested in what you had to tell me, and I think

[1] The South Manchurian Railway Company.   [2] The letter is printed as No. 806.

it was a kind action your going to so much trouble to send me your comments on the present situation. I quite agree with you that currency reform is in the very forefront of needed reforms in China. The poor people have much to put up with, for they are harrassed by tax gatherers, and robbed and blackmailed by the very soldiers who were sent nominally to protect them. Much has to be done, and it will take years to do. It has been calamitous, the directions of energy, not to the accomplishment of needed reforms, but to the acquisition of a throne. The present is full of anxiety, and I have little time for writing letters. If you would be so good as to write to me occasionally I should be grateful.

Chao Erh-hsun[1] I have not seen for a long time, but I had a pleasant letter from him some little while ago. He had not forgotten me, and still remembered an incident which at the time seemed to cause him some surprise, when having given me a cartload of gifts for some service which he considered I had rendered him, I returned the gifts with some heat, saying that the *Times* Correspondent did not accept presents.[2]

With kind regards
Believe me   Very sincerely yours
                                              [G. E. Morrison]

[1] Chao Erh-hsün (1844-1927), Chinese Bannerman and Imperial official, Governor of Hunan (1902-4), Acting President of the Board of Finance (1904-5), and Tartar-General of Manchuria (1905-7). In 1907 he was transferred to be Viceroy of Szechwan, then of Hukuang, then of Szechwan again the following year. He held that post until 1911, when he became Viceroy of Manchuria, and his place in Szechwan was taken by his brother Chao Erh-feng, who was killed by the angry populace of Chengtu in November the same year. With the military support of Chang Tso-lin, Chao Erh-hsün was able to suppress the revolutionaries in Fengtien Province, of which he became the first *Tutu* after the establishment of the Republic. But he soon resigned and retired to Tsingtao, in the German Leased Territory in Shantung. In 1914, as part of his monarchical scheme, Yüan created the Bureau of History of the Ch'ing Dynasty, and Chao Erh-hsün was made Editor-in-Chief, and in the same year a member of the Political Consultative Council. In December 1915, as the enthronement was impending, Yüan conferred upon him the honour of being his equal as one of the 'Four Friends of Sung Shan' (Sung Shan, one of five 'Sacred Mountains' of China, being in Yüan's native province Honan). The other three were Chang Chien, Hsü Shih-ch'ang [q.v.] and Li Ching-hsi. The *Ch'ing shih kao*, or the draft history of the Ch'ing dynasty of which Chao was Chief Editor, was a work of careless scholarship. It was revised under the general editorship of Chang Ch'i-yün (b. 1901) and published in Taiwan in 1962 bearing the imprint of the Ministry of Defence, entitled *Ch'ing shih*, a history of the Ch'ing dynasty, but was equally shoddy and shows the irresponsibility of Chang Ch'i-yün and his colleagues, particularly in view of the scholarly works and other facilities available to them that were not available to Chao and his collaborators.

[2] *See* Letter No. 272, Morrison to Chao Erh-hsün, 15 August 1907, *Correspondence*, Vol. I, pp. 429-30.

817. To Ethel Bell[1]

[Peking] 8 May 1916

Dear Mrs Moberly Bell,

It is a very long time since I wrote to you, and I have much to apologise for.

[...]

We are having an interesting time in Peking. Things have got into an awful mess. In his mad ambition to wear the purple Yuan Shih-kai has wrecked his own career and gravely involved his country. Every warning was given to him. The best men in his employ, and the best friends he had among foreigners, urged him not to take a step so fraught with danger, but family influence and his own ambition were too strong, and he accepted the throne on Dec. 11th,[2] despite the warning that he received on Oct. 28th from the five friendly powers: England, France, Italy, Russia and Japan, Japan, of course, being in the lead in this matter. Things had been going on well. The country had managed to hold its own fairly successfully, and its financial obligations were being met, when everything was thrown out of gear by this monarchical movement. It is difficult to see how the President can now keep his post. Even men in the employment of the Palace itself speak openly of his retirement, and at the Customs College a few days ago there was an open discussion as to what would happen after Yuan Shih-kai withdrew. Should he withdraw, the Vice-President, Li Yuan-hung – a quiet, sensible man, who has been very little in evidence since his election to the Vice-Presidency – will automatically succeed. Money is the chief difficulty, it always is in China, yet the revenue has been coming in well, and China would, but for this present upheaval, have been in a better position to meet her obligations than ever before.

I am afraid that in England very little interest is being taken in China, yet there was a time, not long ago, when China could have rendered material assistance to the prosecution of the war on the side of the Allies. Since you have been in China it may interest you to know that in August 1914, when the attack on Tsingtao was being organised by Japan, China offered to take part, but was dissuaded by Sir John Jordan. In the first days of November last year China again was prepared to join the Allies, but, having met with a rebuff on the first occasion, she made it a condition this time that she should be invited to join by the Allied powers. All were willing to invite her, except Japan. There seems to have been much bungling, much misunderstanding,

[1] The widow of Charles Frederick Moberly Bell (1847–1911), former Manager of *The Times*.
[2] On 11 December 1915 Lu Cheng-hsiang informed the Ministers of Japan, Great Britain, Russia and France in Peking, that the proposed constitutional change from republic to monarchy accorded with the will of the majority of the Chinese people, but that the Chinese Government was proceeding with caution in the matter. The Chinese Foreign Minister had earlier, on 1 November, rejected the advice contained in the *note verbale* of Russia, Japan and England.

but the net result was that Japan refused to join with the other Allies in inviting China to take part on their side.

It seems to me, and to many others in the Far East, that up to quite recently the Japanese were quite confident that Germany would be victorious in Europe, but now they realise it is only a question of time, and that nothing can stay the success of the Allies. Japan has acted in a very unusual way for an ally, for when China was prepared to join, as I have no doubt told you, Japan prevented her from doing so. Had China joined, the blow to Germany would have been a very serious one, and must have hastened the termination of the war.

With kind regards
Believe me

Very sincerely yours
[G. E. Morrison]

818. From J. M. Allison

[London] 11 May 1916

My dear Morrison,

Your letter of the 1st April reached me about a week ago in Rome.[1] [...] [...]

Porter[2] has just returned from Japan, having arranged for the publication of a regular Japanese Supplement and, even if I had not received a letter from you, I would be writing to you now with more definiteness than has hitherto been possible. [...]

You say in your letter that my project of spending £50,000 over two years is far too ambitious. I am not surprised that you and your friends take this view because the sum is undoubtedly a large one. I have always been anxious, when *The Times* did tackle the Chinese supplement, that it should be done in such a way that there could be no possible question whatever as to its effect in improving the trade relationships of the two countries. I outlined my plan, as I told you before, in some detail to the Chinese Ambassador here, and mentioned the sum of £50,000 to ensure a Supplement of noble proportions, a Supplement which would be sure to do the work which it was intended it should do. The Ambassador did not express any surprise at the sum mentioned and left me under the impression that on the whole he was favourable

---

[1] Not printed.
[2] Robert Percival Porter (1852-1917), American journalist who joined *The Times* in 1904. He had previously worked for various papers in America, including the *New York Tribune* and *Philadelphia Press* (1884-7), and was co-founder of the *New York Press* (1887). He had also served with the United States Government. His special field with *The Times* was Japan, on which he wrote a number of books, among them *The Full Recognition of Japan* and *Japan, The Rise of a Modern Power*, both published posthumously in London in 1918.

to the project. If, however, the Chinese Government consider the proposal too ambitious, there is no reason why a start should not be made upon less ambitious lines.

It has been my experience that every Government, which has co-operated with us in the publication of these special Supplements, has started somewhat nervously and, in a sense, with some degree of scepticism. It has also been my experience that the longer we continued to issue Supplements, the greater was the effect, and as time went on we found less difficulty in renewing our contracts and increasing their scope. Russia is a case in point. The first efforts of the Russian Government were somewhat timid; supplements have been issued at irregular intervals for some years but about nine months ago, I arranged for a regular monthly Russian Supplement and that contract has within the last few months been renewed so that the publication of the Russian Supplement has been ensured for the next twelve months.

We would, however, be quite agreeable to entertain a smaller Supplement and we are not particularly interested in the size of it so long as we make a start, although, of course, it must be big enough and regular enough to make a good impression here. [...]

The new trade problems which will confront us after the war, are stupendous and I firmly believe that *The Times* is rendering a great national service by publishing regular Supplements dealing with the resources and the requirements of great countries like Russia, Japan, China and Italy. China is practically unknown in the British Empire and yet everyone one meets who knows China, seems to deplore the fact that our political and commercial relationships are not closer.

So much for the Supplement which I will now leave in your hands and upon which I await your wire.

I have noticed the activities of the *Manchester Guardian* with, I confess, a certain feeling of irritation. This newspaper has not the physical difficulties to contend with that *The Times* has. The actual white paper necessary to produce a China Supplement of the *Manchester Guardian* is a trifle compared to the amount of paper necessary to produce a Supplement of *The Times*. The *Guardian* is in the same position in this respect as *The Times* used to be when it was a 3d paper.

The *Guardian* does not publish circulation figures but I have not very much doubt that the circulation of *The Times* is ten times as large as that of the *Guardian*, so that you will understand the raw material problem is not nearly so acute with them as it is with us.

As for the influence of the paper compared with that of *The Times*, you are qualified to form your own opinions. The remark of the correspondent[1] is simply typical cynicism of the Manchester school. It is deplorable to think that the accredited representative of what, after all, is an important English

[1] Edward Manico Gull.

newspaper, should be in a position to spread such a malicious doctrine as that which characterises his statement about England with respect to the integrity of China.

The influence of *The Times* seems to me to be greater than ever, which I suppose is only natural when one considers the enormous increase in its circulation. When I recently visited the Continent, I found that in official circles it was supreme. Although perhaps my opinion is prejudiced, I consider that the manner in which Northcliffe has used the paper to speed up the conduct of the war has been magnificent.

[...]

London is full of Australian soldiers – Anzacs, as they call them, and they are winning golden opinions everywhere. 12,000 are now in France and it is extraordinary to witness their glee that at last they are having a chance of a 'go' at the Germans.

[...]

Yours very sincerely
J. Murray Allison

819. To O. M. Green

[Peking] 17 May 1916

My dear Green,

For some time I have been intending to write to you to tell you how glad I was to hear that you had returned to China, and I do hope that you will take an opportunity this year of coming to Peking and having a look round.

I was glad to see your strenuous attack upon the insane folly of Liang Shih-yi, for it was really he, and not the Cabinet, who decreed the Moratorium of last Thursday evening.[1] The Minister of Finance[2] only learned of this suicidal act the next morning. Mazot,[3] a very intelligent Frenchman who is called Adviser in the Ministry of Finance, only heard of it in the course of the day after the act had been committed. His opinion was then asked, and he suggested that it was like inviting the physician to attend to a case after it was dead. Liang Shih-yi has been the evil genius of China. In the four years of my service, no scheme with which he has been connected, and he has been

---

[1] On 12 May, Yüan Shih-k'ai ordered the Bank of China and Bank of Communications to suspend redemption of their notes. The Shanghai branch of the Bank of China then managed by Chang Chia-ao, who later played a significant role in the Nationalist Government, was alone in disregarding the order on the advice of Passeri. For this Chang was censured by the Government, but received credit from later historians.

[2] Sun Pao-ch'i was at this time Minister of Finance. He absented himself on the excuse of illness three days after this letter was written, on 20th, when Chou Tzu-ch'i acted for him, but Chou resigned three days later when Sun's resignation was formally gazetted, and Ch'en Chin-t'ao was appointed in his place.

[3] Henri Mazot, French economist. He was appointed to the Audit office in connection with the Five-Power or Reorganisation Loan of 1913.

connected with nearly all, has been a success, and where success was possible, under common-sense, straightforward guidance, success was impossible under his tortuous and medieval methods. The monarchy ought to have been abandoned, and the promise was made that it should be abandoned, on the 8th of February, but to the Chinese mind it seemed less a loss of face to abandon it by stages – postponement first, cancellation afterwards. The result was disastrous. I can see very little hope.

You will have no doubt heard that Sir John is leaving, and that his successor is coming from the Foreign Office. It is not stated who is the successor, but there seems little doubt that it is Alston, and of all the men who have held charge in my time in Peking he seems to me the most unfitted for this important post. If it should be a fact, the appointment is a 'job' of the worst kind, for we want a Minister of capacity, not merely an amiable nincompoop who has a pull in London. It may be, however, that it is not Alston, though the Japanese say that it is. His appointment will date, I understand, from the 26th October.[1] The Chinese regarded Alston as somewhat of a buffoon, but he has a very charming wife, and she may help him to take more interest in his work.

There is one thing that I would like to mention to you. More than once a reference has been made to the possibility of Sir Richard Dane resigning. These reports come from the Chinese, and they have no foundation in fact, but to the Chinese mind it seems that reports of this kind can in some way create ill-feeling between the British and Japanese. Dane has no intention of resigning, nor has he ever had such an intention. He has done good work. He has impressed his personality upon the Chinese, which is so important, and he carries on a very effective administration with the help of only 38 foreigners, whereas in the Customs there are 45 times this number, producing a revenue 12 million dollars less than that produced by the Salt. Sir Richard is paid the equivalent of £7,350 per year, a salary nearly approaching that of Aglen, who gets 4,000 Haikuan taels a month, and this year receives his septennial bonus of an additional one year's full pay.

Write to me some day if you have time.

Please remember me very kindly to Mrs. Green. We are living in the country, and I come in every day to do my work.

With best wishes

Sincerely yours
[G. E. Morrison]

[1] This statement proved to be premature. Jordan's appointment was renewed. He merely went on home leave, during which time Francis Beilby Alston was Chargé d'Affaires.

820. To W. R. Hughes

[Peking] 18 May 1916

My dear Hughes,

Yesterday I scribbled a short note to thank you for your very full and careful statement,[1] which is of great value to me, as it makes me able to answer the strictures of the Japanese Minister, and to help others to answer them.

Apparently the British policy is – at any rate while the war lasts – to become more and more subservient to Japan. Not only without protest, but actually by subsequently giving them support, we have connived at the Japanese illegal action in withholding from China the payment of the Salt surplus. How far the present crisis is due to this you can possibly surmise. The Japanese action in Shantung is the most outrageous of anything done by a foreign power in China since China first had intercourse with foreign powers.

I hope to see you this summer. My wife and children are going over to Japan for the summer on the 30th of this month, and will be away until the end of September. I may take this opportunity of going up to the North while they are away, and if so should hope to see you. I wonder are you going to Hulutao.

With best wishes to you

Very sincerely yours
[G. E. Morrison]

821. To G. W. Prothero

[Peking] 22 May 1916

Dear Dr. Prothero,

I am much obliged for your letter of April 21st.[2]

[...]

Yuan Shih-kai is still in office, but his position is daily becoming more difficult. He is prepared to retire, but has considerable anxiety as to his personal safety, I believe. A conference of the southern provinces has been held in Canton, and another has been called for Nanking,[3] and by the decision of the latter the President will, I believe, abide, but there are difficulties in the way of the meeting of this second conference, and altogether the position is

---

[1] Not printed.   [2] Not printed.

[3] The Military Governors and their representatives from the seventeen provinces met in Nanking on 17 May at the invitation of Feng Kuo-chang to discuss the monarchy question and the position of Yüan Shih-k'ai. The majority favoured Yüan's retirement but some were in favour of his retaining the Presidency, and the meeting ended on 21st without an agreement being reached. As to the Canton conference, Morrison may have been referring to the assembly of various anti-Yüan factions in Chao-ch'ing, Canton, which set up there, on 8 May, a military government under Ts'en Ch'un-hsüan and Liang Ch'i-ch'ao with T'ang Chi-yao as titular head.

very confused. In the meantime the Japanese are renewing their activity, although the speech just published, of Baron Kato, shows that Japanese statesmen now realise that Germany is a defeated country.

I am convinced that there is no German money behind the trouble in China. Japan is the *agent provocateur*. A delegate of the American Legation, sent to make independent enquiries in Shantung, has just returned with the report that the statements published by the papers regarding Japan's provocative action, Japanese assistance to the rebels, and Japanese co-operation with rebels, are in no way overstated.

You will no doubt have heard before this that Sir John Jordan is leaving. His successor has been appointed. He is Mr. Beilby Alston, C.B., Chief Clerk of the Foreign Office, who has been in charge of the China section for some time past. Twice already he has been Councillor of our Legation here, and Chargé d'Affaires. He now comes for the third time as Councillor, arriving here at the end of July, and taking Sir John's post when that Minister retires in October. It is not too much to say that in making this appointment Sir Edward Grey has done a serious dis-service to British interests in the Far East. Alston is a pleasant, amiable man, of suitable age, but with little diplomatic experience, and unprepossessing appearance, who stammers, and entirely lacks that repose in manner which is necessary in dealing with the Chinese. Of all the men who have been in charge of our Legation here during the last 18 years he is the one who proved himself to be most unfitted for the post. In saying this I am speaking without any personal prejudice. It is, I know, the view held by every prominent Englishman in Peking. This morning one of the two or three most prominent Englishmen here spoke to me as to whether it would not be possible to get the China Association to take action and prevent the appointment of Mr. Alston, which he regarded as a catastrophe. There is no more important post under the British Government than Peking, and there are many able men in the Diplomatic Service. To go outside the Service and appoint one who entered the Foreign Office by a side door, who has never shown himself possessed of any other quality than social amiability, is not fair to the British community in the Far East. It is a 'job' of the worst kind. In other ways he has shown singular unfitness for the post, and had himself talked about in a manner unbefitting a *Chef de Mission*.

The explanation of the appointment is given that Sir Arthur Nicholson[1] takes but little interest in Far Eastern affairs, and that he would be guided by Sir Walter Langley,[2] who would naturally wish to help a personal friend, but

---

[1] Arthur Nicolson (1849-1928), 1st Baron Carnock, British diplomat, at the time referred to Permanent Under-Secretary of State for Foreign Affairs (1910-16), and previously British Ambassador to Russia (1905-10). From 1876 to 1878 he was Second Secretary at the British Legation in Peking.
[2] Walter Louis Frederick Goltz Langley (1855-1918), British diplomat, Assistant Under-Secretary of State for Foreign Affairs since 1907. He was Private Secretary to successive Parliamentary Under-Secretaries of State for Foreign Affairs from 1887 to 1898.

it is not fair, at such a critical time, when the situation is daily becoming more complex, and when the ability of even a highly-trained diplomatist might be taxed to its utmost, that so arrant a 'job' should be perpetrated as the sending of this amiable nincompoop to Peking.

I will see that the *Far Eastern Review* is sent to you every month. I am quite sure that Donald will be glad to do this.

You thank me for the trouble I have taken. What I have done has been really no trouble, and it gives me pleasure to do anything I can for the Editor of so great a British institution as the *Quarterly Review*.

With best wishes
Believe me

Very sincerely yours
[G. E. Morrison]

822. From J. R. Muir

Pengshanhsien, Sze[chwan] 23 May 1916

Dear Dr Morrison,

I write to you this evening from the 'other side of the fence'.[1] Your very kind letter of April 27th reached me Sunday morning last at which time the important step was being taken in Chengtu.[2] Mr J. L. Smith,[3] the Consul, had written me that morning in anything but a reassuring tone. However it appears that the inevitable happened some time on Sunday. As yet all we know is that the Postal Commissioner sent the information through the P.O. runner who passed through today. There can be no mistake about it. And though the wires are down so that Chengtu is isolated you will have had the news before this reaches you.

You received my former letter[4] so kindly that I make bold to accept your invitation and write again. There is very little that one may say at this time. I have refrained from writing to any but close friends during this crisis. You will agree with me that it is better for us to remain 'neutral' in the strictest

---

[1] Peng-shan-hsien, Szechwan, from where J. R. Muir was writing, was then under the control of the anti-Yüan Shih-k'ai forces.

[2] On 22 May Ch'en Yi (b. 1869), the Military Governor of Szechwan, joined the anti-Yüan Shih-k'ai forces by declaring the independence of the province at the provincial capital, Chengtu. Ch'en Yi was a graduate of Japan's Shikan Gakkō. Believed to be a trusted supporter, being a relative of Yüan by marriage, the stand he took against Yüan was greatly deplored by him. A protégé of Li Yüan-hung who succeeded Yüan as President on 7 June 1916, Ch'en was transferred to become Military Governor and concurrently Civil Governor of Hunan Province in July 1916, but did not take up the post. He became instead a member of the Military Council, serving as military adviser to the President.

[3] John Langford Smith (b. 1877), British consular official, at the time referred to Acting Consul-General in Chengtu. He later served as Consul in Ichang, Kiukiang and Chefoo.

[4] Printed as No. 806.

sense. Still I must confess now that I had very little doubt from the beginning in January and I am not surprised at the outcome.

It appears that the Magistrate of Kwanhsien wrote to all of his colleagues in the *Hsiens* throughout the province urging them to exhort the Governor to declare Independence. We do not know how many responded, but the report is that it was unanimous. I can quite believe it. The people here for several weeks have considered it inevitable and they have waited with almost breathless suspense from day to day. I have heard not a single expression of even regret at the passing of Yuan Shih Kai.[1] All took it for granted that his course was run. Naturally none of them are inclined to be as charitable as we are.

I wonder as I write if this will reach you while the *status quo* is maintained in Peking. Need I urge the necessity of the all important step that has been voiced so often during the past weeks? All I will need to say is this: We are quite confident that from a condition of terrorism this province will settle down almost immediately to quietness and normal conditions. The soldiers that have been drawn up against each other for weeks will now be liberated to care for the bandits and other unruly elements. There is plenty of authority and plenty of material to accomplish all that. And, furthermore, the crisis being over for us we have nothing further in the way of Revolution to look forward to.

As we are quite sure that every other soul in China feels in heart as those of us do who are now 'Independent' it is worse than folly for Mr. Yuan to expect anything else for himself. He has been strong, but he was strong only when the *people were behind him*. If I could tell you the sentiment I found in 1911 in his favour I could more readily explain the sentiment now that is against him. Like Samson of old his strength has departed from him, but he 'knows it not'. The people have left him and there is nothing for him, but to withdraw.

Or possibly there may be another outcome. I expect to spend my days in Szechwan and as I am sure that the step taken will be permanent I make bold to throw in my lot with the rebels who have defied Peking. He may be able to hold some of the Northern provinces, but if he does it will mean a division of the country. Surely, Dr. Morrison, no sane man in China wants that. We all waited to see if Mr. Yuan could keep Szechwan in line. Now that it has gone the other side will have strength enough to defy Peking forever. And there is no idea of taking a single back step. It means independence forever, not of Peking, but of Yuan Shih Kai. If Peking means Yuan Shih Kai then we are in another country from you.

I am almost enough of a fatalist to believe that it will be done, but it will mean the disintegration of the Chinese nation. You do not want me to discuss

---

[1] As Yüan Shih-k'ai did not die until 6 June 1916, the reference must be to the abandonment of the monarchical scheme.

that now and Europe has troubles of her own so the time is not immediate. However, I hope and pray that we will not see two nations carved out of this magnificent people by the vanity of one man. Get him out of it by all means as quickly as possible.

Your friendship for Yuan Shih Kai was not merely a thing on paper that we know. But the Yuan Shih Kai of 1911 and the Yuan Shih Kai of 1916 are two different men as we know them. As I stated in my other letter[1] it is unspeakably sad to see the eclipse of such a brilliant character. The country still needs him, but the country will not have him. If your circumstances change with his and you should become to us once more the honoured *Times* Correspondent we will rejoice for having known you in a position where your influence has told. May it tell now in one last attempt to save China from destruction.

Very sincerely yours
John R. Muir

823. To Ts'ai T'ing-kan

[Peking] 27 May 1916

My dear Admiral,

Herewith I return you these four letters.[2] They are not genuine letters. They are faked letters. There is no firm in Shanghai known as Thomas, Davis & Ross.

On the envelope is written Alf Ross & Co. 39 Canton Road. No such firm as Alf Ross & Co. occurs in the Directory and it is at least a curious coincidence that 39 Canton Road is the address of Mr. Thaddeus C. White[3] who is now in Peking. He is the husband of the Princess Der Ling[4] [...]

Best wishes to you

Very sincerely yours
[G. E. Morrison]

[1] Letter No. 806.
[2] Only the two printed here were found.
[3] An American adventurer, who had worked as marshal of the American Court in Shanghai. He subsequently undertook many shady dealings as a commercial agent, and was involved in the attempted sale of Palace treasures from the Manchu Palace in Mukden.
[4] A daughter of Yü-keng, Chinese Bannerman and Minister to Japan (1895-8) and to France (1899-1902), Der Ling (Te-ling) and her sister Yung-ling served at one time as ladies-in-waiting and interpreters for the Empress-Dowager Tz'u-hsi. In 1911 Der Ling published her experiences in the Manchu Court in a book entitled *Two Years in the Forbidden City* and another book, *Son of Heaven*, was published in 1935 (New York and London). A volume of memoirs by Yung-ling, who married a Chinese general, T'ang Pao-ch'ao, was published in 1957 in Peking entitled *Ch'ing-kung so-chi* (miscellaneous notes on the Ch'ing court).

Enclosure I to Letter No. 823: *From Thomas, Davis & Ross, Shanghai 21 April 1916*

Dear Sir,

We trust that you will excuse the liberty that we venture to take in thus addressing you concerning the present apparent unquiet condition of affairs, which has agitated, and is agitating, the minds of merchants in China locally and elsewhere, by the disturbing rumors of revolt against the Central Government.

Might we presume to submit our counsel, it would be, that you should give little, or no heed to the wild utterances so abundantly and freely made by the various provincial guilds of this port, especially the Cantonese Guild, as we have generally found these corporations of men of low degree of intelligence and of somewhat lax political principles.

For example, Mr. Tang Shao-yi, during the Manchy Dynasty, was employed in a subordinate capacity under Yuan Shih Kai, in Corea, many years ago, prior to the China–Japanese war: and it was only by and through the latters influence that the former attained the high official rank and position which he subsequently achieved. During the first revolution, at Hanyang, the Manchu Government appointed Yuan Shih Kai to negotiate on their behalf, terms of peace with the revolutionaries: and Yuan Shih Kai, at this juncture, employed Tang Shao-Yi as his collegue. Tang evidently made his pile out of this negotiation but he was unable to subject his accounts in connection therewith to a satisfactory audit: and, in consequence, was forced to leave Yuan Shih Kai's service. These circumstances are familiar to the entire world. And they are alone sufficient to demonstrate to all foreigners how faithful and trustworthy Cantonese of such a character are.

Our primary object in addressing you at this crisis is to enlist your active sympathy and co-operation in the preservation of peace in Shanghai and its neighbourhood, for we fervently believe that, by thus acting, you will obviate years of trouble for China. In the event of Independence being declared in this province, the Japanese, who are eagerly anticipating such a course of action will seize the opportunity to enter the Yangtse Valley for they are duly prepared for it and are in tacit agreement with the revolutionaries.

We crave leave, furthermore, to exhort you to write to the various Consular bodies, to request them to direct the newspapers concerned in such work to cease further publications of wild rumors in their papers, on pain of suppression.

In our humble opinion, Yuan Shih Kai is the one man at present capable of saving China. And should the revolutionaries obtain access to Peking and introduce and adopt *their* system of Government under the aegis of Japan, with whom they have already a secret agreement, the result will be the destruction of China, to the permanent gain of Japan.

Earnestly soliciting your consideration of the foregoing, and hoping you will conjointly labor with your fellow provincial collegues for the salvation of your country.

We have the honour to be, Sir

Your obedient servants
[Thomas, Davis & Ross]

Enclosure II to Letter No. 823: *From Thomas, Davis & Ross to Yüan Shih-k'ai, Shanghai 20 May 1916*

Your Excellency,

Our object in addressing you is to urge you to pay no attention to the wild and clamorous rumors circulated by interested factions for ends of their own in order to disrupt the present Government, and to maintain your position in the state. For notwithstanding such disturbing reports, given out as authentic by agitators, the majority of the people are still at heart for you: out of a population of, say, four hundred million people, the minority against you are less than a million.

Moreover, foreigners in China have faith only in yourself as the one man who possesses the requisite qualifications to guide and steer the state through the present crisis: for they appreciate what you have hitherto done since your inauguration as President, and are gravely apprehensive that, with your abdication, succeeding Governments would involve disastrous consequences to their business.

In the event of your really being desirous of abdicating the Presidency, the only individual whom we believe would be capable to succeed you, without further commotion, is the late Emperor Hsuan Tung. We have indeed already heard that it is your intention to resign the Presidency into his hands. But such a course must be brought about voluntarily by yourself, not as the result of popular pressure. By thus acting you will obviate all troubles and disturbances.

In the meantime, we beg to urge you to devise and take prompt and strenuous measures to frustrate Tang Shao-yi and the members of the Cantonese Guild from executing their base plot of sinking steamers, as already exhibited in the recent sinking of the S.S. *Hsin-Yu*.

As representatives of more than six hundred thousand citizens of this country, profoundly concerned in the fate of the state, we have thus taken the liberty of addressing you in the foregoing terms, as well as to the Governors of the various provinces, alleged to have declared their Independence, to cease their struggle and, if possible, to restore harmony and peace.

We enclose here with a copy of a telegram,[1] in Chinese, addressed and

---

[1] Not found.

despatched on the 18th inst. to Premier Tuan Chi-jui, to Feng Kuo-chan,[1] Nanking; to Nee Zu-chuen,[2] and to Chang Hsun. This telegram was carefully devised and prepared after due consultation and deliberation with various foreign lawyers and merchants, and fully represents and embodies your point of view that will be submitted by your delegates at the forthcoming Nanking Conference which will be held on the 26th instant.

With our best wishes for your ultimate success

We have the honour to be

Your Excellency's servants
Thomas, Davis & Ross

824. From Ts'ai T'ing-kan

[Peking] 1 June [1916]

My dear Doctor,

[...]

I saw the President who phoned for me this morning and received me in his bed room. He is truly sick but not dangerously ill. He said: I heard all the Legations think I should or would resign. I said: All think you should take a rest which you badly need. The Financial outlook is not rosy and difficulties are increasing rather than decreasing. I said every body is anxious for his health.

Yours sincerely
Tsai Ting Kan

825. From W. R. Giles[3]

Peking 6 June 1916

Dear Dr Morrison,

The report that two thousand five hundred of General Chang Hsun's troops had arrived in Peking is untrue. As far as I can learn not one of his men is to be found in this city. The report is supposed to have been placed in circulation through some of the Chinese mistaking the troops from French Indo-Chine for those of Chang Hsun's.

[1] Feng Kuo-chang was at this time Military Governor of Kiangsu at Nanking. He was soon to become Vice-President upon Li Yüan-hung's accession to the Presidency.

[2] Ni Ssu-ch'ung (1868–1920), Chinese soldier. A subordinate of Yüan Shih-k'ai he rose to become the Military Governor of his native Anhwei Province replacing the southern republican Sun To-sen at the time of the 'Second Revolution' in July 1913. He held this post, except for the period July 1916 to July 1917, until his death. In spite of being one of the staunchest supporters of Yüan Shih-k'ai's monarchical scheme, he survived Yüan's downfall to become a forceful supporter of his fellow provincial Tuan Ch'i-jui and the Anfu Government.

[3] William R. Giles (?b. 1878), British soldier and journalist. A former sergeant with the Royal Welsh Fusiliers, he was at this time Correspondent of the *Peking and Tientsin Times* and Special Correspondent of the *Chicago Daily News* in Peking.

Some thirty or forty Chinese soldiers attempted to cause a disturbance near the Hou Men[1] last night but were quickly dispersed by the police.

I am told that the French doctor[2] remained in the palace all last night and that he has suggested calling in further foreign medical opinion.

With regards

Sincerely yours
William R. Giles

[1] The main northern city gate of Peking.
[2] Dr Bussière, physician to the French Legation in Peking.

June 1916 – June 1917

Yüan Shih-k'ai died on 6 June 1916. Having dominated the Chinese political stage for almost six years he left a sudden vacuum on his death. Li Yüan-hung, who had never been allowed to play any significant role in the nation's affairs in his capacity as Vice-President, now stepped into his place, but could not quite fill it. The real power was in the hands of the military governors who, with the exception of those from the disaffected provinces in the South, were all Yüan's supporters. Having exercised emergency powers in Yüan's name within the provinces and territories under their control, they now upon his death gathered these powers into their own hands. Independently or in concert, they soon set about carving up the country amongst themselves and ultimately reduced China to a nation in name only.

In the central government by far the most powerful figure was Tuan Ch'i-jui. Together with Wang Shih-chen, the Chief of Staff, and Feng Kuo-chang, the Military Governor of Kiangsu Province, Tuan had formed a triumvirate under Yüan. However, he had soon outdistanced the other two in national politics when he was chosen by Yüan to be his Army Minister in the first Republican cabinet. This post, which he successfully held down in spite of rapid cabinet changes, not only gave him a measure of control of the military – the most important single factor in the early years of the Republic – but also enabled him before long to assume the seat of Prime Minister, and so gain an even stronger hold on the policy-making apparatus. The fact that he had in the previous year temporarily retired from politics on account of his disagreement with the monarchist clique only added to his prestige and influence when, after the abandonment of the monarchical plan, he was finally invited by Yüan to return on his own terms. Having won from such an autocrat as his late master the power to act as head of the first responsible cabinet since the founding of the Republic, Tuan now set about running things his own way and would brook no interference from any quarter. President Li Yüan-hung, however, supported and urged on by the members of the resurrected parliament, claimed the power of balance and restraint which he considered his official due. This difference in the interpretation of their respective constitutional roles soon led to a conflict between the new President and his Prime Minister, which was to have far-reaching and unexpected repercussions.

The immediate question that touched off the dispute was whether or not

China should participate in the European war. Yüan Shih-k'ai had offered at the outbreak of European hostilities to join the war on the side of the allied powers, in the hope of increasing his prestige by retrieving from Germany the territory in Shantung she had forcibly taken from China in 1897. The offer was rejected by Japan for reasons already apparent in the foregoing correspondence. China had then declared her neutrality, 'a wise policy' as Morrison at the time described it. However, as the war progressed, Morrison changed his views and in so doing tried to persuade the Chinese Government to review the question in the light of new developments. Both in conversation with the Chinese and in the numerous memoranda he sent them, he pointed out the various benefits that would accrue if China were to declare war on Germany, including that of gaining a seat at the Peace Conference subsequent to victory. Of all the potential advantages of such a course of action, Yüan and his followers were especially attracted by the prospect of China's being able to obtain desperately needed financial assistance from the Allied powers.

Japan, however, persisted in her strong objection to China's participation in the war, and England, now a weakened ally, could do nothing but acquiesce. Baron Ishii, Foreign Minister in the Okuma Cabinet, gave the reason for Japanese opposition when in November 1915 he was officially approached by the representatives of England, France and Russia in Tokyo, asking that Japan join them in inviting China to declare war on their side. On this occasion he was reported to have said: 'The Japanese Government could not accept responsibility for awakening the activity of 400 million people.'

With the demise of Yüan Shih-k'ai, who had not been in good odour with the Japanese, Morrison thought he might be able to help smooth out the difficulties. He took the opportunity, while holidaying with his family in Japan in August 1916, to see Katō Takaaki – the Japanese Foreign Minister at the time of the Twenty-One Demands – to find out from him the real reasons for Japan's objections and to see what he could do to overcome them. But notwithstanding Katō's sympathetic reception, Japan refused to shift from her position. That she finally relented was not, as Morrison thought at the time, because her generals had come to the conclusion that Germany could not win. She did so only after she had obtained from England in February 1917 and in the following month from France, what the Japanese Foreign Ministry described as 'fresh proof of the close ties' that united the Allies – an assurance that at the Peace Conference the two would support Japanese claims regarding her acquisitions in Shantung. Of all the side effects of the European war and in view of the serious repercussions it provoked, this Anglo-French undertaking came second only in magnitude to the decision to establish a Jewish home in Palestine, which was made in November of the same year.

Moves for China's participation in the war were also greatly assisted by

America's entry, since Paul Reinsch, the American Minister in Peking, was at last in a position to use all his influence in support of Morrison's advocacy. By that time, however, the Chinese government under Tuan Ch'i-jui needed little persuasion. The insurgent southern provinces were not showing signs of submission and Tuan and his chief advisers considered that with the financial support it would bring, China's declaration of war would greatly strengthen his position. It was for precisely this reason that the move was opposed by the southern party whose members dominated Parliament. To break the deadlock Tuan recommended that the President dissolve Parliament, but this the new President was unwilling to do. Lest the President and Parliament should take the threatening words of the military governors among his supporters merely for distant thunder, Tuan summoned the military governors to Peking for a demonstration of strength, and at the meeting they unanimously declared in favour of China's entry into the war. At the same time the government sponsored the so-called 'Citizen Groups' to lay siege to Parliament, threatening to incarcerate its members in the building until they had passed the bills approving a declaration of war.

It was at this juncture that Japan's duplicity was revealed. It was discovered that though she had withdrawn her objection to China's participation in the war, she had continued her clandestine support of the southern party's opposition to such entry, while supplying Tuan Ch'i-jui's government with funds. The money was furnished by the Japanese Government through the Yokohama Specie Bank and other semi-government banks in exchange for important industrial and political concessions. Parliament, which had been kept in ignorance of this, was incensed and passed a vote of no confidence in Tuan. This culmination of a chain of events which Tuan's activities had set off finally compelled Li Yüan-hung to remove him from his post on 23 May 1917.

The dismissal was, however, contested by Tuan on the grounds that the decrees were without his signature and therefore illegal. In the circumstances, he declared, he could no longer be held responsible for any consequences. This hint was readily taken up by his supporters among the northern militarists, who responded by declaring the secession of their provinces from the central government. They threatened to remain severed until Tuan was reinstated and parliament dissolved. As a warlike gesture they also established a joint headquarters in Tientsin, to which city Tuan had retired.

Like the Chinese themselves, foreign well-wishers were also divided on the question of China's participation in the war. While Morrison's stand was never in question, he did not always take kindly to those with views differing from his own. Material demonstrating his zeal to pursue and persecute 'subversive' elements – a role he also played during the Russo-Japanese War of 1904–5 and during the reign of Yüan Shih-k'ai – has been largely omitted, but the picture of him as a fanatical 'war-monger' is much in evidence.

826. From O. M. Green

Shanghai 8 June 1916

Dear Morrison,
[...]
So Yuan is no more. What a tragedy that monarchical movement was! To think that his great statesmanship should have slipped up so badly at the last. The strength of the feeling it aroused has amazed me. Now the position of the revolutionaries down here is quite comical. They have been so busy shouting 'Yuan must go' that they have hardly spared thought for what they would do if he went, and the wind is completely taken out of their sails. They have got what they pretended to clamour for, and Li president etc., and now they don't know what to do with it. It doesn't please them a bit. If there were a spark of genuine patriotism among 'em, one would call the death of Yuan Heaven's own providence. So it may yet be. But I'm sick of politicians. I love China, the ordinary Chinese one comes across, the great country, and I believe in her yet. If Britain plays any fool tricks, standing in with Japan in any way, it will be the most criminal and the blindest folly. But all the same these modern reformers[1] (!!) I hate.
[...]

Yours sincerely
Owen M. Green

827. To Ts'ai T'ing-kan

Peking 10 June 1916

My dear Admiral,
Yesterday by appointment Dr. Ariga, Mr. Willoughby[2] and Prof. Jenks and I were received by the new President.[3] Our reception was a very agreeable one and the impression created by the President, by his evident sincerity, his modesty and his simplicity was most pleasing.

Opportunity being given me I expressed the hope that the services of the Foreign Advisers would be utilised to the utmost. In the past our experience was that our advice was rarely asked and still more rarely followed. Our interests were bound up with the interests of the country of our adoption whose success and prosperity we most earnestly desired. Our one wish was to

[1] Apparently a reference to the republicans in the south.
[2] William Franklin Willoughby (1867–1960), American Jurist. A graduate of Princeton University and according to Morrison, 'very like Woodrow Wilson', he was Professor of Jurisprudence and Politics at Princeton at the time of his appointment in 1914 as adviser to the Chinese Government on the drafting of the constitution, in succession to J. F. Goodnow who left to become President of Johns Hopkins University. Willoughby held the post until 1916 when, on leaving China, he became Director of the Institute for Government Research (1916–32) at his *alma mater*.
[3] Li Yüan-hung.

be given work to do and to be associated with every effort by which China would strive to raise herself to a place among the strong nations of the world.

Dr. Willoughby said that he hoped the Political Council would be re-established and the President without committing himself seemed to indicate that when the favourable time came it would be re-established.

Speaking to Dr. Ariga the President reminded him that he had known him 20 years before in Japan when he was a Professor of Law.[1]

Dr. Jenks at once adopted the tone of flattery. So reassured were the people by the succession of His Excellency that the paper notes had risen in value more than 15% in the last two days an omen he thought of happy augury for the future.

Aglen I know also takes this view but undoubtedly a contributory cause is the expectation of the people that large reserves of Salt monies will now be released and that large loans can now be negotiated in America.

Personally I do sincerely hope that there will be the least possible borrowing from abroad. Already the country is overburdened with foreign debts. Every source of Revenue is more or less hypothecated.

As regards the Salt I am informed by Sir Richard Dane that the total amount available for release is $7,000,000 of which $2,000,000 are earmarked for Ssu-ch'uan. In his opinion the remaining $5,000,000 can safely be handed over to the Chinese Government (whose money it is by law and right) if certain guarantees easily forthcoming can be given. But the question is what guarantees will the Japanese require what conditions will they impose? You will probably have already heard. I will see Sir Richard on Monday. This week-end I could not go out to stay with him.

I hope that you will continue to work with the new President. Everyone wishes that you will do so. Your influence is wholly good and conciliatory and with your personal popularity you can greatly facilitate the harmonious establishment of the new Regime especially in its relations with foreigners.

Last Summer I wrote to Mr. Liang Shih-yi a short resumé of the recent history of China.[2] An unhappy chapter has now to be added to that record. What is to be the future? Work must be done. Actual work must take the place of the everlasting talk of the intention to do work. If we can become united and all strive together Chinese and foreign alike in the service of the Government we can recover much that now seems irretrievable we can create a new and powerful China of consideration among the nations.

Again you will have seen that President Roosevelt has denounced the policy of President Wilson and the most opprobrious term he can find to use in his denunciation is that 'this college sissy is Chinafying America' reducing his country to impotence among the powers.

[1] Li Yüan-hung must have met Ariga in 1897 when he was sent by Chang Chih-tung, then Viceroy of Hukuang, to Japan in connection with the new army he was establishing in Hupeh. Ariga was then Professor of International Law at the Imperial University in Tokyo.   [2] A reference to Morrison's letter of 12 July 1915, printed as No. 770.

That reforms can be effected completely changing the attitude of the world towards China I have no doubt whatever but such reforms can never be possible so long as their execution is entrusted to the hands of those who do not understand the foreigner and foreign methods.

China has every conceivable advantage in her favour, territorial extent, varied climate, fertile soil, abundant waterways, an intelligent and industrious people. But she lacks up to date government and up to date methods of administration. In her contest with the highly trained nations of the west her strength is that of the bow and arrow fighting with the quick-firer.

Many things have to be accomplished. Working unitedly we can accomplish them.

1. Recovery of Independence, fiscal independence, military independence by the removal of foreign military guards, independence from foreign dictation.
2. Delimitation of her frontiers in Yunnan, Tibet, Hsin chiang and Mongolia and adequate policing of those frontiers.
3. Recovery of her position in Tibet by the Signature of the Anglo-Tibetan Agreement.
4. Negotiation of Commercial Treaties permitting the increase of Customs duties.
5. Financial Reorganisation and separation of the Bank of China from Government interference.
6. Reform of the Land Tax Collection by the Chinese themselves in conjunction with foreign expert guidance on the same lines as the Salt Tax has been reorganised by the Chinese in co-operation with foreign expert experience. It need never be forgotten that the Chinese with the assistance of 38 foreigners collect a Salt revenue $12,000,000 greater than that collected by the Maritime Customs with the assistance of 1750 foreigners.
7. Roads must be built and railways reorganised. So long as the present mismanagement continues every day brings nearer the time when there will be a demand for the foreign control of those railways in which foreign capital is invested.
8. Finally and yet foremost China by one bold stroke can and must raise herself among the nations and place her relations with foreign countries upon a new footing. And she can do this by *joining the Allies*. This can be done. I am confident and I could help her to accomplish it.

Think over the foregoing. We must work towards the fulfilment of these aims and aspirations.

Very sincerely yours
[G. E. Morrison]

P.S. I hope that now you will find time to complete your biography of the late President.[1] I also have many notes of my experiences. Looking back over these I recall vividly many of the endearing qualities of the famous ruler, his generosity, his kindness, his loyalty to his friends, his consideration for others, his invincible good humour and courage under difficulties. The most striking characteristic as I observed then of his relations with the foreigner was his caution, his unwillingness ever to give full confidence, his invariable withholding of the essential fact. Thus he never could be given a well-balanced judgement because he never submitted the full facts of the case. During my four years intercourse November 1911 – May 1916 never once was I given complete information and this was specially striking in all financial questions in the Chandless Batouieff case[2] in the Tibetan Case and in the case of the Japanese demands information regarding which first came to me from Donald. I fancy this will always be the difficulty in rendering effective service – this inveterate distrust of the foreigner. The same characteristic is very noticeable in Mr. Liang Shih-yi, in Mr. Lu Tseng-tsiang and even in men of a younger generation like Alfred Sze and Wellington Koo.

It would be very interesting to read your study and compare notes. My letter is already too long.

828. From Ts'ai T'ing-kan

[Peking] 12 June 1916

My dear Doctor,

Thank you for your very instructive letter. It gives ample food for thought.

I am trying to make up my mind – to begin with 'Yuan Shih Kai, the man' – or to start writing my 'Concubiniad', a work at once interesting and instructive – a key to the social life of the upper class (wealthy) Chinese.

Yours sincerely
Tsai Ting Kan

829. To Li Yüan-hung[3]

Peking 19 June 1916

To His Excellency the President of the Republic of China

We the undersigned, advisers to your Excellency, being convinced that the

---

[1] Ts'ai T'ing-kan had helped Morrison with articles on Yüan Shih-k'ai for *The Times* after Yüan's recall in 1911 following the Wuchang Uprising. Ts'ai had told Morrison that he intended to write a life of Yüan Shih-k'ai. *See* Letter No. 374, Morrison to Ts'ai T'ing-kan, 5 April 1911, *Correspondence*, Vol. I, pp. 592–3.

[2] *See* Letter No. 712, Morrison to Ts'ai T'ing-kan, 9 July 1914.

[3] A draft of this letter in Morrison's handwriting is among the papers of W. F. and W. W. Willoughby, of which the present Editor was allowed to make a photocopy when he examined the Willoughby Papers at the Willoughby home in Washington. It is identical to the copy in the Morrison Papers, which is reproduced here.

sovereign people of China, have spoken indubitably in favour of a government under the Nanking Constitution, strongly advise that an immediate proclamation be issued by Your Excellency, countersigned by the Premier and Ministers of State, affirming that the Nanking Provisional Constitution is recognised as in full legal force,[1] and that in pursuance thereof a parliament will be convened as soon as possible in order that not only may necessary laws be constitutionally enacted but also steps may be taken for the establishment of a permanent Constitution.

This immediate action we advise in order that peace may be restored and a permanent union be established throughout all China.

Geo. Ernest Morrison
N. Ariga
W. W. Willoughby

830. From Kuo T'ai-ch'i[2]

Office of the President 21 June 1916

Dear Dr Morrison,

I wish to inform you and your colleagues, Drs Ariga and Willoughby, that your joint memorandum to the President regarding the constitutional question was duly shown to His Excellency after having been translated into Chinese. The President was highly gratified at your unanimous decision. A copy of the translation of the document has been sent to the Cabinet. It is expected that a Presidential proclamation on the subject will be issued in the course of a few days.

With my best regards to Drs Ariga and Willoughby and your good self

Sincerely yours
Quo Tai Chi

[1] This is a reference to the Provincial Constitution passed by the Senate in Nanking and announced by Sun Yat-sen, President of the Provisional Government in Nanking, on 11 March 1912. As a result of Yüan Shih-k'ai's acceptance of this Provisional Constitution he was made Provisional President in succession to Sun Yat-sen.

[2] Kuo T'ai-ch'i, otherwise Quo Tai-chi (1889–1952), Chinese diplomat. An American-trained political scientist, he became Secretary to Li Yüan-hung upon his return to China soon after the Wuchang Uprising, the post he was holding at the time of this letter. He left Li's service in July the following year upon Li's dissolution of Parliament and went to Canton where he became a secretary to Sun Yat-sen after the establishment of the Canton Government. Kuo was one of China's more prominent professional diplomats during the period of Nationalist rule in Nanking serving, among other posts, as the first Chinese Ambassador to Britain when the Legation was raised to an Embassy in 1935. He held the post until 1941 when he was made Foreign Minister, and represented China at many international conferences.

831. To Beatrice Brownrigg

[Peking] 10 July 1916

Dear Lady Brownrigg,

Last week I sent you a photograph of my two little boys which I had just received from my wife, who is now having a summer in Japan. I am leaving for Japan myself next Saturday, so write you a few lines before I go.

Things here are not very bright, but actual fighting is only taking place in Canton Province, where forces under various brigands are attacking the greatest brigand in China: Lung Chi-kuang, a Miaotze savage who Yuan Shih-kai placed in the important position of Military Governor of Canton Province. I sincerely hope he will meet his death soon. He has done every conceivable injury to his country. Needless to say, he has greatly enriched himself while holding office, and he has purchased property in Hongkong amounting, at a conservative estimate, to not less than ten million dollars.

Yuan Shih-kai solved the difficulty about his retirement in the best possible way by dying. His mad ambition to become Emperor not only wrecked his own career, but very nearly wrecked his country. I was always opposed to the movement, and the consequences were largely what I anticipated. The new President is beginning well, and the impression that he has given is a good one.

The Japanese attitude towards China seems to have undergone some modification, which is attributed to the European situation. Up to quite recently the Japanese were quite confident that Germany would be victorious in Europe, but now they realise it is only a question of time, and that nothing can stay the success of the Allies. Japan has acted in a very unusual way for an ally, for when China was prepared to join, as I have no doubt told you, Japan prevented her from doing so. Had China joined, the blow to Germany would have been a very serious one, and must have hastened the termination of the war.

With kind regards
Believe me

Very sincerely yours
[G. E. Morrison]

832. From T. A. Rustad

Ninghsiafu,[1] Kansu 16 August 1916

Dear Dr. Morrison,

I have now been travelling in this district since the 8th of June, date on which I arrived here after a lengthy and enforced stay at the catholic mission at Santaoho. The robbers were operating in great numbers in this province

[1] Ning-hsia-fu became the Provincial Capital of Ningsia when the province was created in 1925 but was at this time under the jurisdiction of Kansu Province. Its name later reverted to Yin-ch'uan, as it was known in Sung times (960-1286).

537

then, and in the Ordos, [...] The soldiers of Ma-Fu-Hsiang from Ninghsiafu finally routed the brigands who retired into the mountains called Leang-Shan, where they have since been staying with an occasional outing now and then just to make the inhabitants in that poor district remember that they are still to be reckoned with. Now the Kansu soldiers under General Ma-Fu-Hsiang have a good reputation amongst the chinese who live in these disturbed districts. They do realy try and kill the robbers whenever they get a chance and they are said to have accounted for a great number. Also the brigands do really fear General Ma's troops. [...] General Ma-Fu-Hsiang sent for me when I arrived and asked me all kinds of questions about the different officials in Peking, also if I knew who would realy be the governing man under Li-Yuan-Hung. Of cource I could not tell him. He seemed to think that Li-Yuan-Hung was not much of a man and that somebody else would take all the power. Ma-Fu-Hsiang is well spoken off amongst people here. The only thing I have heard against him is that he is very fond of money. By which I suppose they mean that he squeeces them whenever he gets a chance. There is realy some dicipline amongst his troops, who are mostly mohamedans. The general has also armed other mohamedans in this district, made some sort of volunteer army out of certain well known people who can be trusted with a rifle. Of course the mohamedans stick together. Before Yuan-Shih-Kai's death, Ma-Fu-Hsiang is reported to have said that he would not fight *bona fida* revolutionaries, but he would fight any and all robbers and do his utmost to keep peace in his district. No revolutionaries showed themselves up this way, so he did not have to show his cards, but he has certainly kept his word in holding down the robbers. Also these brigands keep out of his territory and rob only in territory which is under the Kuei-Hua-Cheng General who does not seem to be able to do anything to them. I suppose it is the same old fellow in Kuei-Hua-Cheng,[1] the man who fights immaginary battles and kills more robbers than there ever were. His officers and men gets the decorations or rather got them so I suppose everybody is satisfied. [...]

With kind regards
Yours sincerely

T. A. Rustad

[1] P'an Chü-ying.

833. To W. Conyngham Greene[1]

Chuzenji [Tochigi, Japan] 21 August 1916

Dear Sir Conyngham,

I send you herewith two copies of the note I made of my conversation with Viscount Kato[2] last Wednesday. Written the same evening I believe it correctly represents the substance of our conversation.

On the previous Saturday I saw Mr. Kroupensky.[3]

Regarding the Japanese attitude towards China's joining the Allied Powers he said that on his way home to Russia he had travelled with Mr. Ijuin, formerly Minister to Peking: they had discussed this question, and Mr. Ijuin had said that he was of the opinion that it would have been good policy for Japan to join in the invitation to China. No indication however had been given to Mr. Kroupensky that this represents the view of the Japanese F.O. He thought their views may change. He had spoken to Viscount Kato – I judged without success although he did not say so – and he would speak to him again. Everything he admitted, depended upon Japan. He confessed that he could not understand her policy except on the supposition that she believed Germany would not be defeated.

When speaking to Viscount Kato I was not aware that the railway contract to which I referred as having been signed by the Americans was even more important than I believed.[4] It has been signed since I left Peking. This contract provides for the construction on favourable terms of a railway more than 1100 miles in length from Feng Chen north of Shansi to Ninghsiafu, with an extension to Lanchow, the capital of Kansu. The Engineers are due to arrive in Yokohama today.

Surely American activity in China and the immense extension of the American Pacific fleet necessitated by Japanese policy in China must induce Japan to reconsider her attitude towards the China question.

I was struck by Viscount Kato's hostility to Professor Ariga, the Constitutional Adviser in Peking. I said that I had recommended the appointment, having been advised that he was the most distinguished of Japanese Jurists. He said he *never was that*. Yet Ariga was attached as adviser to

[1] William Conyngham Greene (1854–1934), British diplomat, at this time British Ambassador to Japan (1912–19). He had previously been Minister to Switzerland (1901–5), Rumania (1905–10) and Denmark (1910–12).
[2] Katō Takaaki (or Komei) was forced to resign his post as Foreign Minister in the second Ōkuma Cabinet in August 1915 following criticism of his handling of Japan's Twenty-One Demands. He remained however one of the most powerful political leaders in Japan. He was a supporter of Ōkuma's aggressive policy towards China under Yüan Shih-k'ai.
[3] Basil Kroupensky, who had been Russian Minister to China, became Russian Ambassador to Japan earlier the same year, succeeding Nicylas Malewsky-Malèwitch.
[4] A reference to the Agreement signed on 17 May 1916 by the Chinese Government with Siems & Carey for the construction of five railway lines. A supplementary Agreement was signed on 29 September 1916.

Oyama[1] during the China Japan war and to Nogi[2] during the Russo-Japanese war and capitulation of Port Arthur, and when appointed by Yuan Shih-kai the Japanese Minister insisted that he should be given a salary of £4,000 a year and a five years contract. Viscount Kato even attacked his moral character and suggested that his integrity was doubtful.[3]

With kind regards

Very sincerely yours
[G. E. Morrison]

Enclosure to Letter No. 833: *Notes on a Conversation with Viscount Katō, Tokyo 16 August 1916*

This afternoon at 2.30 by appointment I called upon Viscount Kato at his private residence. He was punctual. He was dressed in Japanese clothes. Three years ago he was in Peking when Ijuin was Minister, and we had discussed affairs in China.

At the beginning he spoke slowly in a low voice, carefully weighing his words, but as time went on he grew interested and animated.

1. I spoke of the change in tone of the Japanese press, so welcome after the acrimony of the attacks made during last year upon Englishmen in China. He said the Japanese papers were largely irresponsible; they were sensational and exaggerated. Home affairs they discussed with equal irresponsibility. Their tendency was to follow American models. He regretted it. Small incidents were magnified.

I said in China English papers were often to blame, but they were angered by the attacks in the Japanese papers and indulged in recrimination. The paper with the highest sense of responsibility was the *North China Daily News*, but this was due to the personality of the editors, and not to any influence exercised by the British authorities, who were always reluctant to interfere with the liberty of the press. In Shanghai there was great bitterness

---

[1] Ōyama Iwao (1842–1916), Japanese soldier. He was Commander of the Japanese Second Army during the first Sino-Japanese War (1894–5), and Commander-in-Chief of the Japanese Army during the Russo-Japanese War (1904–5). Ariga was Legal Adviser to the Japanese Army Headquarters during both of these wars.

[2] Nogi Maresuke (1849–1912), Japanese soldier. As Commander of the Japanese Third Army during the Russo-Japanese War, he had been responsible for the capture of Port Arthur, and had invited Morrison to participate in the ceremony after its occupation. The article which Morrison wrote about the fall of Port Arthur was considered by many to have been responsible for changing European views about Japanese military power. Nogi committed *seppuku* (suicide by disembowelment) following the death of Emperor Meiji, and is revered by the Japanese as a model of loyalty.

[3] Ariga had incurred Katō's strong hostility because as the emissary of Yüan Shih-k'ai to the *Genrō* or Japanese Elder Statesmen following the presentation of Japan's Twenty-One Demands, he was held by Katō to have been responsible for arousing the strong dissatisfaction of the *Genrō* with Katō's handling of this issue, resulting in Katō's replacement as Foreign Minister in August 1915.

at the attacks made by Professor Uyeno[1] in the Japanese Shanghai paper[2] on the question of the English in Tsingtau – the result was the placing of the Japanese candidate for the Municipal Council at the bottom of the poll. Relations improved, and at the next election the British placed the Japanese at the head of the poll.

2. We spoke of Yuan Shih-kai, and, while I admitted that the President had gone mad in his ambition to be Emperor, I defended him against what I thought was the harsh and unjust criticism of the Japanese press. Personally I had seen evidence of his desire to be on terms of friendship with Japan, and I cited in support this case: One day the Japanese Minister sent Midzuno, the Counsellor, to see me to sound me as to whether it would not be possible to induce Yuan Shih-kai to open as Trade Marts[3] or Treaty Ports Lung K'ou, on the Shantung coast opposite Dairen, and five towns including K'uei-hua-ch'eng and Taonanfu, along the borders of Inner Mongolia. I thought the proposal a good one, lay the matter before Yuan Shih-kai, telling him that the opening of these new trade marts would be in the best interests of both countries. He agreed, and in a few days issued the Mandate declaring them open.

He remembered the case, and said personally he regarded Yuan Shih-kai as a statesman of capacity, but his countrymen judged him by Japanese standards, by sentimental standards. Cognate peoples, the Japanese regarded the Chinese as possessed of a similar civilisation to their own, and believed they had, or ought to have, similar reverence for the throne and the person of the sovereign. Yuan Shih-kai betrayed his Emperor in 1898:[4] he also

[1] Ueno Iwatarō (1867–1925), Japanese journalist and newspaper publisher. He had been Correspondent of the Tokyo *Asahi Shimbun* in Vladivostok and was later a Correspondent in Manchuria covering the Russo-Japanese War. He was the publisher of the *Shin Kōron* (*New Public Opinion*) and was the founder of the Nisshi Kyōdō Tsūshin (Sino-Japanese News Agency), and Managing Director of the *Shun-tien shih-pao*.
[2] Possibly the *Shanghai Mercury*, at this time Japanese-owned, and under the editorship of Sahara Tokusuke.   [3] *See* p. 258 n. 1.,
[4] Yüan Shih-k'ai, at that time in charge of the New Army stationed in Hsiao-chan near Tientsin, and regarded by the reformers as their sympathiser and supporter, was summoned on 16 September 1898 and again the following day, to an audience with the Emperor Kuang-hsü during which Yüan reaffirmed his support for the reform movement. The audience was followed by a visit to him on the night of 17 September by T'an Ssu-t'ung (1865–98), one of the reformers who had been appointed by Kuang-hsü as a secretary in the Grand Council, to carry out reform measures. During the course of his visit T'an revealed to Yüan the reformers' plan and handed him the Emperor's authority to carry it out. According to this, Yüan was to go to Tientsin and put to death Jung-lu (1836–1903), the Viceroy of Chihli, chief supporter of the Empress-Dowager Tz'u-hsi, and then return to Peking with his troops to eliminate the Empress-Dowager and the conservative clique supporting her. Yüan, who feigned obedience to the Imperial order, revealed the whole plan to Jung-lu as soon as he returned to Tientsin on 20 September. Jung-lu then hurried to Peking to warn the Empress-Dowager who in a *coup d'état* the following day made the Emperor a prisoner in his own palace where he was to remain until his death ten years later, in November 1908. Six reformers were put to death and

betrayed the reformers, and his action drove Kang Yu-wei[1] and Liang Ch'i-ch'ao and others into exile. Again at the time of the Revolution in 1911 he had come back to power trusted by the Imperial Family to save them; he had the means to suppress the Revolution had he wished, but he had done otherwise. He had counselled abdication. The advice may have been good, and his action may have been justifiable had he stood aside and resigned when the abdication was accomplished. But what did he do? Acting against all Japanese ideas of honour and loyalty he had caused himself to be created ruler instead of the Emperor whose abdication he had counselled, and later had aspired to be Emperor.

He went on in these words: – 'European and American residents in China – with few exceptions – come to China to make money. That is their main endeavour. Their moral standards they leave at home. No ruler who acted as Yuan Shih-kai had done would be tolerated in Europe or America; in Japan his life would be taken. Yet Americans and Europeans were uninfluenced by his record. He was a Chinese, they contended, and could not be judged by their standards. But the Japanese did not so regard him. They considered him treacherous and disloyal – faithless to his pledges. They insisted upon judging him by their standard as Japanese. They attacked him fiercely in the press. Naturally (and I would have felt the same) Yuan Shih-kai resented these attacks, and everything he could refuse the Japanese he did refuse.'

---

many others cashiered and exiled, while the two leaders K'ang Yu-wei and Liang Ch'i-ch'ao, assisted by British and Japanese diplomats, managed to escape. Morrison was the medium through which Yüan Shih-k'ai, soon after the outbreak of the Revolution, in an attempt to absolve himself from the accusation of betrayal, made known to the outside world his version of the event. Morrison's article entitled 'Yuan Shih-k'ai on the Crisis. A Limited Monarchy or a Republic. The Danger of Disruption' was published in *The Times* on 21 November 1911. A Diary purported to have been kept by Yüan at the time, but obviously put together at a later date, and discussed in *Ku hung mei k'o pi-chi* (notes of the studio of the ancient red plum) by Chang I-lin, Yüan's Secretary, who had probably helped to compose or doctor it, was reprinted under the title *Wu-hsü jih-chi* (the diary of 1898) in a collection of sources on Modern Chinese history edited by Tso Shun-sheng and published in Shanghai in 1938. The Japanese, like everyone else, were convinced of Yüan Shih-k'ai's guilt even before Hayashi Gonsuke, who was Japanese Chargé d'Affaires in Peking at the time and who helped in the escape of Liang Ch'i-ch'ao to Japan, published his version in his memoirs *Waga shichijū nen wo kataru* (an account of my seventy years) (Tokyo 1935). This belief was exploited by Japanese adventurers both in their support of Sun Yat-sen and also in their conspiracy with the monarchists.

[1] K'ang Yu-wei (1858–1927), Chinese scholar and leader of the 1898 Reform Movement. He fled the country with the help of the British Government after the *coup d'état* of 21 September 1898, and did not return to China until 1913. A committed constitutional monarchist, he became thereafter an opponent of the Republic. In less than a year after this interview took place he emerged as a principal conspirator in the Imperial Restoration of 1 July 1917 engineered by Chang Hsün. Of his many works, *Ta t'ung shu*, written largely during his long exile abroad and published posthumously (English translation by L. G. Thompson, London 1958) is one of the best known.

'Several times I spoke to the Editors, especially to the Editors of the *Osaka Mainichi* and the *Nichi Nichi*, and pointed out the effect of their policy, but they could not be induced to see the case from the view point of the practical statesman.'

'But,' I said, 'Yuan Shih-kai is dead and buried, and with him is buried this animosity.'

Then we spoke of the present situation.

3. I spoke of American activity in China, of the vast claims Americans were pegging out for their posterity, of the Railway Concessions they were obtaining – the railway from Feng Chen north of Shansi to Ninghsia in Kansu for example; of the Road Concession signed on June 14th; of the contracts for the dredging of the Grand Canal from the town of Techow in Shantung to the Yangtse River; the loans provided for the work being secured on the tolls of the canal and the revenues to be derived from the land reclaimed: of the vast Huai River Basin reclamation scheme to be financed by the American Red Cross Society and to cost millions of pounds sterling, the security being the taxes leviable on the 17,000 square miles of territory to be reclaimed, etc., etc., etc.[1]

I spoke of other American enterprises, of American industrial activity in China, the coming of the American contractors due here on the 21st, led by F. W. Carey,[2] and of the eagerness of the Americans to lend money to China in return for industrial advantages, and I submitted that this formidable trade activity could not be to the advantage of Japan. I spoke of the favour shown to Americans, who were regarded by the Chinese as the most friendly of the Powers, and of the profit they were obtaining by the exploitation of this friendliness. For example I cited the case of the manufacture of China's Banknotes by the American Banknote Company, who had secured an order – completed last June – for the manufacture of Banknotes of the face value of $869,000,000 at a cost of £257,000.

4. I now asked the Viscount's permission to speak of the question in China which seemed to me of the highest importance and to tell him how it appeared to an English observer who had seen a good deal during the last three years, and who could not understand the attitude of the Japanese

---

[1] During the course of April and May 1916, the United States concluded no less than four Agreements with China for extensive industrial concessions. These were the Lee, Higginson & Company Loan of 7 April, the Agreement for the South Grand Canal of Shantung Province 7% Improvement Gold Loan of 19 April, the Agreement for the Huai River Conservancy Grand Canal Improvement 7% Gold Loan of 13 May, and the Agreement for Railway Construction of 17 May, the last relating to concessions for railways in the six provinces of Hunan, Kwangsi, Shansi, Kansu, Kwangtung and Chekiang, amounting to 1,500 miles in all.

[2] William Francis Carey (1878–1951), American engineering contractor, President of the construction firm of Siems & Carey Railway & Canal Company, and Vice-President of the China Corporation, a firm having extensive railway concessions in China. It was Carey who signed on behalf of his firm the Agreement mentioned in the preceding note.

Government. I referred to China's joining the Alliance, and to Japan's objection to her doing so. With deference I would like to point out what seemed to me to be the advantages that Japan can derive from a reconsideration of this question. He was glad to hear me.

5. I began by speaking of German activity in China, of the abundance of money with which German agents in China are furnished, of the press campaign they are maintaining, the distribution of *The War* published in Shanghai among prominent Chinese throughout China and among all neutral missionaries scattered throughout the country, of the activity of their agents travelling everywhere throughout the interior, and of the preparations they are making for the resumption and expansion of commercial enterprise after the war. Every day China paid Germany £6,000 sterling on account of the Boxer Indemnity, various Railway Loans and the Quintuple Loan, and a large proportion of this money was being devoted to the campaign of sedition and of preparedness. The Counsellor of the German Legation in Peking boasted that the German authorities in China had never before been so well provided with funds.

Only temporarily had we checked German trade in China: we ought to crush out for ever German power of competition on terms of equality. Looked at from the Japanese standpoint it seemed certain that Japan must derive material advantages from the course of action proposed – namely the admission of China into the Alliance and the termination of China's relations with Germany and all its consequences. Her opposition to this policy was difficult to understand.

Briefly I recounted the circumstances as I knew them – the offer to China to join in the operations on Tsingtau, the advice of the British Minister that abstention would be preferable, the refusal of Yuan Shih-kai to make a second offer but his willingness to accept an invitation to do so if presented by Japan and the Allied Powers. I stated that the terms the President required were:

(a) Resumption by China of the German Concessions at Tientsin and Hankow, and of the Austrian concession at Tientsin.
(b) Settlement of the Extradition question at Shanghai (A question which has since been settled.)
(c) Guarantee by the Allied Powers against future reprisals on the part of Germany.
(d) Representation at the Peace Conference if one were ever held. This condition was implied rather than specified. China as one of the belligerents would naturally expect a seat at the Conference.

I said that Japanese had told me that this last named concession placing China as it appeared to do, on an equality with the Allies could not be assented to by Japan. But such Conference would never be called upon to reconsider questions between China and Japan already settled before the Conference: what then could be the disadvantage to Japan?

Yet Japan refused her assent although the advantages obtainable seemed many and obvious.

7.[1] I cited some of the advantages. China in the first place, by terminating diplomatic relations with Germany, would confiscate Germany's share of the Boxer Indemnity, which amounts to £13,500,000 plus the Austrian share of £600,000 being 141 millions of dollars of fixed value of 10 – £1.

With this sum as security China could if need be raise even £10,000,000 from the Allied Powers whose hold over China's finances would be increased by that amount. None but the Allied Powers could lend money on this security. America, a neutral country, could not do so without displaying unfriendliness to Germany. It seemed better that Japan should take a leading part in this transaction which did not add to China's financial burden for the security is the Customs revenue which is entirely under foreign control – than that America should increase China's financial indebtedness by lending money to Peking upon security, the development of which would bring the United States into more acute competition with Japan.

8. In the Maritime Customs by the removal of Germans 118 vacancies would be created. Who would fill them? Mainly Chinese and Japanese. Since the War began there had been 58 vacancies in the Customs, of which 15 had been filled with Japanese and 43 with Chinese.

9. In the Salt Gabelle, the second highest post is filled by a German.[2] Japan would have an undisputed claim to fill this vacancy.

10. China having denounced her treaties with Germany, new treaties would be negotiated after the War. From these the clause providing for Most Favoured Nation treatment would be excluded. Germany would be excluded from participation on equal terms in China trade. Surely it would be to the advantage of Japan – this elimination or handicapping of a very formidable European competitor.

11. A deadly economic blow would be dealt to Germany. All Germany would be stricken with alarm on learning that this field, upon the future exploitations of whose resources she based so great hopes, this great field of China had been closed to her.

12. Then there was the Mahommedan question – a question of great importance to England and Russia. China is a Mahommedan power of consider-

[1] Morrison has obviously numbered his points incorrectly.
[2] E. A. W. von Strauch, German soldier, formerly of the German Imperial Guard. He had been a military instructor to the New Army under the Viceroy Chang Chih-tung in Wuchang before he entered the service of the Imperial Chinese Maritime Customs in 1899. A Chinese-speaker, he did important work for the Central Government at the time of the Revolution, when he was Commissioner of Customs in Chungking. Following the Reorganisation Loan of 1913 von Strauch was transferred to the Salt Administration and became Deputy Inspector-General. Morrison knew von Strauch well and praised him highly for his part in the defence of the foreign legations during the Siege of Peking in 1900.

able importance. There are Mahommedans in every province of China. In Chinese Turkestan the population is mainly Mahommedan. In all there are from 15 to 20,000,000 Moslems in China. For years the Sultan of Turkey has been interested in these Moslems, and has frequently sent holy Teachers from Constantinople to visit the Mosques and preach to the faithful. Since 1908 these Turkish preachers and other Turkish subjects are provided with German passports, Turkey having no treaty with China. In nearly every considerable Moslem community in China some Chinese headman has made the pilgrimage to Mecca via Constantinople.

The campaign of calumny carried on by Germans in China largely was directed towards influencing the Mahommedans of China against Great Britain. For the trade relations between the Mahommedans of China and their co-religionists in India are quite intimate. Virtually the whole frontier trade of India with Chinese Turkestan is monopolised by Mahommedans as is the trade with Russian Turkestan, Persia and Afghanistan. The fact that China, a Mahommedan Power which is still regarded in Central Asia as a mighty power, had joined the Allies would have a marked effect upon Mahommedan feeling in India, in Persia and in Mesopotamia. And surely China's defiance of Turkey would cause far-reaching dismay throughout the Ottoman Empire.

13. To the foregoing statement Viscount Kato listened intently, asking me now and then to repeat figures or give explanations, and then he said:

Last year he was not in office when the three Ambassadors[1] brought up the question of China's renouncing neutrality, and he could not speak now with intimate knowledge. He only knew what he had 'overheard' but he believed the case had not been presented in the way I had just presented it. As he had understood, a proposal had been made that China should join the Alliance. But the distrust of Yuan Shih-kai was deep-seated. His (Kato's) countrymen had seen in this proposal a subterfuge on the part of the President for obtaining recognition of himself as Emperor from the Government of Japan which had taken the leading part in trying to restrain him from his mad desire to occupy the throne.

And then the Military ridiculed the offer of China to reconstruct her arsenals and supply arms to the Allies. What arms, they asked, could China supply?

14. 'But,' continued Viscount Kato, as if commenting on what he had just said, 'the case now appears in a different light. Circumstances have changed, and the question might be approached anew.'

15. I explained that while China had undoubtedly made a foolish proposal regarding a loan for Arsenals, the advantages to Russia should China renounce neutrality were that Dairen, Tientsin, and other ports would be opened to the allied transports shipping arms and munitions to Russia, the congestion at Vladivostok would be relieved, and in the case of Dairen the

---

[1] A reference to the Ambassadors of England, France and Russia.

Japanese South Manchuria Railway would be benefitted. Also the camel caravan trade route across the desert of Gobi from Kalgan to Urga and Kiakhta and the Siberian Railway would be opened for the transport of arms and munitions delivered at ports now closed to such traffic. Thousands of camels were available, the cost of transport to the Russian Railway being estimated at £12 per ton. Congestion on the Siberian Railway would thus be relieved.

16. Viscount Kato repeated that the case had not been stated in this detail.

17. I continued: If now the case were reopened, Japan would have to take the lead and herself induce China to join the Alliance and terminate relations with Germany. Surely it is to Japan's advantage to do so. The reply given by Baron Ishii to the Ambassadors was conclusive,[1] but circumstances have changed, and surely Japan can now lead China to take this important step.

18. Viscount Kato said: 'You have set forth the case in a new and interesting light. You will have no objections to my bringing your views before the Ministers? With the death of Yuan Shih-kai circumstances have changed. Besides there is another point. At the time of which you speak (last November) there was in the minds of many of my countrymen considerable uncertainty as to the future of the war. We had to be careful not to raise up dangerous antagonism for the future. The uncertainty is now less.' And he repeated his words about giving the matter reconsideration.

19. We spoke then of other things. I ventured to say that the selection of Baron Hayashi[2] to proceed to Peking was an excellent choice. He will surely

[1] On 23 November 1915 Ishii Kikujirō (1866–1945), at the time Japan's Foreign Minister (October 1915 – October 1916), at a conference with the Ambassadors of England, France and Russia, refused to support an invitation to China to enter the war on the side of the Allies. He had served as First Secretary in the Japanese Legation at the time of the Boxer Uprising. Appointed Vice Foreign Minister in 1909, he became in 1912 Ambassador to France, holding the post until his recall in October 1915 to take up the Foreign Affairs portfolio. It was he who, as Japanese Ambassador Extraordinary and Plenipotentiary on Special Mission, in November 1917 signed the Agreement with Robert Lansing (q.v.), American Secretary of State, regarding extra-territorial rights in China.

[2] Hayashi Gonsuke (1860–1939), Japanese diplomat. He had served at various posts in China, including Peking where he was First Secretary and Chargé d'Affaires at the time of the Coup d'Etat in 1898, before being appointed Japanese Minister to Korea the following year. There he was responsible for the negotiation of the Treaty of 17 November 1905 which led eventually to Japan's annexation of Korea five years later. He returned to Peking as Japanese Minister in 1906, holding the post until his appointment two years later as Ambassador to Italy. He was sent back to Peking once more, in July 1916, when Terauchi Masatake succeeded Ōkuma Shigenobu as Prime Minister, and Hayashi was chosen to implement the new Japanese policy of economic penetration of China. In this mission he was handicapped rather than helped by Nishihara Kamezō (q.v.), Terauchi's personal agent, and he resigned his post in October 1918 after the fall of the Terauchi cabinet. He was then appointed Governor-General of the Japanese-occupied territory of Kwantung Peninsular in Manchuria, in April 1919, and became Japanese Ambassador to Great Britain the following year (1920–5). After the overthrow of the Chang Tso-lin controlled Peking Government by the Nationalists, Hayashi was selected by Prime

be made Ambassador? Viscount Kato laughed; 'You would have us Dean of the Diplomatic Body as well as the guide of China.' I said assuredly that was Japan's role. Everyone expected the Minister would be made Ambassador. He said that would depend upon what the other Powers did. I said in 1914 Yuan Shih-kai wished it, and I added that I believed America will raise her Legation to an Embassy.

20. We spoke of other matters, for example of Professor Ariga, whose appointment Viscount Kato thought regrettable and whose retirement he would welcome: of the *Tarif Minimum* in Indo-China and of many other things of insufficient interest to be recorded.

I left at 4 p.m.

834. To J. W. R. Macleay[1]

[Peking] 13 September 1916

My dear Macleay,

I enclose you herewith a copy of the memorandum I made of an interview given to me on the 16th of August in Tokyo by Viscount Kato.[2]

It seems to be generally agreed that Kato is the most powerful man in Japan. At any rate, he has the most influence over Japan's foreign policy. He is not in office as you know, but the Minister of Foreign Affairs is his nominee,[3] the Vice-Minister is his brother-in-law,[4] and two of the chief permanent

---

Minister Tanaka Giichi as Special Representative to Chang Hsüeh-liang (b. 1898) who had taken over, after the assassination by Japanese of his father Chang Tso-lin, as overlord of Manchuria, in an attempt to prevent Chang accepting the authority of the Central Government in Nanking. As Japan's trouble-shooter diplomat in China, Hayashi was able to record many interesting anecdotes in his memoirs *Waga shichijū nen wo kataru* (*op. cit.*) including those concerning the *coup d'état* of 1898 and his rescue of the Reform leader Liang Ch'i-ch'ao, and Chang Hsün's *coup* in 1917, on which occasion he gave asylum to President Li Yüan-hung in his Legation. The book however reveals little of the inside story of Japanese policy with which he was associated for more than a quarter of a century, being published, as it was, on the eve of full-scale Japanese aggression against China.

[1] At this time British Chargé d'Affaires in Peking in the absence of Sir John Jordan on home leave.
[2] The memorandum was the same as that enclosed in the previous letter.
[3] Ishii Kikujirō. He held the post until the fall of the second Ōkuma cabinet in October 1916.
[4] The Vice-Minister at this time was Shidehara Kijurō (1872-1951). In 1903 he married Iwasaki Masako, the daughter of Iwasaki Yataro (q.v.), founder of the Mitsubishi Combine, thus becoming the brother-in-law of Katō, who had married Masako's elder sister, Haruji, in 1886. First entering the foreign service in 1896, Shidehara began his diplomatic career under Ishii Kikujirō in Korea and, having served in various foreign posts, returned to become Vice-Foreign Minister when Ishii became Foreign Minister. He retained this post under Terauchi Masatake, Motono Ichirō, Gotō Shimpei (q.v.) and Uchida Yasuya, until his appointment as Japanese Ambassador to the United States in

officials are his son-in-law[1] and his private secretary. I have known him for several years and thought it better to speak to him than to any other high official. Before seeing him I saw the British Ambassador who quite approved of my having a talk with him. I may say that I did not see Marquis Okuma[2] although I could have done so for I had also met him several times during recent years, but he is so garrulous and so indiscreet that I thought it wiser to make an excuse for not meeting him.

You are leaving for home so shortly that I have only time to jot down a few suggestions or rather reminders that occur to me in connection with Japan.

I. As regards Germany, the Japanese attitude is one of neutrality. The Germans in Japan carry on their business as usual. German business houses are still active. German banks are still open. There is no restriction – or rather only a very modified restriction upon the movements of Germans throughout Japan. Two explanations are given of this attitude. The military party in Japan, indoctrinated with German militarism, have never up to quite recently admitted the possibility of Germany's defeat in this war. British merchants will tell you that the benevolent treatment of Germans is due to the fear of further revelations regarding the navy scandals in which Germans and the great firm of Mitsui have been implicated. Still another explanation is given – which seems to be widely credited – that a bargain has been struck between the Germans and the Japanese which permits freedom of German action in Japan in return for immunity of Japanese shipping from German submarines. Up to the present only one Japanese steamer of any importance has been sunk by a German submarine.

II. There is widespread antagonism to the English Alliance. Even Tokutomi,[3] the most powerful publicist in Japan, editor of the *Kokumin*

1919, in which capacity he took part in the Washington Conference. In June 1924 he was made Foreign Minister when his brother-in-law, Katō Takaaki, formed his cabinet. He held the same post in the first and second cabinets of Wakatsuki Reijirō (1866–1949) (January 1926 – April 1927 and April–December 1931) and the cabinet of Hamaguchi Osachi (1870–1931) (July 1929 – April 1931). In 1932 Shidehara, who was regarded as having a conciliatory attitude towards China, withdrew from active politics after Japan invaded Manchuria, and did not emerge until after Japan's defeat in 1945, when he became Japan's first post-War Prime Minister (October 1945 – April 1946).

[1] A reference to Okabe Nagakage (b. 1884), at the time a temporary clerk in the Foreign Ministry. He was the son of Okabe Nagamoto (1854–1925), the last feudal lord of the Kishiwada clan who after the Restoration became the first Governor of his erstwhile domain. Nagakage in 1912 married Yoshiko, the only daughter of Katō Takaaki, who had been a colleague of the elder Okabe in the Foreign Ministry. After holding various posts, Okabe Nagakage became Minister of Education (April 1943 – July 1944) in the Wartime cabinet of Tōjō Hideki (1884–1948).

[2] At this time Prime Minister. He was replaced by Terauchi Masatake some three weeks after this letter was written.

[3] Tokutomi Ichirō, better known by his pen-name, Tokutomi Sōhō (1863–1937), Japanese publicist. As founder in 1890 of the *Kokumin Shimbun* and its Chief Editor, he was an advocate of extreme nationalism and an aggressive foreign policy for Japan. After he sold

Shimbun, a trusty supporter of the late Prince Katsura who was a foremost advocate of the Anglo-Japanese Alliance, now describes the Alliance as one of the horse and the rider, Japan being the horse. This statement he published actually while I was in Japan. You may have seen the reference. It is an error to attribute hostility solely to irresponsible journalists. The hostility is much deeper.

III. The Japanese military are re-adjusting their opinions regarding the ultimate success of Germany. The Minister of War[1] told Krupenski on or about the 5th August that Germany's decline had set in, having been precipitated by the irretrievable blunder of the attack upon Verdun.[2]

IV. The Japanese have no intention of restoring the Marshall Islands[3] to Australia, although the Australians are nursing a belief that Japan undertook to do so. The islands have already been placed under Japanese civil administration, a civil governor has been appointed, and Japanese administrative machinery introduced. Parties of the islanders, including King John, are brought to Japan and shown the majesty of the Japanese Empire. On the day I was in Yokohama a party of 21 arrived. I have photographs of the group. The islands are referred to also as 'our South Sea Island possessions'. The harbour of Jaluit is being fortified, and a powerful naval base will there be created. What will be the effect on Australia?

V. The Japanese boast, and are continually boasting – and in support of their boasting they quote the subservient English press, as to what they have

---

the *Kokumin Shimbun* he became a contributor to the Osaka *Mainichi Shimbun* and the Tokyo *Nichinichi Shimbun*, continuing his nationalist propaganda, and strongly supported the Japanese military adventure in China. He was the author of a history of modern Japan which has been considered a great work by many Japanese. He was the elder brother of Tokutomi Kenjirō (1868–1927), the well-known Japanese writer of liberal views, from whom he was estranged for many years.

[1] Ōshima Ken'ichi (1858–1947), Japanese soldier. He had studied in Germany and France and fought in the first Sino-Japanese War (1894–5) and the Russo-Japanese War (1904–5). He was Deputy Chief of General Staff of the Japanese Army, when he was appointed Minister of War in the second Ōkuma Cabinet, in March 1916 and continued to hold the post in the succeeding Terauchi Cabinet, until September 1918. He then became Commander-in-Chief of the Japanese forces in Tsingtao and was later made a member of the House of Peers.

[2] The Battle of Verdun, which lasted from February to the end of June 1916, was considered by many to be the most unnecessary as it was the most costly battle in the European War, fought on political rather than military grounds. It resulted in the removal of both General Joffre and General Erich Georg Anton Sebastian von Falkenhayn (1861–1922) from their posts of Commanders-in-Chief of the opposing French and German forces. Henri Philippe Omer Pétain (1856–1951) was made a hero by the French for losing some 310,000 men in holding the line; the loss by Germany of some 280,000 men helped to turn the tide of the fortunes of the war against herself.

[3] Japan, who had taken over the former German colony of the Marshall Islands, succeeded in obtaining an undertaking by the French and British Governments in 1917 to recognise her claim to the former German possessions north of the Equator, including the Marshall Islands.

accomplished during the present war for the Alliance. Apparently they claim that they have shown the highest qualities of *bushido*. If *bushido* means that they have refrained from attacking their friends and allies their claim is justified. By the help of the Alliance their financial equilibrium has been restored. From the verge of bankruptcy they have been saved and are now in a position of affluence, thanks to the supply of arms to the Allies at a vast profit to themselves. It is preposterous to speak of the services rendered by their navy. Did their navy save Craddock's fleet?[1] Did their navy assist in the battle of the Falkland Islands?[2] Have they no commerce of their own to protect? One would think when one reads of the wonderful services they have rendered in policing Far Eastern seas that they are doing this solely in the interests of British commerce. Did they check the depredations of the *Emden*?[3] Or was a bargain struck that the activities of this raider would not be interfered with so long as they did not molest the Japanese flag? Whatever their boast the fact remains that the Japanese have not exchanged a single shot with any enemy ship.

VI. Regarding Japan's attitude towards the admission of China into the Alliance, was it a friendly act or a service rendered to the Allies to prevent at a critical time in the history of the war material help being given to the Allies? Will it ever be forgotten that when China was willing to give assistance to Great Britain Japan forbade such assistance being given?

VII. In the operations at Tsingtau, a fort of very inferior strength defended by 6,000 Germans hastily gathered together and containing a large percentage of clerks, pot-bellied cooks and such like was after a short siege reduced by a gigantic Japanese force whose casualties were quite insignificant. Ever since this incident the Japanese Government have sedulously exaggerated the importance of the military operations which brought about the downfall of this weakly defended 'fortress'. They have in recognition of

[1] Admiral Sir Christopher George Francis Maurice Cradock (1862-1914), British sailor, who had been naval commander of the Allied forces at the taking of Taku from the Chinese in 1900. He was appointed Commander of the British Fleet of the North America and West Indies Station in 1913, and on the outbreak of the European War the following year was given the task of keeping the Atlantic free for British trade, but his fleet was overwhelmed in an engagement with a German squadron under Admiral Maximilian von Spee (1861-1914) off Coronel and Cradock went down with his flagship on 16 October 1914.

[2] Having won his victory over Admiral Cradock, the squadron under Admiral von Spee proceeded to the Falkland Islands with the aim of destroying the British wireless station there, but instead encountered the British battle cruisers sent by Churchill and Fisher after the Cradock disaster. In the ensuing encounter which took place on 8 December 1914 all except one of the five German ships were sunk, together with their commander Admiral von Spee.

[3] A light German cruiser which achieved a spectacularly successful record in naval history by sinking and capturing, during a six-week period from 10 September 1914, twenty-one enemy vessels in the Indian Ocean. She bombarded Madras and raided warships in Penang Harbour, before being driven aground on the Cocos reefs by the Australian cruiser *Sydney* on 9 November 1914.

their services thus rendered created two baronies, Kamio[1] and Oka.[2] They have given 145,000 medals to the soldiers who took part. They have promoted many hundreds of officers. They have decorated 380 nurses. They have given high decorations and gifts of money to every foreign minister in the service of Japan who could be described as even remotely connected with the operations. Every cabinet minister has received high honour and gifts of gold ornaments. Every Member of Parliament similarly to a lesser degree. So extravagant has been the awarding of honours that for the first time in Japan's history three Members of Parliament have declined to receive the imperial gifts on the ground that they had done nothing to deserve such honour. What is the object of doing all this? Is it not to impress the people with the mighty services rendered by Japan to the subjugation of mighty Germany?

VIII. You will notice that when I was speaking to Kato I referred to American activity in China and to its success largely due to America's policy of friendliness to China. Such a reference appealed a little to the Japanese because in Korea a similar display of friendliness on the part of America to the Koreans obtained for Americans concessions which the Japanese Government regarded with covetous eyes, valuable gold mines, copper mines, electric tramways, water works, to mention a few. Some of these they have succeeded in buying back for large sums, but the gold mines, which are immensely productive, are still in American possession. The fact, too, that America, wholly distrustful of Japan's policy in China, is now spending 315,000,000 dollars gold upon an increase to her navy, which increase will call for a corresponding increase in expenditure on the part of the Japanese Government if the balance is to be preserved, has made many Japanese realise that their policy of adventure has led them into danger.

IX. You will have seen in the papers that General Aoki, who was for many years military attache in Peking,[3] has been appointed adviser to the Chinese army. The step is a very serious one, one that must cause us English considerable misgiving. He will have great influence, and we will have no counter-acting influence. To some degree the fault lies with our Foreign

---

[1] Kamio Masutomi (1855–1927), Japanese soldier. As an Intelligence Officer for some fifteen years (1882–97) stationed mostly in Tientsin, he greatly helped the Japanese General Staff in its planning during the first Sino-Japanese War, in which he also took part, serving under General Ōyama Iwao. He distinguished himself in the Russo-Japanese War and played a prominent role in the taking of Port Arthur. In 1914 he led the Japanese forces in the taking of Tsingtao and became its Military Commander, a post he held until May the following year, when he was made Garrison Commander in Tokyo. In 1916 he was promoted to a full General and made a Baron.

[2] Oka Ichinosuke (1860–1916), Japanese soldier. He had taken part in the first Sino-Japanese and the Russo-Japanese Wars, as well as serving with the Japanese Expeditionary Forces during the Boxer Uprising. As War Minister (April 1914 – March 1916) in the Second Ōkuma Cabinet he was directly responsible for the Japanese seizure of the German Leased-Territory of Kiaochow in Shantung Province, for which he was made a Baron.

[3] Aoki Nobuzumi was to hold this position until shortly before his death in 1923.

Office. Some three years ago when Colonel Bruce[1] was leaving the Shanghai police I suggested to Yuan Shih Kai that he would be able to render useful service to the Chinese Government in the organisation of the gendarmerie. He was a man of high character, of excellent ability, and had had many years' experience in China. At Yuan Shih Kai's request I asked Bruce on what conditions he would enter Chinese service. These conditions were accepted, and, as you know, he was appointed as adviser in the Police. This was a voluntary appointment on the part of the Chinese. For some reason that I have never been able to understand the Foreign Office took exception to the appointment. As Alston said to me it was 'a hole and corner appointment and the British Government would not stand it'. The result was that difficulties were placed in the way of giving Bruce leave to accept the appointment. Everything was done to make the Chinese lose face in the matter, and only after a month or more spent in negotiations was the appointment sanctioned after it had been hedged round with various restrictions. The result was inevitable. Bruce was never given any work to do of any kind whatever. Nor was he even consulted. Some time later on the suggestion of Colonel Robertson[2] that it was important that there should be an Englishman in the Chinese army in some capacity I spoke to Yuan Shih Kai on the subject, but the President brushed the suggestion aside with the words 'What! and be treated in the same way as we were treated in the case of Bruce!'

X. In my memorandum of the talk with Viscount Kato I did not note, because I was giving a copy to Sir Conyngham Greene, that Kato said that none of the three ambassadors seemed to know much about the case. He said it a little stronger than this, adding that the Russian Ambassador seemed to know a 'little more than the British'.

Excuse the foregoing somewhat discursive observations. I am convinced that China ought to join the Alliance, and that her adherence would be the most serious economic blow that could be dealt to Germany. I am convinced that she would join the Alliance if the matter were properly handled, and I am convinced that Japan can be persuaded to join in bringing China into the Alliance. It is absurd for us to be boasting of what we have done to check German activities in China. We have caused the Germans a temporary loss of trade in China, but we have done nothing to prevent the prosecution of this trade with immensely increased vigour after the war.

[1] Clarence Dalrymple Bruce, whose appointment by the Chinese Government as Police Adviser was objected to by the British Legation on the grounds that Bruce, having been Commissioner of Police in the International Settlement in Shanghai, should have had his appointment negotiated through the British Legation. The real reason was that the British Government feared that Bruce's intimate knowledge of the inside working of Shanghai's International Settlement might be detrimental to British interests there. One of the conditions insisted on by the British authorities, when he was eventually appointed, was that he should not operate in or near Shanghai.

[2] David Stephen Robertson, British soldier, Military Attaché with the British Legation in Peking (1913-19).

I wish you a pleasant journey home. I will always recall with pleasure our intercourse in Peking. Your future success I look forward to with confidence. You see you belong to the very best Australian stock,[1] and every Australian will be proud to know that the man whose forbears rendered such inestimable service to Australia has reached the highest rank in the diplomatic service.

All good wishes to you

Very sincerely yours
[G. E. Morrison]

P.S. Baron Hayashi told me today that he was always in favour of China's joining the alliance, that he had telegraphed to Kato when the latter was still Foreign Minister urging him to bring China into the alliance. He said Baron Motono[2] was of the same opinion. 'Now this is your time to act' I suggested. Hayashi told me this 'confidentially'. He said Kato had sent him a report of my conversation of August 16th.

835. To J. W. Robertson Scott[3]

[Peking] 15 September 1916

Dear Robertson Scott,

[...]

I came back to Peking on Saturday, having stayed some days in Korea and run across to the Kongo San – really a delightful trip.

You will be deeply interested to know what is being done in Korea. Japanese colonisation in regard to the settling of men on the land may have been a failure, but there is no question as to the admirable efficiency of the Japanese administration and of the many reforms introduced in an incredibly short time into that benighted land.

After all these years there are still only 300,000 Japanese resident in Korea. It was hoped that Korea would be able to absorb a surplus population of 682,000 *per annum* from Japan. The Koreans under Japanese government are developing and multiplying, and absorbed into the Japanese people they will

---

[1] Macleay was descended from two well-known Australian families, having among his ancestors John Macarthur (1767–1834), an army officer who arrived in New South Wales in 1790 and became the colony's foremost farmer, being responsible for the introduction of merino sheep, so vital to the wool industry. His high-handed methods and truculence towards several of the early Governors, especially Philip Gidley King (1758–1808) and William Bligh (1754–1817), dominated the early pages of the colony's history. On the other side, Macleay was descended from Alexander Mcleay (1767–1848), a Scottish entomologist who was Colonial Secretary for New South Wales (1825–37).

[2] Motono Ichirō was Japanese Ambassador to Russia (1906–16) at the time of his appointment as Foreign Minister in the Terauchi Cabinet less than two months after this letter was written.

[3] British journalist, founder and Editor of the *New East*, an English-language journal published in Japan.

be, I think, a very healthy infusion of new blood. They have many fine qualities. Physically they are a fine race, capable of great muscular exertion. They are born linguists, and I believe are capable of a very high degree of intellectual development. You must go there and see for yourself. You would thoroughly enjoy the trip.

[...]

Very sincerely yours
[G. E. Morrison]

836. To H. A. Gwynne

[Peking] 15 September 1916

Private

My dear Gwynne,

My wife and I will not hear of you sending anything to our boy.[1] We have everything we require and while the war is on you must not send away clothing to China.

I have just returned from Japan where I have discussed with prominent Japanese the question of China's joining the Alliance. The Japanese Minister here[2] professes to be a supporter of this view, Japan herself is acting in regard to Germany as a neutral power, and not as an enemy Power. Germans have every freedom to trade in Japan. German business houses are undisturbed. And German banks are open. The fact is, I believe, that the intimate relations, not always of the most honourable kind, subsisting for many years between the Mitsui Company, who are all powerful in Japan, and the Germans cannot easily be terminated without revelations, at any rate without loss to the former.

China ought to join the Alliance. China ought to terminate her treaty relations with Germany. By doing so she can confiscate the German share of the Boxer indemnity, amounting to £13,500,000 and the Austrian share amounting to £600,000. Then when making her new treaties after the war with Germany she can exclude from the treaties the most favoured nation treatment clauses.

We have done very little to destroy German trade in China. We have temporarily caused inconvenience to German traders, but their activities will be renewed with increased vigour after the war unless we can now take steps to frustrate them.

I wish you could have a talk with Macleay, Counsellor of Embassy, who left here yesterday and is to be in the Foreign Office. I did not think at the time of giving him a letter to you. I wish now that I had done so. He would

---

[1] In his letter to Morrison dated 9 August 1916 (not printed), Gwynne, who was godfather to Morrison's second child, Alastair, had offered to send some clothing as a gift.
[2] Hayashi Gonsuke.

give you a lot of interesting information as he has full knowledge of the views I have expressed (not that my views are worth a damn) of the Japanese and of the Chinese. The case itself is interesting and Macleay would have the most up to date information that you could obtain. He is a very pleasant fellow.

I do not like to write more. All good wishes to you. My wife and I are genuinely proud of having you as god father of our kid.

Best regards to Mrs Gwynne

Ever your attached friend
[G. E. Morrison]

837. To Zumoto Motosada[1]

Peking 3 October 1916

Dear Mr. Zumoto,

I am obliged to you for sending me a copy of the *Herald of Asia* containing a leading article showing that you are not in agreement with the Cabinet's present Chinese policy.

I was sorry not to see you when I was in Tokyo and have a talk with you over affairs, for I have always held you in high regard and greatly admire the brilliant gifts with which you have been endowed. But I was also under the impression – evidently the mistaken impression – that you were a foremost advocate of the policy of your government which has caused such immense distrust in China and such serious misgiving among the allies and in America.

When the Peace Conference is subsequently held what plea will the Japanese Envoy seated with the envoys whose nations have been bled white in the cause of civilization present in justification of the action of his country during this devastating war? What contribution will he be able to claim that his country made towards its successful persecution and its triumphant conclusion? He will admit that Japan never exchanged a shot at sea with an enemy ship, that the whole burden of protecting Japanese commerce on the seas where there were enemy ships was left to England, that she did nothing to save the fleet of Craddock, nothing to suppress the depredations of the *Emden*. Her military effort consisted in the capture of Tsingtau, a weakly defended fort garrisoned by an untrained mob of German Bank clerks and potbellied pastry cooks and out of all proportion to the effort were the immense advantages thereby obtained in China. The envoy will further explain that the chief expense Japan was put to by this military operation was the purchase of countless medals and decorations and trophies and money

---

[1] Zumoto Motosada (1862–1943), Japanese journalist and newspaper publisher, formerly a Correspondent of the *Japan Mail*, he became in 1895 private secretary to Itō Hirobumi and in 1906 accompanied Itō to Korea upon Itō's appointment as Japan's Resident General there. Zumoto was the founder, in 1897, of the *Japan Times* and in 1909 of the Oriental Information Bureau and the *Oriental Review*. He was at this time Proprietor and Editor of the *Herald of Asia*.

gifts to reward the 150,000 men who took part in this desperate venture which cost the lives of nearly one company of her soldiers.

While Japan's chief claim to the admiration of her Allies is that she supplied them with arms as America supplied them how can they forget that she effectively prevented China from rendering them assistance, that in fact she did all that in her lay to prolong the war in order to show her 'constant devotion to her allies' to whom she was supplying arms at a vast profit to her revenues.

Moreover, throughout the first year and a half of the war in order to show her chivalrous spirit she did in the most violent manner attack the British Alliance, and carry on a campaign of calumny against the British to whom she owes her present position among the nations and treat German traders of all classes in Japan not as enemies but as friends.

It is truly a fine record wherewith to appeal to the world to prove that the spirit of chivalry is not dead in Japan.

Do you a patriotic Japanese think that it will ever be forgotten that at a critical time when China's entry into the alliance and her expulsion of Germans from China and the prevention of their intrigues against the British in India would have had a material effect in shortening the war, do you think it will ever be forgotten that despite the repeated request of England Russia France and Belgium, Japan – greatly in the interests of Germany who at that time she believed would be victorious – refused to allow that assistance being given.

Please forgive me for writing to you so frankly. A new and powerful ministry is coming into power. Will they carry on the policy of the past two years or will they render effective help to the allies other than merely continuing to supply them with arms – at a profit.

With kind regards

Very sincerely yours
[G. E. Morrison]

838. To J. McCall[1]

[Peking] 4 October 1916

My dear Sir John,

[...]

Japan's attitude throughout this war has created lively misgivings among us out here. She has taken very little real part in the war. It is true that she did not join with our enemies, and in that way indirectly rendered us a service. Such argument put forth in defence of her attitude presupposes her

---

[1] John McCall (1860–1919), Australian politician, member of the Tasmanian House of Assembly (1883–93), and Chief Secretary of the State Government (1903–4). In 1909 he was appointed Agent-General for Tasmania in London, the post he was holding at this time.

capability of doing such an act of gross treachery. Her fleet have never exchanged a single shot with any enemy ship. Her fleet did nothing to check the depredations of the *Emden*.

She has profited enormously by the war. Her finances are most flourishing, thanks to the profits derived from the sale of arms and munitions to the Allies, and to her prosperous overseas trade. The policing of the danger waters has been left entirely to Great Britain. Three only of her ships have been sunk since the war began. When she could have rendered material help by bringing China into the Alliance she flatly refused to do so.

Her treatment of Germans has ignored her obligations to her allies. Germans have been allowed to trade without any restriction whatever since the war began. Only within the last three weeks has the German Bank in Japan been closed, and its closure was due not to any representation from the British Government but to publicity given in the London press.

I have always understood that Japan promised to return the Marshall Islands to Australia, but a recent visit to Japan convinces me that she has no such intention. She calls the Islands her colonial possessions. She has introduced Japanese civil government there. She is putting the harbour of Jaluit into a state of defence. In the future it will be a submarine base. Relays of Marshall Islands people are being brought to Japan. I have a photograph of 21 who arrived there on the 21st September. King John and other 'potentates' from the Islands have been treated in Japan as honoured guests. I am sure there will be a serious question about this in the future.

China will come into this war if she be invited to join the Allies. But Japan as I say has hitherto refused to join in extending the invitation. We have temporarily stopped German trade in China except that which goes on *via* Japan, but we ought to exclude German competition in China in the future, and that can only be done by inducing China to terminate her treaties with Germany and exclude from any future treaty the most favoured nation treatment clauses. German activity is great in China preparing for the future. Large funds are available, for the Chinese Government pay to the German Bank £2,150,000 *per annum* (£6,000 per day) on account of various indemnities and loans owing to Germany. This money is used largely for carrying on a campaign of sedition in the Far East, in India, and in the Mohammedan section of China against Great Britain. These payments would cease if China joined the Alliance, but Japan prevents that junction being effected. It is deplorable to think that our own ally is preventing the earlier termination of the war.

[...]

Very sincerely yours
[G. E. Morrison]

839. To L. G. Fraser

[Peking] 12 October 1916

My dear Fraser,

It is a very long time since we had any communication with each other, but I constantly read your work. Not less than once a week an article of yours is published in our chief Peking Paper, and no doubt many other articles of *The Times* also republished here have been written by you.

You have rendered services of inestimable value and I am proud to be able to boast that there was a time when I knew you well.

I am now writing to you about a matter in which you can, if you wish, render, should you see fit, opportune help to a cause that I and nearly every other Englishman out here with whom I have spoken have very much at heart. It is this. Why should China not be brought into the Alliance?

You may have considered this question. You will surely have heard of the attempt made last November and of its failure, and of the professed indignation of the Japanese that there should be any question of the admission of China into the ranks of the Allies. Assuming you have heard something of what took place in London I will tell you what happened at this end.

That it would be to the advantage of Great Britain that China should join the Alliance I have never had any doubt whatever. It was equally to the advantage of France, Russia and Belgium. It was unquestionably to the advantage of China. Assuming that Japan was sincere in her declaration to maintain the integrity and independence of China, it was also to the advantage of Japan. Serious Japanese with whom I have discussed this question have admitted that it would be to the advantage of Japan, but these men represent more the non-military section of the Japanese, and, as you know, the Japanese military have been very much under German influence and have from the beginning of the war up to the failure of Verdun been convinced that Germany was invincible.

In August 1914 (at that time I was on my way to China and I did not know of this until later) when Japan prepared to attack Tsingtau Yuan Shih-kai offered to join in the operations by land, placing if need be 50,000 troops for this service. He communicated this offer to Sir John Jordan, the dean of the Diplomatic Body, the most trusted of the Foreign Ministers, one whom he had known for nearly thirty years, and Sir John without consulting his colleagues, saw fit to advise the President to keep quiet and do nothing. It was a serious rebuff. It was a diplomatic blunder of the very worst kind, and whatever may be said about it in London I do know that here indignation, almost violent, was expressed by the Russian and French Ministers when more than a year afterwards they learned of the action or rather inaction of their British colleague. At least they ought to have been consulted, they contended.

For a long time no other opportunity presented itself. On January 18th,

1915, the famous Twenty-One Demands were presented to China by the Japanese Government, Baron Kato now Viscount Kato being the Minister of Foreign Affairs at the time. It is not necessary to remind you that the Japanese Government at that time saw fit to deceive their Allies and to communicate to them an expurgated edition of their peremptory communication from which the more undesirable section had been omitted.

Report says that the perfidy of Japan at this time gave Sir Edward Grey many anxious moments. David Fraser was likewise deceived. I had considerable difficulty in inducing Yuan Shih-kai to make known the full text of the Twenty-One Demands, but eventually he did so, and I sent an early copy to Steed.[1] I presume it reached him although I received no acknowledgement. I also induced the President to have the actual dispatch photographed so that had occasion arisen and the Demands had been persisted in a photograph could have been communicated to the Powers interested. Owing to the publicity given to the Demands China got off much more lightly than at one time seemed possible. You have no doubt got the text of the Agreement[2] signed on May 25th last year.

Early in the summer of last year began that mad movement for the elevation of the President to Sovereign which eventually resulted in his overthrow. On October 28th, 1915, the three Powers, England, France and Russia tendered to China their advice – very proper and opportune advice that the monarchy movement ought to be postponed. I had myself warned Yuan Shih Kai that such advice was bound to be tendered. To me and to others he had professed his determination not to accept the throne. That is another story.

Immediately after this advice had been tendered I considered it opportune to urge Yuan Shih-kai that China should join the Alliance. It was then I learned that in August of the previous year he had offered to join the Alliance. He professed himself in favour of joining the Alliance. He admitted that the memorandum I submitted to him pointing out the advantages of China joining the Alliance was cogent and powerful,[3] and he declared his willingness to join provided that he would not be exposed to another rebuff such as he had experienced on the first occasion. He said he was prepared to join the Alliance on three conditions, viz., Guarantee against reprisals on the part of Germany in the future, the occupation by China of the concessions held by Germany in Tientsin and Hankow and by Austria in Tientsin, and an arrangement regarding the extradition of political offenders from Shanghai (an arrangement satisfactory to him was subsequently agreed to). He

---

[1] *See* Letter 737.
[2] A reference to the Agreement regarding Japan's Twenty-One Demands.
[3] The memorandum here referred to was handed to Li Yüan-hung during Morrison's interview with him on 15 July 1916. Its contents were similar to that of a memorandum Morrison submitted through Ts'ai T'ing-kan to Yüan Shih-k'ai (printed here as the enclosure to Letter No. 784), and is therefore not printed.

expected of course that if China joined the Alliance that her representative would have a seat at the Peace Conference. This went without saying.

The Japanese subsequently alleged that in discussing this matter with Yuan Shih-kai – for it became known that I had discussed it with the President (it is almost impossible to keep such things secret in Peking) – that I was acting in collusion with Sir John Jordan. Nothing could be more untrue. Sir John Jordan was the chief opponent of anything being done. In discussing the matter academically fear of Japan dominated all other considerations in his mind. Nothing was to be done of which there might be any fear that Japan would disapprove. Even he has risked the position of the Deputy Inspector General of Customs being given to a Japanese rather than have an Englishman appointed whom justice and right ought to be appointed for fear that the Japanese might be offended.[1]

You will understand that Yuan Shih-kai when he decided to join the Alliance made it a proviso that he had to be invited to join, and that Japan was to be one of the inviting Powers. This was quite right and reasonable and proper. Then with the characteristic Chinese timidity he conceived that it would be better to force Germany to declare war against China rather than China should declare war against Germany. He thought that if China were to give military assistance to the Allies in the shape of placing her arsenals at the service of the Allies that Germany would regard this as a *casus belli* and would declare war. On the 6th November a formal proposal was made by Yuan Shih-kai that the arsenals should be re-constituted under foreign supervision, mainly British, that a loan of £2,000,000 repayable within three years should be granted for this service, and that the product of the arsenals should be purchased by the Allies. This proposal of Yuan Shih-kai was telegraphed home by Sir John Jordan the same evening and was communicated at once to the Allies. It was communicated in London on Sunday the 7th to Marquis Inouye.[2] It was of course telegraphed to Japan and at once communicated to the Japanese ambassadors abroad. No doubt acting under instructions Baron Chinda,[3] the Ambassador in Washington, communicated the proposal to the President. Indignation was expressed here that this leak should have occurred in Washington. It was attributed to the State Department, but it is known now that the State Department did not

[1] T. D. Moorehead, the Commissioner of Customs at Mukden, was appointed to take charge of the Customs at Tsingtao after Japan captured the city, but on Japan's insistence that a Japanese be appointed, Tachibana, the Commissioner of Customs at Dairen, was appointed in his stead. See Letter No. 720, Morrison to Macleay, 11 December 1914.
[2] Inoue Katsunosuke, at the time referred to, was Japanese Ambassador in London.
[3] Chinda Sutemi (1856–1929), Japanese diplomat, a returned student from the United States. He had served as a consular official in the United States, Korea and China and Minister to Brazil, Russia (1900–2) and Germany (1908–11) before being appointed Ambassador to the United States in 1912. In 1916 he succeeded Inoue Katsunosuke as Japanese Ambassador in London, a post he held until 1920. He was a Japanese Delegate to the Paris Peace Conference in 1919.

make the communication but that it was Baron Chinda now Ambassador to London.

On the 23rd November the three Powers, England, France and Russia formally requested the Japanese Government (Baron Ishii now Viscount Ishii being Minister of Foreign Affairs), to join with them in inviting China to join the Alliance, to place her arsenals at the service of the Allies and to expel the Germans who were carrying on serious intrigues in China especially prejudicial to British rule in India. Baron Ishii declined. The question of arsenals he said had been brought up in connection with the Twenty-One Demands on January 18th. China had given an unfavourable response. As regards the Germans each case ought to be settled on its merits. As regards China joining the Alliance the Japanese Government could not accept the responsibility of awakening the activities of 400 million people. There the case ended.

The three ambassadors, I may tell you, were unfortunately badly informed. They did not know their case. None of them had ever been in China, and in confining themselves to the three points they gave Japan the opportunity of a refusal of which she took advantage.

During the next three months nothing could be done except to wait. By July, however, it was obvious that a change of sentiment had occurred in Japan: the military party had had their confidence in the invincibility of Germany shaken. As a matter of fact on or about the 7th August the Minister of War in Japan, speaking to one of the foreign ambassadors, admitted that Germany's decline had set in, and that it dated from the irretrievable blunder of the unavailing attack upon Verdun.

On July 15th I again brought up the question with the new President, pointing out to him the advantages that China would derive from her admission into the Alliance, and I submitted a memorandum to him in writing, reciting these advantages. On the 17th July I went to Japan in order to discuss the question with the Japanese. I did not see Marquis Okuma. He is too garrulous and too indiscreet. I saw the man whom I most trusted, Viscount Kato, knowing that at any rate in foreign affairs he was the most powerful man in Japan, and that he was likely to be Prime Minister in succession to Okuma.[1] I saw him on August 16th and stated the case to him.

On my return to Peking I saw Baron Hayashi, the Japanese Minister, who was formerly ambassador to Italy, and who would be the first ambassador to China were the legations to be raised to embassies. Baron Hayashi took the opportunity to tell me that he was in favour of China's joining the Alliance, that he had communicated his opinion in this sense when he was ambassador to Rome, but Baron Kato, who was then Foreign Minister, said that his views did not coincide with the views of the Japanese Government.

[1] Ōkuma was not succeeded by Kato but by Terauchi. Kato did become Prime Minister, but not until June 1924.

Hostility to Yuan Shih-kai, distrust of Yuan Shih-kai, unwillingness to do anything which might help Yuan Shih-kai towards the fulfilment of his ambition to be Emperor, were no doubt at the root of his Government's opposition to the proposal. He told me, moreover, that Baron Motono, ambassador to Petrograd, was also in favour of China's joining the Alliance. I knew also from unimpeachable sources that Baron Ijuin, the new ambassador to Italy, was also in favour of China's entering the Alliance. Ijuin told the Russian Ambassador Kroupensky when they were travelling together, and Kroupensky told me.

Now it happens that a new government has come into power in Japan. The new Foreign Minister is Baron Motono, and another cabinet minister is Baron Goto,[1] who is Home Secretary. He, I have reason to believe, favours the admission of China into the Alliance. Another minister, Makino, is brother-in-law of Ijuin, and I have reason to believe that he is of the same opinion. The time thus seems to be opportune, the military party in Japan having at last become convinced (there is every indication of this) that the defeat of Germany is now inevitable.

I say now that Japan can be induced, provided the British Government will act with reasonable firmness, to join in inviting China to become a member of the Alliance, to terminate her treaties with Germany, to expel Germans from China, and I have not the shadow of a doubt that Japan agreeing to do this there will be no difficulty in obtaining the acquiescence of China. Surely the advantage would be inestimable.

We boast that we have checked German trade in China, and it is true that we have done so, but it is a temporary check only. A certain communication from German firms in China lamenting the loss that they will sustain by the enforcement of the British blockade and the Trading with the Enemy Act fell into the possession of the British authorities. This was communicated to the Chambers of Commerce. The check, however, is only a temporary one, and this must be repeated. We must prepare this great unexploited field for the activities of our merchants subsequent to the war. The Germans in China have never been more active than at present. There are probably 200 Germans travelling throughout China at the present time. They are abundantly supplied with money. China pays in to the Deutsch-Asiatische Bank in

---

[1] Gotō Shimpei (1857–1929), Japanese politician. A medical graduate from Germany, he distinguished himself as Chief Inspector of Army Hygiene during the first Sino-Japanese War of 1894–5. In 1901 he was selected as Chief Civil Administrator of Formosa under Kodama Gentarō (1852–1906), the Governor General of Formosa. In 1906 he became President of the newly founded South Manchurian Railway Company, and two years later Minister of Communications, a post he held again in 1913. At the time referred to he was Minister of the Interior in the Terauchi Cabinet (October 1916 – April 1918). He then succeeded Motono Ichirō as Foreign Minister. He was to become Minister of the Interior again, from September 1923 to January 1924. Gotō had come to know Morrison serving as President of the South Manchurian Railway.

China at present £6,000 per day on account of the Boxer Indemnity, the 1896 and 1898 Anglo-German Loans, the Hukuang Railway Loan, the Tientsin–Pukow Railway Loan, and the Quintuple Re-organisation Loan. This money is used in China largely for carrying on a propaganda against Great Britain especially among Mahommedans, and particularly among the Mahommedans of Far Western China who are in constant intercourse with the Mahommedans of India.

The Germans subsidise native papers. More ingeniously they publish papers in English: the *Peking Post* in Peking, the *Tientsin Sunday Journal* in Tientsin, the *Hankow Daily News* in Hankow, and *The War* in Shanghai. These papers, distinguished by their scurrility and infamy, are subsidised by the Deutsch–Asiatische Bank, the most scurrilous articles in the Northern papers being written by a renegade Englishman named Eggeling, manager of the Deutsch–Asiatische Bank in Peking. It is this Bank which is in such close relations with the Hongkong and Shanghai Bank, but of this later.

Surely you can help to induce the British Government to adopt a new and more resolute attitude both in Tokyo and in Peking. In neither place will the authorities act except under definite and clear instructions. In Tokyo the Ambassador[1] accustomed throughout his whole diplomatic career to European posts has never realised that in dealing with the Asiatic pusillanimity is the worst quality to display.

German trade has continued in Japan as if no state of war existed. Germans have been treated not as enemies but as friendly neutrals. Only last week was the Deutsch–Asiatische Bank closed in Japan. It had remained open and had continued its operations in Japan ever since the war began. There can be little doubt that its closure was due not to protest from the British Ambassador but to exposure from the *Daily Telegraph* correspondent, Putnam Weale.

Here in Peking we are unfortunately represented by a Minister of quite exceptional timidity of character. He is not old, only 63, but he is thoroughly brain weary. There never was a more devoted servant of the British Government. He has never spared himself. Go into his office any day during the last ten years when he was in charge and you would find him surrounded by mountains of boxes of memoranda and papers most of them of the most trivial importance dealing with paltry questions, questions of *likin* and of evasions of the Opium Agreement and such like at the various places where British trade is carried on in China. He could never see the wood for the trees. He is a terrible pessimist. Speaking to a prominent Englishman the other night in an almost weeping state he said that France was bled white,

---

[1] William Conyngham Greene from his post of Third Secretary in Athens in 1880 to his appointment as successor to Sir Claude MacDonald in Tokyo in 1912 had served in Germany, Holland, Belgium, Switzerland, Rumania and Denmark. He had, however, also served as Secretary of the Legation and Chargé d'Affaires in Teheran from 1893 to 1896 and was British Agent with the rank of Chargé d'Affaires in Pretoria in South Africa from 1896 to 1899.

that upon England now fell an ever increasing burden in the conduct of the war, that the time was coming when we would have to make the best terms we could. Such words coming from him would in ordinary circumstances cause the community here considerable anxiety, but so confident are we all of the glorious victory that is to be ours that we regard his words rather with contempt and indignation than with dismay.

Some time ago the British Government recognised that the time had come when a younger and fresher man should be in charge of our Legation here. We all approve of this decision. At the same time Sir John has been told by our Government that he can remain as long as he likes, and he has got into that attitude of mind in which he believes himself indispensable. Alston, his successor, arrived here in the first week of August, and it was understood that Sir John was to leave in September, but he is still here and is now making plans for Christmas.

We have shelved our aged and decrepit generals. Surely in a time of national crisis like this we ought to shelve our aged and decrepit ministers. Sentiment ought not to stand in the way.

Sir John sees Baron Hayashi frequently. They have known each other for nearly twenty years, but there is no intimacy between them. Hayashi never discloses to him the demands he is submitting with regard to the latest incident, what is known as the Chenchiatun incident,[1] nor does Sir John ever speak to him about China joining the Alliance. But if Sir John were instructed to speak to him he would do so faithfully and well, for there is no question, as I have said before, he will most faithfully carry out whatever instructions are given him. But he is thoroughly worn out. These instructions had better be given to Alston, who must command the confidence of the Foreign Office to have been given this very important post without any of the hard diplomatic training which other ministers have to go through.

I repeat that I am confident that an arrangement could be come to. I am confident that Japan can be induced to come into line with us. I am confident that China, despite German intrigue and despite German money, can be induced to come into line.

Japan has done nothing for the Alliance. In the September number of *The Nineteenth Century* you will see that Robert Macrae[2] states the case for

---

[1] Following the shooting incident between Chinese and Japanese troops in Chengchiatun in Fengtien Province which took place on 13 October 1916, a week before presenting his credentials, Hayashi handed to the Chinese Government a series of demands, including the right to establish police stations in many towns in Southern Manchuria and Eastern Mongolia, and a demand for an undertaking by the Chinese Government to employ Japanese military instructors.

[2] Robert Machray (1857–1946), Canadian churchman, journalist and author. A graduate of Cambridge, he was ordained in 1883 and served under his uncle, the first Archbishop of Rupert's Land, until 1889 when a throat infection forced him to abandon the career of a preacher and he took up writing and journalism. He worked as War Editor of the *Daily Mail* (1904–5) and foreign affairs critic for the *Saturday Review* (1924–5) and was the

Japan. This ex-soldier of fortune, this ex-canon who wrote the somewhat lurid *Night Side of London*, points out the great services which Japan has rendered during the war. What are these services? She has never exchanged a single shot with an enemy ship. She has sold arms and munitions to the Allies at a vast profit. The policing of the enemy waters where there is danger is entirely left to England. But as Macrae points out the case would have been serious if Japan had joined our enemies at the outbreak of war. No doubt the case would have been serious for us. It would also have been very serious for Japan. It would have been the greatest act of infamy committed by any Power except Germany since the world began. Every ship that she had upon the overseas would have been lost. America would have become our ally. Etc.

[...]

[G. E. Morrison]

840 From R. Dane

Peking 14 October [1916]

Dear Morrison,

I return the Memo[1] with many thanks. Personally I think you have overestimated the value to the Allies of Chinese cooperation. Persia appears to have been brought into line and outside Persia the Amir of Kabul[2] is the only personage who counts, and he appears (fortunately for us) to have

---

author of many books on eastern Europe. *The Night Side of London* was published in London in 1902. In the article referred to, which appeared in the September number of the *Nineteenth Century* (pp. 531–42) entitled 'Japan's Part in the War' he repeatedly stressed the important role which Japan had played and said, 'During the war our people and our interests in China have owed their security to the loyalty of Japan to the Anglo-Japanese Alliance and the Entente. That same alliance postulates the independence and integrity of China and the "open door".'

[1] Dane seems to be referring to the memorandum Morrison wrote to Li Yüan-hung on 15 July 1916 (*see* Diary vol.), which he must have borrowed when he visited Morrison on 11 October 1916.

[2] Habibullah Khan (d. 1919), Amir of Afghanistan (1901–19), the son of Abdur Rahman, the previous Amir. He declared the neutrality of his country at the outbreak of the European War and confirmed it on 3 October 1914. But he became restive when Turkey entered the War and Germany tried to persuade the Amir through bribery to give passage to their troops to attack India. Both the British Government and the Government in India also offered him large sums of money to keep Afghanistan neutral. In a Treaty signed on 24 January 1916 Germany promised to supply the Afghan Government without obligation with a large quantity of arms but the British Agent in Kabul was assured by Habibullah of his neutrality, which was maintained in spite of revolts among his people on the border areas. Habibullah had demanded from Britain as the price of his country's remaining neutral a seat at the Peace Conference, but this was refused on the grounds that Afghanistan was not a belligerent. Habibullah was assassinated some three months after the end of the European War on the night of 19/20 February 1919 in Kalla Gush.

decided to remain neutral. I doubt also if he would be impressed by any action taken by China.

I confess also that I think the policy you favour is of very problematical advantage for China. Poor China cannot afford to make powerful enemies. The present solidarity of the Allies is not likely to continue. The jellyfish attitude maintained up to date appears to me to be the wisest course in China's own interest. However as you know, I do not concern myself with high politics.

Yours sincerely
R. Dane

841 To Beatrice Brownrigg

[Peking] 14 October 1916

Dear Lady Brownrigg,

Your letter of August 10th[1] I got shortly after I returned from Japan.

I had a rotten time there. It rained nearly every day. The hotel was inferior and I was in a constant state of discontent. Chuzenji is a God-forsaken place in which to spend the summer. At least I found it so, although it did my wife and my children good, but it is a long and expensive way to go in order to have a holiday.

Although the weather was shocking, there was a very agreeable company at the hotel, most of the leading residents of Shanghai being there, viz., the Ezras, the Benjamins, the Judahs, the Rehemiahs, the Toegs, the Kadoories (Kadoorie is a Bagdad Turk and therefore an enemy subject: he has been unavailingly endeavouring to get registered as a British subject ever since the war began: he used to speak to me about the homeland, meaning Surrey not Mesopotamia) the Nysshims, etc. I was afraid if we remained much longer that my boy would be speaking Yiddish.

You no doubt know that Japan's attitude during the war has been much open to suspicion. [...]

We have scrapped some of our useless generals, and yet we retain in this important post in Peking a doddering, muddle-headed Minister, whose timorousness is proverbial. He ought to be scrapped. The Foreign Office have sent his successor to Peking, but apparently they do not like to tell Sir John bluntly to go, and he has got into that condition of mind in which he thinks he is indispensable. His influence on the British community is most depressing. The other day speaking to one of the two or three most prominent Englishmen in Peking he expressed the view in the most lugubrious terms that France was bled white, that the whole burden of sustaining the war was more and more having to be borne by England, and that peace at the best terms we could get was inevitable. Fortunately, none of us are influenced

[1] Not printed.

by such talk. Moreover, we know that Japan now recognises that her belief in the invincibility of Germany was a mistaken belief, and if the Foreign Office care to bring pressure to bear upon Japan it can be brought more easily now than it could have been a year ago.

Please give my best remembrances to Douglas.
With all good wishes to you and yours
Believe me

Ever faithfully yours
[G. E. Morrison]

842   From A. H. Smith

T'ung Chou [Chihli] 4 January 1917

Dear Dr Morrison,
Thank you for your letter received yesterday, and for the volume which came this morning. I am much interested in your good opinion of the President. It is rare enough to find a man in Chinese public life of whom any one can say that he is both honest and unselfish.

From what I know the Parliament seems hopeless. Our American experience shows that the number once fixed can never be reduced, so that we are condemned to age long inefficiency. Thank you very much for the trouble which you have been at in regard to my pamphlets, &c. I shall be glad to get rid of them all, as I am giving my books to be used for an intermission loan library.

I remain cordially yours

Arthur H. Smith

843.   To Tiao Tso-ch'ien[1]

[Peking] 7 February 1917

Dear Mr. Tyau,
Please pardon the delay in answering your letter of the 3rd.[2]

I am so intensely desirous that China should not let slip this opportunity of joining the nations who are henceforth to control the destinies of the world that I have been bending all my energies towards inducing the Authorities to accept without delay the heaven sent opportunity now given them by America.[3]

[1] Also known to his Western friends as Philip K. C. Tyau (b. 1880), Chinese diplomat and jurist. A graduate from Cambridge and London Universities, he held many diplomatic posts and was at this time a Secretary in the Chinese Ministry of Foreign Affairs and concurrently a Secretary in the Cabinet Office.
[2] In a letter to Morrison dated 3 February 1917, which is not printed, Tiao asked Morrison about 'a certain Georges Padoux'.
[3] On 3 February 1917 the United States, having severed her diplomatic relations with Germany, urged the Chinese Government to take the same course.

A few days ago you would have noticed a letter in the *Peking Gazette*[1] suggesting that the foreign advisers should be got rid of and that their salaries should be applied towards the improvement in the condition of the rickshaw coolies. One of these advisers thus referred to is Georges Padoux, about whom you ask me. You know that I have always been anxious to be associated with China in the recovery of her complete independence and in the raising of her position among the nations. Two examples are always before us, the example of Japan and the example of Siam. In 1893 Siam was completely crushed. It appeared to have lost all vestige of independence, yet by the action of its wise rulers and by the help of foreign advisers the country so far re-established itself that by 1907 it had recovered even its extra-territorial rights and had obtained jurisdiction over all foreigners within its territory.

One of the men associated with this work for a number of years was Padoux, a distinguished member of the French diplomatic service, an authority on Mohammedan law who was for several years in Tunis. Shortly after my own appointment I submitted to Yuan Shih-kai the suggestion that he should appoint as legal adviser this well known jurist. As legislative adviser in Siam M. Padoux had been given an opportunity to render important services, and he had rendered them, with the result that we all know. He was accordingly appointed by China, not however in any legal capacity, as I suggested but as auditor, a branch of work that had never previously engaged his attention. His one wish has been to render to China similar service to that he rendered to Siam. He has never been given the opportunity. He re-drafted the Penal Code of Siam, and is a lawyer of so much distinction as to be given the rank of minister plenipotentiary in the French service. I am surprised

[1] A reference to a letter to the Editor of the *Peking Gazette* from an apparently foreign reader signing himself 'Friendship', published on 29 January 1917. It was provoked by the 'Report of the Committee for the Relief of Rickshaw Coolies etc' which had appeared in the paper two days previously. Several examples of the living conditions of a cross-section of the poverty-stricken in the Chinese capital were given. In one case the Committee found that 'one court of miserable little rooms back of an old grain shop contains sixteen families of rickshaw coolies few of whom had any bedding or even a straw mat on the *k'ang* in one instance. Rarely was there any coal or meal in the house. The older children were out gathering half burned coal balls for fuel; the younger ones huddled together over the fire trying to cover their naked limbs with the one upper garment they wore, and hoping there would be something to eat before the day was over. Many of the women simply hibernate during the winter. They cannot go out of doors for lack of clothes and there is nothing to do indoors, nothing to cook, nothing to sew, nothing to wash; though too often there is a baby to feed and warm if possible.' The correspondent who had been moved to write said in his letter that 'the calls on the foreign community have been heavy and are increasingly so these days, but foreigners are helping as they can. It would be good to know that our Chinese friends and especially the Government were also doing what they could.' He went on to suggest: 'Perhaps some of the highly salaried "advisers" could help to solve the problem if they would, or better still the Government might give these salaries and start reproductive and improvement work instead.'

that you have not read his work on the Penal Code of Siam.[1] It is in French. When you give me the pleasure of coming to my library I will show it to you.

I certainly think it would be to your advantage to have a talk with M. Padoux. He speaks English excellently, and is only one of several advisers of similar ambitions now engaged by the Chinese Government who are scrupulously prevented from doing any work which might be of service to the Chinese Government. The most notable case, I should think, is that of Dr. Hirai, a member of the House of Peers, permanent head of the Japanese railways before entering the Chinese service, a railway administrator known to every railwayman in the world, the representative of Japan at various international railway conferences, a graduate of Harvard, who, since his engagement three years ago, has never been asked a question of any kind whatever. An administrator of the high moral qualities of Hsu Shih-ying,[2] whose only idea of managing a ministry is to sell every job in the gift of that ministry, would scorn to accept the trained service of a highly qualified foreign expert.

So too with Mr. Sherfesee. So too with Dr. Willoughby.

With best wishes to you

Very sincerely yours
[G. E. Morrison]

844. To Beatrice Brownrigg

[Peking] 8 February 1917

Dear Lady Brownrigg,

[...]

We have been having an interesting time here. America has invited China to join with her in severing diplomatic relations with Germany, and we are doing everything we possibly can to induce her to accept this invitation. Unfortunately our Legation is not well served.

[1] *Code pénal du royaume de Siam promulgué le 1er juin 1908, entré en vigueur le 22 septembre 1908* (Paris 1909).
[2] Hsü Shih-ying (1872-1964), Chinese Imperial official and Republican politician, at this time Minister of Communications (July 1916 - May 1917) in the cabinet of his fellow-provincial Tuan Ch'i-jui. He was one of the few who flourished in high offices in three successive regimes - the Imperial Manchu Government, the Warlord regime in Peking and the Nationalist Government in Nanking. He also served as Minister of Justice (July 1912 - September 1913), Interior (June-July 1916), Governor of his native Anhwei Province (September 1921 - February 1923) and was for two and a half months Prime Minister, from December 1925 to February 1926. He was Chinese Ambassador to Japan at the outbreak of the second Sino-Japanese War in 1937, and on his return became Chairman of the Tibetan and Mongolian Commission (1937-49), holding the post until he fled with the Nationalist Government to Taiwan. He then served, until his death, as an adviser to Chiang Kai-shek. Beginning his career under the Manchus in the judicial administration, he became according to Morrison one of the most corrupt officials in the Republic.

By the system adopted in the Legation much responsibility is placed on the shoulders of the chief interpreter, who is called the Chinese Secretary. Often we have had a Chinese Secretary of high ability who has had an excellent influence over the policy of the Minister. At present our Chinese Secretary is a man named Barton, 40 years of age, a narrow-minded man who has had no experience outside of the consular service in China, and who is much dominated by his wife, a lady of high social pretensions.[1] Her father was a bankrupt merchant who became head of Jardine's in Shanghai and realised a fortune. Barton is equally unpopular with the Chinese and with the British community. Thus through his unfitness for the post the Legation has very little influence with the Chinese, both directly because it is not in touch with the Chinese and indirectly because it does not encourage but rather alienates the support of the British people who have dealings with the Chinese.

The Chargé d'Affaires is a man from the Foreign Office named Alston, a pleasant fellow, 48 years of age, who is regarded by the Chinese rather as a buffoon. He stammers and has a curiously unreposeful and undignified manner, but he is anxious to do well and if he had better assistance from his interpretorial secretary he would do better. Naturally he is ambitious to retain the post in succession to Sir John Jordan.

The next man to Alston is a man of fine presence named Lampson,[2] who was for some time in Japan, and no doubt you know him well. He has created a very favourable impression here. He seems to have realised the defects of the Legation and is taking a keen interest in his work. He and his wife are both learning Chinese.

[...]

Ever faithfully yours
[G. E. Morrison]

845. To Tuan Ch'i-jui[3]

Peking 8 February 1917

Memorandum for His Excellency the Prime Minister

In the strongest possible manner I urge that China accept with alacrity the invitation extended to her by America to join with America in severing

[1] Sidney Barton married in 1894 Mary Ethel Winifred (d. 1945), the eldest daughter of Alexander Palmer MacEwen, a Shanghai merchant.
[2] Miles Wedderburn Lampson (1880–1964), later 1st Baron Killearn, British diplomat, at this time First Secretary of the British Legation in Peking. In 1926 he became British Minister to China, a post he held until 1933 when he was appointed British High Commissioner and later Ambassador to Egypt and the Sudan, remaining there until March 1946. As one of the trustees of the Morrison Papers, he, together with the others, turned down the proposed publication of a selected edition of the Diary. See p. 214 note 3.
[3] No covering letter has been found.

diplomatic relations with Germany. It is a heaven sent opportunity. It is the greatest opportunity ever given to China.

I suggest the following procedure:

Firstly. The severance of diplomatic relations, the sending of passports to the German Minister in Peking and to the German consuls in China, and the withdrawal of the Chinese Minister and the Chinese consuls from Germany. Consuls in China are on a somewhat different footing from consuls in other countries. Extraterritoriality in China gives them judicial functions over their subjects. It is essential that when passports are being sent to the German Minister that passports should also be sent to the German Consuls in China. Steps will have to be taken for the Chinese to exercise jurisdiction in place of the German consular jurisdiction.

Secondly. Safe transit must be given to the German Minister and to the German Consuls to the nearest point of territory under the jurisdiction of Germany or of her allies. I suggest that they be sent to Port Said in Egypt. From that port they could find a Greek vessel which will take them to Asia Minor, where they will be on Turkish territory.

Thirdly. In the German concession at Tientsin and the German concession at Hankow the Chinese must enter into occupation and must continue the municipal administration. I suggest that this be done in co-operation with the foreign residents of these two concessions. The Municipal Council should consist of a Chinese chairman and of a certain proportion of Chinese and of representatives of foreigners resident in the Concession of allied or of neutral nationality.

Fourthly. Instructions must at once be given to discontinue the payment of any Chinese Government moneys into the German bank, Customs moneys or Salt moneys or Postal moneys. Instructions must also be issued through the proper authorities to the Bankers Commission in Shanghai instructing them to make no further payments to Germany on account of the German share of the Boxer Indemnity or of any German railway or other loan in China. In case of the Boxer Indemnity, payments will be discontinued for all time. In the case of the railway and other Loans payments are suspended only until peace has been signed after the war.

Fifthly. Immediate steps must be taken to issue a Presidential Mandate declaring that all non-treaty Powers shall henceforth pay Customs duties in China of three-tenths *ad valorem*. This will be the first step towards China recovering her tariff autonomy. She begins by recovering her tariff autonomy with one of the European Powers, namely, Germany, which will become one of the non-treaty Powers, for the severance of diplomatic relations in this case must be interpreted by China to mean the termination of her treaty engagements with Germany.

Sixthly. Germans in the employ of the Chinese Government, in the Customs, in the Salt, and in the Post Office, and in Government institutions must be given notice of the termination of their agreements, for as soon as a state of war exists they must be removed. Those of military age may be interned, but I suggest the advisability of allowing those who have been in the service of the Chinese Government to proceed to Japan or to America or to accompany if they desire the German Minister and Consuls on their enforced pilgrimage to Asia Minor.

Seventhly. Later the question will arise as to the internment of Germans of military age. Those in China at the present time under this category number several hundreds. A considerable proportion of the German population of China was taken prisoner at Tsingtao and is now in Japan. It is believed that there are 3,500 German subjects remaining in China.

Eighthly. I would point out the necessity of stringent precautions being taken in the case of the arsenals and military establishments.

[G. E. Morrison]

846. From O. M. Green

Shanghai 11 February 1916 [1917][1]

Dear Morrison,

I must apologize for not writing before but the week since my return has been the busiest I ever remember.

[...]

You did give me a splendid and most useful time in Peking. It was good all the way round, and I think I laid some useful foundations for the supplement.[2] I never asked you but would you write for it? Would it be possible in your position to do so? I leave the choice of a subject wholly to you. But I should like to have you in the thing.

I suppose before, long before, that special number comes out China and ourselves will be allies! I am dancing with joy over that Note.[3] The whole situation is, of course, utterly different from what it would be if we invited China to come in. Japan cannot possibly object to her doing what she is doing, and as the logical outcome of this note appears to be war China is represented at the peace conference, and in that way England France and Russia can help her against Japan as they could not possibly do by any other

[1] This letter was wrongly dated. The year should have been 1917.
[2] A reference to a special supplement on China in the *North China Daily News*.
[3] On 3 February 1917 the United States, having broken off diplomatic relations with Germany, invited China to take the same step, and on 9 February China made a protest to Germany against the blockade of the Chinese coast by German submarines. The protest was rejected on 19 February and so on 14 March China formally broke off diplomatic relations with Germany. Owing to the opposition by a majority of members of Parliament and by the southern republicans, however, President Li Yüan-hung refused to sanction the move to enter the war. This led to great constitutional and political upheaval, and China did not declare war on Germany until five months later on 14 August 1917.

means. Altogether it seems to me to be about the most brilliant diplomatic stroke that China has ever achieved. The authorities down here are rather haggard about possible Hun aggressions. But could they really be such fools, desperate as their position will be? [...]

Yours sincerely
Owen M. Green

847. To F. B. Alston

[Peking] 13 February 1917

My dear Alston,

Yesterday morning Padoux, De Codt, Ariga and myself were called to the Kuo Wu Yuan[1] and we were asked our opinion as to the procedure to be followed in the event of a rupture of diplomatic relations taking place.

Afterwards we met at my house and we drew up a memorandum which we all signed and which I sent to the Waichiaopu last evening. I will send you a copy as soon as I have it made.

You have no doubt been told that the Chinese were more than pleased with the verbal communication made to the Premier by Yoshizawa[2] the day before yesterday and by the communication made to the Chinese Minister in Tokyo by Viscount Motono. The latter expressed satisfaction at the action taken by China and expressed the hope that China would go further and rupture diplomatic relations with Germany. It is about this I am writing to you.

It seems to me from talking to many Chinese that there would be no particular difficulty now in inducing China to sever diplomatic relations. This is a consummation devoutly to be wished. It can be brought about if a

[1] Cabinet Office.
[2] Yoshizawa Kenkichi (1874–1965), Japanese diplomat, at this time Counsellor (1916–19) at the Japanese Legation in Peking where he was chief aide to Hayashi Gonsuke in his dealings with the Anfu Government. He had previously served at various consular posts in China as well as in London. In 1919 he became Director of the Political Bureau of the Foreign Ministry and when this post was abolished as a result of reorganisation in October the following year he was made Director of the Bureau of Asia as well as that of America and Europe. He returned to China as Japanese Minister in 1923, holding the post until 1929, and was at the centre of the intrigues with the three successive warlord cliques that were in control, in its last days, of the Peking regime. He then became Minister to France and represented Japan at the League of Nations during the debate following the so-called 'Manchurian Incident' of 18 September 1931. He was Foreign Minister in the Cabinet of Inukai Tsuyoshi, from January 1932 until Inukai's assassination in May the same year. After the Japanese seizure of the Dutch East Indies, Yoshizawa became Japanese Special Envoy there. He survived the Second World War to become in 1952 at the age of 78, Japanese Ambassador to Chiang Kai-shek's Nationalist Government in Taiwan. He had thus one of the longest and unrivalled records of association with his country's policy in China.

joint representation could be made to the Waichiaopu by the representatives of the Allies.

It is not sufficient to have removed the opposition of Japan. It is very necessary to obtain her active support of her lead in extending this invitation. I am confident that if it were efficiently handled the Chinese could be definitely brought into the Alliance. Such an invitation would be much more satisfying to their pride and dignity than the invitation of America. We, the Allies, ought to take a leading part in influencing China. At present our Governments seem disposed to regard the question too much as if it were an academic question, and to leave to America the privilege of guiding China.

Compared with the great sacrifices of money which all of us Allies are making in the present war the advantage which China hopes for in case of finance relief is insignificant. China will ask for delay in the payment of the Boxer Indemnity until after the war. She will ask for the immediate raising of the Customs tariff to an effective five per cent *ad valorem*. All the Powers have already agreed to this except Russia and Japan, Russia wishing to stipulate that Vladivostok should be treated as a port of China and have the advantage of an interport customs tariff, and Japan opposing any increase in the duties now being levied on cotton fabrics and I believe – I am not quite sure – on silk fabrics also.

It is quite certain that you will be spoken to on this question and also that representation will be made to you by the Chinese that there shall be some relaxation of the rule arising from the Protocol of the 7th September, 1901,[1] that Chinese troops shall not be permitted within a certain distance of Tientsin.

What the Chinese who come to see me emphasise is the need of doing something to give face or to placate the military who are undeniably responsive to a considerable extent to German military influence or tradition.

China's accession to the Alliance would be of such unquestionable value not only actual but moral that I feel that the effort of every Englishman, whether official or un-official, should be directed towards helping this movement.

We have had no one in the Chinese Army for many years past. When I spoke to Yuan Shih-kai about employing an Englishman in the Ministry of War he dismissed the suggestion somewhat angrily I thought with the words 'And be treated by the British Legation as we were treated in the case of Bruce', whose appointment to the police I had brought about.

If the opportunity should occur, and it will occur, for China to join the Alliance it will be infinitely wiser for her to employ an English high military officer trained in modern warfare than to depend upon a Japanese intriguing

[1] By Article ix of the 'Conditions for the Dissolution of the Provisional Government of Tientsin' which had been set up by the occupying forces of the Powers, signed on 15 July 1902, Chinese troops were forbidden to come within 20 Chinese *li* (6⅔ English miles) of the city of Tientsin where foreign troops were stationed.

general who has had no experience of the conditions of this great war in Europe.

Excuse this long screed. The Chinese are pretty sure to approach you to-morrow.

Very sincerely yours
[G. E. Morrison]

848. From F. E. Taylor

Shanghai 10 March 1917

My dear Morrison,

It will be many years before China finds herself in such a position as the present, when she really has a chance to make a fair start on the road of progress to wealth and security. May I give my views of what I conceive her attitude should be in view of the invitation tendered to her to join the Allies. I do not see that China should join unless she can gain substantial benefits; but she has something to offer in exchange, and what she can offer will benefit herself as much as the concessions she may receive.

Revision of the Import Tariff is apparently to be conceded to her; but it is Mackay's absurd proposal that is contemplated. An import Tariff should be based upon practical and scientific grounds. To charge luxuries and necessaries a flat rate of $12\frac{1}{2}$ per cent all round is childish and harmful. It is too high for the one and too low for the other. Moreover, we know the results of Tariff negotiations by our previous experience, when the promised 5 per cent[1] was whittled down to $4\frac{1}{2}$ per cent. China should demand the right of drawing up her own Tariff in her own interests. If this is denied she should demand the Japanese Tariff, which has fulfilled the aim of building up an immense industrial trade, and would do the same for China. If the Allies refuse this also, then China can know she is simply being exploited.

China should also demand the remission of the balance of the Boxer indemnity. This will have to be remitted before long, as it is too unjust to be allowed to continue for many years longer. Why should the Chinese all have to pay for the crime of the Manchus whom they have kicked out, when almost the whole of China was kept quiet by Chinese officials? It is a heavy tax on China, but amounts to as much as England alone spends in one day on the war!!

---

[1] By Article VIII of the Sino-British Commercial Treaty of 5 September 1902, China was to be allowed to levy a surcharge not exceeding one and a half times the stipulated 5% *ad valorem* on imported goods, in exchange for the abolition of *likin* and other transit dues. The reduction of the stipulated 5% rate here referred to was due primarily to exchange fluctuations. This Treaty or Convention is often referred to by the name of its British signatory, Sir James Lyle Mackay (1852–1932), later 1st Earl of Inchcape, British civil servant. At the time of his appointment as British Special Commissioner to China in 1901 Mackay was in the service of the Indian Government and held various posts in India both before and after his China mission. He was also a Director of the Bank of England, Royal Bank of Scotland and National Provincial Bank.

In return for these concessions China should abolish all taxation of every description on goods in transit, and do away with all barriers. She should abolish export duties and coast trade duties and transit dues. She should agree that within a specified time, say two years, she will with the assistance of foreign experts establish a uniform national currency and also draw up practical mining regulations. Finally, there should be an understanding that the Boxer indemnity will be reimposed, and the present Tariff reverted to, unless in two years China has redeemed her promises about the currency and mining, and if it is proved that goods in transit are taxed.

I assert most positively that such an arrangement would be the commencement of an enormous expansion of trade, by which all parties would benefit. Possibly Japan will not see it, as the papers say that the cotton spinners in Osaka are already agitating against any increase of duties on cotton goods. But Japan protects her cotton industry by high import duties: why should not China do the same.

If China cannot get her terms, she would be wise to declare benevolent neutrality and invite the vessels of all the Allies to make use of Chinese waters. Otherwise the Japanese will take advantage of U.S. vessels leaving. I think this is not doubtful.

Yours very truly
F. E. Taylor

[...]

849. To G. Padoux

Peking 18 March 1917

Dear Monsieur Padoux,

I regret that I cannot sign the memorandum.[1] I am of course open to conviction and your persuasive tongue may convince me that I am wrong, but knowing the Chinese as I do, it seems to me that it would be discouraging to them if we, the foreign advisers now suggest that the German concessions of which they have resumed possession should be placed under the direction *réelle* of a foreigner.

The Chinese would never agree to this. One of the rewards promised to them – promised I mean, not officially but promised by those who advocated this step – for entering the war was the resumption of the German Concessions. With commendable promptitude they have taken this step which may, I understand, be really interpreted into an act of war and if now they are to be advised by their foreign counsellors to place the control of the concessions so taken in foreign hands not only will the advice be disregarded but all of our advice in the future will be looked upon with suspicion.

[1] The memorandum (not printed) was one drafted by Padoux in the name of all the foreign advisers, suggesting to the Chinese Government that the Allied Powers should be given control of the German concessions that had reverted to China.

The proposal does not seem to me fair to the Chinese. I wish you would reconsider the matter. Before sending on the memorandum to Dr. Ariga, I would like to consult with you. So if convenient to you, I will come over and see you to-morrow morning at 9.30.

With kind regards

Very sincerely yours
[G. E. Morrison]

[...]

850. From R. Gilbert[1]

Peking 23 March [1917]

Dear Dr. Morrison,

I have been asking a number of Chinese friends about taxation of various sorts in and out of Peking and am confirmed in the belief that I expressed to you the other day, that the residents of cities (in the North at any rate) pay no direct taxes into what might be called municipal treasuries. They see no reason why they should; it has never been done. All public improvements, measures for sanitation, police administration, and the like, either come out of the rural land tax and the special federal taxes or are financed by public subscription. For the most part the countryside bears the expenses of the city which administers its affairs, and the residents of cities pay nothing unless they own arable land outside their city walls. The injustice of this is not apparent to any Chinese until he has been told of foreign systems. That the farmers beyond the walls should contribute the funds which keep up the schools, streets, police forces, and public buildings, not to mention the various organs of the government, for the benefit of those who happen to live within the walls seems quite natural. This seems to explain clearly enough why the farmer ranks socially next to the scholar and why the merchant has always been held in contempt. In his relation to the state the city merchant has always been a parasite.

Improvements in cities, not provided for by the public funds, have always been carried out by local subscription. This system prevails in Peking now. Street lighting, the handling of garbage etc etc, are in the hands of the police

[1] Rodney Yonkers Gilbert (b. 1889), American journalist, formerly with the *Chicago Tribune*, he took on various jobs including investigation missions to West China on behalf of the American Government after arriving in China. Like many foreign journalists at the time he was deeply involved in Chinese politics and was reputedly author of the 'Apologia', otherwise attributed to Ku Hung-ming, which Chang Hsün had had published in the Peking papers on 11 July 1917 before taking asylum in the Dutch Legation. Gilbert, who had earlier worked for the *Far Eastern Review*, became the journal's Editor in the absence of W. H. Donald and L. Pratt. He was author of *What's Wrong with China?* (N.Y. and London 1926), *The Unequal Treaties: China and foreigner* (London 1929) and *The Indiscretion of Lin Mang* (London 1929).

department and the municipality is only indirectly responsible for them. The police in each district keep up as efficient a system as public subscription, pledged annually and paid monthly, will permit and where there is no subscription there is neither light nor sanitation. Many of the poor give nothing while the wealthy, under the pressure of public opinion give liberally.

There is no tax upon merchants for local purposes. They contribute to federal funds through the stamp tax on documents, the *likin*, the salt, wine and tobacco taxes, etc. etc., but pay no fixed rates to the community on any basis. Permits to open shops here in Peking are obtained from the bureau in charge of such matters in the Nei Wu Pu.[1] There is no charge, but a small fee accelerates matters for small shops and a larger fee for larger commercial enterprises. Those who have friends in the department pay nothing. Such contributions as are made through this medium are not likely to reach the municipal exchequer. On the sale and transfer of properties, there are no taxes unless a measurement of land and the writing of a new deed are entailed, and land once acquired within the city walls pays no taxes whatever.

The country folk pay the land tax twice a year. The assessment is roughly fixed per *mou* over large areas, belts of fertile land paying a little more and arid land paying a little less. In these big areas with a fixed taxation there is of course poor land which pays too much and good land which pays too little. I do not think, from the little that I have heard at various times that the average through the North runs higher than 6 or 8 tael cents per *mou per annum*. I know very little about this however and as there have been books and pamphlets published on the subject of the land tax it is easy enough to get more accurate information. A man who owns land in Honan however gave me the following figures. His land is worth from 6000 to 16,000 cash a *mou* according to its location and fertility. It produces to the *mou* from 7 to 13 *tou* of wheat at the 5th Moon harvest and late crops of equal value in the 8th or 9th Moons. His wheat sells in various years from 500 to 800 cash per *tou*, and the tael exchange is capable of variation from 1400 to 1800 cash. He pays on all of his land a fixed tax of $4\frac{1}{2}$ tael cents per *tou* in the 5th Moon and $4\frac{1}{2}$ tael cents in the autumn. The first tax is known as *fen yin* – division of silver – and the second as *fen mi* – division of grain. In some provinces the second tax is actually paid in kind into government granaries. This landowner estimates that he pays an average of one per cent on the value of his crops *per annum*, or of nearly one and a half per cent on the value of his land. You will see at once that the annual yield from land is worth more than the soil itself. This is not so much because land is cheap as because it is virtually priceless. A landowner never sells unless the hardest conditions drive him to it, so the estimated value put upon land is the price it will sell for under the most adverse conditions. A farmer in easy circumstances will not sell unless he gets two or three times this famine price, and the small holder, who depends upon a few

[1] Ministry of the Interior.

acres for his living will sell the members of his household before he will part with his fields.

In every village community there is a professional extractor of squeeze who is known as the *kuan ching chi*. He is appointed by the *hsien* magistrate, is supposed to have a salary and to act in the service of the country people as surveyor, notary public, and recorder of deeds. His chief occupation however is that of go-between. He is the middleman at land sales and at village markets, and contrives to get a percentage out of the selling of grain, horses, houses, and land. These fees are regarded as public tribute and stand in the light of taxes but do not find their way to the magistrate. In the ordinary measurement of land and fixing of boundaries in cases of dispute the *kuan ching chi* acts free of charge. Where a transfer of property is in question however, he measures the land, writes the deed and records it, helps the persons concerned to come to terms, and takes a percentage, often as high as ten per cent, from the seller. This, or part of it, does go to the district treasury. Once a year, in company with the local gentry, this official goes about the country side and gathers in his cumshaw, the poor giving nothing, the well-to-do giving according to their means. This of course is not a tax but a graceful attestation of value of the land measurer's public services. Apart from these exactions and whatever unjust squeezes the officials have the courage to impose from time to time upon those who can bear it, there are no taxes other than the land tax which are direct. Roads, bridges, dams, irrigation courses etc are cared for by public subscription or are put up by benevolent individuals or by officials for their own convenience or the public good. There are no fixed school taxes, road taxes, military taxes or anything of the sort. A certain amount of labour or animals and carts, may be required for military purposes in certain districts. For instance a man with a cart may be required in case of need to do hauling once a year over a journey not exceeding say 20 days. These matters are determined locally and such services, known as *chai-shin*, may not be requisitioned over periods of many years in some districts while in others they may be a continual burden. This of course is not a tax but a saving of the public revenues. I do not think it ever prevails in cities except in times of siege, when each citizen is supposed to carry so many stones onto the wall or perform some similar service. Here again the burden falls on the farmer.

This is about all that I have learned about taxes. If anything else comes up I shall add a note for your benefit. There is of course all the material in printed form anyone needs about the federal taxes of various products, of which the people at large are ignorant and blissfully unconscious. It might be suggested, if you were in a position to do so, that the police department's supervision of public services which are supported by subscription in each police district is an extravagance, because greater efficiency at less cost could be obtained if the whole system were under one central bureau and were supported by a very light property tax. In many parts of Peking the work is not carried out because settlements are thin and poor, while in other districts the cost of maintaining the system is small out of all proportion to the wealth of the community, and is probably much less than the funds actually subscribed – the profits in these cases going to the district supervisers.

Yours faithfully
Rodney Gilbert

851. From F. E. Taylor

Shanghai 5 April 1917

My dear Morrison,

I was very glad to get your letter of the second,[1] as I was beginning to fear that you found my ideas too unpractical. But I am quite in earnest about them. I have been preaching to the Chinese all along that a twelve and a half flat rate will be absolutely harmful, and urging them not to make any change until they are in a position to negotiate a *scientific* tariff. This is the position that they should place themselves in at the present crisis. I want you to consider an aspect of this matter that seems to me quite serious. To my mind the Chinese have two genuine grievances against foreigners: the import tariff and having missionaries shoved down their throats. The second is of course open to argument, but as I am convinced that the story of the synoptic gospels is a myth on a par with the fables about Attis, Adonis, Osiris and Buddha, etc., I think it rough on the Chinese that an extra superstition should be forced on the ignorant populace under the threat of hell-fire and against the will of the Government; especially as the presence of uneducated and tactless fanatics in the interior often causes serious embarrassment. But about the import tariff there can be no argument at all. China has seen Japan grow from a poverty-stricken and negligible country outside the pale of civilization into a world power: her progress being due to the creation, in spite of the lack of natural resources, of huge industrial enterprises fostered by Government and assisted and protected by a scientific tariff. The fact that Japanese cotton magnates are now protesting against any increase in the import duties is proof that they know they could not compete with a Chinese cotton industry without the help of the absurd Chinese fiscal system. In other words, the objections to a revised import tariff are based on the desire to keep China from producing goods for herself: which means keeping her back and preventing her from attaining to wealth and power and freedom. (Incidentally, I ought to say that I am a convinced free-trader in theory: but perfect as the theory is I see that unless it is universally applied, it would seem to need adaptation to surroundings.)

Now one of the objects for which the Allies profess to be fighting is said to

[1] Not found.

be the protection and liberty of weak nations. Apparently this does not reach as far as China! Suppose the Chinese ask to be allowed to adopt the Japanese tariff in order that they too may make industrial progress, offering at the same time the reforms that I set out in my letter of the 10th March. The Powers would certainly refuse: but what reasons could they give for the refusal that would not be a refutation of what they profess and expose the contemptible cant with which we try to obscure our true object. We English are fighting for England and for England's interests and safety, and for nothing else as a fundamental cause of war: and quite good enough too. But we don't want it advertised that self-interest is at the bottom of our efforts and sacrifices, as it looks much better to say that we are fighting to save Belgium, etc: If in the interests of Manchester, etc, we deny the Chinese the right of building up their industries (a most short-sighted policy), they will be in a position to show us up to neutrals and place a useful weapon in the hands of the Germans. I admit that to allow the Chinese to draw up their own tariff would be fraught with impossibilities: they are too ignorant of political economy and the negotiations with the Powers would certainly prove so full of snags that the matter would probably be hung up for years. That is why I suggest the adoption of the Japanese tariff that has been already tested. We ought to look 50 years ahead in these matters, and consider what the effect on China would be if the suggestions in my last letter were all carried out. No doubt certain trades would suffer in competition with Chinese manufactures, but think of the enormous potential market presented by a China humming with industrial activity. Japan is an example. See how the imports into Japan have increased with the expansion of her industries. Help China to become wealthy and she will increase the wealth of the world.

I have been doing some useful work here. I have brought the British Chamber of Commerce into close touch with the Chinese Chamber of Commerce, and Committees are being appointed on both sides to discuss trade matters: more especially the question of increasing the exports.

[...]

Yours very truly
F. E. Taylor

852. To F. B. Alston

Peking 11 April 1917

My dear Alston,

On the 13th February I wrote to you to tell you of a visit paid to me that afternoon by Lu Tseng-tsiang. A similar visit had been paid on the same afternoon to Padoux, and a copy of his memorandum which agreed in the main with the statement made to me, I sent to you.[1]

[1] Not found.

When China presented her demands on March 14th[1] I was puzzled to reconcile the communication then made with the communication previously made by Lu. I could not understand why the demands had been so excessively increased. I believe I have discovered the reason, and it is only another instance of the perfidy of the Japanese. It will be within your recollection that some time ago an agent of the Japanese Government came here on a 'secret' financial mission. His name was Kamezo Nishihara[2] (a Chosen *ronin*[3] and a confidant of Count Terauchi[4]). He came here in order to negotiate a loan of Yen 5,000,000 with the Bank of Communications, the security being certain mining rights in the Yangtsze Valley and certain rights in regard to the smelting of brass cash. Before the loan contract was actually signed the money was paid over to the Chinese Government. This money was paid over by the Yokohama Specie Bank, but it was not Yokohama Specie Bank money. As a matter of fact, it was Japanese Government funds, and the transaction was entered into without the knowledge of the Japanese Parliament. Unquestionably this money has been the lever used to obtain all those advantages of which we have read so much in regard to advantageous (advantageous to the Japanese) contracts for railway material, etc., agreed to by the corrupt Minister of Communications.[5]

Nishihara was provided with credentials by Viscount Motono, and as the agent of the Japanese Government he led the Chinese to believe that the Japanese Government were prepared to support China in those demands which were submitted to the Allied Powers on the 14th March and the

[1] On 9 February China protested to Germany against the blockade of Chinese ports by German submarines. This protest was rejected by the German Government ten days later, on 19 February. Accordingly on 14 March the Chinese Government severed diplomatic relations with Germany and recalled her Ambassador Yen Hui-ch'ing (better known as W. W. Yen) (1877–1950).

[2] Nishihara Kamezō (?1872–1954), Japanese financial broker and adventurer, formerly a priest of the West Honganji Sect of the reformed Buddhist Church of Japan. He was with Terauchi when the latter was Governor-General in Korea, and when Terauchi succeeded Ōkuma as Prime Minister in October 1916, he became Terauchi's Special Emissary to China, negotiating with the Tuan Ch'i-jui Government, independently of the Japanese Minister in Peking, loans through the Government-controlled Banks of Chōsen, of Taiwan, and the Industrial Bank of Japan, in exchange for extensive industrial concessions. Nishihara's version of his activities during those years is given in his memoirs, *Yume no shichijū yo nen* (seventy-odd years of dreaming) (Kyoto 1949).

[3] From the original meaning of '*samurai* without a master', *rōnin* came to mean, in the context of Japanese aggression in China, a ruffian-adventurer.

[4] Terauchi Masatake (1852–1919), Japanese soldier and politician. A returned student from France, he became Minister of the Army in the first Katsura Cabinet in 1902, a post he held for the next ten years until his appointment as Governor-General in Korea and was responsible for completing the annexation of the country. In October 1916 he was appointed Prime Minister. His policy of economic penetration of China by means of large loans to the Anfu Government in exchange for extensive industrial and political concessions contributed to the downfall of the Anfu Clique which he sought to support.

[5] Hsü Shih-ying.

acceptance of which by the Powers was incorrectly and misleadingly stated to Parliament by Tuan Chi-jui. Unquestionably this *demarche* was made with the knowledge of Hayashi, who has now a quarrel with Motono and is exchanging acrimonious telegrams with him because Nishihara has been used for another secret mission, this time without Hayashi's knowledge. Nishihara came for the second time in order to negotiate a loan of 20,000,000 yen, the security being the Chinese Land Tax.[1]

A few days ago Motono in Tokyo declared to a friend of mine that Japan would not consent to any increase in the customs duties above an effective five per cent. Even in regard to this he has given no promise to the Japanese merchants of Osaka and Nagoya who are so energetically in the cotton duties, both Nakashoji,[2] Minister of Communications, and Shoda,[3] Minister of Finance, have publicly declared that they would uphold the interests of Japanese commerce, which means that they will oppose even an increase in the customs to an effective five per cent.

Thus the Chinese have once more been fooled by the Japanese just as before they were fooled by the Japanese into believing that Japan would give her support to the monarchical movement in China. It serves China right for dealing with these secret emissaries whose missions can be repudiated by their government and not dealing through the proper responsible diplomatic authorities.

I am, dear Sir

Yours sincerely
[G. E. Morrison]

[1] The only loan of 20,000,000 yen at this time was one for which an Agreement was concluded by a syndicate representing three Japanese banks, the Industrial Bank of Japan, the Bank of Chōsen and the Bank of Taiwan, in association with the so-called Exchange Bank of China (which was in fact also a Japanese Bank) on the one side, and the Chinese Government represented by Ts'ao Ju-lin, concurrently Minister of Communications and of Finance, on the other, on 30 April 1918, ostensibly for the improvement of Chinese telegraph lines using as a security installations and property of the Telegraph Administration.

[2] Nakashōji Ren (1866-1924), Japanese politician. A returned student from England he had been Vice-Minister of Communications in the first Saionji Cabinet (1906). At this time he was Minister of Agriculture and Commerce (October 1916 - September 1918) in the Terauchi Cabinet, a post he had held earlier (December 1913 - February 1914) in the third Katsura Cabinet. He was never Minister of Communications, the post being occupied at this time by Den Kenjiro (1855-1930).

[3] Shōda Kazue (1869-1948), Japanese politician, Minister of Finance in the Katsura Cabinet. Joining the Ministry of Finance in 1895 he became Vice-Minister of Finance in the first Yamamoto Cabinet in 1912, and later President of the Bank of Chōsen. In October 1916 he again became Vice-Minister of Finance and two months later Minister in the Terauchi Cabinet, holding the same portfolio again in 1924 in the Cabinet of Kiura Keigo (1850-1942). A supporter of the military clique, he withdrew from the Seiyūkai in 1932. In 1939 he became a Counsellor to the Cabinet and contributed much to Japan's war effort.

853. To F. B. Alston

Peking 11 April 1917

My dear Alston,

I may tell you in confidence that Willoughby who is leaving in May will be succeeded by Professor McElroy[1] and the duties of his office extended to education. Both men are well known to Woodrow Wilson. Much stress is laid by Americans on the advantage to America of educating Chinese along American lines. At present there are 1,350 Chinese students at American Colleges and Universities and the number is increasing at every term.

Should Dr. Reinsch[2] leave – and I think it is very probable that he will leave long before his term of office expires, he will, I feel sure be succeeded by one of the professorial class of the type of Willoughby or McElroy. As you will remember Wilson appointed John R. Mott of the Y.M.C.A. Minister to Peking in succession to W. J. Calhoun but after consideration Mott declined the appointment.

Nothing in this war is more hopeful than its effect in bringing together the British and the Americans. I do not know whether you or any of the legations have met Willoughby or McElroy. Both have been strong supporters of the allied cause. Willoughby's only son has been with an ambulance in France and after a brief visit to Peking has returned to the front. McElroy's lectures all down the coast of China have been an eloquent defence of the cause of the allies and must have had a considerable effect on public opinion.

Willoughby's brother[3] who was here before him and was a man of considerable distinction called on the legation but I fancy from his disappointment that no one then thought it worth while to show him any attention. He has now got a high position in Washington and has been offered but has declined the post of taking over and reorganising the newly acquired Danish West Indies.

Tsai Ting-kan has returned,[4] it seems to me with views modified by contact with the officials encountered on his journey not one of whom was in favour of China's entering the war. He found every where fear of what revenge Germany might take in the future – fear of famine from the export

[1] Robert McElroy (1872–1959), American historian, who studied at Leipzig, Berlin and Oxford after graduating from Princeton, where he taught American History from 1901. He was appointed in 1925 Professor of American History at Oxford (1925–38), and was the first American Exchange Professor to China (1916–17).
[2] Reinsch did not leave China until 1919 when he was succeeded by Charles Crane (q.v.).
[3] Westel Woodbury Willoughby (1867–1945), American political scientist, a graduate of Johns Hopkins University where he was Professor of Political Science from 1897 to 1933. He succeeded his brother here referred to, W. F. Willoughby, as Constitutional Adviser to China (1916–17) and was Technical Adviser to the Chinese Delegation at the Washington Conference (1921–2) and at the Geneva Conference (1924–5).
[4] Ts'ai T'ing-kan had just returned from a visit to Chungking in Szechwan.

of food stuffs – indignation at the Lao-hsi-kai outrage,[1] the French still retaining possession of the land forcibly seized from China – and heard the opinion expressed that 'aggression' on the part of England in Tibet, of Russia in Mongolia and of Japan in Manchuria has a definite policy in pursuance of an agreement previously come to between the three powers.

No doubt misrepresentation for which I believe the Japanese are the chief offenders, misrepresentation regarding demands respecting Tibet which are wholly fictitious are to blame for the attitude of many.

Dr Reinsch is still hesitating to muzzle Gilbert Reid,[2] yet this crank is most active in furthering the cause of Germany.

[...]

Did I ever tell you that in speaking to Rockhill, Conty laid down the axiom that a Minister (presumably to China) ought never to be *persona grata*!

Very sincerely yours
[G. E. Morrison]

[...]

854. To F. E. Taylor

Peking 17 April 1917

My dear Taylor,

Many thanks for your letter of the 5th April. [...]

Japan has played false with China again. It was Japan who induced China to make her proposals of the 14th March, leading China to believe that these proposals would be acceptable to the Allied Powers. It is Japan herself who is most strongly opposed to the most important of these proposals, viz., the increase of the tariff to an effective five per cent. Have you read the *Asahi* articles dealing with this? China will not be allowed tariff autonomy in our time. That is sure. It is not within practical politics.

[...]

---

[1] On 17 October 1916 the French Consul-General in Tientsin, following instructions from the acting French Minister in Peking, served an ultimatum on the Governor of Chihli Province demanding the cession of the district in Tientsin, known as Lao-hsi-k'ai, adjoining the French concession. On the same day the French forcibly seized the district, taking into custody nine Chinese policemen who were not released until 19 November. There was a great outcry, particularly in Tientsin, and the Chinese employees in the French concession struck in protest. The strain on Sino-French relations was to last for many months.

[2] Gilbert Reid (1857–1927), American missionary, who first went to China in 1882, working in Shantung Province for ten years. With a view to converting the more privileged class of Chinese he founded in 1894 the International Institute of China and became its Director. He was proprietor and editor of the *Peking Post*. Contrary to the general opinion among the Allied nationals he was strongly opposed to China's entering the European War, and was condemned by Morrison as a traitor to the Allied cause. He expounded his views in his book *China, Captive or Free? A Study of China's Entanglements* (London 1922).

This is for your own private ear. Tsai Ting-kan told me the other day that prominent Chinese had frequently urged him to have a Japanese appointed as D.I.G.[1] They are considering now whether the balance-sheet of the Customs should be published or not. The Chinese think that the British Government is opposed to its publication, whereas I believe the contrary is the case.

[...]

Yours very sincerely
[G. E. Morrison]

855. From F. E. Taylor

Shanghai 21 April 1917

Private

My dear Morrison,

I am much obliged to you for your kind letter of the 17th [...]

You have, I think, rather missed my point about China being allowed tariff autonomy. If she claims it on the basis of our professed war aims and we refuse, while the Americans perhaps jump at the chance of currying favour, we shall miss making on China the good impression we made in Japan where we were the first to grant it (and, incidentally to agree to the abolition of extraterritoriality), and we shall stultify ourselves and raise doubts in the minds of the Chinese regarding the genuineness of our friendship. Don't you think the Chinese may see the debate[2] about Manchester wanting to oppress the cotton industry in India, and being turned down by our Government? If the duties are raised in China it will not hit Manchester's trade, because Japan is taking care to monopolise all the class of trade that would be affected. It would be the Japanese cotton industries that would suffer from the competition of the Chinese mills. And a good job too. Better a rich and progressive China, with no designs on her neighbours, than an aggressive Japan enabled to make war with the wealth she has acquired by filching the trade of her ally and keeping back the industries of her great but sluggish neighbour.

[...]

Yours very sincerely
F. E. Taylor

[1] Deputy Inspector-General. In the event no Japanese was appointed to the post.
[2] In a debate in the House of Commons on 14 March 1917 on the offer by the Indian Government of a contribution towards the cost of the War of a sum of one hundred million pounds, which was 'gratefully accepted' by the British Government, several speakers, in discussing the extra taxation to be imposed in India as a result, stressed the need for protection of the Manchester cotton industry against competition from India. *Hansard* 1917, Vol. XCI, cols. 1137-1241.

856. To J. Robertson Scott

[Peking] 30 April 1917

My dear Robertson Scott,
I owe you an apology for delaying so long to answer your various letters. [...]

It was somewhat disconcerting to me to learn that I was a *bête noire* in Tokyo, and I appreciate your kindly wish to bring me in touch with officials by means of this junior official on the Railways, who is a promising young fellow.[1]

In my daily intercourse with Japanese officials in Peking – I suppose I know every prominent Japanese in Peking – and rarely a day passes without my having a talk with them, no indication has been given of my being a *bête noire*. On the contrary they always treat me with unusual consideration and apparent friendliness, recognising the services I have rendered to their country during so many years, which services gained me the honour of the offer of a high Japanese decoration and the honour of a private audience with the Emperor.[2]

A few days ago I received a letter from a clergyman in Sydney[3] telling me that there is a growing spirit of distrust in regard to Japan in Australia, and that a committee has been appointed of the congregational denomination for the purpose of encouraging fraternal feelings with the people of Japan. I have written to the clergyman telling him that the movement has my sympathy, and if you will allow me I will recommend him to get into touch with you. The Church has a considerable membership and a growing influence in one of the Sydney suburbs, and it may have some influence in removing the distrust which has become so widespread, especially in Australia and in Canada.

[1] Kanai Kiyoshi (b. 1884), Japanese official. A graduate of Tokyo Imperial University, his career was largely connected with railway administration in both Japan and China. He served on the South Manchurian Railway as chief construction officer at Harbin, and was railway superintendent of the inter-allied control of the Russian Siberian Railway in 1919. In 1921 he was a technical adviser with the Japanese delegation to the Washington Conference, and also attended the Economic and Financial Conference in Geneva the following year. In 1932 he represented the South Manchurian Railway on the investigating commission under Lord Victor Alexander George Robert Lytton (1876–1947) who was sent by the League of Nations to Manchuria following Japanese aggression in Manchuria in what is known as the 'September 18 Incident' the previous year. Kanai had been introduced to Morrison by Robertson Scott who apologised for doing so and added, 'but you are such a *bete noire* that I feel that it is a good thing to let official Japanese come in touch with you'. Morrison, in his Diary entry for 29 April 1917, recorded his indignation at being introduced to a person he regarded as so insignificant.

[2] In his letter of 16 December 1907, Hayashi Gonsuke, the then Japanese Minister in Peking sounded out Morrison with a view to offering Morrison the Third Class Order of the Rising Sun, which Morrison declined. *See* Letter No. 275, Morrison to Hayashi Gonsuke, *Correspondence*, Vol. 1, p. 433. It was on 26 May 1909 that Morrison in the company of Chirol was received in audience by the Japanese Emperor.

[3] The letter, dated 13 February 1917, from the Rev. Parkin, is not printed.

This distrust is attributed to Japan's attitude towards the Allies since the war began, Japan being held to have done nought in any way commensurate with her duty to her Allies, no ship of hers having been called upon to exchange a hostile shot with any German ship, and her mercantile fleet having enjoyed an immunity from submarine attack, which is at least remarkable, not to say suspicious. The object of the Committee in Sydney is to remove the impression created by Japan's action in preventing for example China from joining the war and in her failure to put into operation any adequate Enemy Trading Act (Such an Act has been promulgated last week.).

I wonder if in your Magazine[1] you will deal with the question of Nishihara and his secret mission to Peking? which again seems to have had the effect of increasing the distrust. And are you going to deal with the Japanese morphia trade in China, the traffic in Japanese women, the contraband trade in salt, and such like things, all of which will require to be explained away before the distrust can be removed.

I am meeting Baron Hayashi twice this week at dinners given by my Japanese friends, and I will have a chat with him about your magazine.

China will probably come into the war this week under the aegis of America. She will look to America for support at the Peace Conference.

With regard to the names of Chinese officials, I must say I cannot agree with you that there is much confusion regarding them in Japan. I read three of the foreign daily papers published in Japan, and I have been struck with the accuracy with which they discuss the activities of Chinese officials. In Japan itself when talking to Japanese officials I have been impressed with the knowledge they displayed of Chinese officials. I fancy that as you have, owing to your other work, not been able to give so much attention to the China side of politics you are apt to fear that others have given equal inattention to this serious subject.

In Peking you seemed rather to give the impression intentionally that you had not devoted any time to the consideration of the Chinese case, and you seemed to be unfamiliar with the names of the high Chinese officials who are referred to almost daily and quite accurately in the foreign papers published in Japan. Several of us were somewhat impressed by this, and for that reason we wonder what attitude you are going to adopt towards political questions between China and Japan.

As soon as your Magazine is published I will send a copy to Australia.
With best wishes
Believe me   Very sincerely yours
                                                                                                          [G. E. Morrison]

[1] The *New East*.

857. From Chang Min-chih

Peking 5 May 1917

Confidential

Dear Dr. Morrison.

[...] at the end of last March, an unknown Japs. gentleman, Mr. Yoshida, who claims himself to be the confidant of a new financial group organized by Baron Shibusawa,[1] Mr. Okura[2] and others at Tokio for the development of Chinese resources called on me together with a Chinese friend of mine and discussed with me about the existing friendship between the Tuan Chi-jui and the Terauchi Cabinets and the absolute necessity of co-operating between China and Japan for checking further aggrandizement of the Westerners in Eastern Asia. This Japs. friend then informed me about the great development of news agency in Japan resulting in the purchase of the rights of the Reuters Company in that Country and that he would be exceedingly glad to render me whatever assistance I then desire. I told him about the satisfactory condition of the 'National News Agency' so that I am not in want of assistance from friends. Mr. Yoshida finally talked with me about the popularity of evening and afternoon papers in the U.S.A. and we hit upon the scheme of starting an afternoon *Anglo-Chinese Times* in Peking more for commercial and economical than for political purposes as nearly all existing Chinese journals devote their entire energy and vigilance to political questions and parties and also there is no afternoon paper in China at present. [...] This Japs. gentleman entirely endorsed this plan and said that he would advise his

[1] Shibusawa Eiichi (1840–1931), Japanese banker and industrialist. It has been said that to write his life story would be to write the history of Japanese industry and banking of the Meiji and Taishō eras, since he was a founder of what later became the Daiichi Bank, the Yokohama Specie Bank, the Bank of Japan, Nippon Yūsen Kaisha, and Tokyo Railway Company, as well as having major interests in insurance, mining, steel manufacturing, ship building, printing, textile manufacturing, gas and electrical industries, paper making, petroleum, fisheries, hotels and numerous other enterprises. His money was behind the Japanese invasion of the neighbouring countries of Korea and China. In 1878 his Daiichi Bank opened a branch in Pusan which in time developed into a kind of central bank of Korea and its bank-notes became the legal tender of the country. In 1909 he helped to establish the Bank of Chōsen, later a creditor of the Peking Government. In 1903 he built the railway from Pusan to Seoul which proved a timely service for the Japanese Army during the Russo-Japanese War. In the previous year (1902) Shibusawa founded the Steam Company of Hunan, which became the Sino-Japanese Steamer Company five years later, dominating Chinese river and coastal navigation. Then in 1909 he founded the East Asia Industrial Development Company, and he was one of the forces in 1914 behind the establishment of the Sino-Japanese Industrial Development Company, an enterprise in which Sun Yat-sen, as titular head, became a willing tool of Japanese capitalism. This company was later taken over by the Peking Government, Sun being replaced by Yang Shih-ch'i and later by the notorious pro-Japanese official Lu Ts'ung-yü (q.v.). Together with its sister organisation, the so-called Exchange Bank of China of which Lu Ts'ung-yü was also titular head, it played an important part in Japan's economic and industrial invasion of China.   [2] Ōkura Kihachirō.

employers to subscribe, to the amount of five thousand dollars or one set of printing machinery (for printing papers only) as capital. The management of the proposed paper will be entirely in my hands so as to enable me to devote my full attention and energy for its success; but to publish Japs. commercial news in Chinese in both my news agency reports and the said paper as it may be sent to me from time to time from various Japs. firms. There will be no interest on the capital during the continuance of the European War but there will be six per cent interest after the restoration of general peace, or the price of the machinery be then paid by yearly instalments against guarrantee. The above are the rough outlines of our draft agreement, details of which are to be mutually arranged at Shanghai.

As you know, personally, I hate the Japs. and I have not the least intention of co-operation with any of them. The change from a military to a non-militaristic policy by the Terauchi Cabinet towards this Country is equally not a good omen for China, I firmly believe and a Japs. economical conquest of China means the domination of my fatherland and loss of her national independence. I shall be a national traitor to my Country if I assist the Japs. brutes to achieve their plots. The Japs. papers and news agencies established in this Country are not trusted by the majority of the Chinese people though they publish nonsense everyday so that they wish to utilize my journalistic services among the Chinese.

The British supremacy in commerce in this Country should be maintained not only to the advantage of Great Britain, but also to China and Peking is the seat of the Chinese Government, if you think Mr. E. Little[1] of the British Chamber of Commerce or any other prominent British residents at Shanghai would like to contribute one set of printing machinery as capital and I will supply the working expenses, I will call on them this time and discuss with them about the starting of the proposed bi-lingual newspaper. I have only written to Mr. S. Barton[2] briefly about this and nobody else.

Yours sincerely
Michie C. L. Chang

[...]

858. To F. E. Taylor

[Peking] 9 May 1917

My dear Taylor,

Many thanks for yours of the 4th[3] and the information therein contained. The tariff question in China is now largely dependent upon Japan. Britain,

---

[1] Edward S. Little, British businessman in Shanghai and a member of the Municipal Council of the International Settlement there. A friend of T'ang Shao-yi, he played host to T'ang during the peace negotiations held in Shanghai after the Wuchang Uprising in 1911. As a champion of Chinese residents' rights he unsuccessfully proposed at a meeting of the Municipal Council in 1920 that Chinese rate-payers be represented on that body.

[2] Sidney Barton.   [3] Not printed.

France and Russia are prepared to grant to China the increase in her tariff that she is asking for, but they make it a condition that this shall come into operation after China has entered upon the war and of course they will require that all the other Powers shall agree to the increase.

Japan has played China false once more. At the time of the monarchical movement secret negotiations were made by the Japanese Government in which they promised Yuan Shih-kai that they would support his ambition to become Emperor. When the time came these promises, which Yuan Shih-kai was very foolish ever to have listened to, were repudiated by the Japanese.

I do not know whether you have heard what has happened in this second case. China sent a Note to America and to Germany on February 9th.[1] A few days later she sounded the Allied Ministers as to their willingness to agree to the raising of the tariff of an effective five per cent. Baron Hayashi had gone to Japan. Yoshizawa was in charge. On February 14th there arrived in Peking a secret envoy from Terauchi named Kamezo Nishihara. Nishihara got the Chinese to believe that very much more ample terms than China had asked for would be agreed to by Japan, who would use her influence with her Allies to obtain their assent also. Deceived by these promises Tuan Chi-jui on March 8th announced in Parliament that the Powers had agreed in the event of China joining the war to the increase of the Customs tariff, the postponement of the payment of the Boxer Indemnity for ten years, the withdrawal of the guards from Peking and from the railway.

This communication made on March 8th was the first news received by the Allied Ministers of what the Premier alleged were the promises given by Allied Ministers. These oral promises having been given and the Chinese having been foolish enough to accept them, Tuan Chi-jui found himself in the position of having deceived Parliament unintentionally, for Japan has repudiated the promises given by Nishihara and not only is Japan opposing the increase of the customs duties beyond five per cent, but there is very strong pressure being used to induce the Japanese Government to refuse the increase even to the effective five per cent. That is where we are at present. Parliament has been misled, and Parliament resents it.

Japanese intrigue against China's coming into the war has been temporarily effective, and she is now doing what she can to induce continued resistance on the part of the southern people. At the same time the Germans are spending money freely in Parliamentary quarters.

I take it that England cannot consent to the tariff increase unless the other Powers consent. As you say, she gained credit in Japan by being the first to grant to Japan tariff autonomy, but I believe I am right in saying that until all the Powers came to the same view tariff autonomy was not exercised.

It is difficult to know if we gain anything by trying to curry favour with the

[1] This refers to China's protest to Germany over the blockade of Chinese ports by German submarines.

Chinese. Look at what we have done for the University in Peking. Through the British Legation machinery to the value of £15,000 has at the urgent entreaty of the University been supplied gratis by British manufacturers. Before this machinery can reach Peking the University is abolishing the department of engineering. At the request of the University authorities picked British teachers were obtained. There was every indication that these appointments would be permanent. Now as you know these contracts have been terminated, in one case two years before the end of the three years of the engagement.

The same is happening in the Telegraphs, where the foreign staff after many years service are being offered increases of 25 taels per month on re-engagement. All this is disheartening.

[...]

Very sincerely yours
[G. E. Morrison]

859. To O. M. Green

[Peking] 17 May 1917

My dear Green,

Thanks for your letter of the 7th. My wife and I both thank you very much for your kind congratulations.[1]

Gilbert[2] came in yesterday evening to tell me that he had got a telegram from you. I presume that he succeeded in getting the photographs, otherwise he would have communicated with me. The difficulty in getting photographs of the Ministers is now considerable, because three-fourths of them have resigned.[3]

The position is one of considerable difficulty. The crux of the difficulty is the antagonism between the President and the Premier, and the determination of the Kuomintang not to have Tuan Chi-jui as Premier. The President is still under some German influence. Curiously enough, Miss Carl[4] has

---

[1] Not printed. The congratulations were for the birth of Morrison's third child, Colin George Mervyn, on Saturday 21 April 1917. Morrison noted in his Diary: 'Glad for the day selected. Same day Saturday 21 April 1883 completed my walk across Australia.'

[2] Rodney Gilbert.

[3] There were frequent ministerial changes in Tuan Ch'i-jui's Cabinet immediately preceding his dismissal which occurred about a month after this letter was written. Eight out of the nine ministries in the cabinet were held by the Vice-Ministers in an acting capacity, or else by other Ministers concurrently, including those of Foreign Affairs, Interior, Finance, Justice, Education, Agriculture and Commerce, Communications, and Navy. The only exception was that of the Army, which was held concurrently by Tuan himself.

[4] Katherine Augusta Carl (d.1938), American portrait painter, daughter of Francis Augustus Carl (1861–1930), an American employee of the Chinese Maritime Customs who first joined in 1881, serving as Commissioner at various ports until 1921. He was

considerable influence and she is the most loquacious of the enemies of the Allies. Her father was a German refugee. She says he was a general. He may have been a lieutenant, who fled to America in 1848.

All of us were astonished at David Fraser's letter defending the Dutch Consul-general[1] and still more at his letter in support of the Opium Combine. In connection with the former case, the opinion of the five advisers consulted by the Kuo Wu Yuan was unanimously in favour of refusing the claim of the Dutch to exercise jurisdiction over German subjects.[2] The concession was granted without adequate thought by C. C. Wu, who was acting for his father at the time, and I may tell you that it was because of his action, his unpatriotic action as it was claimed by the Government, that he was not appointed Vice-Minister.[3] He is considerably under the influence of Dr. Reinsch, who, I understand, favoured the view that jurisdiction should be entrusted to the Dutch. He took a most liberal view of the conditions brought about by China's suspension of diplomatic relations.

Dr. Reinsch has also had considerable difficulty in making up his mind whether China would be wise to take the third step or not. Influences like these help to make the Chinese vacillate. Never have I known any Legation in Peking exercise quite the same influence with the Chinese that the American Legation is able to exercise. Both Reinsch and Tenney[4] have exceptional influence, and I think justly so. They are both able men, both animated with a sincere desire to assist China while of course not neglecting the interests of their own country.

[...]

Evidence is accumulating against Chen Chin-tao. Even in the case of the Opium deal he does not come out with clean hands. It was he who, on the recommendation of C. C. Wu, appointed the son of Sassoon's opium hulk compradore, to be the Special Envoy of the prohibition of the opium sales in

---

actually born in America. Miss Carl had painted portraits of the Empress-Dowager Tz'u-hsi, P'u-yi, and Li Yüan-hung among others.

[1] J. H. de Reus, Dutch Consul-General in Shanghai. He was involved in April 1917 in a case in which an ex-German marine was apprehended in connection with some lawbreaking and turned over to him as the protector of German interests in Shanghai. He instead turned the prisoner over to the Germans still living in Shanghai and the prisoner was acquitted. This caused an outcry among the Allied nationals there.

[2] Contrary to the advice tendered by Morrison and his colleagues to the Kuo-wu yüan, or Cabinet Office, the Dutch Legation was allowed to look after German interests in China after China severed diplomatic relations with Germany.

[3] Wu Ch'ao-shu, the son of Wu T'ing-fang, then Foreign Minister, was at the time a Counsellor in the Ministry of Foreign Affairs (1915–17). Soon afterwards he followed his father and resigned to join Sun Yat-sen's government in Canton in July 1917.

[4] Charles Daniel Tenney (1857–1930), American missionary and diplomat. He abandoned his missionary work in 1886 to found the Anglo-Chinese School in Tientsin and became its first Principal (1886–1895). While in Tientsin he became acquainted with Li Hung-chang and was a tutor to his sons. In 1895 he became President of the Imperial Chinese University in Tientsin, a post he held until 1906. He then joined the American

the three provinces.¹ All the Foreign Advisers are unanimously of the opinion that the contract is invalid. In view of the effort made towards recognising the opposition of Parliament it is preposterous to think that a Cabinet can commit China to the payment of 21,000,000 taels for opium without any reference to Parliament. Had the Combine not forced the price of opium to such an exaltant height the opium would have been sold a long time ago. I wonder if you have seen the Opium Agreement.

Best wishes to you

Very sincerely yours
[G. E. Morrison]

860. From Chang Min-chih

Peking 3 June 1917

Dear Dr. Morrison,

Owing to the sudden rising of the *Tuchuns* and the route was impassable beyond Hsuchow, I went as far as Tientsin and then returned here. I will leave for Shanghai when matters are settled down in North China. I have much pleasure in sending you some private information concerning the situation. Chang Hsun will not come now because the Provinces do not want mediation.

President Li's position is tottering and a petition will be presented to him by the Peking Military men requesting him to resign his seat.²

With best wishes

Yrs sincerely
Michie Chang

Enclosure to Letter No. 860: *Plots and Counter-plots, 3 June 1917*

Confidential

Liang Chi-chao, Tang Hua-lung and some other moderates have presented suggestions to those *Tuchuns* who have severed their political connexions with Peking as follows:

---

diplomatic service and was Chinese Secretary at the United States Legation in Peking from 1908 until his retirement in 1921, during which time he served also as Consul in Nanking (1912–14).

[1] Wang Chih-jui. As Special Envoy for the Prohibition of the Sale of Opium in Kiangsu, Kiangsi and Kwangtung, he was one of the three Chinese signatories to the agreement for the purchase by the Chinese Government of the residue of the stock of Indian opium remaining in the hands of the Shanghai Opium Combine, signed on 28 January 1917, with Supplementary Agreements signed on 29 January 1917 and 11 June 1918.

[2] Following the dismissal by Li Yüan-hung of the Prime Minister Tuan Ch'i-jui on 23 May 1917, the thirteen northern provinces under the militarists sent a joint telegram to Li on 1 June demanding his resignation, and established a General Headquarters in Tientsin the following day with Lei Chen-ch'un (q.v.) as Chief of Staff in charge. As a result Li was compelled to resort to the mediation of Chang Hsün, and to accede to Chang's demand for the dissolution of Parliament ten days after this letter was written.

1. This internal strife should be called 'constitutional revolution' without using the word 'independent'.
2. If this strife is to be called a revolution then it is better for the Provinces to not recognize the existing Provisional Constitution on the ground that if they recognize the existing Provisional Constitution, then they are themselves to be called rebels.
3. If the existing Provisional Constitution is discarded, then through revolution, the President, the Vice-President, the Parliament and all their subordinate offices become invalid legally and they are to be entirely reconstructed as in 1911 at Nanking.
4. Each Province is to elect four or five members to form a National Convention in Peking just the same as the Tsan-yi Yuan[1] in Nanking had done in 1911 to draw up a Provisional Constitution for the Republic of China.
5. The existing Chief Executive should resign his seat and he shall be treated nearly the same as the ex-Taching Emperor.
6. If the Provinces think their present action in opposing the Peking Government for its illegal and unconstitutional act in issuing the Mandates on the twenty-third May, 1917 depriving Marshal Tuan Chi-jui from his dual-post of Premier and Minister of War is right and lawful, then the fundamental law (provisional constitution) will lose its effectiveness and becomes invalid legally otherwise the *Tuchuns* and their supporters are rebels who must be suppressed by force of arms.
7. The headquarters of the Provinces are to be established in Tientsin under the leadership of ex-Premier Hsu Shih-chang with General Nei Cheng-chun,[2] late Chief of the Peking Martial Court, as military chief of staff.

The measures adopted by Peking are to excite Kuangtung, Kuanghsi, Yunnan, Hunan and those Generals who do not favour this revolution to oppose the independent Provinces by circulating the rumour that the northern army is plotting the restoration of the ex-Manchu Emperor. This is untrue because this will do more harm to the Manchus than good, and Chang Hsun absolutely denies it.

[1] The Senate.
[2] Lei Chen-ch'un, Chinese soldier, Military Commander of North Kiangsu under the Manchu Government. In December 1910 he was cashiered for bribing Tsai-hsün, the younger brother of the Prince Regent and at the time Minister of the Navy. However, with the outbreak of the Revolution and the return of Yüan Shih-k'ai to power he came once more into favour and was made Chang Hsün's deputy as a commander of the army forces of the Yangtze District. A staunch monarchist, he supported Yüan's Imperial scheme, becoming in 1915 Director of the Martial Court in Peking. A fellow provincial of Tuan Ch'i-jui, he was prominent among the northern military leaders in attacking President Li Yüan-hung for his dismissal of Tuan as Prime Minister on 23 May 1917, and he became the Chief of Staff and actual head of the Military Headquarters set up in Tientsin by the northern militarists. He was one of the leading supporters of the Imperial Restoration which Chang Hsün brought about four weeks after this letter was written, on 1 July 1917, becoming Minister of War in the short-lived government. He was taken prisoner by the forces that overthrew the Restoration Government but was later pardoned

861. From L. H. Drakeford[1]

Newchwang [Fengtien] 14 June 1917

Dear Doctor,

The most interesting local news since last I saw you is of course the revolt of the local *Tuchun*.[2] The first we heard of the matter was on 30th ult., when the local *Taoyin*, Yung hao,[3] invited my colleague Mr Ma[4] to a meeting of the principal officials, at which the news of the independence of Fengtien was given out.[5]

Besides control of the funds in the Bank of China and the Bank of Communication, including the salt revenue, the *Taoyin* asked that we should agree not to make any transfers to the Group Banks for the time being, explaining that the *Tuchun* had no idea of using the salt revenue for any other purpose, but was anxious that it should not reach Peking. The demands of the seceding

[1] L. H. Drakeford (?b. 1876), Australian employee in the Chinese Salt Administration, at this time District Inspector of the Salt Revenue of Fengtien Province at Newchwang, and later of Shansi Province at Ta-t'ung. Morrison first met Drakeford in 1914. Before entering the Chinese service he was Editor of *Social Shanghai*.

[2] Chang Tso-lin (1873–1928), Chinese soldier, whose fortunes started with the Russo-Japanese War when he with his private band of armed men rendered the Japanese forces assistance by harassing the Russian troops. His troops were then reorganised into the regular government forces. After the outbreak of the 1911 Revolution it was he who, together with Feng Te-lin (1866–1925), assisted Chao Erh-hsün, the Viceroy of Manchuria, in suppressing the revolutionaries there. His power expanded so rapidly and greatly that by the time of Yüan Shih-k'ai's monarchical attempt he was in a position to challenge Tuan Chih-kuei, Yüan's appointee as Civil and Military Governor of Fengtien Province, and had himself appointed in April 1916 in Tuan's stead. He was holding this post at the time of this letter. By a series of manoeuvres and because of the peculiar circumstances of Manchuria as a buffer between and target of the contending powers of Japan and Russia, Chang soon gained control not only of all the Manchurian provinces but, from this base, launched out over the Great Wall, and played an important role in subsequent Republican politics. He sided with the Chihli Clique in 1920 in toppling the Anfu Government and four years later, with the assistance of defectors from the Chihli camp drove his erstwhile allies from Peking, becoming as a result the arbiter of North China. In 1928, however, he was forced to withdraw into his base, Manchuria, but was killed by a mine laid by the Japanese Kwantung Army, which wrecked his train. The semi-independent state of Manchuria, which he had created and which his son Chang Hsüeh-liang inherited, fell in 1931 to the Japanese, whose rule there through the Puppet Government under P'u-yi, the last Manchu Emperor, was to last until 1945.

[3] Jung-hou, a Manchu, was at this time *Taoyin* (Regional Commissioner) of the southern region of Fengtien Province (June 1914 – September 1919). In May 1921 he was appointed Finance Administrator of Heilungkiang Province, but before long was transferred to the same position in Kirin Province (1921–4).

[4] Possibly Ma T'ing-liang, Foreign Affairs Commissioner for Fengtien Province from August 1915 until his removal in 1917.

[5] In support of protests by his fellow militarists against the dismissal of Tuan Ch'i-jui as Prime Minister on 23 May, Chang Tso-lin declared the independence of Fengtien Province five days later, on 28 May.

Tuchuns were said to be the reinstatement of Tuan Chi-jui and the dissolution of Parliament, which latter might be reassembled later on.

Mr Ma of course said that he could do nothing without first consulting me, which he did. We told the *Taoyin* that the salt collections could not be considered the property of the Government until released after due process by the Group Bankers, and that if he wanted us to do anything he had better send in an official letter.

We at once wrote the Chief Inspectors[1] *re* the matter, and next day got the *Taoyin*'s letter, giving the *Tuchun*'s instructions to negotiate with the foreigners concerned *re* control of the monies in their hands. There was a statement that the salt revenue would on no account be touched on 'for the time being'. We sent this on to the C.I.'s.

Before our first letter reached Peking the Chief Inspectors wired reminding us that we were responsible for the safety of the revenue, and ordering us to put it into the foreign (Group) banks. It was not clear whether or not they wanted us to stop lodging the revenue in the Bank of China, but we inferred there would be no objection to depositing it there, provided we could transfer it whenever we wanted to.

However, as there was a considerable sum available for transfer we instructed the Bank of China to make a transfer, and were told that they could not comply, on account of the *Tuchun*'s orders. On this we ordered the Bank to cease receiving revenue, and made arrangements with the Yokohama Specie Bank to act temporarily as receiving bank. At the urgent request of the Manager of the Bank of China we went with him to see the *Taoyin*, and explained what action we were taking. The *Taoyin* said that if we did as proposed there would probably be great trouble with the local military officers, who would not stand seeing hard cash slip out of their control. As we insisted, the *Taoyin* asked us at least to wait till he had time to report to the *Tuchun*, promising to urge him to cancel his instructions so far as they concerned the salt revenue. The *Taoyin* also pointed out the risk of danger to our outlying Collectorates and to monies in transit in case we crossed the military men. Eventually we agreed to suspend action till we had placed the situation before the Chief Inspectors – the *Taoyin* promising our wires would get through the censorship he had already established. We reported at length, and asked for a time limit to be fixed for the cancellation of the *Tuchun*'s order.

On 2nd we got a reply that if the *Tuchun* would cancel his order before the 4th, and guarantee safety of our collectorates and revenues in transit, things might go on as before, otherwise our proposal to appoint the Japanese Bank as Collecting Bank was to be adopted and enforced. On getting this news the *Taoyin* was very reluctant to communicate it to the *Tuchun*, but when we

---

[1] A reference to the Chief Inspector and Deputy Chief Inspector, at this time Richard Dane and W. R. Strickland respectively.

assured him that on Tuesday morning we should proceed to act as instructed he gave way, and on Monday night the *Tuchun*'s embargo was lifted. Since then we have made several transfers, and things are going on smoothly in the old way.

There was an attempt to get control of the Customs revenue, but as that goes direct into the Yokohama Specie Bank there was no trouble in rejecting it.

I'm sorry to see that the *Tuchuns* have got their way *re* dissolution of Parliament. President Li will lose in reputation by his action, and old Mr Wu Ting-fang will be the hero of the hour.[1]

Although Parliament had not been a very brilliant success it at least held the germs of future improvement. A new Parliament elected under the shadow of the *Tuchuns*' successful demands is not likely to be any more satisfactory than that just done away with – except, of course, to the militarists. Yet even they can hardly expect to get more out of the country than the late parliament gave them. If there were only an outstanding figure that could control the *Tuchuns* the situation would not seem so bad, but there seems to be no such personality available, and what the future of the country will be, with 18 or 20 or more *Tuchuns* to decide things, Heaven only knows.

I notice it is reported that you urged the President not to agree to dissolution, and that Dr Ariga took the opposite course. All the intelligent Chinese here agree with your view, and deplore the turn things have taken. I sincerely hope it does not lead to a fourth revolution, but from what one knows of the South there seems nothing else to expect. The one consolation is that things political in China seldom go the way they should do according to common-sense reasoning, so one is encouraged to hope for the best.

[...]

I am, Dear Doctor

Yours faithfully
L. H. Drakeford

862. To O. M. Green

[Peking] 19 June 1917

My dear Green,

Many thanks for your letter of the 12th[2] [...]

Your letter interested me, especially in what you said about Tuan Chi-jui.

---

[1] On 13 June 1917 President Li Yüan-hung, in the face of pressure from the militarists and in compliance with the request by Chang Hsün who made it a condition for his intervention as mediator, issued a decree dissolving Parliament. Wu T'ing-fang, the Foreign Minister who had been appointed Acting Prime Minister on 23 May upon the dismissal of Tuan Ch'i-jui, refused, however, to countersign the Presidential Decree. The President therefore dismissed him and appointed Chiang Chao-tsung (1863–1943), the Military Governor of Peking, as Acting Prime Minister in order to obtain his signature and give the Decree an appearance of legality. [2] Not printed.

The situation here is quite complex. We are working in vicious circles, to declare war upon Germany the assent of Parliament is necessary. Now that there is no Parliament there can be no declaration unless the military act unconstitutionally. They have already been informed by the American Minister that if they do so they can expect no financial assistance from America, nor presumably from their allies.
[...]

Very sincerely yours
[G. E. Morrison]

863. From O. M. Green

Shanghai 26 June 1917

Dear Morrison,
[...]
Has *Millard's Review*[1] reached you. Most attractive to look at and poisonous beyond words. I've been going for him baldheaded to-day. He's a loathsome creature. In the early days of the war he got the China Press blacklisted for his violent anti-Britainism. He's far more dangerous than Gilbert Reid because cleverer.
[...]
The Chinese press here has lately announced that the Navy has revolted against the *Tuchuns*. There's not a word of truth in it. The press in Shanghai is just now badly under the control of Sun Yat sen and his crowd. I haven't see Quo Tai-chi yet but will try to find time to get in touch with him.
[...]
With all good wishes

Yours sincerely
Owen M. Green

[1] In June 1917 T. F. F. Millard, the American journalist, launched the first issue of the review that bears his name. *Millard's Review*, with a subsidy from the Nanking Government, was to become one of the most influential English-language journals in China during the Republican period, serving as a tool of the Chinese as well as of the American interests which supported it, and was also the means by which Millard himself became an influential figure. The journal, later known as the *China Weekly Review*, remained in circulation, with a brief interruption, until July 1951.

July 1917 – November 1918

On 1 July 1917, the citizens of Peking awoke to find themselves once more the subjects of an Empire. So sudden indeed was the turn of events that many were caught by surprise, amongst them the President of the Republic and those in the tailoring trade. The latter, with the demand for instant dragon flags and court costumes, became overnight the most sought-after men. With the fiasco of Yüan Shih-k'ai's monarchical plan still freshly in mind, there were few who thought anyone would risk a similar attempt; yet this dramatic climax to the recent crisis was not altogether unexpected. The central figure in this drama was General Chang Hsün.

A soldier of fortune, Chang Hsün had risen to his exalted position from the ranks. Known for the fierceness of his troops as well as for his monarchist sympathies, he went so far as to insist that his soldiers retain their queues even after the founding of the Republic and so won for his army the nickname of 'pig-tail savages'. It was his army which in September 1913, during the capture of Nanking from the revolutionaries, was responsible for the massacre in which three Japanese lost their lives. Japan's protest at this incident resulted in his being removed from his post of Governor of Kiangsu. He repaired to Hsü-chou in the North of the province and from this strategic base exercised virtually autonomous power over a large border area of the three provinces of Kiangsu, Anhwei and Shantung. This geographical position on China's eastern seaboard, between the Northern plain and the Yangtse to the south, aptly reflected his position amongst the militarists. As one of the few remaining strongmen of the old school, he was something of an odd-man-out and did not belong to any of the cliques into which the supporters of Yüan Shih-k'ai were divided after their master's death. He was sought after as much as he was feared. His balancing role and monarchist sympathies soon made Hsüchou a meeting place of Northern militarists as well as a centre of the monarchist movement.

When the eight provinces declared their secession from the central government in Peking as a protest against the dismissal of Tuan Ch'i-jui at the end of May 1917, Chang Hsün, allegedly by agreement with these militarists, feigned a kind of neutrality. This stand immediately attracted the attention of President Li Yüan-hung, to whom Chang let it be known that he would, if so requested, come to Peking to mediate. Desperate because of the worsening situation, Li grasped at the hint and Chang entered Peking with his colourful troops on 14 June. On the previous day, as a condition of his intervention, Parliament had been dissolved by Li, the man whose earlier refusal of a similar demand by Tuan Ch'i-jui had brought about the present crisis. Li soon found, however, that he had bought a bad bargain, but before he had time to retrieve the situation, Chang Hsün engineered a *coup* on the last night of June, proclaiming the restoration of the eleven-year-old P'u-yi, the deposed Hsüan-t'ung Emperor.

Chang Hsün was, however, himself misled. He had apparently been given to understand by Tuan Ch'i-jui's emissaries that Tuan would support his plan to restore the monarchy. But only five days after the *coup*, Tuan accepted reappointment as Prime Minister from the very man who had dismissed him only six weeks earlier. He appeared at the head of the army 'to save the Republic' and on 12 July re-took Peking.

The comical aspects of the 'Chang Hsün Restoration' did not mitigate the effect the incident had on subsequent events. The immediate question of the President *versus* the Prime Minister came once more to the fore. But it was now the old dispute with a difference. Li Yüan-hung, President at the time of the *coup*, refused to resume his duties and moved directly from the Japanese Legation in Peking, where he had taken refuge during the crisis, to the foreign concession in Tientsin (as many Chinese politicians in similar circumstances had done and were to do). His place was taken by Feng Kuo-chang. As the leader of the Chihli clique of Northern militarists, Feng was not willing to be the mere rubber-stamp Tuan had tried to make his predecessor. The confrontation between these two powerful figures immediately created a dangerous situation. Having emerged as the 'Saviour of the Republic' and having, at long last, got his way by declaring war on Germany on 14 August, 1917, Tuan now prepared to strengthen his position with the support of various right-wing groups of financiers and politicians, as well as Japanese money. To this end, a political organisation known as the Anfu Club – most of its leaders were from Tuan's native province Anhwei – was founded at the beginning of 1918. Because of its subsequent manipulation of parliament, its shady dealings with the Japanese and its many adherents who in the 1930s and 1940s were to become collaborators with Japan's occupation forces in China, this club won for itself in the history of modern China a reputation synonymous with corruption and treason. The foundation and activities of the Club had the immediate effect of sharpening and intensifying not only the power struggle between the two dominant Northern cliques of Anhwei and Chihli, often disguised as constitutional disputes between the President and the Prime Minister, but also the conflict with the forces in the South, which in September 1917 set up a Government in Canton under Sun Yat-sen – a conflict leading eventually to open warfare.

At the beginning of November 1917, while the struggle was still going on, Morrison left for a six-month visit to Australia and New Zealand. One of the purposes of the trip, as he told his friends, was to see for himself whether Australia was a place where he and his family might settle. In preparation for such an eventuality and as a reflection of his gloomy view of the situation in China, he succeeded, before he left, in selling his collection of books on China for £35,000 to Baron Iwasaki of Japan, one main stipulation being that it be kept intact and known as the 'Morrison Library'. He had previously turned down similar offers from America, because he had decided that, failing a buyer who would keep the collection in China, it should at least remain in the Far East. The Japanese guardians of this collection, however, have since re-named the library in which the collection is housed in Tokyo the Tōyō Bunko, or Oriental Library, though to many scholars it continues to be known by the name Morrison wished for it. This collection of books remains to this day one of the best of its kind in the world.

The transfer of Morrison's library from Peking to Tokyo caused an outcry among Chinese and foreign scholars and other interested parties. A prominent Chinese, feeling 'deep sorrow' at the fact that the 'unique collection could not be kept in this city where it should be kept', registered 'a protest against those whose duty it is to attend to such matters',[1] while a foreign resident, bemoaning 'the loss which Peking is sustaining', considered 'it is but one more sign of China's wastefulness, when she had the opportunity, but did not avail of it, to secure such a valuable library'.[2] The sale was not only reported at great length in newspapers and journals in China and abroad, but also formed the topic of editorial comments. In a lengthy leader in the *Peking Daily News* (11 August 1917), the writer expressed 'a thousand pities that it should ever have been within the realm of conceivability that such an instrument for the study of China and things Chinese should be allowed to leave the country. The library is unique, and there is really only one fitting place for it' – Peking. Though he admitted that the state of national finances was 'not such as to warrant waste on luxuries, a library of this kind,' he asserted, 'would not be a luxury'. Scholars, for reasons quite unconnected with national pride, felt the loss the most keenly. Nowhere was the feeling more poignantly expressed, in a voice bordering on despair, than in the brief note (printed below) from the author of *A Dictionary of Chinese Mythology*. They were not consoled by Morrison's argument, not altogether sincerely expressed, that what China needed was not a specialist library such as his but a general reference library. Whatever the truth of this, the loss to China of this library has not been made good, nor is it ever likely to be, unique as this collection remains today.

Morrison does not seem to have been particularly enthusiastic at the prospect of returning to settle in his native land. He did, however, see and talk to a great many people in Australia and New Zealand, and in both countries he

[1] Wang Ching-ch'un to Morrison (10 August, 1917), not printed.
[2] Robert R. Gailey to Morrison (8 October 1917), not printed.

was well received. His central topic of conversation, as well as in correspondence, was the rising menace of Japan. We include here a few examples of his exchanges with politicians there, even though in part repetitious of letters he had earlier written to various different quarters, to illustrate his attempts at influencing opinion in those two countries.

864. To Jennie Morrison[1]

Shanhaikuan [Chihli] 1 July 1917

My dearest Jennie,

Leaving on Saturday morning reached Chin Wang Tao in comfort. Stayed at the Rest House and spent an interesting time with La Touche[2] the ornithologist who, 35 years in China with world wide reputation, is still Deputy Commissioner under a nonentity named Maze[3] who has been 21 years in China, for 10 of which he has been full commissioner. Such is justice!

[...]

This morning I came through to Shanhaikuan and had a most hearty reception from Capt Cattarinich[4] who asked warmly after you and the children. I share a table with Wu Ting-fang who may not be a brilliant Premier but has good table manners. I sent post cards to the children. They're not

[1] At this time staying with their children at the seaside resort of Pei-tai-ho.
[2] John David Digues La Touche, British ornithologist and employee of the Chinese Maritime Customs, at this time Deputy Commissioner of Customs at Chinwangtao. He was the author of *A Handbook of the Birds of Eastern China* (London 1925).
[3] Frederick William Maze (d. 1959), British employee of the Chinese Maritime Customs, a nephew of Sir Robert Hart, and the son of Hart's favourite sister Mary. His spectacular promotion within the service was strongly condemned by Morrison as the worst case of nepotism on the part of Hart, Robert Bredon, the brother-in-law of Sir Robert Hart, being another case. Maze entered the service in 1897 and within two years became Acting Audit Secretary in the Inspectorate-General in Peking, in 1900 Acting Commissioner, Deputy Commissioner the following year and a full Commissioner within ten years, in 1906, an event Morrison did not fail to comment upon. After serving as Commissioner in many major cities in China, including Chinwangtao and Tientsin, where he was at this time, he was appointed Deputy Inspector-General in 1928 and in 1929 Inspector-General, a post he held until 1943, serving besides in an advisory capacity on many boards and committees of the Chinese Government, and was the recipient of many Chinese and European decorations, including the K.C.M.G. in 1944 after he retired from service with the Chinese Government. Morrison had a poor opinion of his ability and elsewhere described him as 'half-witted'.
[4] Alexander Clement Cattarinich, Austrian hotelier. An ex-officer of the Austrian army, he spent some years in the Indo-Chinese Opium trade between Tonkin and Yünnan before coming to China. Apparently a gifted linguist, speaking, according to Morrison, eleven languages, he was at this time the manager of the Railway Hotel in Shanhaikuan. Morrison first came to know him in Siam, and in 1913, when Sun Yat-sen's party passed through Shanhaikuan and threatened to take action against Cattarinich for an alleged slight, it was to Morrison Cattarinich had appealed to put his case to the Chinese Government.

striking and I can get none coloured. Tomorrow I'll go on to Newchwang. Its been raining all yesterday and today. I walked to the seaside and saw the cottages.

Nothing to record. All well. My best love to you and the children

Your ever loving husband
Ernest

P.S. [...] I had just finished when your telegram came in '*Emperor Restored two o'clock Donald*'. I have shown this to Wu Ting-fang. He cannot believe it. He is obviously much agitated. I have wired to Donald asking him for confirmation saying '*Wu Ting-fang incredulous*'. If it is confirmed I will have to return to Peking at once by the 10.15 a.m. train, or if the reply comes too late, by the night train. I will of course wire you. You need have no anxiety about my contract.[1]

G.E.M.

865. To Jennie Morrison

Peking 4 July 1917

My dear Jennie,

I was too busy to write yesterday. Everything is very quiet here and my old boy tells me that the change is welcomed by the people and that Chang Hsun has acted wisely.

There will however be powerful opposition and I should think the monarchy is already trembling, in a week it will totter and in a fortnight fall.

I was glad to get my salary for June. At the present moment the treasury has $6,000 in hand cash and with this inadequate sum has to meet $28,000,000 of notes to be increased in a few days to $33,000,000. Government is in fact living upon notes. Trains from Peking to Tientsin are crowded, the exodus may even include Tsai Ting-kan.

The Foreign Office is wholly under German high influence.[2] This is the last flicker. There is nothing to worry about. I am going to the cottage this evening. Last evening I dined with Chang,[3] the Priv. Sec. of Liang Chi-chao.

[1] A reference to Morrison's contract of employment with the Chinese Government. *See* p. 398 n. 1.
[2] Morrison was undoubtedly referring to Liang Tun-yen (q.v.), who was appointed Foreign Minister in Chang Hsün's Restoration Government, Li Ching-mai, the son of Li Hung-chang and formerly Chinese Minister to Austria (1905–7), who was appointed Senior Vice-Minister, and Ku Hung-ming (q.v.) who was made Senior Counsellor in the Ministry.
[3] Chang Chia-shen, better known to Chinese as Chang Chün-mai and to foreigners as Carson Chang (b. 1886), Chinese scholar and Republican politician. A returned student from Japan and Germany, he spent a great many years in the latter country at different times in his life, first as a student and then as a lecturer. A follower of Liang Ch'i-ch'ao, he had been Liang's emissary to Chang Hsün and Feng Kuo-chang during the crisis following the launching by Yüan Shih-k'ai of his monarchical scheme, and in the months

Li Yuan-hung is in the Japanese Legation, whither he went after being refused admittance by the damned fool sisters of the French hospital, Bussière[1] arriving a few minutes too late to prevent the misfortune.

My new office is somewhat overcrowded but has the advantage of requiring no stove to keep it warm in this weather. My boy will be able to toast the bread at the window, perhaps even boil the kettle. However there is always the library which is quite cool.

[...]

Love to you all

Ever your affectionate husband
G. E. Morrison

866. To Liang Tun-yen

[Peking] 5 July 1917

Dear Mr. Liang,

Our friendly acquaintance extending now over so many years must be my excuse for writing to you.

I am one of those Englishmen who can never forget the services you rendered to us in 1900 in the framing of the Yangtse Compact whereby the

---

preceding Chang Hsün's Restoration in July 1917, when Liang sought to play a role in the Government. In 1919 Chang accompanied Liang to attend the Paris Conference and went on to Germany to study Philosophy at Jena, not returning to China until 1922. The following year, a lecture he delivered at Tsinghua University provoked heated debate involving some of China's leading intellectuals, on the theme of science *versus* metaphysics, a notable event in the intellectual movement that began with the 'May Fourth' Movement in 1919. A social democrat, he was an opponent of the one-party system, making him suspect in the eyes of the Kuomintang which came to power in Nanking in 1927. After a short imprisonment Chang was compelled to flee the country and went to Germany for the third time, remaining there until 1931. The following year he started a political party among the intellectuals, adopting the unfortunate name of Nationalist Socialist Party (Kuo-she tang) and was as a result greatly misunderstood and maligned. It bore no relation to the German party of the same name, however, but resembled more the British Labour Party (one of the works of whose high priest, Harold Joseph Laski (1892–1950), he translated). Until 1938 he sought to eke out a living by teaching under the protection of various provincial authorities in opposition to the Central Government. After the outbreak of war against Japan in 1937, though his party was recognised by the Central Government, his activities were much circumscribed. In 1941 his party combined with the other small parties to form what later became known as the China Democratic League gaining a large following among the intellectuals in the Kuomintang controlled area. However with the renewal of civil war between the Communists and the Kuomintang after the Japanese surrender, the China Democratic League became divided and unlike many of his friends he chose a life of exile after 1949 and went to live in America, where he devoted himself to writing, mostly on Chinese philosophy. His autobiography, *The Third Force*, was published in New York in 1952.

[1] Bussière was the physician to the French Legation in Peking.

Imperial Edicts were disregarded which decreed the death of all foreigners in China.[1]

As *Times* correspondent, I had frequent opportunities to be grateful to you for your kind assistance.

There is no Chinese in China who was more generally respected by foreigners than you. It was then with the most painful feelings that I learned you had seen fit to ally yourself with this insane attempt to restore to China a Government of reaction. I deeply regret your decision.

So great is the indignation against you, for you are an enlightened man, of a different stamp from the illiterate barbarian Chang Hsun, and the feeling of resentment against you is all the greater thereby, that you are, I am afraid, in great danger, and as a friend I write to urge you before it is too late to resign your office and get away from Peking.

There is not the faintest possibility of your Government continuing. There is not the faintest possibility of your obtaining any money other than the small sum which can be paid by the German Bank. Your action has invited foreign intervention, for no one can know better than you the terms of the Protocol of September 5th, 1901, and the terms of the Quintuple Loan Contract, 1913.[2]

Yesterday a prominent Chinese[3] wished that you should be warned, and I send you a warning to urge you to escape from Peking while there is still time.

Believe me

Very sincerely yours
[G. E. Morrison]

867. To Liang Tun-yen

[Peking] 7 July 1917

Private

Dear Mr. Liang,

The day before yesterday I wrote to you to warn you of the danger you were incurring by remaining in your impossible post in Peking.

---

[1] At the time of the Boxer Uprising, Liang was Secretary-Interpreter to Chang Chih-tung, the Viceroy of Hukuang. 'Yangtze Compact' refers to the assurance given jointly by Chang Chih-tung and Liu K'un-yi (1830–1902), the Viceroy of Liangkiang (1890–1902), to the foreign powers that they would undertake to protect the lives and properties of foreigners under their jurisdiction provided no foreign troops were landed. This compact was supported by other provincial authorities, among them Li Hung-chang, at this time Viceroy of Liangkuang, and Yüan Shih-k'ai, Governor of Shantung.

[2] The 1901 Protocol provided for intervention by the foreign Powers on the grounds of security for their nationals in the Chinese capital, while the Five-Power or Reorganisation Loan of 1913, stipulated in Article IV that 'No loan, charge or mortgage shall be raised or created which shall take precedence of or be on an equality with this loan'. This made it difficult for the Chinese Government to contract any other loan.

[3] Not identified.

Yesterday I learned of your visit to the Japanese Minister.

I now write to you again to urge you to escape from Peking while there is yet time. Misty as your faculties have become by the prolonged use of opium, you are surely not too muddled to realise how dishonourable is your conduct in causing the issue of an Imperial Decree appointing Tsai Ting-kan 'Deputy Imperial Commissioner of the Customs Administration', a loyal friend to you ever since you were together in America.[1] To make it appear now, as this edict does, that he is willing to serve in the present insane Government is to do that which you know to be untrue. Telegrams will be sent to-day to try to counteract the evil you are trying to do your friend.

Unless you escape, disaster will quickly overtake you. Friends of mine witnessed the 'battlefield' of last evening and the flight of the pig-tailed barbarians who are now your only supporters.

I again urge you to leave Peking at once. You can take with you that crazy lunatic in the pay of the Germans, the enemies of your country, whom you have made chief councillor.[2]

Hoping that you will be wise in time

Yours very sincerely
[G. E. Morrison]

[1] The Decree of the Restoration Government merely confirmed Ts'ai T'ing-kan in the post he was holding, adding the word 'Imperial' to his existing title. Like many who were appointed by Chang Hsün in their absence and without their consent, Ts'ai did not take up the post. He in fact asked for sick leave and went to stay in the Wagons-Lits Hotel in the Legation Quarter. Morrison apparently attributed Ts'ai's appointment to Liang. Ts'ai and Liang were among the first group of Chinese students sent to study in the United States in 1872.

[2] The reference is to Ku Hung-ming (1857–1928), a Chinese scholar whom Morrison more than once described in his Diary as a 'lunatic'. A returned student from Britain and Germany, he was to become one of the most colourful intellectuals of his time. His attacks on missionaries and his defence of traditional Chinese culture made him unpopular with many foreigners. However, his intellect was widely recognised and admired, and a work of his translated into German became required reading for German students of philosophy. His eccentricity attracted the interest of foreign scholars and writers, among them Somerset Maugham, who made him the subject of one of his sketches in 'On a Chinese Screen' (1922). Ku was for twenty years, from 1885 to 1905, on the staff of Chang Chih-tung whose views on the relative values of Chinese and Western cultures were attributed to Ku's influence, and it was while in Chang's service that Ku came to know Liang who was Chang's Secretary of Foreign Affairs in Wuchang. A committed Monarchist, Ku preferred poverty to serving the Republic after the overthrow of the Manchu Dynasty in 1911, and after the abortive Restoration attempt in which he served as Senior Councillor in the Foreign Ministry under Liang he went back to teaching and writing. He remained as uncompromising as ever until the end of his life, and left his family destitute when he died.

868. To Jennie Morrison

Peking 8 July 1917

Dearest Jennie,

Yours of the 5th just in,[1] the first I have received since the trouble began. Do not be excited or worried. Things are very quiet and I have never seen Peking in better order or discipline. The conduct even of Chang Hsün's braves is without reproach. At present they are in great anxiety because rain is about to fall and they dislike rain or water of any kind as much as a cat does.

This morning there was firing outside the East Wall and I understand that there was one casualty, a ricksha coolie, being hit by a stray bullet. I heard the rattle quite distinctly at 4 a.m. a very long way away.

Yesterday three bombs were dropt inside the Palace, one only exploding, another fell in the lake, a third fell harmlessly.[2] Two men were wounded but not seriously and are now in the London Mission Hospital.

Since I came to Peking on Monday evening I have dined at the Hotel de Pekin twice and have lunched with Lucas[3] and others. Domestic arrangements have been excellent and I am in excellent health and thankful beyond measure that you and the children are not here in this annoying time of rumour. There is absolutely no danger.

Donald and Roy Anderson were out this morning at Fêng-t'ai and found the Republican forces there in good force maintaining excellent order. Peking is now surrounded and Chang Hsün and his pig tailed savages are cornered. Within two days the Republic will be re-established and all will be well once more and I will still be in the service of the President.

Last night the Mandate of abdication was ready for signature. Chang Hsün has resigned, and his mischievous activities finished. After all the Restoration may have done much good.

Kang Yu-wei is in hiding and Liang Tun-yen has asked protection from Tenney.[4] He was resolved to die for the monarchy but changed his mind. I wrote him two letters telling him of his danger and scared him a good deal. The result was good. I have kept copies to show you.

It was delightful to picture the two little boys bathing. How I wish I were with you.

[...]

[1] Not printed.
[2] This was the first time an aircraft was used in fighting in China, and Peking residents were reported to have crowded into the streets to watch the spectacle.
[3] Sydney E. Lucas, formerly Branch Manager of the Chartered Bank of Australia, India and China in Peking. He became on Morrison's recommendation Assistant Manager of the Bank of China in which position he refused Chang Hsün's demand for funds.
[4] Upon the overthrow of the restoration government K'ang Yu-wei was granted asylum in the United States Legation in Peking and left for Shanghai escorted by a United States Legation Guard five months later. Liang Tun-yen too took refuge in the same Legation, and later retired to Tientsin. Both men were unshaken in their monarchist convictions and remained staunch critics of the Republic.

Keep carefully the *Gazette* of Monday as I cannot get a copy anywhere in Peking.

My warmest love to you all

Ever your affectionate husband
G. E. Morrison

869. From J. D. D. La Touche

Chinwangtao [Chihli] 9 July 1917

Dear Doctor Morrison,

Thank you very much for your kind letter of the 5th, received last night. You must indeed have had an anxious time, but I am glad to hear the old brigand has fled and I hope that quiet and peace have by this time been restored. Here we naturally have been quiet. The cutting of the railway and the news of the expected fighting made the Peking ladies anxious about their husbands, and now, the interruption of the traffic between this and Mukden is holding up our home mails which are anxiously expected every week.

It was most kind of you to put in a good word for me. You are giving me an undeserved reputation I fear, although, certainly bug-and-bird hunters are not numerous among the members of the Customs. But perhaps, the authorities think, if they are too polite to say it outright, that they have no use for bird hunters and that stern, strong officials with a keen eye to business and the prevention of smuggling are much more in their line ... All the same, it is deplorable to see the paucity of men having intellectual or scientific hobbies in China. Everywhere else in the East and Far East, learned societies, museums and workers, official and private, are in evidence. Only in China does the club bar and the race course etc., appear to be the sole amusement of the immense majority. We adapt ourselves to our surroundings and howl with the wolves and the absolute indifference of John Chinaman to anything which does not concern his pocket or belly reacts upon us all. That a country with the immense resources that China has should be without some govt. scientific institution is a disgrace to the rulers of the country.

I fancy that complete sets of *The Ibis*[1] are rather rare and must be very expensive. There is one at Sikawei.[2] But £115 seems to me rather stiff. At the

[1] *The Ibis*, a quarterly journal of ornithology published in London by the British Ornithologists Union since 1859.
[2] Sikawei, Siccawei, or in French, Zikawei, was the rendering in the local Shanghai dialect of Hsü-chia-hui, formerly a village and now part of Shanghai's western suburb, chosen in 1874 by the Jesuit missionaries as the headquarters for their work in South China. It was made famous not only by the museums, libraries and the Université l'Aurore, or Chen-tan ta-hsüeh, the leading Catholic university in South China established there, but even more by the scholarly works published there. Its counterpart in North China in this aspect was Ho-chien-fu (or Hokienfu) in Chihli, later Hopeh Province. *See also* Letter No. 892, p. 65.

same time the greater number of the volumes being out of print, two pounds a volume is perhaps not excessive.

With kind regards, and again many thanks for your kindness

Yours sincerely
La Touche

870. To Jennie Morrison

Peking 9 July 1917

My dearest Jennie,

Your telegram came in at 11.15 this morning. I am sorry that you should be in any way anxious. There is not the slightest need to be disturbed. Everything is quiet. I am very well and would be quite happy but for the heat and for my absence from those I love at Pei tai ho.

The Diplomatic body today asked that Chang Hsün's braves should be disarmed. Liang Tun-yen resigned and I think will go into the American Legation having asked Tenney for protection. In my letters to him I referred in as gentle a way I could to the 'haziness of his faculties due to the long continued use of opium'.

If disarmament is effected I will come down in a few days. Mrs Fraser went down to Pei tai ho. It was amusing to hear her dissatisfaction with Mrs Warren. Today I lunched with Mrs Jackson Fleming and her husband. She is a most delightful woman who has done work in Europe since the war began in Alabama in Paris and in London. On social questions she is an authority. I showed them our house and they were ecstatic in their expressions of admiration for you. So by the way was Mrs Newman the other day who spoke of you quite affectionately as being so charming and beautiful, my eye! –

[...] Everyone has come in from the racecourse. The soldiers around Peking are behaving in an exemplary manner. You need have no anxiety at all. Normal communication will be restored in a day or two.

The Japanese put their money on Chang Hsün, of that I am sure and have been hoist with their own petard.

All my love to you and the kids

Ever your affectionate husband
G. E. Morrison

871. To Jennie Morrison

Peking 10 July 1917

My dearest Jennie,

Another day has passed without a letter from you. I write every day. This morning I sent Nurse a small gift in recognition of her services to us during the last 3 years. I bless the day you secured her.

Nothing new. Lucas who has done admirable work throughout this crisis and saved the Bank of China from pillage was with Chang Hsün this morning for a long time. He had a very interesting interview, Chang Hsün demanding money, Lucas refusing to give even one dollar without the authority of Chiang Chao-tsung[1] and Wang Shih-chen,[2] two 'Heroes of the Revolution'.

Many of Chang Hsün's men are bereaving themselves of their queues. Out of one group today of 15 I noticed that 4 had been shorn.

Have no fear. This thing will fizzle out. I will go to the Cottage in a day or two.

Best love to you and the kids

Ever your loving husband
G. E. Morrison

872. From T. Knox[3]

Melbourne [Victoria, Australia] 10 July 1917

O my prophetic Soul, my Uncle!

Did you expect the Republic to come to an end when you got that group taken? To my mind the Asian is not republican minded, be he Aryan or Turan or Mongol. He likes a healthy democracy – and that means a despot at

[1] Chiang Ch'ao-tsung (1863–1943), Chinese soldier, Deputy Commander of the *Gendarmerie* in Peking. It was he who counter-signed the Presidential Decree for the dissolution of Parliament, having been appointed by Li as Acting Premier on 12 June 1917 for that express purpose. He served briefly as Commander of the *Gendarmerie* in the Chang Hsün Restoration Government. By virtue of his position, which he continued to hold in successive governments, he was to act as a caretaker when Peking changed hands from one regime to another. He was made Chairman of the 'Peace Maintenance Committee' by the Japanese when they occupied Peking in 1937, and later served as mayor of the city under them.

[2] Wang Shih-chen (?1861–1930), Chinese soldier, the least successful of the three chief lieutenants of Yüan Shih-k'ai, the other two being Feng Kuo-chang and Tuan Ch'i-jui. Wang's role in the contending factions of this period was one of mediator, serving as caretaker between the changing regimes rather than a holder of real power in his own right. In May 1915, following Tuan Ch'i-jui's resignation from his posts of Minister of War and Chief of the General Staff because of his disapproval of Yüan's monarchical scheme, Wang Shih-chen was appointed to these posts, holding them until Tuan's reappointment in April the following year. He was in Peking during Chang Hsün's Restoration and was appointed Chief of the General Staff. He was also to become briefly Acting Caretaker Prime Minister in November 1917, until March 1918 when the rift occurred between his erstwhile colleagues, Feng Kuo-chang and Tuan Ch'i-jui. He and Chiang Ch'ao-tsung were responsible for maintaining order in the Capital before the forces under Tuan Ch'i-jui took charge of the city after defeating Chang Hsün in July 1917.

[3] Thomas Knox, Australian journalist, at this time working for *The Age*, a Melbourne daily. Replying to Knox on 27 August 1917 Morrison wrote: 'I hope you will write to me again ... but to speak frankly, it is useless writing to me unless you can do so in a handwriting that is legible or on a typewriter. I can speak with some feeling in the matter because my own handwriting is described as infernal. For that reason I use the typewriter to save me from the anathema of my friends.'

the top, and the rest practically on a level, with a gambling chance for everyone to rise. With justice short and sharp, no matter how erratic; but be done with it. Give him that sort of life, and so he goes about his business happy.

We get most of the China news through the *Morning Post* man at Tientsin. Who is he? Anyhow he is intently anti-monarchical. When at Oxford old Legge[1] was Chinese Professor there. What [?From] what I could make out after wading thro' his *Analects*, the Chinese prefer as national representative a sort of Boss Joss, no matter who, but with heredity behind him, if possible. Saves trouble. Then the custom of self-accusation in public acts as well as any conventional constitution. Parliaments no. Only so many more to be bribed, instead of one. The people who used to blame the old Duke of Cambridge[2] wailed much when their much demanded War Council came into being and five men proceeded to promote their friends.[? Now] the War Council is composed of x members, and they all are at the job and the men at the front are forgotten, but the men who never leave England rise rapidly. One man became a lt col in a year, but then his wife was a popular leg-show lady.

[...]

What in the name of all the wild cats keeps the Japanese on the Eagle's gizzard? The Yankee seems to spend all his time thinking when the wily Jap will jump on his chest. I conclude it is due to the fact that he has been meditating something against the Jap. *Honi soit qui mal y pense* sort of thing.

Anyhow the reality of war – America hasn't grasped it yet – has begun to make some Americans think in what a fools' paradise they have been living. It's enlivening to hear of munition works, even Govt. navy yards going up in the air. When the American really gets spy mania, there will be the devil to pay, for he will catch it badly, very badly, I hope, for then there will be fewer hyphenates in the land of the living. Telegraph and telephone posts are numerous and handy in the States, to say nothing of the accommodation the overhead railway can give along the track.

[...]

Funny gentleman Chang Hsun; our cables say he admits his move was premature. Want of cash? Who got Old Buddha's[3] treasure after all? Is there

---

[1] James Legge (1815–97), British missionary and scholar. He is best known as the English translator of Chinese Classics in which he collaborated with the Chinese scholar and modern press pioneer Wang T'ao (1828–97). In 1876 Legge became the first Professor of Chinese at Oxford, holding the post until his death.

[2] George William Frederick Charles, 2nd Duke of Cambridge (1819–1904), British soldier, a first cousin of Queen Victoria. He was Commander-in-Chief of the British Army from 1856 to 1895.

[3] The translation of *Lao Fo-yeh*, an appellation for the Empress Dowager Tz'u-hsi, by which she was addressed by her eunuch-servants, and sometimes referred to by her subjects. As Tz'u-hsi liked to be known as a devoted Buddhist, this name was used to flatter her, indicating that she must have been a Buddha in an earlier incarnation, cruel and ruthless though she was.

any man of nerve who wont hesitate to do 'heads off' on either side, or are they all [? simply] too afraid of their precious skins and won't go the whole hog? Evil result of contact with Western civilisation. For, once in a time the Chinaman sailed in, and damn the consequences. A Chinese Parliament to me is a joke, the Chinaman being practical and quite capable of seeing the hideous mess of western democracy and how democratic Parliaments are worked.
[...]

Yours truly
T. Knox

873. To Jennie Morrison.

[Peking] 14 July 1917

My dearest Jennie,

I'll try and come down on Monday. We had an interesting time on Thursday. Firing was terrific. Some 30,000 or 40,000 troops were engaged in a struggle to the death in a confined area.

Casualties were 29 killed (14 combatants and 15 non-combatants) and several wounded. You never heard such a terrific banging. In my district several thousands fought and one was slightly wounded. I'll tell you the thrilling story when I see you.

The heat is very severe and I'll be thankful to get away. This afternoon I go to my cottage. Yesterday there were no trains.

All my love to you and the children. I'll have very little baggage I think.

Your devoted husband
G. E. Morrison

874. From L. H. Drakeford

Newchwang [Fengtien] 18 July 1917

My dear Doctor,

I delayed replying to your welcome letter of 22nd ulto,[1] expecting to see you in person here. Now the political pot has boiled over once more, perhaps you wont be able to get here at all.

As you found my previous narrative of the interferences of our worthy *Tuchun*[2] so interesting, you might like to hear of his latest?

On 7th instant he wired dismissing the Salt Commissioner, Mr Chen Shih-hua,[3] who by the way is a western-educated medical man, and appointing a certain Mr Tseng Yu-yi[4] in his stead. This gentleman was a member of

---

[1] Not printed.   [2] Chang Tso-lin.
[3] Salt Commissioner for Manchuria from October 1916. until his dismissal in 1917.
[4] He was not appointed Salt Commissioner but on 27 July 1917 became Supervisor of Customs at Shanhaikuan, holding the post until September 1920. He was a Member for Fengtien Province in the 1913 House of Representatives (Chung-yi yüan), and retained his membership when Parliament was revived in 1922.

the defunct Parliament, representing Fengtien, and is said to be a Secretary of the *Tuchun*. He 'achieved merit' during the revolt of the *Tuchuns* by carrying messages between the Premier (Tuan) and Chang Tso-lin.

On hearing of the *Tuchun*'s action Messrs. Ma and Kono[1] and myself at once lodged a strong protest with the *Taoyin*,[2] warning him that until we heard from the Chief Inspectors we would not recognise the *Tuchun*'s appointee. The *Taoyin* admitted the irregularity of the action, and said he'd telegraph the *Tuchun* advising him to withdraw. The same night Mr Tseng arrived, but on the *Taoyin*'s advice decided not to take over at once.

On Monday we sent in a written protest, and warned the *Tuchun*, through the *Taoyin*, that persistence in his course – till we got instructions from headquarters anyhow – would result in total stoppage of salt revenue collections and releases of salt throughout Manchuria and that such a result would probably lead to his embroilment with the foreign Banks and diplomatic authorities. Tseng tried to take over, but in view of what we had told him, the *Taoyin*, who had been appointed by the *Tuchun* to superintend the transfer of seals, refused to act, so Tseng went back to Mukden for consultation.

I should say that Commissioner Chen said he had no option but to take the *Tuchun*'s instructions, though of course he knew the thing was grossly irregular. Most people advised him to leave Yingkou at once, as they feared the *Tuchun* would make things hot for him if he did not. However, he decided to hold his ground, being willing to surrender his seals at any time formalities were complied with.

After learning what a fix the *Tuchun* might get into if we did not recognise his man, the *Taoyin* became very anxious lest Mr Chen should actually depart. At 1 a.m. on 11th we got a message from him that Mr Chen intended flight, and had already sent his baggage and family away. The *Taoyin* said he'd have to stop the departure by force, and urged us to persuade Mr Chen not to go. I told the *Taoyin* that if Chen did really leave, it would be entirely due to the *Tuchun*'s action, and that if the latter wanted him to remain it would be well to cancel his order of dismissal.

We had wired to Peking for instructions on 7th, and on 12th got a reply saying active protest was unnecessary, and that the Yen Wu Shu would take action in due course. We communicated this to the *Tuchun*, or rather the *Taoyin*, warning him at the same time that as the meaning was not very clear, if Mr Tseng took up the post we'd have to wire for further orders.

On 13th Mr Tseng returned, and on 14th Mr Chen gave up his seals. On hearing of this we wired to Peking saying we purposed working with Mr Tseng as if the appointment were regular, and asking for confirmation,

---

[1] Kōno Iwao, Japanese employee of the Chinese Salt Administration, which he joined in September 1913. He had been a Counsellor in the Japanese Foreign Ministry before going to China, and was at this time assistant manager of the Bureau of Salt Gabelle of Fengtien Province at Newchwang. [2] Jung-hou.

which up to tonight has not come. Mr Chen intended leaving for Tientsin on 15th, to consult with his intimate friend General Chin,[1] now adviser to Premier Tuan and formerly *Tuchun* of Shantung, who had got Mr Chen his appointment here. On the night of 14th a telegram came from the *Tuchun* accusing Mr Chen of having been bribed with a hundred thousand dollars to connive at smuggling. I don't know if he was put under arrest, but there were armed police outside his door when I called that night. However, he learned from Tientsin that the accusation of bribery was merely an afterthought of the *Tuchun*, to give some appearance of justification for his action. Evidently the matter was not serious, as Mr Chen left here yesterday.

During the last few days we heard privately that the Premier had appointed a certain Mr Chin,[2] a former *Taotai* of Hankow, to the position of Salt Commissioner here. What is going to happen I don't know, but I suppose it all depends on the amount of value Tuan places on Chang's support, whether or not the latter gets a snub for his officiousness.

However, that was not the only caper cut by the *Tuchun*. He also dismissed the Superintendent of Customs, a Mr Chang,[3] son of ex-viceroy Chang Jen-chun[4] of the Liang-Kiang, who happened to be away when the restoration was accomplished, appointing the *Taoyin*, Yung Hao, who is a Manchu, in his stead. The Commissioner of Customs, Mr C. E. S. Wakefield,[5] lodged a strong protest, and before the C.I.[6] wire came through to us, the *Taoyin*, and perhaps the *Tuchun*, got cold feet and returned the Commissioner's seal. I hear, however, that he has since taken it over again, in pursuance of proper instructions from Peking, but am not sure as to that.

I have heard nothing from headquarters *re* the line of action taken by us, but suppose it will be endorsed, as it is hardly likely either the Central Government or the foreign powers interested would permit interference with salt administration affairs by any provincial officer.

[1] The reference is to Chin Yün-p'eng (b. 1877), Chinese soldier. A follower of Tuan Ch'i-jui, he was Military Governor (*Tuchün*) of Shantung province from August 1913 to May 1916. He was at the time of this letter Co-Director of the Bureau of War Preparation, headed by Tuan, a post he held until his replacement by Hsü Shu-cheng in September 1918. (For his further career, *see* p. 783 n. 3.)

[2] Chin Ting-hsün, who had been Acting *Taotai* of Chiang-han at Hankow, was appointed Acting Salt Commissioner for Manchuria succeeding Ch'en Shih-hua, a post he held until September 1920.

[3] Chang En-yen, a son-in-law of Yuan Shih-k'ai. He was Superintendent of Customs at Shanhaikuan from September 1915 until his removal on 27 July 1917.

[4] Chinese Imperial official. He was successively Governor of Shantung (1901–2), Honan (1902–3, 1906–7), Kwangtung (1903–5), and Shansi (1905–6), becoming Viceroy of Liang-kiang at Nanking in August 1907, and remaining in the post until 2 December 1911, when he fled the city on its fall to the Revolutionary forces. His resignation was formally gazetted on 23 January 1912. He was the nephew of Chang P'ei-lun (1849–1903), the scholar son-in-law of Li Hung-chang.

[5] British employee of the Chinese Maritime Customs. He later served as Commissioner of Customs at Swatow.   [6] Chief Inspector.

The *de facto* Commissioner has never held an official post of any kind – unless his membership of Parliament is so regarded – and is perfectly ignorant of salt matters. However, he is accompanied by two ex-secretaries of earlier Salt Commissioners, of unsavoury reputation, and will doubtless soon be put up to all the devices essential to the making the best of a post that is no longer as good as it used to be.

You and all other Peking residents have been having a lively time of it, and I understand that you personally have been very busy in trying to unravel the tangle things have got into. I am glad peace is restored, if only for the moment. I suppose your family remained at Peitaiho?

[...]

I'd like a chat with you, especially *re* the British Trade Bank, which I see has got its charter, and will presumably invade the China field.

Kind regards from

Yours very sincerely
L. H. Drakeford

875. To G. G. S. Lindsey[1]

Peking 27 July 1917

My dear Lindsey,

Two days ago I returned from the seaside and to my great pleasure yesterday received a letter from you dated June 26th.[2] By the same post there came a letter to my wife from Mrs. Lindsey which I took the liberty of opening before sending on to her. It gave me the greatest pleasure to read these two letters. [...]

Here in China things are in considerable confusion, but a cabinet that can be called strong has been formed by Tuan Chi-jui, and I am hoping now that inasmuch as nearly every member of it has committed himself to support the declaring of war against Germany before you receive this letter war may have been declared.

Two years ago I urged that Siam should come into the war. I thought the effect in China would be good. Siam is a country in which I spent more than one year when correspondent of *The Times*, and I have a considerable knowledge of the local conditions along the northern frontier. It seemed to me inevitable that Siam should come into the war in order to check German intrigue in Northern Siam. You can imagine how pleased I was then to read

---
[1] George Goldwin Smith Lindsey (1860–1920), Canadian lawyer and a cousin of William Lyon Mackenzie King (1884–1950), later Prime Minister of Canada (1921–30, 1935–48). Morrison met Mackenzie King when the latter was attending the International Opium Conference in Shanghai in 1909 as Canadian representative and it was through him that Morrison came to know Lindsey. Lindsey was Morrison's host when Morrison stopped at Toronto on his way to attend the Paris Conference in 1919.
[2] Not printed.

in the Reuter's telegrams two days ago that this brave little country had taken its courage in both hands and had cast out the Germans.

For shame's sake China must now do the same, if for no higher motive. I feel confident that it will be done. Japan now is in favour of a declaration of war. I mean really in favour. Before, she professed to be in favour while doing everything she could to thwart such a declaration. Japan has not acted wisely. In 1915, in November of that year, she prevented China from coming into the war for her own ends and so prolonged this great conflict, but prolonged it too far, prolonged it until America came in. Statesmen in Japan realise their mistake. Of that I am sure. It must be their policy now to have this war brought to a conclusion as quickly as possible before America can reach a very high stage of preparedness.

American policy here, I think, must meet with general approval. Mr. Lansing's note[1] communicated to China on June 6th urging the Chinese to settle their differences provoked vehement recrimination in Japan. It was looked upon as an interference with the domestic affairs of this country. Apparently Japan wished it to be thought that only she had the right to interfere in the domestic affairs of China. The Note was a wise one. It contained only one blemish that I could see, and that was a curious lapse to occur in a carefully worded state document of high political importance. In one of the paragraphs reference was made to the European war and the view was expressed that China's entry into it was a question of secondary consideration. It was impossible to expect that the Powers would give assent to a dictum so entirely in conflict with both their views and their acts during the past three years. They could not subscribe to the view that the war was of secondary importance, when as a simple matter of fact it is a war of paramount importance. This was the only part of the Note that seemed to me to be open to question. My view is that America was wholly justified in making the communication and that the effect will ultimately be good.

Japan is now sending a mission to the United States. That mission is

---

[1] Robert Lansing (1864-1928), American politician, Secretary of State from June 1915 to February 1920. On 4 June 1917 he instructed Paul Reinsch, the United States Minister in Peking, to inform the Chinese Government that his Government considered China's entry into the War, the issue which was the immediate cause of the rift between the President Li Yüan-hung, and the Prime Minister, Tuan Ch'i-jui, as being of secondary importance compared with the unity and peace of China. Lansing at the same time proposed to the governments of Japan, France and Great Britain that they should take concerted action to remonstrate with the Chinese Government in the same sense. While the British Government was hedging in its reply the Japanese Government expressed 'irritation' and 'surprise' that Reinsch should have communicated the Note to the Chinese Government before the Japanese Government had replied. In a communication to the State Department Japan said that she had understood the Note to the Chinese Government was to be a 'joint' and 'identical' representation and she regarded the action of the American Minister in China as an 'interference' in China's 'internal politics and a further indication of objectionable activities of the [United States] Legation at Peking'. For details see *Foreign Relations of the United States, 1918*, Vol. 1, pp. 48-58.

headed by Viscount Ishii, a weak man of no intellectual distinction. He has been, it is true, Ambassador to Paris, after being Vice-Minister of Foreign Affairs, and he has been Minister of Foreign Affairs but was a mere puppet in the hands of the more masterful Baron Kato. A poor speaker, he has little following in Japan, and as a national representative he is not in the same street with Balfour[1] or Viviani.[2] He has a tricky, subtle mind, but my impression is that his mission will be a failure.[3] He will be looked upon with suspicion *ab initio* because of his close association with Kato who was responsible for the presentation of the Twenty-One Demands to China in January 1915 and the subsequent ultimatum by which acceptance of four-fifths of them was exacted from China.

[...]

Ever faithfully yours
[G. E. Morrison]

876. From L. H. Drakeford

Newchwang [Fengtien] 7 August 1917

My dear Doctor,

Many thanks for your letter of 27th ulto. I am glad to hear we may yet see you this summer. [...]

The currency muddle in Manchuria is to be intensified on 16th instant by the introduction of large dollar notes. There are to be given out – it is said to all applicants – in exchange for small-coin dollar notes, $120 of the latter to $100 in the new (Peiyang) dollar notes. As there is no more silver available

---

[1] Arthur James, 1st Earl of Balfour (1848-1930), British politician, Conservative Member of the British House of Commons (1874-1922), First Lord of the Treasury from 1895 to 1902 when he succeeded Salisbury as Prime Minister (1902-5). He was at this time Foreign Secretary (1916-19) in the Coalition Cabinet headed by Lloyd George. It was Balfour who entered into a secret undertaking with the Japanese Government in February 1917 pledging British support for the Japanese claim to the former German concessions in Shantung Province which Japan had wrung from Germany in November 1914.

[2] René Raphaël Viviani (1863-1925), French politician, a socialist Deputé of the French National Assembly from 1893 until his defeat in 1904, but was re-elected in 1906. In 1902 he was co-founder with Jean L. Jaurès (1859-1914) of *l'Humanité* and of the United Socialist Party. He became in October 1906 Minister of the newly-created Labour portfolio in the Cabinet of Georges Clemenceau (1841-1929), and was also a member of the Cabinet of Aristide Briand (1862-1932), but resigned in 1910. In 1913 he was made Minister of Education in the Cabinet of Paul Doumer (1857-1932), and became Prime Minister as a result of the June 1914 elections. As the head of a radical socialist ministry, he was associated with all the steps that led France into the European War. In October the following year he was replaced by Briand, and he served as Minister of Justice in the new Government until March 1917. He was French representative at the League of Nations in 1920 and in 1921 a member of the French delegation, headed by Briand, at the Washington Conference.

[3] Contrary to Morrison's prediction, Ishii was successful in his mission which resulted in the signing of the Lansing-Ishii Agreement (q.v.) of 2 November 1917.

than before, this will effect no real improvement in the financial situation, but may tend to increase the cost of living.

The Japanese at Mukden are to have $40,000 of the new notes exchanged for silver every day, as against the $80,000 small coin notes they are now getting coins for. As the discount on small coin notes is today $8\frac{1}{2}\%$, Westerners are beginning to press for equal treatment, and I understand the British Consul is giving support to the nationals. This is only right, as if one's Japanese competitor has an 8% advantage over you in this single item, it is easy to see that British trade must go to the wall. But while the discount is now unusually heavy, the Japanese have had this exclusive advantage for several years.

I think the Japanese here are quietly inciting the Chinese to all kinds of muddling in finances, with a view to forcing a currency adviser on them ere long. The *Far Eastern Review* article on this question was a good one, but nothing seems to have been made of the point that the primary cause of the difficulty is the reckless issue of notes by the Chinese banks, chiefly to the benefit of the officials in control. Owing to the present discount on notes we may have to increase our rate of exchange for Mexican dollars again soon, and that will simply mean an increase of taxation so far as the common people are concerned.

Hoping to see you ere long, and with best wishes
Believe me Dear Doctor

Very sincerely yours
L. H. Drakeford

877. From Ariga Nagao

Shiohara, Tochiki, Japan 8 August 1917

My dear Dr. Morrison,

On the 20th of July, when I left Pekin you were at Petaiho, I do not know where you are now, so I send you this care of British Post, Pekin.

As I told you in my last note, I had notice on the 17th of July, from the Premier Tuan, that he decided to renew my contract for another year. I said I wish the Chinese Government address itself to the Japanese Government, for this time it was necessary for me that the Japanese Government is in favour of the renewal. My position is this. I am already too long away from Japan, so that people think that I am a man greedy for money, which makes me forsake scholarly life for the sake of material gain. Hence in order to save my reputation as a scholar, it is necessary that I can say: 'I renewed the contract, because the Japanese Government says that it is for the good of the country that I should do so.' Please understand my situation, good Dr. Morrison.

On returning to Tokio, I find that the whole Government, including Count Terauchi and Viscomte Motono, are in favour of the renewal.

But curiously enough, the Chinese Government has since then changed its attitude, because of, it is said, opposition coming from the side of the Japanese Legation, Pekin. (This is a great secret which I hope you will never divulge for the sake of Japan). But I cannot really understand this. I am on cordial terms with Baron Hayashi. We never differ. I am rather helping him in his aims and this he ought to know. Hence only two suppositions are possible. (1st) It may be that some of the secretaries still hate me on account of my having stood in the way of their success at the time of the Sino-Japanese negotiation three summers ago. (2nd) It may be that Baron Hayashi is honestly thinking that some more active person had better be in my place. But I am really very active in my own sphere and the Baron simply does not know how much I am doing in secret for the Chinese Government, drafting, revising laws and regulations. If I stand aloof from active diplomacy, it is on purpose that I do so. Besides, China will never consent to change of man.

I write to you these in order that you may kindly see how the land lies in case the question comes up within the sphere of your influence. I am here till the end of August.

Yours most sincerely
N. Ariga

878. To Ting Wen-chiang[1]

[Peking] 8 August 1917

Dear Mr. Ting,

Some little time ago you asked me if my library had been sold. At that time it had not been. It was under offer to the Japanese, but it was of course uncertain whether the offer would be acceptable or not. To-day, however, the

---

[1] Ting Wen-chiang, or, as he signed himself, V. K. Ting (1887-1936), Chinese scientist, a graduate of Glasgow University. He was China's first and foremost geologist and a versatile scholar. It was he who in 1916 undertook the first Geographical Survey of China, for which he sought through Morrison the support of the Chinese Government. The work resulted in the publication in 1934 of the first modern map of China. In 1922-3 he was a central figure in the famous Science *versus* Metaphysics debate with Chang Chia-shen. A book he wrote about the northern warlords whom he came to know in the course of his geographical work is a useful guide to the contending factions of the time. He also undertook and supported anthropological and archaeological research. A follower of Liang Ch'i-ch'ao, the Chinese publicist, Ting published, after Liang's death, a draft chronology of his life and work which has become an indispensable source book on modern China. In 1934 Ting became the General Secretary of the Academia Sinica and was responsible for its reorganisation. Aware of the lack of library facilities for the work to be done on China, Ting Wen-chiang, who first came to know Morrison soon after his return to China from Britain, was a great admirer of Morrison's collection of books on China and like Morrison's many other Chinese acquaintances was most anxious for it to remain in China.

transaction has been completed, and my library in due course will be transferred to Tokyo.

I have made it a condition that the Library shall be open as in the past to all serious students. It will remain intact and will be called after me. More than this it will be kept up to date.

Its purchaser is the famous Baron Iwasaki,[1] who purchased Max Muller's Library,[2] although that is a very inferior one.

I am sorry to part with my library, but the strain of keeping it up is too severe both upon my time and my pocket. I should have liked if it could have remained in Peking, but that is not possible.

The climate here is ideal for book collecting.

I have kept my catalogue, and if ever the Government should decide upon starting a Library of their own I will be very glad indeed to help in acquiring one. But to keep a Library worth £35,000 in Peking uninsured with incidents such as those of the 12th July[3] occurring round about one is a risk that ought to be borne not by an individual but by a corporation.

With kind regards

Believe me

Very sincerely yours

[G. E. Morrison]

[1] Iwasaki Hisaya (1865–1955), Japanese businessman. He was created Baron in 1885 upon the death of his father Iwasaki Yatarō (1834–85), founder of the Mitsubishi *Zaibatsu* which, under the guiding hand of Iwasaki Yanosuke (1850–1908), his uncle, and then of his cousin Iwasaki Koyata (1879–1945), became and remains to this day one of the most powerful forces in Japan's finance, industry and politics. In purchasing Morrison's Library, Hisaya was following the example of his uncle Yanosuke, who ten years earlier, in 1907, purchased through Shigeno Yasutsugu (1827–1910), the well-known scholar of Chinese classics and founder of the Japanese History Section of Tokyo University, the famous collection of Lu Hsin-yüan (1834–94), the Ch'ing bibliographer and scholar. This collection, which included 120 Sung and 100 Yüan editions as well as rare books printed after Ming, amounting to some 40,000 *chüan*, is preserved in the Iwasaki Library, the Seikadō Bunko, in Tokyo. The Morrison collection is now preserved in the Tōyō Bunko, the Oriental Section of the National Diet Library.

[2] Friederich Max-Müller (1823–1900), German-born British scholar. A Sanskrit student, he was Taylorian Professor of Modern Languages at Oxford (1854), Corpus Professor of Philology (1858) and Editor of *Sacred Books of the East*. After his death his library was sold in 1901 to Baron Iwasaki Hisaya, who donated it to Tokyo University, but the whole collection was destroyed in the earthquake of 1923, without having been catalogued. This fact was said to have persuaded Baron Iwasaki not to donate the Morrison collection to any institution. The result was the establishment of the Tōyō Bunko.

[3] The reference is to the fighting in Peking between the forces of Chang Hsün and those under Tuan Ch'i-jui, before the latter took the city. *See* Morrison to Willoughby, 31 October 1917, Letter No. 886.

879. From E. T. C. Werner[1]

Peking 11 August 1917

Dear Morrison,
[...]
I congratulate you on the successful disposal of your library, but !!!!!!!!!! these are my tears!

Yours sincerely
Edward Chalmers Werner

880. To F. E. Taylor

[Peking] 13 August 1917

My dear Taylor,
Many thanks for your letter of the 9th August.[2]

I am indeed sorry to part with my library, but I know that I am doing the right thing in selling it, for I have to think of others who are dependent upon me.

My library is, as you will have seen from the papers, to continue to bear my name, to remain intact, and to be open to serious students as heretofore. The verification of its contents will begin this week, and as soon as the money is paid into the Bank the library will become the property of the purchaser.

Carefully invested, £35,000 ought to produce me a comfortable income, even after the deduction of the income tax which at present, having no domicile in England, I am not called upon to pay.

[...]

More and more it seems hopeless to expect the Chinese to learn. They are willing to pay, for example, their advisers large salaries and are quite happy never to consult them. I have not yet seen the present President[3] – my august master!

[1] Edward Theodore Chalmers Werner (1864-1954), a New Zealander in the British consular service, and scholar. Beginning his career in 1884, he served for the next thirty years in various parts of China, retiring in 1914 as Consul in Foochow. He later lectured at Peking University. Among his published works are *A Dictionary of Chinese Mythology* (Shanghai 1932) and *Descriptive Sociology – Chinese* (Part IX of the series *Descriptive Sociology; or groups of sociological facts* (classified and arranged by Herbert Spencer, London 1873-1934)). His autobiography *Autumn Leaves* was published in Shanghai in 1928.   [2] Not printed.
[3] Feng Kuo-chang (1859-1919). One of the chief lieutenants in the New Army under Yüan Shih-k'ai, he replaced Chang Hsün in December 1913 as Military Governor of Kiangsu Province at Nanking. In this position he built himself up into the most powerful provincial authority, having subordinates of his in control of Kiangsi and Hupeh along some 700 miles of the Yangtze, China's richest region. In 1916, after the death of Yüan Shih-k'ai, he was elected to the Vice-Presidency, retaining his position of Military Governor of Kiangsu and continuing to reside at Nanking. However when Li Yüan-hung, Yüan's successor as President, refused to resume his post after Chang Hsün's

My present idea is to make all the provision I can for the future and then go down to Australia on leave at first. Whether I shall go there permanently I will have to decide on my return. My wife would prefer to go to England where the education of our children would be superior.

I will do all I can with regard to your retirement. You would not, of course, retire so long as silver is at its present abnormal elevation. Aglen has good reason to expect this year that his salary will be well over £12,000. Even Bowra[1] with $2,100 a month and his advantages is receiving a salary considerably higher than that of the British Minister.

Paid in gold as I am, I am losing heavily. Last month I received only Ts 1,600 [?] whereas for the corresponding month two years ago I received Ts. 2,900 [?]. I will try to sell my freehold property in Peking now that silver is high.

[...]

All good wishes to you

Ever faithfully yours
[G. E. Morrison]

881. From C. W. Kinder[2]

Near Farnham Surrey [England] 15 August 1917

My dear Morrison,

Awfully glad to get yours of 22nd June[3] and to hear you and yours are still going strong in spite of the usual assorted revolutions and scraps among the

---

coup on 1 July 1917, and retired to the French Concession in Tientsin, Feng went to Peking to take up the post of Acting President, having arranged for his subordinate, Li Ch'un, formerly Military Governor of Kiangsi, to succeed him at Nanking. As the leader of what is known as the Chihli Clique of militarists, Feng soon came into conflict with the Anfu Clique headed by Tuan Ch'i-jui, the Prime Minister, who had him replaced by Hsü Shih-ch'ang by means of Hsü's election by a rigged Parliament controlled by the Anfu Clique in October the following year. Feng died some six months before he could witness Tuan Ch'i-jui's overthrow by his followers as a result of the first war between the Anfu and Chihli Cliques in July 1920.

[1] Cecil Arthur Verner Bowra (1869–1947), British employee of the Chinese Maritime Customs which he joined in 1886. In 1910 he became the Chief Secretary of the Inspectorate-General, a post he held until 1923. He was then appointed the administration's London Secretary serving there until his retirement in 1927. He was the father of Sir Cecil Maurice Bowra (1898–1971), the well-known scholar and writer, for many years Warden of Wadham College, Oxford (1938–1970).

[2] Claude William Kinder (1852–1936), British railway engineer, who had been General Manager and Engineer-in-Chief of the Imperial Chinese Railways for thirty-one years. While in that position he was the subject of diplomatic wrangling between Britain and Russia, and Morrison as *Times* Correspondent was deeply involved in his case and later became Kinder's champion in his dispute with his Chinese employers. Kinder, who resigned his post to return to England in 1906, had been highly critical of Chinese and the Chinese Government.   [3] Not printed.

Chinese in and around Peking. I did not know that you had so many sons. You must be regarded as quite a big boss amongst the natives.

I see in *Times* that you have sold your library for £35,000 so it is about time you retired, came here and gave beans to all and sundry. If I ever go to China again it will be to apologise to the Chinese for having given them hell so often as I find that they are really no worse than the average European of today when rascality of every kind infests everything. The ruffians one now sees everywhere rolling in ill-gotten gains is a caution and war-profiteering is *the* thing.

Always great talk about putting it down but nothing is actually done, just like the old Peking game only on a far larger scale. Thank Heaven the Germans are just as bad or we should have long since been licked. Do you take in *The New Europe* if not do so, it is published weekly and is the only publication that really indicates conditions in this part of the world.

[...] Very sorry my land at P.T.H.[1] went to a beastly Fritz. I left it to Doney & Co. to sell as I wanted to bring all my money etc. to England and save all the bother over income tax etc. Five bob in the £ makes a big hole in the dollar bag, but I have all I want in spite of it, so cannot grumble. You fellows out East are lucky to be free from all such charges and the Ry. men seem to be having a real good time and probably agree with the wife with a big separation allowance who said the 'War is too good to last'. It is a perfect scandal this allowance and most females marry anyone in Khaki in order to get it plus pension if husband is wiped out. My maid was only 8 days with her new husband and gets 15/– a week plus the good pay she has from me. None of them save anything and all is spent on pleasure dress and jewellery. The Yanks are wiser and give no allowances to women married to soldiers after declaration of war unless they have children. Fritz is encouraging all women to have kids married or otherwise if the latter it is call[ed] 'official child birth' or pregnancy – I wonder if we shall come to that?

But for the universal use of 'preventitives' we should at least double our birthrate, especially the illegitimate type as morals have ceased to exist in almost all classes of society. We are on Devonport rations and manage alright as female servants don't eat as much as men so I get more than my share. If Germans put 300 U boats into the water next Spring I think it likely we shall run short of grub and have trouble with the 'poor workingman' class that has become accustomed to live far better than the proverbial Lord. We have howled for years for the appointing of 'business men' to regulate government affairs, but before such men have been in a warm berth for a month they become just like the old red-tape article and adopt all the old rotten obstructive methods and impossible English in their notices and correspondence. The chief aim of all is to shove the blame for any action or delay upon some

---

[1] Pei-tai-ho, the seaside resort on the Gulf of Pechili, south of Shanhaikwan, favoured by foreign diplomats and residents in and around Peking.

other Dept. and the devil himself does not seem to relish the hindermost as they still hang on or get promoted.

I am now on the Food Control business, and am to run Controllers about in my car, whenever these gentlemen turn up. The pay is 1/6 a day which about pays for the water for washing the car, but I don't mind that so long as it is useful work. The d——d newspapers make such a fuss over Ramsey Macdonald,[1] Snowdon[2] and such bounders, they would be utterly unheard of unless thus advertised and cease to give any trouble. They are only out for cheap notoriety like most of the wind-bags in and out of Parliament.

Russia is playing Cain and it is lucky we have the Yanks to help us to finish Fritz. Kerensky[3] does not know the Russians, if he did he would go about with a Cross and run the religious game, that is the only way to make them pull together. Personally I wish Roosevelt would go to Moscow, as a thorough-bred Republican President he would have greater influence than anyone else and might point out successfully the difference between anarchy and freedom. The Russian is a sentimental kid and must be handled as such. Preach a crusade to him and he will roll up in millions, and fight like the devil. I am lost in admiration of our troops, I never thought it possible such men could be made of the rotten material we had. The semi-effeminate public school boy has become an air-man of the best and his pluck an eye-opener to us all. The Australian and New Zealanders are the best men all round. The Canadians too are tip top but 80% of them have been born in England.

I expect you are cussing me for worrying you with this long letter. Anyhow

[1] James Ramsay MacDonald (1886–1937), British politician. In 1924 he was to become the first Labour Prime Minister, a position he again held from 1929 to 1935, when he became Lord President of the Council in the Coalition Government.

[2] Philip Snowden (1864–1937), 1st Viscount, British politician. He was a Labour Member of the British House of Commons from 1906 to 1918 and from 1922 to 1931 and Chancellor of the Exchequer in the first Labour Government in 1924 and again from 1929 to 1931.

[3] Alexander Fedorovitch Kerensky (1881–1970), Russian politician who played a leading part in the overthrow of the Czarist regime in February 1917, becoming successively Minister of Justice (March–April 1917), Minister of War and of the Navy (May–September 1917), and then Prime Minister (July–November 1917) in the Provisional Government. Some three weeks after this letter was written, on September 9, he succeeded in putting down the military revolt led by General Lavr Georgyevich Kornilov (1870–1918), Commander-in-Chief of the Russian forces and former Russian Military Attaché in Peking (1907–11). But Kerensky was deposed in the take-over by the Bolsheviks led by Vladimir Ilyich Lenin (1870–1924), two months later, on 7 November, and he fled to France, living there and in England until 1940, when he moved to Australia, and in 1946 to the United States, where he became a lecturer and a regular contributor to newspapers and magazines. He gave his version of the Russian Revolution in his books, *The Prelude to Bolshevism: the Kornilov Rebellion* (London 1919), *The Catastrophe* (London 1927) and *The Road to the Tragedy* (London 1935).

drop me a line before long as I never get any news from China and most people there have forgotten me.

With best wishes to you and yours

Yours very sincerely
C. W. Kinder

882. To O. M. Green

[Peking] 27 August 1917

My dear Green,

It was a pleasure to receive your letter of the 24th August.[1]

Last night I returned from Peitaiho and to-day I completed the transaction for the sale of my library.[2] The money has been ordered to be paid over, and the keys will be handed over to-morrow to the representative of Baron Iwasaki.

It would be absurd to pretend that I do not feel deeply parting with this hobby. The collection of the books have given me pleasure and happiness, and up to quite recently comparatively little anxiety. It is a curious coincidence that only since I handed over the catalogue to the Japanese on the 21st April have I lost books by enemy action at sea. All consignments have reached me safely until last May when on the 4th and the 29th May two consignments were sent to the bottom; where has not been disclosed to me.

My own movements are quite uncertain. Now that China has come into the war I feel a certain measure of satisfaction, and no doubt I will have more strongly as time goes on a feeling of freedom to which I have been a stranger for some years. Once I knew that the library could be sold for £35,000 I have had considerable anxiety lest any hitch should occur in the transaction, for although I feel deeply parting with my collection it would not be right that I, 55 years of age, with a young wife and three young children and with an uncertain income should retain in my possession so valuable a white elephant as a £35,000 collection of books.

I still retain of course my English books, and no doubt from time to time I will add to my collection of English illustrated works of the early '60s.[3]

[1] Not printed.
[2] The contract for the sale of the Library was signed, according to Morrison's Diary, by Morrison and Odagiri, the representative of the Yokohama Specie Bank in Peking, on behalf of Baron Iwasaki Hisaya on 28 and not 27 July. In his Diary entry for 28 July 1917 Morrison wrote: 'This morning at 10 Odagiri came to my office and signed the contract for the purchase of my library. He signed *ad referendum* but I think he was furnished with adequate authority. At the same time I handed him a letter by which I undertook to add to the library those books etc. I have received since April 21 – amounting to more than 500 items. So I have acted generously and I hope now that the transaction will be completed quickly.'
[3] Among the English books which Morrison retained, probably the most valuable was his collection of rare editions of *Robinson Crusoe*, considered by experts to be one of the best in the world. This collection went to his second son, Alastair, after the death of Jennie Morrison, and was sold by him during the Second World War.

I will now endeavour to sell my old property and it may be that I will go down to Australia this year. If not this year, certainly early next year, on six months' leave of absence. Paid in gold, I lose heavily by the high rate of exchange, but the amount of work I am called upon to do is not worth the salary paid for it, yet if I were asked to take up such an appointment again I would require a much higher salary than the one which in my enthusiasm I was willing to accept in 1912. To think of what I have refused in the mistaken belief that by so doing I would improve my standing with the Chinese, and to think how little this availed me, the thought is irritating. A man joins the service as I did full of enthusiasm, believing that he would succeed where others had failed. This is the way with all foreign advisers who are worth anything. The experience of all of us is the same. The first year enthusiasm. The second year pessimism. The third year indifference.

During the conferences that were held in February and March much useful work was done by the five chief foreign advisers. I found our meetings most instructive, and I look back with pleasure to my association with men like Padoux and Willoughby. The memoranda which we then drafted for the Chinese Government are the memoranda which have been used to a large extent in China's subsequent action, but essential portions of our advice have been disregarded, especially the portion dealing with the internment of Germans, which we all consider absolutely imperative, and the taking over of full jurisdiction over all German subjects. To allow Germans to go about as they are going about now is to render farcical China's declaration of war. I am convinced that it is timidity which is at the back of China's feeble action and that as she feels her ground she will act more strongly.

I have very little news to give you. Sir John Jordan is leaving England at the end of this month, returning to Peking via Canada, to remain here until the end of the war. Alston's movements are uncertain. He may return. He may be willing to remain on in the hope of the succession. My own belief, and one about which I spoke to you when you were in Peking, is that the Japanese Legation here will be raised to an embassy, and so of course will the Chinese Legation in Tokyo, that America will follow suit, and that England will do likewise. In that case Sir John Jordan would remain here as ambassador. He is old and feeble, much older than his years, petulant and difficult to discuss with dispassionately. His outlook is narrow: his speciality of a very restricted type. Still he works faithfully, will carry out strenuously any instructions given him. He has no views of his own where government policy is concerned and is thus a docile servant such as a government likes. But it is an advantage having him as doyen. He has at any rate prestige and dignity, which poor Alston, under the domination of Mrs. Barton, completely lacks. [...]

Yours very sincerely
[G. E. Morrison]

883. To A. E. Wearne

[Peking] 6 September 1917

My dear Wearne,
[...]
Things are going slowly. China at last came into the war. The date of the declaration, as you may have noticed, was the 14th August, the anniversary of the date upon which the Peking Legations were relieved in 1900.
[...]
China, will, I believe, if she is permitted to do so, send troops to the front. There is no question that there is a desire in China to do so. Whether they will be permitted to do so is another question. The financial difficulty could be solved, but the question of transport is a serious one. Although it seems strange to say so another serious question is: Who are to be the foreign officers attached to the Chinese troops? Japan would insist upon Japanese officers accompanying the force. My impression is that China in that case would refuse to send a force chiefly on the ground that Japan has not yet sent a single soldier to the front and if there are to be foreign officers they ought to be English or French or American.

The Japanese are considerably exercised by the prompt and determined way in which Americans are following up their declaration of war. They have come into it with both hands and with both feet, and will, I feel confident, gain many glorious triumphs over the common enemy of mankind.
[...]
Our chief concern now is the subject of exchange. The Mexican dollar to-day in Peking is worth 3/6½, and there is every indication that it will rise to 4/-. We who are paid in gold are suffering severely. On the other hand the Customs are thriving amazingly. Aglen's pay for example is at present £1,050 per month plus 14% *per annum* bonus plus a multitude of other advantages. Bowra is getting over £5,500 a year. Passeri is getting nearly £6,000 a year. I do not know whether it was in your time or later that men began gambling in roubles. Vast stores of roubles are held in Peking. One friend of mine holds 13,000 which he purchased at 90. To-day he could sell them for 18, and there seems to be some prospect of their going still lower. Frodsham said to me a day or two ago that he proposed to buy roubles when they were at $10.

What is to happen in regard to Russia we are quite unable to foresee. Kroupenski, who is now Ambassador in Tokyo and who only lost getting the Embassy in London owing to a change in the Foreign Office in Petrograd, is fearfully pessimistic about his own position. Great estates are being torn up and anarchy continues to pursue its devastating course. Here the Russian Minister is an amiable man named Prince Koudacheff.[1] All that has happened is a fearful loss of face to him.

[1] Prince N. A. Koudacheff, Russian diplomat, who succeeded Basil Kroupensky as Minister

[...]
No time for more. All good wishes to you and good luck. I am proud of the way you have earned the commendation of your superior officers.
Best wishes

Very sincerely yours
[G. E. Morrison]

884. To Liang Ch'i-ch'ao[1]

[Peking] 3 October 1917

Dear Mr. Liang,

I must apologise for having to trespasss upon your time in asking you to be so kind as to look into a small private matter which concerns those foreign members of the Chinese Government Service who are paid in gold. I understand that some of my colleagues have already spoken on this subject, and I wish to join them.

The question is one affecting Monsieur Padoux (French), Monsieur Konovaloff (Russian),[2] Monsieur de Codt (Belgian), General Aoki and Professor Ariga (Japanese), the successor of Dr. Willoughby (American), Sir Richard Dane, Mr. Lucas and myself (British). It may be that there are one or two others, but I do not know for certain.

We are all paid in gold. Our contracts provide that we shall be paid in gold. The Chinese Government has faithfully fulfilled its obligations towards us. None of us has any legal claim. We signed these contracts and we are in duty bound to carry them out, but a situation has arisen which was not foreseen, and it is to consider this unforeseen situation that we are asking Your Excellency's attention.

Owing to the War, the price of silver in relation to gold has changed so seriously that we who are paid in gold are receiving little more than one half

---

to China in March 1916. In 1917, after the Bolsheviks seized power in Russia, he ignored instructions sent to him by Leon Trotsky (1879-1940), Commissar for Foreign Affairs, to carry out the policy of the Soviet Government or resign. In September 1920, following the Soviet Government's undertaking to relinquish all Russian concessions and treaty rights in China, permission was granted by Yen Hui-ch'ing (otherwise W. W. Yen) (1877-1950), then Chinese Foreign Minister (August 1920 – December 1921) for Dzevaltovsky (*alias* Yourin) to establish himself as the Russian diplomatic agent in Peking. On 24 September 1920 Koudacheff, who had been informed by the Chinese Government the previous day of the withdrawal of recognition of his credentials and those of the Russian consuls in China, announced the termination of his mission and left China in January 1921.

[1] At this time Minister of Finance (July–November 1917).
[2] N. A. Konovaloff, formerly Russian employee of the Chinese Maritime Customs which he joined in 1897. He was appointed an auditor in connection with the Five-Power Reorganisation Loan in 1913, a position he was still occupying at the time of this letter. He had been Private Secretary to Sir Robert Hart in 1900 and was Commissioner of Customs at Newchwang during the Russian occupation there. In 1906 he became the first Commissioner of Customs in Harbin.

the salary that we were formerly paid. In my own case, for example, my salary last month was only Taels 1,368, a salary less than that received by most Commissioners of Customs in the Chinese service.

It is a great satisfaction to all the foreign employees paid in gold to know that the Chinese Government is profiting so greatly by this increased price of silver. Would it not be possible for Your Excellency to arrange for payment to be made to us in future half in gold and half in silver at the fixed and normal rate of ten dollars to the English pound. In this way relief would be given which would cost the Government but little, and would be of great advantage to the foreign members, for the dollar now purchases less than it did formerly. Similar provision to this is made in the case of all Chinese Government railway employees, by foreign Governments in the case of their employees in China, and by the foreign banks in China. In the case of the railway employees the concession made is even more advantageous to the employee than a payment half [. . .][1]

[G. E. Morrison]

885. From Ishida Mikinosuke[2]

Tokyo 30 October 1917

Dear Sir,

Tokyo was visited early in the morning of the 1st inst., by a severe typhoon, which left serious damage in its track and was the cause of a tidal wave quite unexpected by anybody. The valuable books forming the 'Dr. G. E. Morrison Library' (which I am proud to have escorted to Japan) only arrived at the Capital a few days prior to the catastrophe, and were then lying in one of the Mitsubishi Godowns at Fukagawa on their way to their final destination, but notwithstanding that they were thus protected, part of them unfortunately suffered damage as the result of the abnormal weather. Although the damage done to the books was generally speaking slight, I had the intention of reporting to you on the matter, in detail, much earlier than this, in the hope of relieving you of any anxiety you may have entertained as regards their fate, but my whole time having been devoted to the care of the damaged books, acting under the keen impulse to do so created by their great value, I regret that I have not had the opportunity to write you before now. However, I believe you will readily make allowances, in view of the many difficulties I have had to contend with in the meantime. I am given to understand that

[1] The continuation of this letter has not been found.
[2] Ishida Mikinosuke (1891–1974), Japanese scholar, a specialist in Chinese history, and later Professor at Nihon Daigaku in Tokyo. He was in charge of the transfer of the Morrison Library to Tokyo, becoming Curator of the Tōyō Bunko, in which Morrison's library was housed, on its establishment in 1924, and was the author of many books on Chinese history.

Mr. Inouye,[1] President of the Yokohama Specie Bank, has been asked in a cable message from Mr. Odagiri[2] to enquire after the books, and although I learn that a reply has already been wired back, I think I should not, even so, lose a single moment in reporting to you fully on the matter.

The typhoon which visited us on the 30th ult., was of a very severe nature, in fact unprecedented in living memory, and its violence was at its greatest intensity at 2 a.m. next morning, when a tidal wave formed in Tokyo Bay, which flooded a corner of the Metropolis and paying no respect to the above named godown where the books were temporarily stored, a part of them got soaked with water although still in the cases. I may mention that this godown was specially selected for the storage on account of its being reckoned a safer place than any other from every point of view. But who can tell! This safe place turned out to be unsafe after all *vis à vis* an Act of God! As a matter of fact, the godown is perfectly waterproof, and is situated at a distance of about one and a half mile from the sea; but the progress of the tidal wave was so swift that the servants on duty there were utterly unable notwithstanding their utmost efforts to take any steps to check the rush of water. I might also add that the packing can hardly be blamed, though water made its way through the broken seams of the tin lining of the cases. As was to be expected under the circumstances, some of the godown servants were on the alert and soon noticed what was taking place, but on account of there being insufficient hands available, they could do nothing to protect the books at the moment. Besides it being in the depth of night, with a severe storm raging outside, and with the suspension of any handy means of communication due to the derangement of the telephonic system by the typhoon, any call for help was impossible. The cases had, therefore, to be left at the mercy of the water (two and a half feet deep) for about two hours, after which the flood began gradually to subside. At last with great effort the servants succeeded in

[1] Inoue Junnosuke (1866–1932), Japanese politician and banker. He joined the Bank of Japan after graduating from the Imperial University in Tokyo in 1896 and rose to become its Governor. At this time he was the Managing Director of the Yokohama Specie Bank. He was Minister of Finance in 1923 in the second Yamamoto cabinet and again in 1929 in the cabinet of Hamaguchi Osachi (1870–1931) retaining the portfolio in the second cabinet of Wakatsuki Reijirō (1866–1949) formed in 1931 after the assassination of Hamaguchi. Inoue himself was assassinated during the election that took place after the assassination of Inukai Tsuyoshi. Inoue became one of the six trustees of the Tōyō Bunko on its foundation in 1924.

[2] Odagiri Masunosuke (1868–1934), Japanese diplomat and banker. He was Acting Consul-General then Consul-General in Shanghai from 1897 to 1905 when at the request of the Yokohama Specie Bank he became its representative in Peking. In this position he was responsible for Japanese financial activities in China and under his direction the Bank became the chief single creditor of the Chinese Government. In 1919 he accompanied Marquis Saionji to the Paris Conference as adviser and visited Morrison during his last illness while in England. It was Odagiri who negotiated the purchase of Morrison's library by Baron Iwasaki in 1917 and he became a trustee on the foundation of the Tōyō Bunko in 1924.

removing the damaged cases, thus saving a lot of the valuable books in them, amounting [to] some eight thousand in number, from being soaked. As soon as day broke, the entire lot of the cases were removed to the compound of the Mitsubishi Buildings near Tokyo Station, where the highest experts were consulted and every available means called into assistance, while no expense nor labour was spared in order to attain an immediate amelioration of the situation. (As regards details of the methods we adopted in this connection, I trust I may find an opportunity to give them to you later on.) In fact, a lot of people were hired to assist in the salvage and subsequent necessary operations. Many professors of the Imperial University, *inter alia*, Messrs. Taki,[1] Uyeda,[2] Matsubara,[3] Nagaoka,[4] Tamba[5] and other gentlemen also came in person and lent their inestimable help to our work, giving valuable service and important information as to the best means of overcoming the various difficulties. Prof. Sayce[6] too, who is now in Kyoto, was likewise kind enough to enlighten us through Prof. Hamada,[7] on the treatment of books in such an emergency. We found, after careful and minute examination, that about two thirds of the books were more or less damaged, including a few thousands of those in pamphlet and magazine form. However, thanks to the careful packing, about 85% of these books were only spoiled cover deep, the damage not penetrating any further, so that these can easily be restored to their original

---

[1] Taki Seiichi (1873–1945), Japanese art historian and critic, Professor of Fine Arts at Kyoto University then at Tokyo University, where he was at the time of this letter.

[2] Ueda Kazutoshi (1867–1937), Japanese scholar. A graduate of the Imperial University in Tokyo, he also studied in Germany and France. He was at this time Professor and Dean of Literature at his *alma mater*. In 1924 he was made a trustee of the Tōyō Bunko on its foundation.

[3] Matsubara Kōichi (1872–1955), Japanese scientist, a pioneer in the field of organic chemistry in Japan. He became a professor of the Imperial University in Tokyo in 1909 three years after his graduation. In 1929 he was to become the Dean of the Science Department.

[4] Nagaoka Hantarō (1865–1950), Japanese scientist. He studied in Japan and Germany. He became Professor of Physics at Tokyo Imperial University in 1896, and in 1931 the first President of Osaka University.

[5] Tamba Keizō (1854–1927), Japanese scientist, a specialist in hygiene and forensic chemistry. After spending three years studying in Germany he returned in 1887 to become a Professor at Tokyo Imperial University and was the founder in the following year of the Pharmacological College in Tokyo.

[6] The Reverend Archibald Henry Sayce (1845–1933), British scholar. Reader of Comparative Philology at Oxford from 1876 to 1890, he became Professor of Assyriology there in 1891, a post he held until 1919. A specialist on the early history of south-western Asia and northern Africa, he wrote extensively on Assyrian, Babylonian and Egyptian cultures.

[7] Hamada Kōsaku (1881–1938), Japanese archaeologist. He was responsible for the introduction of modern scientific archaeological research into Japan. A specialist in the art and religions of ancient China, Japan and Korea, in all of which three countries he carried out extensive archaeological work, he became in 1917 Professor at Kyoto University, of which he was made President twenty years later, in 1937.

state by rebinding. The remaining 15%, to our great regret, were soaked to a fair extent and some, depending on the nature of the paper used were completely saturated. The majority of these being old, and therefore rare and costly books, it is idle to say that we were the more grieved about them, but consulting the opinions of several professors and judging from our own experiences, we are convinced that, should they be washed with fresh water and then carefully dried, they also will be brought to such a state of restoration as will make it well worth while to keep them. I am therefore acting accordingly, and of course they will be most carefully re-bound in due time.

You will now understand from the above details, that after all there was no great substantial damage done to the books on the whole, except to those printed in art papers, which are almost hopeless of repair. Still these being of comparatively recent publication, we may console ourselves with the hope of being able to purchase substitutes sometime.

I must not let this opportunity pass without mentioning that Baron Iwasaki, who is exceedingly grieved at the damage done to the books, is taking a personal and daily interest in all matters connected with them. And as for me, being persuaded that I am one of those who keenly appreciate the value of the 'Library,' and feeling and taking a special interest in it owing to my familiarity with the books, shall, needless to say, spare no pains to take the best care of them, in future as well as in the present.

With kind regards

Yours very truly
M. Ishida

P.S. For the periodicals and magazines you have been subscribing to the 'Library,' I have already placed my orders with the publishers for a future supply to us, and shall never neglect to obtain any new books worth purchasing to reinforce the 'Library'. It is gratifying to me to be able to inform you at the same time that I have been succesful in procuring some works on your 'Wanted books' List, including A. Pozdnieef's work in Russian on Mongolian Literature &c.

886. To W. W. Willoughby

[Peking] 31 October 1917

My dear Willoughby,

Your letter of the 12th of July[1] reached me a long time ago. I am ashamed to have allowed so long a time to pass without replying to you. Please forgive me.

Interesting things were happening as you wrote your letter. The astonishing restoration of the monarchy took place on the 1st of July, and on the 12th of July we residents in Peking were witnessing one of the most mighty

[1] Not printed.

combats that ever took place on earth – an encounter between Chang Hsun's men and the men of a stalwart monarchist upholder of the Republic, General Tuan Chih-kuei.[1] Total casualties on both sides amounted to 25 killed, mostly by stray shots. I should imagine that not less than 50 million shots were exchanged. Large bodies of men were engaged on both sides. Round my old house the shooting was most intense. No bird of passage could safely pass over Peking on that date. Nearly all the shots were fired into the air. Chang Hsun's residence, the point of attack, was on the bank of the canal just inside the Imperial City and on the same line as my old house. Firing began about 5 o'clock in the morning and continued steadily until midday, and then intermittently until 3 o'clock in the afternoon. In the lane passing behind my house serried masses of men were stationed, and they fired with machine-guns at Chang Hsun's residence. Millions upon millions of shots were fired. Distance was 150 yards, but there was a wall 30 ft. high and 6 ft. thick between. None of the shots struck the wall. What damage was done was done to harmless wayfarers two miles distant. A knowledge of ballistics is not an essential equipment as yet of the modern Chinese army. Now an American writer, Rodney Gilbert, is urging the restoration of the bow and arrow. His view is that a man with a rifle, who does not know how to use it, is not nearly so dangerous as a man with a bow and arrow who does know how to use his weapon. A Chinese soldier with a rifle is no great menace at more than 25 yards, while a practised hand with a bow and arrow may be a real menace up to 300 yards. That is his contention. He thinks that if the bow and arrow could be re-introduced it would be impossible with bows and arrows for two forces to remain two miles apart and waste sufficient money to establish a university or hospital. He thinks that the introduction of the bow would help to stamp out rebellions, because rebellions would then be dangerous.

During the bombardment of the 12th my house escaped damage. Since

[1] Tuan Chih-kuei (1869–1925), Chinese soldier. He had served during the Manchu Dynasty as Inspector-General of Police Forces of the Southern Section of Tientsin and in April 1907 acted briefly as Governor of Heilungkiang, allegedly as a result of bribing Prince Tsai-hsün, later the Minister of the Navy. A fellow provincial of Tuan Ch'i-jui, whose close associate he was, he was also a staunch supporter of Yüan Shih-k'ai and a ready tool in his political manoeuvres. In February 1914 he replaced Li Yüan-hung as Military Governor of Hupeh, holding the post until August 1915 when he was sent to Mukden as Military Governor of Fengtien Province, the loyalty of Chang Tso-lin having become suspect. However, Chang was able to capitalise on Yüan's worsening situation on the southern front against the republican forces in Yunnan under T'ang Chi-yao, and Tuan Chih-kuei was compelled to relinquish his post. His resignation was gazetted soon after Yüan's death in 1916. Though a supporter of Yüan's Imperial scheme, and involved in Chang Hsün's Restoration attempt, he escaped censure because of his relationship with Tuan Ch'i-jui, and even emerged as a saviour of the Republic, leading Tuan's army which occupied Peking on 12 July 1917. He was made Commander-in-Chief of the Garrison Forces in the Capital, a post he held until the overthrow in July 1920 of the Anfu Clique Government. He was concurrently Minister for the Army from December 1917 to January 1919.

the restoration of the Republic we are a Republic chiefly in name. Manoeuvring is now going on with a view to bringing about a reconciliation. Nothing is being accomplished.

China declared war on Germany on the 14th of August. She has given passports to the German and Australian [Austrian] Legations, she has dismissed various German employees, and in return she has made a very good bargain by getting far-reaching financial advantages. What is to happen now we do not know. Fourteen German and Austrian ships have been interned and made over to a private company in which many prominent officials are interested, and these ships, having been chartered at a small price, are to be re-chartered at a high price to the profit of the individual shareholders of the favoured company. The Minister of the Navy is the same old buster who was Minister under Yuan Shih-kai, and who became a Duke, I believe, on the restoration of the monarchy in Yuan's time.[1] His son is compradore to a German firm. There has been considerable difficulty in obtaining the use of the ships for the common cause against Germany.

Liang Chi-chiao, 'a man of high ideals', is Minister of Finance. The outlook is obscure. Feng Kuo-chang is still only Acting President, and by insisting upon having only an acting post his position is stronger than if he were *de facto* President in the present chaos.

Tuan Chi-jui, the Prime Minister, appears to have considerable capacity. He seems to bear resemblance to Terauchi, the Prime Minister of Japan. The two know each other and are much akin.

The Minister of Finance, Liang Chi-chiao, the Minister of Communications, Tsao Ju-lin, and the powerful military leader Hsu Shu-ch'êng,[2] Vice-Minister of War, are all strongly pro-Japanese. Their action is causing

[1] Liu Kuan-hsiung, Minister of the Navy through successive cabinet changes until June 1916, after Yüan Shih-k'ai's death, when he was removed for his support of the Imperial scheme which had earned him a dukedom from Yüan. He was recalled to the same portfolio by Tuan Ch'i-jui after Chang Hsün's abortive Restoration attempt in July 1917, and he held the post until January 1919.

[2] Hsü Shu-cheng (1880–1925), Chinese soldier and Republican politician, chief lieutenant of Tuan Ch'i-jui and co-founder of the Anfu Club in March 1918. From the time of his appointment as Deputy Secretary of the Cabinet under Tuan in 1916 he became a dominant and disruptive force in the Government. He was largely responsible for intensifying the conflict between Tuan and Li Yüan-hung. As Vice-Minister of War from May 1914 to June 1915, and again from August to November 1917 during which time China declared war on Germany, he played a leading role in the negotiations with Nishihara Kamezō for the loan to reorganise and equip Tuan's army. It was his activities as Commissioner for North-Western Frontier Development and Commander-in-Chief of the North-Western Frontier Defence Forces in the western part of Manchuria, which Chang Tso-lin regarded as his sphere of influence, that compelled Chang to throw in his lot with the Chihli Clique, and this helped in the overthrow of the Anhwei Clique in the civil war of July 1920. In December 1925 he was intercepted while on the train from Peking to Tientsin, by troops of Feng Yü-hsiang who had him shot to avenge the death of Lu Chien-chang, a relative of Feng whom Hsü had had summarily executed in 1918.

great anxiety. There never has been such an invasion of Japanese as is now to be seen in Peking. Ex-Ministers, Members of Parliament, military officers, engineers, financiers – it is really an organised campaign. A large part of the time of the Chinese officials is now occupied in giving entertainment to Japanese.

A National Council has been summoned, and its members are now being elected or selected, but no heed is being given to this Council by the Southern leaders. A separate mock parliament is being held in Canton under the leadership of Sun Yat-sen, that enlightened warrior who once proposed to lead an army of five million men into Russia, and to reform the finances of China by the issue of an inconvertible paper currency unsupported by bullion. His emergence as Generalissimo provokes derisive laughter, but is one of the most serious indications of the trend of Chinese politics. He has the support of a considerable number of enlightened men. How many we do not know, because very little is allowed to be known of what is passing in Canton. I am going down there in a few days to see for myself.

Now in reply to your various questions.

Eugene Chen is in Shanghai, doing work for the *China Press*, and writing manifestos to foreign countries. Chen Chin-tao[1] is still in durance vile on a bribery charge, sentenced to imprisonment for several years, the sentence having been confirmed today on appeal.

[...]

You are quite right in what you say about the Parliament and about the drafting of the permanent Constitution, which will have to be begun from the beginning.

[...]

Since you left, the foreign Advisers have had very little to do. On Saturday evening several of them dined with me: Ariga, Aoki, de Codt, Padoux, Konovaloff, and one or two more. Dr. Reinsch tells us that your successor is to be William Cullen Dennis.[2] You may be sure that we shall all give him a hearty welcome. [...]

You will have heard that I sold my library to the Japanese. Several years ago I made a promise that I would give them the first refusal, and when I found that I could get an offer for £35,000 from America, under certain conditions, I offered the collection to the Japanese for this price, making the condition that the library should remain intact, should continue to bear my

---

[1] Accused of accepting a bribe, Ch'en Chin-t'ao was dismissed from his post of Minister of Finance on 16 April 1917 and was arrested two days later. He was not cleared of the charge and released from prison until 5 February 1918. The charge against him had been inspired by Tuan Ch'i-jui and Liang Shih-yi.

[2] William Cullen Dennis (1878–1962), American lawyer. He had taught Law at Stanford, Columbia and George Washington Universities from 1904 to 1909 and was in private practice from 1911 to 1917, when he was appointed Legal Adviser to the Chinese Government succeeding W. W. Willoughby, remaining until 1919.

name, and should be kept in a building associated with the University, or with the Imperial Library, or with an institution devoted to Oriental learning. It was always to be open for the use of serious students. An arrangement was come to, the money was paid, and the library duly shipped to Japan, and there it has been ruined, irretrievably ruined. For three days the books were under water. They were packed in straw, in badly-made tin-lined cases, the lids of which were not sealed. I understand the collection will have to be rebound, and as one of its chief merits was the fact that every book was in the original binding, you can see what damage re-binding will do to the value – especially Japanese re-binding.

I am leaving for Australia the day after to-morrow. I shall be absent six months. The Chinese have treated me well, and have even contributed something towards the expense of my holiday – in Chinese bank-notes, which now stand at 74. My wife and children remain here. I am very much interested to see the conditions in Australia, and a good many Australians have expressed the wish that I should go down there and speak to them of the conditions in the Far East, especially in regard to Japan.

I do not know whether you will have come in contact with either of the two Japanese Commissions which are now in America. Ishii was Minister of Foreign Affairs when Japan flatly refused to join her Ally in inviting China to enter the war. His action led to a prolonging of the war, the prolongation continuing until America entered. The thought of his ill-considered statecraft must often make him furiously think. The last thing on earth that Japan wished for was the entry of America into the war. Now England and America must unite and act together throughout future ages.

In Megata's mission[1] you will note that one of the chief members is Koike,[2] who calls himself Managing-Director of the Kuhara Copper Syndicate. When head of the political bureau of the Foreign Office in Tokyo he was the author of the 21 demands. He had been Consul-General in Mukden, and later Councillor to the Japanese Embassy in London. On his return to Tokyo, and his appointment to this high post in the Foreign Office, he had sufficient influence to force his views upon Kato, and to inspire him with the belief that Japan could rush these 21 demands.

[1] Megata Tanetarō (1853–1926), Japanese financial expert, a returned student from America. He was Director of Taxation in 1894 and was in charge of finance in the first Sino-Japanese War (1894–5) and again during the Russo-Japanese War ten years later. He was appointed Financial Adviser to the Government in Korea and became the *de facto* financial overlord of this Japanese-occupied country.

[2] Koike Chōzō (1873–1921), Japanese diplomat. He had been Consul-General in Mukden (1908–11), and later as Director of the Political Bureau of Japan's Foreign Ministry he was the architect of the Twenty-One Demands presented to China in January 1915. In 1916 he resigned to become a Director of the Kuhara Mining Company, and in September 1917, at the invitation of the Terauchi Government, he became a member of the mission to the United States here described. His contribution to the success of the mission won him high rewards on his return to Japan.

With best wishes to you and to your daughter, and trusting that you have good news of your son, in all of which my wife joins me
I am

Very sincerely yours
[G. E. Morrison]

887. From H. Goffe[1]

Yunnanfu [Yunnan] 20 November 1917

My dear Morrison,

I was very glad to see your fist again, after such a long time. Your Japanese friend has not turned up yet, but I shall be very glad to see him and do all I can for him when he does.[2] The Japanese are paying great attention to this province, much to the annoyance of the French; they even object to my activities here, looking upon it as entirely a French preserve, if not part of Tonkin.

[...] I am going to do my utmost to retire when I do go home; I am fed up with China, from every point of view. The Chinese do the same silly things they have done for the last 25 years, and our men have no idea beyond routine work; to anything else they pay no attention and just like to go on in the old grooves, without any policy at all. The British empire is the most fearful and wonderful of God's works; I wonder it survives at all; it surely must have something inherently vital in it and be based on internal principles, otherwise we could never muddle through as we do. How long O Lord?

China seems to be in a nice mess again and Heaven only knows how it will all pan out. Tuan Chi Jui seems to be the great stumbling block. To my mind China will never do any good until they change the capital to Nanking or Wuchang, the latter for preference; the Peking atmosphere is too strong for Chinese as well as foreigners. They all disregard entirely what happens outside the walls of Peking and imagine that when they have settled something to their liking round a table in Peking that the last word has been said. The actual facts are very far from that, but nothing short of an earthquake will make Peking Chinese or foreigners realise it.

The French cripple this province with their transit dues in Tonkin and their differential railway tariff. At the Peace Conference China ought to demand free access to the sea, if Yunnan is not to become a second Serbia; the Powers ought to see to it in the re-mapping of the world, as it is in their

[1] Herbert (later Sir Herbert) Goffe (1870–1939), British consular official, Consul-Genera in Yunnan-fu from 1912 until his transfer to Tientsin in 1918. He later became Consul-General in Hankow and in that position it was he who negotiated with Ch'en Yu-jen, Foreign Minister in the Wuhan Government, the retrocession to China of the British Concession in Hankow.
[2] Kanai Kiyoshi, an employee of the Imperial Railways of Japan who had been introduced to Morrison by J. W. Robertson-Scott, Editor of the English-language journal in Japan, the *New East. See* p. 588 note 1.

interests just as much as in justice to China. We might insist upon our goods being free of transit dues and not subject to discriminatory railway tariffs if we chose; the London Chamber of Commerce reports shew the way. I have written to Peking about it, but of course get no answer. It is pretty hopeless and most discouraging.

Hope you'll have a good trip and come back full of vigour.[1]

Very sincerely yours
H. Goffe

888. To D. S. Robertson[2]

Manilla [The Philippines] 22 November 1917

My dear Robertson,

I ought to have written to you from Canton, but I was too pressed for time.

It seems to me from what I can hear along the coast that there are still a number of missionaries and lay brothers who would be willing if they were called upon, to go to the Front with the coolies.[3]

[...]

I arrived at Canton at a time when most of the Politicians were absent at Wuchow at a conference with Lu Yung ting.[4] I did not think it worth while

[1] A reference to Morrison's impending visit to Australia and New Zealand.
[2] David Stephen Robertson, British soldier, Military Attaché with the British Legation in Peking (1913–19).
[3] In May 1916 Liang Shih-yi, capitalising on his position, founded a company named Hui-min kung-ssu to recruit Chinese labourers for the European War. This company under the direction of Liang Ju-ch'eng, manager of the Bank of Communications, signed a contract on 14 May with the representative of the French Government, Colonel Truptil. As China was still a neutral country, Truptil was camouflaged under the title of 'Agricultural Engineer', to avoid international complications. By this contract, China for the next two and a half years was to send some 200,000 men from the four ports of Tientsin, Pukow, Tsingtao and Hong Kong to France and her colony Algeria, to work in factories as well as on the battlefield, digging trenches and servicing transport. The French example was followed by Russia at Harbin and by Britain at Weihaiwei. Men of these nationalities were invited to be interpreters and to take charge of the Chinese workers so recruited, referred to here as 'coolies'. Liang and his associates were severely criticised for profiting from the War and the misfortune of these labourers, a great many of whom never saw their homeland again.
[4] Lu Yung-t'ing (1856–1927), Chinese soldier, a brigand who rose to become overlord of his native Kwangsi Province until he was ousted in 1921. He was at this time joint Deputy Generalissimo together with T'ang Chi-yao of Yunnan Province, in the Military Government set up in Canton on 1 September 1917 under the leadership of Sun Yat-sen, who assumed the title of Generalissimo. In July the following year he was to force the reorganisation of the Government which resulted in the removal of Sun from his supreme position. Lu's rule in Canton was strongly resented by the local warlords who were advocating 'Canton for the Cantonese', and this led to warfare in 1920, ending in the expulsion from Kwangtung of the Kwangsi forces.

to see Sun Yat Sen who is generalissimo in all his glory in the Cement Works of Canton.[1] The saying is there that his jurisdiction does not extend outside the wall of the compound.

[...]

Believe me

Very sincerely yours
[G. E. Morrison]

P.S. It will be of interest to you to know that there is on board here a man of whom I have known for many years, and of whose correctness of information I have no doubt, and he tells me this – in Tsingtao there are now sixteen thousand Japanese. There were twenty two British but now one or two less. The Enemy Trading Act came into force on June 1st. Despite this Act the Japanese Government purchased on August 31st, and paid cash for them, the three hotels in Tsingtao. They purchased them from Angustessen the agent for Sietas Planbeck, paying $450,000, approximately Yen 750,000. They have been sold to Amano for Yen 120,000, which includes one hotel sold out right (the best one) and the lease duty and rent free for ten years of the two other hotels.

This Amano, a broker from Osaka, is a kinsman of Col. Koizumi[2] who was Military Administrator under General Otani[3] and now under General Hongo.[4] As you know the civil administration of Tsingtao has been taken over (October 1st) by Dr. Akiyama[5] who, curiously enough is full brother, but adopted into another family, of Col. Koizumi. Nominally the administration of Tsingtao is civil, actually the administration is, as it always has been, under the military, the present officer in command being General Hongo who succeeded Otani, who again succeeded Kamio.[6]

[1] The headquarters of the Military Government under Sun Yat-sen in Canton.
[2] Koizumi Masayasu (d. 1917). A former Military Attaché with the Japanese Legation in Peking, he had taken part in the Russo-Japanese War (1904-5) and then became Garrison Commander in Formosa.
[3] Ōtani Kikuzō (1855-1923), Japanese soldier who took part in both the first Sino-Japanese War (1894-5) and the Russo-Japanese War. Garrison Commander of the Japanese forces in Tsingtao (May-1915 August 1917), he led the Japanese Expeditionary Forces to Siberia in 1918 and was created a Baron for his services.
[4] Hongo Fusataro (1860-1931), Japanese soldier, Vice-Minister of War in 1912, he was appointed to succeed General Ōtani at Tsingtao in August 1917, and in 1918 became a Member of the War Council.
[5] Akiyama Masanosuke (1866-1937), Japanese diplomat. He joined the Japanese Foreign Ministry after graduating from the Imperial University in Tokyo, becoming a Counsellor in 1897, but transferred to the War Office in 1904. He represented Japan at a number of international conferences and was made Governor of Tsingtao in 1917. He later became President (1933-4) of Hōsei University.
[6] Kamio Mitsutomi (1855-1927). Garrison Commander of Tsingtao upon its occupation by the Japanese forces, he held the post until May 1915.

Another little item which is worth noting is that Col. Taga[1] whose name is occasionally in the paper as Military Adviser to the *Tu-chun* of Nanking (formerly Feng Kuo chang, and now Feng's successor), is the brother of the Japanese retired military officer who led the Wei hsien insurrection of 1916.[2]

The Japanese are simply pouring into Hongkong and Canton. This ship[3] is full of hard headed business men returning from Japan where they have been buying vast quantities of goods formerly supplied by Germany and Austria. One and all think there will be a terrific slump after the war.

889. To W. H. Donald

S.S. *Aki Maru* 23 November 1917

My dear Donald,

Yesterday I spent a day at Manilla, and tomorrow we are due at Zamboanga when I will post this note to you.

This ship is filled with commercial travellers returning from a round trip to Japan. None of them have been to China proper although one or two stayed over in Shanghai and one or two visited Canton. One man informed me last night of the impossibility of buying amber and showed me an imitation cigarette holder of which he had purchased 10,000 in Japan. He was much astonished when I told him amber was one of the most widely distributed products of China and that amber ornaments are among the most beautiful of China's cheap curios. I told this particular man to put himself

[1] Taga Muneyuki (1872–1935), Japanese soldier and intelligence officer who spent thirty years in China. In 1902 he became Adviser to Yüan Shih-k'ai, and was Chief Military Instructor at the Paoting Military Academy, remaining in China until 1910. Upon the outbreak of the Revolution in 1911 he was sent back to Peking by the Chief of Staff, and there conspired with the Japanese Police Chief of Peking, Kawashima Naniwa (b. 1865) – allegedly the adoptive 'father' of a daughter of Prince Su (Shan-ch'i) (?1866–1922), Kawashima Yoshiko, the notorious secret agent before and during the second Sino-Japanese War (1937–45) – to prevent the revolutionary takeover and to set up a separate state in North China with the child-Emperor P'u-yi at its head. When this failed following the assassination of Liang-pi and the flight of Shan-ch'i under Kawashima's protection, Taga joined other Japanese military adventurers in fomenting the revolt of the Mongols in Inner Mongolia and Western Manchuria against the new Republic. In 1914 Taga, who was with the Japanese occupation army in Shantung, was sent as a spy to Nanking, where he was appointed, in 1917, an adviser to Feng Kuo-chang, then to Feng's successor Li Ch'un, and later to Ch'i Hsieh-yüan (1879–1946).

[2] On 4 May 1916, with the encouragement and active support of the Japanese occupation forces in Shantung, the Republicans under the command of Chu Cheng, acting on the instructions of Sun Yat-sen, attacked Weihsien and several neighbouring districts in Shantung. The Japanese not only rejected the protests of the Chinese Government but demanded the withdrawal of the Chinese garrison forces. A list of Japanese who took part in this incident, known as the Weihsien Insurrection, is given in *Tōa senkaku shishi kiden* (Tokyo 1935) Vol. II, Chapter 34, pp. 612–24.

[3] S.S. *Aki Maru*.

into communication with Archibald Rose C.I.E., Professor of Dancing and Deportment in the Department of Commerce, c/o British Legation, Peking.[1]

Another man who has been to Japan to purchase drugs was astonished when I told him how great were the possibilities of the purchase of drugs in China. He had a copy of the *Far Eastern Review* he had read with some [?pride]. He represents Felton & Grimwade,[2] Melbourne. I enjoined upon him the necessity of advertising in the *Far Eastern Review* as well as subscribing to it.

Another man told me that in the matter of men's socks he was unable to obtain the size he wanted in Canton and apparently he did not know how to approach the manufacturers, but that socks similar to those costing $1.00 or $1.50 he could sell in thousands from 6/6 to 9/6.

Friend Suttor has far too big a field to cover. Are you in touch with any advertising agents in Australia. The *Far Eastern Review* ought to be known in Australia especially as it is edited by an Australian.[3] I will do what I can to boost your papers, quite conscientiously, because it seems to be by far the best advertising medium for the Australian manufacturer and Colonial Governments.

I cannot learn anything about what I can do in Australia about steamer and railway communication, etc. You ought to have a special Australian number devoted to the advertising of their products and possibility of their sale in the China market.

Why not take up this case and write a series of papers upon the possible interchange of products between Australia and China? Ignorance is, as I told you before, colossal on both sides.

[...]

Australians are spending thousands in Japan and are ignorant of the existence of China. They are even importing Japanese blankets into Australia!

I am going to advocate the appointment of a High Commissioner of the Commonwealth to reside in Shanghai with proper official rank to take precedence immediately after the British Minister and to get a number of young men and have them trained in the language and conditions existing in the country. Many men are available. The Customs and Consular services ought to be schools for the training of men to be employed in the development of British trade. This is the American plan, but hitherto has not been the British one. Men are discouraged from leaving the services, whereas they ought to be encouraged to do so and enter into business. Sydney Mayers is a good example of what can be done.

Felton & Grimwade have products just as popular as Pink Pills for Pale

---

[1] Archibald Rose was at this time Commercial Attaché with the British Legation in Peking.
[2] A firm of wholesale druggists founded by Alfred Felton (1831–1904) with F. S. Grimwade in 1866.
[3] W. H. Donald.

People, and if they only realised the vast fortunes made by pills they would not neglect China.

[...]

With best wishes

[G. E. Morrison]

890. To W. H. Donald

S.S. *Aki Maru* 26 November 1917

My dear Donald,

[...]

It was a fine surprise that Mr Lansing gave to us all. The Exchange of notes of Nov. 2nd was published in Hongkong when I was there.[1] Heintzlemann[2] in Canton told me privately that relays of Chinese had thronged to see him all sounding one note – that they had been betrayed by America. After all her valiant protestations, what earthly good did America gain by making such a concession to Japan, giving recognition to that which every American and Englishman in China had been endeavouring to prevent. Carried to its logical conclusion this agreement gives recognition not only to Japan's 'special interests' in Manchuria, but also in Fu Chien Province which lies in 'geographical proximity' to Formosa. Surely the British will now claim recognition of their special interests in Yunnan Province, and France similarly in Kwangsi Province. It is all very deplorable.

Ishii seems to have completely hoodwinked America. I am confident that the Japanese appeal for the removal of the ban to the export of steel was a blind. Japan has got stocks of steel ample for all requirements during any reasonable continuation of the war. Steel plates which she purchased for $120 per ton are lying unsaleable at £60 per ton. Yards are clogged with steel. Japan has no wish to purchase more steel, for this would add to the inevitable loss that will come to her after the war. Japan has gambled to such an extent that if the war were to come to an end quickly a large section of her people would be ruined.

We are due to arrive at Thursday Island on Friday morning. What I have heard on board has not increased the cheerfulness of the prospect of revisiting my country after an absence of fifteen years. I hear nothing but

[1] On 22 November 1917 Robert Lansing, United States Secretary of State, and Ishii Kikujirō, Special Japanese Ambassador, exchanged Notes relating to the mutual interests of their two countries in China, by which the United States recognised 'that territorial propinquity creates special relations between countries, and, consequently, [. . .] that Japan has special interests in China, particularly in the part to which her possessions are contiguous'.

[2] Percival Stewart Heintzlemann (1880–1942), American consular official. He had served at various consular posts in China, as well as in the State Department, and was at this time Consul-General in Canton (1916–18). He later served at Tientsin (1918–19) and at Hankow (1920–25).

loafing and slacking and the disloyalty of Archbishops preaching open sedition,[1] and of men holding up their country at one of the most critical stages of the war.

I visited the Canton Christian College and I had opportunities given to me of speaking to a considerable number of that class who provide teachers to young China. There seemed to be a unanimity of feeling about them that the British as represented by Monkey Jamieson[2] and by the Government of Hongkong were wholly unsympathetic with the case of Young China.

In Monkey Jamieson we seem to have a very undesirable representative, foul mouthed, drunken, turbulent, but he is not wanting in ability and if he were properly directed he might serve his country well. I believe that he does not know personally and will not receive in the consulate any of the class of C. T. Wang.[3] Things seem to be in great confusion and there is no unity of purpose. They appear to be looking to the leadership of an ex-brigand, Lu Yung ting, who is a champion Facing Bothways. Most of the leaders were at Wuchow with Lu Yung ting who had come over from Nanning. Sun Yat Sen I would judge has no following outside the Cement Works, where he main-

---

[1] The reference is to Daniel Mannix (1864–1963), Irish-born Catholic Archbishop of Melbourne, Australia from 1917 until his death, and previously Co-adjutor Archbishop (1912–17). He was known for his anti-conscription stand against the then Prime Minister William Morris Hughes (1864–1952) in that hotly debated issue in Australia during the First World War. His stand swung the crucial Irish voters, normally supporters of Hughes, resulting in victory for the anti-conscription faction and the defeat of the Government in the two plebiscites held in October 1916 and November 1917. Mannix was regarded as unpatriotic for his stand in the highly jingoistic wartime atmosphere, and on his way to Ireland had been intercepted by a British gunboat because of his allegedly pro-German sympathies.

[2] James William Jamieson (1867–1946), British consular official, at this time Consul-General in Canton (1909–19). Before his retirement from the service in 1930, he also officiated as Consul-General in Shanghai from 1919 to 1920, and in Tientsin from 1926 to 1929. He was popularly called Monkey Jamieson because his unusually long upper lip was thought to resemble that of a chimpanzee.

[3] Wang Cheng-t'ing (1882–1961), Chinese Republican politician. A returned student from Japan and America, he was accidentally drawn into Republican politics soon after arriving back in China after the Wuchang Uprising. He became a delegate from Hupeh Province to the Senate in Nanking, and after the Manchu abdication, Deputy President of the Senate. He was made Acting Minister of Industry and Commerce in the first T'ang Shao-yi Cabinet, in place of Ch'en Ch'i-mei, who had refused to take up the post. In June 1917, after Parliament was dissolved for the second time, Wang went to Canton where he was at the time referred to Deputy Speaker of the Parliament there. From then on he was to play a prominent part in China's foreign relations, being a Chinese delegate to the Paris Conference and the Washington Conference, and many times Foreign Minister in the Peking Government and in the Nationalist Government from 1928 to 1931. He was responsible for the negotiation of some of the most important treaties with Russia and Japan, including those regarding the Chinese Eastern Railway, the retrocession of Shantung, and China's tariff autonomy. After 1931, he played no further role in Chinese politics apart from serving briefly as Ambassador to the United States (May 1937 – September 1938).

tains a mockery of state. No doubt I could have seen him had I had the time, but I got a bad cold in Canton and was fit for little.

Monkey Jamieson was absent. I wonder whether you met him in Peking. He announced that he was going to Peking to bring about a compromise. The day I was in Manila I read a Reuter's telegram which said that a coalition government is being formed.[1]

I hope you will write to me. I will be in the vicinity of Melbourne certainly until the middle of February. [...]

With best wishes to you

I am [G. E. Morrison]

891. From W. H. Donald

Peking 28 December 1917

My dear Doctor,

I hear that you arrived in Australia on the 7th (Sydney, I suppose) and that you are being treated as a distinguished visitor. That is what I expected. [...]

Re your letter from Thursday Island.[2]

[...]

I was in Tokyo when the Notes signed between Japan and America were published.[3] I took quite a different view from the one you take, and when I saw them I was delighted, because I read into them the fact that America had, to use an Americanism, completely 'put one over' Japan. Ishii went to America to get acquiescence in Japan's predominance in China, to get America to agree that Japan should establish a so-called 'Munroe Doctrine', and above all to get America to admit Japan's hegemony of the Pacific. He got neither. Instead, he had to reaffirm adherence to the previous undertakings – undertakings which were disregarded when Japan put in her 21 Demands. And in addition he had to agree that *no* power was to have exclusive rights in China.

What happened was this: Ishii went to the States, was asked what he had to say, said he wanted to talk of China, and was politely asked to come for a walk while the weather was fine. They showed him round the dockyards where battleships, submarines, etc. were being built, round the vast munition factories, through the camps of the new army. He was then asked back, and

---

[1] On 22 November 1917, a so-called coalition government was formed by Wang Ta-hsieh (1859–1928), formerly Chinese Minister to England (1905) and Japan (1910–13), who as Foreign Minister in the Tuan Ch'i-jui Cabinet in July 1917, became Acting Prime Minister upon Tuan's resignation. His 'coalition government' included four members of the so-called 'Research Clique', but the Government lasted only a week, and Wang Ta-hsieh was replaced on 30 November by Wang Shih-chen.

[2] A reference to the preceding letter which was written on board the S.S. *Aki Maru* and posted from Thursday Island.   [3] The Lansing-Ishii Agreement.

was told that now they could discuss China. When he was asked if Japan still stood by the old declarations regarding China's sovereignty, territorial integrity, etc., the open door and equal opportunity, he could say but one thing, and that was: Yes. Had he even hesitated he would have been asked chop chop what Japan's game was, and with the memory of the dockyards, the arsenals, and the camps in mind he could do nothing but say that Japan's game was a square one. Likewise with the memory of American preparedness in mind he could not ask about the Munroe Doctrine, nor about Predominance, though he spoke of 'special interests'. And when the Americans entrusted with the job got Ishii to reaffirm the old undertakings and add a new clause about exclusive rights they succeeded, without anything else, in preventing Japan from having predominance, or any other thing that any other nation has not got. 'Special interests' are geographical, and what Japan got as a result of the Demands in Manchuria. They mean no more generally than the interests China has in Japan, or that Britain (or Burma) has in China, or that Russia has in China, or that France (Indo-China) has in China. To me it reads as a complete defeat of Japan's ambitions. She cannot and dare not do one thing now that she realises that America is furbishing her sword and is getting her armour shined. I prognosticate that history will show that the documents Lansing signed with Ishii will be among the most important brought about during the war. They settle this Pacific question to a certainty, for Japan can do nothing to assert predominance in China without breaking all the articles in the document. If she starts to interpret the 'special interests' as meaning that she can dictate what China can do she will be hauled up sharply and will have poked under her nose her recognition of China's sovereignty. And she will be told a few other things. I am convinced that Ishii has told his Government what he has seen and has warned them to keep off the grass. The papers are dumb on the whole matter. There is no jubilation about the 'special interests' because they happen to be impossible of fulfilment while the other clauses stand. If the Government had not the closure on the press Ishii would have got a hostile reception when he returned, something reminiscent of the hostile reception accorded to the peace delegates when they returned from the Portsmouth Conference.

These are my sentiments, and I may say that I was the only one in Tokyo to hold them. I never expressed them to the Japanese, of course, but all foreigners with whom I conversed held the view you take. I hold to the opposite one, because it seems to me that America would not sign any note giving Japan anything tangible in China. First, there is no need for such a thing now that she is armed to the teeth, and secondly she is acting with Great Britain or John Bull, in this matter, and we are not likely to throw things to Japan after the 21 Demands.

I may be wrong, but I feel it in me somewhere that my reading will prove to be right. I hope I am right anyway. It would be a sorrowful thing if

America and Great Britain should knuckle under to Japan at this stage of the war.

[...] I agree with what you say. Our officials do not care a damn about Young China, and are out of touch with the whole situation. Also I agree with what you say ought to be our policy with regard to the fostering of trade. I had an experience this afternoon on similar lines. The representative here of Thorneycroft, the big British Manufacturers of machinery, recently went to Szechuan and at the salt wells at Tzeliutsing made an arrangement with the producers to instal a modern system for raising the brine at the expense of Thorneycroft, merely to try it out. The producers said they would set aside a well for the experiment and if it proved feasible would instal plants at all their wells. The machinery is now on the way. I told the chap he ought to have a talk with Sir Richard,[1] and today I went to ask Sir Richard if he would see him. I said 'Sir Richard a well-known British firm has undertaken at its own expense to try and solve brine raising at Tzeliutsing. I have suggested to the representative that he see you, since it is a matter of very great importance to British interests.' Hardly had I got this far when the old man burst out: 'I don't want to be dragged into anything of the kind. The Government cannot do anything, and I do not want to have anything to do with it.' I explained carefully that the man was not trying to interest the Government at all, that he had arranged everything with the producers, that I suggested that he should talk with him, and so on. After much argument the old man said 'Alright, tell him to come to my place at 9.15 one morning and I can give him 15 minutes.' So, what can be said! I was staggered to say the least at the reluctance that seems to be shown to help any reputable British concern.

The other night I was at dinner at the Legation with Wilton and the gentleman you described as the Professor of Deportment at the Legation.[2] In the course of conversation I was asked what was the reason for the feeling against the Legation outside. I told them without mincing any words, pointed out that the entertainment of Americans like Rankin, representing the trading firm of Anderson & Meyer, etc., to the exclusion of Representatives of British firms, was noticed by all British residents and was commented upon. The Professor asked me what British representatives were not properly treated. I named several, and as the Professor could not disprove what I said, I added: 'And what about the representative of Paulings?' Wilton smiled, but the Professor said: 'Pauling's representative – I did not know that they had a representative!' Wilton naturally laughed outright, and so did I. The Professor colouring up a little, asked: 'Who is Pauling's Representative?' I suggested that he ought to consult the records of the Legation, which seemed to me to be the duty of the Com. Attache, seeing that he ought to know every British firm interested in China, and their representative. Wilton could not suppress his amusement, and enlightened the Professor by

[1] Sir Richard Dane.   [2] Archibald Rose.

saying 'Why, you are talking to Pauling's representative.' Naturally the Professor could only ejaculate: 'Well, I'm damned.'

I merely recount this to further add to your comment about the failure of our people properly to deal with this field and the interests that we ought to be developing in it. It is amazing that we have gone three years through the war and have not yet learned anything about reorganizing in one of the greatest potential markets that is left to us in the world. Someday we will wake up and learn that while we were asleep the Teutons were preparing for the after-the-war war.

As to politics in China, I can tell you nothing. The situation is more complex than ever it has been. In the days of Yuan one could fairly judge possible events. Now that there is no central figure and those that do exist have no defined policy it is useless to try and judge what the future is likely to be. Feng[1] flounders, the Peiyang *Tuchuns* yell war to the finish and intrigue for a compromise, while the South does not know what to do. We are trying to persuade Li Chun to get together 100,000 men, train them and then set out to whallop all the *Tuchuns* and the professional revolutionists and set things in order by creating a properly organised civil service under foreign jurisdiction, or rather, advice. So far he has listened favourably. He claims to be opposed to military interference with politics and if he maintains that view he will be a useful member of society. We are trying to convince him that the man to save China is the man who will knock the military ninepins over and set up in their stead a properly organized civilian government, to which the military must be subservient. To effect this the bulk of the existing army must be sent to the war fronts to help where possible in guarding communications, etc. to fight, or to do coolie labour, the balance to be turned into *Gendarmerie*. A new model force to be created under British or Allied instruction to be at the service of the State, and not to be the instrument or tool of any one general, or group of generals.

Li Chun seems to be appreciative of the necessity for drastic reform and reorganization, and may be you will see him wake up and do something. The only thing against that is that he is a Chinaman.

In all probability the present trouble between North and South will be compromised. The reason that is likely is that Feng wants the southern vote at the next Presidential election. The Southerners are favoring Li Chun. He

[1] Feng Kuo-chang, the Acting President, had advocated a policy of peaceful unification of the country by negotiation with the republicans as opposed to the war policy of the Prime Minister Tuan Ch'i-jui. Tuan was compelled to resign on 20 November 1917, just over a month before this letter was written, following the reverses of the northern troops of Hunan and Szechwan in October and early November. Tuan's supporters in the northern provinces, referred to here as the Peiyang *Tuchüns*, or northern Military Governors, however, continued to press for an aggressive policy towards the south. Feng was unable to resist pressure from them and was obliged to recall Tuan some three months after this letter was written.

will probably be made Vice-President, to go on with, and later will be President. But none can prophesy. I am trying to persuade the intelligent members of the Government to pave the way for the Peace Conference and maybe you will get a letter asking you to go to London. They ought to send men who know China both to Washington and London to do nothing but missionary work – to educate people who count on the Far Eastern Question. The Minister of Foreign Affairs appreciates that and is considering the matter. If Li Chun ever becomes President I'll bet something will be done in the way of a general sweep-up. Anderson has been in Nanking for a week past. I left him there two days before Christmas, and he is not back yet. We are trying to form a secret society of the leading intelligents to oust the corruptionists, the military, the ancients, the reactionaries, and all who are not for giving protection to the life and property of the mere citizen. And I think in time something will happen to shake the do-nothing element to its foundations.

Everything here is as when you left. Much wind this winter – and dust. Very unpleasant. Dane is planning a trip to Turkestan with Strickland.[1] Chang Hsun is still in the Dutch Legation,[2] refusing to go to Madagascar; Kangyuwei[3] is in Tsingtao; Sunyatsen is still in the cement works, alone, pretty well; Wutingfang[4] has returned unable to do anything; much talk of another monarchical restoration – but hot air; Chinese troops are in charge of Harbin, having ousted the Russians, and China is lifting her tail a little higher in the air as a consequence. The anarchists got charge of the place, were given an ultimatum by the Chinese, fired on a body of Chinese troops, and the end was the anarchists had to go. The Japs are now rubbing their eyes. I do not think of any real news to tell you.

[...]

I hope that your impressions of Aus[tralia] have altered after landing, that the vote against conscription is not really against continuance of the war, and that our countrymen will conduct themselves as citizens of the Empire.

With best regards, and with remembrances to any inquirers

Very sincerely
W. H. Donald

[1] W. R. Strickland, British employee of the Chinese Salt Administration. A lawyer, he first went to China in 1908, and was at this time Deputy Chief Inspector of the Salt Administration.

[2] After the abortive Restoration attempt, Chang Hsün was granted political asylum in the Dutch Legation in Peking, where he remained until his pardon by President Hsü Shih-ch'ang on 23 October 1918. He refused offers of a public office and died in retirement in Tientsin in September 1923.

[3] K'ang Yu-wei, who took refuge in the American Legation after the abortive Restoration attempt, remained there until December 1917 when he left Peking under the protection of a United States Legation Guard.

[4] Wu T'ing-fang, Foreign Minister and Acting Prime Minister at the time of Chang Hsün's Restoration, left to join the Government set up by Sun Yat-sen in Canton and played no further role in the Peking Government.

892. To R. D. Meagher[1]

Melbourne [Victoria, Australia] 5 January 1918

Dear Mr. Meagher,

Many thanks for your letter of the 21st December,[2] which reached me last evening, the delay having been due to its reaching Father Robinson at a time when he was suffering from the gout.

[...]

There is a very extensive Catholic literature on China. The *Lettres édifiantes*,[3] which were the chief source of information of conditions in China during two centuries, dating back, I speak from memory, to 1602, have been continued down to the present day, although now they appear under the title of *Annales de la Propagation de la Foi*.[4] They are published in Lyons. There are several series. On them was based the monumental work by du Halde,[5] published in Paris in 1735. You have no doubt read Isaac Disraeli's *Curiosities of Literature*;[6] in one passage he refers to this important work of du Halde

---

[1] Richard Denis Meagher (1866-1931), Australian lawyer and politician of Irish Catholic descent, described by a contemporary Sydney journalist as 'the premier perjurer of our public life and champion criminal of the continent'. His unprofessional behaviour during a murder trial resulted in his being struck off the rolls in 1895, and he had to resign his seat as a member of the N.S.W. Legislative Assembly, to which he had only recently been elected. But as a reflection of the man's resourcefulness and of Australian politics of the time, he succeeded, in spite of his record, in having himself re-elected to the State Legislative Assembly three years later, in 1898, and with a short interruption remained a member until 1917, becoming in 1910 Chairman of Committees (1910-13), in 1913 Speaker (1913-17), and in 1917 a Member of the State Legislative Council (1917-20). During this time he was concurrently an Alderman of Sydney (1901-20), and Mayor, (1916-17). Shortly before his retirement as Mayor of Sydney Meagher gave a reception to Morrison, who lamented in his Diary of 12 December 1918: 'Although his record is bad he is the only citizen of N.S.W. who has at the same time been Lord Mayor of Sydney and Speaker of the House! In both positions he has shown efficiency, but a laxity of public decency – this appointment to two of the highest offices in the State of a disbarred solicitor and a public crook.' Some of the more colourful incidents in his career are described in a social history of that period by Cyril A. Pearl, entitled *Wild Men of Sydney* (London 1958). [2] Not printed.
[3] The full title of the collection was *Lettres Edifiantes, et Curieuses, Ecrites des Missions Etrangères, par quelques Missionaires de la Compagnie de Jésus*, published in Paris (1702-76). The reports in this collection by Jesuit missionaries in China were to exercise a great influence on some of the leading thinkers of the 18th century, prior to the French Revolution.
[4] *Annales de l'Association de la Propagation de la Foi, Recueil périodique des Lettres des évêques et des missionaires des missions des Deux Mondes et de tous les documents relatifs aux Missions et à l'Association de la Foi*. This periodical, the first number of which appeared in Lyon in 1827, was a continuation of *Lettres Edifiantes*.
[5] Jean-Baptiste du Halde (1664-1743), French Jesuit priest and scholar. He was the author of *Description Géographique, Chronologique, Politique et Physique de l'Empire de la Chine et de la Tartarie Chinoise, Enrichée des Cartes Générales* (Paris 1735).
[6] Isaac Disraeli (1766-1848), British author. His work *Curiosities of Literature* was published in two volumes in London in 1792-3. He was the father of Benjamin Disraeli (1804-1881), the British politician.

written with an intimate knowledge of China by a Priest who had never been ten leagues from Paris. The very accurate account published in 1719 of China in the *Further Adventures of Robinson Crusoe*[1] is also taken from the *Lettres édifiantes*. Our knowledge of Mongolia is mainly derived from the reports of the Belgian Missionaries, our knowledge of Chinese Turkestan is due largely to the Dutch Missionaries. The two other serials, apart from the *Annales de la Propagation de la Foi*, dealing with the condition in China as reported by the Catholic Missionaries are the *Missions en Chine et au Congo*[2] and the *Missions Catholiques*.[3] You no doubt know that the first complete account of the manufacture of Chinese porcelain was given in one of the letters from Père Courrejolles,[4] published in the *Lettres édifiantes*. I am writing from memory and cannot give you the exact date.

In China at the present time the two chief centres for the publications by Catholic Missionaries are Hokienfu in the south-eastern part of Chili Province and Siccawei in Shanghai, both under the Jesuits.

The greatest dictionary yet published in China is the work of Père Couvreur,[5] S.J. of Hokienfu. The author is still alive at the age of eighty five. In Siccawei an important series of monographs have been published by the Jesuit Fathers, both Chinese and foreign entitled *Variétés Sinologiques*.[6] They now number some forty or more volumes, deal with such questions as Marriage customs, the Nestorian Tablet, Superstitions etc. etc., and are of the highest value.

In regard to Chinese servants in Peking I think I told you at the time of

---

[1] The book, entitled *The Farther Adventures of Robinson Crusoe, being the second and last part of his Life, and of the strange surprizing accounts of his travels round three parts of the globe etc. written by himself*, was published in London in 1719.

[2] An illustrated magazine of the Congrégation du Coeur Immaculé de Marie, at Scheut-les-Bruxelles in Belgium. The first number appeared in 1889.

[3] A weekly illustrated bulletin of the Propagation de la Foi, published in Lyon and Paris. The first number appeared in 1868.

[4] Morrison must have meant François Xavier d'Entrecolles (also spelt d'Antrecole or d'Antrecolles) (1662-1741 according to Louis Pfister; 1652-1741 according to Joseph Dehergne), French Catholic Missionary. He first went to China in 1681, and became the third Father Superior of the Jesuit Mission there in 1706. He wrote two accounts, in 1712 and 1722, of the manufacturing of porcelain at the famous Ching-te-cheng in Kiangsi Province, near where he first established his mission station. These accounts appeared in *Lettres Edifiantes*, Volume 18, pp. 224-96, and Volume 19, pp. 173-220. Both accounts reappeared in a work by the French sinologue Stanislas Julien, *L'histoire de la fabrication de la porcelaine chinoise* (Paris 1855).

[5] F. Séraphin Couvreur (1835-1919), French Jesuit missionary. Born in Picardy, he entered the Society of Jesus in 1853 and arrived in China in 1870. He was the author of *Dictionarium Lingua Sinicae Latinum, cum brevi interpretatione Gaelica ex radicum ordine dispositum* (Hokienfu 1877), and *Dictionnaire Classique de la langue Chinoise* (Hokienfu 1904).

[6] An occasional monograph series which numbered 45 at the time of the sale of Morrison's library. Publication ceased in 1937 with the 65th issue, upon the Japanese occupation of Shanghai.

your visit to Peking that it is the custom in China for a servant always to be recommended, which means also to be guaranteed, by another well known servant. Nearly all house servants employed by foreigners in Peking after 1860 were servants who had been trained by the Catholic Missions, and these servants were Catholic. When I went to Peking in 1897 and engaged servants for myself they were of course Catholics, guaranteed by other Catholic servants. Nearly all house servants employed in Peking prior to 1900, outside of the Protestant Mission were Catholics. At present my head servant is a Catholic of the eighth generation, his family having been Catholic for more than two centuries. His mother, his brother, and many other relatives and connections were killed during the Boxer trouble in China in 1900. His children are Catholics of the ninth generation. I believe that on the border of Shansi Province there are Catholics of the eleventh generation. Shansi Province one may remember was the seat of the Bishopric of the learned Lexicographer, Basilio Brollo di Gemona,[1] who completed a manuscript dictionary in Chinese and Latin in 1705. A copy of this dictionary was in my library. A copy was given to my namesake Robert Morrison,[2] the first Protestant Missionary to China, on his arrival in Canton in 1807 and was an important help to him in the compiling of his monumental encyclopedic dictionary published in six volumes between 1815 and 1822.

I do not know if there is any more information I can give you, but if there is I will be only too glad if you will write to me and tell me so. I am leaving on Monday for Tasmania and New Zealand, but will be back in Melbourne about the 20th of February, and I return to China by a Japanese steamer leaving Sydney about the middle of March.

Please remember me most kindly to Mrs. Meagher and with best wishes for the New Year to you all

Believe me

Very sincerely yours
[G. E. Morrison]

[1] Basilio Brollo di Gemona (1648–1706), Italian Franciscan missionary. He had taught theology at Padua in 1678 before leaving for China in 1680. After studying Chinese first in Siam he moved to Canton in 1684 and in 1700 was consecrated Bishop of Shensi in its capital Sian, where he died four years later. He is best known for his Chinese–Latin Dictionary which contained more than 9,500 characters. The first dictionary of such scope and learning ever compiled by a European, it served for over a century as an indispensable tool in Chinese studies. In 1813 it was printed in Paris by order of Napoleon with the name of 'des Guignes' given as the author. This plagiarism was discovered by Jules Henri Klaproth (1783–1835), who compiled a supplement to the Dictionary (Paris 1819), and Jean Pierre Abel Rémusat (1788–1833), professor of Chinese at the Collège de France from 1814.

[2] Robert Morrison (1782–1834), British Protestant missionary who arrived in China in 1807. His work was entitled: *A Dictionary of the Chinese Language*, in Three Parts, published in Macao, 1815–23.

893. From Ariga Nagao

Pekin 10 January 1918

Dear Dr. Morrison,

My last letter was dated 7th December.[1] Since then a Christmas and a New Year have come and gone.

On the 10th of December last, the French chargé d'affaires[2] saw the Foreign Minister Lou Tseng tsiang[3] and asked the Chinese Government to take over to itself the protection of the Manchurian railway against the ravages of the Russian socialists and the Chinese Government has already sent out one division, which is doing very well in Harbin.

On the 18th Dec. Tuan-chi juai[4] was made Director of the War Participation Bureau. He took up the post willingly, and in this way a complete rupture between him and the President could be avoided.

Wan-shi-chen[5] resigned Minister of War, in order to devote himself to Premier's work, Tuan chi-kwei[6] succeeded him as Minister of War.

For some days it seemed as if the Government was in earnest, preparing for expedition against the South. Soldiers were sleeping in their cars ready to start. But days and nights went by without the order to start being issued. On the 24th of December it became apparent that the President and the Premier really had no intention to fight. On the 25th stopfighting order was issued. *Tuchuns* like Nishichung,[7] Saokun[8] etc. were much disappointed. But they remained quiet. Indeed there was no clear reason why they must fight – beyond the necessity of keeping up the prestige of the Pei-yang party.[9]

On the 25th December, Baron Hayashi left Pekin for Tokyo on two weeks leave of absence. It is still uncertain whether he will return to his post or not. The fall of the Tuan Cabinet was a severe blow to him. I think he will return, and if change comes, it will come only after some months.

The fact that the Southern leaders will not stop fighting, is going to introduce new atmosphere and perhaps some disquiet in the immediate future.

[1] Not printed.
[2] Viscomte de Martel, French diplomat, whose official post at this time was First Secretary.
[3] Lu Tseng-hsiang.   [4] Tuan Ch'i-jui.   [5] Wang Shih-chen.
[6] Tuan Chih-kuei.   [7] Ni Ssu-ch'ung.
[8] Ts'ao K'un (1862–1938), Chinese soldier, at this time *Tuchün* of his native Chihli Province (September 1916 – October 1923). Next to Feng Kuo-chang the most senior figure in the Chihli Clique of warlords, he became its leader after Feng's death in December 1919, and in July 1920, with the support of the Manchurian warlord Chang Tso-lin, he defeated the Anhwei Clique headed by Tuan Ch'i-jui. In May 1921 he and Chang fell out, however, and this led to the First Chihli–Fengtien War. The resulting victory of his subordinate, Wu P'ei-fu, gave Ts'ao control of the Government in Peking. In October 1923 he had himself elected President by means of wholesale bribery of members of parliament. A year later, however, the Chihli forces were defeated by the Manchurian troops in the Second Chihli–Fengtien War through the defection of Wu's subordinate, Feng Yü-hsiang, and Ts'ao K'un was held a prisoner in Peking until 1926. In 1927 he retired to Tientsin, where he died eleven years later.
[9] The 'northern militarists'.

The authority of the President has been much shaken by the fact that his words are not heeded by the South. The Southern leaders say that he is insincere in appointing Tuan-chi juai Director of the War Participation Bureau and Tuan chi-kwei, Minister of War. The *tuchuns* who were quiet after the stopfighting order, will not be quiet at seeing the Southern leaders march north. They say the President's policy is courting death itself. Should the Southern armies march to Pekin or occupy such strategical points as are necessary for the safety of the vital lines of communication required for the north, not only will their position be endangered, but their very lines will be in danger. They are holding Conference in Tientsin at this very moment.

In the meanwhile our colleague, Mr. Dennis has arrived from America. I already saw him twice, a young man of thirty-six, but very earnest and well meaning. I enclose a cutting from *P.D. News* giving his biography.[1]

Yours very sincerely
Dr. N. Ariga

894. From Ariga Nagao

Pekin 31 January 1918

Dear Dr Morrison,

My last letter was dated Jan 10th. The situation remained the same for about two weeks. The President and the Premier[2] insisted on not issuing the general order to fight and the militant *Tu-chuns* kept on pressing them to issue that order, without which they will not send out their troops. In the meanwhile the South continued gathering its forces around Yuechow (spelt Yochow in the papers) until its fall became inevitable. The influence of the President subsided more and more, and finally it became dangerous for him to remain in the same attitude any longer. Whispers were even heard of plot against him, when on the 25 he had Conference with Shu shi chang[3] and Tuan Chi juai in Shu shi chang's house and promounced his intention of

---

[1] Not printed.
[2] Ch'ien Neng-hsün (1870–1924), Chinese Imperial official, Governor and Republican politician. He replaced Tuan Ch'i-jui as Prime Minister on 10 October following the military reverses of the northern Army in Hunan and Szechwan, holding the post until June the following year. A *chin-shih*, or Metropolitan Graduate, he had served under the Manchus as Commissioner of Justice for Shensi, becoming Acting Governor of the Province in October 1911, but he fled Sian when the province declared its independence after the Wuchang Uprising. He entered Republican politics serving as Vice-Minister of the Interior in the Hsiung Hsi-ling Cabinet in October 1913 and became Under-Secretary of State under Hsü Shih-ch'ang when the Cabinet was abolished and the office of Secretary of State created as part of Yüan Shih-k'ai's monarchy scheme. He was then made President of the Administrative Court and in November 1917 was appointed Minister of the Interior in the Cabinet of Wang Shih-chen, a post he held also in the Cabinet of Tuan Ch'i-jui, whom he replaced as Prime Minister. [3] Hsü Shih-ch'ang.

going to the South himself. At first it was not clearly known what he really intended to do. Many thought he was fleeing out of Pekin. But it was not so. He left Pekin at 8.20 p.m. 26th arrived in Tientsin at midnight and had a conference with Tsao-kun with whom he left Tientsin for Chinang[1] at 4.50 a.m. 27th. He arrived at Chinang at 4 p.m. 28th, had conference with Chang Huai-chi,[2] with whom he proceeded to Shu-chow where general Chang-chin-yao[3] met them at the station. After a few minutes interval they all proceeded to Peng-pu (a place in An-hui on the Tientsin–Pukou line). Here Li-shun[4] was supposed to be waiting for them. But Li-shun did not leave Nanking on the pretext of illness and sent his confidential generals as his representatives. The conference of the generals at Peng-pu was not entirely fruitless, in so far as misunderstandings between the generals were removed and Tsao-kun and Chang-huai-chi will no longer obstinately require a mandate for the general resumption of hostility and Li Shun will no longer obstruct the passage of their troops through his province. This done, the President immediately broke up his journey and returned to Pekin at 1.45 p.m. 29th January. Reinforcements will now be sent to Hupeh and the marching of the southern troops upon Hankow and Wuchang will be prevented. Great consternation however reigns at the two towns and the danger at Wuchang is particularly serious. Great panic reigns there. Today Mandate for so-called partial resumption of hostility has been issued, i.e. against the

[1] Tsinan, the provincial capital of Shantung.
[2] Chang Huai-chih (b. 1860), Chinese soldier, who rose from the ranks, having fought in the first Sino-Japanese War, to become Garrison Commander at Tientsin at the time of the Wuchang Uprising and was ruthless in his suppression of revolutionary activities in the north. He was then transferred to Pao-ting and in 1915 became Military Governor of Chahar Special District. A supporter of Yüan Shih-k'ai and his monarchical scheme, he was appointed Military Governor and concurrently Civil Governor of Shantung in May 1916 and was one of the northern *Tuchüns* who denounced Li Yüan-hung's dismissal of Tuan Ch'i-jui in May 1917. In June 1918 he was appointed Commander-in-Chief of the northern troops against the republicans in Canton, and became in the following year Chief of General Staff and then Commander-in-Chief of Metropolitan Forces, a post he held until 1924.
[3] Chang Ching-yao (1880–1933), Chinese soldier, a subordinate of Tuan Ch'i-jui. He came into prominence in 1914 in a campaign against the White Wolf and was made 'Commander-in-Chief of Bandit Suppression' in the border areas of four provinces of Kiangsu, Anhwei, Shantung and Honan. Soon after this letter was written he was appointed Commander-in-Chief of the advance troops against the Republican forces in Hunan, and in spite of suffering reverses he was appointed Military Governor and concurrently Civil Governor of Hunan after the troops of Wu P'ei-fu had successfully recovered the greater part of the province from the Republican forces. His appointment thus caused an open split between the Chihli Clique of militarists headed by Ts'ao K'un and Wu P'ei-fu and the Anhwei clique headed by Tuan Ch'i-jui, to which Chang belonged. He held these posts until the overthrow of the Anfu Government in 1920. Later he served with various anti-Chihli Clique forces but retired, after the Republican army occupied Peking in 1928, to Tientsin where he was assassinated five years later by secret service agents (under the direction of Tai Li (1895–1946)), of the 'Blue Shirts', one of the most feared fascist organisations of Chiang Kai-shek. [4] Li Ch'un.

Southern troops marching upon Hankow and Wuchang only. With the fall of Wuchang and then of Hankow, a new phase of contest will set in between the North and the South, and there is already much talk in Japan of mediation. Baron Hayashi was to leave Tokyo for Pekin on the 29th, but his departure has been postponed *sine die*. Pekin is quiet, but pneumonic pest prevails around Sui-yuan, Tatung and Fengchen. Active measures of prevention are taken by the Chinese, Japanese and European and American doctors.

Yours most sincerely
Dr. N. Ariga

895. To J. Allen[1]

Melbourne [Victoria, Australia] 22 February 1918

My dear Sir James,

I returned to Melbourne the day before yesterday. News from China in regard to the extension of the pneumonic plague is somewhat disquieting to me, the last report stating that it had appeared at Paotingfu, a city only 80 miles from Peking, with frequent daily train connection. I am, therefore, expediting my return. I have cancelled my passage on the Japanese steamer and am leaving for China on Saturday the 9th of March by the British steamer *Changsha*.

Pneumonic plague is I believe the most serious epidemic in the world. It is the 'Black Death' that spread over Europe in the middle ages. Defoe's[2] account purporting to be written by an eye witness is an accurate description. In November of 1910 the disease broke out in North Manchuria, having travelled from Russian Central Asia. It was known as Tarbagan plague, having attacked men engaged in the trapping of the Tarbagan or Marmot. I know something about the epidemic for I went to investigate it on behalf of *The Times*.[3] There was no known case of recovery, although there were some cases of immunity. I saw one Chinese house set apart as a lazarette, in which

---

[1] James Allen (1855–1942), New Zealand politician. At this time Minister of Defence, he had previously served, between 1912 and 1920, as Minister of Education and of Finance, and Acting Prime Minister during the absence of the Prime Minister W. F. Massey (q.v.). In 1920 he became New Zealand High Commissioner in London, holding the post until 1926.

[2] A reference to the *History of the Plague*, written in 1722 by the British author Daniel Defoe (1659–1731).

[3] Morrison's telegram on the subject, entitled 'The Plague in China. Real Extent of the Epidemic', appeared in *The Times* on 15 March 1911. It was followed by two articles, 'The Plague in China. Its Origin and Course. Part played by the Marmot' (22 March 1911), and 'The Plague in China. Course of the Epidemic. The Work of the Doctors' (23 March 1911). An editorial based on these articles, under the heading, 'The Plague in the East', appeared in *The Times* on 12 March 1911. Morrison had visited the plague centre when returning from England by rail via Siberia to China in 1911.

1,400 patients were admitted and from which 1,400 corpses were taken out while two caretakers, elderly men living in contact with the stricken, both escaped infection. Naturally, therefore, I am anxious about the plague, for if once it were to take hold in China and Japan the destruction would be appalling.

[...]

I am now going to write you at some length about various things. Please forgive me if I am somewhat discursive, but I may not have another opportunity of writing to you before I leave for China. In the first place you may remember that we spoke regarding the Japanese–American Agreement of November 2nd. I then said to you that I could not understand why America should enter into such an engagement at the present time, and I told you that when I heard first of this engagement I was in Canton, and that the American Consul General[1] there had taken the same view of the Agreement that I had done, and had condemned it as being in conflict with America's previously declared policy. Moreover the Consul General told me that many Chinese had come to see him and had openly stigmatised the Agreement as a 'betrayal'. After this I wrote to a friend of mine[2] in whom I have confidence, who is in close relations with both Chinese and Japanese. I have his reply before me. You will see that he does not agree with my view and I sincerely hope that he is right, and that I am wrong. His letter is dated December 28th and is written from Peking in answer to a letter of mine written from the Philippines on November 23rd, where also the opinion was the same as that I expressed to you.

[...][3]

The Viscount Ishii referred to in my friend's letter, has I see, since been made Japanese Ambassador to Washington. I have known him for many years. We were in Peking together during the siege. I did not form a high opinion of his ability, nor have I ever heard any of my Japanese friends speak of him other than as a mediocrity. Yet I see in the paper to-day that the American Press speak of him as 'the most outstanding figure in Japan to-day'. This is certainly an exaggeration. On the other hand Captain Brinkley,[4] who was in his time the leading authority on Japan and the Japanese, (he was the *Times* Correspondent in Tokyo), had a high opinion of Ishii, and could not praise too highly the services he rendered to *The Times*

---

[1] Percival Stewart Heintzlemann.   [2] W. H. Donald.
[3] What is omitted here is a *verbatim* reproduction of a portion of the letter from W. H. Donald on the Lansing–Ishii Agreement, printed as Letter No. 891.
[4] Francis Brinkley (1841–1912), British soldier and journalist. After serving in Hong Kong he was sent to Japan as a Lieutenant then as Captain of the British troops in Japan in 1867. After the Restoration of 1868 he became attached to the military school in Tokyo, and in 1881 became Proprietor and Editor-in-Chief of the *Japan Mail*. As the *Times*' Tokyo Correspondent, he was frequently criticised by Morrison for his pro-Japanese bias in his reports on matters relating to Sino–Japanese relations. He was married to a Japanese, and died in Tokyo.

during the war between Japan and Russia, when he was director of the Political Bureau in the Foreign Office in Tokyo. Willingness to serve, however, the chief London newspaper at the time of war, when England was holding the field for Japan would not necessarily imply the possession of exceptional ability.

Ishii, it must never be forgotten, was Minister for Foreign Affairs at Tokyo when Japan refused to permit China [to] join the Allied cause. On November 23rd 1915 when the British, French and Russian Ambassadors in Tokyo approached the Japanese Government with a request that Japan would join with them in bringing China into the Alliance, if her doing so would be acceptable to the Allies, Ishii on behalf of the Japanese Government peremptorily refused his consent. In other words at a critical time during the war when the entry of China into the war would have been of material assistance to the Allies, the Japanese Government through Ishii refused to permit that assistance being given. This surely can never be forgotten.

There is a curious feature in connection with the other Japanese mission now in America – the financial mission headed by Baron Megata, who, after the war between Japan and Russia, reorganised the finances of Korea. The real director of this mission is not Megata but Koike, described as Managing Director of the Kuhara Copper Mining Company, and his name always put modestly at the bottom of the list of members of the Commission. Koike was formerly the Consul General in Moukden, later counsellor to the Embassy at London and later Director of the Political Bureau in the Foreign Office in Tokio. While holding this last named post he was the author and framer of the 21 Demands submitted to China, without the knowledge of the Allies, by the Japanese Government on January the 18th 1915. Rarely has a more indefensible act been done by one ally to another ally. These demands were submitted to the President Yuan Shih-kai under threat of punishment if they were disclosed to the Allies. It was with the greatest difficulty that I helped to secure their disclosure. The Japanese Government faced with exposure and asked by the British Government as to what demands had been submitted, handed as you know to their Ally the British Government an expurgated edition of the 21 Demands, omitting the whole of Section five comprising 7 articles of the most far reaching significance. In deference to protest these articles have not been pressed but they remain in abeyance, to be settled by subsequent negotiations.

We have been very forgiving and while Japan has been acting in this dishonourable way to the Ally to whom she owes everything in the world, we in Australia and New Zealand are under strict injunctions to say of the Japanese nothing but good. This is a mistaken policy. The Oriental does not understand this policy, he attributes it to fear. Press attacks in Japan upon Great Britain are still permitted. I have seen in the November issue of one of the chief magazines in Japan an article by Lieutenant General Horiuchi,[1] in which he speaks as follows:— 'France is truly fighting to her full capacity, but this cannot be said of England, which seems to be very anxious to conserve her human resources as much as possible. For the sake of her own honour England should not ask for the assistance of the Japanese army until her own resources are utilised to their limits.' Horiuchi argues that Japanese troops should not be sent to the front on the ground that the sending of the Japanese troops 'will simply invite the ravages of the German submarine. The ultimate result will be only to hurt the prestige of the Japanese army, and prostrate the expectation of the Allied Countries.' He goes on to deprecate any assistance being asked by America adding 'I sincerely hope that America will be able to make a decisive exhibition of her power in order to hasten the end of the war. I think it will rather be a disgraceful reflection to the credit of great America if she will be obliged to ask for the assistance of so small a nation as Japan in order to accomplish her purpose.'

I have not yet had time to obtain a copy of the *New East*, in which a Japanese professor explains why the Japanese military sympathises with Prussian militarism.[2] When I return to China I will send you some papers showing you what is the attitude of the Japanese people towards their Allies.

In Auckland I read again the paper in the *Nineteenth Century* for September 1916, in which the writer Robert Machray, who is employed as a publicist by the Japanese Government states the case for Japan. Machray is, I believe, a de-canonised Canon of Toronto Cathedral. He is the author of *The Night Side of London* a book illustrated by Tom Browne,[3] not usually seen in good English libraries.

That paper makes three points. Firstly Japan did not join our enemies. That is one would think, rather a left handed compliment. In other words Japan did not turn upon the country to which she owes her present standing among the nations. Suppose she had done so. She would have done the most infamous act in history. She would have been ruined by it. When war broke out in 1914 Japan was in considerable financial embarrassment. The war has raised her to a pinnacle of prosperity such as she could never have aspired to had peace continued. Had she joined our enemies her whole overseas marine would have been swept from the seas within a fortnight.

Secondly Japan supplied arms and munitions to the Allies. That is true,

[1] Possibly Horiuchi Bunjirō, Japanese Soldier, who became a Lieutenant-General in May 1916 and had been on the reserve list since August of that year. The article referred to here has not been traced.

[2] Anesaki Masaharu (1873–1949), Japanese scholar. Professor at the Imperial Tokyo University, he wrote widely on the religions of Japan and his book on Buddhism has been translated into a number of foreign languages.

[3] Tom Browne (1872–1910), British artist. His works include *Tom Browne's Comic Annual* (London 1899), *The Khaki Alphabet Book* (London 1901) and *Tom Browne's Cycle Sketch Book* (London 1904, 1905).

but she squeezed us unmercifully in doing so. She supplied arms at a profit, a very large profit indeed to herself. I do not know whether I told you what Kroupensky, the present Russian Ambassador to Tokyo told me. While Minister in Peking in 1915 he made no secret that some at any rate of the disasters encountered by Russian arms on the German frontier were due to the inferiority of the guns, arms and ammunition supplied by the Japanese to the Russians at that time. Largely these supplies consisted of Russian arms and ammunition captured during the war of 1904–5, the guns and rifles being refurbished and then sold back to corrupt Russian Agents.

The third point made is that Japan has rendered assistance to the Allies in the convoying of Australian and New Zealand troops. I wonder whether you think I am prejudiced against the Japanese. I try to believe that I am not. I have a great admiration for their administrative efficiency, I early believed in their attaining a great position among the nations and as correspondent to *The Times* I was on their side while they were fighting for the attainment of this position. The administrative order which they have introduced into Korea I rank as equal to anything that has been done by Great Britain in Egypt or in Burma, America in the Philippines or by France in Indo-China. So I maintain I am not prejudiced, and thinking dispassionately I consider that the third claim to consideration, namely that of convoying our troops through peaceful waters on their way to lay down their lives in the trenches in France in order that Japan may have the freedom of the seas, is the most contemptible claim ever put forth by any nation for the world's consideration. In this convoying have they lost a single ship, have they lost a single man? Has one of their ships ever exchanged a shot with an enemy ship? 'Convoying' is not the correct word to use. Even 'escorting' would be too great a claim. 'Accompanying' is the proper term. When the Japanese cruisers arrived in New Zealand and left with the New Zealand contingent on October 16th 1914, relief was felt by many, but there need have been no anxiety for on that day Admiral Von Spee's squadron was off the coast of South America and on November 1st sunk with grave loss of life the ships of Craddock's squadron. The Japanese claim that they were policing Australian waters. Did they do anything to stop the depredations of the *Emden*. The *Emden* sank 17 British ships worth $2\frac{1}{4}$ million pounds. Did it sink any Japanese ship? Did not Japanese ships at that time traverse the water of the Indian Ocean unafraid of the *Emden*. Are we not justified in suspecting that Japanese protection to German trade in China and Japan, and Japanese immunity from German submarines were in some way related. What was the amount of policing done in the case of the *See Adler*. The fact remains that it has been to Japan's commercial advantage, this destruction of British shipping. Every British ship sunk has increased the value of the Japanese mercantile marine. The few Japanese ships that have been sunk have in the great majority of cases if not all cases, been under charter at the time to the Allied countries.

An exception may be cited in the case of the *Yasaka Maru* sunk on December 21st 1915 in the Mediterranean, which was loaded with British war material for Egypt. The loss to Great Britain was a very serious one, very much more serious than the loss to Japan, assuming in the latter case that there was any loss at all and that the ship was not insured in British companies.

Nothing has been more curious to me than the contrast between the way in which we in the Far East regard Japanese action, and the way in which Japanese action is regarded in New Zealand. We speak with indignation of Japan's failure to carry out her obligations as an Ally. In New Zealand many seemed to think that Japan has fulfilled her obligations and speak with gratitude of Japan's action in sending two ships to New Zealand to protect New Zealand troops against German cruisers, which German cruisers fleeing from H.M.A.S. *Australia* were then off the coast of South America.

In China perhaps we see Japanese action too close. In the case of Tsingtao Bay for example, British troops rendered assistance in the taking of this weakly defended 'fortress', with its hastily gathered garrison of German reservists from all over China. The facts regarding this incident must not be forgotten. These are the facts as officially cited. Thirty thousand Japanese troops were allotted the task of capturing this 'stronghold'. The attack on Tsingtao began on the 15th October, the fortress capitulated on November 7th. The Japanese casualties were, officers killed 12, wounded 40, rank and file killed and wounded 1,472, prisoners taken 222 officers, 4,426 rank and file. Expense of the expedition 65,000,000 yen, value of booty captured 70,000,000 yen. Japan lost only one warship during the war, namely the third class cruiser *Takachiho* sunk with a loss of 280. For the taking of Tsingtao medals were given to 140,000 Japanese soldiers, two Baronies were created and so many decorations were distributed that for the first time in Japanese history three Japanese members of Parliament asked that they should be permitted to decline the decorations offered to them by their Emperor. I made a note of the decorations distributed but I have left it behind in Peking.

One other point and I have finished with Japan. When Japan refused to allow China to take part in the war the campaign of calumny directed against Great Britain began in the Japanese Press, and continued until the German failure at Verdun. Japan's attitude towards Germany has caused us the gravest misgiving. Since ever the war began German trade in China and Japan continued under Japanese auspices. The enemy trading act was only put into operation on June 1st 1917, and then only nominally, for on August 31st 1917 the three large hotels owned in Tsingtao by a German firm, Sietas, Planbeck & Co., were purchased by the Japanese for $450,000, approximately at the time £75,000. Before the Japanese invested Tsingtao there were resident in the town 25 British and some 150 Japanese, a large number of whom were what is euphemistically known as 'women of a certain class'. On the first of January this year there were 16 Englishmen in Tsingtao and 16,000 Japanese.

You will no doubt have noticed the publication in the *Manchester Guardian* referred to in the cable published in New Zealand on February 9th, of the correspondence between Krupensky the Russian Ambassador in Tokyo and his Foreign Office, regarding the retention by Japan of the South Sea Islands.[1]

I have written you at some length thus putting into writing some of the things I said to you in conversation. It gave me the greatest pleasure in the world to meet you in New Zealand. My intercourse with you and with your family is among the pleasantest memories I take back with me to China. If ever I could do anything to help to throw light upon any question in which you are interested I would be proud if you would give me the opportunity of doing so.

Please remember me most kindly to your daughter and to Mr Montgomery[2] and to your Secretary, Mr Dixon,[3] and with all good wishes

Believe me

Very sincerely yours
[G. E. Morrison]

P.S. Since writing the foregoing I have received a letter from my brother[4] who, since the beginning of the war has been fighting against the Germans in Africa. His letter is dated from Dar es Salaam, December 4th. He is a mining engineer, who, enlisting as a private is now Sergeant. He says 'The affair has pretty well fizzled out in German East Africa, and the latest we hear is that Von Lettow[5] and two or three hundred Germans with a few thousand Askaris have crossed to Portuguese East Africa. This means prolonging the campaign as the Portuguese are a miserable and deceitful lot and can't

---

[1] The reference to the undertaking by Russia to Japan, similar to that given to the Japanese Government by Britain and France that Russia would support Japan's claim to German interests in Shantung and German possessions north of the Equator. This assurance was contained in a note from Basil Kroupensky, then Ambassador in Tokyo, to the Japanese Foreign Minister Motono Ichirō on 20 February 1917.

[2] William Hugh Montgomery (b. 1866), New Zealand politician who had been a Member of the New Zealand House of Representatives, and a member of the Board of Governors of Canterbury College.

[3] George Finlay Dixon, New Zealand civil servant since 1915 and Private Secretary to Sir James Allen, Minister of Defence.

[4] Arthur R. M. Morrison (b. 1868), Australian engineer, a younger brother of Morrison who was for several years mining gold in the Transvaal and was at this time a Regimental Sergeant Major fighting in German East Africa.

[5] Paul Emil von Lettow-Vorbeck (1870–1964), German soldier. As Commander of troops in German East Africa from 1913 to 1918, he successfully withstood the Allied offensive there without help. He recounted the story of those years in *Meine Erinnerungen aus Ostafrika* (Leipzig 1920) and *Was mir die Engländer über aus Ostafrika erzählten* (Leipzig 1932).

"fight for nuts".' They are suspected and rightly too I fancy, of supplying the Germans with supplies and ammunition for a long while back.

Russians, Portuguese and Japanese – we have much to be proud of in our Allies!

896. From Lin Hsiung-ch'eng[1]

Singapore 8 March 1918

Sir,

I have the honour to address you the following:

I am the author of *How China ought to be governed*, and I have addressed the British Chargé de Affaires (Sir John Jordan was on leave) on the book, and Mr. Alston replied that he would be pleased to see me at the British Legation.

In May last I took a trip to China, and when I reached Shanghai I saw Dr. Sun Yat Sen who gave his opinion that if the book was accepted, China would lose sovereignty.

I also saw the ex-Premier Tang Shao Yi, who expressed sympathy with the book, but said there were something which could be discussed later on (probably to every English magistrate or judge, a Chinese is to sit together to represent sovereignty). This might be given in in order to shorten discussion. A political trouble in Peking then broke out, and he told me that nothing could be done then until there was a proper government. I also received a letter from Mr. Alston advising me not to come up to Peking, but to return home to Singapore as he could not do anything then on account of the political situation at Peking.

In the meantime if you can prepare the way of the British Minister and make his path straight your work would be memorable in the history of new China. I would beg that you will be pleased to advise the President and his cabinate to recognise and employ the genius of the work – the pure work of a Chinaman without much delay, and that any idea like that expressed by Tang Shao Yi would cause the correspondents of foreign newspapers to report to their respective paper the coming greatness of China, although only one prefecture to be selected and converted into a Switzerland which is to act as a centre for training. [...]

As soon as China has a Switzerland, there will be no more revolutionists, as they would come and live there and become peaceful citizens, and would do their best to help the progress of that place, instead of continuing to waste further blood and property and come to nothing.

You will find men who would give Dr. Sun's opinion, and I believe you will find men who would give Tang's opinion. Moreover, the raising of a

[1] A Chinese clerk serving with the Singapore Government.

really efficient army would take place at once which can be placed in any battlefield.

If China has no leader, she says so – but if China has one, what will she do with him? I therefore earnestly hope that you may be a co-worker of the scheme, and to obtain an early favourable reply from you, and

I have the honour to remain Sir

Your most obedient servant
Lim Yong Seng

897. To W. Irvine[1]

Sydney [New South Wales, Australia] 14 March 1918

Dear Sir William,

I regret that while I was in Melbourne I had no time to give you in writing a résumé of certain matters concerning the Far East and especially China and our policy there which we discussed in various conversations that it was my privilege to have with you. I try now to do in Sydney what I ought to have done in Melbourne, and in the following letter which I am afraid you will find rather lengthy I set down for your reference a chronological statement regarding China's participation in the war, a subject more than once alluded to or dwelt on in our discussion. The Far Eastern Question naturally interests me greatly and if I can at any time help to throw light upon anything relating to the country whose service I entered five and a half years ago I will be only too happy to do so.

To begin then:—[2] In August 1914 when war broke out I was in England and although I left by the first steamer I did not arrive in Peking until the 14th September. In the meantime still in August, Yuan Shih-kai the powerful President of China, had offered to join in the operations for the investment of Tsingtao, the German headquarters in Shantung Province in China and had

---

[1] William Hill Irvine (1858–1943), Irish-born Australian politician. He had taught at Geelong College, where Morrison's father was Principal and Morrison went to school, before entering politics. He became a Member of the Legislative Assembly of Victoria in 1894 and served as Attorney-General in 1899, becoming Victorian Premier in 1902 and holding concurrently and successively the posts of Attorney-General, Solicitor-General and Treasurer. In 1906 he entered Federal politics by becoming a Member of the Australian House of Representatives and held his seat until 1918. During this time he was Attorney-General in 1913. In 1918 he became Lieutenant-Governor and Chief Justice of Victoria, retiring in 1936.

[2] Though phrased differently, a good deal of what follows appeared in Morrison's letter to Lovat Fraser of some 18 months earlier (12 October 1916) and in the memorandum submitted to Yüan Shih-k'ai on 1 November 1915. This letter is another illustration not only of Morrison's remarkable memory, writing as he was without recourse to any of his diaries or notes, but also of his obsession with the events here related. This is a much shortened version of the original very lengthy letter, a copy of which is also to be found in the Archives of the National Library of Australia.

undertaken to detach 50,000 troops for this service. He communicated this offer to Sir John Jordan, the British Minister and doyen of the diplomatic body in Peking, and Sir John without consulting his colleagues saw fit to advise the President to keep quiet and do nothing. It was a serious rebuff to the President. It was what the Chinese call a grave 'loss of face', for it told the Chinese who had offered help that their help was not needed. It was a diplomatic blunder of the worst kind, and I know that indignation quite outspoken was expressed by the Russian and French Ministers when, more than a year afterwards, they heard for the first time of the action of their British colleague. At least they ought to have been consulted, they contended.

Naturally on my return to China I wished to use what influence I could to bring the country, in whose service I was, into the arena of the war on the side of my own country. But for some time there was no possibility of doing anything. Feeling against Japan was too bitter. No President would have dared at that time to take action which favoured rendering assistance to Japan. For, early in 1915, when relations between China and Japan were still outwardly friendly, the Japanese Government (Baron Kato who had signed the Anglo-Japanese Treaty of July 13, 1911 being Foreign Minister) instructed their Minister in Peking, E. Hioki to ask for a Private audience with Yuan Shih-kai and at the audience to present a series of demands far reaching in their nature. He was to insist on immediate compliance. He was to insist on secrecy. Especially was no disclosure to be made to the British.

On January 18th, 1915, Hioki having obtained a private interview with the President communicated to him in writing the famous 'Twenty-one Demands'. They were in five sections, the fifth section being the most important. They were probably the most far reaching demands ever submitted during a time of peace by one friendly power to another.

Secrecy is difficult to keep in Peking. Almost immediately it became known that the Japanese Minister, under threat of punishment for disclosure, had made very serious demands upon China. Disclosure was China's only safeguard, yet it was with the greatest difficulty that I could induce Yuan Shih-kai to reveal the text of the document. Only on the 23rd January was I able to help in the publication of the essential features of these demands and to hand them to the British Minister who, in accordance with the Anglo-Japanese Treaty aforesaid, ought to have been kept fully and frankly informed by his Japanese colleague of so important a proceeding.

An outcry arose throughout China and in America. Questions were asked by the British Government. And in reply to these questions the Japanese saw fit to communicate to their Allies to whom they owe their position among the Nations, an expurgated edition of the demands, omitting the highly important Section V. A copy of this section I append to this letter.[1] Report says that the perfidy of Japan at this time gave Sir Edward Grey many anxious

[1] Not printed.

moments. The Japanese Government when pressed for further explanation declared that Section V represented not demands but *desiderata*, and they suggested that German machinations were at the root of the misunderstanding. *The Times* accepted the Japanese official view, although I sent them a copy of the official text.[1]

In defence of his good faith I advised Yuan Shih-kai to have the document photographed. There was a precedent for such action in the case of the Fournier Convention of 1885 when there was a question as to whether erasures, as contended by Li Hung-chang, had been made in the document or not, and the Chinese had indisputably proved by Photograph that the erasures had been made.[2] A copy of the photograph of the Japanese demands was sent to the President of the United States. Had need arisen and Japanese misrepresentation been persisted in a photograph would have been published throughout the world, but this was not necessary. Owing to the publicity given to the demands and the sympathy thus invoked China escaped more lightly than at one time seemed possible.

But China eventually had to yield to the demands submitted in the first four sections. On May 7th the Japanese delivered an ultimatum to China requiring her immediate compliance with Japanese wishes and China yielded: and on May 25th an agreement was signed between the plenipotentiaries of the two countries whereby the four sections were accepted by China and the fifth section was left over for subsequent negotiations. You can imagine that bitterness was great and how possible it was to suggest to China at that time even the possibility of an alliance in which Japan would be one of the Allies.

Shortly after the signature of the agreement there began in China that ill-advised movement for the elevation of the President to Emperor which eventually resulted in his overthrow. On October 28th, 1915 the three Powers, Japan England and Russia, followed by France and Italy, tendered to China their advice, very proper and opportune advice – that the monarchy movement should be postponed. More than once I had warned Yuan Shih-kai that such advice would be tendered. To me and to others he had expressed his determination never to accept the throne, but that is another story. When this advice was tendered intense indignation was aroused among the Chinese at what they regarded as an inexcusable interference with their domestic affairs.

I saw that the opportunity had come to take advantage of this indignation. You may think it strange that such a time should be chosen but it seemed to me to be opportune to turn this indignation to the advantage of the Allies. Accordingly on October 30th in a prolonged audience with Yuan Shih-kai I suggested to him that the time had come when China should take action to

[1] *See* Letter No. 739. Morrison to Steed, 24 February 1915.
[2] *See* the enclosure to Letter No. 742.

guard herself from exposure to the repetition of such a humiliating experience as was implied in the tendering of advice to an independent country by other independent countries. Repetition could be avoided by his joining the Alliance. I urged him to join with the four Powers by whose territories China is bounded. I pointed out to him and gave him in writing a detailed statement showing the advantage his country would gain were she to join the Allies.[1]

The main points of my communication upon which I laid emphasis were:—

The stimulating effect upon the national character. Chinese have only recently awakened to a consciousness of nationality and their new born patriotism would be animated by the knowledge that their country was allied in a struggle for civilization with the great nations of the world.

China would become an ally of the four Powers by whom she is surrounded, namely England, France, Russia and Japan.

China would obtain a fair share of the profits to be obtained by the manufacture of arms for the Allies, and the supply of munitions of war.

Her arsenals would be reorganised and equipped with modern and up-to-date machinery.

China after the war would have a voice at the Peace Conference when her destinies would be involved. Hitherto it has been the rule when treaties have been signed regarding China between other countries, that China has not even been consulted.

Joining the Allies would facilitate the settlement of China's various frontier questions.

China without violating international law could confiscate the German and Austrian shares of the Boxer Indemnity, amounting in all to £14,100,000.

China would suspend payment during the war of the service of various Railway and Reorganization loans obtained from German financiers requiring together with the service of the Boxer indemnity a payment of £6,000 per day.

China would recover possession of the German and Austrian concessions at Tientsin and Hankow.

China would be able to recover her Treaty independence, and after the war would be able to make treaties with Germany and Austria of reciprocal advantage and not as in the past unilateral in their advantage. From these treaties China could exclude the objectionable clauses providing for most favoured nation treatment.

China no longer neutral, trade routes across her territory would be open for the passage of munitions of war and other goods now held to be contraband. Dalny and the South Manchurian Railway would be available for such

---

[1] There is no entry in Morrison's Diary for 30 October 1915, recording the 'prolonged audience' referred to here by Morrison as having taken place on that day. He did however note elsewhere: 'Nov. 1st. Saw President. Handed in my written Memo', namely, that printed above as the enclosure to Letter No. 784.

trade as well as the trade route across the Gobi Desert from Peking to Urga.

Large numbers of Chinese would be employed in Russian territory from which they are now excluded.

On the other hand should China remain apart and be unable to preserve her neutrality she would sink lower still. She would be exposed to outside menace. She would be regarded with increasing distrust.

She would again witness agreements drawn up by other countries disposing of her rights without having a voice in the disposal of those rights.

At present the Allies could not but be dissatisfied with the way in which China had failed to preserve her neutrality. German intrigue had been rampant in China. Resentment had been felt by the Powers in consequence of this, and it is always China that suffers. Chinese are held responsible, and China has to pay.

The President listened to me patiently and then disclosed to me what I did not know before that in August of the previous year he had offered to join the Alliance and had been advised by the British Minister to take no action. He admitted that the arguments I submitted to him were cogent and powerful, and he declared his willingness to join provided he was spared such another rebuff as that which he had experienced on the first occasion. He said he was prepared to join the Allies on three conditions; firstly, a guarantee against reprisals on the part of Germany and Austria in the future; secondly, the occupation by China of the concessions held by Germany in Tientsin and Hankow and by Austria in Tientsin; and thirdly a satisfactory arrangement to be made regarding the extradition of political offenders from the international settlement of Shanghai (In regard to this last stipulation an agreement satisfactory to the President was subsequently agreed to by the Powers). He expected, of course, that if China joined the Alliance her envoy would have a seat at the Peace Conference. This went without saying.

The Japanese allege that in discussing this matter with Yuan Shih-kai (for it became known that I had discussed it with him – it is almost impossible to keep such things secret in Peking) I was acting in collusion with Sir John Jordan, the British Minister. Nothing would have been more untrue. Sir John Jordan was the chief opponent of anything being done. In discussing the question academically the fear of Japan dominated all other considerations in his mind. Nothing was to be done of which there might be any fear that Japan would disapprove.

When therefore Yuan Shih-kai expressed his willingness to join the Alliance he made it clear that he must not be exposed to a second rebuff, that China's entry into the Alliance was to be acceptable to the Powers, that China, in fact, was to be invited by the four Powers of England, France, Russia and Japan to join with them in fighting Germany. This was reasonable and proper. Negotiations were accordingly set on foot to bring England, France and Russia into line in extending this invitation to China. It was then that indignation was expressed by the Russian and French Ministers who heard for the first time of the action of Sir John Jordan in August 1914.

An agreement having been reached, the three ambassadors to Japan of England, France and Russia, the Russian being doyen, on November 23rd 1915 at an audience with Viscount Ishii who had in the meantime become Foreign Minister for Japan in succession to Kato, formally requested the Japanese Government to join with them in inviting China to declare war on the side of the Allies, to place her arsenals at the service of the Allies and to expel the Germans who were carrying on intrigues in China especially prejudicial to British Rule in India.

The Ambassadors were not well informed. Not one of the three had any knowledge of China. The British Ambassador, Sir Conyngham Greene was conspicuously incompetent. His claim to this important embassy had been based not upon knowledge but upon seniority. Without any previous experience of Asia he had been transferred from Copenhagen to Tokio. Three arguments only were the Ambassadors able to submit to the Japanese Government.

First, should China join the Alliance, Chinese arsenals would be placed at the disposal of the Allies.

To this Ishii replied that Japan had already submitted to China a proposal regarding arsenals, (it was one of the 'Twenty-one Demands' of January 18, 1915) and to this proposal China had given an unfavourable reply.

Secondly, German sedition in China would be suppressed.

To this Ishii objected that each case of alleged sedition should be tried on its merits.

'But' said the Russian Ambassador, who appears to have been less ill-informed than his colleagues, 'there is extra-territoriality in China. The chief offender is the German Minister. Who is to try him?'

Thirdly, China's throwing in her lot with the Allies would be an economic blow to Germany. To this Ishii replied that Japan could not regard with equanimity the liberation of the activities of 400,000,000 people.

Thus the reception given to the proposals of the Ambassadors was unfavourable, and this refusal on the part of Japan to further the cause of the Allies was confirmed within a few days in writing.

In the meantime, it is worth recording, Dr Reinsch, the American Minister, a learned professor who had been appointed to Peking by President Wilson because of his special knowledge of the Far Eastern Question, was consulted unofficially by the Chinese and he gave it as his personal opinion that her entry into the Alliance would be the 'salvation of China'.[1]

No sooner, however, had the refusal of Japan been communicated to the Allied Ambassadors than there began a vigorous campaign in the Japanese papers tolerated if it were not fostered by the Japanese Government attacking

---

[1] Reinsch gave his version of the story in *An American Diplomat in China, op. cit.*

Great Britain and the Alliance, and this continued throughout the winter of 1915–16.

Nothing could be done in China but wait.

Beginning however in the middle of April, 1916, there was a marked improvement in the tone of the Japanese papers. Improvement synchronised with and was attributable to the German failure at Verdun. The effete Russian Ambassador in Tokio was recalled and in his place there was sent from Peking the Russian Minister to China, Kroupensky, who thus became the youngest Ambassador in the service of his Government. Kroupensky had known of the negotiations in Peking and was well equipped with knowledge of China.

The Japanese change of attitude was noticeable in Peking. On June 6th, Yuan Shih-kai died and was succeeded by the Vice President.[1] As soon as the new President was formally established in office and Parliament had reassembled, the attitude of Japan in the meantime having become still more friendly, I saw the President and submitted to him in writing a memorandum similar to that which I had given to his predecessor.

This was on July 15th. I suggested to him that I should go over to Japan and lay the matter before the Japanese authorities and endeavour to remove Japan's objections to China's entering the Alliance. A good excuse was available for my going, as my wife and children were at Chuzenji and it was reasonable that I should go there to bring them back. Accordingly with the President's approval I went to Japan on July 17th and at Chuzenji saw Sir Conyngham Greene, and with his consent I arranged to have an interview with Viscount Kato. At this time Kato was out of office but he was the leader of the most powerful party in Japan.[2] He had been Ambassador in London where he had signed the Anglo–Japanese Treaty of Alliance of July 13th, 1911. He had been Foreign Minister when the 'Twenty-one Demands' were submitted to China and there was reason to believe that he would be the next Prime Minister. In his knowledge of Foreign Affairs he was held to be without a rival in Japan, and he was a trustworthy and discreet man unlike the garrulous old Okuma who at this time was Prime Minister. I had known Kato for seventeen years and on his last visit to Peking had discussed the situation with him with much intimacy. My interview with him was on August 16th. It is necessary now to read the following three papers, (1) my letter to the British Ambassador; (2) the detailed report of my interview with Kato; and (3) the acknowledgement of the British Ambassador, this being a veritable curiosity left furtively in the evening by the Ambassador at my hotel when I was out, so non-committal that to be completely so it ought to have been written in invisible ink.[3]

[1] Li Yüan-hung.   [2] The Kenseikai, formerly the Rikken Dōshikai.
[3] There were three enclosures, the first and second of which are omitted, being copies of Morrison's letter to Greene of 21 August 1916 and his attached interview with Katō dated

[...]

On my return to Peking in the beginning of September I saw Baron Hayashi[1] the Japanese Minister who was formerly Ambassador to Italy and who would be the first Ambassador to China were the Legations in Peking to be raised to Embassies. I had known Hayashi for nearly eighteen years, and had close relations with him when he was Minister to Korea and I was *Times* correspondent.

He told me he had received a despatch from Kato reporting the conversation I had with him on August 16th. He took the opportunity to tell me that he was in favour of China's joining the Alliance, that he had communicated his opinion in this sense when he was Ambassador to Rome, but Viscount Kato who was then Foreign Minister replied that such views did not coincide with the views of the Japanese Government. Hostility to Yuan Shih-kai, unwillingness to do anything which might help Yuan Shih-kai towards the fulfilment of his ambition to be Emperor, were no doubt at the root of his Government's opposition to the proposal. He told me, however, that Baron Motono, Ambassador to Petrograd, was also in favour of China's joining the Alliance. I knew also that Ijuin the new Japanese Ambassador to Italy who was for many years Minister to Peking, was also in favour.

Nothing however was done. Expressions of sympathy were not followed by action. Copy of my letter to Greene and of my interview with Kato I sent by our Counsellor to Embassy[2] who was returning to duty at the Foreign Office on September 13th, 1916. In my covering letter to the Counsellor, I wrote for his consideration the following notes. Regarding item IX of these notes I will write you again about this deplorable blunder which prevented us from having a British officer in the Chinese Army. The blunder was due to the incapacity and ignorance of Chinese affairs of the Senior Clerk from the Foreign Office, Mr. Beilby Alston whom Sir Edward Grey had sent to be Chargé d'Affaires of our important interests in China in the absence of Sir John Jordan.

[...][3]

In my memorandum of the talk with Viscount Kato I did not note, because I was giving a copy to Sir Conyngham Greene that Kato said that none of the three ambassadors seemed to know much about the case. He said it a little stronger than this, adding that the Russian Ambassador seemed to know a 'little more than the British'.

The next step after September 1916 was taken by America. On February 2,

---

16 August 1916 (*see* p. 540). The third enclosure, Greene's reply to Morrison of 22 August 1916, read: 'I had hoped to call at the Hotel today to thank you for your kind letter and its enclosure, but heard you had gone to Enomoto for the day. I beg therefore to send you my best thanks by letter instead. C.G.' [1] Hayashi Gonsuke.

[2] James William Ronald Macleay.

[3] What is omitted here is a *verbatim* reproduction of the memorandum Morrison sent to Macleay on 13 September 1916, printed here as the enclosure to Letter No. 834.

1917, America severed diplomatic relations with Germany and on the same day telegraphed to China inviting China to support America's action and join with her in upholding the rights of neutrals.

This telegram reached Peking on Sunday February 4th, 1917. Now clearly the time had come when China need no longer fear to act in opposition to Japan.

I was in the country on this day, but returned to Peking late in the evening, too late to see the President who was already in bed.

Early on Monday morning I saw him and urged him to accept the invitation extended by America and act at once. I found him weak, vacillating and tremulous, obsessed with the idea that Germany would be victorious. The Germans, he said to me, would shortly be in Odessa. How far he was speaking in order to be able to obtain from me replies that he could give to those opposed to his taking action I do not know.

During the day the American Minister having been told by me exactly what passed at my interview saw the President and during the next three or four days both the American Minister and myself with all the assistance we could engineer did what we could to induce China to take action. Yielding to our advice China consented so far as to take modified action. She decided first to send a warning letter to Germany promising the American Minister that if the warning were disregarded she would sever diplomatic relations. She sent the warning letter on February 9th and the threat having been disregarded she severed diplomatic relations on March 14th. Later, on August 14th, she declared war against Germany and against Austria. Before doing so she made terms with the Allies.

In recognition of her action she has obtained certain advantages from the Powers. The chief opposing force to the granting of these advantages was Japan, as one would expect.

These advantages are:

First, payment on account of the Boxer indemnity has been postponed for five years.

Second, promise has been given that the Customs tariff will be raised to an effective five per cent *ad valorem*, the present tariff, although nominally five per cent being based on obsolete prices, is actually less than four per cent.

Third, relaxation has been permitted of certain clauses in the Protocol following the Boxer uprising which forbad China to station troops in Tientsin. And there the matter stands at present.

In the meantime large numbers of Chinese coolies have been sent to the war working behind the lines on the Western Front where they have done highly efficient work. Many have lost their lives, probably not less than 3,000. More than 550 were drowned when the M.M.S. *Athos* was sunk.[1] German

---

[1] A French ship of the Messageries Maritimes Line which was sunk after leaving Kwangchow-wan with the loss of 543 lives.

ships have been confiscated and most of them have passed into the hands or under the control of Japan. What the present status of this question is I will not be able to know until I return to China.

It seems to me that in considering this Far Eastern Question it must always be borne in mind that from the beginning of the war up to April 1916 Japan's policy in the Far East was based on the belief held by the military in Japan that Germany was invincible and that England would emerge from the present war seriously shaken as a world power, with her strength as a Far Eastern Power irretrievably impaired.

Since the days of Verdun there has been a considerable change of opinion. Belief in the defeat of England was succeeded by a period of doubt and then by a certain measure of confidence that England cannot be defeated but after the war will be more mighty than before.

The Japanese Government which is now guided by Count Terauchi, a Military Officer of high distinction who was trained in France and not in Germany as have been the majority of Japanese officers: who was Minister for War during the war with Russia and who has been Governor General of Korea where his work will bear comparison with the work of Cromer[1] in Egypt, can be counted upon to support the Alliance. He must realise that the policy of his country under his predecessors first in submitting demands to China of the most far reaching importance, knowledge of the most important of which she concealed from her ally Great Britain; and secondly in refusing to allow China to come to the support of Great Britain at a most critical time of the war, is bound to have a certain effect upon Japan's foreign relations in the future or at any rate upon her relations with Great Britain.

Other matters I will leave over for a second letter.[2]

Believe me

Very sincerely yours
[G. E. Morrison]

898. From Lin Shih-yüan[3]

Wellington, New Zealand 19 March 1918

Dear Sir,

I beg to acknowledge the receipt of your letter of the 10th ultimo for which

---

[1] Evelyn Baring (1841–1917), 1st Earl of Cromer, British colonial official and politician. He had been successively British Agent, Consul-General and Pro-Consul in Egypt (1885–1907).

[2] Morrison wrote again to Sir William Irvine after he returned to China, but the letters are not printed.

[3] Chinese diplomat, a graduate of the Foochow Naval College and a great-grandson of Lin Tse-hsü (1785–1850), Viceroy of Kwangtung, whose burning of British opium was used by the British as a *casus belli* in the First Anglo–Chinese War (1839–40). Lin Shih-yüan was at this time Chinese Consul in New Zealand (1917–22). He had previously been Consul in Vancouver (1914–17).

I have to express my very cordial thanks.[1]

I propose at the next session of the New Zealand Parliament to make representations to the New Zealand Government for a removal of the £100 poll-tax which all Chinese, without discrimination, have to pay besides having to pass the education test if they wish to remain in New Zealand permanently.[2]

Since the education test was passed by Act of Parliament in 1908, not more

[1] Not found.
[2] The anti-Chinese legislation in New Zealand dated back to the gold-rush days when Chinese started to enter the country first from Australia and later directly from China. The immigration laws were designed solely as a measure against Chinese immigrants who, though constituting the only Asiatic immigrants to the Dominion, accounted in 1880 for less than one per cent of the country's population. Practically every noted New Zealand politician for some ninety years since the poll-tax of £10 was first introduced in 1881, had been an advocate or supporter of the anti-Chinese Legislation. When Seddon became Prime Minister in 1893, a suggestion was made that the poll-tax should be raised from £10 to £500. However £100 was finally settled for. In addition to the poll-tax, a Chinese Immigration Amendment Bill enlarging upon the language test principle of 1899 was introduced on 12 November 1907 by Sir Joseph Ward (q.v.) 'to restrict further the immigration of Chinese', although the Chinese population in the country had decreased in that year by nearly half from 4,814 in 1874 to 2,570. The Bill proposed 'the imposition of an education test, the reading of 100 words of English, the test to be carried out by the Collector of Customs, selected at his discretion'. The reason for the test, he explained, was that to impose a complete stoppage of Chinese immigration, as many people had urged, and Ward himself favoured, could involve difficulties with the British Government, and he thought the proposals contained in the Bill would 'effectively achieve the desire... to have the purity of our race maintained in our country and to restrict the immigration of Chinese'. When the poll-tax of £500 was again mentioned by a Member who argued that 'the presence of 50 Chinese women in the Dominion made it imperative for Parliament to do something about the matter', it was explained that by imposing such a heavy tax the Chinese would have to remain in New Zealand all their lives in order to earn sufficient to repay it, and so defeat the purpose of the tax – their exclusion. As a result of this new legislation the Chinese population in New Zealand fell further, to 2,147 at the outbreak of the European War, during which anti-Chinese agitation subsided somewhat. But with the unemployment that accompanied the return of the ex-servicemen at the end of the War, anti-Chinese feelings again ran high, and in spite of the proposed action of the Chinese Consul, as outlined in this letter, the treatment of Chinese did not improve. On the contrary, an Immigration Restriction Act was introduced by the Prime Minister, W. F. Massey (q.v.) in order, in his own words, 'to keep the race as pure in this Dominion as it is possible to keep'. It was supported by Sydney George Holland (1893-1961), later Prime Minister (1949-57), who, however, advocated the abolition of the reading test, maintaining that to raise the education test would be worse than lowering it because the Chinese 'would not be selling fruits at every street corner' but 'they would be entering into active competition in every profession and even become labour agitators'. There was to be more anti-Chinese agitation and legislation, becoming fierce during the period of the depression, and the poll-tax was not abolished until 1944 when other more subtle restrictions were introduced in its place. It was not until 1947 that any Chinese was granted a permit for permanent residence. (For further details see *The Chinese in New Zealand: A Study in Assimilation*, by Ng Bickleen Fong (Hong Kong 1959).

than fifteen Chinese (women and children of naturalised Chinese excluded) have landed in New Zealand. This small number for the past 10 years is solid proof that the education test is an effective barrier against an influx of Chinese into the Dominion; and if the New Zealand Government fears that if the poll-tax was raised, there would be a great influx of Chinese into the Dominion, my Government, I believe, would be prepared to consult with the Dominion Government limiting the number of Chinese immigrants into New Zealand yearly. My chief desire is to maintain the dignity of my country.

The poll-tax of £100 which is imposed only on the Chinese is clearly an unjust discrimination against my countrymen, and in these critical times when China has shown and is showing her sympathy in a material way with the cause of the British Empire in the present war, the Government of New Zealand should remove this indignity.

The proper course to follow before making application to the local Government on the matter is to request the Chinese Minister in London to make representations to the Secretary of State for the Colonies, but in view of the multitudinous affairs the latter have to attend to on account of the war, and also in view of the authority for granting such a concession being entirely in the hands of the Government here, I feel reluctant to trouble them, and I therefore propose in June next or thereabouts to make direct representations to the New Zealand Government; but should they fail to give favourable consideration to my representations, I will then appeal to my Government for assistance. But as you exercise a very strong influence on the Government officials and people of this country as was evidenced by your recent visit, no one could be in a better position to assist me than yourself; and since you have so kindly offered to help me in any way you can, I would feel deeply gratified if you could use your personal influence in the matter as would contribute to the removal of the indignity above referred to.

Yours respectfully
Lin Shih-yuan

899. From J. Allen

Wellington [New Zealand] 10 April 1918

Dear Dr Morrison,

Your letter of the 22nd February has been read by me with much interest.

I hope the pneumonic plague was not so troublesome as you anticipated and that the Chinese Medical Authorities have been able to cope with it.

[...]

Thank you very much for sending me an extract from your friend's letter dealing with the Japanese American Agreement of November 2nd.[1] Your opinion seems to differ from your friend's, but I hope that your friend is right.

[1] A reference to the Lansing–Ishii Agreement.

Since your letter arrived I have looked through the text of the Agreement and see no reason to differ from the opinion expressed by your friend. I have read through the report in the *New York Times* of November 7th 1917, and it seems to me that this backs up your friend's opinion. I quote one paragraph from *The [New York] Times* which is as follows:—

'There was a disposition in some quarters here today to attribute to the agreement the recognition of a Japanese Monroe Doctrine, but in authoritative quarters this was corrected, with the assertion that the agreement applies rather the principle that on this hemisphere is known as Pan Americanism. The Monroe Doctrine, it was contended, was based on the principle of national safety – the national safety of the United States – while Pan Americanism was altruistic in that it was based on preserving the integrity of all the nations involved, and was therefore international. The principle of the Monroe Doctrine, it was said, was not applied to China by the Lansing–Ishii agreement, but it contained a recognition of the principle that all the nations concerned were to see that the territorial integrity of China was respected.

It should be explained, however, that there is no authoritative statement embodying this interpretation.

High officials preferred to let the agreement, with Secretary Lansing's accompanying statement, speak for itself. Japan's special interests in China were likened to the special interests the United States has in Mexico, on account of the geographical proximity of the two countries.

Officials at the Chinese Legation declined to comment on the exchange of notes between Secretary Lansing and Special Ambassador Ishii.'

Probably you have read Secretary Lansing's statement, but as I happen to have it before me I quote a paragraph:—

'The visit of Viscount Ishii and his colleagues has accomplished a great change of opinion in this country. By frankly denouncing the evil influences which have been at work, by openly proclaiming that the policy of Japan is not one of aggression, and by declaring that there is no intention to take advantage commercially or industrially of the special relations to China created by geographical position, the representatives of Japan have cleared the diplomatic atmosphere of the suspicions which had been so carefully spread by our enemies and by misguided or overzealous people in both countries. In a few days the propaganda of years has been undone, and both nations are now able to see how near they came to being led into the trap which had been skilfully set for them.

Throughout the conferences which have taken place Viscount Ishii has shown a sincerity and candor which dispelled every doubt as to his purpose and brought the two Governments into an attitude of confidence toward each other which made it possible to discuss every question with frankness and cordiality. Approaching the subjects in such a spirit and with the mutual desire to remove every possible cause of controversy, the negotiations were marked by a sincerity and good-will which from the first insured their success.

Principle of Non-Interference: The principal result of the negotiations was the mutual understanding which was reached as to the principles governing the policies of the two Governments in relation to China. This understanding is formally set forth in the notes exchanged and now made public. The statements in the notes require no explanation. They not only contain a reaffirmation of the "open door" policy, but introduce a principle of non-interference with the sovereignty and territorial integrity of China, which, generally applied, is essential to perpetual international peace, as clearly declared by President Wilson, and which is the very foundation also of Pan Americanism, as interpreted by this Government.

The removal of doubts and suspicions and the mutual declaration of the new doctrine as to the Far East would be enough to make the visit of the Japanese Commission to the United States historic and memorable, but it accomplished a further purpose, which is of special interest to the world at this time, in expressing Japan's earnest desire to cooperate with this country waging war against the German Government. The discussions, which covered the military, naval, and economic activities to be employed, with due regard to relative resources and ability, showed the same spirit of sincerity and candor which characterized the negotiations resulting in the exchange of notes.'

I dare say Secretary Lansing has put his own ideas about Ishii's actions into the Press and for his own reasons. I was interested to read what you have to say about Ishii's policy and can well understand the reason why the American Press speaks of him as 'the most outstanding figure in Japan today'. Exaggeration is sometimes used for a purpose.

Your account of the financial mission headed by Baron Megata, but the real director of which is Koike, is very interesting.

I think you know that I have not much faith in the Japanese and have had it in my mind for many years that ultimately we shall have to face them in the Pacific. I am surprised, therefore, at what happened with regard to the 21 Demands submitted to China, and I think the Empire must be grateful to you that you secured their disclosure and ultimately their modification.

You touch on a very delicate subject when you allude to the attitude of Australia and New Zealand towards Japan at the present time. We have had our instructions as you know and must be very careful in any action we take which might prejudice the Imperial Government's relationship with Japan. As we are so much at the mercy of Japan in the Pacific, it would seem that the

Imperial Government's policy is correct. I understand you to think, however, that a bold policy which would indicate that the Empire would not allow certain things would have a greater effect than submission to circumstances as they exist today. You may be quite right, but from my point of view when I tell a man he must do this or he must not do that I want to have the power to make him do as I wish.

I have also read with interest what you have to say about the Japanese Press and attacks that are still taking place therein upon Great Britain. You say you will send me some papers showing the attitude of the Japanese people towards their Allies. I shall be only too pleased to have them.

Our Parliament met yesterday for a short Session prior to the Prime Minister[1] and Sir Joseph Ward[2] leaving for the War Council. Finance will be the only subject to be dealt with and I expect the Session will end in about 2 weeks.

. . . . .

7 May 1918

The dictation of this letter had to be put aside owing to pressure of other work.

The Prime Minister and Sir Joseph Ward are now well on their way to the United Kingdom and I am Acting Prime Minister.

Since beginning to write this letter I have seen the paper *Policy in China* presented to both Houses of Parliament[3] in January 1918 (Cd. 8895). Mr Lansing's Note to Viscount Ishii is in accord with the extract I have already quoted. Viscount Ishii's reply to Mr Lansing confirms the statement made.

Industrial peace reigns in New Zealand for the time being, but we had had some disturbances recently by a portion of the Second Division League of Reservists. This League is composed of married men who are now liable to be called up under the Military Service Act. In Christchurch there has always been a good deal of unrest. The members of the Second Division League there who are opposed to military service have been active and have led astray the loyal members by passing a resolution that they would not go into camp unless their demands were conceded. Three of them are about to be prosecuted for sedition and I hope this will end the trouble. It is becoming increasingly difficult to carry out our conscription measure because so many men are away. At the end of last month we balloted for 10,000 men of Class B of the Second Division, i.e. married men with one child. The balance of the

---

[1] William Ferguson Massey (1856–1925), New Zealand politician. A member of the New Zealand Parliament (1896–1925), and for thirteen years Prime Minister, from 1912 to his death, holding at different times various portfolios concurrently. He represented New Zealand at the Imperial War Cabinet and Conference (1917–19) and was a representative at the Paris Conference.

[2] Sir Joseph Ward (1856–1930), Prime Minister of New Zealand (1906–12, 1928–30). He was a Member of the Imperial War Cabinet (1917–18), and represented New Zealand at the Paris Conference. [3] The British Houses of Parliament.

Class will be gazetted at an early date. The country at heart I believe is sound and we shall get over our difficulty.

We also have an interesting problem with regard to the Maoris. Voluntary enlistment has been splendid from all the Tribes except one – the Waikatos – who have some ancient grievances about land. The Waikatos were warned that if they did not find their fair share voluntarily conscription would be applied to them. They have taken no heed of the warning and were balloted some few days ago. We may have some sport with them, but I do not anticipate any serious difficulty.

I trust that your wife escaped the dangers of the plague, and that you yourself have reached your home safe and well.

Yours sincerely
J. Allen

[...]

900. To J. Allen

[Peking] 9 May 1918

Dear Sir James,

Last week I arrived back in Peking after an absence of exactly six months from Nov. 1st to April 30th. [...]

Things in China are not going well. Japan has made enormous progress. The Report on the Trade of China for 1917[1] just issued is really a Report on the Trade success of Japan. In every direction Japan has strengthened her hold over China. As Rodney Gilbert who is editing the *Far Eastern Review* said to me the other day China is ladling out concessions to Japan with both hands. Chinese are inveterate borrowers. Japan is the only country that has money to lend. She lends to China freely on terms disastrous to China. China is a silver country. Silver is very high. All monies lent by Japan are lent in gold. For a loan of Yen 10,000,000 China receives 6,000,000 Mexican dollars. When the time comes for repayment she may have to pay 10,000,000 to 12,000,000 dollars.

I will write you again when I am more fully informed. In the meantime I am sending you a copy of the paper by Prof. Anesaki of the Imperial University of Tokyo about which I spoke to you in New Zealand. When in New Zealand I was taken to task for referring in a talk at Dunedin on January 21st to certain pro-German sympathies of the Japanese Army. The correctness of this statement would never be questioned in the Far East, but Sir John Findlay[2] and others who spoke to me thought it impolitic to give even

[1] This annual report, highly praised by Morrison, was by F. E. Taylor, Statistical Secretary of the Chinese Maritime Customs.
[2] Sir John George Findlay (1862–1929), New Zealand lawyer and politician. A former Attorney-General, he was at the time Morrison met him a Judge of the Supreme Court. In his Diary for 3 January 1918, Morrison described him as 'a fine scholar who carries a

guarded expression to such views while the war was on. This paper was published in the Magazine *The New East* in June 1917 in the third year of the war.

I will write again soon.
All good wishes to you

Very sincerely yours
[G. E. Morrison]

901. From F. E. Taylor

Shanghai 21 May 1918

My dear Morrison,
Many thanks for your letter. I am glad you like the Trade Report. [...]
As to the Japanese, I am told that they demand, in exchange for surrendering the islands in the Pacific they took from Germany, that the Inspector General of Customs be a Japanese, and I think this may be true and that they will gain their point. At any rate there will almost certainly soon be a Japanese Deputy I.G. It seems to me that this would be regrettable so far as British prestige in China is concerned, but, provided precautions were taken against differentiation in favour of Japanese goods, it would certainly be to the ultimate advantage of China and trade in general, and a great improvement on present conditions. A Japanese I.G. would interest himself in trade and in the development of industries, and he certainly would try to persuade the Chinese to modify a fiscal system that hinders both. Aglen takes no interest in trade matters, and his policy is deplorable. He makes no attempt to lighten the burdens trade has to bear in this country, and he leaves the decision on all questions of duty treatment to the Shui Wu Ch'u, and he resents any broadminded suggestion that would forego a small collection of duty for the sake of nourishing enterprise that would bring in a larger revenue later on. [...]

Yours very truly
F. E. Taylor

902. To H. Dering[1]

Peking 24 June 1918

My dear Dering,
I am sending a letter of introduction to you to a close friend of mine who may never come to Bangkok, but who in the event of his doing so desires

---

Horace in his pocket and was a Professor, is a good climber and I believe has climbed Mt. Cook'.

[1] Sir Herbert Guy Nevill Dering (1867–1933), British diplomat who had served during the Boxer Uprising in Peking where he came to know Morrison. He was at this time British Minister in Bangkok (April 1915 – December 1919).

above all things to have the opportunity of meeting you. He is an American named Forsythe Sherfesee, Vice-President of the American Asiatic Association, held in much esteem by the American and British communities in Peking. He was Director of Forestry in the Philippine Islands, and is now employed as Adviser in Forestry by the Chinese Government. A month ago he left Peking, and for the next six months he is to be *en mission* in connection with war work to report upon the possibilities of the supply of timber needed in China, now that the American supplies have been cut off. He seeks especially for a timber which could be substituted for Oregon pine. He will go from the Philippines to the Dutch East Indies and other Tropical places.

This is his 'official' duty, but actually, I may tell you *in confidence*, he is detached in the conjoint interests of the American and of the Chinese Governments to make various investigations, the nature of which he will no doubt disclose to you. He is a thoroughly trustworthy man of high character, and if he should come to Bangkok, you will, I feel sure, find his information both instructive and enlightening.

Conditions in China are in a parlous state. Elections for both Houses of Parliament have been proceeding for some time past.[1] The President has to be elected by the 10th July, and his inauguration will take place on the 10th October. There are three candidates now in the field. The one most likely to be elected is Hsu Hsih-chang, who in your time in Peking was one of Yuan Shih-kai's staff at his camp near to Tientsin. He rose under the Manchus to be the first Viceroy of Manchuria. He has held many high posts, and was one of the 'Four Friends' of Yuan Shih-kai. To the foreigner he appears to have every possible disqualification for such a post, and it is deplorable to think that the Republic should have such a President. The other two candidates are the Acting President, Feng Kuo-chang and Tuan Ch'i-jui, the present Prime Minister. Either of them would make a less unworthy President than Hsu. It is difficult to believe that with the reassembling of Parliament strife will cease in China, for a large section of the people of China will still regard the election as illegal.

[...]

The chief topic of interest here now among the foreigners has been the fiasco in connection with the failure to deport the Germans. How admirably everything regarding the Germans was managed in Siam – the Declaration of War, their internment! How badly mismanaged everything has been in China! No wonder constant references are made to the contrast. Your work in Siam makes an important chapter in the history of that delightful country. You will probably see in the Confidential Reports what were the reasons of the failure. There was much mismanagement, much want of cohesion, and at the end there were the threats of reprisals upon unfortunate Belgians and

---

[1] A reference to the election rigged by the Anfu Clique in the fourteen provinces. It was considered illegal by the southern republicans who set up a rival Government in Canton the following month under Sun Yat-sen.

Frenchmen whose liberty is at the mercy of the Germans. While there was inevitably a loss of face in our failure, the three ships being all ready to carry away 1,500 Germans, these ships can now be used to transport 2,000 Czecho-Slovaks across to America. There are not less than 50,000 of them in Siberia, anxious to go and fight against Germany.

There are few changes here since your visit. Sir John is feeling the summer badly. Alston and his charming wife are still waiting for the succession. Lampson and Head[1] are both flourishing.

I hope the day is not far distant when we shall meet again. I shall always follow your career with deep personal interest, and wishing you continued success,

Believe me

Very sincerely yours
[G. E. Morrison]

903. From A. J. Moore-Bennett

Peking[2] 26 June 1918

Dear Dr Morrison,

Being a citizen of London anything that I may say there is naturally held in less esteem than anything said by one who is not a citizen and by one who has the world wide reputation of yourself hence I set down here my convictions in case that you seeing eye to eye with me in any of them might be moved to press for those changes I have tried so hard to get accomplished.

Today a debt averaging £200 odd on every life in Britain is being piled up. Every railway road factory and public and private enterprise is being strained to the point of scrapping in an endeavour to win the war. Every lawyer with a gift of oratory is striving to attain a place in a government which being above responsibility and censure, protected by a bomb proof censorship gives its members and higher employees complete immunity from all mishaps arising from ignorance, negligence or carelessness. Lastly over two millions of our best and greatest in heart and body have been killed and over six hundred thousand hopelessly maimed and crippled altho' these never at any time had any say in the direction of the government.

In addition the health of the people is being seriously jeopardized doctors are scarce, women and young girls are worked for long hours in factories put up without any of the prewar regulations, food is scarce and hard to get and chaos such as I believe never existed since the early seventeenth century now holds sway in Britain.

[1] Sir Robert Pollock Somerville Head (1884-1924), at this time Second Secretary with the British Legation in Peking, having been transferred from St Petersburg the previous year. Before that he had served as Third Secretary in Peking (1911-14).
[2] Moore-Bennett, who left Britain in February 1917 after a visit there, was caught up in the revolution in St Petersburg in March, and had only just arrived back in Peking.

The Unions most of which were founded after years of bitter struggling by the workmen have been made to relinquish all their hard-won priviledges, the press world has been made to give up many of its most cherished ideals of free speech, and open comment not only on things military but on things diplomatic and economic, a postal censorship exists which secretly operates against all modern ideas and ideals of personal freedom and one set of laws exist for the governed and another for the governing in every walk of life.

Immorality of every kind has crept into British public life, the buyers of the immense quantities of munitions are mostly men against whom either suspicion existed in the South African war or against whom actual peculation was proven, or they are men who by their early life and training know nothing whatever about the business they are engaged upon. Business men, great engineers, great organizers going into Government departments giving their time and money wholly free to the country's service have been dismissed and permitted to resign at the instigation of subordinate members of the permanent departments concerned. Great soldiers and Staff officers admirals and engineers have been moved out of the combatant services to allow the entry of someone often wholly unacquainted with the work to be done: utterly useless Inspectors of the great munition works have been appointed who have squandered the country's money and resources like water and done more to lose us the war than any other one thing and generally an unbelievable state of affairs exist where waste, wanton destruction, carelessness and ignorance seem to dance in one great orgy.

To blind the people a press bureau is working actively aided by the Latin activities of the Italian and French chancellories, and pressed on by the Japanese Embassy Press bureau. News wholly misleading frequently appears, the days seem to have left us when reliance could be put on the pledges or spoken words of cabinet ministers and Parliament is snubbed unmercifully and the shibboleth of 'pro-Germanism' hurled against anyone who asks questions or really strives to pierce the veil of secrecy. Members [...] who dare question our policies are called into the Whips office and straightly told that steps to curtail their personal freedom will be taken if they do not control their tongues and bankers are threatened with an enhanced subscription to the war loan if they dare raise their voices too high. Insistent criticisms are met with the creations of 'Committees' of which there were Dec. 1917 over 318 sitting by rewards by punishments where parties are weak enough and the evil day of reckoning held off by so called 'reforms'. [...]

This is the internal situation – which can be seen by anyone sufficiently interested in men and facts who will study them – comes now an inner situation not so easy to appreciate and only glimpsed rarely by accident through the action of finance and groups.

The main policy seems to be that China and the East generally with Australia are to be left to their fate. That Africa is to be made to take the place of China and that a great Union of Africa is to be made where the Rand crowd of magnates and gold field owners will rule. As a large proportion of these magnates are of German extraction or birth their friends and relatives are protected in the most amazing manner right in the heart of the city. A movement financed and engineered by them has already moved the 'popular' will in the press to protest against any handing over of South West Africa, G.E.A.[1] and other German African colonies to Germany and I actually had it put to me before I left that I should support a movement to bring pressure on Portugal to make her part with her East African colonies.

On five or six occasions when not looking for evidence I found capitalists bemoaning the fact that the opium business had ceased and so made China 'uninteresting'. I heard leading Frenchmen expound the theory in all solemnity that if Japan took China she should no longer cast her eyes Tonkinwards and once I found a Member of the War Cabinet who stated that in Africa we should find relief for our losses in Asia and Russia.

In the Foreign Office I found a state of mental hand to mouth existence. No definite strong policy could be seen, no attempt to take any intelligent anticipation in the future could be found and only by Sir John Simon's[2] hard campaign towards universal suffrage could any really futuristic constructive policy be really found that was in accord with the pressing needs of the times.

One group of people on the side – the workers in the engineering trades and the sailors and fireman's union – controlled through their organized ability to enforce demands and one group – namely the great international banking and finance groups – at the other end of the pole controls things, the latter by their power of refusing credit as the workmen refuse labour and the great middle class together with the professional and 'business' classes are utterly without the cohesive power to either object or make their objections effective.

In order to avoid the necessity for any real permanent change of procedure which would weaken their position the permanent officials – who without doubt are today the real rulers in Britain – of various government departments have from time to time instituted so called 'Reforms' which movements have been much advertised in the press and certainly in some departments juniors have been dismissed and an effective camouflage made which more often than not attains the desired end – of causing criticism to cease.

The movement which I have most interested myself in of late years was

[1] German East Africa.
[2] Sir John Allsebrook Simon (1873–1954), Viscount Stackpole Elidor, British politician, Liberal Member of the British House of Commons since 1906. He was Solicitor-General (1910–13), then Attorney-General with a seat in the Cabinet (1913–15). He became Home Secretary in 1915. From 1931 for the next fifteen years he held the successive portfolios of Foreign Secretary (1931–5), Home Secretary (1935–7), Chancellor of the Exchequer (1937–40), and Lord Chancellor (1940–5).

the improvement of our trade services abroad, as I have taken as my axiom of belief that whereas twenty eight million of our population live on the production of our industries and mines, and whereas national debts can only be paid by the balance of exportable values over import values, and that therefore every worker in Britain is as an economic soldier entitled to the best training, working and living conditions as a military soldier [...]

I tried first of all the press. The result was disastrous. The great financial groups sat down upon me hard. Merchant Houses – so-called 'British' who pay nothing to the upkeep of the constitution, whose head offices have thoughtfully been placed abroad out of the way of the British tax-gatherer, have been ever since war started pressing forward the wares of foreign countries upon our most essential markets teaching foreign producers the goods acceptable, sent their representatives to our Minister here who reported last year in England that I had 'socialistic tendencies and was dangerous'. I then tried the Chambers of Commerce and they took up the matter with a will till something happen in the middle of 1917 and they stopped dead never to start again. I got Samuel Samuel[1] and others in the House to speak on the subject and they were roundly rated for daring to suggest such a thing by their party whips and the former stated that he would never try it again, I saw all the leaders of thought at Home and many declared they believed in my gospel and would do what they could but always there was a block and lastly my own manufacturers were lead by pressure to ask me to do nothing more.

Then at the last I tried the Unions. I saw Henderson[2] and told him all I have told you – and more. [...]

Dr. Morrison, the people that are paying most for the war are those that have never had any say whatever in the determination of their own destinies. The people that are saying the most are those that may be British in name but are anything but British at heart. The country at home is a mass of financial international intrigue, of hidden intrigues both political and economic with half a dozen great controlling groups all of them above or outside the law. It is not a question of why the Prime Minister does so badly – but rather a question of how he is allowed to do anything at all. Money he must have to carry on the war – and money he can only get by agreement to things that must be most distasteful to him or any other Britisher.

[1] Samuel Samuel (1855–1934), British politician and financier. A Conservative Member of the British House of Commons since 1913, he was a partner in the firm of merchant bankers M. Samuel & Company, and founded with Lord Bearsted the Shell Transport & Trading Company Limited, of which he became a Director. He was also a Director of many other companies including the Anglo-Saxon Petroleum Company Limited and Lloyds Bank.

[2] Arthur Henderson (1863–1935), British politician. Leader of the Labour Party in the House of Commons from 1908 to 1910 and again from 1914 to 1917. President of the Board of Education (1915–16), Postmaster General (1916), and Minister without Portfolio in the War Cabinet (1916–17), he later became Home Secretary in the first Labour Cabinet in 1924, and Foreign Secretary from 1929 to 1931.

I have failed – been squeezed to extinction in Britain – by these same cliques and today my only hope lies in the Labour Unions. It would be quite easy to fan a revolution into flames in Britain. Personally I believe this lies in my power because there are twenty or thirty incidents any one of which might succeed in doing this – quite well known and provable by me to the right people – but whether such a revolution would not do more harm than good is the one recurring thought to me and one I finally decided before leaving home last year – not to consider. A revolution may quite well come for all that – there are today probably thirty or forty thousand local zealots who are hardly likely to see far into the future and certainly less likely to weigh the consequences of any such action – resident in the Midlands ardently preaching the 'cause': there are two thousand three hundred con[scientious] objectors some of whom have been as cruelly tortured as ever was done in the middle ages by the Inquisition and some of whom are well protected and fattened by their powerful friends all very ripe for mischief. There are fifty or sixty thousand maimed men and soldiers discharged without pensions for technical offences that are very ripe fruit and lastly there are the disgruntled Irish, three millions of women labourers on high rates to go back to penury when Union laws again are enforced or alternatively four million angry unionists demanding the acceptances of pledges the Government will be powerless to enforce.

Sir John Simon has seen what is coming. With a silver tongue he has cajoled and wiled the Reform Act through parliament and if a general election takes place before the end of the war then we may be saved – but if the old gang go through and enforce their own ideas of the peace terms on Britain – then I think you will find there will be a revolution indeed and what has happened in Russia will quite well be surpassed in Britain for all our so called democracy.

I possess no politics. I belong to no side of the House. Like greater men I can see no ways beyond the veil but you are going home – you might quite well go home, it's an interesting trip these days and you might work the miracle in my optimism I hoped to work when nine years ago I started out to improve from the top our trade advantages which is the life of our Empire.

You could succeed for many reasons the first being by virtue of your position here no one would doubt your word. By virtue of your position you are above their cavil. By virtue of your knowledge you could prove your facts.

You have seen the logic of their present methods – seen the foreign office do everything to make China our enemy whilst appointing society men like Alston to be a representative of our taxpaying community here, of Fox[1] as a

---

[1] Harry (later Sir Harry) Halton Fox (1872–1936), British consular official. Having acted as Consul-General in Yünnan, Chengtu and Hangkow, and worked in the Foreign Trade Department in the Foreign Office from 1916 to 1917, he was appointed in April 1917 Commercial Attaché with the British Legation in Peking. In the following year he was appointed a British delegate on the International Commission for the Revision of Chinese

representative of our manufacturing classes and Rose of our industrial communities, to cajole the Chinese into favouring our nationals' handicrafts.

For myself I am at the parting of the way – here in this country lies ease and comfort and a competence – at home penury and a difficult fight against almost overwhelming odds but I do not know yet whether I have the pluck for the latter course.

But only by much suffering shall we ever reach any better state and never I think shall we do it whilst there is one law for the people and another for the government – hence if the four points I tried to make could be generally acceptable to our people – then I think we might tread in future an happier road to our destiny.

Yours very sincerely
Arthur J. Moore Bennett

[...]

904. To G. G. S. Lindsey

[Peking] 28 June 1918

My dear Lindsey,

I am ashamed to have delayed so long in answering your letter of December 21st,[1] which both my wife and I read with the greatest of pleasure. [...]

The reason of the delay in answering your letter is partly this. On November 1st I left Peking on six months leave of absence, and went down to Australia and New Zealand. [...]

Things in China are very bad indeed. For two years China was prevented from coming into the War, partly by the incapacity of the British representative, but mainly by the action of Japan. Japan, in 1911, was signatory of a Treaty, by which she undertook to assist in the maintenance of peace in the Far East.[2] Again, when sending her Ultimatum to Germany on August 15th, 1914, she declared that her object was the maintenance of order in the Far East. So far from fulfilling these obligations, she has been the chief agent for the provocation and prolongation of disorder in China, the largest country in the Far East. Money supplied by Japan has permitted the continuance of civil strife which is wrecking a large part of this distracted country; and the money is lent always on the security of mines or railways or taxes, the administration of which would involve certain interference with the sovereign rights of China.

Japan is a signatory to the forbidding of the importation of morphia into China.[3] Yet no trade is more flourishing than the importation of Japanese

---

Import Tariffs, sitting in Shanghai with which work he was intermittently involved as the British Delegate until his retirement in 1930.   [1] Not printed.
[2] The reference is to the Anglo-Japanese Alliance Treaty of 1902 which was renewed for the second time on 13 July 1911.
[3] A reference to the International Opium Convention of 23 January 1912, to which Japan was a signatory.

morphia into China. Japan, by Article 26 of the Regulations of 1871, engaged herself not to traffic in Chinese brass cash.[1] Yet no trade has been more lucrative than the illegal export of this brass cash to Japan, and its smelting down there.

Japan has recognised China as a Republic. An article of the Constitution of China provides that all Treaties shall be ratified by Parliament. Yet Japan, knowing this, is signing almost every day new agreements and conventions with China, ratification of which cannot be given by Parliament, because Parliament does not exist. So we are in a state of constant anxiety, lest before the War terminates, all valuable resources of China shall have been mortgaged to Japan.

It is true that Japan is the only country that has money to lend at present. But she is in that favoured position because her Allies, chief of whom is England, are fighting in Europe, spending all their energies, their blood and treasure, upon the destruction of Prussian militarism. After this war, Japan will be the only military autocracy in existence. I claim – and this view is bound to prevail – that inasmuch as Japan has obtained all her advantages in China, because her Allies are engaged elsewhere, and she is free, taking no part in the War, all Agreements entered into by Japan with China, by reason of this fact, must be held to have been obtained by Japan for the good of the common cause for which the Allies are fighting, and must be shared with the Allies. Why should she, alone among the Allies, profit, when all her Allies are being bled white?

I should like very much to come to Canada and talk over the Pacific question with you and your friends. Such opportunities were given to me in Australia, and I fancy that I was able to remove various misconceptions. It may be that next year I shall come to Canada. [...]

The wish was expressed, I believe, that I should go to England this year, but everything is in such a parlous state in China – the Acting President will be out of office in a few days[2] – that there was no Government with which to come to an understanding as to the object of my suggested mission.

I hope you will write me again before long.

With all good wishes to you and Mrs. Lindsey, in which my wife joins

Very sincerely yours
[G. E. Morrison]

[1] Article 26 of the 1871 Treaty read: 'The copper coins of each country shall not be exported, except to another port in the same country in accordance with the regulations on this subject. Should any merchant secretly trade in such copper money he shall be arrested and the coins in question shall be confiscated.'

[2] Under pressure from the militarists of the Anfu Clique headed by Tuan Ch'i-jui, and from its political wing, the Anfu Club, which now dominated the Parliament, Feng Kuo-chang, the Acting President, was finally forced to vacate his Presidential seat. Although Hsü Shih-ch'ang was not elected until three and a half months later, in October 1918, the outcome was already a foregone conclusion.

905. To G. Morrison[1]

[Peking] 28 June 1918

My dear George,

Your letter of the 11th March I found waiting here on my return from Australia on the 30th April. Please forgive me for having delayed so long in sending you an answer.

There are no statistics in China as to the percentage of people who can read, but both estimates – the one as low as 5 per cent, and the other as high as 30 per cent – might be correct in the experience of different individuals speaking of different parts of China. That a vastly larger percentage of men can read than women is a fact, and it is also a fact that a rapidly increasing number of men can read. By 'read' I mean those who can read the newspapers would be able to read the classics.

That the number of those who can read is always increasing, is shown by the constant increase in the number of daily papers. Not many years ago, in my time, there were five daily Chinese newspapers in Peking and Tientsin. Yesterday I had occasion to send out for some Peking dailies, and thirty seven different daily papers were brought to me. Some are still to be got. In Peking and Tientsin, these two northern cities, there are not less than sixty daily newspapers printed in Chinese. I should think that in the capital cities 30% of the males could read the daily paper, but this is only guess work. There has been a very large extension of educational facilities, both missionary and native, during the last few years.

Education is compulsory, but that word is not to be taken in such a literal sense as it would be in England, for there is an immense amount of opium smoking still, although opium has been forbidden. And although the unbinding of the feet is 'compulsory', I went across China only a few years ago and did not see a single woman who did not have small feet, except a small number in three mission compounds.

This letter is somewhat negative in its information, but as I repeat once more, statistics in China are always untrustworthy.

With all good wishes to you

Your affectionate cousin
[G. E. Morrison]

[1] George H. Morrison, British churchman, son of Morrison's uncle, Thomas who had been Principal of the Free Church Normal School in Glasgow, George Morrison was Minister of the Wellington Church, Glasgow.

906. To Liang Shih-yi[1]

[Peking 12 July 1918][2]

Dear Mr Liang,

Three years ago today I addressed a long letter to you[3] in reply to a communication made to me by you. I then briefly summarised the position in China, and I pointed out how gloomy was the outlook unless something was done quickly by the Government in power. I quoted from Lord Curzon who is at present one of the leading members of the British Government,[4] as to the condition into which China had been reduced during the 20 years preceding her war with Japan, and I sketched briefly what were the further losses sustained by China since Lord Curzon wrote his criticism. As you know, early in November of 1915, I urged the President to come into the War. I pointed out to him what were the advantages of doing so, and I think I can claim that every one of the conditions that I then stated, was conceded to China in return for her coming into the War on the side of the nations who will in the future dominate the world. What has been done since?

China came into the war on the 14th August 1917. By her action in ranging herself alongside of the Allies, she has recovered possession of the German Concessions in Tientsin and Hankow, and of the Austrian Concession in Tientsin. She has recovered her Treaty independence in regard to these two countries. She has acquired control over Austrian and German subjects in China. She has cancelled the German share of the Boxer Indemnity. She has dismissed a number of Germans from her service, and in a large number of cases the vacancies have been filled – as they ought to have been filled – by the employment of Chinese subjects. She has obtained a postponement of the payment of the Boxer Indemnity for 5 years. She is obtaining a revision of the Customs Tariff to an effective 5%; she has obtained a relaxation of the rule which forbade Chinese soldiers to traverse Tientsin city. She has confiscated 13 German ships, which are now being used in the service of the Allies.

In return for all these great advantages, what has China done to support the cause of the Allies? For nearly 4 years past England, France and Belgium have fought for the cause of right to overcome the most ruthless Prussian militarism. Their soldiers have been killed by hundreds of thousands. They have poured out treasure to the amount of thousands of millions of pounds sterling. Their sufferings have been greater than have ever been sustained by warring nations in this world. Russia for nearly 3 years also fought on the side of right, but the country has fallen into a state of anarchy even greater than

---

[1] Liang Shih-yi was at this time Minister of Communications. On 22 August 1918 he was to become Speaker in the Anfu-dominated Parliament.
[2] This letter was undated, but three years to the day would make it 12 July 1918 if Morrison is to be taken literally in his opening sentence.   [3] Printed as Letter No. 770.
[4] Curzon was at this time Lord President of the Council in the War Cabinet (1916–19), and Leader of the House of Lords (1916–24).

the anarchy which now prevails in China. Russia is no longer a mighty power.

Early last year America came into the War, and her entry finally disposed of all possible hopes of Germany obtaining a victory. Her men are moving to France at the rate of 50,000 per week. The whole energies of her people have been bent towards the winning of the war. After this war is finished, America will be not only one of the two greatest naval Powers in the world, but she will be one of the greatest of military Powers. While all these countries have fought and suffered, Japan alone among the Allies has, by remaining outside of the operations of war, been able to acquire vast wealth, even though it has been won in the face of the contempt of all the Allies who have actually been fighting. No Japanese soldiers have gone to the front. There is no possibility that any Japanese soldiers will go to the front. They do not know what modern warfare means. They would fail just as the Indian troops failed. This is openly admitted by their own statesmen. They dare not enter the fray. They remain outside, and profit by the sufferings of their Allies. You who read the newspapers well, know that Japan claims to have deserved the consideration of the Allies:

(1) because she did not join our enemies;
(2) because she can supply arms and ammunition to the Allies at a vast profit to herself;
(3) because in the early stages of the war, she convoyed Australian troops proceeding from Australia to Egypt, but in this convoy she incurred no danger. She escorted troops through peaceful waters.

Until America came into the war, when Japan sent some ships to the Mediterranean, she never exchanged a shot with an enemy ship. And the ships that she has sent to the Mediterranean have, as you are no doubt aware, displayed the highest inefficiency. Troopships actually under their convoy have been torpedoed by enemy submarines. Yet this was the power which prevented China from coming into the war, to whom China has looked for guidance, and is now looking for guidance. It is to this Power, which after this mighty conflict will be regarded as a third-rate Power, that China is pledging the securities of her dominions.

You no doubt know that at the present moment there are 165,000 Japanese in China, everyone of whom is entitled to extra-territorial protection, is under the exclusive jurisdiction of the Japanese consuls, whose sense of justice may be gauged from the fact that so far as is known, there has never been a case in dispute between Chinese and Japanese in which the Japanese Consul has considered his Japanese subject to be in the wrong.

To this country then, China has looked for guidance. By an Agreement between Japan and the other Powers, Japan stands for the maintenance of peace in the Far East as regards the territorial extent of China, and so far from maintaining or helping to maintain peace in China, it is Japanese action which has provoked and prolonged disorder throughout China. Never has any nation in this world had a greater opportunity of raising itself among the nations than China has had during this European conflict. Yet during the 4 years of this war, look how China has fallen materially and morally. Large parts of China, some of the fairest portions of China in Hunan province for example, have been devastated, women ravished, men massacred, children carried away into captivity; and this devastation, these ravishings, these massacres, have been done, not by a ruthless enemy invader like Germany, but by the Chinese themselves in the plenary exercise of their sovereign rights. Could anything be more terrible?

Owing to the enhancement of the price of silver, China has had a gift made to her by the Allies the equivalent of hundreds of millions of dollars, her foreign indebtedness having been decreased by 50%. Ordinary patriotism, ordinary commonsense, would have seized the occasion to pay off portion of her foreign debts as Japan has been able to do. This is not the way of your countrymen. Instead of reducing their debts by taking advantage of this heaven sent opportunity, they have enormously increased their burden. At a time when silver is dearer than it has been at any time for the past 40 years, China has incurred vast debts in silver, so that when the time comes for redemption, for every dollar she has borrowed, she will have to repay not less than two dollars.

Every resource open to Chinese enterprise has been mortgaged to the Japanese, and the money used not for the development of the resources of the country to the building of roads and railways and telegraphs and the restoration of waterways, but to the payment of savage troops preying upon the Chinese and destroying Chinese lives and property

I take it then, calmly surveying the present position in China, calmly considering the recent opium deal by which China has sunk so deeply in the estimation of the world,[1] that the outlook in China is now ten times blacker than it was when I wrote to you three years ago. There is not a province which has not been blighted. Whole provinces of China are under the sway of brigands like Chang Tso-lin and Lung Chi-kuang, to mention the two most conspicuous of the leaders who bring shame to their countrymen. Resources of provinces as far distant as Yunnan and Kirin have been pledged

[1] The reference is to the purchase of opium by the Chinese Government from the Shanghai Opium Combine, the Agreement for which was signed on 11 June 1918 by the Combine and Ts'ao Ju-lin, Minister of Finance, as a supplement to the Agreement signed by Feng Kuo-chang and the Opium Combine on 29 January the previous year. This caused such a scandal that the British Government declined to authorise the registration of these Agreements, and two Presidential Decrees were issued some five months after this letter was written, on 3 and 4 December 1918 by Hsü Shih-ch'ang, declaring that the remaining stock of purchased opium was to be burned. When this eventually took place it was described by a foreign observer as a 'very expensive bonfire', the purchase having cost the Chinese Government 25 million taels.

to Japan in the belief – the incredible belief – that Japan holds the balance of power in the world.

Americans are being chided because they do not lend money to China, but should they lend money to continue the present unrest in China? The declaration made by the American Minister to China that money borrowed would be used for reproductive purposes is an untruth of such appalling magnitude that it brings dishonour to the country.

What claim then has China to be heard at the Peace Conference? What help has she rendered to the Allied Cause? The Allies would ask: Have Germans been interned in China? Or have they been allowed their full liberty to intrigue against the Allies? Has China sent any troops to Europe? Has China helped the Allies who are actually fighting, or has she mortgaged her resources to the Ally that has cunningly kept herself out of the war? Has China any moral regeneration in regard to the growth of opium. Has China preserved order within her own confines? Has China, having been given this great opportunity, done anything to reform her internal administration of her currency or her communications? Is not the present administration of China more discreditable now than it has been ever in the past? etc., etc. [...][1]

[G. E. Morrison]

907. From A. J. Moore-Bennett

Peking 2 September 1918

Dear Dr. Morrison:—

Enclosed copy my last letter to Pears.[2] The idea is not new I do not suggest that – but I believe that it could be carried out *if we knew our own mind* about it.

Pears was as you may know 40 years in Constantinople and has sent me a message cordially hoping that Japan will not be employed in the Siberian movement. As he is a friend of Mr Asquith's I have hoped that he will put the enclosed views forward.

The trouble here is that every Britisher I know has entirely divergent views upon the same situation. Many here as you know are credited with a much more gifted idea of the international situation than perhaps they have any right to. Pears says that there are only about thirty people in all Britain he can find who have either knowledge or power to influence opinion and no one seems to know what policy if any we possess herewards.

[1] The copy of this letter amongst the Morrison Papers is without an ending.
[2] Sir Edwin Pears (1835–1919), British journalist and lawyer who went to Constantinople in 1873 and established a legal practice there. In 1876, as Correspondent of the *London Daily News*, his exposure of Turkish atrocities in Bulgaria attracted international attention to the explosive situation in the Balkans, which was the subject of the Berlin Conference two years later in 1878. Knighted in 1909, he was forced in 1914 to leave Constantinople. He returned there in April 1919 however, and died seven months later.

I have taken the trouble to lay on paper what steps might be taken and if you ever knew anyone of influence liable to be moved by a cut and dried scheme which would result in the financial and political regeneration of China – I should like to put before him my ideas – which I have sufficient faith in to offer to leave everything else to carry through if the necessary backing is forthcoming.

Yours sincerely
Moore-Bennett

Enclosure to Letter No. 907: *From A. J. Moore-Bennett to E. Pears, Peking 1 September 1918*

Dear Sir:—

A note of yours [to?] my father-in-law after reading one of my letters has lead me to the indiscretion of writing.

I have sincerely regretted not having called upon you when I was in London last year – after having been in Petrograd and seen during March and April the beginning of the trouble.

Here we are most of us oppressed by the information and knowledge which a wise and beneficent Censor effectually keeps from our Home folk and it is upon this aspect I would briefly touch on.

The war has materially enriched but one nation – and that nation is as militaristic in temperament, government and psychology as Germany. Her rulers and thinkers express much the same ideas as the Pan-Germans and today she is insiduously preaching a Pan-Asianism as hardly as Germany every preached Pan-Germanism.

If we were informed of the matter I should have nothing to say, if our people realized what a united militaristic Asia with 1000 million people meant I should be silent and content to wait and see but you know as well as I do that they do not so know and I am unwilling to accept the responsibility of permitting them to be brought up against an impasse as difficult as they were in 1914 if anything I can do or say will change matters.

So long as America was not openly with us, I agreed to the policy of 'saying nowt' because I realise quite as well as others that Hongkong, the Straits, Java, Australia and the Islands not to speak of India would be the price we should pay if this new and Eastern pupil of Germany's idealism went over to her side. Today however the situation has changed, and with that change we should without delay inaugurate a positive policy in the East instead of the negative policy which has been our undoing.

Whatever the rulers and thinkers of this new Germany think and say is seldom or never reported correctly by our British papers. I saw Lord Northcliffe last year twice and done my best to make him see the potential danger ahead but without result. The *Times* correspondent here is notoriously unsympathetic to the Chinese and the *Manchester Guardian*'s representative is pro-Japanese hence these facts coupled with the ominous but well known fact that the greatest British trading house[1] here is pro-Japanese spell for our people one of the greatest and most far reaching results that could possibly accrue in this century.

Mr Wilson is well aware of the designs and idealisms of our Eastern neighbour and was consequently loath to give them any lead in Siberia. Mr Asquith I have not seen, but in Feb 1915 when Japan first gave the world an open idea of her designs on China first as a prelude to Asia, I wrote Mr Asquith and Sir Edward Grey very fully and begged that they in view of their experiences with Germany would nip in the bud other attempts at world domination.

Mr. Lloyd George will not move, being as I believe unduly pressed both by one financial group and also by Lord Northcliffe's views hence if any thing is to be done it must be done by the Anglo-American section of our community.

I would ask for a definite move forward in conjunction with America towards the settling of the Eastern question today while it is yet possible. I would ask that steps be taken to remove from office the Japanese elected Government of Peking. To arrange a scheme whereby China should be set on her feet independently of any one power's influence. That a financial administration be brought into being consisting of an Anglo-American-Franco-Japanese Board controlling and administrating China finances for a period of say 50 years. That only a cleanly elected government should be granted the sinews of Government by this Financial Board and that the country should be cleansed of the Japanese *agents provocateurs* and others who are at this time actively engaged in stirring up strife and preventing China giving that aid to the Allies that she otherwise would. In other words I ask that we should take up the white man's burden and do our work well to the end that a great artistic nation of 400 million souls shall not be perverted to the views and aims of a military power but rather that she shall be educated and guided into a path that will make her our friend rather than a source of danger to us and become a sister democracy to us with a great friendship towards us.

I ask you not to think this is a dream of an idealist – it is on the contrary a perfectly feasible scheme lacking only the leader to bring it into being.

China today consists of 18 provinces whose 18 military leaders are much in the position of the Rhine Barons of the middle ages. They are played upon now by our Eastern neighbour who desires above all things a weak China and one against the other they are being played by as dark and as astute a diplomacy as the middle ages ever gave birth to. They are being financed and

---

[1] Jardine Matheson & Co.

urged to fight one against the other and chaos and misery reign supreme as ever it did when we aided misery with our Opium Policy.

The people are oppressed in a thousand ways and Sir I ask you to see Mr Asquith if possible and put before him my views. The people here are far different to the Indian races. All they desire is peace in which to trade and farm the land. The malcontents who cause the trouble are less than an half of one per cent of the population and 25,000 well equipped troops maintained at Peking: Hankow: Canton and Nanking could not only give an insurance that there should be peace but they would give an example to China of what troops should be used for.

An international finance control, with the necessary force to maintain its decisions and enforce its rules would result in a great nation being built up from the chaotic muddle China is in. It would bring into being and foster all that is great and good in this wonderful race – instead of accentuating the evil elements that Japan's influence is now cultivating. It would help remove from our country the Black memory of our Opium policy and would save the world from that Armageddon of white and yellow that far seeing men of two generations have feared.

Briefly the choice is open to us to have a nation of 400 million upright friends or the same number of evilly taught enemies and the price today of the one is merely that we should openly approach Mr Wilson and endeavour through him and his Government to have a cut and dried positive policy ready for the Peace Conference.

Our people can see but one thing and one enemy – I ask you in all sincerity and open mindness to help them see the Eastern view at the same time.

With all good wishes and many thanks for your kindness

Yours sincerely
[A. J. Moore-Bennett]

908. To Ts'ai T'ing-kan

[Peking] 14 September 1918

My dear Admiral,

It is a long time since I have had any communication with you. I hear on every side praise of the work you have done in Shanghai. I hope that the Government will reward you for what you have done.[1]

I have not yet seen the new President,[2] but I am to see him on Monday

[1] A reference to the Tariff Revision Commission which met in Shanghai in 1918, at which Ts'ai T'ing-kan, replacing Tung Shih-ch'i, had acted as Chairman. On his return to Peking Ts'ai was appointed to his former position in the Presidential Office, with the title of Assistant Grand Master of Ceremonies. But he soon gave this up, devoting himself full-time to his position of Associate Director of the Bureau of Repatriation of Enemy Subjects.

[2] Hsü Shih-ch'ang, who was elected President by the Anfu-controlled Parliament on 4 September 1918 but did not assume office until 10th of the following month.

afternoon at 5.30. It is my intention then to make a suggestion to him with regard to inviting the good offices of the President of the United States of America in mediating between the contending factions in China.[1]

The state of the country is deplorable. The war news is good,[2] and there is every reason to believe that the Peace Conference will be held next year. Even this year it may be that preparations will have to be made for the Peace Conference. Suppose peace were to take place now. Mr. Lu Tseng-tsiang[3] were he appointed, as he will be, Chinese plenipotentiary to the Conference, the Southern Government would immediately issue a proclamation that he was not regarded by them as their representative, and this would greatly impair the efficiency and prestige of the delegate.

I have always believed that the present difficulty in China could only be solved by arbitration, the arbitrator to be selected by the President of the United States. It was the United States which brought China into the war. America was the first country to recognise the Republic of China. An invitation to the President to arbitrate is an invitation extended to the head of an allied country. There are many precedents for such action.

It is certain that the North would object to make any proposal for arbitration because arbitration might be held to imply recognition of the Southern Government as a belligerent, and to this the present Prime Minister[4] would never consent, but if the President of the United States were asked to mediate then it is possible that such a course would commend itself to the North as well as to the South and also to the Yangtsze.

How long are you remaining in Shanghai? I propose to go to Shanghai next month. Will you still be there? Professor Willoughby wants me to go with him to Canton, and if it can be arranged I would like very much to do this. I do not wish to miss seeing you, and I would like to arrange that I shall go to Shanghai while you are there.

[1] In his reply dated 21 September 1918 Ts'ai T'ing-kan wrote: 'Your suggestion about mediation is good. Last November I proposed to the British, American and Japanese Legations to offer their good offices but the South was then too much divided! The time may be opportune now. Success to you in the project.'

[2] By September 1918, the German offensive launched by General Erich von Ludendorff (1865-1937) against the Allied positions had failed and the German line was being hard-pressed by the counter-offensive of General Foch (q.v.), the Supreme Commander of the Allied forces. The German Army which had thrown in all its might for the victory Ludendorff had promised them was greatly demoralised, and so shaken was Ludendorff himself that he urged the German Government to open peace negotiations just two weeks after this letter was written. Another four weeks after that he was forced to resign his post, and fled to Sweden in disguise. Ludendorff later became a supporter of Hitler, and was an unsuccessful National Socialist (Nazi) candidate in the Presidential Election held in 1925.

[3] In the event Lu Cheng-hsiang did become the leader of the Chinese Delegation to the Paris Peace Conference. A compromise was reached with the republican south by including one of their members, Wang Cheng-t'ing, in the delegation.

[4] Tuan Ch'i-jui.

Things are going well with me except of course that I lose every month quite a considerable sum of money. My salary, which normally ought to be $3,300 a month, is now reduced to $1,750. Had I planned my expenditure for the latter amount I could have lived within it, but unfortunately I took up obligations which require my spending no less than from $2,000 to $2,500 per month, so I am not having a very cheerful time financially, especially this month when I have to pay $1,250 as my contribution to the Red Cross.
[...]

Very sincerely yours
[G. E. Morrison]

909. To J. Allen

[Peking] 15 September 1918

Dear Sir James,

Your long letter dated April 10th was delivered to me in duplicate through the Japanese Post Office. Both enclosures were delivered by the same post, both had been opened and no doubt read by the Japanese authorities. One had not even been closed when it was handed to me.

It is not reasonable that letters written in New Zealand addressed to an Englishman in China should have to pass Japanese inspection. It is of course quite reasonable that the British authorities should exercise censorship over such letters. Consequently, I have been in communication with the Director General of the Chinese Post Office in order to ascertain what remedy there may be for such an absurdity. The Director General is a Frenchman. By agreement between France and China dated April 10, 1898, this position must be held by a Frenchman.[1] From him I learn that while the Chinese Post Offices of exchange make a point of closing direct mails to the important offices in Australia (where letters will be retransmitted to New Zealand) only one Australian office, namely, Adelaide, has so far closed a few direct mails for the Chinese offices of Shanghai and Canton. Letters sent from Australia or from New Zealand addressed to China come mainly by Japanese steamers because the majority of steamers on these routes are Japanese. All letters sent by Japanese steamers are censored with the exception of those enclosed in closed bags to Hongkong and as far as possible the Japanese Post Office retains possession of these letters to the point of their destination.

---

[1] An Agreement was signed by France and China on 10 April 1898 for a railway concession from Tonkin to Yunnan, the lease of Kwangchow-wan and the organisation of the Chinese Postal Service. Clause 3 in the Agreement stated: 'When the Chinese Government organises a definite Postal Service and places a high functionary at its head, it proposed to call for the help of foreign officers, and declares itself willing to take account of the recommendations of the French Government in respect to the selection of the Staff.' A Frenchman, A. Théophile Piry, was appointed head of the Posts and Telegraphs when they became separated from the Customs. He held the job until 1917 when another Frenchman, H. Picard-Destelan, succeeded him in August of that year.

Complaints against the Japanese Post Office are common. For foreigners the post office is the most inefficient service in Japan. For years before the war foreign letters from Japan have been censored, not openly but secretly. And so long as Australian and New Zealand mails are sent as at present it should be known that every letter is examined by the Japanese either on the steamer or subsequently in the Japanese Post Office.

The remedy is to send all letters in closed bags to the Hongkong Post Office. Such letters of course will during the war be censored, but they will be censored by British and not by Japanese. The relations between the Hongkong Post Office and the Chinese Post Office are excellent, and letters handed from the Hongkong Post Office to the Chinese Post Office are dealt with purely by the Chinese, who do not censor foreign letters.

Since I last wrote to you many interesting things have happened. It can safely be prophesied that we are within reasonable distance of a revolution in Japan. The recent riots have been of a kind never before known in Japan. Not tens of thousands rioted, but hundreds of thousands. I do not know whether your attention is ever drawn to articles appearing in the foreign papers published in Japan. If so, you will have heard of the address given by Dr Ebina,[1] the leading Christian pastor of Japan, at Karuizawa on August 5th. This is an extract from what he said:

> 'The principles of American democracy had great influence on the revolution of 1867 which destroyed feudalism in Japan. The German system was introduced some twenty years later, superseding these democratic ideas. It made Japan very conservative. In certain aspects Japan even went beyond German Kaiserism and overtook Roman Kaiserism, introducing a kind of Emperor worship.
>
> 'Now Japan has entered the war as an ally of the great democratic nations... The greatest crisis in Japanese history is impending. The defeat of German militarism and imperialism on the battlefields of Europe means the defeat of these doctrines all the world over.'

It is surprising that a Japanese who has a large following among young Japanese of the thoughtful class should have spoken in this way. It is a hundred times more significant that the papers should have been allowed to publish such a pronouncement.

In China things are not doing well. A new president has just been elected, and we hope that a movement now on foot may result in the effecting a reconciliation between the North and the South.

An Anglo-American Association has been started in Peking under happy

---

[1] Ebina Danjō (1856–1937), Japanese educationalist and Christian leader. He was the founder of the magazine *Shinjin* in which he propagated the fusion of Shintō ideas with the Christian doctrine. From 1920 to 1928 he was the President of Dōshisha University, a Christian institution in Kyoto of which he was a graduate.

auspices, and discussions have taken place among its members with a view to making suggestions to the British and American Governments regarding some constructive policy in China. At a gathering held on July 13th at Wo Fo Ssu, a beautiful temple near to Peking, under my chairmanship, which was attended by prominent English and American residents including Sir Charles Eliot, the principal of the Hongkong University, the heads of the Hongkong and Shanghai Bank and other British corporations, Putnam Weale, the well known writer, and a number of equally prominent Americans, various suggestions were made which were afterwards embodied in a paper and this having been passed unanimously by the committee of the Anglo-American Association was sent to the British and American Ministers. I enclose you a copy of this paper as it may interest you.[1] It was sent to the British Foreign Office on August 30th, the British Minister having delayed sending it owing to there having been no precedent for such action. He is one who is entirely guided by precedent.

It is felt here among the allies that the policy of Japan in fostering the continuance of disorder in China by providing money and arms to the Northern people to wage war against the southern people has been in direct conflict with the terms of her treaties with foreign countries by which she engages to provide for the 'consolidation and maintenance of the general peace in the regions of Eastern Asia'.

The Japanese Minister[2] has just returned to Japan leaving here last Sunday. He is believed to be in favour of the restoration of the monarchy in China. Yet such a policy seems almost fatuous, and can only be inspired by the hope that such a restoration might arrest the weakening authority of the monarchy in Japan.

The war news is good, and the situation in Siberia is satisfactory. There has been no fighting to speak of. Putnam Weale reflects the opinion generally held among the allies in a message published in the *Shanghai Gazette* on September 6.[3]

Recently I have received letters from New Zealanders who have gone to Japan for business, but none of them have come to China. This is most regrettable. I should have thought that very large orders could have been obtained at the present time for New Zealand blankets and warm clothes of all kinds. Tenders are being called for in the Far Eastern papers for blankets and such things for use by the large bodies of troops now in Siberia. Condi-

[1] Not printed.
[2] Hayashi Gonsuke. Following the replacement of Terauchi Masatake as Prime Minister of Japan by Hara Kei, who sought to initiate a more conciliatory policy towards China by abstaining from direct interference in Chinese internal politics through the financing of rival military cliques, a policy which Terauchi had sent Hayashi Gonsuke to China to implement, Hayashi was withdrawn and Obata Yukichi (Torikichi) was appointed in his stead as Japanese Minister in Peking.
[3] The journal was not available for identification.

tions in Siberia during the winter are very severe, and warm clothing of all kinds is essential. English firms find that it pays to send travellers with samples of their cloth even to Peking, yet merchants here in the North tell me that they have never seen a traveller from Australia or New Zealand. The rugs which I myself brought for my own use from New Zealand have been greatly admired not only for the beauty of their texture and their lightness but for their exceeding cheapness. Surely it is a favourable time for the Chinese to purchase, using as they do a silver currency, their standard coin being the Mexican dollar. At normal times ten Mexican dollars are needed to buy one sovereign. To-day I can buy one sovereign for $5.35.

This letter has grown to too great length, so I must stop. Please remember me most kindly to Mr and Mrs Montgomery, and with my best wishes
Believe me

Very sincerely yours
[G. E. Morrison]

910. To W. A. Watt[1]

[Peking] 17 September 1918

My dear Watt,

When I had the pleasure of meeting you in Melbourne you indicated to me that you would not object to my communicating with you should occasion arise. I therefore take the opportunity to write you about two or three things which I think are deserving of your consideration.

[...]

Firstly, you are probably not aware that letters sent from Australia to Australians resident in China are censored by the Japanese in all cases unless these letters are sent in closed bags to the Hongkong Post Office [...]

It is intolerable for example, that if you should write to me your letter will, unless this precaution be taken, be handed to me censored by the Japanese through the Japanese Post office in Peking.

[...]

Secondly, I would again point to the necessity of sending to China a commission or a High Commissioner with diplomatic rank to inquire into the conditions of China trade. There seems to be a complete misconception in Australia of the importance of the China market. I enclose you a picture of a

[1] William Alexander Watt (1871–1946), Australian politician. He became a Member of the Legislative Assembly of the State of Victoria in 1897 and Postmaster General in 1899. From 1909 to 1914, he served first as Treasurer and then concurrently as Premier in the Victorian State Government. He then entered Federal politics as a Liberal (Conservative), and became in 1917 a member of the Cabinet, serving successively as Minister of Works and Railways, Treasurer, and Minister of Trade and Customs. In 1919 he acted as Prime Minister during the absence of William Morris Hughes who was attending the Peace Conference in Paris.

new departmental store which has just been opened in Shanghai under the direction of Australian trained Chinese.[1] Appended to this advertisement in the American newspapers is the announcement that seven-eighths of the goods in the store come from the United States. This is only one of several departmental stores. Two or three times I have written to the Chairman of the Melbourne Chamber of Commerce pointing out to him the possibilities for the sale of Australian products in China. Australian lead is used in China tea chests. For Australian silver there is a demand which ought to be met by direct purchase between China and Australia and not by the round about way that the sale is now conducted, giving profits to middlemen which ought to go to the producer. There is a great demand in China for cloth of all kinds. Probably every year some tens of thousands of Chinese adopt foreign costume, and the only cloth that I can learn of in the market is of English manufacture made from Australian wool sent to England.

Several English firms send travellers to China four times a year. The chief tailor in Peking informs me that he receives visits from English travellers but he has never seen an Australian traveller. A military expedition to Manchuria and Siberia is now in progress. The troops will be there during the winter. Warm clothes are required, yet I never hear of Australian blankets or Australian rugs or other Australian woollen fabrics, though the rugs I brought from Australia and New Zealand are looked upon as beautiful in texture, light and economical.

Chemists in Peking tell me that they have great difficulty in getting foreign medicines, even American medicines. I have written to the Chairman of the Melbourne Chamber of Commerce telling him that the tooth paste I obtain

[1] The reference is to a new departmental store named Hsien-shih kung-ssu, or Sincere Company Limited, which an Australian Chinese merchant Ma Ying-piao (or as he spelt it in his native Cantonese dialect Ma Ying Piu) and a group of fellow merchants from Australia and America had opened first in Hong Kong in 1900 and then on Shanghai's Nanking Road in 1917. It was the first Chinese-owned store of its kind, distinguished by its business methods (its principle of no bargaining being responsible for the subsequent wide currency of the term '*pu erh chia*', or 'no two prices') but also by the wide range of activities that were carried out on its premises. It housed, besides the usual wares, a multitude of entertainments including theatres, traditional operas, variety shows, cinemas, restaurants, tea-houses, dancing and story-telling, making it one of Shanghai's chief centres of amusement. Before long 'Hsien-shih kung-ssu' became a household word, conjuring up for countless people outside the metropolis something of the material millennium vaguely connected with the so-called *hsin wen-ming*, a hybrid culture with all kinds of vulgar trimmings from the two worlds of East and West, of which Hong Kong is a living example. To those who were able to make the pilgrimage, a ride in the elevator, the first to be installed by a Chinese enterprise, was a lift towards the material ultimate for the growing ranks of aspiring middle and lower bourgeoisie, what with the roof-garden full of novel diversions, and the 'hundreds-of-goods' – hence *pai-ho kung-ssu*, the term by which departmental stores have since become known in Chinese. As the Company expanded its activities into other fields, its example was emulated in Shanghai and elsewhere.

from Melbourne costing me landed here 1/6 per tube is in my opinion much superior to the American tooth paste for which I have to pay 2/10. These are things that have come under my own observation.

China produced a tough silk which is well adapted for use in Australia in the summer in all parts and in the tropical part of Australia throughout the year, yet the trade in this silk with Australia is comparatively unimportant, though the bartering of commodities is the most lucrative trade as regards revenue.

This question is one which ought not to be delayed. China is a silver using country, and her finances are benefitted enormously by the enhanced price of silver. It is only four years ago that I had to pay $12.44 Chinese currency for an English sovereign and now I can buy an English sovereign for less than $5. There is every indication that this enhancement of price will continue for a long time to come.

As regards the political situation, things in China are unsatisfactory, but with the election of the new President there is a hope that a reconciliation will be effected between the North and the South.

In Japan conditions have been most serious. The riots which have only recently been suppressed involved not thousands of rioters but hundreds of thousands. In this connection I would draw your attention to what I think is the most significant address delivered in Japan during recent years. The view of Dr. Ebina is held by most thoughtful men in the Far East that revolution is impending in Japan.[1] This revolution will have a marked effect upon the position in China. For this reason also it is important that we should have a High Commissioner to look after our Australian interests. The Australian Government ought to have a representative upon this allied commission that is now functioning in Siberia. Canada will send troops and even if Australia does not send troops she ought to send a delegate whose voice can be listened to and who can guide the Australian Government in a way that it is not being guided now by the British Minister,[2] an amiable old gentleman, who is retained here not because of his efficiency but because if he were to retire a Dutchman[3] who is not believed to be too friendly to the Allies would be the dean of the diplomatic body.

I must ask you to keep this letter confidential as I have written to you quite

---

[1] *See* Letter No. 909, Morrison to Allen, 15 September 1918.   [2] Sir John Jordan.

[3] F. Beelaerts van Blokland (b. 1872), Dutch diplomat, at this time Dutch Minister in Peking where he had first arrived in 1909; he was, therefore, the second longest serving foreign envoy in the Chinese capital, after Sir John Jordan who was appointed in 1906. He later became Dutch delegate to the Washington Conference and then Minister to Belgium. In 1927 he was appointed Dutch Foreign Minister, holding the post until 1933, and in 1936 he became Minister of State. When Holland fell during the Second World War he went to London and served as Chairman of the Extraordinary Advisory Council there from 1942 to 1944, and was a Member of the Control Commission of the League of Nations, from 1944 to 1946.

frankly. I hope soon to go to Hongkong, where I shall make some inquiries with regard to the appointment of an Australian agent in Hongkong. I will write to you from there.

It gave me profound pleasure to return to Australia after so many years of absence. I saw much while I was down there and heard many speakers but nothing stands out more clearly in my recollection than the noble speech delivered by you while I was in Sydney.[1]

With best wishes
Believe me

Very sincerely yours
[G. E. Morrison]

911. To Lu Cheng-hsiang[2]

[Peking] 25 September 1918

Dear Monsieur Lu,

I venture to write a few lines to your Excellency in regard to China's joining the movement for the establishment of a Home for the Jewish people in Palestine.[3]

On June 6th, when your Excellency was on leave at the seaside, the Jewish Community of China, through their representative body, the Shanghai Zionist Association,[4] appealed to your Excellency as Minister of Foreign Affairs to support the declaration of sympathy conveyed to the leader of the Zionist Federation in Great Britain, Lord Rothschild, by Mr. Balfour on behalf of the British Government on November 2nd, 1917, in regard to the establishment in Palestine of a National home for the Jewish people.

The Declaration of the British Government has since been followed by similar declarations from all of the Allied Nations, the last Government to associate itself with this movement being the Government of Siam.

---

[1] On 12 December 1917, the day after he arrived in Sydney, Morrison was entertained to a luncheon given by the Lord Mayor, during which Morrison and W. A. Watt were speakers. In his Diary for that day, Morrison recorded Watt's having made 'a really fine speech', in which 'Watt spoke of the lifelong admiration he had for me and compared me with Cecil Rhodes as an Empire builder and extolled the work I had done in China. It was all very surprising to me.'

[2] At this time Foreign Minister (December 1917 – August 1920).

[3] Morrison wrote this letter in answer to an appeal from Eleazer Silas Kadoorie (b. 1867), and Nissim Ezra Benjamin Ezra, respectively President and Secretary of the Zionist Association of Shanghai, to him to use his influence with the Chinese Government to support the Jewish call for a homeland in Palestine. A Baghdad Jew who came to China in 1881, Kadoorie, like Ezra, started his career with the leading opium firm, David Sassoon & Company, in Hong Kong. He soon, however, set up his own business and eventually became a prominent opium merchant in Shanghai. He received honours from both the French and British Governments for his charity works in the Middle East.

[4] The letter from the Shanghai Zionist Association to Lu is not printed.

[...]¹

The Association hope that your reply will be in English so that it may be telegraphed to the Zionist Associations in other countries, 'bringing joy and cheer to millions of Jewish people throughout the world', and they hope that your Excellency will send them some such words as these:—

'The Chinese Government expresses its complete accord with the Declaration of Sympathy with Jewish Zionist aspirations pronounced by the British Government on November 2nd, 1917, and view with favour the establishment in Palestine of a national home for the Jewish people, and will use their best endeavours to facilitate the achievement of this object, it being clearly understood that nothing shall be done which may prejudice the civil and religious rights of existing non-Jewish communities in Palestine or the rights and political status enjoyed by Jews in any other country.'²

It would, I think, be a considerable advantage to China if such a declaration could be made at the present time, showing as it would sympathy with the aspirations of a people who regard the Declaration of Mr. Balfour as the greatest event in the history of the Jews since their dispersion. Such a Declaration now by China, so soon after the great British victories in Palestine, would be received with enthusiasm and with gratitude.

With best regards

Very sincerely yours
[G. E. Morrison]

912. From Wu Ch'ao-shu[3]

Canton 29 September 1918

Dear Dr. Morrison,

I heard of your going to Australia and subsequent return to China. I am sorry that we didn't get an opportunity of seeing each other to talk over things.

There are one or two things I should like to write to you about. First as regards the political situation in China. The stand that the Constitutionalists have taken is unassailable. We uphold the Constitution which is admitted even by the Northerners to be the fundamental law of the country, and we uphold the Parliament which is still the legal representative body of the people though twice illegally dissolved. The Northerners have a Parliament of their own creation composed of members elected with bare-faced corrup-

---

[1] Omitted here are a letter addressed by Arthur James Balfour, British Foreign Secretary, to Lord Rothschild, President of the Zionist Association in England, dated 2 November 1918, and one from Prince Devawongse, the Siamese Minister of Foreign Affairs, to E. S. Kadoorie, dated 22 August 1918, supporting the Zionist case for a Jewish home in Palestine.

[2] China's support in the sense Morrison indicated here was conveyed in a letter, not printed, from Lu Cheng-hsiang to E. S. Kadoorie dated 14 December 1914.

[3] At this time Vice-Foreign Minister in the Canton Government.

tion and bribery. It is not difficult for an impartial judge to decide which is the real and which is the false Parliament of China. But the Northerners happen to be in possession of the Capital of the country and on that account, and it seems to me on that account alone, the Powers continue their dealings with them. The Constitutionalists on the other hand besides the great asset of legality possess all the elements of at least a belligerent power. They are in full possession of five rich and strategic provinces. They have armies in seven or eight others, and two of these, Fukien and Shensi, bid fair according to the latest bulletins to come entirely under their control. They have formed a Government of prominent and respected leaders, whose authority over the Constitutionalist provinces and armies, I make bold to say, is greater than what the Peking Government can boast of in its jurisdiction. They have therefore all the requisites for recognition by the Powers. The only possible reason that I can see why there is delay in according recognition is perhaps that the Powers fear that recognition of the Constitutionalists would prolong the Civil War. At first sight this may seem true. On further consideration I believe, however, that, paradoxical though it may seem, recognition, instead of prolonging, will shorten the war. The Northerners realize that they cannot hope to crush us with force alone. They rely considerably on foreign support, financial, material and moral. Recognize us and they will perceive that they can no longer rely on foreign assistance. The last vestige of hope of victory will be gone. Nothing will remain for them but to come to reasonable terms with us. These terms have been declared in the same way that the Allies have declared their peace terms to the Central Powers and consist of nothing selfish but simply the legal and constitutional demand of the reconvocation of the illegally dissolved Parliament and the strict observance of the Constitution. Therefore, foreigners who have the best interests and welfare of China at heart, among the foremost of whom I would place your goodself and Sir John Jordan, should do everything in their power to bring this about. With the improved conditions of trade and commerce the restoration of peace in China will not be only a blessing to China but also to the interests of foreigners as well.

I noticed a short time ago a report in the Chinese press that there was a possibility of Great Britain and America offering their good offices to bring about reconciliation between Peking and the Constitutionalists. How much truth is there in this report? I believe that we are ready to entertain a proposition of this kind, confident as we are that the Governments of the great British and American democracies will appreciate the principles for which we are fighting and will recognize the similarity of these principles with those for which they themselves are fighting in the bloody plains of France.

The bogus Parliament has elected a President.[1] The Chinese press reports

[1] A reference to the election of Hsü Shih-ch'ang by the Anfu Clique Parliament on 4 September 1918.

that foreign diplomats have offered their congratulations to him. It may be asked, if the Constitutionalists are anxious for peace as they declare themselves to be, why should they not take this occasion to bring about peace and conciliation? The answer is simple. The President-elect derives his title from a Parliament against whom and against the principles for which it stands we have been fighting for fifteen months. It would be a criminal inconsistency for us to recognize the acts of that so called Parliament, particularly an act which is the exercise of such a high function. We owe it to ourselves and to those who have suffered in this fratricidal war that our attitude be consistent and logical.

A rumour circulated a couple of weeks ago that the Military Government intended to take over the Maritime Customs in these provinces by force if necessary. An official *dementi* has already been published. You may rest assured that so long as experienced men are in charge of foreign affairs here no such action will be taken. On the other hand we see that the Customs revenue has now a large surplus, owing to the suspension of the Boxer Indemnity payments and to the favourable rates of exchange for the discharge of other obligations, charged on the Customs. This large surplus is turned over to the Peking Government which directly or indirectly employs the funds for administrative or military purposes. I understand that the Customs surplus is supposed to be ear-marked for the service of the domestic bonds recently issued and alleged to be used in payment of debts owing by the Peking Government to the Banks of China and Communications. This use of the Customs surplus does not detract from the truth of my statement that it is used for administrative or military purposes of the Peking Government in as much as this use either creates new sources of revenue to the government or else releases funds which would otherwise have to be employed for the payment of its debts. The enormous depreciation of the Peking bank notes, by the way, is an instructive indication of the manner in which the two banks employ the money paid to them by the Peking Government. Now a large share of the Customs revenue is contributed by the independent provinces; out of a total collection of Tls 37,500,000 in 1916 the ports of Kwangtung alone contributed Tls. 4,200,000. It means therefore that money from these provinces are being sent to fill the war chest of our political enemies. Small wonder that commanders asked why this is so when money is badly needed to pay troops whose pay is in some cases months in arrears. The Military Government has therefore proposed that while the Constitutionalist provinces should bear their portion of the foreign national obligations charged on the Customs, they should likewise retain a proportionate amount of the balance after the discharge of those obligations. This offer is fair and just while at the same time it does not jeopardize in the least the security of foreign creditors. We moderates are doing everything we can to calm the excitement and restrain the zeal of the soldiers and I think that the foreign diplomats should not increase our difficulties but do everything in their power to facilitate our task.

I notice a very fair article in the last issue of the *Far Eastern Review*[1] on the political situation, you have no doubt seen it yourself. With the disgusting incompetence of the Peking Authorities, their absolute lack of patriotism amounting in case[s] almost to treason, their revival of the dying opium traffic, their auction of the assets of the country bit by bit, their corruption open and rampant, it is really difficult to see what there is in them which can secure the continued support of the foreign governments. The only possible explanation so far as I can see is that they are nominally the Allies of the Entente Powers. You who know the real inside history of China's ranging herself on the side of the Allies will not be misled by the false 'inside history' published by a Shanghai weekly. The war policy of China, the fruits of which the Peking Government is at present garnering was as you very well know inaugurated by men who are now in the Military Government. After all, what has the Peking Government done in active execution of that policy? It has received benefits from the Allies but has done nothing to help them and suffer with them. In short it has prostituted the far-sighted war policy conceived by us to their selfish ends. I have more than once wondered if the world war were to end today what figure China would cut at the Council Table tomorrow. Even in our present circumstances and with our resources we should like to do something for the Allies' cause. We should like to do it in the name of China as a whole. We should not be currying favour with the Entente Powers merely to secure possible advantages for ourselves but we should be doing it for the highest interest of China as a whole, for the North as well as for the South, for the future diplomatic position of China among the States of the world.

I am writing to you frankly and without reserve as a friend to friend. While titularly you are adviser to the Peking Government I would rather consider you adviser to China. I believe that all patriotic Chinese either in the North or in the South as well as all well-wishers of China should work for the same end. I being in touch with the Constitutionalist leaders write to you who are in touch with the foreign representatives in Peking. I am sure you will exert to the utmost your good influence for China's greatest good. I am willing to do my best to collaborate with you. Between us I hope something can be done.

With kindest regards to Mrs. Morrison from Mrs. Wu who has joined me down here, and myself, and best wishes for your goodself

I am

Yours sincerely
Chao-Shu Wu

[1] A reference to an article published in the September 1918 number of the journal, entitled 'A Republic with two Parliaments? It gave the views of both the Peking Government and the break-away government at Canton.

913. From Lin Hsiung-ch'eng

Singapore 5 November 1918

Dear Dr. Morrison,

I am in receipt of your letter of the 6th September for which I thank you. I send you herewith two copies of my photograph.

I was in the service of the Straits and Federated Malay States Governments for twenty-one years, during which time I was chiefly employed as Interpreter and have a general knowledge of the works of all government departments. I had also served as an articled clerk to a practising barrister with a view of being called to the local bar, but as I did not serve up the time I was not entitled to present myself for examination. Last year I received a letter from Mr. Alston saying he would be pleased to see me at the British Legation and I left my government post at Kelantan and went to Shanghai where I was advised to come home owing to the political situation at Peking, and on my return to Singapore I took up the post of acting reporter to the *Singapore Free Press*. When I was in school I began to think of one subject, that is, How China ought to be governed, and have been studying that one subject all my life, and the book has taken as it says eighteen years to finish.[1]

The Chinese Government may say that they have many Chinese who have passed high examinations in Europe and America, but the Government does not know that in Europe and America however high an examination a man has passed, when he leaves college he has to serve as an apprentice, and he is nobody. The Government would think that if they can finance, a Chinese engineer who has returned from Europe or America can be entrusted with the building of a railway bridge across the Yang-tse-kiang, or if he is a barrister he can advise the government on legal matters.

When a cadet who has passed high examination arrives in the Straits to serve the Government, he is given a bungalow to live in, a bedroom with a bed and a couple of chairs and a hall with a few other furniture, and his salary is what a senior clerk gets and his position is not much better than a senior clerk who can teach him what government routine is. Twenty years after when he might be eligible for the post of a Governor. I have the lengthy service and practical experience and can the wealth of Peking purchase them if the Government require my services, and if it is considered that China can be saved?

With regard to the post of Director, I do not mind if I may go third or fourth in the Reformed Prefecture if Government can appoint someone for the

---

[1] Lin's book *How China Ought to be Governed* has not been traced. He had previously sent a complimentary copy to Morrison together with the letter printed as No. 896. Morrison in his reply dated 6 September 1918 wrote: 'Without in any way wishing to discourage you from aspiring to so distinguished a position, I think to myself there must be some difficulties in giving effect to such a suggestion. International jealousy counts for a great deal in China, and, however desirable such a project may be, I fear that there will be opposition to any such attempt to hand over the Government of China to a British subject from Singapore.'

post, provided he can deal with all the English minute papers placed before him by the Chief Secretary, and if he has never seen an English minute paper and unable to direct the Chief Secretary he may have to quit the Director's chair within 48 hours. Perhaps a Co-Director may be appointed, the one a thoroughly experienced man, and the other a nominal Director. If there will be no frictions well and good, but will the Chief Secretary be willing to serve two masters? Moreover, if a so-called Director is appointed the Chief Secretary who is a foreigner will be the real Director, and the Allies will say that an Englishman is the chief ruler of the prefecture. If they say this their claims would reasonably come in, but my argument is, if China has a Chinese who is a genuine Director in the fullest sense of the title, why should the Allies interfere with China's internal government. The Allies do not interfere with the Russian internal affairs.

The Allies asked themselves what was the object of the war – to win the victory, and they appointed a French general to be Commander-in-Chief of the Allied forces. If China thinks she can be saved she should waive the question of the author being a British subject.

If I be appointed Director I will sit in all courts from the lowest to the highest, and hear eminent barristers pleading before me with a view of making law reports which will be employed in the courts of the Reformed Prefecture, otherwise the English decisions will be applicable, and thus give laws to the people. In drafting ordinances I will not leave the Advocate-General to do them entirely himself, but will direct him what to do, for he will not know what suit the Chinese and what do not. Some laws will be drafted by myself.

I will always be accompanied by a private secretary who writes shorthand, and whatever lectures or teachings I will deliver at one place of education will be disseminated to other places of education, such as High School, College and University. Such buildings I will visit from time to time apart from my administrative work and bring the students up under the Director's *kultur* chiefly to consist of four parts – force of character, reliableness, duties towards God, and duties towards man. The Chinese value the teachings of ancient Confucius, and they may have to venerate the teachings of a modern Confucius. The students will be dealt with as if they were the Anglo-Saxons a thousand years ago and their shortcomings made up. It is a great mistake to educate them as if they were modern Anglo-Saxons, and for this reason, the book says Oxford and Cambridge may not educate. The Reformed Government will not have confidence in those foreign educated Chinese, and if any of them is employed, he must consider himself very lucky.

I will undertake the organisation of the Army itself, and will be an honorary captain of a company of a regiment which will be known as the Director's company, and whatever lecture, teaching I deliver will be disseminated by the private secretary to every regiment, and ever soldier must hear it. The Government thinks if a man is given a gun he is a soldier, a man may never have held a gun and yet he is a soldier. Drill, military instruction and manoeuvre will be left to the generals. I have been a volunteer here for two years. Singapore has a garrison for me to study.

In general, the Director will supervise all departments himself, and not leave heads of departments alone. I am 52 years of age. The line and principle are now fully established and any alterations or amendments should not impair or vitiate them. I have been studying the subject all my life, and in my head there is inexhaustible store to deliver. If I be not appointed Director, all the above will be lost since it is not the invention of another Director. If I be appointed, and when I die, the Chief Secretary will keep up my principle.

In conclusion, the world will deem your success as a miracle.

I am

Very faithfully yours
Lim Yong Seng

914. To G. Woodhead

[Peking] 6 November 1918

Private

My dear Woodhead,

[...]

I understand that the Japanese will insist upon Obata's coming here.[1] The Chinese dare not raise any objection. After all his manners towards them are mild and conciliatory compared with the studied rudeness of Barton. I have always noticed that the Chinese judge a Legation not by the attitude of its Minister so much as by the attitude of the interpreters through whom they communicate with the Minister. The Japanese interpreters are specially friendly with the Chinese. Our interpreter, Barton, never refers to the Chinese except as 'swine', and he acts towards them as if they were, and the Chinese know it.

It was a pleas[ure] to us to see you in Tientsin.

With kind remembrances

Very sincerely yours
[G. E. Morrison]

915. From T. F. Millard

Shanghai 11 November 1918

Dear Dr Morrison,

I am sorry that I did not have a further talk with you before I left Peking, as there were some matters about which I would like to have your views.

[1] Obata Yūkichi (Torikichi), while Counsellor with the Japanese Legation in Peking during the negotiations relating to Japan's Twenty-One Demands, was an advocate of an aggressive policy in China and was well-known for his bullying manner. In the event he did become Japanese Minister, and held the post until 1923.

Especially, I wanted to urge the necessity for China to have some kind of an organisation at the Peace Conference whose task will be to see that her side of matters gets adequate publicity. I have urged the necessity for this upon the Foreign Office at Peking, but one never knows how much of an impression is made. My idea, roughly, was that they should have attached to the official delegation (perhaps semi-officially) a sort of Information Bureau, through which news could be given out to the press correspondents, and which would serve as a center for information. I think it would be well to have a Chinese as the nominal head of this Bureau – Hollington Tong[1] would do very well – he has a good address and makes a good impression, and as a Chinese editor he would be enough of a novelty to attract interest. Or it may be that there are other Chinese journalists who would do even better than Tong. This Bureau should be provided with all reference books, etc, and other matter useful to pressmen; and have a location so that it would be always accessible to them. Of course, some assistants, typists, etc. would be needed.

As aids to the Bureau, there should be a number of foreign journalists who are acquainted with conditions in the Far East, of proven friendship for China, and who have some reputation in connection with eastern affairs as publicists, if possible. One or more British Americans and French should be included. It has been Welling[ton] Koo's idea that I should attend the Conference in this capacity, because I am known to the American press fraternity as a writer about Eastern affairs, and also I have a wide personal acquaintance among the men who will act as correspondents on this occasion.

[1] Tung Hsien-kuang, known to foreigners by his anglicised name, Hollington K. Tong (1887–1971), Chinese journalist and Republican politician. A graduate in Journalism from the University of Missouri, he had worked on the staff of the *New York Times* and the *New York Evening Post* before his return to China in 1912. After leaving his post of Assistant Editor of the *China Republican* in Shanghai, he went to Peking as a correspondent for papers in Shanghai and New York, serving at the same time as an Editor of the *Peking Daily News* and an English secretary in the Senate. In 1914 he became a secretary in the National Petroleum Administration and in 1917 the Chinese representative of the Standard Oil Company. He later held various Government posts, while continuing to work as a journalist, and became closely associated with T. F. F. Millard, serving as Peking Correspondent of *Millard's Review* when it was first founded in 1917. In 1931 he became Managing Director of the *China Press*, and in 1935 Managing Director of the *China Times*, *Ta-wan pao* and the Shun-shih (Shen-shih) News Agency, owned by K'ung Ling-k'ai, the son of K'ung Hsiang-hsi, organs which were in fact an unofficial mouthpiece of the Chiang Kai-shek clique in the Nationalist Government. He was on particularly close terms with Sung (Soong) Mei-ling, the wife of Chiang Kai-shek, and through her influence became Vice-Minister, then Minister of Information, one of whose functions was the censoring of foreign news in the wartime Government in Chungking. After fleeing to Taiwan with the Nationalist Government in 1949 he became Managing Director of the Nationalist Government Broadcasting Corporation, and in 1952 was made Taiwan's Ambassador to Japan, and in 1956 Ambassador to the United States, where he remained after his retirement in 1958. He was the author of the official biography of Chiang Kai-shek, published in 1937, and his experiences during the war years are recorded in a book entitled *Dateline: China* (New York 1950).

On the British side, men like yourself and Simpson[1] would be especially useful – although in your own case, you may attend in an official capacity, attached to the Plenipotentiaries as adviser. My idea is to have a few foreign journalists there, not officially connected with China's representatives, but who can serve as a connecting link with the foreign press. I am willing to go in such a capacity, as probably others will be willing too. The men who are fitting for this work are comparatively few, unfortunately.

I probably have written enough to outline my idea about this matter. With any Government except that of China, it would be a foregone conclusion that this matter would be attended to; but in view of the strong probability that pressure will be exerted to prevent China from having an adequate organization at the Conference, and China's own ineptness, there is a possibility that nothing may be done. This is why I suggest that you will use your influence to bring the need of this particular matter to the attention of the officials who are able to decide what will be done. This will require funds, of course, but the cost is as nothing in comparison with the issues at stake.

Another matter: I heard at Peking that Wellington Koo is soon to be recalled, and replaced at Washington by a new minister. While Koo has about completed his regular turn in that post, it seems to me that the present time is very inopportune to make a change. Koo is known at Washington, is quite favorably regarded; and there is a serious risk in replacing him just now by any man, however able, who is not known and who is not in touch with events in America. It may be, of course, that Koo is designated as a member of the delegation for China at the Conference (there will, in addition to the Plenipotentiaries be quite a number of Secretaries and minor officials I presume), and he would be useful in that capacity I think. But a man who understands things should be on watch at Washington.[2]

I hope that you will let me know if you receive this letter, and that you will lend your influence to helping to get a publicity organization for the time coming.[3]

With regards I remain

Yours truly
Thomas F. Millard

[1] Bertram Lenox Simpson, or Putnam Weale, who from the time of Japan's Twenty-One Demands had been championing China's cause.
[2] Ku Wei-chün, Chinese Minister in Washington since July 1915, had just returned to China after the death of his first wife, and was appointed a Chinese delegate to the Paris Conference. He was then sent as Minister to Britain, and the former Chinese Minister in London, Shih Chao-chi, took his place in Washington. Ku remained in London until his appointment as Foreign Minister in August 1922.
[3] On the margin of this letter Morrison wrote: 'Letter unanswered. Already Millard about Nov. 25th appointed head of Publicity Bureau in connection with the Chinese Delegation.'

November 1918 – May 1920

It was exactly one month and a day before the European conflagration came to an end that China found herself with a new President – Hsü Shih-ch'ang. One of the last Grand Secretaries and Imperial Guardians of the defunct Manchu dynasty, Hsü, holding fast to his Confucian code of ethics, had refused to serve the Republic and had retired in the company of many other prominent monarchists to the German-controlled territory of Tsingtao. In 1914, when his old friend Yüan Shih-k'ai decided to proceed with the monarchical scheme, Hsü yielded to his appeal and accepted appointment as the first Secretary of State, the post to which the Prime Ministership had been converted. But as an expression of his unshaken loyalty to the old dynasty and for the sake of his philosophical purity, he allegedly refused all emoluments. That such a man should now have been chosen for and have accepted the Presidency of the Republic tells of the complexity and treacherous uncertainty of Chinese politics during those troubled times.

The choice of Hsü, full of absurdities and contradictions though it was, was intended as a compromise between diverse conflicting interests; or so it was meant by his sponsors, the Anfu clique, which by means of a rigged parliament now dominated the Government. Indeed, peace by negotiation between the main contending factions, the North and the South, for which the whole nation was clamouring, suddenly became a possibility when Hsü succeeded Feng Kuo-chang to the Presidency. The conclusion of the European War also helped to bring the prospect nearer. The Western Powers were now able to revive their interest in China for the first time in four years. This seemed to some extent to inhibit the Japanese Government, particularly as more and more of the secret dealings it had had with the Anfu Government became known. The exposure of these, and the nation-wide agitation which resulted from it, put in turn a temporary check on the Anfu Government and made Tuan Ch'i-jui and his followers, who had failed to win the day by arms, more amenable to negotiation.

At about the same time as the Paris Conference was assembling, a Peace Conference between the North (the central government) and the South (the revolutionary government) took place in Shanghai. But it was to end in failure. Not only were the two parties unable to agree, but friction and dissension arose within the ranks of both. In the South it was to end in the dissolution of the revolutionary government, while in the North it was to lead in the autumn of 1920 to war between the Chihli and Anhwei cliques, culminating in the temporary eclipse of the latter.

Morrison was to hear of all this only from a distance. He had left Peking in December 1918 as a technical adviser to the Chinese Delegation at the Peace Conference, having been initially ignored, not so much through a deliberate slight as because in the confusion of a general scramble for appointments as delegates to the Conference, he was simply overlooked. This fact nevertheless reflected the diminishing influence of the Political Adviser with his employers, who had changed four times in less than the same number of years.

Though asked by the Foreign Minister and the Head of the Chinese Delegation to arrive in Paris in early February, Morrison took his time, spending a while in Canada on the way, and arrived in Paris only on the last day of February 1919. It may have been partly for this reason that the Chinese Foreign Minister asked him on his arrival whether he preferred to be attached to the Chinese Delegation or to attend the Conference in a private capacity. At any rate, his arrival was most timely. The central issue for China was the recovery of what Japan had forcefully wrung from her during the War in one way or another, particularly the former German Leased Territory in Shantung. Like the injured party facing an indifferent court and an ill-informed jury, the Chinese were prone to overstate their case with arguments couched in flowery style, aimed to appeal to sentiment and emotion rather than to reason. Morrison considered this the wrong approach. He felt that China had a clear case. All that she needed to do was to present it with moderation, in tone as well as in substance. And Morrison made his great contribution to China's cause by his ruthless weeding and pruning of the documents which various Chinese members of the Delegation prepared. Among those in his debt were Ch'en Yu-jen, who was to become known as the 'revolutionary diplomat', 'a firebrand but clear-headed' as Morrison described him, and Liang Ch'i-ch'ao, who was probably China's best known publicist. A Chinese reader of Morrison's Diary during this period would be enlightened to learn that it was after having corrected and edited Liang's famous statement of China's case that Morrison was inspired to comment that 'these men are all astonishingly ignorant of the history of their own country'.

Only two examples of Morrison's handiwork at the Peace Conference are given here. They were both key documents which were eventually presented by the Chinese Delegation. In both cases the version given here for the first time, complete with Morrison's pruning and comments, is the original one, and is quite different from that which has hitherto been known. They give an insight into the process of formulation of the Chinese case in Paris.

But Morrison was soon struck down by an illness from which he was not to recover. As though he felt something ominous was portending, he recorded at the end of his Diary for 1918, a few days after he left Peking, his prayer 'that Luck and Happiness be ours during 1919'. But just the opposite occurred. He became ill after hardly five weeks in France, and this illness, pancreatitis, finally forced him to leave Paris in early May for a nursing home in England. He did not, however, take leave of the Chinese Delegation until after he had learnt that in spite of his efforts China had lost her case, betrayed by America, in whom Morrison and the Chinese had come to place such faith, and her other allies. When this news reached China, as Morrison was about to cross the English Channel for the last time, it sparked off a nation-wide protest initiated by students in Peking. This protest has become known, after the day the first demonstration took place, as the 'May Fourth Movement'. It was to develop into more than a mere protest against the injustice China had suffered at Versailles. It was the expression of an intellectual and political awakening. In the course of it some Chinese for the first time came to see in Communism (which Morrison described in July 1919 as 'a serious danger to China') an alternative path to the one along which Morrison and his friends had tried to steer China in the course of salvation.

Meanwhile, from his sick bed, Morrison continued to fight for China as he was fighting for his life. As if by fate, men whom he had known at the beginning of his career in China, but from many of whom he had grown distant, now crowded into his final hours as China herself fast receded into the distance. It was almost symbolic that Morrison should have had these former colleagues and Old China Hands – themselves not far from death – draw about him as his world drew to a close.

916. From W. H. Donald

[Shanghai] 29 November 1918

My dear Doctor,

I have your letter,[1] for which many thanks. [...]

I agitated quite a bit before I left Peking, and Anderson got Li Shun[2] to wire Peking that you must be at the Conference. I got a letter yesterday from Peking saying that you and Willoughby[3] were going. Last night I talked to Green about it and he wrote a leader, saying he would also advocate the utilization of Dane's knowledge. I have not yet read the article.

I hear from several here that Millard is going for the Chinese in publicity work. He told someone that he had given them a plan of publicity operations, and led them to understand that he had been selected to carry out the scheme.

[1] Not found.   [2] Li Ch'un, at this time Military Governor of Kiangsu Province.
[3] In the event W. W. Willoughby did not go to Paris as a Technical Adviser to the Chinese Delegation because of objection by the State Department.

So far as I am concerned I would be no use at the Conference, I mean associated with the outside work thereof, and furthermore this government would do anything before they would ask me to go seeing that I have been hammering them so badly.

Financial troubles worry them considerably and they had to go to a foreign bank and raise a loan to send the delegates they had selected. Further I am too tied down here to go even if they wanted me to do so – which they don't.

I think that you ought to get together something on the question of China's entrance into the war. You have the dates of different incidents in connection with the matter, and I would like to have them at least. All hands and the cook, including Liang Chi-chiao,[1] are writing about how China got into the war and not one of them gives the actual inside information about it.

The Cabinet refuses to resume payment of that advertising amount to us on the ground that we do not help the Central Government as it is at present constructed – nor do we, of course, nor would we if they paid five hundred times as much. The suggestion is that if we will stop attacking they will resume. Well, I won't do that till they are out. Then when it is useless further to attack them I will desist – not before. Or, until they change their policy I will keep up a campaign against them.

I hope by this time you have been definitely appointed for the Peace Conference. Anderson will stir up Li Shun if the Peking crowd have side-stepped in any way, as also will Wen.[2] But my letter from the President's Palace says that it has been decided you go with Willoughby. We are wondering if Fergy[3] has been appointed. Hope to see you about the fifth or sixth.

Yours sincerely
W. H. Donald

917. From Wu Ch'ao-shu

Canton 7 December 1918

Dear Dr. Morrison,

I have been disappointed in not hearing from you since your return to Peking. I expect you have been too busy to write.

The peace movement in China has made great strides forward since your visit south. Both sides have ordered cessation of hostilities. The Constitutionalists have made the offer of a direct peace conference at Shanghai and the principle has just been accepted by Peking though they differ in regard to the

[1] Liang Ch'i-ch'ao went to Paris not as a Delegate to the Peace Conference but as an official observer with a large grant from the Government. His writings on China's entry into the European War, and his records of his European sojourns, *Ou yu hsin-ying lu*, are to be found in his collected works, *Yin-ping-shih ho-chi* (Shanghai 1936).
[2] Wen Tsung-yao, at this time in Shanghai, where he was the representative of the southern republicans, succeeding T'ang Shao-yi, at the conference between the north and the south.   [3] John Calvin Ferguson.

locality. The Powers have made representations to both sides though I consider and shrewdly guess them to be more intended for Peking than for Canton. This is all to the good. But the real hard work will be at the peace conference in reconciling divergent principles and in effecting a just and lasting peace for the country which is the aim of the South.

The European Peace Conference will commence, in all probability, next month. For the North to appoint a delegation alone cannot be said to represent the whole country. Even if the Powers accept it, the members will not be able to speak with full effect. As, owing to the dilatoriness with which things are done, it is highly improbable that a settlement which can give at least an appearance of unity to the country can be arrived at before the meeting of the European Conference, what is the way out of the dilemma? I have a suggestion. Let the North designate a certain number of nominees, say three, and let the South designate a similar number. After ascertaining that the nominees of each are acceptable to the other, let each officially appoint both groups of nominees, the South undertaking to submit the whole delegation to Parliamentary approval, if necessary, according to the Provisional Constitution which requires envoys to be so submitted. Such a way would produce a delegation which represents in fact the whole country, is constitutionally appointed, and would be able to speak with effect at the Conference. This is my personal suggestion only, but I believe it would be favourably considered by the Constitutionalist Government. I have spoken of this solution to both Mr. Jamieson and Mr. Pontius[1] and they think it a good idea.

Reuter says that owing to the opposition of your Ally, you would not be a member of the Chinese delegation. Is it true? With your unique knowledge of Chinese affairs, I consider it a great misfortune if you are really not to go. But then there is more than one way always of arriving at one's aims. I don't suppose it was ever intended that you should be an official member of the delegation, but be an advisory member of it. Well, as you are not too busy just now in Peking, why dont you obtain six months' furlough, to be prolonged if necessary, and spend it in *Paris*?

Has Mr. Lu[2] been officially appointed China's chief delegate and has been accepted by the Powers?

Hoping to hear from you soon, and with kind regards

Yours sincerely
Chao-shu Wu

[1] Albert William Pontius (1879–1923), American consular official. He had served in various posts in China and was at this time United States Consul in Canton.
[2] Lu Cheng-hsiang.

918. To Ju Jen-ho

[Peking] 11 December 1918

Dear Mr. Ju,

After the conversation I had on Monday with his Excellency the President when you gave such efficient help as interpreter I arranged with you that I would send you a brief résumé of the subject of our conversation.

I ought to have done that yesterday but unfortunately yesterday I was taken suddenly ill and could not possibly do any work having to lie down. Today I am much better. And I herewith send you the note.

With kind regards

Very sincerely yours
[G. E. Morrison]

Enclosure to Letter No. 918: *Memorandum of a Conversation with the President on 9 December 1918*

In the course of conversation with His Excellency the President on Monday afternoon the 9th December I made the following observations regarding the Peace Conference:—

1. I suggested that at a Conference of such vast importance it was essential that China should send the best representatives available. Every foreigner interested in China knows of Mr. Liang Chi-chao and of the powerful following he has among the Chinese both at home and overseas. His inclusion would lend distinction to the Conference.

And inasmuch as questions of extraterritorial protection would be brought before the conference it would be an advantage that the presentation of the case should be entrusted to one who has a greater knowledge of this subject than any member of the delegation so far appointed.

Dr. Wang Chung-hui[1] has won for himself a great reputation in the world of law. Intellectually he is one of the most remarkable men in any country. His translation of the German Code into English was a remarkable achievement. He is well known to the Jurists of England, America and France and no one is so well fitted as he to explain what has been done and what is being done in China to reform the judicial system and bring it into accord with that of other nations as provided in the Treaties with England, America and Japan of 1902 and 1903.[2]

---

[1] Wang Ch'ung-hui was at this time Chairman of the Law Codification Commission in Peking. He did not go to Paris, but was appointed Chief Justice of the Supreme Court in 1920. As China's leading jurist, however, he participated in the 1921 Conference on the revision of the League of Nations Covenant and was also a Chinese Delegate to the Washington Conference. *See also* p. 191 n. 2.

[2] The reference is to Article XII of the Sino-British, or Mackay Convention of 5 September 1902; Article XV of the Sino-U.S. Treaty of 8 October 1903; and Article XI of the Sino-Japanese Treaty of 8 October 1903.

Dr. Wang Chung-hui by his work on the Law Codification Commission has done more than any other man in China to prepare the way for the abolition of Extraterritoriality. To leave him out of the delegation seems a serious mistake which it is not too late to rectify.

2. Speaking further of the conference I pointed out what a prejudicial effect it must have upon the consideration given to the Chinese delegation the appointment of Mr. Millard as chief of publicity.

Mr. Millard is an American journalist who edits a monthly paper in Shanghai which is subsidised by the Chinese Government. He is regarded as unfriendly by both the British and the French. It was unwise to make an appointment of this kind and then announce in the papers that the appointment has been made. Mr. Millard is a strong advocate for China against Japan and if he were the representative of independent American papers at the Peace Conference he could render help to China but being known as the paid publicity agent of China any help he could now give would be unimportant.

It would have been better to appoint in such a capacity a Chinese writer like Mr. M. T. Z. Tyau[1] who writes English with great force and eloquence.

3. I spoke of the surprise felt in Peking especially by the French and Belgians that M. Lu Tseng-tsiang should take as his chief French assistant Mr. Wang Ching-chi[2] who is not received at either the French or Belgian legations. The foreign papers have commented adversely upon this appointment pointing out that the conference will be held in France that the Councillor Mr. Wang Ching-chi will be brought into contact with French officials and the fact that he is not received at the French Legation will also make him unwelcome in France.

4. I enclose you the card of Mr. J. C. Ferguson 'Adviser to the President of China'. The president expressed his doubt and surprise that the card should be inscribed 'Adviser to the President of China' when Mr. Ferguson is not an Adviser.

5. His Excellency expressed the wish that I should go to the Conference and give what help I could to Mr. Lu Tseng-hsiang. I said I would be very pleased to do what I could to help China at this important juncture and that I would leave as soon as possible after the new year either in the same steamer

---

[1] Tiao Ming-ch'ien (b. 1888), who signed himself M. T. Z. Tyau, Chinese jurist and journalist. An LL.D. from London University, he was at this time Editor of the *Peking Leader* which he founded in 1917. He taught Law at Tsinghua College in Peking and assisted in many important diplomatic negotiations. He was the author of a number of books in the English language on China's legal and diplomatic questions.

[2] Wang Ching-ch'i (b. 1884), Chinese diplomat. A returned student from France, he had served in 1915 as a Secretary with the Chinese Delegation in the Tripartite Conference between China, Russia and Mongolia in Kiakhta. He was selected by Lu Cheng-hsiang as his assistant during the Paris Conference. He later became Minister to Belgium (1921-7). He also taught at universities in Peking and Shanghai, and was the author of several books, two of them in French.

with Mr. Yeh Kung-cho[1] or earlier and I would go via Canada and see the Canadian authorities.

His Excellency expressed his wish that I should give him a note of my expected expenses which he would be glad to provide.[2] This I will do as soon as possible. I presume that the treatment will be the same as that given me by His Excellency Yuan Shih-kai in 1914.

919. From O. M. Green

Shanghai 19 December 1918

My dear Morrison,

I enclose herewith the slips of your admirable article. It has caused quite a sensation down here – as well it might. I ventured on one small alteration, which was to leave out the names of the firms you mentioned.[3] I was compelled to do this as a matter of common prudence. As it is, all the local Japanese merchants are much exercised over the article. Since then some of the missionaries have been to me and want to know who it was who wrote the article, so that they may get further information, which they propose to lay before that very much-enduring body, the Peace Conference. I told them that I could not possibly disclose the writer's identity without his consent. I leave it, of course, entirely to you to decide. In point of fact, as you may gather from the leader in to-day's paper, I have not very much sympathy with these gentlemen. They are trying all the time to get a whipping post. Formerly, of course, they had Great Britain, and made the most of her. Now they are eagerly catching at Japan. No one, of course, defends Japan, but the revival of cultivation in the provinces, as reported far and wide by our correspondents, is at least as serious a matter. Of course the foreign anti-opium party realize very well the difficulty of any solid amendment in that direction.

You say you are going Home by the *Nanking* on the 16th. Can't you postpone it until the *Empress of Japan* leaves here on January 25, by which steamer – vastly to my surprise – I have got leave to make a flying trip Home. I am going to do, all being well, a sort of Jules Verne's round the world in 80

[1] Yeh Kung-ch'o (b. 1881), Chinese politician. A leader of the 'Communication Clique', he owed his political rise to Liang Shih-yi, with whose major enterprises he was associated. He was many times Vice-Minister, then Minister of Communications (August 1920 and again in December 1921). In 1918, having quarrelled with Ts'ao Ju-lin, at that time Minister of Communications and leader of the so-called 'New Communication Clique', he resigned his position as Vice-Minister and was sent as Commissioner to study industry and communications in post-war Europe. A scholar of traditional learning, he was renowned for his calligraphy.
[2] In a subsequent letter to Ju Jen-ho on 12 December, Morrison gave an estimate of his travel and living expenses for 6 months, a sum of $9,900.
[3] In his Diary entry for 11 December 1918 Morrison mentioned Suzuki and Mogi as being the names of the Japanese involved in the opium and morphia trade, but these names were excluded from the printed article for fear of legal complications.

days,[1] only if possible I shall do it in less, catching up a wife and family on the road. It's a wild idea, but the prospect of being able to sleep unlimitedly from here to Vancouver is attractive. Do come by the *Empress*, and I shall have some inducement to stop awake. It'll get you Home just as soon as the *Nanking* and San Francisco.[2]

Yours sincerely
O. M. Green

Enclosure to Letter No. 919: *The Japanese Opium Trade with China: A scandal calling for instant and drastic repression*[3]

In the *North China Daily News* of September 15, 1915, a correspondent explained in some detail the large proportions to which had attained Japan's morphia traffic with China. He expressed his belief that the morphia trade was the most lucrative of all trades conducted by Japanese in China. He pointed out that the trade with Tairen [Dairen] alone in 1913 amounted to six and a quarter tons of morphia, and that between the price at which this morphia made in Europe was purchased in Japan, and the price ultimately paid for it by the consumer, there was a margin, that is to say there was a profit to the intermediary in the six and a quarter tons, of $8,400,000.

That morphia trade still flourishes. It is a larger trade now than it was in 1913. Morphia, however, can no longer be purchased in Europe. The seat of industry has been transferred to Japan and morphia is now manufactured by the Japanese themselves. Although Japan is a signatory to the Agreement which forbids the import into China of morphia or of any appliances used in its manufacture or in its application, the traffic, inasmuch as it has the financial support of the Bank of Japan as explained by your correspondent, is carried on with the direct approval and encouragement of the Japanese Government. In no other country in the world has there ever been known such a wholesale contraband traffic. Literally tens of millions of yen are transferred annually from China to Japan for the payment of Japanese morphia. The chief agency in the distribution of morphia in China is the Japanese post office. Morphia is imported by parcels post. No inspection of parcels in the Japanese post offices in China is permitted to the Chinese Customs Service. The Service is only allowed to know what are the *alleged* contents of the postal packages as stated in the Japanese invoices, and yet morphia enters China by this channel by the ton.

A conservative estimate would place the amount of morphia imported by the Japanese into China in the course of the year as high as 18 tons and there

---

[1] A reference to the work by the French writer, Jules Verne (1828–1905), which first appeared in *Le Temps* in 1872 entitled *Le Tour du Monde en quatre-vingts jours*.

[2] Morrison eventually left on 3 January 1919 by way of Yokohama, on the S.S. *Fushimi Maru* bound for Toronto.

[3] This article was published as 'From a Correspondent' in the *North China Daily News* on 17 December 1918.

is evidence that the amount is steadily increasing. Wherever Japanese are predominant there the trade flourishes. Through Tairen [Dairen] morphia circulates throughout Manchuria and the provinces adjoining; through Tsingtao morphia is showered over Shantung province, Anhui and Kiangsu, while from Formosa, so favoured by geographical propinquity, morphia is carried along with opium and other contraband by motor-driven fishing boats to some point on the mainland, from which it is distributed throughout the province of Fukien and the north of Kuangtung. Everywhere it is sold by Japanese under exterritorial protection. How efficient is that protection may be gauged by the fact that no Japanese has ever yet been punished for dealing in contraband in China. When Chinese police raid the morphia shops along the Tsinanfu railway in Shantung, as they have a right to do, for the traffic is illegal, Japanese *gendarmerie* rescue the arrested and exact a fine, not from the guilty be it understood, but from those who attempted to uphold the law. In recorded instances known to American investigators the magistrate himself has been compelled to pay the fine.

In South China morphia is sold also by Chinese peddlers each of whom carries a passport certifying that he is a native of the Island of Formosa and therefore entitled to Japanese protection. Japanese drug stores throughout China carry large stocks of morphia. Japanese medicine vendors look to morphia for their largest profits. Everywhere Japanese prostitution, the systematic extension of which from Yunnan city even to Urga is such an inspiring evidence of the business activities of our Asiatic Allies, goes hand in hand with the sale of morphia.

Morphia, no longer purchasable in Europe, is manufactured now in well-equipped laboratories in Japan and in Formosa. During recent years the bulk of the Persian opium coming into the market has been purchased by Japan for conversion into morphia, for Persian opium yields a larger percentage of morphia than Indian opium. Opium grown in Korea, the cultivation of which, it is interesting to note, followed immediately upon the closing of the opium shops in Shanghai, Japanese officials providing the seeds, and opium grown under Japanese protection in Manchuria, is an ever expanding source of the supply of morphia, and, it may be added, of opium required by the administration of Formosa.

But while the morphia traffic is a large one, there is every reason to believe that the opium trade, upon which Japan is now embarking with such enthusiasm, is likely to prove even more lucrative. In the Calcutta opium sales Japan has become one of the considerable purchasers of Indian opium. She purchases for Formosa, where the opium trade shows a steady growth and where opium is required for the manufacture of morphia. She purchases for import into Japan. Sold by the Government of India, this opium is exported under permits applied for by the Japanese Government, is shipped to Kobe, and from Kobe is transhipped to Tsingtao. Large profits are being made in this trade, in which are interested some of the leading firms of Japan.

One must emphasize that this opium is not imported into Japan. It is transhipped in Kobe harbour to Tsingtao, from which point of vantage, assisted by the Japanese-controlled railway to Tsinanfu, it is smuggled through Shantung into Shanghai and the Yangtze Valley. Opium purchased in Calcutta for Rs. 3,500 per chest – about Tls. 1,000 – costs, delivered in Kobe Harbour, all told well under Tls. 1,200 per chest. This opium – Tsingtao opium – is sold in Shanghai at $500 a ball of 40 balls to the chest – a total of $20,000 per chest. China's failure to sell 'for medicinal purposes' her opium at $27,000 per chest, the price asked by the opium ring, is thus explained. The price is undercut by the Japanese. The dimensions that the traffic has already assumed are noteworthy. There is reason to believe that between January 1 and September 30 of this year 1918, not less than 2,000 chests of opium purchased in India were imported into Tsingtao via Kobe.

Upon this amount the Japanese authorities levy a tax which does not appear in the estimates equivalent to Tls. 4,000 per chest, a total for the 2,000 chests at the present rate of exchange of two million pounds sterling. The acquisition of this immense profit from a contraband traffic would explain the origin of those immense sums now being lavished upon the development of Tsingtao and the establishment there of Japanese commercial supremacy.

It may be asked how it is possible that at Tairen [Dairen], where the morphia traffic is greatest, and at Tsingtao, which is the chief centre of the Japanese opium trade, the importation of this contraband continues without the knowledge of the Chinese Maritime Customs. But at both Dalny and Tsingtao, the Chinese Maritime Customs are wholly under the control of the Japanese and manned by them. Japanese military domination would forbid in both ports any interference with a traffic in which the Japanese authorities were interested, either officially or unofficially. In Dalny the highest civic dignity has been conferred upon the chief dealer in morphia and opium. Moreover in the case of Tsingtao by the agreement which relinquished to Japanese the exclusive charge of the Chinese Maritime Customs, any trade in which the Government is interested, contraband or not, can be carried on without the official knowledge of the Customs. Article 13 of the Agreement of December 2, 1905, perpetuated in the Agreement of August 6, 1915, provides that any goods landed in Tsingtao under 'certificates of government' shall be free from customs examination.[1] The way has thus been opened, not

[1] Article 13 of the 'Ordinance Regulating Procedures in Customs Matters in Kiaochow Territory', signed by A. Mumm, German Minister to China, and Sir Robert Hart, Inspector-General of Customs, on 2 December 1905, stipulated that 'the personal luggage of the passengers, declared as not containing either dutiable or contraband goods, is passed free of Duty and, as a rule, without examination; but the right of examination is reserved to the Customs in cases where it may be considered specially necessary'. This, and other concessions granted by China to Germany regarding Shantung and Tsingtao,

only for the illegal import of opium, but of contraband arms, by which the bandits of Shantung province are provided with the means of harrying and looting and murdering the peaceful peasants of the most sacred province of China.

The Maritime Customs returns of 1917 show that 45 piculs of boiled opium were admitted into Tsingtao in 1917. The actual amount was probably 50 times greater. The balance enters in cases stamped *Chun yung p'in* ('military stores'), and boxes so stamped are to be seen commonly in the Japanese drug stores along the Shantung railway. In 1917 morphia to the amount of nearly two tons is recorded as having entered Tairen for use in the Leased Territory, but no morphia is recorded as having entered Manchuria from the leased territory during the year, nor does any entry of morphia appear in the Tsingtao Customs returns for 1917. Yet a competent witness Dr. Wu Lien-teh[1] states that 'Almost every Japanese drug dealer or peddler in Manchuria (and Shantung he might have added) sells morphia in one form or another, and does so with impunity, because no Japanese can be arrested without first informing the Consul.'

Your readers will remember that not long ago efforts were being made by the Japanese to remove from the control of any but Japanese subjects the Chinese Customs of Antung and of Newchwang. It would perhaps be unjust to say that the chief object sought for in the removal of these stations from foreign control other than Japanese is the removal of obstruction to Japanese contraband traffic, but none the less the effect of such removal would be this desirable end.

---

was transferred to Japan by an Agreement signed by Hioki Masu, Japanese Minister to China, and F. A. Aglen, Sir Robert Hart's successor, on 6 August 1915, regarding 'the reopening of the office of the Chinese Maritime Customs at Tsingtao, and its functioning in the territory leased to Germany and now in consequence of the German Japanese War under the military government of Japan'. Article 2 of this Agreement stipulated that 'The agreement about the establishment of a Maritime Customs Office at Tsingtau signed at Peking on the 17th April, 1899, by the German and Chinese representatives for their respective Governments and the Amendment to the same signed similarly at Peking by the German and Chinese representatives on the 1st December, 1905, with the replacement of the term "German" by "Japanese" wherever the principle of this Agreement demands such change, shall be held operative between the Governments of China and Germany in regard to the reopening of the Chinese Maritime Customs Office at Tsingtau and in regard to its regulations and procedure.'

[1] Wu Lien-te (1879–1960), Chinese medical practitioner. A graduate from Cambridge, he first made his name as a fighter against plague in Manchuria in 1911, and his autobiography entitled *The Plague Fighter* was published in Cambridge in 1959. Morrison came to know Wu well when he was Director of the Peiyang Army Medical College in Tientsin.

920. From C. D. Bruce[1]

The Hague 3 March 1919

My dear Morrison,

Lunching with Sir Charles[2] at the Hong Kong Bank not long ago he told me you were on your way home for the Paris meeting [...]. Addis said China had sent a large staff over to Paris, why he could not say, except that it was like them. Over 200 altogether which seems extraordinary considering they do not represent any of the great five, nor even of the lesser ten, nations who count.

[...]

I know all about the new Shanghai settlement scheme and heard it hotly discussed in London at a gathering of Old China hands! However Shanghai is always capable of looking after itself but what of poor old China?[3] Are they anywhere nearer a solution of all the crying evils and burning questions which have rent her so long? It does not seem like it from what I have heard and read of the last two or three years.

One thing I imagine is clear and that is with America armied and navied as she should have been all along, Japan must fall into line at last. Dare she go to extremes in threatening Peking any longer?

You have not had a bed of roses these last four years I imagine, and I shall be most interested to hear all about it when we meet. [...]

Ever yours very sincerely
C. D. Bruce

[1] Bruce had left his post of Police Adviser to the Chinese Government on the outbreak of the European War and was taken prisoner soon after. He became after the war ended Director of Repatriation in Holland, the post he was holding at the time of this letter.
[2] Sir Charles Stewart Addis.
[3] Probably a reference to the arbitrary action by the municipal authorities of the International Settlement of Shanghai in building roads out of the settlement into the Chinese territory known as the Western Suburbs of Shanghai, and then claiming land along both sides of the roads so constructed. While this encroachment on Chinese territory involved the demolishing of many dwellings, Chinese ratepayers within the Settlement had no voice in the municipal matters that affected them. The request for Chinese representation on the Council was in fact put informally to Bruce by Morrison when Bruce was still Police Commissioner in Shanghai, and through him to the municipal authorities, when the question of extension of the International Settlement was raised. Later, this request was put formally by the Chinese Government but it was strongly resisted by what Bruce here refers to as the Old China Hands who controlled the Council. A few months after this letter was written, Edward S. Little, a British member of the Council, formally proposed that representatives of the Chinese Ratepayers should be admitted to the Council, but his motion was defeated by a majority of three to one.

921. From Wang Cheng-t'ing[1]

Délégation Chinoise, Paris 4 March 1919

Dear Dr Morrison:

The Drafting Committee, of which you have been asked to be a member, will meet this afternoon (Tuesday) at 2 at Hotel Lutetia.[2] We trust you will find it possible to be present.

Herewith a copy of the matter under consideration.

Yours sincerely
Chengting T. Wang

Enclosure to Letter No. 921: *The Claims of China submitted by the Chinese Delegation: Preamble*[3]

Not [*Must not begin with the word not*][4] the least weighty of the major implications involved in the collapse of the German system of power is the general repudiation of Imperialism as a rule of action in the transactions of nations.

This repudiation finds its typical expression in the statement of principles known as the Fourteen Points, which define the American and Allied conception and application *of the new justice* – 'of justice to all peoples and their right to live on equal terms of liberty and safety with one another, whether they be strong or weak'.

On the assumption that the Peace Conference is to apply this rule of justice in order to work out a settlement of the affairs of nations which will prevent or minimize the chances of war in the future, it is submitted that China has a strong claim to a consideration and adjustment of the group of issues known

[1] Wang Cheng-t'ing, who at the time of the Armistice was in America, where he had been sent by the Canton Government to secure its recognition by the United States Government, was appointed one of the five Delegates to the Paris Conference as a result of the compromise between the North and the South. The Canton Government had selected Wu Ch'ao-shu, but Lu Cheng-hsiang, the head of the Delegation, refused to make a change, on the grounds that the list had already been submitted. The three members of the Delegation representing the south were Wang Cheng-t'ing, Wu Ch'ao-shu and Ch'en Yu-jen.
[2] The headquarters of the Chinese Delegation to the Peace Conference.
[3] This was the original draft presented by Ch'en Yu-jen from which China's subsequent submission of her case to the Conference was made. Commenting on Ch'en's draft Morrison said: 'The enclosed lucubration is by Eugene Chen. It is so shockingly bad that one feels resentment against an educated man who could endeavour to induce the Chinese Delegation to use a document designed so surely to do injury to their cause. Every case of good sense, of taste, of truth, of sincerity, is violated in this preamble.'
[4] The following conventions have been used in printing this and the subsequent document (the enclosure to Letter No. 922):
 (i) italicized words within square brackets are Morrison's comments or suggestions;
 (ii) italicized words without square brackets are his deletions;
 (iii) words in normal type in square brackets are his insertions;
 (iv) capitals represent emphasis in the original;
 (v) foreign words in the text of these documents are not italicized.

as the Chinese question, in terms consistent with the new standards of right guiding the Conference and just to a people claiming only the right to live untrammelled and unthreatened by the *alien* [predatory] imperialism hitherto hindering her legitimate development.

And this claim is *not a little* re-inforced in its appeal by the assurance communicated in the *British* [allied] reply to the circular note of the Chinese Government, announcing the existence of a state of war between China and the Central Powers. The same reads in part: '...His Britannic Majesty's Government have pleasure in assuring them (the Chinese Government) of their solidarity, of their friendship, and of their support. His Majesty's Government will do all that rests with them to ensure that CHINA SHALL ENJOY IN HER INTERNATIONAL RELATIONS THE POSITION AND THE REGARD DUE TO A GREAT COUNTRY;' [*France and Italy replied in the same sense if not in the same words.*]

The Chinese Question

Stripped of its minor features, the Chinese Question may be said to centre on the preservation of the independence and integrity of China, which has been guaranteed in a series of conventions and agreements concluded by Great Britain, France, Russia and the United States with Japan.

The necessity of these international guarantees springs from the inability of China to prevent assaults on her sovereignty owing largely to the weakness marking the transition of a state in the process of re-adjusting its life to the demands of a new environment. [*but practically all these 'assaults' were committed prior to 1911 when the revolution broke out.*] *But it is well to remember that in the course of a continuous national life of nearly 5000 years, China developed a polity that secured her administrative efficiency and political stability before she was brought definitely within the orbit of the West by the transaction of Nanking in 1842.* [*I suggest elision. China cannot look with pride upon the past.*]

[Domestic question between Manchus and Chinese]

Since that date [At present] a process of adjustment and adaptation *has been* [is] at work in China, seeking to harmonize the features of her old life with the needs and exigencies of the new conditions of existence set up around her by foreign pressure and intercourse. This process was necessarily slow and imperfect up to the abdication of the Manchus in 1912, because these foreign rulers of China viewed the modernization of the Chinese nation in a sense inimical to the permanence of their dynasty. [*What do these words mean?*]

Under the Manchus, therefore, a policy of alien hostility prevailed which yielded the rights of intercourse to the foreigner grudgingly and mostly under diplomatic and political pressure exercised by the Powers in treaty relation with the Manchu–Chinese government. [*Nearly every one of China's foreign Treaties was signed not by a Manchu but by the leaders of the nation Chinese like Li Hung-chang.*] As a result of the operation of this international system in China, based on Manchu hostility and on alien pressure, the Chinese nation found itself, at the abdication of the Manchus, enmeshed in a network of foreign 'rights, interests and privileges' so inconsistent with the independence and integrity of a full-sovereign state that, perhaps, the right phrase to use in describing these burdens is to say that they constituted and still constitute a system of alien servitudes in China. [*This foolish paragraph must be redrawn.*]

Since the establishment of the Chinese Republic however, a foreign policy has been pursued by China which is the opposite of the one under the Manchu. The country is ruled by Chinese; and, in spite of internal *perturbations* [*perturbations a euphemism for anarchy*] over the type of political fundamentals which perturb even the settled democracies of the Occident, the governing class in China to-day realize the necessity of foreign co-operation in order to effect administrative modernization and the introduction of the apparatus and processes of modern life conditioning China's claim to political and economic equality with the great democracies of America and Europe.

This complete change of attitude vis-à-vis the foreigner was strikingly shewn during the great revolution of 1911–12 which won us freedom from the Manchu yoke. [*Complete liability of Chinese Recognition of all that China did, even established usages*] Hardly a foreigner lost his life in spite of months of fierce fighting; and the same can be said of the other revolutionary transactions in 1913 and 1916 when the Chinese democracy again fought in order that the republic might live. Today, it is the entire truth to say that the foreigner is neither the unwelcomed guest nor the enemy that he was during the Manchu days of isolation and hostility. He is being increasingly regarded as the bringer of the things [?] that will assist China to revive, may-be, the glories of a past famous at times for its achievements, in the regions of the mind and action.

With one *momentous* exception, it may be said that the states in treaty relation with the Chinese Republic have responded largely in a sympathetic spirit to this new Chinese policy and attitude towards foreigners. And it is mainly in this sense and as typical of the sentiment of the other Powers that the Chinese people understand the inspiring assurance expressed in the British reply already quoted. [*You cannot play off one power against another. It won't work.*]

Basing the claims of China on the politics and ethics of the new order under creation in the League of Nations and presenting these claims to the

Powers who have already evinced their sympathetic interest in the Chinese Republic, the Chinese Delegation are without misgiving regarding the impartiality and justice that shall mark the decision of the Conference on these claims. [*Is it a decision?*]

And the heart of China is also untroubled because she rests in the high hope that the day is come when a new vision and a creative statesmanship will right the alien wrongs fettering her free development along those great lines of progress always traversed by nations in quest of the sources of a new life. [*Balls!*]

The Claims of China

The claims of China [*It's not a claim, it's something she has.*] under presentation by the Chinese Delegation deal with (a) articles and provisions to be inserted in the Preliminary Treaty of Peace with the Enemy relating to and as between the latter and China; (b) the cancellation or fundamental revision of the Treaties, Declarations and Notes signed, made and exchanged by and between China and Japan as a result of the Twenty-one Demands and the Japanese ultimatum of May 7, 1915; [*b must be decided now.*] and (c) the readjustment of the *alien servitudes* or body of foreign rights, interests and privileges affecting or impairing the sovereignty of the Chinese Republic in respect of (1) its territorial integrity (2) its political independence and (3) its fiscal autonomy.

These claims are submitted in separate Memoranda for the consideration of the Conference.

922. From Wang Cheng-t'ing

[Paris 19 March 1919] Wednesday Morning

Dear Dr Morrison,

I am sending you a copy of the Memorandum on the 'Twenty one Demands'.[1] We will take it up this afternoon. Can we meet at 2.30, i.e. half an hour earlier.

Yours sincerely
Chengting T. Wang

Enclosure to Letter No. 922: *Memorandum submitting for abrogation or other revisionary action by the Peace Conference the treaties, declarations and notes made and exchanged by and between China and Japan on May 25, 1915, as a single entity or transaction arising out of and connected with the war between the Allied and Associated States and the Central Powers. Filed March, 1919*

[1] This was the memorandum, written by Ch'en Yu-jen, from which the subsequent Chinese submission was made. Morrison commented on his copy of the document: 'This is the original document submitted to us for revision. It had passed the Chinese and been

I Introductory

In the course of a great cycle of national life, the Chinese People worked out a civilization and culture which expressed itself in many a fruitful theory and deed and in many a rare thing of art and of letters. And their existence to-day as a sovereign people, who have fought autocracy in order that the Republic shall live in China, witnesses to the power and vitality inherent in Chinese life and thought.

It is the continued existence of this people as a Republican nation that is ultimately involved in the issue submitted in the present claim.

The Treaties of 1915

2. This claim submits for abrogation or other revisionary action by the Peace Conference the set of treaties, declarations and notes made and exchanged by and between the Chinese Government and the Japanese Government on May 25, 1915 (*vide Appendix XVI to the Memorandum relating to Kiaochow, filed by the Chinese Delegation, for an English translation of these treaties and documents*).

These treaties and other documents – hereinafter referred to as the 'Treaties of 1915' – were signed by the Chinese Government under pressure of the series of demands known as the TWENTY-ONE DEMANDS presented by the Japanese Government on January 18, 1915, and *reinforced* [enforced] by the Japanese ultimatum delivered to the Chinese Government on May 7, 1915. [?]

3. *Appellate action by the Peace Conference in respect of these Treaties of 1915 is claimed by China for reasons which are* [subsequently] *elaborated, in Part V of this Memorandum and succinctly tabulated in Part VI, section 1.* [?]

Briefly summarised here, these reasons are that the Treaties of 1915 constitute and embody a single transaction, dealing with matters arising out of and connected with the war between the Allied and Associated States and the Central Powers and, consequently incapable of being settled except by the Peace Conference.

Besides this vice of procedure infecting them the Treaties seriously impair the territorial integrity as well as the political and economic independence of the Chinese Republic and, also manifestly contravene the new standards of right under application by the Peace Conference in its work of re-settlement. [?]

Further the Treaties were concluded in circumstances of harassment and compulsion exercised by the Japanese Government which entirely prevented the Chinese Government from being a free and consenting party thereto.

---

approved by E. T. Williams head of the China Section of the American Delegation'. In his Diary entry of 19 March 1919 Morrison wrote: 'Sat up very late tearing to pieces the appallingly bad document prepared by Eugene Chen (of all unsuitable men)...blind to realities he wishes to appear himself before the Conference and submit and defend the paper...The document – it deals with the 21 Demands – as now erased and lined and corrected is quite a curiosity.' For the printing conventions used *see* p. 728 note 4.

And added to these reasons deriving their force from justice and equity, there is a final argument in support of the present claim which is to be found in the revisionary authority exercised by the Congress of Berlin in respect of the treaty of San Stefano and in the action of the three continental Powers who insisted on the revision of the Treaty of Shimonoseki.

A Note of Explanation

4. Dealing as the present claim does with a settlement vitally affecting the independence and integrity of China, it is inevitable that its adequate presentation must involve a consideration of the policy hitherto pursued by the Japanese Government vis-a-vis China in terms of a criticism inspired by a sense of realities but withal dispassionate and without animus.

And it is well to emphasise the fact that the interpretation of Japanese policy submitted in this Memorandum does not necessarily carry with it the implication that Japan will, in the future, adhere to the aims hitherto pursued by her in China.

It is believed that the influences at work in the creation of the League of Nations are certain to react on these aims and lead the Japanese Government to a revision of the same more consistent with the right of China to live and develop as a full-sovereign state.

The hope, therefore, is expressed that the Japanese Government of to-day – which has been repeatedly represented as a ministry of democracy – will meet the present claim of China in the sense of a settlement which, liberating her from the meshes of a policy already expressed in the annexation of Korea, shall lay the foundation of relations not a little calculated to yield Japan the economic assistance necessary for her legitimate development as a Great Power dedicated to the interests of peace.

II 'First Instructions' to Mr Hioki

1. On December 3, 1914, the Japanese Minister at Peking, Mr. Hioki, was handed at Tokyo the text of the *demarche* [document] known as the TWENTY-ONE DEMANDS for presentation to China. An English translation of these demands, *based on* [from] the *original* Chinese text, will be found in Appendix XII *to the Memorandum relating to Kiaochow, under submission to the Peace Conference.*

2. In the 'First Instructions' given by Baron Kato [then Japanese Minister for Foreign Affairs][1] to Mr. Hioki – *officially gazetted* [published in the official Gazette] at Tokyo on June 9, 1915, (vide Appendix)[2] – the latter was informed that 'in order to provide for the readjustment of affairs consequent on the

[1] The brackets only, not the wording within them, were added by Morrison.
[2] No appendices are printed.

Japan–German war and for the purpose of ensuring a lasting peace in the Far East BY STRENGTHENING THE POSITION OF THE EMPIRE, the Imperial Government have resolved to approach the Chinese Government with a view to conclude treaties and agreements mainly along the lines laid down in the first four Groups of the appended proposals (i.e. the Twenty-one Demands) ...Believing it absolutely essential, FOR STRENGTHENING JAPAN'S POSITION IN EASTERN ASIA as well as for the preservation of the general interests of that region, to secure China's adherence to the foregoing proposals, the IMPERIAL GOVERNMENT ARE DETERMINED TO ATTAIN THIS END BY ALL MEANS WITHIN THEIR POWER. You are therefore, requested to use your best endeavour in the conduct of the negotiations, which are hereby placed in your hands.'

As regards the proposals contained in the fifth Group, Mr. Hioki was informed that they were 'presented as the wishes of the Imperial Government' but 'you are also requested to exercise your best efforts to have our wishes carried out'.

It is necessary, however, to state that the proposals in this fifth group were presented to the Chinese Government as demands and not as 'wishes'.

Meaning of the [The] 'First Instructions'

3. Attention is directed here to these instructions because [a study of them reasonably leads to the interference that] *they define* Japan's dominant aim in entering the war against the Central Powers. *That aim* was to strengthen 'Japan's position in Eastern Asia' and the Japanese Government were 'determined to attain this end by all means within their power'. *The attainment of this end might or might not have involved, also, the decisive defeat of Germany, although the first of the Twenty-one Demands assumed that the end of the war would find Germany in a position to negotiate separately with Japan regarding the 'disposition' of the German system of 'rights, interests and concessions' in the province of Shantung, including the leased territory of Kiaochow.* [Elide]

And the same assumption is emphasised in the last sentence but one of the 'First Instructions' to Mr. Hioki, in which the possible restoration of Kiaochow is indicated 'in the event of Japan's being given free hand in the disposition thereof as the result of the coming Peace Conference between Japan and Germany'. [Elide]

A Necessary Reference

4. This reference to Japan's *dominant* war-aim is a necessity if all the facts are to be placed before the Peace Conference in order that a right and just decision should be rendered on the pending claim of the Japanese Government for 'the unconditional cession of the leased territory of Kiaochow

together with the railways and other rights possessed by Germany in respect of Shantung province'.

If the *primary* object for which Japan entered the war was less the destruction of German Imperialism than the creation of a situation enabling her to strengthen her own 'position in Eastern Asia... by all means within *the* [her] power *of the Japanese Government*', it is *a right of argument* [legitimate] for China to urge the rejection of the Japanese claim on the ground that Japan entered the war and envisaged its end in a sense *greatly* at variance with the principles for which the *Western Allies and America have* [war has been] fought and *conquered* [won].

III Presentation of the Twenty-One Demands

1. Six weeks had elapsed [from the time when the Japanese Minister was given his instructions] when it was decided that a suitable opportunity had occurred for the presentation of the Twenty-one Demands. [*To recast.*] This took place on January 18, 1915, following swiftly on the communication of a note from the Chinese Minister for Foreign affairs in reply to a despatch from the Japanese Minister at Peking, refusing to recognise the Chinese declaration cancelling the special military zone voluntarily created by the Chinese Government in the nature of a war-measure to facilitate the operations of the British and Japanese forces besieging the German garrison at Tsingtao, the port of Kiaochow. [*Incorrect Tsingtau fell on 7/11/14*]

This note from the Chinese Minister for Foreign Affairs is the last of a series of six notes passing between him and the Japanese Minister at Peking. These notes dealt with the protest of the Chinese Government against the forcible and unnecessary seizure by the Japanese of the trans-Shantung railway, which pierces the heart of the province and dominates it, as well as with the special military zone created and delimited by the Chinese Government. [*anti-climax*]

The whole of this series of notes is important because the same, in a sense, directly connects the Twenty-one Demands with the situation developed in Shantung by and through the excessive elaboration of the Japanese plan for the reduction of a weakly [*held by a small German garrison reinforced by German reservists summoned from the ports of China*] fortified 'place in the sun,' *garrisoned by a couple of thousand of German Clerks and traders. These notes are included in the Appendices to the Memorandum on Kiaochow and are numbered VI, VII, VIII, IX, X, and XI. Leave is craved to incorporate them here by reference, subject however to a brief summary of the sixth note above referred to.*

This [The] sixth note pointed out that the two months had 'elapsed since the capture of Tsingtao; the basis of German military preparations *have* [has] been destroyed, the troops of Great Britain have ALREADY [*lower type*] been, and those of your country [are being] *been* gradually withdrawn. This shows clearly that there is no more military action in the special area, and that the said area ought to be cancelled admits of no doubt...As efforts have always been made to effect an amicable settlement of affairs between your country and ours, it is our earnest hope that your Government will act upon the principle of preserving peace in the Far East and maintaining international confidence and friendship...'

2. Within 36 hours of the expression of this earnest hope of the Chinese Government, Mr. Hioki presented – not to the Chinese Minister for Foreign Affairs who is, according to diplomatic practice, the proper official to deal with in such a case – but to the President of the Chinese Republic a series of demands which *the Chinese nation compared, in their frank invasion of the sovereignty of the State and their practical subjection of China to Japan as suzerain*, [may reasonably be compared] to the Austrian ultimatum to Serbia which precipitated the Great War.

IV Analysis of the Twenty-One Demands

1. *The briefest* [An] examination of these Twenty-One Demands *on China* shows that their ruling purpose was to impose on China a settlement not unlike in principle to the one imposed on Korea during the short period preceding the extinction of Korean independence. [?]

Group I

2. *Analysing these Demands it will be seen that* Group 1 deals with the province of Shantung which, *incidentally it may be noted*, is greater in population and in area than the whole of England, besides being *a living piece of China* [the sacred province of China] packed with memories of Confucius and hallowed as the cradle of Chinese culture.

3. The first demand insists on Chinese recognition of the right of Japan to succeed to the system of 'rights, interests and concessions' established by Germany in 1898 as 'compensation' for the death of two German missionaries who were killed in the province. This German system embraced the leased territory of Kiaochow, the trans-Shantung railway known as the Tsingtao–Chinan Railway and other railway and mining rights in the province. [*Quoted*]

The transfer of this German system to Japan would mean that the latter could continue to use Kiaochow or the strategic section of it as a point d'appui for the political and economic penetration of the province as Germany had done. It would also mean the Japanese possession of the trans-Shantung railway which dominates the entire province; and in the event of war *such an alien* [its] possession would enable an enemy not only to over-run Shantung but the great province of Chih-li in which the national Capital, Peking, is situated.

Railway Domination of North China

4. *And if* [If] this right of succession to the German system also *vested* [vests] in Japan the 'other railway rights' included in it, the following formidable situation would be created.

Through the trans-Shantung railway, with its western or inland terminus at the provincial capital of Chinanfu where it flanks the northern section of the Tientsin–Pukow Railway – built by the Germans – Japan would at once dominate the whole of Shantung as well as this northern half of the great trunk line connecting Tientsin, which is the port of Peking, with the maritime reaches of the Yangtze river in Central China. Then, by exercising one of the 'other railway rights' – i.e., the projected line from Kaomi, [*Kaomi to Hsuchow*] a point on the trans-Shantung railway, to a point strategically dominating the southern or British constructed section of the same Tientsin–Pukow Railway – Japan would practically master the great railroad which forms one of the two highways linking Peking and North China with the Yangtze valley and Southern China.

Next, by exercising another of the 'other railway rights' – another projected line practically extending the trans-Shantung railway from Chinanfu where it would bisect the Tientsin–Pukow line to a point westward on the Peking–Hankow Railway – Japan would flank the other of the two trunk lines connecting Peking and North China with Central and Southern China. Although this railway situation is stated subjunctively, [*hypothetically*] it ought to be noted that Japan has actually 'exercised' these 'other railway rights' whose serious meaning is discussed in the text. By a preliminary agreement made on September 24, 1918, Japan has secured – or rather (since the Conference is now considering the question of Japan's claim to succession to the German 'system' in Shantung) has attempted to secure – the German 'rights' to finance the construction of the two lines connecting the trans-Shantung railway with the Tientsin–Pukow or, more accurately, the Tientsin–Pukow–Nanking–Shanghai railway at the important strategic point known as Hsuchow in the adjoining province of Kiangsu as well as with the other trunk-line of the Peking–Hankow railway. The text of the agreement is given in Appendix 20 to the Memorandum on Kiaochow, and as stated in the said Memorandum at B., 9, the agreement was concluded under pressure of the alarming situation created by the Japanese Government who had stationed armed troops along the entire length of the trans-Shantung railway, against the repeated protests of the Chinese Government, and had also established – without a shadow of right and against also the strenuous protests of the Chinese Government – a system of civil administration [?] under Japanese officials responsible to Tokyo at Tsingtao with 'branches at the provincial capital, Chinan, and in two other cities in the province'. [*What earthly value is this?*] [*Must be replied to*]

And when it is borne in mind that Japan also controls the railway systems in South Manchuria and Eastern Inner Mongolia – through which lies the 'historic road of invasions' into China – the *completeness* [extent] of Japan's railway domination of the *whole of* [north of] China *north of the great line of the Yangtze* will be realised.

There is [This] also *a significant corollary of this railway domination that must be noted. It is* [means] the isolation of Peking which would be cut off from Central and Southern China not only by land but by the sea-route, owing to the Gulf of Pechihli – through which Peking can be reached via its port of Tientsin – being strategically dominated by the Japanese at Port Arthur.

The 'Strategic Rear' of Weihaiwei

5. And it is further interesting to note the connexion between the third demand in Group I with this strategic situation based on Japan's contemplated railway domination in Northern China. The demand requires 'the Chinese Government to agree to Japan's building a railway connecting Chefoo or Lungkow' with the trans-Shantung railway.

Look at a map of Shantung and you will at once see that, lying obliquely opposite to Port Arthur, is the leased territory of Weihaiwei which Great Britain occupied in order to redress the 'balance of Power' in China when Russia seized Port Arthur. It is apparent that the strategic value of Weihaiwei could be seriously impaired if the power in possession of Port Arthur were to control either Chefoo or Lungkow, both of which lie to the 'strategic rear' of the British leasehold. [*? Therefore England ought on no account to be permitted to withdraw from Wei Hai Wei.*]

Group II

Annexation at Work

6. The seven demands in Group II, relating to South Manchuria and Eastern Inner Mongolia, may [thus] be summarised in a single sentence. They exact in favour of Japan and her nationals a series of preferential rights, interests and privileges in those rich regions of *extramural* China *peculiarly* calculated to increase *and intensify the conditions already* [the difficulties which now] render*ing* effective Chinese administration in those two areas impracticable, if not impossible, and withal developing a situation that facilitates the extension thereto of the specific territorial system which has transformed Korea into a Japanese province. [*At the same time a situation is developed facilitating the extension of that territorial system which has. . .*]

Group III

Japan's Iron Policy in China

7. Besides involving the violation of the territorial integrity and sovereignty of China in Shantung, South Manchuria and Eastern Inner Mongolia, the Twenty-one Demands *also* encroach on Chinese economic independence by their exaction in Group III of an undertaking with respect to the Han-Yeh-Ping Company which *seriously fetters the free development of the greatest iron works in the Yangtze Valley.* [*Here quote*] Indeed, the undertaking is worded in terms well calculated to lead to ultimate Japanese acquisition of the most important industrial enterprise in the country, *practically controlling as the same does the largest iron and coal areas in China. And there is the further objection that the undertaking conflicts with the policy of the Open Door.* [*Yangtse Valley*]

Two Japanese Statements

8. *The economic policy expressed in this Han-Yeh-Ping undertaking is not at all obscure in view of two recent Japanese statements.* In a pamphlet lately issued and circulated in Paris by Baron Makino, then acting senior member of the Japanese Peace Delegation, the declaration is made that 'China has the raw material; we have need for raw material and we have the capital to invest with China in its development for use by ourselves as well as by China.' This same point *is* [was] expressed *in a more urgent sense* in an address delivered by Viscount Uchida, Japanese Minister for Foreign Affairs, at the opening of the Diet at Tokyo last January. 'We have to rely', the Minister declared, 'in a large measure, upon rich natural resources in China in order to ASSURE OUR OWN ECONOMIC EXISTENCE'.

China does not admit that her natural resources are necessary to assure the economic existence of Japan any more than the 'natural resources' of Alsace–Lorraine were necessary to assure the economic existence of *a* Germany *that had not profited greatly from the business of war. But these natural resources of France, of course, were necessary to a Germany that was 'determined' to capture power which her own natural resources denied her.*

Group IV

9. The single demand included in Group IV required the Chinese Government to 'engage not to cede or lease to any OTHER Powers any harbour or bay on any island along the coast of China'. [*It may have been possible that this was done to prevent Germany from obtaining a harbour.*]

In insisting on this demand, Japan represented her object to be the more effective preservation of 'the territorial integrity of China'. It will be seen, however, that the demand is worded in a sense that seems to exclude Japan from the category of Powers in whose favour the Chinese Government engage not to violate the territorial integrity of China. Apart from this point, the demand inspired not a little resentment on account of the implication of political tutelage that Japan appeared to have assumed in making it. [*Anticlimax.*]

Group V

10. Finally, we come to the set of seven demands known as Group V, *which it appears, was rightly considered by Japan to reveal a policy of such serious meaning that its suppression was deemed expedient when the Japanese Government replied to an enquiry of the Great Powers regarding the nature and terms of the demarche.*

11. [By these demands] 'Influential Japanese' were to be engaged by the Chinese Government as 'political, financial and military advisers'. 'The police in localities (in China) where such arrangements were necessary' was to be placed under joint Japanese and Chinese administration, or Japanese to be employed in police offices in such localities. 'China' was 'to obtain from Japan the supply of a *certain* [*To quote correctly*] quantity of arms, or to establish an arsenal in China under joint Japanese and Chinese management and to be supplied with experts and materials from Japan'.

In other words the Chinese army [with its limitless possibilities in manpower] practically was to be organised and controlled by influential Japanese *generals acting as* 'military advisers' and was to be equipped and supplied with arms and munitions of Japanese pattern and manufacture.

In this connexion it is useful to point out that the population of China is so vast that EVERY FOURTH MAN IN THE WORLD IS A CHINESE *and her natural resources are of such variety and richness that not even an Allied blockade of fiercer intensity than that which starved Germany to submission could affect her war-capacity in the event of her man-power and resources being centred in the directing hands of an efficient military power.* [*Must elide this.*]

Further, the Japanese schoolmaster and the Japanese priest were to be granted rights and privileges enabling them – if and when they chose–to turn into political propagandists, teaching and preaching ideas subserving a policy that might be inconsistent with the independence and integrity of China. [?]

12. Railway rights were also demanded which *violated* [conflicted] the terms of certain railway agreements [previously concluded] with the British in the Yangtse valley. [?]

Meaning of 'Reserved for Future Discussion'

13. It is true that, with the exception of a demand relating to the important province of Fukien, this Group v was 'reserved for future discussion'

and its acceptance was not demanded in the ultimatum by which Japan on May 7, 1915, *closured* [stopped] further discussion of the Twenty-one Demands *on the part of China* and insisted on the acceptance of the demands in Groups I, II, III and IV, subject to verbal variations of a more or less unimportant nature. [?]

Although this postponement *of the evil day* regarding Group V was *explained* [alleged] by the Japanese Government *in the sense of* [to be] 'a mark of their good will towards the Chineae Government', it is known that this course *was deemed expedient in view of* [followed] representations made to Japan by *the* other Powers *guaranteeing the independence and integrity of China. Be this as it may, it is to be noted that the* [The] Japanese Government [nevertheless] insisted *on* [that] the Chinese Government – *who had intimated their intention of accepting the ultimatum in general terms* – [should] specifically *stating* [state] in their reply that Group V had been 'reserved for future discussion'.

This statement of the case would *lack completeness* [be incomplete] unless it were *further* noted that since the date of the *said* ultimatum, and more so within the past fifteen months, the manifestation of Japanese policy in China seems to be in accordance with the specific principles worked out in the demands in Group V which have been 'reserved for future discussion'.

M. Krupensky's Testimony

14. What Japan means by reserving Group V 'for future discussion' is made *abundantly* plain by M. Krupensky, Russian Ambassador at Tokyo, in two despatches written by him to his home Government. These despatches were included among the documents found in the archives of the Russian Foreign Office and published by the Russian Revolutionary Government on November 22, 1917. *The English text quoted here is reproduced from a volume of 'The Secret Treaties' by F. Seymour Cooks; London.*

15. M. Krupensky's first despatch is dated October 16, 1917, and reads as follows:—

> 'In reply to my question as to the credibility of the rumours alleging that Japan is prepared to sell to the Chinese Government a considerable quantity of arms and munitions, Viscount Motono confirmed them, and added that the Peking Government had promised not to use the arms against the Southerners. It was evident from the Minister's words, however, that this promise possessed only the value of a formal justification of this sale, infringing as the latter does the principle of non-intervention in the internal Chinese feuds, proclaimed by Japan herself, and that the Japanese Government was in this instance deliberately assisting the Tuan Chi-jui Cabinet in the hope of receiving from it in return substantial

advantages. It is most likely that the Japanese are aiming principally at obtaining the privilege of arming the entire Chinese army, and at making China dependent in the future on Japanese arsenals and the supply of munitions from Japan. The arms to be supplied are estimated at 30,000,000 yen. At the same time, Japan intends establishing an arsenal in China for the manufacture of war materials.' [*First part ends.*]

M. Krupensky's Second Despatch

16. The other despatch written by M. Krupensky is dated October 22, 1917. It is a document of exceptional value. [written as it is.] No leader of statesmen in America or Europe can read it without being convinced of the reality of the continental policy that has hitherto aimed at the inclusion of China within the system already holding Korea in its grip. Here we have the testimony of one of the ablest members of the Russian Diplomatic Service, with a great knowledge of both Chinese and Japanese affairs, having been Russian Minister at Peking for many years before he was appointed to the Tokyo Embassy. *And he is reporting secretly to his Government, without a thought that his grave envisagement of Japanese policy vis-à-vis China will be read by other eyes than those of his Chief at Petrograd.*

After remarking that the American recognition of Japan's special position [as was then contemplated] in China will 'inevitably lead in the future to serious misunderstandings between us (Russia) and Japan', the document continues:—

'The Japanese are manifesting more and more clearly a tendency to interpret the special position of Japan in China, inter alia, in the sense that other Powers must not undertake in China any political steps without previously exchanging views with Japan on the subject – A CONDITION THAT WOULD TO SOME EXTENT ESTABLISH A JAPANESE CONTROL OVER THE FOREIGN AFFAIRS OF CHINA. [It will be remembered that one of the decisive acts preceding the annexation of Korea was the conclusion of the Korea–Japan Treaty of *1904* [Nov 17 1905] vesting in the Japanese Government the direction and control of the foreign affairs of Korea].[1] On the other hand, the Japanese Government DOES NOT ATTACH GREAT IMPORTANCE TO ITS RECOGNITION OF THE PRINCIPLE OF THE OPEN DOOR AND THE INTEGRITY OF CHINA, regarding it as merely a repetition of the assurances repeatedly given by it earlier to the other Powers and implying no new restrictions for the Japanese policy in China. It is therefore quite possible that at some future time there may arise in this connection misunderstanding between the United States and Japan. The Minister for Foreign Affairs confirmed to-day in conversation with me that in the negotiations by Viscount Ishii the

---

[1] The brackets only, not the wording within them, were added by Morrison.

question at issue is not some special concession to Japan in these or other parts of China, but JAPAN'S SPECIAL POSITION IN CHINA AS A WHOLE.'

Japan and the United States

17. It is necessary to add here a quotation from another despatch written by M. Krupensky to the Russian Government if the full significance of his foregoing despatch is to be understood. The despatch is dated November 1, 1917, and indicates what the Japanese Government thought regarding the possibility of misunderstandings between the United States and Japan touching the proper interpretation of the Lansing–Ishii Agreement. [*Rewritten*] The document reads in part:

> 'To my question whether he did not fear that in the future misunderstandings might arise from the different interpretations by Japan and the United States of the meaning of the terms "special position" and "special interests" of Japan in China, Viscount Motono replied by saying that... (gap in original) NEVERTHELESS, I GAIN THE IMPRESSION FROM THE WORDS OF THE MINISTER THAT HE IS CONSCIOUS OF THE POSSIBILITY OF MISUNDERSTANDINGS IN THE FUTURE, BUT IS OF THE OPINION THAT IN SUCH A CASE JAPAN WOULD HAVE BETTER MEANS AT HER DISPOSAL FOR CARRYING INTO EFFECT HER INTERPRETATION THAN THE UNITED STATES.'

'A Foreign Power' in Fukien

18. *A precise grasp of the issues involved in the Twenty-one Demands calls for a* [A] short reference [must be made] to the demand relating to the province of Fukien *whose* acceptance [of which] is included in the Japanese ultimatum, although – according to the 'First Instructions' to Mr. Hioki – it was to be presented not as a demand but as a 'wish'.

The province happens to be the part of China lying nearest – but at some distance – from the island of Formosa which was ceded to Japan as a result of her successful war against China in 1894–5. This geographical propinquity is serving as a basis for certain Japanese claims respecting Fukien. One of these claims is that Japan has a sort of right of vetoing any attempt on the part of China to utilise and develop, with foreign capital, the natural facilities on any part of the Fukien coast as a 'shipyard, military coaling station, naval station, or any other military establishment'.

In the Japanese note relating to Fukien and included in the series of documents embodying the settlement demanded by the Japanese ultimatum, specific reference is made to a reported intention of the Chinese Government, permitting 'a foreign power' to build a shipyard, etc., in the province. It is well-known that the 'foreign power' referred to is the United States.

V Abrogation or Revision of the Treaties of 1915

1. It is submitted that the treaties, Declarations and Notes signed, made and exchanged by and between the Chinese and Japanese Governments on May 25, 1915, as a result of the negotiations connected with the Twenty-one Demands and of the Japanese ultimatum of May 7, 1915, are and constitute a transaction or settlement arising out of and connected with the war between the Allied and Associated States and the Central Powers.

2. *These Treaties of 1915 embody the settlement demanded in the Twenty-one Demands and exacted in the ultimatum delivered by the Japanese Government to the Chinese Government on May 7, 1915.*

An essential feature of this [transaction or] settlement *is expressed in the demands massed under Group I of the Twenty-one Demands, relating* [relates] to the province of Shantung and *insisting* [insists] on the right of Japan to succeed to the leased territory of Kiaochow and the other 'rights, interests and concessions' of Germany in the provinces.

On the face of it [That] this essential feature *of the single transaction embodied and worked out in the Treaties of 1915 deals with a matter that* can only be settled by the Peace Conference – *namely, the final disposition of Kiaochow and the other rights of Germany in Shantung.*

This is clearly admitted by the Japanese Government because they have submitted to the Five-Power Council a claim for 'the unconditional cession of the leased territory of Kiaochow together with the railways and other rights possessed by Germany in respect of Shantung province'.

It follows, therefore [that] the entire transaction or settlement of which this Shantung claim of Japan forms an essential feature is a *war*-matter [directly arising out of the War and] within the purview of the Peace Conference and necessarily subject to its revisionary action.

War Character of the Treaties of 1915 emphasized

3. The war-character of these Treaties of 1915 is further attested by the opening sentence of the 'First Instructions' to Mr. Hioki. The same reads: 'In order to provide for the readjustment of affairs consequent on the Japan–German war and for the purpose of ensuring a lasting peace in the Far East by strengthening the position of the Empire, the Imperial Government have resolved to approach the Chinese Government with a view to conclude treaties and agreements mainly along the lines laid down in the first four Groups of the appended proposals.'

The Japanese ultimatum of May 7, 1915, also begins with a sentence, emphasizing that the demarche is due to the desire of Japan 'to adjust matters to meet the new situation created by the war between Japan and Germany and of strengthening, in the interest of a firm and lasting peace in the Far East, the bond of amity and friendship between Japan and China...'

Treaties of 1915 signed under Duress

4. The fact that these Treaties of 1915 were signed by China does not remove them from the *ambit* [purview] of the revisionary authority of the Peace Conference. Nor can the same operate as an estoppel against China in her claim to be released from them. These Treaties were signed by the Chinese Government under the duress *and coercion* of the Japanese ultimatum of May 7, 1915, and in circumstances entirely excluding any suggestion that China was a free and consenting party to *a* [the] transaction *which in every one of its terms, transgressed the Allied formula of justice expressed in President Wilson's statement of the principles guiding the Peace Conference in its work of re-settling the affairs of nations.*

5. *And in its rough assault on the things for which the Allied and Associated States have fought and their manhood have died, the Japanese work at Peking in 1915 may be compared to the Austro-German work done at Bucharest on May 5–7, 1918 – not to speak of the transaction of Brest-Litovsk negotiated two days before.*

At Bucharest, the Central Powers imposed on Rumania, a State associated with the Allies, a settlement contravening Allied principles and dealing with a situation arising out of and connected with the war in a sense designed to remove the same from the ultimate consideration of the Peace Conference.

At Peking, Japan imposed on a state, since associated with the Allies, a settlement also contravening Allied principles and dealing in a similar sense with a war-situation that was and is properly a Conference interest.

The fact that the Central Powers are the enemy of the Allies, and Japan is one of the latter, leaves the analogy unfalsified, since the point of it lies in the attempt of the Central Powers and of Japan to deal in advance with matters that could only be settled by the Peace Conference.

And on this ground of similarity between Bucharest and Peking, it is submitted that the same revocatory action applied to the former ought to be exercised in respect of the latter.

Abrogation invokes no Injustice or Unfairness to Japan

6. The abrogation of the Treaties of 1915 necessarily carries with it the rejection of the pending Japanese claim for the unconditional cession of the German system in Shantung.

On this point the submission is made that no injustice *or unfairness* will be *worked on* [done to] Japan in denying her claim to *continue and* perpetuate *the* German *work* [aggression] [*!*] in Shantung, *unless indeed the settlement of the affairs of nations to be worked out by the Peace Conference is to be in terms of the 'old Imperialism'.*

Nor in this connection would Japan be justified in accusing China – who simply insists on regaining the lost things of her sovereignty – of a lack of appreciation of the services involved in the Anglo-Japanese reduction of Tsingtao and the subsequent Japanese occupation of the leased territory of Kiaochow unless, also, China or non-Europe is to be excluded from the new international order which is to heal the wounds of the nations. [The abrogator of treaties]

7. Whilst there is no intention to modify the expression of China's appreciation of these services, which occurs in the Memorandum relating to Kiaochow, *a full knowledge of the facts of the case inspires or rather suggests a repetition here of the view that Japan warred against Germany mainly because the Japanese Government were determined to secure for Japan the succession to the German system of political and economic servitudes in Shantung, in order to develop a situation enabling them to strengthen 'Japan's position in Eastern Asia...and to attain this end by all means within their power'.*

8. It is also submitted as not an unfair suggestion that but for *this strong desire* [the attitude] of Japan *to replace Germany in Shantung*, China would have been associated with the Allies in August 1914 or in November 1915 in the struggle against the Central Powers and, not improbably, the situation would not have arisen which forms the issue submitted in this Memorandum. (*vide, Appendix 2). [footnote]*[1]

Nor further is it [Further, it is] *now un*reasonable to point out that, if Japan had not occupied it, the leased territory of Kiaochow would have [been directly restored] *certainly formed the subject of a clause in the Armistice concluded with Germany, ordering its direct restitution* to China as one of the Associated States in the war, *assuming that China had not previously regained possession of it. Just as Germany has been disarmed in German East Africa and compelled to withdraw her forces beyond the Rhine, suffering her territory to be occupied by the armies of the Allies and America without the discharge of a further single shot, so, in the event supposed, it must be evident that any German garrison in Tsingtao would have been disarmed, to be followed by a Chinese occupation of Kiaochow.*

The Congress of Berlin

9. The submission is also made that, in addition to the foregoing reasons [there are precedents] justifying the abrogation of the Treaties of 1915, [by the Peace Conference] *there exist others warranting the Peace Conference in applying the Bucharest precedent to them.*

There are precedents affirming the right of political expediency, if not the juristic right of the Great Powers as a collective whole or as a Group of some, acting collectively, to revise and amend a treaty between two states. The Congress of Berlin is an instance of the Great Powers, acting as a whole and collectively, revising a treaty concluded between Russia and Turkey for a variety of *political and international* reasons but mainly because *a vital*

---

[1] These square brackets were added by Morrison.

British interest, in the shape of the independence and integrity of the Ottoman Empire, was gravely affected *by the settlement dictated by the Tsardom at San Stefano.*

The Treaty of Shimonoseki

10. *But a* [A] precedent of [still greater] *singular aptness and* relevancy is the revision of the Treaty of Shimonoseki which, Baron Makino's recent pamphlet reminds the public, was effected by the 'force majeure' of a 'protest from France, Germany and Russia'.

It will be remembered that the [The] Treaty of Shimonoseki ceded to Japan 'in perpetuity and full sovereignty' the Liao-tung Peninsula, *besides the island of Formosa and the Pescadores Islands, and also imposed on China a war-indemnity whose payment first started that disorganisation of Chinese finances which – next to the issues centring on the Treaties of 1915 – is to-day the most disturbing problem connected with the administrative modernisation of the Chinese Republic.* The Powers named viewed the *forcible* cession of the Peninsula to Japan as an act demanding their intervention and insisted on its retrocession to China. Japan obeyed but regained the Peninsula ten years later *in the second of the two successful wars which ranked her among the Great Powers of the world.* [as a result of the successful war with Russia.]

A Ruling of the *Five-Power Council* [Conference]

11. *Added to these reasons deriving their force from the new principles under application by America and the Allies to the transaction of Bucharest as well as from the 'old' principles applied by the Great Powers to the treaties of San Stefano and Shimonoseki, there* [There] are two other arguments against the validity of the Treaties of 1915. One is based on *the* [a] ruling of the *Five-Power Council* [Conference] and the other on the lack of finality affecting the treaties.

12. *It will be seen that by* [By] Article 1 of the 'Treaty respecting the Province of Shantung', the Chinese Government engage to recognise any Agreement concluded between Japan and Germany respecting the disposition of the latter's *servitudes or* 'rights, interests and concessions' in the province; and in the notes exchanged regarding Kiaochow, Japan subjects the restoration of the leased territory to *a* [the] eondition [that, *then quote*] *enabling her to establish a separate settlement in a locality to be designated by the Japanese Government.* (*vide Appendix* XVI *to the Memorandum on Kiaochow for the treaty and notes*).

As regards this article 1 of the Shantung treaty, it is important to *underline* [emphasize] the objection that Japan is debarred from negotiating separately with Germany in respect of the latter's servitudes in Shantung *owing to the principle of procedure adopted by the Five-Power Council in 'dealing'* – these are the words used in [In] the course of a hearing of the Japanese claim to the German *system* [Rights etc.] in the province at the Quai d'Orsay on January 28 last – 'with the territories and cessions previously German without consulting Germany at all'. [*President Wilson*] This ruling was made in the form of a direct comment on Baron Makino's statement that Japan had taken Kiaochow 'by conquest from Germany' and 'before disposing it to a third party it was necessary that Japan should obtain the right of free disposal from Germany'.

It is plain, therefore, that Japan *cannot – in the sense of the article under notice –* [is not in a position to] agree with Germany regarding the 'free disposal' of Kiaochow, *even assuming that Germany has (which is not at all the case) the right freely to dispose of it to Japan.*

In these circumstances the articles in question must be deemed *and treated as* an inoperative provision. *And it is legitimate to urge that, since it is an essential term of the entire transaction expressed in the treaties of 1915, the latter are necessarily affected by this specific objection to the validity of the article.*

An Illusory Restoration of Kiaochow

13. *The same objection applies to the notes exchanged, in addition to the illusory character of the restoration of Kiaochow contemplated in them.* The chief value of Kiaochow lies partly in the *port* [harbour] of Tsingtao and partly in an area [dominating the finest anchorage of that harbour] delimited by the Japanese Government and already reserved for exclusive Japanese occupation under Japanese jurisdiction. [no one other than Japanese being permitted to hold land within its boundaries.] *This delimited area is so situated and is under present development in such a manner that the importance of Tsingtao as the eastern terminus of the trans-Shantung railway – which connects the provincial capital of Chinanfu with the sea – can be transferred to it without much difficulty.*

If the question of Kiaochow be setted in terms of the notes exchanged, there can be little doubt that Japan will select, certainly, the delimited area and, probably, Tsingtao as the [This delimited area is the] 'locality to be designated by the Japanese Government' for a separate settlement under the exclusive control and jurisdiction of Japan. [The restoration of Kiaochow with the retention of the area dominating it is the 'restoration of the shadow with the retention of the substance'.] *And even if the selection were limited to the delimited area, the transaction would be accurately described as one in which Japan would be retaining the substance while foregoing the shadow of Kiaochow in favour of China.*

In this connection it is important to direct attention to the reply of the Japan-

ese Premier Hara to an interpellation in the Diet on *January 21 last, when he declared that there was 'no reason why China should demand the return of Tsingtao'.*

Lack of Finality

14. *Referring to the impermanent character of the Treaties of 1915, there is evidence showing that – since the date of the transaction – even* [Since the date of the Treaties of 1915] Japan has acted on the assumption [that they lacked finality.] *of an absence of finality in the business done at Peking on May 25, 1915.*

This appears in the Japanese diplomacy which secured (a) the two treaties concluded between Japan and Russia in the summer of 1916, (b) the assent of Russia and others to support Japan's claim to succeed to the German system in Shantung as the price of Japanese consent to China's intervention in the war on the side of the Allies and the United States, as indicated in a despatch written by M. Krupensky to the Russian Government under date of February 8, 1917, and (c) the Lansing–Ishii Agreement of November 2, 1917.

15. It is evident that the scheme worked out in the Twenty-one Demands and incorporated, in certain essential features, in the Treaties of 1915, demanded for its permanence the assent of the Great Powers with whom Japan was and is under agreement touching the independence and integrity of China. And to secure this assent, the Japanese Government appear immediately to have thought out a diplomacy which first addressed itself to the Tsardom.

The Russo-Japanese Treaties of 1916

As a result of negotiations pursued, it seems, in the sense of this diplomacy, the two treaties referred to in section 14 (a) hereof were concluded between Japan and Russia. [In 1916 two Treaties were concluded between Japan and Russia. They had direct bearing upon the Twenty-one Demands embodied in the Treaties of 1915.] One was made public, and before its signature, was communicated to the British Government. But the other was a secret treaty, consisting of six articles, of which the last provided that the 'PRESENT CONVENTION SHALL BE KEPT IN COMPLETE SECRECY FROM EVERYBODY EXCEPT THE TWO HIGH CONTRACTING PARTIES.' (vide App. 3.)

Commenting on the treaties of its issue of December 24, 1917, a great organ of British public opinion pointed out that there were considerable differences between the public and secret documents; 'The public treaty professes to aim at maintaining a lasting peace in the Far East and makes no specific reference to China; the Secret Treaty is not concerned with Peace, but with the "interests" of both contracting Powers in China... The public treaty indicates consultation between the contracting parties as to the measures to be taken, the Secret Treaty points to military measures and is definitely a military alliance.'

16. *A further comment may be added to explain the bearing and connexion of this transaction with the settlement based on the Twenty-one Demands and embodied in the Treaties of 1915.* Article 2 of the Public Treaty provides for consultation between Japan and Russia should their Territorial rights or SPECIAL INTERESTS in the Far East be threatened. The specific reference to China in the Secret Treaty shows that the 'special interests' of the parties contemplated are those recognised by each other as existing in China.

There can be no question *whatever* that, [should the Treaties of 1915 remain undisturbed] *under the Treaties of 1915*, Japan has acquired [by them] valuable territorial rights and special interests in China, particularly in *the extramural regions of* South Manchuria and Eastern Inner Mongolia *and in the intra-mural province of Shantung between which the great province of Chihli, with Peking in its heart, lies like a helpless prey within the jaws of a 'strategic pincers'.*

17. *Emphasis has also been laid on the fact that the Secret Treaty refers to other secret agreements concluded between Japan and Russia on July 30, 1907, July 4, 1910, and July 8, 1912, to all of which the treaty is made supplementary. Similar emphasis has been laid on the wording of article 1 of the Secret Treaty, which* is significant in that, whilst it provides against the 'political domination' of China 'by any THIRD POWER', it fails to provide against the political domination of the same country by either or both Japan and Russia.

Further Negotiations with Russia

18. *The diplomacy which had yielded the Russo-Japanese Treaties of 1916 also found expression in the further* [Further] negotiations with Russia [are] reported in another despatch written by M. Krupensky to Petrograd under date of February 8, 1917.

The Ambassador is reporting on his effects to induce Japan to withdraw her *then well-known* opposition to China's entry into the war on the side of the Allies – *see App. 2* – *mainly, it may now be stated, because it was feared that such an intervention would have entitled China to admission to the Peace Conference and to secure a hearing of her case for the direct restitution of the leased territory of Kiaochow among other claims in which Japan was interested.*

After stating that he never omitted 'an opportunity for representing to the (Japanese) Minister for Foreign Affairs [Viscount Motono] the desirability, in the interests of Japan herself, of China's intervention in the war' *and that the Minister had promised 'to sound the attitude of Peking without delay'*, M. Krupensky reported that 'on the other hand, the Minister pointed out the necessity for him, in view of the attitude of Japanese public opinion on the subject, as well as with a view to safeguard Japan's position at the future

Peace Conference, if CHINA SHOULD BE ADMITTED TO IT, of securing the support of the Allied Powers to the desires of Japan, in respect of Shantung and the Pacific Islands. These desires are for the SUCCESSION TO ALL THE RIGHTS AND PRIVILEGES HITHERTO POSSESSED BY GERMANY IN THE SHANTUNG PROVINCE and for the acquisition of the islands to the north of the equator which are now occupied by the Japanese. Motono plainly told me that the Japanese Government would like to receive at once the promise of the Imperial (Russian) Government to support the above desires of Japan.'

'In order to give a push,' the Ambassador added persuasively, 'to the highly important question of a break between China and Germany I regard it as very desirable that the Japanese should be given the promise they ask...'

19. It is reasonable to suggest that if Japan had at this date regarded, in a sense of finality, the settlement imposed on China in 1915 – *with its mandatory clause requiring China to Recognise in advance Japan's right of succession to the German servitudes in Shantung* – there would have been no necessity for Japan to insist on Allied support of her claim in the matter vis-à-vis China [at the future Peace Conference.]

The latter's [Japan's] treaty undertaking on the point was either final or not final in the sense that the settlement was subject to revisionary action by the Peace Conference. If it were final there was no necessity for Japan to demand Allied assistance as a price for her assent to China's active association with the Allies in the war. If, however, the settlement was not final, there was of course good reason for the price exacted.

The Lansing–Ishii Agreement

20. *It seems that, in further pursuance of the diplomacy that had yielded the desired assent of Russia to the settlement embodied in the treaties of 1915, the Japanese Government despatched a mission to the United States in the autumn of 1917. The party was headed by Viscount Ishii who eventually concluded with the American Government the understanding known as the 'Lansing–Ishii Agreement'.* [*Why weaken the case by this!*]

In Part IV, sections 16 and 17, two important despatches are cited, written by M. Krupensky to his home government, in which he indicates the far-reaching interpretation placed by the Japanese Government on the American recognition of Japan's 'special position' and 'special interests' in China.

Disclaimer by Chinese Government

21. [Moreover] *In addition to this envisagement of the Treaties of 1915 as lacking in finality, which is disclosed in the Japanese diplomacy that was intended to cure this defect,* there can be no doubt that the Chinese Govern-

ment clearly indicated their sense of the *impermanence* [lack of finality] of the entire transaction.

Although *harassed and* threatened by the presence of large bodies of troops despatched by the Japanese Government to South Manchuria and Shantung – whose withdrawal, the Japanese Minister at Peking declared in reply to a direct enquiry by the Chinese Government, would not be effected 'until the negotiations could be brought to a satisfactory conclusion' – the Chinese Government issued an official statement on the negotiations immediately after this 'satisfactory conclusion' had been *secured* [effected] *under pressure of the ultimatum of May 7, 1915, containing the declaration* [declaring] that they were 'constrained' to comply in full with the terms of the ultimatum, but in complying the Chinese Government disclaim any desire to associate themselves with any revision, which may thus be effected, of the various conventions and agreements concluded between other Powers in respect of the maintenance of China's territorial independence and integrity, the preservation of the status quo, and the principle of equal opportunity for the commerce and industry of all nations in China.'

A 'Unilateral Negotiation'

22. The foregoing declaration was preceded by an account of the manner in which the negotiations had been conducted or, more accurately, dictated by Japan. It was shown how, faced by these Twenty-one Demands of a powerful Government 'determined to attain this end by all means within their power' and at a selected moment when three of the Powers, with whom Japan had severally guaranteed the independence and integrity of China, were engaged in a deadly struggle with the Germanic Kingdoms, China was compelled to enter into a singularly unequal negotiation with Japan.

It was a negotiation in which the number and *almost* [virtually the] personnel of China's representatives were *practically* dictated to her. It was a negotiation in which Japan refused to have, *according to custom and practice*, official minutes of the proceedings kept as suggested by China, with the result that the Japanese and Chinese representatives differed in their respective records of important declarations made by the latter, and, on the basis of some of these differences, the Japanese Government in their ultimatum accused the Chinese Government of 'arbitrarily...nullifying' statements alleged to have been made – but in fact never made – by the senior Chinese representative. It was a negotiation in the course of which – these are the words of the Chinese official statement issued at the time – 'the Japanese Minister twice suspended the conferences, obviously with the object of compelling compliance with his views on certain points at the time under discussion'. In a word, it was a negotiation in which Japan dominated and dictated the course and the terms of the discussion, *and in which even China's policy of acquiescence in order to avert a war with Japan and to prevent the creation of a situation compelling a dispersion of Allied war-energies into the Far East, failed to arrest the development of the negotiations into a phase enabling the Japanese Government to deliver their ultimatum of May 7, 1915, to the Chinese Government.*

Protest by the Government of the United States

23. [Presumably it] *It* was *these features* [this element] of harshness in the negotiations [which led] *and other considerations of high policy that seem to have led* the Government of the United States [four days before the signature of the Treaties to send on May 11, 1915 the following identic note to China and Japan:] *to notify its refusal to recognise the validity of the settlement embodied in the Treaties of 1915.*

This refusal was communicated on May 11, 1915 – within 72 hours of China's complete submission to the Japanese utimatum – in an identic note cabled to the Chinese and Japanese Governments, reading:—

'IN VIEW OF THE CIRCUMSTANCES of the negotiations which have taken place and which are now pending between the Government of China and the Government of Japan and of the agreements which have been reached as a result thereof, the Government of the United States has the honour to notify the Government of the Chinese Republic that it cannot recognise any agreement or undertaking, which has been entered into between the Governments of China and Japan impairing the treaty rights of the United States and its citizens in China, the political or territorial integrity of the Republic of China or the international policy relative to China commonly known as the Open Door Policy. An identical note has been transmitted to the Japanese Government.'

VI Conclusion

1. Summing up the foregoing arguments, it is submitted that they establish the claim of China for the abrogation of the Treaties of 1915 *because the same are*:—

(a) [because they] *are and* constitute one entire transaction arising out of *and connected with* the war and *seek or* attempt to deal with matters whose *proper* determination is entirely a right and interest of the Peace Conference;
(b) *manifestly* [because they] contravene the Allied formula of justice which *finds expression in President Wilson's statement of principles* now serving as the guiding rules of the Peace Conference in its task of working

out a settlement of the affairs of nations in order to *prevent or* minimise the chances of war in the future;

(c) *specifically* [because they] violate the territorial integrity and political independence of China as guaranteed in the series of conventions and agreements severally concluded by Great Britain, France, Russia and the United States with Japan;

(d) [because they] were negotiated in circumstances of intimidation and concluded under the duress of an ultimatum *completely disabling the Chinese Government from exercising a free and un-coerced judgment in the matter or acting as a consenting party thereto;*

(e) [because they] were *envisaged even by Japan as* lacking in finality [being even so regarded by Japan who sought to forestall inevitable opposition by entering into a series of secret agreements at variance with the principles now guiding the Peace Conference;] *which the latter sought to cure by exacting Allied support in a set of secret agreements wholly at variance with President Wilson's statement of principles and necessarily annulled by the Belligerents' acceptance of those principles as the basis of the Armistice arranged and of the peace treaty to be concluded;*

[*make them final by negotiating a set of secret agreements at variance with the principles acceptance by the Belligerents as the basis of the peace*]

(f) [*because they*] *are subject both to the principle of the Allied and American decision regarding the treaty of Bucharest and the principles of political expediency applied by the Congress of Berlin to the Treaty of San Stefano and by the Three Continental Powers to the Treaty of Shimonoseki.*

The Barrier to Friendship between China and Japan

2. *The adequate presentation of the present claim has rendered it necessary to define the framework of Japanese policy in China and rightly to group and fix within it the salient facts in which that policy has expressed itself over a period of years.*

This treatment of the subject has involved a process of analysis and explanation which had to be frank and objective in order to secure accuracy and clearness. But the caution must be registered that nothing has been set down in this Memorandum which was not strictly demanded by the necessities of argument.

Whilst it would be obviously insincere to suggest that the preparation of this claim has not evoked many an unpleasant memory of the harshness and unfairness hitherto characterizing Japan's dealings with China, the interests of peace as well as the future of the two countries, as co-workers in Far Asia have counselled a statement of China's case, on the issue of these Treaties of 1915, which would make it not impossible for the two nations to live as authentic friends in the new age whose dawn is on the horizon.

But realities must be faced. Even in a world chastened by the ideals and chari-

ties of the League of Nations, friendship between China and Japan would hardly be possible if the barrier of the Treaties of 1915 should be left standing.

These Treaties are not merely the symbol but the concrete expression of an Imperialism which has enabled Japan – so we interpret it in China – to wage two successful wars, emerging out of them the greatest power in Far Asia, and then to annex Korea. And be it false or not, it is the conviction of the Chinese nation that the march of that Imperialism will not cease until China shares the fate of Korea.

But these Treaties not only prohibit friendship between China and Japan, but their continued existence must deny the reality of Japan's adhesion to the Covenant of the League of Nations and her membership in the League. It is not possible to reconcile the net-work of 'rights and privileges' with which they enmesh China with the postulate of a nation's liberties underlying the League of Nations.

As we see it all in China, there lies ahead a road packed with contentions and disputes between China and Japan unless the great wrong of 1915 be redressed in terms of the new order under inauguration to-day in Paris. League or no League of Nations, that wrong – unrighted – will fester and [will] breed the things for whose extinction men have lately died on the soil of France.

923. To H. A. Gwynne

London 9 May 1919

My dear Gwynne,

I am sorry to have to tell you that I became ill in Paris and that my illness developed into a severe attack of jaundice. I was ordered back to London – arrived here on Wednesday evening, was examined yesterday by a specialist and today I am going to the country to that cottage we have taken at Forest Row.[1] I am dictating this letter to my wife.

I have just been reading your issue of today, and really heartily congratulate you upon the high level which your leaders attain.[2] In Paris the Chinese lost their case entirely. They were spurred on by the Americans to put their trust in the President, and they were left in the lurch, just as from the very beginning I warned them they would be. Of course, being in close contact with the Chinese I heard a good deal of what was passing.

On the evening of the 6th May, immediately after the closing of the Plenary Session, the chief Chinese Delegate[3] who was present at the Session and who speaks French with the utmost purity and correctness, came to see

[1] Forest Row in Sussex, England, where Morrison had rented a cottage from his sister and brother-in-law, Violet and Lance Gaunt, the latter a lawyer with a practice in Singapore.
[2] A reference to the *Morning Post*, of which Gwynne was at this time editor (1911–37).
[3] Lu Cheng-hsiang.

me, to tell me of what Foch[1] had said, and I noted it at the time. Foch spoke to the members on the subject of the defence of the Rhine. He spoke gravely–said the defences were inadequate and he must enter a protest against them, and he protested that *he had not seen the terms of the Peace Treaty relating to the military defence of the Rhine frontier*. Fancy these politicians drafting military clauses relating to the safe guarding of France's future without reference to the highest military authority in France!

President Wilson completely befooled the Chinese. In order to buy off Japan's opposition to a League of Nations which did not include words stipulating for national equality, he made a bargain, and in return for Japan's not pressing her claim, he undertook to support in their entirety all Japan's claims in regard to China. The result has been that Japan has obtained in China far more than ever she could have hoped for and more than she would have accepted as adequate. Now the President is endeavouring to cajole the Chinese into believing that he was their champion throughout but that the opposition of Mr Lloyd George[2] and of the French was such that in order to save his precious League of Nations he had to yield.

I hope I can see you soon. There is much that I would like to tell you, but at present I am not fit to be seen with this startling colour[3] which ill-luck has given to me, but which I hope is only temporary.

[...]

Ever faithfully yours
[G. E. Morrison]

924. From Ting Wen-chiang[4]

Paris 14 May 1919

My dear Dr. Morrison,

I went to MacMahon Hotel a few days ago and to my grief I found that you had gone back to England. Let us hope that the pure air of Sussex will do you good and make you recover rapidly.

You asked me the other day the economic consequences of the Japanese victory[5] – Well I think they are more important than many people can

[1] Ferdinand Foch (1851–1929), French soldier. As Commander-in-Chief of the Allied forces, his success in holding off the offensive launched by Field-Marshal von Lüdendorff was responsible for turning the tide of the War. He was prominent as the French delegate to the Paris Conference.
[2] At this time leading the British Delegation to the Paris Conference.
[3] Morrison was struck down the previous month by pancreatitis from which he never recovered, dying from it just a year later.
[4] At this time in the entourage of Liang Ch'i-ch'ao in Paris.
[5] A reference to the endorsement by the Great Powers at the Paris Peace Conference of Japan's claims to the former German concessions in Shantung. This was embodied in the Peace Treaty subsequently signed on 28 June 1919. By Article 156 'Germany renounces, in favour of Japan, all her rights, titles and privileges – particularly those concerning the

imagine and will certainly affect other countries than China. Japan, in spite of her organisation, is a country without resources. Nothing made her realise her impotence more than when America prohibited the export of steel in entering the War. As you well know, in recent years great efforts have been made to secure her needs at the expense of China. The Peace Conference has given her 3-4,000,000 tons of good iron ore and more than one billion tons of good coal, all near to the railway, the extension of which will traverse three more coal fields, containing billions of tons of coking coal. Thus Japan has secured her monopoly of Chinese iron industry.

There can be no doubt that in the near future Japan will be able to build as many ships as she likes with her own steel. Then she will assume a different attitude towards such questions as racial equality. Besides for the first time the Powers give formal recognition to what is known as the Japanese equivalent to the Monroe doctrine. Here in a treaty to be signed by practically all the countries of the world Japan is allowed to act as arbitrator between China and Germany. Kiouchow [Kiaochow] is to be returned to China not directly by Germany with whom China is also at War, but through the hands of Japan. Henceforth Japan can regard herself as the only spokesman of Asia.

I wonder how many Englishmen understand the mental attitude of the Japanese towards India. I remember vividly that in 1903 the Indian students in Tokyo organised an evening party at which I was fortunate enough to be present. There many prominent Japanese spoke openly against England and told the Indians that *as soon as Japan was strong enough* India would be cleared of Englishmen. And they were prolongedly applauded. During the whole period of the World War, every little incident in India was carefully exaggerated in the Japanese Press. Even after the armistice many articles on India appeared in the Japanese papers which were extremely unfriendly to England (to put it mildly). You yourself must have been aware of the intimate connections between the prominent Indian agitators and many responsible Japanese statesmen, notably Count Okuma. Now so far Japan has remained passive (apparently at least) because she is fully aware of her weakness in resources, but when she can produce 5,000,000 tons of steel instead of 500,000 she will only wait for a favorable opportunity to become your enemy instead of your ally, and not only India, but even Australia will not be safe without a large navy.

In thinking over these things I cannot help becoming a fatalist. It seems that fate is with Japan in her effort to dominate Asia, for at the Paris confer-

---

territory of Kiaochow, railways, mines and submarine cables – which she acquired by virtue of the treaty concluded by her with China on 6 March 1898, and of all other arrangements relative to the Province of Shantung.' In addition, by Article 157, Japan was to be granted 'the movable and immovable property owned by the German State in the territory of Kiaochow, as well as all the rights which Germany might claim in consequence of the works or improvements made or of the expenses incurred by her, directly or indirectly, in connection with this territory.'

ence Great Britain, who, of all nations, should have opposed Japan in her own interest, vigorously supported her claims. It is Fate that has whispered to Lloyd George in favour of her protégé or is it simply ignorance?

I am leaving Paris tomorrow for Normandy and hope to go to Bilbao afterwards. But I am compelled reluctantly to give up my projected trip to Rio Tinto[1] as the communication is too difficult.

Hoping to have good news from you soon

Yours sincerely
V. K. Ting

925. From V. Chirol[2]

[Devon, England] 25 May 1919

My dear Morrison,

I am distressed at the contents of your letter.[3] I wish you could have sent me more cheerful birthday greetings, but I hope and pray the operation will not confirm Sir Thomas'[4] worst apprehensions – not only for your own sake, but for that of your wife and children, who have, I know, brought you and received from you so much happiness.

I am so glad we were able to meet again in Paris and restore the old cordiality of our friendship. It is more than twenty years now since I dug you out at Bangkok[5] to the advantage, I feel sure, of all concerned. Your letter has reached me at Sir Ernest Satow's[6] where I have been enjoying a week of wonderful weather and most peaceful surroundings.

[1] Morrison had worked as a medical officer with the Rio Tinto Mining Company in Spain from May 1888 to August 1889, and might have suggested that Ting, as a geologist, should visit the mines there.

[2] Sir Valentine Chirol (1852–1929), British journalist. As Foreign Editor of *The Times*, he was involved in Morrison's appointment and had had close relations with him until their difference over the paper's policy on the question of China and Japan led to an open breach between them in 1911. They did not meet again until the Paris Conference when Chirol was there with the British Delegation.

[3] Morrison's letter to Chirol of 20 May 1919 is not printed.

[4] Sir Thomas Jeeves Horder (1871–1955), later 1st Baron Ashford, British physician, a Consultant at St. Bartholomew's Hospital and Physician to various members of the British royal family.

[5] Morrison's first contract with *The Times* was for a period of six months, subsequently extended to a year, during which time he wrote over twenty long articles for the paper, mainly on Indo-China. His work so impressed the Manager, C. F. Moberly Bell, and his colleagues that they proposed that he should proceed as their Correspondent to Peking. Morrison was instructed to meet up with Chirol, who was then on a trip to the Far East, in Bangkok. There Chirol, on behalf of *The Times*, signed the contract with Morrison which is printed as Letter No. 7 in Vol. 1 of the *Correspondence*. Chirol is therefore somewhat overstating his contribution to the making of Morrison's career as *Times* Correspondent. *See also* Morrison to Moberly Bell, 8 June 1904, printed as Letter No. 1 in Vol. 1.

[6] After his retirement the former British Minister to Japan and China Satow went to live at Ottery-St-Mary in Devonshire, England, close to the seaside town of Sidmouth where Morrison was to spend his last days.

This is the most bucolic part of the most bucolic county in the S. of England, and just now with its broad and intensely green pasture lands, its deep-set lanes and hedges all atwinkle with little wild flowers, and its billowing pink and white orchards, it affords a picture of placid abundance and content which makes it hard to realise that there are still Peace (?) Conferences and Huns and Bolshevists making mischief all the world over.

I return to town tomorrow, and if I can come and see you there before your operation, please let me know. I want very much to make your wife's acquaintance. [...]

With heartfelt wishes for a happy issue to your trouble

Yours very sincerely
V.C.

926. From W. R. Strickland

Peking 20 June 1919

Dear Dr. Morrison,

It was extremely kind of you to write to me in the cheering and sympathetic terms of your letter dated 11.5.19, received this morning.[1] I am most sorry that you have been unwell.

[...] The post of Foreign Chief Inspector[2] here is, as you know, one of great difficulty and tribulation, as the Chinese have not (and, I believe, never have had) any intention of introducing reforms which will benefit the people at large. Any suggestions in this direction by foreigners are regarded as admirable in sentiment but not seriously intended.

The situation has been rendered one of greater difficulty for the reason that, when loans are made, the terms are left to financiers to decide (and financiers are by profession 'without soul'). If only our Legation would take an interest in the broader issues of humanity and not confine their efforts to spasmodic intervention when a high appointment is at stake, foreigners would be able to produce permanent beneficial results and could check the undoubted increase of anti-foreign sentiments among the very poor population of the country who will one day direct the policy of the country. At the present time they have the one 'right' quoted by Hobbes[3] in the *Leviathan*,

[1] Not printed.
[2] The post of Foreign Inspector in the Salt Administration, of which W. R. Strickland was Associate Foreign Inspector, was at this time held by Sir Reginald Gamble (1862-1929) who had succeeded Sir Richard Dane in 1918.
[3] Thomas Hobbes (1588-1679), British political philosopher, whose book, *Leviathan, or the Matter, Forme and Power of a Commonwealth Ecclesiasticall and Civill*, appeared in 1651. Much of the argument expressed in it was the direct result of Hobbes' own observations of the Civil War in England which raged from 1642 to 1651. The words he used were actually 'Right of Rebellion', not 'Revolution'.

'the right of revolution'. This they will exercise sooner or later and we shall call it Bolshevism.

Their present existence is again (if I remember correctly) rightly described by Hobbes as nasty solitarry(?) poor brutish and short'.[1]

What is called the 'people of China' in the press does not include in its connotation these 'starving millions', who live merely to create others in their own likeness and then die.

The conclusion then is that the foreign advisers should 'function' as the representatives of this enormous and potentially powerful class. At present the advisers are servants of Mammon by the terms of their charter and they cannot serve another master. (Here the tone of the missionary creeps in.) This is all well known to you, but it renders the post of Chief Inspector unattractive in itself. What can be said of an Administration under which a pound of salt in a tropical country costs far more than a man's daily wage? Only that it is not the fault of the foreign Adviser. This is true today in large areas of the country, mainly owing to the existence of Military Governors who are not paid by the Central Government (as they should be) owing to its poverty and, quite apart from the question of honesty or dishonesty, must find money to keep their troops reasonably quiet. Meanwhile, our Administration is in increasing danger of collapse.

The dilatory attitude of America both in China and more especially in Siberia is inexplicable. Non-intervention does not mean respecting the rights of the people: it is only by intervention that they can get any rights at all.

I have sent a number of paper extracts to my young brother in the Guarantee Trust, calculated to show that as things are going now a mandate might as well be given at once to the Japanese to 'civilize' the country.

It is in fact doubtful if it will not come to this and it is in fact doubtful if this course will not benefit China in the end.

And yet it is a shortsighted policy, for China is one of the few countries where money is still to be made. America especially often barred out from older countries by Protective Tariffs will require China as a field of investment for her hoarded war profits. Here indeed is the main ground for hope. Then get U.S.A. gold in, and we may trust the financiers to rouse the U.S.A. from the Conspiracy of Dreams and to bring their Government into the arena like a hooked minnow. Meanwhile of course we must not forget that we are still at war with Germany.

This is awful gas but there is no news.

[1] The paragraph from which this quotation was made reads: 'Whatsoever therefore is consequent to a time of Warre, where every man is Enemy to every man, the same is consequent to the time, wherein men live without other security, that what their own strength, and their own invention shall furnish them withall ... In such conditions ... there is no Society; and which is worst of all, continuall feare, and danger of violent death; and the life of man, solitary, poore, nasty, brutish, and short' (*Leviathan*, Part 1, Chapter 13)

Kung Hsin Chen[1] is acting Premier, a 'good' man. The Anfu Club[2] put him in as a temporary stop gap and is now unable to agree upon a permanent man. The students' movement is a splendid sign.[3] The danger is

[1] Kung Hsin-chan (1868–1943), Chinese Republican politician, a returned student from England. He had served in various diplomatic and financial posts, including Director of Finance of his native Anhwei Province. In January 1919 he was made Minister of Finance and became Acting Prime Minister in June upon the resignation of Ch'ien Neng-hsün, holding both posts until the overthrow of the Anfu Clique, to which he belonged, in September the same year. When Tuan Ch'i-jui returned once again to power in November 1924, Kung was made Minister of the Interior, and then in December the following year Minister of Education, a post he held until Tuan's fall in April 1926. In 1896, Kung Hsin-chan was a student in London living with his uncle, Kung Chao-huan, Chinese Minister in London (1893–7), when the kidnapping of Sun Yat-sen took place. As nephew of the Minister he was said to have interrogated Sun and to have ill-treated him. This incident was recalled and commented upon when in 1925 Kung as Minister of the Interior (November 1924 – December 1925) was delegated by Tuan Ch'i-jui, then Chief Executive or Head of State, who absented himself on the excuse that he could not put his shoes on because of swollen feet, to attend the funeral of Sun Yat-sen who had died in Peking on 12 March, 1925. Morrison, who strongly condemned the appointment of Kung by his fellow-provincial, the new Finance Minister Chou Hsüeh-hsi, to succeed Chang Hu as Director-General of the Salt Administration in May 1915, changed his mind when Kung called on him and greatly impressed him as a man of ability.

[2] The political wing of the northern militarist clique headed by Tuan Ch'i-jui, which formally came in being on 7 March 1918. The club derived its name from Anfu Hutung, a lane in Peking into which the Club's headquarters were located. Its leading members were mostly, but not exclusively, fellow-provincials of Tuan from Anhwei. It was through the Club that Tuan and his followers manipulated the elections in the fourteen provinces under their political control for the new Parliament which came into being in August 1918 and which elected their candidate Hsü Shih-ch'ang as the new President. The Anfu Clique while in the control of the Government in Peking was known as a tool of Japanese imperialism and was the main target of the student protest during what has become known as the 'May Fourth' Movement in 1919. After its army was defeated by that of Chihli in the first Anfu–Chihli war in July 1920, the Club was dissolved by the order of the very President it had helped to elect. Many members of the Club came back to Power with the return of Tuan Ch'i-jui at the end of 1924, but the Club itself was not revived although Tuan's followers were still described as members of the Anfu Clique. After Tuan's removal in April 1926, soon followed by the overthrow of the Peking Government and the establishment of the Nationalist Government at Nanking, most Anfu leaders retired to live under Japanese protection, only to re-emerge as collaborators in Japan's aggression, first in Manchuria (Ting Shih-yüan and others) and then in northern and central China (Wang I-t'ang, Chu Shen (1879–1943), Liang Hung-chih, Li Ssu-hao (b. 1879) and others). The Club as a result came to be synonymous, to many Chinese, with corruption and treason, and gave the very mention of Anhwei Province an odious ring.

[3] The reference is to the protest movement which students launched in Peking on 4 May 1919, directed against the decision of the Versailles Treaty on Shantung, and against the Anfu Government, whose dealings with Japan had been used by that country to influence the decision in her favour. As the protest spread to other parts of China, the Movement widened its scope. It marked the beginning of a new cultural awakening in China, and was celebrated during the Nanking phase of the Republican period as the 'Day of Youth'.

that it will be captured by the Chinputang[1] for political ends and thus lose its moral force.
[...]

Yrs very sincerely
W. R. Strickland

927. From W. R. Giles[2]

Peking 1 July 1919

My dear Dr Morrison,
You will no doubt think me remiss for not having written to you before this, but when you learn that I have been for three months in Korea, during which time I contracted double pneumonia and pleurisy you will understand my silence. [...]

Korea: Although my illness interfered with my original plans for carrying out an investigation of the Japanese atrocities in Korea, I had a very interesting time both before and after it. I saw thing[s] with my own eyes, interviewed so many people Koreans and foreigners, and did a certain amount of photography, that I am fully able to confirm anything I write.

The cruelties and atrocities committed are beyond the imagination of the people in Europe and America. Useless murder and brutalities, rape and torture, have occurred in all parts of Korea. The Government in Korea[3] have tried to make the world believe that the demonstrations were of such small importance that they need not be considered, yet they sent in another ten thousand troops, and only a few days ago the Korean Government [Governor] General issued statistics showing that more than 17,000 were prosecuted as main agitators, of whom about 8,00[0] have been released as minor offenders, the rest, 9,059 in all, being still detained in custody. The above statistics were

[1] The Chin-pu tang, or Progressive Party, combined a number of middle-of-the-road parties, standing between the Kuomintang, or southern republicans, on the one side, and the northern militarist factions on the other. Though mainly conservatives and former constitutional monarchists and reformists, its leaders regarded themselves as a third force in Chinese politics of the time, and as such their collaboration with the Peking regime was used by Yüan Shih-k'ai and his successors to give an appearance of a wider base of democratic support. Hsiung Hsi-ling's Cabinet (July 1913 – February 1914) under Yüan Shih-k'ai and the participation by Liang Ch'i-ch'ao, T'ang Hua-lung and Lin Ch'ang-min (q.v.) in the Tuan Ch'i-jui Government in 1917 were notable examples of such collaboration. Their occasional criticism of and opposition to some of the more extreme measures of the Peking regime, such as Yüan's monarchical scheme, lent these fundamentally conservative opportunists a claim to being spokesmen for the popular will. By far the most articulate and vocal of the population, they presented themselves to a great many people, particularly students and intellectuals, as the champions of the nation's cause.

[2] Correspondent of the *Peking and Tientsin Times*, and Special Correspondent of the *Chicago Daily News*. He had just returned from a trip to Korea to investigate the allegations of Japanese atrocities there following the so-called 'March First' Movement of 1919.

[3] The Japanese Government in Korea.

published by the Tokyu News Agency under date of June 25. If the Japanese admit this number, it can be taken for granted that the total is a much larger one.[1]

The people are being tortured much in the same manner as they were during the conspiracy trial.[2] The Prisons are crowded in the most awful manner. I saw in the Prison from thirty to forty crowded into a room twelve feet by six – it may have been smaller but it could not have been larger than that. The prisoners were unable to sleep as there was only room for them to sit crammed in together. The worst tortures, however, take place in the police stations where they are first examined after arrest. The Japanese treat men and young school girls alike. In fact the Japanese are acting in Korea worse than the Germans did in Belgium. It must be remembered that there is not a firearm in the country. All the demonstrations have been pacific, and the only time that the Koreans have turned around on the mob has been when the Japanese were shooting and beating a crowd of women. So far there is only evidence of three Japanese being killed, although a number have been roughly handled. The movement is being used to crush Christianity in Korea, an influence greatly feared by the Japanese. I visited and photographed a number of the burnt down villages and churches, finding in the majority of instances that the inhabitants had sought refuge in the mountains. I also visited one village where the non-Christian villagers had been forced to drive the Christians out otherwise the Japs threatened to burn down the village. The Koreans are the most oppressed people in the world today. Now I think I have given you enough news about Korea. The only means by which it is possible for the foreign governments to get a true

[1] On 1 March 1919, as the culmination of a call for the liberation and independence of Korea by Koreans in America, China and elsewhere, following the cessation of the European War, the Koreans in Seoul launched a large demonstration in defiance of the Japanese Government in Korea with a declaration signed by thirty-three of the country's leading citizens headed by Son Chung-hee. There was a massive response throughout the country, which brought on severely repressive retaliatory action by the Japanese authorities, with large-scale imprisonment, killing and other brutal measures which continued, as did the Movement, known as the 'March First' Movement, for many years. According to Japanese statistics, more than 1,316,000 people were involved in the Movement, over 6,700 of whom were put to death and some 53,000 imprisoned.

[2] In January 1912, following the discovery in the previous month of a plot for the assassination of Terauchi Masatake, successor to Itō Hirobumi as Japanese Resident-General in Korea, 105 suspects, almost all of them Christians, were arrested. At the end of their prolonged trial on 28 December 1912, they were all convicted on the basis of their confessions, allegedly obtained by torture. The confessions were, however, withheld from the court hearing. The procedures of the court which convicted them were called into question, even in Japan, and in the following year the sentences of seven of the convicted men were reduced after an appeal, and the rest acquitted. The allegation of torture was the subject of several letters to the Editor of *The Times* in 1913, in which evidence revealed by the correspondents helped to substantiate the allegation. This became known as the '105 Incident'.

understanding concerning the state of affairs in Korea is for them to send out a commission that will make its own private investigations. But under the existing state of things it is impossible to expect this to be done.

The Boycott:[1] When I got back to Peking, I found things in their usual state of chaos and uncertainty. The cabinet was again on the verge of being wrecked on account of the activities of the pro-Japanese organization, the Anfu Club, the latter being supported by the military clique. A few days before my return it had become known that the Peace Conference had determined to hand over Germany's Shantung concessions to Japan. This was the cause of the present boycott against the Japanese. All the educational institutions struck, formed processions and marched around the city. They intended to hold a mass meeting in the Central Park, but the police and military drove them back and made numerous arrests. This was the greatest mistake the government could have made, for if the students had been allowed to hold the meeting they would not have had the opportunity of making themselves martyrs. A large crowd of the students then went to the residence of Tsao Ju-lin,[2] Lu Chung yu[3] and another pro-Jap official[4] and began

[1] Responding to the call of students from Peking and elsewhere, the business community started a boycott against Japanese goods in major sea ports and cities all over China.

[2] At this time Minister of Communications (July 1917 – June 1919). In this position and in that of Minister of Finance, which he held concurrently from March 1918 to January 1919, he was responsible for the financial deals with Japan negotiated through Nishihara Kamezō, the personal representative of Terauchi Masatake, then Japanese Prime Minister. These agreements, concluded only shortly before the end of the European War, were used by the Japanese Delegation at the Paris Conference to counter the arguments put forward by the Chinese Delegation that the concessions China had granted to Japan were made under coercion. Ts'ao managed to escape by a back door when the students stormed his house on 4 May 1919.

[3] Lu Tsung-yü (?1875–1941), Chinese Republican politician. A graduate of Waseda University in Tokyo, and one of the best-known pro-Japanese officials in the Peking Government. He was appointed Minister to Japan in December 1913, remaining in the post until June 1916 when he was succeeded by his friend, another pro-Japanese official, Chang Tsung-hsiang (q.v.). On returning to China he was put in charge by Ts'ao Ju-lin of the loan negotiations which the Tuan Ch'i-jui Government was then conducting through Nishihara Kamezō. At this time his official position was Director-General of the Currency Bureau, to which he was appointed in October 1918. Together with Ts'ao Ju-lin and Chang Tsung-hsiang he became the main and immediate target of the student demonstration that took place in Peking on 4 May 1919. He was dismissed from his post, as were the other two from theirs, on 10 June following the nation-wide demand for their death.

[4] Chang Tsung-hsiang (1879–?1963), Chinese Republican politician. A Law graduate from Tokyo Imperial University, he was Director of the Bureau of Codification in the Presidential Office after the establishment of the Republic and then Chief Justice of the Supreme Court. In February 1914 he became Minister of Justice, a post he held until June 1916 when he was appointed Chinese Minister to Japan, succeeding his friend Lu Tsung-yü. At this time he was in Peking having returned there in April for consultation, and he was at the home of Ts'ao Ju-lin on 4 May when students stormed Ts'ao's house. Too slow in escaping, he was beaten unconscious by the demonstrators, being accused, together with Ts'ao and Lu, of betraying his country to Japan.

hunting for the owners. Tsao managed to escape unhurt, and Lu was wounded as he was escaping.

During the next few days excited students could be seen in small parties in every street of Peking, working themselves into a state of delirium by telling the passers-by of the indignities being thrust upon them through the fault of the pro-Japanese members of the Cabinet, whom they rightly stated were nothing more than the paid agents of Japan. The Government tried to get them to go back to their schools but with no success. They eventually camped outside of the Presidential Palace until he saw fit to see their representative, which finally he was forced to do. These men demanded the dismissal of Tsao Ju-lin and Lu Chung-yi, and further that the Government should not sign the Peace Treaty without reservations concerning Shantung.[1] So strong had their movement become, the Chambers of Commerce and merchants supporting them, that the President finally accepted the resignation of Tsao Ju-lin and Lu, who had tendered their resignation under the belief that the President dared not to accept it. Then followed further political manoeuvring. The Anfu Club furious at Tsao's resignation being accepted and knowing they had the support of the military party behind their organization, tried to undermine the President. The latter at first was against signing the treaty without reservations. But the Anfu Club at that time fearing that it would interfere with their financial schemes with the Japanese urged him to sign it under any conditions. They promised him their full support. Finally he was won over and sent instructions to the Chinese Delegates to sign. When the students' trouble arose they saw that it was likely to interfere with their political standing, so they sent a circular despatch to all the provinces to the effect that they were opposed to the signing of the treaty without reservations. This naturally through [threw] all the responsibility upon the shoulders of the President.

The President finding himself in this position sent in his resignation to Parliament, and his resignation was followed by that of the cabinet. The parliament the following day sent back the President's resignation, stating that it was impossible for them to accept it, as there was no provision in the constitution governing the resignation of the President. The President only accepted the resignation of the President [?Premier] the remainder being requested to remain in office until a new premier had been appointed. That was two weeks ago and no one has yet been found to accept the position. Chou Shu-mu,[2] a friend of the President was selected by him for the posi-

---

[1] Their demand that the stipulation regarding Shantung should be reviewed and revised having been refused by the Conference, the Chinese representatives abstained from the signing of the Peace Treaty which took place three days before this letter was written, on 28 June 1919, in the Salle des Glaces in the Palace at Versailles.

[2] Chou Shu-mu (1860–1925), Chinese Imperial official and Republican politician. A Hanlin scholar, he was Governor of Heilungkiang at the outbreak of the 1911 Revolution. In May 1914, at the invitation of Yüan Shih-k'ai, he became President of the Administrative

tion, but the Anfu Club stated that they would not support his nomination unless they were given the Ministries of Finance and Communication, forty 'first grade positions' for members of their organization, and a guarantee that the War Participation troops would not be disbanded. They are still looking for a premier.

But to come back to the boycott. This movement is the strongest move of its kind that the Chinese have made. The *Tatsu Maru* and the 1915 boycotts sink into insignificance beside it.[1] Not only has it spread all over China, but in Australia, Singapore, Hongkong, Vladivostok, and even as far as America. Already it has caused great alarm in Japan. This boycott is different to all others. On previous occasions it has been the Chinese merchants who have been the mainstay of such attempts, but this time it is the *consumer* who is carrying it on. The students not only shamed the people into a refusal not to purchase Japanese goods, but each one of them took a certain part of a street and explained why they should not. Another thing the students did was to show the people and merchants that there were articles made in China equal to those of the Japanese, if not better, and that they would be encouraging their own industrial expansion by purchasing them. Lectures are being given all over the country encouraging manufacturers and merchants to open up new industries, with the result that millions of dollars have been collected to start making the articles which have heretofore been purchased from Japan. It will not surprise me if this boycott within the next eighteen months does not cost the Japanese four hundred million dollars. A member of the Japanese Legation told me that the *Tatsu Maru* boycott cost them over two hundred million dollars. Basing my estimate on that I think you will agree with me that I am not overstating the case.

The New Consortium:[2] With reference to this new financial group, the

---

Court, but in October resigned in disapproval of Yüan's monarchical scheme. After Yüan's death he was reappointed in July 1916 to the same position, holding it until February 1917. In the event Chou did not become Prime Minister.

[1] In December 1908 a Japanese steamer, the *Tatsu Maru*, was captured by the Chinese Navy for carrying firearms and munitions in Chinese waters off Macao. Both the Japanese and Portuguese Governments protested against the ship's seizure, maintaining that it was in Portuguese territorial waters when it was intercepted. As a result the Japanese presented to the Chinese Government a series of demands including compensation and punishment of the Chinese naval officers involved. Having failed to induce Japan to submit the case to arbitration, China gave way to Japan's demands under the threat of military reprisals. When this became known it sparked off the first boycott movement against Japanese goods which soon spread from Canton to Hong Kong, Shanghai and other Chinese cities, and to the Chinese communities in South-East Asia. The movement subsided only towards the end of the year after repeated Japanese warnings and requests for suppressive measures by the Chinese Government. The boycott movement of 1915 referred to here was started following Japan's Twenty-One Demands.

[2] A reference to the new financial consortium which came to be formed in 1919 by the financial representatives of Britain, France, Japan and the United States. The old consortium, which consisted of Britain, France, Japan, Russia and Germany, ceased to

action of the Japanese in playing a double game is only a repeat performance of previous ones. While the Japanese representatives in Europe are telling the other powers that they are willing to enter the consortium, they are using all their influence in Peking to prevent its accomplishment. The *Shun Tien Shih Pao* in an issue a few days ago made a most violent attack on the scheme. They attacked both Great Britain and America in the most abusive manner. They told the Chinese that this consortium was a scheme of Britain and America to secure control of China financially, economically and industrially. They appealed to the Chinese to fight it for all they were worth, calling all those in favour of it traitors etc. etc. The organ of the Japanese Legation followed this up with an equally violent attack the next day and appealed to the Parliamentarians to knock it on the head. But this is not the only way they are opposing it. They work through the Anfu Club and the militarists and use them to start agitations against it. Among the Anfu Club members are those who have contracted all the Japanese loans, and as the Japanese are said to be financing the club, it is pointed out that this financial support will not be forthcoming should the consortium come into being. The Anfu Club at the present moment controls both Houses of Parliament, the Speaker of the Lower House Wang I-tang, being the head of the Club. This has resulted in a number of members of parliament sending in an interpellation to the Government in which is expressed their opposition to China accepting the Consortium's terms. The Military who have heretofore depended on Japanese money to hold their position are also opposing it. Standing behind them all is Japan who fears that the Consortium will force the publication of numerous deal[s] which have as yet been kept secret.

Anti Anglo–American agitation of the Japanese: The Japanese papers both in Japan and here are carrying on a strong agitation against Britain and America. I know that full reports of this are reaching the State Department in America but how much our people at home know I have not the slightest idea. A few days ago the Legation Police captured in the Legation a ricksha containing many thousands of leaflets containing the most violent charges against Britain and America. It stated that Britain and America were acting in conjunction to partition China and that the question of Shantung was a mere flea bite in comparison. Britain had applied to Wai Chiao-pu pressure to force China to include in Tibetan territory the whole of Szechuan, Kansu, and Hsiangkiang. The Chinese were exhorted to oppose this foreign invasion. Under cross examination the ricksha stated that he had brought the papers from a certain large Japanese firm. The next day, in the Japanese concession, men were caught distributing similar documents.

Now, Doctor, I think that I have given you everything that is likely to

---

function on the outbreak of the European War, for the duration of which Japan was allowed to dominate the supply of money to China. The Japanese representative in the new consortium, as in the old, was the Yokohama Specie Bank.

interest you, unless it is that the news of the signing of peace was received here without the slightest excitement, although three days have elapsed nothing official or otherwise has been done in the way of celebration. I am afraid that you will have to proof-read this yourself, it being rather more than I can tackle. I have just written it off in a rough and ready manner as I wanted to tell you as much as I could in the limited time at my disposal.

[...]

Sincerely yours
William R. Giles

[...]

928. From V. Chirol

London 4 July 1919

My dear Morrison,

I am very sorry to hear you are making but slow progress. I shall try to run down and see you before I go away North at the end of the month. My plans are still rather uncertain – in fact more so than when I saw you.

I can't understand why China refused to sign the Treaty, for I can't see that it would have worsened her position as against Japan, and her refusal creates an awkward situation for herself and for everybody and does not tend to gain her much sympathy. It seems to me she has been badly advised. I wrote a leader on Chino-Japanese relations the day after I saw you, and as Steed couldn't make room for it then, I reshaped it a few days ago after China had declined to sign, supplementing it with a short 'Special Article' on the Chino-Japanese Treaties. However it still hangs fire.[1]

[1] The 'Special Article' referred to here appeared in *The Times* on 9 July 1919, entitled 'China and the Peace Treaty. The Agreement with Japan. Hopes of Revision', in which Chirol gave a summary of the background, as he saw it, of China's refusal to sign the Peace Treaty. He chided China for her claim, saying she 'did not come into the war until August 1917 and her actual participation in it, valuable as it proved in many indirect ways, was mainly confined to the supply of large and very efficient labour corps for France'. She had little claim to the retrocession to her of rights in Shantung formerly conceded by her to Germany, and less to demand the revision of the agreement of May 1915 between her and Japan regarding Japan's Twenty-One Demands. Chirol gave a distorted description of how these Demands had come about by saying that it was in order to settle the conditions under which Japanese would allow 'China to benefit by the elimination of German power [in Shantung], which she had never attempted to resist during the war' that negotiations were opened between Peking and Tokyo, and that 'as they proceeded too slowly, the Japanese Government forced the pace by laying down a series of demands, with which China had at the time no option but to comply'. China's claim that she had been coerced into acquiescence to the Japanese Demands was, Chirol maintained, invalidated by the fact that agreements signed by China with Japan shortly before the end of the European War had confirmed her concessions to Japan in May 1915. A *Times* leader of the same day supported Chirol's arguments maintaining that China had no case for abstaining from the signature of the Peace Treaty simply because the Confer-

You must be glad anyhow to be back in your own home again, and I suppose after such a severe operation[1] you can hardly expect to recover strength very rapidly.

With kind remembrances to your wife

Yours
V.C.

929. From M. van Lerberghe[2]

Agen [France] 4 July 1919

My dear friend,

Excuse me for having left China without saying good bye to the excellent friend you have always been to me, but you remember the trouble I had: all the kids having a terrible dysentry and one of them having to be buried.

When I arrived in France, I went of course with my regiment and, really, I could not find one occasion to write to you. But now the peace has been signed at last, a very poor peace which leaves France in a pitiable condition. My first thought is for you and I have jumped on my typewriter to send you this short letter.

Shall I give you some news from France? The life here is awfully expensive. For instance, one egg which used to cost *un sou* before de war, cost actually fifty centimes or half a franc. Is it not frightfull? And we do not see anything in the futur to bring a better state of conditions. On the contrary, the salary of the workmen having been increased and the duration of the working day shortened, it is absolutely certain that the futur will be impossible for everyone except the working classes which are on the top presently and do not care for anything but themselves. There is some frightfull selfishness which is bound to bring a lot of trouble. Beside that, the financial

---

ence had ratified Japan's claim to the former German rights and concessions in Shantung It urged America not to endorse China's plea for a revision of the 1915 Treaties, and exhorted Japan to be 'magnanimous' in defining her intentions, and in conclusion sounded this warning note: 'We cannot bring ourselves to believe that China seriously intends to persevere in a wilful course of which one of the most unfortunate results for herself would be to cut her off from original membership of the League [of Nations], since the covenant of the League is part and parcel of the Treaty she has declined to sign.' It was precisely such pro-Japanese sentiments as were expressed in this Article and Leader that had caused the difference between Chirol and Morrison when both were on the staff of *The Times*, prior to 1911.

[1] On 2 June 1919, after a diagnosis of carcinoma of the pancreas, Morrison underwent a laparotomy operation which, however, did nothing to improve his condition.

[2] Marcel van Lerberghe, French journalist. He was Editor of *Le Courrier de Tientsin* from 1905 to 1911, and then became Editor of the French-language *Journal de Pékin* until his return to France in July 1918. He was joint author with Alphonse Monestier of *Notes, documents et considérations pour servir à l'histoire de la révolution chinoise, 1911–1913* (Peking 1915).

situation of France is somewhat critical; you may have an idea of it by seeing the exchange rate.

In fact this war has been a tremendous calamity etc. and its effects are far from being at end. I do not see any hope of a normal state of affairs in the near futur; I simply wish that the catastrophe started in Russia will not happen here; but it is only a wish. God knows what to morrow reserves to us!

The damned German have really ruined the world and put everything upside down. They may be proud of such devastating work.

A revolution seems to me very probable in all the old Europe. Happy will be those who shall remain abroad. Actually, already, a workman, the worst, is earning bigger wages than a magistrate, a lawyer, a general, a juge, a prefect, and still the workmen are not satisfied. Eight hours work a day are still too much. Twenty francs a day are still not sufficient. What they want, it seems, is no work at all and a perpetual strike with plenty of money.

You should get pale to see what everyone is able to see. The *bourgeois* are starving, having scarcely enough to bring up there children. They dare not buy a pair of shoes nor a suit; they look just like beggars. During that time, the workmen without work buy the dearest things. Nothing is dear enough for them. They are dressed in silk with varnish shoes and in the evening they never miss the balls which are numerous. It looks like a *sarabande*, everybody running joyfully to the end of everything.

And the peace has changed absolutely nothing. On the contrary the prices are increasing considerably. You just imagine what a kind of rest I have with all my kids!

And it makes me laugh when I read the beautyfull speeches about the end of every war in the futur. Do you remember what I told you a few years ago about Japan? Do you see now clearly the next big conflict between Japan on one side and United States, China and Britain on the other side? This conflict will burst soon, believe me, and there will be no pact of nations to prevent it. We may see by that time Japan allied to Germany and Russia. That is the show of tomorrow. You will see it as I told you often.

But there is nothing to do. There is a fatal power which the humanity is not able to fight against.

A good shake hand and best wishes

M. van Lerberghe

930. To V. Chirol

Sussex [England] 7 July 1919

My dear Chirol,

Many thanks for your letter.[1] I believe I am now doing fairly well. On Saturday the 28th inst. I weighed for the first time since leaving the nursing

---

[1] A reference to the letter printed as No. 928.

home, and was discouraged to find that I had if anything lost weight. I had certainly gained nothing. But I believe I am now gaining in weight, and today I feel encouraged. I am about 8 st. 9 lbs.

I'll certainly be up in town before you leave, and will call upon you, having arranged a time beforehand, and have a chat over this Far Eastern situation.

The full text of the Peace Treaty is more disastrous for China than she had been led to expect. I do not believe that there is any Chinese living of any standing with sufficient hardihood to sign the Treaty unless some definite assurance acceptable to the Chinese can be given by America. But America left them in the lurch before, and the Chinese may be more chary than before of accepting American guidance. It is an astonishing Peace Treaty which punishes China who gave considerable help to the Allies and would have given more – would have indeed entered the war at the very beginning if Japan had not prevented her. The Chinese will never be able to understand why Mr. Balfour promised so far back as Feb. 17, 1917 to support Japan in her claim to perpetuate German aggression in China.[1] Mr. Balfour, it is always said, has explained that he was 'blackmailed' into giving that promise – given fourteen days after it was certain that America was coming into the war, when Japanese pretensions or claims or threats would lose much of their force. Mr. Balfour on the other hand could never understand why the Chinese came to the Peace Conference with high hopes of having their case against Japan given sympathetic consideration – at any rate by the British Delegation.

I believe that the British Govt. could, if it acted with wisdom and discrection, become the dominating force in the Far East. We have immense interests in China, not less than ten times greater than Japan has got. China is the largest unexploited area in the world at present. Germany had great interests there – nothing comparable to ours, however, and yet we are content to hand over these interests to Japan and in a greatly extended form. A German railway traversing Shantung Province meant that the capital was German, that the Chief Engineer and a few of the Chief officials, Accountant, Traffic Manager, etc. were German, just as on the British railways in China they are British, and all the employés, the station-masters, ticket collectors, etc. were Chinese. A Japanese railway through Shantung Province means:

Every employé on the railway from top to bottom except a few station coolies working even in their case under Japanese red-caps is Japanese.

[1] This refers to Britain's assurance to Japan that 'on the occasion of the Peace Conference' Britain would support 'the claims of Japan in regard to the disposal of Germany's rights in Shantung and positions in the islands north of the Equator'. This assurance was conveyed to Motono Ichirō, Japanese Foreign Minister, by Sir Coyngham Greene, then British Minister to Japan, in a Note of 16 February 1917. This was followed by a similar undertaking by the French Government in a Note to the Japanese Government some two weeks later, on 1 March 1917.

The Railway is policed by Japanese.

There is preferential treatment of Japanese goods.

Every station is a centre for the smuggling of opium, morphia and salt.

So really the Chinese in Shantung are worse off through the Peace Treaty than they were under the Germans. It is difficult to convince them otherwise. And convinced as they are of the injury the Peace Treaty has done them, I cannot, I repeat, believe there is any Chinese who would dare to sign it unless permitted to sign it under protest or under some reservation.

You will notice in *The Times* today a telegram from Tokyo which gives indication of what I spoke to you in Paris.[1] Most significant is the warning of the *Mainichi*, a very widely circulated paper: 'A day of reckoning is coming for those who are not thinking of the welfare of the people'.

The *Yamato*,[2] speaking of a 'powerful anti-Japanese movement in China instigated by a *certain Allied country*', refers undoubtedly to Great Britain. This paper on Dec. 10, 1915, in a contemptuous leader regarding Great Britain, expressed its opinion that '*after the war England's position would be that of China today*'.

I must say I am surprised that *The Times* continues to give so little attention to China. It publishes about one telegram every three weeks from David Fraser. There was a very significant passage in his telegram published in *The Times* on June 23.[3] 'An endeavour is being made', he says, 'to divert attention from Japan by the circulation of pamphlets in Peking making all sorts of accusations against Britain.' The pamphlets he refers to are Japanese pamphlets, written of course in Chinese. This is not clear to the casual reader.

Best wishes to you, and again my grateful thanks for your encouragement and sympathy during my illness. The wound healed perfectly, and I am now almost of a normal colour, but still as thin as a scarecrow.

Very sincerely yours
[G. E. Morrison]

[1] The telegram was entitled 'Gloomy Background to Peace Festivities'. 'The Peace Celebrations', it was stated, 'are the subject of general Press comment and serve as an introduction to the discussion of graver matters, domestic and foreign, which are now facing Japan. The *Hochi* pointed out that the war benefits conferred upon Japan have undeniably aroused jealousies in other countries and provoked a spirit of persecution of Japan in China which is clear proof of foreign ill-feeling.'

[2] The *Yamato Shimbun*, established in Tokyo in 1868, was a right-wing nationalistic organ with Government connections. Among its backers were Yamagata Aritomo, Katsura Tarō, Gotō Shimpei and Ōkura Kihachirō. It held the view that Japan's war efforts had been insufficiently rewarded. The quotation Morrison gave here was from the message from Tokyo referred to in the preceding note.

[3] The article referred to was entitled 'Chinese Militarists All-Powerful. Cabinet Reconstruction'. Morrison's quotation was from the last paragraph.

931. To G. W. Prothero

Sussex [England] 14 July 1919

Dear Dr. Prothero,

Your note of the 11th reached me on Saturday.[1] I will endeavour to answer your question. Energy still fails me. I believe I am making progress, although often discouraged. I am very weak still and much emaciated. Yesterday the Chinese Minister and two of his assistants came down to see me.[2]

No doubt you read in *The Times* of July 11 a letter signed Eugene Chen. That letter is correct and authoritative.[3]

The reason why China could not sign the Peace Treaty with Germany is to be found in her refusal to acquiesce in her own despoilment. China wished to sign *under reservation* and a precedent was furnished her by Professor John Bassett Moore, the international jurist.

The avowed object of the war was the destruction of Prussianism, but to use the words from the Chinese protest cabled to the American Congress: 'The Treaty of Peace transfers to Japan all Germany's iniquitous rights in the Chinese province of Shantung without conditions and free from all charges. This means that whilst Prussianism is to be destroyed in every other part of the world America and the Allies have decided to perpetuate it in China in the interests of Japan.' *Times* 27/5/19.

On March 6 1898 under pressure of an ultimatum China was compelled to cede to Germany Kiaochow Bay,[4] the finest harbour – although at that time undeveloped – on the coast of China north of the Yangtze and extensive railway and mining rights and preferential advantages throughout the Province of Shantung, a territory larger than England, the most sacred province in China.

China is now called upon to agree despite her protest to the transfer of this harbour and of all these rights and privileges to Japan without any condition whatever. There is no Chinese who would dare to sign such a treaty.

War broke out on Aug. 4. 1914.

On August 15 Japan delivered in the form of 'Advice' an ultimatum to Germany to hand over Kiaochow to Japan with a view to its 'eventual restoration to China'. Operations followed and after a feeble resistance Kiaochow was captured by the Japanese.

[1] Not found.
[2] According to his Diary entry for 13 July 1919, among Morrison's visitors that day were 'Alfred Sze, Eugene Ch'en and Kuo [T'ai-ch'i], priv. sec. to C. T. Wang'.
[3] The letter was published in *The Times* under the title 'The Shantung Question'. It attributed China's abstention from signing the Peace Treaty to the refusal by the Peace Conference to modify the wording of the Treaty to allow China to ask, at a suitable moment, for a reconsideration of the Shantung question. This letter was intended to correct the reasons put forward by Chirol, writing as 'a Correspondent', in his article published in *The Times* on 9 July 1919. See p. 768 n. 1.
[4] This concession was made in a Convention signed by China and Germany in Peking on 6 March 1898. For the full text *see* MacMurray, *op. cit.*, Vol. I, pp. 112–18.

In these operations China desired to take part; participation would have meant China's entry into the war with her unlimited manpower on the side of the Allies. The British Minister, Sir John Jordan, acting under the influence of the Japanese and presumably with the approval of Sir Edward Grey, advised her to take no action. Again a second time in Nov. 1915 China desired to enter the war and Great Britain, France and Russia wished her to do so, but Japan on Nov. 23 1915 vetoed her participation. Japan prevented China from rendering assistance to the Allies. This action of Japan should be remembered because during the Peace discussions in Paris Mr. Balfour more than once reproached the Chinese for their tardiness in rendering help and contrasted to their disfavour the more active participation of Japan.

Kiaochow was captured by the Japanese on Nov. 7, 1914, the Japanese losses being insignificant.

On May 25, 1915 China, while still at peace with Japan, was compelled by the pressure of an ultimatum to agree to a series of demands which the Chinese contend are as detrimental to their sovereignty as were the demands submitted to Serbia by Austria in July 1914.[1]

The Big Four maintain that China is bound by 'this solemn treaty' although it was forced from her by a threat of war, and China is asked to sign now a Peace Treaty which accepts the validity of some of the most important clauses of this forced compact. To accept the validity of any clause means the acceptance of the validity of all clauses – and some of the clauses are of the most far reaching kind. How could China acquiesce in the impairment of her own sovereignty even though pressed thereto not by her enemy but by her Allies to whose success she contributed in as great measure as was permitted her.

China has not signed the treaty with Germany. Technically she is still at war with Germany, but this state can be terminated by Parliamentary action in Peking. Parliament declared war; surely it will be legal for Parliament to put an end to the state of war. There is nothing that Germany would desire

[1] Japan, after presenting China with the Twenty-One Demands on 18 January 1915, broke off negotiations on 20 April, having had twenty-four sessions of talks with Chinese representativesw ithout a final agreement being reached. A lull ensued, during which, while the *Genrō* were called in to discuss possible modifications to some of the demands, large reinforcements of Japanese troops, which had earlier been landed both in Shantung and Manchuria as a threatening gesture, were intensifying their warlike activities, and finally on 7 May, Japan gave an ultimatum to China requesting that a satisfactory answer be received within forty-eight hours. China was compelled to give in on 9 May, a day which was observed throughout the Republican period, as the 'Day of Humiliation'. The date here mentioned, the 25th of May, was the date of signature of the Treaty embodying the Twenty-One Demands. The European example Morrison gives as a comparison was the ultimatum which the Austrian Government delivered to Serbia on 23 July 1914 following the assassination of Archduke Ferdinand by Gavrilo Princip on 28 June. The Austrians also allowed Serbia forty-eight hours to give satisfaction to all their demands and though Serbia replied within the set time the reservations contained in her reply were considered unsatisfactory by Austria, who declared war on Serbia the day after the reply was received, on 28 July 1914.

more than peace with China and the resumption of tradal relations with China. Then, or even without waiting till then, China, who becomes one of the League of Nations by signing as she will do the Peace Treaty with Austria, will bring the Shantung case before the first meeting of the League of Nations in Washington in October.

An attempt is now being made and I understand that Lord Curzon[1] may approach Marquis Saionji[2] in the matter to induce the Japanese to consider whether it would not be to their advantage to make an official declaration to the Big Four, or to Great Britain alone, that the restoration of Kiaochow to China will be effected within a certain specified time, and that the restoration will be in such a form etc. – thereby attempting to remove some of the distrust which her actions in the past have engendered.

Mr. Balfour's treatment of the Far Eastern question since he became Foreign Minister has been quite inexplicable except on the assumption that he has been blackmailed by Japan. Look at the dates.

On Feb. 3, 1917 it was manifest that America was coming into the War.

On Feb. 9, 1917, it was manifest that China was to follow America in coming into the war.

On Feb. 16, 1917, Mr. Balfour pledges Great Britain to support Japan in obtaining at the subsequent Peace Treaty German rights in China.

On April 6, 1917, America entered the war.

On Aug. 14, 1917 China entered the war, thereby with the approval of all the Allied Powers terminating all German rights in China. You will read the rest in Eugene Chen's letter in *The Times*.[3]

I may tell you that Mr. Lansing expressed to Wellington Koo, the Chinese Minister to Washington, one of the Peace Delegates, his approval (presumably his private approval) of the Delegates' action in absenting themselves from the Salle des Glaces on June 28th.

I wish I could have a talk with you, and when I am better I will come one day and if it will not bore you, will give you some sidelights on the Far Eastern question.

It is most strange that both the F.O. and *The Times* are so neglectful of our interests in the Far East. We sadly lack the sense of proportion.

Best wishes

Very sincerely yours

[G. E. Morrison]

[1] At this time Secretary of State for Foreign Affairs (October 1919 – January 1924).

[2] Saionji Kimmochi (1849-1940), Japanese politician, at this time leader of the Japanese Delegation to the Paris Peace Conference. He was twice Prime Minister (1906-8 and 1911) and served in various other ministerial capacities under Itō Hirobumi, whose supporter he was. He was the founder of the Meiji Law School, and succeeded Itō as leader of the Seiyūkai, which he had helped Itō to found in 1900. He was made a Prince after his return from Paris, and continued to exercise an influence on Japanese politics as a *Genrō* in his retirement.

[3] A reference to Ch'en Yu-jen's letter published in *The Times* on 11 July 1919.

932. From Beatrice Brownrigg

Northallerton [Yorkshire, England] 16 July [1919]

My dear Dr. Morrison,

I should very much like some news of you? Please let me know how you are? [...]

I should like to know if the Chinese Delegates acted upon your advice in not signing the Treaty? I think they were perfectly right not to do so unless their relations with Japan had been cleared up to their satisfaction – and the present situation certainly does not square with the ideals of the League of Nations!

We are surrounded by 'strikes' up here – strike in the collieries and strike on the North Eastern Railway. The latter is really preposterous, an engine-driver being proved to be colour blind was removed, and so all the rest of the engine drivers came out on strike, and say they refuse to return to work unless the colour blind driver is allowed to return to his engine! You notice that the safety of the public is not to be considered. I sometimes despair of the working man, for four generations of education does not seem to have developed simple common sense.

My love to you and always good wishes

Yours affectionately
Beatrice Brownrigg

933. From Ch'en Yu-jen

c/o Chinese Legation [London] 17 July 1919

Dear Dr. Morrison,

I have just handed the *Times* a short screed along the lines suggested.[1] A member of the staff, who interviewed me, promised publication.

The first sentence reads: 'You once had a famous correspondent at Peking whose despatches were said to be at once a history of China and a guide to British policy in Far Asia.'

Yours sincerely
Eugene Ch'en

934. From V. Chirol

[London] 19 July 1919

My dear Morrison,

I am very sorry I shan't after all be able to get down to Forest Row before I go North this day week. [...]

The rain is spoiling the fireworks tonight, but we have had a very fair day,

[1] Ch'en enclosed a copy (not printed here) of his letter to *The Times*, published the following day, in which he praised the reports by the paper's Washington correspondent on the U.S. Senate's debate on the Peace Treaty.

especially for the procession of which I got quite a good bird's eye view from the top of the Athenaeum. I can't say I feel much attuned to these peace celebrations when there is still so little peace in the world and not much even at home. But I cheered Foch[1] and Beattie[2] and Haig[3] for all I was worth and the fine fellows who stood for so much heroism and for such appalling sacrifices by land and water. Is it conceivable that we should muddle the fruits of it all away?

Kind remembrances please to your wife

Yrs
Valentine Chirol

935. To Ch'en Yu-jen

Sussex [England] 23 July 1919

Dear Mr Chen,

I was up in town to day to see the doctor, and intended coming to see you at the Legation, but I was too tired. I wanted to draw your attention to the mischievous telegram from David Fraser, published in *The Times* of this morning.[4] I wish to draw attention to his mention of 'the iniquitous scheme in course of preparation'.

He does not know the Mongolian Agreements. Outer Mongolia, where China proposes at present to take action against the extension of Bolshevism is 'under the suzerainty of China', being so recognised by Russia in the Agreement by the Russian Minister Kroupensky, recently Ambassador at Tokyo, on November 5, 1913. Similarly by an Exchange of Notes of the same date Russia recognises that '*Outer Mongolia is part of Chinese territory*'.[5]

Bolshevism is, everyone knows, a serious danger to China. It has penetrated from Siberia into Outer Mongolia. China is rendering a service not only to Outer Mongolia, but to Allied interests, in preventing the establishment of

[1] Ferdinand Foch.
[2] Admiral Sir David Beatty (1871–1936), 1st Earl, British sailor. He succeeded Admiral John R. Jellicoe (1859–1935), as Supreme Commander of the British fleet after the Battle of Jutland in 1916.
[3] General Sir Douglas Haig (1861–1928), 1st Earl Haig of Bemersyde, British soldier, who became Commander-in-Chief of the British forces in France in December 1915, succeeding Sir John French (1852–1925).
[4] Fraser's telegram sent from Peking on 17 July 1919 was published under the heading 'Militarist China. Projected Expedition to Mongolia. Anti-Japanese Feelings.' It claimed that Chinese troops and weapons were being amassed at Kalgan ready for an advance on Urga. 'The excuse for these preparations,' the message said, 'is that the Bolsheviks... are threatening a descent on Mongolia, and, Russia being powerless, China must act as the protector of Mongolia'.
[5] A reference to the Declaration and Exchange of Notes by Russia and China on 5 November 1913. China's suzerainty over Mongolia was confirmed in a Treaty signed by China, Russia and Mongolia on 7 June 1915 at Kiakhta.

anarchy in part of her own territory by the Power most interested next to China herself in the maintenance of the integrity of Outer Mongolia. Russia is now powerless to act. China is acting in the interests of Russia, of China and of the Allied States, in sending an expedition to restore order in Outer Mongolia. It is in the interests of the Mongols themselves and to say that 'the Mongolians are greatly alarmed and do not know which way to turn' is a statement which is entirely at variance with the information upon which the Chinese Govt. is acting. It is not fair to prejudice China's case in the eyes of Englishmen by describing this wise act of the Suzerain power as being 'an iniquitous scheme to tear up the Tripartite Kiachta Convention', which, signed on June 7, 1915 confirms China's 'suzerainty over Outer Mongolia' and 'recognises that Outer Mongolia forms part of Chinese territory'.

You must also point out how close are now the relations between Kalgan and Urga. A well equipped motor service in which the Chinese and Mongol authorities are interested, has brought Urga and Kalgan within 4 days of each other. One can now cross the Gobi Desert at 20 miles an hour, where until within recent years the only effective transport was by camel cart, taking 24 days on the journey.

I hope you will tackle this problem quickly.

Very faithfully yours
[G. E. Morrison]

936. To Ch'en Yu-jen

Sussex [England] 30 July 1919

Dear Mr Chen,

This morning I went up to town, partly to see the doctor, who by the way has given me an encouraging report, and partly to see you upon a matter of urgency. I went to the Legation, but could learn nothing of you. The Minister[1] was out at the time, but came in later, when I handed him a letter on the subject which I had intended to bring to your notice.

This morning I received from Dr Prothero, the Editor, a copy of the *Quarterly Review* for the third quarter, July, issued to the public today. You will read the leader, which in the case of the *Quarterly Review* is always the last article, with vivid interest. I draw your attention to pages 253-4, wherein the *Review* demonstrates that 'the tacit recognition of the arrangements (of May 25, 1915) is one of the most grievous blots on the Treaty of Versailles'.[2]

You will agree, I am sure, that no pronouncement by any English public organ could be more important than this, or more opportune, or carry

[1] Shih Chao-chi, or Alfred Sze.
[2] The article by Prothero was entitled 'Peace with Germany'. Prothero was referring to the recognition by the Great Powers of Japan's claim to German interests in Shantung.

greater weight. The *Quarterly Review* is admittedly the leading Review in the British Empire, and possibly the leading Review of the world. It is a Review of world-wide importance. Dr G. W. Prothero, the Editor, is in the forefront of living British historians. He is the Editor of the Cambridge Historical Series, and co-Editor of the *Cambridge Modern History*. He was the expert in history attached to the British Peace Delegation throughout the Conference, and it may be added, for a long time previously attached to the British Government. He is the elder brother of Lord Ernle,[1] who has just retired from the Ministry of Agriculture.

I was obliged to you for telling me that the Legation had transmitted to China at considerable length the speech made in the House of Commons the other evening by Colonel Murray.[2] I fear that the name of Colonel Murray does not carry much weight. No London paper even referred to his speech. Still it was, I think a prudent act to give importance to his comments. Of still greater importance – of very real importance – would be the giving of wide publicity to this Editorial of our Leading British Review. I suggested to Mr Sze that the most economical way of handling a message of this kind would be through Reuter. They would cable it to the United States and to China. A carefully prepared *précis*, quoting the more salient passages would be an interesting news item, and could be sent by them as news, the Legation in that case not requiring to pay anything for its transmission.

I have written to the Editor of the *London & China Express* drawing his attention to the article, and no doubt he will publish the extract word for word, but his paper will not reach China for 7 weeks, and early action is necessary.

I am sorry that you probably will not receive this letter till the day after

[1] Rowland Edmund Prothero (1851-1937), 1st Baron Ernle, British politician and author. He was Editor of the *Quarterly Review* from 1894 to 1898, when he was succeeded by his brother George Walter Prothero. In 1914 he became a Member of the British House of Commons for Oxford University (1914-19), and was President of the Board of Agriculture from 1916 to 1919.

[2] Arthur Cecil Murray (1879-1962), 12th Baron Elibank and 3rd Viscount of Elibank, British soldier and politician, Liberal Member of the British House of Commons since 1908. He was Private Secretary to the Under-Secretary of State for India (1909) and to Sir Edward Grey, Secretary of State for Foreign Affairs from 1910 to 1914, when he volunteered for the War, and was employed in the Ministry of Munitions. He was Assistant Military Attaché with the British Embassy in Washington (1917-18), and on his return served in the Political Intelligence Department and Foreign Office. Entering the Army in 1898 he had served with the British Expeditionary Forces to China during the Boxer Uprising. During a debate on the Treaty of Peace Bill in the House of Commons on 21 July 1919 Lt.-Col. Murray made a speech in which he spoke on China's case in the question of Shantung. Murray argued that, China being a participant in the War on the side of the Allied Powers, these former German concessions in Shantung should have reverted to China. He took particular exception to the phrase in the Treaty 'all the rights which Germany might claim' as the basis for the transfer of the former German rights to Japan, arguing 'how do we know what these are and what limit will be placed on the rights of Japan'. See *Hansard*, Vol. CXVIII, p. 1018 *et seq.*

to-morrow. If I knew of a more direct address, I should be glad to use it. Is there not a Post office near you to which I could send letters *Poste Restante*?

With best wishes to you

Very sincerely yours
[G. E. Morrison]

937. From W. J. Garnett[1]

[London] 30 August 1919

Dear Morrison,

Some recent articles in *The Times*[2] on Mongolia – the last was I think on or about August 10 – have turned my attention to my old love and I have written two articles on the subject which *The Times* may publish.[3] [...]

The world is busy examining and settling the future status of most of its component parts and though interested in several I am interested in none so much as Mongolia. It was so easy in 1907 to predict what was likely to happen: Russia had learnt nothing from the failure of her Manchurian venture: she was busy pressing everywhere along the line from Vladivostok to the Carpathians and no matter how much she was held in check at these two extremities she 'bulged' on the Mongolian and Persian fronts: and in both places endeavoured through her Consular office and banks to obtain a paramount position and a mortgage on land and to oust existing rights. My written warning with regard to Mongolia is still in existence: with regard to Persia you may remember that I was at Teheran from 1911 to 1914 (after Petersburg): there we had an uphill fight the whole time to keep Russia at bay and to check the 'orgy of Russian Consular indiscipline' as the Russian Minister (Poklewsky)[4] himself described it. So long as Poklewsky was there our task was a pleasant though difficult one but with the advent of Korostovetz such a strain was placed on Anglo-Russian relations that had the Germans delayed the outbreak of war for a year the whole Anglo-Russian *entente* would have

[1] William James Garnett (b. 1878), British diplomat. He had served as Third then First Secretary of the British Legation in Peking from June 1905 until he was transferred to St. Petersburg in March 1909. After his term in Teheran (August 1911 – March 1915), he served in Sofia and Tangier, resigning from the Foreign Service in 1920. While in China he made a journey to Mongolia.

[2] Garnett may have been referring to an article by David Fraser entitled 'Mongolian Anxiety. Aspirant for League Protection. The Land of Caravans' published in *The Times* on 11 August 1919, and also to David Fraser's telegram published on 23 July 1919 referred to above on p. 777 n. 4.

[3] An article was published in *The Times* on 17 September 1919 entitled 'Mongol Princes at Home. Walled Towns Impregnable. Fox-Hunting with an Eagle.' It was prefaced by a statement that 'a correspondent interested in our recent articles on Mongolia sends the following account of a journey in the country'.

[4] Polish-born Russian diplomat, at this time Russian Minister in Teheran. A millionaire, it was said of him that he had virtually made Persia a Russian dependency.

been in great jeopardy. Enough about Persia. With regard to Mongolia the Russian intrigues to displace China were more successful and the Russians hoped to be able to eat up the unprotected lamb at their leisure. The gift of independence to Mongolia was a snare and a menace to that simple nomad people. However they have survived the great collapse of Russia. Nothing can put all the broken bits of Russia together again though stable Government may eventually be formed in different sections such as Siberia. What is Mongolia's future to be? She cannot in my opinion stand permanently by herself without foreign advisers. She must lean either one way or the other. She has discarded Chinese tutelage. But foreign politics abhor, like nature, a vacuum, and the vacuum created by the removal of Russian influence in countries contiguous to the late Empire has got to be filled – *vide* the latest Anglo–Persian agreement.[1] Who is to fill the vacuum – whether large or small – at Urga? Siberians, Japanese or Englishmen lent by China? On that may depend the peace of Asia because whatever foreign influences arise in Mongolia or Tibet – and some must arise in Mongolia – ultimately affect India most vitally.

Forgive my butting in on your holiday in this way, but of what the heart is full the mouth speaks (or in this case the pen writes). [...]

Yours sincerely
W. J. Garnett

[...]

938. From Beatrice Brownrigg

Maidenhead [Berkshire, England] 4 September [1919]

My dear Dr. Morrison,

I should much like some news of you – tell me how you are? I hope well again, and recovering your strength.

Are you anxious at the latest reports from China? I can't understand the delay – or the difficulties of settling the question of Shantung. If there is to be any peace in the future it is certain that Shantung must be Chinese. And Japan's claims are preposterous – it is not even logical that because Japan took Kiao-Chow from the Germans that therefore she has any *right* to succeed to the German position in Shantung. If this was to be allowed the whole principle of the League of Nations crumbles – not that *I* believe in the League of Nations but the Conference accepts it as part of the Peace Treaty. It is all wrong that Japan should be encouraged to develop herself in China in any different ways from other nations. If she does it will be to her own

---

[1] A reference to an Agreement signed by Britain and Persia on 9 August 1919, by which Britain was to provide Persia with a loan of £2,000,000 at 7% redeemable in 20 years. The full text was given in *The Times* on 16 August 1919.

eventual undoing. It seems to me a cause of regret that Japan and Greece and America are the three nations who have made a great deal of money out of the war.

[...]

Douglas[1] is in Glasgow a good deal these days – the sudden stoppage of work on warships has created some industrial difficulties in the shipyards. I feel dreadfully anxious at this reluctance to work which pervades the country, and though I never dreamt I should live to change my views entirely and become an enthusiast for Free Trade I have come to recognise that free imports – cheap foreign goods poured into the country – is the only spur which will prick the British labourer to wake up to the very critical situation into which his ignorance and laziness is leading us.

Write to me please and tell me about yourselves. I hope your wife and boys are having a happy time.

Ever yours affectionately
Beatrice Brownrigg

939. From A. E. Wearne

Peking 11 October 1919

My dear Morrison,

Many thanks for your long and very interesting letter. All your old friends were delighted to hear of you and to learn that you were on the way to recovery. [...]

My scheme for the establishment of an international race club is rapidly assuming concrete form. The Peking Club has now come forward with the suggestion that the internationals should purchase the land opposite the Club grandstand, erect there first-class grand stands and other necessary buildings, improve the present course and form a straight on the other side of the course, the two clubs to use the new buildings and old course on their respective racing days. The Club's present buildings would then be turned into a Country Club for the exclusive use of its members. [...]

There has been a lot of sickness in North China this year due probably to the wretched weather. The winter I thought bad but the Spring was appalling and the Summer the worst I've known in Peking. Cholera raged in Manchuria and selected occasional victims in Chihli. [...]

Stevens[2] has just come to Peking. He stayed four days at Mukden and saw quite a lot of Chang Tso-lin, who, he is convinced, intends to declare the

[1] Beatrice Brownrigg's husband, Rear-Admiral Sir Douglas Brownrigg.
[2] John F. Stevens (b. 1853). American civil engineer. Involved in the construction of many American railways, he was best known as the Chief Engineer of the Panama Canal. In 1917 he led the American Railway Mission to Russia (1917–18) and became in 1919 Chairman of the Inter-Allied Technical Board supervising the Siberian Railway, a post he held until 1923.

independence of the Three Eastern Provinces, perhaps under the suzerainty of Japan. For some years now Chang Tso-lin has spent every spare hour in studying the language and the manners and deportment of a gentleman. He is no longer a Coolie. Little Hsu[1] recently has been intriguing with Chang Tso-lin and has lost much of Tuan Chi-jui's[2] favour thereby. The new Premier General Chin Yung-peng[3] is very antagonistic to little Hsu. Tuan and the President appear to be working closely together. This was essential for Tuan, for without real political power he could do nothing against Chang Tso-lin who has been dictating more and more to the Government. Tuan has only about 15,000 troops now whereas Chang has 125,000.

Wang I-tang[4] left here amid a flourish of trumpets to negotiate peace with

[1] Hsü Shu-cheng, at this time Commander-in-Chief of the North-West Frontier Defence Forces, Tuan Ch'i-jui being the Director-General of the Frontier Defence Bureau which was established on 24 June 1919, replacing the Bureau of War Preparation. In this position it was Hsü who forced the cancellation of the autonomy of Outer Mongolia on the Mongols at Urga in November 1919. Chang Tso-lin, the overlord of the Manchurian Provinces, was offended by Hsü's activities which he considered impinged on the territory under his influence. This led to Chang's siding with the Chihli Clique in the first Anhwei-Chihli War in July 1920, which resulted in the removal of the Anfu Clique. Wearne and his informant were therefore incorrect in their assessment of the relation between Hsü and Chang and between Hsü and his superior, Tuan Ch'i-jui. Hsü had intrigued with Chang Tso-lin during the previous year in order to force the hand of the then Acting President, Feng Kuo-chang, in order to have Tuan Ch'i-jui restored as Prime Minister which duly occurred on 23 March 1918. But as Vice-Commander-in-Chief of the Fengtien Army within the Great Wall, a title he had persuaded Chang to confer on him in 1918, he had overreached his authority, and his appointment was revoked by Chang, the Commander-in-Chief, resulting in a deterioration in their relations.

[2] Tuan, having resigned his Premiership in accordance with a previous agreement with Feng Kuo-chang that both would withdraw upon the inauguration of Hsü Shih-ch'ang as President on 10 October 1918, held the nominal title of Director-General of the Frontier Defence Bureau, but in fact possessed the real military and political power controlling the Peking Government at this time.

[3] Chin Yün-p'eng who was replaced as Co-Director of the Bureau of War Preparation, headed by Tuan, by Hsü Shu-cheng in September 1918, was appointed Minister of the Army in January 1919 and became concurrently Acting Prime Minister on 24 September, some two and a half weeks before this letter was written. In November he became substantive Prime Minister holding concurrently the Army portfolio and retaining both posts until May 1920. In spite of his former relationship with Tuan Ch'i-jui, he was chosen as a compromise by the Fengtien and Chihli Cliques to fill the positions he had held prior to the Anhwei-Chihli War, those of Prime Minister and concurrently Minister of the Army. He held both posts until December 1921.

[4] Wang I-t'ang (1878-1946), Chinese Republican politician, best known as the co-founder with Hsü Shu-cheng of the Anfu Club, and for his collaboration with the Japanese Occupation Forces in North China during the second Sino-Japanese War (1937-45). Brought up with a traditional Chinese education gaining a *chin-shih* degree, he also studied in Japan, and in 1911, through the introduction of Hsü Shih-ch'ang, he became a Secretary of Yüan Shih-k'ai. He first came into prominence in 1913 as an organiser of the Chinpu tang. An active force in the Peking Government, he served as a member of the Committee that helped to draft the Constitution giving Yüan life-long tenure of the Presidency

the South at Shanghai. He is still waiting at Shanghai for the Southerners to meet him which they declare they will not do. Tang Shao-yi resigned the leadership of the Southern delegation but it has not been officially accepted. Either Tang or Wang must go.

The Nishihara banks[1] have been lulling China into a sense of false financial security for some weeks by the offer of six monthly instalments of $4,000,000 each without security. Last Wednesday when the Chinese applied for the first advance, the Japs put forward some conditions about Shantung which the Government could not accept, and that scheme is high up in the air. The present outlook appears to give some hope for the new Consortium, for the Japs dare not throw down the gauntlet and attempt to finance China independently. The general opinion is that we are at the cross roads: if the Japs decide on a lone hand they will have a war on their hands some years earlier than otherwise. Their effrontery in Siberia is surprising. They are carrying on there as though they were a Germany that had won the great war and yet it ought to be patent to Europe and America that Japan is putting up the greatest bluff in history.
[...]

Sincerely yours
A. E. Wearne

940. From A. J. Moore-Bennett

Peking 19 October 1919

Dear Dr Morrison,

I heard with very deep regret [...] that you were ill. [...]

China needs you badly – brace up and get well to come back to us. With

---

with dictatorial powers. In April 1916 he was appointed Minister of the Interior in the Tuan Ch'i-jui Cabinet, after serving briefly as Governor of Kirin Province. As the co-founder of the Anfu Club he was the chief architect of the rigged Parliament which came into being in 1918, and became its Speaker. One of the men most wanted for his misdeeds, Wang had to flee to Japan when the Anfu Government was overthrown in 1920, and stayed there until Tuan's return to power in November 1924, when he was appointed Governor of his native Anhwei Province, a post he held, however, for less than six months. He then retired to the Japanese Concession in Tientsin, devoting himself to the study of Buddhism, until he and other known pro-Japanese officials were asked by the Nanking Government to assist in its attempt to block the Japanese advance into north China from Manchuria. But he became instead one of the chief collaborators of the Japanese Occupation Forces and was executed for treason in 1946. His appointment as the chief delegate, succeeding Chu Ch'i-ch'ien, of the Peking Government to the peace conference in Shanghai was opposed by the southern delegation resulting in the breakdown of negotiations.

[1] A reference to the Bank of Chōsen, the Bank of Taiwan, Industrial Bank of Japan, and the Exchange Bank of China, which furnished the loans to the Tuan Ch'i-jui Government concluded through Nishihara Kamezō in 1917 and 1918.

Wilson and you both ill we are indeed left to the mercy of those whose code allows no mercy.[1]

For the news there is none say [?save] the usual riot of extravagant borrowing, with the Japanese *agents provocateurs* stirring up province against province and N. against S. That China should allow it is past all belief, but the student movement shows an awakening of public spirit that is actually beginning at last to force a respect for some show of public decency from the corrupt ones. This student movement is to me the most hopeful sign of all – but it is largely confined unfortunately to the coast and the coast never yet controlled China. I have been in nine provinces this year and in the interior there is an industrial awakening at least worth noting but if Steel-Maitland[2] failed to make the F.O. appreciate it I know I can do no better.

With all good wishes

Yours ever sincerely
Moore Bennett

941. To A. E. Wearne

London 10 January 1920

My dear Wearne,

I have been having a bad time since I wrote to you,[3] going steadily down hill, emaciated to a degree, and losing strength continuously. [...]

The Chinese have treated me with extraordinary kindness, and I am in close touch with the Chinese Legation. Thus I keep myself fairly well informed, but all my plans in connection with *The Times* have come to naught, simply because of my physical incapacity.

The Chinese have been indignant at the action of Woodhead in selling to Yamamoto,[4] the Japanese, for 10,000 Yen, a half share in the *China Year Book*. The great mass of information in this valuable book has been communicated to Woodhead by the Chinese, and they think that at least they might have been approached by Woodhead before he sacrificed his independence to the Japanese of whose policy in China he has been an unsparing critic. If it is not too late, Woodhead ought to reconsider his attitude in this matter.

[...]

Lu Tseng-tsiang has returned to China. He postponed his return as long as

[1] President Wilson fell ill on 25 September 1919 at Pueblo, Colorado. He was threatened with a total physical collapse and was ill for many months.
[2] Sir Arthur Herbert Drummorne Ramsay Steel-Maitland (1876–1935), British politician, Parliamentary Under-Secretary of State for the Colonies (1915–17) then for Foreign Affairs (1917–19). He was to become Minister of Labour under Stanley Baldwin (1867–1947) in the Conservative Government from 1924 to 1929.
[3] Letter not identified.
[4] Yamamoto Tadasaburō, principal of the Japanese firm Shosho Yoko of Tokyo.

possible, for he was alarmed by the publication of his despatches to Tuan Chi-jui, in which, far from showing himself a 'national hero' as David Fraser fantastically described him in one of his telegrams because he refused to sign the Peace Treaty in Paris, he proves himself to have been strongly in favour of signing this document.[1]

[...]

Ever faithfully yours
[G. E. Morrison]

942. From A. C. W. Harmsworth

Bournemouth [Hampshire, England] 26 January 1920

My dear Morrison,

I have thought much and deeply about you since our meeting.

Are you trying all the resources of medical skill? Are not our best men often narrow and ill informed of what has been discovered elsewhere, in the United States for example?

In October last I said *adieu* to Lord Grey[2] on his departure for the U.S. He was very nearly a totally blind man. Last week I saw an entirely different Grey and *he saw me*. Why? because Wilmer[3] the great American oculist at once discovered that Grey's trouble was not eyes, but *teeth*. Grey is younger by 10 years. Our eye men are very angry about this damnably convincing proof of their ignorance. It is a miracle.

Have you been out? Have outings had any ill effect upon you? Are there methods of feeding by skin absorption?

If you continue to debilitate, are there not other treatment and men? I don't know your men so have no feelings about that.

What I do feel is that there is yet plenty of time for you to get well and that your recovery may *be brought about by your own action* in taking your case in hand while you have strength to travel, if travel be necessary.

It may seem to you an impertinence on my part. It is meant only as a demonstration of affection and interest my dear fellow.

Most sincerely yours
Northcliffe

[1] In the telegram published in *The Times* on 12 July 1919, entitled 'China's Refusal to Sign Popular Approval,' Fraser commented: 'Needless to say there have been no Peace celebrations in China, for the whole country is exasperated by the Shantung arrangement. There is vast delight however, because the delegation refused to sign the fateful document, and the delegates will go down to history as national heroes.'

[2] Edward Grey went to the United States towards the end of 1919 ostensibly to consult an eye doctor. While there he sought to influence Congress to ratify the Paris Peace Treaty which Wilson had signed on behalf of America.

[3] William Holland Wilmer (1863–1936), American ophthalmologist, at this time Professor at Georgetown University (1906–25). He was later Director of the Wilmer Ophthalmological Institute, Johns Hopkins Hospital and Professor at Johns Hopkins University (1925–34).

943. To Shih Chao-chi

[London] 30 January 1920

Dear Mr. Sze,

Since I saw you I have had a long talk with Mr. Steed, the Editor of *The Times*, with Lord Northcliffe and with one of their chief assistants. I feel confident that the Far Eastern question will take its due place in our chief paper after this long period of quiescence. Difficulties are very considerable. Messages are long retarded. Expenses are three-fold of what they formerly were. *The Times* were impressed by the messages you sent them regarding the Customs collection, and as I said before they will be still more impressed when they read the results of the Salt Collection for last year. I do hope that Peking will send you these figures, and that you will allow me to give them adequate publicity. For this reason I now write to you again, because, as you will see in the *London and China Express*, the figures circulated in regard to the Salt Collection are many million pounds sterling short of the proceeds actually paid into the Chinese Treasury. [...]

My best wishes to you

Very sincerely yours
[G. E. Morrison]

944. To F. T. A. Ashton-Gwatkin[1]

London 2 February 1920

My dear Gwatkin,

I have read your paper.[2] It is not only exceedingly well written, but it is a contribution to knowledge of serious importance. [...]

There is one blemish in your paper which must be removed. [...] The last paragraph is not only unjust, but in a high degree impolitic. You cannot cast a slur upon the British communities in the Far East. The Japanese are working for the hegemony of Asia. Everywhere throughout Asia is observable the movement against European world predominance. British communities are narrow, often ignorant and ill-informed, but I think they are free from jealousy. They are fine sturdy bodies of Englishmen, speaking generally of high rectitude and of a high sense of honour. They have set an example, it seems to me, to the Asiatic, of fair dealing and of honesty in their business

---

[1] Frank Trelawny Arthur Ashton-Gwatkin (b. 1889), British diplomat, who rose to become Assistant Under-Secretary of State for Foreign Affairs in 1947, was at this time employed on Special Service in Singapore. Before this he had served with the British Legation in Tokyo in 1913, first as Student Interpreter, then Second-Class Assistant, becoming Pro-Consul in Yokohama in 1917.

[2] Morrison seems to be referring to an article which was subsequently published in the *Quarterly Review* (No. 464, July 1920), entitled 'Japan and the War', the name of the author not being given. It was one of several articles in the issue discussing the conduct and aftermath of the European War in various countries.

transactions. That they have resented the unscrupulousness of their Japanese competitors must be admitted, but your words, 'Their (Japanese) sentiments are not particularly anti-British. It is a wonder that they are not more so, considering the ridiculously hostile and jealous attitude of British communities throughout the East towards their Japanese competitors,' would be both resented and repudiated by Britishers in Japan, and would do you injury as an historian. Not only does Japan owe 'some gratitude' to Great Britain, but Great Britain has laid Japan under the deepest debt of gratitude any nation ever owed to any other nation. Japan's position in the world today is due to Great Britain. At the end of the Russian War, Japan was literally at her last gasp. It was England's action in holding the field for Japan that saved Japan from disaster. We will talk about this when we meet.

In the meantime I can only congratulate you upon a really excellent paper which ought to help in your advancement. I return you the General's interesting letter.[1] I do not know what Japanese paper he refers to as publishing virulent articles advocating the expulsion of Europeans from Asia.

Very sincerely yours
[G. E. Morrison]

Enclosure to Letter No. 944: *From D. Ridout[2] to F. T. A. Ashton-Gwatkin, Singapore 29 October 1919*

My dear Gwatkin,

Your kind letter of 19 September found me here! All I can get out of the War Office is regrets that they cannot tell me when I am to be relieved. [...]

I must now cast about for some one who can take on the careful watching in this part of the world. It all depends upon the attitude of the W.O. [War Office] in sending me a G.S.O. [General Staff Officer] 3 who has or has not Japanese qualifications. I took no action until I knew whether there was a likelihood of your returning here. In any case, even if my G.S.O. 3 has Japanese qualifications, there is room for someone who would deal with nothing else.

Cardew[3] has been through. I am sorry that I had very little opportunity of speaking at length with him. He is on deputation to the Far East to study its questions for 'India' to whom he has been appointed Adviser on Far East questions.

[1] A reference to the enclosure.
[2] Major-General Sir Dudley Howard Ridout (1866–1941), Canadian soldier, at this time Commander-in-Chief of British troops in the Straits Settlements and concurrently a member of the Executive and Legislative Councils there (1915–21). He had served as an Intelligence Officer in South Africa from 1900 to 1902.
[3] Sir Alexander Gordon Cardew (1861–1937), British colonial official. He held the posts of Under-Secretary in the Madras Government (1885–90), Member of the Legislative Council (1906–19) and Member of the Executive Council (1914–19).

At the time Cardew was here I had Maj. Piesse[1] (pronounced Peace) here from Australia. He was at one time head of a Branch, similar to our MI5, of the Commonwealth Section of the Imp[erial] Gen[eral] Staff. He was sent through the Far East to study its problems, particularly the Japanese question. Subsequent to his departure from Australia, he was appointed to be head of a Separate Branch of the Prime Minister's Office to study similar questions (but again more particularly the Japanese one), his sphere of action taking in the Pacific. He is now head of the 'Pacific Section'. He is a very earnest man who found Singapore gave him so much to think about that he stayed here a month, and was very active the whole time. He was kind enough to say that Australia admired our industry in threshing and thrashing out the Japanese question, but that's your part. I hope your ears tingle. He told me the Commonwealth viewed the whole question as one requiring constant and careful thought. Apparently Jellicoe[2] has told them that the centre of pressure has shifted to the Pacific and Far East. The new Admiral for the China Station, Duff,[3] with his vigorous Chief of Staff, Henderson,[4] think likewise, and we (the C. of S. [Chief of Staff] and myself) have had long talks together.

Lord Fisher[5] I see writes guardedly and ambiguously, but points to Asia being the future area for trouble. Meanwhile, while we are taking this view secretly, a certain vocal section of the Japanese are writing virulent articles in *Ajia Jiron*[6] [in] which they point out that Europeans *must* be driven from Asia. And there is the same demand for Malacca and Sunda Straits[7] as has

[1] Edmund Leolin Piesse (1880–1947), Australian civil servant, Director of Intelligence in the Defence Department of the Australian Government (1906–19), and Director of the Pacific Branch of the Prime Minister's Department (1919–23). In 1933 he became Editor of the *Australian Law Institute Journal*, and was President of the Law Institute of Victoria (1943–4). He was author of *Japan and the Defence of Australia* (1935).
[2] John Rushworth Jellicoe (1859–1935), later 1st Earl, British sailor. As Commander-in-Chief of the British fleet he was criticised for his handling in May 1916 of the Battle of Jutland during which the British fleet suffered heavy losses. He was removed from his command, his place being taken by Admiral David Beattie, but was promoted to First Sea Lord. In 1920 he became Governor of New Zealand. Jellicoe had come to know Morrison while serving with the British Far Eastern Squadron in 1899, and the following year he took part in the relief of the Peking Legations.
[3] Admiral Sir Alexander Ludovic Duff (1862–1933), British sailor, at this time Commander-in-Chief of the China Station (1899–1922). He had taken part in the Battle of Jutland and was Assistant Chief of Naval Staff (1918–19).
[4] Reginald Guy Hannan Henderson (1881–1939), British sailor. Chief of Staff to the Commander-in-Chief of the China Station (1919–21), he was to become Third Sea Lord and Controller of the Navy in 1934, and was made an Admiral in 1939.
[5] John Arbuthnot Fisher. He published in this year his reminiscences in two volumes, entitled *Memories* (London 1919) as well as a series of articles reprinted from *The Times*.
[6] A magazine published monthly by the extreme right-wing nationalist organisation, the Black Dragon Society, in Tokyo.
[7] Here Morrison commented in the margin: 'The Japanese Expansionists not content with the Formosa Channel as the southern gateway to the Japanese Pacific wish now to push forward and further south to the gateway here indicated.'

been so often expressed. And so we go round the Mulberry Bush, and work in a vicious circle. The *Ajia Jiron* says conflict will come in 10 years, my figure.

Meanwhile there is a feeling of resentment among Japanese because we are sending recent ships to China, with a fair number of destroyers late pattern submarines. The idea of the Navy is that for six weeks we shall be in the air unless they strengthen this Station.

[...] Mikami[1] told me that the Boycott had damaged, and was still doing so, the trade of Japan in these parts, but that they were able to obtain any amount of raw material through brokers. Their attitude towards the Chinese is studiously polite.

We have lighted upon some fresh discoveries of anarchical propaganda among the Chinese. I will send you a note on it, it is too long for a letter.

23rd November. I apologize for having kept this letter over. I had hoped to have written on subjects which I know interest you, but my time has been very fully occupied, and has left me no opportunity for finishing my letter.

I was glad to have met Saionzi and Makino.[2] The first with his secretary, Sadao Saburi,[3] called, and I took the opportunity of saying good-bye to him on the steamer. The local Govt. had taken umbrage at Saionzi's conduct when going to Paris, and rather resented the tone of the Consul General's[4] letter asking for free motors and entertainment.

I detailed Colonel Tyler,[5] a bemedalled man with charming manners, to meet the party and bear lead them, for which they were most grateful. Prithi Chand was placed in charge of his (Saionzi's) safety for which they feared. Saionzi received me on board when he was going and had a spread on deck. He couldn't speak English, but Saburi, a charming man, conveyed my speeches to the Delegate. We toasted Emperors and Kings, and I hear the party was gratified that some one had come to say goodbye. Admiral Takeshita[6] was on board. I was very glad to see him. He too is

[1] Possibly Mikami Yoshitada, Japanese sailor. A Rear-Admiral in 1923, he retired the following year.
[2] Saionji Kimmochi and Makino Nobuaki, two of the Japanese delegates to the Paris Peace Conference, were at this time on their way back to Japan.
[3] Saburi Sadao (1879–1929), Japanese diplomat, a member of the Japanese Delegation to the Paris Conference and in 1921 to the Washington Conference. He had travelled widely in China and in 1929 was appointed Japanese Minister there. The same year, however, while back in Japan for consultations, he committed suicide.
[4] Although Japan raised her Consulate in Singapore to a Consulate-General in May 1919, the Consul-General, Ukita Gōji, was not appointed until August 1921, and the office was in the charge of Yamazaki Heikichi, who had been Japanese Consul in Singapore since January 1917. Yamazaki acted as Consul-General from May 1919 to April 1921.
[5] Possibly James Arbuthnot Tyler (1867–1945), British soldier. He had won many decorations for his services in the South African War (1899–1902) and the European War.
[6] Vice-Admiral Takeshita Isamu (1869–1949), at this time a member of the Naval Council. He became Commander-in-Chief of the First Combined Fleet in 1922, and was made a full Admiral the following year.

charming. Chisaka[1] came down to say good bye to the Governor,[2] a graceful compliment.

I found Makino who came through on 28/8 a much more live[ly] man, who, speaking good English, discoursed on many subjects of real gripping interest. He and I sat and talked for over an hour. I could not help thinking the Japanese were leaving the Conference with a tinge of bitterness and regret. He spoke very freely from the Japanese point of view, and with an insistence which showed that they considered themselves equal to the best, and not content to be dictated to in anything by anyone. He was a real live man. Kimoura Eitchi,[3] his secretary, was a charming man too. Makino had much to say about our delegates whom he thought wonderful men, especially Balfour.

Now I really must close. I hope that we shall get someone to look after the Japanese question, but whoever comes, he will be unable to present the same unbiassed reports as you did.

They [the Japanese] are acquiring many important places, among them St. James in the Harbour, you know the blob standing out near the P. & O. Wharf. It is where our Command Telephone lines go. They are also trying to acquire the Sultan's property on Johore which encircles and will stifle Johore Bahru.

If you get a chance try and get Paske Smith's[4] report about the Japanese activities in the Philippines. He sent it to me quite recently. (The number is 43 Secret, 21 Oct. 1919). I can't give the date. It is most interesting reading, and one begins to see the plan on which they are working. [...]

Yours very sincerely
Dudley Ridout

[1] Vice-Admiral Chisaka Tomojiro, Japanese sailor, at this time Commander of the Second Fleet based on Singapore. He later became Principal of the Naval College.
[2] Sir Arthur Henderson Young (1854-1938), British soldier and colonial official. He was Governor of the Straits Settlements in Singapore and British High Commissioner to the Federated Malay States from 1911 to 1919, when he was succeeded by Lawrence Nunns Guillemard (1862-1951).
[3] Kimura Eiichi (b. 1879). He later served as Counsellor in the Japanese Embassy in Washington, and in 1925 became Director of the Bureau of Asia in the Ministry of Foreign Affairs. From 1927 to 1929 he was Minister to Czechoslovakia and in 1930 became a Director of the South Manchurian Railway.
[4] Montague Bentley Talbot Paske-Smith (d. 1946), Canadian-born British consular official, who served from the beginning of his career in 1907 until 1932 in Japan and the Philippines. Starting as Student Interpreter in Japan in 1907, he held various posts in that country until 1915, when he was transferred to Manila, becoming Acting Consul-General in 1919, the post he was holding at the time of this letter. He was sent back to Japan in 1921, and served in Kobe, Nagasaki and Osaka until 1930, when he was once more Acting Consul-General in Manila. In 1931-2 he was Consul-General in Talien (Dairen).

945. To A. C. W. Harmsworth

[London] 5 February 1920

Dear Lord Northcliffe,

My wife and I were touched by your kind letter of the 26th January, and we have given it much attention. [...]

I am determined to follow the suggestion made to me by you and to go across to America when the warmer weather comes round. In the meantime I am doing all I can to sustain my strength, or rather to check the wastage which has been going on now almost uninterruptedly for several months past.

Since you were so kind as to come and see me I have had my usual ups and downs. Some days I felt much encouragement. Then this uncontrollable diarrhoea would seize me, and I would fall back. I am thoroughly comfortable in this Home.[1] Everything that can be done is done for me. My present doctor is Dr A. P. Beddard,[2] of Guy's Hospital, one of the Examiners in Medicine of the University of Cambridge, a man of independent mind, a well trained bacteriologist, who has made a special study of pancreatitis. He is only too glad to call in any outside assistance.

I thank you again most warmly for your kind and affectionate letter which gave me much solace in this horrible calamity which had overtaken me. I wish to get well, for never have I felt a keener interest in what is going on around me, nor have I ever felt a keener desire to keep myself in touch with the Far East, especially with the Chinese, who, ever since I was taken ill, have treated my wife and myself with such extraordinary kindness and consideration.

You will, I am sure, excuse a type-written letter, typed by my wife, and again thanking you, and with all good wishes

Believe me

Ever faithfully yours
[G. E. Morrison]

946. To W. S. Scott[3]

[London] 18 February 1920

Dear Mr. Scott,

I know the interest you take in Far Eastern affairs, and I am writing to suggest to you that you would bring about a meeting between your City Editor and a Japanese of great power and influence in Japan and China, who is returning to Japan next Saturday. You may probably already know him. I refer to Mr. M. Odagiri,[4] of the Yokohama Specie Bank, who was formerly

---

[1] The reference is to Mrs. Bateman's Nursing Home in Cavendish Square, London.
[2] Arthur Philip Beddard (d. 1939), British physician. A graduate of Cambridge and Guy's Hospital, he was physician and lecturer in Medicine at the latter institution.
[3] Walter S. Scott of *The Times*.
[4] Odagiri Masunosuke. He was visiting England after attending the Paris Peace Conference as an adviser to Saionji, and called on Morrison in his London nursing home.

the Consul-General for Japan in Shanghai, and would now be of the rank of Ambassador had he remained in the Diplomatic Service. As you know he is the Japanese representative in the Consortium of Banks in China – a Consortium which is now in process of reformation. I think he is the most powerful member of the group. His relations with English people have always been very friendly, with Bland in Shanghai, and with myself especially.

Odagiri is leaving for Japan on Saturday by the *Imperator* via America. He is at present staying at the Hyde Park Hotel. His great wish is to see Mr. Steed, the Editor, but I have told him that it was almost impossible to arrange a meeting at such short notice, for it was only yesterday that he decided to return to Japan. I believe Mr. Steed would find it very interesting to meet him, and a telephone message sent to him to the Hyde Park Hotel would bring him along at any time. He is an intimate personal friend of Chinda,[1] the Ambassador. Of course he knows all the inner workings of the Consortium, and he would explain the situation to the City Editor[2] quite lucidly and well, for he speaks good English. In view of the possible great importance of Consortium developments in China, dealing as they will with the construction of thousands of miles of railway at a cost of millions of pounds sterling, I believe it would be to the advantage of Mr. Chisholm to have a talk with him.

In Japan Odagiri goes to meet Lamont,[3] of Pierpont Morgan's, who, with his publicity agent, Martin Egan,[4] leaves San Francisco to-morrow for Japan and China. The American Group has been extended from a body of four New York Banks to thirty-seven financial institutions representative of the Middle West and of California as well as of Wall Street.

[1] Chinda Sutemi, at this time Japanese Ambassador in London (1916–20).

[2] Hugh Chisholm (1866–1924), British journalist, at this time Director of *The Times* Publishing Company (1913–14), and Financial Editor of *The Times* (1913–20). He was Editor of the 10th, 11th and 12th editions of the *Encyclopaedia Britannica*.

[3] Thomas William Lamont (1870–1948), American banker, a member of J. P. Morgan & Company since 1911. He became a Director of the Company in 1940 and Chairman of Directors in 1943. He was also a director of many other companies, including the United States Steel Corporation. His visit to China was eagerly awaited by the Chinese in the hope that it would be followed by a flow of funds which would not only help China out of her perennial difficulties but deliver her from the financial grip of Japan. Pierpont Morgan, the American investment bank founded by John Pierpont Morgan (1837–1913), was one of the chief banking houses in the American Group, which was actively interested in Chinese loans and railways before the Group's withdrawal from the Six-Power Consortium in 1913.

[4] Martin Egan (1878–1932), American journalist. He had served with the Associated Press in various countries, including China, and was Editor of the *Manila Times* from 1908 to 1913. In 1914 he joined the staff of J. P. Morgan & Company in New York and became the Personal Assistant to Henry Pomeroy Davison (1867–1922), Chairman of the Company's Board of Directors. In 1918 he became Civilian Aide to General John J. Pershing (1860–1948), Commander-in-Chief of the American forces in France, but after the War returned to work with the firm as its public relations officer.

The British and American Governments insist that if the Consortium is to have their support Japan must bring into the common pool all railways in China not yet constructed, the construction of which has been granted to Japan, including those in South Manchuria and in Eastern Inner Mongolia. And there is the difficulty! The Japanese view, as I understand it, is that she will bring all these railways into the pool if all railways, the concession for the construction of which has been granted to British and to French are also brought into the pool.

At present the big railway concession of George Pauling,[1] who is hostile to the Hongkong and Shanghai Bank, is not brought in, and in France the two immense concessions extending to some three thousand miles, obtained by the Banque Industrielle de Chine, do not come in. For the Banque Industrielle is hostile to the Banque de l'Indo-Chine which is the French representative in the Consortium, and as you know, the Banque Industrielle has much influence, for its Director-General, or at any rate the most influential of its directors is Berthelot,[2] a brother of the Berthelot of the Foreign Office in Paris.[3]

I do not wish to appear obtrusive in writing in this way, but naturally I take a vivid personal interest in *The Times*, and I do think if you could arrange that Mr. Chisholm had a talk with Odagiri before the latter left London either in the Hyde Park Hotel or in the City Office of *The Times*, the knowledge gained would not be without its advantage in the future. I would write to Mr. Chisholm direct only I am not sure if I am correct in believing that he is in

[1] Founder and Managing Director of the Pauling Railway Construction Company which, through its representative in China, Lord ffrench, was involved in the railway scheme in Manchuria in cooperation with the American Group represented by Willard Straight. The scheme failed, however, owing to the opposition of Russia and Japan. Pauling later conducted many negotiations for railway construction with the Chinese Government, most of which came to nothing.

[2] André-Marcel Berthelot (1862-1938), French banker and politician. A Director of the Pekin Syndicate and of the Banque Industrielle de Chine which he co-founded with the Belgian financier Edouard Empain in 1911, he was active in the politics of Paris where he was a member of the City Council, and was responsible for the city's electrification. Shortly before this letter was written he presented himself as a candidate for the Senate, but was not elected owing to the scandal surrounding the failure of his Bank. A son of Pierre-Eugène-Marcelin Berthelot (1828-1907), the noted French chemist and politician, he was a man of great versatility, being a noted historian and geographer. He had also served as a diplomat in Holland and Italy, Editor of the *Grande Encyclopédie* of Paris, Editor for a period of the newspaper *Le Matin*, and had written about the Boxer Uprising.

[3] Philippe-Joseph-Louis Berthelot (1866-1934), French diplomat and younger brother of André-Marcel Berthelot. As Aide to Clemenceau he had played an important role in the Paris Peace Conference the previous year. Director of the Political Department at the Quai d'Orsay since 1914, he was made its Secretary-General in 1919, a post specially created for him with Ambassadorial rank and which he held until the year before his death, except for a period of 18 months between 1922 and 1924 when he was temporarily removed owing to the scandal surrounding the failure of his brother's bank, the Banque Industrielle de Chine, in which he was also involved.

charge of your City department. Of course if Mr. Steed could see Odagiri, it would give a pleasant impression both in Japan and at the Embassy here.

With kind regards

Very sincerely yours
[G. E. Morrison]

947. From H. W. Steed

The Times 1 March 1920

Private & Confidential

My dear Morrison,

The enclosed from Nagai,[1] the Counsellor to the Japanese Embassy, explains itself. I should be glad to have your opinion on it, if you can give it me briefly and without tiring yourself. I have merely acknowledged it, and have said that as my chief leader writer on Far Eastern affairs is absent I must hold up the matter for a day or two.

Is the *Ishihpao* by any chance a Japanese organ?

Yours ever
Wickham Steed

Enclosure to Letter No. 947: *From Nagai Matsuzō to H. W. Steed [London] 1 March 1920*

My dear Mr. Steed,

The psychological moment to give China a 'push' to accept the Shantung offer of Japan seems to have arrived. We learn from the first hand source that those who are at the helm in Peking are very much desirous of entering into direct negotiations with Japan. The statesmen outside the Government are no less anxious than those who are in power not to let the opportunity slip by. The advisability of accepting the invitation is forcibly advocated also by the newspapers published in Peking, such as the *Peking Times*, the *Ishihpao*, etc. It is significant that these papers give that advice as they were not in favour of the Shantung settlement in the Treaty when the discussion was still in progress in the Peace Conference. They are generally recognised as organs of foreign residents in China. No less remarkable fact is that even in Shanghai where the influence of the South is much felt, foreign papers, such as the *Shanghai Times*, are pointing out the futility of relying upon the suggestion to refer the whole question to the League of Nations, and urging that the negotiations should at once be commenced.

[1] Nagai Matsuzō (b. 1877), Japanese diplomat, at this time Counsellor at the Japanese Legation in London. He later became Minister to Denmark, Norway, Sweden and Finland (1825–8), and Minister to Belgium and Luxembourg (1928–31). In 1933 he became Ambassador to Germany.

Why then, don't the Government take the course of securing the German rights reinstated? Because, they are afraid that some untoward development may follow coming as it did before from the quarters where students can lay their hands to agitate against the decision of the Government. The South would be watchful to make political capital out of any new situation. This is another reason for which the North is hesitating.

It is, however, reported that the sway the students have had on the public mind appears to be on the wane and the Southern influence may not count so much as one might fear. The *Ishihpao* is now reprimanding the attitude of students by whose agitation the disturbances have been generated and much injury and harm was caused to the public. The paper doubts whether their movement is really worthy of the banner they carry in the name of patriotism. Their chauvinistic activities do not seem to the paper to have earned any sympathy and approbation of the sensible people in that country. In short, the paper is strongly in favour of the direct negotiation with Japan.

Though the Government may be apprehensive of the pressure that the South and the students may bring to bear, the Chinese papers have considerably altered their attitude, a calmer and saner consideration becoming more prevalent, no doubt due to the influential counsels the foreign papers published in China are now giving as mentioned above.

Under such circumstances it is, no doubt, more than advisable to give China a push and tender her encouragement from outside the country, much more so from the country which China takes as a disinterested and impartial adviser. I do not doubt that an editorial in so esteemed a paper as yours will have profound impression upon the public mind of China and give a speed to her progress towards the acceptance of Japan's offer. The approval by *The Times* of the views the foreign press in China has maintained will give it the strength and courage in exercising its influence to lead the public.

It is more than two months since Japan's offer was made, (*The Times* of January 29th has a statement) and nothing has since developed officially. Japan is assuredly appreciative of the timely advices your paper gave some time ago and is anxious to be right and just in dealing with China. Japan however must be given an opportunity to do so by a speedy acceptance of Japan's invitation to open negotiations by China.

I should have come to you on Saturday to have a talk on this subject personally. Unfortunately, however, more visitors from my country than usual are staying here and took much of my time. I could not come, therefore, to my great regret. Hence this writing.

We have not received here any official information of the dissolution of Diet. Telegrams from Tokyo are so horribly delayed these days. I shall

---

[1] The Japanese Diet was dissolved on 26 February 1920 following a series of riots and strikes demanding universal suffrage which was opposed by the Government. The Hara Kei Government was returned in the ensuing election, which took place on 10 May.

inform Mr. W. Scott and explain the whole situation upon the receipt of information.

If I can be of any service to you in your writing the editorial above mentioned in supplying you any further information or otherwise, I shall be happy to be so commanded by you.

Believe me

Very sincerely yours
M. Nagai

948. To H. W. Steed

[London] 2 March 1920

My dear Steed,

I have to acknowledge the receipt of your letter written yesterday with its important enclosure which I herewith return to you.[1] Please excuse my not acknowledging it at once, but to-day I was given permission to be out most of the day and I returned quite tired. I will send you a memorandum tomorrow.

The enclosure you sent me is most significant. You can, I think, from it deduce with certainty the conviction that there is grave industrial and political unrest in Japan. Every one of the three papers mentioned in Nagai's letter is either under Japanese control or, in the case of the *Shanghai Times*, is Japanese property. To cite those three papers as examples of the opinion of foreigners in China and of enlightened Chinese requires, to say the least, some hardihood.

Undoubtedly in Japan there is grave unrest. It is absurd to think the Japanese Embassy are not informed of it. Telegrams from Japan sent to the Foreign Office usually come through without delay. It is only since this disorder broke out or became more serious that there has been an interruption of communication between Tokyo and the Foreign Office. That the Japanese in London are being fully informed I have no doubt whatever, for they have in addition to the cable service highly efficient wireless installations.

The Japanese Government are being attacked for their mishandling of the Shantung question. The Chinese boycott has been quite serious and has been a contributory cause to the dissatisfaction in Japan and the consequent disorder.

I will write to you fully to-morrow. My object in writing these few lines is

[1] In his Diary entry for 2 March 1920 Morrison wrote: 'I received an important communication from Wickham Steed enclosing in strict privacy a letter from Nagai of the Japanese Embassy, the extraordinary effrontery of which, asking *The Times* to publish a leader bringing pressure on China, shows how intimate are the relations between the Japanese, our most formidable and unscrupulous trade competitors, and *The Times*, our great national institution whose position should be above all pressure. On getting up I went over to the Chinese Minister and received some information which I will embody in my reply.'

to return the letter which was enclosed in your private and confidential communication.

Very sincerely yours
[G. E. Morrison]

949. To H. W. Steed

[London] 3 March 1920

My dear Steed,

Yesterday I wrote to you a brief note to say that I was convinced that there was serious trouble in Japan – much more serious than we have been permitted to know. For a long time past observers have noticed that a serious change was coming. The fact that telegrams dealing with the agitation in regard to suffrage and the disturbances outside and inside the Diet were permitted to come through, and then a sudden censorship was instituted, is at best an ominous fact. The rice riots in Japan in October, 1918,[1] affected not a few tens of thousands of people but hundreds of thousands. Nothing impressed me more when I was in Japan in January, 1919, than the forebodings I heard expressed by thoughtful Japanese in regard to the future. There had been immense profiteering. There has been an immense increase in the cost of living. All the staple commodities of the people had increased in price three or four fold – rice, chickens, flour, fish, eggs, seaweed – and while there had been an increase in wages, it was in no degree commensurate with the increase in the cost of living.

Another thing that struck me very much was the kind of foreign literature most in evidence. It seemed to me that the book which was having the largest sale was Henderson's *The Rights of Labour*.[2]

But before this an incident had occurred which I do not think was referred to in any English paper, and yet it was of very grave significance. The foremost Christian pastor in Japan, Dr. Danjo Ebina, speaking at a great missioary gathering at Karuizawa on August 5th, 1918, said:

> 'The principles of American democracy had great influence on the revolution of 1867 which destroyed feudalism in Japan. The German system was introduced some twenty years later, superseding these democratic ideas. It made Japan very conservative. In certain aspects Japan even went beyond German Kaiserism and overtook Roman Kaiserism, introducing a kind of Emperor worship.

[1] Following a sudden and drastic rise in the price of rice, which brought trading to a standstill in Osaka on 18 July 1918, and in Tokyo on 31 July, riots broke out on a large scale, in Nagoya, Kyoto and thirty-five other big cities, and in over 250 towns and villages in Japan, involving several hundred thousand people, of whom nearly 8,000 were arrested and prosecuted.

[2] The correct title of this book by Arthur Henderson is *The Aims of Labour*, published in London in 1917 and reprinted in 1918.

'Now Japan has entered the war as an Ally of the great democratic nations ...The greatest crisis in Japanese history is impending. The defeat of German militarism and imperialism on the battlefields of Europe means the defeat of these doctrines all the world over.'

Commenting on this, a Review, widely read in Japan, said: –

'If the War continues, the people of Japan, as distinguished from the rulers of the country, must become more and more inspired by the ideals for which the Allies are fighting, and the result must be changes and modifications in the Government of Japan.'

More significant than the words of Dr. Ebina was the fact that these words were permitted publication in Japanese papers.

While the Paris Conference was sitting, a body of Japanese as you no doubt know, some twenty eight in number, who had come from Japan to watch the course of the Conference, held a meeting and passed a resolution which was telegraphed to Japan, urging the adoption of a Constitutional Government, taking the British Constitution as the model.

Since the Conference the relations between China and Japan have not been satisfactory. The Chinese resented the way they were treated over the secret treaties regarding Shantung, especially the promise given by the British Government on the 17th February, 1917, to Japan to support her claims against China at the subsequent Peace Conference. The Chinese could not understand why a country, that stands for all that is just like Great Britain, should prejudge a case in this way. They have been told it is an axiom with the British never to prejudge a case – to hear both sides before coming to a decision – and it was not until April 22nd, 1919, that an explanation was given to them, and unwisely, by Mr. Lloyd George.

At a conference on that date at which were present Mr. Lloyd George, President Wilson, Monsieur Clemenceau,[1] and two Chinese delegates, the senior of whom was that uncommonly clever Wellington Koo, Mr. Lloyd George explained that at the time when Mr. Balfour gave his undertaking, England was being hard pressed by Japan. The English were lacking in torpedo destroyers in the Mediterranean. They asked for the assistance of Japanese destroyers, and the Japanese made 'a very hard bargain'. Of course Wellington Koo, with the textual memory that is one of the chief Chinese characteristics, made a report of this to his Government. A day or two later Sir Maurice Hankey,[2] who was present, gave a resumé of the proceedings to

---

[1] Georges-Benjamin Clemenceau (1841-1929), French politician, at the time referred to French Prime Minister and Minister of War, and Chairman of the Paris Peace Conference.

[2] Maurice Pashal Alers (later Lord) Hankey (1877-1963), British official and politician – 'man of secrets' – successively and concurrently Secretary to the Committee of Imperial Defence (1912-38), Secretary to the War Cabinet (1916-18) and to the Cabinet (1919-38). He had played an important role in the policy decision of the British Government for more than two decades. Created a Baron in 1938, he served in various ministerial posts in the War Cabinet during the Second World War, from 1939 to 1942.

the British, the American and the French representatives, and this précis was promptly communicated by President Wilson to the Chinese.

Later President Wilson acted in a way which the Chinese could only stigmatise as a betrayal of their interests which he had undertaken to protect. It was for this reason that China submitted her whole case with all the documentary proof she could furnish to Henry Cabot Lodge,[1] and the Republican leaders thereupon gave China the support which she had found lacking in President Wilson. China was then inspired with the hope that her only redress could be obtained from the League of Nations – her only hope of obtaining a modification of the Japanese demands, or at any rate of obtaining a settlement which would be binding upon Japan.

This question has done much to bring about union among the Chinese, for while there is no question that there is a Japanese party in China, the general feeling of the nation has been against a direct settlement with Japan. Dissatisfaction with Japan has been manifested by a boycott which has been in existence now for very nearly one year, dating from the earliest days of the Peace Conference. Accentuated later, it showed signs last October of being on the wane, when the incident occurred in Foochow which gave fresh impetus to the movement, and the boycott has continued ever since.

In the Foochow case you will remember the Japanese Government sent warships to Foochow to make a demonstration in support of the Japanese police who, acting *ultra vires*, had come in conflict with the Chinese students in regard to the Japanese boycott.

The boycott has been of the most far reaching kind. Throughout 1919 a Japanese line of steamers between Shanghai and Hankow on 230 trips carried an average only of 71 tons of cargo, whereas the British line of steamers of the same kind on the same run carried on an average 327 tons per trip. This boycott has seriously affected a very considerable section of the Japanese people who believe that the boycott will continue until a Shantung settlement has been reached by their Government and satisfactory relations with China have been restored. They blame the Government, and hence I think you will find the reason why Nagai is anxious through *The Times*, which has a name much honoured throughout China, to bring pressure on the Chinese Government to force them into yielding to Japan's insistence that the negotiations shall be carried on direct and shall not be referred to any League of Nations. Nagai under instructions is obviously seeking the assistance of *The Times* to divert attention from the situation in Japan and to persuade the Japanese people that their interests in China are being successfully protected by the Japanese Government.

[1] Henry Cabot Lodge (1850–1924), American politician, Republican Senator for Massachusetts since 1893. Leader of the Republicans in the Senate, he was one of the most powerful political figures of the time. His opposition led to the refusal by Congress to ratify the Treaty of Versailles. China had sought through him to influence American opinion in her favour.

That there is much misunderstanding cannot be doubted, nor can it be questioned that there is almost universal distrust in China of Japan. Take this instance for example. Nagai in his letter to you referred to the statement in the issue of *The Times* of January 29th last. This statement was published by *The Times* under the caption: 'Japan's Shantung Offer'. In the third paragraph the statement as published in the foreign papers contained these words, the liberality of which was favourably commented upon by foreign readers:—

> '(The Japanese Government) are prepared to effect the withdrawal (of the Japanese forces stationed along the Shantung Railway) not only when an agreement is concluded but even previously, provided that the Chinese police forces are completely organised and ready to take over the duties of safe-guarding the railway operation.'

I do not know whether it was pointed out to you, but the words 'but even previously' down to 'railway operation' were not included in the communication addressed to the Chinese Government, and when Obata, the Japanese Minister to Peking, had his attention drawn to this important omission, he explained the insertion of the words in the English communication by saying that they were due to an error in the decodification.

When these representations were made to China, Chinese Ministers abroad were asked to give their opinions as to what reply should be sent. The Chinese Minister in London consulted Sir John Macdonnell[1] I understand – or at any rate a jurist of equal reputation – and China was advised to reply in this way: – (1) polite acknowledgement; (2) expression of desire that the unsatisfactory condition of things should be settled; (3) a courteous request that Japan should state the basis upon which the negotiations were to be conducted.

What decision was come to in Peking in regard to this advice sent from London I do not yet know, but I do know that what might be described as the Southern Party, the party whose leaders are Tang Shao-yi, a graduate of Columbia University,[2] Wu Ting-fang and his son Wu Chao-chu, both barristers of Lincoln's Inn, and Wang Cheng-ting, graduate of Yale, declare that the South will not agree to direct negotiations between Japan and China in regard to this Shantung question until Peking has published for the information of the country all the secret agreements entered into between the North, when the Japanese party in Peking was in power, and the Japanese Government.[3] The Japanese forbid the publication of these agreements even though the Peking Government were prepared to publish them.

[1] Sir John Macdonnell (1846–1921), British lawyer, Queen's Professor of Comparative Law, University College London (1912–20), first Dean of the Law Faculty of London University and concurrently Master of the Supreme Court from 1889 to 1920.
[2] T'ang Shao-yi attended Columbia University in New York but returned to China without completing his course.
[3] A reference to the loan agreements concluded between the Tuan Ch'i-jui Government and Japan in 1917 and 1819. The 'Japanese party' here refers to Ts'ao Ju-lin, Lu Tsung-yu, Chang Tsung-hsiang and their collaborators.

I venture to suggest that no good can come by your bringing pressure upon China. On the contrary much dissatisfaction would be felt if, on behalf of Japan, the leading power in the British newspaper world were to intervene in a matter which affects solely those two countries. I venture further to suggest that we can look with equanimity upon the growth of industrial unrest in Japan. The Japanese are our most formidable trade competitors. The struggle between militarism and industrialism in Japan can have only one ending, namely the victory of industrialism, the development of constitutional government, and the weakening of Japan's power as the great aggressive, military power of Asia who aspires to the hegemony of Asia.

During the war the Japanese profited enormously by our misfortunes. They grew rich at our expense. Let them now have their reward. There will be a revolution in Japan as certain as anything can be in this world. Enlightened and progressive people like the Japanese cannot continue under the guidance of a Mikado and four octogenarian statesmen.[1] Jokingly we often say, and have said now for two years past, that the next applicant for a villa at Twickenham will be the Emperor of Japan.

I have burdened you with a long letter. I ought to condense it, but I am still in very feeble health, and even the dictation of this 'private and confidential' letter has caused me some effort.

All good wishes to you. I am proud to think that the greatness which I always knew you would achieve has been won by you at an age when you are best able to enjoy your triumph.

Ever faithfully yours
[G. E. Morrison]

P.S. The *Ishihpao* is a Japanese organ namely a Chinese newspaper under the control of the Japanese. The chief Japanese organ in Peking is the *Shuntien Shih pao*. It is openly Japanese edited by Japanese (Y. Washizawa[2] in succession to R. Kamei). The *Peking Times* is under Japanese control. In no sense can it be called a forcible advocate, in no sense can it be considered as representing any foreign opinions other than those of Japan. It has a very meagre circulation mostly gratuitous.

The *Shanghai Times* was purchased outright by the Japanese from Dr. J. C. Ferguson an American. It has no influence whatever.

The *Shanghai Mercury* a reputable old-established English paper regis-

[1] Only three who were in their eighties in this year could be identified: Matsukata Masayoshi, born in 1835, and Yamagata Aritomo and Ōkuma Shigenobu, both born in 1838. Morrison may also have had in mind Saionji Kimmochi who, though only born in 1849, was one of the last three surviving *genrō*, or Elder Statesmen, along with Matsukata and Yamagata.

[2] Washizawa Yoshiji (1883–1956), Japanese journalist and politician. He first went to China as Correspondent of the Tokyo *Jiji Shimbun* in Peking and later succeeded Kamei Rokurō as Editor of the Japanese Government-subsidised Chinese-language newspaper the *Shun-tien shih-pao*. In 1919 he became a Member of the Japanese Diet.

tered as English is under the control of the Japanese, the Japanese Editor and director being T. Sahara.

Japan has by purchase obtained the support of or has directly established Chinese newspapers in several cities as well as two other English papers namely *Tientsin Daily News* and the *China Advertiser* published also in Tientsin.

[G. E. M.]

950. From G. D. Gray

Peking 14 March 1920

My dear Morrison,

I was indeed glad to hear from you (though your letter took 3 months to come!) but am still more keen to get some news of your post-operative progress. [...]

I expect you see the China papers and as I am rather outside the pale of Chinese political doings I hesitate to write about them to such a one as you! But, briefly, the main features at present are a growing resentment against the Anfu Club and all its members, and an equally strong growing resentment against the Japanese. The students of all the Government Colleges are trying to organize a big national strike and are gradually working towards it, as an evidence of their country's deep feeling over the Shantung question: they do not wish anything in the shape of direct negotiation to take place for they feel that it would only end in Japan's favour. Hsu Shih-chang is not showing himself a strong leader: Parliament is a farce and its opening has been postponed. The clamour increases for the breaking up of the Anfu Club. You may have heard that Dr. Reinsch is coming out as an Adviser at a salary of $30,000 gold![1] The recent Japanese Loan of $9,000,000[2] was a very unpopular one among the populace and was fiercely criticized in the Chinese Press. Sir John Jordan will no doubt be seeing you – he had a most remarkable series of farewell functions and tributes by the President, Premier etc. to his able guidance and help to the Govt. He was feasted every night for over a fortnight and he always made good sound replies, by no means limiting himself to empty complimentary thanks. [...] I met quite a number of Chinese officials while attending Sir John's Farewell Dinners and had many enquiries among them about you. You have made a great name for yourself

---

[1] After his retirement as American Minister to China in August 1919, Reinsch was appointed Legal Adviser to the Chinese Government, a position he held until his death in 1923. Although the latter post was a non-resident one, he made several trips to China during the period, and died while in Shanghai.

[2] The loan was contracted in February 1920 on the security of the Salt Revenue surplus, with additional security for the full payment to come from a loan then being negotiated with the Four Power Consortium.

among them – it's a name that reflects very creditably on us British – among the host of international Advisers of varying competence.

We had a big medical missionary Conference in Peking – over 270 doctors. I was rather struck with the number of Chinese foreign trained doctors who read scientific papers and took part in the Discussions in fluent easy English. Most of them had been in America. As far as the Educational conquest of the Far East is concerned America clearly leads the way. France is also making efforts to attract Chinese students. Our policy seems to be that they can come to England if they like, otherwise they can stay away. Beyond the Hongkong University (which is not going ahead as it should) we British are doing very little and it is going to react on our trade and other interests later on. [...]

The new Hotel de Pékin is open – it is a great rendezvous every afternoon for Dancing teas. All rooms occupied and they tell me it is very well run, lots of our Community dine there. [...]

Ever yours sincerely
Geo. Douglas Gray

951. From W. P. Thomas[1]

Peking 17 March 1920

Dear Dr. Morrison,

[...]

Your salary for January and February being still unpaid I felt it necessary to take some drastic action, so indited a letter (copy enclosed) to President Hsü Shih-ch'ang, and requested Mr. Ju to present the same to the President, if he thought fit. You will see from two notes from Mr. Ju (also enclosed)[2] what has transpired, and now I am waiting to hear the result, which of course I shall at once communicate to you. Am very sorry that so far I have been unable to let the house and the racecourse cottage; do wish I had some definite news of your return.

[...] For the past few days we have been enjoying magnificent weather. Please forgive me for mentioning the fact.

With kindest regards from wife and self

Yours sincerely
W. P. Thomas

[1] William Porter Thomas, who entered the British Foreign Service in 1898 and was appointed Student Interpreter to China in the same year. He was forced to retire through illness, however, in August 1901. Through Morrison's introduction he came to be employed by the Spanish Legation in Peking and was in charge of Morrison's interests during the latter's absence from the Chinese capital.

[2] Only one is printed here.

Enclosure I to Letter No. 951: *From Ju Jen-ho to W. P. Thomas, Peking 11 March 1920*

Dear Mr. Thomas,

In reply to your letter of the 7th inst.[1] I regret very much to say that inquiry from the Ministry of Finance that they cannot see their way to pay Dr. Morrison's salary until a few days later. It is true that they are in a very stringent position and have not paid out yet salaries for February (including myself though I got mine for January a few days ago). Moreover the Minister is not taking up work owing to his contemplated resignation.[2] Really I do not know what to do unless Dr. Morrison directly communicates with the President.

I return you herewith Dr. Morrison's picture which appeared to me as if it were a stranger. I think he must be very weak.

Yours sincerely
J. H. Ju

P.S. You may be surprised to know that the Ministry of Fin[ance] has not paid into the President's Treasury for about half a year!

Enclosure II to Letter No. 951: *From W. P. Thomas to Hsü Shih-ch'ang, Peking 12 March 1920*

Monsieur le President:—

When Dr. G. E. Morrison, Political Adviser to Your Excellency, left Peking for Europe more than a year ago, he entrusted to me the management of certain of his affairs, one of my duties in this connection being to see that his salary was paid regularly each month into the credit of his account with the Hongkong & Shanghai Banking Corporation, and to sign, on his behalf, receipts for the same for the Ministry of Finance. Since his departure the Ministry of Finance has gradually grown more and more dilatory in the matter of payment, and I have constantly been obliged to appeal for the kind help of Mr. Ju, of the Department of the Grand Master of Ceremonies, in order to obtain payment. Now it is nearly the middle of March, and the salary of Dr. Morrison both for January and for February of this year is still unpaid. As Your Excellency is doubtless aware, Dr. Morrison's return from England is unavoidably postponed by reason of illness, an illness which, as Dr. Morrison has pointed out in a private letter to myself, was incurred in the service of the Chinese Government. Dr. Morrison is an old and faithful servant of the Chinese Government, and it is scandalous that there should be this constant delay in paying the due remuneration for his services. Therefore I beg Your Excellency to be so good as to take steps to ensure that the salary of Dr. Morrison for the two months now overdue is paid without further delay, and

[1] Not printed.
[2] The Minister of Finance at this time was Li Ssu-hao, who held the post until 24 July.

also that in future it is paid into the Bank promptly at the end of each month.

Thanking Your Excellency in anticipation

I have the honour to be Your Excellency's most obedient humble servant

[W. P. Thomas]

952. From H. Porter

London 20 March 1920

Dear Dr Morrison,

Many thanks for your very kind letter and for the trouble you have taken in writing to Mackennal on my wife's behalf.[1] [...]

We had tea with Lady Jordan at her house in East Putney (of all places!) last Sunday and met the ffrench's there. He seems to have given up China for good and is head of some sort of issuing house in the city and talks of juggling in millions. I suppose Pauling rather burnt his fingers in China and I rather gathered from Keswick[2] – of the opposition – that ffrench had not been considered particularly capable.

It must be an immense relief to you to be out of Queen Anne Street at last and in the country for a change[3] and I hope it wont be long before you are quite fit again and out in China. I suppose it is indiscreet to say so and still more to write it but I haven't much faith in the new regime which is coming on in China and a man like you will be needed to oil the wheels a bit. I wish I had as much belief in my own service, but I have long been of opinion that we are more or less anachronisms in these days of modern progress. So long as our functions vis à vis the Chinese authorities are practically limited to efforts to maintain by diplomacy rights which were exacted at the point of the sword, and many of which are palpably unfair to the Chinese, we merely retard progress by fostering an attitude of mutual hostility. The Chinese know we are futile and will never fight them again and the time has long since come in my opinion when we ought to revise our whole attitude and try and meet them on common ground and give them a fair deal. Apart from the 1900 business China has never done us any harm and we have lived and traded there on extraordinarily favourable terms. There ought to be more Chinese representation abroad, Chinese banks, Commercial Houses or Chambers of Commerce ought to be represented in the principal European countries – if not by Chinese then by Europeans knowing them and with Chinese understudies who could eventually take charge. I would much rather do that sort of thing than spend many more years of my life fighting *lekin* cases and trying

---

[1] Morrison had written to Bertram Mackennel (1863–1931), the Australian sculptor then in London, on behalf of Harold Porter's wife who had remained in London hoping to continue her study of sculpture.   [2] Henry Keswick.

[3] Having tried various nursing homes, Morrison finally moved with his wife and children to Sidmouth in Devonshire on 18 March 1920.

to cure the remoter symptoms of deeplying evils which are left unremedied.

I am afraid this is a long letter which may bore you, but the temptation of my wife's new typewriter has proved too strong for me. With renewed grateful thanks from us both and with kindest regards to Mrs Morrison from us both

Yours sincerely
Harold Porter

953. From W. R. Strickland

Peking 26 March 1920

Dear Dr Morrison,

[...]

I fully appreciate your remark *re* the advertisement of Salt Revenue.[1] We paid over 80 million into the Banks, an increase of some 9 million over the previous year, some 75 million being surplus revenue (including 4 million from the reserve). Of this sum various local authorities kept 26 million. This is a good result but there is no reason to proclaim that the security is over good. The retention of revenue by local authorities is at the moment a matter of indifference. They do as much good with it as the Central Government and they will fix it up when proper provincial budgets are secured as the result of pressure by foreign Powers on the Central Government. The danger lies in the fact that a single general astride a rider can kill the revenue of a whole Province by levying a tax on salt boats. No one can stop him.

For instance at Kweifu on the Yangtse there are two generals Li[2] and Wang[3] who take between $3 and $4 off each bag of Szechuan salt going into Hupeh. Result Szechuan salt is not coming down. The Ichang money market is therefore ruined and there is no money to finance Szechuan external trade. The Hupeh *Tuchun*[4] then takes a hand and brings in Tientsin salt on his own,

---

[1] In his letter to Strickland dated 7 February 1920 Morrison wrote: 'Towards the end of January I asked the Chinese Minister to telegraph to Peking asking for a statement in regard to the Salt Collection of last year. I told him to enquire especially what was the gold equivalent of the silver collection and what was the actual amount paid into the foreign Banks. I wanted the statement to come from Sir Reginald Gamble as a few days before a statement had come from Sir Francis Aglen. In every way it would have been a good advertisement both for the British administration and for the credit of the Chinese Government.' [2] Unable to identify.

[3] Possibly Wang Tsang-hsü (b. 1888), Chinese soldier, later Governor of Szechwan. He had served for a period as Salt Commissioner of his native Szechwan province. It might also be Wang Ling-chih (b. 1885), Chinese soldier, a follower of Liu Hsiang (1890-1938) *Tuchün* of Szechwan (December 1920 – May 1924 and again in May 1925 – July 1926). Wang Ling-chih had been Garrison Commander of Chungking and was to become acting *Tuchün* (for Liu Hsiang) in 1922.

[4] Wang Chan-yüan (1861-1934), Chinese soldier, Military Governor of Hupeh since December 1915, a post he held until August 1921 when he was forced by Wu P'ei-fu to retire. He re-emerged in 1926 to serve as an Adviser to his former subordinate Sun

but instead of selling it at Tls 4 he sells it at Tls 9.80 a bag. The revenue of Ichang thus decreased by a million in 1919. This may happen anywhere. For two years the *Tuchun* has kept all the revenue and at times has sold salt at Tls. 14 a picul. The Cabinet and Premier[1] are willing to remove him but the President[2] refuses. The Hupeh *Tuchun*'s political views are uncertain, therefore both parties court him for the time being. For these reasons we ourselves are forced to take a hand in the game of politics (which suits me well) and we try to play one off against another and so get a good deal of money. But it is a wearing game and uncertain.

The [   ][3] I was told by a Chinese is now doing stunts to raise money which actually shock some of its oldest denizens.

Still, when all is said, there is perfect security for the present loan[4] and for another equally large, unless the country breaks into Bolshevism. This security is our great *bête noire*. How can we claim to interfere in the salt when the loan is paid from the Customs. Yet, if we do not interfere, the Chinese perpetuate all forms of abuse – gather them on to the foreigners. There is not and I doubt if there ever has been any desire to reform at all. Only compulsion will produce the result, but at present the Foreign Chief Inspector[5] is a suitable Daniel in the Lion's den, waiting for the Lion's dinner hour.

The question now coming to the front is whether when making a loan only the value of the security is to be considered and not the effect of the Administration on public opinion. If the first, then no change in the Agreement is required, but if the second element is important then the foreigners must have equal power with the Chinese, and I hope that Sir R. Dane will not (with recollections of H. E. Yuan Shih Kai in his mind) say to the contrary in his Book. If he does there may be difficulty in securing a suitable foreign Chief Inspector.

Advertisement therefore is a double edged weapon. If the situation is painted too bright, we shall not get the power. I doubt if we shall any how.

All Chinese eyes are focussed on Lamont (of Pierpont Morgan) now in Tokyo or arriving at Shanghai today. The rice bowls are greedily held out for more. The question is 'can Lamont accomplish anything?' If his terms are properly stringent the Anfu Club will run to the Japs for help. Hence, I imagine, Lamont's two weeks in Japan. If he can bind the Japanese in advance, the Anfu Club will be thrown on the scrap heap.

Personally I would like to see the few Hsiung Hsi Lings[6] come to the fore.

Ch'uan-fang (1885–1935), then Commander-in-Chief of the Five Provinces of Kiangsu, Chekiang, Anhwei, Kiangsi and Fukien. In 1928 he became an army commander under Chang Tso-lin.

[1] Chin Yün-p'eng.   [2] Hsü Shih-ch'ang.   [3] Unable to decipher.   [4] *See* p. 803 n. 2.
[5] Sir Reginald Gamble (1862–1929), British employee of the Chinese Salt Administration. He succeeded Sir Richard Dane as Foreign Chief Inspector in 1918.
[6] Hsiung was one of the promoters of the Peace Conference between the North and the South held in Shanghai in 1919–20.

Lin Chang Ming[1] (now on his way to London) is also a good man, I believe. If these two came to the front Liang Shih Yi would get Communications and Chang Hu Agriculture and Commerce.[2] This can't be helped.

At the present the Government is in the melting pot allright. The Anfu Club (Hsu Shu Chen and Co) control the Cabinet and Parliament. The Premier Chin Yung Peng stands alone and the President sits down.

Chin is trying to coquette with Chang Tso Lin, the uncrowned king of Manchuria. Chang Tso Lin is, I suspect, dallying with Tang Chi Yao of Yunnan (tho' this has not yet come out). Tang Chi Yao would like to down Kwangsi (Lu Ying Ting) and Kwangtung *Tuchun*[3] who are in alliance for the moment, and Lu Yung Ting is whispering to Hsu Shu Chen. Honan and Hupeh are intensely strong strategic positions and Hunan is the danger zone. The Anfu Club recently tried to capture the Honan post, but failed and after a slight scrap at Chengchow (the Peking Hankow and Lenghai Junction) they gave it up without coming to grips. The general opinion is that the Anfu Club will be downed after three months, probably by the Students and U.S.A.[4]

Lamont of Pierpoint Morgans is now in Japan and coming to China. He favours Chow Tze Chi and Hsu En Yuan of the Bank.[5] I guess that Lamont

---

[1] Lin Ch'ang-min (1876-1925), Chinese Republican politician. He was at this time on his way to England where he was to come into contact with Fabian socialism. He later attempted to introduce it into the Chinese Constitution, in the drafting of which he was to be engaged on his return. A returned student from America, he was a middle-of-the-road politician with liberal views. His official career was largely connected with the drafting of the Constitution and the promotion of a parliamentary system of government in China. As a member of the so-called 'Research Clique', which supported Tuan Ch'i-jui in 1917, he served briefly in that year as Minister of Justice. His articles on the decision of the Paris Peace Conference regarding Shantung were said to have contributed to the launching of the student protest movement in May 1919. He held no further cabinet post.

[2] Liang Shih-yi was favoured by Chang Tso-lin as Prime Minister after the overthrow of the Anfu Government, but his candidacy was opposed by Wu P'ei-fu. As a result he held the post for only one month (December 1921). The portfolio of Communications was held briefly by his chief lieutenant, Yeh Kung-ch'o. Chang Hu was to hold the post of Minister of Finance from December 1921 to April 1922, and again from August to November 1923.

[3] Mo Jung-hsin (b. 1851), Chinese soldier. A subordinate of Lu Yung-t'ing, he became Garrison Commander of Canton and Waichow (Hui-chou) after the removal of Lung Chi-kuang as Military Governor of Kwangtung Province, holding the post until the Kwangsi forces were compelled to withdraw into their own province by the Kwangtung Army under Ch'en Chiung-ming in November 1920. Prior to this he had served as the representative of Lu Yung-t'ing in the Canton Government and concurrently Minister of the Army.

[4] As it transpired, it was overthrown by the army forces of the Chihli Clique three and a half months after this letter was written.

[5] Chou Tzu-ch'i, who had earlier served as Finance Minister (February 1914 - March 1915, and May-June 1916), became Acting Minister of Finance in August 1920, holding the post until May 1921. Hsü En-yüan, who had been Director of the Department of Audit, was Governor of the Bank of China, having succeeded Sa Fu-mao in June 1916.

will do a business deal with Japan for the joint development of Manchuria and Inner Mongolia. Japan will then modify her attitude to China and the Consortium will go through in the summer on the Wine and Tobacco Tax, with the Salt as (perhaps) additional security. It is dangerous to prophesy. I hope to see you in England.

With very kind regards to you and Mrs Morrison and best wishes for your health

Yours very sincerely
W. R. Strickland

954. To W. G. Max-Müller

Sidmouth [Devonshire, England] 29 March 1920

My dear Max-Muller,

I was touched by your kind letter.[1] [...]

I had no idea that you were still in London. I knew, of course, that you had been appointed Minister to Constantinople, and I have often reproached myself for not having written to you to congratulate you upon your appointment.[2] It is one of the most difficult posts in the Diplomatic Service. Your appointment met with universal approval – the best tribute that could be paid your ability. I suppose no one can tell very exactly when you will be able to take up your duties. Had the post been Peking instead of Constantinople, there would, I venture to say, have been even greater approval. Nothing could be more unfortunate than the selection that has been made for that most important post. British interests are too great in China to be trifled with in this way, and these interests are bound to become infinitely greater. Personally, of course, and socially, nothing can be said against the appointment of Alston, but apart from being a pleasant, amiable gentleman, he has not a single qualification befitting this important position. I have never known such widespread dissatisfaction. The appointment was known as far back as 1916. It was received with incredulity at first, and then with ridicule. The desire of the British communities in China to have the Legation raised to an Embassy was inspired partly by a wish to retain Sir John Jordan, but still more by the hope that Alston would then be ineligible to remain in the post.[3]

[1] Not found.
[2] Max-Müller was appointed British Minister to Turkey, but did not proceed, and in November 1920 was made Minister to Poland (1920–8).
[3] Francis Beilby Alston was appointed Minister to Peking on 1 March 1920, succeeding Sir John Jordan. The British Legation in Peking was not raised to an Embassy until June 1935, when Sir Alexander Montagu George Cadogan (1884–1968) became the first British Ambassador to China. In his reply to Morrison on 4 April 1920, Max-Müller wrote: 'Strictly *entre nous* I may say that I share to a great extent your disapproval of the appointment to Peking though like yourself, only on national, not in any way on personal grounds. I knew that it was coming and did what I could to prevent or at all events to defer it, but as I was supposed to be interested in running for the post myself, I was placed in a very difficult position.'

In these days when thousands of Chinese are studying English, it is absurd to appoint as Minister a man who stammers like Alston, and has such difficulty in expressing himself even in ordinary conversation. The Chinese regard him as a mountebank, with his silly grimaces, his sticking out his tongue, his playing as he himself describes it 'the giddy goat'.

The British Minister ought to be one able to address gatherings of his fellow-subjects – still more to be able to address gatherings of English-speaking Chinese students – and now for four years we are to be debarred from this means of influencing the new Chinese, who are to be the rulers of their country. The Chinese expect dignity and repose in the British Minister. They are not impressed by seeing that Minister get up in the middle of dinner and dance. I speak in this way, and in doing so represent the views of the immense majority of British residents in China, whose opinion is worth having. There is no personal animosity, for no one has anything but a friendly regard for both Alston and his charming wife, but when I think of his ignorance, his weakness, his frivolity, his unwillingness to learn, I am appalled that such a selection should have been made.

Everyone interested in the Far East is specially interested in the question of the continuance of the Anglo-Japanese Alliance.[1] Telegrams from Australia would indicate that the Australian and New Zealand Governments have been asked for an expression of their opinion. The Melbourne *Age*, one of our leading papers, is in favour of a continuance. Personally, the extension of the Alliance seems to me quite inconsistent with the League of Nations. We have now a good opportunity, either of terminating the Alliance altogether, which I am strongly of the opinion ought to be done, or of drastically amending it in our favour. It stands in the way of our better understanding with America. However, there is no use discussing this in a letter. If you are still in London when I return there, I hope that we may have an opportunity of meeting and speaking on this subject, regarding which I have collected a good deal of material and made many notes.

You will be interested to hear that we have entered our boys for Summerfields.[2] My wife was charmed with the school, and your name which you gave us liberty to use, was a passport in itself.

During my illness I have read again, *India : What can it teach us ?*[3] having been able to buy a copy of the first edition, the generous type of which added to the pleasure of reading. I regard the book as a classic. Would that some great teacher could arise, who would do for China what your father did for India.

[1] In the event the Alliance was not renewed, and was formally terminated on 17 August 1923.
[2] In the event Ian and Colin attended Winchester School, and Alastair, Malvern College. All three then went on to Trinity College, Cambridge.
[3] A book by Max-Müller's father, Friedrich Max-Müller, based on a course of lectures he delivered at the University of Cambridge, and published in London in 1883.

All good wishes to you, and again thanking you for your letter, which cheered me in my unhappiness

Very sincerely yours
[G. E. Morrison]

955. To D. S. Fraser

Oriental Club, London[1] 2 April 1920

My dear Fraser,

My wife and I were deeply touched by your kind and sympathetic letter from Harbin, dated the 28th January.[2] It reached me this morning at Sidmouth, by the seaside, in Devonshire, where I have come from the nursing home in the hope that the milder air in the south of England might do me good. Unfortunately, so far the weather has not been good, and to-day is as cold as any day we had in London. Curiously enough, only two doors from me is Wilfranc Hubbard,[3] who was for fifteen years *The Times* Correspondent in Rome. His wife is a Flemish lady, who knew well the wife of Lou Tseng-tsiang,[4] the highly inefficient Minister for Foreign Affairs, who showed quite exceptional unfitness for the post of Senior Delegate to the Peace Conference. He seemed to think that his duties there were to be social only. Other Delegates of China, especially Wellington Koo, C. T. Wang and Alfred Sze, acted quite up to the level of the delegates of other countries.

[...]

Although the information reaching us is somewhat meagre, and in your letter you explain why it is meagre, a good deal of interest is taken in the Shantung question, and the action of the Japanese Government in exercising a rigid censorship over messages from Tokyo, exaggerated probably the belief now widely held in England that domestic trouble of a very serious kind, even revolutionary in character, is impending in Japan. There is much about this that I should like to tell you from the point of view of those at home, but I must defer this to another occasion.

You know, of course, that the question of the continuance, the discontinuance or the radical modification of the Anglo-Japanese Treaty is now

---

[1] Morrison was using this as his forwarding address.   [2] Not printed.
[3] Wilfranc Hubbard, British journalist and author, who joined the Foreign Department of *The Times*, then directed by his friend Valentine Chirol, shortly before the Boer War. In 1902 he was sent to Rome to take the place of Henry Wickham Steed as *Times* Correspondent, and remained there until 1914. He was the author of a number of books, among them *Donna Lisa; an Italian Idyll* (New York 1924), and *Orvieto Dust* (London 1915).
[4] In 1899 Lu Cheng-hsiang, then a Secretary in the Chinese Legation in St Petersburg, married the Belgian Eugénie Bertha Bovy (1855-1926), daughter of General Frédéric Bovy, aide-de-camp to Leopold I. She had gone to St Petersburg as Governess to the children of her cousin, M. Leghait, the Belgian Minister to Russia. Lu Cheng-hsiang and his wife were in fact known to be rather retiring, and while in Peking tended to shun society.

under discussion, and I believe that Lord Curzon, who is under no illusion as to the meagre assistance rendered to us by our Allies during the war, can be safely trusted to protect our interest in this vital question. Personally I take the view that the Treaty ought to come to an end. It has served its purpose in the interests of both countries, and its continuance is quite inconsistent with the existence of a League of Nations. [...]

I should think it certain that the Alliance will be continued, although surely with modifications. I understand that both the War Office and the Admiralty are in favour of its continuance, and to judge from the tone of the Australian papers I would hazard the guess that the Colonial Department will also be in favour, for they have apparently asked for the opinions of the Overseas Governments.

Now I am going to tell you something about myself. For just over one year I have had an appalling time of misery. It has been like a nightmare to my wife and to myself. I was taken ill on the 25th March, 1919, when on my way over from Paris, attacked with acute infective jaundice, which led to many complications, and required me to undergo an operation, the opening of the abdomen of exceptional severity. It was thought I had cancer, and I was prepared for death, but the operation disclosed that my condition, though grave enough, was not malignant. Since that operation on the 2nd June I have gone steadily down hill – have spent months in nursing homes – have been subjected to experimental treatment at the hands of many specialists. Now I have left the last nursing home, and have come to the seaside, weighing round about 7 stone 10 lbs, weak and emaciated to a degree past belief. Lying in bed this morning, I received your kind letter, offering to help me in Peking, and I am really deeply grateful to you. There is nothing that I know of that can be done for me in Peking. W. P. Thomas has been looking after my affairs with extraordinary devotion and solicitude. Naturally I have found my income shrinking, but a material loss of that kind is insignificant compared with this disastrous sapping of my life's energy. I came home with everything that a man could wish for, and even now I have everything that a man could wish for except health. My salary in Peking has fallen to about Tls. 750 a month, and my house rent is 250 dollars a month plus the wages of my servants. Naturally no one will take my house at a rent which, expressed in sterling, is so very high a one, but I am paying 250 dollars a month for the place. The improvements I put into it were worth 150 dollars a month, and I ask for the place furnished only 250 dollars a month. If you would be so kind as to look round and see my house, I should be much obliged. I nurse the hope that I may be able to return to China, leaving Vancouver by the *Empress of Russia* on July 29th. I have felt a little stronger during the last two weeks, and I do hope that I may be able to get across to Canada on or about the 15th of June.

Ever faithfully yours
[G. E. Morrison]

956. To Hester J. Hart[1]

Sidmouth [Devonshire, England] 7 April 1920

Dear Lady Hart,

Your letter dated March 31st was only delivered this morning. It had gone to the Hotel, and had there been forwarded to a Mrs Morrison who lives at Exeter, and by her had been sent back to the hotel.

I shall be only too glad to do what I can to help you. In my opinion far the best man you could get to address the Asiatic Society at Oxford would be Mr Eugene Ch'en. He is a man of exceptional gifts. He is an ardent and patriotic Chinese, a pure Chinese although born in Trinidad, and not speaking Chinese, but he has a mastery over English which is quite exceptional. During the Paris Conference he rendered exceptional services to the Chinese Peace Delegation, and he has since been active in keeping informed American and other public opinion in regard to political questions in the Far East. I do not know whether this idea would commend itself to you, but personally I think he would be the best man you could get. Some years ago he addressed the Central Asian Society. If you like, I will communicate with Eugene Ch'en, but I will wait to hear from you first. I am not quite sure whether he is still in London.

Your kind message gave me much pleasure. Unfortunately the weather at the seaside has been as severe as it was in London.

All kind remembrances

Very sincerely yours
[G. E. Morrison]

957. From J. N. Jordan

London 26 April 1920

My dear Morrison,

I got your address from McLeavy Brown[2] to-day and wish merely to write a word to assure you that I have felt a very sincere sympathy for you and Mrs Morrison in your illness. Brown tells me that you are mending and that you have definitely decided to start for China in June – which is very encouraging and cheering news. I do hope that the improvement will continue and that you will soon be yourself again.

I returned about ten days ago but was laid aside by a cold for part of the time. It was a big wrench to say good-bye to China and to part with so many friends and familiar surroundings but the break had to come some time. I can never forget all the kindness and consideration I received from the British communities in China and from Chinese of all classes from the highest to the lowest.

Very little interest seems to be taken in the Far East in this country and the

[1] Hester Jane Hart, *née* Bredon, who in 1866 married Robert Hart, then Inspector-General of the Imperial Chinese Maritime Customs.
[2] At this time Counsellor at the Chinese Legation in London.

affairs of places like Torsken[1] attract far more attention in the Press than China does. But China will come into her own sooner or later.

Pray remember us most kindly to Mrs Morrison and believe me

Yours sincerely
J. N. Jordan

958. To G. D. Gray

Sidmouth [Devonshire, England] 4 May 1920

My dear Gray,

This morning I had the great pleasure of receiving your long and interesting letter of March 14th, telling me the news of Peking and of my old and faithful boy. But in some measure your letter astonished me. Who could have made the mistake I do not know, but a message was sent not only to China, but to Australia and India, saying that I had undergone another operation, gladly though I would incur the risk if thereby health could be restored to me.

[...][2]

Sir John Jordan has arrived in England, and I heard from him a few days ago. A few days after his arrival, *The Times* published a panegyric of him, written by David Fraser,[3] curiously unbalanced, for if he were such an immense authority in China, why did he accomplish so little. *His policy of Anglo-German co-operation, which was first broken down by the Crisp Loan, was singularly unwise and shortsighted. His pusillanimity kept China out of the War* for two years. His apathy kept the Deutsch–Asiatische Bank going full swing ahead until the exposure in the London *Times* of October, 1918;[4] and now he withdraws from China, having settled nothing except the Opium Agreement, and the only success he had was the appointment of Sir Richard Dane as head of the Salt, such an appointment having been rendered possible only because of the Crisp Loan, which he in the interests of Anglo-German co-operation, had vehemently attacked.

Quite close to where I am there is living Sir Ernest Satow. He has been twice to see me, and I have been over to see his beautiful place. I can imagine no more delightful old age. He is in good health, still active mentally and physically. He has a beautiful house, which I believe you have visited – a

---

[1] A port in northern Norway.
[2] Morrison's detailed description of his illness is omitted.
[3] The 'panegyric' refers to an article which appeared in *The Times* on 28 April 1920, written by 'Our Own Correspondent' in Peking, entitled 'Sir John Jordan. Our Greatest Specialist in China.' It read in part: 'His influence here has been unique among Chinese as well as Europeans. All had confidence in him, for they trusted his knowledge and ability and believed in his sincerity ... Close, often fierce critic of the Chinese officials, he has nevertheless won their respect in a greater measure than any other foreigner has.'
[4] A reference to an article published in *The Times* on 30 October 1918 entitled 'German Influence in China. Bank not Liquidated.' Morrison had contributed to the exposure.

delightful garden. He is surrounded by books, and he is doing literary work, which occupies pleasantly several hours a day. He has just finished the record of his first five years in Japan.[1] When I saw him the other day, he was studying Russian. He spoke very kindly about you. [...] I had an impression that all of you in the Legation were receiving compensatory allowances, and I am very sorry indeed to hear that this is not so in your case. You could make any amount more in private practice than ever you can in the Government Service. A Shanghai doctor here now, Hanwell, lately retired, tells me that if he were in Shanghai at the present time, he would, after paying all his expenses, be in a position to remit to England £5,000 *per annum*.

I would like the old Boy[2] to come and meet us in Shanghai. I would dearly like to see the old fellow again, and I can imagine the extremely depressing speech which he will make when he sees me so wasted. I will arrange with Thomas about giving him money.

All good wishes from my wife and myself to you and Mrs. Gray and Anna
Believe me

Ever faithfully yours
[G. E. Morrison]

959. To J. N. Jordan

Sidmouth [Devonshire, England] 6 May 1920

My dear Sir John,

Both my wife and I highly appreciated your kind note of April 26th. We thank you very much.

Although I have definitely decided to return to China, I am in such a state of emaciation and weakness that I am often despondent as to whether I shall ever be able to get there. Unhappily, there is no mending in my case. [...] I underwent a dreadful operation on June 2nd, and although I recovered from the actual operation, proving myself indeed to be endowed with unusual powers of resilience, I have not made any recovery from the disease itself, and there is no use blinking the fact that I am living on the very verge of death. [...]

Since I have been associated with Peking for so many years, since my property is there, and my interests are there, I have a great longing to go back, and this longing is shared by my wife, who thinks, as I think, that climatic conditions and our comfortable home in Peking must have a better effect upon me than the cold, raw and severe climate of England.

I have been under many doctors. Generally they agree as to my having pancreatitis, but methods of treatment vary in a way that show me how inexact still is our scientific knowledge of this intractable disease. So there I

---

[1] The book was published after Morrison's death, under the title *Diplomat in Japan. The inner history of the critical years in the evolution of Japan when the ports were opened and the monarchy restored* (London 1921). [2] Sun T'ien-lu, Morrison's head servant.

have told you all about myself, and this will explain to you why I am dictating my letter to you and not writing to you in my own hand.

You probably know that Sir Ernest Satow lives quite close to here, at Ottery St. Mary. I can imagine no happier old age than that of Sir Ernest. [...]

Here in Sidmouth itself we have several men associated with China. Sir Pelham Warren[1] often looks in to see me. He also has preserved his health and vigour, and I find it curiously interesting talking to him about his experiences in Formosa, and that most interesting experience of all when in August, 1884, he witnessed the bombardment of the Min Forts by Admiral Courbet.[2] He of course feels the silver exchange very much, but he tells me that his son, who was in Peking during the last few years, has a salary equivalent now to £3,500 a year. How fortunate are those men who are paid in silver! Aglen's pay last year was well over £25,000. Men like Cox[3] and Ricketts[4] have salaries nearer £7,000 a year than £6,000. For a considerable time Sir Reginald Gamble has been drawing an income at the rate of £16,000 a year, and his assistant, Strickland, at the rate of £6,000. A gardener, like Purdom,[5] who in England was getting £2.5 a week, was for a long time drawing at the rate of £2,250 a year, and so on through hundreds of employees of the Chinese Government. I, on the other hand, paid in gold, have in the matter of exchange lost enormously. That has been the least of my worries.

[...]

I have seen a good deal of *The Times* people. Steed, the present editor, is a friend of mine of many years' standing. Lord Northcliffe wished me to go over to America some time ago and try whether the American doctors might not succeed where our own doctors have failed. I see a good deal of C. W. Campbell,[6] who appears to have done excellent work in the Foreign Office. One day, to my pleasure, Cockburn[7] came to see me, and curiously enough,

---

[1] Pelham Laird Warren (1845–1923), British consular official in China, retiring from the service as Consul-General in Shanghai (1901–11). He was Acting Consul in Taiwan in 1883–4, during the Sino-French War, and again in 1886.

[2] Amédée-Anatole-Prosper Courbet (1827–85), French sailor. In 1883, he was Commander of the French fleet in Indo-China, and his attack on Hué brought about the surrender by the Emperor of Annam. He was then appointed French Commander-in-Chief in Tonkin, and fought against the Chinese army under Liu Yung-fu at Sontay. He led the French naval bombardment of Foochow, the occupation of Keelung in Formosa and the occupation of Pescadores. He died soon after peace was signed.

[3] A. G. Cox, British engineer-in-chief of the Canton–Hankow Railway.

[4] D. Poyntz Ricketts, British engineer-in-chief of the Chinese Northern Railways.

[5] William Purdom, British Adviser in the Chinese Bureau of Forestry.

[6] Charles William Campbell, who had retired in 1911 from the British Consular Service as Chinese Secretary in the British Legation in Peking, was at this time employed in the Foreign Office as a Temporary Clerk (1918–24).

[7] Henry Cockburn, former Chinese Secretary in the British Legation in Peking, where Morrison had come to know him. He retired as British Consul-General in Korea and was at this time living in England.

in one week I met three of our Military Attaches, Pereira, Willoughby[1] and Ducat,[2] and was in communication with General Brown,[3] who would have come to see me could I have remained a day or two longer.

I am leaving for China with my family on June 11th, sailing from Liverpool for Quebec. We will spend one month in Canada, and catch the *Empress of Russia* from Vancouver on July 29th. I return to London on Thursday, June 3rd, and will stay at the Oriental Club, Hanover Square. Perhaps you will come there one day and take lunch with me.

With kindest regards from us both to you and Lady Jordan

Very sincerely yours
[G. E. Morrison]

960. From C. R. Crane[4] to Jennie Morrison

S.S. *Nanking* 8 May 1920

My dear Mrs Morrison,

Your letter[5] came just as we were leaving – Thank you! I hope that you received my message sent through the Whytes.[6] I cannot get at all reconciled

[1] Brig.-Gen. Michael Edward Willoughby (1864–1939), British soldier. He was with the British Expeditionary Forces in China in 1900–1, and in 1907 returned to the British Army station in North China (1907–8). In 1909 he became British Military Attaché in Peking. He later served in Sikkim and Tibet and was in Special Service in France after the outbreak of the European War.
[2] Col. Charles Merewether Ducat (1860–1934), British soldier. He was with the British Expeditionary Forces sent to China in 1900–1, and was British Military Attaché in Peking from 1902 to 1905. He later served in India and retired in 1913.
[3] Maj.-Gen. George Fitzherbert Browne (1851–1935), British soldier, Military Attaché in Peking from 1896 to 1902. In 1910 he became a Colonel in the Northamptonshire Regiment, and retired in 1913.
[4] Charles Richard Crane (1858–1939), American businessman and diplomat. A supporter of President Wilson, he was appointed by him American Minister to China succeeding Paul Reinsch, and attended the Paris Peace Conference before taking up his post in Peking. While in the French capital he was a frequent companion of Morrison and his wife. As Chairman of the Finance Committee for the election of Wilson in 1912, Crane had been Wilson's choice as American Minister to China on Wilson's becoming President in 1913, but the appointment was revoked because of Crane's indiscretion in press interviews before leaving America, and Paul Reinsch, whom he was now succeeding, was appointed in his place. Crane had only a very short term in Peking, because no sooner had he arrived than the Republicans won the election and Jacob Gould Sherman (1854–1942), the President of Cornell, was selected by President Harding (1865–1923) as the new Minister to China in June 1921.   [5] Not found.
[6] Alexander Frederick Whyte (1883–1970), British journalist and politician. He was founder and joint Editor of *The New Europe* (1917–18) and Liberal Member of the British House of Commons (1910–18). In 1919 he covered the Paris Peace Conference for the London *Daily News*. He was President of the Legislative Assembly of India (1920–25) before becoming Political Adviser to the Nationalist Government in Nanking (1929–32). He was the author of *Asia in the Twentieth Century* (London 1926), *China and Foreign Powers* (London 1927) and *The Future of East and West* (London 1932). The message referred to here has not been found.

to going to Peking without hope of finding the Morrisons there. They are the most essential element in the composition I have pictured there. We have been very warmly received on the way by both Americans and Chinese in San Francisco and Honolulu. This voyage across the Pacific is of course the finest sea voyage in the world and Mrs Crane and I are thoroughly enjoying it. I shall go quite directly to Peking, possibly stopping a day at Shanghai and a day at Nanking en route. If you and Ernest are not coming out soon, please ask him to prepare me a little 'who's who' of wise men whom he trusted for me to consult with when I find the water getting too deep. Our Embassy at London will see that the letter gets to me intact.

But please also communicate with me yourself once in a while and let me have the family news. If you decide to go to Peking I shall be on the lookout for you and give you the warmest kind of welcome.

Affectionate greetings to you, everyone, especially to Ernest

Yours always sincerely
Charles R. Crane

961. From F. Sherfesee

Peking 12 May 1920

Dear Dr. Morrison,

It was a very great pleasure to all your friends in Peking to see the recent cablegram, published in all the papers in China, telling of your convalescence and of your intention to return during the present year to Peking – which we like to think that you regard as your permanent home. It would be futile for me to attempt to tell you how very greatly and constantly you have been missed, and what a wide gap your and Mrs. Morrison's absence has made, and continues to make, in the very extensive circle of your friends, Chinese and foreign: and I can assure you that no one returning to Peking could receive a more sincere and spontaneous welcome that yours will be when you arrive. The first cabled news of your illness came as a very depressing shock both to your personal friends and, almost equally, to all who had at heart the success of China's cause in Paris – and our sympathy for China was second only to that we felt for you yourself and for Mrs. Morrison.

I'm afraid that, on your return, you will find little cause for optimism in the political situation here – unless some very sudden change for the better takes place in the meantime. I would say that the political and financial situation – and the international situation also – could not be worse, had we not all thought so a year ago, and then seen it deteriorate steadily – always to lower levels. The gradual process of political and social evolution – or the quicker and more drastic changes brought about by revolution – seem the only things to look forward to – and as to the latter, there are no important signs on the horizon. There is, of course, enormous and very wide-spread discontent, evidencing itself chiefly in the student movement – which, however, at least ostensibly and superficially seems to have been more or less cowed by the all-powerful military; but even the students' demands seem more negative than positive, and so far there is apparent no strong, definite force with a positive program to insist upon a real change for the better. The *Tuchuns* have ceased to attempt to exact money from Peking – knowing its hopelessness for Peking has been sucked dry – and support themselves and their troops from the unlucky provinces they govern in true feudal-baron style: and Peking, on its side, receives not a cent from any province except a pittance from Shantung, eking out a disgraceful livelihood on the salt surplus, with perhaps an occasional windfall of part of a Japanese loan, or, chiefly, from usurious borrowings from native money-lending banks. Its prestige is as low as its finances.

Just as I was writing the above I received a telephone message from Mr. Thomas telling of your expected return on the July *Empress of Russia*. I am *delighted* to hear it, and I congratulate you most heartily on the recovery such news implies. Any attempt to send you political or personal news from Peking would now be ridiculous, partly because you will soon find for yourself that my political prognostications are, I'm afraid, like most other foreigners', all wrong.

I hope that you will all have a wholly delightful voyage, and I look forward with the keenest pleasure to seeing you all again within a few weeks.

Very sincerely
Forsythe Sherfesee

962. To W. P. Thomas

[Sidmouth, Devonshire, England] 14 May 1920

My dear Thomas,

I have to acknowledge the receipt of your letters dated March 17th, March 24th, March 26th and March 29th.[1] There was a great deal of interest in your letters. The letter you sent to the President on March 12th[2] was an admirable letter, exceedingly well expressed, and appropriate for the occasion.

[...]

Please disabuse yourself of the idea that Sun Tien-lu[3] abused you in any way. If he did, I have not heard a word of it. It is unlikely that he would abuse one who was so loyally helping the master with whom he had served since February 1898. No doubt my servants have squeezed me, but 'squeeze'

---

[1] Thomas' letter of 17 March is printed as Letter No. 951. Those of 24, 26 and 29 March are not printed.   [2] Printed as Enclosure II to Letter No. 951.
[3] Morrison's head servant.

is permissible in China, and so long as it does not exceed five per cent is permitted by the Catholic Church, as you doubtless know, who have recognised it as an ineradicable custom that has come down from the remotest antiquity, and speaking from an experience of both hemispheres, I would say that it is nothing like as great in China as it is in England and in France.[1] Here the squeezing, the corruption, the shirking of labour, really make one despair of the future of the country.

[...]

Ever sincerely and gratefully yours
[G. E. Morrison]

963. To Jennie Morrison

[undated]

My dearest Jennie,

I was lying in the easy chair in the court yard thinking of you always thinking of you when your kind note came. It is impossible that sometimes I shall not feel dispirited when I think how unworthy I am of you and when I contrast your bright young life with what I see of myself. Oh God how I love you. I never knew before what it was to love and worship as I love and worship you my dear. What can I do to make you happy, that is all I think about, and make you contented and show you my devotion.

May God Bless you always my dear and shield you and guard you from all harm and give you all the happiness possible in the world.

Ever your loving
Ernest

---

[1] Catholic converts had a monopoly of positions on the household staffs of foreign residents in Peking, a tradition that dated from the establishment of the Jesuit Mission in Peking in the seventeenth century. Such positions also tended to be hereditary.

June 1920 – December 1920

Morrison died on 30 May 1920. He was 58 years old. His last hours are described below in a letter from his wife, Jennie, to his mother, Rebecca Morrison.

Jennie Morrison was 31 when her husband died. She was left with three children, Ian, Alastair and Colin, aged seven, five and three. Unlike her husband, she was no great lover of China or the Chinese way of life, but she was a remarkable woman.

Of her, Morrison wrote in his Diary exactly a week before his death and on the eighth anniversary of their engagement in 1912: 'Seven years of happiness for Jennie and one year of tribulation borne with exemplary patience and devotion.'

This devotion was to continue after his death. The correspondence she has left behind reveals her indefatigable efforts to make of her husband's papers something worthy of his name. But before she could realise this, she succumbed to overwhelming grief over her husband's death and died, after a brief illness, in 1923. She had married, as a fortune-teller had predicted, a famous man. Now she died, also as the fortune-teller had predicted, in her 34th year. Her eldest child was then not yet ten.

Of the three children, Ian, born in 1913, was to die in 1953 in Korea covering the war there for *The Times*. Alastair, born in 1915, became an administrator and student of Malaysia. He later joined the Australian Government in Canberra after many years with the British Colonial Service in Sarawak. Colin, the youngest of the three, was born in 1917. He became a schoolmaster at Winchester in England. Morrison's references to his wife and children, and the notes and drawings they sent him during his long illness, are among the most touching documents in the whole of the Morrison Papers.

Of the China Morrison left behind, no more needs to be said. Included at the end of the Volume, however, is an exchange in a protracted correspondence recording the difficulties the Chinese Government had in paying the three months' salary it offered to Jennie Morrison by way of condolence. For a government which Morrison had spent the best years of his life helping to extricate from perennial financial embarrassment, there can be no more fitting or sadder final comment.

964. From Jennie Morrison to Rebecca Morrison[1]

London 20 June 1920

Dear Mrs Morrison,

Forgive me for not having written earlier to you, but I have felt too crushed and ill to attempt it, and I felt I could think better and tell you all you wished to know if I waited for a little. Your grief must be as deep and bitter as mine, and I long to be with you. We were the dearest beings to him in this world, and only we can truly realise what a truly great and noble man the world has lost. For him we cannot grieve. He had suffered too much, and Death came as a Deliverer. Indeed I was grateful when the dear Spirit was allowed to leave the poor, tortured body. We could not have wished him to live – it was too inexpressibly sad to see him suffering so. But we had so hoped that he might regain sufficient strength to return to his beloved Peking, and, if he had to die, that he might die in his own home amid the old surroundings and friends that he had so loved. But Fate decreed otherwise, and I feel that perhaps I have been spared a worse ordeal and he worse suffering if he had died at sea or in the train.

I feel that great, noble Mind and Spirit cannot be quenched, and that he will adventure splendidly in the Beyond and carry on all his activities and interests. I feel too he must go on loving his dear ones, and try to help and guide them. But of course for us there is the terrible loneliness and desolation, and the *having* to go on without him. Even the fact of having faced all this for so long does not seem to make the pain less, and I should so like to lie down and join him. I feel too worn out and broken after this terrible year of anxiety.

I feel he will come to me if he can, and the morning after he died, when I was lying in bed awake, a great peace and happiness came over me, and I felt that beloved Presence was near, trying to comfort me. I have not felt it since – perhaps it is impossible for him – but that experience has comforted me so, and I now have such faith and confidence that I shall one day rejoin my darling. Half the agony of seeing him so ill was the thought of losing him for ever, but now I *know* that I shall see him again. We had such great happiness together, and there was much to live for. He was such a true tender Husband and Father, and I feel I have been blessed and privileged above most women in having been the wife of such a truly great and noble man and the mother of his sons. As for the boys he has left them a great heritage in his name. I had high ideals of marriage, and I can say, as few women can say, that I lost no illusions during those wonderful years in Peking, and I have only wonderful memories of our life together.

It has filled me with sad pride to read the noble tributes to him in all the papers, and I have had hundreds of letters and telegrams from all over the world, which I shall always treasure. I am going to make copies of some of the

[1] Morrison's mother, at the time living in Melbourne, Australia.

letters for you, and I am also collecting the cuttings for you. As one man in *The Times* wrote, George Meredith's words about a dead friend, so truly applied to Ernest:—

> 'The tender humour, and the fire of sense,
> In your good eyes; how full of heart for all
> And chiefly for the weaker by the wall.'

He was ever the champion of the weak and the friend of the poor. He did not wait until after he was dead to do kind actions. He was so full of goodness and generous impulse and benevolence. His mind and intellect were great, but his big heart was greater still.

Up to the week before he died he was so anxious and hopeful about returning to China. On the 14th May he had a relapse, rigours, high fever, and a severe bleeding from the tongue, and was in bed for several days and I slept in the room at nights. We thought he had caught a chill through sitting out of doors, and though much shaken and looking terribly frail, he insisted on my going up to London much against my will, to make final arrangements with the shipping Co. and passport people for our return to China on the 23rd June. I hated going, but he was so insistent, and got into such a state of nervous irritation that our arrangements would be so rushed at the end, that to please him, and against my better judgment, I went up to London on the 22nd May. On Thursday morning on the 27th May just as I was dressing I got a telegram to return to Sidmouth at once. I caught the first train and got there at 3 o'clock in the afternoon. He had a haemorrhage, and I could see that the end was near. I never left him until he died on Sunday afternoon, May 30th, at 4.40. Nothing could be done, and I would not let the doctors do anything which would simply prolong his sufferings. On Sunday morning at 9 o'clock I brought the boys in to say good-bye, and about 10 o'clock he lost consciousness, which he never regained, though just at the last he tried to open his eyes and smile at me. He died in my arms, and his last words were that he loved me. Maxwell Prophit[1] I had wired the day before, and he was in the room when he died, also Nurse (my nannie) and his faithful valet, Willmer. He looked so beautiful and noble in death, and there was such a sweet expression on the dear wasted features.

No man could have stood the strain of this terrible diarrhoea, and he had had it now since last September. It was wonderful that he had fought so long, but the terrible disease conquered him at last.

Maxwell Prophit has been goodness and kindness itself and I can never forget all he did for me. He made all the arrangements for the funeral and for people coming down from London with such thought and care, and he was so full of heart and sympathy and affection for Ernest. I am staying with him

[1] Maxwell Grant Prophit (?1859–1924), British banker. He had been Governor of the Bank of Bengal, and in 1919 became a Director of the Chartered Bank of India, Australia and China. Related to Morrison by marriage, he helped to look after Morrison's family's financial interests after his death, being one of the executors of his will.

now for a few days, as he was one of Ernest's trustees, and he is so good and helpful.

I think Nurse has already sent you a copy of the funeral service and the notice in the paper. It was a glorious day of sunshine, and we had chosen a beautiful spot in the peaceful, little Sidmouth Cemetery, right on the top of the hill, looking over Salcombe Hill and the Valley. Such reverence was shown going to the Cemetery. Not a poor labourer that did not take off his hat in respect to the memory of a good man. Many people came from London to pay the last tribute of affection to a dear friend, and there were many beautiful flowers. The little chapel was beautifully decorated, and the grave was lined with flowers. It was all so beautifully done, with such simplicity and dignity, worthy of our Dear One. You will see in the paper the names of those present. The Rev. Mr. Phillips is the clergyman who married us – he now lives near Sidmouth.

I did not take the children, because I did not wish to sadden their little lives, but the next day I took them all to see the flowers, and they were so happy in that beautiful spot. I told them that God was so sad to see dear Daddy suffering so, and had said that he would not let him suffer any longer, and had taken him to a place where he will be very happy. So that we are not grieving for Daddy, it is just because we are so sad and lonely without him, and miss him so. Poor mites, they seem to understand, a little, but they can never realise what they have lost, just at the age when they so require a father's care and guidance. My heart seems so dead that I find it difficult even to take an interest in the boys just now, but I suppose that later, when time has deadened the pain a little, the old interest and enthusiasm will return. I am all they have now, and I feel the burden of a great responsibility in their education and training.

Frederick Greenwood[1] came at once, directly he got the news, and has been very kind. I feel he will be a friend to us. Cicely came too,[2] and told me she was writing to you.

Ernest did so love you, and he used to speak with such pride and affection to everyone of his 'dear old Mother'. He did not write because he had so little cheering news he could give you, and he knew I wrote and told you all I could about him and the children. His thoughts were often with you, I know, and he always looked back with happiness to the time he had with you at Coriyule.[3]

---

[1] James Frederick Greenwood, a cousin of Morrison's mother, Rebecca Morrison *née* Greenwood. According to Morrison he was a successful owner of cloth mills near Oxenhope in Yorkshire.

[2] In his Diary for 9 February 1920 Morrison wrote: 'Cicely Fawcett called – kindly plain red-nosed spinster who will be 51 next month.' She told Morrison about the wealth and miserliness of James Frederick Greenwood. She was made a Trustee of the Morrison Papers.

[3] The name of Morrison's former family home in Geelong. It was also used by Rebecca Morrison for her house in Fulham Avenue, South Yarra, a Melbourne suburb, after the family sold the property in Geelong.

Now, I have to try and make plans for the future. I have taken a tiny furnished house at Sidmouth for a year, and am leaving Nurse there with the governess and children. It will be a week or two before I can get our affairs straight here, but on July 28th I am sailing for China via Canada, and shall be away until the Spring. It all depends on how long it will take to get things settled at Peking. I dread the long dreary journey alone, and the break up of our beloved home, but there is no one else who can do the work, and I know my Darling wished me to go. I am leaving the children at Sidmouth in this dear little cottage, and I know they are absolutely safe with Nurse and the governess, Miss Bebbington, a very sweet girl, with a true love of children, and a proper kindergarten training. Everyone has been so extraordinarily kind. We have made so many friends at Sidmouth, and the children have nice little friends there that I do not wish to take them away from such a pretty healthy place. We shall probably stay there until October 1921, by which time I shall hope to have got my furniture home and to have found a tiny house in London somewhere. I want to stay in London, so that I can keep in touch with all Ernest's friends for the children's sake, and I should like to make my home a little centre for all those who knew and loved him, both in the Far East and in England and in Australia. I don't quite know how we stand as regards money yet, but I think there is enough to enable me to live very quietly in London and give the boys a first class education at Winchester and Oxford as Ernest wished. But with death duties which are very crippling, we shall have to go very slow for a year or two until they are paid off. So the little cottage at Sidmouth has been a godsend. Indeed I cannot imagine how we managed to get it – it really must have been kept for us, as there is not a lodging or house to be got there for over a year.

When you get this, perhaps you will write to me, c/o British Legation, Peking. I shall reach there about the middle of September.

Dear Ernest, in a last letter of instructions to me, asked me to make certain gifts to the museums in Melbourne and Australia, and I am writing a letter to Mary Alice[1] about this, and she will speak to the Curators about it. But of course everything is in China, and it will be perhaps a year before things can be sent off.

I want to give you a little piece of Sir George Prothero's letter. He is editor of the *Quarterly Review*, and one of the great literary figures of London:

'It will always be a precious memory to me to have known your husband; his friendship I always felt to be both an honour and an invaluable possession; and I am profoundly saddened by the thought that I shall not see him again. Nor can I ever forget the splendid courage and patience with which he faced his illness and the prospect of death – it was indeed a noble example, to be admired but never excelled.'

[1] A sister of Morrison's, and wife of Henry Bournes Higgins, Justice of the High Court of Australia (1906-29).

From Mr Buckle, late Editor of *The Times*:

'I am very sorry that I was unable to get down to Sidmouth yesterday, so as to pay the last tribute of respect to a great man – an honoured friend of many years standing. There was no correspondent in my day at *The Times* in whom we placed greater confidence. It is indeed grievous that so valuable a life should have been cut off in its prime...

It must be some comfort to you I think in your affliction to read the universal appreciation shown of your husband's services alike to the British Empire and to China, and the widespread regret expressed for this untimely end.'

I will try to get the letters typed for you, but you will understand just now how overwhelmed I am with work and business, and I have been writing every night up to two or three o'clock. I cannot sleep, and it is a comfort to write. I have had hundreds of letters and telegrams, many from people I have never heard of, and I feel I must answer them in my own hand.

I am really heartbroken, and I know I can never get over this. The light has gone out of my life, and it is so long still before I can hope to join my Beloved. The only thing is to set one's teeth and go on, but it is so hard. We were such true mates and friends. He told me everything, and his life was the dominating interest and happiness of my life. Some day I am going to bring out his life. There are all the Diaries and notes of so many years, and it will be a great work for me to do. At least I am not capable of doing it by myself, as I have no literary gift, but I could be of great assistance in going through all the material, and shedding light on various matters.

Good-bye, dear Mrs Morrison. All my loving thoughts and sympathy are with you too, and I think of you constantly in the midst of my own sorrow, for I know what Ernest was to you too. And I feel only a very good woman could have been the mother of such a man.

Ever yours affectionately
[Jennie Morrison]

Forgive a typewritten letter, but I simply cannot write any more in my own hand – my hand is too tired, and I can write more fully like this. Willmer is keeping all the cuttings for you, and I hope you will send me the Australian ones.

Nurse's name is Miss Toovey, and if you want to write to Sidmouth, the new address for one year is 4 Millford Avenue, Sidmouth, Devon.

965. From Ju Jen-ho to W. P. Thomas

Peking 11 June 1920

Dear Mr. Thomas,

In reply to your letter of the 6th inst. I beg to inform you that regarding Mrs. Morrison's request on safeguarding her property I have asked our

Grand Master of Ceremonies[1] to see that proper actions be taken whenever necessary.

The President in expressing his recognition of Dr. Morrison's services has granted our request for an allowance of an amount equivalent to three months' salary to his family. This together with the overdue salaries we have already written officially to the Ministry of Finance and I will see that they be paid promptly.

With kind regards I am

Yours sincerely
J. H. Ju

966. From Jennie Morrison to Chou Tzu-ch'i[2]

Peking 2 December 1920

Dear Mr. Chow Tzu-chi,

As you will see from the enclosed note[3] from the Hongkong and Shanghai Bank, the cheque you sent me yesterday has been returned by the Salt Industrial Bank, marked 'Insufficient Funds'.

I therefore return you the cheque, and should be much obliged if you would kindly send me a fresh cheque, instructing the Bank to meet the payment.

With kind regards

Sincerely yours
[Jennie Morrison]

[1] Huang K'ai-wen, Chinese Imperial and Republican official. Brother of Huang K'ai-chia and a protégé of his fellow provincial from Kwangtung, T'ang Shao-yi, he became through T'ang Director of the Bureau of Industry under Hsü Shih-ch'ang, the first Viceroy of Manchuria (1907–9). In this post he was known for his incompetence and corruption. After working for a time with the Tientsin-Pukow Railway, he was appointed by Yüan Shih-k'ai in 1912 to the lucrative post of Superintendent of Customs at Hankow, which he held until 1914 when he was made Yüan's Grand Master of Ceremonies, becoming a fervent supporter of his monarchical scheme. He survived the débâcle, however, and served once more as Grand Master of Ceremonies under his erstwhile master Hsü Shih-ch'ang, when Hsü succeeded to the Presidency of the Republic in 1918.
[2] At this time Acting Minister of Finance (August 1920 – May 1921).
[3] Not found.

Glossary

This Glossary lists identifiable Chinese, Japanese and Korean personal and place names, terms and expressions, as well as some Tibetan and Mongolian names and terms which have a Chinese rendering. Surnames are given first, however they might appear in the text.

Each entry is spelt as in the text, followed by its rendering, for Chinese, in the Wade–Giles system and, in the case of place names, by any variant forms, earlier and modern names, and the province (in italics) in which it is to be found, and for Japanese, in the Hepburn system.

Many place names spelt according to the Postal system of the time, such as Peking, Tientsin, Shanghai, Nanking, Amoy, Canton, Mukden etc., have not been included, nor are characters supplied for the names of provinces.

In the case of such names as Lu-Han Railway and Chiao-t'ung Bank, only the Chinese component is supplied with characters, not 'Railway', 'Bank' etc. There are, however, exceptions to this, such as Kiangnan (or Shanghai) Arsenal, for which, in view of the repeated mistakes historians have made, the full Chinese name is given.

No characters are supplied for the Chinese names adopted by many foreign enterprises, unless those names actually appear in the text. Hence characters are given for T'ai-lai, the Chinese name of Telge & Schroeter, but not for Messrs Butterfield & Swire (T'ai-ku), Jardine, Matheson & Company (I-ho, Ewo), or Hongkong & Shanghai Banking Corporation (Hui-feng), etc.

Abe Moritarō 阿部守太郎

Administrative Bureau (Japan) 總務局

Administrative Court (President of). See Ping-Cheng yüan (院長)

Ah-wang-lo-pu-tsang-t'u-pu-tan-chia-ts'o-chi-chai-wang-ch'ü-ch'üeh-le-lang-chieh 阿旺羅布藏吐布丹甲錯濟塞汪曲郤勒郎結

Aigun (Hei-ho, *Heilungkiang*) 璦琿, 艾輝;(黑河)

Aimak 愛瑪克(盟)

Aisin-Gioro 愛新覺羅

Aki Maru, S. S. 秋九

Akiyama Masanosuke 秋山雅之助

Aksu (*Sinkiang*) 阿克蘇雅蘇

Altai Mountains 阿爾泰山

Amano 天野

Amban 參贊辦事大臣

An Myŏng-gŭn 安明根

An-shan (*Fengtien*) 鞍山

An-ting men (Peking) 安定門

Anching (An-ch'ing, *Anhwei*) 安慶

Anesaki Masaharu 姉崎正治

Anfu clique 安福系

Anfu Hutung 安福胡同

Anking. See Anching

Annam (French Indo-China) 安南

Ansi (An-hsi, *Kansu*) 安西

Antung (An-tung, *Fengtien*) 安東

Aoki Nobuzumi 青木宣純

Aoki Shuzō 青木周藏

Aoyagi Katsutoshi 青柳勝敏

Ariga Nagao 有賀長雄

Ariyoshi Akira 有吉明

Army Inspector in Yangtse Valley 長江巡閱使

Asahi Shimbun 朝日新聞

Audit, Board of 審計院

Bakan (Japan) 馬關

Bandit suppression, Commander-in-Chief of 剿匪督辦

Banzai Rihachirō 坂西利八郎

Barga (*Heilungkiang*) 巴爾虎

Batang (Pa-t'ang, *Szechwan, Ch'uan-pien, Sikang*) 巴塘

Baxat (Pai-chai, *Yunnan*) 白寨

Bhamo (Burma) 八莫

Black Dragon Society 黑龍會

Black Flags 黑旗

Black Smoke 烏片煙

'Blue-Shirts' 藍衣社

Bureau of Codification 法制局

Bushidō 武士道

Cabinet Office 國務院

Censorate. See Su-cheng t'ing

Central Audit Office 審計處

chai-shin (*ch'ai-hsin*) 柴薪

Chamdo (*Szechwan, Ch'uan-pien, Sikang*) 察擦多・察木多昌都

Chang Chen-fang 張鎮芳

Chang Chen-wu 張振武

Chang Ch'i-huang 張其鍠

Chang Chi-Shih 章繼詩

Chang Ch'i-yün 張其昀

Chang-chia-k'ou (*Chahar*) 張家口

Chang Chia-sen 張嘉森

Chang Ch'ien 張謇

Chang Chih-tung 張之洞

830

Chang Ching-yao 張敬堯
Ch'ang-ch'un (*Kirin*) 長春
Chang Chün-mai 張君勱
Chang Chung-liang 張仲良
Chang Hsi-luan 張錫鑾
Chang Hsin Tien (Ch'ang-hsin-t'ien, *Chihli*) 長辛店
Chang Hsüeh-liang 張學良
Chang Hsün 張勳
Chang Hu 張弧
Chang I-lin 張一麐
Chang I-shu 張翼樞
Chang Jen-chün 張人駿
Chang Ju-mei 張汝梅
Chang Jung 張搈
Chang Min-chih 張敏之
Chang Ming-ch'i 張鳴岐
Chang P'ei-lun 張佩綸
Chang Ping-lin 章炳麟
Chang Po-hsi 張百熙
Chang Po-ling 張伯苓
Chang Shao-tseng 張紹曾
Chang Shih-heng 張士珩
Ch'ang-te-fu (*Hunan*) 常德府
Chang Te-yi 張德彝
Chang Tso-lin 張作霖
Chang Tsung-hsiang 章宗祥
Chang Yao-tseng 張耀曾
Chang-yen pao 昌言報
Chang Yi 張翼
Chang Yin-huan 張蔭桓
Chang Yin-mao (Chang Yen-mou) 張燕謀
Chang Yin-t'ang 張蔭棠
Chang Yü-ch'üan 張煜全

Chang Yü-chün 章逷駿
Chang Yün-shan 張雲山
Chang Yün-yen 張允言
Ch'angli (Ch'ang-li, *Chihli*) 昌黎
Changsha (Ch'ang-sha, *Hunan*) 長沙
Changte-fu (Chang-te-fu; An-yang, *Honan*) 彰德府（安陽）
Chao Erh-feng 趙爾豐
Chao Erh-hsün 趙爾巽
Chao-ho 肇和艦
Chao Ju-kua 趙汝适
Chao Kung fu [? 趙公府]
Chao Ping-chün 趙秉鈞
Chao Shu-ch'iao 趙舒翹
chao yo (*tsao yao*) 造謠
Chaoch'ing (Chao-ch'ing, *Kwangtung*) 肇慶
Chapei (Cha-pei, Shanghai) 閘北
Chefoo (Chih-fu; Yen-t'ai, *Shantung*) 芝罘（煙台）
Chemulpo (Korea) 鎮南浦
Chen an fu. *See* Chinan
Chenan. *See* Chinan
Ch'en Ch'i-mei 陳其美
Ch'en Chia-keng 陳嘉庚
Chenchiatun (Cheng-chia-t'un; Liao-yüan, *Fengtien*) 鄭家屯（遼源）
Ch'en Chin-t'ao 陳錦濤
Ch'en Ching-hua 陳景華
Ch'en Chiung-ming 陳炯明
Ch'en I-fan 陳貽範
Ch'en King-wa. *See* Ch'en Ching-hua
Ch'en Kung-po 陳公博
Ch'en Kuo-fu 陳果夫

Ch'en Lan-pin 陳蘭彬
Ch'en Li-fu 陳立夫
Ch'en Lu 陳籙
Ch'en Luan 陳鑾
Ch'en Pi 陳璧
Ch'en Shih-hua 陳世華
Chen-tan ta-hsüeh 震旦大學（院）
Ch'en T'ing-hsün 陳廷訓
Ch'en Tu-hsiu 陳獨秀
Ch'en Yi 陳宧
Ch'en Yu-jen 陳友仁
Cheng-chou (Honan) 鄭州
Cheng Ju-cheng 鄭汝成
Ch'eng-shun-tsan-hua-hsi-t'ien-ta-shan-tzu-tsai-fo 誠順贊化西天大善自在佛
Ch'eng Te-ch'üan 程德全
Chengting-fu (Cheng-ting-fu, Chihli) 正定府
Chengtu (Ch'eng-tu, Szechwan) 成都
Chi-chin hui 急進會
Ch'i Hsieh-yüan 齊燮元
Ch'i-hua men (Ch'ao-yang men, Peking) 齊化門（朝陽門）
Chi-ning (Suiyuan) 集寧
Ch'i-shan 琦善
Chia-ch'ing 嘉慶
Chia-ho 嘉禾
Chia-yü-kuan (Kansu) 嘉峪關
Chiamdo. See Chamdo
Chiang Chao-t'ang 江召棠
Chiang Ch'ao-tsung 江朝宗
Chiang-chün 將軍
Chiang Kai-shek 蔣介石

Chiang Kuei-t'i 姜桂題
Chiang-lai chu-jen weng 將來主人翁
Chiao-t'ung pu 交通部
Chiao t'ung Bank 交通銀行
chien 健
Chien-ch'ang (Szechwan; Sikang) [?間昌]
Ch'ien-lung 乾隆
Ch'ien men (Peking) 前門
Ch'ien-men ta-chieh (Peking) 前門大街
Ch'ien Neng-hsün 錢能訓
Chien Shu-fen 錢樹芬
Chien-t'ang River (Ch'ien-t'ang Chiang, Chekiang) 錢塘江
Ch'ien Wen-hsüan 錢文選
Chientao (Chien-tao, Kirin) 間島
Chih Feng (Ch'ih-feng; Hata, Jehol) 赤峯（哈塔）
chih-fu 知府
Chih Hua Men. See Ch'i-hua men
Chih-li chou 直隸州
Chih-yüeh (Chih-jui) 志銳
Chihli clique 直隸系
chin-chin (ch'ing-ch'ing) 請請
Chin-chou (Fengtien) 金州
Chin-koku Manyū Nikki 清國漫遊日記
Chin-liang 金梁
chin-shih 進士
Chin Ting-hsün 金鼎勳
Chin-wei chün 禁衛軍
Chin Yün-p'eng 靳雲鵬
Chin Yung 金永
China Democratic League 中國民主同盟

Chinan (Chi-nan, *Shantung*) 濟南

Chinchow (Chin-chou, *Fengtien*) 錦州

Chinda Sutemi 珍田捨巳

Ch'ing, Prince (*see also* I-K'uang) 慶親王

Ching-chou (Chiang-ling, *Hupeh*) 荊州（江陵）

Ch'ing-hua jih-pao 清華日報

Ch'ing-hua Yüan (Peking) 清華園

Ch'ing-kung so-chi 清宮瑣記

Ching-shan 景善

Ch'ing shih 清史

Ch'ing shih kao 清史稿

Ching-te-cheng 景德鎮

Chining (Chi-ning, *Shantung*) 濟寧

Chinkiang (Chen-chiang, *Kiangsu*) 鎮江

Chinkiang pu (Ch'ing-chiang-p'u, *Kiangsu*) 清江浦

Chinputang (Chin-pu tang) 進步黨

Chinwangtao (Ch'in-huang-tao, *Chihli*) 秦皇島

Chisaka Tomojirō 千坂智次郎

Ch'iu Chin 秋瑾

Chiu, Moses (Ch'iu Ch'ang-k'ang) 〔？邱長康〕

Chōsen (Korea) 朝鮮

Chōshū clan 長州藩

Ch'ou-an hui 籌安會

Chou Ch'ang-ling 周長齡

Chou En-lai 周恩來

Chou Fu 周馥

Chou Hsüeh-hsi 周學熙

Chou Mien 周冕

Chou Shou-ch'en 周壽臣

Chou Shu-mo 周樹模

Chou Tzu-ch'i 周自齊

Chu 朱

ch'u 處

Chü Cheng 居正

Chu Ch'i 朱淇

Chu Ch'i-ch'ien 朱啟鈐

Chu-Ching Fu (Ch'ü-ching-fu; Nan-ning, *Yunnan*) 曲靖府（南寧）

Chü Hung-chi 瞿鴻禨

Chü-jen 舉人

Chu Jui 朱瑞

Chu Kam-wing 〔？朱金榮 朱錦榮〕

Chū-Nichi Jitsugyō Kabushiki Kaisha 中日實業株式會社

Chu Pao-k'uei 朱寶奎

Chu Shen 朱深

Chuan-Han (Ch'uan-Han) 川漢

Ch'üan-hsüeh pien 勸學篇

chuan pan 專辦

Ch'uan-pien 川邊

chuang-yüan 狀元

Chūgoku Kōgyō Kabushiki Kaisha 中國興業株式會社

Chuguchak (T'a-ch'eng, *Sinkiang*) 塔城

Chumbi (*Tibet*) 春丕

Ch'un, Prince 醇親王
 (1st, *see* I-huan)
 (2nd, *see* Tsai-feng)

Chün-chi ch'u 軍機處

Ch'un-chiu 春秋

Chün yung p'in 軍用品

Ch'ung-hou 崇厚

833

Chung-hua ko-ming tang 中華革命黨

Chung-hua min-kuo k'ai-kuo wu-shih nien wen-hsien 中華民國開國五十年文獻

Chung-hua pao 中華報

Chung-kuo kuo-min tang 中國國民黨

Ch'ung-li 崇禮

Chung-t'ang 中堂

Chung-wai jih-pao 中外日報

Chung Wen-yao 鍾文耀

Chung-yung 中庸

Chunghsiang (Chung-hsing) 中興

Chungking 重慶號

Chungking (Ch'ung-ch'ing, *Szechwan*) 重慶

Chusan Archipelago 舟山群島

Chūzenji (Japan) 中善寺

Citizen Groups 公民團

Civil Governor 巡撫, 民政長, 巡按使, 省長, 省主席

Codification, Bureau of 法制局

Colonisation of Tsinghai and Sinkiang Provinces, Commissioner for 新疆青海墾屯使

Communication Clique 交通系

Consultative Council 參政院

Council of Generals 將軍府

Currency Bureau 幣制局

Customs, Superintendent of 關監督

Da Lai Wang 達賴王

Da Lama 大喇嘛

Dairen (Ta-lien, *Fengtien*) 大連

Dalai Lama 達賴喇嘛

Darg Angar (Dariganga, *Chahar*) 達里岡愛・達里岡厓・達爾岡愛

Den Kenjirō 田健次郎

Der Ling (Teh-ling) 德齡

Diplomatist Clique 外交系

Doihara Kenji 土肥原賢二

Dolon-nor (*Chahar*) 多倫泊

Dōmei 同盟

Domestic Loans, Bureau of 內國公債局

Ebina Danjō 海老名彈正

Eitaki Hisakichi 永瀧久吉

Examination Yüan 考試院

Exchange Bank of China 中華滙業銀行

Fa shan (Fo-shan; Nan-hai, *Kwangtung*) 佛山（南海）

Fakumen (Fa-k'u-men, *Fengtien*) 法庫門

Fan-t'ai 藩臺

Fang Chao-ying 房兆楹

Fang Wei 方維

Fatshan. *See* Fa shan

Fei-chih 菲支

Fei-chou 菲洲

fen-mi 分米

fen-yin 分銀

Feng Chen (Feng-chen, *Suiyuan*) 豐鎮

Feng-kang chi-men ti-tzu 鳳岡及門弟子

Feng Kuo-chang 馮國璋

Feng Lin-k'o 馮麟閣

Feng-shan 鳳山

feng-shui 風水

Feng Te-lin 馮德麟

Feng Yü-hsiang 馮玉祥

834

Fengtai (Feng-t'ai, *Chihli*) 豐台
Five Provinces, Commander-in-Chief of 五省聯軍總司令
Foochow (Fu-chou, *Fukien*) 福州
Foreign Affairs Commissioner 特派交涉員
Four Friends of Sung Shan 嵩山四友
Freedom League 自由大同盟
Frontier Defence Bureau 西北籌邊使事務處
Fu 府
Fu-lin 福臨
Fukien People's Government 福建人民政府
Fukuoka (Japan) 福岡
Fukushima Yasumasa 福島安正
Fukuzawa Yukichi 福澤諭吉
Fung Wa-chun [? 馮華春]
Fushimi Maru, S.S. 伏見丸
Fushun (Fu-shun, *Fengtien*) 撫順
Futan 復旦
Futupan 副督辦
Gartok (*Tibet*) 噶大克
Gendarmerie, Commander of 步軍統領
General Staff, Chief of 參謀總長
Genrō 元老
Giamdu. *See* Chamdo
ginseng 人參
Gotō Shimpei 後藤新平
Grand Canal 運河
Grand Council 軍機處
Grand Master of Ceremonies 大禮官 *also* 禮官長

Great *Tutuh* (Generalissimo) 大都督
Gunbatsu 軍閥
Gyantse (*Tibet*) 江孜
Ha-mi (*Sinkiang*) 哈密
Hai-nan 海南
Hai-san-kung 海三公
Haicheng (Hai-ch'eng, *Fengtien*) 海城
Haichow (Hai-chou; Tung-hai, *Kiangsu*) 海州（東海）
Haikwan (Hai-kuan) 海關
Haimun, S.S. 海門號
Hamada Kōsaku 濱田耕作
Hamaguchi Osachi 濱口雄幸
Han 漢
Han Chün 漢軍
Han Kuo-chün 韓國鈞
Han-ta Chin-wang 汗達親王
Han Tan Hsien (Han-tan-hsien, *Chihli*) 邯鄲縣
Han-Yeh-P'ing 漢冶萍
Hanchuang (Han-chuang, *Shantung*) 韓莊
Hang Hsin-chai 杭辛齋
Hangchow (Hang-chou, *Chekiang*) 杭州
Hankow (Han-k'ou, *Hupeh*) 漢口
Hanlin Yuan (Han-lin yüan) 翰林院
Hanyang (Han-yang, *Hupeh*) 翰陽
Hara Kei (Satoshi) 原敬
Haraguchi Kaname 原口要
Haraoka Isamu 原岡武
Hata (Ch'ih-feng, *Jehol*) 哈塔（赤峯）
Hatamen (Ha-t'a men, Peking) 豁達門 哈達門
Hatsuse 初瀨
Hayashi Gonsuke 林權助
Hayashi Senjūrō 林銑十郎

835

Hayashi Tadasu 林董

Heiho (Hei-ho; Aigun, *Heilungkiang*) 黑河（愛琿）

Hibiya 日比谷

Hing-ho (Hsing-ho, *Suiyuan*) 興和

Hingan Mountains 興安嶺山脈

Hioki Eki 日置益

Hirai Seijirō 平井晴二郎

Hirohito 裕仁

History of Ch'ing Dynasty, Bureau of 清史館

Ho Ch'ang-ch'ing 何長清

Ho Chien fu (Ho-chien-fu, *Chihli*) 河間府

Ho Kai (Ho Ch'i) 何啟

Ho-kou (Ho-k'ou, *Shensi*) 河口

Ho-k'ou (*Yunnan*) 河口

Ho-shên 和珅

Hōchi Shimbun 報知新聞

Hochien-fu. *See* Ho Chien fu

Hokienfu. *See* Ho Chien fu

Honanfu (Ho-nan-fu; Lo-yang, *Honan*) 河南府（洛陽）

hong 行

Hongkew (Hung-k'ou, Shanghai) 虹口

Hongō Fusutarō 本鄉房太郎

Hongwanji 本願寺

Hori Yoshiatsu 堀義貴

Horiuchi Saburō 堀內三郎

Hōsei Daigaku 法政大學

Hou K'ou. *See* Ho-kou

Hou Men (Peking) 後門

Hsi-hu (*Sinkiang*) 西湖

Hsi-liang 錫良

Hsi-po 錫伯

Hsi-Tzu-Men (Hsi-chih men, Peking) 西直門

Hsiang-chün 湘軍

Hsiang-yang (*Hupeh*) 襄陽

Hsiao-ch'in 孝欽

Hsiao-ting 孝定

Hsiaochang (Hsiao-chan; Ko-ku, *Chihli*) 小站（葛沽）

Hsieh-ho i-hsüeh yüan 協和醫學院

Hsieh Ling 協領

Hsieh Tsan-t'ai 謝讚泰

Hsien 縣

Hsien-feng 咸豐

Hsien I Huei (Hsien I-hui) 縣議會

Hsien-shih kung-ssu 先施公司

Hsin-hai ko-ming 辛亥革命

Hsin-min chung-pao (*Hsin-min ts'ung-pao*) 新民叢報

Hsin Min Tun (Hsin-min-t'un, *Fengtien*) 新民屯

hsin wen-ming 新文明

Hsin Yang Chou (Hsin-yang-chou, *Honan*) 信陽州

Hsinching (Hsin-ching; Ch'ang-ch'un, *Kirin*) 新京（長春）

Hsinminfu (Hsin-min-fu, *Fengtien*) 新民府

Hsiung Hsi-ling 熊希齡

Hsiung K'e-wu 熊克武

Hsiung Yüeh-shan 熊越山

Hsu Ching-ch'eng 許景澄

Hsü Ch'ung-chih 許崇智

Hsü En-yüan 徐恩源

Hsü Fu 徐鄜

Hsü Kuo-chen 徐國楨

Hsü Pao-chen 徐寶楨

836

Hsü Pao-shan 徐寶山
Hsü Shih-ch'ang 徐世昌
Hsü Shih-ying 許世英
Hsü Shu-cheng 徐樹錚
Hsü Ting-hsiang 徐鼎襄
Hsü Ying-k'uei 許應騤
Hsü Yung-i 徐用儀
Hsüan-tsang 玄奘
Hsüan-tsung 宣宗
Hsüan-t'ung 宣統
Hsüan-yeh 玄曄
Hsuanfu shih (Hsüan-fu shih) 宣撫使
Hsuanhua-fu (Hsüan-hua-fu, *Chahar*) 宣化府
Hsüchowfu (Hsü-chou-fu, *Kiangsu*) 徐州府
Hsün-an-shih 巡按使
Hsün-fang-tui 巡防隊
Hu Ching-yi 胡景伊
Hu Chün 胡鈞
Hu Han-chang 胡漢章
Hu Han-min 胡漢民
Hu pu 戶部
Hu Shih 胡適
Hu-t'o-t'ou 虎頭陀
Hu Wei-te 胡惟德
Hu Ying 胡瑛
Hu Yü-fen 胡燏棻
Hu Yün-mei 胡芸楣
Hua Chang Antimony Company 〔華昌錦礦公司〕
Huach'ing hui (Hua-hsing hui) 華興會
Huai River (Huai Ho) 淮河
Huai Su 懷素

Huang Chung-kuei (Huang Chung-hui) 黃中慧
Huang Fu-sheng 黃復生
Huang Hsing 黃興
Huang-hua-kang (Canton) 黃花崗
Huang K'ai-wen 黃開文
Huang-shang wan-sui wan-wan-sui 皇上萬歲萬萬歲
Huang Shao-ming. *See* Wang Chao-ming
Huang Sheng. *See* Huang Hsing
Huang-tsao-pa (Huang-ts'ao-pa; Hsing-i, *Kweichow*) 黃草壩 (興義)
Huang Tsun-hsien 黃遵憲
Huang Yi-ou 黃一歐
Huangpu River (Huang-p'u Chiang, *Kiangsu*) 黃浦江
Hui-min kung-ssu 惠民公司
Hui Ning (Hoeryong, Korea) 會寧
Huichow (Hui-chou, *Kwangtung*) 惠州
Huili Chou (Hui-li-chou, *Szechwan, Ch'uan-pien, Sikang*) 會理州
Hukow (Hu-k'ou, *Kiangsi*) 湖口
Hukuang (Hu-kuang) 湖廣
Hulutao (Hu-lu-tao, *Fengtien*) 葫蘆島
Hung-hsien 洪憲
Hung Hsiu-ch'üan 洪秀全
hung hu-tzu 紅鬍子
Hung-li 弘曆
Hung Liang-chi 洪亮吉
Hung Shu-chu (Hung Shu-tsu) 洪述祖
Hutukhtu (Khutokhtu) 呼圖克圖
I-chu 奕詝
I-hsin (Prince Kung) 奕訢
I-huan (1st Prince Ch'un) 奕譞

837

I-k'uang (Prince Ch'ing) 奕劻
I-li-pu 伊里布
I-ning (Sinkiang) 伊寧
I-shih pao 益世報
Ichang (I-ch'ang, *Hupeh*) 宜昌
Ienaga Toyokichi 家永豐吉
Ijūin Hikokichi 伊集院彦吉
Ijūin Yoshiko 伊集院芳子
Ike Kyōkichi 池亨吉
Ikeda Tsunetarō 池田常太郎
Ili (I-li, *Sinkiang*) 伊犂
Imperial Bank 大清銀行
Imperial Chinese University (Tientsin) 北洋大學
Inagaki Manjirō 稻垣萬次郎
Inchon (Korea) 仁川
Industry, Bureau of 勸業道
Inoue Junnosuke 井上準之助
Inoue Kaoru 井上馨
Inoue Katsunosuke 井上勝之助
Inukai Tsuyoshi 犬養毅
Investigating Commissioner 查辦使
Ishida Mikinosuke 石田幹之助
Ishii Kikujirō 石井菊次郎
Itagaki Seishirō 板垣征四郎
Itagaki Taisuke 板垣退助
Itō Hirobumi 伊藤博文
Ito Hirobumi Hiroku 伊藤博文秘錄
Itō Jukichi 伊藤壽吉
Iwasaki Haruji 岩崎春治
Iwasaki Hisaya 岩崎久彌

Iwasaki Koyata 岩崎小彌太
Iwasaki Masako 岩崎雅子
Iwasaki Yanosuke 岩崎彌之助
Iwasaki Yatarō 岩崎彌太郎
Jao Meng-jen 饒孟任
Jarkent (Yarkand, Soche or Sha-che, *Sinkiang*) 莎車
Jebtsun Damba Khutokhtu 哲卜尊丹巴呼圖克圖
Jehol (Je-ho; Ch'eng-te, *Jehol*) 熱河（承德）
Jen K'o-ch'eng 任可澄
Jen-tsung 仁宗
Jih Chao (Jih-chao, *Shantung*) 日照
Jihk'atse. See Shigatse
Jiji Shimbun 時事新聞
Jiji Shimpo 時事新報
Ju Jung-hao (Ju Jen-ho) 汝人鵠
Judicial Yüan 司法院
Jui-cheng 瑞澂
Jung-hou 榮厚
Jung Hung 容閎
Jung-lu 榮祿
k'ai-ch'üeh 開缺
K'ai Lu (K'ai-lu, *Fengtien*) 開魯
Kaifeng-fu (K'ai-feng-fu, *Honan*) 開封府
Kaiping (K'ai-p'ing, *Chihli*) 開平
Kaishintō 改進黨
Kaiyuen (K'ai-yüan, *Fengtien*) 開原
Kaiyuen (K'ai-yüan; A-mi, *Yunnan*) 開遠（阿迷）
Kalgan. See Chang-chia-k'ou
Kamio Mitsuomi 神尾光臣

Kanai Kiyoshi 金井清
k'ang 炕
K'ang-hsi 康熙
Kang-yi 剛毅
K'ang Yu-wei 康有為
Kao Chiao (Kao-ch'iao, *Fengtien*) 高橋
Kao-tsung 高宗
kaoliang (kao-liang) 高粱
Kaomi (Kao-mi, *Chihli*) 高密
Kashgar (K'a-shih, Shu-fu, *Sinkiang*) 喀什，喀什噶爾，疏附
Katō Kōmei (Takaaki) 加藤高明
Katō Yoshiko 加藤悦子
Katsura Tarō 桂太郎
Kawakami Toshihiko 川上俊彦
Kawashima Naniwa 川島浪速
Kawashima Yoshiko 川島芳子
Keelung (Chi-lung, *Taiwan*) 基隆
Kenseikai 憲政會
Kenseitō 憲政黨
Khailar (*Heilungkiang*) 海拉爾
Khalka (Mongolia) 哈拉哈
Kherah (Yü-t'ien, *Sinkiang*) 于闐
Khingan Mountains. *See* Hingan Mountains
Khobdo (Mongolia) 科布多
Khotan (*Sinkiang*) 和闐
Kiakhta (Mai-mai-ch'eng) 恰克圖（買賣城）
Kiang-fei-t'ing (Chiang-pei-t'ing, *Szechwan*) 江北廳
Kiangnan (Shanghai) Arsenal 江南製造局
Kiangyin (Chiang-yin, *Kiangsu*) 江陰

Kiaochow Bay (Chiao-chou Wan, *Shantung*) 膠州灣
Kiating (Chia-ting; Lo-shan, *Szechwan*) 嘉定（樂山）
Kido Kōin 木戶孝允
Kimura Eiichi 木村銳市
Kinchow (Chin-chou, *Fengtien*) 金州
King Kung-pa (Chin Ch'ung-p'o, or Chin Shao-ch'eng) 金鞏伯（金紹城）
Kishimoto Hirokichi 岸本廣吉
Kishiwada (Japan) 岸和田
Kitada Masahira 北田正平
Kiukiang (Chiu-chiang, *Kiangsi*) 九江
Kiungchow (Ch'iung-chou, *Kwangtung*) 瓊州
Kiura Keigo 木浦奎吾
k'o 可
Ko Chiao. *See* Kao Chiao
K'o Hung-lieh 柯鴻烈
Ko lao hwei (Ko-lao hui) 哥老會
Ko-ming wen-hsien 革命文獻
Kodama Gentarō 兒玉源太郎
Kōfuku Gingō 廣福銀號
Koike Chōzō 小池張造
Koizumi Masayasu 小泉正保
Koko Nor (*Tsinghai*) 青海
Kokumin Shimbun 國民新聞
Kokumintō 國民黨
koming (ko-ming) 革命
Komura Jutarō 小村壽太郎
Komura Shunzaburō 小村俊三郎
Kongmoon (Chiang-men, *Kwangtung*) 江門
Kongo San [?] 金剛山]

839

Kōno Iwao 河野農男

Koo, Wellington. *See* Ku Wei-chün

Kou Pang Tzu (Kou-pang-tzu, *Fengtien*) 溝幫子

kow-tow (*k'ou-t'ou*) 叩頭

Ku hung mei ko pi chi 古紅梅閣筆記

Ku Hung-ming 辜鴻銘

Ku Wei-chün 顧維鈞

Kuan Cheng tze (K'uan-ch'eng-tzu, *Kirin*) 寬城子

Kuan Chiung (Kuan Chiung-chih) 關烱（關烱之）

Kuan-hsien (*Szechwan*) 灌縣

kuang 侊

Kuang-fu 廣福

Kuang-hsü 光緒

Kuang-hsü shih-lu 光緒實錄

Kuang Hsüan hsiao-chi 光宣小記

Kuang-hua pao 光華報

Kuchar (*Sinkiang*) 庫車，苦叉

Kucheng (Ku-ch'eng-tzu; Ch'i-t'ai, *Sinkiang*) 古城子（奇臺）

Kuei-ch'ün 桂春

Kuei-hsiang 桂祥

Kuei-Hua-Cheng (Kuei-hua-ch'eng; Kuei-sui, Hu-ho-hao-t'e, *Suiyuan*) 歸化城（歸綏，呼和浩特市）

Kuei-hua T'ing (Kuei-hua-t'ing; An-shun, Tzu-yün, *Kweichow*) 歸化廳（安順，紫雲）

Kuei tzu lai le, tsai tei mieh t'a men i hui 鬼子來了，再得滅他們一回

Kuei-yang-fu (*Kweichow*) 貴陽府

Kuenlun Mountains (K'un-lun Shan, *Sinkiang*) 崑崙山

Kuhara 久原

Kuldja (Hui-yüan I-li, I-ning, *Sinkiang*) 惠遠，伊里，伊寧

Kulun Nor (*Heilungkiang*) 呼倫泊，呼倫諾爾

K'un-kang 崑岡

Kung, Prince (*see also* I-hsin) 恭親王

Kung Chao-yüan 龔照瑗

Kung-ho 共和

Kung Ho Tang (Kung-ho tang) 共和黨

K'ung Hsiang-hsi 孔祥熙

Kung Hsin-chan 龔心湛

Kung Kuan 公館

K'ung Ling-k'an 孔令侃

K'ung T'ien-tseng 孔天增

Kung-pao 宮館

Kunming (K'un-ming, *Yunnan*) 昆明

Kuo Ch'ung-kuang 郭重光

Kuo-feng pao 國風報

Kuo-min chün 國民軍

Kuo-min kung-tang 國民公黨

Kuo-she tang 國社黨

Kuo Sung-t'ao 郭嵩燾

Kuo T'ai-ch'i 郭泰祺

Kuo Tzu-hai ?〔郭子海〕

Kuo-wen pao 國聞報

Kuo-wu yüan 國務院

Kuomintang 國民黨

Kurachi Tetsukichi 倉知鐵吉

Kurino Shin'ichirō 栗野慎一郎

Kuroda Kiyotaka 黑田清隆

Kurosawa Reikichi 黑澤禮吉

kwan pan (*kuan-pan*) 官辦

840

Kwang-cheng-tzu. See Kuan Cheng tze

Kwangchow-wan (Kuang-chou Wan, *Kwangtung*) 廣州灣

Kwangfu party 光復黨

Kwanhsien (Kuan-hsien, *Szechwan*) 灌縣

Kwangtung Peninsular (Kuan-tung Pan-tao, *Fengtien*) 關東半島

Kweifu (K'uei-fu; Feng-chieh, *Szechwan*) 夔府 (奉節)

Kweihwacheng. See Kuei-Hua-Cheng

Kweilin (Kuei-lin, *Kwangsi*) 桂林

Kyōto Shimpo 京都新報

Lan T'ien-wei 藍天蔚

Lanchow (Lan-chou, *Kansu*) 蘭州

Lanchow (Luan-chou, *Chihli*) 灤州

Land Survey, Bureau of. 經界局

Langfang (Lang-fang, *Chihli*) 廊房

Lao Fo-yeh 老佛爺

Lao-hsi-k'ai (Tientsin) 老西開

Laokay (Indo-China) 勞開 老撾, 老街

Lappa (La-p'u, Macao) 拉普

Lau Chu-pak (Liu Chu-po) 劉鑄伯

Leang-Shan (Liang Shan) 梁山

Legislative Council (1915) 立法院

Legislative Yüan (1928 and after) 立法院

Lei Chen-ch'un 雷震春

Leichow (Lei-chou, *Kwangtung*) 雷州

Lenghai. See Lunghai

li 里

Li-chi 禮記

Li Chia-chü 李家駒

Li Ching-fang 李經芳
Li Ching-hsi 李經羲
Li Ching-mai 李經邁
li-ch'uan hui-shou 利權回收
Li Chun 李準
Li Ch'un 李純
Li Chung-chüeh 李鍾珏
Li Hung-chang 李鴻章
Li K'ai-shen (Li K'ai-hsin) 李開侁
Li Keng-yüan 李根源
Li Lieh-chün 李烈鈞
Li Lien-ying 李蓮英
Li Long (Li-lang-ch'ang, *Kwangtung*) 李朗場
Li Ming-chung 李鳴鐘
Li Ping-heng 李秉衡
Li P'ing-shu 李平書
Li Po 李白
Li Sheng-to 李盛鐸
Li Shih-wei 李士偉
Li Ssu-hao 李思浩
Li Sum-ling (Li Hsin-ling) 李心靈
Li T'ai-po 李太白
Li Te-shun 李德順
Li Teng-hui 李登輝
Li T'ing-yu 李廷玉
Li Tsung-huang 李宗黃
Li Yüan-hung 黎元洪
Li Yuan-yun 李完用
Liang Chen-tung 梁震東
Liang Ch'eng 梁誠
Liang Ch'i-ch'ao 梁啟超
Liang Hsing Hsien (Liang-hsiang-hsien, *Chihli*) 良鄉縣

841

Liang Hung-chih 梁鴻志
Liang Ju-ch'eng 梁汝成
Liang Ju-hao 梁如浩
Liang-kuei 良桂
Liang Meng-t'ing 梁孟亭
Liang-pi 良弼
Liang Shih-hsü 梁士詡
Liang Shih-yi 梁士詒
Liang Tun-yen 梁敦彥
Lianghuai 兩淮
Liangkiang (Liang-chiang) 兩江
Liangkwang (Liang-kuang) 兩廣
Liao River (Liao Ho, *Fengtien*) 遼河
Liaotung Peninsula (Liao-tung Pan-tao, *Fengtien*) 遼東半島
Liaoyang (Liao-yang, *Fengtien*) 遼陽
Lien Ch'üan 廉泉
Lien-fang 聯芳
Lien-yü 聯豫
Lien-yün (*Kiangsu*) 連雲
Lienchow (Lien-chou; Ho-fu, *Kwangtung*) 廉州（合浦）
Lienchow (Lien-chou; Lien-hsien, *Kwangtung*) 連州（連縣）
Lifa yüan (Li-fa yüan) 立法院
likin (*li-chin*) 釐金
Lin Ch'ang-min 林長民
Lin-ch'eng (Hsüeh-ch'eng, *Shantung*) 臨城（薛城）
Lin Cheng (Lin-ch'eng, *Chihli*) 臨城
Lin Hsiung-ch'eng 林雄成
Lin Shih-huan 林軾垣
Lin Tze-hsü 林則徐
Lin Wen-ch'ing 林文慶
ling-ch'ih 凌遲

Litang (Li-t'ang, *Szechwan, Ch'uan-pien, Sikang*) 裏塘
Liu Ch'eng-en 劉承恩
Liu Ching-jen 劉鏡人
Liu Hsiang 劉湘
Liu Hsien-shih 劉顯世
Liu Kuan-hsiung 劉冠雄
Liu K'un-yi 劉坤一
Liu Kung tao (Liu-kung Tao, *Shantung*) 劉公島
Liu-li ch'ang (Peking) 琉璃廠
Liu Ming-chuan 劉銘傳
Liu-shih nien lai Chung-kuo yü Jih-pen 六十年來中國與日本
Liu Yü-lin 劉玉麟
Liu Yung-fu 劉永福
Liuchiu Islands (Liu-ch'iu Ch'ün-tao) 琉球群島
Lo Ch'ang 羅昌
Lo Feng-lu 羅豐祿
Lo Shan (Lo-shan, *Honan*) 羅山
Lo Wei-hsin 樓韋新
Lolo 玀玀
Lu Cheng-hsiang 陸徵祥
Lu Chien-chang 陸建章
Lu Chuan-lin 鹿傳霖
Lu Chung-ch'i 陸鍾琦
Lu-chün 陸軍
Lu-chün (Hsiao) Hsüeh-t'ang 陸軍（小）學堂
Lu Hai-huan 呂海寰
Lu Hsin-yüan 陸心源
Lu Hsün 魯迅
Lu Jung-t'ing 陸榮廷
Lu Liang-ch'en 陸亮臣
Lu Mu-ch'en 盧慕貞

Lu Tsung-yü 陸宗輿
Luhan 蘆漢
Lukouchiao (Lu-kou-ch'iao, *Chihli*) 蘆溝橋
Lun-ch'uan chao-shang-chü 輪船招商局
Lun-yü 論語
Lung Chi-kuang 龍濟光
Lung Chien-chang 龍建章
Lung Ch'in-kuang 龍覲光
Lung-chou (Lung-chin, *Kwangsi*) 龍州（龍津）
Lung K'ou (Lung-k'ou, *Shantung*) 龍口
Lung-yü 隆裕
Lung Yü-kuang 龍裕光
Lung Yün 龍雲
Lunghai 隴海
Lushan (Lu-shan, *Kiangsi*) 廬山
Ma Chien-chung 馬建忠
Ma Fu-hsiang 馬福祥
Ma Fu-lu 馬福祿
Ma Hung-k'uei 馬鴻逵
Ma Hung-pin 馬鴻賓
Ma Liang 馬良
Ma shi wen-t'ung 馬氏文通
Ma Soo 馬素
Ma Ying-piao (Ma Ying Piu) 馬應彪
Mainichi Dempō 每日電報
Mainichi Shimbun 每日新聞
Makino Nobuaki 牧野伸顯
Man 滿
Manchukuo 滿洲國
Manchuli (Man-chou-li, *Heilungkiang*) 滿洲里
Mao Tse-tung 毛澤東

Maotze (Mao-tsu, *Yunnan*) 茂租
Martial Court 軍法庭
Masampo (Korea) 馬山浦
Matsubara Kōichi 松原行一
Matsudaira Tsuneo 松平恒雄
Matsui Iwane 松井石根
Matsui Keishirō 松井慶四郎
Matsukata Masayoshi 松方正義
Matsuoka Yōsuke 松岡洋右
Megata Tanetarō 目賀田種太郎
Mei Tung-yi 梅東益
Meiji Emperor. *See* Mutsuhito 明治天皇
Meng-tzu (*Yunnan*) 蒙自
Meng-tzu 孟子
Mengtse. *See* Meng-tzu
Metropolitan Forces, Commander-in-Chief of 京畿衛戍司令
Miao-tzu (*Honan*) 廟子
Miaotze (Miao-tzu) 苗子
Mien-yü 綿愉
Mikami Yoshitada 三上良忠
Military Council. *See* Council of Generals
Min-cheng pu 民政部
Min-cheng-ssu 民政司
Min-kuo hsin-wên 民國新聞
Min-ning 旻寧
Min pao 民報
Mint, Director-General of 造幣總廠總裁
Mirs Bay 大鵬灣
Mitsubishi 三菱
Mitsui Bussan Kaisha 三井物產會社

843

Miyazaki Torazō (Tōten) 宮崎寅藏（滔天）
Mizuno Kōkichi 水野幸吉
Mo Jung-hsin 莫榮新
Mochizuki Jitsutarō 望月實太郎
Mochizuki Keisuke 望月圭介
Morrison, George Ernest 莫理循，磨禮遜，馬立孫，磨理遜，穆禮循，莫利循，莫利遜，磨禮遜
Motono Ichirō 木野一郎
mou (mu) 畝
Mu-tsung 穆宗
Muroran (Japan) 室蘭
Mussart Pass (Sinkiang) 莫扎爾特山口
Mutsu Munemitsu 陸奧宗光
Mutsuhito 睦仁
Na-t'ung 那桐
Na Wang 那王
Na-yen-t'u 那彥圖
Nabeshima Naohiro 鍋島直夫
Nagai Matsuzō 永井松三
Nagaoka Hantarō 長岡半太郎
Nakashōji Ren 仲小路廉
Namquan (Nan-kuan, Chekiang) 南關
Namti (Nan-ch'i Ho, Yunnan) 南溪河
Nan-fang pao [？ 南方報]
Nanchang (Nan-ch'ang, Kiangsi) 南昌
Nankai (Nan-k'ai, Tientsin) 南開
Nank'ang (Nan-k'ang, Kiangsi) 南康

Nankow Pass (Nan-k'ou, Chihli) 南口
Nanning (Nan-ning, Kwangsi) 南寧
Nansiang (Nan-hsiang, Kiangsu) 南翔
National History, Bureau of 國史館
National Petition Association 變更國體全國請願聯合會
National Petroleum Bureau, Director of 全國石油礦事務督辦
National Rehabilitation Council (1925) 善後會議
Nawa Matahachirō 名和又八郎
Nei-wu pu 內務部
Nen River (Nen Chiang) 嫩江
New Communication Clique 新交通系
Newchwang (Niu-ch'uang, Fengtien) 牛莊
Ni Ssu-ch'ung 倪嗣冲
Nichinichi Shimbun 日日新聞
Nieh-t'ai 臬臺
Nikkō (Japan) 日光
Nimrod Sound (Hsiang-san Chiang, Chekiang) 象山港
Ning T'iao-yüan 甯調元
Ninghsiafu (Ning-hsia-fu, Kansu, Ningsia) 寧夏府
Ningpo (Ning-po, Chekiang) 寧波
Ninguta (Kirin) 寧古塔（寧安）
Ningyuan (Ning-yüan; Hsi-ch'ang, Szechwan, Ch'uan-pien, Sikang) 寧遠（西昌）
Ninshiafu. See Ninghsiafu
Nippon (Nihon) Yūsen Kaisha 日本郵船會社

Nishihara Kamezō 西原龜三
Nisshi Kyōdō Tsūshin 日支共同通信
Nogi Maresuke 乃木希典
North China Daily News 字林報
North China Herald 北華捷報
North China Political Council 華北政務委員會
North-Eastern Army, Commander-in-Chief of 中華革命軍東北軍總司令
North-West Frontier Defence Forces, Commander-in-Chief of 西北邊防軍總司令
Obata Yukichi (Torikichi) 小幡酉吉
Odagiri Masunosuke 小田切萬壽之助
Ōishi Masami 大右正巳
Oka Ichinosuke 岡市之助
Okabe Nagakage 岡部長景
Okabe Nagamoto 岡部長職
Okabe Saburō 岡部三郎
Okamura Yasuji 岡村寧次
Ōkubo Toshimichi 大久保利通
Ōkuma Shigenobu 大隈重信
Ōkura Kihachirō 大倉喜八郎
Ordos (*Suiyuan*) 車臣汗（翁都爾汗）
Ōsaka Mainichi 大坂每日
Ōshima Ken'ichi 大島健一
Ōtani Kikuzō 大谷喜久藏
Ou-Lan-Hua (U-lan-hua, *Suiyuan*) 烏蘭花
Ou-yang Wu 歐陽武
Overseas Chinese Affairs Bureau, Director-General of 僑務局總裁

Ōyama Iwao 大山巖
Ōyama Sutematsu 大山捨松
Ozaki Yukio 尾崎行雄
Pacification Commissioner 宣撫使
Pagoda Anchorage (Lou-hsing Tao, *Fukien*) 羅星島
Pai Ch'ung-hsi 白崇禧
pai-ho kung-ssu 百貨公司
Pai Lang 白狼
P'ai Lou (p'ai-lou) 牌樓
Pai Wen-wei. *See* Po Wen-wei
Pai Yung-ch'eng 白永成 (also 白永丞)
Paise (Po-se, *Kwangsi*) 百色
Pakhoi (Pei-hai, *Kwangtung*) 北海
Pao-an hui 保安會
Pao Huang Hwei (Pao-huang hui) 保皇會
Pao-i 寶頤 (or Pao Tzu-kuan 寶子貫 寶子觀)
Pao-kun 寶崑
Pao-Tou (Pao-t'ou, *Suiyuan*) 包頭
Paoshan (Pao-shan, Shanghai) 寶山
Paoting-fu (Pao-ting-fu, *Chihli*) 保定府
Patou. *See* Pao-Tou
Peace Maintenance Committee 治安會
Pei-ching jih-pao 北京日報
Pei-ching pao 北京報
Pei-hua pao (Pai-hua pao) 白話報
Peitaiho (Pei-tai-ho, *Chihli*) 北戴河
Peitang (Pei-t'ang, Peking) 北堂
Peiyang 北洋

845

Peking & Tientsin Times 京津時報

Peking Daily News 北京日報

Pench'i (Pen-ch'i-hu, Fengtien) 本溪（本溪湖）

Peng-pu (Anhwei) 蚌埠

P'engshanhsien (P'eng-shan-hsien, Szechwan) 彭山縣

Pen-shih-hu. See Pench'i

People's Political Consultative Conference 人民政治協商會議

Petuna (Hsin-ch'eng-tzu, Fu-yü, Kirin) 新城子，扶餘

Pi Kuei-fang 畢桂芳

Pien Chün 邊軍

Picnma (P'ien-ma, Yunnan) 片馬

Pin-Hei 濱黑

P'ing-cheng yüan 平政院

Ping Hsiang (P'ing-hsiang, Kiangsi) 萍鄉

Ping-hsü 丙戌

p'ing-jen 聘任

Ping-ting-chow (P'ing-ting-chou, Shansi) 平定州

Pitozewo (Pi-tzu-wo, Fengtien) 貔子窩

Po Hai 渤海

Political Affairs, Director of (Japan) 政務局局長

Political Consultative Council (1914) 參政院

Political Consultative Council (1913) 政治會議

Pootung (P'u-tung, Shanghai) 浦東

Po-se. See Paise

Po Wen-wei 柏文蔚

Provincial Legislative Assembly 參議會

Provisional Government (Nanking 1912) 南京臨時政府

Provisional Political Consultative Council (1925) 臨時參政院

Pu-chen shih 布政使

P'u-chien 溥健

P'u-chün 溥儁

pu erh chia 不二價

P'u-hsü 溥煦

P'u-jun 溥儒

P'u-kuang 溥侊

P'u-lun 溥倫

P'u-t'ung 溥侗

P'u-yi 溥儀

Pukow (P'u-k'ou, Kiangsu) 浦口

Pusan (Korea) 釜山

Pyongyang (Korea) 平陽

Quo Tai-chi. See Kuo T'ai-ch'i

Red River (Hung Ho) 紅河

Reform Government 維新政府

Regional Commissioner 道尹

Relief and Rehabilitation, Director-General of 賑務督辦

Research Clique 研究系

Revenue, Board of 稅務處

ri 里

Rikken Dōshikai 立憲同志會

Rikken Seiyūkai 立憲政友會

rōnin 浪人

Ryūkyū Islands. See Liuchiu Islands

Sa Chen-ping 薩鎮冰

Sa Fu-mao 薩福懋

Sa-yin-tu 薩蔭圖

Saburi Sadao 佐分利貞夫

Sahara Tokusuke 佐原篤介

846

Saigō Takamori 西鄉隆盛
Saigō Tsugumichi 西鄉從道
Sain Noin 桑音訥顏
Sainam (Hsi-nan, *Kwangtung*) 西南
Saionji Kimmochi 西園寺公望
Salachi (Sa-la-ch'i, *Suiyuan*) 薩拉齊
Samsah (San-sha, *Fukien*) 三沙
Samshui (San-shui, *Kwangtung*) 三水
San Liu-ch'iao 三六橋
San-shui Liang Yen-sun hsien-sheng nien-p'u 三水梁燕孫先生年譜
San-Tao-Ho (San-tao-ho; Teng-k'ou, Kuang-hsing-yüan, *Kansu*, *Ningsia*) 三道河（磴口廣興源）
Sanmoon Bay (*Chekiang*) 三門灣
Santaoho. See San-Tao-Ho
Santo 三多
Santō Maru 山東丸
Satō Yasunosuke 佐藤安之助
Satsuma clan 薩磨藩
Secretary of State 國務卿
Seikadō Bunko 靜嘉堂文庫
Seiyūkai 政友會
Semba Tarō 仙波太郎
sen 錢
Senate. See Tsan-yi yüan, Tsan-cheng yüan
seppuku 切腹
Shaberte (Shabartai, *Chahar*) 什巴爾台・沙伯爾特
Shameen (Sha-mien, Canton) 沙面
Shan-ch'i (Prince Su) 善耆

shang pan 商辦
Shang pu 商部
Shang Wu Chu (Shang-wu ch'u) 商務處
Shanghai Mercury 文滙報
Shanghai Times 泰時報申報
Shanhaikwan (Shan-hai-kuan, *Chihli*) 山海關
Sharasume (Ch'eng-hua, A-shan, A-le-t'ai, *Sinkiang*) 承化・阿山・阿勒泰
Shashe (Sha-shih, *Hupeh*) 沙市
Shen Chin 沈藎
Shen K'e-ch'eng 沈克誠
Shen pao 申報
Shen Shou-chih 沈受之
Shen Yün-p'ei 沈雲沛
Sheng-ching (Mukden, Shen-yang, *Fengtien*) 盛京（瀋陽）
Sheng-ching pao 盛京報
Sheng-ching shih-pao 盛京時報
Sheng Hsüan-huai 盛宣懷
Sheng-tsu 聖祖
Shi Pien men (Hsi-pien men, Peking) 西便門
Shiba Gorō 柴五郎
Shibusawa Eiichi 澁澤榮一
Shidehara Kijurū 幣原喜重郎
Shieh Fu Ma Ta Chieh (Shih-fu-ma ta-chieh, Peking) 石駙馬大街
Shigatse (Tibet) 日喀則
Shigeno Yasutsugu 重野安繹
Shih Chao-chi 施肇基
Shih-ching 詩經
Shih-hsü 世續
Shih-lu 實錄

847

Shih-shu hsin-pao [? 世俗新報 時事新報]

Shih-tsu 世祖

Shih-tsung 世宗

Shih-wu jih-pao 時務日報

Shih-wu pao 時務報

Shihchiachuang (Shih-chia-chuang; Shih-men, *Chihli*) 石家莊

Shikan Gakkō 士官學校

Shimbu Gakkō 振武學校

Shin Kōron 新公論

Shiohara (Japan) 鹽原

Shōda Kazue 勝田主計

Shōwa Emperor. *See* Hirohito 昭和天皇

Shu-ching 書經

shu hui li chuan (shou hui li ch'üan) 收回利權

Shui-wu ch'u 稅務處

Shun-chih 順治

Shun-shih News Agency (Shen-shih tien-hsin she) 申時電訊社

Shun-t'ien shih-pao 順天時報

Shunfang (*Hsün-fang*) 巡防

Shuntefu (Shun-te-fu, *Kwangtung*) 順德府

Sia Tien-bao 夏

Sian(fu) (Hsi-an-fu, *Shensi*) 西安(府)

Siccawei (Hsü-chia hui, Shanghai) 徐家滙

Signan. *See* Sinyang chow

Sik'ang (Hsi-k'ang) 西康

Sikawei. *See* Siccawei

Sincere Company. *See* Hsien-shih kung-ssu

Sing Tai [? 邢泰]

Singanfu (Hsin-an-fu, *Honan*) 新安府

Sining (Hsi-ning, *Tsinghai*) 西寧

Sinyang chow (Hsin-yang-chou, *Honan*) 信陽州

Soejima Giichi 副島義一

Son Chung-hee 孫重熙

Soochow (Su-chou, *Kiangsu*) 蘇州

Soong, Charles. *See* Sung Chia-shu

Soong, T. V. *See* Sung Tzu-wen

sōshi 壯士

Ssu-ma Kuang 司馬光

Ssu p'ai lou (Peking) 四牌樓

Su, Prince (*see also* Shan-ch'i) 肅親王

Su-cheng T'ing 肅政廳

Suchowfu (Su-chou-fu; Chiu-ch'uan, *Kansu*) 肅州府 (酒泉)

Sui-t'ing hsien (Sui-ting-hsien, *Sinkiang*) 綏定縣

Suifu (Sui-fu; Sui-chou, I-pin, *Szechwan*) 敘府 (敘州宜賓)

Suiting-hsien. *See* Sui-t'ing hsien

Suiyüan 綏遠

Sun Chi-ch'ien [? 孫繼賢]

Sun Fo. (Sun K'o) 孫科

Sun Pao-ch'i 孫寶琦

Sun To-shen 孫多森

Sun Wen 孫文

Sun Wu 孫武

Sun Yat-sen 孫逸仙

Sung Ai-ling 宋靄齡

Sung Chia-shu 宋嘉樹

Sung Chiao-jen 宋教仁

Sung Ch'ing-ling 宋慶齡

Sung Fa-hsiang 宋發祥

Sung Mei-ling 宋美齡
Sung Shan (*Honan*) 嵩山
Sung Shan ssu-yu 嵩山四友
Sung Tzu-an 宋子安
Sung Tzu-liang 宋子良
Sung Tzu-wen 宋子文
Supao 蘇報
Swatow (Shan-t'ou, *Kwangtung*) 汕頭
Sze, Alfred. *See* Shih Chao-chi
Szemao (Ssu-mao, *Yunnan*) 思茅
Ta ching (Ta-Ch'ing) 大清銀行
Ta-hsüeh 大學
Ta-jen 大人
Ta-kung pao 大公報
Ta Tsung-tung (*Ta ts'ung-t'ung*) 大總統
Ta-t'ung shu 大同書
Ta-wan pao 大晚報
Ta Wang Miao (Ta-wang-miao, *Jehol*) 大王廟
Tabol (*Jehol*) 塔布爾
Tachibana Masaki 立花政樹
Tachienlu (Ta-chien-lu; K'ang-ting, *Szechwan*) 打箭爐 (康定)
Tach'ing Ho (Ta-ch'ing Ho, *Shantung*) 大清河
Tae Islands (T'ai-shan Lieh-tao) 臺山列島
tael 兩
Taga Muneyuki 多賀宗之
Tai Chi-t'ao 戴季陶
Tai Chuan-hsien 戴傳賢
Tai K'an 戴戡
Tai Lai (T'ai Lai) 泰來
Tai Li 戴笠

T'ai-pei (*Taiwan*) 臺北
Tai-shing-hsien (T'ai-hsing-hsien, *Kiangsu*) 泰興縣
T'ai-tzu p'ai 太子派
Tai-yuan-fu (T'ai-yüan-fu, *Shansi*) 太原府
Taichow (T'ai-chou; Lin-hai, *Chekiang*) 台州 (臨海)
Taihu (T'ai Hu, *Kiangsu* and *Chekiang*) 太湖
T'aikuhsien (T'ai-ku-hsien, *Shansi*) 太谷縣
Taiping (T'ai-p'ing) 太平
Taishō Emperor. *See* Yoshihito 大正天皇
Taiyuan. *See* Tai-yuan-fu
Takachiho 高千穂
Takasan (Ta-ku-shan, *Fengtien*) 大孤山
Takata Shinzō 高田慎藏
Takeshita Isamu 竹下勇
Taki Seiichi 瀧精一
Takoshina. *See* Sa-yin-tu
Taku (Ta-ku, *Chihli*) 大沽
Talien-wan (Ta-lien Wan, *Fengtien*) 大連灣
Talifu (Ta-li-fu, *Yunnan*) 大理府
Tamba Keizō 丹波敬三
T'an Jen-feng 譚人鳳
T'an Khan-kan. *See* Ch'en Chia-keng
Tanada 棚田
Tanaka Giichi 田中義一
T'ang Chi-yao 唐繼堯
T'ang Chüeh-tun 湯覺頓
T'ang Hsiang-ming 湯薌銘
T'ang Hua-lung 湯化龍
T'ang Jui 湯叡

T'ang Pao-ch'ao 唐寶潮

T'ang Shao-yi 唐紹儀

T'ang Shou-ch'ien 湯壽潛

T'ang T'ing-shu 唐廷樞

T'ang Ts'ai-ch'ang 唐才常

T'ang Yüan-chan 唐元湛

T'angku (T'ang-ku, *Chihli*) 塘沽

T'angshan (T'ang-shan, *Chihli*) 唐山

Tanling (Tan-leng, *Szechwan*) 丹稜

Tao-kuang 道光

Tao-tsang 道藏

Taoch'ing (T'ao-ch'ing) 洮清

Taonanfu (T'ao-nan-fu, *Kirin*) 洮南府

Taotai (*Tao-t'ai*) 道臺

Taoyin (*Tao-yin*) 道尹

Tapienling (Ta-pien-ling, *Fengtien*) [？大邊嶺]

Tarbagatai (T'a-ch'eng, Mongolia) 塔城

Tashi Lama 大智喇嘛

Tashihchiao (Ta-shih-ch'iao, *Fengtien*) 大石橋

Tatsu Maru 辰丸

Tatung (Ta-t'ung, *Shansi*) 大同

Tayeh (Ta-yeh, *Hupeh*) 大冶

Te-chou (*Shantung*) 德州

Te-tsung 德宗

Tei Eishō 鄭永正

Teng Hsiao-hsien 鄧孝先

Teng P'ing-shu 鄧平書

Tengyueh (T'eng-yüeh, *Yunnan*) 騰越

Terao Tōru 寺尾亨

Terauchi Masatake 寺內正毅

Terauchi Seiki 寺內正記

Teshima Sutematsu 手島捨松

T'i-t'ai 提臺

Tiao Min-ch'ien 刁敏謙

Tiao Tso-ch'ien 刁作謙

Tibetan Affairs, Special Commissioner for. *See* Hsuanfu shih

T'ieh-liang 鐵良

Tieling (T'ieh-ling, *Fengtien*) 鐵嶺

T'ien Chen-pang 田振邦

T'ien Chih-chìng [？田志清]

Tien-ling-sse (T'ien-ning-ssu, Peking) 天寧寺

t'ien-ming 天命

Tien-tse-pai (T'ien-chih p'ai) 天知派

T'ien Ya-hsin, ?T'ien-Ya-chün, [?T'ien Yu-heng 田亞贇 田又橫]

T'ien Yü-shan [？田玉山]

Tienshan Mountains (T'ien Shan, *Sinkiang*) 天山

Tiger Hill (Hu-t'ou-yai, *Shantung*) 虎頭崖

Tihuafu (Ti-hua-fu, *Sinkiang*) 迪化府

Ting 廳

t'ing-chi 廷寄

Ting Pao-ch'üan 丁寶銓

Ting Shih-yüan 丁士源

Ting, V. K. *See* Ting Wen-chiang

Ting Wen-chiang 丁文江

Tōa senkaku shishi kiden 東亞先覺志士記傳

Tochiki (Japan) 栃木

Tōgō Heihachirō 東鄉平八郎

Tohoro 托活絡

Tōjō Hideki 東條英機

850

Tokugawa Ieyasu 德川家康
Tokutomi Ichirō 德富一郎
Tokutomi Kenjirō 德富健次郎
Tokutomi Sōhō 德富蘇峯
Tokyo Semmon Gakkō 東京專門學校
Tokyu (Tōkyū) 東急
Tonami Tatsuaburō 外波辰三郎
Tong Kai-son (T'ang Chieh-ch'en) 唐介臣
Tong, Y. C. See T'ang Yüan-chan
Tongnip Sinmun 獨立新聞
Tongshan. See T'angshan
tou 斗
T'oung pao 通報
Tōyama Mitsuru 頭山滿
Tōyō Bunko 東洋文庫
Tōyō Jiyū Shimbun 東洋自由新聞
Tsai-chen 戴振
Ts'ai-ch'un 戴淳
Ts'ai-fa 財閥
Tsai-feng (2nd Prince Ch'ing) 戴澧
Tsai-fu 戴搏
Tsai-hsün 戴洵
Tsai-i 戴漪
Tsai-lan 戴瀾
Tsai-lien 戴濂
Ts'ai Nai-huang 蔡乃煌
Ts'ai O 蔡鍔
Ts'ai Shao-chi 蔡紹基
Tsai-t'ao 戴濤
Tsai-t'ien 戴湉

Ts'ai T'ing-kan 蔡廷幹
Tsai-tse 戴澤
Ts'ai Yüan-p'ei 蔡元培
Tsan-cheng yüan 參政院
Tsan-yi yüan 參議院
Tsang Chow (Ts'ang-chou, *Chihli*) 滄州
Ts'ao Ju-lin 曹汝霖
Ts'ao Kai-cheong (Ts'ao Chia-hsiang) 曹嘉祥
Ts'ao K'un 曹錕
Tsaochow fu (Ts'ao-chou-fu; Ho-tse, *Shantung*) 曹州府（菏澤）
Tse-chou fu (Tse-chou-fu; Chin-ch'eng, *Shansi*) 澤州府（晉城）
Ts'en Ch'un-hsüan 岑春煊
Ts'en Hsüeh-lü 岑學呂
Ts'en Yü-ying 岑毓英
Tseng-ch'i 增祺
Tseng Chi-tse 曾紀澤
Tseng Ching-yi 曾敬貽
Tseng Kuang-ch'üan 曾廣銓
Tseng Kuo-fan 曾國藩
Tseng Tsung-kien (Tseng Tsung-chien) 曾宗鑒
Tseng Yu-yi 曾有翼
Tsinan-fu. See Chinan
Tsinghua (Ch'ing-hua) 清華
Tsingtao (Ch'ing-tao, *Shantung*) 青島
Tsining. See Chining
Tsitsihar (*Heilungkiang*) 齊齊哈爾
Tso-chuan 左傳
Tsou Chia-lai 鄒嘉來
Tsou Jung 鄒容

851

Tsuji Karoku 辻嘉六

Tsung-li (ko-kuo shih-wu) ya-men 總理(各國事務)衙門

Tu Yüeh-sheng 杜月笙

Tuan Ch'i-jui 段祺瑞

Tuan Chih-kuei 段芝貴

Tuan-chin 端錦

Tuan-fang 端方

Tu-chün 督軍

Tumen River (T'u-men Chiang, *Kirin*) 圖門江

Tun Fang (T'un-fang, Peking) 囤房

T'ung-chih 同治

T'ung Chou (T'ung-chou, *Chihli*) 通州

Tung Fu-hsiang 董福祥

Tung-hai (T'ung-hai, *Yunnan*) 通海

Tung Hsien-kuang 董顯光

Tung Kuan (T'ung-kuan, *Shensi*) 潼關

T'ung-kuan-shan (*Anhwei*) 銅官山

T'ung-meng hui 同盟會

Tung pa li chuang (Peking) 東八里莊

T'ung-wen kuan 同文館

Tungchow. See T'ung Chou

Turin (*Mongolia*) 吐林

Tutu (Tu-tu) 都督

Tutung (Tu-t'ung) 都統

Tzeliutsing (Tzu-liu-ching, *Szechwan*) 自流井

Tzu-cheng yüan 資政院

Tzu-chih t'ung-chien 資治通鑑

Tzu-chou (Sui-te, *Shensi*) 子州 (綏德)

Tzu-chou (Tzu-chung, *Szechwan*) 資州 (資中)

Tz'u-hsi 慈禧

Tzu-i chü 諮議局

Uchida Ryōhei 内田良平

Uchida Yasuya 内田康哉

Ude (Wu-te, *Chahar*) 烏得

Ueno Iwatarō 上野岩太郎

Ukita Gōji 浮田鄉次

Uliassutai (*Mongolia*) 烏里雅蘇台

Ulugshat (*Sinkiang*) 烏魯克恰提

Uo-Lan-Hua (U-lan-hua, *Suiyuan*) 烏蘭花

Urga (Ulanbator, K'u-lun, *Mongolia*) 烏蘭巴托 (庫倫)

Urianghai (*Mongolia*) 唐努烏梁海

Urumchi. See Tihuafu

Waga shichijū-nen wo kataru わが七十年を語る

Wai-chiao pu 外交部

Wai-wu pu 外務部

Wai Wu Sze (Wai-wu shih) 外務司

Waichow (Hui-chou; Hui-yang, *Kwangtung*) 惠州 (惠陽)

Wakatsuki Reijirō 若槻禮次郎

Wan, B. C. See Wen Ping-chung

Wan-hsien (*Szechwan*) 萬縣

Wang Chan-yüan 王占元

Wang Chao-ming 汪兆銘

Wang Ch'eng-pin 王承斌

Wang Cheng-t'ing 王正廷

Wang Chih-ch'un 王之春

Wang Chih-hsiang 王芝祥

Wang Ching-ch'un 王景春

Wang Ching-wei 汪精衛
Wang Ch'ung-hui 王寵惠
Wang Fu Ching Tachieh (Peking) 王府井大街
Wang I-t'ang 王揖唐
Wang K'ai-yün 王闓運
Wang K'ang-nien 汪康年
Wang K'e-min 王克敏
Wang Ling-chi 王陵基
Wang *Pan-ch'eng* 王半城
Wang Shih-chen 王士珍
Wang Ta-hsieh 汪大燮
Wang Tsuan-hsü 王纘緒
Wang Ts'un-shan 王存善
Wang T'ung 王同 (also 王統)
Wang Tzu-chan 王子展
Wang Wen-shao 王文韶
Wang Yang-ming 王陽明
Wang Yün-sheng 王芸生
War Participation Bureau, Director of 參戰督辦
Waseda 早稻田
Washizawa Yoshiji 鷲澤與四二
Watanabe Kikujirō 渡邊菊次郎
Wei Ch'ung-shu 魏冲叔
Wei Hsien (Wei-hsien, *Shantung*) 濰縣
Wei Kuang-t'ao 魏光燾
Wei Yi 魏易
Weiyuan (*Wei-yüan*) 委員
Weihaiwei (Wei-hai-wei, *Shantung*) 威海衛
Wen-Kuan (*wen-kuan*) 文官
Wen Ping-chung 溫秉忠
Wen-tsung 文宗

Wen Tsung-yao 溫宗堯
Wenchow (Wen-chou; Yung-chia, *Chekiang*) 溫州（永嘉）
Weng T'ung-ho 翁同龢
Wenhsiu fu (Wen-su-fu, *Sinkiang*) 溫宿府
West River (Hsi Chiang) 西江
Western Hills Clique 西山派
Whangpoo River. *See* Huangpu River
Wo Fo Ssu (Wo-fo-ssu, *Chihli*) 卧佛寺
Wo ti ch'ien pan sheng 我的前半生
Wong Chu-shwui (Wang Chih-jui) 王之瑞
Wong Kai-kai (Huang K'ai-chia) 黃開甲
Woosung (Wu-sung, *Kiangsu*) 吳淞
Wu-ch'ang (*Hupeh*) 武昌
Wu Ch'ao-ch'u (Wu Ch'ao-shu) 伍朝樞
Wu Chih-ying 吳芝瑛
Wu Ch'ung-hsi 吳重熹
Wu-han (*Hupeh*) 武漢
Wu-hsü jih-chi 戊戌日記
Wu Juin-pah (Wu Yin-po, Wu Chin-pao) 吳藎拍，吳進寶
Wu Lien-te 伍連德
Wu Lu-chen 吳祿貞
Wu Mao-ting 吳懋鼎
Wu Ming-fu 吳銘福
Wu P'ei-fu 吳佩孚
Wu Shih-ying 武士英
Wu-su (*Sinkiang*) 烏蘇
Wu T'iao-ching 吳兆卿
Wu T'ieh-ch'eng 吳鐵城
Wu T'ing-fang 伍廷芳

Wu Yü-lin 吳毓麟

Wu Yüeh 吳越

Wuchang (Wu-ch'ang, *Hupeh*) 武昌

Wuchow (Wu-chou, *Kwangsi*) 梧州

Wuhan (Wu-han, *Hupeh*) 武漢

Wuhu (Wu-hu, *Anhwei*) 蕪湖

Wutai 烏泰

Wutai-shan (Wu-t'ai Shan, *Shansi*) 五臺山

Ya Hsi Ya Po (*Ya-hsi-ya pao*) 亞細亞報

Yalu River (Ya-lu Chiang) 鴨綠江

Yamagata Aritomo 山縣有朋

Yamamoto Gombei (Gonnohyōe) 山本權兵衛

Yamamoto Tadasaburō 山本唯三郎

Yamane Takeyoshi 山根武亮

Yamato Shimbun やまと（日出國）新聞

Yamaza Enjirō 山座圓次郎

Yamazaki Heikichi 山崎平吉

Yamen 衙門

Yang Ch'eng 楊晟

Yang Ch'ing-ch'ang 楊慶昶

Yang Jui 楊銳

Yang Shih-ch'i 楊士琦

Yang Shih-hsiang 楊士驤

Yang Tseng-hsin 楊增新

Yang Tsuan-hsü 楊纘緒

Yang Tu 楊度

Yangampo 龍岩浦

Yangchow (Yang-chou, *Kiangsu*) 揚州

Yangtsun (Yang-ts'un, *Chihli*) 揚村

Yano Fumio 矢野文雄

Yao Hung-fa 姚鴻發

Yasaka Maru 八坂丸

Yashima 屋島

Yasukawa Keiichirō 安川敬一郎

Yatung (Ya-tung, *Tibet*) 亞東

Yeh Kung-ch'o 葉恭綽

Yehonala 葉赫那拉

Yen, Duke (K'ung Ling-i, K'ung Yen-t'ing) 燕（孔令貽，孔燕庭）

Yen, Hawkling (Yen Ho-ling) 嚴鶴齡

Yen an fu (Yen-an-fu; Fu-shih, *Shensi*) 延安府（膚施）

Yen Chang (Yen-ch'ang, *Shensi*) 延長

Yen-chih 延祉

Yen Fu 嚴復

Yen Hsi-shan 閻錫山

Yen Hsiu 嚴修

Yen Hui-ch'ing 顏惠慶

Yen-tu pao 燕都報

Yen Wu Shu (Yen-wu shu) 鹽務署

Yen-yeh Bank 鹽業銀行

Yen Yüan Hsien (Yen-yüan-hsien, *Szechwan, Ch'uan-pien, Sikang*) 鹽源縣

Yenan-fu. *See* Yen an fu.

Yenchow-fu (Yen-chou-fu; Chien-te, Tzu-yang, *Shantung*) 兗州府（建德，滋陽）

Yih-hsien (I-hsien; Lai-chou, *Shantung*) 掖縣（萊州）

854

Yih-hsien (I-hsien, *Shantung*) 嶧縣
Yihchow Fu (I-chou-fu; *Shantung*) 沂州府（臨沂）
Yin-ch'ang 廕昌
Yin-chen 胤禎
Yin ping shih ho chi 飲冰室合集
Yinchuan (Yin-ch'uan; Ning-hsia, *Kansu, Ningsia*) 銀川（寧夏）
ying 應
Ying-hsien (*Shansi*) 應縣
Ying K'uei-ch'eng 應夔丞
Ying Kuei-hsiang 應桂馨
Ying-t'ai (Peking) 瀛臺
Ying-tak (Ying-te, *Kwangtung*) 英德
Yingchow (Ying-chou; Fou-yang, *Anhwei*) 潁州（阜陽）
Yinkow (Ying-k'ou, *Fengtien*) 營口
Yokohama Specie Bank 橫濱正金銀行
Yokosuka (Japan) 橫須賀
Yoshida Shigeru 吉田茂
Yoshihito 嘉仁
Yoshiwara (Tokyo) 吉原
Yoshizawa Kenkichi 芳澤謙吉
Yü Ho-te 虞和德
Yü Hsia-ch'ing 虞洽卿

Yü-hsien 毓賢
Yü-hua-t'ai (Nanking) 雨花臺
Yü-keng 裕庚
Yü-lang 毓朗
Yu Ya Ching. *See* Yü Hsia-ch'ing
yüan 院
Yüan Ch'ang-k'un 袁長坤
Yüan K'e-ting 袁克定
Yüan Shih-k'ai 袁世凱
Yüan Ta-hua 袁大化
Yüan Yün-t'ai 袁雲臺
Yüanming-yüan (Yüan-ming yüan, Peking) 圓明園
Yuechow (Yüeh-chou; Yüeh-yang, *Hunan*) 岳州（岳陽）
Yüeh-Han 粵漢
Yume no shichijū yo nen 夢の七十餘年
Yün, C. K. *See* Yüan Ch'ang-k'un
Yun Ch'i-ho 尹致昊
Yung Lo 永樂
Yung-cheng 雍正
Yung-ling (Yü Yung-ling) 容齡（裕容齡）
Yung-yen 顒琰
Yunnanfu (Yün-nan-fu, Yunnan) 雲南府
Zaibatsu 財閥
Zumoto Motosada 頭本元貞

Index

Abdur Rahman Khan (1844-1901), Amir of Afghanistan, 566 n.1
Abe Moritarō (1872-1913), Japanese diplomat, 222 + n.3
Abignente, Filippo (1814-87), Italian politician, 74 n.2
Abignente, Giovanni (1854-1915), Italian scholar, 74 n.2
Abugaida Wang, Mongol leader, 230, 266
Academia Sinica, 621 n.1
Acland, Francis Dyke (1874-1939), British politician, 75 + n.3, 126, 127
Addis, Charles Stewart (1861-1945), British banker, 34 + n.2, 54 n.2, 55, 66, 71, 317 n.3, 727 + n.2;
letter from, 253
Addison, Joseph (1879-1953), British diplomat, 77 + n.1, 78
Affleck, John Barr (1878-1941), British consular official, 268 + n.3;
letter to, 268
Afghanistan: Amirs of (*see* Abdur Rahman Khan; Habibullah Khan); and World War I, 546, 566-7
Aglen, Francis Arthur (1869-1932), British employee of Chinese Maritime Customs, 55 + n.3, 82, 239 n.3, 271 n.1, 288, 316, 354, 356, 402, 533, 624, 629, 725 n.1, 807 n.1, 817;
letter to, 475;
letters from, 353, 493
Ainscough, Thomas M. (?b. 1886), British government official, 135 + n.1;
letter to, 167
letter from, 135
Akiyama Masanosuke (1866-1937), Japanese diplomat, 641 + n.5
Alcock, Rutherford (1809-97), British diplomat, 413 + n.3
Alexeiev, Evgeni Ivanovich (1843-1918), Russian sailor, 58 n.3
Allen, James (1855-1942), New Zealand politician, 657 + n.1, 663 n.3;
letters to, 657, 680, 699;
letter from, 676
Allison, James Murray (1877-1929), Australian Advertising Manager of *The Times*, 409 + n.2;
letter from, 516
Alston, Francis Beilby (1868-1929), British diplomat, 152 + n.1, 170, 297 + n.2, 342-3, 353 n.2, 519 + n.1, 521-2, 571, 628, 664, 672, 687, 710, 810 + n.3, 811;
letters to, 574, 582, 585
Alston, Hilda (*née* Gream) (d. 1945), wife of F. B. Alston, 519
Amano, Japanese financial broker, 641
Anderson, Frederick A., British businessman, 313 n.3, 339 + n.1
Anderson, Robert van Vleck (1884-1949), American geologist, 503 + n.2
Anderson, Roy S., American political and financial agent, 119 + n.2, 482, 609, 650, 717, 718
Anderssen, Johann Gunnar (1874-1960), Swedish geologist, 415 + n.1, 416
Anesaki Masaharu (1873-1949), Japanese scholar, 660 + n.2, 680
Anglo-Japanese Alliance. *See under* Japan; Treaties, agreements etc.
Angustessen, German commercial agent, 641
Aoki Nobuzumi (1859-1923), Japanese soldier, 92 n.2, 124 + n.1, 343 n.1, 475 n.1, 509, 552 + n.3, 630, 637
Aoyagi Katsutoshi (1879-1934), Japanese soldier and adventurer, 211 + n.2
Ariga Nagao (1860-1921), Japanese jurist, 99 + n.2, 332, 338, 532, 533 + n.1, 536, 539, 540 + n.1, n.3, 548, 574, 578, 599, 621, 630, 637;
letters from, 620, 654, 655
Ariyoshi Akira (1876-1937), Japanese diplomat, 189, 290 + n.1
Armed forces and soldiery, Chinese, 18, 120, 148-9, 159-61, 167-8, 203-5, 259-60, 265-6, 269-70, 291, 295, 304, 308-9, 329 + n.2, 333, 343, 362 n.1, 380 + n.1, 406, 487, 497, 500-1, 541 + n.4, 553, 575, 601, 609 n.2, 611, 612, 614, 649, 693, 742; Council of Generals,

Armed forces and soldiery (cont.) 86 n.1, 522 n.2. *See also* Tuchün revolt; Yüan Shih-k'ai: and New Army; anti-monarchist movement (Nanking conference of militarists)

Arsenals in China, 471–2, 546, 561, 562, 573, 670; Kiangnan (Shanghai) Arsenal, 116 n.2, 181+n.2, 251+n.1, 438 n.1, 469, (attack on) 208, (*see also* Ch'en Ch'i-mei; Revolution *1913*); Nanking Arsenal, 104 n.2

Ashton-Gwatkin, Frank Trelawny Arthur (b. 1889), British diplomat, 787 n.1; *letters to*, 787, (from R. Ridout) 788

Asquith, Herbert Henry (1852–1928), British politician, 223+n.1, 344+n.2, 489 n.3 (490), 694, 696, 697

Astor, John Jacob (1886–1971), 1st Baron Astor of Hever, proprietor of *The Times*, 373 n.1

Australia: racial policy, 220+n.2; Chinese in, 316 n.1, 348–9, 675 n.2; trade possibilities, 642–3, 702–5; postal links, 699–700; and Japan, 220+n.2, 550, 588–9, 659–60, 661, 678–9, 757; and World War I, 518, 645+n.1, 650

Austria in China, 464, 466, 544, 545, 555, 560, 636, 642, 775

Backhouse, Edmund Trelawny (1872–1944), 2nd Bart, British adventurer and author, 83+n.3, 157, 330 n.5 (331), 376

Bagada Lama. *See* Jebtsun Damba Khutukhtu

Bailey, Frederick Marshman (1882–1967), British colonial official, 428+n.1

Bailey, George, 156

Baldwin, Stanley (1867–1947), British politician, 785 n.2

Balfour, Arthur James (1848–1930), 1st Earl, British politician, 489 n.3 (490), 619+n.1, 705, 706+n.1, 771, 774, 775, 799

Bande, R. L. P., employee of Chinese Salt Administration, 480+n.2

Banks, financial houses and consortia:
- consortia, 244–51, (Four Power) 766 n.2; (Four Power, 1919) 766+n.2–767, 784, 793+n.3, 803 n.2, 808–10; (Five Power) (*see* Loans: Quintuple); (Six Power) (*see* Loans; Sextuple); American Group, 793+n.3; Nishihara Banks (*see* Bank of Chosen, Exchange Bank of China, Industrial Bank of Japan, Bank of Taiwan);
- individual banks etc: Anglo-Russian Trust (Bank), 33 n.2, 66 n.1; Bank of Bengal, 824 n.1; British Bank of Foreign Trade, 33 n.2; British Trade Bank, 617; Central Trust Co., 405 n.2; Chartered Bank of India, Australia and China, 57 n.4, 96, 249, 298, 299, 310, 324, 338 +n.3–339, 407, 609 n.3, 824 n.1; Bank of China, 244 n.2, n.3, 248, 305 n.3, 310, 318 n.1, 339, 404+n.2, 496 n.1, 518 n.1, 597, 598, 609 n.3, 612, 708, 809+n.5; Bank of Chōsen, 583 n.2, 584 n.1, n.3, 590 n.1, 784 n.1; Commercial Guarantee Bank of Chihli, 300; Bank of Communications (Chiaotung Bank), 79 n.2, 244 n.2, 311+n.2, 518 n.1, 583, 597, 640 n.3, 708; C. Brich Crisp & Co., 192 n.2, (*see also* Loans: Crisp Loan); Daiichi Bank, 590 n.1; Deutsch-Asiatische Bank, 44 n.3, 71, 82 n.1, 244 n.2, 300, 302, 333, 375, 469, 563–4, 572, 607, 815+n.4; Bank of England, 34 n.2, 298, 576 n.1; Exchange Bank of China, 584 n.1, 590 n.1, 784 n.1; Hongkong & Shanghai Banking Corporation, 27, 34 +n.2, n.3, 37, 44–6, 54 n.2, 55+n.1, 65–6+n.1, 68, 69, 70, 71, 72, 96, 105, 286, 297–303, 305, 308, 315, 316, 317 +n.1, n.2, n.3, 337, 407–8, 564, 701, 727, 794, 805, 828; Banque de l'Indochine, 300, 303, 305, 794; Industrial Bank of Japan, 583 n.2, 584 n.1, 784 n.1; Bank of Industrial Development, 361+n.2; Banque Industrielle de Chine, 80 n.1–81, 300, 302, 303, 305+n.3, 794 +n.2, n.3; Bank of Japan, 415, 632 n.1; Kuhn Loeb & Co., 405 n.2; Lloyds Bank, 46+n.1, 65, 298, 686 n.1; London City Safe Deposit Co., 285; Bank of Montreal, 54 n.2; J. P. Morgan & Co., 793 n.3, n.4, 808, 809; National Bank of Egypt, 55 n.1; National Provincial Bank, 576 n.1; Russo-Asiatic Bank, 55, 315; Russo-Chinese Bank, 91; Royal Bank of Scotland, 576 n.1; Bank of Salt Revenue 14 n.5 (15), 79 n.2 (80); Banque Sino-Belge, 67 n.1; Ta-ch'ing Bank, 52; Bank of Taiwan, 93, 583 n.2, 584 n.1, 784 n.1; Yen-yeh Bank, 79 n.2 (80); Yokohama Specie Bank, 93, 432 n.1, 531, 583, 590 n.1, 598, 599, 627 n.2, 632+n.1, n.2, 766 n.2 (767), 792;
- moratorium on Chinese banks, 244 n.2, 518+n.1; Chinese financial agent in Europe, 255–7;
- Bankers Commission Shanghai, 572; British Institute of Bankers, 34 n.2; Berlin Bourse, 309; New York Stock

858

Banks (*cont.*)
Exchange, 405 n.2; Paris Bourse, 309; Shanghai Stock Exchange, 403
Banzai Rihachirō (b. 1870), Japanese soldier, 92 + n.2, 124 n.1, 343 n.1
Baring, Evelyn (1841–1917), 1st Earl of Cromer, British colonial official, 342 n.1, 674 + n.1
Barnardiston, Nathaniel Walter (1858–1919), British soldier, 424 + n.3
Barnes, Ernest, British soldier and financial agent, 68 + n.1
Barnes, Frederick Dallas (1842–99), British businessman, 68 + n.2
Barnes, Thomas (1785–1841), British journalist, Editor of *The Times*, 13 + n.4
Barse, German employee of Chinese government, 71 n.1
Barton, Mary Ethel Winifred (*née* McEwen) (d. 1945), wife of S. Barton, 571 + n.1, 628
Barton, Sidney (1876–1945), British diplomat, 277 + n.1, 286, 571 + n.1, 590, 591 + n.2, 712
Bate, Reginald, British journalist, 313 + n.1
Batouieff, Russian adventurer, 336
Bearsted, 1st Visct. *See* M. Samuel
Beattie, David (1871–1936), 1st Earl, British sailor, 777 + n.2, 789 n.2
Bebbington, Miss, British governess to the children of G. E. Morrison, 826
Beddard, Arthur Philip (d. 1939), British medical practitioner, 792 + n.2
Beelaerts van Blokland, Frans (b. 1872), Dutch diplomat, 704 + n.3
Belgium in China, 67, 68 + n.3, 100, 118–19, 286 + n.2, 298–9, 333 n.3, 465, 468, 473. *See also* Banks, financial houses and consortia; Loans; Missionaries; Powers in China; Railways: Peking–Hankow; Treaties, agreements etc.
Bell, Charles Alfred (1870–1945), British colonial official and author, 428 n.2
Bell, Charles Frederick Moberly (1847–1911), British journalist, Manager of *The Times*, 515 n.1, 758 n.5
Bell, Ethel (*née* Chataway), wife of C. F. M. Bell, 515 + n.1; *letter to*, 515
Bell, Henry Thorburn Montague (1873–1949), British journalist, 88 + n.2
Benjamin, Shanghai businessman, 567
Benn, William Wedgwood (1877–1960), 1st Visct Stansgate, British politician, 75 n.3

Berthelot, André-Marcel (1862–1938), French industrialist, financier and author, 80 n.1, 794 + n.2, n.3
Berthelot, Philippe-Joseph-Louis (1866–1934), French diplomat, 794 + n.3
Berthelot, Pierre-Eugène-Marcelin (1828–1907), French chemist and politician, 794 n.2
Bevan, Louis R. O., British educationalist, 68 n.5
Binsteed, G. C. (d. 1917), British soldier, 50 + n.4, 143 + n.2
Bintu Wang, Mongol leader, 230
Birchal, Edward Frank (1852–1920), British financial agent, 65 + n.1
Bismarck-Schönhausen, Otto, Prince von (1815–98), German politician, 117 n.2, 380 n.2
Bland, John Otway Percy (1863–1945), British journalist and author, 1, 45, 54 n.2, 83 + n.2, n.3, 113 + n.3, 192–3 + n.1, 226 + n.1, 272 n.1 (273), 313 n.3, 330 + n.3, 333, 335, 793
Bligh, William (1754–1817), British sailor and colonial official, 554 n.1
Bogdo Khan. *See* Jebtsun Damba Khutukhtu
Bouchard, Raoul-Paul-Alexandre (1851–1916), French soldier and adventurer, 80 + n.1–81
Bovy, Eugénie Bertha (1855–1926), Belgian wife of Lu Cheng-hsiang, 15 n.1 (16), 812 + n.4
Bovy, Frédéric, Belgian soldier, 812 n.4
Bowra, Cecil Arthur Verner (1869–1947), British employee of Chinese Maritime Customs, 624 + n.1, 629
Bowra, Cecil Maurice (1898–1971), British scholar, 624 n.1
Boxer Uprising, 29 n.2, 30, 58, 59 n.5, 68 n.5, 90 n.2, 105, 106 n.2 (107), 148, 202 n.1, 394 n.4, 395 n.1, 438, 474 n.1, 491 n.2, 545 n.2, 547 n.1, 551 n.1, 552 n.2, 607 + n.1, n.2, 629, 653, 779 n.2, 794 n.2, 806, 818 n.1, n.2; indemnity, 76 + n.1, 79, 82, 133 n.2, 238 n.1, 261, 276, 288, 316, 330 n.5–331, 334, 344, 355, 380 n.2, 466, 471, 491 n.2, 544, 545, 555, 564, 572, 575, 577, 607 + n.2, 668, 673, 691, (American indemnity) 56
Braham, Dudley Disraeli (1875–1951), British journalist, 32 + n.1, 50 n.4, 97 n.1, 115 + n.1, 135 n.1, 140 + n.3, 141, 296 + n.3, 373 n.1; *letters to*, 33, 87, 99, 121, 123, 228
Brailsford, John Annesley (d. 1918), New

859

Brailsford (*cont.*)
Zealand journalist and author, 94 + n.1
Brambilla, Guiseppe, Italian diplomat, 73 n.2
Bredon, Lily Virginia (*née* Crane), wife of R. E. Bredon, 449 + n.1
Bredon, Robert Edward (1846–1918), British employee of Chinese Maritime Customs, 271 + n.1, 289, 362, 449 n.1, 604 n.3
Briand, Aristide (1862–1932), French politician, 619 n.2
Bright, John (1811–1889), British social reformer and politician, 439 + n.3
Brinkley, Francis (1841–1912), British journalist, 658 + n.4
Brissaud-Desmaillets, Georges-Henri (1869–1948), French soldier, 123 + n.2, 233, 343
Britain: social and political conditions during and after World War I, 425–6, 460, 499, 625–6, 683–8, 776, 781–2; peace celebrations, 777
Britain: in China, 26–30, 35, 36, 44–5, 64–71, 77–9, 120, 297–303, 324–5, 344, 407–8, 694–7, 806;
- and Revolution *1911*, 67, 82;
- recognition of Chinese Republic, 6 n.2, 30 + n.1, 34, 35, 36, 41, 42, 62 n.2, 78, 89, 130, 223–4;
- style of diplomacy, 41, 43 + n.2, 46, 47, 68 + n.4, 69, 71–2, 77, 82, 270–1, 286, 342–3, 437, 449, 519, 521–2, 564–5, 567–8, 571, 628, 648–9, 712, 806, 810–11, 815; Chinese Legation in London, 357 + n.1;
- Parliament on China, 40 + n.1, 63, 75 + n.3–76, 109, 125–31, 139, 210 + n.2, 345, 467, 799 + n.2;
- press and China, 26, 36, 44, 328 + n.1– 329, 330, 339–41, 373 + n.1–377, (*see also* Times);
- concessions, 27, 69 + n.2, 468; Hankow, 43 n.3 (44); Kiukiang, 43 n.3 (44); Shameen, Canton, 467 + n.2; Shanghai, (*see* Shanghai: International Settlement);
- finance and trade, 27, 30, 33 + n.2–34 + n.1, n.4, 37, 40 + n.1, 41, 44–6, 47, 63, 64–84 + n.1, 70, 72–3, 135 n.1, 271 n.1, 297–303, 344, 353–7, 591, 648–9, 703; (*see aslo* Banks, financial houses and consortia; Commerce, Chambers of; Commercial and industrial companies and corporations; Loans; Railways; Treaties, agreements etc.);
- opium trade, 26 n.1, 69 + n.1, 70 + n.2, 75 + n.3–76, 78, 125–31, 153 n.1, 344,

(*see also under* Conferences and institutions, international; Opium and morphia; Wars);
- Tibet, (*see* Conferences and institutions, international; Tibet; Treaties, agreements etc.); Yunnan (Pienma) frontier, 41, 151–3, 154, 156–7, 158, 171, 534; Mongolia, 81, 262;
- personnel in Chinese service, 68 + n.4, n.5, 69, 71, 82, 553 + n.1, 649, (*see also* Customs and excise in China; Salt Gabelle; and entries for individuals);
- China's entry into World War I, 466, 468, 471, 532, 684–5, 687–8, 688, (*see also* World War I);
- and Japan: policy compared, 324–7; Anglo-Japanese Alliance (*see under* Treaties, agreements etc.); and Twenty-one Demands, 365, 371 + n.1–372 + n.1, 373 + n.1 – 377, (*see also* Twenty-one Demands);
- *See also* G. E. Morrison: Powers in China; *Times*; Yüan Shih-k'ai
British and Chinese Corporation. *See under* Commercial and industrial companies and corporations, etc.
British India: land revenue, 412 n.2, 457–9; frontier with China, 104–5, 151, (*see also* Tibet); opium export (*see under* Opium and morphia); and Japan: (Anglo-Japanese Alliance) 445; (Japanese aspirations) 421, 757, (Indian students in Japan) 421; German incitement of Mohammedans and threat, 468, 471, 557, 558, 562, 564, 566 n.2, 670; cotton industry, 125 n.1, 587 + n.2; and World War I, 587 n.2.
British Parliament and China. *See under* Britain in China
Brittain, Harry Ernest (1873–1974) British politician and entrepreneur, 65 + n.3
Brollo, Basilio, di Gemona (1648–1706), Italian Catholic missionary, scholar and author, 653 + n.1
Broome, Louis E., British railway engineer, 304 + n.1;
letter to, 503
letter from, 304
Broome, Mrs, wife of L. E. Broome, 304
Brown, John McLeavy (1842–1926), British employee of Chinese Maritime Customs and of Chinese diplomatic service, 25 + n.3, 46, 65, 158 n.1, 338, 814 + n.2
Browne, George Fitzherbert (1851–1935), British soldier, 818 + n.3

860

Browne, Tom (1872-1910), British illustrator, 660+n.3; *The Night Side of London*, 660+n.3
Brownrigg, Beatrice (*née* Clementi Smith) (d. 1952), wife of D. E. R. Brownrigg, 120 n.2, 424+n.1, 425 n.2, 787 n.1;
letters to, 537, 567, 570
letters from, 424, 447, 776, 781
Brownrigg, Douglas Egremont Robert (1867-1939), British sailor, 424 n.1, 425+n.2, 568, 782+n.1
Bruce, B. D., British employee of Chinese Maritime Customs, 239+n.2
Bruce, Clarence Dalrymple (1862-1934), British soldier and policeman, 180+n.2, 181, 208 n.3, 363 n.2, 553+n.1, 575+n.2, 727+n.1;
letters to, 180, 207, 214, 269, 277, 290, 362
letters from, 186, 208, 289, 291, 727
Bryan, William Jennings (1860-1925), American politician, 499+n.1; *Letters to a Chinese Official*, 499+n.1
Bryce, James (1838-1922), 1st Visct Bryce of Dechmont, British diplomat, politician and scholar, 168+n.4, 410
Buckle, George Earle (1854-1935), British journalist and author, Editor of *The Times*, 13+n.2, n.3, n.4, 14 n.1, n.2, 827;
letter from, 13
Buckle, Mrs, wife of G. E. Buckle, 14
Bussière, French medical practitioner, 528+n.2
Butler, Nicholas Murray (1862-1947), American educationalist, 23+n.6

Cabinet, Chinese;
letter to, 184
letter from, 172
Cadogan, Alexander Montagu George (1884-1968), British diplomat, 810 n.3
Calhoun, William James (1848-1916), American diplomat, 24, 585
Cambridge, George William Frederick Charles (1819-1904), 2nd Duke, British soldier, 613+n.2
Campbell, Charles William (1861-1927), British consular official, 28+n.2, 78 n.3, 91, 103+n.3, 104, 817+n.6;
letter to, 41
letter from, 77
Campbell, W. L., British soldier and colonial official, 428+n.2
Canada: Asiatic question, 314; Mounted Police, 265
Cantlie, James (1851-1926), British medical practitioner and teacher, 200 n.2, 216+n.3
Canton: Notes, 304+n.4, 310, 322+n.1; under Lung Chi-kuang, 217+n.2, 308-9, 310, 537; British concession in Shameen, 467+n.2
Capper, John Brainerd (1855-1936), British journalist, Assistant Editor of *The Times*, 57 n.4, 214+n.3;
letter from, 214
Cardew, Alexander Gordon (1861-1937), British colonial official, 788+n.3, 789
Carew, Reginald Pole (1849-1924), British sailor, 26+n.5
Carey, William Francis (1878-1951), American railway entrepreneur, 543+n.2
Carl, Francis Augustus (1861-1930), American employee of Chinese Maritime Customs, 593 n.4
Carl, Katharine Augusta (d. 1938), American artist, 593+n.4
Carnegie, Andrew (1835-1919), American manufacturer, 23 n.1; Carnegie Foundation, 20+n.1-24, 100
de Cartier et de Marchienne, Emile (1871-1946), Baron, Belgian diplomat, 85+n.2, 118, 119;
letter to, 276
letter from, 85
de Castellane, Marie-Ernest-Paul Boniface (1867-1932), Marquis, French politician and author, 106 n.2
Castello, Antonio Paterno (1852-1914), Marquese di San Giuliano, Italian politician, 74+n.1
Cattarinich, Alexander Clement (b. 1852), Austrian hotelier, 604+n.4
Causton, Richard Knight (1843-1929), 1st Baron Southwark, British politician, 335+n.1
Cecil, Robert Arthur Talbot Gascoyne (1830-1903), Visct Cranborne, 3rd Marquess of Salisbury, British politician, 436 n.3, 619 n.1
Chang Chen-fang (b. 1865), Chinese Imperial official, Republican politician, Provincial Governor, 14+n.5-16, 361+n.1
Chang Chen-wu, Chinese soldier, 118+n.4
Chang Ch'i-huang (1877-1927), Chinese Republican politician, Provincial Governor, 311+n.1
Chang Ch'i-yün (b. 1901), Chinese Republican politician and cultural entrepreneur, 514 n.1; editor, *Ch'ing shih*, 514 n.1

861

Chang Chia-ao (b. 1888), Chinese Republican politician, 244 n.2, 518 n.1

Chang Chia-shen (Chün-mai) (b. 1886), Chinese Republican politician and scholar, 605 + n.3, 621 n.1; science *versus* metaphysics debate, 621 n.1

Chang Ch'ien (1853–1926), Chinese industrialist and Republican politician, 200 n.4, 514 n.1

Chang Chih-tung (1837–1909), Chinese Imperial official, Viceroy Grand Councillor, 386 n.4 (387), 533 n.1, 607 n.1, 608

Chang Ching-yao (b. 1880), Chinese soldier, 656 + n.3

Chang En-yen, Chinese Republican official, 616 + n.3

Chang Hsüeh-liang (b. 1898), Chinese soldier, 7 n.1, 547 n.2 (548)

Chang Hsün (1854–1923), Chinese soldier, 14 n.5 (15), 85 n.3, 86 n.1, 120, 141 + n.1, 142 + n.1, 198, 206 n.1, 214 + n.3–215, 222 + n.3–223, 237 n.3, 252 n.1, 269, 289, 291, 386 n.4 (387), 439 n.1, 487, 527, 542 n.1, 578 n.1, 595 + n.2, 596 + n.2, 601–2, 605 n.2, n.3 (606), 607, 608 n.1, 609 + n.3, 611–13, 622 n.3, 623 n.3, 635 + n.1, 636 n.1, 650 + n.2; *see also under* Governments in China; Monarchist movement; Revolution 1913;
telegram from, (to Yüan Shih-k'ai) 142

Chang Hsün Restoration. *See under* Monarchist movement

Chang Hu (b. 1875), Chinese Republican politician, 161 n.2, 404 + n.1, 761 n.1, 809 + n.2

Chang Huai-chih (b. 1860), Chinese soldier, 656 + n.2

Chang Hung-shun, Chinese Republican official, 142

Chang I-lin (1867–1943), Chinese scholar and Republican politician, 439 n.1, 541 n.4 (542)

Chang I-shu (b. 1885), Chinese Republican official, 151 + n.3

Chang Jen-chün, Chinese Imperial official, Viceroy, 616 + n.4

Chang, L. *See* Chang Yü-chün

Chang, Michie C. L. *See* Chang Min-chih

Chang Min-chih (Chung-liang), Chinese journalist and newspaper entrepreneur, 423 + n.1;
letter from, 423, 590, 595

Chang Ming-chi, Chinese Imperial official, Viceroy, Republican politician, Governor, 18 + n.2, 217 n.2

Chang P'ei-lun (1848–1903), Chinese Imperial official, 616 n.4

Chang Ping-lin (1868–1936), Chinese revolutionary and scholar, 182 n.1

Chang Shao-tseng (?1869–1928), Chinese soldier, Provincial Military Governor, 118 n.1, 319 + n.3, 320

Chang Shih-heng, Chinese Imperial official, 438 + n.1

Chang Tso-lin (1873–1928), Chinese soldier, 7 n.1, 43 n.3, 47 n.3 (48), 64 n.2 (65), 79 n.2 (80), 474 n.1, 514 n.1, 547 n.2, 597 + n.2, n.5–599, 614–17, 635 n.1, 654 n.8, 693, 782, 783 + n1,. 809 + n.2

Chang Tsung-hsiang (b. 1879), Chinese Republican politician, 764 + n.3, n.4, 801 n.3

Chang Yin-huan (1837–1900), Chinese diplomat, 90 n.2, 217 n.1

Chang Yin-t'ang, Chinese diplomat, 90 + n.2, 427, 428 + n.2

Chang Yü-ch'üan, Chinese Republican official, 404 + n.2

Chang Yü-chün (Chi-shih) (L. Chang), Chinese soldier, 129 + n.2;
letters from, 129, 264

Chang Yu-tang, Chinese brigand, 167

Chang Yün-shan, Chinese soldier and secret society leader, 401 + n.3

Chanless, American adventurer, 336

Chao Erh-feng (d. 1911), Chinese Bannerman, Imperial official, Viceroy, 136 + n.1, 514 n.1

Chao Erh-hsün (1844–1927), Chinese Bannerman, Imperial official, Viceroy, Republican politician, 136 n.1, 514 + n.1, 597 n.2; editor, *Ch'ing shih kao*, 514 n.1

Chao Ju-kua, Chinese official of the Sung Dynasty, 214 n.1

Chao Ping-chün (d. 1914), Chinese Imperial official and Republican politician, 4 + nn.1–5, 64 n.2, 110, 112 n.2, 138 n.1, 172, 173, 184, 185, 186, 195, 510 n.2;
letter from, (to Yüan Shih-k'ai) 173

Ch'en Ch'i-mei (1876–1916), Chinese politician, 10 n.3, 116 + n.4, 150, 163, 181 + n.2, 189, 208 + n.2, 209, 392, 394 n.2, 645 n.3

Ch'en Chin-t'ao (1870–1939), Chinese Imperial official and Republican politician, 254 + n.1–257, 338, 339–40, 518 n.2, 637 + n.1;
letter to, 254

Ch'en Ching-hua (Chen King-wa) (d. 1913), Chinese Imperial and Republican official, 217 + n.2
Ch'en Chiung-ming (1878-1933), Chinese soldier, 395 + n.2, 809 n.3
Chen, Eugene. *See* Ch'en Yu-jen
Ch'en I-fan (Ivan Chen), Chinese Republican official, 90 n.2 (91), 149 + n.1, 150-3, 158, 169-71, 198 + n.2, 227; *letters from*, 239, 408
Chen, Ivan. *See* Ch'en I-fan
Chen King-wa. *See* Ch'en Ching-hua
Ch'en Kung-po (?1892-1946), Chinese Republican politician, 395 n.2
Ch'en Kuo-fu (1892-1951), Chinese Republican politician, 116 n.4 (117), 388 n.1
Ch'en Li-fu (b. 1900), Chinese Republican politician, 116 n.4 (117), 388 n.1
Ch'en Lu (1878-1939), Chinese diplomat, 281 + n.1
Ch'en Luan (b. 1865), Chinese Imperial and Republican official, 485 + n.1
Ch'en Shih-hua, Chinese Republican official, 614 + n.3, 615, 616 n.2
Ch'en T'ing-hsün, Chinese secret society leader, 209 + n.4
Ch'en Tu-hsiu (1879-1942), first leader of the Chinese Communist Party, 395 n.2
Ch'en Yi (b. 1869), Chinese soldier, Provincial Governor, 167, 487 + n.4, 488 n.2, 522 n.2
Ch'en Yu-jen (Eugene Chen) (1878-1944), Chinese Republican politician, 43 + n.3-44, 56 + n.2, 375, 382-5, 637, 639 n.1, 716, 728 n.1, n.3, 731 n.1, 773 + n.2, 775 + n.3, 776 + n.1, 814; *letters to*, 384, 777, 778
letter from, 776
Chenery, Thomas (1826-84), British journalist, Editor of *The Times*, 13 + n.4
Cheng Ju-cheng (d. 1915), Chinese sailor, 113 n.3, 269 + n.3, 289-90, 291, 308 + n.1, 469 + n.1
Ch'i Hsieh-yüan (1879-1946), Chinese soldier, 642 n.1
Chiang Ch'ao-tsung (1863-1943), Chinese magistrate, 599 n.1, 612 + n.1, n.2
Chiang Kai-shek (1887-1975), Chinese soldier and Republican politician, 7 n.1, 20 n.3, 43 n.4 (44), 116 n.4 (117), 166 n.2, 169 n.3 (170), 199 n.1, 206 n.2 (207), 211 n.2, 305 n.3, 343 n.1, 388 n.1, 393 n.1, n.2, 394 n.1, n.2, 415 n.4 (416), 474 n.1, 477 n.3, 477 n.4 (478), 570 n.2, 574 n.2, 656 n.3, 713 n.1

Chiang Kai-shek, Mme. *See* Sung Mei-ling
Ch'ien-lung, Emperor. *See* Hung-li
Ch'ien Neng-hsün (1870-1924), Chinese Imperial official and Republican politician, 655 + n.2, 761 n.1
Ch'ien Wen-hsüan (b. 1873), Chinese Imperial and Republican official, 480 + n.1;
letter from, 480
Chin Ting-hsün, Chinese Republican official, 616 + n.2
Chin Yün-p'eng (b. 1877), Chinese soldier, 616 + n.1, 783 + n.3, 808 + n.1
Chin Yung, Chinese Republican official, Provincial Governor, 479 + n.2
China Association. *See under* Societies, learned, professional or otherwise
China Merchants Steam Navigation Company, 201 n.1, 304-8, 326; (loan) 307
China Year Book, 88 + n.1, n.2, 785
Chinda Sutemi (1856-1929), Japanese diplomat, 561 + n.3, 562, 793 + n. 1
Ch'ing, Prince. *See* I-kuang
Chirol, Valentine Ignatius (1852-1929), British journalist and author, 1, 32 n.1, 97 n.1, 214 n.3 (215), 296 n.2, n.3, 373 n.1, 588 n.2, 758 n.2, n.5, 768 n.1, 773 n.3, 812 n.3;
letter to, 770
letters from, 758, 768, 776
Chisaka Tomojirō, Japanese sailor, 791 + n.1
Chisholm, Hugh (1866-1924), British journalist, 793 + n.2, 794
Ch'iu Chin (1875-1907), Chinese revolutionary martyr, 388 n.3
Chou Ch'ang-ling (Chou Shou-ch'en, Shouson Chow) (1861-1959), Chinese Imperial official and entrepreneur, 307 + n.2
Chou Fu (1837-1921), Chinese Imperial official, Viceroy, 161 n.2
Chou Hsüeh-hsi (1866-1947), Chinese Republican politician, 55, 161 + n.2, 403, 404 n.2, 407 + n.2, 439 + n.2, 761 n.1
Chou Mien (?b. 1844), Chinese Imperial official and land-owner, 58 + n.2, 59
Chou Shu-mu (1860-1925), Chinese Imperial official, Provincial Governor and Republican politician, 765 + n.2
Chou Tzu-ch'i (1868-1923), Chinese Republican politician, 67 n.1, 120 n.1, 141 + n.1, 161 n.2, 237 n.3, 310, 318 + n.2, 333, 342 n.2, 356 n.1, 360, 361,

863

Chou Tzu-ch'i (*cont.*)
  362, 403, 510 n.2, 518 + n.2, 809 + n.5, 828 + n.2;
  letter to, 356, (from Jennie Morrison) 828
Chow, Shouson. *See* Chou Ch'ang-ling
Chu, Marquis, a descendant of the Ming ruling family, 33 n.1, 83, 216
Chü Cheng (1876–1951), Chinese Republican politician, 393 + n.2
Chu Ch'i (d. 1931), Chinese newspaper entrepreneur, 376 + n.3
Chu Ch'i-ch'ien (b. 1871), Chinese Imperial official and Republican politician, 237 n.3, 318 n.2, 510 + n.2, 783 n.4 (784)
Chu Jui (1883–1916), Chinese soldier, Provincial Governor, 11 + n.2, 198
Chu Shen (1879–1943), Chinese Republican politician, 761 n.2
Ch'un-ch'iu, 426
Chung-yung, 462
Chungar, Prince, Mongol leader, 474, 475
Churchill, Randolph Henry Spencer (1849–1895), British politician, 106 n.2
Churchill, Lady Randolph. *See* J. Jerome
Churchill, Winston Leonard Spencer (1874–1965), British politician, 426 + n.1, 551 n.2
Clemenceau, Georges (1841–1929), French politician, 619 n.2, 794 n.3, 799 + n.1
Cobden, Richard (1804–65), British politician and reformer, 439 n.3
Cockburn, Henry (1859–1927), British consular official, 285 + n.1, 817 + n.7;
  letter to, 285
Cockerell, Samuel Pepys (1880–1915), British diplomat and financial agent, 192 + n.2, 298 + n.3;
  letter to, 236
  letter from, 192
de Codt, Henri, Belgian jurist, 100 + n.4, 173 + n.1, 277 n.2, 574, 630, 637
Collins, Robert Muirhead (b. 1867), American journalist, 24 + n.1;
  letter from, 24
Collins, William F., British mining engineer, 301 + n.1
Commerce, Chambers of: Bradford Dyers Association, 135 n.1; British Chamber of Commerce (Shanghai), 127 n.3 (128), 423, 582, 591; Canadian Chamber of Commerce, 334; Chinese Chamber of Commerce (Shanghai), 582; Chinese General Chamber of Commerce (Peking), 423; Hong Kong Chamber of Commerce, 310 n.1; London Chamber of Commerce, 127 n.3, 331–2 + n.1, 334, 335, 640; Manchester Chamber of Commerce, 334; Melbourne Chamber of Commerce, 703
Commercial and industrial companies and corporations, etc: American Banknote Co., 361; Anderson & Meyer, 648; Anglo-Saxon Petroleum Co. Ltd, 686 n.1; Armstrongs, 302, 335, 340, 357, 432; Bethlehem Steel, 296; J. P. Bisset & Co., 305, 307–8; British and American Tobacco Co., 47 n.1; British and Chinese Corporation, 44 n.2, 45 + n.1, 54 n.2, 55 n.1, 70, 286 + n.3, 301, 313 n.3, 338 n.1, 417; Butterfield & Swire, 306; Carlowitz, 302; Chanless & Batouieff, 336, 337–8, (case of) 535; China Conservation & Development Co., 66 n.2, n.3; China Corporation, 543 n.2; China Industrial Development Co. Ltd. (Chūgoku Kōgyō Kabushiki Kaisha), 476 n.1; De Beers, 55 n.1; Doney & Co., 625; Dunn Fischer & Co., 66, 285; East Asia Industrial Development Co., 590 n.1; Hanson, McNeil & Jones, 188; Hsien-shih kung-ssu (Sincere Co.), 703 + n.1; Felton & Grimwade, 643 + n.2; Hong Kong & Yaumati Ferry Co., 310 n.1; Hudson's Bay Co., 336 n.1; Hudson's Consolidated Ltd, 336 n.1; Hui-min kung-ssu, 640 n.3; Hunan Steam Ship Co., 590 n.1; Japanese Government Iron Works, 432 n.1; Jardine & Co., 127 n.3, 571; Jardine Matheson & Co., 697 + n.1; Kawasaki Dockyard, 93; Krupp's, 161, 438 n.1; Kubana Copper Mining Co., 638 + n.2, 659; Lloyds, 275, 287; Luzac & Co., 224 + n.3; Marconi Telegraph Co., 183 n.1, 340, (case of) 183 + n.1; Matheson & Co., 127 n.3; Mitsubishi, 476 n.1, 548 n.4, 622 n.1, 631, 633; Mitsui Bussan Kaisha, 93, 358, 476 n.1, 549, 555; Nippon Yūsen Kaisha, 590 n.1; Ōkura & Co., 93, 476 n.1; Panama Co., 185 + n.2, (Canal), 328; Pauling Railway Construction Co., 191 n.1, 648, 649, 794 n.1; S. Pearson & Co., 503 n.2, Pekin Syndicate 4, 69 + n.1, 135 n.5, 285 n.1; Ransomes & Rapier, 376 n.2; Rio Tinto, 758 + n.1; Alf Ross & Co., 524; Sassoons, 70 + n.2, 594; D. Sassoon & Co., 705 n.3; E. D. Sassoon & Co., 361 n.3; Shanghai

corporations (*cont.*)
Tramway Co., 303; Shell Transport & Trading Co. Ltd, 686 n.1; Siems & Carey, 539 n.4, 543 n.2; Sietas Planbeck & Co., 641, 662; Sino-Japanese Industrial Development Co. (Chū-Nichi Jitsugyō Kabushiki Kaisha), 476 + n.1, 590 n.1; Sino-Japanese Steamer Co., 590 n.1; Standard Oil Co., 296, 713 n.1; Suez Canal Co., 212 n.2; Takata & Co., 405 n.1; Telge & Schroeter (T'ai-lai), 340, 358 + n.1; Thomas, Davis & Ross, 524; Thorneycroft, 648; Tokyo Railway Co., 590 n.1; United Steel Corporation, 793 n.3; Upper Yangtze Steam Navigation Co., 69 n.3; James Veitch & Sons, 508 n.3; Vickers, 78, 302, 335, 340, 376 n.1, 432; Western Union Telegraph Co., 106 n.2, 405 n.2; Williams & Norgate, 461, 481 + n.2; Syndicat de Yunnan, 300, 301 + n.1

Conferences and institutions, international: Congress of Berlin (*1878*), 694 n.2, 733, 746–7, 754; Geneva Conference (*1924-5*), 585 n.3; Genoa Conference (*1922*), 588 n.1; Hague Peace Conference (*1907*), 28 n.3; Imperial Press Conference (*1909*), 65 + n.1; Institute of Pacific Relations conferences, 51 n.1; Kiakhta Conference (*see under* Mongolia); League of Nations, 347 n.1, 574 n.2, 588 n.1, 619 n.2, 704 n.3, 720 n.1, 755, 775, 776, 781, 795, 800, 811, 813, (covenant) 768 n.1 (769); Opium Conferences (Shanghai, *1909*), 120 n.2, 617 n.1, (Hague, *1911*) 120 n.2; Paris Peace Conference (*see* separate entry); Permanent Court of International Justice, Hague, 52, 191 n.2, 252 n.4 (253), 279 + n.2; Portsmouth Conference (*1905*), 58 n.3, 133 n.2; Simla Conference (*see under* Tibet); United Nations Conference, San Francisco (*1945*), 357 n.1; Washington Conference (*1921–2*), 53 n.3 (54), 252 n.4, 548 n.4 (549), 585 n.3, 619 n.2, 645 n.3, 704 n.3, 720 n.1, 790 n.3

Conger, Edwin Hurd (1843–1907), American diplomat, 59 n.5

Constitutions, Chinese: drafting of, 226–7 + n.1, 228, 233–6, 264, 637, 721, 809 n.1; Codification Bureau, 721; Provisional Constitution, Nanking (*1912*), 396 n.1, 536 + n.1, 596, 689, 706–8; Constitution (*1 May 1914*), 450. *See also* Governments in China; Parliaments in China

Conty, Alexandre-Maurice-Robert, French diplomat, 81, 82 + n.2, 300 + n.1, 357, 586, 666, 670

Cook, Joseph (1860–1947), Australian politician, 220 n.2

Cooks, F. Seymour, British author, 741; *The Secret Treaties*, 741

Cordes, Heinrich, German diplomat, financial agent, 82 + n.1

Cormack, James A., British teacher in China, 68 + n.4

Cormack, James Grieve (b. 1864), British missionary and medical practitioner, 129 + n.1

Courbet, Amédée-Anatole-Prosper (1827–85), French sailor, 817 + n.2

Courrejolles, Père. *See* F. X. d'Entrecolles

Couvreur, F. Séraphin (1835–1919), French Catholic missionary, 652 + n.5

Cox, British journalist, 268

Cox, A. G., British railway engineer, 817 + n.3

Cradock, Christopher George Francis Maurice (1862–1914), British sailor, 551 + n.1, n.2, 556

Crane, Charles Richard (1858–1939), American businessman and diplomat, 585 n.2, 818 + n.4; *letter from*, (to Jennie Morrison) 818

Crane, Mrs, wife of C. R. Crane, 819

Crewe-Milnes, Robert Offley Ashburton (1858–1945), 1st Marquess of Crewe, British politician, 90 + n.1, 126

Crisp, Charles Birch (1867–?1948), British financier, 33 n.2, 37, 40, 46, 55, 65–6, 298 + n.2, 300

Cromer, 1st Earl of. *See* E. Baring

Cromwell, Oliver, English soldier, 425 n.6

Crossley, British commercial agent, 305 + n.1

Curzon, George Nathanial (1859–1925), 1st Marquess of Kedleston, British politician and colonial official, 342 n.1, 436 + n.3–437, 440, 459, 691, 775 + n.1, 813

Customs and excise in China:
- Chinese Maritime Customs, 55 + n.3, 56 n.1, 82, 153, 213 n.2, 214 n.1, 231, 239 n.3, 242, 261, 271 n.1, 275–6, 282, 283, 284 n.1, 285, 287 n.1, 288, 316, 317 + n.3 (318), 342, 357, 363 n.3, 377 n.1, 399, 402, 404 n.3, 407 n.1, 414–15, 437, 439, 449 n.1, 468, 515, 519, 534, 545, 561 + n.1, 572, 575, 577, 587, 593 n.4, 604 + n.2, n.3, 610, 616 + n.3, n.5, 624, 629, 630 n.2, 631, 673, 681, 691,

Customs and excise in China (*cont.*) 708, 723–6, 808, 828 n.1; Tsingtao customs, 351, 353–6, 360, 725;
– Shui-wu ch'u, 3 n.1, 271 n.1, 399, 681;
– *See also* Salt Gabelle; Tariff revision and autonomy; Taxation in China

Da Lai Bese (Da Lai Wang), Mongol leader, 49 + n.3
Da Lai Wang. *See* Da Lai Bese
Da Lama. *See* Tsening Chimet
Dalai Lama, 13th. *See* Thub Idan rgya mtsho
Dane, Louis William (1856–1946), British colonial official, 412 + n.4, 457, 459–60
Dane, Richard Morris (1854–1940), British inspector of Chinese Salt Administration, 84 n.1, 170, 193 + n.3, 241, 242, 254, 288, 313, 316, 317, 407, 412 + n.4, 459, 460, 480 + n.3, 519, 533, 566 n.1, 598 + n.1, 616 + n.6, 630, 648 + n.1, 717, 759 n.2, 808; *letter from*, 566
Darwin, Charles Robert (1809–82), British naturalist, 450
Davis, George T. B., American missionary, 155 + n.1, 156; *letter from*, (to Yüan Shih-k'ai), 155
Davison, Henry Pomeroy (1867–1922), American financier, 793 n.4
Dawlish, Hope. *See* F. T. Piggott
Dawson, George Geoffrey. *See* G. G. Robinson
Deakin, Alfred (1856–1919), Australian politician, 220 n.2
Defoe, Daniel (1659–1731), English author, 657 + n.2; *The Farther Adventures of Robinson Crusoe*, 562 + n.1
Dehergne, Joseph, French scholar, 652 n.4
Delane, John Thadeus (1817–79), British journalist, Editor of *The Times*, 13 + n.4
Den Kenjirō (1855–1930), Japanese politician, 584 n.2
Denmark in China, 468. *See also* Posts and telegraphs, Chinese
Dennis, William Cullen (1878–1962), American jurist, 637 + n.2, 655
Der Ling. *See* Yü Te-ling
Dering, Herbert Guy Nevill (1867–1933), British diplomat, 681 + n.1; *letter to*, 681
Dessiner, Lieut, French soldier, 167
Devawongse, Prince, Siamese politician, 706 n.1
Devos, Robert, financial representative, 67 n.1

Dickens, Charles John Huffam (1812–70), British writer, 12 n.1
Dickinson, F. W., British businessman, 257 + n.2, 258
Dickinson, Goldsworthy Lowes (1862–1932), British scholar, 499 n.1; *Letters from John Chinaman*, 499 n.1
Disraeli, Benjamin (1804–81), 1st Earl of Beaconsfield, British politician, 13 n.2, 14 n.2, 651 n.6
Disraeli, Isaac (1766–1848), British author, 651 + n.6; *Curiosities of Literature*, 651 + n.6
Dixon, George Finley, New Zealand civil servant, 663 + n.3
Doihara Kenji (1883–1948), Japanese soldier and adventurer, 92 n.2 (93), 206 n.1
Donald, William Henry (1875–1946), Australian journalist, 7 + n.1, 151, 163 + n.1, 222, 333, 352, 369, 372, 373, 378, 391, 472, 491, 522, 535, 578 n.1, 605, 609, 643 + n.3, 658 + n.2, n.3; *letters to*, 642, 644 *letters from*, 7, 17, 221, 646, 717
Donaldson, H. Beaumont, British commercial agent, 78 + n.1
Dorjieff, Agvan (1853–1938), Mongol adventurer, 85 + n.1, 89
Doumer, Paul (1857–1932), French politician and colonial official, 619 n.2
Dragon-bone. *See under* Yüan Shih-k'ai
Drakeford, L. H. (?b. 1876), Australian employee of Chinese Salt Administration, 597 + n.1; *letters from*, 597, 614, 619
Drummond, William Venn (?1842–1915), British lawyer, 188 + n.1
Ducat, Charles Merewether (1860–1934), British soldier, 818 + n.2
Duff, Alexander Ludovic (1862–1933), British sailor, 789 + n.3
Dugenne, Alphonse-Jules (1841–1887), French soldier, 381 + n.1,
Duncan Chesney (b. 1854), British journalist, 112 n.3, 231 + n.1, 238
Duncan, Moir (?1861–1906), British educationalist, 68 n.5
Dundas, Lawrence John Lumley (1876–1961), 2nd Marquess of Zetland, Earl of Ronaldshay, British politician and author, 342 + n.1; *letter to*, 342
Durbet Wang, Mongol leader, 266
Dzevaltovsky, Ignatius (*alias* Yourin), Russian diplomatic agent, 629 n.1 (630)

Ebina Danjō (1856–1937), Japanese Christian leader and educationalist, 700 + n.1, 704, 798–9
Education in China, 68–9, 267, 331, 344, 690, 804, (Christian education) 343–5, (medical) 804;
- Chinese students sent abroad, 3 n.1, 243 + n.2–244, 480 n.1, 487, (America) 3 n.1, 307 n.2, 347, 386 n.4, 506, 585, 804, (England) 347, 506, (Germany), 469, (Hong Kong) 243 + n.2, Japan) 100, 101, 136, 157, 211 n.2, 347, 412, 415 n.4, 480, 506;
- institutions: (Australia), Brisbane Grammar School 131 n.1, Geelong College 664 n.1, Maryborough Grammar School 131 n.1, University of Sydney 131 n.1;
- (Britain), Aberdeen University 131 n.1, University of Cambridge 127 n.3 (128), 348 n.1, 565 n.2, 568 n.1, 711, 726 n.1, 792 + n.2, Edinburgh University 129 n.1, Eton 127 n.2, n.3 (128), Free Church Normal School Glasgow 690 n.1, Glasgow University 621 n.1, King's College London 313 n.3, 345 n.1, 489 n.3, Leeds University 383 n.1, Lincoln's Inn 149 + n.1, 233 n.2, 801, London School of Economics and Political Science 318 n.1, University of London 489 n.3 (490), 568 n.1, 801 n.1, Malvern College 811 n.2, Manchester University 383 n.1, University of Oxford 83 n.3, 127 n.2, 131 n.1, 168 n.4, 243, 330 n.5 (331), 489 n.3 (490), 585 n.1, 613 + n.1, 622 n.2, 633 n.6, 711, 779 n.1, Royal Naval College Greenwich 358 n.2, Sandhurst 27 n.3, School of Oriental and African Studies 224 n.2, Sheffield University 243 n.1, Summerfields 811, Trinity College Cambridge 811 n.2, University College London 801 + n.1, Wadham College Oxford 624 n.1, Winchester School 811 n.2, Worcester College Oxford, 131 n.1;
- (China), Anglo-Chinese College Shanghai 508 n.1, Anglo-Chinese School Tientsin 594 n.4, Canton Christian College (Ling-nan ta-hsüeh) 311 n.3, 645, Canton Military Academy 311 n.2, Customs College 515, Futan University 112 n.1, Gordon Missionary Theological Seminary 98 n.2, Imperial Chinese University Tientsin 594 n.4, McTyeire School 478, Naval College Tientsin 3 n.1, 404 n.2, North China Union College Tung-chou 478, North China Union Women's College 388 n.3, Paoting Military Academy 642 n.1, Peking Normal University 238 n.1, Peking University 243 + n.2, 361 n.2, 593, 623 n.1, St John's College Shanghai 478 + n.2, Shansi University 68 + n.5, 330 n.5 (331), Tongshan Engineering College 68 + n.4, Tsinghua College 238 n.1, 254 n.1, 491 n.2, 605 n.3 (606), 721, Union Medical College Peking 69, 83 n.3 (84), 129 n.1, Université l'Aurore (Chen-tan ta-hsüeh) 610 n.2;
- (Finland), Helsinki University 50 n.3;
- (France), Collège de France, 653 n.1;
- (Germany), Berlin University 585 n.1, Jena University 605 n.3 (606), Leipzig University 585 n.1;
- (Hong Kong), College of Medicine 216 n.3, University of Hong Kong 243 n.1, n.2, 310 n.1, 701, 804;
- (Italy), University of Bologna 74 n.3, Istituto Medio ed Estremo Oriente 233 + n.1, Istituto Orientale di Napoli 232 n.1, 233 n.1, University of Rome 74 n.3;
- (Japan), Dōshisha University 700 n.1, Hōsei University 641 n.5, Kyoto University 633 n.1, n.7, Meiji Law School 775 n.2, Nihon Daigaku 631 n.2, Osaka University 633 n.4, Pharmacological College Tokyo 633 n.5, Shikan Gakkō 42 n.2, 135 n.2, n.7, 166 n.2, 209 n.3, 310 n.3, 393 n.4, 394 n.1, n.2, 522 n.2, Tokyo Higher Commercial School 355, Tokyo Imperial University 99, 133 n.2, 354 n.3, 396 n.1, 533 n.1, 588 n.1, 622 n.1, 632 n.1, 633 + nn.1–5, 638, 660 + n.2, 764 n.4, Tokyo Semmon Gakkō 6 n.1, Waseda University 6 n.1, 764 n.3;
- (Korea), Anglo-Korean School 508 n.1;
- (New Zealand), Canterbury College, 663 n.2;
- (U.S.A.), Boston University 19 n.1, University of California 95 n.1, University of Chicago 5 n.3, Columbia University 5 n.3, 23 + n.5, n.6, 98 n.2, 214 n.1, 254 n.4, 279 n.2, 637 n.2, 801 + n.2, Cornell University 270 n.2, 818 n.4, Emory College 508 n.1, George Washington University 637 n.2, Georgetown University 786 n.3, Harvard University 20 n.1, 133 n.2, 570, Jewish Theological Seminary 405 n.2, Johns Hopkins University 453 n.1, 532 n.2, 585 n.3, 786 n.3,

Education in China (cont.)
Massachusetts Institute of Technology 23+n.4, University of Missouri 713 n.1, Oberlin College 478, Princeton University 585 n.1, 532 n.2, University of Southern California 19 n.1, Stanford University 637 n.2, Vanderbilt University 508 n.1, Washington University St Louis 23 n.4, Wellesley College 477 n.2, Wesleyan College, 479, Wilmer Opthalmological Institute 786 n.3, University of Wisconsin 296 n.1, Yale University 386 n.4 (387), 478, 801

Edwards, A. H. F., British employee of Chinese Maritime Customs, 55 n.3

Effendi, Russian Mussulman, 63 n.1

Egan, Martin (1872-1938), American journalist and publicity agent, 793+n.4

Eggeling, A. J., journalist and banker, 564

Eliot, Charles Norton Edgcumbe (1862-1931), British diplomat and scholar, 243+n.1, n.2, 701;
letters from, 243

Eliot, Charles William (1834-1926), American educationalist, 20+n.1, 100; *letter to*, 142
letters from, 20, (to T'ang Shao-yi) 21

Empain, Edouard, Belgian banker, 794 n.2

Empress-Dowager Tz'u-Hsi. See Hsiao-ch'in

d'Entrecolles, François Xavier (1652(?62)-1741), French Catholic missionary and author, 652+n.4

Ernle, 1st Baron. See R. E. Prothero

Extraterritoriality in China, 276, 547 n.1, 572, 670; Most-Favoured Nation Clause, 545, 555, 558. See also the individual powers in China; Shanghai: International Settlement

Ezra, Nissim Ezra Benjamin (b. 1880), Shanghai opium dealer, 361+n.2, 567, 705 n.3

von Falkenhayn, Erich Georg Anton Sebastian (1861-1922), German soldier, 455 n.2, 550 n.2

Fang Chao-ying (b. 1908), Chinese scholar, 98 n.2

Fang Wei (d. 1912), Chinese soldier, 118+n.4

Fawcett, Cicely Deborah, Executor and Trustee of Jennie Morrison's Will, 825+n.2

Felton, Alfred (1831-1904), Australian businessman, 643 n.2

Feng Kuo-chang (1859-1919), Chinese soldier, 209 n.2, 291, 361 n.2, 382 n.1, 488+n.2, 520 n.3, 527+n.1, 529, 605 n.3, 612 n.2, 623+n.3, 636, 642 n.1, 649+n.1-650, 654 n.8, 655-6, 682, 689 n.2, 693 n.1, 715, 783 n.1, n.2

Feng Te-lin (1866-1925), Chinese soldier, 597 n.2

Feng Yü-hsiang (1882-1948), Chinese soldier, 43 n.3, 206 n.2, 224 n.2, 401 n.1, 474 n.1, 636 n.2, 654 n.8

Ferguson, John Calvin (1866-1945), American missionary and adventurer, 19+n.1, 279, 718+n.3, 721, 802;
letter from, 19

ffrench, Charles Austin Thomas Robert John Joseph (1868-1955), 6th Baron, British commercial agent, 191+n.1, 192, 301, 794 n.1, 806

ffrench, Mary Margaret (*née* Corbally) (d. 1944), wife of C. A. T. R. J. J. ffrench, 806

Financial conditions in China, 254, 340-3, 315-19, 343, 356+n.1-357, 473, 533; Chinese budget (*1913*), 210+n.1; Bank moratorium, 224 n.2, 518+n.1;
– See also Banks, financial houses and consortia; Boxer Uprising; Indemnity; Customs and excise in China; Loans; G. E. Morrison: and China's finances; Tariff revision and autonomy in China; Taxation in China

Findlay, John George (1862-1929), New Zealand lawyer and author, 680+n.2

Fisher, John Arbuthnot (1841-1921), 1st Baron of Kilverstone, British sailor, 425 n.5, 426+n.1, n.2, n.3, 551 n.2, 789+n.5

Fleming, Jackson, Mr and Mrs, 611

Foch, Ferdinand (1851-1929), French soldier, 698 n.2, 756+n.1, 777+n.1

Fong, Ng Bickleen, Chinese author, 675 n.2

Foreign advisers, 20-4, 87, 97, 99-100, 142-3, 148, 173, 180+n.2-183, 186-91, 213-14, 232-4, 269-70, 343+n.1, 363 n.2, 392, 408, 414, 415+n.1, n.2, 509, 518-19, 532-4, 535-6, 553+n.1, 569 +n.1, 570, 574-6, 577+n.1-578, 585, 594, n.2-595, 620-1, 623, 628, 630-1, 637, 682, 760, 803; (salaries) 569+n.1, 623, 630-1, 817

Forster, John, British adventurer, 279, 338+n.1

Fournier, François-Ernest (1842-1934), French sailor, 380+n.3, 381

Fox, Harry Halton (1872-1936), British consular official, 687+n.1

868

France: in China, 27, 79, 80+n.1–81, 82, 119, 247, 286+n.2, 299–303, 305, 309, 343, 357, 366, 468, 471, 586+n.1, 639, 647; Lao-hsi-k'ai incident, 586+n.1; post-World War I conditions, 769–70. *See also* Powers in China

Franz Ferdinand (1863–1914), Archduke of Austria, 774 n.1

Fraser, David Stewart (1869–1953), British journalist, 31 n.4, 33+n.2, 54+n.1, 87, 89, 93–4, 97+n.1, n.3, 122+n.2, 169 n.1, 222, 240, 241, 242, 252+n.2, 275, 295–6, 315, 317, 319 n.1, 333, 352, 372+n.1, 385 n.2–386, 391, 406, 410, 411, 464, 560, 594, 696, 777+n.4, 780 n.2, 786+n.1, 815+n.3;
letter to, 812
letter from, 41

Fraser, Mrs, 611

Fraser, Everard Duncan Home (1859–1922), British consular official, 70+n.1

Fraser, Lovat George (1871–1926), British journalist, 34+n.4, 35+n.1, n.2, 43 n.2, 88+n.5, 97, 665 n.2;
letters to, 35, 140, 332, 559
letters from, 108, 330

French, John Denton Pinkstone (1852–1925), British soldier, 425+n.1, 508 n.1, 777 n.3

Fukuzawa Yukichi (1834–1901), Japanese educationalist, 508 n.1

Gailey, Robert R., American missionary, 388 n.1, 477+n.1, 603+n.2;
letter from, 477

Gallina, Giovanni, Italian diplomat, 74 +n.4

Gamble, Reginald Arthur (1862–1930), British employee of Chinese Salt Administration, 759 n.2, 807 n.1, 808 n.5, 817

Garnett, William James (b. 1878), British diplomat, 780+n.1, n.2, n.3;
letter from, 780

Gaunt, Lancelot O., British lawyer, 755 n.1

Gaunt, Violet (*née* Morrison), sister of G. E. Morrison and wife of L. Gaunt, 755 n.1

di Gemona. *See* Basilio Brollo

George III (1738–1820), King of England, 274 n.1

George V (1865–1936), King of England, 156, 307

Germany in China:
– occupation of Kiaochow and interests in Shantung: 44 n.3 (45), 247, 371+n.1, 465, 514, 530, 715, 756+n.5, 757, 773;

railways (*see* Railways: in Shantung, Tientsin–Pukow, Tsingtao–Tsinan etc.; Treaties, agreements etc);
– concessions, (Hankow and Tientsin), 464, 466, 472, 544, 572; retrocession of, 560, 577+n.1;
– Boxer Indemnity, 466, 471, 544, 545, 555, 564, 572; Customs, 282, 468, 545, 572–3, (Tsingtao Customs) 282, 351, 353–6, 360, 725; Salt Gabelle, 27, 545, 572–3; Telegraphs, 467; trade, 69, 262, 545, 555, 563, 564; loans, 27, 300, 302, 305, 309, 454, 464, 469, 471, 472–3 (*see also* Banks, financial houses and consortia; Loans);
– Revolution *1911*, 69; military advisers, 343+n.1, 575; missionaries, 119, 465; interests in Mongolia, 122, 124, 262;
– World War I: China's plan to recover Kiaochow, 467, 469, 471, 530; Morrison's advice on China's entry (*see under* G. E. Morrison); diplomatic rupture, 468, 547, 555, 563, 565, 572, 573+n.3, 574, 583+n.1–584, 586, 594, 774–5; treatment of German diplomatic personnel and nationals, 367, 375, 467 +n.2, 468–9, 544, 572–3, 594 n.1; influence of returned students, 375, 469, 546; press influence, 375, 544, 564, (Gilbert Reid) 586+n.2; bribing parliamentarians, 592; incitement of Mohammedans in China and elsewhere, 468, 471, 545–6, 564; alleged letter to Yüan Shih-k'ai, 379+n.1, 380, 381–2;
– Loss of concessions (*see* Japan; Japan in China: Shantung; Paris Peace Conference; Versailles Treaty)

Gilbert, Rodney, American journalist, 578+n.1, 593+n.2, 635, 680;
letter from, 578

Giles, William R. (?b. 1878), British soldier and journalist, 527+n.3, 762 +n.2;
letters from, 527, 762

Ginnell, James, British railway engineer, 476+n.2

Gladstone, William Ewart (1809–98), British politician, 380 n.2

Goffe, Herbert (1870–1939), British consular official, 639+n.1;
letter from, 639

Goodnow, Francis Johnson (1859–1939), American jurist, 100+n.1, 142, 233, 234, 235, 301+n.1, 332, 338, 450, 451, 453+n.1, n.2, n.3, 532 n.2;
memorandum, 235–6, 450, 451, 453 +n.1, n.2, n.3

869

Goodrich, Chauncey Shafter (1836–1925), American Protestant missionary, 98 +n.2, 442 n.2 (443)
Goodrich, Mrs, wife of Chauncey Goodrich, 98+n.2
Goodrich, Luther Carrington (b. 1894), American scholar, 98 n.2
Gotō Shimpei (1857–1927), Japanese politician, 548 n.4, 563+n.1, 772 n.2
Gould, Anna (?1875–1961), American heiress, 106+n.2
Gould, Jason (Jay) (1836–92), American railway tycoon, 106 n.2
Governments in China:
- Constitutions (*see* separate entry);
- Monarchy *versus* republic, (*see under* Monarchist movements); nepotism, 403–4; corruption, 570;
- administration reform, 438; Administrative Council, 264; Law Codification Commission, 721; Censorate, 440+n.1; Examination Yüan, 393 n.1; Judicial Yüan, 393 n.2; Legislative Yüan, 57 n.1, 392 n.2, 477 n.4, 478, (*see also* Constitutions; Parliaments);
- Manchu Government (Prince Ch'ing cabinet) 386 n.4 (387), (Yüan Shih-k'ai cabinet) 386 n.4 (387), 450, 535 n.1, 596 n.2;
- Wuhan Revolutionary Government (*1911*), 394 n.3;
- Nanking Provisional Government (*1912*), 8 n.1, 112 n.2, 191 n.2, n.3; 215 n.2, 254 n.1, 358 n.2, 363 n.2, 393 n.2, 396 n.1, 536 n.1, (*see also* Sun Yat-sen);
- Hung-hsien Government, (*see* Yüan Shih-k'ai: monarchy scheme);
- Chao-ch'ing military government (*1916*), 10 n.1, 395 n.1, 505 n.2 (506), 520 +n.3;
- Militarist Headquarters, Tientsin (*1917*), 595 n.2;
- Chang Hsün restoration government, (*see* Monarchist movement);
- Canton Military Government (*1917*), 56, 57 n.1, n.2, 254 n.1, 392 n.2, 394 n.2, n.4, 395 n.1, n.2, 534 n.2, 536 n.1, 594 n.3, 602, 637, 640+n.3–641+n.1, 645, 650 n.4, 682 n.1, 706 n.3, 709 n.1, 719, 728 n.1, (*see also* Sun Yat-sen);
- Peace negotiations between Central Government and southern republicans, (*see* separate entry);
- National Government, Canton (*1925*), 477 n.4;
- Wuhan Government (*1926*), 43 n.3, 57 n.1, 639 n.1;
- Nationalist Government, Nanking (*1927*), 43 n.3 (44), 57 n.1, 79 n.2 (80), 145 n.2, 166 n.2, 191 n.2, 199 n.1, 225 n.2, 252 n.4 (253), 348 n.1, 388 n.1, 392 n.2, 393 n.2, 394 n.1, n.2, 477 n.4 (478), 478 n.2, 536 n.2, 547 n.2 (548), 570 n.2, 600 n.1, 605 n.3 (606), 713 n.1, 761 n.2, n.3, 818 n.6; (Presidential election *1947*), 393 n.2; 'Four Grandee Families', 388 n.1;
- People's Government, Fukien (*1933*), 43 n.3;
- People's Government (*1949*), 510 n.2;
- Nationalist Government, Taiwan (*1949*), 237 n.3, 393 n.2, 574 n.2, 713 n.1;
- Japanese-sponsored puppet governments: 'Manchukuo' (*1932*), (*see under* Manchuria); Peace Maintenance Committee, Peking (*1937*), 612 n.1; Provisional Government of the Republic of China (Wang K'e-min, *1937*) and North China Political Council, Peking (*1940*), 305 n.3, 783 n.4 (784); Reform Government of the Republic of China (Liang Hung-chih, *1938*), 10 n.1, 254 n.1, 281 n.1; National Government of the Republic of China (Wang Ching-wei, *1940*, 10 n.1, 395 n.2

Graham, John Anderson (1861–1942), British missionary and author, 484
Grant, John Peter, Canadian adventurer, 336+n.2, 338
Gray, Anna, daughter of G. D. Gray, 816
Gray, George Douglas (d. 1946), British medical practitioner, 5 n.4, 14+n.4, 31 n.1, 367 n.2;
letter to, 815
letters from, 14, 367, 803
Gray, Lucy, wife of G. D. Gray, 31+n.1, 816;
letter to, 31
Green, Owen Mortimer, British journalist, 64+n.1, 290, 323, 403 n.1;
letters to, 64, 168, 409, 518, 593, 599, 627
letters from, 72, 251, 460, 532, 573, 600, 722
Green, Mrs, wife of O. M. Green, 519
Greene, William Conyngham (1854–1934), British diplomat, 553, 671+n.3, 771 n.1, 539+n.1;
letter to, 539
Greenwood, James Frederick (?b. 1854), British manufacturer, executor and trustee of G. E. Morrison's will; a cousin of his mother, 825+n.1, n.2

870

Gregory, John Duncan (1878–1951), British diplomat, 45 + n.3, 297 + n.3
Grey, Edward (1862–1933), 1st Visct Fallodon, British politician, 2, 26 + n.4, 31, 40 n.1, 72, 78, 95, 126, 127, 171, 193 + n.2, 297, 342, 345, 406, 413, 467 + n.2, 468, 472, 489 + n.2, n.3 (490), 490 n.1, 521, 560, 666, 672, 696, 774, 779 n.2, 786 + n.2
Grimwade, F. S., Australian businessman, 643 n.2
Griswold, Alfred Whitney (1906–1963), American historian, 60 n.1
Guillemard, Laurence Nunns (1862–1951), British colonial official, 791 n.2
Gull, Edward Manico (b. 1883), British journalist, 403 + n.1, 696;
letter to, 403
Gwatkin. *See* F. T. A. Ashton-Gwatkin
Gwynne, Helen, wife of H. A. Gwynne, 26, 556
Gwynne, Howell Arthur (1865–1950), British journalist, 26 n.1, n.2, 455 n.1, 555 n.1, 755 n.2;
letters to, 26, 555, 755
letter from, 455

Habibullah, Amir of Afghanistan (1872–1919), 566 + n.1
Hackman, German employee of Chinese Government, 71 n.1
Hai-san-kung, Mongol leader, 48 + n.3, 49–52, 204, 219 n.2, 230, 231, 266
Hai Yung-pu, Mongol leader, 219 + n.1
Haig, Douglas (1861–1928), 1st Earl of Bemersyde, British soldier, 127 n.2, 777 + n.3
du Halde, Jean-Baptiste (1674–1743), French scholar, 651 + n.5–652
Hall, L. M. C., British author, 131 n.2
Hamada Kōsaku (1881–1938), Japanese archaeologist, 633 + n.7
Hamaguchi Osachi (1870–1931), Japanese politician, 548 n.4 (549), 632 n.1
Hamilton, Ian Standish (1853–1947), British soldier, 316 + n.1
Han Kuo-chün (?1858–1942), Chinese Republican politician, Provincial Governor, 269 + n.2
Han-ta chin-wang, Mongol leader, 48 + n.2, 49, 51–2, 58 n.3, 91, 174
Hankey, Maurice Paschal Alers (1877–1963), British politician, 799 + n.2
Hankow: redevelopment, 304 n.4 (305), 511; retrocession of British concession, 43 n.3 (44); German concession, 464, 466, 472, 544, 572, 577 + n.1; Japanese concession, 307, 472
Hanwell, British medical practitioner, 816
Hara Kei (Takashi) (1856–1921), Japanese politician, 701 n.2, 749
Haraoka Isamu, Japanese employee of Chinese Maritime Customs, 407 + n.1
Harding, Rev., British missionary, 484
Harding, Warren Gamaliel (1865–1923), 29th President of the United States, 818 n.4
Harmsworth, Alfred Charles William (1865–1922), 1st Visct Northcliffe of St Peter, British newspaper publisher, proprietor of *The Times*, 14 n.1, 373 n.1, 425 + n.3, 460, 695, 696, 787, 817;
letter to, 792
letter from, 786
Harris, A. H., British employee of Chinese Maritime Customs, 363 + n.3, 377 + n.1;
letter to, 377
letters from, 363, 404
Hart, Hester Jane (*née* Bredon), wife of Robert Hart, 814 + n.1;
letter to, 814
Hart, Robert (1835–1911), British Inspector-General of Chinese Maritime Customs, 55 n.3, 92 n.1, 213 + n.2, 271 n.1, 449 n.1, 604 n.3, 630 n.2, 725 n.1, 814 n.1
Harvey, Thomas Edmund (1875–1955), British politician, 128 n.2
Hauptmann, Gerhart Johann Robert (1862–1946), German writer, 43 n.3 (44)
Hay, John Milton (1838–1905), American politician, 23 n.1, 59 + n.4
Hayashi Gonsuke (1861–1939), Japanese diplomat, 476 n.1, 505 n.2, 541 n.4 (542), 547 + n.2, 554, 555 + n.2, 562, 565, 574 n.2, 584, 588 n.2, 589, 592, 621, 654, 657, 672 + n.1, 701 + n.2; *Waga shichijūnen wo kataru* 541 n.4 (542), 547 n.2 (548)
Hayashi Senjūrō (1876–1943), Japanese politician, 463 n.1
Head, Robert Pollock Somerville (1884–1924), Bart, British diplomat, 683 + n.1
Heintzlemann, Percival Stewart (1880–1942), American diplomat, 644 + n.1, 658 + n.1
von Hellfeld, Alfred, German adventurer, 333 + n.3, 337, 338
von Hellfeld, Hans, German adventurer, 333 n.3

871

Henderson, Arthur (1863-1935), British politician, 686+n.2, 798+n.2; *The Aims of Labour*, 798+n.2

Henderson, Reginald Guy Hannam (1881-1939), British sailor, 789+n.4

Henle, Father, German Catholic missionary, 465

Henningsen, H. F., Danish employee of Chinese Telegraph Administration, 114+n.1, 115, 284

Henry, Patrick (1736-99), American politician, 500+n.1

Hertslet, Lewis (1787-1870), British archivist and author, 387 n.2; *Commercial Treaties* (London 1827-1925), 387 n.2

Higgins, Mary Alice (*née* Morrison), sister of G. E. Morrison and wife of H. B. Higgins, 826+n.1

Higgins, Henry Bournes (1851-1929), Australian judge, 826 n.1

Hillier, Edward Guy (1857-1924), British banker, 34+n.3, 71+n.2, 82, 105, 286, 300, 302, 317+n.3, 416; *letters to*, 84, 240, 317, 378 *letters from*, 241, 379

Hillier, Walter Caine (1849-1927), British consular official, 313 n.3

von Hintze, Paul (1864-1941), German sailor and diplomat, 375+n.1, 670

Hioki Eki (Masu) (1861-1926), Japanese diplomat, 351, 355+n.2, 360, 368, 373, 377-8, 379, 380, 463 n.1, 507, 508, 520, 666, 725 n.1, 733, 734, 736, 743, 752

Hirai Seijirō (1856-1926), Japanese railway engineer, 334+n.3-335, 338, 570

Hirohito, Emperor Shōwa of Japan (b. 1901), 220 n.1

Hirth, Friedrich (1845-1927), American scholar, 214+n.1

Hitler, Adolph (1889-1945), Austrian-born German dictator, 698 n.2

Hjalmarson, Gen., Swedish soldier, 414

Hobbes, Thomas (1588-1679), English philosopher, 759+n.3, 760; *Leviathan*, 759+n.3, 760

Hoeppli, Reinhard (1893-1973), Swiss parasitologist, 83 n.3

Holland, Sydney George (1893-1961), New Zealand politician, 675 n.2

Hongō Fusutarō (1860-1931), Japanese soldier, 641+n.4

Horace (Quintus Horatius Flaccus) (65-8 B.C.), Roman poet, 680+n.2 (681)

Horder, Thomas Jeeves (1871-1955), Bart, British medical practitioner, 758+n.4

Hori Yoshiatsu (b. 1885), Japanese diplomat, 494+n.1, 495

Horiuchi Bunjirō, Japanese soldier, 660+n.1

Hosie, Alexander (1853-1925), British consular official, 331, 410+n.2

Hosie, Florence. *See* F. Soothill

de Hoyer, L., Russian banker, 72+n.1, 315

Hsi-liang (1853-1917), Mongol Bannerman, Viceroy, 53 n.3

Hsiao-ch'in, Empress-Dowager Tz'u-hsi (1835-1908), 29+n.1, n.2, 122 n.4, 225 n.2, 264, 395 n.1, 505 n.2, 524 n.4, 541 n.4, 593 n.4 (594), 613 n.3

Hsieh Tsan-t'ai (Tse Tsan-tai) (b. 1872), Australian-born Chinese compradore, 148+n.1, n.2, 456-7; *The Creation - The Real Situation of Eden and the Origin of the Chinese*, 456-7; *Proofs of The Creation and The Deluge*, 456-7; *letters to*, 148, 456 *letters from*, 159, 197, 456

Hsien-feng, Emperor. *See* I-chu

Hsiung Hsi-ling (1870-1942), Chinese Republican politician, 40 n.2, 64+n.2, 80+n.1-81, 242+n.1, 254+n.2, 255+n.1, 262-3, 655, 762 n.1, 808+n.6; *letter to*, 229

Hsiung K'e-wu (b. 1881), Chinese soldier, 393-4+n.1

Hsiung Yüeh-shan (d. 1913), Chinese revolutionary, 181+n.1

Hsü, C. F., Chinese official, 15

Hsü Ch'ung-chih (1887-1965), Chinese soldier, 394+n.2, 395

Hsü En-yüan, Chinese Republican official, 318+n.1, 496+n.1, 809

Hsü Pao-chen, Chinese soldier, 198+n.3

Hsü Pao-shan, Chinese soldier, 181+n.3, 189, 198+n.3

Hsü Shih-ch'ang (1855-1939), Chinese Imperial official, Viceroy, Grand Secretary, Republican politician, President, 361 n.2, 381+n.3, 386 n.4 (387), 439 n.1, 504, 514 n.1, 596, 655+n.2, n.3, 682, 689 n.2, 693 n.1, 697+n.2, 700, 704, 707+n.1, 708, 715, 718, 720, 721, 761 n.2, 765, 783+n.2, n.4, 803, 804, 805, 808+n.2, 828+n.1; *letter to*, (from W. P. Thomas) 805

Hsü Shih-ying (1872-1964), Chinese Imperial official and Republican politician, 254 n.1, 570+n.2, 583+n.5

Hsü Shu-cheng (1880-1925), Chinese soldier and Republican politician, 401 n.1, 616 n.1, 636+n.2, 783+n.1, n.3, n.4, 809

Hsu, Tiger. *See* Hsü Pao-shan

Hsü Ting-hsiang, Chinese Republican official, 404 n.3

Hsüan-tsung, Emperor. *See* Min-ning

Hsü Ying-k'uei (d. 1903), Chinese Imperial official, Viceroy, 394 n.2

Hsüan-yeh, Manchu Emperor K'ang-hsi (Sheng-tsu) (1654–1722), 408+n.2, 458

Hu Ching-yi (1877–1925), Chinese soldier, Provincial Governor, 135+n.2

Hu Chün, Chinese educationalist, 68 n.5 (69)

Hu Han-min (1876–1936), Chinese Republican politician, Provincial Governor, 117 n.1, 169–71, 216+n.2, 393, 395+n.2

Hu Shih (1891–1962), Chinese scholar, 395 n.2

Hu Ying (1884–1933), Chinese Republican politician, 394+n.3

Huang Fu-sheng (?1882–1948), Chinese revolutionary, 181 n.3

Huang Hsing (1874–1916), Chinese Republican politician, 8+n.1, 110, 112 n.2, 116+n.4, 142+n.1, 150, 163, 165, 187+n.2–188, 209, 212, 392, 394 n.4

Huang K'ai-wen (Wang K'ai-wen), Chinese Republican politician, 828+n.1

Huang Yi-ou (b. 1893), Chinese Republican politician, 392+n.2

Hubbard, Charles F., American missionary, 442 n.2

Hubbard, Wilfranc, British journalist, 812+n.3

Hughes, William Morris (1864–1952), Australian politician, 220 n.2, 645 n.1, 702 n.1

Hughes, Willoughby R. (d. 1918), Australian civil engineer, 512+n.2; *letters to*, 512, 520

Hung-li, Manchu Emperor Ch'ien-lung (Kao-tsung) (1711–99), 274 n.1, 408+n.2

Hung Liang-chi (1746–1809), Chinese scholar, 138 n.1

Hung Shu-tsu (?1858–1919), Chinese Imperial and Republican official, 112 n.2, 138+n.1

Hutukhtu. *See* Jebtsun Damba Khutukhtu

Huxley, Thomas Henry (1825–95), British naturalist, 303+n.2, 450

I-chu, Manchu Emperor Hsien-feng (Wen-tsung) (1831–61), 29 n.2

I-kuang (Prince Ch'ing) (1836–1916), Manchu Imperial Clansman, Grand Councillor, 53 n.2, 332+n.2

I-li-pu (?1771–1843), Manchu Bannerman, Viceroy, 118 n.2

I-tsung (1831–89), Manchu Imperial Clansman, 491 n.2

Ienaga Toyokichi (1863–1936), Japanese publicist, 5+n.3, 6

Ijūin Hikokichi (1864–1924), Japanese diplomat and politician, 82+n.3, 101 n.4, 102, 123+n.3, 124, 207, 211, 273 n.1, 506–7, 539, 563, 672; *letter to*, 273

Ijūin Yoshiko (*née* Ōkubo), wife of Ijūin Hikokichi, 101 n.4, 273

India. *See* British India

Inoue Junnosuke (1866–1932), Japanese banker and politician, 632+n.1

Inoue Kaoru (1835–1915), Japanese politician, 132 n.2, 472 n.1

Inoue Katsunosuke (1860–1929), Japanese diplomat, 472+n.1, 561+n.2, n.3

Inukai Tsuyoshi (1855–1932), Japanese politician, 132+n.6, n.7, 222 n.3, 396 n.1, 508 n.1, 574 n.2, 632 n.1

Irwin, J. O'Malley, British journalist, 469 n.2, 484+n.1, 503; *letter from*, 484

Irvine, William Hill (1858–1943), Australian politician, 665+n.1, 674 n.2; *letter to*, 665

Isaacs, Godfrey Charles (d. 1925), British businessman, Managing Director of Marconi's Wireless Telegraph Co. Ltd, 183+n.1

Isaacs, Rufus Daniel (1860–1935), 1st Marquess of Reading, British politician, 183 n.1

Ishida Mikinosuke (1891–1974), Japanese scholar, 631+n.2; *letter from*, 631

Ishii Kikujirō (1866–1945), Japanese diplomat and politician, 530, 547+n.1, 548 n.3, n.4, 562, 619+n.3, 638, 644 n.1, 646, 658, 659, 670, 677–8, 679, 751; mission to U.S., 547 n.1, 618–19, 644, 646–8, 678

Ismail Pasha (1830–95), Khedive of Egypt, 212+n.2

Itagaki Seishirō (1885–1948), Japanese diplomat, 92 n.2 (93)

Italy in China, 73–5, 85, 119, 232–4, 468

Itō Hirobumi (1841–1909), Japanese politician, 101 n.3, 132 n.2, 556 n.1, 763 n.2, 775 n.2

Iwasaki Haruji. *See* Katō Haruji

Iwasaki Hisaya (1865–1955), Japanese entrepreneur, 274 n.1, 603, 622+n.1, n.2, 627+n.2, 632 n.2, 634

873

Iwasaki Koyata (1879–1945), Japanese entrepreneur, 622 n.1
Iwasaki Masako. *See* Shidehara Masako
Iwasaki Yanosuke (1850–1908), Japanese entrepreneur, 622 n.1
Iwasaki Yatarō (1834–85), Japanese entrepreneur, 548 n.4, 622 n.1

Jackson, Abraham Wendell (b. 1855), American financier, 65 + n.2, 66 + n.3
Jackson, Henry Bradwardine (1855–1929), British sailor, 426 + n.3
Jameson, C. D. (b. 1855), American civil engineer, 200 + n.4;
letter from, (to E. J. Williams) 200
Jamieson, George (1843–1920), British consular official, 44 + n.2, 65, 313 n.3, 458
Jamieson, James William (1867–1946), British consular official, 645 + n.2, 646, 719
Jao Meng-jen, Chinese Republican politician, 233 + n.2;
letter to, 234
Japan, Emperor Meiji of. *See* Mutsuhito
Japan, Emperor Shōwa of. *See* Hirohito
Japan, Emperor Taishō of. *See* Yoshihito
Japan: internal conditions, 131–4, 218, 219–20, 704; fiscal reform, 101 n.3; rice riots, 704, 798 + n.1; trade success, 680;
- Political groups in, (*see under* Political groups);
- Pan-Asianism and Monroe Doctrine in Asia, 211 n.2, 420–1, 422, 646–7, 677; extreme nationalism, 150 n.1, 222 n.3, 549 + n.3;
- and World War I, 350, 406–7, 473, 548–51, 556–8, 565–6, 589, 629, 644, 660–3, 680, 700; profiteering, 557, 558; reaction to Peace Treaty, 722 + n.1, n.2;
- and Powers: Treaty Revision, 6 n.1, 25 n.2; Australia (*see under* Australia); Britain, 219–20, 365, 389, 421, 507, 519, 532, 541, 557, 659, 664, 691 n.1, 757–8, 767, 787–8, 789–91, 799, (*see also* Treaties, agreements etc.: Anglo-Japanese Alliance); France, 370 + n.1, 444 + n.3, 476 n.1, 530, 550 n.2, 771 n.1; Germany, 219–20, 350–1, 364, 365, 366, 547, 549, 555, 556–8, 563; Russia, 661, 663 + n.1, 741, 742–3, 749–51, 784; U.S., (*see under* United States);
- *See also* Japan in China
Japan in China:
- and reformers, 505 n.2;
- and Revolution *1911*, 69, 99, 100, 181 + n.1, 194 n.1, 302;
- as *agent provocateur* and supporter of Sun Yat-sen and southern republicans, 38–9, 101, 108 + n.3, 123–4 + n.1, 132 n.7 (133), 134, 150, 157, 180–3, 186–91, 198, 199, 207, 209–12, 251–2, 289–90, 314, 323–8, 389–91, 392–8, 452, 476 + n.1, 487, 506, 541 n.4 (542), 590 n.1, 642 n.1, n.2;
- and Yüan Shih-k'ai, (*see under* Yüan Shih-k'ai);
- financial and industrial penetration, 39, 93 + n.1, 296, 307, 326, 357–60, 386 + n.1, 396 n.2, 547 n.2, 583–4, 590 n.1, 591 n.1, 620, 642, 689, 693–4, 739, 764 n.2, n.3, n.4, 784 + n.1; Nishihara Mission (*see* Nishihara Kamezō); tariff revision and autonomy (*see* separate entry);
- aggression: 1st and 2nd Sino-Japanese Wars (*see under* Wars); Boxer Uprising (*see* separate entry); Chientao, 386 + n.3–387, 506; *Tatsu Maru*, 38–9, 366 + n.1; Ch'ang-li, 218 + n.2; Chen-chia-t'un, 365 + n.1; Manchurian incident (*see under* Manchuria);
- Formosa and Pescadores, 437, 644, 747; (opium smuggling) 96–7, 402, 724; as strategic threat, 789 + n.7;
- Fukien, 377, 421, 644, 724;
- Manchuria (*see under* Manchuria);
- Mongolia, 102, 122, 123–5, 211 + n.2–212, 262, 377, 386 + n.2, 541 n.4 (542), 565, 642 n.1, 781, 794, 810;
- Yangtse Valley, 39, 296, 307, 326, 358, 377, 386 + n.1, 396 n.2, 472, 739;
- Yunnan, 493–5;
- Twenty-one Demands (*see* separate entry);
- and World War I (*see under* Japan); China's entry into World War I, 471, 516, 530, 537, 539–48, 551, 554, 557, 558, 559–66, 573, 592, 618, 619, 659, 662, 665–74; occupation of Tsingtao, 350–1, 402, 424 + n.3, 431, 438 + n.2, 551–3, 556–7, 561 n.1, 641 + nn.3–6, 773–4; (British assistance) 424 + n.3; claim to German rights in Shantung, 101 n.4 (102), 337, 360–1, 452, 463 n.1, 475–6 + n.1, 520, 619 n.1, 641–2 + n.1, n.2, 622, 725 + n.1–726, 731–55, 756–8, 771–2, 773, 781; (Tsingtao Customs) 351, 353–6, 360;
- Powers and Japan, and support for her claims at the Paris Peace Conference: Britain, 530, 550 n.2, 771 + n.1, 775,

874

Japan in China (*cont.*)
799; France, 530, 550 n.2, 771 n.1;
Russia, 661, 663 + n.1, 741, 742–3,
749–51; U.S., 644, 646–8, 658, 717,
742–3, 751, 755–6; *see also* Powers in
China; Treaties, agreements etc.
- propaganda against China, 5 n.1, n.3,
25, 101, 475 n.1, (*see also* Newspapers,
Journals, Press Agencies etc.); attempt
to influence *Times*, 795–803; Liang
Shih-yi's reply to *Asahi*, 418–22,
(Morrison's comments on Liang's reply)
429–46;
- secret service in China, 92 n.2 (93),
149–50, 475 n.1;
- in Chinese employment: military
advisers, 92 n.3 (93), 124 n.2, 211 n.2,
343 n.1, 552 + n.3, 630, 637, 642 + n.1;
Customs, 587, 681 (*see also* Customs
and excise in China); Post Office, 699,
702;
- Chinese students trained in Japan (*see
under* Education);
- Chinese collaborators in Japanese
aggression, 10 n.1, 236–8, 254 n.1, 281
n.1, 287 n.2, 305 + n.3, 347 + n.1, 395
n.2, 584 + n.1, 590 n.1, 636, 761 n.2,
n.3, 764 + nn.2–4, 765, 767, 783 + n.4
(784), 800, 801 + n.3;
- Anti Japanese demonstrations and
boycotts, 133–4, 423, 446 + n.1, 449,
591, 722, 763–6, 790, 797, 800;
- *See also* Banks, financial houses and
consortia; Customs and excise in China;
Japan; Loans; Manchuria; G. E.
Morrison; Opium and morphia; Powers
in China; Salt Gabelle; Treaties,
agreements etc.; Twenty-one Demands;
Yüan Shih-k'ai
Japan in Korea. *See* Korea
Jasaktu Khan, Mongol leader, 49 + n.8
Jaurès, Jean Leon (1859–1914), French
socialist leader, 619 n.2
Jebtsun Damba Khutukhtu (Bagada Lama,
Bogdo Khan, Hutukhtu) (1870–1924),
Mongol leader, 49, 62 + n.3, 90, 121–2
+ n.2, 169, 174, 175, 178, 179, 204, 260,
268 + n.1
Jefferson, Thomas (1743–1826), 3rd
President of the United States, 500 n.1
Jellicoe, John Rushworth (1859–1935), 1st
Earl, British sailor, 777 n.2, 789 + n.2
Jen K'o-ch'eng, Chinese Republican
politician, 481 n.3
Jenks, Jeremiah Whipple (1856–1929),
American economist, 270 + n.2–272, 279,
284–5, 533

Jerome, Jeannette (1854–1921), American
heiress, 106 n.2
Joffre, Joseph Jacques Cesaire (1852–
1931), French soldier, 447 + n.3, 550
n.2, 662
John, King of the Marshall Islands, 550,
558
Jones, Rev. Josiah Towyn (1858–1925),
British politician, 128 n.2
Johnston, Reginald Fleming (1874–1938),
British scholar and colonial official,
206 n.1, 224 + n.2, 459, 462, 481;
*Kinship in China and its relation to
Confucianism*, 462;
letter to, 511
letters from, 224, 461, 481
Jordan, Anne Howe (*née* Cromie), wife of
J. N. Jordan, 806, 818
Jordan, John Newell (1852–1925), British
diplomat, 31 + n.2, 41, 43 n.2, 50, 51,
69, 72, 77, 78 + n.3, 85, 87, 89, 90 + n.2
(91), 95 n.2, 105, 114, 152 + n.1, 251,
271, 273, 278, 281, 286, 297, 336 n.2,
337, 342 n.4, 392, 426, 463 n.1, 471
+ n.1, 476, 482, 488, 507, 509, 515,
519 + n.1, 521, 544, 548 n.1, 559, 561,
564–5, 567–8, 571, 624, 628, 664, 666,
669, 671, 683, 701, 704 + n.3, 707, 774,
803, 810 + n.3, 815 + n.3;
letters to, 43, 57, 297, 345, 368, 371, 453,
469, 816
letters from, 47, 454, 814
Ju Jen-ho, Chinese Republican official,
192 + n.1, 209, 210, 258, 398, 454 + n.2,
722 n.2, 804, 805;
letter to, 720
letters from, (to W. P. Thomas) 805, (to
W. P. Thomas) 827
Ju Jung-hao. *See* Ju Jen-ho
Judah, Shanghai merchant, 567
Julien, Stanislas (1797–1873), French
scholar, 652 n.4
Jung-hou, Manchu Bannerman, Republican official, 597 + n.3, 615 + n.2,
616
Jung-lu (1836–1903), Manchu Bannerman,
Grand Secretary, Viceroy, 541 n.4

Kadoorie, Eleazer Silas (b. 1867),
Shanghai opium dealer, 567, 705 n.3,
706 n.1, n.2
Kamei Rokurō (1871–1923), Japanese
journalist, 475 + n.1, 476, 802
Kamio Mitsutomi (1855–1927), Japanese
soldier, 552 + n.1, 641 + n.6
Kanai Kiyoshi (b. 1884), Japanese government official, 588 + n.1, 639 + n.2

K'ang-hsi, Emperor. *See* Hsüan-yeh
K'ang Yu-wei (1858–1927), Chinese scholar and reformer, 122 n.4, 505 n.2, 541 n.4 (542), 542 + n.1, 609 + n.4, 650 + n.3
Katō Haruji (*née* Iwasaki), wife of Katō Takaaki, 548 n.4
Katō Takaaki (Kōmei) (1860–1926), Japanese politician, 132 n.5, n.7 (133), 355 n.2, 385 n.3–386, 419, 475, 530, 539 + n.2–548, 548 + n.4–549, 552, 553, 554, 560, 562 + n.1, 619, 638, 666, 670, 671 + n.3, 672, 733; interview with Morrison, 539 + n.2–548
Katō Yoshiko. *See* Okabe Yoshiko
Katsura Tarō (1847–1913), Marquis, Japanese politician, 101 + n.2, 132 + n.4, n.7, 133 n.2, 135 + n.5, 550, 584 n.2, n.3, 772 n.2
Kawashima Naniwa (b. 1865), Japanese adventurer, 642 n.1
Kawashima Yoshiko, Sino-Japanese spy, 642 n.1
Ker, William Pollock (b. 1864), British consular official, 302 + n.2
Kerensky, Aleksandr Fedorovich (1881–1970), Russian politician and author, 626 + n.3
Keswick, Henry (1870–1928), British businessman and politician, 127 + n.3, 128 n.2–129, 806 + n.2; speech in House of Commons on opium, 128 n.2
Keswick, John Henry (b. 1906), British businessman, 127 n.3 (128)
Keswick, William (1835–1912), British businessman and politician, 127 n.3
Keswick, William Johnston (b. 1903), British businessman, 127 n.3 (128)
Khalachin, Prince, Mongol leader, 203
Kiakhta Conference. *See under* Mongolia
Kido Kōin (1833–77), Japanese politician, 132 n.2
Kimura Eiichi (b. 1879), Japanese diplomat, 791 + n.3
Kinder, Claude William (1852–1936), British railway engineer, 624 + n.2; *letter from*, 624
King, Louis Magrath (1886–1949), British consular official, 153 + n.2
King, Philip Gidley (1758–1808), British sailor and colonial official, 554 n.1
King, William Lyon Mackenzie (1874–1950), Canadian politician, 617 n.1
Kirton, Walter, British journalist, 66 + n.2, n.3

Kishimoto Hirokichi (b. 1883), Japanese employee of Chinese Maritime Customs, 355 + n.1
Kiura Keigo (1850–1942), Japanese politician, 584 n.3
Klaproth, Jules Henri (1783–1835), French scholar, 653 n.1
Knox, Thomas, Australian journalist, 612 + n.3; *letter from*, 612
K'o Hung-lieh, Chinese Republican official, 135 + n.4
Kodama Gentarō (1852–1906), Japanese soldier, 563 n.1
Koike Chōzō (1873–1921), Japanese diplomat, 638 + n.2, 659, 678
Koizumi Masayasu (d. 1917), Japanese soldiers, 641 + n.2
Komura Jutarō (1855–1911), Japanese diplomat and politician, 133 + n.2, 476 n.1
Kōno Iwao, Japanese employee of Chinese Salt Administration, 615 + n.1
Konovaloff, N. A., Russian employee of Chinese Maritime Customs, 630 + n.2, 637
Koo, Wellington. *See* Ku Wei-chün
Korea: Japan's annexation of, 101 n.2, 132 n.7 (133), 133 n.2, 324 n.2, 419, 513, 547 n.2, 736; Japan in, 25 n.2, 60, 363–4, 373, 433, 440–1, 442, 507–8, 547 n.2, 554–5, 583 n.2, 590 n.1, 638 n.1, 674, 733, 742, 755, 762–4; '105 incident' (*1912*), 440–1, 508 n.1, 763 + n.2; 'March 1st' movement (*1919*), 324 n.2, 762 + n.2, 763 + n.1; U.S. in, 60, 441, 443–4
Kornilov, Lavr Georgyevich (1870–1918), Russian soldier, 626 n.3
Korostovetz, Ivan Iakovlevich, Russian diplomat, 48 n.2, 58 + n.2, n.3, 59 n.2, n.3, 140, 158 n.3, 174, 780; *letter to*, 143 *letter from*, 134
Korostovetz, Mme, wife of I. Ia. Korostovetz, 144
Koudacheff, N. A., Prince, Russian diplomat, 629 + n.1
Krieger, Dr, German journalist, 467
Kroupensky, Basil N., Russian diplomat, 62 + n.4 (63), 72, 85, 103 + n.2, 123, 124 + n.3, 144 + n.1, 174, 175, 180 + n.1, 228 n.1, 253, 286, 459, 463 n.1, 509, 539 + n.3, 550, 553, 563, 629 + n.1, 661, 663 + n.1, 666, 670, 671, 672, 741, 742, 743, 749, 750, 751, 777

876

Ku Hung-ming (1857–1928), Chinese scholar, 578 n.1, 605 n.2, 608+n.2
Ku Wei-chün (Wellington Koo) (b. 1887), Chinese diplomat and politician, 139, 252+n.2, 279, 535, 713, 775, 799, 812; *letters to*, 252, 270, 284, 385, 386
Kuan Chiung (Kuan Chiung-chih), Chinese Imperial and Republican official, 188+n.2
Kuang-hsü, Emperor. *See* Tsai-t'ien
Kung Chao-huan, Chinese diplomat, 761 n.1
K'ung Hsiang-hsi (1881–1967), Chinese Republican politician, 388+n.1, 477+n.2–480; views on Sun Yat-sen and Japanese, 388–91; *letter from*, 388
K'ung Hsiang-hsi, Mme. *See* Sung Ai-ling
Kung Hsin-chan (b. 1868), Chinese Republican politician, 404 n.1, 761+n.1
K'ung T'ien-tseng, Chinese journalist, 112+n.1, 113 n.3; *letters from*, 112, 348
Kuo Ch'ung-kuang, Chinese Imperial and Republican official, 42+n.2
Kuo Sung-t'ao (1818–91), Chinese diplomat, 104 n.2
Kuo T'ai-ch'i (1889–1952), Chinese diplomat, 536+n.2, 600, 773 n.2; *letter from*, 436
Kurachi Tetsukichi (1870–1944), Japanese diplomat and industrialist, 476+n.1
Kuroda Kiyotaka (1840–1900), Japanese soldier, 6 n.1, 132 n.2
Kurino Shin'ichirō (1851–1937), Japanese diplomat, 370 n.1
Kurosawa Reikichi (b. 1868), Japanese employee of Chinese Maritime Customs, 354+n.2, 355
Kuzminsky, Mikhail Nikolaevich, Russian consular official, 104+n.1, 105
La Touche, John David Digues, British ornithologist and employee of Chinese Maritime Customs, 604+n.2; *letter from*, 160
Lagerholm, Swedish engineer, 267
Lamont, Thomas William (1870–1948), American financier, 793+n.3, 808, 809
Lampson, Miles (1880–1964) 1st Baron Killearn, British diplomat, 214 n.3 (215), 353 n.2, 571+n.2, 683
Lan T'ien-wei (d. 1921), Chinese soldier, 319 n.3
Langeback, H. T., Danish employee of Chinese Telegraph Administration, 103+n.2

Langley, Walter Louis Frederick Goltz (1855–1918), British diplomat, 521+n.2
Lansdowne, Marquess of. *See* H. C. K. Petty-Fitzmaurice
Lansing-Ishii Agreement. *See* Treaties, agreements etc.: U.S.–Japanese
Lansing, Robert (1864–1928), American politician, 618+n.1, 619 n.3, 644+n.1, 647, 677, 678, 679
Lao-hsi-k'ai incident. *See* France in China
Larson, Frans August (b. 1870), Swedish missionary and trader, 47+n.2, 90, 102, 104, 153–4, 203, 204, 205, 219, 229, 230, 231, 260, 262–3, 265, 266, 269, 280, 281–2
Laski, Harold Joseph (1893–1950), British scholar, 605 n.3 (606)
Lau Chu-pak. *See* Liu Chu-p'o
Lau Tak-po, Chinese entrepreneur, 310 n.1
Lavino, William, British journalist, 296 n.2
Law, Andrew Bonar (1858–1923), British politician, 425 n.5
League of Nations. *See under* Conferences and institutions, international
Lee, Richard Henry (1732–94), American politician, 500 n.1
Legendre, Aimé François (b. 1867), French medical practitioner and author, 167+n.2
Legge, James (1815–97), British missionary and scholar, 613+n.1
Leghait, Belgian diplomat, 812 n.4
Lei Chen-ch'un, Chinese soldier, 595+n.2, 596+n.2
Lenin (Ulyanov), Vladimir Ivanovich (1870–1924), Russian revolutionary, 626 n.3
Lenox Simpson, Bertram. *See* B. L. Simpson
Leopold I (1790–1865), King of the Belgians, 812 n.4
van Lerberghe, Marcel, French journalist, 769+n.2; *letter from*, 769
de Lesseps, Ferdinand (1805–94), French engineer, 185 n.2
von Lettow-Vorbeck, Paul Emil (1870–1964), German soldier, 663+n.5
Lew Yuk Lin. *See* Liu Yü-lin
Li, General, Chinese soldier, 807
Li-chi, 462
Li Ching-fang (?1855–1934), Chinese diplomat, 306–7+n.1, 336 n.2 (337), 338+n.2

Li Ching-hsi (1860-1925), Chinese Imperial official, Viceroy, and Republican politician, 284 n.2, 514 n.1
Li Ch'ing-mai, Chinese Republican official and diplomat, 605 n.2
Li Ch'un (1871-1920), Chinese soldier, 119 n.2 (120), 209+n.2, n.3, 623 n.3 (624), 642 n.1, 649-50, 656+n. 4, 717 +n.2, 718
Li Han-chang (1821-99), Chinese Imperial official, Viceroy, 305 n.3
Li Hung-chang (1823-1901), Chinese Imperial official, Grand Secretary, Viceroy, 57 n.2, 202 n.1, 305 n.3, 336 n.2, 380+n.2, n.3-381, 438+n.1, 594 n.4, 605 n.2, 607 n.1, 616 n.4, 667
Li K'ai-shen, Chinese Republican politician, Provincial Governor, 309 +n.1
Li Keng-yüan (?1879-1965), Chinese soldier, 393+n.4, 395+n.1
Li Lieh-chün (1882-1946), Chinese soldier, Provincial Governor, 166+n.2, 195, 197 n.1, 209 n.3, 211+n.2, 269 n.3, 395, 493+n.1
Li Ming-chung, Chinese soldier, 474 n.1
Li Shih-wei (d. 1927), Chinese Republican politician, 404 n.2
Li Ssu-hao (b. 1879), Chinese Republican politician, 761 n.2, 805+n.2
Li Teng-hui (b. 1872), Chinese educationalist, 112 n.1
Li T'ing-yü, Chinese soldier, 203+n.2, 205, 229
Li Yüan-hung (1864-1928), Chinese soldier, Republican President, 3 n.1, 43 n.3, 57 n.2, 85+n.3, 86 n.1, 118 n.4, 138 n.1, 287 n.2, 309 n.1, 324+n.2, 381 n.3 (382), 482, 504, 515, 522 n.2, 529, 531, 532+n.3-534+n.2, 537, 538, 547 n.2 (548), 560 n.3, 562, 566 n.1, 568, 573 n.3, 593+n.4 (594), 595+n.2, 599+n.1, 601, 602, 606, 612 n.1, 623 n.3, 635 n.1, 636+n.2, 656 n.2, 671 +n.1;
letter to, 535
Li Yuan-yun, Korean politician and collaborator with Japanese, 324+n.2
Liang Cheng (Liang Chen-tung), Chinese diplomat, 217+n.1;
letter from, 217
Liang, Chentung. *See* Liang Cheng
Liang Ch'i-ch'ao (1873-1929), Chinese scholar, publicist and Republican politician, 244 n.3, 439 n.1, 452, 505 +n.2, 520 n.3, 541 n.4 (542), 547 n.2 (548), 595, 605+n.3, 621 n.1, 630 n.1, 636, 716, 718, 720, 756, 762 n.1;
letter to, 630
Liang Hung-chih (1883-1946), Chinese Republican politician, 10 n.1, 254 n.1, 281 n.1, 761 n.2
Liang Ju-cheng, Chinese banker, 640 n.3
Liang Ju-hao (Mou-t'ing) (b. 1860), Chinese Imperial official and Republican politician, 53+n.2, n.3, 54 n.1
Liang Mou-t'ing. *See* Liang Ju-hao
Liang-pi (1877-1912), Manchu Bannerman and soldier, 118+n.2, 642 n.1
Liang Shih-hsü (b. 1879), Chinese soldier, 311+n.2
Liang Shih-yi (1869-1933), Chinese Imperial official and Republican politician, 55 n.3, 79+n.2, 117+n.1, 161 n.2 (162), 222 n.1, 228, 229, 233, 237 n.3, 254 n.1, 258 n.1, 284 n.2, 306 n.2, 311+n.2, 318 n.2, 352, 418-422, 454, 485, 488, 505, 510 n.2, 518, 533, 535, 637 n.1, 640 n.1, 691 n.1, 722 n.1, 809+n.2; and *Asahi Shimbun*, 418-22, 429-46;
letter to, 429, 691
Liang Tun-yen (1872-1924), Chinese Imperial official and Republican politician, 386+n.4, 469, 605+n.2, 608+n.1, n.2, 609+n.4, 611;
letters to, 606, 607
Liao, General, Chinese soldier, 168
Libraries, galleries, museums and herbaria: Arnold Arboretum, Harvard, 508 n.3; Australian National Library, Canberra, 83 n.3 (84), 665 n.2; British Museum, London, 484, 503; Kew Gardens, London, 508 n.3; Morrison Library, Tokyo, 274 n.1, 603, 622 n.1, n.2, 631 n.2, 632 n.1, n.3, 633 n.2, (*see also* Morrison: library); National Diet Library, Japan, 622 n.2, 628; National Gallery, London, 127 n.2; Seikadō Bunko, Tokyo, 622 n.1; Semitic Museum, Harvard, 405 n.2; Tate Gallery, London, 127 n.2; Thomas Fisher Rare Book Library, Toronto, 54 n.2; Tōyō Bunko (Oriental Library), Tokyo (*see above,* Morrison library)
Lien Ch'üan, husband of Wu Chih-ying, 388 n.3
Lien-yu, Manchu Bannerman, Imperial official, 427+n.2-428
Lim Yong Seng. *See* Lin Hsiung-ch'eng
Lin Ch'ang-ming (1876-1925), Chinese Republican politician, 762 n.1, 809+n.1.
Lin Hsiung-cheng (Lim Yong Seng) (?b. 1866), Singapore government clerk,

Lin Hsiung-c'eng (*cont.*)
664+n.1, 710–12; *How China Ought to be Governed*, 664+n.1, 710–12;
letters from, 664, 710
Lin Shih-yüan, Chinese diplomat, 674 +n.3;
letter from, 674
Lin Tse-hsü (1785–1850), Chinese Imperial official, Viceroy, 674 n.3
Lincoln, Abraham (1809–65), 16th President of the United States, 59 n.4
Lindsey, George Goldwin Smith (1860–1920), Canadian lawyer, 617 n.1;
letters to, 617, 688
Lindsey, Mrs, wife of G. G. S. Lindsey, 617, 689
Lister-Kaye, John Pepys (1853–1924), Bart, British financier and concession hunter, 69+n.1, n.2
Little, Archibald John, British missionary and businessman, 69+n.1, n.3
Little, E. S., British businessman, 591 +n.1, 727 n.3
Liu, Chinese compradore, 358
Liu Ching-jen, Chinese diplomat, 368 +n.1
Liu Chu-p'o (Lau Chu-pak) (1866–1922), Chinese entrepreneur, 310+n.1
Liu Hsiang (1890–1938), Chinese soldier, 807 n.3
Liu Hsien-shih (d. 1927), Chinese Republican politician, Provincial Governor, 495+n.2
Liu Kuan-hsiung (b. 1858), Chinese sailor, 358+n.2, 636+n.1
Liu K'un-yi (1830–1902), Chinese Imperial official, Viceroy, 607 n.1
Liu Ming-ch'uan (1836–95), Chinese Imperial official, Provincial Governor, 138 n.1
Liu Yü-lin (Lew Yuk Lin) (b. 1862), Chinese diplomat, 56+n.1, 79, 120, 285, 335, 338;
letter to, 60
Liu Yung-fu (1837–1917), Chinese soldier, 380 n.1, 817 n.2
Lloyd, George Ambrose (1879–1941), British banker and politician, 46+n.1, 65
Lloyd George, David (1863–1945), British politician, 183 n.1, 223+n.1, 344–5, 460, 489 n.3 (490), 619 n.1, 696, 756, 758, 799
Lo Ch'ang, Chinese Republican official, 57+n.3
Lo Wei-hsin, Chinese politician, 189+n.1
Loans, 39, 44–6, 54 n.2, 64–8, 80, 81, 82, 105, 111, 137, 192–4, 297–303, 315–17 +n.3 (318), 319 n.1, 333–5, 335–7, 338–40, 341, 343, 356+n.1–362, 402–3, 416–18, 423, 469, 471, 561, 572, 668, 689, 820;
– Anglo-Belgian Loan, 67+n.1, 298–9, 333 n.3; Anglo-German Loans: (2nd China Loan, *1896*) 564, (3rd China Loan, *1898*) 564; Carlowitz Loan, 302; Central China Railway Loan, 66; China Merchants Steam Navigation Co. Loan, 307; Crisp Loan, 33 n.2, 34 n.4, 37, 39, 40 n.1, 41, 44–6, 47, 55+n.2, 64–8, 245, 249, 298–9, 319 n.1; Currency Loan, 34, 245; (*see also* Quintuple Loan); Hongkong & Shanghai Bank Loan, (*1894*) 317+n.1, (*1895*) 317+n.2; Huai River Loan, 296; Hukwang Railway Loan, 564; Industrial Gold Loan (*1924*) 80 n.1, 327+n.1; Japanese Loans, 184+n.1, 803+n.1, 808 (*see also* Banks, financial houses and consortia: Nishihara banks; Nishihara Kamezō); Marconi Loan, 340; Pin-Hei Railway Loan, 504; Quintuple Loan, 63, 71, 72–3, 84+n.1, 85, 86+n.2, 111, 137, 144, 244+n.4–251, 298+n.1–299, 302, 309–10, 316–17, 322+n.1, 340, 361, 407, 467, 518 n.3, 544, 564, 597, 607 +n.2 (*see also* Currency and Reorganization Loans); Reorganization Loan, 93, 193, 249, 250, 315 (*see also* Quintuple and Sextuple Loans); Sextuple Loan, 34 n.1, 40+n.1, n.2, 65, 66, 67, 70, 71, 72, 79, 80–1, 108+n.1, n.2, 121 n.1, 398 n.1, 763 n.3 (opposition of southern republicans) 11+n.3–12, 14 n.5 (15)–16; Telge & Schroeter Loan, 340; Tientsin-Pukow Railway Loan, 66, 564. *See also* Banks, financial houses and consortia; Railways
Lockhart, James Haldane Stewart (1858–1937), British colonial official, 224+n.5, 225
Lodge, Henry Cabot (1850–1924), American politician, 800+n.1
Loeb, Theresa. *See* T. Schiff
Loh Wei-sen. *See* Lo Wei-hsin
Longford, Joseph Henry (1849–1925), British author, 131 n.2
Louba, Victor Fedorovich, Russian consular official, 50+n.2
Lowry, Hiram Harrison (b. 1843), American missionary, President of Peking University, 442 n.2 (443)
Lu, Chinese cobbler in Calcutta, 428–9
Lu Cheng-hsiang (1871–1949), Chinese diplomat and politician, 4 n.1, 15+n.

Lu Cheng-hsiang (*cont.*)
1–16, 50 n.4, 51, 53 n.2, 56+n.3, 62, 77, 100+n.2, 103, 114, 123, 124, 139, 153, 154+n.1, 169+n.2, 175, 177, 180+n.1, 232+n.2, 281 n.1, 368, 381+n.2, 463 n.1, 535, 582, 654+n.3, 698+n.3, 705 n.2, 716, 719+n.3, 721+n.2, 728 n.1, 755+n.3, 785, 812+n.4;
letter to, 705
Lu Cheng-hsiang, Mme. *See* E. B. Bovy
Lu Chien-chang (1872–1918), Chinese soldier, 401+n.1
Lu Hsin-yüan (1834–94), Chinese bibliographer and scholar, 622 n.1
Lu Hsün (1881–1936), Chinese writer, 415 n.4 (416)
Lu Mu-ch'en, 1st wife of Sun Yat-sen, 477+n.4
Lu Ts'ung-yü (b. 1875), Chinese politician and diplomat, 590 n.1, 764+n.3, n.4, 765, 801 n.3
Lu Yung-t'ing (1856–1927), Chinese soldier, 42 n.2, 244 n.3, 395 n.1, 640+n.4, 645, 809+n.3
Lucas, Sydney E., British banker, 324, 336 n.1, 338 n.3 (339), 609+n.3, 612, 630
von Ludendorff, Erich (1865–1937), German soldier, 698 n.2, 756 n.1
Lun-yü, 462
Lung Chi-kuang (1860–1921), Chinese soldier, Provincial Governor, 117 n.1, 217 n.2, 244 n.3, 308+ n.2–309, 310+n.2, 311 n.1, 395 n.2, 487+n.1, 488 n.2, 493+n.2, 495+n.1, 496, 537, 693, 809 n.3
Lung Chien-chang, Chinese Republican politician, 284+n.2, 495 n.2, 636 n.2
Lung Chin-kuang, Chinese soldier, 310+n.2, 493+n.2
Lung Yü-kuang, Chinese soldier, 310+n.2
Lung Yün (1888–1962), Chinese soldier, Provincial Governor, 42 n.2
Luther, Martin (1483–1546), German religious reformer, 159
Luzac, Cornelis Gerbrand (1862–1903), Dutch bookseller, 224 n.3
Luzzatti, Angelo, Italian concession hunter, 69 n.1
Luzzatti, Luigi (1841–1931), Italian politician, 73+n.2, 74, 232
Lytton, Victor Alexander George Robert (1876–1947), 2nd Earl, British politician, 588 n.1

Ma Fu-hsiang (1876–1932), Chinese soldier, 474+n.1, 538
Ma Hung-k'uei (b. 1893), Chinese soldier, Provincial Governor, 474 n.1
Ma Hung-pin (1883–1960), Chinese soldier, 474 n.1
Ma Soo, Chinese-French journalist, 9, 11, 112 n.3, 238, 239, 339
Ma T'ing-liang, Chinese Republican official, 597+n.4, 598
Ma Yi-ting, Chinese soldier, 167, 168
Ma Ying-piao (Ma Ying Piu), Chinese businessman, 703+n.1
Ma Ying Piu. *See* Ma Ying-piao
Macarthur, John (1767–1834), British soldier and colonist, 554 n.1
Macartney, George Halliday (1867–1945), British consular official, 104+n.2
Macartney, George Macartney (1737–1806), 1st Earl, British politician and colonial official, 274+n.1; journals, 274+n.1
Macartney, Samuel Halliday (1833–1906), British employee of Imperial Chinese government, 104 n.2
McCall, John (1860–1919), Australian politician, 557+n.1;
letter to, 557
MacDonald, Claude Maxwell (1852–1915), British soldier and diplomat, 335+n.2, 382 n.2, 449
MacDonald, James Ramsay (1866–1937), British politician, 626+n.1
Macdonnell, John (1846–1921), British judge and educationalist, 801+n.1
McElroy, Robert (1872–1959), American historian, 585+n.1
MacEwen, Alexander Palmer, British merchant, 571 n.1
MacGlade, Miss A. B., secretary to G. E. Morrison, 215+n.3, 314
Machray, Robert (1857–1946), Canadian journalist and author, 565+n.2, 566, 660; *The Night Side of London*, 565 n.2, 566, 660
Mackay, James Lyle (1852–1932), 1st Earl of Inchcape, British banker and official, 576+n.1
Mackennal, Bertram (1863–1931), Australian painter, 806+n.1
McKinley, William (1843–1901), 25th President of the United States, 23 n.1, 59 n.4
Macklin, W. E., Canadian medical practitioner, 215+n.2
McLeay, Alexander (1767–1848), British colonial official, 554 n.1
Macleay, James William Ronald (1870–1943), British diplomat, 353+n.2, 454,

880

Macleay, James William Ronald (*cont.*) 476, 548 + n.1, 554 + n.1, 555–6, 672 + n.2; *letters to*, 353, 548 *letter from*, 355
McMahon, Arthur Henry (1862–1949), British colonial official and author, 172 n.2, 342 + n.5. *See also* Tibet
de MacMahon, Marie Edme Patrice Maurice (1808–93), French President, 236 + n.1
MacMurray, John van Antwerp (1881–1960), American diplomat and author, 28 n.1, 58 n.2, 352; *Treaties and Agreements with and concerning China 1894–1919*, 352
Macoun, J. H., British employee of Chinese Maritime Customs, 71 + n.2
Makino Nobuaki (1862–1949), Japanese politician, 82 n.3, 101 + n.4, 124 n.2, 133 + n.3, 563, 739, 747, 748, 790 + n.2, 791
Malewsky-Malewitch, Nicylas, Russian diplomat, 124 + n.3, 509 + n.1, 539 n.3
Mamen, O., Norwegian trader, 53 + n.1
'Manchukuo'. *See under* Manchuria
Manchurian Incident. *See under* Manchuria
Manchuria: Revolution (*1911*), 514 n.1, 596 n.2, 597 n.2;
– Political conditions, 783; cholera and plague, 657 + n.3–658, 726 n.1, 782;
– Japan in Manchuria, 163 n.1, 176, 211 n.2, 247, 252 n.4 (253), 273 n.1, 282, 299 n.1, 350, 363–4, 377, 386 n.3, 404–5, 430, 512–13, 541 n.4 (542), 565, 574 n.2, 586, 588 n.1, 597 n.2, 642 n.1, 644, 723–4, 783, 794, 810;
– Kwantung Leased Territory, 273 n.1; Kwantung army, 597 n.1;
– Manchurian Incident (*September 18 1931*), 252 n.4 (253), 574 n.2, 588 n.1, 761 n.2;
– 'Manchukuo' Puppet Government, 163 n.1, 205 n.2, 206 n.1, 224 n.2, 347 n.1, 597 n.2;
– Russia in Manchuria. *See under* Russia in China;
– *See also* Japan in China; Railways; Treaties, agreements etc.; Wars: Russo–Japanese War
Mandl, German commercial agent, 438 n.1
Mannix, Daniel (1864–1963), Irish-born Catholic Archbishop of Melbourne, 645 + n.1
Mao Tse-tung (1893–1976), Chinese Communist leader, 477 n.3

de Margerie, Pierre (1861–1942), French diplomat, 82 n.2
Markham, Violet Rosa (d. 1959), British social worker and author, 205 + n.1; *letter from*, 205
Marshall Islands, 550 + n.3, 558
de Martel, Vicomte, French diplomat, 654 + n.2
de Martens, Frederic Frommhold (1845–1909), Russian jurist, 99 + n.3
Massey, William Ferguson (1856–1925), New Zealand politician, 657 n.1, 675 n.2, 679 + n.1
Matsubara Kōkichi (1872–1955), Japanese chemist, 633 + n.3
Matsudaira Tsuneo (1877–1949), Japanese diplomat, 211 n.1
Matsui Iwane (1878–1948), Japanese soldier, 124 n.1
Matsukata Masayoshi (1835–1924), Japanese politician, 101 + n.3, 132 n.2, 802 n.1
Matsukawa, Japanese adventurer, 182
Maugham, William Somerset (1874–1965), British writer, 608 n.2
Max-Müller, Friedrich (1823–1900), German scholar, 78 n.3, 622 + n.2, 811 + n.2; *India: What can it teach us?*, 811 + n.2
Max-Müller, William Grenfell (1867–1945), British diplomat, 78 n.3, 810 + n.2, 811 n.3; *letter to*, 810
Maxim, Hiram Stevens (1840–1916), American-born British engineer, 2, 148 + n.2–149, 159, 160, 161
May Fourth Movement, 237 n.3, 505 n.2 (506), 605 n.3 (606), 717, 722, 761 + n.2, n.3, 764 nn.2–4, 785, 796, 803, 820
Martin, William Alexander Parsons (1827–1916), American missionary, 442 n.2 (443)
May, Francis Henry (1860–1922), British colonial official, 17 + n.2, 244 + n.1; *letters to*, 309, 412 *letter from*, 17
May, Helena (*née* Barker), wife of F. H. May, 311
Mayers, F. J., British employee of Chinese Maritime Customs, 353 n.1
Mayers, Sidney Francis (1873–1934), British consular official and commercial agent, 45 + n.1, 71, 286 + n.3, 416, 417
Maze, Frederick William (d. 1959), British employee of Chinese Maritime Customs, 604 + n.3

Mazot, Henri, French economist, 518 +n.3
Meagher, Richard Denis (1866–1931), Australian politician, 651+n.1, 705 n.1; *letter to*, 651
Meagher, Mrs, wife of R. D. Meagher, 653
Megata Tanetarō (1843–1926), Japanese government official, 638+n.1, 659, 678
Meiji, Emperor (*see* Mutsuhito); Era, 132 n.2, 549 n.1, 658 n.4
Meng-tzu, 462
Meredith, George (1828–1909), British writer, 824
Messina Earthquake, 215+n.1
Meyer, Carl (1851–1922), 1st Bart, German-born British financier, 55+n.1, 65
Meyer, Frank Nicholas (d. 1918), American botanist, 411+n.1
Mikami Yoshitada, Japanese sailor, 790+n.1
Mill, John Stuart (1806–73), British philosopher, 134, 450; *On Liberty*, 134
Millard, Thomas Franklin Fairfax (1868–1942), American journalist, 145+n.1, n.2–147, 600+n.1, 713 n.1, 717, 721; *letter from*, 712
Miller, Aleksandr Iakovlevich, Russian consular official, 134+n.1
Milner, Alfred (1854–1925), 1st Visct, British politician and colonial official, 14+n.1, n.3
Min-ning, Manchu Emperor Tao-kuang (Hsüan-tsung) (1782–1850), 225 n.2, 491 n.2
Miner, Luella, American missionary, 388+n.3
Ming, William, British claimant to the Chinese throne, 2, 32+n.2–33, 83 +n.1–84, 216+n.1, n.2; claim to the Chinese throne: 32–3, 83–4, 216; *letter to*, 216 *letters from*, 32, 83
Mining in China, 377, 378, (Mining Bureau) 415+n.2, n.3–416, (regulations) 432, (China Mining & Metal Co.) 301, (Chung-hsing Coal Mine, Shantung) 510 n.2, (Fu-Shun Coal Mine, Fengtien) 296 n.2, 432, (Han-yang Iron Works) 306, 296 n.2, (Han-yeh-p'ing Mines) 39, 396, 326, 386+n.1, 396 n.2, 739, (Hua-ch'ang Antimony Co.) 439, (Kiang-fei-t'ing Mining Co. Ltd, Szechwan) 69 n.3, (Pen-ch'i-hu Iron Mines, Fengtien), 358, 396 n.2, (P'inghsiang Collieries) 386, (Ta-yeh Iron Mines) 307, 358, 386, (T'ung-kuan-shan Iron Mines, Anhwei) 358, 360–1, 432, (Yen-ch'ang Petroleum Concession) 326. *See also* Twenty-one Demands; Britain in China

Minority nationalities in China: Lolo, 168, 483; Miao, 487+n.1, 537; Mohammedans, 468, 471, 545–6, 558, 564, 569; Sain Noin, 49 n.7

Missionaries, 93 n.2–94, 148;
– Nestorian Tablet, 652;
– Catholic missionaries, 16, 106–8, 118–19, 167, 276, 610 n.2, 651–3, 821+n.1, (in Mongolia) 267, 276, (Belgian in Inner Mongolia and elsewhere) 118–19, 473, 652, (in Kweichow) 495+n.3, (Dutch in Sinkiang) 652, (French in Szechwan and elsewhere) 89, 119; (German) 119, 465; (Italian) 119;
– publications: *Annales de la Propagation de la Foi*, 651+n.4, 652; *Lettres Edifiantes*, 652+n.3; *Missions en Chine et au Congo*, 652+n.2; *Variétés Sinologiques*, 652+n.2;
– Protestant missionaries, 16, 94+n.1, 155–6, 159, 442+n.2–443, 497, 653, 722;
– societies etc.: American Board of Commissioners of Foreign Missions, 97 n.2, 98 n.2, 388; Association for the Protection of Women and Children, 388 n.3; British and Foreign Bible Society, 47 n.2, 90, 102; China Inland Mission, 129 n.1, 484, 497 n.1; Chinese Christian Church, Tokyo, 479; Congrégation du Cœur Immaculé de Marie, 652 n.2; English Baptist Mission, 400 n.2, 401+n.2; International Institute of China, 586 n.2; Jesuits, 651+nn.3–5, 652+nn.2–5, 653+n.1, 821 n.1; London Missionary Society, 345 n.1; Missions Etrangères, 495 n.3; Pocket Testament League, 155, 156; Propagation de la Foi, 652 n.3; Union Foreign Church, 442 n.2; World Council of Churches, 98 n.1; World Sunday School Convention, 156, Y.M.C.A., 98 n.1, 477 n.1, 478, 585, (in Peking) 477 n.1, (in Tokyo) 478;
– individuals (*see* separate entries)

Mixed Court. *See under* Shanghai
Miyazaki Torazō (1870–1922), Japanese adventurer, 150+n.1, 396 n.1
Mizuno Kōkichi (1873–1914), Japanese diplomat, 90+n.1, 102 n.1, 124, 258 n.1

Mo Jung-hsin (b. 1851), Chinese soldier, 809 + n.3
Mogi, Japanese opium dealer, 722 + n.3
Molunga, Mongol soldier, 280
Monarchist movements: 206–7, 212, 225–6, 234–6, 264;
- Monarchy versus republic 206–7, 212, 225–6, 234–6, 264, 809 n.1; Confucianism and monarchy, 462; Chinese kinship, 461–2;
- Yüan Shih-k'ai's monarchy scheme (*see under* G. E. Morrison; Yüan Shih-k'ai);
- Chang Hsün Restoration (*1917*), 14 n.5, 86 n.1, 206 n.1, 386 n.4 (387), 542 n.1, 547 n.2 (548), 578 n.1, 596 n.2, 601–2, 604–9, 611–14, 622 n.3, 634–9, 650 + n.2, n.3;
- Powers and, 462–3 + n.1, 467, 488, 515 + n.2
Monestier, Alphonse, French author, 769 n.2
Mongolia:
- Outer Mongolia: secession, 28, 29, 30, 37–8, 39, 47–53, 56, 61, 62 + n.4, 72, 90–2, 102–5, 108, 111, 121 + n.2–122, 123–5, 134, 140–1, 143–4, 153–4, 157 + n.1, 158 + n.2, 162–3, 168–9, 173–80, 202–5, 219 + n.1, n.2, 228 + n.1, 229–30, 231, 233–4, 258–63, 269, 275–6, 280, 281–4, 300, 364, 442, 534; Russia in, 48–53, 58 + n.3, 61, 63, 81, 85 + n.1, 90–2, 102–5, 121–2, 123–5, 134, 140, 143–4, 157 n.1, 168–9, 173–80, 203–4, 228 + n.1, 229–30, 234, 247, 258–62, 266, 268, 275–6, 281–4, 364, 586, 777–8, 780–1; (Buriats) 50 + n.1; (*see also* Treaties, agreements, etc.: Sino-Russian, Russo-Mongolian, Sino-Russo-Mongolian); Kiakhta Conference, 281–4, 721; Chinese Parliament and, 158, 168, 177, 180; Sun Yat-sen and southern republicans and, 435;
- Inner Mongolia: 319–21, 473–5, 537–8; taxation, 320–1; railway proposal, 267–8; trade marts, 258 + n.1–262, 268, 275–6; missionaries, 118–19;
- Relations between Outer and Inner Mongolia, 283–4; Mongolian and Tibetan Affairs Commission, 474 n.1, 570 n.2;
- Japan and, 122, 123–5, 157, 211 n.2, 262, 377, 386 + n.2, 541 n.4 (542), 565, 642 n.1, 794, 810;
- Morrison and, 37–8, 53, 102–5, 111, 168–9, 143–4, 173–80, 202–5, 219–21, 229–30, 233–4, 252–3 + n.1, 258–62, 262–3, 265–8, 269, 280, 281–4; suggestions for reorganization of Inner Mongolia, 258–62, 265–8; suggested use of Mongolian cavalry against White Wolf, 280–1

Montagu, Edwin Samuel (1879–1924), British politician, 128 n.2
Montgomery, Mrs, wife of W. H. Montgomery, 702
Montgomery, William Hugh (1866–1958), New Zealand politician, 663 + n.2, 702
Monypenny, William Flavelle (1866–1912), British journalist and author, 13 n.2, 14 + n.2
Moore, John Bassett (1860–1947), American jurist, 279 + n.2, 773
Moore-Bennett, Arthur J., British businessman, 482 + n.1, 495 n.2, 683 n.2; *letters from*, 482, 483, 493, 683, 694, 784, (to E. Pears) 695
Moorehead, R. B., British employee of Chinese Maritime Customs, 354 n.1
Moorehead, T. D., British employee of Chinese Maritime Customs, 354 + n.1, 561 + n.1
Morgan, John Pierpont, Jnr (1837–1913), American financier, 793 n.3
Morgenthau, Henry (1856–1946), German-born American diplomat, 213 + n.1
Morley, John (1838–1923), 1st Visct Morley of Blackburn, British politician, 26 + n.3, 210 + n.2
Morrison, Alastair Robin Gwynne (b. 1915), 2nd son of G. E. Morrison, 83 n.3 (84), 455 n.1, 520, 537, 555 + n.1, 604 + n.1, 624, 627 n.3, 758, 811 + n.2, 822, 825
Morrison, Arthur R. M. (b. 1868), Australian mining engineer, younger brother of G. E. Morrison, 663 + n.4
Morrison, Colin George Mervyn (b. 1917), 3rd youngest son of G. E. Morrison, 593 n.1, 604 + n.1, 624, 758, 811 + n.2, 822, 825
Morrison, George (1830–98), Australian schoolmaster, father of G. E. Morrison, 664 n.1
Morrison, George H., British clergyman, cousin of G. E. Morrison, 690 + n.1; *letter to*, 690
Morrison, George Ernest (1862–1920), 7 n.2, 18 n.3, 59 n.8, 66 n.2, 68 n.5 (69), 73 n.2, 77 n.1, 83 n.3 (84), 93 n.1, 99 n.4, 120 n.1, 122 n.1, n.3, 124 n.2, n.4, 126, 161 n.2, 164 n.1, 169 n.3 (170), 188 n.1, 214 n.3, 227 n.1, 233 n.1, 244 n.1, 251 n.1, 258 n.1, 285 n.1, 301 n.1, 304 n.3, 311 n.3 (312), 313 n.3, 315 n.1, n.2, 317 n.3, 318 n.1, 323 n.1, 330 n.5

Morrison, George Ernest (*cont.*)
(331), 332, 336 n.2, 342 n.2, 348, 403 n.1, 423 n.1, 438 n.1, 442 n.2 (443), 510, 593 n.1, 663 n.4, 772 n.3, 807;
- early connections: Geelong College, 665 n.1; Rio Tinto, 758 n.1;
- *Times* correspondent, 59 n.1, 87, 93, 113 n.3, 115 n.1, 122 n.3, 140+n.1, 144, 154, 202 n.1, 222, 232 n.1, 271, 341, 413-14, 514+n.2, 541 n.4 (542), 607, 617, 624 n.2, 657 n.3, 672, 758 n.2, n.5, 776, 827; journey across Central Asia, 491 n.1, n.2; leaving *The Times*, 1; later relations with *The Times*, 33-4, 94, 95, 228, 296, 373-9, 792-5, 795-803; letter to *The Times*, 25+n.1; *The Times*, opinion on, 25 n.1, 32 n.1;
- Political Adviser: reactions to appointment, 1-2, 3, 5-7, 12, 13, 17, 19, 20, 24-5, 31+n.3; contract, 4+n.1, 5, 286, 392, 398+n.1, 408, 510+n.1-511, 605 +n.1; salary, 5 n.4, 13, 19, 31, 286, 699, 804-6, 813, 817, 828; decorations, 55, 151+n.1, 154+n.3, 161+n.1, 406; as Adviser, 87, 251, 273, 286, 296, 347, 408, 411-12, 454+n.3, 518-19, 624, 722, (frustration), 151, 154, 161, 196, 221-2, 286, 511-12, 569, 574-6, 577-8, (retirement plan) 287;
- and Yüan Shih-k'ai, 38, 137-8, 142-3, 154, 161, 164, 166, 226, 251, 258, 262, 265, 286, 322-3, 328-9, 335-41, 345-6, 399+n.1, 413, 451, 454, 469, 485-9, 496-7, 502-3, 504, 507, 509, 511 n.3-512, 515, 520-1, 524, 535, 537, 541 n.4 (542);
- and southern republicans, 111, 138-9, 180-3, 186-91, 191-2, 209-12, 314; and murder of Sung Chiao-jen, 138, 172-3, 183-6;
- publicity and press censorship, 35, 36, 37, 60-1+n.1, 76-7, 111, 114-16, 139, 140-1, 145-7, 164+n.2, 196, 209-10, 222-4, 228-9, 230-1, 238-9, 240-1, 254-7, 257-8, 270-2, 284-5, 313-14, 322-4, 328-9, 331-3, 334+n.1-340, 341+n.1, 382-5, 391, 409-11, 516-18;
- and British policy in China, 26-30, 34, 35, 64-72, 297, 303, 330-1, 342-3, 521-2, 567-8;
- and Mongolia, (*see under* Mongolia);
- and Tibet, (*see under* Tibet);
- and China's finances, 37, 40, 44-6, 55-6, 63, 64-8, 161-2, 254-7, 315-19, 333-41, 356-60, 360-2, 403-4, 416-18, 469, (*see also* Customs and excise in China; Loans; Salt Gabelle);
- and Japan, 351-6, 358, 360-1, 365-6, 368, 369, 530, 539-48, 548-54, 554-5, 566-8, 588+n.1, n.2; (Twenty-one Demands) 351-2, 364-6, 368, 369-70, 371-2, 373-6, 377-9, 380, 383, 385-7, 391-2, 398-9, 406-7, 470, 472, 530, 666-7, (interview with Katō Takaaki) 539-48; (*see also* Japan in China);
- and Yüan Shih-k'ai's monarchy scheme, 451-3+n.2, 454, 456-7, 462-3, 470, 485-9, 496-7, 502-3, 505, 515;
- and China's entry into World War I, 454, 463+n.2, n.3, 464-7, 467-8, 471-3, 509, 515-16, 530, 531, 534, 537, 543-7, 551, 553, 555, 558, 559-66+n.1, 568, 570, 571-3, 574-6, 585, 586 n.2, 617-18, 665-74;
- in Australia and New Zealand, 602-3, 704-5+n.1;
- and Paris Conference, 716-22, 727-55, 771-2;
- illness, 717, 755, 756+n.3, 758, 769 n.1, 770-1, 784, 786, 792, 805, 806, 813, 814, 815+n.2, 816, 819; death, 822-8;
- opinions on: *Evening News*, 25 n.1; *Westminster Gazette*, 25 n.1; G. E. Buckle, 827; G. W. Prothero, 826;
- and/on his contemporaries: T. M. Ainscough, 135 n.1; F. B. Alston, 152 n.1, 238, 342-3, 519, 521-2, 571, 810+n.3, 811; S. Barton, 277 n.1; G. C. Binsteed, 50 n.4; J. O. P. Bland, 113 n.3; F. Brinkley, 658 n.4; J. McLeavy Brown, 25 n.30; B. Brownrigg, 424 n.1, 120 n.2; C. D. Bruce, 180 n.2; J. Bryce, 168 n.4; J. B. Capper, 214 n.3; E. de Cartier, 85 n.2; A. L. Cattarinich, 604 n.4; Ch'en Yu-jen, 43+n.3-44, 56+n.2, 382-3, 384-5, 716, 728-55, 814; V. I. Chirol, 758 n.2, n.5, 768 n.1 (769); R. M. Collins, 24 n.1; J. G. Cormack, 129 n.1; C. R. Crane, 818+n.4-819; R. M. Dane, 566 n.1; H. G. N. Dering, 681 n.1; W. H. Donald, 7 n.1; L. H. Drakeford, 597 n.1; C. N. E. Eliot, 243 n.1, n.2; C. W. Eliot, 20 n.1; J. C. Ferguson, 19 n.1; J. G. Findlay, 680 n.2; D. S. Fraser, 33-4, 41, 87, 89; F. J. Goodnow, 451; Gotō Shimpei, 563 n.1; H. A. Gwynne, 26 n.1, n.2, 555 n.1; Hsieh Tsan-t'ai, 148 n.1; Hsü Shih-ch'ang, 720-2; Ijūin Hikokichi, 82 n.3, 273; W. H. Irvine, 665 n.1; J. R. Jellicoe, 789 n.2; J. N. Jordan, 41, 43-6, 47, 628, (*see also* Britain in China: style of diplomacy); Ju Jen-ho, 192 n.1; Kamei

Morrison, George Ernest (*cont.*)
Rokurō, 475 n.1; Katō Takaaki, 539-48; C. W. Kinder, 624 n.2; W. L. Mackenzie King, 617 n.1; Ku Weichün, 252 n.4 (253); K'ung Hsiang-hsi, 388+n.4; K'ung T'ien-tseng, 113 n.3; Li Yüan-hung, 568; Liang Ch'i-ch'ao, 716; Liang Shih-yi, 422, 429-46, 533, 691-4; Liang Tun-yen, 606-8; W. G. Max-Müller, 810 n.3; F. W. Maze, 604 n.3; R. D. Meagher, 651 n.1; T. F. F. Millard, 131 n.1, 145-7, 712-14; Mizuno Kōkichi, 91-2; J. Murdoch, 145 n.2; Nogi Maresuke, 540 n.2; Odagiri Masunosuke, 632 n.2, 792+n.4-793; G. Reid, 586 n.2; W. W. Rockhill, 20 n.2; C. A. W. Rose, 57 n.4; E. M. Satow, 28 n.3, 758; C. Sforza, 73 n.1; A. H. Smith, 97 n.3, 98 n.3; H. W. Steed, 373 n.1, 797 n.1; W. P. Thomas, 804 n.1; Ting Wen-chiang, 621 n.1; Tsai-lan, 491+n.2; Ts'ai O, 310 n.3 (311); Ts'ai Ting-kan, 3 n.1, 136 n.2, 164, 697-9; Tuan Ch'i-jui, 571-3; Yamaza Enjirō, 102 n.1;
– Papers, 39, 57 n.4, 182 n.1, 185 n.3, 214 n.3-215, 356 n.1, 424 n.1, 535 n.3, 571 n.2, 588 n.2, 593 n.1, 627 n.2, 668 n.1, 680 n.2, 722 n.3, 758 n.5, 822, 825 n.2, 827;
– library, 41, 82 n.3, 214, 243 n.1, n.2, 273-5, 287, 296-7, 410-11, 511 n.3, 603, 622-3, 625, 627+n.2, n.3, 631-4, 637-8, 652, (collection of Robinson Crusoe editions) 627+n.3; Morrison Library (Tōyō Bunko) (*see under* Libraries, galleries and museums etc.)
– marriage, 24+n.2, 35, 825;
– family (*see* A. R. G. Morrison; C. G. M. Morrison; I. E. M. Morrison; J. Morrison);
– miscellaneous: and Hulutao scheme, 512 n.2; and Zionist movement, 361 n.3, 705-6
Morrison, George Noel Irving (b. 1893), nephew of G. E. Morrison, 348+n.2
Morrison, Ian Ernest McLeavy (1913-50), eldest son of G. E. Morrison, 158+n.1, 192, 206, 212, 226, 287, 314, 520, 537, 604+n.1, 624, 758, 811+n.2, 822, 825
Morrison, Jennie Wark (*née* Robin) (1889-1923), wife of G. E. Morrison, 13+n.1, 24+n.2, 39+n.1, 64, 73, 79, 86, 109, 121, 206, 212, 226, 243, 254, 279, 286, 314, 335, 362, 379, 454, 485, 520, 537, 604+n.1, 624, 627, 758, 811, 813, 814, 816, 818 n.4, 819, 822 (*see also* G. E. Morrison: papers); *letters to*, 604, 605, 609, 611, 614, 821, (from C. R. Crane) 818
letters from, (to Chou Tzu-ch'i) 828, (to Rebecca Morrison) 823
Morrison, Rebecca (*née* Greenwood) (1836-1932), mother of G. E. Morrison, 510+n.3, 822, 823, 825+n.1, n.3, 827; *letter to*, (from Jennie Morrison), 823
Morrison, Reginald H. (b. 1864), Australian medical practitioner, brother of G. E. Morrison, 348+n.2
Morrison, Robert (1782-1834), British Protestant missionary, 653+n.2
Morrison, Thomas, British schoolmaster, uncle of G. E. Morrison, 690 n.1
Motono Ichirō (1862-1918), Japanese politician, 101 n.4, 124+n.2, 548 n.4, 554 n.2, 563+n.1, 574, 583, 584, 621, 663 n.1, 672, 741, 743, 750, 751, 771 n.1
Mott, John R. (1865-1955), American Protestant clergyman, 98+n.1, 585
Muir, John R. American Protestant missionary, 497+n.1, 522 n.1; *letter to*, 513;
letters from, 497, 522
Mumm, Philipp Alfons (1859-1924), Freiherr von Schwarzenstein, German diplomat, 92 n.1, 725 n.1
Munthe, J. W. N., Norwegian soldier, 362+n.1, 414
Murdoch, James (1856-1921), British historian, 131+n.1, n.2, 132; *A History of Japan*, 131+n.2; *letter from*, 131
Murray, Arthur Cecil (1879-1962), British soldier and politician, 779+n.2
Murray, C. Wyndham (1844-1928), British soldier and politician, 382+n.2
Mushuitin, Russian journalist, 91
Mutsu Munemitsu (1844-97), Japanese politician, 133 n.2
Mutsuhito, Emperor Meiji of Japan (1852-1912), 25 n.2, 132+n.1, 220 n.1, 588+n.2

Na Beileh. *See* Namsarai
Na Wang. *See* Namsarai
Na-wang-yeh. *See* Namsarai
Na-yen-t'u, Mongol Bannerman and Republican politician, 203+n.1, 205
Nagai Matsuzō (b. 1887), Japanese diplomat, 795+n.1, 797+n.1, 800, 801
Nagaoka Hantarō (1865-1950), Japanese physicist, 633 n.4
Nakashōji Ren (1866-1924), Japanese politician, 584+n.2

Nall, Australian journalist, 221
Nam-serai Wang. *See* Namsarai
Namnan-surun, Mongol leader, Khan of the Sain Noin tribes, 49 n.7
Namsarai, Mongol leader, 49 + n.2, 52, 204, 219, 230, 258–9, 263, 280
Napoleon Bonaparte (1769–1821), Emperor of the French, 455, 653 n.1
Nawa Matahachirō (1863–1928), Japanese sailor, 208 + n.3
Netherlands and China, 92
New Zealand: Chinese in, 675 + n.2–676; and Japan, 659, 661–2, 678–9, 701–2; and World War I, 518, 679–80; Maoris, 680
Newman, B. Leigh, British adventurer, 336 + n.1, 338
Newman, Mrs, 611
Newspapers, journals, press agencies, etc:
- Chinese press, 101, 145–7, 270–1, 590–1, 600, 690; (revolutionary press), 198, 199, 393 n.1, n.2; foreign press on China, 26, 36, 44, 255, 257–8, 328 + n.1–329, 330, 339–41, 373 + n.1–377; (*see also* Times); Japanese press, 101, 390–1, 475 n.1, 541, 542, 589, 647, 662, 679, 680, 757, 767; (Japanese infiltration of Chinese press) 590–1; U.S. press, 658, 678; Chinese publicity abroad, (in Belgium) 270–2, 337–8; (in U.S.A.), 270–2, 590, (*see also under* G. E. Morrison), Millard's proposal for, 145–7, 712, 714; Reuters service, 257–8;
- (Australia), *Age* 612 n.3, 811; *Bulletin* 221, 222; *Daily Telegraph* 221, 296 n.3;
- (Belgium), Agence de l'Extrême Orient 270, 337, *Revue Jaune*, 270, 271, 272;
- (Britain), *Chinese Review* 341; *Contemporary Review* 127 + n.1; *Daily Chronicle* 30; *Daily Mail* 425 n.3, 565 n.2; *Daily News* 30, 694 n.2, 818 n.6; *Daily Telegraph* 31 + n.3–32, 40, 114–15, 122, 125 n.1, 295, 328 n.1, 332 + n.1, 334, 335, 339, 341, 374, 383, 391, 472, 564; *Eatanswill Gazette* 12 + n.1; *English Review* 489 + n.3 (490); *Evening News* 25 n.1; *Financial News* 54 n.2; *The Ibis* 610–11; *Illustrated London News* 2; *Jewish Chronicle* 361 n.3; *Lancet* 367 + n.2; *London and China Express* 423 n.1, 779, 787; *Manchester Guardian* 30, 36, 403 + n.1, 411, 461, 663, 696, (China supplement), 517; *Morning Post* 26 n.1, 317 n.3, 334, 460, 613, 755 n.2; *Nation* 383 n.1; *New Europe* 625, 818

n.6; *Nineteenth Century* 565 + n.2 (566), 660; *Observer* 64 n.1, 140, 330 n.3, 333; *Pall Mall Gazette* 35 n.1, n.2, 36, 43 n.3, 108, 237, 374 n.2, 382; *Quarterly Review* 470, 489 + n.1, 490 + n.1, 502, 522, 778 + n.2, 779 + n.1, 787 + n.2, 826, Reuters News Agency 1, 24 n.1, 26 n.1, 31 n.4, 40 + n.2, 75, 77, 87, 89, 105, 123, 152, 211, 221, 229, 252, 253 n.1, 257–8, 268, 290, 376, 464, 590, 618, 646, 770; *Saturday Review* 565 n.2; *Slavonic Review* 489 n.3 (490); *Standard* 26 n.1; *The Times* (*see* separate entry), *Westminster Gazette* 25 n.1;
- (Canada), *Toronto Globe* 498, 499;
- (China), *Anglo-Chinese Times* 590; *British Chamber of Commerce Journal* 403 n.1, Bureau of Economic Information 7 n.1; *Central China Post* Hankow, 93 + n.2–94 + n.1, 423 n.1; *China Advertiser* Tientsin 803; *China Gazette* 8, 10; *China Mail* 7 n.1, 9 n.2; *China Press* 9, 94 n.1, 145 + n.2, 312, 383 n.1, 637, 713 n.1; *China Republican* Shanghai 11–12, 17, 112 + n.3, 163, 184, 230, 231 n.1, 238, 713 n.1; *China Times* Tientsin 313 + n.1, 423 n.1, 713 n.1; *China Tribune* Tientsin 313; *China Weekly Review* 145 n.2, 600 n.1; *Chinese Public Opinion* 376 n.3; *Chinese Social and Political Science Journal* 238 n.1; *Courrier de Tientsin* 769 n.2; *Far Eastern Review* 7 n.1, 12, 163 + n.1, 334, 484, 522, 578 n.1, 620, 643, 681, 709 + n.1; *Hankow Daily News* 564; *I-shih pao*, 795, 796, 802; *Israel Messenger* Shanghai 361 n.3; *Journal de Pékin* 79, 769 n.2; *Manchuria Daily News* 476; *Millard's Review* 145 n.2, 600 + n.1, 713 n.1; *Min-kuo hsin-wen* 6 + n.4; *Municipal Gazette* Shanghai 187; National News Agency 590; *National Review* 66 n.2, 193, 383 + n.1; *North China Daily News* 9, 12, 87, 113 n.3, 241, 275, 323, 369, 432 n.1, 460 + n.2, n.3, 540, (China Supplement) 573 + n.2, 723 n.3; *North China Daily News & Herald* 64 n.1, 403 n.1; *North China Herald* 323; *North China Star* 383 n.1; *Ostasiatische Lloyd* 467; *Pei-ching jih-pao* 376; *Peking Daily News* 46, 56, 58, 81, 87, 94 n.1, 96, 97 n.3, 138, 376 + n.3, 383 n.1, 467, 603, 655, 713 n.1; *Peking Gazette* 43 n.3, 230, 235, 238, 280, 321, 365, 366, 375, 384, 569 + n.1, 610; *Peking Leader* 721, Peking News Agency 423 n.1; *Peking Post* 564, 586

886

Newspapers, ournals, press agencies, etc. (cont.)
n.2; *Pekin & Tientsin Times* 484, 527 n.3, 762 n.2; *Peking Times* 795, 802; *Republican Advocate* 112 n.1; *Shanghai Gazette* 701; *Shanghai Mercury* 5 n.1, 9 n.1, 383 n.1, 541 + n.2, 802; *Shanghai Recorder* 9 n.2; *Shanghai Times* 9, 12, 383 n.1, 795, 797, 802; *Sheng-ching shih-pao* 5 n.1, Shun-shih (Shen-shih) News Agency 713 n.1; *Shun-tien shih-pao* 157, 475 + n.1, 541 n.1, 767, 802 + n.2; *Social Shanghai* 597; *Su-pao* 182 n.1; *Ta-wan pao* 713 n.1; *Tientsin Daily News* 803; *Tientsin Sunday Journal* 564; *The War* Shanghai 544, 564; *Ya-hsi-ya pao* 395 n.3;
- (France), *Humanité* 619 n.2; *Le Matin* 794 n.2; *Revue des Deux Mondes* 106 n.2 (107); *Le Temps* 373, 723 n.1
- (Germany), *Frankfurter Allgemeine Zeitung* 2;
- (Hong Kong), *South China Morning Post* 148 n.1, 423 n.1; *Telegraph* 9 n.2;
- (Japan), *Ajia Jiron* 789 + n.6, 790; *Asahi Shimbun* 418, 422 + n.1, 429, 430, 509, 541 n.1, 586, Dōmei News Service 494 n.1; *Herald of Asia* 556 + n.1; *Hōchi Shimbun* 772 n.1; *Japan Gazette* 131 n.1; *Japan Mail* 556 n.1, 658 n.4; *Japan Times* 556 n.1; *Jiji Shimbun* 475 n.1, 802 n.2; *Jiji Shimpo* 5 n.1; *Kokumin Shimbun* 549 + n.3–550; *New East* 554 n.3, 589 + n.1, 639 n.2, 660, 681; *Nichi Nichi Shimbun* 543, 549 n.3 (550); Nisshi Kyōdō Tsūshin 541 n.1; *Oriental Review*, 556; *Osaka Mainichi* 207 + n.1, 543, 549 n.3 (550); *Shin Kōron* 541 n.1; *Shinjin* 700 n.1, Tōkyū News Agency 763; *Yamato Shimbun* 772 + n.2;
- (Korea), *Tongnip Sinmun* 508 n.1;
- (the Netherlands), *T'oung Pao* 214 n.2;
- (the Philippines), *Manila Times* 793 n.4;
- (Russia) *Novoe Vremya* 91;
- (Singapore), *Singapore Free Press* 710;
- (South Africa), *Johannesburg Star* 14 + n.1, n.2;
- (U.S.A.), Associated Press 24 n.1, 369, 370, 373, 793 n.4; *Chicago Daily News* 403 n.1, 527 n.3, 762 n.2; *Chicago Tribune* 578 n.1, Far Eastern Information Bureau 270–2, 284–5; *New York Evening Post* 403 n.1, 713 n.1; *New York Herald* 7 n.1, 222, 295, 333; *New York Press* 516 n.2; *New York Times* 192 n.1, 209 + n.1, 210, 341 + n.1, 677, 713 n.1; *New York Tribune* 516 n.2; *New York World* 106 n.2; *Philadelphia Press* 516 n.2; *Times Democrat* 403 n.1

Ni Ssu-ch'ung (1868–1920), Chinese soldier, Provincial Governor, 199 n.1, 527 + n.2, 564 + n.7
Nicholas II (1868–1918), Czar of Russia, 48 n.2, 174, 375 n.1, 447 n.2
Nicolson, Arthur (1849–1928), 1st Baron Carnock, British diplomat, 521 + n.1
Nielson, A. *See* Voretzsch
Nies, Father, German Catholic missionary, 465
Nihei Hyōji, Japanese consular official, 494 n.1
Nikolai Nikolaevich (1856–1929), Grand Duke of Russia, 447 + n.2
Ning T'iao-yüan (1884–1913), Chinese revolutionary, 181 + n.1
Nishihara Kamezō (?1872–1954), Japanese adventurer, 547 n.2, 583 + n.2, n.4, 584, 589, 592, 636 n.2, 764 n.2, n.3, 784 + n.1
Noel-Buxton, Noel Edward (1869–1948), 1st Baron of Aylsham, British politician, 490 n.1
Nogi Maresuke (1849–1912), Japanese soldier, 540 + n.2
Norman, Henry (1858–1939), British journalist and author, 374 + n.2
Northcliffe, 1st Visct. *See* A. C. W. Harmsworth
Norway in China, 468
Nysshim, Shanghai merchant, 567

Obata Yūkichi (1873–1947), Japanese diplomat, 462, 463 n.1, 507 + n.2, 508, 701 n.2, 712 + n.1
O'Connor, William Frederick Travers (1870–1943), British soldier and colonial official, 27 + n.2, 428 + n.3
Odagiri Masunosuke (1868–1934), Japanese diplomat and financial agent, 368, 627 n.2, 632 + n.2, 792 + n.4, 793, 794, 795
Ohl, Josiah Kingsley (d. 1920), American journalist, 295 + n.1; *letter to*, 295
Oi Kentarō (1833–1922), Japanese politician, 222 n.3
Ōishi Masami (1855–1935), Japanese politician and publicist, 391 + n.2
Oka Ichinosuke (1860–1916), Japanese soldier, 552 + n.2
Okabe Nagakage (b. 1884), Japanese politician, 549 + n.1

887

Okabe Nagamoto (1854–1925), Japanese head of Kishiwada clan and government official, 549 n.1
Okabe Yoshiko (*née* Katō), wife of Okabe Nagakage, 549 n.1
Okamura Yasuji (b. 1884), Japanese soldier, 92 n.2 (93)
Ōkubo Toshimichi (1831–78), Japanese politician, 82 n.3, 101 n.4
Ōkuma Shigenobu (1838–1922), Japanese politician, 6+n.1, 100, 132 n.7, 150 n.1, 323+n.1, 324, 371, 385 n.3, 421, 422, 445, 509, 530, 539 n.2, 548 n.3, 549+n.2, 550 n.1, 552 n.2, 562+n.1, 757, 802 n.1
Ōkura Kihachirō (1837–1928), Japanese industrialist, 93 n.1, 396+n.2, 590 +n.2, 772 n.2
'Open Door' policy. *See under* United States
Opium and morphia, 39, 69–70, 75+n.3– 76, 78, 93–7+n.3, 97–9, 125–9, 129–31, 139–40, 153+n.1, 361+n.2, 400–1, 594, 608, 674 n.3, 690, 693+n.1, 694, 705 n.3;
– Indian opium traffic, 26 n.1, n.3, 41, 93 n.2, 125+n.1, 126 n.1, 128 n.1, 130, 139, 140 n.1, 344, 604 n.4; Indian Government and opium trade, 125+ n.1, 127 n.1, 128 n.1, 130;
– Japanese smuggling of in China and Korea, 363–4, 367–8, 402–3, 405, 414–15, 589, 688–9, 722–6, Japanese Formosan Government and Chinese opium trade, 96–7, 402, 724;
– Anching incident (*1912*), 69+n.4–70, 126–7, 130; in foreign concessions, 130, (Hankow) 312, (International Settlement Shanghai) 311–12, (Soochow) 312, (Tientsin) 312; Foreign Opium Combine, Shanghai, 361 n.3, 595+n.1, 693 n.1;
– cultivation in China, 93–6, 97–9; Mongolia 320;
– prohibition, 125–31, 288, 311–12, 414, 594–5+n.1; British Anti-Opium Board, 125+n.1; China Association and opium, 78; International Reform Bureau, 311 n.3 (312); British Parliament debate on opium traffic, 128 n.2. *See also under* Conferences and institutions, international; Treaties, agreements etc.; Wars
O'Shea, John (b. 1869), British journalist, 9+n.1
Ōshima Ken'ichi (1858–1947), Japanese soldier, 550+n.1
Ōtani Kikuzō (1855–1923), Japanese soldier, 641+n.3, n.4

Ou-yang Wu, Chinese soldier, 209 n.2, n.3
Overseas Chinese, 148 n.1, (in Australia) 316 n.1, 348–9, 675 n.2; (in Canada) 316 n.2; (in France) 47 n.3–48, 640 +n.3, 755; (in New Zealand) 675 +n.2–676; (in Transvaal) 18+n.1; (in U.S.A.), 30 n.2, 42, 146, 316 n.1
Owen, George (d. 1914), British Protestant missionary, 345+n.1
Ōyama Iwao (1842–1916), Japanese soldier, 540+n.1, 552 n.1
Ozaki Yukio (1858–1954), Japanese politician, 132–3+n.1

Paderewski, Ignacy Jan (1860–1941), Polish pianist and national leader, 43 n.3 (44)
Padoux, George, French jurist, 99+n.4, 436+n.1, 569–70+n.1, 574, 577 n.1, 582, 628, 630, 637;
letter to, 577
Pai Lang. *See* Pai Yung-ch'eng
Pai Chung-hsi (1894–1966), Chinese soldier, 64 n.2 (65)
Pai Wen-wei. *See* Po Wen-wei
Pai Yung-ch'eng (Pai Lang, White Wolf), Chinese soldier, 14 n.5, 280+n.1–281, 289–91, 304+n.2, 317 n.3 (318), 328 n.1 (329), 361+n.1, 440, 656 n.3
P'an Chü-ying, Chinese soldier, 319+n.2, 320, 321, 474+n.2, 475, 538+n.1
Pao-i, Manchu Bannerman, Imperial official, 188
Paris Peace Conference, 15 n.1, 43 n.3 (44), 54 n.2, 57 n.1, 82 n.3, 101 n.4 (102), 220 n.2, 238 n.1, 252 n.4, 273 n.1, 357 n.1, 419, 440, 468, 472, 505 n.2 (506), 530, 556, 560, 561+n.3, 589, 605 n.3 (606), 617 n.1, 632 n.2, 639, 645 n.3, 650, 668, 679 n.1, n.2, 694, 697, 698 n.3, 702 n.1, 712–14, 715–22, 727–59, 761 n.2, n.3, 764, 768–9, 790 n.2, 792 n.4, 795, 799+n.1, 800, 809 n.1, 812–13, 814, 818 n.4, n.6;
– Chinese claims, 716, 717, 728–55; Chinese publicity, 712–14;
– Peace Treaty, 756+n.5, 761 n.2, 765, 768+n.1, 771–2, 773–5, 776, 778–9+ n.2, 781, 786+n.1, n.2, 800 n.1;
– *See also under* G. E. Morrison
Parkin, Australian Clergyman, 588+n.3
Parliaments in China: Constitutions (*see* separate entry)
– Tzu-cheng yüan (*1907*), 203 n.1, 225 n.2;
– Nanking Senate (*1911–12*), 596+n.1;

888

Parliaments in China (*cont.*)
- Parliament (*1913*), 14 n.5 (15), 116 n.2, 117, 118 n.4, 121, 122, 124, 135, 136, 137, 157, 158+n.2, 225 n.1, 226 n.1 (227), 614 n.4, (dissolution of) 196, 264, 439 n.1, 645 n.3;
- Political Council (*1913*), 533; Resurrected Parliament (*1916-17*), 531, 568, 592, 595, 596, 615, (dissolution of) 536 n.2, 598, 599+n.1, 600, 601, 602, 612 n.1; Political Consultative Council (*1914-16*), 14 n.5 (15), 135 n.2, 203 n.1, 225 n.2, 309 n.1, 451;
- Canton Rump Parliament (*1912-22*), 637, 645 n.3, 706-7, 719;
- Anfu Parliament (*1918*), 623 n.3 (624), 682+n.1, 691 n.1, 697 n.2, 706-7+n.1, 761 n.2, 765, 767, 774, 803, 809;
- National Rehabilitation Council (*1925*), 203 n.1;
- Provisional Political Consultative Council (*1925*), 225 n.2;
- Provincial Assemblies: 226 n.1 (227), 512; (in Honan) 14+n.4, n.5-16; (in Hupeh) 439 n.1; (in Szechwan) 135; (Hsing-ho District Consultative Assembly) 119+n.1

Paske-Smith, Montague Bentley Talbot, Candian-born British diplomat, 791 +n.4

Pasquier, Pierre-Victor, Belgian Catholic missionary, 495+n.3

Passeri, G., Italian employee of Bank of China, 244+n.2, 518 n.1, 629; *letter from*, (to T'ang Jui) 244

Pauling, George, British Railway contractor, 794+n.1, 806

Peace negotiations between Central Government and southern republicans: (*1911-12*) 10 n.1, 20 n.3, 57 n.2; (*1919-20*) 10 n.1, 510 n.2, 654-7, 698+n.1, 704, 706-9, 715-16, 718 +n.2-719, 728 n.1, 783+n.1-784, 796, 801, 808 n.6

Pearl, Cyril Altson (b. 1906), Australian journalist and author, 651 n.1

Pears, Edwin (1835-1919), British journalist and lawyer, 694+n.2; *letter to*, (from A. J. Moore Bennett) 695

Peking Syndicate. *See under* Commercial and industrial companies, etc.

Peking: Anfu Hutung, 761 n.2; Ch'ing-hua yüan, 491 n.2; foreigners in post-war Peking, 782; Hotel de Pékin, 609, 804; Hotel Wagons-Lits, 608 n.1; Legation quarter police behaviour, 268-9; Pekin Club (Peking Country Club), 782; tramways, 303; Wang-fu ching ta-chieh (Morrison Street), 286; destruction of Yüan-ming yüan by Anglo-French forces (*1860*), 436 n.2; taxation and municipal administration, 578-9; 581

Pereira, George (1865-1923), British soldier, 42+n.1, 818; *letter from*, 42

Pernotte, A. J., French banker, 80 n.1

Perry-Ayscough, Henry George Charles, British employee of Chinese Postal Administration, 121+n.3, 122, 143

Pershing, John J. (1860-1948), American soldier, 793 n.4

Persia: and World War I, 471, 546, 566; Anglo-Russian rivalry in, 780-1

Pétain, Henri Philippe (1856-1951), French soldier, 550 n.2

Petersen, Vilhelm, Danish employee of Chinese Telegraph Administration, 491+n.1; *letter to*, 491

Petty-Fitzmaurice, Henry Charles Keith (1845-1927), 5th Marquess of Lansdowne, British politician, 433+n.2, 434

Pfister, Louis Aloys (1833-91), French scholar, 652 n.4

Phillips, Rev., British clergyman, 825

Pi Kuei-fang, Chinese Republican politician, Provincial Governor, 281+n.1

Picard-Destelan, H., French employee of Chinese Postal Administration, 699 n.1

Pichon, Stéphan Jean-Marie (1857-1933), French diplomat and politician, 370 n.1

Pienma. *See under* Britain in China

Piesse, Edmund Leolin (1880-1947), Australian intelligence agent, 789+n.1

Piggott, Francis Taylor (1852-1925), British judge, 2, 18+n.3-19, 71

Piry, A. Théophile (d. 1918), French Postmaster-General of Chinese Postal Administration, 284+n.1, 699+n.1

Plehve, Vyacheslar Konstantinovich (?1846-1904), Russian politician, 115 n.1

Po Wen-wei (?1874-1947), Chinese soldier, 199+n.1, 394

Poklewsky, Russian diplomat, 780+n.4

Pokotilov, Dmitri D. (d. 1908), Russian diplomat, 58 n.3

Political groups: China, 164-6; Anfu Clique, 79 n.2 (80), 101 n.4 (102), 161 n.2, 273 n.3, 287 n.2, 358 n.2, 510 n.2, 527 n.2, 574 n.2 583, n.4, 597 n.2, 602, 623 n.3 (624), 635 n.1, 636 n.2, 654 n.8,

889

Political groups (*cont.*)
656 n.3, 682 n.1, 689 n.2, 715, 809,
(Anfu Club) 347 n.1, 636 n.2, 689 n.2,
761+n.1, n.2, 764, 783 n.1, n.4, 803,
808; Blue Shirts, 656 n.3; China
Democratic League, 605 n.3 (606);
Chihli Clique, 86 n.1, 209 n.2, 319 n.3
(320), 381 n.3 (382), 597 n.2, 602, 623
n.3 (624), 636 n.2, 654 n.8, 656 n.3,
783 n.1, n.3, 809 n.4; Chin-pu tang,
111, 762+n.1, 783 n.4; Ch'ou-an hui,
415 n.4 (416), 450-1, 453, 457; Chung-
hua ko-ming tang, 393 n.3, 394 n.2;
Chung-kuo kuo-min tang (*see also*
Kuomintang below), 6 n.3, 111, 145
n.2, 169 n.3 (170), 252 n.4 (253), 393
n.1, n.2, 395 n.3, 415 n.4 (416), 474 n.1,
477 n.4 (478), 547 n.2, 605 n.3 (606);
Communication Clique, 79 n.2, 237
n.3, 318 n.2, 510 n.2, 722 n.1;
Communist Party, 388 n.1, 393 n.1, n.2,
394 n.1, 395 n.2, 477 n.3, n.4 (478);
Diplomatist Clique, 15 n.1 (16);
Hua-ch'ing hui, 8 n.1, 10; Kuo-min
kung-tang, 10 n.1, n.2; Kuomintang
(*see also* Chung-kuo kuo-min tang
above), 6 n.3, 64 n.2, 110, 111, 112 n.2,
n.3, 116-17+n.1, 119, 122, 135, 138,
139, 141, 150, 157, 162-3, 164-6, 177,
195, 196, 198, 199, 240, 593,
(proscription of) 253+n.3, 264; Kuo-she
tang, 605 n.3 (606); Kung-ho tang,
13+n.3; monarchist faction, 118 n2,
(*see also* Monarchist movement); New
Communication Clique, 237 n.3, 722
n.1; Research Clique, 646 n.1, 809 n.1;
T'ai-tzu p'ai (Crown Prince Clique),
477 n.1 (478); T'ung-meng hui, 6+n.3,
7-13, 17, 42, 110, 112 n.2, 116 n.3,
118 n.1, 393 n.2, 394 n.3, n.4; Western
Hills Clique, 393 n.1, n.2;
- Japan: Black Dragon Society, 789 n.6;
Chōshū clan, 132+n.2, n.3, 472 n.1;
Gunbatsu, 132 n.3, 220, 563; Kenseikai,
132 n.4, n.5, 671+n.2; Kenseitō, 132
n.6; Kishiwada clan, 549 n.1; Rikken
Dōshikai, 132 n.4, n.5, 391 n.2 (392),
671 n.2; Rikken Kaishintō, 6 n.1, 132
n.7; Rikken Kokumintō, 132+n.6, n.7,
391 n.2 (392); Satsuma clan, 132+n.2;
Seiyūkai, 132 n.7 (133), 463 n.1, 584
n.3, 775 n.2;
- elsewhere: Labour Party, Britain, 605
n.3 (606), 626 n.1, n.2; National
Socialist Party, Germany, 698 n.2;
United Socialist Party, France, 612 n.2
Political and religious movements and
sects: Buddhism, 319 n.3, 660 n.2,
(West Honganji Sect) 583 n.2, (*see also*
Dalai Lama); Confucianism, 112 n.1,
206 n.2 (207), 462, 711; communism,
393 n.1, n.2, 505 n.2 (506), 717, 760,
777-8, (*see also* May Fourth Movement;
Reform, revolts and revolutions:
Russia in China); Fabian socialism,
809 n.1; fascism in Italy, 73 n.1; Islam,
167, 468, 471, 545-6, 558, 564, 569;
New Life movement, 206 n.2 (207);
Nazism in Germany, 698 n.2; socialism
in France, 619 n.2; Taoism (and *Tao-
tsang*), 381 n.3 (382); Zionist movement
(see separate entry); *See also* Political
groups
Pontius, Albert William (1879-1923),
American consular official, 719+n.1
Pope Pius X. *See* G. M. Sarto
Porter Harold (1879-1938), British
consular official, 135+n.5, 806 n.1;
letter from, 806
Porter, Mrs, wife of H. Porter, 806+n.1,
807
Porter, Robert Percival (1852-1917),
American journalist, 516+n.2
Portugal: in China, 468; and World War I
663-4
Posts and telegraphs, Chinese: posts, 27,
121 n.3, 238, 284, 437, 491 n.1, 522,
699+n.1-700, 702; telegraphs, 66 n.3
(67), 103+n.2, 114 n.2, 115, 263+n.1,
284+n.1, 404 n.2, 473, 491 n.1, 584
n.1, 593; Eastern Extension Telegraph
Co., 92; Great Northern Telegraph
Co., 92
Powers in China:
- recognition of the Republic, 6+n.2,
116+n.2;
- rivalry, 28, 64-72, 79, 81-2, 85-92,
104-5, 105-19, 210+n.2, 244-51, 261,
275-6, 297-303, 322+n.1, 356-60, 366,
367, 370, 373, 380 n.2, 406, 413, 414-15
+n.3, 418-22, 429-46, 465-7, 468, 471,
472, 491 n.2, 496, 555, 559, 563, 576-7,
581-2, 587, 591-3, 618, 695-7, 729,
780-1, 807-8
- Extraterritoriality, (*see* separate
entry);
- and Yüan Shih-k'ai's monarchical
scheme, (*see* Yüan Shih-k'ai: monarchy
scheme); and China's entry into World
War I, (*see under* Wars: World War I);
- *See also* entries for individual powers;
Banks, financial houses and consortia;
Loans; Railways; Treaties, agreements
etc.

890

Pozdnieef, Alexei M., Russian scholar, 634; *Lectures on the History of Mongol Literature*, 634
Pratt, Frederick Lionel (b. 1872), Australian journalist, 9+n.2, 11, 12, 221, 323 n.1, 578 n.1;
letters to, 158, 323
letters from, 149, 162, 198, 199, 208
Primrose, Archibald Philip (1847-1929), 5th Earl of Rosebery, British politician, 409+n.1
Princip, Gavrilo (1894-1918), Slav nationalist, 774 n.1
Pritchett, Henry Smith (1857-1939), American astronomer, 23+n.4
Prithi Chand, Singapore policeman, 790
Prophit, James Maxwell Grant (?1859-1924), British banker, Executor and Trustee of G. E. and Jennie Morrison's wills, 824+n.1
Prothero, George Walter (1848-1922), British historian, 778, 779+n.1, 826; co-editor, *Cambridge Modern History*, 779;
letters to, 470, 502, 505, 520, 773
letter from, 489
Prothero, Rowland Edmund (1851-1937), 1st Baron Ernle, British politician, 779+n.1
P'u-jun, Manchu Imperial Clansman and official, 178+n.2
P'u-lun, Manchu Imperial Clansman, 225+n.2
P'u-yi (1906-67), Manchu Emperor Hsüan-t'ung (1908[9]-12), 163 n.1, 206+n.1, 212, 224 n.2, 225 n.2, 381 n.3 (382), 491 n.2, 526, 593 n.4 (594), 596, 597 n.2, 602, 642 n.1
Purdom, William, British botanist, 508+n.3, 817+n.5

Quo Tai Chi. *See* Kuo T'ai-ch'i

Rahman, Abdur. *See* Abdur Rahman Khan
Railways in China, 168, 194, 200, 299, 301, 304+n.3, 370, 402-3, 416-17, 430, 431, 437, 471, 486, 539, 544, 588 n.1, 645+n.3; Central Administration, 79 n.2; nationalization, 306 n.2; Szechwan railway riots, 514 n.1; (*See also* Sun Yat-sen: and railways); in Chekiang, 338 n.1; in Inner Mongolia, 237 n.2, 267-8, 738; in Kweichow, 301, 350; in Manchuria, 153, 237 n.2, 654, 738, 794+n.1; in north China, 738; in Shantung, 351, 353, 358, 360+n.3, 736, 737, 738, 748, 801;

– Canton-Chungking-Lanchow Railway, 191 n.1, 301; Central China Railways, 66, 402; Chefoo-Lungkow Railway, 413 n.2; Chefoo-Tsinan Railway, 431; Chefoo-Weihsien Railway, 413+n.2, 475; Chinese Eastern Railway, 59 n.1, 103, 645 n.3; Fengchen-Ningsia-Lanchow Railway, 543; Hsinminfu-Aigun Railway, 70; Hsin-yang-Pukow Railway, 286+n.2, 402, 416, 417, 487; Hukwang Railway, 564; Kaomi-Hanchuang Railway, 366 n.3; Kaomi-Hsüchou Railway, 737; Imperial Northern Chinese Railways, 53 n.3, 624 n.2; Lung-hai Railway, 299 n.1; Lungkow-Weihsien Railway, 475; Peking-Hankow Railway, 68+n.3, 299+n.1, 347 n.1, 360, 485, 737; Peking-Kalgan Railway, 440; Peking-Mukden Railway, 307+n.2; Peking-Suiyuan Railway, 347 n.1; Pin-Hei Railway, 504+n.3; Shanghai-Nanking Railway, 737; South Manchurian Railway, 5 n.1, 299 n.1, 364, 370, 476 n.1, 513+n.1, 547, 563 n.1, 588 n.1, 688, 791 n.3; Tientsin-Pukow Railway, 44+n.3, 66, 69, 105, 120+n.1, 141, 299 n.1, 360, 385 n.1, 485, 564, 737, 828 n.1; Tsinan-Pukow Railway, 385, 417 n.1; Tsinan-Shuntefu Railway, 366 n.3; Tsingtao-Tsinan Railway, 360, 413 n.2, 725, 736; Yunnan-Chentu Railway, 300; Yunnan-Chungking Railway, 301;
– elsewhere: North-Eastern Railway (Britain), 776; Seoul-Pusan Railway, 590 n.1; Siberian Railway, 103, 402, 415, 504, 588 n.1, 782 n.2
Ramsay, Alexander, British journalist, 376
Ramstedt, Gustaf John (1873-1950), Finnish scholar, 50+n.3
Rankin, American commercial representative, 648
Rea, George Bronson (1869-1936), American journalist, 7 n.1, 163+n.1, 334, 335
Rees, John David (1854-1922), British politician, 128+n.1, n.2
Reform, revolts and revolutions:
– in China, 487; Canton Uprising (*1895*), 148 n.1, 197+n.3; Constitution Protection Movement (*1917*) 395 n.1; Constitutional Reform Movement (*1909-11*), 439 n.1; Huang-hua-kang Uprising (*1911*), 8 n.1; Kalgan Troop Mutiny (*1912*), 329+n.2, 333; Lanchow Revolt (*1911*), 118 n.1; Northern

Reform (*cont.*)
 Expedition (*1926-27*) 64 n.2 (65);
 Reform Movement and Coup d'Etat
 (*1898*), 90 n.2, 122 + n.4, 264, 505 + n.2,
 541 n.4-542 + n.1, 547 n.2; Revolution
 1911 (*see* separate entry); Revolution
 1913 (*see* separate entry); Second
 Revolution (*see* Revolution (*1913*);
 Sian Incident (*1936*) 7 n.2;
 Supao case (*see* separate entry);
 Szechwan Railway riot (*1911*) 514 n.1;
 Taiping Revolution, 206 n.2; *Tuchün*
 Revolt (*1917*) (*see* separate entry);
 Waichow Uprising (*1900*), 150 n.1;
 Weihsien Insurrection (*1916*), 393 n.2,
 642 n.2; Wuchang Uprising (T'ang
 Ts'ai-ch'ang, *1900*) 244 n.3; Wuchang
 Uprising (*1912*), (*see* Revolution
 1911);
 – elsewhere: American Revolution, 500
 n.1; French Revolution, 651 n.3;
 Mexican Revolution, 264, 442 + n.1;
 Russian Revolution, 368 n.1, 447 n.2,
 455 n.2, 626 + n.3, 629 + n.1, 654,
 691-2, 695, 759; (Powers' intervention
 in Siberia) 641 n.3, 704, 784, (American
 railway mission to Siberia) 782 n.2,
 (Allied control of Siberian Railway) 782
 n.2; in Mongolia, 777 + n.4-778
Rehemiah, Shanghai merchant, 567
Reid, Gilbert (1857-1927), American
 Protestant missionary, 586 + n.2
Reinsch, Paul Samuel (1870-1923),
 American scholar and diplomat, 20 n.2,
 296 + n.1, 451, 478, 531, 585 + n.2, 586,
 594, 618 n.1, 637, 670, 673, 694, 701,
 803 + n.1, 818 n.4; *An American
 Diplomat in China*, 670
Rémusat, Jean Pierre Abel (1788-1833),
 French scholar, 653 n.1
de Reus, J. H., Dutch consular official,
 594 + n.1
de Reuter, Auguste Julius Clemens
 Herbert (1852-1915), 1st Bart,
 Managing Director of Reuter Telegram
 Company, 257 + n.1, n.2, 376;
 letter from, (to A. E. Wearne) 257
Revolution *1911*, 3 n.1, 8, 42 n.2, 57 n.2,
 85 n.3, 94, 124 n.1, 135 n.7, 148 n.1,
 150 n.1, 182, 202, 237, 264, 292, 306
 n.2, 307 n.2, 310 n.3, 316, 319 n.3,
 393 n.4, 394 n.1, n.2, n.4, 395 n.1,
 396 n.1, 415 n.4, 450, 491 n.2, 534 n.2,
 535 n.1, 542, 591, 645 n.3, 656 n.2, 730;
 and Manchus, 118 n.2, 381 n.3,
 (abdication) 79 n.2 (80), 206 n.1, 287
 n.2, 729; in Canton, 18; in Honan,
 14-16; Lanchow revolt, 118 n.1; taking
 of Nanking, 394 n.2; in Kweichow,
 42-3; in Manchuria, 514 n.1, 596 n.2,
 597 n.2; in Szechwan and Ch'uan-pien,
 135-6, 167-8, 514 n.1; in Shantung,
 53 n.2; in Yunnan, 42 n.2; Powers'
 compensation claims, 82, 279, 302, 309;
 W. Ming's claim to Chinese throne
 (*see* W. Ming)
Revolution *1913* ('Second Revolution'),
 8 n.1, 42 n.2, 110-11, 116 + n.4, 149-51,
 162-4, 166 + n.2, 169-71, 180 + n.2-181,
 191, 195-6, 197-202, 203 n.2, 205-12,
 214-15, 237 + n.1, n.3, 269 n.3, 270
 + n.1, 287 n.2 (288), 324 + n.1, 333,
 393 + n.1, n.2, 394 n.2, n.4, 395 n.1,
 n.2, 396 n.1, 405, 439 n.1, 476 n.1,
 527 n.2; in Shanghai, 149-51, 162-4,
 195, 198-9, 208, 209, 251-2; sacking of
 Nanking by Chang Hsün and Japanese
 claims, 214 + n.3-215, 222 + n.3-223,
 237 n.3, 252 + n.1, 253. *See also under
 Japan in China*
Rhodes, Cecil John (1853-1902), British
 politician and industrialist, 705 n.1
Richard, Timothy (1845-1919), British
 missionary, 68 n.5
Ricketts, D. Poyntz, British railway
 engineer, 817 + n.4
Ridge, Sheldon, British journalist, 383
 + n.1
Ridout, Dudley Howard (1866-1941),
 Canadian soldier, 788 + n.2;
 letter from, (to F. T. A. Ashton-Gwatkin)
 788
Robertson, David Stephen, British soldier,
 553 + n.2, 640 + n.2;
 letter to, 640
Robertson Scott. *See* J. W. R. Scott
Robin, Jennie Wark. *See* Jennie Morrison
Robin, Robert, New Zealander, father-in-
 law of G. E. Morrison, 32 + n.3
Robinson, Father, Australian Catholic
 priest, 651
Robinson, George Goeffrey (later G. G.
 Dawson) (1874-1944), British journalist,
 Editor of *The Times*, 13-14 + n.1,
 330 + n.1, 373 n.1, 410 + n.1, 460
Rockhill, Edith Howell (*née* Perkins), wife
 of W. W. Rockhill, 286
Rockhill, William Woodville (1854-1914),
 American diplomat, 20 + n.2, 21, 24,
 58 n.2, 213 n.1, 214 n.1, 279 + n.3, 286,
 444 + n.2, 586;
 letter from, 213
Rolin-Jacquemyns, Gustave (1835-1902),
 Belgian jurist and politician, 100 + n.4

Rolland, Romain (1866-1944), French writer, 43 n.3 (44)
Ronaldshay, Earl of. *See* L. J. L. Dundas
Roosevelt, Theodore (1858-1919), 26th President of the United States, 23 n.1, n.3, 59 n.4, 481+n.5, 533, 626
Root, Elihu (1845-1937), American politician, 23+n.1
Rose, Charles Archibald Walker (1879-1961), British consular official, 57+n.4, 58, 153+n.3, 643+n.1, 648-9, 688
Rosebery, Earl of. *See* A. P. Primrose
Rosen, Henry P., financial agent, 67 n.1
Rossi, Lugi (b. 1867), Italian educationalist and politician, 74+n.3, 232
Rothschild, Gustave de, British financier, 127 n.2
Rothschild, Lionel Walter (1868-1937), 3rd Bart and 2nd Baron, British financier, 705, 706 n.1
Rothschilds, the, 148 n.2
Rump, C., German employee of Chinese Salt Administration, 71+n.1
Russell, Lindsay (1870-1949), American lawyer and author, 382+n.1-383, 384
Russia in China:
– Czarist, 27-8, 68, 79, 85, 119, 179, 300, 366, 369, 468, 471; territorial concession, 437; in Manchuria, 58-9, 597 n.2; (*see also* Railways: Chinese Eastern Railway, Pin-Hei Railway); in Mongolia, (*see under* Mongolia); in Sinkiang, 63+n.1, 72, 74, 104-5, 158, 178-9, 364, 534, 546; in Tibet, 28; China's withdrawal of recognition of Czarist Russia, 629 n.1 (630);
– Soviet mission to China, 629 n.1 (630);
– *see also under* Japan in China; Loans; Railways; Powers in China; Treaties, agreements etc.
Rustad, T. A., Norwegian trader, 47+n.1; *letters from*, 47, 319, 473, 537
Rutten, Père, Belgian Catholic Missionary, 118+n.5

Sa Chen-ping (1858-1952), Chinese sailor, 289+n.1-290, 291
Sa Fu-mao (b. 1874), Chinese Republican official, 244 n.3, 404+n.2, 809 n.5
Sa-yin-t'u (Takoshina), Mongol Bannerman and diplomat, 178 n.2
Saburi Sadao (1879-1929), Japanese diplomat, 790+n.3
Sahara Tokusuke (1874-1932), Japanese journalist and publicist, 5+n.1, 541 n.2, 803;
letter to, 218;

letters from, 5, 206, 212, 225
Saigo Takamori (1827-77), Japanese politician, 132 n.2
Saigo Tsugumichi (1843-1902), Japanese politician, 132 n.2, 396 n.2
Saiki, Japanese adventurer, 182
Saint-Pierre, H. M. R., French banker, 303+n.3
Saionji Kimmochi (1849-1940), Marquis, Japanese politician, 584 n.2, 632 n.2, 773+n.2, 790+n.2, 802 n.1
Salisbury, Marquess of. *See* R. A. T. G. Cecil
Salt Gabelle, 27, 56 n.1, 84+n.1, 85, 105, 161, 172, 193, 240-1, 242, 254 n.1, 255, 288, 298, 300, 309-10, 315, 317, 361, 404 n.1, 416-18, 437, 459, 480+nn. 1-3, 498, 501, 519, 520, 533, 534, 572-3, 579, 597-9, 614-17, 650+n.1, 759, 760, 761 n.1, 787, 803 n.2, 807 +n.1-808+n.3; Japanese salt smuggling, 589
Samuel, Marcus (1858-1927), 1st Visct Bearsted, British businessman, 686 n.1
Samuel, Samuel (1855-1934), British politician, 686+n.1
San Giuliano, Marquese di. *See* A. P. Castello
San Liu-ch'iao. *See* Santo
Santo (San Liu-ch'iao) (b. 1876), Mongol Bannerman, Imperial and Republican official, 47+n.3-48, 51+n.1, 90, 144, 177, 260, 428
Sarto, Guiseppe Melchiorre (1835-1914), Pope Pius X (1903-14), 106
Sassoon, Albert Abdullah David (1818-96), 1st Bart, Baghdad-born British opium merchant, 127 n.2
Sassoon, Edward Albert (1856-1912), 2nd Bart, British politician, 127 n.2
Sassoon, Philip Albert Gustave David (1888-1939), 3rd Bart, British politician, 127+n.2
Satow, Ernest Mason (1843-1929), British diplomat, 5 n.4, 28+n.3, 344+n.1, 758+n.6, 815-16, 817
Saunders, George (1859-1922), British journalist, 296+n.2
Saunderson, British newspaper manager, 375
Sayce, Archibald Henry (1845-1933), British philologist, 633+n.6
Sazanoff, Sergei Dimitrievich (1866-1927), Russian politician, 455 n.2
Schiff, Jacob Henry (1847-1920), American financier, 405+n.2

Schiff, Mortimer Loeb (1877-1931), American financier, 405 n.2
Schiff, Theresa (*née* Loeb), 405 n.2
Scopes, John T., American teacher, 499 n.1
Scott, J. W. Robertson, British journalist and publicist, 554+n.3, 588 n.1, 639 n.2;
letters to, 554, 588
Scott, Walter S., British journalist, 792 +n.3, 797;
letter to, 792
Second Revolution. *See* Revolution 1913
Secret Societies, 394 n.4, 401, 415 n.4 (416)
Seddon, Richard John (1845-1906), New Zealand politician, 675 n.2
Serembo, Mongol soldier, 280
Seton-Watson, Robert William (1879-1951), British historian, 489+n.3, 490 n.1
Sforza, Carlo (1872-1952), Count, Italian diplomat and politician, 73+n.1, n.2, 74, 233
Shan-ch'i (Prince Su) (?1866-1922), 642 n.1
Shanghai:
- International Settlement, 8+n.2, 38, 111, 113 n.2, 116 n.3, 127 n.3 (128), 138 n.1, 146, 180 n.3, 186-91, 199, 208, 306, 541, 553 n.1; extension, 277-9, 727+n.3; Chinese representation, 591 n.1, 727+n.3; Chinese political refugees, 149-51, 162-4, 180-3, 186-91, 277 n.2-278; government detective service, 149-51, 163-4; Mixed Court question, 116 n.3, 182+n.1, 187, 188, 189, 277-9, 405; Japanese activities, 207, 208, 289-90, 291;
- French Concession, 112 n.3, 151 n.3;
- *See also* Arsenals: Kiangnan Arsenal; C. D. Bruce; Ch'en Ch'i-mei; Political groups in China: Kuomintang; Revolution *1911*; Revolution *1913*
Sharman, Lyon, American author, 323 n.1
Shaw, George Bernard (1856-1950), British writer, 43 n.3 (44)
Shen, Samuel. *See* Shen Shou-chih
Shen Shou-chih (Samuel Shen), Chinese Republican official, 263+n.1
Shen Yün-p'ei, Chinese Imperial official and Republican politician, 417+n.1
Sheng Hsüan-huai (1849-1916), Chinese Imperial official, 305 n.3, 306+n.2, 308
Sherfesee, Forsythe, American botanist, 508+n.2, 570, 682;
letter from, 819
Sherman, Jacob Gould (1854-1942), American educationalist and diplomat, 818 n.4
Shibusawa Elichi (1840-1931) Baron, Japanese industrialist and financier, 476 n.1, 590+n.1
Shidehara Kijurō (1872-1951), Japanese diplomat and politician, 548+n.4
Shidehara Masako (*née* Iwasaki), wife of Shidehara Kijurō, 548 n.4
Shigeno Yasutsugu (1827-1910), Japanese scholar, 622 n.1
Shih Chao-chi (Alfred Sze) (1877-1958), Chinese diplomat, 357+n.1, 391+n.1, 516, 535, 773+n.2, 778+n.1, 801, 812;
letter to, 787
Shih-ching, 462
Ships: S.S. *Aki Maru*, 646 n.2; M.M.S. *Athos*, 673+n.1; *Audacious*, 447+n.4; H.M.A.S. *Australia*, 662; *Changsha*, 657; *Chao-ho*, 116 n.4 (117); *Devenha*, 279; *Emden*, 551+n.3, 556, 661; *Empress*, 342; *Empress of Japan*, 722; *Empress of Russia*, 813, 818, 820; *Flora*, 126, 215; S.S. *Fushimi Maru*, 723 n.2; S.S. *Hsin-yu*, 526; *Imperator*, 793; *Lusitania*, 400+n.1, 448, 465; S.S. *Nanking*, 722, 818; *See Adler*, 661; *Sydney*, 551, n.3; *Takachiho*, 662; *Tatsu Maru* (*see under* Japan: in China); *Titanic*, 5+n.2; *Yasaka Maru*, 662
Shōda Kazue (1869-1948), Japanese politician, 584 n.3
Shorrock, A. G., British missionary, 401+n.2
Shu-ching, 462
Siam, 100, 387+n.1, 569-70, 617, 705, 706 n.1; abolition of extraterritoriality, 569; and World War I, 617-18, 682; Anglo-French rivalry, 387 n.2
Sikkim, Maharajkumar of, 428+n.3
Silver: currency and price, 402-3, 620, 624, 629, 630-1, 680, 693, 702, 704; mint, 404 n.2
Simla Conference. *See under* Tibet
Simon, John Allsebrook (1873-1954), 1st Visct Stackpole Elidor, British politician, 685+n.2, 687
Simpson, Bertram Lenox (Putnam Weale) (1877-1930), British journalist, 31+n.3- 32, 40, 114-16, 140-1, 237, 295, 333, 341, 374, 383, 449, 564, 701
Sinclair, Upton Beall (1878-1968), American writer, 43 n.3 (44)

Sinkiang. *See under* Russia in China
Smith, Arthur Henderson (1845–1932), American missionary and author, 93 n.2, 97 + n.2, n.3–99;
letters from, 97, 568, (to Editor of *The Times*) 98
Smith, Cecil Clementi (1840–1916), British colonial official, 120 + n.2, 424 + n.2;
letter to, 406
letter from, 120
Smith, Earl Hamilton, American journalist, 271 + n.2, 285
Smith, J. A. Creasey, British missionary, 400 + n.2;
letter from, 400
Smith, John Langford (b. 1877), British consular official, 522 + n.3
Snowball, Jabez B., Canadian politician, 54 n.2
Snowden, Philip (1864–1937), 1st Visct Ickornshaw, British politician, 626 + n.2
Societies, learned, professional or otherwise: American Asiatic Association, 286, 682; Anglo-American Association, Peking, 700–1; Asiatic Society, Oxford, 814; British Engineers Association, 376 n.2; British Ornithologists Union, 610 n.1; Central Asian Society, 814; China Association, 78, 108 n.3, 127 n.3, 313 + n.3, 316, 521; China National Goods Association, 423; China National Medical Association, 367 n.2; Finno-Ougrienne Society, 50 n.3; Freedom League, 415 n.4 (416); Law Institute of Victoria, 789 n.1; Japan Society, Great Britain, 382–3; Japan Society, New York, 382 + n.1, n.2; National Petition Association, 417 n.1; Pilgrims Society of London and New York, 382 n.1, 383; Red Cross, 543, 699; Royal Society of Tropical Medicine and Hygiene, 216 n.3 (217); Seamen's Hospital Society, 216 n.3; Sino-Japanese Society, Peking, 101
Son Chung-hee, Korean patriot, 763 n.1
Soong Family. *See* Sung
Soothill, Florence, 410 n.2
Soothill, William Edward (1861–1935), British missionary, 68 n.5, 330 + n.5, 410 n.2;
letter to, 331
letter from, 343
Sosita-gung, Mongol leader, 52
Southwark, 1st Baron. *See* R. K. Causton
Spain in China, 468

Spandau fund. *See* Wars: Franco-Prussian War
von Spee, Maximilian Johannes Maria Hubert (1861–1914), Reichsgraf, German sailor, 551 n.1, n.2, 661
Spencer, Herbert (1820–1903), British philosopher, 450, 623 n.1
Steed, Henry Wickham (1871–1956), British journalist and author, 330 + n.2, 373 + n.1, 460, 490, 560, 768, 787, 793, 795, 797 n.1, 812 n.3, 817;
letters to, 373, 377, 797, 798, (from Nagai Matsuzō) 795
letter from, 795
Steel-Maitland, Arthur Herbert (1876–1935), British politician, 785 + n.2
Stephen, A. G., British banker, 317 + n.3
Stevens, Durham White (1852–1908), American diplomat, 25 + n.2
Stevens, John F. (b. 1853), American civil engineer, 782 + n.2
Stewart, Murray, British financial broker and journalist, 108 + n.3
Stokes, Claude Bayfield (1875–1948), British soldier, 315 + n.1; *letter to*, 315
Stokes, Frederick Wilfred Scott (1860–1927), British civil engineer and financial agent, 376 + n.2
Straight, Willard Dickerman (1880–1918), American diplomat and financial agent, 60 n.1
von Strauch, E. A. W., German employee of Chinese Maritime Customs, 545 + n.2
Straus, Oscar Solomon (1850–1926), American diplomat, 23 + n.3
Strickland, W. R., British employee of Chinese Salt Administration, 598 + n.1, 650 + n.1, 759 n.2, 807 n.1, 817;
letters from, 759, 807
Su, Prince. *See* Shan-ch'i
Su-kung, Mongol leader, 230
Sugden, Arthur Henry (1863–1947), British employee of Chinese Maritime Customs, 353 + n.1
Sun Ch'uan-fang (1885–1935), Chinese soldier, 807 n.4
Sun Fo. *See* Sun K'o
Sun K'o (Sun Fo) (b. 1891), Chinese Republican politician, 477 + n.4
Sun Pao-ch'i (1867–1931), Chinese Imperial official, Provincial Governor and Republican politician, 53 + n.2, 169 n.2, 228 n.1, 231, 237 + n.2, 239 + n.2, 285, 313, 346, 518 + n.2;
letter to, 231
Sun T'ien-lu, Morrison's Chinese head servant, 606, 815, 816, 820

Sun Wen. *See* Sun Yat-sen
Sun Wu (?1877-1940), Chinese Republican politician, 86+n.1
Sun Yat-sen (Sun Wen) (1866-1925), Chinese revolutionary leader: 7+n.1, n.3, 38, 42 n.2, 43+n.3 (44), 57 n.1, n.2, 118 n.4, 150, 216, 231 n.1, 323+n.1, 324, 328, 339, 358 n.2, 388 n.1, 664;
- revolutionary career, 112 n.2, 148 n.1, 163, 165, 169 n.3, 197+n.3, 209-10, 212, 393-6, 536 n.2, 600; (abduction in London) 197 n.3, 216 n.3, 761 n.1; (and reformers) 505 n.2 (506);
- Provisional President, 191 n.2, 215 n.2, 254 n.1, 536 n.1;
- and railways, 17 n.1, 101 n.1, 163, 191-2, 200+n.2, 301, 604 n.4;
- and Mongolia, 435, 445;
- and Yüan Shih-k'ai, 7-13, 17+n.1, 110-11, 163, 187 n.2, 191 n.1, 200 +n.2, 209-10, 390, 439 n.1, 500+n.2;
- and Japan, 101+n.1, 132 n.7 (133), 134, 150+n.1, 199, 323-8, 389-91, 392+n.1, n.2, 395-8, 476+n.1, 541 n.4 (542), 590 n.1; (alleged letter to Ōkuma) 323-8, (alleged agreement with Japan) 392-8
- marriage to Sung Ch'ing-ling, 477-80; death, 761 n.1
Sun Yat-sen, Mme. *See* Lu Mu-chen; Sung Ch'ing-ling
Sun Yi-ching (1826-90), Chinese Imperial official, Imperial Tutor, father of Sun Pao-ch'i, 53 n.2
Sung, Chinese political intermediary, 142
Sung Ai-ling (Regina) (b. 1890), wife of K'ung Hsiang-hsi, 191 n.3 (192), 388 n.1, 477+n.2-480
Sung Chiao-jen (1882-1913), Chinese Republican politician, 4 n.1, 10 n.3, 64 n.2, 101 n.1, 110, 112+n.2-13, 116-17, 123+n.1, 136+n.2, 138+n.1, 142, 166 n.2, 172-3, 183-6; 187 n.2, 195, 200 n.2, 386 n.3, 394 n.4, 510 n.2
Sung Chiao-shun (Charles Soong) (1866-1918), Chinese preacher and businessman, 477 n.2, 479
Sung Ch'ing-ling (Rosamonde) (b. 1892), 2nd wife of Sun Yat-sen, 191 n.3 (192), 477+n.3-480
Sung Fa-hsiang (Far T. Sung), Chinese Republican politician and diplomat, 256+n.1, 361+n.1
Sung Mei-ling (Mayling) (b. 1897), wife of Chiang Kai-shek, 191 n.3 (192), 388 n.1, 713 n.1

Sung Tzu-an (d. 1969), Chinese Republican politician, 478 n.2
Sung Tzu-liang, Chinese Republican politician, 478 n.2
Sung Tzu-wen (T.V. Soong) (1894-1971), Chinese Republican politician, 388 n.1, 478+n.2
Supao case, 38, 182 n.1
Suttor, John Bligh (b. 1859), Australian Trade Commissioner, 219+n.4, 221
Suzuki, Japanese opium dealer, 722+n.3
Sweden: in China, 468; Geographical Survey, 416; War Trade Board, 503 n.2
Sze, Alfred. *See* Shih Chao-chi

Ta-hsüeh, 462
Tachibana Masaki (b. 1865), Japanese employee of Chinese Maritime Customs, 354+n.3, 355
Taga Muneyuki (1872-1935), Japanese soldier, 642+n.1
Tai Chi-t'ao (Ch'uan-hsien, T'ien-ch'ou) (1891-1949), Chinese Republican politician, 392-3+n.1
Tai K'an (1880-1917), Chinese soldier, Provincial Governor, 495+n.2
Tai Li (1895-1946), Chinese secret police chief, 656 n.3
Taishō, Emperor. *See* Yoshihito
Takata Shinzō (1852-1921), Japanese financier, 405+n.1
Takeshita Isamu (b. 1870), Japanese sailor, 790+n.6
Taki Seiichi (1873-1945), Japanese scholar, 633+n.1
Talleyrand-Périgord, Duc de (d. 1937), 106 n.2 (107)
Tamba Keizō (1854-1927), Japanese pharmacologist, 633+n.5
Tan Jen-feng (?1860-1920), Chinese Republican politician, 394+n.4, 395
T'an Ssu-t'ung (1865-98), Chinese reformer and martyr, 541 n.4
T'an Chung-lin (?d. 1905), Chinese Imperial official, Viceroy, 305 n.3
T'an Yen-k'ai (1879-1930), Chinese Republican politician, 305 n.3
Tanaka Giichi (1863-1929), Japanese soldier and politician, 132 n.7 (133), 547 n.2 (548)
T'ang Chi-yao (?1882-1927), Chinese soldier, Provincial Governor, 42+n.2, 310 n.3, 452, 481 n.3, 495 n.2, 520 n.3, 635 n.1, 640 n.4, 809
T'ang Hsiang-ming, Chinese sailor and Republican politician, 488 n.2

T'ang Hua-lung (1874-1918), Chinese Republican politician, 439+n.1, 595, 762 n.1

T'ang Jui (Chüeh-tun) (1878-1916), Chinese Republican politician, 244+n.2, n.3, 404 n.2;
letter to, (from G. Passeri) 244

T'ang Pao-ch'ao, Chinese soldier, 524, n.4

T'ang Shao-yi (1860-1938), Chinese Imperial official and Republican politician, 4 n.1, 10 n.1, n.3, 15 n.1, 20+n.3, 38, 53 n.3 (54), 64 n.2, 79+n.1, n.2, 90 n.2, 110, 116 n.4, 118+n.3, 141, 142, 166 n.2, 252 n.4, 357 n.1, 423, 525, 526, 591 n.1, 664, 645 n.3, 718 n.2, 784, 801+n.2, 828 n.1

T'ang Ts'ai-ch'ang (1867-1900), Chinese reformer and martyr, 244 n.3

T'ang Yüan-chang (Y. C. Tong), Chinese Imperial and Republican official, 66+n.3

Tariff revision and autonomy in China, 284-5, 287-9, 572, 576+n.1-577, 581-2, 586, 587, 591-3, 645 n.3, 673, 697 n.1; Tariff Commission, 55 n.3, 697+n.1. *See also* Customs and excise in China, Salt Gabelle; Taxation in China; Treaties, agreements etc.: Mackay Treaty

Tatsu Maru case, 38-9, 766+n.1

Taxation in China, 320-1, 439, 480, 486, 501, 514, 534, 578-81; Land tax and Survey, 310 n.3, 412-13, 457-60, 579-81, 584+n.1; *likin*, 288, 321, 501, 576 n.1, 579, 806-7. *See also* Customs and excise in China; Salt Gabelle; Tariff revision and autonomy in China

Taylor, Francis Edward (b. 1855), British employee of Chinese Maritime Customs, 287+n.1, 680;
letters to, 402, 504, 586, 591, 623;
letters from, 287, 399, 576, 581, 587, 681

Taylor, Theodore Cooke (1850-1952), British manufacturer and politician, 125+n.1, 127 n.1, 128 n.2, 129, 139+n.1, n.2, 140;
letter from, 125

Tenney, Charles Daniel (1857-1930), American missionary and diplomat, 594+n.4

Terao Tōru (1858-1925), Japanese lawyer and adventurer, 396+n.1

Terauchi Masatake (1852-1919), Japanese soldier and politician, 101 n.4, 440-1, 508 n.1, 547 n.2, 548 n.4, 549 n.2, 550 n.1, 554 n.2, 562 n.1, 563 n.1, 583+n.2, n.4, 584 n.3, 590, 591, 592, 621, 638 n.2, 674, 701 n.2, 763 n.2, 764 n.2

Terstappen, J., Belgian Catholic missionary, 473+n.2

Teshima Sutematsu (1863-1924), Japanese consular official, 207 n.1

Thomas, D., Australian teacher in Tongshan Engineering College, 68+n.4

Thomas, Davies & Ross;
letters from, 525, (to Yüan Shih-k'ai) 526

Thomas, William Porter, British consular official, 804+n.1, 813, 816;
letters to, 820, (from Ju Jen-ho) 805, 827
letters from, 804, (to Hsü Shih-ch'ang) 805

Thub Idan rgya mtsho (1876-1933) 13th Dalai Lama, Tibetan head of Yellow Sect Buddhism, 29+n.1, 62, 75, 76, 85 n.1, 89, 227, 428-9

Thwing, Edward Waite, American missionary, 311+n.3, 320, 363, 442 n.2 (443);
letter from, 311

Tiao Min-ch'ien (Tyau, M.T.Z.) (b. 1888), Chinese educationalist and journalist, 453 n.2, 721

Tiao Tso-ch'ien (Philip K. C. Tyau) (b. 1880), Chinese educationalist and diplomat, 568+n.1, n.2;
letter to, 568

Tibet: Sino-British dispute regarding, 10 n.1, 27-30, 31, 34, 37-8, 39, 62+n.2, 75+n.1, n.2, 76-7, 79+n.2, 85, 88, 89-90, 109, 135+n.7, 149+n.1, 152-3, 169-71, 210+n.2, 239-41, 247, 333, 334, 342 n.5, 345-6, 362-3, 408-9, 426-9, 442, 534, 535, 586;
– Younghusband's expedition, 27-8, 37, 89, 428 n.1, 436 n.3; Sino-British Tibetan Treaty, (*see under* Treaties, agreements etc.);
– Simla Conference, 149+n.1, 152-3, 169, 170, 171, 210, 227, 239+n.1-240, 342 n.5; Simla Treaty, (*see under* Treaties, agreements etc.); McMahon Line, 342 n.5;
– Chinese Expedition, 135-6; Chinese proposal, 426-9;
– Morrison and, 27-30, 62, 75, 76-7, 80, 89-90, 169-71, 210, 227, 240-1, 345-6, 362-3, 426-9;

Tibet (cont.)
- Mongolian and Tibetan Affairs Commission, 474 n.1, 570 n.2
Tiger Hsu. See Hsü Pao-shan
Times, The, 1, 35 n.1, 54+n.1, 56, 61, 64 n.1, 65, 66 n.1, 76, 87, 93+n.2-94+n.1, 97+n.3, 98 n.3, 108+n.2, n.3, 113 n.3, 115, 120, 122 n.3, 125, 140+n.1, 143, 144, 158 n.1, 169, 193, 214 n.3, 222, 223, 224, 226+n.1, 227, 228, 232, 240+n.1, 252+n.2, n.3, 255, 275, 285, 295, 296+n.2, n.3, 314, 315, 316 n.1, 317, 319 n.1, 327, 328+n.1, 329+n.2, 330, 332, 340, 341, 352, 376, 377, 409-11, 422, 424 n.1, 425+n.3, 444, 460, 471, 472, 514, 515 n.1, 516+n.2, 518, 535 n.1, 559, 607, 617, 624 n.2, 625, 657, 658, 661, 672, 696, 758 n.2, n.5, 763 n.2, 772+n.1, n.3, 773, 775+n.3, 776+n.1, 777+n.4, 780+n.2, n.3, 785, 786 n.1, 787, 789 n.5, 792 n.3, 793 n.2, 794, 796, 800, 801, 812+n.3, 815+n.3, n.4, 817, 822, 824, 827; and Twenty-one Demands, 369+n.1, 370, 371+n.1, 372+n.1, 373+n.1, 377-8, 391, 406, 667, 768, n.1; *China Supplement*, 516-18; *Russian Supplement*, 517; editors, 13+n.2, n.4-14+n.1
Ting Shih-yüan (W. S. Y. Tinge) (1879-1945), Chinese Republican politician, 304 n.4 (305), 347+n.1, 761 n.2;
letter to, 347
letters from, 511, 512
Ting Wen-chiang (V. K. Ting) (1887-1936), Chinese geologist, 621+n.1, 756+n.4, 758 n.1; science *versus* metaphysics debate, 621 n.1; Geographical survey of China, 621 n.1;
letter to, 621
letter from, 756
Ting, V. K. See Ting Wen-chiang
Tinge, W. S. Y. See Ting Shih-yüan
Toeg, Shanghai merchant, 567
Tōjō Hideki (1884-1948), Japanese soldier and politician, 549 n.1
Tok-tan-tai-chi, Mongol brigand, 49+n.4, 91, 103, 203
Tokutomi Ichirō (Tokutomi Sōhō) (1863-1937), Japanese publicist, 549+n.3
Tokutomi Kenjirō (1868-1927), Japanese writer, 549 n.3 (550)
Tong, Hollington. See Tung Hsien-kuang

Toovey, Sarah Jane, nurse to G. E. Morrison's children, 824, 825, 826, 827
Tower, Charlemagne (1848-1923), American diplomat, 23+n.2
Tōyama Mitsuru, Japanese adventurer, 222 n.3, 392 n.1
Trade Marts and Treaty Ports. See Treaty Ports and Trade Marts
Treaties, agreements etc:
- China and the Powers: Boxer Peace Protocol (*1901*), 380 n.2, 575+n.1, 607+n.2; Mackay Treaty (*1902*), 285, 415+n.3, 576+n.1, 720+n.1; Reorganization (Quintuple) Loan, 93, (*see also* Banks, financial houses and consortia; Loans); China and Foreign Opium Combine Agreement (*1915*), 414 n.3; (*28.1.1917*) 595 n.1; (*29.1.1917*) 595 n.1, 693+n.1; (*11.6.1918*) 595 n.1, 693+n.1;
- Sino-British: Nanking Treaty (*1842*), 729; Adhesion Convention – Tibet (*1903*), 240; Tibetan Agreement (*1906*), 10 n.1, 28+n.1, 79 n.2; Tibetan Trade Regulations, 90 n.2 (91); Opium Treaty (*1911*), 75 n.3 (76), 93 n.2, 95+n.2, 125 n.1, 139; Hsin-yang–Pukow Railway Loan Agreement, 286+n.2;
- Sino-British-Tibetan: Simla Convention (*1914*), 149 n.1, 239-40, 346 n.1, 363+n.1, 426-7, 534;
- Sino-French: Tientsin Treaty (*1858*), 416+n.1; Li-Fournier Treaty (*1884*), 380; Fournier Convention (*1885*), 667; Treaty (*1898*), 699+n.1;
- Sino-German: Kiaochow Treaty (*1898*), 756 n.5 (757), 773+n.4; Tsingtao Customs Agreement (*1905*), 92+n.1, 725+n.1;
- Sino-Japanese: Treaty (*1871*), 689+n.1; Shimonoseki Treaty (*1895*), 437, 733, 747, 754; Commercial Treaty (*1903*), 507+n.1; Exchange of Notes on Railways in Manchuria and Inner Mongolia (*1913*), 237 n.2; Han-yeh-p'ing Loan Contract (*1915*), 432+n.1; Twenty-one Demands Agreement (*1915*), 667; Shantung Agreement (*1915*) 725+n.1;
- Sino-Russian: St Petersburg Treaty (*1881*), 63 n.1, 168, 178 n.1; Tseng-ch'i-Alexeiev Agreement (*1900*), 59 n.2; Chou Mien-Korostovetz Agreement (*1901*), 58 n.2, 59 n.2; Mongolian Agreement (*1913*), 157+n.1, 158+n.2, 162, 168-9, 228 n.1, 252-3+n.1; Exchange of

Treaties: Sino-Russian (*cont.*)
Notes (*1913*), 777+n.5; Urga Telegraph Convention (*1916*), 504 n.2;
- Sino-Russian-Mongolian: Kiahkta Treaty, 281 n.1, 777 n.5, 778;
- Sino-U.S.: Commercial Treaty (*1903*), 30 n.2; Grand Canal Agreement (*1916*), 543+n.1; Huai River Agreement (*1916*) 543+n.1; Lee Higginson Agreement (*1916*), 543+n.1; Siems and Carey Railway Agreement (*1916*), 539+n.4, 543+n.1;
- Afghanistan-German Treaty (*1916*), 566 n.2;
- Anglo-Afghanistan Treaty (*1905*), 459;
- Anglo-German: Yangtse Agreement (*1898*), 27, 305+n.2;
- Anglo-Japanese: Alliance Treaty, 125, 407, 408, 419-20, 422, 429, 430, 433+n.1-435, 441, 445, 476 n.1, 509, 549-51, 666, 671, 688+n.2, 811+n.1, 812-13; Exchange of Notes (*1917*), 530, 550 n.2, 771+n.1, 775, 799;
- Anglo-Persian Agreement (*1919*), 781+n.1;
- Anglo-Russian Agreement (*1899*), 27+n.1;
- Anglo-Siamese: Chiengmai Treaty (*1883*), 387+n.2; Treaty (*1909*), 387 n.2;
- Franco-Japanese: Agreement (*1907*), 370+n.1, 444+n.3, 476 n.1; Exchange of Notes (*1917*), 530, 550 n.2, 771 n.1;
- Japanese-Korean: Treaty (*1904*), 375; Annexation Treaty (*1905*), 444+n.1, 476 n.1, 547 n.2;
- Russo-Japanese: Portsmouth Treaty (*1905*), 58 n.3; Agreement (*1907*), 476 n.1, 750; Agreement (*1910*), 750; Agreement (*1912*), 750; Treaty (*1916*), 750;
- Russo-Mongolian: Urga Convention (*1912*), 48 n.2, 58 n.3, 59+n.3, 61, 62+n.4, 63, 72, 79, 87, 91, 103, 105, 122, 158+n.3, 168, 173-80, 282-3;
- U.S.-Japanese: Treaty (*1889*), 25, 476 n.1; Lansing-Ishii Agreement (*1917*), 547 n.1, 618+n.1, 619 n.3, 644+n.1, 646+n.3-648, 658+n.3, 676+n.1-678, 679, 743, 749, 751-2;
- U.S.-Korean Treaty, 60, 443-4;
- International: Treaty of San Stefano (*1878*), 733, 747, 754; Hague Convention (*1899*), 448; International Telegraph Convention (*1908*), 115; International Opium Convention (*1912*), 688+n.3; Versailles Peace Treaty (*see* separate entry)

Treaty Ports and Trade Marts, 275-6, 306; (Inner Mongolia) 258+n.1-262, 268, 275-6; (Lungkow) 353; (Pukow) 385

Trotsky, Leon (Lev Davidovich Bronstein) (1879-1940), Russian revolutionary, 629 n.1 (630)

Truptil, Col., French soldier, 640 n.3

Ts'ai Ao. *See* Ts'ai O.

Tsai-feng (Second Prince Ch'un) (1883-1951), Manchu Imperial Clansman and Prince Regent, 92 n.2 (93), 206 n.1, 327, 596 n.2

Tsai-hsün, Manchu Imperial Clansman, 596 n.2, 635 n.1

Tsai-i (Prince Tuan), Manchu Imperial Clansman, Grand Councillor, 491 n.2

Tsai-lan, Manchu Imperial Clansman, 491+n.1, n.2, 492;
letter from, 492

Tsai-lien, Manchu Imperial Clansman, 491, n.2.

Ts'ao O (Ts'ai Ao) (1882-1916), Chinese soldier and Republican politician, 310+n.3-311, 412+n.2, 413, 452, 459 n.2, 483, 493 n.1, 494

Tsai-t'ien, Manchu Emperor Kuang-hsü (Te-tsung) (1871-1908), 29 n.1, 122+n.4, 206 n.1, 428 n.3, 505 n.2, 541 n.4, 542

Ts'ai T'ing-kan (1861-1935), Chinese Imperial official and Republican politician, 1, 3+n.1, 22, 50 n.4 (51), 56 n.2, 62+n.1, 124 n.4, 191 n.3, 192+n.1, 209 n.1, 229, 243 n.1, 323 n.1, 328 n.1, 346, 356 n.1, 379 n.1, 388 n.4, 429 n.2, 453+n.2, 454, 560 n.3, 585+n.4, 587, 605, 608+n.1, 697 n.1;
letters to, 36, 40, 53, 55, 58, 62, 63, 73, 75, 76, 79, 114, 118, 137, 138, 145, 151, 156, 161, 166, 169, 173, 183, 191, 200, 202, 209, 210 (2), 219, 258, 262, 275, 279, 304, 313 (2), 322, 333, 360, 364, 369 (2), 373, 379, 382, 385, 391, 398, 416, 420, 422, 426, 446, 457, 462, 464, 467, 468, 485, 496, 510, 524, 532, 697
letters from, 3, 39, 136, 137, 154 (2), 164, 186, 251, 262, 362, 364, 366, 372, 381, 384, 392, 398, 418, 453, 463, 469, 484, 527, 535

Ts'ai Yüan-p'ei (1868-1940), Chinese Republican politician and educationalist, 10 n.3

Ts'ao Chia-hsiang (Ts'ao Kai-cheong), Chinese sailor, 220 + n.1, 277 + n.2, 278;
letters to, 222, 227, 230, 233, 265
letter from, 164
Ts'ao Ju-lin (1976-1966), Chinese Imperial official and Republican politician, 237 + n.3, 354, 381, 584 n.1, 636, 693 n.1, 722 n.1, 764 + n.2, n.3, n.4, 765, 801 n.3
Ts'ao Kai-cheong. *See* Ts'ao Chia-hsiang
Ts'ao K'un (1862-1938), Chinese soldier and Republican politician, President of the Republic, 654 + n.8, 656 + n.3
Tse Tsan-tai. *See* Hsieh Tsan-t'ai
Ts'en Ch'un-hsüan (1861-1933), Chinese Imperial official, Viceroy, and Republican politician, 10 n.1, 393 n.4, 394-5 + n.1, 505 n.2 (506), 520 n.3
Ts'en Hsüeh-lü, Chinese author, 79 n.2 (80)
Ts'en Yü-ying (1829-89), Chinese Imperial official, Viceroy, 395 n.1
Tseng-ch'i, Manchu Bannerman, Military Governor, 59 + n.2
Tseng Chi-tze (1839-90), Chinese diplomat, 202 n.1
Tseng Ju-cheng. *See* Cheng Ju-cheng
Tseng Kuang-chuan, Chinese Imperial official, 202 + n.1
Tseng Kuo-fang (1811-72), Chinese Imperial official, Grand Secretary, Viceroy, 202 n.1, 206 + n.2
Tseng Tsung-chien (T. K. Tseng) (b. 1881), Chinese diplomat 348 + n.1
Tseng Yu-yi, Chinese Republican official, 614 + n.4, 615
Tseng, T. K. *See* Tseng Tsung-chien
Tsening Chimet (Da Lama), 48 n.3, 49 + n.1, n.7
Tso-chuan, 462
Tso Shun-sheng (b. 1893), Chinese politician and author, 541 n.4 (542)
Tsou Chia-lai, Chinese Imperial official, 95 n.2
Tsou Jung (1885-1905), Chinese revolutionary, 182 n.1
Tsuji Karoku, Japanese soldier, 396 + n.3, 397
Tu Yüeh-sheng (1888-1951), Chinese secret society leader, 415 n.4 (416)
Tuan, Prince. *See* Tsai-i
Tuan Ch'i-jui (1865-1936), Chinese soldier and Republican politician, 14 n.5, 43 n.3, 57 n.2, 79 n.2 (80), 86 n.1, 101 n.4 (102), 118 n.4, 237 n.3, 254 n.1, 287 + n.2, 291, 347 n.1, 358 n.2, 439 n.1, 505 n.2 (506), 527 + n.2, 531, 570 n.2, 583 n.2, 584, 590, 592, 593 + n.3, 595 n.2, 596, 597 n.5, 598, 599 + n.1, 601, 602, 612 n.2, 616 + n.1, 617, 618 n.1, 620, 635 n.1, 636 + n.1, n.2, 637 n.1, 639, 646 n.1, 654 + n.4, 655 + n.2, 656 n.2, n.3, 682, 689 n.2, 698 + n.4, 715, 741, 761 n.1, n.2, 783 + n.1, n.2, n.3, n.4, 786, 801 n.3, 809 n.1;
letter to, 571
Tuan Chih-kuei (1869-1925), Chinese soldier and Republican politician, 86 n.1, 287 n.2 (288), 597 n.2, 634 + n.1, 654 + n.6, 655
Tuan-fang (1861-1911), Manchu Bannerman, Viceroy, 191 n.3
Tuan Jung (d. 1913), Chinese Christian convert, 119, 276
Tuchün revolt (*1917*), 531, 595-6, 597-9, 600, 601, 614-17
Tuckey, T. W. T., British railway engineer, 45 + n.2
Tung Fu-hsiang (1839-1908), Chinese soldier, 474 n.1
Tung Hsien-kuang (Hollington Tong), Chinese journalist and Republican politician, 384 + n.1, 713 + n.1
Tung Shih-ch'i, Chinese Republican politician, 697 n.1
Turkey: Sultan of, 546; and China 546; conditions in, 213; and World War I, 546, 566 n.2
Turner, George, British financier, 54 + n.2;
letter to, 54
Turner, Peter, Canadian builder, 54 + n.2; *letter to*, 54
Twenty-one Demands, 6 n.1, 7 n.1, 237 n.3, 351-2, 355 n.2, 364-6, 368-92, 396 n.2, 398-401, 404-5, 406-7, 413 n.1, 418, 423, 432 n.1, 442-3, 446 n.1, 451, 463 n.1, 470, 472-3, 507, 530, 535, 539 n.2, 540, 560 + n.2, 596, 619, 638 n.2, 659, 666, 670, 688, 696, 712 n.1, 731 + n.1-755, 766, 768 n.1, 774 + n.1; (and *Genrō*) 540. *See also* Hioki Eki: Japan in China; Katō Takaaki; Koike Chōzō; Morrison: and Twenty-one Demands; Obata Yūkichi; Ōkuma Shigenobu; *Times*: and Twenty-one Demands
Twigge, H. C., British adventurer, 336 n.1
Tyau, M. T. Z. *See* T'iao Min-ch'ien
Tyau, Philip K. C. *See* T'iao Tso-ch'ien
Tyler, James Arbuthnot (1867-1945), British soldier, 790-n.5

Ts'u-hsi, Empress-Dowager. *See* Hsiao-ch'in

Uchida Yasuya (1865-1936), Japanese diplomat and politician, 476 n.1, 548 n.4, 739
Ueda Kazutoshi (1867-1937), Japanese scholar, 633 + n.2
Ueno Iwatarō (1867-1925), Japanese journalist, 475 n.1, 541 + n.1
Ukita Gōji, Japanese consular official, 790 n.4
United States: in China, 56, 59-60, 121 + n.1, n.2, 145-7, 213-14, 296, 344, 468, 471, 491 n.2, 530-1, 542, 543 + n.1, n.2, 561-2, 568 + n.3, 570, 573 n.3, 585, 618 + n.1, 644, 646-8, 658, 659, 728 n.1, 760, 773, 800 n.1; 'Open Door' policy, 20 n.2, 59 + n.4-60, 371 + n.1, 419, 444, 565 n.2 (566), 647, 678, 739, 753; racial discrimination, 30 n.2, 42, 136 n.1, 146; Chinese boycott, 30 n.2, 42; recognition of the Chinese Republic, 6 n.2, 30, 116 + n.2; withdrawal from China Loan, 108 n.2, 121 + n.1, 244 n.4, (*see also* Loans);
– and World War I: China's entry, 530-1, 570, 571, 573, 575, 594, 618 + n.1, 775; abandonment of Chinese cause, 644, 646-8, 658, 717, 742-3, 751, 755-6; (*see also* Powers in China; Treaties, agreements, etc.: Sino-U.S., U.S.-Japanese); profiteering, 468, 760;
– and Japan, 60 + n.1, 421 + n.1, 751-2, 753, 767, (*see also* Ishii Kikujirō; Megata Tanetarō; Treaties, agreements etc.: U.S.-Japanese);
– *Foreign Relations of the United States* (1915), 453; railway mission to Russia, 782 n.2; Texas Rangers, 265

Verne, Jules (1828-1905), French writer, 722-3 + n.1
Versailles Peace Treaty, 717, 756 + n.5, 757, 761 n.3, 768 + n.1-769, 771, 773 + n.3, 774-5, 776 + n.1, 778 + n.2, 779 n.3, 781, 786 + n.1, n.2, 795, 800 n.1, 813
Vickers, Douglas (1861-1937), British manufacturer, 376 + n.1
Victoria (Alexandrina Victoria) (1819-1901), Queen of the United Kingdom of Great Britain and Ireland, Empress of India, 613 n.2

Vitale, Guido Amedo (1872-1918), Baron, Italian diplomat and teacher, 232 + n.1
Viviani, René (1863-1925), French politician, 619 + n.2
Voretzsch (*alias* A. Nielson), German consular official, 375

Wakatsuki Reijirō (1866-1949), Japanese politician, 548 n.4 (549), 632 n.1
Wakefield, C. E. S., British employee of Chinese Maritime Customs, 616 + n.5
Waldersee, Alfred von (1832-1904), German soldier, 59 n.5
Wallenberg, G. O., Swedish diplomat, 414 + n.1
Wallenberg, Knut Agathon (1853-1938), Swedish politician, 414 n.1
Walter, Robert (d. 1959), British colonial official, 224 + n.4
Wang, Chinese compradore of the opium dealers Sassoons, 594
Wang, Dr, Chinese medical practitioner, 164
Wang, Chinese Republican official, 167
Wang Chan-yüan (1861-1934), Chinese soldier, 807 + n.4
Wang Ch'eng-pin (1874-1936), Chinese soldier, Provincial Governor, 86 n.1
Wang Cheng-t'ing (1882-1961), Chinese Republican politician, 10 n.3, 645 + n.3, 698 n.3, 728 + n.1, 773 n.2, 801, 812; *letters from*, 728, 731
Wang Chih-jui, Chinese Republican official, 594-5 + n.1
Wang Ching-ch'i (b. 1884), Chinese diplomat, 721 + n.2
Wang Ching-ch'un (1882-1956), Chinese Republican official, railway administrator, 603 + n.1
Wang Ching-wei (1883-1944), Chinese Republican official, 10 n.1, 395 n.2
Wang Chung-hui (1881-1958), Chinese Republican politician, 10 n.3, 191 + n.2, 720 + n.1, 721
Wang I-t'ang (1878-1946), Chinese Republican politician, 287 n.2, 510 n.2, 761 n.2, 767, 783 + n.4, 784
Wang K'ai-wen. *See* Huang K'ai-wen
Wang K'ai-yün (1833-1916), Chinese scholar, 415 n.4
Wang K'e-min (1873-1945), Chinese Republican politician, 305 + n.3
Wang Ling-chi (b. 1885), Chinese soldier, 807 + n.3

Wang Mou-tao, Chinese diplomat, 270+n.3, 271, 337+n.1
Wang Shih-chen (1861–1930), Chinese soldier and Republican politician, 529, 612+n.2, 646 n.1, 654+n.5
Wang Ta-hsieh (1859–1928), Chinese diplomat and Republican politician, 646+n.1
Wang T'ao (1828–97), Chinese journalist, 613 n.1
Wang Tsang-hsü (b. 1888), Chinese soldier, 807+n.3
Wang Tung, Chinese revolutionary, 393+n.3
Wang Tz'u-ch'ang (Ch'un-shan), Chinese Imperial official, 305+n.3
Wang, W. C., Chinese resident in London;
letter from, 331
Wang Yang-ming (1472–1528), Chinese neo-Confucian scholar, 206 n.2 (207)
Wang Yun-sheng (b. 1899), Chinese journalist and author, 323 n.1
Warburg, Felix, American financier, 405 n.2
Ward, Joseph (1856–1930), Australian-born New Zealand politician, 675 n.2, 679+n.2
Warren, Pelham Laird (1845–1923), British consular official, 817+n.1
Warren, Mrs, 611
Wars: Afghan War, 26 n.5, 382 n.2; Anglo–Chinese War (1st Opium War), 118 n.2, 225 n.2, 674 n.3; Anglo–French expedition (2nd Opium War), 436+n.2, 437; Anhwei–Chihli War (*1920*), 597 n.2, 602, 783 n.1, n.3; Balkan War, 81; Chihli–Fengtien War (1st), 654 n.8; Chihli–Fengtien War (2nd), 654 n.8; English Civil War, 759 n.3; Franco–Prussian War (*1870*), 117 n.2, (Spandau fund, 117+n.2); Napoleonic Campaign, 328; North and South war in China, 602; Russo–Japanese War, 59 n.6, 91+n.1, 92 n.2, 115 n.1, 133+n.4, 185 n.3, 208, 211 n.2, 316 n.1, 350, 351, 396 n.1, 438+n.2, 440, 461 n.2, n.3, 465, 506, 531, 540+n.1, n.2, 541 n.1, 550 n.1, 552 n.1, n.2, 590 n.1, 597 n.2, 638 n.1, 658–9, 661, 788, (Chinese neutrality in) 59 n.7, (surrender of Port Arthur) 185 n.3; Sino–French War (*1884*), 380–1, 437, 817+n.1, n.2, (occupation of Formosa) 381 n.1, (Battle of Lanson) 381 n.1; Sino–Japanese War (*1894–5*), 93, 161 n.2, 208 n.3, 350, 380 n.2, 437+n.2–438, 525, 540+n.1, n.2, 550 n.1, 552 n.1, n.2, 563 n.1, 656 n.2, 743, 783 n.4; Sino–Japanese War (*1937–45*), 43 n.3 (44), 124 n.1, 201 n.1, 206 n.1, 547 n.2 (548), 570 n.2, 605 n.3 (606), 638 n.1, 641 n.3, 652 n.6, 761 n.2, (Nanking massacre) 124 n.1; South African (Boer) War, 26 n.5, 684, 788 n.2, 790 n.5, 812 n.3;
– World War I, 31 n.4, 123 n.2, 192 n.2, 342+n.2, n.3, 348, 349, 350, 365, 370, 376, 400, 406–7, 414 n.1, 419, 422, 424–6, 430–1, 435–6, 447–9, 454, 455–6, 463+n.2, n.3, 464–9, 470, 489+n.3–490+n.1, 492, 494, 516, 518, 524, 549, 550+n.2, 551+n.1, 559–67, 571–8, 591, 619 n.2, 665–74, 675 n.2, 682–3, 698+n.2, 727 n.1, 757, 774+n.1, 818 n.1; Balkan question, 126, 213; Dardanelles campaign, 425 n.5, 426+n.1, 494; East African campaign, 663+n.4, n.5–664; Falkland, Battle of, 551+n.2; Jutland, Battle of, 777 n.2, 789 n.2, n.3; the Marne, Battle of, 447 n.3; Neuve Chapelle, Battle of, 448; Campaigns in Poland and Russia, 455+n.2; Verdun, Battle of, 550 n.2, 559, 562, 662, 671, 674; China and, 463+n.2, n.3, 464–9, 470–3, 509, 516, 530–1, 543–7, 559–67, 571–8, 581–3+n.1, 586 n.2, 588–9, 618, 628, 629, 630, 636+n.2, 640+n.3, 665–74, 691, 774, 775, 783+n.1, n.2, n.3; (Powers and China's entry) 466, 530–1, 546+n.1, 547 n.1, 557, 559, 562, 565, 570, 571, 573, 574–6, 576–7, 594, 618+n.1, 667, 691–4, 774, 775, (Chinese labour forces) 47 n.3–48, 640+n.3, 755;
– World War II, 73+n.1, 106 n.2 (107), 180 n.2, 489 n.3 (490), 574 n.2, 704 n.3, 799 n.2; prediction of, 770
Washington Conference. *See under* Conferences and institutions, international
Washington, George (1732–99), 1st President of the United States, 197
Washizawa Yoshiji, Japanese journalist, 802+n.2
Watanabe Ikujirō, Japanese author, 323 n.1
Waterways and conservancy in China, 148–9, 201, 486–7; Chefoo Breakwater, 353, 413; Chihli, 413, 486; Grand Canal, 201+n.1, 543+n.1; Huai River

Waterways and conservancy in China (*cont.*)
scheme, 148–9, 200 n.4, 201, 296, 413, 486, 543 + n.1; Hulutao Harbour project, 413, 512 n.2; Kwangtung, 486; Liao River, 413; Newchwang, 413; Yellow River, 201 + n.1
Watt, William Alexander (1871–1946), Australian politician, 702 + n.1, 705 n.1; *letter to*, 702
Weal, Putnam. *See* B. L. Simpson
Wearne, A. E., Australian journalist, 1, 31 + n.4, 40, 123, 139, 152–3, 210, 211 n.1, 229, 253 n.1; *letters to*, 81, 629, 785, (from H. de Reuter) 257
letter from, 782
Wellwood, J. M., American Protestant missionary, 167 + n.8
Wen Ping-chün, Chinese Imperial official and Republican politician, 191 + n.3, 479 + n.1
Wen Tsung-yao (b. 1876), Chinese Imperial official and Republican politician, 10 + n.1, n.2, 152 + n.2, 718 + n.2
Werner, Edward Theodore Chalmers (1864–1954), New Zealand-born British consular official, 603; *A Dictionary of Chinese Mythology*, 603, 623 + n.1;
letter from, 623
Wheler, Aubrey S., British mining engineer, 415 + n.2
White, Thaddeus C., American adventurer, 524 + n.3
White Wolf. *See* Pai Yung-ch'eng
Whitehead, Thomas Henderson (1851–1933), British banker, 338
Whyte, Alexander Frederick (1883–1970), British journalist and publicist, 818 + n.6
Wilde, Oscar Fingal O'Flahertie Wills (1854–1900), British writer, 162 + n.1; 'Libertatis Sacra Fames', 162 + n.1
Wilhelm II, (1859–1941), Kaiser of Germany, 345, 464
Wilkinson (later Wilkinson-Guillemard), Walter Hugh John (1874–1939), British colonial official, 172 + n.1, n.2;
letter to, 172
Williams, Edward Thomas (1854–1944), American diplomat, 95 + n.1, 200 n.4, 406, 731 n.1 (732);
letter to, (from C. D. Jameson) 200
Willmer, valet of G. E. Morrison, 824, 827

Willoughby, Michael Edward (1864–1939), British soldier, 818 + n.1
Willoughby, Westel Woodbury (1867–1945), American political scientist, 585 n.3, 630, 637 n.2, 698, 717, 718; papers of, 535 n.3;
letter to, 634
Willoughby, William Franklin (1867–1960), American jurist, 532 + n.2, 533, 536, 570, 585 + n.3, 628; papers of, 535 n.3
Wilmer, William Holland (1863–1936), American ophthalmologist, 786 + n.3
Wilson, Thomas Woodrow (1956–1924), 28th President of the United States, 20 n.2, 98 n.1, 108 n.2, 116, 121 + n.1, 143 + n.1, 156, 213, 279 n.3, 296 n.1, 532 n.2, 533, 670, 678, 696, 697, 698, 748, 754, 755, 756, 785 + n.1, 786 n.2, 799–800, 818 n.4
Wilton, Ernest Colville Collins (1870–1952), British consular official 153 + n.1, 346 + n.2, 482 + n.3, 648–9
Wise, Bernard Ringrose (1858–1916), Australian politician and adventurer, 336 n.2 (337)
Wollenborg, Leone (1859–1932), Italian politician, 74 + n.5
Woodhead, Henry George Wandesforde (1883–1959). British journalist and author, 88 + n.1, 138–9, 230, 785;
letter to, 712
Woodward, Robert Simpson (1849–1924), American astronomer, 23 + n.5
World War I. *See under* Wars
World War II. *See under* Wars
Wouters, E. d'Oplinter, Belgian jurist, 100 + n.3
Wu, Chinese political intermediary, 142
Wu, C. C. *See* Wu Ch'ao-shu
Wu Ch'ao-shu (Ch'ao-ch'u) (1887–1934), Chinese Republican politician and diplomat, 57 + n.1, 62, 88 + n.4, 227 n.1, 477 n.4 (478), 594 + n.3, 706 + n.3, 728 n.1, 801;
letter to, 226;
letters from, 706, 718
Wu, Mrs, wife of Wu Ch'ao-shu, 709
Wu Chih-ying, Chinese calligrapher, wife of Lien Ch'üan, 388 n.3
Wu Lien-te (1879–1960), Chinese medical practitioner, 367 n.2, 726 + n.1
Wu Lu-chen (1879–1911), Chinese soldier, 118 + n.1, 280 n.1, 319 n.3, 386 n.3
Wu Ming-fu (Shih-ying) (d. 1913), Chinese hired assassin, 113 + n.2

903

Wu P'ei-fu (1874-1939), Chinese soldier, 311 n.1, 319 n.3, 654 n.8, 656 n.3, 807 n.4, 809 n.2
Wu Shih-ying. *See* Wu Ming-fu
Wu T'ieh-cheng (1888-1953), Chinese Republican politician, 477 n.4 (478)
Wu T'ing-fang (1842-1922), Chinese diplomat and Republican politician, 57 + n.1, n.2, 59 + n.5, 62, 88, 172, 173, 183, 184, 185, 186, 423, 594 + n.3, 599, 604, 605, 650 + n.3
Wuchang Uprising. *See* Revolution *1911*
Wutai, Prince, Mongol leader, 122, 203

Yamagata Aritomo (1838-1922), Japanese soldier and politician, 101 n.3, 132 + n.2, n.3, 772 n.2, 802 n.1
Yamagata Isō, Japanese scholar, 131 n.1
Yamamoto Gombē (1852-1933), Japanese politician, 82 n.3, 132 n.7, 273 n.1, 584 n.3
Yamamoto Tadasaburō, Japanese businessman, 785 + n.4
Yamaza Enjirō (1866-1914), Japanese diplomat, 102 + n.1, 189 + n.2, 207, 237 n.2, 355 n.2, 507
Yamazaki Heikichi, Japanese consular official, 790 + n.4
Yang Ch'eng, Chinese diplomat, 290 + n.2
Yang Shih-ch'i (1861-1917), Chinese Republican politician, 476 n.1, 590 n.1
Yang Tu (1875-1931), Chinese Republican politician, 304 n.4 (305), 415 + n.2, 416, 450, 454
Yano Fumio (1850-1931), Japanese diplomat, 354 n.2
Yasukawa Keiichirō (1849-1934), Japanese industrialist, 392 + n.1
Yates, M. M.,
 letter from, 106
Yeh Kung-ch'o (b. 1881), Chinese Republican politician, 237 n.3, 722 + n.1
Yen-chih, Manchu Bannerman, Imperial official, 48 + n.1
Yen Ho-ling (Hawkling Yen) (1879-1937), Chinese Republican official and educationalist, 238 + n.1;
 letter to, 238
Yen, W. W. *See* Yen Hui-ch'ing
Yen Hsi-shan (1883-1960), Chinese soldier, 64 n.2 (65)
Yen Hui-ch'ing (W. W. Yen) (1877-1950), Chinese diplomat and Republican politician, 583 n.1, 629 n.1 (630)
Yin, Chinese detective, 479
Yin-ch'ang (1860-?1928), Manchu Bannerman and soldier, 118 n.1

Yin Ch'ang-heng (b. 1884), Chinese soldier, Provincial Governor, 135 + n.7-136
Yin-chen, Manchu Emperor Yung-cheng (Shih-tsung), 408 + n.2
Ying K'uei-ch'eng (Kuei-hsiang), Chinese conspirator, 113 + n.2
Ying Kuie-hsiang. *See* Ying K'uei-ch'eng
Yoshida, Japanese financial agent, 590
Yoshihito (1879-1925), Emperor Taishō of Japan, 107, 220 + n.1, 324 n.2, 424 n.3, 802
Yoshizawa Kenkichi (1874-1965), Japanese diplomat, 574 + n.2, 592
Young, Arthur Henderson (1854-1938), British colonial official, 791 + n.2
Younghusband, Francis Edward (1863-1942), British colonial official, 27 + n.3, 89, 343, 428 n.1, 436 n.3
Yourin. *See* Dzevaltovsky
Yü-keng (d. 1905), Chinese Bannerman, diplomat, 524 n.4
Yü Te-ling, lady in-waiting to Empress-Dowager Tz'u-hsi, 524 + n.4
Yü Lien-san, Chinese Imperial official, Provincial Governor, 138 n.1
Yu-wei-to, Chinese Republican official, 321
Yü Yung-ling, lady-in-waiting to Empress-Dowager Tz'u-hsi, 524 n.4
Yüan K'e-ting (Yün-t'ai), eldest son of Yüan Shih-k'ai, 503 + n.2
Yüan Shih-k'ai (1859-1916), Chinese Imperial official, Viceroy, Republican politician, President of the Republic, 2, 3 + n.1, n.3, 4 n.1, 10 n.1, 13, 14 n.5, 18 n.2, 20 n.2, n.3, 30, 38, 39 + n.1, 41, 55, 56 n.2, 58, 64 n.2, 65, 89, 91, 99, 101 + n.1, 114, 118 n.2, n.3, 138 n.1, 139, 153, 206, 212, 219, 226, 273 n.1, 277 + n.2, 278, 279, 280 + n.1, 287 n.2, 288, 290, 291, 304, 306 n.2, 310 + n.3, 311 + n.1, 313, 314, 318 n.2, 322, 328 n.1 (329), 333, 335, 336, 338, 342, 379, 381-2, 383, 436, 454, 461, 469, 616 n.3;
– in Korea, 525; and New Army, 61, 92 + n.2, 124 n.1, 287 n.2, 362 n.1, 541 n.4, 612 n.2, 623 n.3, 642 n.1, 682; and Reform Movement (*1898*), 541 + n.4-542; Governor Shantung, 607 n.1; Viceroy Chihli, 92 n.2, 195, 454; last Imperial Chancellor, 386 n.4 (387), 450, 535 n.1, 596 n.2;
– President, 3 n.3, n.4, 4, 6, 7-8, 30 n.1, 66 n.3 (67), 78-9, 86, 87, 110, 112 + n.2, 115, 116 n.2-117, 122, 129, 143 + n.1, 193, 196, 205 n.1, 220 n.1, 223,

904

Yüan Shih-k'ai, President (*cont.*)
224+n.2, 225+n.1, 226 n.1, 227, 233-4, 240+n.1, 241, 325, 326, 330, 332, 342 n.2, 352, 358 n.2, 362, 391, 395 n.1, 401 n.1, 409, 410, 439 n.1, 450, 453, 462, 476 n.1, 481+n.4, 486, 511+n.3, 636, 722, 783, 808; (weekly Political Conference) 511+n.3;
- and Sun Yat-sen and southern republicans, 7-13, 17+n.1, 110-11, 119-20, 137-8, 141, 163, 166+n.2, 169-71, 180-3, 186-91, 195-6, 197, 199, 200+n.2, 201, 253+n.3-254, 319 n.3, 390, 393 n.2, 394 n.4, 395 n.2, 439 n.1;
- and World War I, 413, 463+n.3, 507, 509, 530, 546, 547, 559, 560-1, 563, 575, 665-71, 672, 691;
- and Japanese, 99, 211, 222-3, 351, 451, 452, 493-5, 503-10, 521, 539 n.2, 541+n.4 (542)-543, 560-3, 592; and Twenty-one Demands, 368, 374, 379, 406, 413, 659 (*see also* Japan in China; Twenty-one Demands);
- monarchy scheme, 14 n.5, 42 n.2, 86 n.1, 135 n.2, 142-3, 188 n.1, 203 n.1, 206-7, 212, 225 n.2, 237, 284 n.2, 309, 318 n.2, 381 n.3, 386 n.4 (387), 401 n.1, 415 n.4, 417 n.1, 439 n.1, 440 n.1, 449, 450-5, 456-7, 460-1, 462-3+n.1, 467, 469-70, 474-5, 481, 482-9, 492-500, 502-3, 504-5, 510 n.2, 511-12, 515+n.2, 518-19, 520, 524-7, 532, 537, 543, 560, 563, 592, 597 n.2, 601, 605 n.3, 635 n.1, 655 n.2, 656 n.2, 667, 672, 715, 762 n.1, 765 n.2, 828; dragon bone, 469 n.2, 484+n.1, 503;
- anti-monarchist movement, 10 n.1, 116 n.2, 215, 244 n.3, 310 n.3, 393 n.4, 394 n.1, 480, 481+n.3, 482-9, 493-502, 505-6, (in Hunan) 505, (in Kwangsi) 244 n.3, (in Kwangtung) 503+n.1, 505, (Nanking conference of militarists) 520+n.3, (in Shantung) 393 n.2, (in Szechwan) 493-502, 522-4, (in Yunnan) 10 n.1, 452, 480, 481+n.3, 482, 488, 493+n.1, n.2-496, 502, 522-4;
- abandonment of monarchy, 452, 502-3, 504-6, 509, 515, 518-19;
- illness, 164, 166, 454, 527; death, 452-3, 523+n.1, 529, 532, 538, 671;
- and Dalai Lama, 29 n.1; and 'Four Friends of Sung Shan' (Chang Ch'ien, Chao Erh-hsün, Hsü Shih-ch'ang, Li Ching-hsi), 514 n.1; and Liang Shih-yi, 79 n.2; and T'ang Shao-yi, 79+n.1, n.2-80, 141; and Ts'ai T'ing-kan, 3 n.1, 535+n.1;
- and Morrison (*see under* Morrison); and foreign advisers, 154, 161, 164, 251, 258, 262, 265, 341, 345-6, 399;
- *letters to*, 322, 328, 335, 339, 496, (telegram from Chang Hsün) 142, (from Chao Ping-chün) 173, (from G. T. B. Davis) 155

Yüan, Mme, wife of Yüan Shih-k'ai, *letter to*, 226

Yun Ch'i-ho (1867-1945), Korean clergyman and patriot, 508+n.1

Yung-cheng, Emperor. *See* Yin-chen

Yung Hao. *See* Jung-hou

Zionist Movement: Shanghai Zionist Association, 361 n.3, 705+n.3, n. 4-706+n.1; Zionist Federation in Great Britain, 705, 706 n.1; *Israel Messenger*, 361 n.3; *Jewish Chronicle*, 361 n.3; *Jewish Encyclopaedia*, 361 n.3; Jewish Theological Seminary, 405 n.2; National home for the Jewish people in Palestine, 530, 705+n.3-706+n.1

Zumbrum, 304

Zumoto Motosada (1862-1943), Japanese publicist, 556+n.1; *letter to*, 556

Lightning Source UK Ltd.
Milton Keynes UK
UKHW01f0435240518
323138UK00001B/94/P